THE HARVARD CLASSICS
EDITED BY CHARLES W. ELIOT, LL.D.

The Editor's Introduction
Reader's Guide
Index

TO THE FIRST LINES OF POEMS,
SONGS *and* CHORUSES, HYMNS *and* PSALMS

General Index
Chronological Index

With a Frontispiece
Volume 50

P. F. Collier & Son Corporation
NEW YORK

CONTENTS

                                                                    PAGE
THE EDITOR'S INTRODUCTION TO THE HARVARD CLASSICS............   3

READER'S GUIDE TO THE HARVARD CLASSICS.......................   18
  CLASS I A THE HISTORY OF CIVILIZATION....................   19
           B RELIGION AND PHILOSOPHY........................   29
           C EDUCATION   36
           D SCIENCE   39
           E POLITICS   42
           F VOYAGES AND TRAVELS............................   45
           G CRITICISM OF LITERATURE AND THE FINE ARTS......   47
  CLASS II A DRAMA   51
           B BIOGRAPHY AND LETTERS..........................   53
           C ESSAYS   55
           D NARRATIVE POETRY AND PROSE FICTION.............   58

AN INDEX TO THE FIRST LINES OF POEMS, SONGS AND CHORUSES,
  HYMNS AND PSALMS..   63

GENERAL INDEX 117

CHRONOLOGICAL INDEX 453

THE
EDITOR'S INTRODUCTION
TO THE
HARVARD CLASSICS

MY PURPOSE in selecting The Harvard Classics was to provide the literary materials from which a careful and persistent reader might gain a fair view of the progress of man observing, recording, inventing, and imagining from the earliest historical times to the close of the nineteenth century. Within the limits of fifty volumes, containing about 22,000 pages, I was to provide the means of obtaining such a knowledge of ancient and modern literature as seems essential to the twentieth century idea of a cultivated man. The best acquisition of a cultivated man is a liberal frame of mind or way of thinking; but there must be added to that possession acquaintance with the prodigious store of recorded discoveries, experiences, and reflections which humanity in its intermittent and irregular progress from barbarism to civilization has acquired and laid up. From that store I proposed to make such a selection as any intellectually ambitious American family might use to advantage, even if their early opportunities of education had been scanty. The purpose of The Harvard Classics is, therefore, one very different from that of the many collections in which the editor's aim has been to select the hundred or the fifty best books in the world; it is nothing less than the purpose to present so ample and characteristic a record of the stream of the world's thought that the observant reader's mind shall be enriched, refined, and fertilized by it.

With such objects in view it was essential that the whole series should be in the English language; and this limitation to English necessitated the free use of translations, in spite of the fact that it is impossible to reproduce perfectly in a translation the style and

flavor of the original. The reader of this collection must not imagine that he can find in an English translation of Homer, Dante, Cervantes, or Goethe, all the beauty and charm of the original. Nevertheless, translations can yield much genuine cultivation to the student who attends to the substance of the author's thought, although he knows all the time that he is missing some of the elegance and beauty of the original form. Since it is impossible to give in translation the rhythm and sweetness of poetry—and particularly of lyric poetry—far the larger part of the poetry in The Harvard Classics will be found to be poetry which was written in English.

While with very few exceptions every piece of writing included in the series is complete in itself—that is, is a whole book, narrative, document, essay, or poem—there are many volumes which are made up of numerous short, though complete, works. Thus, three volumes contain an anthology of English poetry comprising specimens of the work of over two hundred writers. There is also a volume of memorable prefaces, and another of important American historical documents. Five volumes are made up of essays, representing several centuries and several nationalities. The principal subjects embraced in the series are history, biography, philosophy, religion, voyages and travels, natural science, government and politics, education, criticism, the drama, epic and lyric poetry, and prose fiction—in short, all the main subdivisions of literature. The principal literatures represented in the collection are those of Greece, Rome, France, Italy, Spain, England, Scotland, Germany, and the United States; but important contributions have been drawn also from Chinese, Hindu, Hebrew, Arabian, Scandinavian, and Irish sources. Since the series is intended primarily for American readers, it contains a somewhat disproportionate amount of English and American literature, and of documents and discussions relating to American history and to the development of American social and political ideas.

Chronologically considered, the series begins with portions of the sacred books of the oldest religions, proceeds with specimens of the literature of Greece and Rome, then makes selections from the literature of the Middle Ages in the Orient, Italy, France, Scandinavia, Ireland, England, Germany, and the Latin Church, includes a considerable representation of the literature of the Renaissance in Italy,

France, Germany, England, Scotland, and Spain, and, arriving at modern times, comprehends selections derived from Italy, three centuries of France, two centuries of Germany, three centuries of England, and something more than a century of the United States.

Nothing has been included in the series which does not possess good literary form; but the collection illustrates the variations of literary form and taste from century to century, the wide separation in time of the recurrent climaxes in the various forms of literary expression in both prose and verse, and the immense widening of the range and scope of both letters and science during the seventeenth, eighteenth, and nineteenth centuries.

At the very outset of the work unexpected difficulties arose, some of which, although almost mechanical, proved to be insurmountable. Many famous books were too long to be included in the set, that is, they would have taken a disproportionate number of the fifty volumes. Thus, the English Bible could not be included as a whole, because it was too long; and for the same reason only selections from Shakespeare, and the first part of "Don Quixote," could be included. Many famous and desirable books on history had to be excluded because of their length. The works of living authors were in general excluded, because the verdict of the educated world has not yet been pronounced upon them.

Finally, the whole of nineteenth century fiction, with two exceptions, was excluded; partly because of its great bulk, and partly because it is easily accessible. It proved to be possible, however, to represent by selections complete in themselves the English Bible, Shakespeare, and some other works of the highest order. Some authors whose greatest works were too long to be included in the series could be represented by one or more of their shorter works. It was hard to make up an adequate representation of the scientific thought of the nineteenth century, because much of the most productive scientific thought has not yet been given a literary form. The discoverers' original papers on chemistry, physics, geology, and biology have usually been presented to some scientific society, and have naturally been expressed in technical language, or have been filled with details indispensable from the scientific point of view but not instructive for the public in general.

Although a good part of the reading provided in The Harvard Classics may fairly be called interesting, there are also volumes or portions of volumes which make hard reading, even for a practised student. In the literature of other days some of the topics treated are unfamiliar, and, moreover, the state of mind of the authors is apt to be strange to the present generation. The sentiments and opinions these authors express are frequently not acceptable to present-day readers, who have to be often saying to themselves: "This is not true, or not correct, or not in accordance with our beliefs." It is, however, precisely this encounter with the mental states of other generations which enlarges the outlook and sympathies of the cultivated man, and persuades him of the upward tendency of the human race. The Harvard Classics, as a whole, require close attention and a resolute spirit on the part of the reader. Nevertheless large parts of the collection were undoubtedly composed just to give delight, or to show people how to win rational pleasures. Thus, the real values of almost all the tales, dramas, fiction, and poetry in the series are esthetic, not didactic, values. The interested reader ought to gain from them enjoyment and new power to enjoy.

There is no mode of using The Harvard Classics which can be recommended as the best for all readers. Every student who proposes to master the series must choose his own way through it. Some readers may be inclined to follow the chronological order; but shall they begin with the oldest book and read down through the centuries, or begin with the youngest and read backward? Another method would be to read by subjects, and under each subject chronologically. A good field for this method is the collection of voyages and travels. There is also merit in the chronological order in reading the documents taken from the sacred books of the world. Still another method is that of comparison or of contrast. The collection gives many opportunities of comparing the views of contemporaneous writers on the same subject, and also of contrasting the prevailing opinions in different nations or different social states at the same epoch. In government and politics, for example, the collection supplies much material for comparing the opinions of writers nearly contemporary but of different nationality, and for contrasting the different social states at the same epoch in nations not far apart

geographically, but distinct as regards their history, traditions, and habits.

Another way of dealing with the collection would be to read first an essay or a group of essays on related subjects, and then to search through the collection to discover all the material it contains within the field of that essay or group of essays. The essays in the collection are numerous, and deal with a great variety of topics both old and new. Whoever should follow the various leadings of the essays in the collection would ultimately cover far the greater part of the fifty volumes.

The biographies, letters, and prefaces contained in the collection will also afford much good guidance to other material. The student who likes the comparative method will naturally read consecutively all the dramas the collection contains; and it will not make much difference at which chronological end he begins, for some persons find the climax of drama in Shakespeare, but others in the Greek tragedies.

The anthology of English poetry is one of the most important parts of the collection, in respect to its function of providing reading competent to impart liberal culture to a devoted reader; but those volumes should not be read in course, but rather by authors, and a little at a time. The poems of John Milton and Robert Burns are given in full; because the works of these two very unlike poets contain social, religious, and governmental teachings of vital concern for modern democracies. Milton was the great poet of civil and religious liberty, Puritanism, and the English Commonwealth, and Burns was the great poet of democracy. The two together cover the fundamental principles of free government, education, and democratic social structure, and will serve as guides to much good reading on those subjects provided in the collection. The poetry contained in The Harvard Classics from Homer to Tennyson will by itself give any appreciative reader a vivid conception of the permanent, elemental sentiments and passions of mankind, and of the gradually developed ethical means of purifying those sentiments and controlling those passions.

In order to make the best use of The Harvard Classics it will be desirable for the young reader to reread those volumes or passages

which he finds most interesting, and to commit to memory many of the pieces of poetry which stir or uplift him. It is a source of exquisite and enduring delight to have one's mind stored with many melodious expressions of high thoughts and beautiful imagery.

I hope that many readers who are obliged to give eight or ten hours a day to the labors through which they earn their livelihood will use The Harvard Classics, and particularly young men and women whose early education was cut short, and who must therefore reach the standing of a cultivated man or woman through the pleasurable devotion of a few minutes a day through many years to the reading of good literature.

The main function of the collection should be to develop and foster in many thousands of people a taste for serious reading of the highest quality, outside of The Harvard Classics as well as within them.

It remains to describe the manner in which The Harvard Classics have been made up. I had more than once stated in public that in my opinion a five-foot shelf would hold books enough to give in the course of years a good substitute for a liberal education in youth to any one who would read them with devotion, even if he could spare but fifteen minutes a day for reading. Rather more than a year ago the firm of P. F. Collier & Son proposed that I undertake to make a selection of fifty volumes, containing from four hundred to four hundred and fifty pages each, which would approximately fill my five-foot shelf, and be well adapted to accomplish the educational object I had in mind.

I was invited to take the entire responsibility of making the selection, and was to be provided with a competent assistant of my own choice. In February, 1909, I accepted the proposal of the publishers, and secured the services of Dr. William A. Neilson, Professor of English in Harvard University, as my assistant. I decided what should be included, and what should be excluded. Professor Neilson wrote all the introductions and notes, made the choice among different editions of the same work, and offered many suggestions concerning available material. It also fell to him to make all the computations needed to decide the question whether a work desired was too long to be included. The most arduous part of his work was the

final making up of the composite volumes from available material which had commended itself to us both.

It would have been impossible to perform the task satisfactorily if the treasures of the general library and of the department libraries of Harvard University had not been at our disposal. The range of the topics in the series was so wide, and the number of languages in which the desired books were originally written so great, that the advice of specialists, each in some portion of the field, had frequently to be sought. We obtained much valuable advice of this sort from scholarly friends and neighbors.

We are under obligations to the following Harvard professors and instructors, whose advice we obtained on questions connected with their several specialties:

Crawford Howell Toy, Hancock Professor of Hebrew; George Herbert Palmer, Alford Professor of Natural Religion; William James, Professor of Philosophy; William Morris Davis, Sturgis-Hooper Professor of Geology; Ephraim Emerton, Winn Professor of Ecclesiastical History; Charles Rockwell Lanman, Wales Professor of Sanscrit; Edward Laurens Mark, Hersey Professor of Anatomy; George Foot Moore, Frothingham Professor of the History of Religion; Edward Stevens Sheldon, Professor of Romance, Philology; Horatio Stevens White, Professor of German; Josiah Royce, Professor of the History of Philosophy; Harold Clarence Ernst, Professor of Bacteriology; Herbert Weir Smyth, Eliot Professor of Greek Literature; Frank William Taussig, Henry Lee Professor of Economics; Albert Bushnell Hart, Professor of History; Morris Hicky Morgan, Professor of Classical Philology; Theobald Smith, George Fabyan Professor of Comparative Pathology; Albert Andrew Howard, Pope Professor of Latin; George Lyman Kittredge, Professor of English; Samuel Williston, Weld Professor of Law; Charles Hall Grandgent, Professor of Romance Languages; Hugo Münsterberg, Professor of Psychology; Leo Wiener, Assistant Professor of Slavic Languages and Literatures; Heinrich Conrad Bierwirth, Assistant Professor of German; Theodore William Richards, Professor of Chemistry; George Pierce Baker, Professor of English; James Haughton Woods, Assistant Professor of Philoso-

phy; Irving Babbitt, Assistant Professor of French; Charles Jesse Bullock, Professor of Economics; Edwin Francis Gay, Professor of Economics; Charles Burton Gulick, Professor of Greek; William Zebina Ripley, Professor of Political Economy; Thomas Nixon Carver, David A. Wells Professor of Political Economy; William Guild Howard, Assistant Professor of German; Fred Norris Robinson, Professor of English; Charles H. C. Wright, Assistant Professor of French; William Rosenzweig Arnold, Andover Professor of the Hebrew Language and Literature; John Albrecht Walz, Professor of the German Language and Literature; Jeremiah D. M. Ford, Smith Professor of the French and Spanish Languages; Edward Kennard Rand, Professor of Latin; Oliver M. W. Sprague, Assistant Professor of Banking and Finance; Jay Backus Woodworth, Assistant Professor of Geology; George Henry Chase, Assistant Professor of Classical Archæology; William Scott Ferguson, Assistant Professor of History; Roger Bigelow Merriman, Assistant Professor of History; Ralph Barton Perry, Assistant Professor of Philosophy; Louis Allard, Instructor in French; Harold de Wolf Fuller, Instructor in Comparative Literature; Lawrence Joseph Henderson, Assistant Professor of Biological Chemistry; F. W. C. Hersey, Instructor in English; F. W. C. Lieder, Instructor in German; C. R. Post, Instructor in Romance Languages; R. W. Pettengill, Instructor in German; H. W. L. Dana, Assistant in English.

Many other scholars answered specific questions which we laid before them, among whom should be mentioned:

Jefferson Butler Fletcher, Professor of Comparative Literature, Columbia University; A. A. Young, Professor of Economics, Leland Stanford Jr. University; G. R. Noyes, Assistant Professor of Slavic, University of California; Lucien Foulet, Professor of French, University of California; Francis B. Gummere, Professor of English, Haverford College; Curtis Hidden Page, Professor of English Literature, Northwestern University; William Draper Lewis, Dean of the Law Department, University of Pennsylvania; James Ford Rhodes, LL.D. (Harvard), Historian; Henry Pickering Walcott, Chairman of the Massachusetts Board of Health; William Belmont Parker, New York; John A. Lester, Ph.D., the Hill School, Pennsylvania; Alfred Dwight Sheffield, Cambridge, Massachusetts.

The staff of the Harvard Library have also given valuable assistance.

In illustrating the volumes with portraits and facsimiles the publishers are under great obligations to the following owners of valuable prints, manuscripts, and autograph letters, who kindly permitted the publishers to use precious objects from their collections:

J. Pierpont Morgan, Esq.; R. H. Dana, Esq.; Wymberley Jones De Renne, Esq.; Harvard University Library; New York Public Library; Boston Public Library; Library of Congress; Library of the Metropolitan Museum of Art; Fogg Art Museum of Harvard University.

The elaborate alphabetical index is intended to give any person who knows the art of using indexes or concordances, or will acquire it in this instance, immediate access to any author or any subject mentioned in the entire collection, and indeed to any passage in the fifty volumes to which the inquirer has a good clue. This full index should make The Harvard Classics convenient books of reference.

March 10, 1910

Charles W. Eliot

THE EDITOR'S
SECOND INTRODUCTION

IN seven years The Harvard Classics have demonstrated their fitness for the special work they were intended to do. They were to provide from famous literature, ancient and modern, an ample record of "the stream of the world's thought"; so that a careful reader of the collection might in the course of years attain the standing of a cultivated man or woman, making up through this long course of reading any deficiencies which might have existed in the early education of the reader. I hoped, too, that in spite of the serious character of the entire collection, an interested and patient reader would gain from the collection much enjoyment and a new power to enjoy.

The experience of seven years has proved that the sale of The Harvard Classics has been large and, on the whole, increasing in amount.

Most owners of the set select occasional reading matter from it; but some have read the fifty volumes through, and a few have read the entire set through twice. I have been surprised to see how often I turn to the collection to enjoy pieces of permanent literature, in contrast with the mass of ephemeral reading matter which I am obliged to go through. Many people might use it in this way to advantage. It has also turned out that the collection, through its excellent index, has value as a book of reference for the general reader, and can be especially helpful to teachers, journalists, and authors.

In the original fifty volumes, for reasons which have turned out not to be of permanent effect, fiction in the modern sense was only slightly represented. To-day a supplement of twenty volumes of modern fiction—The Harvard Classics Shelf of Fiction—provides an ample representation of that new force in the world which the modern historical romance, the novel, and the short story exert. With this supplement The Harvard Classics may fairly be said to provide a permanent record in high literary form of the powers and achievements of "man thinking" down to the end of the nineteenth century, sufficiently comprehensive to illustrate well the chief powers and achievements of the race.

The last half of the nineteenth century and the opening of the twen-

tieth show a strong tendency to discard the study of the Greek and Latin languages as an indispensable part of American secondary and higher education. This study is to be replaced in part by the study of modern languages, which have many uses in the literary, scientific, and business life of to-day. It is the confident belief of the educational reformers that young people brought up in this new way need not lose the substantial values of ancient thought; because they can get them through translations. The Harvard Classics contain six and a half volumes of choice material for this purpose. The collection contains also three volumes and two half volumes of famous writings belonging to the Middle Ages, writings, which can only be made known to the present generations through translations. The reader who makes himself familiar with these ten volumes and a half, with the Confessions of St. Augustine, and with the two volumes of Sacred Writings, may feel sure that he has followed the course of the best thinking of mankind down to the Italian Renaissance.

From these volumes, the thorough reader may learn valuable lessons in comparative literature. He can see how various the contributions of the different languages and epochs have been; and he will inevitably come to the conclusion that striking national differences in this respect ought in the interest of mankind to be perpetuated and developed, and not obliterated, averaged, or harrowed down. The comparative method has in the study of literature a value similar to that it has recently exhibited in the study of art, government, science, and religion.

One may hope that the collection will endure for some decades to come, not only as a monument or milestone, but also as an active force toward the sound mental equipment of American reading people, both the young and the mature.

February 1, 1917

Charles W. Eliot

LIST OF VOLUME NUMBERS

AS DESIGNATED IN THE FOLLOWING INDEXES

Volume I   Benjamin Franklin, John Woolman, William Penn

Volume II   Plato, Epictetus, Marcus Aurelius

Volume III   Bacon, Milton's Prose, Thomas Browne

Volume IV   Complete Poems in English, Milton

Volume V   Essays and English Traits, Emerson

Volume VI   Poems and Songs, Burns

Volume VII The Confessions of St. Augustine, The Imitation
of Christ

Volume VIII Nine Greek Dramas

Volume IX   Letters and Treatises of Cicero and Pliny

Volume X   Wealth of Nations, Adam Smith

Volume XI   Origin of Species, Darwin

Volume XII Plutarch's Lives

Volume XIII Æneid, Virgil

Volume XIV Don Quixote, Part I, Cervantes

Volume XV   Pilgrim's Progress, Donne and Herbert, Walton

Volume XVI The Thousand and One Nights

Volume XVII Folk-Lore and Fable, Æsop, Grimm, Andersen

Volume XVIII Modern English Drama

Volume XIX Faust, Egmont, etc., Goethe, Doctor Faustus,
Marlowe

Volume XX   The Divine Comedy, Dante

Volume XXI I Promessi Sposi, Manzoni

Volume XXII The Odyssey, Homer

Volume XXIII Two Years Before the Mast, Dana

Volume XXIV On the Sublime, French Revolution, etc., Burke

Volume XXV J. S. Mill and Thomas Carlyle

Volume XXVI Continental Drama

Volume XXVII English Essays, Sidney to Macaulay

Volume XXVIII   Essays, English and American
Volume XXIX   Voyage of the Beagle, Darwin
Volume XXX   Faraday, Helmholtz, Kelvin, Newcomb, etc.
Volume XXXI   Autobiography, Cellini
Volume XXXII   Montaigne, Sainte-Beuve, Renan, etc.
Volume XXXIII   Voyages and Travels
Volume XXXIV   Descartes, Voltaire, Rousseau, Hobbes
Volume XXXV   Froissart, Malory, Holinshed
Volume XXXVI   Machiavelli, More, Luther
Volume XXXVII   Locke, Berkeley, Hume
Volume XXXVIII   Harvey, Jenner, Lister, Pasteur
Volume XXXIX   Famous Prefaces
Volume XL   English Poetry, 1
Volume XLI   English Poetry, 2
Volume XLII   English Poetry, 3
Volume XLIII   American Historical Documents
Volume XLIV   Sacred Writings, 1
Volume XLV   Sacred Writings, 2
Volume XLVI   Elizabethan Drama, 1
Volume XLVII   Elizabethan Drama, 2
Volume XLVIII   Thoughts and Minor Works, Pascal
Volume XLIX   Epic and Saga
Volume L   Introduction, Reader's Guide, Indexes

READER'S GUIDE

READER'S GUIDE TO THE HARVARD CLASSICS

THE following lists have been prepared in order to enable the reader more easily to choose and arrange for himself such courses of study as have been suggested in the Introduction. They fall into two classes, the first being selected with respect to subject-matter, as History, Philosophy, or Science; the second with respect to literary form, as the Drama or Essay. Within each group the arrangement is in general chronological, but this has been occasionally departed from when it seemed wise to introduce national or geographical cross-divisions. While most of the volumes can be most profitably read in some chronological or other sequence, many others, such as the collections of English Poetry and of Essays, are equally suited for more desultory browsing.

These lists are not intended to relieve the reader from the use of the General Index, which has purposely been made so ample that it is possible by its intelligent use to track almost any line of interest through the entire set of volumes.

CLASS I

A

THE
HISTORY OF CIVILIZATION

THE following list is by no means confined to works regarded by their authors as history, but includes letters, dramas, novels, and the like, which, by virtue of their character, period, or scene, throw light upon social and intellectual conditions, enriching and making vivid the picture of human progress which is outlined in the more strictly historical narratives.

Professor Freeman's essay, which is suggested as a general introduction to this division, deals in a highly illuminating fashion with the much misunderstood term, "Race"; and by definition and illustration brings out the elements according to which the historian and the anthropologist determine the relationships among the families of mankind.

The oldest civilization with which the ordinary reader has any acquaintance is that of Egypt, and his knowledge of this is usually confined to the dealings of the Egyptians with the Israelites, as narrated in the first books of the Old Testament. The account of Egypt by Herodotus gives a picture of this people from the point of view of a Greek, and is made entertaining by the skill of one of the best story-tellers in the world. A glimpse of life in the days of the patriarchs, in the countries surrounding Palestine, is given in the narrative portions of "The Book of Job," where Job himself is concerned as a powerful and wealthy sheik.

With Homer we come to the civilization which, more than any other, has affected the culture of modern Europe. The wanderings of Odysseus in the "Odyssey" and the account of the fall of Troy in the "Æneid" contain, of course, a large mythical element; but they

leave, nevertheless, a vivid picture which must represent with much essential truth the way of life of the Greeks before the historic period. The two poems by Tennyson named here were suggested by the "Odyssey," and express with remarkable power and beauty the modern poet's conception of the Greek hero's character, and the mood of reaction from the life of effort and suffering. The pieces by Wordsworth and Landor are modern retellings of stories from the same treasure-house from which the Greek tragedians drew the plots of those great dramas which, with the dialogues of Plato, represent the height of intellectual achievement in the ancient world. The five Greek lives by Plutarch give portraits of a group of the most distinguished men of affairs in the same period.

Plutarch again, in his "Lives" of famous Romans, brings before us several of the greatest figures of Republican Rome. His main interest was in personality; but incidentally he gives much information as to the political history of this period. For the years immediately preceding the end of the Republic, the "Letters" of Cicero give a detailed picture of Roman politics from the inside. In spite of the frequent allusions to events and persons now known only to the scholar, the general reader may easily find interest in the similarities between the political methods of antiquity and those of our own day. Dryden's "All for Love" is a thorough making-over of Shakespeare's "Antony and Cleopatra," which in turn is based on Plutarch's "Life of Antony." It is interesting, not only as an excellent example of Dryden's work as a dramatist, but as affording, along with Shakespeare's tragedy, a suggestive study of two of the most picturesque figures of ancient times. From the Alexandrian scenes one can gain an impression of the luxury that was beginning to sap the foundations of the old Roman virtue.

Pliny's "Letters" picture the life of a cultivated Roman under the Empire. Among them, special interest attaches to that giving a graphic account of the eruption of Vesuvius which destroyed Pompeii, and in which the elder Pliny perished, and to those in which Pliny as proconsul consults with the Emperor Trajan about the policy of persecuting the early Christians. The story of the "Æneid" does not deal with this period; but its patriotic purpose makes it important in judging the spirit of the times. Tennyson's tribute to

Virgil is a superb appreciation of the literary quality of the Roman writer, with whom the Englishman had many points of kinship. In the writings of the Emperor Marcus Aurelius and the slave Epictetus, the moral philosophy of paganism reaches its highest level.

The condition of our Teutonic ancestors during the period of Roman supremacy is admirably described by the historian Tacitus in his account of Germany. The description is external, but well-informed, and is the work of an acute and highly trained observer of society and politics. More intimate are the poems that have come down from the early period of Germanic culture, represented here by the Old English "Beowulf," and the Icelandic "Song of the Volsungs." These stories deal with incidents and personages whose historic bases belong to continental Europe, though the earliest extant literary poems of both happen to be insular. "Beowulf" is the more circumstantial as a picture of life and manners; the Volsung story in its various versions, through the "Nibelungenlied" down to Wagner's operas, has made a more profound appeal to the imagination. The splendid though grotesque specimen of Irish saga-writing given in "The Destruction of Dá Derga's Hostel" belongs to nearly the same period. In the case of all three, the material represents a stage of culture considerably earlier than the date of writing, and still essentially pagan.

The books from the New Testament are selected to give the story of the founding of Christianity; St. Augustine's "Confessions" exhibit the development, after a few centuries, of Christian doctrine, Christian standards of conduct, and Christian ways of thinking; while the Hymns of the Early Church, East and West, represent the lyrical expression of the devotional feeling of the young religion.

While Christianity was gradually overcoming the paganism of Europe, Mohammed appeared in Arabia; and from the chapters of the "Koran," which he claimed to have received by inspiration, we can form an idea of the teaching which, with the aid of the sword, so rapidly conquered the East. "The Arabian Nights" are Mohammedan in background, the multiplicity of angels and genii which the

Prophet admitted into his system playing a large part in the mechanism of the tales. The representation of the social life of the East is, however, more important than the religious element in these. Omar Khayyám is the free-thinking philosopher in a Mohammedan society, and his quatrains are given here in the free paraphrase of Fitzgerald, a work which ranks higher as an original poem than as an exact translation.

The Middle Ages denotes a period with somewhat vague boundaries; and some of the books already touched on might well be placed within it. Here it includes representative literary products of Western Europe from the time of Charlemagne to the middle of the fifteenth century. "The Song of Roland" begins, on a slight historical foundation, the great structure of French epic, and is itself a simple and vigorous celebration of heroic loyalty. In the passages from the Norse "Saga of Eric the Red" which describes the discovery of America by Icelanders about 1000 A. D., we get a glimpse of the hardy life of the Vikings. In "The Divine Comedy" Dante summed up the essential characteristics of the spiritual and intellectual life of the Middle Ages, and by his emotional intensity and the extraordinary distinctness of his imaginative vision gave his result an artistic preeminence that makes it the supreme creation of the epoch.

The pageantry and pomp of the military and court life of this age are seen at their best in the pages of Froissart; and in Marlowe's "Edward the Second" a dramatic genius of the next period interprets a typical tragedy of the medieval contest between king and nobles. Drayton, Marlowe's contemporary, celebrates, in one of our greatest war-songs, the victory of Agincourt. In contrast with these pictures of the more exciting sides of medieval life is the exquisite series of portraits of typical English men and women which give Chaucer's "Prologue" its unique place among the works, literary and historical, of the time.

Malory, Tennyson, and Morris deal with parts of the great Arthurian legend, the most wide-spread and characteristic of the themes which entranced the imagination of the Middle Ages, and one which continues to attract the modern writer. Romantic in tone,

historical in incident, Rossetti's poem on the death of James I. of Scots is one of the most successful modern attempts to render a medieval theme in ballad form; yet its essential literary quality will be apparent at once when it is compared with the popular tone of the genuine traditional ballads.

Our list of the productions of the Renaissance naturally begins with Italy, the country in which the great revival of interest in pagan antiquity first showed itself, and from which came in large measure the impulse to throw off the traditional bonds that had fettered the human spirit in the Middle Ages, and to seek a fuller scope for individual development. Machiavelli and Cellini represent respectively the political and the artistic sides of the Italy of this period; and the impression to be derived from them may be made more distinct by Browning's pictures of the scholar, the painter, and the worldly ecclesiastic, and by Webster's and Shelley's dramas, with their lurid light on the passion and crime which reigned in much of the courtly life of the time. A pleasing contrast is afforded by Roper's Life of the saintly Sir Thomas More, and by More's own "Utopia," with its vision of a perfect society. Later in the sixteenth century came the struggle of Spain to subjugate the Netherlands, an incident of which forms the plot of Goethe's "Egmont." Sir Walter Raleigh, compiling in his prison his vast "History of the World," prefixed to it a long preface which gives us a most interesting conception of the attitude of an Englishman who had lived and thought not only upon the history of past times, but upon the whole problem of man's relation to God and the universe. About the same time, in Spain, the great novelist, Cervantes, was showing in his masterpiece how quickly the world was passing from under the domination of the chivalrous ideals of the previous age.

So far we have been enumerating documents representative of the secular Renaissance. But a religious revolution had also taken place, and in the works of Luther, of Calvin, and of Knox, we have a statement in the words of the leaders themselves of the fundamental principles of the Protestant Reformation.

In Science also a new beginning had been made. In the "Journeys" of Ambroise Paré we have, incidentally, a picture of the armies of

the sixteenth century in the field, and also, of more importance to posterity, the beginnings of a new and more humane surgery. Copernicus introduced his revolutionary theory by which the sun took the place of the earth as the center of our system, and Columbus, Vespucci, and the great English navigators opened up the Western world and circumnavigated the globe.

In England itself this exploration of the West brought on the conflict with Spain celebrated with fiery patriotism in the poems by Drayton, Macaulay, and Tennyson. How Englishmen lived at home is told in intimate detail in Harrison's "Description," and more dramatically represented by Dekker, Jonson, and Beaumont; while in Keats's lines we have a later poet harking back to those literary triumphs which are perhaps the most permanent of the achievements of the "spacious times of great Elizabeth."

In the seventeenth century we find ourselves in what may be regarded as modern times, though the picture of the plague in Manzoni's great novel still suggests a period far remote from modern science. In the "Areopagitica," however, Milton is arguing for that freedom of the press which is a very living question in many modern states; and in the poems of Marvell and Scott we have echoes of the struggle for constitutional liberty through which modern Britain came into existence. Voltaire's "Letters" reflect not only the impressions derived by an acute Frenchman from a visit to England, but describe many important phases of the life and thought of the eighteenth century. Burke's "Reflections" recall the excesses through which some of the things which Voltaire envied the English were achieved by France; and Goethe in his exquisite idyl, "Hermann and Dorothea," lets us hear the echoes of the great Revolution in the quiet life of a German village. In Byron's famous lyric we have a lament over the spirit of liberty not yet reawakened in Greece. Throughout all these later pieces there appear, more or less distinctly, evidences of the gradual spread over the world of the struggle for freedom and equality.

Of this struggle in America the records collected in the "American Historical Documents" and the other works here enumerated need no interpretation.

Subject and Author	Vol.	Page
Race and Language:		
Edward Augustus Freeman	28	227
Ancient Egypt:		
Herodotus, Egypt	33	7
The East in Patriarchal Times:		
The Book of Job	44	71
Ancient Greece: *Legendary*		
Homer, the Odyssey	22	9
Dramas of Æschylus	8	7
Sophocles	8	209
Euripides	8	303
Fall of Troy, Virgil's Æneid, Book II	13	100
Tennyson, Ulysses	42	977
The Lotos-Eaters	42	993
Landor, Death of Artemidora	41	902
Iphigeneia	41	903
Wordsworth, Laodamia	41	662
Ancient Greece: *Historic*		
Plato, The Apology of Socrates	2	5
Plutarch, Life of Pericles	12	35
Life of Themistocles	12	5
Life of Aristides	12	78
Life of Alcibiades	12	106
Life of Demosthenes	12	191
Ancient Rome: *Republican*		
Plutarch, Life of Coriolanus	12	147
Life of Cicero	12	218
Cicero, Treatises and Letters	9	9
Plutarch, Life of Cæsar	12	264
Life of Antony	12	322
Dryden, All for Love	18	23
Ancient Rome: *Imperial*		
Pliny the Younger, Letters	9	187
Virgil, Æneid	13	73
Tennyson, To Virgil	42	1014
Marcus Aurelius, Meditations	2	193
Epictetus, Golden Thoughts	2	117

SUBJECT AND AUTHOR	VOL.	PAGE
GERMANIC PEOPLES IN PRIMITIVE TIMES:		
Tacitus, Germany	33	93
Song of the Volsungs	49	257
Beowulf	49	5
IRELAND IN PRIMITIVE TIMES:		
Destruction of Dá Derga's Hostel	49	199
THE EARLY CHRISTIAN CHURCH:		
The Gospel according to Luke	44	353
The Acts of the Apostles	44	423
The Epistles to the Corinthians	45	491
St. Augustine, Confessions	7	5
Hymns of the Greek Church	45	541
Hymns of the Latin Church	45	546
THE MAHOMMEDAN EAST:		
Koran	45	879
The Arabian Nights	16	15
Rubaiyat of Omar Khayyám	41	943
THE MIDDLE AGES:		
The Song of Roland	49	95
Voyages to Vinland	43	5
Dante, The Divine Comedy	20	5
Marlowe, Edward the Second	46	7
Froissart, Chronicles	35	7
Chaucer, Prologue to Canterbury Tales	40	11
Drayton, Agincourt	40	222
Malory, The Holy Grail	35	105
Tennyson, Morte d'Arthur	42	986
Galahad	42	1002
William Morris, Defence of Guenevere	42	1183
Rossetti, The King's Tragedy	42	1153
A Gest of Robyn Hode	40	128
Traditional Ballads, especially	40	51
The Battle of Otterburn	40	88
Chevy Chase	40	93
Johnie Armstrong	40	101
Kinmont Willie	40	108
THE RENAISSANCE:		
Machiavelli, The Prince	36	7

Subject and Author	Vol.	Page

THE RENAISSANCE:

Macaulay, Machiavelli	27	363
Benvenuto Cellini, Autobiography	31	5
Browning, A Grammarian's Funeral	42	1083
Andrea del Sarto	42	1087
The Bishop Orders his Tomb	42	1075
Webster, The Duchess of Malfi	47	755
Shelley, The Cenci	18	281
Sir Thomas More, Utopia	36	135
Roper, Life of Sir T. More	36	89
Goethe, Egmont	19	253
Raleigh, Preface to History of the World	39	66
Cervantes, Don Quixote	14	17
Luther, Ninety-five Theses	36	251
Address to the German Nobility	36	263
Concerning Christian Liberty	36	336
Calvin, Dedication of the Institutes	39	27
Knox, Preface to History of the Reformation in Scotland	39	58
Paré, Journeys in Diverse Places	38	9
Copernicus, Dedication of Revolutions of Heavenly Bodies	39	52
Columbus, Letter Announcing Discovery of America	43	21
Amerigo Vespucci, Account of his First Voyage	43	28
Cabot, Discovery of North America	43	45
Sir H. Gilbert's Voyage to Newfoundland	33	263
Sir Francis Drake Revived	33	129
Drake's Famous Voyage Round the World	33	199
Drake's Great Armada	33	229
Raleigh, Discovery of Guiana	33	311
Drayton, To the Virginian Voyage	40	226
Macaulay, The Armada	41	915
Tennyson, The Revenge	42	1007
Harrison, Elizabethan England	35	217
Dekker, The Shoemaker's Holiday	47	469
Jonson, The Alchemist	47	543
Beaumont, Letter to Ben Jonson	40	319
Keats, The Mermaid Tavern	41	874

MODERN EUROPE:

Manzoni, I Promessi Sposi	21	7
Milton, Areopagitica	3	189
Marvell, Horatian Ode upon Cromwell's Return	40	372

Subject and Author	Vol.	Page
MODERN EUROPE:		
Scott, Here's a Health to King Charles	41	754
Bonny Dundee	41	752
Voltaire, Letters on the English	34	65
Burke, Reflections on the French Revolution	24	143
Goethe, Hermann and Dorothea	19	337
Byron, The Isles of Greece	41	812

(For the history of recent European thought, see under headings, "Science," "Religion and Philosophy," "Politics," "Education," and the various literary types.)

AMERICA:		
First Charter of Virginia	43	49
And the later items in volume of American Historical Documents	43	5
Franklin, Autobiography	1	5
John Woolman, Journal	1	169
Dana, Two Years before the Mast	23	7
Bryant, The Death of Lincoln	42	1223
Emerson, Concord Hymn	42	1245
Boston Hymn	42	1261
Longfellow, Evangeline	42	1300
Paul Revere's Ride	42	1295
Whittier, Randolph of Roanoke	42	1341
Massachusetts to Virginia	42	1344
Barbara Frietchie	42	1362
Holmes, Old Ironsides	42	1366
Lowell, The Present Crisis	42	1370
Ode Recited at Harvard Commemoration	42	1379
Abraham Lincoln	28	429
Whitman, War Poems	42	1402
Pioneers	42	1404
Poems on Death of Lincoln	42	1412

B

RELIGION AND PHILOSOPHY

IN THIS division are represented the sacred writings of the chief religions of the world, and characteristic works of the most important philosophers, so far as these can be expected to be intelligible to readers without technical training in philosophy. Here, as elsewhere in The Harvard Classics, the interest and profit of the reader have been preferred to formal completeness; yet it has been possible to bring together a selection of the attempts of thinkers to solve the problems of life for twenty-five centuries, with surprisingly few important omissions.

In Class I, A, of the Reader's Guide we noted the historical interest of the narrative setting of "The Book of Job." The speeches themselves show the Hebrew mind wrestling with the problem of reconciling the justice of God with the misfortunes of the righteous. "Ecclesiastes" consists mainly of a collection of pungent and, for the most part, pessimistic comments on life, interspersed with passages of a more inspiring nature, which may be due to a different author. Both books are marvels of literary beauty. "The Psalms" gave utterance to the religious emotions of the people of Israel through many generations, and have appealed to the devout of races and periods far beyond the limits of their origin.

Plato is at once a philosopher and a great man of letters; and the three dialogues given here not only present some of the main ideas about conduct and the future world which he received from Socrates or developed himself, but also draw a distinct and attractive portrait of his master during the closing scenes of his life. The plays of the Greek tragedians, though ostensibly dramatic entertainments, deal profoundly and impressively with some of the vital questions of religion, as these presented themselves to the Greek mind.

In Marcus Aurelius and Epictetus we have the loftiest expression

of the Stoic doctrine in its application to the conduct of life; and in the treatises of Cicero the working philosophy of a great lawyer and politician.

The "Sayings" of Confucius, like these Roman writings, are ethical rather than religious; and while to the Western mind they appear curiously concerned with ceremonial, they still appeal to us through their note of aspiration toward a lofty and disinterested scheme of life. Equally remote in their religious and philosophical background are the examples of Hindu and Buddhist teaching, but here again there is much that is inspiring in the moral ideals.

In the previous section, "The Gospel of Luke," "The Acts of the Apostles," and "The Epistles to the Corinthians" were regarded as giving the history of the founding of the Christian Church. Here they should be read as giving a statement of its principles as laid down by its Founder and His immediate followers. Its development after four centuries is shown in the "Confessions" of one of the greatest of the Fathers; and the height of medieval devoutness is beautifully exhibited in "The Imitation of Christ," ascribed to Thomas à Kempis, one of the most widely circulated books in the history of literature. The Hymns of the Early Churches bring out those features of Christian belief which obtained prominence in public worship.

Mohammedanism, with its curious borrowings from Hebrew and Christian scripture and tradition, is more interesting as the religion of many millions of people than as a source of spiritual inspiration. An interesting comparison may be made between Omar Khayyám in his relation to Mohammedanism and the author of "Ecclesiastes" in his relation to Judaism.

With the Reformation opens a new chapter in the history of religion, and the figures of Luther, Calvin, and Knox appropriately represent militant Protestantism in Germany, Switzerland, and Scotland. Raleigh is a Protestant layman, a man of action rather than a theologian or philosopher, yet his "Preface" is a remarkably enlightening presentation of the attitude of a detached thinker at the beginning of the seventeenth century. His poems, with those of Southwell, Habington, Rowlands, Herbert, Donne, Quarles, Vaughan, Crashaw, Drummond, Wotton, Watts, Addison, and Christopher

Smart, and the collection of modern hymns, still further express, with varieties of emphasis and shade of opinion, the more popular aspects of modern Christianity. In Walton's "Lives" of George Herbert and John Donne, Christian ideals are exhibited in the history of two men of strongly marked character and lofty spirituality. Sir Thomas Browne was a member of the Church of England and a physician, and the splendid prose of his "Religio Medici" conveys a quaint mixture of orthodoxy and independent thought. "The Pilgrim's Progress" is the great popular presentation of Puritan theology in imaginative form; and this theology is again the background of the great religious lyrics and epics of John Milton.

Roman Catholic thought on religion and life is brilliantly represented in the writings of Pascal, one of the most acute minds and most intensely religious spirits of his age. The "Thoughts," collected and arranged after his death, suffer from lack of sequence; but their fragmentary nature cannot disguise from the careful reader the astounding keenness of the intellect behind them.

In the "Fruits of Solitude" of William Penn, and in John Woolman's "Journal," we have a representation of the views and ideals of the Quakers, who contributed so important a stream of spiritual influence to the Colonial life of America.

Modern philosophy is often said to begin with Bacon, and, though the fresh attack upon the problems of the universe made in the seventeenth century can not be credited to any one person, Bacon as much as any has a right to be regarded as the herald of the new era. The prefatory documents listed here indicate not only the nature and scope of his intellectual ambitions, but present in considerable detail his program for the conquest of nature and his "new instrument" for the advancement of science. The "Essays" deal with a thousand points of practical philosophy; and "The New Atlantis" outlines his view of a model state and foreshadows the modern research university.

For philosophy in its more technical sense Descartes is more important than Bacon, and his influence on succeeding thought is more clearly traceable. Hobbes, Locke, Berkeley, and Hume carried on the quest for philosophical truth in England, and were able to express their views in language that is still intelligible to the ordi-

nary man. Pope, in his "Essay on Man," put into polished and elegant verse, the more obvious principles of a group of thinkers of his day; but the ideas are more memorable on account of their quotable form than their profundity or subtlety.

Voltaire, writing on many aspects of English life, includes in his "Letters" a condensed account of the philosophy of Locke and the investigations of Newton. Rousseau in his "Discourse," one of the earliest of his writings, expounds the fundamentals of that social philosophy which he expanded later in the "Social Contract" and elsewhere, and which had so important a place among the influences leading up to the French Revolution. Lessing, clinging much closer to essential Christianity than Voltaire or Rousseau, elaborates in his "Education of the Human Race" the views he upheld in opposition to the less liberal theologians of Protestant Germany.

With Kant and his successors philosophy becomes more a professional subject, and with an increase in depth and subtlety it loses in breadth of appeal to the world at large. Yet the treatises mentioned in this list will yield to the reader who cares to apply his mind an idea of a view of ethics of immense possibilities of influence over his thought and conduct.

A large part of the remaining titles are of poems whose philosophical bearing it is scarcely necessary to point out. More and more during the last hundred years poetry has been made the medium of serious thought on the problems of life; and if one wishes to learn what earnest and cultivated people have thought on such matters in our day and that of our fathers, as much is to be gained from the poets as from the professional metaphysicians or moralists. In Carlyle and Emerson we have two writers who can not be regarded as systematic philosophers, and who yet have been among the most influential of modern thinkers. Mill has a more definite place in the history of philosophy; but in his fascinating account of his own development, and in his essay "On Liberty," we need have no fear of technical jargon, and may find a clear picture of a mind finely representative of English thought in the middle of the nineteenth century, and an abundance of ideas capable of application to the problems of our own day.

	Vol.	Page
SUBJECT AND AUTHOR		
HEBREW: The Book of Job	44	71
Ecclesiastes	44	335
The Psalms	44	145
GREEK: Plato, Apology of Socrates	2	5
Phædo	2	45
Crito	2	31
The Greek Drama: Æschylus, Sophocles, Euripides	8	7
ROMAN: Marcus Aurelius, Meditations	2	193
Epictetus, Golden Thoughts	2	117
Cicero, On Friendship	9	9
On Old Age	9	45
CHINESE: Confucius, Analects or Sayings	44	5
HINDU: Bhagavad-Gîtâ, or Song Celestial	45	785
Buddhist Writings	45	577
CHRISTIAN: *Primitive and Medieval*		
The Gospel of Luke	44	353
The Acts of the Apostles	44	423
The Epistles to the Corinthians	45	491
St. Augustine, Confessions	7	5
The Imitation of Christ	7	205
Hymns of the Early Churches	45	535
MOHAMMEDAN: The Koran	45	879
Rubaiyat of Omar Khayyám	41	943
CHRISTIAN: *Modern*		
Luther, Ninety-five Theses	36	251
Address to the German Nobility	36	263
Concerning Christian Liberty	36	336
Calvin, Dedication of the Institutes of the Christian Religion	39	27
Knox, Preface to History of the Reformation in Scotland	39	58
Raleigh, Preface to History of the World	39	66
Poems	40	203
Southwell, The Burning Babe	40	218
Habington, Nox Nocti	40	252

Subject and Author	Vol.	Page

Christian: *Modern*

Rowlands, Our Blessed Lady's Lullaby 40   256
Walton, Life of George Herbert 15   373
Herbert, Poems 40   341
Walton, Life of John Donne 15   323
Donne, Hymn to God the Father 40   304
Quarles, Poems 40   341
Vaughan, Poems 40   346
Crashaw, Saint Teresa 40   363
Drummond, St. John Baptist 40   326
Wotton, Character of a Happy Life 40   288
Sir Thomas Browne, Religio Medici 3   253
Bunyan, The Pilgrim's Progress 15   13
Milton, Ode on the Nativity 4   7
    Ode on the Passion 4   23
    Paradise Lost 4   87
    Paradise Regained 4   359
Pascal, Thoughts 48   9
    Minor Works 48   365
Penn, Fruits of Solitude 1   321
Watts, True Greatness 40   398
Addison, Hymn 40   400
Smart, Song to David 41   484
Woolman, Journal 1   169
Hymns of the Modern Churches 45   557

Modern Philosophers:

Bacon, Prœmium, Epistle Dedicatory, Preface and
    Plan of the Instauratio Magna 39   116
    Preface to the Novum Organum 39   143
    Essays 3   7
    The New Atlantis 3   145
Descartes, Discourse on Method 34   5
Hobbes, On Man (Bk. I of the Leviathan) . . . 34   311
Locke, Some Thoughts on Education 37   9
Berkeley, Three Dialogues 37   189
Pope, Essay on Man 40   406
Voltaire, Letters on the English 34   65
Rousseau, Discourse on the Causes of Inequality . . 34   165
Lessing, Education of the Human Race 32   185
Hume, Enquiry concerning Human Understanding . 37   289
Kant, Fundamental Principles of the Metaphysic of
    Morals 32   305

SUBJECT AND AUTHOR   VOL. PAGE

MODERN PHILOSOPHERS:
Kant, Transition from Popular Moral Philosophy to the
   Metaphysic of Morals 32   318
Wordsworth, Ode on Intimations of Immortality . . 41   595
          Ode to Duty 41   649
          Lines Written above Tintern Abbey . 41   635
          Character of the Happy Warrior . . 41   656
Shelley, Adonais 41   856
     Written among the Euganean Hills . . . 41   835
Mill, Autobiography 25   7
    On Liberty 25   195
Carlyle, Characteristics 25   319
Emerson, Essays 5   5
    Poems 42   1241
Tennyson, The Higher Pantheism 42   1004
    Flower in the Crannied Wall 42   1005
    Wages 42   1005
    Maud 42   1015
    Crossing the Bar 42   1057
Thackeray, The End of the Play 42   1058
Browning, Prospice 42   1065
    Abt Vogler 42   1100
    Rabbi Ben Ezra 42   1103
    Epilogue 42   1109
Emily Brontë, Last Lines 42   1110
     The Old Stoic 42   1111
Clough, Poems 42   1119
Arnold, Rugby Chapel 42   1130
    Dover Beach 42   1137
    The Better Part 42   1138
    The Last Word 42   1139
Henley, Invictus 42   1210
Stevenson, The Celestial Surgeon 42   1212
Bryant, Thanatopsis 42   1213
Whittier, The Eternal Goodness 42   1338
Holmes, The Chambered Nautilus 42   1365
Lanier, How Love Looked for Hell 42   1398
Whitman, One's-Self I Sing 42   1402

C

EDUCATION

THE earlier discussions on education differ from most modern writings on the subject in one important respect: the author had his eye on the single youth, the son of a family of birth and wealth, who was to be educated alone; while the educational theorist of to-day, even when he is not dealing with popular elementary education, is usually concerned with institutions for training pupils in large groups. This distinction has inevitably a profound effect upon the nature of the principles laid down.

Montaigne, Locke, and Milton are all examples of this earlier kind of discussion. It is assumed that all resources are at command, and the only questions to be settled are the comparative value of subjects and the best order and method of learning. On these points the opinions of these men are still valuable; and all three, but especially Locke, give incidentally much information on the manners and state of culture of their times.

The five "Essays" by Bacon named here do not form an attempt to construct a scheme of education, but deal suggestively with single points of importance in the training of children. "The New Atlantis" describes in "Solomon's House" an elaborate institution for advancing knowledge, which anticipates in many respects the departments for research in modern universities.

Swift's so called "Treatise" deals lightly with social rather than intellectual culture; and the chapter on the "Education of Women" by his contemporary, Defoe, shows how long it is since some views which we are apt to regard as entirely modern have been put forward.

Lessing's treatise is more philosophical than educational in the ordinary sense, being rather an interpretation of history as the record of the development of the race than a plan for the future. The

letters in which Schiller discussed the "Æsthetic Education of Man" contain the essence of his views on art.

It is characteristic of American democracy that the lectures by Channing should be on the elevation of the laboring classes, and should take up an educational problem at the end of the social scale most remote from that where Montaigne and Locke found their interest.

Mill's "Autobiography" is an account of great interest of the education of a remarkable son by a remarkable father; and though containing much that has no direct bearing upon the training of the average child, it is valuable as showing what extraordinary results can be achieved under exceptional conditions.

Newman's discussion of "The Idea of a University" deals with the ultimate aims of university education, and some of the more important considerations affecting the means of attaining them. Carlyle's address, delivered at Edinburgh while he was Lord Rector of his own University, is a sort of summary of an old man's wisdom on questions of a student's use of his time and the choice of his reading. Ruskin's well-known lectures, "Sesame and Lilies," deal in very different, but equally characteristic fashion with similar topics.

In "Science and Culture," Huxley presents from the point of view of the scientist his side of the standing question of modern education: the comparative value of science and the classics as a means of culture.

Subject and Author	Vol.	Page
Montaigne, Of the Institution and Education of Children	32	29
Bacon, Of Travel	3	46
Of Nature in Men	3	96
Of Custom and Education	3	98
Of Studies	3	122
Of Parents and Children	3	19
The New Atlantis	3	145
Milton, Tractate on Education	3	235
Locke, Some Thoughts on Education	37	9
Swift, Treatise on Good Manners and Good Breeding	27	99
Defoe, Education of Women	27	148
Lessing, On the Education of the Human Race	32	185
Schiller, Letters upon the Æsthetic Education of Man	32	209

D

SCIENCE

THE writings of ancient times on physical science are now mainly of historical and curious interest; but from Greek times have come down these two interesting formulas to which the name of Hippocrates is attached, which show how loftily a conception the ancient physician held of his function, and which form the basis of the professional ethics of the modern doctor.

The army surgeon is a modern official. In the sixteenth century, even an officer who wished medical or surgical attendance had to take his personal doctor with him, or trust to the quacks who swindled the rank and file. Paré was such a personal surgeon to several distinguished generals through many campaigns; and the account of his improvements in the treatment of wounds vies in interest with his description of the battles themselves.

Few single scientific discoveries have influenced the world so profoundly as that which showed that the earth was not the center of the universe. The treatise in which Copernicus put forth the new theory is filled with arguments which are often preposterous, so that for the true explanation of the motions of the heavenly bodies the book is practically useless. But from his "Dedication" we gather something of the spirit of the man who led the way in this momentous reform. The "Principia" of Newton has immeasurably greater scientific value, but the reasoning is highly technical, so that the ordinary reader is glad to get the great physicist's own statement of the purpose and method of the work which first expounded the law of gravitation.

The papers by Harvey and Jenner are landmarks in the history of physiology and medicine, the one explaining for the first time the true theory of the circulation of the blood; the other putting forward the method of vaccination which has relieved the world of the scourge of smallpox.

Faraday was not only a great investigator but also a great teacher, and these two books by him are classical expositions of fundamental laws in physics and chemistry.

Dr. Holmes's paper is an interesting scientific argument, which proved of immense value in saving life; it is also an inspiring instance of the courage of a young scientist in risking professional disaster by attacking the practices and prejudices of his colleagues.

The theories which lie behind Lord Lister's application of the antiseptic principle in surgery are expounded in the fascinating papers in which Pasteur makes the original argument for the germ theory of disease, and founds the science of bacteriology.

In the chapters included in the following list from Sir Charles Lyell's "Principles of Geology," he combats the notion that to explain the present condition of the earth it is necessary to assume a series of great catastrophes. A more comprehensive view of a modern geologist's theory of how the physical world arrived at its present form is given in Geikie's essay on "Geographical Evolution."

The great German physicist, von Helmholtz, is here represented by a lecture on the fundamental principle of the conservation of energy, and one on the theory of glaciers, while his colleague in Britain, Sir William Thomson, Lord Kelvin, expounds the wave theory of light and the movement of the tides.

It was on the voyage of the "Beagle" that Darwin collected the material which suggested to him the great generalization later set forth in "The Origin of Species," and gave currency to a theory of development that has proved to be the most pervasive and influential force in the intellectual progress of modern times.

How enormously modern astronomical investigation has increased our notion of the universe, of which we form so minute a part, is expounded by Newcomb in his essay on "The Extent of the Universe."

Thus in the scientific section of these volumes the reader may gain from the pens of the leaders and discoverers themselves an idea of many of the most important conceptions in the sciences of Medicine, Surgery, Physiology, Biology, Bacteriology, Physics, Chemistry, Geology, and Astronomy.

SUBJECT AND AUTHOR	VOL.	PAGE
The Oath of Hippocrates	38	3
The Law of Hippocrates	38	4
Paré, Journeys in Diverse Places	38	9
Copernicus, Dedication of Revolutions of the Heavenly Bodies	39	52
Harvey, On the Motion of the Heart and Blood of Animals	38	75
Newton, Preface to the Principia	39	150
Jenner, The Three Original Publications on Vaccination against Smallpox	38	145
Faraday, The Forces of Matter	30	7
The Chemical History of a Candle	30	86
Holmes, The Contagiousness of Puerperal Fever	38	223
Lister, On the Antiseptic Principle in the Practice of Surgery	38	257
Pasteur, The Physiological Theory of Fermentation . . .	38	275
The Germ Theory and its Applications to Medicine and Surgery	38	364
On the Extension of the Germ Theory to the Etiology of Certain Common Diseases	38	371
Lyell, Prejudices which have Retarded the Progress of Geology	38	385
Uniformity in the Series of Past Changes in the Animate and Inanimate Worlds	38	398
Von Helmholtz, On the Conservation of Force	30	173
Ice and Glaciers	30	211
Darwin, The Voyage of the Beagle	29	11
The Origin of Species	11	23
Kelvin, The Wave Theory of Light	30	251
The Tides	30	274
Newcomb, The Extent of the Universe	30	311
Geikie, Geographical Evolution	30	325

E

POLITICS

FROM the point of view that "history is past politics," it is evident that such historical documents as those in the "Lives" of Plutarch and the "Letters" of Cicero and Pliny are also of value from the political point of view. Many of the problems of politics change their form rather than their essence from age to age, and in these records of the political struggles and principles of antiquity there are many illuminating parallelisms to the conditions of our own day. Even the contrast to modern democratic ideas of government which the theories of Machiavelli afford is suggestive; and in the institutions of Elizabethan England as described by William Harrison we may often find the germ of practices which persist here to-day.

More's "Utopia" and Bacon's "New Atlantis" have the value belonging to any sketch of ideal conditions drawn up by men of capacity and experience; and, with much that is fantastic, both books still afford considerable practical suggestion for political progress. Those of Bacon's "Essays" which touch political topics contain abundance of acute observations on the conduct of public men, though the advice is sometimes, but not always, more suited to forming politicians than statesmen.

Though dealing with the special subject of unlicensed printing, Milton, in his "Areopagitica," handles with a noble eloquence many of the fundamental questions affecting free government. Defoe's pamphlet treats in ironical strain the situation during a later period in the progress of England towards freedom and equality—in this case, religious equality; while Voltaire, coming from France a few years later, expresses his admiration for English tolerance. Of Rousseau's "Discourse" we have already spoken (I. A).

"The Wealth of Nations" may be regarded as founding the mod-

ern science of political economy; and it remains the greatest general treatise on the subject. The present edition has been relieved of those passages which are out of date and no longer of value.

In Burke's eloquent "Reflections" we get the view taken by an English constitutionalist of the principles of the French Revolution while it was still in progress; and in his "Letter to a Noble Lord" a vivid glimpse of the workings of politics in England at the same period.

Mill's treatise "On Liberty" is a classical argument on the relation of the individual to the state.

The poetry of the nineteenth century contains much political as well as philosophical thinking; and the pieces by Goldsmith, Wordsworth, and Tennyson are favorable examples of the impassioned treatment of these themes in verse.

The interest and importance of the American Documents here collected are obvious; and a careful study of these alone will go far to give a basis for an intelligent understanding of contemporary politics.

Subject and Author	Vol.	Page
Plutarch, Lives of Greeks and Romans	12	5
Cicero, Letters	9	81
Pliny the Younger, Letters to Trajan	9	356
Machiavelli, The Prince	36	7
Macaulay, Machiavelli	27	363
More, Utopia	36	135
Harrison, Elizabethan England	35	217
Bacon, The New Atlantis	3	145
Essays: Of Unity in Religion, Of Great Place, Of Nobility, Of Seditions and Troubles, Of Empire, Of Counsel, Of Delays, Of Cunning, Of Innovations, Of Despatch, Of the True Greatness of Kingdoms and Estates, Of Plantations, Of Ambition, Of Usury, Of Negotiating, Of Followers and Friends, Of Suitors, Of Faction, Of Judicature, Of Vicissitudes of Things	3	7
Milton, Areopagitica	3	189
Defoe, The Shortest Way with Dissenters	27	133
Voltaire, Letters on the English	34	65
Rousseau, Discourse on the Causes of Inequality	34	165

SUBJECT AND AUTHOR	VOL.	PAGE
Smith, The Wealth of Nations	10	9
Burke, Reflections on the French Revolution	24	143
Letter to a Noble Lord	24	381
Goldsmith, The Deserted Village	41	509
Wordsworth, Political Sonnets	41	675
Tennyson, Locksley Hall	42	979
Maud	42	1015
Sydney Smith, Fallacies of Anti-Reformers	27	225
Mill, On Liberty	25	195
Emerson, Politics	5	239
Lowell, Democracy	28	451
The Present Crisis	42	1370
American Historical Documents, especially		
The First Charter of Virginia	43	49
The Mayflower Compact	43	59
The Fundamental Orders of Connecticut	43	60
The Massachusetts Body of Liberties	43	66
Winthrop, Arbitrary Government Described	43	85
The Instrument of Government	43	106
Sir Henry Vane, a Healing Question	43	118
Declaration of Rights	43	147
Declaration of Independence	43	150
Constitution of the United States	43	180
The Federalist, I and II	43	199
Opinion of Chief Justice Marshall	43	208
Washington, First Inaugural Address	43	225
Washington, Farewell Address	43	233
The Monroe Doctrine	43	277
Lincoln, Gettysburg Address	43	415

F

VOYAGES AND TRAVELS

THE story of travel has always held a general fascination; and little is needed to introduce to the reader such a list as follows. Beginning with the account of ancient Egypt by Herodotus, the collection gives the narratives of the early voyages to America of Leif Ericsson, Columbus, Amerigo Vespucci, and Cabot; the campaigns followed by the French surgeon, Ambroise Paré, in the sixteenth century; the voyages, partly for exploration, largely for plunder, of the great seamen of Elizabeth's time, Drake, Gilbert, and Raleigh; and, in striking contrast, John Eliot's "Brief Narrative" of his travels in the attempt to propagate the Gospel among the American Indians. Goldsmith's "Traveller" describes many scenes in eighteenth century Europe; and in Dana's absorbing "Two Years Before the Mast" we have the double interest of a picture of life on a sailing vessel two generations ago, and an admirable account of California as it was under the Spaniards, and before '49.

Darwin's "Voyage of the Beagle," apart from its scientific importance, is a highly interesting and modestly told story of exploration in remote seas. Emerson's "English Traits" is a penetrating description and criticism of England, its people and its institutions, as the American philosopher saw it in the middle of the nineteenth century.

SUBJECT AND AUTHOR	VOL.	PAGE
Herodotus, Egypt	33	7
Voyages to Vinland from Saga of Eric the Red	43	5
Paré, Journeys in Diverse Places	38	9
Columbus, Letter Announcing Discovery of America	43	21
Amerigo Vespucci, Account of his First Voyage	43	28
Cabot, Discovery of North America	43	45
Sir Francis Drake Revived	33	129
Drake's Famous Voyage Round the World	33	199
Drake's Great Armada	33	229

G

CRITICISM OF LITERATURE
AND THE FINE ARTS

WILLIAM CAXTON, the first printer in England, took a much more personal interest in the productions of his press than does the modern publisher. He himself made several of the translations which he printed; and to other books he attached Prologues and Epilogues, which, if not quite literary criticism after the modern manner, are yet interesting indications of the qualities which made the works which Caxton selected for publication the favorite reading of the end of the Middle Ages.

Of the three critical writings selected from the sixteenth century, Montaigne's is a delightful talk on his personal tastes (see essay by Sainte-Beuve below); Sidney defends imaginative literature against the assaults of an extreme Puritan; and Spenser explains to his friend Raleigh the plan and purpose of "The Faerie Queene."

Shakespeare, as is well known, paid no attention to the printing of his plays; and it was left for two of his fellow actors to make the first collected edition of them, seven years after his death. The unique importance of the volume makes the address of its editors to the readers a matter of curious interest. Of more real significance are the opinions, friendly yet candid, which Ben Jonson has left of his great fellow dramatist, and of his patron, Bacon.

But it is with Dryden that we come to the first English critic on a large scale; and in his discussions on Chaucer and on Heroic Poetry we have him, both for style and matter, at his best. Swift's "Advice" is slighter, and, like all his work, displays his ironic temper. Fielding, in a prefatory chapter, defines and expounds his idea of a novel. Dr. Johnson's famous essay on Shakespeare originally formed the Preface to his edition of the plays; and it remains one of the most

important estimates of the genius of our greatest writer. In the "Life of Addison," Johnson was dealing with a subject where his eighteenth century limitations hampered him less, and the result is a delightful piece of appreciative criticism.

So far the criticism in this list has been wholly literary. The next four writers are concerned with æsthetic principles in general, with, perhaps, a special interest in painting and sculpture. Goethe, in this manifesto of a new periodical to be devoted to the Fine Arts, gives impressively his view of the fundamentals of artistic training. Schiller, on a more extensive scale, treats of the cultivation of taste and the nature of the pleasure to be derived from art; while Hume and Burke deal with similar problems from different points of view.

The "Prefaces" of Wordsworth and Hugo express in different but equally characteristic terms the revolt of the romantic poets of England and France respectively against the classical conventions that dominated poetry and the drama. Coleridge discourses in his own profound and often illuminating fashion on the essentials of poetry, as does Shelley in his eloquent and philosophical "Defense." Those who know Shelley only as the most exquisite of lyric poets will find that this essay will increase enormously their respect for his intellectual power. In the essay "On the Tragedies of Shakespeare" Lamb utters some of the most penetrating criticism ever passed upon the tragedy of "King Lear," and presses to an extreme his view of the inferiority of the stage to the study for the enjoyment of Shakespeare.

Thackeray's lecture on Swift is a fine example of the biographical essay, and may be compared with Carlyle's estimate of Scott with interesting results. Both men deal more with character than style, and both care passionately for moral quality.

Walt Whitman's "Preface," like his poems, stands by itself, the outspoken plea for an astounding extension of the limits of form and matter in poetry. His poems in the third volume of "English Poetry" in The Harvard Classics should be read in connection with this "Preface."

Sainte-Beuve is generally placed at the head of European criticism in the nineteenth century; and the two papers here given are good examples of his manner. Renan, one of the most eloquent of mod-

ern writers in any country, discourses on "The Poetry of the Celtic Races" to which he himself belonged. Mazzini, purest of patriots, is represented by a paper which shows his fine power of generalization and of taking large views. An Italian nationalist in feeling, Mazzini was continental in the range of his intellect. Taine's famous "Introduction" expounds his formula for explaining the characteristics of a literature. Whatever objections may be raised to his theory, there is no question of the brilliance of the presentation.

Few critical writings of our own day have influenced the study of poetry so much as this of Matthew Arnold's. It is an excellent example of his style, and exhibits both the strength and the weakness of his critical thinking.

"Sesame and Lilies" consists of two lectures, largely hortatory, but incidentally containing some notable criticism. Bagehot, best known as a writer on finance, appears here as a specimen of a strong non-literary intellect applying itself to the discussion of a literary topic. At the opposite extreme is the paper in which Poe, a master of the technical side of his art, treats of what he regards as its essence. In three essays, Emerson discourses suggestively, if unsystematically, on "The Poet," on "Beauty," and on "Literature." Finally, in Stevenson's essay on "Samuel Pepys," one of the most expert of literary craftsmen of modern times sketches the personality of the writer who wrote the most remarkable "Diary" in English Literature.

Subject and Author	Vol.	Page
Caxton, Prologue and Epilogue to the Histories of Troy	39	5
Epilogue to Dictes and Sayings of the Philosophers	39	9
Prologue to the Golden Legend	39	13
Prologue to Caton	39	15
Epilogue to Æsop	39	17
Proem to Chaucer's Canterbury Tales	39	18
Prologue to Malory's King Arthur	39	20
Prologue to Virgil's Eneydos	39	24
Montaigne, Of Bookes	32	87
Sidney, Defense of Poesy	27	5
Spenser, Prefatory Letter to Sir Walter Raleigh on the Faerie Queene	39	61
Heminge and Condell, Preface to the First Folio Edition of Shakespeare's Plays	39	148
Jonson, On Shakespeare	27	55

SUBJECT AND AUTHOR	VOL.	PAGE
Jonson, On Bacon	27	56
To the Memory of Mr. William Shakespeare	40	301
Dryden, Preface to Fables (On Chaucer)	39	153
Dedication of the Æneis (On Heroic Poetry)	13	5
Swift, Advice to a Young Poet	27	104
Fielding, Preface to Joseph Andrews (On the Comic Epic in Prose)	39	176
Johnson, Preface to Shakespeare	39	208
Life of Addison	27	155
Goethe, Introduction to the Propyläen (On Fine Art)	39	251
Schiller, Letters upon the Æsthetic Education of Man	32	209
Hume, On the Standard of Taste	27	203
Burke, On Taste	24	11
On the Sublime and Beautiful	24	29
Wordsworth, Prefaces to Various Volumes of Poems	39	267
Appendix to Lyrical Ballads	39	292
Essay Supplementary to Preface	39	311
Coleridge, On Poesy or Art	27	255
Lamb, On the Tragedies of Shakespeare	27	299
Shelley, A Defence of Poetry	27	329
Hugo, Preface to Cromwell (On Romanticism)	39	337
Thackeray, Jonathan Swift	28	7
Carlyle, Sir Walter Scott	25	393
Inaugural Address (On Books and Reading)	25	359
Whitman, Preface to Leaves of Grass	39	388
Sainte-Beuve, Montaigne	32	105
What is a Classic?	32	121
Renan, The Poetry of the Celtic Races	32	137
Mazzini, Byron and Goethe	32	377
Taine, Introduction to History of English Literature	39	410
Arnold, The Study of Poetry	28	65
Ruskin, Sesame and Lilies	28	93
Bagehot, John Milton	28	165
Poe, The Poetic Principle	28	371
Emerson, The Poet	5	161
Beauty	5	297
Literature	5	432
Stevenson, Samuel Pepys	28	285

CLASS II

OF the large variety of literary types represented in The Harvard Classics, only a few of the more prominent have been selected for classification here. Others stand already grouped in the volumes: for, example, the three volumes of English Poetry, along with the works of Milton and Burns, contain most of the Lyric Poetry in the collection; and the Prefaces regarded as independent documents, are in one volume. Still others, such as Allegory, Oratory, the Dialogue, occur in the lists made up according to subject matter; and readers interested in these as forms can easily collect them from the Tables of Contents and the General Index.

A

DRAMA

In dramatic literature the palm of supremacy lies between Greece and England, and it is natural that these two countries should be most fully represented here. Both countries at a culminating point in their history expressed themselves in this form, and much of the intellectual and imaginative vitality of the Age of Pericles in Greece and the Age of Elizabeth in England can be apprehended from these dramas. Eight of the most distinguished masterpieces of the other countries of Europe have been added; so that the present list represents not unworthily the best in this form that the world has produced.

These thirty-seven plays exhibit a great variety of dramatic form —classical and romantic tragedy, satirical and romantic comedy, chronicle history, masque, and cantata. No less varied are the themes; from gods to beggars all types of character appear, and every variety of human motive, human effort, and human suffering is shown. No other literary form could present in so few pages so just and so impressive a reflection of the pageant of human life.

Subject and Author	Vol.	Page
GREEK: Æschylus, Prometheus Bound	8	166
Agamemnon	8	7
The Libation-Bearers	8	76
The Furies	8	122
Sophocles, Œdipus the King	8	209
Antigone	8	255
Euripides, Hippolytus	8	303
The Bacchæ	8	368
Aristophanes, The Frogs	8	439
ENGLISH: Marlowe, Doctor Faustus	19	205
Edward the Second	46	7
Shakespeare, Hamlet	46	93
King Lear	46	215
Macbeth	46	321
The Tempest	46	397
Dekker, The Shoemaker's Holiday	47	469
Jonson, The Alchemist	47	543
Beaumont and Fletcher, Philaster	47	667
Webster, The Duchess of Malfi	47	755
Massinger, A New Way to Pay Old Debts	47	859
Milton, Comus	4	44
Samson Agonistes	4	414
Dryden, All for Love	18	23
Sheridan, The School for Scandal	18	115
Goldsmith, She Stoops to Conquer	18	205
Burns, The Jolly Beggars	6	122
Shelley, The Cenci	18	281
Byron, Manfred	18	407
Browning, A Blot in the 'Scutcheon	18	359
SPANISH: Calderon, Life is a Dream	26	7
FRENCH: Corneille, Polyeucte	26	77
Racine, Phædra	26	133
Molière, Tartuffe	26	199
GERMAN: Lessing, Minna von Barnhelm	26	299
Goethe, Faust	19	23
Egmont	19	253
Schiller, William Tell	26	379

B

BIOGRAPHY AND LETTERS

MOST of the titles in this list have already been the subject of comment; those that remain speak for themselves. Here are a number of records of actual human lives, all of them of notable people, chosen either for their representative or for their intrinsic value. Some of these records are by skilled biographers like Plutarch; in other cases, by letters, or confessions, or in set narratives, the story is told by the man himself; still others are summaries and estimates rather than detailed biographies. Perhaps the formal autobiographies are the most interesting and significant of all; and of these the personal revelations of St. Augustine, of Benvenuto Cellini, of Benjamin Franklin, and of John Stuart Mill stand in the first rank.

Subject and Author	Vol.	Page
Plutarch, Life of Themistocles	12	5
Pericles	12	35
Aristides	12	78
Alcibiades	12	106
Demosthenes	12	191
Coriolanus	12	147
Cicero	12	218
Cæsar	12	264
Antony	12	322
Cicero, Letters	9	81
Pliny the Younger, Letters	9	187
St. Augustine, Confessions	7	5
Benvenuto Cellini, Autobiography	31	5
Roper, Life of Sir Thomas More	36	89
Walton, Life of Dr. Donne	15	323
Life of George Herbert	15	373
Johnson, Life of Addison	27	155
Burke, Letter to a Noble Lord	24	381

C

ESSAYS

THERE is almost no limit to the variety of theme which may be treated in the essay, and few rules can be laid down to regulate its form. Montaigne, who may be said to have originated this type of literature, remains one of the greatest masters of it; and in the specimens from his work in the present list one can find the ease and grace and the pleasant flavor of personal intimacy which constitute much of its charm.

A large proportion of these essays deal with books, and of these something has already been said in the section on Criticism. Some, like those of Milton, Swift, Defoe, Newman, and Huxley, fall also under the heading of Education. A few treat of political matters; such are those of Sydney Smith, Mill, and Lowell. Others, such as some of Montaigne's, Ruskin's, Carlyle's, Emerson's, and Stevenson's, deal with matters of conduct, though not in the formal manner of the ethical philosopher. Bacon's "Essays" are concerned with so great a variety of subjects that classification is difficult; but the largest group form a sort of handbook of the principles on which success in public life was achieved in his time. Yet these more severe themes are mingled with others of more charm, where he chats pleasantly on an ideal palace or garden, or on the contriving of courtly entertainments.

Of all prose forms, the essay is that which gives most scope for pure expression of personality. Those in the present list which rank highest as essays do so, not by virtue of the weight of their opinions, or arguments, or information, but by the spontaneity with which the author gives utterance to his mood or fancy. Thus the delightful essay of Cowley "Of Agriculture" is hardly to be recommended as a guide to farming; but as a quarter of an hour of graceful conversation it is charming. Hazlitt, Leigh Hunt, Lamb, De Quincey,

Thoreau, and Stevenson (in "Truth of Intercourse") all exhibit this individual quality, and reveal personalities of different kinds and degrees of attractiveness, but none without a high degree of interest.

SUBJECT AND AUTHOR	VOL.	PAGE
Montaigne, That We Should not Judge of our Happinesse untill after our Death	32	5
That to Philosophise is to Learne how to Die	32	9
Of the Institution and Education of Children	32	29
Of Friendship	32	72
Of Bookes	32	87
Sidney, Defense of Poesy	27	5
Bacon, Essays	3	7
Milton, Tractate on Education	3	235
Cowley, Of Agriculture	27	61
Dryden, Preface to Fables	39	153
Dedication of the Æneis	13	5
Addison, Westminster Abbey	27	78
Steele, The Spectator Club	27	83
Swift, Hints towards an Essay on Conversation	27	91
On Good Manners and Good Breeding	27	99
A Letter of Advice to a Young Poet	27	104
On the Death of Esther Johnson (Stella)	27	122
Defoe, The Shortest Way with Dissenters	27	133
The Education of Women	27	148
Fielding, Preface to Joseph Andrews	39	176
Johnson, Preface to Shakespeare	39	208
Preface to English Dictionary	39	182
Life of Addison	27	155
Hume, On the Standard of Taste	27	203
Burke, On Taste	24	11
Goethe, Introduction to the Propyläen	39	251
Sydney Smith, Fallacies of Anti-Reformers	27	225
Wordsworth, Preface to Various Volumes of Poems	39	267
Appendix to Lyrical Ballads	39	292
Essay Supplementary to Preface	39	311
Coleridge, On Poesy or Art	27	255
Hazlitt, Of Persons One would Wish to have Seen	27	267
Leigh Hunt, Deaths of Little Children	27	285
On the Realities of Imagination	27	289
Lamb, On the Tragedies of Shakspere	27	299
De Quincey, Levana and Our Ladies of Sorrow	27	319
Shelley, A Defence of Poetry	27	329

SUBJECT AND AUTHOR	VOL.	PAGE
Channing, On the Elevation of the Laboring Classes . .	28	311
Hugo, Preface to Cromwell	39	337
Macaulay, Machiavelli	27	363
Sainte-Beuve, Montaigne	32	105
What is a Classic?	32	121
Thackeray, Jonathan Swift	28	7
Renan, The Poetry of the Celtic Races	32	137
Mazzini, Byron and Goethe	32	377
Newman, The Idea of a University	28	31
Arnold, The Study of Poetry	28	65
Ruskin, Sesame and Lilies	28	93
Taine, Introduction to the History of English Literature .	39	410
Bagehot, John Milton	28	165
Poe, The Poetic Principle	28	371
Carlyle, Characteristics	25	319
Sir Walter Scott	25	393
Whitman, Preface to Leaves of Grass	39	388
Emerson, Essays	5	5
English Traits	5	315
Mill, On Liberty	25	195
Huxley, Science and Culture	28	209
Freeman, Race and Language	28	227
Thoreau, Walking	28	395
Lowell, Abraham Lincoln	28	429
Democracy	28	451
Stevenson, Truth of Intercourse	28	277
Samuel Pepys	28	285

D

NARRATIVE POETRY AND PROSE FICTION

IN this section we have the largest proportion of what frankly professes to be the literature of entertainment. All these titles belong to works which are in the first place good stories; and most of them have lived largely by virtue of this quality. They come from all centuries within the historic period, and from all the countries within our range. They deal with war and peace, love and hate, gods and men and animals, angels and demons, historic fact, modern observation, and pure fancy; some mean no more than they seem to—simple tales of the action and suffering of men; others carry mystical significations hidden under the surface.

But, though they may profess no more than a power to entertain, they, in fact, do far more for us. Each of these tales, in proportion to its truth to human nature and the effectiveness with which it is told, helps to make us more fully acquainted with our kind, broadens our sympathies, deepens our insight, serves us, in fact, as a kind of experience obtained at second hand. No less than the most weighty philosophy or the most informing history or science, then, do these stories in prose and poetry deserve their place among the essential instruments of mental and moral culture.

Subject and Author	Vol.	Page
Homer, The Odyssey	22	9
Virgil, The Æneid	13	73
Æsop's Fables	17	11
Beowulf	49	5
The Song of Roland	49	95
The Song of the Volsungs	49	257
The Destruction of Dá Derga's Hostel	49	199
The Arabian Nights	16	15

Subject and Author	Vol.	Page
Dante, The Divine Comedy	20	5
Chaucer, Prologue to the Canterbury Tales	40	11
The Nun's Priest's Tale	40	34
The Gest of Robyn Hode	40	128
Traditional Ballads	40	51
Malory, The Holy Grail	35	105
Cervantes, Don Quixote	14	17
Drayton, Agincourt	40	222
To the Virginian Voyage	40	226
Milton, Paradise Lost	4	87
Paradise Regained	4	359
Bunyan, The Pilgrim's Progress	15	13
Addison, The Vision of Mirza	27	73
Steele, The Spectator Club	27	83
Goethe, Hermann and Dorothea	19	337
Cowper, The Diverting History of John Gilpin	41	546
Burns, Tam o' Shanter	6	388
Manzoni, I Promessi Sposi	21	7
Wordsworth, Michael	41	615
Ruth	41	607
Laodamia	41	662
Coleridge, The Ancient Mariner	41	682
Christabel	41	709
Love	41	704
Scott, Rosabelle	41	748
Lochinvar	41	751
Hogg, Kilmeny	41	756
Byron, The Prisoner of Chillon	41	801
The Destruction of Sennacherib	41	785
Campbell, Lord Ullin's Daughter	41	773
Battle of the Baltic	41	779
Hohenlinden	41	781
Keats, The Eve of St. Agnes	41	883
Landor, The Death of Artemidora	41	902
Iphigeneia	41	903
Grimm, Household Tales	17	47
Andersen, Tales	17	221
Tennyson, Maud	42	1015
Morte d'Arthur	42	986
The Lady of Shalott	42	967
The Revenge	42	1007
Rizpah	42	1011
Locksley Hall	42	979

Subject and Author	Vol.	Page
Browning, My Last Duchess	42	1074
How They Brought the Good News	42	1066
Macaulay, The Armada	41	915
D. G. Rossetti, The King's Tragedy	42	1153
C. Rossetti, In the Round Tower at Jhansi	42	1183
W. Morris, The Defence of Guenevere	42	1183
Dobell, The Ballad of Keith of Ravelston	42	1114
Poe, The Raven	42	1227
Longfellow, Evangeline	42	1300
The Wreck of the Hesperus	42	1269
Paul Revere's Ride	42	1295
Whittier, Randolph of Roanoke	42	1341
Barclay of Ury	42	1347
Maud Muller	42	1351
Skipper Ireson's Ride	42	1357
The Pipes at Lucknow	42	1360
Barbara Frietchie	42	1362
Lowell, The Courtin'	42	1376
Lanier, The Revenge of Hamish	42	1393

INDEX TO FIRST LINES
OF POEMS

AN INDEX TO THE FIRST LINES
OF POEMS, SONGS AND CHORUSES,
HYMNS AND PSALMS

First Lines	Vol.	Page
A batter'd, wreck'd old man	42	1420
A book was writ of late called Tetrachordon	4	79
A chieftain to the Highlands bound	41	773
A feeling of sadness and longing	28	382
A fig for those by law protected	6	132
A flock of sheep that leisurely pass by	41	680
A garden is a lovesome thing, God wot	42	1148
A good sword and a trusty hand	42	1111
A grief without a pang, void, dark, and drear	25	86
A guid New-year I wish thee, Maggie	6	147
A head, pure, sinless quite of brain and soul	6	325
A heavy heart, Belovèd, have I borne	41	933
A high hall is there	49	297
A Highland lad my love was born	6	126
A hundred, a thousand to one; even so	42	1183
A hundred thousand cycles vast	45	577
A king there was once reigning	19	91
A lassie all alone, was making her moan	6	480
A late lark twitters from the quiet skies	42	1209
A little onward lend thy guiding hand	4	414
A man in prosperity resembleth a tree	16	203
A may of all mays	49	396
A mighty fortress is our God	45	557
A million emeralds break from the ruby-budded lime	42	1018
A moody child and wildly wise	5	161
A pick-axe, and a spade, a spade	46	193
A plenteous place is Ireland for hospitable cheer	41	921
A povre widwe somdel stope in age	40	34
A prince can mak' a belted knight	28	85
A robe of seeming truth and trust	6	95
A Rose-bud by my early walk	6	287
A School for Scandal! tell me, I beseech you	18	113
A simple Child	41	667

First Lines	Vol.	Page
A slave to Love's unbounded sway	6	551
A slumber did my spirit seal	41	672
A sweet disorder in the dress	40	336
A voice by the cedar tree	42	1021
A weary lot is thine, fair maid	41	743
A wet sheet and a flowing sea	41	783
A widow bird sate mourning for her Love	41	848
A wise priest knows he now must reap	45	671
Abide with me! fast falls the eventide	45	566
Abou Ben Adhem (may his tribe increase!)	41	870
Absence, hear thou my protestation	40	313
Abstain from censure; for it will strengthen the censured	16	10
Accuse me not, beseech thee, that I wear	41	929
Adieu! a heart-warm fond adieu	6	215
Adieu, farewell earth's bliss	40	260
Admiring Nature in her wildest grace	6	276
Adopted in God's family, and so	15	354
Adown winding Nith I did wander	6	469
Ae day, as Death, that gruesome carl	6	59
Ae fond kiss, and then we sever	6	428
Afar the illustrious Exile roams	6	290
Afflicted regents of my soul	31	235
Again rejoicing Nature sees	6	192
Again the silent wheels of time	6	255
Again yourselves compose	5	199
Ah, broken is the golden bowl! the spirit flown forever	42	1224
Ah, Chloris! could I now but sit	40	383
Ah, Chloris, since it may not be	6	500
Ah! County Guy, the hour is nigh	41	743
Ah, did you once see Shelley plain	42	1082
Ah, rich in sorrow, thou	19	157
Ah, sun-flower! weary of time	41	584
Ah, wasteful woman!—she who may	28	144
Ah, what avails the sceptred race	41	898
Ah, woe is me, my mother dear	6	24
Airly Beacon, Airly Beacon	42	1060
Alas, 'tis true I have gone here and there	40	280
Alexis, here she stayed; among these pines	40	329
All along the valley, stream that flashest white	42	976
All devil as I am, a damnèd wretch	6	23
All hail! inexorable lord	6	194
All in the Downs the fleet was moor'd	40	402
All people that on earth do dwell	45	539

First Lines	Vol.	Page
A' the lads o' Thorniebank	6	283
All they who thoughtless are, nor heed	45	689
All things are hush'd as Nature's self lay dead	39	323
All thoughts, all passions, all delights	41	704
A' ye wha live by sowps o' drink	6	216
All-conquering have I now become, all-knowing	45	724
All's over, then: does truth sound bitter	42	1069
Altho' he has left me for greed o' the siller	6	415
Altho' my back be at the wa'	6	183
Altho' my bed were in yon muir	6	25
Altho' thou maun never be mine	6	551
Although the Cross could not here Christ detain	15	355
Amang the trees where humming bees	6	479
Amidst the silence of the darkest night	14	331
Among the heathy hills and ragged woods	6	281
An honest man here lies at rest	6	50
An somebody were come again	6	347
An old man bending I come among new faces	42	1408
An ye had been whare I hae been	6	360
Ance crowdie, twice crowdie	6	543
Ance mair I hail thee, thou gloomy December	6	430
An' Charlie, he's my darling	6	489
And I'll kiss thee yet, yet	6	30
And is this—Yarrow?—This the stream	41	629
And maun I still on Menie doat	6	192
An' O for ane an' twenty, Tam	6	415
An' O my Eppie, my jewel, my Eppie	6	348
And therefore if to love can be desert, I am not all unworthy	41	927
And thou art dead, as young and fair	41	785
And will he not come again	46	182
And wilt thou have me fashion into speech	41	928
And wilt thou leave me thus	40	192
And ye shall walk in silk attire	41	580
And yet, because thou overcomest so	41	929
And yet I cannot reprehend the flight	40	220
Anna, thy charms my bosom fire	6	309
Answer me when I call, O God of my righteousness	44	147
Apples were they with which we were beguil'd	15	267
Ariel to Miranda:—Take	41	848
Arms, and the man I sing, who, forc'd by fate	13	73
Art thou pale for weariness	41	847
Art thou poor, yet hast thou golden slumbers?	40	318
Art thou weary, art thou languid	45	544

First Lines	Vol.	Page
Artemidora! Gods invisible	41	902
As a huge stone is sometimes seen to lie	39	304
As cauld a wind as ever blew	6	427
As down the burn they took their way	6	473
As father Adam first was fooled	6	58
As flowers in rich profusion piled	45	754
As Heaven and Earth are fairer far	5	214
As I cam by Crochallan	6	256
As I gaed down the water-side	6	356
As I gaed up by yon gate-end	6	500
As I in hoary winter's night	40	218
As I stood by yon roofless tower	6	480
As I stood by yon roofless tower	6	481
As I was a-wand'ring ae morning in spring	6	25
As I was walking all alane	40	74
As I was walking up the street	6	543
As it fell upon a day	40	283
As Mailie, an' her lambs thegither	6	41
As oft as she names Phædria, you retort	9	127
As on the banks o' wandering Nith	6	411
As one that for a weary space has lain	22	7
As ships, becalmed at eve, that lay	42	1121
As slow our ship her foamy track	41	820
As sunbeams stream through liberal space	42	1253
As Tam the chapman on a day	6	59
As the hart panteth after the water brooks	44	194
As virtuous men pass mildly away	15	338
As virtuous men pass mildly away	40	304
As well might corn, as verse, in cities grow	27	66
As when a wretch, who, conscious of his crime	24	32
As when it happeneth that some lovely town	40	329
As, when the laboring Sun hath wrought his track	3	283
As when 'tis said, 'The tree bears fruit'	45	683
As yielding wax the artist's skill commands	9	302
Ascribe unto Jehovah, O ye sons of the mighty	44	175
Ask me no more where Jove bestows	40	351
Ask not the cause why sullen Spring	40	388
Ask why God made the gem so small	6	404
At Brownhill we always get dainty good cheer	6	413
At Flores in the Azores, Sir Richard Grenville lay	42	1007
At the corner of Wood Street, when daylight appears	41	655
At the last day, men shall wear	5	290
At the last, tenderly	42	1422

First Lines	Vol.	Page
At the mid hour of night, when stars are weeping, I fly .	41	822
At the midnight in the silence of the sleep-time . . .	42	1109
Attend, all ye who list to hear our noble England's praise .	41	915
Auld chuckie Reekie's sair distrest	6	267
Auld comrade dear, and brither sinner	6	334
Avenge, O Lord, thy slaughtered Saints, whose bones . .	4	83
Awake, Aeolian lyre, awake	40	453
Awake, awake, my Lyre	40	365
Awake, my St. John! leave all meaner things	40	407
Away! the moor is dark beneath the moon	41	854
Awa' Whigs, awa'	6	360
Awa' wi' your belles and your beauties	6	469
Awa' wi' your witchcraft o' Beauty's alarms	6	548
Ay flattering fortune look you never so fair	36	124
Ay, tear her tattered ensign down	42	1366
Back and side go bare, go bare	40	190
Balow, my babe, lie still and sleep	40	186
Bannocks o' bear meal	6	490
Bards of Passion and of Mirth	41	873
Be merciful unto me, O God, be merciful unto me . . .	44	211
Be merciful unto me, O God; for man would swallow me up	44	210
Be not dismayed, thou little flock	45	559
Be your words made, good Sir, of Indian ware . . .	40	213
Bear, lady nightingale above	19	86
Beat! beat! drums!—blow! bugles! blow	42	1402
Beauteous Rosebud, young and gay	6	331
Beautiful Evelyn Hope is dead	42	1078
Beauty like hers is genius. Not the call	42	1179
Beauty sat bathing by a spring	40	201
Beauty, sweet Love, is like the morning dew	40	221
Because I feel that, in the Heavens above	42	1236
Because the Few with signal virtue crowned . . .	42	1057
Because thou hast the power and own'st the grace . .	41	938
Because you have thrown off your Prelate Lord . . .	4	80
Beer bring I to thee	49	301
Before the starry threshold of Jove's court	4	44
Behind yon hills where Lugar flows	6	46
Behold, bless ye Jehovah, all ye servants of Jehovah . . .	44	314
Behold her, single in the field	41	654
Behold, how fitly are the stages set	15	294
Behold, how good and how pleasant it is	44	314
Behold, my love, how green the groves	6	503
Behold the hour, the boat, arrive	6	429

First Lines	Vol.	Page
Behold the hour, the boat arrive	6	472
Being your slave, what should I do but tend	40	273
Belovèd, my Belovèd, when I think	41	931
Belovèd, thou hast brought me many flowers	41	940
Below thir stanes lie Jamie's banes	6	58
Beneath these fruit-tree boughs that shed	41	642
Best and Brightest, come away	41	843
Between the dark and the daylight	42	1294
Beyond thee, dearie, beyond thee, dearie	6	403
Bid me to live, and I will live	40	337
Bird of the wilderness	41	767
Birds in the high Hall-garden	42	1028
Bless Jehovah, O my soul	44	271
Bless Jehovah, O my soul	44	272
Bless Jesus Christ, O Cardoness	6	498
Blessed are they that are perfect in the way	44	294
Blessed be Jehovah my rock	44	325
Blessed is every one that feareth Jehovah	44	311
Blessed is he that considereth the poor	44	193
Blessed is he whose transgression is forgiven	44	179
Blessed is the man that walketh not in the counsel of the wicked	44	145
Bless'd be the Day that I began	15	196
Blessings on thee, little man	42	1355
Blest be M'Murdo to his latest day	6	466
Blest pair of Sirens, pledges of Heaven's joy	4	40
Blow, blow, thou winter wind	40	268
Blythe, blythe, and merry was she	6	286
Blythe hae I been on yon hill	6	463
Bonie lassie, will ye go	6	277
Bonie wee thing, cannie wee thing	6	404
Bonnie Kilmeny gaed up the glen	41	756
Borders of kohl enhance the witchery of her glance	16	365
Borgia, thou once wert almost too august	41	904
Bow down thine ear, O Jehovah, and answer me	44	251
Braw, braw lads on Yarrow-braes	6	452
Break, break, break	42	975
Brief life is here our portion	45	548
Bright Star! would I were steadfast as thou art	41	898
Brightest and best of the sons of the morning	45	565
Bring the bowl which you boast	41	754
Build me straight, O worthy Master	42	1280
Burly, dozing humble-bee	42	1246

First Lines	Vol.	Page
Busk ye, busk ye, my bonnie, bonnie bride	41	572
But do not let us quarrel any more	42	1087
But, knowing now that they would have her speak . . .	42	1183
But lately seen in gladsome green	6	503
But only three in all God's universe	41	924
But rarely seen since Nature's birth	6	550
But souls that of his own good life partake	5	133
But warily tent when ye come to court me	6	469
But your allowance, and in that our all	47	943
Buy braw troggin frae the banks o' Dee	6	548
By all I lov'd, neglected and forgot	6	327
By Allah! good sir, I was not a robber	16	130
By Allan stream I chanc'd to rove	6	468
By cool Siloam's shady rill	45	563
By love, and by beauty, by law, and by duty	6	348
By Oughtertyre grows the aik	6	286
By our first strange and fatal interview	27	270
By the cross, on which suspended	45	553
By the rivers of Babylon	44	318
By the rude bridge that arched the flood	42	1245
By what word's power, the key of paths untrod . . .	42	1178
By yon Castle wa', at the close of the day	6	398
Ca' the yowes to the knowes	6	356
Ca' the yowes to the knowes	6	496
Ca' the yowes to the knowes	41	556
Call for the robin-redbreast and the wren	40	322
Calme was the day, and through the trembling ayre . . .	40	229
Can I cease to care	6	532
Can it be right to give what I can give	41	926
Canst thou leave me thus, my Katie	6	509
Captain, or colonel, or knight in arms	4	78
Care-charmer Sleep, son of the sable Night	40	222
Carle, an the King come	6	347
Cast the bantling on the rocks	5	59
Cauld blaws the wind frae east to west	6	299
Cauld is the e'enin blast	6	514
Cease, ye prudes, your envious railing	6	264
Cheer up, my mates, the wind does fairly blow . . .	40	366
Cherry-ripe, ripe, ripe, I cry	40	334
Chiefest glory of deathless Gods, Almighty for ever . .	2	186
Child of Adam, let not hope make game of thee . . .	16	321
Christ is arisen	19	36
Circulate it in the large cup	16	217

First Lines	Vol.	Page
Clarinda, mistress of my soul	6	295
Cold and clear-cut face, why come you so cruelly meek .	42	1018
Cold's the wind, and wet's the rain	40	318
Cold's the wind, and wet's the rain	47	529
Coldly, sadly descends	42	1130
Come all ye jolly shepherds	41	765
Come away, come away, Death	40	268
Come, bumpers high, express your joy	6	413
Come, dear children, let us away	42	1123
Come, gie's sang, Montgom'rie cried	41	568
Come hither, lads, and harken, for a tale there is to tell .	42	1195
Come hither, you that walk along the way	15	137
Come into the garden, Maud	28	162
Come into the garden, Maud	42	1042
Come, let me take thee to my breast	6	470
Come little babe, come silly soul	40	197
Come live with me and be my Love	40	254
Come my tan-faced children	42	1404
Come, rest in this bosom, my own stricken deer	28	384
Come, Sleep; O Sleep! the certain knot of peace	40	213
Come to me, O ye children	42	1279
Come under my plaidie, the night's gaun to fa' . . .	41	577
Come unto these yellow sands	46	412
Comrades, leave me here a little	42	979
Condemn'd to Hope's delusive mine	41	503
Consider mine affliction, and deliver me	44	304
Consider what thou beholdest, O man	16	317
Contented wi' little, and cantie wi' mair	6	507
"Courage!" he said, and pointed toward the land . . .	42	993
Courage, poor heart of stone	42	1048
Crabbed Age and Youth	40	267
Creator Spirit, by whose aid	45	547
Creep into thy narrow bed	42	1139
Criticks, I saw, that others' names efface	39	247
Cromwell, our chief of men, who through a cloud . . .	4	82
Cupid and my Campaspe play'd	40	209
Curse on ungrateful man, that can be pleased . . .	6	257
Curs'd be the man, the poorest wretch in life	6	324
Cyriack, this three years' day these eyes, though clear . .	4	85
Cyriack, whose grandsire on the royal bench	4	85
Daughter of Chaos' doting years	6	332
Daughter of Jove, relentless power	40	450
Daughter to that good Earl, once President	4	79

First Lines	Vol.	Page
Daughters of Time, the hypocritic Days	42	1243
Day of wrath, that day whose knelling	45	551
Dead, long dead	42	1052
Deal bountifully with thy servant, that I may live	44	295
Dear ——, I'll gie ye some advice	6	263
Dear love, for nothing less than thee	40	306
Dear Myra, the captive ribband's mine	6	361
Dear Sir, at ony time or tide	6	329
Dear Smith, the slee'st pawkie thief	6	167
Death, be not proud, though some have callèd thee	40	305
Death stands above me, whispering low	41	905
Degenerate Douglas! oh, the unworthy lord	41	679
Deliberate, and haste not	16	155
Deliver me from mine enemies, O my God	44	213
Deliver me, O Jehovah, from the evil man	44	321
Deluded swain, the pleasure	6	474
Depart from a place wherein is oppression	16	286
Diaphenia like the daffadowndilly	40	228
Did I hear it half in a doze	42	1024
Dire was the hate at old Harlaw	6	545
Dizzied faith and guilt and woe	28	170
Do ye indeed in silence speak righteousness	44	212
Do you remember me? or are you proud	41	904
Does haughty Gaul invasion threat	6	530
Does the road wind up-hill all the way	42	1182
Dost thou not rise, indignant shade	6	447
Doth then the world go thus, doth all thus move	40	327
Doubt thou the stars are fire	46	128
Doubt you to whom my Muse these notes intendeth	40	210
Down in yon garden sweet and gay	41	498
Drink to me only with thine eyes	40	291
Dulcinea here beneath	14	515
Duncan Gray cam' here to woo	6	448
Dweller in yon dungeon dark	6	325
Each altar had his fire	15	343
Earl March look'd on his dying child	41	777
Earth has not anything to show more fair	41	673
Earth'd up, here lies an imp o' hell	6	499
Edina! Scotia's darling seat	6	252
E'en like two little bank-dividing brooks	40	341
Erewhile of music, and ethereal mirth	4	23
Eternal Spirit of the chainless Mind	41	811
Ethereal minstrel! pilgrim of the sky	41	644

FIRST LINES	VOL.	PAGE
Even as the dense and solid rock	45	703
Even as the word of "chariot" means	45	656
Even in a palace life may be led well	42	1139
Even such is time, that takes in trust	40	207
Even let the Fancy roam	41	871
Except Jehovah build the house	44	310
Excuse me, sirs, I pray—I can't yet speak	18	203
Expect na, sir, in this narration	6	211
Faintly as tolls the evening chime	41	819
Fair and fair, and twice so fair	40	217
Fair Daffodils, we weep to see	40	337
Fair Empress of the poet's soul	6	304
Fair fa' your honest, sonsie face	6	253
Fair is my Love and cruel as she's fair	40	219
Fair is my love, when her fair golden hairs	40	250
Fair maid, you need not take the hint	6	267
Fair pledges of a fruitful tree	40	338
Fair stood the wind for France	40	222
Fair the face of orient day	6	340
Fairest maid on Devon banks	6	553
Fairfax, whose name in arms through Europe rings	4	82
False friend, wilt thou smile or weep	18	351
False world, good night! since thou hast brought	40	292
Fare thee well! and if for ever	41	799
Farewell to a' our Scottish fame	6	420
Farewell, dear friend! may guid luck hit you	6	221
Farewell, master; farewell, farewell	46	431
Farewell, old Scotia's bleak domains	6	224
Farewell, rewards and fairies	40	315
Farewell! thou art too dear for my possessing	40	276
Farewell, thou fair day, thou green earth, and ye skies	6	426
Farewell, thou stream that winding flows	6	508
Farewell to the Highlands, farewell to the North	6	362
Farewell, ye dungeons dark and strong	6	297
Farewell, ye green meadows	26	380
Fate gave the word, the arrow sped	6	315
Father of light and life, thou Good Supreme	1	83
Fathers that wear rags	46	253
Fear death?—to feel the fog in my throat	42	1065
Fear no more the heat o' the sun	40	269
Fill me with the rosy wine	6	550
Fintry, my stay in worldly strife	6	379
First time he kissed me, he but only kissed	41	938

First Lines	Vol.	Page
First when Maggie was my care	6	348
Five years have past; five summers, with the length	41	635
Flee with thy life if thou fearest oppression	16	69
Flow gently, sweet Afton! amang thy green braes	6	417
Flower in the crannied wall	42	1005
Fly, envious Time, till thou run out thy race	4	39
Follow thy fair sun, unhappy shadow	40	285
Follow your saint, follow with accents sweet	40	284
For a' that, an' a' that	6	130
For a' that, an' a' that	6	131
For a' that, an' a' that	6	133
For auld lang syne, my dear	6	317
For ever, Fortune, wilt thou prove	40	443
For ever, O Jehovah	44	300
For he that can have good and evil doth choose	14	294
For lack of gold she's left me, O	41	532
For lo! thy law is passed	28	141
For lords or kings I dinna mourn	6	323
For never yet hath any one attained	38	76
For oh, her lanely nights are lang	6	501
For sense, they little owe to frugal Heav'n	6	163
For the tired slave, song lifts the languid oar	23	134
Fortress with turrets	19	42
Forlorn, my Love, no comfort near	6	535
Forget not yet the tried intent	40	192
For us, down beaten by the storms of fate	9	49
For thee is laughing Nature gay	6	295
Fortune, that favours fools, these two short hours	47	542
Four and twenty bonny boys	40	81
Four Seasons fill the measure of the year	41	896
Frae the friends and land I love	6	419
Fresh from the dewy hill, the merry year	41	591
Fret not thyself because of evil-doers	44	186
Friday first's the day appointed	6	215
Friend of the Poet, tried and leal	6	544
Friendship, mysterious cement of the soul	6	167
From Harmony, from heavenly Harmony	40	389
From midst the barren earth, here overthrown	14	391
From Stirling Castle we had seen	41	627
From the forests and highlands	41	823
From the white-blossom'd sloe my dear Chloris requested	6	498
From thee, Eliza, I must go	6	218
From those drear solitudes and frowsy cells	6	485

FIRST LINES   VOL. PAGE

From you have I been absent in the spring 40   278
Full fathom five thy father lies 40   270
Full fathom five thy father lies 46   413
Full many a glorious morning have I seen 40   272
Full well thou know'st I love thee dear 6   553
Fy, let us a' to Kirkcudbright 6   521
Gane is the day, and mirk's the night 6   378
Gat ye me, O gat ye me 6   516
Gather ye rose-buds while ye may 40   335
Gazing from each low bulwark of this bridge 41   911
Gem of the crimson-colour'd Even 41   776
Get up, get up for shame! The blooming morn . . . 40   339
Gie him strong drink until he wink 6   144
Gifts of one who loved me 5   219
Give a man a horse he can ride 42   1149
Give all to love 42   1244
Give ear, O my people, to my law 44   239
Give ear, O Shepherd of Israel 44   245
Give ear to my prayer, O God 44   208
Give ear to my words, O Jehovah 44   148
Give me more love, or more disdain 40   352
Give me my scallop-shell of quiet 40   203
Give me patience, O Allah 16   50
Give me the splendid silent sun with all his beams full-
    dazzling 42   1410
Give the king thy judgments, O God 44   231
Glooms of the live-oaks, beautiful-braided and woven . . 42   1390
Gloomy winter's now awa' 41   594
Glory be to God on high 45   541
Glory of warrior, glory of orator, glory of song . . . 42   1005
Go and catch a falling star 40   307
Go, fetch to me a pint o' wine 6   318
Go from me. Yet I feel that I shall stand 41   925
Go, lovely Rose 40   357
Go not, happy day 42   1033
Go now my little Book, to every place 15   169
Go, Soul, the body's guest 40   204
Go, wanton muse, but go with care 9   248
God be merciful unto us, and bless us 44   222
God is our refuge and strength 44   199
God makes sech nights, all white an' still 42   1376
God moves in a mysterious way 45   562
God prosper long our noble king 40   93

First Lines	Vol.	Page
God standeth in the congregation of God	44	247
Goethe in Weimar sleeps, and Greece	42	1135
Gold and iron are good	5	239
Good-bye, proud world! I'm going home	42	1241
Good-morrow to the day so fair	40	334
Gracie, thou art a man of worth	6	513
Grant me, indulgent Heaven, that I may live	6	459
Great deeds of bale	49	424
Great is Jehovah, and greatly to be praised	44	200
Great spirits now on earth are sojourning	41	897
Green grow the rashes, O	6	47
Grow old along with me	42	1103
Gude pity me, because I'm little	6	121
Gudrun of old days	49	329
Guid-mornin' to your Majesty	6	207
Guid speed and furder to you, Johnie	6	102
Ha! whaur ye gaun, ye crowlin ferlie	6	190
Had I a cave on some wild distant shore	6	467
Had I the wyte, had I the wyte	6	529
Had I wept before she did	16	337
Had we never loved sae kindly	28	87
Hail! beauteous Stranger of the wood	41	570
Hail, famous man! whom fortune hath so blist	14	13
Hail, Native Language, that by sinews weak	4	20
Hail, Poesie! thou Nymph reserv'd	6	409
Hail, thairm-inspirin', rattlin' Willie	6	245
Hail to thee, blithe Spirit	41	829
Half a league, half a league	42	1005
Hallow the threshold, crown the posts anew	40	358
Hame, hame, hame, O hame fain wad I be	41	782
Happy the man, whose wish and care	40	405
Happy those early days, when I	40	347
Happy those which, for more commodity	14	13
Happy were he could finish forth his fate	40	287
Hard Texts are Nuts (I will not call them cheaters)	15	268
Hark, hark, my soul! angelic songs are swelling	45	571
Hark! hark! the lark at heaven's gate sings	40	268
Hark! how all the welkin rings	45	561
Hark! I hear the tramp of thousands	42	1401
Hark the mavis' e'ening sang	6	496
Harp of the North, farewell! The hills grow dark	41	755
Harry, whose tuneful and well-measured song	4	81
Has auld Kilmarnock seen the deil	6	242

First Lines	Vol.	Page
Hast thou a charm to stay the morning-star	41	707
Hasten, ye faithful, glad, joyful, and holy	45	555
Have mercy upon me, O God, according to thy loving-kindness	44	205
Have more than thou showest	46	233
Haymakers, rakers, reapers, and mowers	40	317
He clenched his pamphlet in his fist	6	256
He first by Grace must conquer'd be	15	269
He is dead, the beautiful youth	42	1299
He is gone on the mountain	41	747
He that dwelleth in the secret place of the Most High . .	44	259
He that has and a little tiny wit	46	266
He that is down needs fear no fall	15	242
He that loves a rosy cheek	40	351
He used his lances as pens	16	193
He who of Rankine sang, lies stiff and dead	6	60
He whom we mourned as dead	19	38
He's ower the hills that I lo'e weel	41	560
Health to the Maxwells' veteran Chief	6	422
Hear, Land o' Cakes and brither Scots	6	349
Hear my cry, O God	44	216
Hear my prayer, O Jehovah	44	269
Hear my prayer, O Jehovah; give ear to my supplications	44	324
Hear my voice, O God, in my complaint	44	218
Hear the right, O Jehovah, attend unto my cry . . .	44	158
Hear the sledges with the bells	42	1233
Hear this, all ye peoples	44	201
Hear what God, the Lord, hath spoken	45	563
Hee balou, my sweet wee Donald	6	490
Helen, thy beauty is to me	42	1226
Help, Jehovah; for the godly man ceaseth	44	155
Hence, all you vain delights	40	322
Hence, loathèd Melancholy	4	30
Hence, overshadowing gloom	19	62
Hence, vain deluding Joys	4	34
Hengist had verament	5	276
Her brother is coming back to-night	42	1037
Her daddie forbad, her minnie forbad	6	302
Her flowing locks, the raven's wing	6	110
Her of your name, whose fair inheritance	15	378
Her skin is like silk, and her speech is soft	16	194
Here a little child I stand	40	334
Here, a sheer hulk, lies poor Tom Bowling	41	502

First Lines	Vol.	Page
Here am I laid, my life of misery done	12	377
Here awa, there awa, wandering Willie	6	454
Here Brewer Gabriel's fire's extinct	6	513
Here cursing, swearing Burton lies	6	499
Here, ever since you went abroad	41	899
Here Holy Willie's sair worn clay	6	73
Here is the glen and here the bower	6	483
Here lie Willie Michie's banes	6	265
Here lies a mock Marquis, whose titles were shamm'd	6	499
Here lies Boghead amang the dead	6	50
Here lies John Bushby, honest man	6	488
Here lies Johnie Pigeon	6	120
Here lies, now a prey to insulting neglect	6	484
Here lies old Hobson. Death hath broke his girt	4	26
Here lies our Sovereign Lord the King	40	383
Here lieth Bernardone, ass and pig	31	399
Here lieth one who did most truly prove	4	26
Here, of a loving swain	14	109
Here Souter Hood in death doth sleep	6	50
Here Stuarts once in glory reigned	6	276
Here was a people whom, after their works	16	300
Here, where the Scottish Muse immortal lives	6	494
Here, where the world is quiet	42	1203
Here will I hold. If there's a power above us	1	82
Here's a bottle and an honest friend	6	264
Here's a health to ane I loe dear	6	551
Here's a health to them that's awa	6	449
Here's to the maiden of bashful fifteen	18	152
Here's to the maiden of bashful fifteen	41	554
Here's to the year that's awa'	41	581
Here's to thy health, my bonie lass	6	27
Hey, ca' thro', ca' thro'	6	265
Hey, the dusty Miller	6	300
Hie upon Hielands	40	114
High grace, the dower of queens; and therewithal	42	1181
His face with smile eternal drest	6	325
His foundation is in the holy mountains	44	252
Hnikar I hight	49	289
Hold, mighty man, I cry all this we know	34	144
Hold not thy peace, O God of my praise	44	284
Holy amity! which, with nimble wings	14	238
Holy, holy, holy! Lord God Almighty	45	564
Home they brought her warrior dead	42	973

First Lines	Vol.	Page
Homer, thy song men liken to the sea	22	335
Honest Will to Heaven's away	6	288
Honour, riches, marriage-blessing	46	447
How amiable are thy tabernacles	44	249
How blest the happy solitude	45	628
How can my poor heart be glad	6	494
How cold is that bosom which folly once fired	6	484
How cruel are the parents	6	532
How daur ye ca' me howlet-face	6	427
How delicious is the winning	41	782
How do I love thee? Let me count the ways	41	940
How fresh, O Lord, how sweet and clean	40	344
How good is it to pardon one able to resist	16	65
How happy is he born and taught	40	288
How haps it, Rozinante, thou art so lean	14	13
How hath time made me to tremble	16	195
How lang and dreary is the night	6	501
How, Liberty! girl, can it be by thee named	6	498
How like a winter hath my absence been	40	277
How long and dreary is the night	6	300
How long, O Jehovah? wilt thou forget me for ever	44	156
How many companies have alighted	16	301
How many wretched persons are destitute of ease	16	232
How near to good is what is fair	5	199
How often have I stood in fight	16	301
How pleasant the banks of the clear winding Devon	6	288
How should I your true love know	40	266
How should I your true love know	46	177
How sleep the Brave, who sink to rest	41	476
How soon hath Time, the subtle thief of youth	4	29
How sweet the answer Echo makes	41	821
How vainly men themselves amaze	40	377
How Wisdom and Folly meet, mix and unite	6	338
Humid seal of soft affections	6	318
"Husband, husband, cease your strife"	6	476
I am a Bard of no regard	6	130
I am a fiddler to my trade	6	128
I am a keeper of the law	6	53
I am a mariner to love	14	431
I am a son of Mars who have been in many wars	6	123
I am enamoured of her	16	326
I am monarch of all I survey	41	535
I am my mammy's ae bairn	6	295

First Lines	Vol.	Page
I am not of the noble Grecian race	12	5
I arise from dreams of thee	41	828
I arise from dreams of thee	28	373
I bought my wife a stane o' lint	6	432
I bring fresh showers for the thirsting flowers	41	852
I call no Goddess to inspire my strains	6	354
I Catherine am a Douglas born	42	1153
I coft a stane o' haslock woo'	6	526
I cry with my voice unto Jehovah	44	323
I did but prompt the age to quit their clogs	4	80
I die, and if I cannot be believed	14	331
I do confess thou art sae fair	6	431
I dream'd I lay where flowers were springing	6	21
I dream'd that as I wander'd by the way	41	842
I du believe in Freedom's cause	42	1373
I fear thy kisses, gentle maiden	41	828
I fee'd a man at Michaelmas	6	438
I fill this cup to one made up	28	382
I gaed a waefu' gate yestreen	6	356
I gaed up to Dunse	6	324
I gat your letter, winsome Willie	6	86
I gazed upon the glorious sky	42	1219
I got me flowers to strew Thy way	40	345
I had a dream, which was not all a dream	41	796
I had sax owsen in a pleugh	6	515
I hae a wife of my ain	6	307
I hae been at Crookieden	6	421
I hate the dreadful hollow behind the little wood	42	1015
I hate them that are of a double mind	44	302
I have called with my whole heart	44	304
I have done justice and righteousness	44	302
I have had playmates, I have had companions	41	735
I have heard tell	49	431
I have led her home, my love, my only friend	42	1034
I heard a thousand blended notes	41	643
I heard the trailing garments of the Night	42	1267
I hold it, sir, my bounden duty	6	199
I know a little garden-close	42	1194
I know, Olalia, thou dost me adore	14	82
I know a thing that's most uncommon	40	406
I lang hae thought, my youthfu' friend	6	203
I lift my heavy heart up solemnly	41	925
I like a church; I like a cowl	42	1247

First Lines	Vol.	Page
I lived with visions for my company	41	933
I lo'ed ne'er a laddie but ane	41	576
I long to talk with some old lover's ghost	40	309
I love, and he loves me again	40	293
I love Jehovah, because he heareth	44	291
I love thee, O Jehovah, my strength	44	160
I loved a lass, a fair one	40	331
I met a traveller from an antique land	41	851
I mind it weel in early date	6	258
I murder hate by flood or field	6	378
I must not grieve my Love, whose eyes would read	40	221
I never gave a lock of hair away	41	930
I never saw a fairer	6	444
I once was a maid, tho' I cannot tell when	6	124
I put my hat upon my head	39	288
I rede you, beware at the hunting, young men	6	261
I remember, I remember	41	910
I said, I will take heed to my ways	44	190
I said—Then, dearest, since 'tis so	42	1070
I saw him once before	42	1366
I saw where in the shroud did lurk	41	736
I see a form, I see a face	6	537
I see thine image through my tears to-night	41	935
I sing of a Whistle, a Whistle of worth	6	362
I sprang to the stirrup, and Joris, and he	42	1066
I stood on the bridge at midnight	42	1275
I strove with none; for none was worth the strife	41	905
I struck the board and cried, No more	40	343
I thank all who have loved me in their hearts	41	939
I think of thee!—my thoughts do twine and bud	41	934
I thought of Thee, my partner and my guide	41	679
I thought once how Theocritus had sung	41	923
I tore, I hackt, abolish'd, said and did	14	11
I travell'd among unknown men	41	670
I waited patiently for Jehovah	44	191
I wander'd lonely as a cloud	41	639
I was glad when they said unto me	44	307
I was thy neighbour once, thou rugged Pile	41	605
I was walking a mile	42	1025
I weep for Adonais—he is dead	41	856
I, who erewhile the happy Garden sung	4	359
I, who was late so volatile and gay	18	196
I will bless Jehovah at all times	44	181

First Lines	Vol.	Page
I will cry unto God with my voice	44	238
I will extol thee, my God, O King	44	326
I will extol thee, O Jehovah; for thou hast raised me up	44	176
I will give thanks unto Jehovah with my whole heart	44	152
I will give thee thanks with my whole heart	44	319
I will lift up mine eyes unto the mountains	44	307
I will sing of lovingkindness and justice	44	268
I will sing of the lovingkindness of Jehovah for ever	44	254
I wish I were where Helen lies	40	324
I wonder, by my troth, what thou and I	40	312
I'll aye ca' in by yon town	6	518
I'm now arrived—thanks to the gods	6	237
I'm o'er young, I'm o'er young	6	295
I'm sittin' on the stile, Mary	41	919
I'm three times doubly o'er your debtor	6	107
I'm wearing awa', Jean	41	560
I've heard them lilting at our ewe-milking	41	483
I've seen the smiling	41	482
If age brought nothing worse than this	9	54
If all the world and love were young	40	255
If aught of oaten stop or pastoral song	41	479
If doughty deeds my lady please	41	531
If from the public way you turn your steps	41	615
If I be possessed of wealth and be not liberal	16	201
If I fail any day to render thee due thanks	16	37
If I freely can discover	40	300
If I have faltered more or less	42	1212
If I leave all for thee, wilt thou exchange	41	937
If I, my lord, could show to you the truth	31	244
If it had not been Jehovah who was on our side	44	308
If love were what the rose is	42	1205
If of love we complain, what shall we say	16	63
If one says "No," I answer "No"	9	40
If the red slayer think he slays	42	1243
If thou chance for to find	15	398
If thou must love me, let it be for nought	41	928
If thou should ask my love	6	343
If thou survive my well-contented day	40	271
If to be absent were to be	40	356
If women could be fair, and yet not fond	40	289
If ye gae up to yon hill-tap	6	23
If yet I have not all thy love	40	308
If you rattle along like your Mistress's tongue	6	485

First Lines	Vol.	Page
Ilk care and fear, when thou art near	6	30
Ill-fated genius! Heaven-taught Fergusson	6	431
In a coign of the cliff between lowland and highland . .	42	1207
In a drear-nighted December	41	875
In close intrigue, their faculty's but weak	5	378
In comin' by the brig o' Dye	6	283
In days long gone	49	407
In death for life I seek	14	324
In going to my naked bed as one that would have slept .	40	201
In Jehovah do I take refuge	44	155
In Judah is God known	44	237
In London city was Bicham born	40	84
In Love, if Love be Love, if Love be ours	42	976
In Mauchline there dwells six proper young belles . . .	6	58
In my distress I cried unto Jehovah	44	306
In Politics if thou would'st mix	6	452
In proportion to one's labour, eminences are gained . .	16	235
In Scotland there was a babie born	40	59
In se'enteen hunder 'n forty-nine	6	500
In simmer, when the hay was mawn	6	440
In Tarbolton, ye ken, there are proper young men . . .	6	25
In the downhill of life, when I find I'm declining . . .	41	592
In the greenest of our valleys	42	1225
In the highlands, in the country places	42	1212
In the merry month of May	40	196
In the midway of this our mortal life	20	5
In the sweet shire of Cardigan	41	647
In thee, O Jehovah, do I take refuge	44	177
In thee, O Jehovah, do I take refuge	44	229
In this strange land, this uncouth clime	6	305
In unploughed Maine he sought the lumberers' gang . .	42	1251
In vain to me the smiling mornings shine	39	275
In wood and wild, ye warbling throng	6	466
In Xanadu did Kubla Khan	41	701
In youth, when I did love, did love	46	192
Indeed this very love which is my boast	41	928
Inhuman man! curse on thy barb'rous art	6	339
Instead of a Song, boys, I'll give you a Toast	6	459
Into the proud erected diamond stock	14	519
Inverey cam doun Deeside, whistlin and playin	40	119
Iphigeneia, when she heard her doom	41	903
Is it indeed so? If I lay here dead	41	932
Is it not better at an early hour	41	905

First Lines	Vol.	Page
Is there a whim-inspirèd fool	6	218
Is there for honest Poverty	6	511
Is this thy plighted, fond regard	6	509
It befell at Martynmas	40	103
It fell about the Lammus time	40	88
It fell about the Martinmas time	40	87
It fell upon a holly eve	40	247
It is a beauteous evening, calm and free	41	673
It is a good thing to give thanks unto Jehovah	44	260
It is an ancient Mariner	41	682
It is na, Jean, thy bonie face	6	316
It is not Beauty I demand	41	913
It is not growing like a tree	40	291
It is not to be thought of that the flood	41	675
It little profits that an idle king	42	977
It was a dismal and a fearful night	40	367
It was a lover and his lass	40	263
It was a summer evening	41	732
It was a' for our rightfu' King	6	491
It was fifty years ago	42	1293
It was in and about the Martinmas time	40	68
It was in sweet Senegal that my foes did me enthral	6	437
It was many and many a year ago	42	1239
It was not like your great and gracious ways	42	1112
It was roses, roses, all the way	42	1082
It was the charming month of May	6	504
It was the schooner Hesperus	42	1269
It was the winter wild	4	8
It was three slim does and a ten-tined buck in the bracken lay	42	1393
It was upon a Lammas night	6	44
Ithers seek they ken na what	6	442
Jamie, come try me	6	343
Jehovah answer thee in the day of trouble	44	164
Jehovah, how are mine adversaries increased	44	146
Jehovah, I have called upon thee; make haste unto me	44	322
Jehovah is my light and my salvation	44	172
Jehovah is my portion	44	298
Jehovah is my shepherd	44	168
Jehovah, my heart is not haughty	44	312
Jehovah reigneth; he is clothed with majesty	44	261
Jehovah reigneth; let the earth rejoice	44	265
Jehovah reigneth; let the peoples tremble	44	266

First Lines	Vol.	Page
Jehovah, remember for David	44	313
Jehovah saith unto my lord, Sit thou at my right hand . .	44	286
Jehovah, thou hast been favorable unto thy land	44	250
Jehovah, who shall sojourn in thy tabernacle	44	157
Jenny kiss'd me when we met	41	870
Jerusalem the golden	45	549
Jesu, the very thought of thee	45	550
Jesus, lover of my soul	45	559
Jesus shall reign where'er the sun	45	537
Jesus, Thou Joy of loving hearts	45	550
Jockey's taen the parting kiss	6	544
John Anderson, my jo, John	6	345
John Gilpin was a citizen	41	546
Judge me, O God, and plead my cause against an ungodly nation	44	195
Judge me, O Jehovah, for I have walked in mine integrity .	44	171
Just for a handful of silver he left us	42	1067
Kathrina say	19	161
Kemble, thou cur'st my unbelief	6	498
Ken ye aught o' Captain Grose?—Igo and ago	6	387
Kilmarnock wabsters, fidge an' claw	6	163
Kind gentlemen and ladies fair	19	41
Kind Sir, I've read your paper through	6	375
Know, Celia, since thou art so proud	40	352
Know thou, O stranger to the fame	6	219
Lady Onlie, honest Lucky	6	283
Lady! that in the prime of earliest youth	4	78
Lament him, Mauchline husbands a'	6	120
Lament in rhyme, lament in prose	6	43
Lassie wi' the lint-white locks	6	505
Last May, a braw wooer cam doun the lang glen . . .	6	536
Late at e'en, drinkin the wine	40	115
Late crippl'd of an arm, and now a leg	6	423
Late, late yestreen I saw the new Moon	41	728
Lawrence, of virtuous father virtuous son	4	84
Lay a garland on my hearse	40	321
Lead, kindly Light, amid the encircling gloom . . .	45	567
Lead me, O God, and Thou, O Destiny	2	179
Leeze me on drink! it gies us mair	28	85
Let God arise, let his enemies be scattered	44	223
Let half-starv'd slaves in warmer skies	6	162
Let ignorance a little while now muse	15	127
Let India boast her palms, nor envy we	5	362

First Lines	Vol.	Page
Let me not to the marriage of true minds	40	281
Let me ryke up to dight that tear	6	128
Let my cry come near before thee, O Jehovah	44	305
Let not Ambition mock their useful toil	6	134
Let not Woman e'er complain	6	502
Let other heroes boast their scars	6	225
Let other poets raise a frácas	6	144
Let others sing of Knights and Paladines	40	222
Let schoolmasters puzzle their brain	18	211
Let the Most Blessed be my guide	15	190
Let the toast pass	18	152
Let the world's sharpness, like a clasping knife	41	932
Let thy lovingkindness also come unto me, O Jehovah	44	297
Let us begin and carry up this corpse	42	1083
Let us drink and be merry, dance, joke, and rejoice	40	364
Let us with a gladsome mind	4	15
Life! I know not what thou art	41	555
Life ne'er exulted in so rich a prize	6	395
Life of Life! Thy lips enkindle	41	841
Light lay the earth on Billy's breast	6	487
Like as the culver, on the barèd bough	40	251
Like as the waves make towards the pebbled shore	40	274
Like some brave steed that oft before	9	50
Like to the clear in highest sphere	40	215
Listen, my children, and you shall hear	42	1295
Listen to me, as when ye heard our father	42	1064
Little I ask; my wants are few	42	1368
Little think'st thou, poor flower	40	311
Live in these conquering leaves	40	363
Lo, praise of the prowess of people-kings	49	5
Lo! 'tis a gala night	42	1240
Lo! where the four mimosas blend their shade	41	904
Lo! where the rosy-bosom'd Hours	40	452
Lock the door, Lariston, lion of Liddisdale	41	767
Lone on the bleaky hills the straying flocks	6	292
Long-expected one-and-twenty	41	504
Long fed on boundless hopes, O race of man	42	1138
Long have I sighed for a calm	42	1018
Long have I slept	49	300
Long life, my Lord, an' health be yours	6	205
Long, long the night	6	532
Look not thou on beauty's charming	41	748
Look, Nymphs and Shepherds, look	4	41

First Lines	Vol.	Page
Lord of all being, throned afar	45	570
Lord Thomas and Fair Annet	40	61
Lord, thou hast been our dwelling-place	44	258
Lord, to account who dares thee call	6	459
Lord, we thank, and thee adore	6	460
Lords, knights, and squires, the numerous band . . .	40	396
Loth am I, sister	49	361
Loud blaw the frosty breezes	6	289
Louis, what reck I by thee	6	316
Love bade me welcome; yet my soul drew back	40	341
Love guards the roses of thy lips	40	216
Love in her eyes sits playing	40	402
Love in my bosom like a bee	40	214
Love not me for comely grace	40	325
Love thou thy land, with love far-brought	42	999
Love thy country, wish it well	40	463
Lovely was she by the dawn	6	504
Loving in truth, and fain in verse my love to show . .	40	212
Lythe and listen, gentilmen	40	128
Maid of Athens, ere we part	41	795
Make a joyful noise unto God, all the earth . . .	44	221
Make a joyful noise unto Jehovah, all ye lands . . .	44	267
Make haste, O God, to deliver me	44	228
Maker of all, the Lord	7	156
Mally's meek, Mally's sweet	6	543
Man is his own star; and the soul that can	5	59
Many a green isle needs must be	41	835
Many a time have they afflicted me from my youth up .	44	311
March, march, Ettrick and Teviotdale	41	746
Mark yonder pomp of costly fashion	6	533
Martial, the things that do attain	40	194
Mary! I want a lyre with other strings	41	536
Maud has a garden of roses	42	1031
Maud Muller on a summer's day	42	1351
Maugre the ravings that are set abroach	14	12
Maxwell, if merit here you crave	6	498
May I lose my heart if it cease to love you	16	135
Meet me on the warlock knowe	6	471
Merrily swinging on brier and weed	42	1215
Methought I saw my late espousèd saint	4	86
Milton! thou shouldst be living at this hour	41	677
Mine adventure to the Meek One	43	6
Mine be a cot beside the hill	41	582

First Lines	Vol.	Page
Morning arises stormy and pale	42	1021
Mortality, behold and fear	40	319
Most glorious Lord of Lyfe! that, on this day	40	249
Most sweet it is with unuplifted eyes	41	672
Mother, I cannot mind my wheel	41	901
Much have I travell'd in the realms of gold	41	895
Music, when soft voices die	41	855
Musing on the roaring ocean	6	302
My blessings on ye, honest wife	6	263
My blessin's upon thy sweet wee lippie	6	256
My bonie lass, I work in brass	6	129
My curse upon your venom'd stang	6	239
My days among the Dead are past	41	734
My dear and only Love, I pray	40	358
My faith looks up to thee	45	569
My father was a farmer upon the Carrick border, O	6	38
My future will not copy fair my past	41	940
My girl she's airy, she's buxom and gay	6	58
My God, I love thee; not because	45	556
My God, my God	15	416
My God, my God, why hast thou forsaken me	44	166
My God, where is that ancient heat towards thee	15	379
My godlike friend—nay, do not stare	6	308
My good blade carves the casques of men	42	1002
My hair is gray, but not with years	41	801
My Harry was a gallant gay	6	357
My heart aches, and a drowsy numbness pains	41	876
My heart is a-breaking, dear Tittie	6	346
My heart is fixed, O God	44	283
My heart is sair—I dare na tell	6	510
My heart is wae, and unco wae	6	284
My heart leaps up when I behold	41	600
My heart overfloweth with a goodly matter	44	197
My heart was ance as blithe and free	6	296
My heart's in the Highlands, my heart is not here	6	362
My honor'd Colonel, deep I feel	6	546
My lady's gown, there's gairs upon't	6	262
My letters! all dead paper, mute and white	41	934
My life has crept so long on a broken wing	42	1055
My lord a-hunting he is gane	6	262
My lord, I know your noble ear	6	278
My Love in her attire doth shew her wit	40	325
My love, she's but a lassie yet	6	345

FIRST LINES	VOL.	PAGE
My lov'd, my honor'd, much respected friend	6	134
My lute, be as thou wert when thou didst grow	40	328
My mind to me a kingdom is	40	207
My minnie does constantly deave me	28	89
My mother bids me bind my hair	41	581
My mother, the harlot	19	194
My own Belovèd, who hast lifted me	41	934
My peace is gone	19	148
My Peggy is a young thing	40	401
My Peggy's face, my Peggy's form	6	289
My poet, thou canst touch on all the notes	41	930
My Sandy gied to me a ring	6	343
My Sandy O, my Sandy O	6	344
My sister! my sweet sister! if a name	41	792
My Son, these maxims make a rule	6	183
My soul cleaveth unto the dust	44	296
My soul fainteth for thy salvation	44	300
My soul waiteth in silence for God only	44	216
My spotless love hovers with purest wings	40	220
My sword could not at all compare with thine	14	12
My thoughts hold mortal strife	40	326
My true-love hath my heart, and I have his	40	212
Mysterious Night! when our first parent knew	41	913
Nae gentle dames, tho' e'er sae fair	6	202
Nae heathen name shall I prefix	6	275
Nae shoon to hide her tiny taes	41	918
Nay, with my goodwill	49	387
Nearer, my God, to thee	45	568
Never the time and the place	42	1108
Never trust in women; nor rely upon their vows	16	10
No churchman am I for to rail and to write	6	37
No cold approach, no altered mien	6	443
No coward soul is mine	42	1110
No longer mourn for me when I am dead	40	275
No more of your guests, be they titled or not	6	513
No more, ye warblers of the wood! no more	6	488
No, my own love of other years	41	901
No, no! go not to Lethe, neither twist	41	882
No sculptured marble here, nor pompous lay	6	257
No song nor dance I bring from yon great city	6	371
No Spartan tube, no Attic shell	6	492
No Stewart art thou, Galloway	6	466

First Lines	Vol.	Page
Nobly, nobly Cape Saint Vincent to the North-west died away	42	1069
None keepeth a secret but a faithful person	16	58
Nor grain, nor wealth, nor store of gold and silver	45	676
Not a drum was heard, not a funeral note	41	822
Not, Celia, that I juster am	40	384
Not here and there, but everywhere	9	132
Not marble, nor the gilded monuments	40	273
Not mine own fears, nor the prophetic soul	40	279
Not to know vice at all, and keep true state	40	294
Not unto us, O Jehovah, not unto us	44	290
Now daye was gone, and night was come	39	326
Now haply down yon gay green shaw	6	519
Now in her green mantle blythe Nature arrays	6	509
Now, Kennedy, if foot or horse	6	188
Now Nature cleeds the flowery lea	6	505
Now Nature hangs her mantle green	6	396
Now, Reader, I have told my Dream to thee	15	166
Now Robin lies in his last lair	6	93
Now rosy May comes in wi' flowers	6	471
Now Simmer blinks on flowery braes	6	277
Now sleeps the crimson petal, now the white	42	974
Now spring has clad the grove in green	6	538
Now thank we all our God	45	558
Now the bright morning-star, Day's harbinger	4	39
Now the golden Morn aloft	40	460
Now the last day of many days	41	845
Now this is my first counsel	49	368
Now westlin winds and slaught'ring guns	6	45
Nuns fret not at their convent's narrow room	41	681
O a' ye pious godly flocks	6	63
O angry fate, forbear	16	25
O aye my wife she dang me	6	515
O blithe new-comer! I have heard	41	641
O bonie was yon rosy brier	6	538
O Brignall banks are wild and fair	41	738
O brother, rest from miserable mee	32	85
O cam ye here the fight to shun	6	358
O can ye labour lea, young man	6	438
O Captain! my Captain! our fearful trip is done	42	1412
O could I give thee India's wealth	6	329
O Death, had'st thou but spar'd his life	6	58

First Lines	Vol.	Page
O Death! thou tyrant fell and bloody	6	383
O fairest Flower, no sooner blown but blasted	4	18
O for him back again	6	357
O, for my sake do you with Fortune chide	40	280
O Friend! I know not which way I must look	41	676
O Friends! with whom my feet have trod	42	1338
O give thanks unto Jehovah; for he is good	44	281
O God, keep not thou silence	44	248
O God, the nations are come into thine inheritance	44	244
O God, thou art my God; earnestly will I seek thee	44	217
O God, thou hast cast us off, thou hast broken us down	44	215
O God, why hast thou cast us off for ever	44	234
O Goddess! hear these tuneless numbers, wrung	41	880
O Gowdie, terror o' the whigs	6	94
O gude ale comes and gude ale goes	6	515
O had each Scot of ancient times	6	272
O had the malt thy strength of mind	6	513
O happy dames! that may embrace	40	193
O happy shades! to me unblest	41	542
O happy souls, which from this mortal vale	14	391
O have ye na heard o' the fause Sakelde	40	108
O hearken, ye who speak the English Tongue	49	255
O how can I be blythe and glad	6	304
O how much more doth beauty beauteous seem	40	272
O how shall I, unskilfu', try	6	405
O if thou knew'st how thou thyself dost harm	40	314
O Jehovah, my God, in thee do I take refuge	44	150
O Jehovah, our Lord	44	151
O Jehovah, rebuke me not in thine anger	44	149
O Jehovah, rebuke me not in thy wrath	44	188
O Jehovah, the God of my salvation	44	253
O Jehovah, thou God to whom vengeance belongeth	44	262
O Jehovah, thou hast searched me, and known me	44	319
O ken ye what Meg o' the Mill has gotten	6	456
O Kenmure's on and awa, Willie	6	422
O Lady Mary Ann looks o'er the Castle wa'	6	435
O lassie, are ye sleepin yet	6	517
O lay thy loof in mine, lass	6	550
O leave novels, ye Mauchline belles	6	57
O leeze me on my spinnin-wheel	6	441
O let me in this ae night	6	517
O let the solid ground	42	1028
O let us howl some heavy note	47	821

First Lines	Vol.	Page
O listen, listen, ladies gay	41	748
O Logan, sweetly didst thou glide	6	462
O Logie o' Buchan, O Logie the laird	41	571
O Lord, since we have feasted thus	6	461
O Lord, when hunger pinches sore	6	461
O lovely Polly Stewart	6	413
O lovers' eyes are sharp to see	41	744
O luve will venture in where it daur na weel be seen	6	406
O lyric Love, half angel and half bird	42	1109
O Mary, at thy window be	6	31
O Mary, go and call the cattle home	42	1061
O May, thy morn was ne'er so sweet	6	428
O me! what eyes hath love put in my head	40	282
O meikle thinks my luve o' my beauty	6	415
O merry hae I been teethin a heckle	6	134
O mirk, mirk is this midnight hour	6	454
O Mistress mine, where are you roaming	40	262
O Mother Earth! upon thy lap	42	1341
O mount and go, mount and make you ready	6	344
O my Luve's like a red, red rose	6	482
O never say that I was false of heart	40	279
O Nightingale that on yon blooming spray	4	38
O once I lov'd a bonie lass	6	19
O Philly, happy be that day	6	506
O poortith cauld, and restless love	6	451
O praise Jehovah, all ye nations	44	292
O raging Fortune's withering blast	6	36
O rough, rude, ready-witted Rankine	6	53
O rowan tree, O rowan tree! thou'lt aye be dear to me	41	564
O sad and heavy, should I part	6	430
O saw ye bonie Lesley	6	442
O saw ye my Dear, my Philly	6	501
O saw ye my dearie, my Eppie Macnab	6	414
O saw ye not fair Ines	41	905
O saw ye not fair Ines	28	385
O say what is that thing call'd Light	40	441
O sing a new song to the Lord	6	336
O sing unto my roundelay	41	558
O snatch'd away in beauty's bloom	41	790
O soft embalmer of the still midnight	41	896
O stay, sweet warbling, woodlark, stay	6	531
O steer her up, an' haud her gaun	6	516
O stream descending to the sea	42	1120

First Lines	Vol.	Page
O Swallow, Swallow, flying, flying South	42	974
O sweet and constant hope	14	432
O talk not to me of a name great in story	41	789
O that I had ne'er been married	6	543
O that 'twere possible	42	1049
O that's the lassie o' my heart	6	540
O the month of May, the merry month of May	47	502
O Thou dread Power, who reign'st above	6	238
O Thou Great Being! what Thou art	6	32
O Thou, in whom we live and move	6	428
O thou pale orb that silent shines	6	195
O thou, that sitt'st upon a throne	41	484
O Thou, the first, the greatest friend	6	33
O Thou unknown, Almighty Cause	6	34
O Thou! whatever title suit thee	6	140
O Thou, who in the heavens does dwell	6	70
O Thou who kindly dost provide	6	427
O thou whom Poetry abhors	6	264
O thou with dewy locks, who lookest down	41	584
O Tibbie, I hae seen the day	6	20
O, to be in England	42	1068
O waly waly up the bank	40	323
O wat ye wha that lo'es me	6	540
O wat ye wha's in yon town	6	518
"O well's me o' my gay goss-hawk"	40	69
O were I on Parnassus hill	6	314
O were my love yon Lilac fair	6	464
O wert thou in the cauld blast	6	552
O wert thou, Love, but near me	6	535
O wha my babie-clouts will buy?	6	182
O wha will shoe my fu fair foot	40	65
O wha will to Saint Stephen's House	6	309
O what a plague is love	40	380
O what can ail thee, knight-at-arms	41	893
O when shall I a mansion give	45	779
O when she cam' ben she bobbed fu' law	6	432
O whistle an' I'll come to ye, my lad	6	469
O why should Fate sic pleasure have	6	451
O why the deuce should I repine	6	36
O wild West Wind, thou breath of Autumn's being	41	833
O Willie brew'd a peck o' maut	6	355
O wilt thou go wi' me, sweet Tibbie Dunbar	6	344
O World! O Life! O Time	41	842

First Lines	Vol.	Page
O world of wonders! (I can say no less)	15	69
O worship the King all glorious above	45	540
O ye plants, ye herbs, and ye trees	14	227
O ye wha are sae guid yoursel'	6	184
O ye whose cheek the tear of pity stains	6	50
Obscurest night involved the sky	41	540
Of a' the airts the wind can blaw	6	306
Of all the girls that are so smart	40	403
Of all the numerous ills that hurt our peace	6	49
Of all the rides since the birth of time	42	1357
Of all the thoughts of God that are	41	941
Of Heaven or Hell I have no power to sing	42	1193
Of Lordly acquaintance you boast	6	427
Of man's first disobedience and the fruit	4	88
Of Nelson and the North	41	779
Of old, when Scarron his companions invited	41	505
Of this fair volume which we World do name	40	327
Oft in the stilly night	41	816
Often I think of the beautiful town	42	1290
Oh, a dainty plant is the Ivy green	42	1147
Oh clap your hands, all ye peoples	44	200
Oh come, let us sing unto Jehovah	44	263
Oh for my sake do you with Fortune chide	27	308
Oh Galuppi, Baldassare, this is very sad to find	42	1080
Oh give thanks unto Jehovah, call upon his name	44	275
Oh give thanks unto Jehovah; for he is good	44	293
Oh give thanks unto Jehovah; for he is good	44	316
Oh how love I thy law	44	301
Oh I am come to the low Countrie	6	490
Oh, open the door, some pity to shew	6	455
Oh sing unto Jehovah a new song	44	264
Oh sing unto Jehovah a new song	44	266
Oh, slow to smite and swift to spare	42	1223
Oh that those lips had language!	41	543
Oh, the auld house, the auld house	41	561
Oh, yes! They love through all this world of ours	41	939
Oh! young Lochinvar is come out of the west	41	751
Old Chronos once took queen Sedition to wife	12	37
Old Grahame he is to Carlisle gone	40	121
Old Winter, with his frosty beard	6	475
On a bank of flowers, in a summer day	6	341
On a day, alack the day!	40	266
On a Poet's lips I slept	41	855

FIRST LINES   VOL.   PAGE

On Cessnock banks a lassie dwells   6   28
On either side the river lie   42   967
On his lips Persuasion hung   9   207
On Linden, when the sun was low   41   781
On parent knees, a naked new-born child   41   580
On peace an' rest my mind was bent   6   515
On the brink of the night and the morning   28   89
On the heights peals the thunder, and trembles the bridge   26   380
On the Sabbath-day   42   1146
On the seas and far away   6   495
On these white cliffs, that calm above the flood   41   682
Once did She hold the gorgeous East in fee   41   676
Once fondly lov'd, and still remembered dear   6   221
Once in a cellar lived a rat   19   87
Once upon a midnight dreary, while I pondered, weak and
    weary   42   1227
One day I wrote her name upon the strand   40   251
One more Unfortunate   41   907
One more Unfortunate   28   386
One night as I did wander   6   91
One Queen Artemisia, as old stories tell   6   59
One word is too often profaned   41   850
One's-self I sing, a simple separate person   42   1402
Oppress'd with grief, oppress'd with care   6   197
Or love of understanding quite is void   14   190
Orthodox! orthodox, who believe in John Knox   6   351
Others abide our question. Thou art free   42   1129
Our band is few but true and tried   42   1217
Our bugles sang truce, for the night-cloud had lower'd .   41   770
Our God, our help in ages past   45   538
Our signal in love is the glance of our eyes   16   77
Our thrissles flourish'd fresh and fair   6   360
Out of the depths have I cried unto thee, O Jehovah . .   44   312
Out of the night that covers me   42   1210
Out over the Forth, I look to the North   6   398
Out upon it, I have loved   40   353
Over the mountains   40   379
Pack, clouds, away, and welcome day   40   316
Pardon, oh, pardon, that my soul should make   41   938
Pausanias you may praise, and Xanthippus he be for . .   12   23
Peg Nicholson was a good bay mare   6   376
Phoebus, arise   40   329
Pibroch of Donuil Dhu   41   745

First Lines	Vol.	Page
Pipes of the misty moorlands	42	1360
Piping down the valleys wild	41	584
Poets, like disputants, when reasons fail	18	106
Poor, little, pretty, fluttering thing	40	398
Poor *Little-faith!* Hast been among the Thieves . . .	15	135
Poor naked wretches, wheresoe'er you are	6	248
Poor Soul, the centre of my sinful earth	40	281
Poverty causeth the lustre of a man to grow dim . . .	16	128
Praise waiteth for thee, O God, in Zion	44	219
"Praise Woman still," his lordship roars	6	478
Praise ye Jehovah		
Blessed is the man that feareth Jehovah	44	288
Praise ye Jehovah		
For it is good to sing praises	44	328
Praise ye Jehovah		
I will give thanks unto Jehovah	44	287
Praise ye Jehovah		
Oh give thanks unto Jehovah	44	277
Praise ye Jehovah		
Praise God in his sanctuary	44	331
Praise ye Jehovah		
Praise Jehovah, O my soul	44	327
Praise ye Jehovah		
Praise, O ye servants of Jehovah	44	289
Praise ye Jehovah		
Praise ye Jehovah from the heavens	44	330
Praise ye Jehovah		
Praise ye the name of Jehovah	44	315
Praise ye Jehovah		
Sing unto Jehovah a new song	44	331
Preserve me, O God; for in thee do I take refuge . . .	44	158
Princes have persecuted me without a cause	44	305
Proud Maisie is in the wood	41	746
Proud word you never spoke, but you will speak . . .	41	899
Put forth thy leaf, thou lofty plane	42	1121
Queen and Huntress, chaste and fair	40	299
Ranged thus for battle on the sacred plain	45	785
Rarely, rarely comest thou	41	825
Rash mortal, and slanderous poet, thy name	6	276
Raving winds around her blowing	6	299
Reader! I am to let thee know	15	368
Rejoice in Jehovah, O ye righteous	44	180
Religion! what treasure untold	39	295

First Lines	Vol.	Page
Remember me when I am gone away	42	1182
Remember the word unto thy servant	44	298
Remote, unfriended, melancholy, slow	41	520
Restore to my eyelids the sleep which hath been ravished	16	62
Revered defender of beauteous Stuart	6	266
Riches I hold in light esteem	42	1111
Right, sir! your text I'll prove it true	6	225
Righteous art thou, O Jehovah	44	303
Ring out your bells, let mourning shews be spread	40	211
"Rise up, rise up, now, Lord Douglas," she says	40	51
Rivulet crossing my ground	42	1041
Robin shure in hairst	6	324
Robin was a rovin' boy	6	92
Roman Virgil, thou that singest Ilion's lofty temples robed in fire	42	1014
Round the cape of a sudden came the sea	42	1069
Rudely thou wrongest my dear heart's desire	40	250
Ruin seize thee, ruthless King	40	456
Rusticity's ungainly form	6	248
Sabrina fair	4	67
Sad thy tale, thou idle page	6	272
Sae flaxen were her ringlets	6	497
Sae rantingly, sae wantonly	6	297
Satyr-king, instead of swords	12	70
Save me, O God	44	226
Save me, O God, by thy name	44	208
Say not the struggle naught availeth	42	1119
Say over again, and yet once over again	41	931
Say, sages, what's the charm on earth	6	550
Scorn'd, to be scorn'd by one that I scorn	42	1029
Scots, wha hae wi' Wallace bled	6	472
Search while thou wilt, and let thy Reason go	3	264
Searching auld wives' barrels	6	355
Season of mists and mellow fruitfulness	41	879
See how the flowers, as at parade	40	370
See the Chariot at hand here of Love	40	290
See the smoking bowl before us	6	132
See what a lovely shell	42	1046
See where she sits upon the grassie greene	40	245
See with what simplicity	40	371
Sensibility, how charming	6	426
Shall I compare thee to a summer's day	40	270
Shall I, wasting in despair	40	332

First Lines	Vol.	Page
Shall they who wrong begin yet rightly end	15	46
She came to the village church	42	1025
She dwelt among the untrodden ways	41	670
She is a winsome wee thing	6	444
She is not fair to outward view	41	912
She walks in beauty, like the night	41	789
She was a phantom of delight	41	651
She was so fair	5	277
She which you view, with triple face and sheen	14	514
She's fair and fause that causes my smart	6	328
Shepherd of tender youth	45	541
Should auld acquaintance be forgot	6	317
Shouldst thou think upon me after the length of my age	16	304
Shrewd Willie Smellie to Crochallan came	6	255
Sic a reptile was Wat, sic a miscreant slave	6	485
Sick, am I sick of a jealous dread	42	1026
Sigurd of yore	49	371
Since all that I can ever do for thee	42	1119
Since brass, nor stone, nor earth, nor boundless sea	40	274
Since cruel thou (I publish) dost desire	14	101
Since I am coming to that holy room	15	355
Since, then, such blessings manifold	45	739
Since there's no help, come let us kiss and part	40	228
Sing aloud unto God our strength	44	246
Sing hey my braw John Highlandman	6	126
Sing lullaby, as women do	40	195
Sing on, sweet thrush, upon the leafless bough	6	452
Sir, as your mandate did request	6	186
Sir, o'er a gill I gat your card	6	189
Sir Wisdom's a fool when he's fou	6	125
Sir, Yours this moment I unseal	6	201
Sleep on, and dream of Heaven awhile	41	582
Sleep'st thou, or wak'st thou, fairest creature	6	502
So all day long the noise of battle roll'd	42	986
So dark a mind within me dwells	42	1032
So every spirit, as it is most pure	5	167
So oft as I her beauty do behold	40	250
Soft on the fell	49	298
Some books are lies frae end to end	6	74
Some say the *Pilgrim's Progress* is not mine	15	319
Sometimes thou seem'st not as thyself alone	42	1180
Souls of Poets, dead and gone	41	874
Sound, sound the clarion, fill the fife	41	748

First Lines	Vol.	Page
Spring, the sweet Spring, is the year's pleasant king . .	40	261
St. Agnes's Eve!—ah, bitter chill it was	41	883
Stand close around, ye Stygian set	41	899
Star that bringest home the bee	41	771
Stars of the summer night	42	1273
Stay, my charmer, can you leave me	6	298
Stay, O sweet, and do not rise	40	310
Stern Daughter of the voice of God	41	649
Still anxious to secure your partial favour	6	477
Still to be neat, still to be drest	40	290
"Stop thief!" dame Nature call'd to Death	6	487
Strait is the spot and green the sod	6	269
Strange fits of passion have I known	41	669
Strange, that I felt so gay	42	1040
Streams that glide in orient plains	6	282
Strew on her roses, roses	42	1129
Strive thou, O Jehovah, with them that strive with me	44	182
Sun of my soul, Thou Saviour dear	45	565
Sunset and evening star	42	1057
Sunshine was he	5	57
Sure never were seen two such beautiful ponies . . .	18	132
Surely God is good to Israel	44	232
Surprised by joy—impatient as the wind	41	674
Swallow, my sister, O sister swallow	42	1201
Sweet and low, sweet and low	42	972
Sweet are the banks—the banks o' Doon	6	398
Sweet are the thoughts that savour of content . . .	40	282
Sweet Auburn! loveliest village of the plain	41	509
Sweet, be not proud of those two eyes	40	336
Sweet closes the ev'ning on Craigieburn Wood . . .	6	403
Sweet day, so cool, so calm, so bright	40	342
Sweet dimness of her loosened hair's downfall . . .	42	1180
Sweet Echo, sweetest Nymph, that liv'st unseen . . .	4	50
Sweet fa's the eve on Craigieburn	6	512
Sweet flow'ret, pledge o' meikle love	6	394
Sweet Highland Girl, a very shower	41	652
Sweet naïveté of feature	6	447
Sweet stream, that winds through yonder glade . . .	41	534
Sweetest love, I do not go	40	307
Swiftly walk over the western wave	41	832
Symmetrical, and square in shape	45	688
Take, O take those lips away	40	267
Talk not to me of savages	6	550

First Lines	Vol.	Page
Tam Samson's weel-worn clay here lies	6	245
Tanagra! think not I forget	41	899
Tax not the royal Saint with vain expense	41	678
Teach me, my God and King	40	342
Teach me, O Jehovah, the way of thy statutes . . .	44	296
Tears, idle tears, I know not what they mean . . .	42	972
Tears, idle tears, I know not what they mean . . .	28	390
Tell me, Muse, of that man	22	9
Tell me not, in mournful numbers	42	1264
Tell me not of a face that's fair	40	369
Tell me not, Sweet, I am unkind	40	354
Tell me, thou Star, whose wings of light	41	856
Tell me where is Fancy bred	40	263
Tell me, ye prim adepts in Scandal's school	18	109
Thank Heaven! the crisis	42	1236
That sir which serves and seeks for gain	46	254
That there is a falsehood in his looks	6	499
That time of year thou may'st in me behold	40	276
That which her slender waist confined	40	357
That's my last Duchess painted on the wall	42	1074
The Assyrian came down like the wolf on the fold . . .	41	785
The bairns gat out wi' an unco shout	6	439
The battle on Thermodon that shall be	12	206
The blast from Freedom's Northern hills, upon its Southern way	42	1344
The blear-eyed escapeth a pit into which the clear-sighted falleth	16	122
The blessèd Damozel lean'd out	42	1149
The blude-red rose at Yule may blaw	6	303
The bonie lass made the bed to me	6	528
The Brahman who his evil traits hath banished . . .	45	627
The bride cam' out o' the byre	41	567
The cardin' o't, the spinnin' o't	6	527
The castled crag of Drachenfels	41	798
The Catrine woods were yellow seen	6	109
The clatt'ring thunderbolt that did adorn	14	513
The cock is crowing	41	604
The cod-piece that will house	46	264
The Cooper o' Cuddy came here awa	6	527
The crimson light of sunset falls	42	1199
The curfew tolls the knell of parting day	40	443
The day is cold, and dark, and dreary	42	1273
The day is done, and the darkness	42	1274

First Lines	Vol.	Page
The day is done, and the darkness	28	379
The day is past and over	45	542
The day returns, my bosom burns	6	314
The deil cam fiddlin' thro' the town	6	439
The deil's awa, the deil's awa	6	439
The Devil got notice that Grose was a-dying	6	350
The dusky night rides down the sky	41	501
The earth is Jehovah's; and the fulness thereof	44	169
Th' expense of Spirit in a waste of shame	40	281
The face of all the world is changed, I think	41	926
The fault was mine, the fault was mine	42	1044
The first time that the sun rose on thine oath	41	936
The flame flared at its maddest	49	316
The flower it blaws, it fades, it fa's	6	413
The fool hath said in his heart, There is no God	44	156
The fool hath said in his heart, There is no God	44	207
The forward youth that would appear	40	372
The fountains mingle with the river	41	832
The friend whom, wild from Wisdom's way	6	479
The future hides in it	25	387
The gallant Youth, who may have gained	41	631
The gloomy night is gath'ring fast	6	238
The glories of our blood and state	40	349
The Greeks, when by their courage and their might	12	98
The grief increaseth, and withal the shame	14	315
The Groups break up, and only they, the wise say	45	684
The harp that once through Tara's halls	41	819
The heather was blooming, the meadows were mawn	6	261
The heavens declare the glory of God	44	163
The Hill, tho' high, I covet to ascend	15	45
The isles of Greece! the isles of Greece	41	812
The King of love my shepherd is	45	536
The king our Emperor Carlemaine	49	95
The King shall joy in thy strength, O Jehovah	44	165
The king sits in Dumferling toune	40	74
The King's most humble servant, I	6	460
The Laddies by the banks o' Nith	6	370
The Laird o' Cockpen, he's proud and he's great	41	563
The lamp of day with ill-presaging glare	6	273
The lang lad they ca' Jumpin John	6	302
The lark now leaves his wat'ry nest	40	354
The last and greatest Herald of Heaven's King	40	326
The last time I came o'er the moor	6	461

First Lines	Vol.	Page
The lazy mist hangs from the brow of the hill	6	315
The Lord is only my support	15	208
The lovely lass of Inverness	6	488
The Magadhans hold hitherto a doctrine	45	721
The man, in life wherever plac'd	6	33
The man of life upright	40	286
The man whose mind, like to a rock	45	712
The master, the swabber, the boatswain, and I	46	428
The merchant, to secure his treasure	40	397
The Mighty One, God, Jehovah, hath spoken	44	203
The moon becometh perfect once each month	16	331
The more we live, more brief appear	41	775
The murmur of the mourning ghost	42	1114
The news frae Moidart cam' yestereen	41	564
The night is come, but not too soon	42	1265
The night is come, like to the day	3	328
The night was still, and o'er the hill	6	237
The noble Maxwells and their powers	6	419
The play is done; the curtain drops	42	1058
The poetry of earth is never dead	41	895
The poor man weeps—here Gavin sleeps	6	219
The poplars are fell'd, farewell to the shade	41	534
The red rose whispers of passion	42	1198
The Robin to the Wren's nest	6	542
The rounded world is fair to see	5	223
The sacred lowe o' weel-placed love	28	86
The sea is calm to-night	42	1137
The series which doth bear a fruit	45	683
The shadows lay along Broadway	28	374
The shepherd for the dance was dress'd	19	44
The simple bard, rough at the rustic plough	6	230
The simple Bard, unbroke by rules of art	6	221
The skies they were ashen and sober	42	1230
The small birds rejoice in the green leaves returning	6	305
The smile-dimpled lake woo'd to bathe in its deep	26	380
The smiling Spring comes in rejoicing	6	417
The Solemn League and Covenant	6	512
The soul's Rialto hath its merchandise	41	930
The spacious firmament on high	40	400
The spacious firmament on high	45	535
The splendor falls on castle walls	42	973
The sun descending in the west	41	585
The sun had clos'd the winter day	6	172

First Lines	Vol.	Page
The sun has gane down o'er the lofty Benlomond . . .	41	593
The sun he is sunk in the west	6	22
The sun, in ancient guise, competing	19	18
The sun is warm, the sky is clear	41	827
The sun set; but set not his hope	5	183
The sun, the moon, the stars, the seas, the hills and the plains	42	1004
The sun upon the lake is low	41	754
The sun (which doth the greatest comfort bring,) . .	40	319
The Sundays of man's life	15	416
The Thames flows proudly to the sea	6	342
The thirsty earth soaks up the rain	40	366
The transgression of the wicked saith within my heart . .	44	185
The tree of deepest root is found	45	689
The tryals that those men do meet withal	15	77
The twentieth year is well-nigh past	41	537
The valiant, in himself, what can he suffer	6	224
The valiant warrior famoused for fight	5	110
The victory now hath this illustrious Buddha won . . .	45	622
The wean wants a cradle	6	542
The weary pund, the weary pund	6	431
The whole world was not half so wide	25	438
The wind blew hollow frae the hills	6	400
The winter it is past, and the summer comes at last . .	6	303
The wintry west extends his blast	6	31
The word of the Lord by night	42	1261
The World is too much with us; late and soon . . .	41	678
The world's a bubble and the life of Man	40	348
The world's great age begins anew	41	824
The worthy knight lies there	14	515
The year's at the spring	42	1073
The young May moon is beaming, love	41	821
Their groves o' sweet myrtle let Foreign Lands reckon .	6	534
Then gudewife, count the lawin	6	378
Then hate me when thou wilt; if ever, now	40	276
Then hey, for a lass wi' a tocher	6	548
Then mounte! then mounte, brave gallants all . . .	28	392
Theniel Menzies' bonie Mary	6	283
There ance was a may, and she lo'ed na men . . .	40	398
There be none of Beauty's daughters	41	788
There dwelt a man in faire Westmerland	40	101
There is a flower, the Lesser Celandine	41	614
There is a garden in her face	40	284

First Lines	Vol.	Page
There is delight in singing, though none hear	41	902
There is no flock, however watched and tended . . .	42	1277
There is no writer that shall not perish	16	82
There is not in the wide world a valley so sweet . . .	41	817
There is sweet music here that softer falls	42	994
There lived a carl in Kellyburn Braes	6	436
There lived a wife at Usher's Well	40	80
There shall be seen upon a day	3	92
There they are, my fifty men and women	42	1094
There, through the long, long summer hours	28	380
There was a bonie lass, and a bonie, bonie lass . . .	6	514
There was a boor from Gelderland	47	481
There was a king in Thule	19	119
There was a lad was born in Kyle	6	92
There was a lass, and she was fair	6	464
There was a lass, they ca'd her Meg	6	301
There was a roaring in the wind all night	41	658
There was a time when meadow, grove, and stream . .	41	595
There was a wife wonn'd in Cockpen	6	433
There was five Carlins in the South	6	367
There was once a day, but old Time was then young . .	6	329
There was three kings into the east	6	39
There was twa sisters in a bowr	40	54
There were three ladies lived in a bower	40	58
There were three rauens sat on a tree	40	73
There's a woman like a dew-drop, she's so purer than the purest	18	372
There's a youth in this city, it were a great pity . . .	6	347
There's Auld Rob Morris that wons in yon glen . . .	6	445
There's Death in the cup, so beware	6	513
There's nane sall ken, there's nane can guess	6	518
There's nane that's blest of human kind	6	264
There's news, lassies, news	6	542
There's not a joy the world can give like that it takes away	41	784
There's nought but care on ev'ry han'	6	48
These are the five donations great	45	620
These eyes, dear Lord, once brandons of desire	40	328
They all were looking for a king	42	1118
They are all gone into the world of light	40	346
They bore him barefac'd on the bier	46	181
They made use of their power	16	39
They shot him dead on the Nine-Stone rig	41	769
They snool me sair, and haud me down	6	416

First Lines	Vol.	Page
They that have power to hurt, and will do none	40	277
They that trust in Jehovah	44	309
They told me, Heraclitus, they told me you were dead .	42	1113
Thickest night, o'erhang my dwelling	6	281
Thine am I, my faithful Fair	6	475
Thine be the volumes, Jessy fair	6	552
Think me not unkind and rude	42	1242
This day, Time winds th' exhausted chain	6	372
This Doctrine out of toil begot	45	720
This is he, who felled by foes	5	273
This is no my ain lassie	6	537
This is the forest primeval	42	1300
This is the month, and this the happy morn	4	7
This is the ship of pearl, which, poets feign	42	1365
This is true Liberty when free born men	3	183
This Life, which seems so fair	40	327
This lump of earth has left his estate	42	1032
This morning timely wrapt with holy fire	40	297
This rich marble doth inter	4	27
This Sancho Panza is of body little	14	515
This tale of my sore-troubled life I write	31	4
This winter's weather it waxeth cold	40	188
This wot ye all whom it concerns	6	240
Thou comest! all is said without a word	41	935
Thou flatt'ring mark of friendship kind	6	191
Thou greybeard, old Wisdom! may boast of thy treasures	6	460
Thou hast dealt well with thy servant	44	299
Thou hast left me ever, Jamie	6	473
Thou hast thy calling to some palace-floor	41	924
Thou, Liberty, thou art my theme	6	407
Thou ling'ring star, with lessening ray	6	365
Thou, Nature, partial Nature, I arraign	6	320
Thou of an independent mind	6	526
Thou Power Supreme, whose mighty scheme	28	87
Thou still unravish'd bride of quietness	41	878
Thou that my doleful life didst imitate	14	11
Thou thoughtest well of the days	16	201
Thou unrelenting Past	42	1221
Thou, who thy honor as thy God rever'st	6	403
Thou whom chance may hither lead	6	307
Thou whom chance may hither lead	6	319
Thou, Whose Almighty word	45	572
Thou youngest virgin-daughter of the skies	40	384

First Lines	Vol.	Page
Thou's welcome, wean; mishanter fa' me	6	55
Tho' cruel fate should bid us part	6	92
Though fickle Fortune has deceived me	6	36
Though the day of my destiny's over	41	790
Though the day of my destiny's over	28	389
Though thou art not a peer, thou hast no peer	14	12
Tho' women's minds, like winter winds	6	133
Thoughts, words, and deeds, the Statute blames with reason	6	207
Three poets, in three distant ages born	40	396
Three years she grew in sun and shower	41	671
Three years she grew in sun and shower	28	147
Through and through th' inspir'd leaves	6	264
Through birth and rebirth's endless round	45	624
Through the black, rushing smoke-bursts	42	1126
Thy bosom is endearèd with all hearts	40	271
Thy braes were bonny, Yarrow stream	41	500
Thy hands have made me and fashioned me	44	299
Thy hue, dear pledge, is pure and bright	41	740
Thy testimonies are wonderful	44	303
Thy tomb is fairly placed upon the strand	12	34
Thy word is a lamp unto my feet	44	301
Tiger, tiger, burning bright	41	583
Time consists of two days; this, bright; and that, gloomy	16	16
Timely blossom, Infant fair	40	440
Timon, the misanthrope, am I below	12	377
Tired with all these, for restful death I cry	40	275
'Tis Friendship's pledge, my young, fair Friend	6	541
'Tis that, that gives the poet rage	39	309
'Tis the day of resurrection	45	543
'Tis the last rose of summer	41	818
'Tis the middle of night by the castle clock	41	709
'Tis time this heart should be unmoved	41	815
To be or not to be? That is the question	34	132
To draw no envy, Shakespeare, on thy name	40	301
To fair Fidele's grassy tomb	41	475
To heal his heart of long-time pain	42	1398
To him who in the love of Nature holds	42	1213
To John I owed great obligation	40	398
To make a happy fireside clime	28	86
To me, fair friend, you never can be old	40	278
To Megara some of our madcaps ran	12	67
To Mercy, Pity, Peace, and Love	41	591
To my ninth decade I have totter'd on	41	905

First Lines	Vol.	Page
To my true king I offered, free from stain	41	917
To paint fair Nature, by divine command	27	299
To Riddell, much lamented man	6	514
To see a world in a grain of sand	41	586
To the Lords of Convention 'twas Claver'se who spoke	41	752
To the weaver's gin ye go, fair maids	6	296
To you, sir, this summons I've sent	6	222
Toll for the Brave	41	533
To-morrow is Saint Valentine's day	46	178
Too many leaders are not well; the way	12	384
Toussaint, the most unhappy man of men	41	655
True hearted was he, the sad swain o' the Yarrow	6	455
True Thomas lay o'er yond grassy bank	40	76
Truly, I never have seen the market and street so deserted	19	337
Truly woman is of glass	14	317
Turn again, thou fair Eliza	6	416
Turn all thy thoughts to eyes	40	286
Turn, Fortune, turn thy wheel, and lower the proud	42	976
Turn on the prudent Ant thy heedless eyes	39	294
'Twas at the royal feast, for Persia won	40	391
'Twas even,—the dewy fields were green	6	220
'Twas in that place o' Scotland's isle	6	151
'Twas in the seventeen hunder year	6	524
'Twas na her bonie blue e'e was my ruin	6	534
'Twas on a Holy Thursday, their innocent faces clean	41	590
'Twas on a lofty vase's side	40	462
'Twas on a Monday morning	6	489
'Twas on a Monday morning	41	566
'Twas one of the charmèd days	42	1252
'Twas when the stacks get on their winter hap	6	231
Twenty years hence my eyes may grow	41	898
Two Voices are there, one is of the Sea	41	675
Umbriel, a dusky, melancholy sprite	34	149
Under a spreading chestnut-tree	42	1271
Under the greenwood tree	40	263
Under the wide and starry sky	42	1213
Under yonder beech-tree single on the green-sward	42	1140
Underneath this sable hearse	40	333
Unhappy they, to whom God ha'n't reveal'd	27	67
Unlike are we, unlike, O princely Heart	41	924
Unto thee do I lift up mine eyes	44	308
Unto thee, O Jehovah, do I lift up my soul	44	170
Unto thee, O Jehovah, will I call	44	174

First Lines	Vol.	Page
Up and waur them a', Jamie	6	371
Up from the meadows rich with corn	42	1362
Up in the morning's no for me	6	300
Up the airy mountain	42	1116
Up the streets of Aberdeen	42	1347
Up wi' the carls o' Dysart	6	265
Upon a simmer Sunday morn	6	96
Upon my lap, my Sovereign sits	40	256
Upon that night, when fairies light	6	111
Vane, young in years but in sage counsel old	4	83
Vanity, saith the preacher, vanity	42	1075
Verse, a breeze 'mid blossoms straying	41	703
Victorious men of earth, no more	40	350
Vigil strange I kept on the field one night	42	1403
Virupakkhas, I love them all	45	708
Wae is my heart, and the tear's in my e'e	6	510
Wae worth thy power, thou cursed leaf	6	221
Wailing, wailing, wailing, the wind over land and sea	42	1011
Wake! For the Sun behind yon Eastern bright	41	943
Waken, lords and ladies gay	41	750
Warriors and chiefs! should the shaft or the sword	41	812
We are na fou, we're nae that fou	6	355
We are the music-makers	42	1198
We cam na here to view your warks	6	275
We give thanks unto thee, O God	44	236
We grant they're thine, those beauties all	6	499
We have heard with our ears, O God	44	195
We must resign! heaven his great soul does claim	34	146
We praise thee, O God, we acknowledge thee to be the Lord	45	546
We talk'd with open heart, and tongue	41	602
We trod the steps appointed for us	16	68
We twa hae paidl't i' the burn	28	89
We walk'd along, while bright and red	41	600
We watch'd her breathing thro' the night	41	910
We'll hide the Cooper behint the door	6	527
We're all deluded, vainly searching ways	3	295
Weak-winged is song	42	1379
Wee, modest, crimson-tippèd flow'r	6	193
Wee, sleekit, cow'rin, tim'rous beastie	6	119
Wee Willie Gray, and his leather wallet	6	514
Weep with me, all you that read	40	299
Welcome, wild North-easter	42	1062
Well I remember how you smiled	41	901

First Lines	Vol.	Page
Well! If the Bard was weather-wise, who made	41	728
Were I as base as is the lowly plain	40	314
Were I so tall to reach the pole	40	398
Wha, in a brulyie, will	6	490
Wha is that at my bower-door?	6	48
Wha will buy my troggin, fine election ware	6	548
Whan bells war rung, an mass was sung	40	78
Whan that Aprille with his shoures soote	40	11
Whare are you gaun, my bonie lass	6	361
Whare live ye, my bonie lass	6	433
What ails ye now, ye lousie bitch	6	228
What bird so sings, yet so does wail?	40	209
What can a young lassie, what shall a young lassie	6	406
What can I give thee back, O liberal	41	926
What constitutes a State	41	579
What danger is the Pilgrim in	15	309
What dost thou in that mansion fair?	6	466
What flocks of critics hover here to-day	18	21
What guile is this, that those her golden tresses	40	249
What hath wrought Sigurd	49	391
What have I done for you	42	1210
What I have left, I left not from generosity	16	302
What is our life? The play of passion	40	207
What man his conduct guardeth, and hath wisdom	45	739
What needs my Shakespeare, for his honoured bones	4	25
What needs this din about the town o' Lon'on	6	374
What one would think doth seek to slay outright	15	274
What time my age was twenty-nine, Subhadda	45	643
What was he doing, the great god Pan	41	922
What will I do gin my Hoggie die	6	298
Whatever is, is right. Though purblind man	1	55
When a deed is done for Freedom, through the broad earth's aching breast	42	1370
When all the world is young, lad	42	1062
When at the first I took my pen in hand	15	5
When biting Boreas, fell and dour	6	248
When Britain first at Heaven's command	40	442
When, by a generous Public's kind acclaim	6	260
When chapman billies leave the street	6	388
When chill November's surly blast	6	60
When Christians unto carnal men give ear	15	24
When daisies pied and violets blue	40	264
When dear Clarinda, matchless fair	6	293

First Lines	Vol.	Page
When Death's dark stream I ferry o'er	6	281
When do I see thee most, beloved one	42	1178
When Faith and Love, which parted from thee never	4	81
When first I came to Stewart Kyle	6	57
When first my brave Johnie lad came to this town	6	414
When first the fiery-mantled Sun	41	771
When fortune is liberal to thee	16	202
When God at first made man	40	345
When God willeth an event	16	130
When Guilford good our pilot stood	6	51
When he came to grene wode	28	396
When he who adores thee has left but the name	41	817
When I am dead, my dearest	42	1181
When I consider how my light is spent	4	84
When I consider life, 't is all a cheat	34	134
When I have borne in memory what has tamed	41	677
When I have fears that I may cease to be	41	897
When I have seen by Time's fell hand defaced	40	274
When I survey the bright	40	252
When icicles hang by the wall	40	262
When in disgrace with fortune and men's eyes	40	270
When in the chronicle of wasted time	40	278
When Israel went forth out of Egypt	44	289
When Januar's wind was blawing cauld	6	527
When Jehovah brought back those that returned to Zion	44	310
When Lascelles thought fit from this world to depart	6	487
When Letty had scarce pass'd her third glad year	41	921
When lilacs last in the dooryard bloom'd	42	1412
When Love with unconfinèd wings	40	355
When lovely woman stoops to folly	41	505
When lyart leaves bestrow the yird	6	122
When maidens such as Hester die	41	735
When men shall find thy flow'r, thy glory, pass	40	220
When Morine, deceas'd, to the Devil went down	6	467
When Music, heavenly maid, was young	41	476
When Nature her great master-piece design'd	6	311
When o'er the hill the eastern star	6	443
When on my sickly couch I lay	28	25
When our two souls stand up erect and strong	41	932
When priests are more in word than matter	46	266
When Princes and Prelates	6	450
When rosy May comes in wi' flowers	6	340
When Ruth was left half desolate	41	607

First Lines	Vol.	Page
When Saints do sleepy grow, let them come hither . . .	15	139
When the blest seed of Terah's faithful Son	4	15
When the British warrior queen	41	539
When the drums do beat, and the cannons rattle . . .	6	344
When the hounds of spring are on winter's traces . . .	42	1199
When the hours of Day are numbered	42	1267
When the lamp is shatter'd	41	851
When the pine tosses its cones	42	1249
When the sheep are in the fauld, and the kye at hame . .	41	557
When the voices of children are heard on the green . .	41	590
When to her lute Corinna sings	40	285
When to the sessions of sweet silent thought . . .	40	271
When to the strenuous, meditative Brahman . . .	45	626
When we met first and loved, I did not build . . .	41	937
When we two parted	41	787
When wild war's deadly blast was blawn	6	457
Whenas in silks my Julia goes	40	336
Where are the joys I have met in the morning . . .	6	474
Where are the Kings and the peoples of the earth . . .	16	312
Where art thou, my beloved Son	41	644
Where, braving angry winter's storms	6	288
Where Cart rins rowin' to the sea	6	412
Where did you come from, baby dear	42	1118
Where dost thou careless lie	40	298
Where hae ye been sae braw, lad	6	359
Where is the home for me	8	383
Where lies the land to which the ship would go . . .	42	1122
Where shall the lover rest	41	742
Where the bee sucks, there suck I	46	455
Where the bee sucks, there suck I	40	266
Where the remote Bermudas ride	40	376
Where they once dug for money	28	401
Whereas my birth and spirit rather took	15	385
Whereas the wise who cultivate	45	736
Wherewith shall a young man cleanse his way . . .	44	295
Whether is better, the gift or the donor	42	1253
Which that the sun with his beams hot	40	199
While at the stook the shearers cow'r	6	104
While briers an' woodbines budding green	6	79
While eagerly man culls life's flowers	45	696
While Europe's eye is fix'd on mighty things . . .	6	446
While larks, with little wing	6	467
While new-ca'd kye rowte at the stake	6	83

First Lines	Vol.	Page
While virgin Spring by Eden's flood	6	418
While winds frae aff Ben-Lomond blaw	6	66
While you here do snoring lie	46	426
Whiles in the early winter eve	42	1197
Whither, midst falling dew	42	1222
Who are you, dusky woman, so ancient hardly human	42	1407
Who doth my weal diminish thus and stain	14	237
Who is it worships at my feet	45	706
Who is Silvia? What is she?	40	264
Who is the happy Warrior? Who is he	41	656
Who made the heart, 'tis He alone	28	86
Who shall, Mattio, yield our pain relief	31	168
Who would true valour see	15	301
Whoe'er he be that sojourns here	6	272
Whoe'er she be	40	359
Whoe'er thou art, O reader, know	6	219
Whoever comes to shroud me, do not harm	40	303
Whom will you send to London town	6	520
Whose is that noble, dauntless brow	6	260
Whoso would know the power of God's dominion	31	251
Why am I loth to leave this earthly scene	6	35
Why art thou silent? Is thy love a plant	41	674
Why boastest thou thyself in mischief, O mighty man	44	206
Why, Damon, with the forward day	41	481
Why do the nations rage	44	145
Why dois your brand sae drap wi' bluid	40	56
Why, let the strucken deer go weep	46	155
Why look the distant mountains	41	917
Why so pale and wan, fond lover	40	353
Who standest thou afar off, O Jehovah	44	153
Why weep ye by the tide, ladie	41	741
Why, why tell thy lover	6	536
Why, ye tenants of the lake	6	285
Will ye go to the Hielands, Leezie Lindsay	6	542
Will ye go to the Indies, my Mary	6	201
Willie Wastle dwalt on Tweed	6	434
Wilt thou be my Dearie?	6	479
Wilt Thou forgive that sin where I begun	40	304
Wilt Thou forgive that sin where I begun	15	352
Winds blow and waters roll	5	97
Wishfully I look and languish	6	404
Wi' braw new branks in mickle pride	6	227
With Esop's lion, Burns says: Sore I feel	6	276

First Lines	Vol.	Page
With food and drinks and cunning magic arts	2	249
With his cross-bow, and his quiver	26	428
With how sad steps, O Moon, thou climb'st the skies	40	214
With little here to do or see	41	640
With numerous tribes from Asia's regions brought	12	12
With Pegasus upon a day	6	326
With sacrifice before the rising morn	41	662
With secret throes I marked that earth	6	180
With the same heart, I said, I'll answer thee	41	936
Within the glen sae bushy, O	6	202
Word's gane to the kitchen	40	117
Words of strife heard I	49	418
Work of his hand	5	183
Would that the structure brave, the manifold music I build	42	1100
Would'st thou hear what man can say	40	297
Wow, but your letter made me vauntie	6	366
Ye banks and braes and streams around	6	444
Ye banks and braes o' bonie Doon	6	400
Ye blushing virgins happy are	40	252
Ye distant spires, ye antique towers	40	447
Ye flaming Powers, and wingèd Warriors bright	4	40
Ye flowery banks o' bonie Doon	6	399
Ye gallants bright, I rede you right	6	332
Ye Highlands, and ye Lawlands	40	107
Ye hypocrites! are these your pranks	6	459
Ye Irish lords, ye knights an' squires	6	157
Ye Jacobites by name, give an ear, give an ear	6	420
Ye learnèd sisters, which have oftentimes	40	234
Ye maggots, feed on Nicol's brain	6	265
Ye Mariners of England	41	777
Ye men of wit and wealth, why all this sneering	6	460
Ye sons of old Killie, assembled by Willie	6	242
Ye true "Loyal Natives" attend to my song	6	459
Ye twain, in trouble and distress	19	11
Ye wavering shapes, again ye do enfold me	19	9
Yes, call me by my pet-name! let me hear	41	936
Yes; in the sea of life enisled	42	1128
Yes! let the rich deride, the proud disdain	6	110
Yes, there is holy pleasure in thine eye	41	680
Yestreen I had a pint o' wine	6	377
Yestreen I met you on the moor	6	20
Yet if His Majesty, our sovereign lord	40	198
Yet, love, mere love, is beautiful indeed	41	927

First Lines	Vol.	Page
Yet once more, O ye Laurels, and once more	4	72
Yet, pleased with idle whimsies of his brain	34	143
Yon wandering rill that marks the hill	6	414
Yon wild mossy mountains sae lofty and wide	6	251
You ask me, why, tho' ill at ease	42	998
You brave heroic minds	40	226
You meaner beauties of the night	40	287
You promise heavens free from strife	42	1114
You render me lovelorn, and remain at ease	16	111
You spotted snakes with double tongue	40	265
You'll love me yet!—and I can tarry	42	1073
You're welcome to Despots, Dumourier	6	461
You're welcome, Willie Stewart	6	413
Young Jamie, pride of a' the plain	6	483
Young Jockie was the blythest lad	6	342
Young Peggy blooms our boniest lass	6	108
Your billet, sir, I grant receipt	6	269
Your friendship much can make me blest	6	294
Your hands lie open in the long, fresh grass	42	1179
Your News and Review, sir	6	328

GENERAL INDEX

EXPLANATORY NOTE ON GENERAL INDEX

Titles of books, essays, dramas, poems, etc., are indexed under the significant subject word where there is one (as TRUTH, ESSAY ON, *Bacon's.* IMMORTALITY, ODE ON INTIMATIONS OF).

Where there is no principal subject word, the title is indexed in its proper order, omitting initial articles, prepositions, or interjections (HARP THAT ONCE THROUGH TARA'S HALLS, THE).

Titles of works included in The Harvard Classics *are entered in small capitals* (ÆNEID, THE). *Works discussed in the Classics, but not included therein, are entered in italics (Percy's Reliques), and will be found as a rule only as subtitles under the author's name. Where the author is unknown or uncertain, or where there is a multiple authorship, the work is entered under its own title.*

Titles of many poems are merely the first lines repeated. The exact titles of such poems will therefore be found in the INDEX TO THE FIRST LINES OF POEMS, SONGS, CHORUSES, HYMNS AND PSALMS. *Any other entry likely to be of use has been put into the* GENERAL INDEX.

GENERAL INDEX

Aaron, references to, in Psalms, xliv, 239 (20), 267 (6), 276 (26), 278 (16); beard of, 314 (2); and the golden calf, 437 (40-1); breast-plate of, iv, 150, 384; Calvin on, xxxix, 42; Browning on, xlii, 1099; Mohammed on, xlv, 911

Abaddon, Hebrew for destruction, xliv, 114, note 13; Milton on, iv, 411

Abano, Pietro d', xix, 211, note 35

Abas, in the ÆNEID, xiii, 77, 327, 336

Abascantius, L. Satrius, ix, 361

Abbagliato, Dante on, xx, 122, and note 7

Abbati, Bocca degli, xx, 133, note 8

Abbondio, Don, in THE BETROTHED, meets the bravoes, xxi, 9-15; character and times of, 16-20; tells Perpetua his mishap, 21-4; plans to put Renzo off, 25-6; with Renzo, 27-30; owns truth to Renzo, 31-3; his fever, 33-4; on night of Renzo's intended marriage, 115-20, 127; ordered to go to Lucia, 368-73; with the Unnamed on the way, 373-9; returns with Lucia, 380-8; complained of, by Agnese, 398; with the Cardinal, 407-9; reprimanded by Cardinal, 415-25; during German invasion, 472-81, 487-91; at castle of Unnamed, 493-5; returns home, 496-9; with Renzo on latter's return, 547-50; anxieties about marrying Renzo, 621-2, 627-30; consents to perform ceremony, 631-3; advises Marquis how to aid lovers, 633-6

Abbott, T. K., translator of Kant, xxxii, 297

Abbott, Capt., at Gettysburg, xliii, 385, 387

Abdallah ibn Umm Maktûm, xlv, 885 note

Abd-El-Melik, xvi, 296, 297, 324

Abd-Es-Samad, the sheik, xvi, 299, 324

Abdication, Rousseau on right of, xxxiv, 220

Abdiel, in PARADISE LOST, rebukes Satan, iv, 201-2; leaves the rebel angels, 203; arrival among the faithful, 204-5; com-

bat with Satan, 207-9; in the battle, 213; Bagehot on Milton's, xxviii, 197-8

A Becket (see Becket)

Abel and Cain, Milton on, iv, 330; Mohammed on, xlv, 997; taken from Limbo by Christ, xx, 18; and the tree of Eve, xxxv, 186

Abelard, Carlyle on, xxv, 362-3

ABERFELDY, THE BIRKS OF, vi, 277-8

Aberrant species, xi, 448-9

Abiathar, Winthrop on, xliii, 94

ABIDE WITH ME, xlv, 566-7

Abihu, Browning on, xlii, 1099

Ability, Penn on, worldly, i, 374-7; with humility, i, 392 (247); M. Aurelius on low natural, ii, 223 (5), 243-4 (5), 249 (52), 252 (67), 255 (8); generally accompanied by frankness, iii, 17; certain to make itself felt, v, 286-7

Abîme, the Saracen, xlix, 148-9

Abimelech, and David, xliv, 181

Abindarraez, story of, xiv, 44

Abishag, reference to, xli, 486

Abolitionism, Lowell on, xxviii, 446

Abortion, Hippocrates on, xxxviii, 3

ABOU BEN ADHEM, xli, 870-1

Abra, Pompeia's maid, xii, 271-2

Abradatas, xxvii, 20

Abraham, Milton on, iv, 344-5; and Ephron, x, 30; Bunyan on, xv, 106, 237-8; and Sarah, xxxvi, 272; Paul on, 352; the covenant with, xliv, 275 (9); Stephen on, 435-6 (2-8); Mohammed on, xlv, 904, 910-11, 955, 980; and Iblis, 952, note 5; Pascal on, xlviii, 164 (502), 198, 201, 203, 216 (644), 284 (822), 298; taken from Limbo, xx, 18

Abraxa, early name of Utopia, xxxvi, 172

Abridgments, Swift on, xxvii, 110

Abriorix, Gaulish chief, xii, 284

Abrotonon, mother of Themistocles, xii, 5

Absalom, and David, xx, 118; Psalm when David fled from, xliv, 146-7; Bunyan on, xv, 309; David's grief for, 418

Abscesses, antiseptic treatment of, xxxviii, 263-5

ABSENCE, by Landor, xli, 899
ABSENCE, PRESENT IN, xl, 313
Absence, Lovelace on, xl, 356; Confucius on, xliv, 29-30
Absentees, taxation of, x, 535
Absolutes, Plato on knowledge of, ii, 64-6; participation in, 93-6; further remarks on, 96-8; Schiller on search for, xxxii, 238; Mazzini on, xxxii, 379
Absolution, Luther on unjust, xxxvi, 276; Pascal on, xlviii, 304 (870), 311-2 (904-5), 317 (923)
Abstemiousness, Pliny on, ix, 297-8
Abstinence, Comus on folly of, iv, 63-4; Hindu doctrine of, xlv, 866-7
Abstract ideas, Plato on, ii, 63-6; Epictetus on, 157 (109); Schiller on, xxxii, 238; Rousseau on, xxxiv, 250-1; Berkeley on, xxxvii, 212; Hume on, 411, 413-14 note 3
Abstract names, Hobbes on, xxxiv, 328
Abstract philosophy, Hume on, xxxvii, 290-8, 350
Abstract reasoning, Hume on, xxxvii, 412, 418
Abstract sciences, Pascal on, xlviii, 58-9 (144)
Absurdities, Hobbes on, xxxiv, 333-4
ABT VOGLER, xlii, 1100-1102
Abu Bekr, xlv, 964, note 24
Abu Ghal, xlv, 879, note 3
Abu-l-Abbas El-Khidr, xvi, 323
Abu Laheb, xlv, 989, note 20
Abu Sufiân, xlv, 943, note 2
Abuses, Sidney on, xxvii, 35; Luther on, xxxvi, 309; Dryden on, xxxix, 174, note 36; Pascal on, xlviii, 314 (916)
Abyssinia, salt as money in, x, 28
Academic philosophy, Hume on, xxxvii, 319-20, 407-20
Academics, St. Augustine on the, vii, 73-4; on nature, xxxix, 109
Academy, Milton's design of an, iii, 239-47
Academy of Plato, ii, 3; first formed by Cimon, xxviii, 40-1; Milton on, iv, 401; Newman on, xxviii, 57
Acadie, A Tale of (see Evangeline)
Acamacari, town of, xxxiii, 360
Acception of persons, xxxiv, 409
Accius, works of, lost, xxvii, 344
Acclimatisation, Darwin on, xi, 144-7
Accolti, Benedetto, xxxi, 73, note 2, note 5
Accomplishments, Locke on, xxxvii, 170

Accorso, Francesco, xx, 64 and note 4
Accounting, as part of female education, i, 93; importance of punctual, 98; Locke on knowledge and practise of, xxxvii, 178-9
Accuracy, essential to beauty, v, 210; Hume on, xxxvii, 292-3; Goethe on, xxxix, 256
Accusations, kill innocent names, xviii, 335; Bentham on public, xxvii, 241; in law, Hobbes on, xxxiv, 399-400; of children, xxxvii, 90; Calvin on, xxxix, 28
Accusers, false, in ancient Rome, ix, 296, note 9
Acedophagi, xxxv, 349
Acelin, Count, xlix, 100, 180
Acestes, King of Sicily, xiii, 92; welcomes Æneas, 179; at games, 180; the arrow of, 195-6
Acetate of lead, under voltaic current, xxx, 129 note
Acetate of soda, xxx, 40 and note
Acevedo, Pietro de, on bravoes, xxi, 12
Achæmenides, xiii, 148-9
Achaia, Pliny on, ix, 332
Achaicus, xlv, 514 (17)
Achan, Dante on, xx, 228; Vane on, xliii, 129
Achates, faithful, xiii, 77; references to, 79, 84, 93, 96, 145, 208, 283
Acheloös River, Herodotus on, xxxiii, 11
Acheron, Plato on the, ii, 108-9; sooty flag of, iv, 60; Milton on the, 123; blood-bedabbled peak of, viii, 453; Virgil on, xiii, 211, 217; Dante on the, xx, 15, 60; Homer on the, xxii, 143; Burke on exhalation of, xxiv, 72 (see xiii, 215)
Acherusian Lake, ii, 108, 109
Achievement, Browning on, xlii, 1096
Achillas, and Cæsar, xii, 304-5
Achilles, Socrates on, ii, 17; and Patroclus, iii, 318; xxxii, 77; xlvi, 28; Milton on wrath of, iv, 260; heel of, v, 92; Dryden on, xiii, 8, 14, 26-7; xxxix, 158; father of Pyrrhus, and Priam, xiii, 118; imitated by Alexander, xxxvi, 50; brought up by Chiron, 57; flight from Chiron, xx, 180; in Dante's Hell, 22; javelin of, 127; his quarrel with Ulysses, xxii, 101; Homer on death and funeral of, xxii, 320-2; in Hades, 156-8, 320; Burke on, xxiv, 127; Tom Brown on, xxvii, 313; Shelley on

Homer's, 336; and the twenty-five cities, xxxv, 233; and the captive, xxxix, 239

Achillini, and King Louis, xxi, 466

Achoriens, More on the, xxxvi, 159

Acilius, friend of Pliny, ix, 240; soldier of Cæsar, xii, 277

Acmon, in the ÆNEID, xiii, 326

Acoetes, servant of Pallas, xiii, 356, 358

Aconcagua, volcano of, xxix, 257, 295-6; height of, 250, note 11

Aconteus, in the ÆNEID, xiii, 378

Acoustics, in NEW ATLANTIS, iii, 178

Acquiescence, Burns on, vi, 68; Emerson's doctrine of, v, 60, 147-8; Epictetus on, ii, 126 (26, 29), 130 (37), 136 (58), 138 (61), 143 (71), 148 (84), 164 (131), 165 (133, 134), 167 (138, 139), 172 (152), 174 (159, 160), 179-80 (184), 180 (186); Hume on doctrine of, xxxvii, 368; Jesus on, xli, 490-1; Job on, xliv, 73 (10); Kempis on, vii, 276, 278-9, 301, 303, 317-9; M. Aurelius on, ii, 204 (17), 211 (16), 216 (23), 218 (34), 224 (8), 226 (10), 229 (27), 240 (44), 248 (41), 249-50 (51, 54), 250 (58), 258 (32), 262 (50), 269 (28), 279 (14), 281 (28), 286 (6), 297 (14); Pascal's doctrine, xlviii, 340-1, 352, 372-3; Pascal on Epictetus's doctrine, 338; Pope on, xl, 411, 414-5; Raleigh on, xxxix, 97-8; Rousseau on, xxxiv, 279-80; Tennyson on, xlii, 1020; Thackeray on, xlii, 1059-60.

Acrasia, the enchantress, xxxix, 64

Acron, death of, xiii, 346

Acropolis, propylæa of the, xii, 50-1

Acta Sanctorum, Carlyle on, v, 456-7

Actæon, son of Autonoë, viii, 427; and Artemis, 381; reference to, xlvii, 714 note

Actilius, Caxton on, xxxix, 15

Actinic light, xxx, 260

Actinism, xxviii, 418

Action (see also Acts, Activity); Demosthenes on, iii, 31; the value of, to the scholar, v, 12-15; Kant on principles of, xxxii, 325-50; two ways of, xxxix, 117; Longfellow on, xlii, 1264, 1265; Hindu doctrine of, xlv, 795, 799-801, 805-6, 809-10, 813, 866-8; Webster on want of, xlvii, 757; Pascal on necessity of, xlviii, 51 (131); sources of, 115 (334); and love, 416, 419

Action and reaction (see Polarity)

Actium, battle of, xii, 371-5; Bacon on, iii, 79; Dryden on Antony at, xviii, 32-3; Virgil on, xiii, 290-1

Actius, razor of, iii, 315, note 9

Activity, Cicero on, ix, 51; Epictetus on, and meditation, ii, 125; M. Aurelius on, 268 (16); Hindu Krishna on, xlv, 799; man prone to shirk, xix, 21; in perceptions, xxxvii, 214-15

Actor, the lance of, xiii, 392

Actors, attitude of, toward the drama, xix, 10, 12, 14-15; as teachers, 29; high rewards of, reason for, x, 109; Lamb on, xxvii, 300-8; legal, xxxiv, 413-15; Montaigne on, xxxii, 70; Shakespeare on, xlvi, 139-40, 147-8; Voltaire on, xxxiv, 152-3

Acts, better than knowledge, xv, 85; xxxii, 59; xliv, 9 (24), 370 (47-9); better than words, ii, 177 (175), 279 (16), 288 (15); Browning on, and intentions, xlii, 1071; Confucius on, and words, xliv, 8 (13), 14 (24), 15-16 (9), 48 (29); consequences of, xlviii, 165 (505); effect of, on faculties and habits, ii, 144 (75); explain themselves, v, 67; carry own rewards, 90, 289; hidden, most noble, xlviii, 62 (159); Hindu doctrine of, xlv, 867-8; Hume on, and motives, xxxvii, 353-60, 362 note, 365-6; Kant on moral worth of, xxxii, 308-15, 349-50; Kempis on judgment of, vii, 296; kind of words, v, 164; not motives, to be judged, xxv, 36; our angels, v, 59; our epochs, xviii, 421; our only possessions, xlv, 676; religiousness of, 864; unsocial, ii, 269 (23)

ACTS OF THE APOSTLES, authorship of, xliv, 352, 423-86; editorial remarks on, 422

Acts of settlement, succession, etc. (see Settlement, Succession)

Acuto, Giovanni, xxxvi, 42

Ad, xlv, 891, 905

Adam, awakening of, iv, 180-1; 250; Bacon on fall of, xxxix, 128; Bagehot on Milton's, xxviii, 196; Browne on, iii, 274, 291, 317; Burns on, vi, 142; Chaucer on, xl, 46; confesses his sin and is judged, iv, 294-6; creation explained to, 248; inquiries of, on creation, 228-30, 240; curse of, xxxvi, 332; Dante on, xx, 398-9; earth, kingdoms

of, seen by, in vision, iv, 328-9; Eden, departure of, from, 356-8; Eden, Life in, described by, 250-56; Eden, loss of, dreaded by, 326-7; Eden, sentenced to leave, 321-2; Eve, accused by, 287-90; Eve, discourse with, on laboring apart, 265-70; Eve, love of, for, 256-9; Eve, meeting of, with, 255-6; Eve, supper of, with, 163; Eve, tree of, and, xxxv, 186; Eve, wrath of, at, iv, 312-14; fall of, through own fault, 291; future, vision of, by, 329-55; HAMLET, mentions of, in, xlvi, 191; hides from God, iv, 293; Hobbes on language of, xxxiv, 323; labors of, iv, 186; Lamb on pictures of, xxvii, 312 note; lament of, iv, 309-12; Luther on, xxxvi, 361; Michael, meeting of, with, iv, 324-5; morning hymn, 184-6; Omens, evil, seen by, 323-4; PARADISE LOST, Description of, in, 162-3; supper with Eve, 163; Pascal on state of, xlviii, 184 (560); prayers relieve, iv, 322-3; Raphael discourses with, 192-4; Raphael parts with, 259-60; Raphael welcomed by, 188-90; rest suggested by, 170; retires to rest with Eve, 173; saved by Christ, xx, 18; his place in Paradise, 422; Saviour promised to, xlviii, 215-6; stars, discourse of, on, iv, 171; stars, inquiries of, on, 244; submission advised by, 317-8; tree of knowledge, described to Eve by, 165; wisdom of, xx, 340, note 6; Eve tempts, iv, 282-7; waking, accuses Eve, 287-90

Adam and Eve, Woolman on, i, 214
Adam and Eve's Pools, iii, 170
Adam the First, and his daughters, xv, 73
Adamo of Brescia, xx, 124, note 2; Sinon of Troy, and, 126
Adams, John, Americanism of, v, 67; American independence, and, xliii, 150 note, 154; treaty with England and, 174-5
Adams, John Quincy, treaty of 1814 and, xliii, 255; treaty with Spain and, 268
Adams, Matthew, i, 14
Adams, Samuel, signer of Declaration, xliii, 154; in Articles of Confederation, 167
Adams, Sarah Flower, hymn by, xlv, 568-9
Adams, William, xliii, 255
Adamus, in Utopia, xxxvi, 181-2
Adaptability, Marcus Aurelius on, ii, 239

(39); Montaigne on, xxxii, 57-8; to times, Machiavelli on, xxxvi, 81
Adaptation, in nature, xi, 84-5; examples of, 71-2, 91-2, 198, 224-5; xxix, 467; never perfect, 91; to atmospheric conditions, xxxviii, 338-9; to climate, xi, 145-6
Adder, Harrison on the, xxxv, 344-5
Addison, Joseph, birth and education, xxvii, 155-6; Campaign, 159-60, 182-3; Cato of, 158, 165-8, 178; Cato, quotation from, i, 82; character and habits of, xxvii, 176-80; Commissioner of Appeals, 160; critical abilities of, 196-7; death of, 175-6; defense of Christianity, 173; Dennis on Cato of, 185-96; descriptions of life, 198; The Drummer, 169; Dryden on translations of, xiii, 427; early writings of, xxvii, 157; Esther Johnson and, 123; Freeholder, 171; Hume on, xxxvii, 291; HYMN by, xl, 400; xlv, 535; Johnson on Cato of, xxvii, 184-5; xxxix, 227; Latin compositions of early, xxvii, 157; Letter to Halifax, 158-9, 182; Life and works of, 72; LIFE by Johnson, 155-99; marriage of, 171-2; Old Whig papers, 174, 175; on Chaucer, xxviii, 81; on criticism of art, xxiv, 28; on love of beauty in animals, 38; on the rotund in building, 63 note; papers for the Guardian, xxvii, 168-9; Peerage Bill Pamphlet, 173-4; plans a dictionary, 173; Poems early, 157; poetry of, estimate on, 180-96; Political Papers, 170; Prose, 199; Regent, secretary to, 171; religion, 107; Rosamond, 160, 184; Sainte-Beuve on, xxxii, 131; Secretary of State, xxvii, 172; Shelley on Cato, 341; The Spectator, 83, 162, 164, 169, 170; Steele, relations with, 156, 160-4, 165-6, 173-5; The Tatler, 161-2; Tender Husband, part in, 160; Thackeray on, xxviii, 9; Tragedy on Socrates, xxvii, 172-3; travels, 158; Under-Secretary, 160; VISION OF MIRZA, 73-7; Voltaire on Cato, xxxiv, 135; xxxix, 227; WESTMINSTER ABBEY, xxvii, 78-80; Wharton, Lord, secretary to, 160
Addison, Lancelot, father of Joseph, xxvii, 155
Adeimantus, son of Ariston, ii, 22
Adeimantus, son of Leucolophus, viii, 486
Adeodatus, son of St. Augustine, vii, 3, 96, 146; grief of, over Monica, 155

Ades, reference to, iv, 132

ADESTE FIDELES, xlv, 555-6

Adhibhuta, Adhidaiva, etc., xlv, 822

Adhyâtman, xlv, 822, 834

Adimantus, Athenian general, xii, 143

Admetus, king of Molossians, xii, 26

Administratio, defined, xxxvi, 284

Admirable Crichton, (see Crichton)

Admiral, origin of name, xxxv, 358

Admiralty Cases (U. S.), xliii, 189 (Sec. 2)

Admiration, Byron on, xli, 793; caused by ignorance, xxiv, 52; defined by Hobbes, xxxiv, 341; degrees of, ii, 234 (14); excited by the perilous, ix, 347; inferior degree of astonishment, xxiv, 49; Pascal on love of, xlviii, 60, (150-1); unknown to animals, xlviii, 130 (401)

Admlithe, the jester, xlix, 242

Admonition, Winthrop on use of, xliii, 94

Adœdatus (see Adeodatus)

Adolius, xxxviii, 392

ADONAIS, Shelley's, xli, 856-70

Adonijah, and Solomon, xliii, 94

Adonis, references to, iv, 71, 99, 271

Adoration, David on, xli, 492-5; "pure, which God likes best," iv, 173

Adoxa, Darwin on the, xi, 215

Adramelech, Milton on, iv, 213

Adrastos, viii, 200 note

Adrastus, king of Argos, xii, 240 note; in Hades, xiii, 223

Adrian, Roman Emperor (see Hadrian)

Adrian V, Pope, Dante on, xx, 223-4, note 8

Adrian VI, Pope, xxxvi, 102

Adrian, in THE TEMPEST, xlvi, 417, 418, 443

ADRIAN, DYING, TO HIS SOUL, xl, 398

Adulation, Burke on, xxiv, 148

Adultery in biblical times, xliii, 94; in Dante's Hell, xx, 22-4; in old England, xxxv, 365-6; in old Massachusetts, xliii, 81 (9); in Utopia, xxxvi, 210, 211; Jesus on, xliv, 397 (18); Job on, 119 (9-12); Mohammed on, xlv, 969; punishment of, in ancient Germany, xxxiii, 103

Advancement in Life, Channing on, xxviii, 314-21; Confucius on, xliv, 51 (5); Ruskin on, xxviii, 94-5, 127-8

Adversity, Christ's sake, for, vii, 239 (5), 253-7; Cicero on, ix, 17, 31; despair in, vii, 268, 295 (6), 329, Ecclesiastes

on, xliv, 343 (14); Kempis on, vii, 215, 273 (2), 294 (4); love and, viii, 32-3; Pascal on, xlviii, 47 (107), 354; Penn on, i, 344 (239); prosperity of greatness, v, 290; Raleigh on, xxxix, 67, 96-8; religion and, iii, 44; strength proved by, vii, 220, (4); truth's sake, for, i, 191-2

ADVERSITY, ESSAY ON, Bacon's, iii, 16-17

ADVERSITY, HYMN TO, Gray's, xl, 450-1

Advice, Æsop on interested, xvii, 37; Bacon on, of friends, iii, 70-1, 120; Carlyle on, xxv, 361; Cicero on, ix, 25, 39; in difficulties, xvii, 44; Kempis on giving and receiving, vii, 213 (3); Mill on liberty of, xxv, 295; of parents, xxxvii, 82; Pliny on seeking, ix, 339 (see also Counsel)

Advocates and judges, iii, 132-3

AE FOND KISS AND THEN WE SEVER, vi, 428-9

Æacus, judge in Hades, ii, 29

Æacus, porter in THE FROGS, viii, 453, 457-9, 461-3

Æantodorus, ii, 22

Aëdon, daughter of Pandareüs, in the Odyssey, xxii, 270

Æetes, brother of Circe, xxii, 133

Ægæon, and Jove, xiii, 341 (see also Briareus)

Ægina, in Persian war, xii, 20; Pericles on, 43

Ægisthus, in AGAMEMNON, viii, 71-5; Clytemnestra on, 65; Homer on, xxii, 10, 17, 38, 39-41, 59; in THE LIBATION-BEARERS, viii, 110-13; Orestes on, 90, 117-18

Ægospotami, battle of, xii, 143-4

Ægyptus, in the ODYSSEY, xxii, 21-2

Ælius, Sextus, Cicero, on, ix, 55

ÆLLA, SONG FROM, xli, 558-9

Ælroth, xlix, 132

Æmilianus, Minutius, ix, 200-2

Æmilianus, Scipio (see Scipio)

Æmilius, Papus, ix, 23

Æmilius, Paulus, and the king of Macedon, xxxii, 16; Pascal on, xlviii, 132 (409, 410)

Æneas, adventures related by, xiii, 100-51; Africa, landing of, in, 79-80; Anchises's funeral games celebrated by, 179-97; Anchises rescued by, 122-5; arms of, brought by Venus, 288-92; arms of, made by Vulcan, 282-3; Cervantes on, xiv, 212; Carthage, entered

by, xiii, 87-90; Carthage, prepares to
sail from, 166-7; Carthage, second
warning to fly from, 172; Carthage,
warned to leave, 160-1; Chaonia, voyage of, to, 137; Crete, settles in, 131-3;
Creusa, ghost of, and, 126-7; Dante
places, in Limbo, xx, 19; Dido and, go
hunting, xiii, 157-8; Dido curses, 175;
Dido, first meeting with, 90-1, 94-9;
Dido, love of, for, 152-5; Dido re-
proaches, 163-6; Dryden on Virgil's,
xiii, 9, 18, 19-37; xxxix, 157-8; Evander's aid sought by, xiii, 270-80;
283-7; fire on ships of, 201; Hades
visited by, 211-38; Helenus and Andromache receive, 137-44; hell, visit to,
referred to, xx, 9-10, note 1; Italy,
first landing in, xiii, 145-6; Italy,
warned to seek, 133-4; Jove prophesies
success of, 82; Juno persecutes, 73;
Latium, arrival in, 239-44; Mezentius
and Lausus killed by, 348-54; Pallas,
body of, sent back by, 355-8; parents
of, Venus and Anchises, 95; prayer and
agreement of, 395-6; ships of, turned
to nymphs, 295-8; Sibyl visited by,
207-10; Sicily, driven to, by storm,
178-9; Sicily, first landing in, 147-51;
Sicily, leaves settlement in (cf. Dante,
xx, p. 220), 202-3; Sidney on, xxvii,
10, 18, 23, 28-9; Spenser on, xxxix, 62;
storm overtakes, xiii, 76-7; Strophades,
landing of, in the, 135-7; Thrace in,
129-30; Trojan war, in, 366; trophy
erected by, 355-6; Troy, in sack of,
109-21; Troy, sets sail from, 128; Troy,
withdrawal from, xxxix, 224; Turnus
challenged to single combat by, xiii,
359; Turnus, final combat with, 414-
23; Turnus, prepares for combat with,
393; Turnus, war with, 259-60;
Turnus, war with, renewed, 405-10;
Venus heals, wounded, 404; Venus,
meeting of, with, 84-7

Æneas, palsied man healed by apostles,
xliv, 443 (33-5)

Æneid, The, Dryden's translation, xiii,
73-423; Arguments of, written by
Addison, xxvii, 157; Burke on, xxiv,
20, 54, 60, 72, 135-6; Caxton's Prologue to, xxxix, 24-26; Dryden on machinery of, xiii, 46-50; Dryden on his
translation of, 51-69; Dryden's defence
of, 14-43; editorial remarks on, 3-4;
Homer's influence on, xxxix, 158; Mil-

ton on, iv, 260-1; Montaigne on, xxxii,
90, 92-3; time of, xiii, 43-6; time of
composition, 52; willed by Virgil to be
burned, 18

Ænobarbus, Domitius, xii, 353

Æolus, called Hippotades, iv, 74; in the
ÆNEID, xiii, 75-7; jailer of the winds,
78; Ulysses and, xxii, 130-2

Aeronautics, in NEW ATLANTIS, iii, 178-9

Æschere, xlix, 42, 44, 63

Æschines, the orator, xii, 203, 211; metaphors of, ix, 350; on Demosthenes, xii,
193, 201; ix, 215, 349

Æschines, son of Lysanias, ii, 22, 47

Æschylus, Aristophanes on, viii, 486; on
Artemis, xxxiii, 79; Euripides's dispute
with, in THE FROGS, viii, 462-86; on
the hereafter, ii, 103; HOUSE OF AT-
REUS, viii, 7-165; Hugo on, xxxix,
347; life and works of, viii, 5-6;
Milton on, iv, 413; Montaigne on death
of, xxxii, 13; on Persians, numbers of,
xii, 18; PROMETHEUS BOUND, viii, 166-
206; Shelley on choruses of, xxvii, 332;
Sophocles beats, in contest, viii, 208;
Sophocles and, compared, 208; Suppliants of, xxxix, 341; Taine on, and
Euripides, 426-7; Voltaire on tragedies
of, 364

Æsculapius, son of Apollo, xxxviii, 2;
Æschylus on death of, viii, 45; Jonson
on, xlvii, 615; Virgil on death of, xiii,
265

Æsion, on Demosthenes, xii, 199 and
note

Æsir, northern gods, xlix, 294 note

Æson, son of Tyro, xxii, 151; Medea and,
xli, 664

Æsop, author of Fables, xvii, 8; Bacon on,
iii, 108; Herodotus on, xxxiii, 67

Æsop, the tragedian, xii, 221-2; Cicero
on, ix, 108

Æsop's FABLES, xvii, 11-44; CAXTON's
EPILOGUE TO, xxxix, 17-18; editorial
remarks on, xvii, 8, 9; Emerson on, v,
176; Locke on, xxxvii, 131-2, 160;
Montaigne on, xxxii, 90; Sidney on,
xxvii, 18-19; versified by Socrates, ii,
48-9

ÆSTHETIC EDUCATION, LETTERS ON, Schiller's, xxxii, 207-295

Æsthetics (see Art, Beauty, Taste)

Æstivation, of animals, xxix. 105

Æstyans, Tacitus on the, xxxiii, 118

Æthiops, river, viii, 196, note 56

Ætna, Æschylus on, viii, 179-80; Milton on, iv, 94; Virgil on, xiii, 147

Afer, Domitius, Pliny on, ix, 221; will of, 328

Affability, a source of power, xxxiv, 360

Affairs, great, by what performed, ix, 51

Affectation, Fielding on, xxxix, 180-1; Locke on, xxxvii, 45-7; of simplicity, ii, 288 (15)

Affectation, in speech, i, 383 (121); of wisdom, iii, 64-5

Affection, never wasted, xlii, 1320; "oft the spring of woe," vi, 195; on blind, xl, 301; (see also Love)

Affliction, Browne on, iii, 304; David's prayer in, xliv, 156; Elihu on, 129 (8-11, 15-16); Eliphaz on, 77 (6, 7, 17-19); Emerson on compensation for, v, 102-3; Herbert on, xv, 389-91; Kempis on patience under, vii, 217 (8), 280, 293-4, 300 (2); Longfellow on, xlii, 1277-8; Mohammedan proverb on, xvi, 76; Pascal on temporal, xlviii, 349; "sons of, brothers in distress," vi, 251; wisdom learned by, viii, 14; Woolman on, i, 197-8, 237-8

AFFLICTION OF MARGARET, xli, 644-6

Affronts, Penn on bearing, i, 339-40 (182-5)

Afranius, Lucius, Cicero on, ix, 96, 159; in civil war, xii, 294, 299, 307

Africa, backward state of, cause of, x, 26; Herodotus on, xxxiii, 21; vegetation and animals of, xxix, 92-4

Africanus, Julius, ix, 300

Africanus, Scipio (see Scipio)

After-games, i, 348 (302)

AFTON, SWEET, vi, 417-18

Agabus, xliv, 448 (28), 469 (10-11)

Agace, Gobin, xxxv, 21, 23

Agag, Samuel on, xxxix, 78

Agamemnon, Achilles and, xiii, 14-15; burial of, viii, 94-5; Cassandra foresees death of, 48-59; Homer on return and death of, xxii, 37, 38, 39, 59-60, 154-6; in Hades, 154-7, 320-2; Iphigenia, sacrifice of, by, viii, 15-17; murder of, 60-71; Orestes on, 140-1; Sidney on, xxvii, 17; Spenser on, xxxix, 62; in Trojan war, viii, 9-13, 26-7; xxii, 101; Virgil on death of, xiii, 365

AGAMEMNON, TRAGEDY OF, Æschylus's, viii, 7-75; compared with LEAR, xxvii, 339

Agapetus, Bishop, xx, 306, note 6

Agariste, mother of Pericles, xii, 37

Agassiz, Alexander, on echinodermata, xi, 235, 236

Agassiz, Louis, on amblyopsis, xi, 144; on embryological characters, 437; on embryos, 371, 468; on his first lecture, xxviii, 452; on glacial period, xi, 394; on immutability of species, 348; on movement of glaciers, xxx, 225; on synthetic types, xi, 362; on tertiary species, 336

AGASSIZ [Louis], FIFTIETH BIRTHDAY OF, Longfellow's, xlii, 1293-4

Agatha, St., Kempis on, vii, 309, note 2

Agatharchus, Alcibiades and, xii, 120; Zeuxis and, 49

Agathocles, Machiavelli on, xxxvi, 29, 31-2

Agathon, Aristophanes on, viii, 441; in Dante's Limbo, xx, 236; quoted, ii, 214 (18)

Agathonius, age of, ix, 70

Agave, mother of King Pentheus in the BACCHÆ, viii, 368-436; doom of, 433-6; leader of Bacchanals, 399-402; slays Pentheus, 420-1

Age (see also Old Age); not to be regarded, viii, 279; legal, in Massachusetts, xliii, 73 (53)

Agelaus, in the ODYSSEY, xxii, 281-2, 299, 302, 303, 304

Agents, Bacon on choice of, iii, 118; Hobbes on, xxxiv, 413-14

Agesilaus, Bacon on, iii, 23, 108; Cicero on, ix, 104; on happiness, xxxii, 5

Aggravation, punishment of priests, xxxvi, 308 note

AGINCOURT, Drayton's, xl, 222-6

Agincourt, Macaulay on, xli, 915

Agio, defined, x, 358; of Amsterdam Bank, 256-7

Agis I of Sparta, and Alcibiades, xii, 128

Agis II of Sparta, xii, 210

Agis III, Emerson on, v, 183

Agis the Lycian, xiii, 347

Aglauros, in Dante's Purgatory, xx, 203

Agli, Lotto degli, xx, 57 note

Aglovale, Sir, xxxv, 128

Agnes, St., Luther on, xxxvi, 301, 326

AGNES, ST., EVE OF, Keats's, xli, 883-93

Agnese, in THE BETROTHED (see Mondella, Agnese)

Agnolo, Baccio d', xxxi, 412 note 3

Agnolo, Giuliano di Baccio d', xxxi, 392, 412

Agnolo, Michel, father of Bandinello, xxxi, 14

Agnolo, Michel, the Sienese, xxxi, 55 note 1, 59-60

Agnolo, Michel (Buonarroti) (see Michelangelo)

Agnosticism, Huxley on, xxviii, 208

Agostino, xx, 338 note 31

Agouti, Darwin on the, xxix, 76-7

Agrarian Laws, of Rome, xxxv, 303

Agravaine, reference to, xlii, 1189

Agreeableness, Pascal on, xlviii, 419

Agreement, always silent, xxv, 319; a way of honoring, xxxiv, 364

Agrican, and Angelica, iv, 392

Agricola, Julius, Milton on, iii, 222; Tacitus and, xxxiii, 92

Agricultural schools, Cowley on, xxvii, 65-6; Ticknor on, xxviii, 367

Agricultural systems, of political economy, x, 426-46

Agriculture, capital, best employment for, x, 291, 306

Agriculture, Cicero on pleasures of, ix, 63-6; combinations in, x, 128; effect of, on prices of bread and meat, 151-2; Emerson on, v, 50; European policy not favorable to, x, 6, 131; improvement in, 184-6; in Utopia, xxxvi, 173-4, 178; labor, division of, in, x, 11-12; Locke on, xxxvii, 174-5; Luther on, xxxvi, 332; manufactures compared with, x, 11; manufactures, relation to, 221, 304-7, 444; military spirit and, xxvii, 372-3; Milton on study of, iii, 240; prices in general, x, 192; protective tariffs and, 338; Rousseau on, xxxiv, 178-9, 207-8; skill required in, high, x, 129-30; taxes on profits of, 503; wealth, best source of, iii, 88-9; Woolman's high opinion of, i, 196 note

Agriculture, Essay on, Cowley's, xxvii, 61-9

Agrippa, King, St. Paul and, xliv, 478 (13-27, 1) 481 (27-32)

Agrippa, Cornelius, Emerson on, v, 177; in Faustus, xix, 210; on science, xxvii, 30-31

Agrippa, Marcus, Antony and, xviii, 25; at Actium, xii, 372-3; xiii, 290; Augustus and, iii, 67; marriages of, xii, 388; Octavia and, 348

Agrippa, Menenius, xii, 152; Sidney on, xxvii, 24

Agrippina, daughter of Antony, xviii, 64; daughter of Germanicus, xii, 389

Agrippinus, Florus and, ii, 119

Aguarus, xxxv, 148

Aguecheek, Sir Andrew, Macaulay on, xxvii, 385

Aguilar, Pedro de, xiv, 389; sonnets of, 391

Aguirre, Lope de, xxxiii, 322-4

Ahab, reference to, iv, 368

Ahala, C. Servilius, ix, 65

Ahasuerus, Dante on, xx, 213

Ahauton, the Indian, xliii, 142, 143

Ahaz, Rimmon and, iv, 99-100

Ahenobarbus Domitius, xii, 388

Ahitophel, Dante on, xx, 118

Ahriman (see Arimanes)

Ai, Duke, xliv, 8 (19), 11 (21), 18 (2), 38 (9), 48 (22)

Aias (see Ajax)

Aiguillon, siege of, xxxv, 7, 9

Aiguillon, Duke d', Burke on, xxiv, 249

Aiken, Robert, Burns's inscription to, vi, 134; Epitaph for, vi, 219; references to, vi, 70, 72, 224, 351, note 4

Aims, high, Browning on, xlii, 1089; Johnson on, xxxix, 198

Ainslie, Miss, Epigram to, Burns's, vi, 267

Air, composition of, xxx, 144; elasticity of, 149-50; life without (see Anaërobian Life); needed for combustion, 104-5; pressure of, 145-9; resistance of, 19-20, 147-8; temperature dependent on pressure, 212; weight of, 52, 144-5

Air-burner, the, xxx, 110 note

Airly Beacon, xlii, 1060-1

Ajax (Aias), son of Telamon, xxii, 156, 320; Hector and, v, 93; madness of, xxvii, 17; Socrates on, ii, 29; Ulysses and, xxii, 158-9; son of Oileus, xxii, 58-9

Ajib, King, xvi, 92-3

Akber Khan, pigeons of, xi, 40

À Kempis (see Kempis, Thomas à)

Aladdin (see Ala-ed-Din)

Alæan Twins, xiii, 226-7 (see Ephialtes and Otus)

Ala-ed-Din and the Wonderful Lamp, xvi, 341-424; manuscript of, 3

Alagia, wife of Malaspina, xx, 224 note

Alamanni, Luigi, xxxi, 86 note 4; Cellini and, 86, 91, 259, 260, 261, 276, 299, 319

Alam-ed-in Senjer, xvi, 208

Alaopolitanes, Nephelogetes and, xxxvi, 216

Alāra Kālāma, xlv, 716-7, 722-3

Alaska Purchase, xliii, 432-6

Alaskie, Albert, v, 416

Alba Longa, Virgil on, xiii, 82

Albanians, Freeman on the, xxviii, 264, 266

ALBANY, THE BONIE LASS OF, Burns', vi, 284

Albany, Duke of, in LEAR, xlvi, 215, 217, 219; before battle, 304; Cornwall, war with, 242, 262; Edgar with, 312-3; Edmund with, 308-10; France, war against, 288; Gloucester's wrongs, 285-6; Goneril's death and, 314-5; Goneril denounced by, 311-2; Goneril's letter to, 305; Goneril with, 239-40, 284-6; Lear and Cordelia sent for, by, 314; Lear with, 237-8, 239; plot against, 299; resigns power, 317

Albany Convention, Franklin on, i, 124-6

Albatross, Dana on the, xxiii, 37; food of the, xxix, 167

Albemarle Island, Darwin on, xxix, 380

Alberigo, the friar, xx, 139 and note 4

Alberigo of Como, xxxvi, 44

Albero of Sienna, xx, 122 note 5

Albert I, Emperor, Dante on, xx, 168, 368 notes 5 and 6; Switzerland, conduct of, toward, xxvi, 480-1; murder of, 477-8

Albert, Archbishop of Mayence, xxxvi, 281 note; Luther's address to, 247-9

Alberti, Alessandro and Napoleone, xx, 132 and note 2

Alberto, Abbot, xx, 219, note 8

Albertus Magnus, xx, 327, note 15

Albin, in POLYEUCTE, xxvi, 84-5, 105-8, 119-21, 127

Albinus, Clodius, governor of Britain, xxvii, 8; rival of Severus, xxxvi, 65

Albinus, Spurius, ix, 47

Albinus, D. Brutus surnamed, xii, 316

Albinus, correspondent of Pliny, ix, 282

Albizzi, Girolamo degli, xxxi, 407 and note 1, 408

Al-Borák, reference to, xlii, 1358

Albracca, siege of, iv, 392; xiv, 76

Albret, Perducas d', xxxv, 70, 78

Albuquergues, killed by Don Pedro, xxxix, 84

ALCÆUS, ODE IN IMITATION OF, xli, 579

Alcandrê, her gifts to Helen, xxii, 49

Alcanor, xiii, 316, 332-3

Alcavala, of Spain, x, 540

Alcestis, Milton on, iv, 86; Ruskin on, xxviii, 142; Wordsworth on, xli, 664

ALCHEMIST, THE, xlvii, 541-664; remarks on, 540

Alchemy, Emerson on, v, 297; metal, the, xxxv, 324; punishment of, in Dante's Hell, xx, 122-3

Alcibiades, accused of impiety, xii, 122-3; Andros expedition and, 141; Aristophanes on, viii, 484; Athenian government, attempts to change, made by, xii, 129-31; Athens' power of, strengthened by, 118-9; Athens, return of, to, 138-9; at Potidæa, 111-2; Anytus and, 109-10; Bacon on, iii, 106; birth of, xii, 106; Bithynia and Phrygia, retires to, 144; childhood anecdotes of, 107-8; condemned, 126; CORIOLANUS AND, COMPARED, 186-90; death of, 145-6; Emerson on, v, 265; Eupolis and, ix, 149; excesses of, endured by Athenians, xii, 119-20; General, 131-2; Hipponicus and, 112; league broken by, 116-7; marriage of, 112-3; Montaigne on, xxxii, 58; naval victory of, xii, 132; Nicias's jealousy of, 116-7; Olympic games, success of, at, 114-5; Pericles and, 106, 108, 111; rivals of, in public life, 115-6; Socrates's relations with, 108-12 (see also xlvi, 28); Sparta, life of, at, 127-8; Syracuse, expedition of, to, 120-1, 125-6; Thrasybulus's accusation against, 125; Timon of Athens and, 120, 376; Tisaphernes with, 129, 133; treason of, 126; warns the generals, 143

ALCIBIADES, LIFE OF, Plutarch's, xii, 106-46

Alcidamas, Molière on, xxvi, 215

Alcides (see Hercules)

Alcinous, king of Phæacia, xxii, 81; Poseidon and, 178; descent and marriage of, 91-2; gardens of, iv, 271; Milton on feast of, 22; Ulysses received by, xxii, 94-114; Ulysses sent on way, 174-5

Alcis, German god, xxxiii, 117

Alcmæon, son of Amphiaraus, xxii, 206; Dante on, xx, 192, 300

Alcmena, Heracles's mother, xxii, 151; xl, 242; Homer on, xxii, 24; Herodotus on, xxxiii, 27

Alcohol, produced by fruits in carbonic acid gas, xxxviii, 302-10

Alcoholic fermentation, xxxviii, 275-302, 309 note, 311-6, 339, 345-363

Alcoholic liquors, Burke on taste for, xxiv, 15; Locke on, xxxvii, 19-20

Alda, Roland betrothed, xlix, 94, 153, 186-7

Aldobrandesco, Omberto, xx, 188 note 1

Aldobrandi, Bertino, xxxi, 99

Aldobrandi, Tegghiaio, xx, 66 and note 2

Aldobrandino, Clement VIII called, xviii, 283

Ale, Harrison on English, xxxv, 285

ALE, JOLLY GOOD, AND OLD, xl, 190-2

Alecto, in the ÆNEID, xiii, 250-8; Dante on, xx, 37

Alençon, Earl of, at Cressy, xxxv, 27, 29, 30

Aleotti, Giovanni, xxxi, 120 note 2

Alesia, siege of, xii, 287-8

Alessio, in Dante's Hell, xx, 76; in THE BETROTHED, xxi, 427-8, 429-30

Alethes, in the ÆNEID, xiii, 77, 301, 303

Alexander (see Paris)

Alexander, of Antioch, xii, 358, 359

Alexander, the grammarian, ii, 195 (10)

Alexander the Great, Achilles and, xiii, 27; xv, 368; xxvii, 36; xxxvi, 50; age of, at conquest of Asia, iv, 384-5; Apelles and, ix, 104; Aristotle and, xxxii, 53-4; at Arbela, iii, 74; Athens, orators of, xii, 210; attitude toward arts and sciences, xxxii, 53-4; M. Aurelius on, ii, 206 (3), 236 (24), 254 (3), 270 (29); Browne on, iii, 278; Cervantes on, xiv, 488; chastity and drunkenness of, xlviii, 45 (103); Curtius on, xxxvii, 354; Dante on, xx, 51; Darius's box and, xiv, 51; dogs of, xxxv, 355; Emerson on, v, 202, 265; Hephestion and, xlvi, 28; his wish for more worlds to conquer, xxxix, 316; Pindar and, iv, 78; liberality of, xxxvi, 53; Marlowe on, xix, 237; melancholy of, iii, 49; Montaigne on, xxxii, 13; one of nine worthies, xxxix, 20; Pascal on, xlviii, 51 (132), 235 (701); the Platæans and, xii, 90; reproved for playing well, 36; reason of security of his conquests, xxxvi, 15-17; Sidney on, xxvii, 36; the shower of flame and, xx, 58; supposed prophecy of, xlviii, 248

Alexander, the Jew, xliv, 466 (33-4)

Alexander, king of Macedonia, at Platæa, xii, 92-3

Alexander, the Platonic, ii, 195 (12)

Alexander, the false prophet, xxxvii, 384-5

Alexander, of Syria, xii, 373

Alexander III, Pope, exile of, xxvii, 368

Alexander VI, Pope, Cæsar Borgia, father of, xxxvi, 15; church, aggrandizement of the, 39; frauds of, 58; King Louis and, 13, 14-15, 24; son, efforts to aggrandize his, 23-4, 27

Alexander, James, i, 124

Alexander Pheræus, xxvii, 27-8

Alexander Severus, Machiavelli on, xxxvi, 63, 64, 68

Alexander, Wilhelmina, vi, 181, note 7

Alexander, William, To AURORA, xl, 314-15

ALEXANDER'S FEAST, xl, 391-6

Alexandridas, Montaigne on, xxxii, 45

Alexandrine philosophy, Taine on the, xxxix, 427, 431 note

Alexandrine verse, Dryden on, xiii, 54

Alexas of Laodicea, xii, 378-9; character in ALL FOR LOVE, xviii, 23-106; Antony told by, of Cleopatra's death, 95-6; Cleopatra's messenger, 43-4; Cleopatra denounced, 89-90; on Ventidius, 54; Ventidius with, 28-9; with the priests, 24-6

ALEXIS, HERE SHE STAYED, xl, 329

Alf, son of Hjalprek, xlix, 281-2, 338-9; remarks on story of, 250

Alfonso X (The Wise), Bacon on, iii, 130

Alfred the Great, called the truth-speaker, v, 374; crowned and buried at Winchester, 462; Emerson on, 15; book, how he won the, 403

Algalif, the, xlix, 109, 111, 158, 159

Algarsife, reference to, iv, 36-7

Algebra, Descartes on, xxxiv, 16, 18-19

Ali, in Dante's Hell, xx, 115; quotation from, v, 82; and Mohammed, xlv, 988 note 17

'ALI BABA AND THE FORTY THIEVES, xvi, 424-41

Alichino, the demon, xx, 88, 92

Alicorno, Traiano, xxxi, 92 note, 120, 144, 147

Alidosi, Lito degli, xx, 351 note 12

Alienations, in Massachusetts, xliii, 68 (10, 11, 14, 15)

Alifamfaron, Pentapolin and, xiv, 136-7

Alighieri, grandfather of Dante, xx, 349 note 2

Alisto of Cos, alluded to, ix, 46

ALL FOR LOVE, Dryden's, xviii, 13-106; remarks on, 6; Byron's poem, xli, 789-90

A' THE AIRTS THE WIND CAN BLAW, vi, 306-7

All-Prayer, weapon of Christian, xv, 66-7

Allan, John, Poe and, xxviii, 370

Allan, Dr., on Diodon, xxix, 24; on Holuthuriæ, 468

ALLAN STREAM, BY, vi, 468

Allegories, barbarous nations among, xxiv, 18; Bunyan on, xv, 8; Spenser on, xxxix, 62

Allegretti, Antonio, xxxi, 97 note 5, 163, 166

All mand, François l', xxxi, 281 note

Allen, John, translator of Calvin, xxxix, 1

Allen, Richard, xxxiii, 164-5

Allen, William, i, 106

ALLERLEIRAUH, story of, xvii, 162-6

Alliances, provision for, under Confederation, xliii, 162, 165; under constitution, 186 (10, 3); Machiavelli on, xxxvi, 72-4; More on, 213; Washington on, xliii, 245-6

Alligators, fights of male, xi, 95

Allingham, William, THE FAIRIES, xlii, 1116-1117

Allori, Angelo (Il Bronzino), xxxi, 401 note, 410

Allston, Washington, Coleridge on, v, 319, 320-1

Alluvium, land made of, xxxiii, 11-12; saliferous, in Peru, xxix, 367-8; stratified, in Andes valleys, 319-20

Allworth, Lady, in NEW WAY TO PAY OLD DEBTS, in mourning, xlvii, 863, 866-7; at home, 868-9; with Tom, 869-70; scene with Wellborn, 874-6; welcomes Wellborn and Marrall to dinner, 884-5; after dinner, 887-8; thought to be in love with Wellborn, 890-1; at Overreach's, 905-6, 908, 909; at home, with Lovell, 916-9; reconciliation with Lovell, 928-30; with Wellborn, 931; with Overreach, 932, 933, 934-5, 936-7, 939-40; in final scene, 940, 941

Allworth, Tom, in NEW WAY TO PAY OLD DEBTS, xlvii, with Wellborn at Tapwell's, 862-5; at home, with servants, 867-8; with Lady Allworth, 868-70; shuns Wellborn, 873; parting with servants, 881-2; reconciled to Wellborn, 883; with Lovell on way to Overreach's, 892-5; at Overreach's, 901,

902, 904, 909; discharged from service, 911; as messenger to Margaret, 912; scene with Margaret, 924-8; Lovell on, 929; married to Margaret, 938; in final scene, 940, 942

Almagro, Diego, xxxiii, 317

Almaris, King, xlix, 120, 139

Almasour, in ROLAND, xlix, 123-4, 134

Almeni, Sforza, xxxi, 366 note

Almon, son of Tyrrheus, xiii, 257

Alms, Buddha on, xlv, 593; Krishna on, 866; Mohammed on, 883 note 1, 883-4, 957, 972; never impoverish, v, 27

Alnaschar, story of, xvi, 177-84

Alcæus, and Iphimedeia, xxii, 152

Alonso, king of Naples, in THE TEMPEST, in shipwreck, xlvi, 398, 399; his previous conspiracy with Antonio, xlvi; in island after wreck, 417-22; plot against, 425-6; awakened by Ariel, 426-7; in search for Ferdinand, 439-40; at the banquet, 440-1; denounced by Ariel, 442-3; imprisoned by Ariel, 452-3; in final scene, 454-63

Alonso, Peter, and Don Quixote, xiv, 45

Alonzo III, of Arragon, Dante on, xx, 174 and note 12

Alpha Centauri, distance of, xxx, 316

Alphabet, methods of teaching, xxxvii, 129-30, 131

Alphebo, to Don Quixote, xiv, 12

Alphel, Sir Edmund, xxxv, 83

Alpheus and Arethusa, iv, 42; xiii, 151

Alphonsus of Castile, Bacon on, iii, 130

Alps, Byron on the, xli, 793; Goldsmith on states seen from, 520-1; Helmholtz on the, xxx, 211-14; glaciers of, 215-31

Alps, Witch of the, in MANFRED, xviii, 423-7

Alric, and Eric, v, 344

Alsus, and Podalirius, xiii, 400

Alswid, xlix, 307, 308

Altabin, king of Atlantis, iii, 158

Alternate generation, Darwin on, xi, 458

Alternation, the law of nature, v, 108

Althea, Æschylus on, viii, 102

ALTHEA, TO, FROM PRISON, xl, 355-6

ALTHO' HE HAS LEFT ME, vi, 415

Altmayer, in FAUST, xix, 85-99

Altoviti, Bindo, xxxi, 383 note 2, 385

Altruism, Kant on duty of, xxxii, 334, 341, 351; Locke on, xxxvii, 118; Luther on, 364-6, 369-70; Mill on, xxv, 4-5; More on, xxxvi, 198-9; St. Paul on, xlv, 504 (24)

Alum, crystallization of, xxx, 27, 37; fireproofing qualities of, xxxv, 319

Aluminium, weight of, xxx, 11 note 2

Alva, Duke of, at Metz, xxxviii, 28; EGMONT, character in Goethe's, xix, 253-334; Egmont's arrest planned by, 303-6; Egmont on, 326-7; Egmont with, 307-14; Gomez on, 301-2; in the Netherlands, 252; Netherlands, ruler of, 295-6; Netherlands, sent to, 286, 289-90; Orange, arrest of, planned by, 303-6; Orange thwarts, 306-7; Raleigh on, xxxix, 87

Alypius, student under St. Augustine, vii, 87-8; at the gladiatorial show, 88-9; apprehended as thief, 89-90; as assessor, 91; advises against marriage, 94; as lawyer, 126; his conversion, 115, 136, 142; baptized with Augustine, 145

Amadeus, Cardinal, xxxix, 42

Amadis of Gaul, Arcalaus and, xiv, 114; Cervantes on romance of, 48-9; Don Quixote on, 92, 212; Don Quixote, supposed sonnet of, to, 11; Montaigne on, xxxii, 89; Oriana and, xiv, 116, 212, 218; Sidney on romance of, xxvii, 23; squire of, xiv, 496; sword of, 135

Amadis of Greece, xiv, 49

Amalthea, and Jove, iv, 161; horn of, 380; vi, 321

Amana River, xxxiii, 341

AMANTIUM IRAE, xl, 201-2

Amantius, friend of Cæsar, xii, 305 note

Amapaia, xxxiii, 328-30, 360-1

Amara, Mount, iv, 161-2

Amara, town of, xlv, 577

Amarant, iv, 144

Amaryllis, reference to, iv, 73

Amasis, king of Egypt, xxxiii, 81-90; Ionian guard of, 78

Amastris, city of, ix, 407

Amata, in the ÆNEID, xiii; Æneas, rage against, 251-3; Dante on, xx, 213 note 2; death of, xiii, 410-11; Turnus tries to dissuade, 391

Amaurote, capital of Utopia, xxxvi, 172, 175

Amazon River, discovered by Orellana, xxxiii, 319-20; Thoreau on forests of the, xxviii, 406

Amazons, Æschylus on their war against Athens, viii, 150; home of the, 181 note 25, 192 note 45; Columbus on Indian, xliii, 26; Raleigh on, xxxiii, 326-7

Ambassadors (U. S.), appointed by President, xliii, 188 (2); foreign, received by President, 189; cases affecting, 190 (2); under the Confederation, 162

Amber, Tacitus on, xxxiii, 118-9

Ambiorix, xii, 285 note

Ambition, St. Augustine, St., on, vii, 28, 191-2; Bacon on enviousness of, iii, 24; Burke on, xxiv, 44-5; Burns on, vi, 222, 249, 308; Carlyle on, xxv, 384-5, 420, 448; Epictetus on, ii, 131 (43), 146 (79); Hobbes on, xxxiv, 340, 366, 372; Milton on, iv, 94, 264; Montaigne on, xxxii, 115; Pascal on, xlviii, 411-12, 415; Penn on, i, 381; Pope on, xl, 420; Rousseau on, xxxiv, 224; Ruskin on common, xxviii, 94-5; Shakespeare on, xlvi, 132, 349; Webster on, xlvii, 769

AMBITION, ESSAY ON, Bacon's, iii, 93-5

Amble, in NEW WAY TO PAY OLD DEBTS, xlvii, 866-8, 871, 872-3, 882, 883, 886-7, 916, 941

Amblyrhynchus, Darwin on the, xxix, 389-95, 399

Amboise, Cardinal d', xxxvi, 15, 28

Ambrogio, in THE BETROTHED, xxi, 120, 126-7

Ambrose, St., Augustine, St., on, vii, 76, 81-2; Donne, Dr., comparison of, with, xv, 341-2; Justina persecutes, vii, 146; Luther on, xxxvi, 266; Simplicianus, father of, vii, 119; verses by, 156

Ambrosio, the student, xiv, 85, 86, 98, 104, 108-9

Ameipsias, Aristophanes on, viii, 439

Amendment, Confucius on, xliv, 6 (8), 29 (23), 40 (21); Kempi on, vii, 234-7; Penn on, i, 345 (262)

Amendments, Constitutional, xliii, 191 (5); Lincoln on, 320-1

America, Bacon on ancient, iii, 136, 157-9; Browne on animals of, 275; discovery of original documents concerning, xliii, 5-48; Emerson on, v, 454, 461; English colonies in, first, xxxiii, 226, 227 (see also Roanoke, St. John's); foreign powers in (see Monroe Doctrine); natives of, iii, 159; probable geological changes in, xxix, 136-7; glacial period in, xi, 400; Haies on exploration and settlement of, xxxiii, 263-7; Hunt on, xxvii, 294; Irish monks in, xxxii, 175; Paré on Spaniards in, xxxviii, 32; Senecas's prophecy

of, iii, 90-1, 93; Smith on discovery of, x, 327-8, 397-403; Thoreau on, xxviii, 405-8; zoology of North and South, xxix, 135-7; zoology of, changes in, 178-80 (see also North America, South America, United States)

American art, Emerson on, v, 79

American Civil War, documents of, original, xliii, 313-431; Lowell on, xxviii, 429-33, 442-7; Mill on, xxv, 164-7

American colonies, agriculture and cattle in, x, 186-7; currencies in, 249, 251, 254; documents in history of, original, xliii, 49-105, 138-49; England's trade laws for, x, 424-5; xliii, 148; exportations of meat from, x, 193; Franklin's plan to unite, i, 124-6; Granville on royal government of, 159-60; interest, rates of, in, x, 94; Jefferson on wrongs of, xliii, 151-3; manufactures in, x, 307; newspapers in, i, 19-20; books in, 74; population in, increase of, x, 72; settlement of, motives of, 397-404; settlements in, situation of, 24; slavery in, i, 207-8; trade of, bounties on, x, 407-10; wages in, 71-2; wealth in, progress of, 294; Woolman on state of, i, 261-2

American flag, Haskell on the, xliii, 380; Longfellow on the, xlii, 1286-7

AMERICAN HISTORICAL DOCUMENTS, xliii

American Indians (see Indians)

American literature, Emerson on possibilities of, v, 5, 180; Whitman on, xxxix, 388-409

American mythology, possibilities of an, xxviii, 414-15

American Philosophical Society, founded by Franklin, i, 3, 105, 164

American poets, xlii, 1213-1422

American political institutions, Emerson on, v, 243-6

American Revolution, Burke and the, xxiv, 5-6; Burns on, vi, 51-2; documents of, original, xliii, 150-79; Franklin's part in, i, 4, 76, 165; Franklin's plan of union and, 125; French in the, 136; public libraries, influence of, on, 67; Sheridan on, xviii, 108

AMERICAN SCHOLAR, Emerson's, v, 5-23

AMERICAN WAR, BALLAD ON THE, Burns's, vi, 51-2

Americans, cant of, v, 431; Emerson on interest in, 50; in England, 453-4; faith and hope lacking in, 54-5; ma-

terialism of, 277-8; Mill on political abilities of, xxv, 309; morals and religion of, v, 279-80; Thoreau on, xxviii, 407-8; Whitman on, xxxix, 388-9

Amerigo, the enameler, xxxi, 48

Amerzene, Andrew, first mate on "Pilgrim," xxiii, 398

Ames, Fisher, on republics and monarchies, v, 245

Ames's Mariner's Sketches, xxiii, 5

Amici, Professor, v, 318

AMIENS' SONG, xl, 268

Aminias, the Decelean, xii, 18

Amity, sonnet on, xiv, 238

Ammanato, Bartolommeo, xxxi, 415 note 2, 420-1, 427

Ammon, the Libyan Jove, iv, 161 (see also Amun); Alexander called son of, xx, 58; xl, 411; oracle of, founding of, xxxiii, 33

Ammonia, production of, by moulds, xxxviii, 298 note; test of organisms, 342

Ammonians, Herodotus on the, xxxiii, 27

AMNESTY PROCLAMATION, LINCOLN's, xliii, 416-9

Amompharetus, xii, 95

Amoretta, and Busirane, xxxix, 64

Amos, prophecy of, xlviii, 259

Amphialus, in the ODYSSEY, xxii, 102

Amphiaraüs, Dante on, xx, 82 and note 1; Eriphyle and, 300 note 11; Homer on, xxii, 206; lines on, xii, 81

Amphilochus, son of Amphiaraüs, xxii, 206

Amphimedon, wooer of Penelope, xxii, 302, 303; death of, 303; in Hades, 322-5

Amphinomus, suitor of Penelope, xxii, 225; advises against killing Telemachus, 225, 279; death of, 298; with Odysseus, 248-9, 256; sees ship of conspirators, 224

Amphion, founder of Thebes, xxii, 151; Dante on, xx, 131; reference to, v, 239; Sidney on, xxvii, 6, 11

Amphithea, grandmother of Ulysses, xxii, 267

Amphitrite, references to, iv, 69; viii, 215; xxii, 78-9, 163

Amphitryon, husband of Alcmene, xxii, 151; Herodotus on, xxxiii, 27; name used to express a good host, v, 207

Amposte, chatelain of, xxxv, 41, 46, 58

Amputations, Paré on cauterizing after, xxxviii, 8, 20, 21

Amram, father of Mary, xlv, 952 note 4

Amsanctus, Lake, xiii, 258-9

Amsdorff, Nicolaus von, xxxvi, 260 note

Amun, Zeus called, xxxiii, 27 (see also Ammon)

Amusements, Pascal on, xlviii, 13 (11), 56

Amycla, nurse of Alcibiades, xii, 106

Amyclas, the fisherman, xx, 331 note 16

Amycus, in the ÆNEID, xiii, 81, 319, 407

Amyntas, king of Lycaonia, xii, 369, 370

Amythaon, Homer on, xxii, 151

Anabaptists, Bacon on, iii, 14; of Munster, xxiv, 286-7

Anachronisms, Dryden on, of Virgil, xiii, 34-6; in Shakespeare and Sidney, xxxix, 218

Anacreon, Byron on, xli, 814; in Dante's Limbo, xx, 236 note 7

Anaërobian life, xxxviii, 277 note, 317, 324, 333-5, 337-40, 344, 365-7

Analogical resemblances, xi, 443-8

Analogous variations, xi, 159-63

Analogy, Emerson on, v, 436; Hume on reasoning by, xxxvii, 371-2, 374 (7), 403-4

Analysis, Marcus Aurelius on, ii, 297 (18); Mill on habit of, xxv, 88; Pascal on, xlviii, 421

Ananda, servant of Buddha, xlv, 586, 633-46, 658-60, 701, 713-14, 774, 778

Ananias, husband of Sapphira, xliv, 432 (1-6); Bunyan on, xv, 125; "varlet that cozened apostles," the, xlvii, 588

Ananias, the disciple, and Paul, xliv, 442 (10-18), 472 (12-16); Dante on, xx, 395 note

Ananias, the high priest, xliv, 473 (2), 476 (1)

Ananias, prince of Babylon, xxxvi, 329

Ananias, in THE ALCHEMIST, xlvii, 585-8, 592-9, 638-40, 649, 658-9, 661-2

Anarchy, Sophocles on, viii, 277

Anastasius II, in Dante's Hell, xx, 45 note

Anastasius IV, and Bernard, xxxvi, 339

Anathemas, Burns on, vi, 223

Anatolius, St., hymn by, xlv, 542

Anatomy, Locke on study of, xxxvii, 138, 147; study of, necessary for artists, 293; xxxix, 255-6

Anaxagoras, a native of Ionia, xxviii, 58; Creator, his idea of the, xxxix, 101; Euripides and, viii, 302; in Dante's Limbo, xx, 20; Pericles and, v, 437;
xii, 39-40, 42, 54-5, 69; Socrates on doctrines of, ii, 15, 91-2; Themistocles and, xii, 6; Voltaire on teachings of, xxxiv, 102-3

Anaxarete, Webster on, xlvii, 794

Anaxenor, harper of Antony, xii, 338

Anaxilaus, at Byzantium, xii, 137

Anaximander, on the world, xxxix, 104

Anaximenes, letter to Pythagoras, xxxii, 48; mention of his doctrines, vii, 164; xxxix, 101

Ancestors, Bentham on veneration of, xxvii, 226-8; Huxley on, xxviii, 223; Lowell on, xlii, 1372; More on, xxxvi, 142; Tennyson on, xlii, 1001; Tseng-tzu on, xliv, 6 (9)

Anchemolus, death of, xiii, 334

Anchises, father of Æneas, xiii, 95; Crete, advises settlement of, 131-2; death in Sicily, 151; Dante on, xx, 348; Evander and, xiii, 273; funeral games of, 180-197; ghost of, advises Æneas, 202; in Hades, 230-8; Priam, relationship to, 20; Sidney on, xxvii, 17; Troy, in sack of, xiii, 121-5

ANCIENT MARINER, RIME OF THE, xli, 682-701; Wordsworth on the, xxxix, 268

Ancus, Marcius, Virgil on, xiii, 235

Andersen, Hans Christian, life and works of, xvii, 220; remarks on stories of, 2; TALES OF, 221-361

Andes Mountains, appearance and scenery, xxix, 257-8, 262, 279-80, 322-3, 325-6, 337; Darwin on his passage of, 317-40; geology of, 323-5, 335-7; mines of, 321-2; rain, absence of, in, 328; shingle terraces of, 319-20; snow-line of, 249-50; stone, crumbling, of, 323; torrents of, 320-1; upheaval of, 320, 324-5; vegetation and zoology of, 322, 330-1; winds and storms of, 327-8, 364

Andocides, impiety, accused of, xii, 34; on Themistocles, 34

Andrea, in THE CENCI, xviii, 285, 323

ANDREA DEL SARTO, xlii, 1087-94

Andrew, the apostle, xliv, 368 (14), 424 (13); in PARADISE REGAINED, iv, 372-3

Andrew, the boy, in DON QUIXOTE, xiv, 37-9, 296-9

Andrews, Dr., bishop of Winchester, xv, 339, 383

Andrews, Isaac, Woolman and, i, 181-2

Andrews, Jacob, i, 184

Andrews, Peter, i, 183, 184-6

Androcles, Alcibiades's accuser, xii, 123

ANDROCLES, FABLE OF, xvii, 20-1

Androgeos, death of, xiii, 112-13

Andromache, in Greece, xiii, 137-9, 143-4; dream of, xl, 43; Ruskin on, xxviii, 142

Andromachus, a Syrian, xxviii, 58

Andromeda, constellation, iv, 149

Andronicus, Livius, date of, ix, 63; Sidney on, xxvii, 6

Andros, Themistocles at, xii, 23

Andvari, the dwarf, xlix, 285-6

ANE AN' TWENTY, TAM, vi, 415-6

Anemolians, ambassadors of the, xxxvi, 192-3

Aneurin, Celtic bard, xxxii, 166

Aneurism, defined, xxxviii, 81

ANGEL, THE, a story, xvii, 341-3

Angelica, Agrican and, iv, 392; xiv, 76; Orlando Furioso and, xiv, 12, 213, 226; xxxii, 51 note

Angelo, Michael (see Michelangelo)

Angels, Bagehot on Milton's, xxviii, 200-1; bowers of the, iv, 321; Browne on creation of, iii, 284-5; chorus of, in FAUST, xix, 36-8; creation of, xx, 313 note 9, 407-8 notes; Dante on rank among, xx, 298 note 6; habitation of, iii, 286; in FAUSTUS, xix, 208, 219, 224, 226; in PARADISE LOST, iv, 195-7 (see also Michael, Raphael, etc.); rebellion of the, 198-226 (see also Fallen Angels); love among, 259; Milton on nature of, 212-3; number of, xx, 410-11; Smart on, xli, 487; Tutelary (see Tutelary Angels)

ANGELS, FOOTSTEPS OF, xlii, 1267-9

Anger, Augustine, St., on, vii, 28; Bacon on, iii, 134-6; Collins on, in music, xli, 477; in Dante's HELL, xv, 31-2, 47; Dante's examples of, 213; Ecclesiastes on, xliv, 342 (9); Epictetus on, ii, 144 (75); Hobbes's definition of, xxxiv, 340; Krishna on, xlv, 862; Manzoni on, xxi, 519; Marcus Aurelius on, ii, 201 (10), 204 (16), 229 (28), 239 (26), 280 (25), 291; Pascal on, xlviii, 164 (502); Penn on, i, 346 (270, 271); Plutarch on, xii, 166; Walton on, xv, 328; Webster on, intemperate, xlvii, 788-9

Angle, Guichard d', xxxv, 46, 47, 51

Angles, Tacitus on the, xxxiii, 115

Angrivarians, Tacitus on the, xxxiii, 111

Anguillotto of Lucca, xxxi, 99

Angular figures, not beautiful, xxiv, 94; why unpleasant, 99, 120-1

Angus, in MACBETH, xlvi, 327-8, 383-4

Angustia, Donna, xxiii, 238, 383-4, 385

Aniause, King, xxxv, 164, 172

Anicius, Titus, ix, 117

Animal kingdom, how distinguished from vegetable, xxxviii, 341-2

Animalculæ, perfection of, v, 89; xlviii, 27

Animals, acclimatisation of, xi, 145-6; Bacon's experiments on, iii, 174-5; beauty in, proportion as cause of, xxiv, 77-8; beauty sense of, xxxvi, 203-4; Blake on cruelty to, xli, 587-8; Buddhist ideas of, xlv, 706-9; Burke on cries of, xxiv, 71; Burke on mating of, 38-9; care of, in Massachusetts, xliii, 79; Carlyle on, xxv, 437 note; death, no fear of, in, xxxiv, 177; Descartes on reason in, 47; domestic (see Domestic Animals); Emerson on, v, 229; extinction of large, cause of, xxix, 178-80; fertilisation of, xi, 106-7; habits, diversity of, 116-17; Hume on reason of, xxxvii, 371-4; Locke on cruelty to, 101-2; love of offspring among, xl, 425; Marcus Aurelius on kindness to, ii, 236 (23), 251 (65); Pascal on mind in, xlviii, 117 (340-3); admiration among, 130 (401); plants and, complex relations of, xi, 79-83; Rousseau on distinction between men and, xxxiv, 175-6; size of, disadvantages in, xi, 355; size of, in relation to vegetation, xxix, 91-6; social instincts of, ii, 267 (9); souls of, xxxvi, 227; truth, love of, among, v, 374; Voltaire on souls in, xxxiv, 107; Woolman on kindness to, i, 300 (see also Organic Beings, Species)

Animism, defined, xvii, 7

Animosities, teach value of friendship, ix, 17

Anius, king of Delos, xiii, 131

Anna, St., in Dante's PARADISE, xx, 422; Jesus found by, iv, 365

Anna, the prophetess, xliv, 359 (36-8)

Anna, sister of Dido, xiii, 152-4; Æneas sought for by, xiii, 167-8; at Dido's death, xiii, 176-7

ANNA, THY CHARMS, vi, 309

ANNABEL LEE, xlii, 1239-40

Annas, the high priest, xliv, 360 (2), 429 (6); Dante on, xx, 97 note 7

Annates, Luther on, xxxvi, 278-9, 288

Anne, St. (see Anna)

Annebault, Claude d', xxxi, 321 note 2, 328; Paré and, xxxviii, 12

Anneius, M., legate of Cicero, ix, 135, 137

Annibale, the surgeon, xxxi, 31

ANNIE, FOR, xlii, 1236-9

Annotations, Cervantes on, xiv, 6, 8-9; Hugo on, xxxix, 337; Johnson on, 246, 248

Ansârs, xlv, 949 note 14, 967 note

Anseis, in SONG OF ROLAND, xlix, 98, 120, 135, 146

Anselm, Bacon on, iii, 51; Harrison on, xxxv, 253; in Dante's PARADISE, xx, 338; life of, 338 note 36

Anselmo, Lothario and, story of, xiv, 307-46, 351-5

Anselmo, in the goatherd's story, xiv, 500-4

Anson's Voyages, Mill on, xxv, 11

ANSWER, THE, Scott's, xli, 748

ANT AND GRASSHOPPER, fable of, xvii, 25-6

Antæus, Dante on, xx, 130 note 6; family of, xlix, 268 note; Hercules and, iv, 409; xiv, 19

Antæus, chief of Turnus, xiii, 340

Antagoras, of Chios, xii, 101

Antarctic islands, climate and productions of, xxix, 253-6

Anteia, wife of Helvidius, ix, 339

Antenor, founder of Padua, xiii, 81; xx, 163 note 7

Anteon (see Antæus)

Anterigoli, Piermaria d' (see Sbietta)

Anteros, and Eros, xii, 109 note 3; xviii, 425

ANTHEA, TO, xl, 337

Anthemocritus, xii, 66-7

Anthony, St. (see Antony, St.)

Anthony, the goatherd, xiv, 81-4

Anthores, death of, xiii, 348-9

Anthrax, Pasteur on, xxxviii, 365, 369-70

Anthylla, city of, xxxiii, 48

Antichrist, Browne on, iii, 298; legend of birth of, 282; Luther on, xxxvi, 295; Pascal on, xlviii, 285-6, 293, 295 (846); Paul, St., on, xxxvi, 274

Anticleia, mother of Odysseus, xxii, 147, 148-50; her death of grief, 209

Anticlus, in the Trojan horse, xxii, 53

Antigone, condemned to perish in cave, viii, 281; death of, 282-6, 295-6; fate bewailed by people, 278; in Dante's Limbo, xx, 237; Œdipus with, viii, 253-4; in *The Phœnicians,* xxxix, 341;

Polynices' burial by, viii, 255-8; Ruskin on, xxviii, 142

ANTIGONE, TRAGEDY OF, Sophicles's viii, 255-99

Antigonus, of Judæa, xii, 349; and the Parthians, iv, 393

Antilochus, son of Nestor, xxii, 36; Achilles and, 322; death of, 51; in Hades, 156, 320

Antinous, in the ODYSSEY, xxii, complains of Penelope, 23-4; counsels suitors to heed Telemachus, 280; death of, 296; Irus encouraged by, to fight with Ulysses, 246, 247; contest with the bow, 286, 287, 288, 289, 290-2; Penelope, his gifts to, 252; Penelope rebukes, 226; Telemachus invited to feast by, 29; Telemachus plotted against by, 62, 66, 224-5; Ulysses and, as beggars, 237-40; with Telemachus, 19

Antioch, Christian Church at, xliv, 448 (26-30), 450 (1)

Antiochus of Ascalon, xii. 220

Antiochus, Athenian admiral, xii, 142

Antiochus, king of Commagene, xii, 347

Antiochus Deus, xlviii, 249

Antiochus Epiphanes, and the Jews, iv, 388

Antiochus the Great, Ætolians and, iii, 128; anecdote of, v, 293; prophecy of, xlviii, 249; the Romans and, xxxvi, 11-12, 73

Antiochus Hierax, xii, 84 note

Antiochus, the pilot, and Alcibiades, xii, 113

Antiope, Homer on, xxii, 151; mentioned, iv, 376

Antipater, the Edomite, iv, 382

Antipater, general of Alexander, xii, 213; and the Athenian orators, 214

Antipathies, national, Browne on, iii, 315; Pascal on, xlviii, 103; Washington on, xliii, 243-4

Antiphates, in the ÆNEID, xiii, 316

Antiphates, the Læstrygonian, xxii, 133

Antiphates, son of Melampus, xxii, 206

Antiphates, and Themistocles, xii, 21

Antiphon, Athenian orator, on Alcibiades, xii, 108; condemnation of, 202

Antiphon of Cephisus, ii, 22

Antiphus, son of Ægyptus, xxii, 21; friend of Ulysses, 229

Antipodes, Darwin on the, xxix, 421

Antiquity, Bentham on, xxvii, 226-9; Browne on, iii, 281; Harvey on, xxxviii,

63; Hobbes on, xxxiv, 370; Hugo on, xxxix, 361; Johnson on, 208; More on, xxxvi, 142; Pascal on, xlviii, 106 (301), 437-44; not the rule of belief, 95 (260)

Anti-Reformers, Fallacies of, Sydney Smith on, xxvii, 225-51

Antiseptic principle, Pasteur on the, xxxviii, 381

Antiseptic Principle, Lister's, xxxviii, 257-67

Antisthenes, on detraction, ii, 119 (7), 248 (36); on the piper, xii, 36; with Socrates, ii, 47

Antithesis, Pascal on, xlviii, 17 (27)

Antonia, daughter of Antony, xii, 388; xviii, 64

Antoninus, Marcus Aurelius (see Aurelius, Marcus)

Antoninus, T. Aurelius (Pius), ii, 192; M. Aurelius on, 196 (16), 237 (30)

Antonio, in Duchess of Malfi, xlvii; Ancona, banished from, 806-7; Bosola with, 756-7, 774-5, 780-2, 809-10, 848-50; Bosola on, 800-3; Cardinal, relations with, 762, 837-8, 844-5; Delio, scenes with, 755-6, 757-8, 759-61, 774, 777, 780, 789-90, 833-4, 845-7; Duchess, scenes with, 767-72, 775-6, 777, 793-5, 798, 799-800, 808-9, 810-11; Duchess, steward of, 758; Ferdinand, relations with, 759, 806, 809-10; orders palace closed, 778; son of, born, 780

Antonio, in Tempest, xlvi; Ariel denounces, 441-2; banquet, at the, 440; Prospero and, 402, 454, 456; Sebastian, plot with, 423-6, 440

Antonius, Caius, Roman consul, xii, 226-7; Catiline conspiracy, 231, 236; Mark Antony, relationship to, 328; Cicero mentions, ix, 81

Antonius, Lucius, Cicero on, ix, 172

Antonius, Marcus, the orator, grandfather of Mark Antony, xii, 322; Sidney on, xxvii, 48

Antonius, Marcus, the Triumvir (see Antony)

Antonius, Publius, and Cæsar, xii, 266

Antonius of Florence, xxxvi, 311

Antony, Caius, brother of Marcus, xii, 337

Antony, Mark, Actium, flight from, xii, 372-3; Antiochus, war with, 347-8; appearance and dress of, 324; Artavasdes seized by, 361-2; in Asia, 338-9; Bacon on, iii, 27; his relations with

Octavius, 123-4; burial of, xii, 384; Cæsar and Pompey, contest of, 325-8, 290-1, 297, 300-1; Cæsar, favorite of, 330; after Cæsar's death, 253-4, 331-2, 333; character of, 339; children of, 388; Cicero, relations with, 253-4, 255-6, 259, 322, 335-6; Cicero on his relations with, ix, 93, 177, 178, 180; Cleopatra and, Dryden on, xviii, 13; Cleopatra and sons honored by, xii, 364; Cleopatra, first meeting of, with, 339-44; Cleopatra prevents, from renewing war, 362-3; Cleopatra renews relations with, 349-50; Cleopatra, slave of, charged with being, 367-8; death of, 381-2; Dolabella and, 328, 330; East, campaigns in, early, 323-4; in Egypt after Actium, 376-9; Fulvia, marriage to, 329; in Greece, 337, 346-7; Ides of March, at, 317, 318, 330-2; Italy, driven from, 256, 333; Life of, Plutarch's, 322-89; Lupercalia, at the, 313, 330-1; master of horse, 328; Octavia, marriage of, to, 344-5; Octavia neglected by, 362-3; Octavius and, meet at Tarentum, 348; Octavius, break of, with, 333; Octavius, charges against, made by, 364-5; Octavius, contest with, 367-73; Octavius's growing jealousy of, 346; parentage and youth, 322-3; Parthia invaded by, 349-61; Pompey's house bought by, 329; popularity and liberality of, 324-5; prodigies preceding the war, 368-9 (cf. xviii, 23); Sextus Pompey and, 345-6; statues and honors to, abolished, 259; triumvir, 335-6; Virgil on, at Actium, xiii, 291; war of, with republicans, xii, 336-7 (cf. xviii, 38); world divided by, to triumvirs, 344

Antony, in All for Love, xviii, 21; in Egypt after Actium, 25, 27, 29; his lamentation, 30-1; scene with Ventidius, 31-8; remarks on scene with Ventidius, 20; his reply to Cleopatra's appeal, 40-1; on Octavius, prepares to march, 42-3; receives Cleopatra's gift, 44-5; meeting with Cleopatra, 46-53; with Cleopatra in the palace, 53-4; advised by Ventidius, 55-7; with Dolabella, 57-61; scene with Octavia, 61-5; sends farewell to Cleopatra by Dolabella, 69-70; hears Dolabella's falseness, 77-83; accuses Dolabella and Cleopatra, 84-7; betrayed by Egyptian

fleet, 91; plans to fight it out, 91; hears Cleopatra dead, 95-6; death of, 99-101

Antony, surnamed Creticus, father of Marcus, xii, 322

Antony, the Younger, xii, 388

Antony, St., Augustine on, vii, 127; Burke on pictures of, xxiv, 54; conversion of, vii, 136; Newman on, xxviii, 38

Ant(s), aphides and, xi, 254; Brazilian, xxix, 43; Browne on, iii, 266 (15); Johnson on, xxxix, 294-5; Milton on, iv, 239; Pope on, xl, 427; slave-making instinct of, xi, 264-8; worker castes of, 57, 278-83

Antyllus, son of Antony, xii, 377, 384, 388

Anubis, called the dog, iv, 14; barking deity, vii, 120

Anuruddha, xlv, 646

Anuweekin, the Indian, xliii, 143

Anville, Marshal d', xxxviii, 25

Anxiety, Arabian verses on, xvi, 11; Hobbes on, xxxiv, 374, 376-7; mean and noble, xxviii, 114; physical effects of, xxxviii, 124; Pliny on limits of, ix, 327

Anxur, in the ÆNEID, xiii, 340

Anyder River, in UTOPIA, xxxvi, 175

Anysis, king of Egypt, xxxii, 69, 70

Anything, Mr., in PILGRIM'S PROGRESS, xv, 102

Anytus, Alcibiades and, xii, 109-10; first briber in Athens, 159; Socrates's accuser, ii, 6, 11, 18, 19, 22, 134 (52)

Aorta, Harvey on the, xxxviii, 86-7, 89, 91, 102, 138

Apathy, in Dante's HELL, xx, 13-15; Pope on, xl, 417

Ape(s), intellectual powers of, xi, 224

Apelles, Alexander and, ix, 104; method of, iii, 106; the "Venus" of, ix, 125; xiii, 12

Apemantus, Timon and, xii, 376-7

Aphides, and ants, xi, 254; development of, 462

Aphrodite, Ares and, xxii, 106-8

Aphrodite, in HIPPOLYTUS, viii, 303-4; Cyrene's image of, xxxiii, 89; home of, viii, 384; queen of rapture, 131; "she whom none subdues," 281; (see also Venus)

Apires, Chilian miners, xxix, 344-5

Apis, court of, at Memphis, xxxiii, 77

Aplysia, Darwin on the, xxix, 16

Apocalyptics, Pascal on the, xlviii, 216-7 (650, 651)

Apodictic principles, xxxii, 326

Apollinarian Heresy, vii, 115

Apollinarii, Milton on the, iii, 199

Apollinaris, Domitius, letter to, ix, 265

Apollo, Cassandra and, viii, 47-8, 53-4; Daphne and, xl, 378; Delphi (Phœbus), fourth prophet of, viii, 122-3; Egypt, king of, xxxiii, 72; god of music, iv, 21, 57; viii, 445; Hyacinth and, iv, 18-9; in Egyptian mythology, xxxiii, 78-9; Latona's son, iv, 80; Loxias, called, viii, 100, 119, 123; Lyceian king, 215; Marsyas and, xx, 285; Phlegyas and, 32 note 1; Phœbus, called, viii, 122; Thymbræan god, xx, 191 note; Virgil on, xiii, 157; Zoilus and, xxviii, 383; (see also Delphian Oracle)

Apollo, in THE FURIES, viii, protector of Orestes, 125-6, 129-32; witness for Orestes, 145, 147-9; altercation with the Furies, 151-3

Apollo Belvedere, Cellini on the, xxxi, 318 note; not impossible in life, v, 193

Apollodorus, Socrates's friend, ii, 22, 26, 46-7, 112

Apollodorus, the orator, and Demosthenes, xii, 202-3

Apollodorus, Greek writer, on Chrysippus, xxxii, 31

Apollodorus, the Sicilian, with Cleopatra, xii, 304

Apollonius, Molon, and Cicero, xii, 221; Cæsar and, 265

Apollonius, the Stoic, M. Aurelius on, ii, 194 (8), 199; on self-discipline, 154 (100)

Apollonius, of Tyana, Bacon on, iii, 66

Apollos, the Alexandrian, xliv, 463-4 (24-8); St. Paul on, xlv, 494 (5-6), 495 (6), 514 (12)

Apollyon, and Christian, xv, 60-4

Apologies, Bacon on, iii, 63; Emerson on, v, 67; new actions the only, 190; Pascal on, xlviii, 23 (57)

APOLOGY OF SOCRATES, Plato's, ii, 5-30

APOLOGY, THE, Emerson's poem, xlii, 1242-3

Apostasy, Bunyan on, xv, 154-6

Apostles, Calvin on, xxxix, 44; choosing of the, xliv, 368 (13-16); community of goods among, 431; council of, on circumcision, 455-6; xlviii, 223 (672);

deacons appointed by the, xliv, 434 (1-6); Holy Spirit received, 425; imprisoned and miraculously freed, 433 (17-20), renew teachings, 433 (21-42); in Jerusalem, 439 (1, 14); with Paul, 442-3 (27); Jesus's appearances to, after death, 418 (36-53), 423 (3-11), xlv, 511 (5, 7); Jesus with, xliv, 374 (1, 9), 375 (22-5), 378 (10), 378 (18), 379-80 (43-6), 383 (1), 386 (1), 389 (41), 398 (5-10), 402 (31), 410 (14-40), 412 (45-6); Judas's place supplied, 424; Kempis on the, vii, 286 (4), 295 (6); Lessing on the, xxxii, 198-9; Luther on the, xxxvi, 290, 344; Luther on council, 273; Milton on the, iv, 353, 354; miracles done by, xliv, 427 (43), 432 (12-16); Mohammed on the, xlv, 954, 967, 1006; Pascal on the, xlviii, 268 (770), 277-8, 289 (838); Paul, St., on the, xlv, 495 (9-13); power and authority given to, xliv, 377 (1); sent forth to preach, 377 (2-6)

APOSTLES, ACTS OF THE, xliv, 421-86

Apostles' Creed, xxxix, 47

Apothecaries, Chaucer on, doctors and, xl, 23; profits of, x, 113

Apparel, Penn on, i, 330; Woolman on, 252-4

Apparitions, Hobbes on, xxxiv, 316-7

Apparitor, Chaucer's, xl, 28-9 note 314

Appeal, right of, in Massachusetts, xliii, 72 (36)

Appearances, Emerson on regard for, v, 67; fable of deceptiveness of, xvii, 27; Goethe on, xix, 381; Machiavelli on care of, xxxvi, 59; Marcus Aurelius on, ii, 233 (13); Pascal on, xlviii, 110 (319); Paul, St., on, xxxvi, 276; Schiller on æsthetic, xxxii, 284-9

Appetite, Locke on tempting the, xxxvii, 30

Appius Claudius (see Claudius)

Appius, Marcus, Cæsar and, xii, 282; Cicero and, 240; ix, 120, 127, 142, 146; provincial governor, 131, 142; propylæum of, 151

Applauders, professional, in Rome, ix, 220

Applause (see Praise)

Apple-growing, in Chiloe, short method employed, xxix, 301-2

Apples, Locke on eating of, xxxvii, 21

Appointments, Confucius on, xliv, 41;

Koran on, xxv, 244; Presidential, xliii, 188-9 (2, 3)

Appomattox, terms of surrender at, xliii, 421-2

Apprehensions, Pliny on, ix, 327

Apprenticeships, limitation of, x, 122; long, 122-5; Smith on, 104; unknown to ancients, 125

Appropriations, in Massachusetts, xliii, 77 (78); (U. S.) under the Confederation, 164-5; under Constitution, 184 (12), 186 (7)

Apries, king of Egypt, xxxiii, 81-4

April, Chaucer on, xl, 11; Shakespeare on, 278

Apteryx, wings of the, xi, 177

Apuleius, *Golden Ass* of, xxxix, 350; xlii, 1357

Aquila of Pontus, xliv, 462 (2-4), 463 (18-19), 464 (26)

Aquila, P. Attius, ix, 410

Aquileia, Freeman on, xxviii, 256

Aquilius, Cicero on, ix, 81

Aquilo, charioteer of Winter, iv, 18

Aquinas, Thomas, St., angels, reference to, xx, 408 note; death of, 227 note 11; Hazlitt on, xxvii, 278; Dante places in Paradise, xx, 327; life of, sketch of, 327 note 16; pupil of Albertus Magnus, 327 note 15

Aquinius, Marcus, Cicero on, xii, 240

Arabella, Lady (see Stuart, Arabella)

Arabesques, Cellini on, xxxi, 60-1

Arabian Heresy, iii, 258 (7)

ARABIAN NIGHTS' ENTERTAINMENTS, xvi

Arabs, adopted children among, xlv, 985 note 2, 989 note; beacon-fires of, 1001 note; chase, ideas of, v, 353; divorce among, xlv, 985 note; Emerson on conquests of the, v, 55-6; hospitality among, xlv, 990 note 28; religion of, 876; Schiller on civilization of, xxxii, 237; sheiks, habits of, v, 139; swords as mirrors among, xx, 343 note 22

Arachne, Dante on, xx, 192; reference to loom of, 70

Aratus, Pliny on, ix, 271

Araviscans, Tacitus on the, xxxiii, 108

Arbela, battle of, iii, 74

ARBITRARY GOVERNMENT, Winthrop on, xliii, 85-105

Arbitration, Hobbes on legal, xxxiv, 410; Pascal on international, xlviii, 105 (296); U. S. and Mexico, agreement between, for, xliii, 302-3

Arc, Joan of (see Joan of Arc)

ARCADES, MILTON's, iv, 41-4

Arcadia, Johnson on first inhabitants of, xxxix, 199; Spartan invasion of, xii, 149 note; the "thesmophoria" in, xxxiii, 85

Arcalaus, the enchanter, xiv, 114

Arcas, Callisto's son, xx, 416 note 5

Arceisius, father of Laertes, xxii, 218

Arcens, son of, xiii, 313

Arcesilaus, method of teaching, xxxii, 36; Pascal on, xlviii, 124 (375)

Archander, Herodotus on, xxxiii, 48

Archangels, in FAUST, xix, 18

Archedemus, Aristophanes on, viii, 451, 456

Archelaus, Antony and, xii, 324; the tower of, xxxv, 319

Archenomus, Aristophanes on, viii, 486

Archeopteryx, xi, 342

Archiac, M. d', on changes in species, xi, 359

Archias, the exile-hunter, xii, 214-5

Archibius, Cleopatra's friend, xii, 388

Archidamus, king of Sparta, xii, 66, 69

Archidichē, Herodotus on, xxxiii, 68

Archilochus, banished from Sparta, iii, 194

Archimedes, Huxley on, xxviii, 219; Manzoni on, xxi, 115; Marcus Aurelius on, ii, 241 (47); Pascal on, xlviii, 275

Archipelagoes, Darwin on, xi, 347

Archippe, wife of Themistocles, xii, 33

Archippus, Flavius, ix, 389-90, 399

Architecture, Burke on colors in, xxiv, 69; Coleridge on, xxvii, 262; effects, its means of producing, xxiv, 129; figures in, various, xxiv, 64; Greenough's theory of, v, 317; Hobbes on, xxxiv, 363; Hugo on mediæval, xxxix, 350-1; human body as model in, xxiv, 81-2; light and shade in, 68-9; magnitude in, 64-5; Vitruvius on study of, v, 176; xxxi, 8

Architeles, Themistocles and, xii, 11

Archytas of Tarentum, on isolation, ix, 38; on sensual pleasure, 59

Arcite and Palamon, story of, xxxix, 160, 161, 172

Areius and Octavius, xii, 383-4

AREOPAGITICA, MILTON's, iii, 184-232

Areopagus, Council of, Æschylus on ordaining of, viii, 150-1; Burke on, xxiv, 338; its composition, xii, 44; its powers reduced, 42, 44

Ares, Æschylus on, viii, 23-4; Aphrodite and, xxii, 106-8; Phineus's sons and, viii, 287; worshipped in Egypt, xxxiii, 34, 35, 42; (see also Mars)

Arete, wife of Alcinous, xxii, 91-2; Ulysses with, 93-4, 110, 153; Ulysses's farewell to, 175

Aretheus, Eudamidas and, xxxii, 81

Arethusa, Alpheus and, Milton on, iv, 42; Dante on story of, xx, 104; Jupiter and, xix, 246; Virgil on, xiii, 151

Arethusa, in PHILASTER, xlvii, Bellario sent to, 684, 691; Bellario, scenes with, 691-2, 713, 721, 750; hunt, at, 714; king, scenes with, 708-9, 735; lost in wood, 718; Megra denounces, 697, 744; Pharamond and, 667, 669, 682, 692, 693, 724-5; Philaster, letter to, 704; Philaster, scenes with, 677-81, 710, 721-2, 730, 731, 734

Arethusa, Browne on river, iii, 257

Aretino, Pietro, Milton on, iii, 203 note 43; pictures of, reference to, xlvii, 569; portrait by Titian, xxvii, 272

Argand, Aimé, inventor of hollow wick, xxx, 104, 156

Argas, friend of Orgon, xxvi, 279

Argas, the poet, xii, 194

Argent, Dr., Harvey to, xxxviii, 62

Argenti, Filippo, in Dante's HELL, xx, 33

Argia, in Limbo, xx, 237

Arginusæ, battle of, ii, 20

Argo, Homer on ship, xxii, 163; Milton on ship, iv, 134; Stukeley on, v, 458

Argonauts, date of expedition of, xxxiv, 129-30

Argos, eyes of, references to, iv, 322; xlvii, 567

Argos, Hermes, slayer of, viii, 187 note 37; xxii, 10

Argos, Io and, viii, 187, 190-1

Argos, dog of Ulysses, xxii, 235-6

Argument, Franklin on habit of, i, 15-16, 126-7; Penn on, 335-6 (133-6); Socrates on, ii, 83-4; varieties of, xxxvii, 332 note

Argus, Evander and, xiii, 279; (see also Argos)

Argustus, Eliazar and, xxxv, 154

Ariadne, sister of Minotaur, xx, 49 note 5; placed among stars, 339; Homer on, xxii, 153; Theseus and, xxvi, 136, 143

Ariamenes, Xerxes' admiral, xii, 18

Arians, Bacon on the, iii, 138; Browne on

the, 259 (8); Pascal on the, xlviii, 293, 301; Voltaire on, xxxiv, 83-4

Aricia, mother of Virbius, xiii, 265

Aricia, in PHÆDRA, Hippolytus and, xxvi, 135-7, 148-56, 185, 186-7, 194; Theseus and, 188-9, 196

Ariel, in FAUST, xix, 184, 190

Ariel, in PARADISE LOST, iv, 213

Ariel, in THE TEMPEST, xlvi, at banquet, 441-2; Caliban and, 436-9; Ferdinand and, 412-3, 416; Gonzalo and, 422, 426; Prospero and, 405-10, 445, 449-50, 452-3, 453-4, 455, 459-60, 461, 462-3; Hugo on, xxxix, 354; Hunt on Shakespeare's, xxvii, 294; Shelley on Miranda and, xli, 848-9

Aries, Dante on sign of, xx, 178; sun started in, 6 note 5

Arimanes, in MANFRED, xviii, 431

Arimaspians, Æschylus on the, viii, 195 and note 55; and gryfons, iv, 132

Arimnestus, at Platæa, xii, 89, 97

Ariobarzanes, Cicero and, ix, 136, 142; Plutarch on, xii, 247

Arioch, in PARADISE LOST, iv, 213

Ariosto, Lodovic, Cervantes on, xiv, 50; Dryden on, xiii, 5, 13, 26, 55; Hugo on, xxxix, 351; Hume on, xxvii, 207; Montaigne on, xxxii, 91; Renan on, 160; Sainte-Beuve on, 132; Spenser on, xxxix, 62; Titian's portrait of, xxvii, 272; Wordsworth on, xxxix, 317

Ariovistus, xii, 279-80

Ariphron, guardian of Alcibiades, xii, 106, 108

Aristarchus, friend of Paul, xliv, 466 (29), 467 (4), 481 (2)

Aristarchus of Samos, referred to, xlvi, 80

Aristides, archon, xii, 83; assessment made by, 102; Athenian democracy proposed by, 100; banishment of, 84-5; birth and condition of, 78-9, 103-4, 105; children of, 105; commissioner, as, 100-1; constancy and justice, 81-2, 83-4; death of, 104; Eleutheria proposed by, 99; levy of Greeks proposed by, 99; LIFE OF, Plutarch's, 76-105; Marathon, at, 82-3; Persian wars, in, 16-7, 19, 85-98; public conduct guided by expediency, 103; resentment, freedom from, 189; Themistocles and, 7, 15, 16-7, 19, 22-3, 79-80, 81-2, 84, 86-7, 100, 102, 104

Aristippus, Horace on, xxxii, 58; not with

Socrates in prison, ii, 47; on children, xxxii, 74; quotation from, 63

Aristo, Titus, letters to, ix, 262, 319; Pliny on, 209-10

Aristobulus and Antony, xii, 323

Aristocracy, Channing on, xxviii, 344-5; Mill on government by, xxv, 108; natural and actual, 214; of Europe, v, 214; origin of, xxxiv, 221

Aristocrates, Antony and, xii, 375

Aristodicus, the Tanagræan, xii, 46

Aristogiton, grand-daughter of, xii, 105; Hermodius and, xxxii, 77

Ariston, Claudius, ix, 294

Ariston, of Ceos, xii, 80 note

Ariston, Greek tragedian, xxxii, 70

Aristonicus, death of, xii, 214

Aristophanes, Dryden on, xxxix, 174; Euripides and, viii, 302; THE FROGS, 439-87; Hugo on, xxxix, 347; life and works, viii, 438; Milton on, iii, 194, 206; Samians on the, xii, 63; Socrates on, ii, 7; Taine on comedies of, xxxix, 435

Aristophanes, the grammarian, on Epicurus, xxxii, 64-5

Aristophon, the painter, xii, 120

Aristotle, air and rain, on, xxxviii, 101; Alexander's tutor, iv, 401; xxxii, 53-4; animals, motion of, xxxviii, 134-5; antipater on persuasiveness of, xii, 188; *Art of Poesy*, xxvii, 39; Augustine on *Predicaments* of, vii, 59; Bacon on ostentation of, iii, 128; Browne on, 262 (12), 265, 287, 305, 322; Cicero on, xii, 237; comedy on, xxvii, 46; comets, on, xxxiv, 118; Dante's Limbo in, xx, 20 note 8; death, on, xxxviii, 85; democracy, on, xxiv, 259-60 and note; Don Ferrante on, xxi, 445; drama, on the, xiii, 6; xxxix, 220; Emerson on, v, 152-3; Euripus, flux of, xxxviii, 75; friendship, on, xxxii, 73, 80; heart and blood, on the, xxxviii, 81, 84, 93, 123, 128, 130, 132, 133, 137; human understanding, on, xxxiv, 103; Hume on, xxxvii, 291; imitation, on, xxiv, 43-4; inequality, on, xxxiv, 408-9; Lowell on, xxviii, 452; Luther on, xxxvi, 321; Mill on, xxv, 219; medicine, on study of, xix, 206-7 notes 12 and 13; Milton on Lyceum of, iii, 244; iv, 401; Montaigne on, xxxii, 29; natural selection, his idea of, xi, 9 note; Newman on Lyceum of, xxviii,

58; Pascal on, xlviii, 114; Plato's pupil, ii, 3; poetry, on, xiii, 35; xxvii, 50; xxviii, 79; xxxix, 279, 387; poetry and history, on, xxvii, 19; xxviii, 74; Raleigh on his doctrine of eternity, xxxix, 99, 100, 101, 104; *Rhetoric* of, xxv, 13; ridicule, on, xxxix, 180; soul, on the, 101; space, on, v, 175; state, on members of, xx, 318 note 14; summum bonum of, iii, 331 (15); Taine on, xxxix, 431 note; teacher, profits as, x, 137; taste, on, xxviii, 376; things to be avoided, on, xx, 47 note; tragedy, on, iv, 412; xiii, 8; viper, on the, xxxv, 344-5

Arithmetic, Descartes on, xxxiv, 19; Hobbes on, xxxiv, 363; Hume on, xxxvii, 306; Locke on study of, 153, 154

Arius, Dante on, xx, 343 note 21; Pascal on, xlviii, 288 (832)

Arjuna, Prince (see BHAGAVAD-GITA)

Ark, Browne on story of the, iii, 274; on pigeon sent from, 273; Milton on the, iv, 337

Arkansas River, sediment of, xxxviii, 402

Arkwright, the spinning-jenny and, v, 395

ARMADA, THE, by Macaulay, xli, 915-6

Armadillo, Darwin on the, xxix, 102; Raleigh on the, xxxiii, 353

Armado, fish, xxix, 141

Armagnac, Earl of, xxxix, 95

Armenians, Freeman on the, xxviii, 271

Armgart, in WILLIAM TELL, xxvi, 468, 469-73

Armies, Machiavelli on, xxxvi, 40-1, 48; mediæval Italy, of, xxvii, 374-5; 16th century, xxxviii, 8; standing (see Standing Armies)

Arminians, Bacon on the, iii, 138

Arminius, Milton on, iii, 204

ARMOUR, ADAM, PRAYER OF, vi, 121-2

Armour, Jean, farewell to, vi, 224; lines on, 58, 68-9, 92, 306-7, 316-7; references to, 142 note, 173; Robert Burns and, 15, 16

Arms, Don Quixote on profession of, xiv, 373-5, 377-9; Machiavelli on practice and study of, xxxvi, 40, 48-9; Milton on lack of training in, iv, 347; More on practice of, xxxvi, 144-5; profession of, necessary to empire, iii, 77-8; right of, in U. S., xliii, 194 (2)

Armstead, Gen., at Gettysburg, xliii, 390

Armstrong, Dr., on puerperal fever, xxxviii, 228

ARMSTRONG, JOHNIE, xl, 101-3

Army, U. S., under the Confederation, xliii, 161, 164, 165; under Constitution, 184 (12), 185 (14); President commander-in-chief of U. S., 188 (1)

Army of the Potomac, Haskell on, xliii, 327-8, 402

Arnaces, the eunuch, xii, 20, 87

Arnæus, the beggar, xxii, 245

Arnauld, M., references to, xlviii, 346 note 4, 387

Arnold, Sir Edwin, translator of BHAGAVAD-GITA, xlv, 783

Arnold, Matthew, on culture, xxviii, 213-4; life and writings, 64; POEMS by, xlii, 1123-40; STUDY OF POETRY, xxviii, 65-90

Arnold, Sir Nicholas, xxxv, 328

Arnold, Thomas, Matthew Arnold on, xlii, 1130-5

Arnold, Bishop of Liege, xxxv, 101

Arnold's Battery, at Gettysburg, xliii, 337, 351, 381

Aromaia, Raleigh on, xxxiii, 333-4, 353

Aroras, Raleigh on the, xxxiii, 351

Arouet, François-Marie (see Voltaire)

Arowacai, town of, xxxiii, 349

Arragon, Cardinal of, in DUCHESS OF MALFI, xlvii, 755-855; Antonio, relations with, 759, 762, 883; Bosola, scenes with, 756, 837, 838, 843-5, 851-4; Duchess and, 764-6; Ferdinand and, 762, 786-9, 806, 835, 836-7; Julia and, 783-4, 841-3; keeps watch alone, 847-8; Loretto, at, 807; Malatesti and, 804

Arrangement, Pascal on, xlviii, 16 (22-3)

Arrests, in U. S., xliii, 194 (4)

Arria, wife of Pætus, ix, 242-4; Certus, in case of, 338, 340-1; exile of, 239; Pliny and, 339

Arrian, Epictetus and, ii, 116

Arrianus, Maturus, letters to, ix, 187-8, 251-2, 278-80, 331-2

Arrigo, Cardinal, xx, 336 note 20

Arrigo, Florentine nobleman, xx, 27 note 12

Arrius, Quintus, xii, 230; Cicero on, ix, 88, 93

Arrogance, Dante places, in HELL, xx, 33; Hobbes on, xxxiv, 364, 409; Marcus Aurelius on, ii, 279 (13, 19)

Arrows, Raleigh on poisoned, xxxiii, 352

Arruntius, at Actium, xii, 373 note

Arsaces, Parthian empire, founder, iv, 391

Arsago, Pagolo, xxxi, 27

Art, ancient and modern, contrasted, xxviii, 191; Aurelius on nature and, ii, 287 (10); Browne on, and nature, iii, 268; Browning on, xlii, 1072; Burke on, xxiv, 47-8, 65-6, 87-8; Coleridge on, xxvii, 255-63; Confucius on nature and, xliv, 20 (16), 38 (8); Emerson on, v, 180, 301; Goethe on, xxv, 382; xxxix, 251-66; Goldsmith on blessings of, xli, 522; Greenough's ideas of, v, 316; Hugo on, xxxix, 345-6, 348, 351-2, 355, 356, 364, 367; human and divine, ii, 138 (61); Hume on, xxvii, 207-8; xxxvii, 292-3; "is long" (original saying), xxxviii, 2; Morley on principles of, xxiv, 28; Pascal on, and nature, xlviii, 49 (120); Penn on, i, 343; public attitude toward, xxviii, 119-20; purism in, satirized, xix, 185; Ruskin on, xxviii, 152; Schiller on, xxxii, 209, 212, 231-8, 253-5, 267-9, 268-74; Sidney on nature and, xxvii, 9; Taine on, xxxix, 429, 431, 434; unity the vital requisite of, xxviii, 371; utility and, xxxii, 211; "weaker than Necessity," viii, 185; Whitman on reality in, xxxix, 402 (see also Beauty, Taste)

ART THOU WEARY, xlv, 544-5

Artabanus, Themistocles and, xii, 28-9

Artavasdes, king of Armenia, xii, 350, 351, 361

ARTEMIDORA, THE DEATH OF, xli, 902

Artemidorus, Cæsar and, xii, 316-17; Pliny on, ix, 239-40

Artemis, Actæon and, viii, 381; Atridæ and, 12; Egyptian mythology, in, xxxiii, 79; Bubastis, festival of, 34; oracle of, 42; temple of, 69-70; Homer on, xxii, 83-4; reference to, viii, 215; Thebes, goddess of, 214, 215 (see also Cynthia, Diana)

Artemisia, Burns on, vi, 59

Artemisium, battle of, xii, 12-3

Artemon, the engineer, xii, 63-4

Arteries, Harvey on the, xxxviii, 65-9, 73, 79-81, 88, 89, 102, 109-10, 113, 116, 137, 139

Arthmius of Zelea, xii, 10

Arthur, King, Caxton on, xxxix, 20-4; Cervantes on, xiv, 92, 489; drinking-cup and arms of, xxxii, 145; Eliwlod and, 168-9; Guenevere and, xlii, 1186;

Mordred and, xx, 132 note 3; Renan on, xxxii, 148-9, 155-7; Spenser on, xxxix, 62; university at Cærleon, xxxv, 371; Uther's son, iv, 102

Arthur, King, in HOLY GRAIL, xxxv, 105-6; his custom of adventure, 107; and the marvelous sword, 108; welcomes Galahad, 109, 110; and the Sangreal, 111; his tourney at Camelot, 111-12; at Holy Grail feast, 113; grief at departure of knights, 113-14, 115, 116; orders chronicles of the Grail, 213

ARTHUR, MORTE D', by Tennyson, xlii, 986-92

Arthur, Prince, son of Henry VII, xxxix, 26

Arthur's hunting, xxxii, 153 note 9

Arthurian legends, Caxton on, xxxix, 20-4; Renan on, xxxii, 146, 148-66 (see also HOLY GRAIL)

Artichoke, compared with cardoon, xxix, 125 note 9; Jerusalem, xi, 147

Article, Dryden on the, xiii, 61

ARTICLES OF CONFEDERATION, xliii, 158-68; Lincoln on, 316

Articulate speech, man and nature, the distinction between, xxvii, 256-7

Artificers, in agricultural system, x, 430-6, 439-46; in policy of Europe, 103-4

Artificial, Carlyle on the, xxv, 330

Artisans, anciently inferior to warriors, xxxiii, 83; Socrates on, ii, 10

ARTIST, EPIGRAM TO AN, vi, 263

Artist, Northern, in FAUST, xix, 185

Artists, Browning on, xlii, 1096; Emerson on duty of, v, 50-1; Goethe on training and duty of, 252, 255; xxxix, 260-1, 263, 265; relations to the public, 259

Arts, Burke on the, xxiv, 40, 44, 47-8; Emerson on the, v, 79-80, 304; Raleigh on the, xl, 206; progress in, due to wants, xxxiv, 177-8; relation of various, xxxix, 261 (see also Architecture, Music, Painting, Poetry, Sculpture)

Arulenus, Rusticus (see Rusticus)

Arundel, Earl of, in Crecy campaign, xxxv, 9, 24, 27

Arundel, Thomas of, xxxv, 255

Arundel, in EDWARD THE SECOND, xlvi, 43-6, 50, 59

Aruns, Camilla and, xiii, 383-5; doomed by Diana, 386; his death, 386; in Dante's HELL, xx, 82

Aruspiciny, defined, xxxiv, 382

Arwacas, Raleigh on the, xxxiii, 341, 374

Aryan Races, Freeman on the, xxviii, 240-2; Taine on the, xxxix, 420, 421, 422, 423, 424

Aryans, Tacitus on the, xxxiii, 117

Arybas, the daughter of, xxii, 210-12

Asaf, son of Barkhiya, xvi, 26 note; 27, 308

Asaph, Psalms attributed to, xliv, 144, 203, 232-49

Ascanio, servant of Cellini, xxxi, 185-8, 188-9, 192, 197, 212-14, 258, 261, 265, 277, 278, 279, 304, 327, 335-6, 348, 351

Ascanius (Iülus), in sack of Troy, xiii, 123, 125; Dido's hunt at, 157; Anchises's funeral games, 196-7; in fire of the ships, 200; kills stag of Silvia, 255-6; his fight with Tyrrheus, 257-8; Nisus and Euryalus, with, 301-2; in defence of the town, 313-15, 326; prophecy of his future reign, 82, 269

Ascension Island, Darwin on, xxix, 494-8; rock incrustations at, 19; species of, xi, 414

Ascension Day, Walton on, xv, 403-4

Ascetic goodness, Bagehot on, xxviii, 171-3; disagreeable to women, 182-3

Asceticism, Diogenes on, ii, 180 (187); Epictetus on, 154 (101); pride in, 177 (176); Utopian idea of, xxxvi, 204

Ascham, Johnson on, xxxix, 225

Asciburgium, founded by Ulysses, xxxiii, 94

Asclapo, Roman physician, ix, 154

Asclepius (see Æsculapius)

Ascolano, Aurelio, xxxi, 58

Ascoli, Eurialo d', xxxi, 58 note

Ascot, Duke of, xxxviii, 52, 53, 55, 57

Asdente, Dante on, xx, 84, and note 8

Ashburton, Alexander Lord, xliii, 281

Ashley, Lord, and Locke, xxxvii, 3

Ashtaroth (see Astarte)

Asia, cause of barbarism of, x, 25-6; wealth of ancient, ix, 379 note 1

Asinius, friend of Pliny, ix, 256

Asinius, Pollio (see Pollio)

Ask Me No More, xl, 351

Askew, in Shoemaker's Holiday, xlvii, 471, 472-3, 475, 492

Asmach, Herodotus on the, xxxiii, 20

Asmadai, Asmodai, or Asmodeus, reference to story of, iv, 151; in the battle, 213; lustfulness of, 375

Aspasia, of Miletus, accused of impiety, xii, 68, 69; and the Megarians, 67; Plutarch on, xii, 60-1

Aspasia, concubine of Cyrus, xii, 61

Aspatia's Song, xl, 321

Asphalax, blindness of the, xxix, 59

Asphalion, squire of Menelaus, xxii, 51

Aspirations, worldliness and, xix, 33; inborn in man, 48

Ass, descent of the, as traced by stripes, xi, 162-6; why not improved, 52

Ass, Job's description of the wild, xxiv, 56-7

Ass and Bull, story of, xvi, 11-2

Ass and Horse, fable of, xvii, 42

Ass and Lapdog, fable of, xvii, 15

Ass in Lion's Skin, fable of, xvii, 30

Ass's Brains, fable of the, xvii, 41

Assaracus, in Hades, xiii, 229

Assattha, tree of, xlv, 587

Assent, Dante on haste in giving, xx, 342; Harvey on, xxxviii, 96; Penn on, to please, i, 337 (149)

Assertorial principles, xxxii, 326

Assignats, Burke on the, xxiv, 255-8, 322-7, 364-71

Assimilation, Freeman on, xxviii, 248

Assistance, asking, is honoring, xxxiv, 361; Confucius on, xliv, 52 (15); only to be given by superiors, xviii, 8; willingness to accept, ii, 244 (7)

Associates (see Company)

Association, Burke on effects of, xxiv, 104; Emerson on principle of, v, 259-60; Locke on, as means of education, xxxvii, 36 (49), 40 (58); Mill on education by, xxv, 87-8

Association of ideas, Hume on, xxxvii, 304-5, 327-31

Assurance in children, xxxvii, 52, 53

Assyria, Milton on ancient, iv, 390-1; Raleigh on history of, xxxix, 112

Astarte, Ashtaroth, or Astoreth, Milton on, iv, 13, 99; crescent of, xlii, 1231

Astarte, in Manfred, xviii, 434-6; Manfred on, 425-6; further references to, 420, 424, 444

Astolfo, in Life Is A Dream, with Estrella, xxvi, 21-2; his claim to throne, 22-3; agrees to king's plan to try Segismund, 28-9; Segismund with, 42-3, 44-5; Rosaura and, 67; in the battle, 69-71; reunited with Rosaura, 73

Astonishment, Burke on, xxiv, 49, 50, 128

Astoreth (see Astarte)

Astrologers, in Dante's HELL, xx, 84

Astrology, Augustine, St., on, vii, 103-5; Don Quixote on, xiv, 86; Hobbes on, xxxiv, 363; interest in, reason of, v, -98; unknown in Utopia, xxxvi, 195

Astronomy, Augustine, St., on ancient, vii, 63-4; Dante's, xx, 292-3, 325; Emerson on our ignorance of, v, 80-1; Helmholtz on science of, xxx, 174; Hobbes on, xxxiv, 363; Hume on, xxxvii, 419; Huxley on Greek, xxxviii, 219; Locke on study of, xxxvii, 138, 147, 155; Marlowe's, xix, 225; modern foundation of, xxxix, 52 note; Montaigne on study of, xxxii, 48; Prometheus, originator of, viii, 183

Astur, ally of Æneas, xiii, 327

Astyanax, son of Hector, xiii, 115, 144

Astyochus, Greek admiral, xii, 130

Aswattha, the banyan tree, xlv, 857

Asychis, king of Egypt, xxxiii, 68-9

Asylas, in the ÆNEID, xiii, 312, 327, 378

Asyniur, goddesses, xlix, 300 note

Atabalipa, Milton on, iv, 329; Raleigh on, xxxiii, 303, 317, 319, 321, 330

Atalanta, reference to apple of, xxxix, 138

ATALANTA, chorus from, xlii, 1199-1201

Atarbechis, city of, xxxiii, 26

Atè, Æschylus on, viii, 36, 78, 96, 205; Virgil on, xiii, 348

Athamas, in sack of Troy, xiii, 108; Dante on, xx, 123

Athanasian Creed, Bagehot on, xxviii, 196

Athanasius, St., Pascal on, xlviii, 303 (868); on psalm-singing, vii, 186; on the Trinity, xxxiv, 83

ATHEISM, ESSAY ON, Bacon's, iii, 42-5

Atheism, Berkeley on, xxxvii, 233; Browne on, iii, 272; Browning on, xli, 931; Burke on, xxiv, 227; Burns on, vi, 204; Hume on, xxxvii, 407; Mill on, xxv, 30; Milton on, iv, 422; Molière on charges of, xxvi, 213-14; Pascal on, xlviii, 69 (190), 80 (221), 81 (225), 82 (228); of physicians, iii, 253 note; preferable to superstition, 45

Atheist, in PILGRIM'S PROGRESS, xv, 137-8

Atheists, as witnesses, xxv, 224; Pascal on, xlviii, 69 (190)

Athena, birth of, viii, 149; holder of key to thunderbolts, viii, 156; wardress of Delphi, 123; Egyptian worship of, xxxiii, 34, 42, 86, 80-90; Ruskin on, xxviii, 142 (see also Minerva)

Athena, in THE FURIES, with Orestes and the Furies, viii, 138-42; at trial of Orestes, 144, 145, 150-1; ordains court of Areopagus, 150; casts vote for Orestes, 152-3; appeases the Furies, 155-64

Athenæus, and Cicero, ix, 136

Athenais, Queen, ix, 136

Athene, in THE ODYSSEY, friend of Ulysses, xxii, 10-11

Athenians, prayer of the, ii, 224 (7); Taine on the, xxxix, 412

Athenodorus, the ghost and, ix, 312-13

Athenodotus, Marcus Aurelius on, ii, 195 (13)

Athens, Æschylus on, viii, 160-5; Aristophanes on decline of manhood at, 473-4; and on politics of, 460-61, 484-5; beautifying of, by Pericles, iii, 47-51; books in ancient, xxviii, 56; bounty of ancient, xii, 105; Burke on Areopagus of, xxiv, 338; capital causes in, ii, 25; capital executions in, 45-6; Collins on music in, xli, 479; Dante on, xx, 169-70; economic resources of, xxviii, 43-4; houses and streets of ancient, xxviii, 55; liberty of press in, iii, 193-4; military spirit of, decline of, xxvii, 373-4; Milton on learning of, iv, 401-4; named for Minerva, xx, 206 note 3; Newman on intellectual supremacy of, xxviii, 40-3; population under Pericles, xii, 74-5; religious liberty in, xxxvii, 393; sacred galleys of, xii, 42 note 5; St. Paul in, xliv, 461 (16-34); Schiller on art and liberty in, xxxii, 237; Shelley on golden age of, xxvii, 338-9; on the drama in, 339, 340-1; Spartan policy toward, xxxvi, 18; teachers in, rewards of, x, 136; the Thirty at, xii, 144-5 (for various portions of Athenian history, see PLUTARCH'S LIVES OF THEMISTOCLES, PERICLES, ARISTIDES, ALCIBIADES, DEMOSTHENES)

Athens, Duke of, constable of France, xxxv, 46, 47, 48

ATHENS, MAID OF, xli, 795-6

ATHENS, UNIVERSITY LIFE AT, xxviii, 51-61

Athlete, life of an, Epictetus on, ii, 155 (104)

Athole, Earl of, James I and, xlii, 1161

Atilius, Lucius, called the wise, ix, 11

Atinas, in the ÆNEID, xiii, 409, 413

Atlantic Sisters, Pleiades called, iv, 308

Atlantis, Bacon on, iii, 157-8

ATLANTIS, NEW (see NEW ATLANTIS)

Atlas, Æschylus on, viii, 178-9 and note 21, 182; Homer on, xxii, 10; Virgil on, xiii, 161, 234, 272

ATLI, THE SONG OF, xlix, 407-17; remarks on, 252

Atli, in the VOLSUNG TALE, xlix, 310; his future foretold, 312, 328, 336; Brunhild and, 334; wedded to Gudrun, 340-1; his dreams, 341; sends for Gunnar, 342-3; in the battle, 346-7, 348, 349; Gunnar and, 349-50; his end, 350-3

Atli, in the EDDA, his future foretold, xlix, 378, 383-4, 392; Brunhild and, 379; wedded to Gudrun, 402-4; his dreams, 404-6; sends for Gunnar, 407-8; with Gunnar, 413-4; Oddrun and, 435-7; his eating of his children, 415-6; death, 416-7

Atmosphere, composition of the, xxx, 144; pressure of the, 146-9; resistance of the, 19-20; a blanket for the earth, 212; temperature dependent on altitude, 212-13

Atolls, Darwin on, xxix, 469-72; formed from barrier reefs, 477-81; causes of destruction of, 482-3; absence of, in West Indies, 484; in the Pacific, 406, 456-69

Atom, the universe in the, xlviii, 27

Atonement, commencement of, xviii, 439

ATREUS, HOUSE OF, viii, 7-165

Atreus, Thyestes and, viii, 71-2; Sidney on, xxvii, 17

Atropos, "the blind Fury," iv, 74

Attachments, Pascal on human, xlviii, 156 (471), 158 (479)

Attagis, species of, in South America, xxix, 101

Attainder, bills of, in U. S., xliii, 185 (3), 186 (10)

Attentions, Yu-tzu on, xliv, 6 (13), 25 (2)

Attia, mother of Octavius, xii, 255

Attic Boy, Cephalus called the, iv, 37

Attic comedy, coarseness of, viii, 438

Attica, Newman on, xxviii, 41-2; Rousseau on, xxxiv, 177

Atticus, Titus Pomponius, character of, ix, 80; Cicero's letters to, 81, 83, 85, 94, 100, 133, 141, 169, 171, 172; essays dedicated to, 9-10, 45-6

Atticus, Herodes, xxviii, 59-60

Attila, in Dante's HELL, xx, 52

Attilio, Count, in THE BETROTHED, at Don Rodrigo's, xxi, 73-81, 105-6, 181-3; goes to Milan, 290-1; procures Cristoforo's removal, 299-303; dies in plague, 536

Attinghausen, Baron, in WILLIAM TELL, xxvi, 405-12, 456-61

Attius, Tullus, xii, 218

Attorney, Hobbes on power of, xxxiv, 413-14

Atys, in the ÆNEID, xiii, 196

Aubignac, D', Corneille and, xxxix, 361; Hugo on, 364

Aubigny, Lord d', xxxv, 25, 31

Aubrecicourt, Eustace d', xxxv, 35, 36, 42, 43, 46

Aubrey, on Milton, xxviii, 174

Auburn, the deserted village, xli, 509-19

Auckland Islands, ferns in, xxix, 249

Audacity, Hippocrates on, xxxviii, 5

Audley, James, at Poitiers, xxxv, 43, 44, 48; honored by Prince Edward, 53; his gift to squires, 55; new gift from Prince, 57

Audley, Lord Chancellor, xxxvi, 112, 117, 119, 120, 123, 125, 128, 129, 130, 131

Audrehem, Arnold d', xxxv, 44

Audubon, on the frigate bird, xi, 180; on birds' nests, 254-5; on transportation of seeds, 412

Auerbach's wine cellar, xix, 84-99

Aufidius, death of, xxxii, 13-4

Aufidius, Tullus, Coriolanus and, xii, 167-9, 171-2, 175, 183-5; death of, 185

AUGURIES OF INNOCENCE, xli, 586-90

Augurs, College of, ix, 213 note 4; duties of, 251 note 1; Pliny on, 251-2; seniority among, 68

Augury, defined, xxxiv, 382; among the Germans, xxxiii, 98

AUGUST, SONG COMPOSED IN, vi, 45-6

AUGUSTA, EPISTLE TO, xli, 792-5

AUGUSTA, To, xli, 790-1

Augustan Age, Macaulay on, xxvii, 391

Augustia, Donna, xxiii, 238, 383-4, 385

Augustine, St., Bishop of Hippo, vii, 3-4; Alypius and Nebridius friends of, 87-92; astrology rejected by, 103-6; baptism of, 146; books "on the fair and fit," 56-9; Carthage, in, 31-3; Caxton on teachings of, xxxix, 13; Chaucer on, xl, 16, 46; on Christ, vii, 114-15, 196-7; on Christ and Church, xxxix,

33 note; communistic household of, vii, 96; concubine of, 46, 96; Confessions, 5-198; Confessions, remarks on, xxxi, 1; Confessions, object in writing, vii, 22, 24, 161-3; conversion of, 76-7, 82-4, 118-43; in Dante's Paradise, xx, 420 note 4; De Saci on, xlviii, 393-4; on the dead, xxxix, 92; on death, xlviii, 338; deatl. his fear of, vii, 96; on deception, xlviii, 105 note; Descartes and, 408; disappointments of, vii, 85-7; diviners and, 46-7; Donatists and, xxxix, 34; on doubtful points, 37 note 31; evil, on question of, vii, 101-2, 106; Faustus and, 67-9; friend, loss of, 48-52; on God, 5-7, 27-8, 37-8, 60, 74-5, 98-9, 115, 164, 174, 176-81; on goodness of all things, 110-11; on happiness, 176; Hugo on, xxxix, 345; infancy and boyhood of, vii, 8-20; learning, on his, 59-61; Luther on, xxxvi, 266, 300; on man, xlviii, 32 note; Manichæans, among, vii, 35-45, 63-6, 74-5; marriage, his wish for, 93-5; memory, on the, 166-76; Milan, in, 76; on miracles, 350-1; xlviii, 281 (812); on monks, xxxix, 36 note 25; mother's death, vii, 151-9; Orosius and, xx, 328; Platonists partly convert, vii, 107-14; Pascal on, xlviii, 87, 304 (869); on praise, xxxix, 67; on righteousness, xlviii, 167; Rome, in, vii, 70-3; scriptures, attitude toward, 35, 114-17; studies of, 34; rhetoric, teacher of, 46, 75, 138-41; trials and temptations of, 181-95; truth, his search for, 92-3; Walton on, xv, 336, 341, 353; wills, on two, in man, vii, 131-3

Augustine of Canterbury, Roper on, xxxvi, 130; See of London, changed by, xxxv, 252; Stamford University, suppressed by, 371

Augustus, Æneas, compared with, xiii, 19-24, 36; Æneid saved by, xiv, 99; Agrippa and, iii, 67; Ajax of, iv, 412; arts of, iii, 17; beauty of, 106; Britain's tribute to, xxxv, 315-16; calm nature of, iii, 104-5; censorship of books under, 195; Dante on victories of, xx, 307-8; death of, iii, 10; decree of, in Luke, xliv, 357 (1); diet of, xxxvii, 17; favorites of, xii, 388; Horace and, xxvii, 68-9; xxxix, 164; Herod's son, on, xlviii, 66 (179); Rome, liberator of, iii, 130; M. Aurelius on, ii, 258

(31); motto of, xix, 369; Ovid and, xiii, 36-7, 54-5; Pascal on, xlviii, 51 (132); on pets, xii, 35; pleasure in small children, 368 note 11; postal service of, ix, 369 note; Scribonia, his divorce of, xiii, 37; times of, iii, 45; vestal virgins and, ix, 254 note; Virgil and, xiii, 3, 17-20, 55, 83, 234; xxxix, 164 (see also Octavius)

Auld, William, lines on, vi, 353 note 16; reference to, 228

Auld Farmer's New Year Salutation, vi, 147-50

Auld House, The, xli, 561-2

Auld Lang Syne, vi, 317; Whittier on air of, xlii, 1362

Auld Lichts, Burns on, party of, vi, 16, 63-6, 90-1, 104-7, 183-5

Auld Rob Morris, vi, 445-6

Auld Robin Gray, xli, 557-8

Aulestes, death of, xiii, 400

Auletes, Æneas, ally of, xiii, 328

Aunus, death of, xiii, 381

Aurelia, Regulus and, ix, 229

Aurelia, Cæsar's mother, xii, 269, 271-2

Aurelian, Bacon on, iii, 130

Aurelius, King, v, 374

Aurelius, Marcus, sketch of life and work, ii, 192; Alexander the prophet and, xxxvii, 384; Arnold on, xlii, 1139; Machiavelli on, xxxvi, 63, 68; Meditations of, ii, 193-301; Pope on, xl, 436

Aurelius, Scaurus, xxxiii, 113

Auret, Marquis d', xxxviii, 52-8

Auricles, of the heart, xxxviii, 82-6, 134-5

Aurinia, worship of, xxxiii, 97

Aurochs, deterioration of the, xi, 134

Aurora, Cephalus, the Attic Boy, and, iv, 37; Orion and, xxii, 71; Tithonus and, v, 92; xxii, 68; Zephyr and, iv, 30

Aurora, To, xl, 314-15

Aurora Borealis, Kelvin on, xxx, 264

Austerity, Bagehot on, xxviii, 171-3; not agreeable to women, 182; party spirit and, 186; strength of, lies in itsel', 190

Austin, St., Augustine called, xxxix, 13-14; xl, 16

Austin, Adam, For Lack of Gold, xli, 532-3

Austin, Charles, edits Parliamentary Review, xxv, 76; in debating society, 79-80; Mill on, 51-2, 64; in Utilitarian movement, 67

Austin, John, Mill on, xxv, 49-51; his

friendship with Mill, 44, 49; paper for *Westminster Review*, 63; for *Parliamentary Review*, 76; later years of, 111-12, 161

Australia, Darwin on, xxix, 435-55; European species in, xi, 84, 403; fossil mammals of, 372; glaciers in, 400; marsupials of, 119; native species reduced, 134-5; productions of, reason of inferiority, 111; useful plants, absence of, in, 48

Australians, Darwin on the, xxix, 235, 437-8; dances of the, 454-5; dogs not domesticated by, xi, 258

Austria-Hungary, Freeman on, xxviii, 262-3, 269-70

Authorities, Bacon on, in philosophy, xxxix, 122-3; Emerson on quoting, v, 71; Hugo on citing, xxxix, 387; Raleigh on, 100

Authority, Bacon on vices of, iii, 30, 48; Channing on, in religion, xxviii, 342; Hobbes on legal, xxxiv, 414; Kempis on obedience to, vii, 212; knowledge on, xxxii, 37-9; Lowell on decline of, reverence for, xxviii, 466; Luther on, xxxvi, 274; Mill on limits of, xxv, 203-6, 270-89; Pascal on, and reason, xlviii, 438-44; Pascal on, in religion, 95 (260); Paul on, xxxvi, 274; Pliny's remarks on, ix, 333; truths on, xxv, 229-39

Authors, in law, xxxiv, 414-15, 417; Pascal on egotism of, xlviii, 21 (43); relation of, to public, xxxix, 253-4

Autobiographies, preëminent, xxxi, 3

Autobiography, Cellini on, xxxi, 5; Cicero on, ix, 104; James on influence of, i, 68; Vaughan on, 70-1

Autolycus, xxii, 267-8

Automata, Descartes on, xxxiv, 45-6; Hobbes on, 309

Automedon, in sack of Troy, xiii, 116

Autonoë, in THE BACCHÆ, viii, 399, 421, 427

Autonomy of the Will, explained by concept of freedom, xxxii, 356-7; Kant on, 341-3, 346; the supreme principle of morality, 343, 350-1, 355

AUTUMN, ODE TO, xli, 879-80

Autumn, Burns on, vi, 231-2; Campbell on, xli, 772; Collins on, 481; Longfellow on, xlii, 1304; Shakespeare on, xl, 277-8; Shelley on the, xli, 833-4

Auxerre, battle of, xxxix, 82

Auxiliary troops, Machiavelli on, xxxvi, 45-8

Ava, plant, xxix, 414

Avalanches, cause of, xxx, 214-15

Avalos, Alfonson d', xxxi, 183 note

Avan, province of, xliii, 24

AVARICE, ÆSOP'S FABLE ON, xvii, 32

Avarice, Arabian proverb on, xvi, 201; Arabian verses on, 302; Browne on, iii, 329; Cicero on, in old age, ix, 68; Dante's punishment of, xx, 29-30, 222-4; instances of, 228-9; Dante on, 225 note 1; Epictetus on growth of, ii, 144; Krishna on, xlv, 862; miserliness contrasted with, xxxvi, 51; Mohammed on, xlv, 883-4; Pascal on, xlviii, 164 (502); Penn on, i, 331-2; Shakespeare on, xlvi, 376

AVARICIOUS AND ENVIOUS, fable of, xvii, 32

Avenant, Sir William d', DAWN SONG, xl, 354

Aventinus, son of Hercules, xiii, 262

Avernus, Lake, xiii, 215

Averroes, Dante on, xx, 20 note

Aversion, Hobbes on, xxxiv, 337-40; language of, 344

Avianius, Cicero and, ix, 105

Aviaries, Bacon on, iii, 117

Avicenna, in Dante's Limbo, xx, 20; on tumefaction, xxxviii, 114

Avila, Don Louis de, works of, xiv, 55

Avilion, island-valley of, xlii, 992

Aviones, Tacitus on the, xxxiii, 115

Avitus, letter to, ix, 215

Avoidance, Aurelius on, ii, 236 (20)

AWA', WHIGS, AWA', vi, 360-1

Awe, Confucius on, xliv, 29 (22), 56 (8)

Awood, John, More and, xxxvi, 121-2

Ax, speckled, story of, i, 84-5

Axioms, Montaigne on, xlviii, 392; Pascal's rules for, 405

AYE MY WIFE SHE DANG ME, vi, 515

Ayeshah, wife of Mohammed, xlv, 992 note 1

AYR, THE BRIGS OF, vi, 230-7

AYR, FAREWELL SONG TO BANKS OF, vi, 238-9

Ayrton, William, in Hazlitt's discussion, xxvii, 267-78

Aytoun, Sir William, REFUSAL OF CHARON, xli, 917-18

Azara, Don Felix, on carrion-hawks, xxix, 64, 66; on cattle in Paraguay, xi, 80-1; on hydrophobia, xxix, 357; on ostrich

eggs, 98; on Pampas Indians, 111 note; on plants along new tracks, 124; on wild horses in droughts, 139; on wasps and spiders, 44 note 9; on S. American rainfall, 55 note

Azazel, standard bearer of Satan, iv, 101

Azores, stocked by glaciers, xi, 392-3

Azotos, siege of, xxxiii, 79

Azpetia, Don Sancho de, the Biscaine, xiv, 70

Azûra, Phineas Ibn, xlv, 964 note 24

Azzecca-Garbugli, in THE BETROTHED, xxi, 40, 42-7, 74, 76, 80-1, 406, 637

Azzolino, Dante on, xx, 51, and note 8

Baalim, Milton on, iv, 98

Baal-peor, xliv, 279 (28)

Baba Mustafa, in ALI-BABA, xvi, 429-30, 431-2

Babel, Tower of, Browne on, iii, 275; Hobbes on, xxxiv, 323; Milton on, iv, 105, 343; its builders in Limbo, 147

BABIE, THE, by Miller, xli, 918

Babieca, horse of the Cid, xiv, 13-14; saddle of, 490

Babington, Rev. Dr., lines on, vi, 499

Babrius, Valerius, Æsop and, xvii, 8-9

BABY, by MacDonald, xlii, 1118-19

Babylon, Milton on, iv, 391; Milton on captivity in, 350; psalm on captivity in, xliv, 318; Raleigh on, xxxix, 71

BABYLON; or, BONNIE BANKS o' FORDIE, xl, 58-9

Baçan, Alvaro de, xiv, 386

Baccalaos, Newfoundland called, xxxiii, 281

BACCHÆ, THE, of Euripides, viii, 368-436

Bacchic mysteries, Herodotus on, xxxiii, 42

Bacchus, Amalthea's son, iv, 161; Circe and, 46; Dryden on, xl, 392; Euripides on, viii, 371-2, 382-3, 384

Bacchus, India, return from, xiii, 234; mirth, father of, iv, 30; mother of, xii, 271; Pentheus and, viii, 123; Sophocles on, 293; Thebes, guardian of, 215-16; worship of, described, 399-402; worship of, various forms of, xii, 338 note (see also Dionysus Iacchus)

Bachelors, ancient penalty on, ix, 404 note 1

Bachiacca, the embroiderer, xxxi, 56 note 2, 354 note 5

Bachiacca, the painter, xxxi, 56 note 2, 64, 66

Bachman, on carrion vultures, xxix, 190

Backbite, Sir Benjamin, in SCHOOL FOR SCANDAL, xviii; epigram of, 132; Maria's lover, 119; Sneerwell's, at, 122-6, 131-7; Lady Teazle's, at, after the scandal, 181-5

Backsliding, in religion, xv, 154-6

Bacon, Francis, Emerson on, v, 435-6, 438, 440; ESSAYS, iii, 7-142; remarks on ESSAYS, 4; Hazlitt on, xxvii, 277 note 14; Herbert, George, and, xv, 383; Hobbes and, xxxiv, 308; inquiry, on, xi, 1; INSTAURATIO MAGNA, PREFACE TO, xxxix, 116-42; INSTAURATIO MAGNA, remarks on preface to, 3; Jonson on, xxvii, 56-7; Jonson on times of, v, 437-8; language of, xxxix, 196; LIFE, xl, 348-9; life and works, iii, 3-4, 144; Montaigne and, xxxii, 3; NEW ATLANTIS, iii, 145-81; NOVUM ORGANUM, preface to, xxxix, 143-7; on inquiry, xi, 1; Pope on, xl, 437; on prodigies, xxxvii, 391; Raleigh on, xxxix, 112; on reform, v, 371; on Rome, 362; Shakespeare not mentioned by, xxxix, 317-18; Shelley on, xxvii, 334; on similitudes, 331; Voltaire on, xxxiv, 98-102

Bacon, Sir Nicholas, iii, 3; Jonson on, xxvii, 56

Bacon, Roger, Emerson on, v, 394-5; Newman on, xxviii, 47

Bacteria, absorption of oxygen by, xxxviii, 326-7; air and, 334-5; animal nature of, 342-3; Lister on, 256

Badow, Richard, founder of Clare Hall, xxxv, 381

Baer, Von, on embryos, xi, 459; on standard of organization, 129; on the bee, 370

Bagdemagus, King, xxxv, 116-7; tomb of, 204

Bagehot, Walter, ON MILTON, xxviii, 165-206; life and works of, 164

Baglioni, Malatesta, xxxi, 70 note 5

Baglioni, Orazio, xxxi, 70 note 5, 73-5, 80 and note

Bagot, Charles, correspondence with Mr. Rush, xliii, 265-7

Bahamas, Raleigh on the, xxxiii, 377

Bahia, Darwin on, xxix, 21, 498

Bahia Blanca, Darwin on, xxix, 81-111

Bahrám, reference to, xli, 945

Bail, excessive, forbidden, xliii, 195 (8); right of, in Massachusetts, 69 (18)

Bailiff, Chaucer's, xl, 27-8

Baillie, Lady Grisel, WERENA MY HEART, xl, 398-400

Baillie, Joanna, *Constantine* of, xxv, 15 note

Bailly, M., as mayor of Paris, xxiv, 372-3; on October sixth, 211 note; Burke on death of, 216 note

Bain, Alexander, Mill and, xxv, 152 note 3, 161, 189

Baird, Dr., on Franklin, i, 59

Báithis, sons of, xlix, 241-2

Bajazet, Raleigh on, xxxix, 98; Selymus and, iii, 50-1

Bakbak, story of, xvi, 171-4

Baker, Henry Williams, HYMN, xlv, 536

Baker, Sir Samuel, on the giraffe, xi, 221

Bakewell, the agriculturist, v, 362

Balaam, death of, xxxix, 95; Milton on, iv, 371; prophecy of Rome, xxxvi, 327

Balaam's Ass, Luther on, xxxvi, 272

Balaguet, Emir of, xlix, 123, 134

Balan, Balin and, xxxv, 111

Balance, Penn on, i, 348-9

Balance of Power, Bacon on, iii, 49-50

Balance of Produce and Consumption, x, 369

Balance of Trade, doctrine of, x, 314-30; methods used to make favorable, 330; absurdity of whole doctrine, 359-69; criterions of, 355

Balbo, Girolamo, xxxi, 63 note

Balbus, Cornelius, Cæsar and, xii, 313; Cicero and, ix, 114

Bald Head, Australia, xxix, 453-4

BALD MAN AND FLY, fable of, xvii, 18

Baldini, Bernardone, and the diamond, xxxi, 352-3, 361; and the necklace, 391-2; relations with Cellini, 361, 399, 402, 420

Baldock, in EDWARD THE SECOND, xlvi, 29-31, 38, 55, 62, 64, 65, 66-8

Balducci, Giacopo, xxxi, 109

Baldwin, and the Genovese, iii, 280

Baldwin, son of Ganelon, xlix, 104, 106

Baleen, of whales, xi, 225-9

Baligant, Emir of Babylon, xlix, 184 note

Balin le Savage, xxxv, 111

Baliol, John, Dante on, xx, 368 note 8

Baliol, the devil, in FAUSTUS, xix, 217-8

Ball, John, Froissart on, xxxv, 61-2; in Wat Tyler's Rebellion, 64, 69, 71, 73, 75; death of, 80

BALLADS, TRADITIONAL, xl, 51-186

Ballantine, John, inscription to, vi, 230; reference to, 351 note 3

Ballantyne, James, and Scott, xxv, 429-30

Ballenar, Chili, xxix, 353

Balliol, John, founder of Balliol College, xxxv, 381

Ballmer, George, loss of, xxiii, 38, 40-1

BALLOCHMYLE, FAREWELL TO, vi, 109-10

BALLOCHMYLE, LASS OF, vi, 220-1

Ballot, Burke on the, xxiv, 338; Mill on the, xxv, 159

Balmerino, Burns on, vi, 291

BALOW, xl, 186-7

Balsam of Fierebras, xiv, 74; prepared by Don Quixote, 128

Balsham, Hugh, founder of Peter College, xxxv, 381

BALTIC, THE BATTLE OF THE, xli, 779-780

Balzac, Jean Louis de, Philarchus on, xiii, 60

Ban, King, xxxv, 152

Bancroft, George, and Emerson, v, 463

Band dog, Harrison on the, xxxv, 352-3; cross between bear and, 355

Banda Oriental, province of, xxix, 147-63

Bandaging, Harvey on, xxxviii, 110-4

Bande Nere, Giovanni delle, xxxi, 15 note 1

Bandinello, Baccio, xxxi, 14 note 1; Cellini, relations with, 95, 349, 358-9, 363, 364-5, 367-71, 400, 401-2, 412; choir by, 412; Duke Cosimo and, 345 note 4, 347, 392-3, 416; father of, 14-5; "Hercules" of, 368-70 note 1, 416; knight of St. James, 410 note; "Pieta" of, 419-20

Bandini, Giovan, xxxi, 105 note

Bandini, Don Juan, xxiii, 233-4, 237, 389

Bank failures, Ruskin on, xxviii, 115

BANK OF FLOWERS, ON A, vi, 341-2

Banking corporations, x, 461-2

BANKNOTE, LINES ON A, vi, 221-2

Bank-notes (see Paper Money)

Bankruptcy, Smith on, x, 270

Bankruptcy laws, Ruskin on, xxviii, 115; under control of Congress, xliii, 184 (4)

Banks, power of Congress to incorporate, xliii, 209, 212-15, 222-4

Banks and Banking, Smith on, x, 230-57

BANKS OF AYR, FAREWELL TO, vi, 238-9

BANKS OF THE DEVON, vi, 288

BANKS O' DOON, vi, 398-9

BANKS OF NITH, vi, 342-3

Banks, Sir J., expedition of, xxix, 215

Bannerets, Harrison on, xxxv, 222

BANNOCKBURN, vi, 472

BANNOCKS O' BEAR MEAL, vi, 490

Banquets, Cicero on, ix, 61; skeletons at Egyptian, xxxii, 16, 19

Banquo (in MACBETH), captain of Duncan, xlvi, 323; with witches, 325-7; with king's messengers, 327, 328-9; received by king, 330; at Macbeth's castle, 334; with Fleance, 338; with Macbeth before the murder, 338-9; after murder, 345-7; murder of, 356-7; ghost of, 358-9, 360-1, 369; soliloquy of, 349-50; with Macbeth as king, 350-1; plot to kill, 351-4

Banyan tree, xlv, 857

Baptism, Browne on, iii, 296; Calvin on, xxxix, 50; conversion by, story of, vii, 49; Dante on necessity of, xx, 17, 421; Luther on, xxxvi, 266, 267, 316, 320; Milton on, iv, 353; Pascal on, xlviii, 169 (520), 337; Pascal on, of children, xlviii, 375-6; Paul, St., on, xliv, 464; Quakers on, xxxiv, 66-7

Barabbas, xliv, 414 (18-19, 25)

Baraquan, Orinoco called, xxxiii, 317 note

Barateve, island of, xxxiii, 222-3

BARBARA, by Smith, xlii, 1146-7

BARBARA ALLAN, BONNY, a ballad, xl, 68-9

BARBARA FRIETCHIE, xlii, 1362-4

Barbarians, Milton on invasion of the, iv, 97

Barbariccia, the demon, xx, 88, 90

Barbarossa, Frederick (see Frederick I)

Barbarossa, the pirate, xiv, 386

Barbauld, Anna Lætitia, LIFE, xli, 555; Burns on, vi, 410

Barberry, crosses of the, xi, 104

BARBER'S STORY, in ARABIAN NIGHTS, xvi, 162-89

Barbers, verses on, xvi, 156

Barca, Giacopino della, xxxi, 86-7, 88

Barce, nurse of Sichæus, xiii, 175

Barclay, Robert, Apology of, xxxiv, 73-4; on Quaker faith, 67

BARCLAY OF URY, xlii, 1347-51

BARD, THE, xl, 456-60

BARD'S EPITAPH, A, vi, 218-9

Bardi, Simone dei, husband of Beatrice, xx, 3

Barding, among the Germans, xxxiii, 94

Bardism, Renan on, xxxii, 167-9, 141-2

Bards, ancient title of, v, 176; Renan on Celtic, xxxii, 141-2, 167-9

Barebones, Hugo on, xxxix, 380

BAREFOOT BOY, THE, xlii, 1355-7

Barfleur, capture of, xxxv, 10-11 note; importance of, 13 note 3

Bargaining, Bacon on, iii, 89

Bargello, the, xxxi, 99 note

Bar-Jesus, xliv, 450 (6-11); Pascal on, xlviii, 294

Barking-bird, Darwin on the, xxix, 292

Barlaam and Josaphat, xxvi, 6

Barlass, Kate, xlii, 1153-4, 1155, 1161, 1170-1

Barlow, Gen., at Gettysburg, xliii, 330

Barmekis Feast, xvi, 184-7

Barnabas, at Antioch, xliv, 447-8 (22-6), 456; Jerusalem, mission to, 448 (30), 450 (25), 455; Lystra, men of, and, xxxvi, 297; Paul and, xliv, 442-3 (27), 450 (2-7), 452-4, 457 (36-7)

Barnacle Geese, Harrison on, xxxv, 335

Barnave, on October sixth, xxiv, 211 note

Barnfield, Richard, THE NIGHTINGALE, xl, 283

Barnhelm, Minna von, and Bruchsal, xxvi, 373; Franzisca, scenes with, 313-5, 320-1, 323-4, 343-4, 349-51; Just, scene with, 321-3; landlord, scene with, 315-20, 321; Riccaut de la Marlinière, scene with, 344-9; Tellheim, scenes with, 324-7, 351-8, 362-74

Barnwell, George, xxvii, 305 note, 309-10

BARON OF BRACKLEY, a ballad, xl, 119-21

Baron, origin of word, xxxiv, 368

Barontus, story of, xxxii, 175

Barrande, M., "colonies" of, xi, 350; discoveries of, 345; on palæozoic, animals, 363; on silurian deposits, 361; on succession of species, 359

Barras, Comte de, xliii, 173

Barratry, in Massachusetts, xliii, 71 (34)

Barré, Burke on, xxiv, 396

Barrett, Elizabeth, and Browning, xviii, 358

Barrier-reefs, Darwin on, xxix, 472-81

Barriers, relation of, to species, xi, 379-80

Barry, the actor, xxvii, 275

Barsabbas, xliv, 424 (23), 456 (22)

Bartas, Du, Creation of, xxxix, 317

Barter, human propensity to, x, 18-9; inconveniences of, 27; in relation to division of labor, 20-2

Barterers, in Dante's HELL, xx, 85-6, 89-92

Bartholomew, the apostle, xliv, 368 (14),

424 (13); patron of New Atlantis, iii, 154-5

BARTHRAM'S DIRGE, xli, 769-70

Bartolini, Onofrio de, xxxi, 411 note

Barton, George, xxxiii, 229, 235, 237

Barzanes, in Utopia, xxxvi, 181

Basan and Basil, xlix, 101, 105, 110

Bashan, mountain of, xliv, 224 (15)

Bashfulness, Emerson on, v, 110; Locke on, xxxvii, 51-2, 120

Basil, Council of, xxxix, 42

Basil, St., at Athens, xxviii, 54, 60-1; on use of Homer, iii, 200

Basil, the smith (see Lajeunesse)

Basilio, in LIFE IS A DREAM, relates story of Segismund, xxvi, 23-6; his plan to try Segismund, 26-30; hears of Segismund from Clotaldo, 30-1; with Segismund, 45-52; in the battle, 69-71; resigns crown to Segismund, 72-3

Basilisk, the serpent, xlvii, 680 note

Baskerville, Sir Thomas, xxxiii, 227

Basket, Fuegia, xxix, 212-3, 226-7, 231, 233

Basoche, Hugo on the, xxxix, 351

Basset, Lord, at Crecy, xxxv, 25; at Poitiers, 42; at Poix castle, 18

Bassompierre, M. de, xxxviii, 51

Basstarnians, xxxiii, 119

Bassus, Aufidius, ix, 232 note 3

Bassus, Gabius, Pliny on, ix, 370, 373

BAT, BIRDS, AND BEASTS, fable of, xvii, 21

Batalus, Plutarch on, xii, 193

Batavians, Tacitus on the, xxxiii, 108-9

Bateman, William, founder of Trinity Hall, xxxv, 381

Bates, Mr., on ants, xi, 282; on butterflies, 445, 446

Bath, Knights of the, xxxv, 220

Baths, health, in NEW ATLANTIS, iii, 174; Locke on cold, xxxvii, 13; origin of name, vii, 156

Bathsheba, Winthrop on, xliii, 94

Batrachians, absence of, from islands, xi, 417-8

Bats, Blake on, xli, 587; Collins on the, 479; range of, xi, 418; wings of, 176-7

Bat's-eyes, Mrs., in PILGRIM'S PROGRESS, xv, 187

Battiferra, Laura, xxxi, 427 note

Battista, Giovan (Il Tasso), xxxi, 24-5, 27, 345 note 5, 393

Battle, eyes vanquished first in, xxxiii, 117; not to the strong, xliv, 346 (11)

Batjan, island of, xxxiii, 222-3

Baubo, reference to, xix, 172

Baugé, M. de, at Metz, xxxviii, 25; prisoner to De Vaudeville, 42

Bauhin, Caspar, on the heart, xxxviii, 82

Baumgarten, Conrad (Konrad), in WILLIAM TELL, flight of, xxvi, 382-5; Hedwig and, 457; Rootli League, at, 412-3, 417, 427; Uri, at keep of, 476, 477; Wolfshot killed by, 398

Bavius, Shelley on, xxvii, 358

Bayle, Pierre, Carlyle on, xxv, 446

Bazeilles, the Moine of, xxxv, 25-6

Beagle Channel, xxix, 222

BE NOT DISMAYED, xlv, 559

Beacon, first, in Ireland, xlix, 216

BEAGLE, VOYAGE OF THE, xxix

Beales, Mill on, xxv, 178

BEAR AND TWO FELLOWS, fable of, xvii, 30-1

BEAR AND WILLOW WREN, story of, xvii, 190-2

Bearing, Brynhild on, and forbearing, xlix, 304; Epictetus on, and forbearing, ii, 179 (183); Jonson on, xl, 292-3; Kempis on, vii, 219-20; Penn on, i, 340, 347 (294); (see also Patience)

Bears, Darwin on black, xi, 178; in Egypt, xxxiii, 37

BEARSKIN, story of, xvii, 185-90

Bearwards, Harrison on, xxxv, 306

BEAT! BEAT! DRUMS! xlii, 1402-3

Beatitude, Raleigh on, xxxix, 90

Beatrice, Dante and, xx, 3-4

Beatrice, in DIVINE COMEDY, xx, 10-12, 267-75, 280-417, 419; Arnold on speech of, xxviii, 72; Hugo on, xxxix, 349; Ruskin on, xxviii, 140-1

Beattie, James, Minstrel of, xxxix, 299; references to, vi, 166, 177

Beatty, Mr., with Franklin, i, 142

Beauchamp, Philip, On Natural Religion, xxv, 47-8

Beauchamp, Richard, Earl of Warwick, v, 403; xxxv, 104

Beaujeu, Lord, xxxv, 25, 31, 37

Beaumarchais, Hugo on, xxxix, 357, 383

Beaumont, in EDWARD THE SECOND, xlvi, 27

Beaumont, Francis, sketch of life and works, xlvii, 666; LETTER TO JONSON, xl, 319-21; PHILASTER, xlvii, 667-751; TOMBS IN WESTMINSTER ABBEY, xl, 319

Beaumont, Sir George, Wordsworth on picture by, xli, 605-7

Beaumont and Fletcher, Dryden on, xxxix, 318; editorial remarks on plays of, xlvii, 666; Emerson on plays of, v, 121; Hazlitt on, xxvii, 276; PHILASTER, xlvii, 667-751

BEAUTIFUL, THE SUBLIME AND, xxiv, 29-140

BEAUTIFUL MISS ELIZA J—N, vi, 498

Beautiful Palace, in PILGRIM'S PROGRESS, xv, 49

BEAUTY, BACON'S ESSAY ON, iii, 106-7

BEAUTY, EMERSON'S ESSAY ON, v, 297-310

Beauty, Augustine, St., on, vii, 56, 58; Berkeley on, xxxvii, 228; Burke on, xxiv, 15, 38, 45, 74-104, 119-28; Burns on, vi, 470, 548; Channing on study of, xxviii, 328; Coleridge on, xxvii, 258, 262; Crashaw on, xl, 360-1; Daniel on, 221; Darley on, xli, 913-4; Darwin on, xi, 200-2, 489-90; xxix, 407-8; David, a thing of, xli, 497; Emerson on, v, 100, 140, 167-8, 199, 219; Hugo on, xxxix, 349, 385; Hume on, xxvii, 206; xxxvii, 292-3, 420; Keats on, and melancholy, xli, 883; M. Aurelius on, ii, 205-6, 215 (20); Milton on, iv, 6, 55, 64, 167, 377, 439-40; More on, xxxvi, 203-4, 212; Nashe on, xl, 260; Pascal on, xlviii, 18 (32), 413-14; Plato on, ii, 94; Poe on sense of, xxviii, 376-8; Poe on, and sadness, 382; Raleigh on, xl, 205; Ruskin on, of woman, xxviii, 146-8; Schiller on influence and development of, xxxii, 209, 212, 234-68, 271-4, 281-95; Shakespeare on, xl, 264, 272, 274-5; xlvi, 145; Waller on, xl, 357; Whitman on, xxxix, 394, 395

Beauty and the Beast, Emerson on legend of, v, 348; Hugo on, xxxix, 351

BEAUTY BATHING, xl, 201

BEAUTY, GENIUS IN, xlii, 1179

BEAUTY, THE TRUE, xl, 351

BEAUTY, TIME, AND LOVE, xl, 219-22

Beaver, Harrison on the, xxxv, 342

Bebius, death of, xxxii, 14

Beccaria, Abbot, in Dante's HELL, xx, 134 and note 11

Béchamp, M., xxxviii, 350 note, 356

Becket, Thomas à, Bacon on, iii, 51; Chaucer on, xl, 11; Dryden on, xxxix, 165, note 21; Harrison on, xxxv, 254, 382

Bede, Venerable, sketch of life, xx, 329 note 27; first doctor of Cambridge,

xxxv, 377; in Dante's PARADISE, xx, 329; on Purgatory, xxxii, 179

Bedford, Duke of, Burke and, xxiv, 380; Burke's reply to attack of, 381-421; estates of, v, 404

Bedivere, Sir, xlii, 986-92

Bedr, battle of, xlv, 944 note 4, 948 note 12, 950 note 2, 959-60

Bedr Basim, xvi, 335, 338-40

Bedr-ed-Din, the Gardener, xvi, 123-4

Bedr-el-Budur, the Sultan's daughter, xvi, 365-424

Beds, in old England, xxxv, 297; Locke on, for children, xxxvii, 23

Bedsores, Paré on, xxxviii, 54

Beelzebub, in PARADISE LOST, iv, 91-2, 95, 116-19

Beelzebub, in PILGRIM'S PROGRESS, xv, 29

BEELZEBUB, ADDRESS OF, vi, 205-7

Beer, Harrison on making of, xxxv, 283

Bees, Browne on wisdom of, iii, 266 (15); cell-making instinct of, xi, 268-76; clover and, 101-2; drones and queen, 204; as fertilizing agents, 81-2; Harrison on, xxxv, 346-7; mice and, xi, 82; Milton on, iv, 107, 239; parasitic, xi, 263; Pope on, xl, 427; sting of, xi, 204; Swift on, xxvii, 113; time-saving of, xi, 101; Virgil's description of, xiii, 88; Von Baer on, xi, 370; wax of, 255

Beethoven, his musical setting of EGMONT, xix, 252

Beetles, Brazilian, xxix, 42 and note 7; Collins on, xli, 479; dung-feeding, xxix, 493 note; at Port St. Julian, 175; at sea, xi, 411; xxix, 163-4; springing, xxix, 39-40; without anterior tarsi, xi, 141; wingless, 141-2

Beet-root sugar, Pasteur on, xxxviii, 305 note

Begbie, Ellison, vi, 28 note

BEGGARS, THE JOLLY, vi, 122-33

Beggars, Blake on, xli, 588; Luther on, xxxvi, 313-14; More on, 155

BEGGAR'S SONG, in FAUST, xix, 41

Beginnings, Æsop on, xvii, 16, 22; Goethe on, xix, 350; Hugo on, and ends, xxxix, 354; Machiavelli on, xxxvi, 12; merry, make sad endings, vii, 226 (7); most easy to check, 216

Behavior, Bacon on, iii, 126; Emerson on, v, 215; Epictetus on, ii, 175 (164)

Behemoth, references to, iv, 239; xliv, 137 (15)

Behmen, Jacob, Emerson on, v, 141, 178, 232-3

BEHOLD, MY LOVE, HOW GREEN THE GROVES, vi, 503-4

BEHOLD THE HOUR, THE BOAT, ARRIVE, vi, 429

BEHOLD THE HOUR, THE BOAT, ARRIVE, vi, 472-3

Behring, the navigator, Emerson on, v, 81

Bekkluld, sister of Brynhild, xlix, 306-7

Belacqua, in Dante's PURGATORY, xx, 160-1

Belcher, the devil, in FAUSTUS, xix, 217-18

Belgians, eating custom of, xxxv, 288

Belial, in PARADISE LOST, iv, 100, 111-14, 219-20

Belial, in PARADISE REGAINED, iv, 375-6

Belianis, Don, Burke on romance of, xxiv, 20; Cervantes on romance of, xiv, 51; Don Quixote on, 18, 93; to Don Quixote, 11

Belief, Hobbes on, xxxiv, 347-8; Hume on, xxxvii, 324, 325-31, 332-4, 373, 376-7, 381; Pascal on, xlviii, 35 (81), 42 (99), 90-102, 172 (536); through understanding and will, 400-2

Belisarius, Dante on, xx, 306; Raleigh on, xxxix, 98

BELL, THE, story of, xvii, 357-61

Bell Mountain, Chili, xxix, 260-3

Bellario, in PHILASTER, as Philaster's boy, xlvii, 681-2; sent to princess, 684, 690; with Arethusa, 691; accused as Arethusa's lover, 698, 702; with Philaster, 704-8; Arethusa ordered to dismiss, 709; parting from Arethusa, 713-4; meets Philaster in woods, 717-8; with Arethusa in wood, 721; asleep on bank, 726; wounded by Philaster, 726; taken by Pharamond, 727-8; saved by Philaster, 728-30; with Philaster in prison, 731-3; announces to king marriage of Philaster, 734; denounced by Megra, 744-5; condemned to torture, 746; confesses, 746-51

Bellarmati, Girolamo, xxxi, 328 note 3

Bellarmine, Cardinal, xv, 325

Bellay, M. du, Montaigne on, xxxii, 62, 101

BELLE DAME SANS MERCI, LA, xli, 893-5

Bellefontaine, Benedict, the farmer of Grand-Pré, xlii, 1301; on evening of Evangeline's betrothal, 1306, 1309; at betrothal feast, 1311; on day of exile, 1315, 1316; death, 1317-18

Bellegarde, Abbé, on ridicule, xxxix, 179-80

Bellerophon, reference to, iv, 227

Bellerus, reference to, iv, 76

BELLES OF MAUCHLINE, vi, 58

Belles Lettres, Hume on, xxxvii, 291

BELLING THE CAT, fable of, xvii, 38

Bellona, reference to, iv, 131

BELLS, THE, by Poe, xlii, 1233-5

BELLY AND THE MEMBERS, fable of, xvii, 23; Menenius Agrippa on fable of, xii, 152

Belper, Lord, Mill on, xxv, 52, 67

Belphœbe, Spenser's, xxxix, 63, 65; Burke on Spenser's, xxiv, 136

Beltenebros, name assumed by Amadis, xiv, 212

Belus, father of Dido, xiii, 95

Belus, the god, iv, 106

Belzoni, on inhabitants of Gournou, v, 199

Bembo, Pietro, xxxi, 189

Bembus, Cardinal, patron of poets, xxvii, 40, 50

Benchuca, Darwin on the, xxix, 333

Bendedio, Alberto, xxxi, 52, 269, 271, 272

Bene, Albertaccio del, xxxi, 143, 144, 189, 434-5

Bene, Alessandro del, xxxi, 69

Bene, Ricciardo del, xxxi, 319

Benedetto, Ser, xxxi, 132-3

Benedict, St., Dante on, xx, 379 note 3, 420 note 6

Benedict, Emerson on, v, 291-2

Benedictines, Dante on corruption of the, xx, 380-1

Benedictis, Jacobus de, hymn by, xlv, 553

Benefaction, the rule of good men, v, 190-1

Beneficence, Kant on moral worth of, xxxii, 310; recompense of, xvi, 334

Benefices, of Catholic Church, xxxvi, 280, 286; Luther on, 289, 291

Benefits, Bacon on, common and peculiar, iii, 33; Cicero on, ix, 20, 27; Emerson on, v, 96, 220; Hobbes, of receiving, xxxiv, 371; Tacitus on, xlviii, 30 note (see also Favors)

Benegridran, Welsh chief, quoted, v, 403

Benengeli, Cid Hamete, xiv, 70, 176

Benevento, battle of, xx, 66 note 1

Benevolence, Bacon on, iii, 32-4; Burns

on, vi, 251; Emerson on, v, 27-8, 105, 190-1, 211, 217; Epictetus on, ii, 163 (128); Hobbes on, xxxiv, 340; Kant on, xxxii, 340, 345, 351; Mill, James, on, xxv, 35; More on, xxxvi, 198; Pope on, xl, 439; universality of, ix, 352 note

Benezet, Anthony, i, 102, 285

Bengal, cause of early civilization of, x, 25

Benham, William, translator of IMITATION OF CHRIST, vii

Benincasa of Arezzo, xx, 166 note 2

Benintendi, Niccolò, xxxi, 150-1

Ben-Manasseh, Israel, xxxix, 379-80

Bennett, Harry, xxiii, 401

Bensalem (see NEW ATLANTIS)

Bentham, Jeremy, Mill on, xxv, 39, 43, 44-6, 60-1, 65-6, 74-5, 127, 164; Review of his Book of Fallacies, xxvii, 225-51

Bentham, Sir Samuel, Mill on, xxv, 39

Benthamism, Mill on, xxv, 44-5, 65-73, 136

Bentivoglio, Annibale, xxxvi, 61

Benvegnato, Messer, xxxi, 67-8

Benvenuti, Benvenuto, xliii, 28

Benvenuto (see Cellini)

Benzo of Milan, xxxviii, 32

Beowulf, Breca and, xlix, 19; Daeghrefu and, 73; death of, 79-82, 83, 89; Dragon and, 69, 71, 74-9; Eadgils and, 70; funeral of, 88, 90; Grendel and, 24-7, 62; Grendel's mother and, 40-9, 63; Hetwaras and, 70; Hrethel and, 72; Hrothgar and, 11-23, 30-1, 33; Hygelac and, 59-64, 70, 73; Hygelac's thane, 10; king, 65, 70; Renan on, xxxii, 147; Scyld's son, xlix, 5; sea-adventures, 20

BEOWULF, epic of, xlix, 5-92; remarks on, 3-4

Béranger, Pierre Jean de, Poe on, xxviii, 373

Bérard, J. F., on fruits, xxxviii, 306

Berengario, Giacomo (see Carpi)

Berenger, Raymond, daughters of, xx, 174 note 14, 309 note 27; and Romeo, his steward, 309 note 26

Berengier, in SONG OF ROLAND, xlix, 120, 135, 147, 167

Berenice, daughter of Ptolemy, xlviii, 248

Bergamo, Bartolommeo of, xxxvi, 43

Berkeley, in EDWARD II, xlvi, 72-3, 74

Berkeley, George, sketch of life and works, xxxvii, 186; DIALOGUES, 187-

285; Emerson on anecdote of, v, 264; Emerson on idealism of, 153; Hazlitt on, xxvii, 277; Hume on philosophy of, xxxvii, 412 note

Berkeley, Lord Thomas, at Poitiers, xxxv, 49-50

Berkenshaw, Mr., and Pepys, xxviii, 298-9

Berlinghieri, Berlinghier, xxxi, 101

Bermuda, birds of, xi, 415, 416; Raleigh on, xxxiii, 377

BERMUDA, SONG OF EMIGRANTS IN, xl, 376-7

Bernabo of Milan, xxxvi, 73

Bernard, of Clairvaux, St., Anastasius and, xxxvi, 339; Considerations of, 344; in Dante's PARADISE, xx, 417-24; hymns by, xlv, 550-1; on idleness, xxxix, 13; IMITATION OF CHRIST, attributed to, vii, 200; quotation from, v, 101; on the soul, xxxiv, 103

Bernard, of Morlaix, hymns by, xlv, 548-9

Bernard, of Quintavalle, xx, 332 note 17

Bernard, son of Pepin, xxxix, 80-1, 83

Bernardi, Giovanni, xxxi, 131 note 2

Bernardo da Carpio (see Carpio)

Bernardo, in HAMLET, xlvi, 93-8, 104-7

Bernardone, Pietro, xx, 332 note 21

Berners, Lord, translator of Froissart, xxxv, 1

Berni, Francesco, and the capitolo, xxxi, 237 note 1

Bernice, and Agrippa, xliv, 478 (13), 479 (23), 481 (30)

Bernoulli, on conservation of force, xxx, 175; on comets, xxxiv, 118; on integral calculus, 126

Beroe, wife of Doryclus, xiii, 198

Berreo, Antonio de, xxxiii, 303, 313, 314, 315, 320, 324, 327-35, 369

Berries, Locke on, xxxvii, 20

Bert, Paul, on ferments, xxxviii, 351

Bertha of Bruneck, in WILLIAM TELL, xxvi, 395; with Fürst, 446; with Gessler, 442; Rudenz and, 411, 432-6, 446-7, 463, 475-6, 488-9

Berthelot, M., Pasteur on, xxxviii, 350

Berti, Bellincione, xx, 66 note 1, 350

Berti, Gualdrada, xx, 66 note 1

Bertoldi, Pierfrancesco, xxxi, 422

Bertrand de Born, in Dante's HELL, xx, 118 note

Bessel, on distance of stars, xxx, 316

Bessy, in FAUST, xix, 155-7

BESSY AND HER SPINNIN' WHEEL, vi, 441

Beste, J. R., translator, xlv, 555

Bestia, the tribune, xii, 236; trial of, ix, 100

Bethsaida, Jesus on, xliv, 381 (13)

Betrayers, in Dante's HELL, xx, 140-4

BETROTHED, THE (I PROMESSI SPOSI), by Manzoni, xxi

BETTER PART, THE, xlii, 1138

Bettini, Baccio, xxxi, 177

Beulah-Land, Bunyan on, xv, 156-7, 309

Beuve, Sir, xlix, 157

Beverages, universal use of, xxix, 300

Beverley, John of, xxxv, 377

Bevilacqua, xxxi, 47

BEWARE O' BONIE ANN, vi, 332

BEWICK AND GRAHAME, xl, 121-8

BEYOND THE VEIL, xl, 346-7

BE YOUR WORDS MADE, GOOD SIR, xl, 213

Beza, patron of poetry, xxvii, 40

Bhaddiya, xlv, 776

BHAGAVAD-GITA, THE, xlv, 785-874; remarks on, 784

Bhutas, evil spirits, xlv, 863 note 2

Bianchi, faction of, its origin, xx, 132 note 4; strife with the Neri, 26-7 notes, 101-2 notes

Biarni Heriulfsson, xliii, 5-7

Bias, one of Seven Sages, ix, 30

Bibbiena, Cardinal, Sidney on, xxvii, 40

BIBLE, BOOKS FROM THE, xliv, 69-486; xlv, 489-532

Bible, Apollinarii and the, iii, 199; Augustine, St., on the, vii, 35, 75, 84; Bagehot on the, xxviii, 203; Browne on, iii, 259-62, 271-6, 281; Bunyan on, xv, 230, 303; Calvin on, xxxix, 30-1, 38, 47-8; Dante on, xx, 389, 390, 409; Emerson on, v, 41; xlii, 1248; Hobbes on, xxxiv, 348, 357; Hugo on, xxxix, 352, 353, 354, 386; Hume on, xxxvii, 375, 391; Kempis on the, vii, 210, 354; Locke on, as reading for children, xxxvii, 132, 164; Luther on, xxxvi, 270-1, 325; Mill on, xxv, 243; Milton on, iii, 202-3, 240, 242; iv, 329-52; Mohammed on, xlv, 999; Pascal on, xlviii, 100 (283), 137 (428), 171 (532), 175 (548), 186 (568), 189 (573), 190 (579), 195 (598), 196 (601), 214, 228 (684), 230, 310 (900), 349; Burke on pictures of God in the, xxiv, 59; Rousseau on belief in the, xxxiv, 293-8, 300-2; Ruskin on, xxviii, 104; Swift on, xxvii, 107-8; Winthrop on examples of the, xliii, 96, 103;

Woolman on influence of, i, 170 (see also Gospel, New and Old Testaments)

Bibulus, Calpurnius, consul with Cæsar, xii, 274, 275; Cicero on, ix, 110, 121, 137; edict of, 147; Lucceius and, 88; in Parthia, 147; in Parthian War, xii, 325; Pompey and, ix, 98, 99

BICHAM, YOUNG: a ballad, xl, 84-6

Bigges, Walter, DRAKE'S ARMADA, xxxiii, 226-59

Bigotry, in literature, xxvii, 221; and philosophy, xxxvii, 393

Bikki, in VOLSUNG tale, xlix, 354, 355, 385, 418

Bildad the Shuhite, xliv, 73, 82, 98, 110, 141; Walton on, xv, 337

Bill of Rights, in Constitution, xliii, 194-5

Bills of Credit, under Confederation, xliii, 165; forbidden to states under Constitution, 186 (10)

Bills of Exchange, x, 236, 243

Bimbisāra, King, xlv, 755

Bingham, editor, Mill on, xxv, 63, 73, 74, 76

Bingham, the Kanaka, xxiii, 144

Biography, Bagehot on methods of, xxviii, 166-7; Carlyle on, xxv, 397, 398-9; history made up of, v, 68; Johnson on, xxvii, 175; poetry, compared with, xxxix, 280

Bion, Bacon on, iii, 43

Biorn, son of Karlsefni, xliii, 20

Birago, Francesco, Manzoni on, xxi, 448

Birderg, son of Ruan, xlix, 225-6

Birds, Burns on the haunts of, vi, 45-6; Darwin on color of, xi, 139; fears of, 255; xxix, 405; migratory, iv, 238; nests of, xi, 255; non-flying, 140, 177; of oceanic islands, 415; seeds distributed by, 390, 412; sexual selection among, 96; tame, instances of, xxix, 403

BIRKS OF ABERFELDY, THE, vi, 277-8

Birnam Wood, xlvi, 368, 383-4, 386, 389

Birney, Gen., at Gettysburg, xliii, 348

Birth, Browne on life before, iii, 291 (39); Buddha on, xlv, 662-3; Burke on preference to, xxiv, 190; Hippolytus on, viii, 331; Pascal on accident of, xlviii, 378; on advantages of noble, 111 (322); on respect for, 112 (324), 116 (335, 337); Shakespeare on, xlvi, 112; "a sleep and a forgetting," xli, 596

Birtha, Dame, xx, 343 note 24

BIRTHDAY ODE FOR 31ST DECEMBER, 1787, vi, 290-1

Birthplaces, Plutarch on, xii, 191

Biscop, Benedict, xxxv, 295

BISHOP ORDERS HIS TOMB, xlii, 1075-8

Bishops, Calvin on, xxxix, 41; in Catholic Church, xxxvi, 282, 293; confirmation of, 289; early elections of, 266; Luther on, 302; Ruskin on, xxviii, 108

Bithynia, Pliny's administration of, ix, 365-416

Bitias, in the ÆNEID, xiii, 99, 316, 317

Bitterness, as source of the sublime, xxiv, 72

BIXBY, MRS., LETTER TO, xliii, 420

Bizcacha, Darwin on the, xxix, 129-30

Black, "wisdom's hue," iv, 34

Black, John, Mill on, xxv, 59

BLACK-EYED SUSAN, xl, 402-3

BLACK ISLANDS, THE YOUNG KING OF THE, xvi, 46-54

Black Prince, Audley and, xxxv, 53-4, 56-7; in campaign of Crecy, 7, 12, 13, 24, 27, 30, 32; Froissart and, 5; King John and, 52, 56, 58; in Poitiers campaign, 34-6, 39-46, 52, 56-9

Blacklock, the poet, Burke on, xxiv, 134

BLACKLOCK, DR., EPISTLE TO, vi, 366-7

Blackmore, Sir Richard, xxxix, 172 note, 175 note

Blackness, Burke on effects of, xxiv, 115-9

BLACKSMITH, THE VILLAGE, xlii, 1271-3

Blackwood's Magazine, Carlyle on, v, 321

Blæsus, Velleius, story of, ix, 228

BLAIR, SIR JAMES, ELEGY ON, vi, 273-4

Blake, William, POEMS, xli, 583-92

Blame (see Censure)

Blamire, Susanna, poem by, xli, 580

Blanc, Mont, Byron on, xviii, 409; Coleridge on, xli, 707

Blancandrin, xlix, 96-7, 99, 107-9, 111

Blanche-Taque, battle of, xxxv, 21-2

Blasphemers, in Dante's HELL, xx, 46, 57-9

Blasphemy, in early Massachusetts, xliii, 80 (3); penalized in Athens, iii, 193

Blastus, the chamberlain, xliv, 449 (20)

BLENHEIM, AFTER, xli, 732-4

BLESSÈD DAMOZEL, THE, xlii, 1149-53

Blind animals, Darwin on, xi, 143-4; xxix, 59

BLIND BOY, THE, xl, 441

Blind man, parable of the, xliv, 370 (39)

Blind-man, Mr., in PILGRIM'S PROGRESS, xv, 100

BLINDNESS, Milton, ON HIS, iv, 84

Blindness, Milton on, iv, 137, 416-18; Schiller on, xxvi, 399

Bliss, Hindu conception of perfect, xlv, 815; Hogg on the greatest, xli, 765

Blood, circulation of the (see Circulation of Blood)

Bloodhounds, Harrison on, xxxv, 350

Blood-poisoning, Harvey on, xxxviii, 125

Bloody-man, the giant, xv, 222

Blossius, Gaius, Gracchus and, ix, 22; Lelius and, xxxii, 79

BLOSSOM, THE, xl, 311-12

BLOSSOMS, TO, xl, 338

BLOT IN THE 'SCUTCHEON, A, xviii, 358-404

BLOW, BUGLE, BLOW, xlii, 973

Blundell, Dr., on puerperal fever, xxxviii, 223, 231

Bluntness, Shakespeare on, xlvi, 248

Blushing, Hobbes on, xxxiv, 342

BLYTHE HAE I BEEN ON YON HILL, vi, 463

BLYTHE WAS SHE, vi, 286-7

BOADICEA: AN ODE, xli, 539-40

Boastfulness, Bacon on, iii, 127-9; Kempis on folly of, vii, 211

BOAT SONG, by Burns, vi, 265

Boats, of the Britons, xxxv, 361; in ancient Egypt, xxxiii, 47; of the Germans, 117

Boatswain, in THE TEMPEST, xlvi, 397-9, 459

Bobadilla, Francesco de, Bishop of Salamanca, xxxi, 34 note 2, 38, 41-5

Bobolink, Bryant on the, xlii, 1215-17

Boccaccio, on Arthur, xxxix, 21; Chaucer and, 155, 160, 164, 167, 170-1; Dryden on, 155; Hazlitt on, xxvii, 271; Hume on, 221; Johnson on language of, xxxix, 202; Macaulay on, xxvii, 370; Montaigne on, xxxii, 89; novels of, xiii, 64; Sainte-Beuve on, xxxii, 132; Sidney on, xxvii, 6

Bochartus, on Virgil, xiii, 34

Bodleian Library, Emerson on, v, 417

Body, Browne on the, iii, 289 (37); Descartes on the, xxxiv, 45; Epictetus on care of the, ii, 160 (118), 177 (173), 178 (178); Goethe on beauty of, xix, 380; Hindu doctrine of soul and, xlv, 851-3; M. Aurelius on the, ii, 200 (2), 206 (3), 211 (16), 251 (60), 257 (21); Montaigne on mind and, xxxii, 55; More on pleasures of the, xxxvi,

201-2, 203; Pascal on mind and, xlviii, 32; Pascal on, after death, 338; Paul, St., on the, xlv, 498 (15, 19-20); Penn on the, i, 321 (2); Socrates on the, ii, 54-5

BODY OF LIBERTIES, THE, xliii, 66-84

Boece (see Boëtius)

Boethius, Anicius (see Boëtius)

Boethius, Hector, on the Scotch, xxxv, 271

Boétie, Étienne (Stephen) de la, Montaigne and, xxxii, 108, 111; Montaigne on, 72-3, 78, 84

Boëtius, Anicius Manlius, birth and death of, xx, 328-9 notes 24, 25; Chaucer on, xl, 47; in Dante's PARADISE, xx, 328-9; Sidney on, xxvii, 24, 25

Bœotia, Newman on, xxviii, 41

Bohemia, blind king of (see John of Bohemia)

Boians, Tacitus on the, xxxiii, 108, 116

Boiardo, Dryden on, xiii, 13

Boileau, Addison and, xxvii, 157; on Christianity, xxxii, 160; encomiums and censures of, xxxiv, 145; on human reason, 142-3; on poetry, xxxix, 387; Sainte-Beuve on, xxxii, 123, 131

Boils (see Furuncles)

Bolabola, island of, xxix, 472, 478

Bolas, use of, in S. America, xxix, 52, 117

Boldness, Bacon on, iii, 31-2; Confucius on, xliv, 45 (5); Penn on, i, 334 (119); of saints and wicked men, vii, 225 (3)

Boleyn, Anne (see Bullen)

Bolingbroke, Lord, on Addison's Cato, xxvii, 167; on bishops, xxxiv, 80; Burke on, xxiv, 225, 260; lines to, xxvii, 273; on Marlborough, xxxiv, 99; Pope to, xl, 406-7, 440; Swift and, xxviii, 17; Voltaire on, xxxiv, 156

Bollandists, the, xxxii, 180 note

Bologna, Antonio, in DUCHESS OF MALFI (see Antonio)

Bologna, Giovan, xxxi, 420 note

Bologna, Il (see Primaticcio)

Bologna phials, xxx, 30 note 10

Bombast, defined by Burke, xxiv, 132

Bona Dea, worship of, xii, 271

Bonaparte (see Napoleon)

Bonatti, Guido, xx, 84 note 7

Bonaventura, Father, in THE BETROTHED, xxi, 132

Bond, Thomas, Franklin on, i, 116-7, 137-8

Bones, used as fuel, xxix, 199

BONIE DUNDEE, vi, 256

BONIE JEAN, vi, 464

BONIE LAD THAT'S FAR AWA, vi, 304

BONIE LASS OF ALBANY, vi, 284

BONIE MOOR-HEN, THE, vi, 261-2

BONIE PEG-A-RAMSAY, vi, 514

BONIE PEGGY ALISON, vi, 30

BONIE WAS YON ROSY BRIER, vi, 538

BONIE WEE THING, vi, 404

Boniface, Archbishop, xx, 243 note 4

Boniface VIII, Pope, arrest and death of, xx, 228 note 15; Dante on, 78 note, 279 note 15, 364 note 11, 399 note 3, 410 note 6, 415 note 8; death of, xxxi, 138 note 2; Ghino di Tacco and, xxx, 166 note 2; Montefeltro and, 112-13 notes

Bonnell, Captain, anecdote of Lord Loudoun, i, 153-4

BONNIE BANKS O' FORDIE, xl, 58-9

BONNIE GEORGE CAMPBELL, xl, 114

Bonnivard, Byron on, xli, 811

BONNY BARBARA ALLAN, xl, 68-9

BONNY DUNDEE, xli, 752-4

Booby, Darwin on the, xxix, 20

Book, custom of saving by the, xxxv, 367

BOOKES, ESSAY ON, Montaigne's, xxxii, 87-102

Book-keeping (see Accounting)

BOOK-WORMS, THE, vi, 264

Books, Bacon on, iii, 122; Browne on, 272-3, 276-7 (24); Carlyle on, xxv, 363-4, 373; censorship of (see Censorship); Channing on, xxviii, 337-8; Confucius on, xliv, 10 (9); Ecclesiastes on, 349 (12); Emerson on, v, 8-12, 93, 117-8, 176-8; Epictetus on, ii, 170 (145); Goethe on, xix, 31, 49; Heminge on fate of, xxxix, 148; Hobbes on, xxxiv, 327; Hume on use of, xxxvii, 374 (9); Locke on, for children, 131-3; Milton on, iii, 192-3, 200-2, 203-4; Newman on education by, xxviii, 31-8; Pascal on, xlviii, 121 note 2; Pliny on, ix, 233; prefaces of, xxxix, 3; Rousseau on, xxxiv, 294-5; Ruskin on, xxviii, 93-113, 117-8, 127, 137; Ruskin on, for girls, 150-1; tested by durability, xxxix, 208; transcripts of their times, 410-17, 435-6 (see also Reading)

Boorde, Andrew, verses from, xxxv, 289 note

Boötes, constellation, xx, 416 note 5; mentioned by Homer, xxii, 75

Booth, M. L., translator of Pascal, xlviii

BORDER BALLAD, by Scott, xli, 746

Boreas, Orithea and, xxvii, 270; Virgil on, xiii, 77, 137

Borghild, wife of Sigmund, xlix, 272, 276

Borgia, Cæsar, son of Pope Alexander, xxxvi, 15; Countess of Forli and, 15; cruelty of, 54; Guido Ubaldo and, 71; Macaulay on, xxvii, 388; Machiavelli on, xxxvi, 23-8; Oliverotto and, 31; troops of, 46

BORGIA, LUCRETIA, LINES ON HAIR OF, xli, 904

Borgny, wife of Sigmund (see Borghild)

Borgny, wife of Vilmund, xlix, 431

Borgoignon, Nicolas, xxxiii, 255 note

Borgoo, the negroes of, v, 199

Boric Acid, as antiseptic, xxxviii, 381

Born, Bertrand de, in Dante's HELL, xx, 118 note

Borneil, Giraud de, xx, 253 note 3

Bornoos, language of, v, 200

Boron, Robert de, xxxv, 104

Borromeo, Federigo, in THE BETROTHED, xxi, 351-60; Abbondio and, 415-16; Lucia and, 396-401, 413-14; in Milan famine, 456-8, 465; in plague, 505, 527-8, 531, 533; Unnamed and, 361-72

Borrow, George, and the Gypsies, v, 431

Borrowing, Emerson on, v, 95; Shakespeare on, xlvi, 109

Bors, Sir, in THE HOLY GRAIL, at the abbey, xxxv, 172; birds, omen of, 164, 172-3; at Carbonek Castle, 206-9; at Carteloise Castle, 190-2; chastity of, 160, 164; Galahad and, 106, 110, 181-2, 206, 212-3; gentlewoman and, 167; hermit and, 163; lady's champion, 164-6; Lancelot and, 213; Lionel and, 167, 175-6; Percivale and, 178, 213-14; at Sarras, 211; in ship of Faith, 182, 189; temptation of, 169-72; visions of, 164-5, 173; wounded knight rescued by, 196

Borsiere, Guglielmo, xx, 67 and note 4

Bortolo, in THE BETROTHED (see Castagneri)

Bos, Abbé du, on painting and poetry, xxiv, 52

Bosanquet, reviser of Pliny, ix, 183

Bosola, Daniel de, in DUCHESS OF MALFI, Antonio and, xlvii, 775, 780-1, 848; Cardinal and, 756-7, 837, 843, 851-2; Castruccio and, 772; death of, 854; Delio and, 805; Duchess and, 761,
773, 775, 779, 799, 800-1, 809, 812, 814, 822-3, 830; Ferdinand and, 762-4, 791-3, 805-6, 813-4, 818, 827-30, 835, 852-3; Julia and, 838-9; old lady and, 772-3, 777-8

Bosquet, M., on cirripedes, xi, 342

Bossu, Le, epic code of, xxxix, 385; on heroes of poetry, xiii, 23

Bossuet, on Cromwell, xxxix, 377; Sainte-Beuve, History of, xxxii, 126; Taine on, xxxix, 428

Bostock, Mr., Walton on, xv, 409, 417

BOSTON HYMN, xlii, 1261-4

Boston News-Letter, Franklin on, i, 19

Boswell, James, remarks on Life of Johnson, by, xxvii, 154; Burns on, vi, 310 note 1; Thackeray on, xxviii, 9

Boswell, Robert Bruce, translator of PHÆDRA, xxvi, 131

Botallus, on circulation of blood, xxxviii, 93

Botany, Emerson on science of, v, 297; Locke on study of, xxxvii, 147

Botany Bay, morality of children of, v, 245

Botero, Giovanni, xxi, 447

Botofogo Bay, Darwin on, xxix, 35

BOTTLE, A, AND FRIEND, vi, 264

Bouchardat, M., on fermentation, xxxviii, 351

Bougainville, on the Fuegians, xxix, 232

Bouillon, Godfrey de, in Dante's PARADISE, xx, 362 note 5; "one of nine worthies," xxxix, 20-1

Boulders, in the Azores, xi, 392; erratic, Darwin on, xxix, 191, 252; Helmholtz on, xxx, 227-30

Boullogne, Jean, xxxi, 420 note

Bouncer, Bet, in SHE STOOPS TO CONQUER, xviii, 212, 232

Bounties, Smith, Adam, on, x, 331, 374-88, 407-10, 424

Bountiful, in PILGRIM'S PROGRESS, xv, 232

Bounty, and frugality, i, 327-8; St. Paul on, xlv, 526 (6-7)

Bourbon, Cardinal de, brother of Charles IX, xxxviii, 47

Bourbon, Constable of, his attack on Rome, xxxi, 70; death, 70 note 4

Bourbon, François de, xxxi, 333 note; and Cellini, 333

Bourdeaux, Smith on situation of, x, 263

Bourdillon, M. de, xxxviii, 44

Bourges, surrender of, xxxviii, 46

Bourne, Richard, xliii, 139

Boutron, M., on fermentation, xxxviii, 352

Bowie, Alexander, reviser of Harvey, xxxviii, 59

Bowles, William Lisle, DOVER CLIFFS, xli, 682

Bowring, Sir John, xxv, 60, 62, 83

Bowyer, Sir William, and Dryden, xiii, 426

Boyardo, Matthew, Cervantes on, xiv, 50

Boyd, Rev. Wm., Burns on, vi, 165 note 8

Boyhood, Augustine, St., on, vii, 12; Emerson on, v, 61; Wordsworth on, xli, 596

Boyle, Robert Johnson on, xxxix, 230

Boynton, Sir Edward, house of, v, 398

Braccio, Fortebracci, Machiavelli on, xxxvi, 42, 44

Brachs, defined, xx, 427

Brackenburg, in EGMONT, xix, 265-6, 269-70, 289-90, 315-8, 321-5

BRACKLEY, THE BARON OF, xl, 119-21

Brackly, Lord, in COMUS, iv, 44

Bracy, the bard in CHRISTABEL, xli, 719, 723-4, 727

Bradamant, xxxii, 51 note 44

Braddock, Gen., Franklin on, i, 128-36

Braddock's defeat, i, 135

Bradford, Andrew, Franklin with, i, 22, 26, 27; paper of, 59, 60; as postmaster, 64-5, 98

Bradford, William, i, 22, 26-7

Bradlaugh, Charles, and Mill, xxv, 191

Bradley, James, astronomer, xxx, 319

Bradshaw, John, Milton on, v, 194

Bradwardine, Bishop, Chaucer on, xl, 46; Newman on, xxviii, 47

BRAES O' KILLIECRANKIE, vi, 359-60

BRAES OF YARROW, by Hamilton, xli, 572-6

BRAES OF YARROW, by Logan, xli, 500-1

Brage, Norse god, v, 389

Bragging, Emerson on, v, 390

BRAHMA, Emerson's, xlii, 1243

Brahma, Hindu god, xlv, 800, 821, 822-45, 871-2

Brahma Sahampati, xlv, 721-2

Brahman, Buddha on qualities of a, xlv, 627; virtues of a, 870

Brahmins, Emerson on the, v, 179

Brain, Berkeley on the, xxxvii, 229; in birds, xxxviii, 134; Harvey on the, 100; Pascal on the, xlviii, 26 (70)

Bramador, hill of, xxix, 365

Bramber, Nicholas, xxxv, 78 and note

Bramimonde, Queen, xlix, 114, 183, 184, 186, 195

Bran Galed, horn of, xxxii, 146

Branchiæ, Darwin on, xi, 186-7

Brand, Bishop, xliii, 20

Brandabarbaray, of Boliche, xiv, 137

Brandan, St., Renan on legend of, xxxii, 143, 174-5; and Judas, 148

Brandebourg, Marquis of, at Metz, xxxviii, 31

Brander, in FAUST, xix, 85-99

Brandini, Giovanbattista, xxxi, 410

Branstock, xlix, 260, 261

Brasidas, quoted, xxxiv, 216

Bratius, on hounds, xxxv, 350

Brava Island, xxxiii, 203

Bravery, Confucius on exterior, xliv, 59 (12); fable of, at a distance, xvii, 18

BRAVING ANGRY WINTER'S STORMS, vi, 288

Bravoes, in Lombardy, xxi, 10-13

BRAW LADS O' GALLA WATER, vi, 452

BRAW WOOER, THE, vi, 536

Brawn, boar meat, Harrison on, xxxv, 331-3

Braxfield, Lord, story of, xxv, 428-9

Brazil, Darwin on, xxix, 21-4, 28-46, 498-503; Francis Pretty on, xxxiii, 203-4

Bread, Locke on eating of, xxxvii, 17, 18; price of, compared with meat, x, 151, 154; wheat and oatmeal, compared, 164

Breadalbane, Burns on district of, vi, 277

Breadalbane, Earl of, vi, 205 note

BREAK, BREAK, BREAK, xlii, 975-6

Breathing (see Respiration)

Breca, and Beowulf, xlix, 19

Bredi, the thrall, xlix, 257-8

Breeding, close, diminishes vigor, xi, 103, 134, 304; cross (see Intercrosses)

Brefeld, Oscar, on fermentation, xxxviii, 313-14, 344

Breintnal, Joseph, i, 57, 58, 60, 63

BREMEN TOWN MUSICIANS, THE, xvii, 113

Brennus, reference to, xx, 306

Breton, Nicholas, PHILLIDA AND CORIDON, xl, 196-7

Bretons (see Celtic Races)

Breuer, Thomas, cow of, xxxv, 325

Brevity, "the soul of wit," xlvi, 127; in speech and writing, xxxii, 44-5

Brewing, in old England, xxxv, 281-6

Briareus, in Dante's HELL, xx, 129, 191; Jupiter and, iii, 40; Milton on, iv, 93; Virgil on, xiii, 217 (see also Ægæon)

BRIAR-ROSE, LITTLE, story of, xvii, 137

Bribery, in elections, Plutarch on, xii, 159; a ground of impeachment, xliii, 189 (4); Penn on, i, 354 (384)

BRIDGE, THE, xlii, 1275-7

BRIDGE OF SIGHS, by Hood, xli, 907-10; Poe on, xxviii, 386

Bridges, expense of maintaining, x, 453; made of hide, xxix, 267

Bridgewater, Earl of, president of Wales, iv, 45

Bright, John, on American Civil War, xxv, 166; on woman suffrage, 186-7

Bright, Mynors, Stevenson on, xxviii, 285

BRIGS OF AYR, THE, vi, 230-7

Brisk, Mr., in PILGRIM'S PROGRESS, xv, 230-1

Brissac, M. de, at Perpignan, xxxviii, 15-16

Brissot, Jean Pierre, Burke on, xxiv, 381

Britain, Cæsar in, xii, 284; planted by descendant of Æneas, xiii, 19

British Constitution, Burke on the, xxiv, 376-7; Lowell on the, xxviii, 456; James Mill on, xxv, 61; representation under, xxiv, 319-20; Ruskin on, xxviii, 131

Britomartis, Spenser's, xxxix, 63, 65

Britons, agriculture of the, xxxv, 308; boats of the, 360-1; food of the, 271; houses of the, 293; mirrors among, 322; productions of the, 315-16; use of woad by the, 314-15

Brittany, Arthurian legends in, xxxii, 161-2; Christianity in, 170, 171-3, 174 note 26, 180; English descent on, xxxviii, 13-14; Machiavelli on, xxxvi, 9; Paré on pastimes in, xxxviii, 14-15; Renan on, xxxii, 137, 140

Broca, Paul, objections to natural selection, xi, 211

Brockden, Charles, the scrivener, i, 67, 74

Brocket, defined, xxxv, 343

Brodie, Sir Benjamin, on puerperal fever, xxxviii, 247

Brome, Alexander, THE RESOLVE, xl, 369-70

Bromios, Bacchus called, viii, 123, 372

Bronn, Heinrich, on geological formations, xi, 332, 349; objections to natural selection, 210-1

Brontë, Emily, poems by, xlii, 1110-11

Bronze-casting, Cellini's method of, xxxi, 354 note 1, 376-80

Bronzino, Il (see Allori)

Brooke, Christopher, and Dr. Donne, xv, 327-8

Brooke, Lord, Emerson on, v, 411; Hazlitt on, xxvii, 268-9, 276; Milton on, iii, 227; tombstone of, v, 459

Brooke, Samuel, xv, 327, 357

Brosse, Pierre de la, xx, 166 note 7

Brothels, Luther on, xxxvi, 333

Brotherliness, Burns on, vi, 83, 251, 389, 512

Brothers, Bacon on emulation between, iii, 20; Browning on, and sisters, xviii, 383-4; Montaigne on, xxxii, 74

Brothers of Death, xxi, 270 note

Brougham, Lord, and Edinburgh Review, xxvii, 224; in Edinburgh society, xxv, 80; on English clergy, v, 430; Mill and, xxv, 60; on Milton's Satan, xxviii, 201; and the Times, v, 448

Broughton, Hugh, xlvii, 580 note, 629 note 1

Brouncker, Lord, Voltaire on, xxxiv, 125

Broune, Adam, almoner to Edward Second, xxxv, 381

Brown, Dr., and Franklin, i, 24

Brown, John, Mill on, xxv, 165 and note

Brown, Lieut., at Gettysburg, xliii, 337, 351, 352

Brown, Richard, xxiii, mate of the "Alert," 400-1

Brown, Robert, on classification, xi, 434-5

Brown, Thomas Edward, MY GARDEN, xlii, 1148

Browne, Maurice, xxxiii, 274, 286, 290

Browne, Sir Thomas, on the Bible, iii, 276 (23); Catholic Church, attitude toward, 254 (3), 255 (5); charity of, 311-2, 313-5, 330; Christianity of, 253 (1); on Church of England, 255-6 (5); contentment, dreams, 326-8; on death, 290, 295; on death and burial, his own, 292-3; desires of, 332; disease hated by, 324; Emerson on, v, 433; on faith and reason, iii, 272-4; on the future life, 296-304; on God, 262-5, 280; heresies of, 257-9; Lamb on, xxvii, 268; learning and lack of pride, iii, 321-2; on length of life, 293-5; sketch of life and works, 250; love of the beautiful and harmonious, 323; love of mysteries and miracles, 259-60 (9, 10); on the medical profession, 324-5; his prayers, 319, 329; a Protestant, 253 (2); on providence, 267; RELIGIO MEDICI, 251-332; on religious

disputes, 257; on salvation, 305-9; on spirits, 281-5, 289; on study of nature, 264-7; sympathy of, with all things, 310; tenderness and love of friends, 318-19; toleration of, 256 (6); at variance only with himself, 319-21, 324-5

Browne, William, ON COUNTESS OF PEMBROKE, xl, 333

Brownell, George, i, 10

BROWNHILL INN, EPIGRAM AT, vi, 413

Browning, Elizabeth Barrett, lines to, by Robert Browning, xlii, 1094-1100; poems by, xli, 922-42

Browning, Robert, sketch of life and works, xviii, 358; A BLOT IN THE 'SCUTCHEON, 359-404; SHORT POEMS by, xlii, 1065-1110; SONNET on, by Landor, xli, 902

Brown-Séquard, on mutilations, xi, 141

BRUAR WATER, PETITION OF, vi, 278-81

Bruce, Michael, TO THE CUCKOO, xli, 570-1

Bruce, Robert, Burns on, vi, 374, 472, 111 note 4

Bruchsal, Count von, in MINNA VON BARNHELM, xxvi, 352, 373

Bructerians, Tacitus on the, xxxiii, 111

Brummel, Beau, simplicity of, v, 372

Brunelleschi, Agnello, xx, 104 and note

Brunet, Gustave, xxxii, 107

Brunetto Latini (see Latini)

Brunswick, House of, Burke on title of, xxiv, 163-4

Bruttius, Cicero the Younger on, ix, 174

Brutus, Decimus (Albinus), xii, 316, 317, 330; Bacon on, iii, 67; Cicero on, ix, 11, 178, 179

Brutus, Lucius Junius, first Roman tribune, xii, 152, 158, 313; Corneille on sons of, xxvi, 127; Dante on, xx, 20; death of, ix, 71; Virgil on, xiii, 235

Brutus, Marcus, Cæsar and, xii, 302-3, 310, 314, 318-9, 331-2; ix, 164, 171; after Cæsar's death, xii, 253, 320, 332; Cæsar's ghost and, 321; iii, 91; Cicero and, xii, 255-6, 263; xxxii, 96; Cicero on his relations with, ix, 142-4; letter to, 176-81; in Dante's HELL, xx, 142 and note 1; death and burial, xii, 337; descent of, 313; Hobbes on vision of, xxxiv, 316; Lepidus and, xii, 331; loans of, x, 96; at Marseilles, xx, 219 note 7; Montaigne on, xxxii, 96; at Philippi, xii, 336-7; on virtue, v, 126

Bruyère, La (see La Bruyère)

Bryant, William Cullen, poems by, xlii, 1213-24; JUNE of, Poe on, xxviii, 380-1

Brydone, Patrick, vi, 176 note 10

Brynhild, ending of, xlix, 335-7, 380-6, 394-5; grief of, 321-5, 372-3, 379-80; Gudrun and, 311-12, 318-20; Gunnar and, 317-8, 378-9; at Hindfell, 297-8; Morris on, 256; name of, reason of, 307; Oddrun on, 434-5; Sigurd and, 299-306, 307-9, 326-7, 328, 329-30, 373, 377-8, 392-3; wooing of, 315-17, 371-2, 389-90, 395; remarks on story of, 251

BRYNHILD, FRAGMENTS OF LAY OF, xlix, 391-5; remarks on, 251

BRYNHILD, THE HELL-RIDE OF, xlix, 387-90; remarks on, 251

Bryso, Dante on, xx, 343

Bubastis, the Egyptian Artemis, xxxiii, 79

Bubastis, city of, xxxiii, 34, 37; temple of Artemis at, 69-70

Bubble, Madam, in PILGRIM'S PROGRESS, xv, 307-9

Bubonax, death of, xxvii, 51

Buch, Captal de, xxxv, 36, 42, 47, 50, 58

Buchanan, George, and Montaigne, xxxii, 3, 66; Sidney on tragedies of, xxvii, 46

Buchanan, Robert W., LIZ, xlii, 1199

Buchheim, C. A., translator of Luther, xxxvi, 2

Buck, defined, xxxv, 343

Buckingham, Dukes of (see Stafford, Villiers)

Buckingham, Earl of, in Tyler's Rebellion, xxxv, 67

BUCKWHEAT, THE, story of, xvii, 355-7

Bucolic poets, Shelley on, xxvii, 342

Buddha, on animals, xlv, 706-9; attainment of Buddhaship, 613-24; birth of, 603-12; daily habits, 629-32; death, 633-46; first resolutions to strive for Buddhaship, 577 note 1; on indifference, 712; life of the, 574; Mālunkyāputta sermon of, 647-52; on mendicant ideal, 748-50; Middle Doctrine of, 661-5; Noble-craving Sermon, 713-30; Pasenadi and, 675-6; story of Hare-Mark in Moon, 697-701; story of Husband-honorer, 693-6; on the truth, 657-8; Visākhā and, 754, 770-1, 774, 776-7, 779-81; on way of purity, 702

Buddha-Uproar, xlv, 603

Buddhism, Taine on, xxxix, 424, 432-3

Buddhist priests, ordination of, xlv, 740-7

BUDDHIST WRITINGS, xlv, 573-781
Budli, King, xlix, 310, 315, 317, 321
Budlungs, names of the, xlix, 253
Buenos Ayres, Darwin on, xxix, 126-7; revolution in, 145-6
Buffon, George Louis, on unity in classics, xxxii, 126; on creative force of America, xxix, 178; on evolution, xi, 6, 9; Franklin and, i, 147; Sainte-Beuve on, xxxii, 123
Buford, Gen., at Gettysburg, xliii, 329
BUFFOON AND COUNTRYMAN, fable of, xvii, 43
Bugiardini, Giuliano, xxxi, 86 note
Buhel, Burkhart am, in WILLIAM TELL, xxvi, 412-13, 423
BUILDING, Bacon's ESSAY ON, iii, 108-12
Building materials, demand for, x, 167, 179; supply of, does not limit population, 167; value of, 167
BUILDING OF THE SHIP, xlii, 1280-90
Building rent, by what determined, x, 488
Buildings, as capital, x, 218
Bujamonti, Giovanni, xx, 71 note 7
Bulgarians, Freeman on the, xxviii, 233, 268
Bulimus, Darwin on the, xxix, 351
Bull, why more sublime than ox, xxiv, 56
Bull, Bishop, on angels, xx, 406 note 5
BULL AND ASS, story of, xvi, 11-12
Bull feasts, xlix, 202-3
Bullen, Anne, Henry VIII and, xxxvi, 102, 111, 114; Thomas More and, 121, 122
Buller, Charles, Carlyle and, xxv, 315; Mill on, 67, 82, 122, 123, 135
Bullies, Burns on, vi, 223
Bullion, movements of, x, 325
Bullock, J. C., editor of Adam Smith, x
Bulls, Papal, Luther on, xxxvi, 313
Bulwer Lytton, Emerson on, v, 439
Bumper, Sir Harry, in SCHOOL FOR SCANDAL, xviii, 150-2
Bunau-Varilla, Philippe, xliii, 451
BUNDLE OF STICKS, fable of, xvii, 40
Bunyan, John, sketch of life and works of, xv, 3-4; Franklin on, i, 13, 22; Hazlitt on, xxvii, 275; PILGRIM'S PROGRESS, xv, 5-319; Thoreau on, xxviii, 420
Buonaccorti, Giuliano, xxxi, 196 note 3, 351
Buonacossi, Pinamonte, xx, 83 note 5

Buonaparte, Lucien, on Macpherson, xxxix, 328-9
Buonaparte, Napoleon (see Napoleon)
Buonarroti (see Michelangelo)
Buonaventura, St., in Dante's PARADISE, xx, 334-9; sketch of, 334 note 4
Buondelmonte, Dante on, xx, 356; murder of, 117 note 12, 357 note 31
Buoso of Cremona, xx, 134 note 10
Burchell, on size of animals and vegetation, xxix, 94; on ostriches, 97; on S. African implements, 272
Bürger, Gottfried August, on Percy's Reliques, xxxix, 326-7; Wordsworth on, 326
Burgh, Benet, xxxix, 15
Burghers, in FAUST, xix, 41
Burghersh, Bartholomew de, xxxv, 24, 36, 42, 51, 55
Burgoyne, Gen., Burns on, vi, 51
Burgundy, Machiavelli on, xxxvi, 9
Burgundy, Duke of, in LEAR, xlvi, 216, 221-2
Burials, in ancient Egypt, xxxiii, 42-4; in NEW ATLANTIS, iii, 173
Burians, Tacitus on the, xxxiii, 116
Burke, Edmund, aims and character of, xxiv, 377-8, 402-4; Bagehot on party spirit of, xxviii, 187; Burns on, vi, 52; conservatism of, xxiv, 377-8; on English lawyers, v, 415; Fox and, 211; author of war with France, xxiv, 421; ON FRENCH REVOLUTION, 141-378; generalizations of, v, 438, 441; Goldsmith on, xli, 506; Keppel and, xxiv, 416-17; LETTER TO A NOBLE LORD, 379-421; on liberty, 148-9; life and works, sketch of, 5-6, 28, 142, 380; love of order, 142; on the nobility, 398; Pay-office and Establishment Acts, 386-94; pension of, 380, 383, 401-4; on pensions, 396-7; on his services, 394; ON THE SUBLIME AND BEAUTIFUL, 7-140; ON TASTE, 11-26
Burke, Gen., Mill and, xxv, 179
Burke, Richard, death of, xxiv, 380; Edmund Burke on, 405-6
Burlador, Sonnet of, to Sancho Panza, xiv, 515
Burleigh, Lord, to his son on expenses, v, 394
Burlesque, Fielding on the, xxxix, 177-9
Burn, Dr., on settlement laws, x, 140, 142; on wages, 144
Burnel, the Asse, xl, 47

Burnes, William, father of Robert Burns, vi, 15; epitaph on, 50

Burnet, Bishop, *History of his Own Time,* xxv, 11; on French clergy, xxiv, 283

Burnet, Gov., and Franklin, i, 33, 60

BURNET, MISS, ELEGY ON, vi, 395-6

Burney, Martin, in Hazlitt's discussion, xxvii, 272, 278

BURNING BABE, THE, xl, 218-19

Burns, John, of Gettysburg, xliii, 331

BURNS, MISS, LINES ON, vi, 264

Burns, Robert, POEMS AND SONGS, vi, 19-553; Arnold on, xxviii, 77, 78, 84-9; daughter of, vi, 55-7; death, lines on his own, 60; first book of, 221; elegy on himself, 93-4; Emerson on, v, 21, 123, 304; Hazlitt on, xxvii, 278; Jacobitism of, vi, 281 note; life and works, sketch of, 15-17; possessions, inventory of, 186-8; wife of (see Armour, Jean)

Burton, Sir Richard F., on ARABIAN NIGHTS, xvi, 3; on deserts, xxviii, 411

Burton, Robert, death of, v, 381

Busbacca, the courier, xxxi, 191-4

BUSHBY, JOHN, LINES ON, vi, 488

Bushby, Mr., of New Zealand, xxix, 425-6

Business, character in, v, 185-6; Confucius on, xliv, 5; Emerson on the ways of, v, 45-6; honesty in, iii, 8-9; love and, 28; xl, 311; method in, i, 355 (403); Penn on qualities for, 341-2 (210-12); suspicion bad in, iii, 82; three parts of, 64; time the measure of, 63; Woolman on, i, 180, 195-6 and note, 197, 235-6, 274, 297, 298; youth and age in, iii, 105

Busirane, Spenser's, xxxix, 64

Busiris, city of, xxxiii, 34

Busiris and his Memphian cavalry, iv, 95

Busk, Mr., on avicularia, xi, 237

Buslidius, Hieronymus, xxxvi, 241

Busy-bodies, commonly envious, iii, 23

Butcher, S. H., translator of Homer, xxii

Butchers, excluded from juries, xxxvii, 102

Butes, and Dares, xiii, 190-91; death of, 380-1, 402, 407

Buthrescas, in Utopia, xxxvi, 230

Buti, Cecchino, xxxi, 425

Butler, Joseph, Bishop, Hazlitt on, xxvii, 277; on meaning of "natural," xi, 1; Mill on *Analogy of Religion* of, xxv, 29

Butler, Samuel, Emerson on *Hudibras*

of, v, 433; Voltaire on *Hudibras* of, xxxiv, 147-8

Buto, city of, xxxiii, 34-5, 37; oracle of, 42, 78

Butterflies, in Brazil, xxix, 42; dimorphism of, xi, 57; flocks of, at sea, xxix, 163; imitation by, xi, 446-7; symbol of the soul, xx, 186 note

Button, coffee-house of, xxvii, 179

Button, Jemmy, xxix, 212-14, 222, 223, 225-7, 230-1, 233-4

Butyric acid, production of, xxxviii, 328

Butyric fermentation, xxxviii, 329-40, 341

Butyric vibrios, xxxviii, 327

Buyck, in EGMONT, xix, 253-9

Buys, M., Dutch envoy, xxvii, 101

Buzareingues, Giron de, on fertilization, xi, 311

By-employments, Smith on, x, 119-21

By-ends, in PILGRIM'S PROGRESS, xv, 102-9, 111, 278, 285

Byron, Admiral John, on brutality of Fuegians, xxix, 221; on wolves in Falkland Islands, 198

Byron, George Gordon, Lord, sketch of life and works, xviii, 406; Arnold on, xlii, 1135-6; Carlyle on, xxv, 345, 420, 425; Emerson on, v, 265, 433, 444; Goethe on, xxxii, 128; Hugo on, xxxix, 362; MANFRED of, xviii, 407-50; Mill on, xxv, 93, 95; and Newstead Abbey, v, 399; Poe on lines by, xxviii, 389-90; POEMS by, xli, 784-816

BYRON AND GOETHE, by Mazzini, xxxii, 377-96

Byzantium, Pliny on expenses of, ix, 383; Trajan on, 397-8

CA' THE YOWES TO THE KNOWES, by Burns, vi, 356, 496

CA' THE YOWES TO THE KNOWES, by Pagan, xli, 556

Cabbage, fertilization of the, xi, 105

Cabot, John, account of life, xliii, 45 headnote; account of discoveries, 45-8; Hayes on, xxxiii, 264-5

Cabot, Sebastian, Hayes on, xxxiii, 264-5

Caccia of Asciano, xx, 122 and note 7

Cacciaguida, in Dante's PARADISE, xx, 349-61

Caccianimico, Venedico, xx, 74 and note 2

Cactornis, Darwin on species of, xxix, 383, 399-400

Cactus, Darwin on, xxix, 170 note 9, 265

Cacus, the robber, xiii, 274-5; Burke on, xxiv, 126; Cervantes on, xiv, 8, 26, 50; Dante on, xx, 103; Hercules and, xiii, 274-7

Cadmus, founder of Thebes, viii, 375; Dante on, xx, 104; letters invented by, xxxiv, 322; letters of, Byron on, xli, 814; Milton on, iv, 273; sower of the giant's sod, viii, 378

Cadmus, in the BACCHÆ, viii, 375-6, 381-2, 427-35

Cadwallader, John, Woolman on, i, 269

Cadwallo, Gray on, xl, 457

Cadytis, city of Syria, xxxiii, 80

Cæcilius, C., Pliny on, ix, 256

Cæcilius, Statius, on old age, ix, 54, 58; in Dante's Limbo, xx, 236

Cæcilius, the freedman, and Verres, xii, 223

Cæcilius, the orator, and Cicero, xii, 248; ix, 82-3; on orators, xii, 192

Cæcina, Aulus, letter to, ix, 161

Cæculus, and Æneas, xiii, 340

Cæcus, name of, xii, 157

Cædicus, and Remulus, xiii, 305

Cælianus, Sempronius, ix, 374

Cælius, Marcus Rufus, and Cicero, xii, 248 note, 260-1; ix, 149-50; Pliny on, 205 note 4

Caen, city of, xxxv, 13; defence against Edward the Third, 9, 13-14; capture of, 14-16; importance of, 13 note 3

Cæneus, in the ÆNEID, xiii, 222, 312

Cæpio, Servilius, and Cæsar's daughter, xii, 275; in Germany, xxxiii, 113

Caerleon, ancient see of, xxxv, 252; university of, 371

Cæsar, Caius Julius, reputed ancestor of Æneas, xiii, 18; in African War, xii, 306-8; Alexander and, xiii, 27; xxxvi, 50; ambitiousness of, xii, 273; Analogy of, xxvii, 57; Anti-Cato of, xii, 250-1, 266, 308; Antony's funeral oration on, 332; Atticus and, ix, 151; Bacon on, iii, 104, 130; Blake on laurel crown of, xli, 589; brevity of, xii, 305-6; on British tides, xxx, 279-80; Browne on valor of, iii, 278; Brutus on, ix, 171; Brutus and ghost of, xii, 320-1; Brutus, Decimus, and, iii, 67; Burke on, xxiv, 91; Cæcina and, ix, 161-2; calendar reformed by, xii, 311-12; Calpurnia, wife of, 275; in Catiline conspiracy, 234-5, 269-70; on Cato, ix, 240; Cervantes on, xiv, 8, 488; Cicero, relations

with, xii, 236, 243, 248-9, 250-1, 252, 266, 269-70, 276; Cicero on his relations with, ix, 113, 114, 115, 116, 118, 120, 121, 122, 127-8, 129, 156-7, 162-3, 165, 169, 170, 171, 179; Cicero on character of, 163, 168; Cicero on consulship of, 82, 83; clemency of, xii, 309-10; Cleopatra and, 304-5; xviii, 47, 49-50; Clodius and, ix, 114; conspiracy against, xii, 313-15, 330-2; consulship, first, of, 239, 273-5; consulship, third, 329; consulship, fifth, 330; Curio and, xx, 117 note 11; Dante on, 219 note 7, 252, 307; death, prodigies preceding, xii, 315-16; xlvi, 97; death of, xii, 316-18; death, state of affairs after, ix, 170-1, 177-8; death, signs following, xii, 320-1; death of, Webster on, xlvii, 853; dictatorship of, xii, 309-10; Dryden on, xiii, 15, 16; early offices, xii, 267; Egypt, war in, 303-4, 305; Egyptian priest and, v, 265; Emerson on, 68, 202, 265; extravagance of, xii, 267-8; Fiorino of Cellino and, xxxi, 6; funeral orations on aunt and wife, xii, 267; in Gaul, 276, 279-88; generalship of, 276-9; generosity to the Republicans, 164; as High-Priest, 269; Hugo on, xxxix, 356; kingship desired by, xii, 312-13; Lucceius and, ix, 88; at the Lupercalia, xii, 313-14, 330; Machiavelli on liberality of, xxxvi, 53; Marian party revived by, xii, 268-9; Milton on, iv, 385; Montaigne on history of, xxxii, 97, 99; Octavius, heir of, xii, 255; one of nine worthies, xxxix, 20; Pascal on, xlviii, 51 (132); Pharnaces and, xii, 305; Pharsalia, magnanimity after, 250, 302-3; the pilot and, iii, 100-1; pirates and, xii, 264-5; plans of, 310-11; Pliny on, ix, 205; Plutarch's LIFE OF, xii, 264-321; Pompeia, wife of, 267, 271-2, 241, 242; Pompey, early relations with, 274, 275-6, 282, 284, 285; Pompey, final contest with, 288-303; 248-9, 325-6, 327; and Pompey's statues, 252; Pompey and, Bacon on, iii, 79, 123, 141; Pompey and, Cicero on, ix, 6, 123, 162, 163; Pompey's sons and, xii, 309; Pope on, xl, 434; as prætor, xii, 270-1, 236; Revelius and, 310; Suetonius on, xxxii, 64; Senate, relations with, ix, 124; Shakespeare on portents before death of, xlvi, 97; sick soldier and, xxxii, 21;

Sidney on, xxvii, 21; in Spain, xii, 273; story of the storm, 296; studies at Rhodes, 265-6; Sylla and, 264; iii, 41; Tacitus on, xxxiii, 108; triumphs of, xii, 308, 309-10; Virgil on, xiii, 234; will of, xii, 319; worshipped as a god, 319

Cæsar, Lucius, saved by sister, xii, 336

Cæsarion, son of Cæsar, xii, 305; death of, 384; made king by Antony, 364

Cæsonius, Cicero on, ix, 81

Cæstius, Cicero and the younger, xxxii, 96

Cagli, Benedetto da, xxxi, 204, 231

Cagnano, Angelo da, xx, 116 note 9

Cagnazzo, the demon, xx, 88, 92

Cahors, reference to, xx, 46

Caïaphas, the high priest, xliv, 360 (2), 429 (6); in Dante's HELL, xx, 96

Cain, and Abel, xlvi, 192 note 7; Bacon on, iii, 24; author of BEOWULF on, xlix, 8, 39; Cowley on, xxvii, 64; Milton on, iv, 330; Mohammed on, xlv, 997; tree of Eve and, xxxv, 186

Caïna, first round of Hell, xx, 131-5

Cairns, in old Ireland, xlix, 216

Cairo, Arabian idea of, xvi, 144

Caithness, in MACBETH, xlvi, 383-4

Cajeta, nurse of Æneas, xiii, 239

Cajetan, Cardinal, xxxvi, 341

Calaber, Quintus, Shelley on, xxvii, 349

Calamities, Emerson on compensation of, v, 101-2; limitation of, 131; human delight in, xxiv, 40-3; Montaigne on consolation in, xxxii, 45-6; Woolman on, i, 237

Calandrino, Boccaccio's, xxvii, 385

Calasirians, district of the, xxxiii, 83

Calatinus, Atilius, epitaph of, ix, 67

Calboli, Fulcieri da, xx, 200 and note 13

Calboli, Rinieri da, in Dante's PURGATORY, xx, 199-201

Calc Spar, crystallization of, xxx, 31, 239-40; effect of, on polarized light, 34-5

Calcabrina, the demon, xx, 88, 92

Calchas, the seer, Æschylus on, viii, 13; Landor on, xli, 903; Sinon and, xiii, 103-5; and Trojan War, 106

Calculus, integral and differential, xxxiv, 125-6

Calderon de la Barca, Pedro, sketch of life and works, xxvi, 3-4; LIFE IS A DREAM, 7-74; Shelley on, xxvii, 340

Caldwell, Gen., at Gettysburg, xliii, 346, 349, 392

CALEDONIA: A BALLAD, vi, 329-31

Calendar, Cæsar, reforms, xii, 312

Calendar, Egyptian, xxxiii, 8; Lateran Council, revision of, xxxix, 57

Calentura, Bigges on the, xxxiii, 247

CALF, THE, vi, 225

Caliban, in THE TEMPEST, xlvi, son of Sycorax, 409; Prospero and, 410-12, 427, 436-9, 450-2, 460-2; Stephano and, 429-31, 435-6; Trinculo and, 428, 429; Hugo on, xxxix, 354; Hunt on, xxvii, 294; Johnson on, xxxix, 228

California, admission of, xliii, 306 head-note; Dana on history of, xxiii, 165-6; Dana in (1835), 56-254, 377-8; Dana in (1859), 378-96; Drake in, xxxiii, 213-17; southern boundary of, xliii, 292-3

California, Gulf of, navigation of, xliii, 294

California Rangers, xxiii, 244-7

Caligula (Caius Germanicus), his descent, xii, 388-9; Germans and, xxxiii, 114; wish of, iii, 318 note

Callao, Darwin on, xxix, 369, 371; ruins of old, 372

Callias, Alcibiades and, xii, 111-12; Aristides and, 103-4; Aristophanes on, viii, 452; birth of, xii, 60; at Marathon, 83; Socrates and, ii, 7

Callicles, son of Arrhenidas, xii, 212

CALLICLES, THE SONG OF, xlii, 1126-8

Callicrates, builder of Parthenon, xii, 50; of Athenian wall, 50

Callicrates, the soldier, xii, 95

Callidromus, the slave, ix, 369

Callimedon, called the Crab, xii, 213

Callinicus, meaning of, xii, 156 note

Calliope, mother of Orpheus, iv, 73, 228

Callippides, the tragedian, xii, 138

Callisthenes, Alexander and, xxvii, 36; xxxii, 57; on the Phocian War, ix, 102

Callisto, Diana and, xx, 249; changed to constellation, 416 note 5

Callistratus, the orator, influence on Demosthenes, xii, 194; Melanopus and, 201

Callixtus, Bishop, xx, 400 note 5

Callot, Hugo on, xxxix, 347

Calodera Maculata, xxix, 130

Calonne, M. de, on reign of Louis XVI, xxiv, 266 note 33; on France under the Revolution, 267-8 notes, 318-19, 368 note

Calosoma, instance of, at sea, xxix, 163

Calpurnia, wife of Cæsar, xii, 275; her dream, 315; and Antony, 332

Calpurnia, wife of Pliny, ix, 248 note 5; Pliny on, 258; letters to, 280, 298

Calumniators, punishment of, in Rome, ix, 296 note 9

Calumny (see Detraction)

Calvary, Mount, xliv, 415 note 4

Calventius, Cicero on, ix, 114

Calvin, John, DEDICATION OF THE INSTITUTES, xxxix, 27-51; Knox and, 58 note; life and works, sketch of, 27 note; Pope on, xl, 434; Voltaire on, xxxiv, 84; Wyclif and, iii, 223

Calvinism, doctrines of, xxxix, 47-51; in France, 27-47; Mill on, xxv, 256

Calvinists, debt of, to St. Augustine, vii, 4; in France, xxxix, 83-4; low ideas of human nature, xxviii, 308; Pascal on, xlviii, 270 (777), 301

Calvinus, Domitius, at Pharsalia, xii, 300-1

Calvisius, correspondent of Pliny, letters to, ix, 228, 229, 272, 317, 335

Calvisius, dependent of Cæsar, xii, 367

Calypso, Dido and, xxxix, 157; Odysseus and, xxii, 9, 10, 60, 69-75, 95-6

Cambalu, seat of Cathaian Can, iv, 328

Cambray, peace of, More at, xxxvi, 104-5

Cambrian Period, antiquity of the, xi, 344-5; absence of deposits before, 345-8

Cambridge University, Emerson on, v, 415; Harrison on, xxxv, 371-381

Cambuscan, reference to, iv, 36

Cambyses, expedition against Egypt, xxxiii, 7; Ladikê and, 89; prophecy of, xlviii, 248

Camden, the antiquary, and Ben Jonson, xlvii, 540

Camera Apostolica, xxxi, 41 note 3

Camerinus, Sulpicius, ix, 189 note 5

Camers, son of Volscens, xiii, 340

Camertus, in the ÆNEID, xiii, 397

Camiccione de Pazzi, xx, 133 and note 6

Camilla, in the ÆNEID, xiii, 266-7, 374-7, 379-88; Dante on, xx, 8, 19

Camilla, in story of CURIOUS-IMPERTINENT, xiv, 307-46, 351-5

Camillo, Cardinal, in THE CENCI, at banquet, xviii, 291-2; Beatrice and, 353, 355-6; Bernardo and, 351-2; Count Cenci and, 281-5; with Giacomo, 300-1; at the trial, 342-6

Camillus, Cicero on, ix, 160; Virgil on, xiii, 235

Camino, Gaïa da, xx, 212 note 10

Camino, Gherardo da, xx, 211 note 7, 212

Camino, Riccardo da, death of, xx, 321 note 13; Lombardo and, 209 note; wife of, 177 note 4

Camoëns, Wordsworth on sonnets of, xli, 681

Campana, mountain, xxix, 260-2

Campanella, the physiognomist, xxiv, 106-7

CAMPASPE AND CUPID, xl, 209

CAMPBELL, BONNIE GEORGE, a ballad, xl, 114

Campbell, J., FREEDOM AND LOVE, xli, 782

Campbell, Thomas, poems by, xli, 770-81; Mill on poems of, xxv, 16; on English nobility, v, 413

Campegines, Cardinal, xxxvi, 103, 104

Campion, Thomas, poems by, xl, 284-7

Campistron, Hugo on, xxxix, 360, 364

CAN YE LABOUR LEA, vi, 438

Canace, reference to story of, iv, 37

Canada, invited into the Confederation, xliii, 166

CANADIAN BOAT-SONG, by Moore, xli, 819

CANADIAN BOAT SONG, by Wilson, xlii, 1064-5

Canals, expense of, x, 453-5; Smith on, 150

Canary Islands, Drake in the, xxxiii, 233; Vespucci on, xliii, 30

Candace, queen of Ethiopia, xliv, 440 (27)

CANDLE, CHEMICAL HISTORY OF A, xxx, 86-170

Candle-wood, xxx, 87

Candolle, A. de, on alpine species, xi, 171; on Australian species, 405; on insular plants, 414; on naturalization of plants, 118; on oaks, 62-3; on plants with large seed, 389; on struggle for life, 72; on wide-ranging plants, 65-6, 134, 427; on winged seeds, 150

Candor, Whitman on, xxxix, 402

Candour, Mrs., in SCHOOL FOR SCANDAL, xviii, 120-5, 132-5, 180-5

Candy, Locke on, xxxvii, 21

Canidia, Sidney on, xxvii, 19

Canidius, lieutenant of Antony, xii, 348; in Parthian war, 354-5; in war of Antony and Octavius, 365, 370-1, 372, 374-5, 377

Caninius, letter to, ix, 350

Canneschi, Machiavelli on the, xxxvi, 61

Canning, George, and free trade, xxv, 65; on reform, v, 371

Cannon, known to ancients, iii, 139

Canôbos, city of, viii, 197

Canoes, Columbus on Indian, xliii, 24; Vespucci on, 36

Canon law, Luther on, xxxvi, 305, 307, 323

Canonization of saints, Mill on, xxv, 215

CANST THOU LEAVE ME THUS, MY KATIE, vi, 509

Canterbury, Harrison on the See of, xxxv, 252; archbishops of, 252-3, 255-6

Canterbury, Archbishop of, in EDWARD THE SECOND, xlvi, 14-15, 16-18, 81

Canterbury Tales, Arnold on, xxviii, 76-80; Dryden on, xxviii, 77; xxxix, 164, 165-7; NUN'S PRIEST'S TALE of, xl, 34-51; proem to, xxxix, 18-19; sources of, 159-60, 172

CANTERBURY TALES, PROLOGUE TO, xl, 11-34; Dryden on, xxviii, 77; xxxix, 160, 165-7; editorial remarks on, xl, 10

Cantillon, on wages, x, 69

Cantiron, John de, xxxv, 96

Cantyman, the cacique, xxxiii, 313

Canuri, Raleigh on the, xxxiii, 373

Canute, buried in Winchester, v, 462; Knighton Guild and, xxxv, 314; laws against adultery, 365-6; suppers of, 287

Capaneus, in Dante's HELL, xx, 59

Cape de Verd Islands, Darwin on, xxix, 11-15; Pretty on, xxxiii, 201-3; productions of, xi, 421-2

Capernaum, Jesus on, xliv, 381 (15)

Capet, Hugh, Dante on, xx, 226-7; Raleigh on, xxxix, 83

Capillary Attraction, Faraday on, xxx, 93

Capilupus, Montaigne on, xxxii, 32

Capital, accumulation of, x, 264-77; circulating and fixed, 215-17 (see also Circulating Capital, Fixed Capital); combinations of, to fix wages, 145; defined, 215; distribution of, in agriculture, manufactures, and trade, 305-9; employments of, 287-303; importance of increase of, 270-1; increase of, effect on profits, wages, and interest, 281-2; investment of, 221-2; labor and, relations of, 6, 67-9, 212-13, 260, 333; loans as, 278; naturally seeks domestic industries, 333-5; naturally seeks most profitable industries, 335; profits in relation to, 90, 96-7; revenue and, as determining industry, 262-5; taxes on,

505-11; wages in relation to increase of, 70-5

Capital Causes, in ancient Athens, ii, 25; Bacon on mercy in, iii, 131

Capital Cities, industry in, x, 263-5; virtual universities, xxviii, 36-7, 38

Capital Punishment, in old Massachusetts, xliii, 73 (44, 47), 79-81; More on, xxxvi, 149-50

Capitalists, combinations of, x, 68; Smith on interests of, 209-11

Capitation taxes, Smith on, x, 514-15; in U. S., xliii, 185 (4), 191 (5)

Capitolo, the, xxxi, 237 note

Capocchio, in Dante's HELL, xx, 122-4

Capons, Harrison on, xxxv, 336

Caprara, Cardinal, and Napoleon, v, 208

CAPRICE, MONODY ON, vi, 484

Caprichioso, on Rozinante, xiv, 514

Caprona, surrender of, xx, 87 note

CAPTAIN CAR, a ballad, xl, 103-7

CAPTAIN! MY CAPTAIN, xlii, 1412

CAPTAIN's LADY, THE, vi, 344

Captiousness, Locke on, xxxvii, 123

CAPTIVE RIBBAND, THE, vi, 361-2

Captive, story of the, xiv, 382-423

Captivity in Babylon, Pascal on, xlviii, 212 (637, 639)

Capuchins, Manzoni on the, xxi, 51

Capulets, Dante on the, xx, 169

Capuri, Raleigh on the, xxxiii, 340

Capybara, Darwin on the, xxix, 57-8

Capys, author of the Capuan name, xiii, 326; Privernus and, 312; Trojan horse and, 101

CAR, CAPTAIN, a ballad, xl, 103-7

Caracalla, as a charioteer, iii, 48; Machiavelli on, xxxvi, 64, 65-6, 68

Caracaras, Darwin on, xxix, 63

Caradoc, mantle of, xxxix, 21

Caradosso, Messer, xxxi, 48 note 5, 61-2

Carapana, district of, xxxiii, 325 note 23, 325, 369, 370

Carapana, king of Emeria, xxxiii, 331-2, 334

Caratach, on valor, v, 76-7

Carbo, Gaius, Africanus and, ix, 99; Gracchus and, 24-5

Carbolic Acid, as an antiseptic, xxxviii, 257-66, 381

Carbon, Faraday on combustion of, xxx, 158-9, 160-2, 168-9; Helmholtz on combustion of, 201; tests of presence of, 161

Carbonek Castle, xxxv, 206-7

Carbonic Acid, as gas, liquid, and solid, xxx, 14 note; composition of, 158; method of decomposing, 159-61; heat generated by formation of, 201; made by burning candles, 150-2; natural sources of, 152-3; produced in respiration, 164-8; used by plants, 167-8; properties and weight, 153-5; tested by lime-water, 151-2, 153-4

Carbonic Acid Gas, fermentation in, xxxviii, 302-13

Cardan, Emerson on, v, 177; on dogs, xxxv, 355-6; on pigeons, 336; on rogues in England, 369; on sheep, 329-30

Cardenio, in Don Quixote, xiv, 201-5, 238-51, 264, 268-9, 356-65

Cardin' o't, the Spinnin' o't, vi, 526-7

Cardinals, Luther on, xxxvi, 277

Cardoness, lines on, vi, 498, 499

Cardoon, Darwin on the, xxix, 125-6, 153

Cards, Locke on playing, xxxvii, 176

Care, Burns on, vi, 305; Cicero on freedom from, ix, 26; Cowper on, xli, 542; David on uses of, 491; Goethe on, xix, 33; Milton on, iv, 85; pays not debt, xlvii, 502

Careless, in School for Scandal, xviii, 150-3, 157-62

Carelessness in children, xxxvii, 48, 107-9

Carentan, Edward III at, xxxv, 10; importance of, 13 note

Carew, Thomas, poems by, xl, 351-3

Carey, Dr., Bishop of Exeter, xv, 347

Carey, Henry, Sally in Our Alley, xl, 403-5

Carians in Egypt, xxxiii, 77-8, 82

Caribbean Savages, lack of foresight in, xxxiv, 178; love among, 192

Caricatures, Fielding on, xxxix, 178-9

Cariola, in Duchess of Malfi, xlvii, 761, 766-7, 771, 772, 780, 794-5, 798, 803-4, 811, 819-20, 824-5, 826-7

Carlandrea, in The Betrothed, xxi, 128

Carle, an the King Come, vi, 347

Carlile, Christopher, with Drake, xxxiii, 226, 227, 229, 230, 231, 232, 234; at St. Domingo, 240-1; at Cartagena, 244, 246, 250; at St. Augustine, 254-5; remarks on his services, 253-4

Carlile, Richard, prosecution of, xxv, 58

Carlo, San, body of, in Milan plague, xxi, 522-3; plague named after, 502

Carlo Emanuele I, of Savoy, xxi, 434-6, 466

Carloman, son of The Bald, xxxix, 82

Carloto, and Valdovinos, xiv, 43

Carlovingian Poetry, Renan on, xxxii, 158, 159

Carlovingians, Raleigh on the, xxxix, 81-3

Carlyle, Thomas, on America and Americans, v, 453-4; on art, v, 454; Characteristics, xxv, 319-56; first entry into Edinburgh, 359; Emerson and, v, 3; Emerson on, 21, 315, 321-3, 441; Essay on Scott, xxv, 393-451; French Revolution, 135; heroism in, v, 123; Inaugural Address, xxv, 359-89; remarks on Inaugural Address, 318; life and works, 315-18; Life of Cromwell, xxxix, 415; London Review and, xxv, 129; Mill and, 84, 110; Mill on, 90, 102; reading of, v, 456-7; on unbelief, xxv, 104; Wordsworth on, v, 324-5

Carmagnola, and the Venetians, xxxvi, 43

Carmenta, the prophetess, xiii, 279

Carnal Policy, town of, xv, 21

Carnal Sinners, in Dante's Hell, xx, 21-4, 47

Carneades, an African, xxviii, 58; in Athens, x, 137; Manzoni on, xxi, 115; Montaigne on, xxxii, 54; in Rome, iii, 194

Carnesecchi, Pietro, xxxi, 140 note 6

Carnot, Sadi, on heat, xxx, 195

Caro, Annibale, xxxi, 97 note 5; Cellini and, 163, 166; Giovanni Gaddi and, 97 note 4, 133; language of, xxxix, 202; translator of Virgil, xiii, 55

Caroli River, xxxiii, 355, 357

Caroline, Queen, and the Times, v, 448

Carpathian Wizard, Proteus called, iv, 67

Carpenter, Chaucer's, xl, 21

Carpentry, as recreation, xxxvii, 174

Carpi, Giacomo da, xxxi, 51 and note, 272

Carpigna, Guido di, xx, 202 note 16

Carpino, Plano, x, 311

Carpio, Bernardo del, Cervantes on romance of, xiv, 50, 491; Orlando and, 19, 226

Carr, Sir Robert, Hugo on, xxxix, 380

Carranchas, Darwin on, xxix, 63-4

Carrero, Don Pedro de Puerto, xiv, 388

Carrion Hawks, of South America, xxix, 63-7; smelling-power of, 189-91

Carron Iron Works, Impromptu on, vi, 275

Carrying Trade, capital used in, x, 299,
333-4; encouragement of the, 371-2;
limits of, 302; a sign of wealth, 301
Cartagena, Drake at, xxxiii, 144-5, 156-
60, 244-53, 259
Carthage, Cato on, ix, 51-2; city of Dido,
xiii, 85, 89; loved by Juno, 73-4, 88-9;
Machiavelli on destruction of, xxxvi,
18; mercenaries of, 42; More on mer-
cenaries of, 145; Raleigh on, xxxix, 71,
113; Rome and, xiii, 174, 321; schools
of, vii, 69-70
Carthagena (see Cartagena)
Carthusian Monks, Pascal on, xlviii, 172
(539)
Carus, Metius, Regulus and, ix, 188-9;
Fannia and, 308
Cartwright, William, ON THE QUEEN'S
RETURN, xl, 358
Cary, Henry F., translator of Dante, xx
Casa, Cecchino della, xxxi, 69
Casa, Giovanni della, "book on manners"
(*Galateo*), reference to, xxvii, 162, 163
Casalodi, Alberto da, xx, 83 note 5
Casarita, Darwin on the, xxix, 102
Casati, Father Felice, xxi, 511, 592-5
Casaubon, Isaac, at Oxford, v, 416; on
changes, xxxix, 73-4
Casca, and Cæsar, xii, 317-18
Cascades, in glaciers, xxx, 221-3, 235
Casella, Dante and, xx, 151 and note 5;
Milton on, iv, 81
Cash Credits, in Scotland, x, 236-7, 244-5
Casion, Mount, xxxiii, 80
Casnero River, xxxiii, 360
Caspians, Harrison on the, xxxv, 352
Cassada, Darwin on, xxix, 32
Cassandanê, wife of Cyrus, xxxiii, 7
Cassander, Demades and, xii, 217
Cassandra, in AGAMEMNON, viii, 47-59;
Apollo and, 53; Corœbus and, xiii,
111, 113-14; death of, viii, 65; Homer
on death of, xxii, 155; prophecy of
settlement of Italy, xiii, 134; Ruskin
on, xxviii, 141-2; Trojan horse and,
xiii, 108
Cassavi, a kind of bread, xxxiii, 152,
239
Cassero, Giacopo del, xx, 163 and note 5
Cassero, Guido del, xx, 116 note 9
Cassiodorus, John, on idleness, xxxix, 13
Cassiopeia, reference to, iv, 34
Cassipa, Lake, xxxiii, 358-9
Cassipagotos, Raleigh on the, xxxiii, 354,
356, 358

Cassius, the consul, in Germany, xxxiii,
113
Cassius, Quintus, xii, 326
Cassius, Roman jurist, ii, 169 (144); ix,
310 note 2
Cassius Longinus, Cæsar and, xii, 310,
314-15, 317, 330; ix, 146; Cicero on,
147; conduct after Cæsar's death, xii,
253, 331; in Dante's HELL, xx, 142
and note 1; xiii, 16; flight of, xii, 320;
at Philippi, 320, 336-7
Castagneri, Bortolo, in THE BETROTHED,
xxi, 285-8, 432-3, 542-5, 641
Castalio, Locke on, xxxvii, 71
CASTARA, ROSES IN BOSOM OF, xl, 252-4
CASTAWAY, THE, xli, 540-2
Castello, Guido da, xx, 211 and note 9
Castes, Channing on, xxviii, 343-6; the
four Hindu, xlv, 870-1
Castiglione, Baldassare, the *Courtier* of,
xxvii, 162
Castiglione, Valeriano, xxi, 447
CASTLE GORDON, vi, 282-3
Castlemaine, Lady, xxviii, 296
Castor and Pollux, Homer on, xxii, 152;
in Rome, xii, 149; seamen's term,
xxxiii, 295; Virgil on, xiii, 211; wor-
shipped in Germany, xxxiii, 117
Castor-berry, cultivated in Egypt, xxxiii,
47
Castoro, Francesco, xxxi, 16
Castracani, Castruccio, xxvii, 399
Castration, Harvey on, xxxviii, 110
Castriota, John (see Kastriota)
Castro, Chili, Darwin on, xxix, 281-2
Castruccio, in DUCHESS OF MALFI, xlvii,
758-9, 772, 774, 783, 785, 845
Casualties, of feudal law, x, 506-7
Caswall, E., translator of hymns, xlv,
550, 556
Cat, "turning of the," iii, 59
CAT, ON A FAVOURITE, xl, 462-3
CAT AND FOX, fable of, xvii, 26
CAT-MAIDEN, fable of the, xvii, 42; Bacon
on fable of, iii, 97
Catabaptists, Calvin on, xxxix, 44
Cataclysms, Darwin on, xi, 81, 102-3;
Lyell on, xxxviii, 407, 417
Catalano, in Dante's HELL, xx, 96-7
Catamarans, described, xxiii, 26
Catastrophes, Pope on, xl, 411-12; re-
quire a comic element, xxviii, 177-8
Catastrophism (see Cataclysms)
Catechising, Herbert on, xv, 406
Catechumens, Pascal on, xlviii, 376-7

Categorical Imperative, Kant on the, xxxii, 325-6, 330-43, 363-5, 371, 395

Categories (see Predicaments)

Caterina, mistress of Cellini, xxxi, 305-9, 312-16, 318

Caterpillars, instincts of, xi, 252

Cates, Thomas, xxxiii, 227, 229

Catesby, and Hastings, xxxix, 76

Cathedrals, Burke on grandeur of old, xxiv, 63-4; Hugo on mediæval, xxxix, 350-1; origin of, xxxv, 257

Catherine of Aragon, queen of Henry VIII, xxxvi, 102-5, 114; xxxix, 86

Catholic Church, Roman (see Roman Catholic Church)

Catiline, Lucius, Augustine, St., on, vii, 27; Cicero on, ix, 81, 83; xxvii, 47; conspiracy of, xii, 226-236, 269-70; ix, 5; Pope on, xl, 411; Virgil on, xiii, 290

Catillus, in the ÆNEID, xiii, 262, 372, 379

Cato, Addison's drama of, xxvii, 158, 165-8, 178; Dennis on, 184-96; Johnson on, 185; Shelley on, 341; Voltaire on, xxxiv, 135; xxxix, 227

Cato, Gaius, Cicero on, ix, 97, 99

Cato, Dionysius, alleged author of *Caton,* xxxix, 15

Cato the Censor, on agriculture, ix, 63-5; x, 341; on Carthage, ix, 51; in Cicero's essay on OLD AGE, 10, 45-76; as club member, 61, 240; conciseness of, 205; on dreams, xl, 38, 39; on enemiᵥₛ and friends, ix, 39; Fabius Maximus and, 48-9; on feeding, x, 153; on friendships, ix, 35; Greek literature studied late by, 54; Greek philosophers and, iii, 194-5; knowledge of herbs, xxxv, 240; Livy on, iii, 100; Locke on, xxxvii, 175; Lucius Flaminus and, ix, 60; old age of, 46, 50, 56, 58-9, 61; on orators, 251; *Origins* of, 58, 72; quæstorship of, 48; Sidney on, xxvii, 12, 36-7; son of, ix, 12, 75, 168; Virgil on, xiii, 236; the wise, ix, 11; on yeomen, xxxv, 229

Cato of Utica, Burke on, xxiv, 41, 91; Cæsar and, xii, 270, 273-4, 275, 282, 283, 307-8, 325-6; Cæsar on, ix, 240; during Catiline conspiracy, xii, 235, 270; Cicero and, 236-7, 246-7, 249, 250-1, 261; Cicero's correspondence with, ix, 135, 152, 153; Cicero on, xxiv, 303; on Cicero, xxxii, 62; in Civil War, xii, 249, 250, 298-9, 306; Dante on, xx, 58, 146-8; death of, xii,

307-8; ix, 159; indictment for extortion, 115; Pompey and, 98; xii, 288-9; Rousseau on, xxxiv, 226; as a senator, ix, 88, 99; Sidney on, xxvii, 21; Virgil on, xiii, 17, 290

CATON, PROLOGUE TO, xxxix, 15-16

Catorthóseis, defined, ii, 227 (14)

Cats, breeds of, why impossible to improve, xi, 51-2; correlated variation in, 27, 148; in Egypt, xxxiii, 36-7; flowers dependent on, xi, 82; fruit trees injured by, xxix, 140-1; inherited mental qualities in, xi, 256; Jenner on, xxxviii, 145; in S. America, xxix, 126

Cattans, Tacitus on the, xxxiii, 109-11, 113

Cattinaro (see Gattinara)

Cattle, color of, its importance, xi, 199; crosses between Indian and common, 292; descent of, 33, 41; in old Egypt, xxxiii, 25-6; in Falkland Islands, xxix, 195-6; forests and, x, 170; grassgrowth and, xxix, 124; importation of foreign, x, 339, 342; insects and, xi, 80-1; as medium of exchange, x, 30; new breeds of, xi, 114; Niata, 219; xxix, 150-2; price of, in relation to agriculture, x, 183-4; recognition among, xxix, 150; trees and, xi, 80; as wealth, x, 312

Catullus, Gaius Valerius, Montaigne on, xxxii, 90; pet-bird of mistress of, xii, 368 note

Catulus, Quintus Lutatius, Cæsar and, xii, 269; in Catiline conspiracy, 270; Clodius and, 242

Catulus, teacher of Aurelius, ii, 195 (13)

Caulfield, Capt., xxxiii, 315, 336, 337, 342, 343, 345, 351, 357, 363-4, 369, 372

Cauquenes, mineral springs of, xxix, 267-9

Cause and effect, Berkeley on, xxxvii, 192; in divine matters, xxxix, 104-6; Emerson on, v, 83, 90, 283-4; in human affairs, xxxvii, 352-62; Hume on, 307-18, 320-2, 330, 331, 333-4, 337-43, 346-50, 363-4 and note, 371-2, 396-7, 403 note, 405-6, 415; Hume's doctrine, Emerson on, v, 438; in ideas, xxxvii, 304-5, 327, 329; Lowell on, xxviii, 446; Marcus Aurelius on, ii, 219 (45); in matter, xxxvii, 352-3; Raleigh on, xxxix, 100; Shelley on, xxvii, 338-9

Causes, Berkeley on, xxxvii, 236-7, 257;
Browne on, iii, 265 (14); Burke on,
xxiv, 103-4; definitions of, xxxvii, 348-
9, 364 note; Emerson on, v, 133;
Hobbes on, xxxiv, 374-7; Hume on
ignorance of, xxxvii, 332; Hume on
ultimate, 310; Hunt on, xxvii, 290;
identity of ancient and modern, xxxviii,
385, 417-8; as immediate volitions of
God, xxxvii, 343-5; Lyell on uniformity of secondary, xxxviii, 386; Socrates
on, ii, 89-95; Taine on moral, xxxix,
417; Whewell on, xi, 1

CAUTERETZ, THE VALLEY OF, xlii, 976

Caution, Confucius on, xliv, 22 (10);
Machiavelli on, xxxvi, 82; mountain of,
in PILGRIM'S PROGRESS, xv, 124; Penn
on, i, 334

Cautions, Penn's personal, i, 347-8

Cavalcanti, Cavalcante, Dante on, xx, 41-
2

Cavalcanti, Guido, xx, 42 notes 6 and 7,
189 note 5

CAVALIER, SONG OF THE, xxviii, 392

Cavalletti, Scipione, xxxi, 17

Cava Rumia, in DON QUIXOTE, xiv, 416

Cave, Edward, Gentleman's Magazine of,
i, 147

Cave-animals, blindness of, xi, 142-4

Cavendish, Henry, on gravitation, xxx,
281

Caves, use of, in NEW ATLANTIS, iii, 172-
3

Caviare, to the general, xlvi, 137

Cawdor, thane of, in MACBETH, xlvi, 323,
327, 328, 329

Caxton, William, life and works of,
xxxix, 5, note; PREFACES AND EPI-
LOGUES, 5-26; remarks on prologues
of, 3

Caylen, Darwin on, xxix, 284

Cebes, friend of Socrates, ii, 33; book on
virtue, iii, 240 and note 23; with
Socrates in prison (see PHÆDO, Plato's)

Cecidomyia, Darwin on the, xi, 458

Cecil, Sir Robert, dedication to, xxxiii,
301-4

Cecil, William, xxxiii, 229, 247, 258

Cecilia, St., Dryden on, xl, 390, 395-6

CECILIA'S, ST., DAY, SONG FOR, xl, 389-
96

Celæno, the Harpy, and Æneas, xiii, 136

Celandine, Wordsworth on the, xli, 614-
15

Celano, Thomas à, DIES IRÆ, xlv, 551

Celer, Asinius, surmullet of, x, 182

Celer, friend of Pliny, ix, 305

Celer, Metellus, origin of name, xii, 156;
wife of, 242

Celer, Roman knight, ix, 254

Celestial city, in PILGRIM'S PROGRESS, xv,
156-7

CELESTIAL SURGEON, THE, xlii, 1212-13

Celestine V, Dante on, xx, 14 note 2,
113 note 14

CELIA, by Sedley, xl, 384

CELIA, TO, by Jonson, xl, 291-2

Celibacy, Calvin on, xxxix, 38; Luther
on, xxxvi, 302-5; vows of, 302 note

Cellini, Andrea, xxxi, 8-9, 10

Cellini, Benvenuto, accident to eye, xxxi,
373; Alessandro de' Medici and, 149,
157, 172, 174; Altoviti, bust of, 383,
385; Angelica, the Sicilian, and, 127,
129, 135, 137; Anguillara, Count, and,
54; "Apollo and Hyacinth" of, 372;
arabesques of, 60; arms of, 103; in
artists' club, 55; Ascanio, servant of,
185-9, 212-3, 258, 261, 262, 265, 277-
8, 279, 304, 327, 335-6, 348, 351;
AUTOBIOGRAPHY of, 5-436; AUTOBI-
OGRAPHY of, remarks on, 1-2; Baldini
and, 399; Bandinello and, 364-5, 367-
71; banishment of, 16; Benedetto and,
132-3; Benintendi and, 150-3; birth
and family, 5-9; bronze statues, first,
288-90; brother of, 15-16, 19; brother's
death, 98-106; CAPITOLO ON THE
PRISON, 251-7; Caterina and, 305-9,
312-16, 318; Charles V and, 178, 180-
1; childhood of, 10-11; "Christ" of,
417, 419, 433-4 and note; Clement,
Pope, early relations with, 16, 40-1,
45, 73, 76, 78-80; Clement, in service
of, 86-95, 98, 104, 105-17, 119-26,
133, 135, 139-42; coin designs by, 94-
5, 98, 146, 156-7, 309, 312; Comte de
Saint Paul and, 333; Cosimo de' Medici
and, 341-50, 354-5, 357-68, 372-8,
383, 386-93, 395-404, 405-9, 409-21,
429-31, 433-6; country-house at Tres-
piano, 423 note; daughter by Jeanne
Scorzone, 318-19; dog of, 106, 110,
175, 229; escape from prison, 215-22;
Etampes, Mme. d', and, 292-3, 296-8,
300-1, 310, 322, 325, 328-30; Farnese,
Pier, and, 339-40; Faustina's maid and,
52; in Ferrara, 268-73; Ferrara, Cardinal, and, 201-2, 258-62, 275-6; fever
in Florence, 377-9; Fontainebleau,

work at, 288-9, 294, 295-6, 301, 318-19; France, journey to, 188-195; in France, 195-7, 274-5, 279-82, 299-300, 302-3, 323-4; France, queen of, and, 434-5; Francis First and, 196-7, 201-2, 207-8, 212, 249, 261, 269, 274-5, 278-96, 300, 309-10, 312, 317, 319-35, 348, 350-2, 374; Giovanni Gaddi and, 97, 111, 133-4, 160, 164-6, 167; Galluzzi and, 250; Gambetta and, 355-6; Giacomo da Carpi and, 50-2; Guasconti and, 28-32; Guidi and, 298-9, 422; halo of, 251; Holy Land, intentions to visit, 277-8; Il Bologna and, 310-12, 314; imprisonment of, 203-22; imprisonment, second, 227-50; at the inn, 154-5; Jeanne Scorzone and, 318-19; Julius III and, 385; "Jupiter" of, 279, 282, 288, 324-6; pedestal for "Jupiter," 292, 324, 331; "Jupiter," exhibition of, 324-6; life after 1562, 2; Lippi, Francesco, and, 24, 28; Lo Sbietta and, 421-7, 428-30, 431-3; Lucagnolo and, 35-8; Luigi Pulci and, 62-8; "Mars" of, 295, 310 note 2, 326-7, 331; medals by, 45-6, 48, 61-2, 85-6, 126, 139-40, 157, 174-5, 189-90, 268-9; Medici, Cardinal de', and, 139; Michael Angelo and, 24, 85-6, 384, 386; minor works, 24, 26-7, 28, 34, 35, 42, 51, 61, 90-3, 103, 112, 119, 179, 181-3, 258-60, 279, 289; mistress in Rome, 106; monument to brother, 103; Moro's daughter and, 96-8; musical training, 11, 12, 13, 15, 17-18, 21-2, 39; musician to the Pope, 40-1; "Narcissus" of, 372-3; necromancy, practised by, 127-31; "Neptune" of, 414-21, 423, 427, 428, 434-5; Pantasilea and, 55-6; Pascucci and, 200-1; Paul, Pope, and, 145-6, 159, 163-4, 178-80, 183-5, 202-3, 207-9, 212, 213, 222-3, 225-6, 227-8, 232, 239-40, 243, 244-5, 249-50; Paulino and, 39-40, 42; "Perseus" of, 342 notes 3 and 4, 348, 354, 358, 373, 375-8, 379-83, 397, 400-3, 406-8, 409-12; pilgrimage of thanksgiving, 404-5; Pompeo and, 121, 125-6, 133, 135, 142-4; Pompeo's daughter and, 146-9; Porzia Chigi and, 34-5, 36-7, 38, 45; prophecies of, 176-7, 413-4; reliquary for Mantua, 82; restorations by, 367, 372, 374, 395, 398; robbery of, attempted, 285-7; in Rome, 24-8, 33-4, 174-6, 383-6; among Roman ruins, 49, 50; in sack of Rome, 69-80, 206-7; Salamanca, Bishop of, and, 34, 38, 41-6; in Siena, trouble with postmaster, 263-7; in Siennese war, 392-5, 405-6; sick with plague, 53-4; sister of, 81-2, 267, 341; soldier of Ceri and, 46-7; son of, 364-5; SONNET ON HIS LIFE, 4; SONNET TO CASTELLAN, 244; Taine on memoirs of, xxxix, 435; Torrigiani, relations with, xxxi, 22-4; Vasari and, 172-3; in Venice, 149-53, 356-7

Cellini, Cecchino, brother of Benvenuto, xxxi, 15, 19, 84, 88 note 1; Bargello guard and, 99-100; death of, 102; duel and exile, 15-16; monument, 103

Cellini, Cosa, xxxi, 81-2

Cellini, Cristofano, xxxi, 7-8

Cellini, Giovanfrancesco (see Cellini, Cecchino)

Cellini, Giovanni, father of Benvenuto, xxxi, 8-13, 14, 16, 18, 19, 20-2, 32-3, 39, 41-2, 80-1; death of, 83; the Eight and, 39, 81; the Medici and, 88 note; Pierino and, 17-19

Cellini, Liperata, xxxi, 83-4, 167, 341, 349

Cellini, Luca, xxxi, 7

Cellino, Fiorino da, xxxi, 6

Celsus, Aulus Cornelius, Bacon on, iii, 82; Milton on, 241 note 33; on care of stomach, ix, 354 note

Celsus, governor of Cilicia, xxviii, 60

Celsus, the philosopher, Pascal on, xlviii, 194 (597), 269 (770)

Celtchar, the Luin of, xlix, 238

CELTIC RACES, POETRY OF THE, xxxii, 135-182

Celtic Races, Christianity and, xxxii, 170-81; Emerson on the, v, 338, 342; future of, xxxii, 181-2; Herodotus on the, xxxiii, 22; literature of the, xxxii, 141-70; mythology of, 153-5; Renan on character of the, 137-44

Cemetery Ridge, at Gettysburg, xliii, 336

CENCI, THE, by Shelley, xviii, 281-356; editorial remarks on, 272; story of the, 275-6

Cenci, Beatrice, arrest of, xviii, 334-7; assassins and, 344-51; at banquet, 289-94; Bernardo and, 355-6; Camillo and, 282-3; Count Cenci and, 285, 297-8, 309-13, 320-5; condemned to death, 353-6; Giacomo and, 316-17; Lucretia

and, 294-7, 331-3; madness of, 305-9; Orsino and, 286-8, 309-13; portrait of, by Guido, 278-9; in prison, 346-51; Shelley on character of, 278-9; trial of, 340-6

Cenci, Bernardo, Beatrice and, xviii, 294-7, 346-9, 355-6; Count Cenci and, 298, 322, 332-3; Lucretia and, 294-7; Pope and, 351-2

Cenci, Cristofano, sent to Salamanca, xviii, 285; death announced 289-90

Cenci, Count Francesco, banquet of, xviii, 288-94; Beatrice and, 285, 296, 297-8, 320-6; Cardinal Camillo and, 281-5; chapel built by, 277; Lucretia and, 298-9, 320-2; murdered, 328-30; plots against, 312-16, 319-20

Cenci, Giacomo, accused by Marzio, xviii, 341; Beatrice and, 316-17, 347-51, 354; Camillo and, 300-1; Orsino and, 301-3, 313-20, 337-9

Cenci, Lucretia, accused by Marzio, xviii, 341; arrest of, 334-7; at the banquet, 289; Beatrice and, 295-7, 305-13, 326-30, 331-3, 347-50, 354; Bernardo and, 294; Count Cenci and, 298-9, 320-5; remarks on religion of, 277-8

Cenci, Rocco, son of Francesco, xviii, 285, 289-90

Cenci Palace, Shelley on, xviii, 279

Cennini, Bastiano, xxxi, 158

Censorinus, Plutarch on, xii, 147

CENSORIOUS CRITIC, Burns's REPLY TO A, vi, 276

Censoriousness, Burns on, vi, 183-5; Kempis on, vii, 243 (1, 2); Jesus on, xliv, 370 (41-2); Locke on, xxxvii, 121; M. Aurelius on, ii, 289-90, 297 (12); Molière on, xxvi, 215; Penn on, i, 346 (274), 395; Raleigh on, xxxix, 69; Sidney on, xxvii, 30-1

Censors, duties of Roman, ix, 398 note 2

Censorship, Milton on government, iii, 206-10

Censorship of Press, Milton on, iii, 189-232; Pascal on, xlviii, 314-15

Censure, Browne on, iii, 316-7; Heminge and Condell on, xxxix, 148; man's dislike of, ii, 140-1 (67); Marcus Aurelius on endurance of, 195 (13), 269 (27), 271 (34); Pascal on human dislike of, xlviii, 44-5

Census (U. S.), provisions for taking, xliii, 180-1 (3)

Centano, Andrea, xxxi, 227-8

Centaurs, beginning of their feud with men, xxii, 292; in Dante's HELL, xx, 50; Theseus and, 245 note

Centralization, Mill on, xxv, 120-1, 307-12

Cephalos, the Attic boy, iv, 37

Cephas, Peter called, xx, 377 note 16; Christ's appearance to, xlv, 511 (4)

Cephisophon, in THE FROGS, viii, 484

Cerbaia, Orso da, xx, 166 note 6

Cerbellon, Gabriel, xiv, 388

Cerberus, Æneas and, xiii, 221; in Dante's HELL, xx, 25-6; Hercules and, 38 and note

Cerchi, Veri de', head of Bianchi faction, xx, 27 note 4

Cerealis, letter to, ix, 226

Ceremonies, Browne on religious, iii, 255 (3); Confucius on, xliv, 9 (4), 11 (15); Hume on religious, xxxvii, 328; Locke on excess of, 123-4; Luther on religious, xxxvi, 372-8; Montaigne on, xviii, 14; Pascal on religious, xlviii, 92-3 (250-2); Penn on religious, i, 363 (507), 387 (175); Rousseau on religions, xxxiv, 282-3, 302-3; Shakespeare on, xlvi, 204, note 35, 358; lead to superstition, iii, 45-6; Swift on, xxvii, 100-1

CEREMONIES, ESSAY ON, Bacon's, iii, 124-6

Ceres, daughter of (see Proserpine); Proserpine and, iv, 161; in THE TEMPEST, xlvi, 446-7

Ceri, Rienzo da, xxxi, 46 note 2, 70

Ceroxylus laceratus, xi, 225

Certainty, Descartes on, xxxiv, 29; impossibility of, xlviii, 30, 128 (387), 147 (437); Pascal on, 87-8 (234)

Certus, Publicius, ix, 340-3

Cervantes, Miguel de, author of DON QUIXOTE, xiv; captivity of, 393-4; Galatea of, 54; Hugo on, xxxix, 351; life and works of, xiv, 3-4; Sainte-Beuve on, xxxii, 131-2

Cervolles, Arnaud de, xxxv, 39 note 4, 47

Cesano, Gabriel, xxxi, 259 note 3, 260, 261

Ceserino, Gabbriello, Gonfalonier of Rome, xxxi, 45

CESSATION, THE TRANCE OF, xlv, 731-7

Cethegus, Caius, in Catiline conspiracy, xii, 269, 230-232; executed, 235, 243

Cethegus, Marcus, old age of, ix, 63

Ceylon, slavery not practised in, xxxv, 226 note

Chacao, Chili, xxix, 278-9

Chachidiablo, on Don Quixote, xiv, 515

Chærephon, Plato on, ii, 8

Chæronea, Demosthenes at battle of, xii, 206; iv, 79

Chafing Gear, defined, xxiii, 19

Chagos Islands, xxix, 482

Chagres, river, xxxiii, 143-4

Chalk Formations, Darwin on, xi, 357-8

Chalmers, on the public, xxviii, 126

CHALMERS, WILLIE: a song, vi, 227-8

Chalybe, priestess of Juno, xiii, 254

Chalybes, the, viii, 192 and note 43

Cham, Amalthea and, iv, 161

Chama, shells of the, xxix, 464

Chamavians, Tacitus on, xxxiii, 111

CHAMBERED NAUTILUS, THE, xlii, 1365-6

Chamberland, THE GERM THEORY, xxxviii, 269, 364-70

Chamisso, on coral islands, xxix, 471; on seeds, 459; on transported stones, 465

Chamois Hunter, in MANFRED, xviii, 417-22

Chamois Hunter, song of, in WILLIAM TELL, xxvi, 380-1

Chamouni, glacier of, xxx, 217-19, 222-3

CHAMOUNI, HYMN IN THE VALE OF, xli, 707-9

Champlain, Lake, naval forces on, xliii, 266

Chance, in Chaos, iv, 131-33; Emerson on, v, 83; Hume on, xxxvii, 332, 364; Pope on, xl, 415; providence in, iii, 268-9; Sophocles on, viii, 293; in thoughts, xxxix, 119

Chancellorsville, Haskell on, xliii, 327

Chandos, Sir John, in French invasion, xxxv, 18-19; Lord Clermont and, 40-1; at Crecy, 24; at Poitiers, 43, 45, 52

Ch'ang-chü, Confucius on, xliv, 62 (6)

Change, Carlyle on, xxv, 350-2; Confucius on, xliv, 53 (36), 57 (3); dread of, v, 94-5; Emerson on, xlii, 1261; Goethe on, xxxix, 259; Hooker on, 185-6; the law of the universe, ii, 218 (36), 219 (42, 43), 245-6 (18, 19, 23), 246 (25), 249 (47), 254 (6), 268 (19), 276-7 (7), 278 (11), 279 (18), vi, 502; xxix, 497-8; Lowell on, xlii, 1386-7; Lyell on uniformity of, xxxviii, 398-418; Marcus Aurelius on, ii, 200 (3), 212-3 (3); Pascal on, pleasure of, xlviii, 119-20 (355); Shakespeare on,

xl, 274; tendency to, xi, 345-6, 304; Tennyson on, xlii, 992 (see also Innovation, Vicissitude)

Changelings, legerdemain of, iii, 282

Channa, charioteer of Buddha, xlv, 644-5

Channing, Dr., on puerperal fever, xxxviii, 251

Channing, Edward T., cousin of R. H. Dana, xxiii, 398-9

Channing, William Ellery, Coleridge on, v, 319; life and character of, xxviii, 308; ON THE LABORING CLASSES, 309-367

CHANSON DE ROLAND, xlix, 93-195; Arnold on, xxviii, 70-1

Chanticleer, in NUN's PRIEST's TALE, xl, 35-51

Chao, Duke, xliv, 23 (30) note 8

Chao of Sung, xliv, 20 (14)

Chaos, Descartes on, under natural laws, xxxiv, 36-7; Milton's description of, iv, 131-3

Chapelain, Jean, Corneille and, xxxix, 362-3; Dryden on, xiii, 13

Chapman, George, Arnold on, xxviii, 81; Dryden on, xiii, 62; on man, v, 176

CHAPMAN's HOMER, ON FIRST LOOKING INTO, xli, 895-6

Character, beauty and, v, 310; Browne on outward signs of, iii, 312-3; circumstances and, xxv, 106; concealment of, impossible, v, 285; consistency of, 66; culture and, xxxii, 236-7, 254-5; discernment of, v, 142; education and natural, xxxvii, 44-5; force of, cumulative, v, 67; influence of, in our civilization, 248; Locke on the native, xxxvii, 84-5; maker of its own forms, v, 206; M. Aurelius on, ii, 217 (28), 288 (15); Mill on, xxv, 255; the supreme end, v, 248; talent and, contrasted, 159

CHARACTER, ESSAY ON, Emerson's, v, 183-197

CHARACTERISTICS, Carlyle's, xxv, 319-56; remarks on, 317

Charaxos, and Rhodopis, xxxiii, 67, 68

Charcoal, combustion of, xxx, 158-9

Charesha, island of, xxxiii, 144, 156

CHARGE OF THE LIGHT BRIGADE, Tennyson's, xlii, 1005-7

Charity, Bacon on, iii, 33-4, 90; xxxix, 129; Browne on, iii, 310, 312, 313-14, 330; Dante on, xx, 205-6, 395-7; Dante's allegory of, 265 note 11;

Dante's star of, 177 note 9; David on, xliv, 193-4; Emerson on popular, v, 63; Emerson on relating our, 130; Herbert on, xv, 408; Hobbes's definition of, xxxiv, 340; Kempis on works of, vii, 218-9; Luther on, xxxvi, 248, 254; method or, iii, 256; Milton on, iv, 356; More on, xxxvi, 198; offences against, iii, 314-7; Pascal on, xlviii, 187-8, 220 (663, 665), 274-5 (793) 275-6; Paul, St., on, xlv, 508 (1-13); Penn on, i, 327, 360 (469-70), 396-7; pleasure from, xix, 41; Pope on, xl, 430, 439; pure and sentimental, xviii, 179

Charity, in PILGRIM'S PROGRESS, xv, 54-6

Charity, Mount, xv, 291

Charixenus, and Endamidas, xxxii, 81

Charlatanism, Arnold on, xxviii, 66

Charlemagne, and the Church, xx, 308; in Dante's PARADISE, 362; division of empire of, iii, 139; extinction of race of, xxxix, 80-1; at Fontarabbia, iv, 102; HYMN attributed to, xlv, 547-8; one of nine worthies, xxxix, 20; the Northmen and, v, 342; in Spain, xlix, 94

Charlemagne, in SONG OF ROLAND, xlix, 94

Charles I, of Anjou, abilities of, xx, 173 note 11; Conradine and, 115 note 3, 227 note 10; Machiavelli on success of, xxxvi, 41; Nicholas, Pope, and, xx, 80 note 9; Thomas Aquinas and, 227 note 11; victories in Italy, 66 note 1, 115 notes; wife of, 174 note 14

Charles I, of England ("martyr"), controversy over, iv, 4-5; Drake to, xxxiii, 125; on English law, v, 422; execution of, place of, xxxix, 359; fondness for plays, xxxiv, 153; Harvey and, xxxviii, 60; Marvell on death of, xl, 374; Milton on, xxviii, 187; Swift on reign of, xxvii, 98; Vane on, xliii, 121, 125-6; Voltaire on, xxxiv, 87

Charles II, of England, Emerson on, v, 402; Hobbes and, xxxiv, 308; Milton on restoration of, iv, 5; Presbyterians and, xxxiv, 81; Puritans and, xxvii, 136; Quakers and, xxxiv, 73-4; Shelley on drama under, xxvii, 341-2; Waller and, xxxiv, 145-6

CHARLES II, EPITAPH ON, xl, 383

Charles II of Naples, Dante on, xx, 174 note 13, 227 note 14, 309 note 24, 368 note 11

Charles V, Emperor, Adrian, Pope, and, xxxvi, 102; Clement VII and, xxxi, 114 note 5; on Eraso, xv, 327; France, passage of, through, xxxi, 321 and note; at Landresy, xxxviii, 17; Luther on, xxxvi, 246, 263; melancholy of, iii, 49; at Metz, xxxviii, 23-4, 26, 29-32; More, Thomas, on, xxxvi, 134; the Netherlands and, xix, 252; Raleigh on, xxxix, 86; Rome, visit of, to, xxxi, 178-9; Ruysum in EGMONT on, xix, 255; Seldius and, xxxix, 91; at Therouenne, xxxviii, 34-43; in triumvirate of kings, iii, 50; Valdesso and, xv, 412-3; war with Francis I, xxxi, 68 note, 328 note 1, 334 note 1; wealth of, xxxiii, 307

Charles V, in DR. FAUSTUS, xix, 233, 236-9

Charles VI of France, Duke of Guelders and, xxxv, 100; Voltaire on wars under, xxxiv, 87

Charles VII, organizes national army, xxxvi, 47

Charles IX of France, in Bayonne, xxxviii, 49-50; at Bourges, 46-7; at Havre de Grace, 49; Navarre, King of, and, 47-8; Paré and, 48-9, 50-1, 52; Raleigh on, xxxix, 83; Voltaire on reign of, xxxiv, 87

Charles, Duke of Alençon, xxxv, 27, 29, 30

Charles of Almaine, in Crecy campaign, xxxv, 11-12, 28-9

Charles the Bald, son of Debonnaire, xxxix, 82

Charles of Burgundy, secrecy of, iii, 68

Charles the Fat, xxxix, 82-3

Charles of Lorraine, xx, 226 note 7

Charles of Luxembourg, at Crecy, xxxv, 28-9

Charles Martel, king of Hungary, xx, 315-9

Charles the Simple, xxxix, 82-83

Charles of Valois, and the empire, xx, 309 note 24; in Florentine troubles, 27 note 8, 227 note 12

Charles, Elizabeth, translator, xlv, 559

Charles, Mr., agent of Pennsylvania, i, 159, 162

Charles Island, Galapagos group, xxix, 379

Charles's Wain (see Wain)

CHARLES, KING, HERE'S A HEALTH TO, xli, 754-5

CHARLIE, HE'S MY DARLING, vi, 489
CHARLIE IS MY DARLING, xli, 566
CHARMING MONTH OF MAY, vi, 504
Charmion, maid of Cleopatra, xii, 368;
death of, 387
Charmion, in ALL FOR LOVE, xviii, 39-41,
71-2, 75, 88, 90, 100, 102-5
Charms, Burns on immortal, vi, 289;
origin of term, xxvii, 8-9
Charny, Sir Geoffrey, xxxv, 51
CHARON, THE REFUSAL OF, xli, 917-18
Charon, Æneas and, xiii, 220-1; Dante
on, xx, 15-16; description of, xiii,
217-8; Dirce and, xli, 899; reference
to, viii, 443
Charon, in THE FROGS, viii, 444-5
Charondas, iii, 242 note 46
Charron, Montaigne and, xxxii, 105;
Pascal on, xlviii, 24 (62); on reason,
xxxix, 99-100; on religious creeds,
xxxiv, 284 note
Chartel, Capt., xxxviii, 18
Chartism, and the Times, v, 448-9
Chartist Day, nobility on, v, 408
Charybdis, and Circe's song, iv, 51; de-
scription of, xiii, 141-2; Ulysses at, xxii,
167-8, 172-3
Chase, Mohammed on the, xlv, 994-1004;
Pascal on the, xlviii, 53-4; value of the,
to princes, xxxvi, 49
Chassoygnet, the tree, xxxix, 12
Chaste women, often forward, iii, 22
Chastillon, M. de, xxxviii, 18
Chastisement of children, xxxvii, 34,
35-7, 38-39, 40, 41, 56, 60-63, 65-68,
93-94
Chastisements of heaven, Woolman on,
i, 237
Chastity, beauty and, xlvi, 145; Frank-
lin's rule of, i, 80; Jonson on, xl, 296;
Pascal on, xlviii, 127 (385); Paul, St.,
on, xlv, 499 (25-6); "she that has,"
iv, 55-6; spirit of, in NEW ATLANTIS,
iii, 168; sun-clad power of, iv, 65;
"unblemished form of," 50
Chasuarians, Tacitus on the, xxxiii, 111
Château le Comte, xxxviii, 21-3
Chateaubriand, Carlyle on, xxv, 425; on
criticism, xxxix, 385; Taine on, 414
Chateauneuf, John of, xxxv, 96, 100
Chatelet, court of, Burke on, xxiv, 340
Chatham Island, Darwin on, xxix, 377-9
Chatham, Lord, better than his speeches,
v, 183; on confidence, 371; and the
dictionary, 169; reference to, 167

Chatterton, Hazlitt on, xxvii, 278; SAXON
POEMS of, xxxix, 329; Shelley on, xli,
867; SONG FROM ÆLLA, xli, 558-9;
Wordsworth on, 659
Chaucer, Geoffrey, Arnold, Matthew, on,
xxviii, 76-81; Boccaccio and, xxxix,
171; CANTERBURY TALES, PROLOGUE TO,
xl, 11-34; Caxton on, xxxix, 18-20;
Dido, his picture of, v, 276; Dryden
on, xxxix, 154-5, 159-72; Emerson on,
v, 144, 181, 433; Froissart and, xxxv,
6, on good blood, v, 176; Hazlitt on,
xxvii, 271-2; NUN'S PRIEST'S TALE, xl,
34-51; Ovid, compared with, xxxix,
154, 159-162; reference to, iv, 36-7;
Ruskin on, xxviii, 142; Shakespeare
and, xxxix, 229-30; Shelley on, xxvii,
350; Sidney on, 6-7, 42; sources of his
tales, xxxix, 159-61, 172; Thoreau on,
xxviii, 413; Wordsworth on, xxxix,
330; Wordsworth on language of, 272
note
Chaucians, Tacitus on the, xxxiii, 112
Chaumber, Christopher, xlii, 1161
Chaurias, ii, 259
Chaussier, on puerperal fever, xxxviii, 247
Cheagle, John, i, 182
Cheating, impossibility of, v, 98-9
Chebar, Milton on, iv, 24 (6)
Checks and Balances, Washington on,
xliii, 241-3
Cheek, Sir John, Milton on, iv, 80
CHEER UP, MY MATES, xl, 366
Cheerfulness, in music, xli, 478; Penn on,
i, 334 (119); in prosperity, no credit,
vii, 247 (1)
Cheiron, and Prometheus, viii, 203 note
69
Chemical affinity, capacity of, to do work,
xxx, 200-5; converted to heat and light,
58-9, 201-2, 202; correlation with elec-
tricity, 73-82, 202-4; defined, 47; illus-
trations of, 47-60; measurement of, 208
CHEMICAL HISTORY OF A CANDLE, xxx,
86-170
Chemistry, Huxley on study of, xxviii,
221
Chemmis, island of, xxxiii, 79; worship
of Perseus in, 44-5
Chemos, description of, iv, 98
Ch'en Ch'eng, xliv, 48 (22)
Ch'en Wen, xliv, 16-17
Chenab, sediment of the, xxxviii, 402
Chénier, Marie-Joseph, on reason, xxxii,
125

Cheops, king of Egypt, xxxiii, 63-4

Chephren, king of Egypt, xxxiii, 64-5

Cherbourg, taking of, by Edward III, xxxv, 10, 11 note

Chernubles, in SONG OF ROLAND, xlix, 125-36

Cherries, Locke on eating of, xxxvii, 20-1

CHERRY-RIPE, by Campion, xl, 284

CHERRY-RIPE, by Herrick, xl, 334

Cherubim, the, in Heaven, iv, 40, 10 (11)

Cherubino, Maestro, xxxi, 262, 265-6, 267

Cheruscans, Tacitus on the, xxxiii, 112-13

Chess, among Mohammedans, xlv, 1003 note 12

Chesterfield, Lord, Johnson's letter to, xxxix, 206-7, 182 note; lines ascribed to, 308; on truth in gentlemen, v, 374

Cheucau, Darwin on the, xxix, 292, 282

CHEVALIER'S LAMENT, THE, vi, 305

CHEVY CHASE, xl, 93-101; Johnson on, xxvii, 197-8

Chi, Confucius on the, xliv, 9-10 (1, 6) 20 (22), 34 (16), 54 (1)

Chi Huan, xliv, 61 (4)

Chi K'ang, xliv, 8 (20), 19 (6), 34 (6), 39 (17) note (18, 19), 47 (20)

Ch'i-tiao K'ai, xliv, 15 (5)

Chi Tzu-ch'eng, xliv, 38 (8)

Chi Tzu-jan, xliv, 35 (23)

Chi Wen, xliv, 17 (19)

Chiana, river, xx, 120 note 2, 339

Chicheley, Henry, xxxv, 381

Chicken-pox, and smallpox, xxxviii, 173

Chicken Cholera, Pasteur on, xxxviii, 374

Chickens, counting, before they're hatched, xvii, 42; Harvey on incubation of, xxxviii, 84, 85-6; incubation of, 127; instinctive fears of, xi, 257-8

Chiding of children, Locke on, xxxvii, 40-1, 42-3, 48-50, 60-1, 63-4, 90-1, 94

Chidley, Mr., on Dr. Donne, xv, 343

Chief Justice, presides at impeachment of president, xliii, 182 (6)

Chieh-yü, xliv, 61 (5)

Chieh-ni, xliv, 62 (6)

Chien, Duke, xliv, 48 (22) note

Chigi, Agostino, xxxi, 34 note 4

Chigi, Porzia, and Cellini, xxxi, 34-8, 45

Chih, music-master, xliv, 26 (15)

Chilaway, Job, i, 264-5

Child is father of the man, xli, 600

CHILD, ON A NEW-BORN, xli, 580

CHILD OF QUALITY, TO A, xl, 396-7

CHILD'S GRACE, A, xl, 334

Childbirth, Browne on curse of, iii, 261 (10); Holmes on, xxxviii, 242-3, 251-3; Pasteur on, 380-1

Childeric III, xx, 226 note 7

Childhood, intimations of immortality in, xli, 595-600; shows the man, iv, 400; wisdom sends us to, xlviii, 97 (271)

Children, Arabian proverb on, xvi, 345-6; Bacon on, iii, 21-2, xl, 349; confidence of, v, 61-2; Confucius on, xliv, 5 (6); Dante on, and parents, xx, 317-19; De Quincey on griefs of, xxvii, 320; fable on training of, xvii, 28-9; Goethe on fashioning of, xxxvii, 355; ingratitude of, xxxvii, 355; Jesus on, xliv, 401 (15-17); liberties of, in Massachusetts, xliii, 77-8; Locke on training of, xxxvii, 9-184; memory's voices, viii, 98; Mill on control of, xxv, 302; misfortune made harder by, vi, 224; Montaigne on, and parents, xxxii, 73-5; Penn on training of, i, 384; the Psalmist on, xliv, 310 (3-5); in Utopia, xxxvi, 183-4, 186-7, 192

CHILDREN, by Longfellow, xlii, 1279-80

CHILDREN, DEATHS OF LITTLE, xxvii, 285-288

CHILDREN, INSTITUTION AND EDUCATION OF, xxxii, 29-71

CHILDREN AND PARENTS, BACON'S ESSAY ON, iii, 19-21

CHILDREN'S HOUR, THE, xlii, 1294-5

Chile, climate of, xxix, 250; Darwin on, 257-365; horses in, 158-9; Lyell on earthquakes in, xxxviii, 390; Pretty on coast of, xxxiii, 208-9

Chileus the Arcadian, xii, 10

Chillingworth, Locke on, xxxvii, 159

CHILLON, ON THE CASTLE OF, xli, 811

CHILLON, THE PRISONER OF, xli, 801-811

Chiloe, climate and productions of, xxix, 248-50; Darwin on, 277-82, 295-301; orchard-making in, 301-2

Chimæra, reference to, xiii, 217

Chimæra, statue called, xxxi, 395

Chimango, Darwin on the, xxix, 63-5

Chimborazo, Emerson on, v, 164-5

Chimneys, in Elizabethan England, xxxv, 298

China, ancient government of, xliv, 66 note 1; ancient ordnance in, iii, 139-40; ancient selection in, xi, 45; ancient shipping of, iii, 157; cause of early civilization of, x, 25; inoculation in, xxxiv, 97; law against visitors in, iii,

160-1; Mill on unprogressiveness of, xxv, 266-7; Pascal on history of, xlviii, 192-4; Smith on conditions in, x, 73; state of wealth of, 97-8, 295; women of, xxxvii, 15-16

CHINESE SACRED WRITINGS, xliv, 5-67

Ching, Duke, xliv, 39 (11), 42 (8), 56 (12), 61 (3)

Chioccia, Bartolommeo, xxxi, 304, 313

Chionis Alba, xxix, 101

Chiostra, Ulivieri della, xxxi, 20

Chiromancy, Browne on, iii, 313; Jonson on, xlvii, 560

Chiron, iii, 306; with the Argonauts, xxxiv, 129-30; the Centaur, xxxvi, 57; in Dante's HELL, xx, 50-1; his refusal of immortality, xxxii, 27

Chironomus, asexual reproduction of, xi, 458

Chiu, Duke, xliv, 47 (17) note

Chivalry, Burke on age of, xxiv, 212-13; Cervantes on books of, xiv, 473-7, 481, 487-8; Don Quixote's defence of, 488-94; examples of romances of, 48-54; order of, for girls and boys, xxviii, 157 note; Renan on origin of, xxxii, 158-9; romances of, parodied by Cervantes, xiv, 3, 9; Ruskin on, xxviii, 143-4 (see also Knight-errantry)

Chlorate of potash, experiments with, xxx, 53-4

Chloreus, the priest, xiii, 383-4

Chloride of calcium, experiment with, xxx, 54 note 18

Chloris, in Hades, xxii, 152

Chloris, sonnets to, xiv, 331

CHLORIS, ON, vi, 498

CHLORIS BEING ILL, vi, 532

CHLORIS, INSCRIPTION TO, vi, 541

CHLORIS, Sedley's, xl, 383-4

Choaspes, river, iv, 391

Chochilaicus, Danish king, xlix, 3

CHŒPHORÆ (see LIBATION-BEARERS)

Choiseul, Duke de, Burke on estate of, xxiv, 249

Choler, Bacon on, iii, 93

Chonos Archipelago, Darwin on, xxix, 285-294

Chorazin, Jesus on, xliv, 381 (13)

Chorus, the, in tragedy, iv, 412-13

Chorus of Captive Women (see LIBATION-BEARERS, viii)

Chorus, of Danites (see SAMSON AGONISTES, iv)

Chorus of Frogs (see FROGS, THE, viii)

Chorus of Trozenian Women (see HIPPOLYTUS, viii)

Chorus of Furies (see FURIES, THE, viii)

Chorus of Huntsmen (see HIPPOLYTUS, viii)

Chorus of Initiated Persons (see FROGS, THE, viii)

Chorus of Inspired Damsels (see BACCHÆ, THE, viii)

Chorus of Old Men (see AGAMEMNON, viii)

Chorus of Priests and Suppliants (see ŒDIPUS THE KING, viii)

Chorus of Theban Elders (see ANTIGONE, viii)

Chou, Chinese dynasty, xliv, 9 note 9, 11 (14)

Chou, Duke of, xliv, 21 (5) note, 26 (11), 63 (10, 11)

Chou, Emperor, xliv, 61 note 1, 65 (20), 66 (1) note, 67 note

Chriemhild (see Grimhild)

Christ, Arnold on, xlii, 1138-9; Augustine, St., on, vii, 54-5, 74, 108-9, 114-5, 196-7; Bacon on prophecy of, iii, 91; Bunyan on, xv, 56-7, 212-16, 285-6; Calvin on, xxxix, 48-50; Church doctrine of, xlviii, 328; Clement, St., on, xlv, 541-2; the "Counsellor," iii, 52; Dante on, xx, 311-3, 340 note 6; in Dante's PARADISE, 383-6; as David's son, xliv, 407 (41-4); genealogies of, 190-1; Greek Hymn on, xlv, 541; Hell visited by, xx, 35 note, 49 note; Herbert on, xv, 401-2; Hugo on, xxxix, 343; Jewish rejection of, xlviii, 266-7 (760-2); Jews in NEW ATLANTIS on, iii, 167; John the Baptist on, xliv, 361 (15-17); Keble on, xlv, 565-6; the kingdom of, xxxvi, 276; Lessing on, xxxii, 197-8, 201-2; Luther on, xxxvi, 345, 347, 356-9; Luther on belief in, 346-8, 350-4, 355-6, 358-9; Moses's prophecy of, xliv, 437 (37); Niceta of Remisiana on, xlv, 546-7; Pascal on, xlviii, 155 (466), 159-60 (483), 166 (512), 170 (526-8), 174-80 (543, 545-54), 182, 183, 194 (596), 194 (599-600), 197-8 (607, 609), 220 (665), 220-1 (666, 668), 222 (670), 225-6, 267-9 (764-74), 270 (776) 271 (780, 781-5), 276 (794-7), 277 (800), 284 (822), 295 (846), 332-4, 348-9; Paul, St., on, xxxvi, 366-8; Penn on, i, 359 (456); Platonists on, vii, 107-8; proofs

of, 254-72; prophecies of, xlviii, 186-9, 201, 202 (616-17), 204-5, 214, 215 (644), 218 (656), 219 (659), 219-20 (662), 222 (670), 231, 234-5 (701, 706), 236-8 (707-12), 244 (715), 245 (720), 247-8, 251-9, 263 (744), 263 (749), 264-6 (751-8, 761), 287, 292-3; Quakers on, i, 190; second coming of, xliv, 388-390 (35-59), 399-400 (22-37), 400 (8), 408 (8-11), 409 (25-36); second coming of, Browne on, iii, 277; "unconscious prophecies" of, viii, 197 note 59, 203 note 69; Vane on, xliii, 122 (see also Jesus)

Christ, in PARADISE LOST, iv, 137-46, 195-6, 199, 221-7, 231-43, 292-7, 319-20; Bagehot on Milton's, xxviii, 195-9

Christ, in PARADISE REGAINED, iv, 359-411

CHRIST, IMITATION OF, Kempis's, vii, 201-364

CHRIST'S NATIVITY, ON THE MORNING OF, iv, 7-15

CHRISTABEL, by Coleridge, xli, 709-28

Christian, in PILGRIM'S PROGRESS, xv; ancestors of, 264-5; Apollyon and, 59-64; Atheist and, 137-8; at Beautiful Palace, 49-51, 56-8; in Beulah-land, 156-8; burden of, 13, 42; By-ends and, 102-6; charity and, 54-6; death of, 159-60; in Delectable Mountains, 122-6; at Difficulty Hill, 45-6; in Enchanted Ground, 138-9; Evangelist and, 14-15, 24-8, 89-96; Faithful and, 70-90; Flatterer and, 135-7; Formalist and Hypocrisy with, 43-5; Giant Despair and, 116-22; Good-Will and, 29-32; on Guilt, Mistrust, and Faint-Heart, 133-4; Hold-the-world and, 108-9; Ignorance and, 126-8, 146-52; at Interpreter's House, 32-41; on Little-Faith, 128-32; on Lot's wife, 112-3; at Lucre Hill, 109-11; at Mount Sinai, 24; Obstinate and, 115-7; Piety and, 51-3; Pliable and, 15-19; Prudence and, 53-4; at River of Life, 113-14; Simple and Sloth with, 42; in Slough of Despond, 18-20; Talkative and, 81-9; Timorous and Mistrust with, 46-7; in valley of Humiliation, 59-242; in valley of the Shadow of Death, 65-9; at Vanity Fair, 91-7; Worldly Wiseman and, 21-4

Christian of Troyes, xxxv, 104; on the Bretons, xxxii, 180; on France, xxviii, 76; Renan on, xxxii, 147

CHRISTIAN BROKER, STORY OF THE, xvi, 120-33

Christian Church, Calvin on, xxxix, 40-3, 50; schools of early, xxxv, 269-70

CHRISTIAN CHURCH, HYMNS OF, xlv, 533-72

Christian Holy Days, xv, 403-4

CHRISTIAN LIBERTY, Luther on, xxxvi, 344-78; remarks on Luther's, 246

Christian Morality, Mill on, xxv, 242-6

CHRISTIAN SACRED LITERATURE, xliv, 351-486; xlv, 491-532

Christiana, in PILGRIM'S PROGRESS, xv; at Beautiful Palace, 224-7, 237-9; death of, 310-12; at Difficulty Hill, 218-20; dream of, 200; in Enchanted Ground, 301; Great-Heart and, 211-17; Honest and, 252; ill-favored ones and, 197-9; in Immanuel's Land, 285; at the Inn, 263; at Interpreter's House, 200-12; lions and, 222-3; Mercy and, 186-90, 194-5; at Mnason's Inn, 278-9; pilgrimage of, 180-4; in Slough of Despond, 190-1; song of, 196; Timorus and, 184-7; in valley of Humiliation, 240-3; in valley of Shadow of Death, 245-6; at wicket-gate, 191-2

Christianity, Bacon on, iii, 33; bardism and, xxxii, 168-9; Browne on, iii, 253 (2), 260 (9, 10), 278, 305; Carlyle on modern, xxv, 337-8; Celtic Races and, xxxii, 170-82; Channing on influence of, xxviii, 361; Dante on, and salvation, xx, 367-8; Emerson on, v, 30-7, 81, 155; and freedom of conscience, xliii, 122; Goethe on, xxv, 381; heathenisms in modern, v, 277-8; Hobbes on belief in, xxxiv, 347-8, 379; Hugo on, xxxix, 342-5; Hume on, xxxvii, 375, 391-2; Lessing on, xxxii, 197-202; Luther on, xxxvi, 368-9, 375-6; Manzoni on, xxi, 171; Marcus Aurelius and, xxv, 220-2; James Mill on, 29-31; J. S. Mill on, 235-6, 242-6; paganism in, v, 276; Pascal on, xlviii, 69, 84, 89 (241), 91 (245), 92 (251), 97 (269), 146, 148 (441, 444), 151 (450), 155 (468), 161 (491), 164 (503), 172 (537-8), 173 (542), 174 (544), 181-92, 193 (589), 195-6 (601), 197 (606), 198, 202 (615), 233 (693), 272 (783), 337, 371-2; Pascal on fundamentals of, 181-92; Pascal's proofs of, 102 (289), 260; Penn on, i, 360 (468), 397 (296-99); perpetuity

of, xlviii, 200-5; poetry and, xxxix, 345, 355; porches of, xli, 490; Renan on marvelous element of, xxxii, 160; Rousseau on belief in, xxxiv, 294-9, 300-2; Rousseau on miracles of, 288 note; Ruskin on modern, xxviii, 123-5; rapid spread of, xxxiv, 385-7; Shelley on, xxvii, 345-6; spread without books, iii, 209; Taine on, xxxix, 424-5, 432; in Utopia, xxxvi, 225-6; Vanity Fair opposed to, xv, 97; Wordsworth on, xxxix, 314

Christians, Browne on instability of, iii, 277; disciples first called, xliv, 448 (26); early, forbidden to teach, vii, 124; forbidden to read by Julian, iii, 199; and heathen taxes, i, 218 note; Marcus Aurelius on, ii, 285 (3); Mohammed on, xlv, 996, 999, 1001-2; Pascal on, xlviii, 94 (256), 116 (337-8), 173 (540-1), 223 (671), 311 (903); Pascal on early and later, 374-7; persecutions of, foretold by Jesus, xliv, 408 (12-19); persecution of, in Jerusalem, 439 (1), 448 (1); persecution of, by Marcus Aurelius, ii, 192; Pliny's letter on the, ix, 404-6; attitude towards poetry, xxxix, 314; Trajan on the, ix, 407 and note; Woolman on oppression by, i, 306

Christina, Queen, Pascal to, xlviii, 359-61

Christmas, celebration of, xv, 403; spirits at, xlvi, 98

CHRISTMAS HYMN, xlv, 561-2

Chronology, Hakluyt on, xxx, 325; Hume on, xxxvii, 419; Locke on study of, 138, 153, 156-7; Newton's system of, xxxiv, 126-30

Chryseis, Agamemnon's slave, viii, 65

Chrysippus, ii, 178 (177)

Chrysogonus, Alcibiades and, xii, 138; freedman of Sylla, 219-20

Chrysostom, St., and Aristophanes, iii, 194; in Dante's PARADISE, xx, 338 note 35; Olympias and, xv, 377; Walton on eloquence of, 394

Chrysostom, in DON QUIXOTE, burial of, xiv, 98-100, 108-9; canzone of, 101-4; Marcella and, 85-90, 104-08

Chryssipus, citations of, xxxii, 31; on logic, 63

Ch'ü Po-yü, xliv, 48 (26), 51 (6)

Chung-kung, disciple of Confucius, xliv, 15 note 2, 18 (1), 19 (4), 33 (2), 37 (2), 41 (2)

Church, Burke on an established, xxiv, 228-35; civil authority in the, xliii, 74; Emerson on decline of the, v, 33-4, 275; Emerson on the future of the, 294; Emerson on revivification of, 40-1; liberty and the, xliii, 66; liberties of the, in Massachusetts, 81-4; Mill on an established, xxv, 69; Pascal on early idea of the, xlviii, 374-5; politics and the, xxiv, 151-2; Raleigh on, xl, 205; Ruskin on the true, xxviii, 125; Tennyson on the, xlii, 1053; in Utopia, xxxvi, 232-5

CHURCH, FUTURE PEACE AND GLORY OF THE, xlv, 563

Church Councils (see Councils)

Church Fathers, Calvin on the, xxxix, 35-8; Kempis on the, vii, 220-2

Church Music, Augustine, St., on, vii, 186; Dr. Donne on, xv, 352-3

Church Services, Herbert on, xv, 400-2; Paul, St., on, xlv, 510 (26-35)

Church of England (see England, Church of)

Churchman, John, i, 201, 228, 229

Churchmen, best single, iii, 21; kings and, 51; remuneration of, x, 133-5

Churchyards, Montaigne on, xxxii, 19

Chyle, Harvey on, xxxviii, 126-7

Ci-Devant Genius, in FAUST, xix, 187

Ciacco, the glutton, in Dante's HELL, xx, 26-8

Ciampolo, in Dante's HELL, xx, 90-2

Cianghella, Dante on, xx, 351 note

Ciawani, Raleigh on the, xxxiii, 339

Cibber, Colley, THE BLIND BOY, xl, 441-2; Voltaire on, xxxiv, 139

Cibo, Cardinal, xxxi, 45

Cicero, Marcus, Tullius, the orator, Antony and, xii, 253-4, 256, 259, 322, 333-4, 335; at Athens, xxviii, 52; Atticus and, ix, 85-8, 94-7; made Augur, xii, 247; Augustine, St., on Hortense of, vii, 34; Bestia, case of, and, ix, 99-100; birth and parentage, xii, 218; brother, his love for, ix, 90-4; building ideas, 111; Cæsar and, 113, 114, 115, 116, 117, 118, 120, 121-3, 126, 127, 128, 129-30, 156, 161-3, 164-5, 169, 170-1, xii, 250-1, 252, 266-7, 270, 308, 309-10, 312; conspiracy against Cæsar, 253; after Cæsar's death, ix, 177-80; xii, 253-4; Catiline and, 226-36, 259; xxvii, 47; Cato and, ix, 135, 139, 140-1, 152-4; xii, 308; xxxii, 62; character,

79-80; ix, 101-5, 139-1; xii, 223, 224; 237, 247, 261; iii, 128; in Cilicia, ix, 135-41; xii, 247-8; in Civil War, ix, 162; xii, 248-9, 290; Clodius and, 241-6; 246-8; consulship, ix, 80-3, 84; xii, 226; Crassus and, ix, 128; on death of daughter, ix, 168-9; xii, 253; death, 258-9; at Delphi, 221; DEMOSTHENES COMPARED WITH, xii, 260-3, also 192-3; xxxix, 159; on divination, ix, 161-2; divorce, xii, 253; stories of miraculous dreams, xl, 39-42 note 66; eloquence of, xxxii, 96; exile, ix, 88-90, 92-4, 123-4; xii, 244-6; called father of his country, 227; on fear as a critic, ix, 307; flight, xii, 257; on FRIENDSHIP, ix, 7-44; on public games, 107-8; on gestures in speaking, 226 note; Greek epistles, xii, 238; on right of heirs to prosecute, ix, 173; design for a history, xii, 252; Hume on, xxxvii, 291; on husbandry, xxvii, 61-2; impeachment, xii, 242-4; Jonson on, xxvii, 56; as a lawyer, xii, 230; ix, 89, 109; Lentulus and, 118-20; LETTERS, 80-181; on his library, 100-1, 105-6; life and works, 5-7; Locke on study of, xxxvii, 157, 159, 161; Lucretius and, iii, 195; on study of lyric poets, xxxii, 53; defence of Milo, xii, 246-7; Montaigne on works of, xxxii, 94; Octavius and, xii, 254-6, 259, 334; xlvi, 28; ON OLD AGE, ix, 45-76; as an orator, xii, 221-2; on orators, iii, 109; Pascal on, xlviii, 18 (31); on philosophers, xxxiv, 333; on philosophy, xii, 251; xxxii, 9; on physical knowledge, xxiv, 9; Pliny on, ix, 185, 205, 252, 348; Plutarch's LIFE OF, xii, 218-59; as a poet, xii, 219; iii, 324; Pompey and, ix, 88, 94, 96, 113, 115-6, 120-1, 122, 122-3, 128-9, 161-2; as prætor, xii, 224-6; on his public services, ix, 84-5; quotations from, i, 82; xlviii, 121-2 notes 4, 5, 7, 14; in retirement, ix, 158-60; return from exile, 94-7, 120, 125-6; xii, 246; on Roman success, iii, 44-5; case of Roscius, xii, 219-20; instances of sarcasm, 238-41; 310, 312; case of Satyrus, ix, 82; at school, xii, 219; Senate thanks, ix, 152-4; as Senator, 88, 96, 98, 110; case of Sestius, 99, 100; Shelley on, xxvii, 334; in Sicily, xii, 222; iii, 215; Sidney on, xxvii, 28; principles of statesmanship, ix, 129; with Sylla, xii, 219; travels, 220-1; case of Vatinius, ix, 127-8; case of Verres, xii, 223; on his writings, ix, 114, 130-1, 145

Cicero, Marcus Tullius, 2d (son of the above), birth, ix, 83; Cæstius and, xxxii, 96; Cicero on, ix, 92; as consul, xii, 259; letter to, ix, 89; at school, 146, 171, 172-3, 175

Cicero, Quintus, Atticus and, ix, 85-6; Cæsar and, 113, 114, 118, 127, 129-30; in Clodian troubles, xii, 246; death of, 257; in Gallic wars, 285 note; letters to, ix, 90, 97, 110; in Parthian War, 138; with Pompey, 121-2; Pomponia and, 134; letter of, to Tiro, 175

Cichuil, in DÁ DERGA'S HOSTEL, xlix, 209, 241

Cicones, Ulysses and the, xxii, 116

Cid, The, Cervantes on, xiv, 491; Emerson on, v, 202, 213; excommunication of, xiv, 150

Cieza, Pedro de, xxxiii, 317

Cimabue, Giovanni, Dante on, xx, 189; Hazlitt on, xxvii, 279, 281

Cimaroons, of Central America, xxxiii, 134; Drake and the, 152-5, 165-84, 188, 190, 192, 194; houses of, 168; king's residence, 170; religion of, 169; Spaniards and, 166, 170; town of, 169; weapons of, 167

Cimber, Tullius, and Cæsar, xii, 317

Cimbrians, Tacitus on the, xxxiii, 113

Cimmeria, Homer on, xxii, 145

Cimon, builder of porticoes at Athens, xxviii, 40-1; commissioner to Greek confederacy, xii, 100-1; death of, 46; Emerson on, v, 265; military successes of, xii, 33; Montaigne on, xxxii, 33; at Olympic games, xii, 9; ostracism of, 44-5; Pericles and, 41, 45-6; Plato on, 104; political arts of, 44; sons of, 65; Spartans favor, 23

Cincinnatus, Cicero on, ix, 65; Dante on, xx, 307 note 12; Locke on, xxxvii, 175

CINDERELLA, story of, xvii, 98-104

Cinna, Caius Helvius, death of, xii, 319-20

Cinna, Lucius Cornelius, Cæsar, relationship to, xii, 264; Cicero on supremacy of, ix, 122; Dryden on, xiii, 15

Cioli, Francesco, xxxi, 420 note 2

Cioli, Simone, xxxi, 420 note 2

Cipango, Cabot in, xliii, 47

Circassia, inoculation in, xxxiv, 94-5

Circe, daughter of Helios, xxii, 133-4; Bacchus and, iv, 46; goddess of speech, xxii, 145; Jove, horses of, and, xiii, 248-9; Picus and, 245; songs of, iv, 51; Ulysses and, xxii, 137-44, 162-6; Ulysses's companions and, 135-6; Virgil on, xiii, 239

Circensian Games, Pliny on, ix, 335

Circles, Essay on, v, 149-60

Circulating Capital, defined, x, 215-16; four kinds of, 219; maintenance of, in regard to neat revenue, 226; necessity of, 220; sources of, 220-1

Circulation of the Blood, Descartes on, xxxiv, 39-44; Harvey on, xxxviii, 60, 62, 82-3, 86-139; Pascal on, xlviii, 41 (96)

Circumcision, ancient practice of, xxxiii, 51; the apostles on, xliv, 455-6; Dante on, xx, 421; in Egypt, xxxiii, 23, 24; Emerson on, v, 169; Pascal on, xlviii, 199, 222, 223 (672); Paul, St., on, xlv, 499 (18-19); the Quakers on, xxxiv, 66-7

CIRCUMCISION, UPON THE, iv, 40-1

Circumcision of Christ, feast of the, xv, 403

Circumstances, Emerson on indifferency of, v, 89; independence of (see Independence of C.); Johnson on, xxxix, 225; Lowell on consideration of, xxviii, 437, 442; Mill on doctrine of, xxv, 107; Penn on importance of, i, 346 (278), 347 (293); political institutions, the result of, xxiv, 148; Pope on, xl, 432

Ciriatto, the demon, xx, 88, 90

Cirongilio, of Thracia, xiv, 303-4

Cirripedes, crosses of, xi, 107; development of branchiæ of, 187; first appearance of, 327, 342; larvæ of, 461; parasitic, 151

Cisseus, death of, xiii, 332, 409

Citations, Cervantes on, xiv, 9; Emerson on, v, 71; Hugo on, xxxix, 387; Montaigne on, xxxii, 30-1

Cities, Bacon on, iii, 66; xl, 349; country and, relations of, i, 342-3; v, 203-4; x, 304; Cowley on life in, xxvii, 63-4; Emerson on, v, 224; Goldsmith on, xli, 516-18; Newman on, xxviii, 38-9; pleasures of, iv, 33; poetry and, xxvii, 66; power of inhabitants of, 368-9; Thoreau on life in, xxviii, 397-8; in Utopia, xxxvi, 174-7; Whitman on life in, xlii, 1411-12; Wordsworth on life in, xxxix, 273

Citizens, Confucius on pattern, xliv, 59 (13)

Citizenship, American, xliii, 196, 197, 198

Citizenship, M. Aurelius on, ii, 228 (22), 242 (54), 275 (6), 283 (33)

Cittern, defined, xx, 427

CITY OF BRASS, story of, xvi, 296-325

City of Destruction, xv, 15, 178

City of God, St. Augustine's, vii, 4

Civil Law, Locke on study of, xxxvii, 158

Civil Wars, Pascal on, xlviii, 109 (313)

Civilis, on the gods in war, v, 358

Civility, in children, xxxvii, 48, 103; Locke on, 123-4; Manzoni on, xxi, 489

Civility, Mr., in PILGRIM'S PROGRESS, xv, 23, 27

Civilization, Carlyle on our, xxv, 336-7; Channing on modern, xxviii, 361, 365-6; dependent of power of navigation, x, 24-6; disease and, xxxviii, 145; due to wants of men, xxiv, 178; Emerson on our, v, 80-1, 248; fire-arms and, x, 450; Hugo on progress of, xxxix, 339-45; morality and, xxxiv, 162, 187; Pope on growth of, xl, 426-3 · progress of, in relation to poetry, xxxix, 339-53; Rousseau on beginnings of, xxxiv, 198-208, 227-8; Rousseau on cost of, 169-75; Woolman on, i, 214-5

Clackitt, Mrs., in SCHOOL FOR SCANDAL, xviii, 116, 121

Clara, in EGMONT, Brackenburg and, xix, 265-7, 291-2, 315-18, 320-5; Egmont and, 268-9, 292-6, 332

Clara, Donna, in DON QUIXOTE, xiv, 431-5, 443, 446

Clare, Saint, xx, 296 note 5

Claribel, daughter of Alonso, in THE TEMPEST, xlvi, 418, 424

Claridiane, Alphebo and, xiv, 12

Clarin of Balaguet, xlix, 97

CLARINDA, MISTRESS OF MY SOUL, vi, 295

CLARINDA, VERSES TO, vi, 304-5

Clark, Dr., on Unitarianism, xxxiv, 84

Clarke, Bishop of Bath, xxxvi, 103, 109, 114

Clarke, Edward, Locke to, xxxvii, 5-7

Clarus, Septitius, letter to, ix, 202

CLASSIC, WHAT IS A, xxxii, 121-33

Classics, Arnold on, xxviii, 69; Héricault on, 68

Classical Literature, Augustine on, vii,

16-18; Browne on, iii, 273; the grotesque in, xxxix, 350; Hugo on, 346; Hume on, xxvii, 219-20; Huxley on study of, xxviii, 209-16; Locke on, xxxvii, 77; Milton on study of, iii, 199-200; Shelley on immorality in, xxvii, 336-7; Swift on study of, 110

Classification, Darwin on, xi, 136-7, 431-43; Darwin's theory, effect of, on, 502-4; embryos in, 467-8; Emerson on, v, 7; Hackel on, xi, 452; rudimentary organs in, 475

Claudian, the poet, Shelley on, xxvii, 349; Taine on, xxxix, 426

Claudine, Claudas's son, xxxv, 210

Claudius, name of, xii, 157

Claudius I, Emperor, descent of, xii, 388; famine in reign of, xliv, 448 (28); and the Jews, 462 (2); Nonianus and, ix, 199

Claudius, Appius (Cæcus), old age of, ix, 58; Pyrrhus and, 51

Claudius, Appius, the decemvir, iii, 27; Plutarch on, xii, 165

Claudius, King, in HAMLET, xlvi, 93-211; death of, 208; Gertrude and, 99, 169-70; Hamlet and, 101-2, 141, 147, 172-4, 205-7; Hamlet on, 165-6; Hamlet's father murdered by, 116; Hamlet's friends and, 124-5, 142, 159-60; Laertes and, 100, 179-81, 182-3, 184-8, 197-8, 205-7; marriage of, 99; Norway and, 100, 127; Ophelia and, 177-8; Polonius and, 127-9; remorse of, 160-1

Claudius, Publius (see Clodius)

Clauserus, on poets, xxvii, 50-1

Clausius, on freezing-point, xxx, 232

Clausus, in ÆNEIS, xiii, 263, 333

Claveret, and Corneille, xxxix, 361

Claverhouse (see BONNY DUNDEE)

Clay, Henry, in Treaty of 1814, xliii, 255, 264

Clean Beasts, texts on, interpreted, xv, 83

Cleandrides, and Pericles, xii, 59

Cleanliness, Franklin on, i, 80; Woolman on, 309

Cleante, in TARTUFFE, Damis and, xxvi, 272-80; Orgon and, 208-17, 266, 278-80, 292, 294; Mme. Pernelle and, 201, 203-4, 205-6; Tartuffe and, 262-3, 296; on Valère's marriage, 216-17

Cleanthes, Newman on, xxviii, 51; on philosophy, ii, 169 (142); remark of, xii, 110-1; verses on acquiescence, ii, 179 (184); on the voice, xxxii, 30

Cleanthes, HYMN OF, ii, 186-7

Clearness, less affecting than obscurity, xxiv, 51-4

Cleigenes, Aristophanes on, viii, 460

Cleisthenes, reference to, viii, 452

Cleitophon, pupil of Euripides, viii, 468

Cleitus, son of Mantius, xxii, 206

Clemency, in commanders, xxxvi, 56; More on, 185; pity and, xxxiv, 189; Pliny on, ix, 344; in princes, xxxvi, 53-4

Clemens, Attius, letter to, ix, 195-7, 249-50

Clement, St., of Alexandria, hymn by, xlv, 541-2

Clement, Friar, Bacon on, iii, 98

Clement V, Pope, Dante on, xx, 79 and note 4, 400 note 8, 415 note 7

Clement VII, Pope, bastard son of Medici, xxxi, 84-5 note; Cellini and, 40-1, 45, 73, 75-6, 78, 79-80, 86-7, 88-90, 91-5, 98, 104, 106, 107-9, 111-17, 119-26, 133, 135, 140-2; Charles V and, 114 note 5; the Colonnesi and, 69 note; death of, 142; election of, 33; events of life, 16 note; Foiano and, 237 and note 2; Machiavelli and, xxvii, 384, 399; reputed father of Alessandro de' Medici, xxxi, 174; in sack of Rome, 68, 70, 71, 73, 75-6, 78, 79-80, 206-7; war with Florence, 86

Clement VIII, in THE CENCI, xviii, 275, 281-2, 301, 351-2

Clemenza, Queen, xx, 319 note 1

Cleobuline, Pascal on, xlviii, 14 (13)

Cleocritus, the Corinthian, xii, 86, 98

Cleodora, daughter of Pandareüs, in the ODYSSEY, xxii, 274

Cleombrotus, in Limbo, iv, 147; not with Socrates in prison, ii, 47

Cleomenes, Emerson on, v, 183; and the Samians, xxxii, 61

Cleon, the Athenian, Aristophanes on, viii, 456; dream of, iii, 92; Pericles and, xii, 70, 72

Cleon, in POLYEUCTE, xxvi, 94, 108-9

Cleonice, called Byzantine Maid, xviii, 428

Cleopas, xliv, 417 (18); and Jesus, xv, 407

Cleopatra, at Actium, xii, 371-3; Antony and, 339-46, 349, 362-71, 375-6, 381-2; Antony's soldier and, 379-80; burial and statues of, 388; Cæsar and, 304-5; Cæsar and, Dryden on, xviii, 46-53;

Dante on death of, xx, 308, in Dante's HELL, 22; daughter of, xii, 388; death of, 386-7; death, plans for, 378; monument of, 379; Octavius and, 378-80, 382-3, 384-6; Octavius and, Dryden on, xviii, 51; Pascal on nose of, xlviii, 62-3; revels in Alexandria, xii, 378; Seleucus and, 379; Virgil on, xiii, 291-2

Cleopatra, in ALL FOR LOVE, xviii, 13; Alexas and, 88-93; Antony, her love for, 25, 28, 38-41; Antony, message to, 43-5; Antony, scenes with, 46-53, 53-4, 84-8, 100-2; death of, 103-5; Dolabella and, 58-9, 71-6; Octavia and, 14, 66-8; suicide attempted by, 89; Ventidius on, 76-7

Cleopatra, statue called, xxxi, 318

Cleophantus, son of Themistocles, xii, 33

Cleophon, Aristophanes on, viii, 459, 486-7

Cleremont, in PHILASTER, xlvii, 667-751

Clergy, Dryden on satires on the, xxxix, 164-5; Emerson on the, v, 12, 33-41, 299; Herbert on duties of the, xv, 406-7; Luther on the, xxxvi, 357; Luther on marriage of the, 302-5; maintenance of the, x, 464; More on idleness of the, xxxvi, 180; paid, remarks on a, v, 429; scandal of the, breeds atheism, iii, 44

Clergymen, as examples, xv, 395-6

Clerk, Chaucer's, xl, 19

Clerk, John, manœuvre of breaking the line, v, 358

Clermont, Lord, and Chandos, xxxv, 40-1; death of, 44

Cletus, Bishop, xx, 400 note 4

Cleveland, Grover, and Hawaii, xliii, 437 note

CLEVER ELSIE, story of, xvii, 121-3

Clifford, Lord Thomas, xxxv, 24

Clifton, John, and street-lamps, i, 120

Climate, adaptation to (see Acclimatization); æsthetic disposition and, xxxii, 283; compensations of, v, 86-7; enjoyment of life and, xxix, 258; influence of, in struggle for existence, xi, 78, 85; industry and, xxxiv, 177; jurisprudence and, xlviii, 104; martial disposition and, iii, 139; of northern and southern hemispheres, xxix, 253-4; reacts on man, xxviii, 407; relation of, to productions, xi, 378-9; Taine on effects of, xxxix, 424; variations due to, xi, 139

Climbing Plants, development of, xi, 241-3; various methods of, 185-6

Climorin, xlix, 114, 144

Cline, Henry, on inoculation, xxxviii, 198-9

Clinias, father of Alcibiades, xii, 106

Clinton, Sir Henry, Burns on, vi, 51

Clinton, Gov., story of, i, 106

Clisthenes, Aristides and, xii, 79; Plutarch on, 37

Clitandre, Molière on, xxvi, 215

Clitumnus River, Pliny on the, ix, 318

CLOAK, THE OLD, xl, 188-9

Cloanthus, in the ÆNEID, xiii, 91, 95, 182-6

Clocks, gravity, xxx, 178-9

Clodia, and Cicero, xii, 241-2; called Quadrantia, 242

Clodius, Publius, Antony and, xii, 323; Cæsar and, 276; ix, 114; Cæsar's wife and, xii, 241, 271-2; Cicero and, 242-6; ix, 6, 96, 124; death of, xii, 246; Pompey and, ix, 98, 99; trial of, xii, 241-2; widow of, 329; the soldier, and Antony, 334

CLOE, by Prior, xl, 397-8

Clœlia, reference to, xiii, 289

Clonius, in the ÆNEID, xiii, 312, 347

Clotaldo, in LIFE IS A DREAM, in battle, xxvi, 69-70; escape and recapture, 61, 68; Rosaura and, 18-21, 67-8; Segismund and, 30-1, 37-41, 52-6, 73

Cloth, garments of, xlv, 581 note 9

Clothing, demand for materials of, x, 168, 178; Locke on, xxxvii, 10-11, 15, 29; materials of, do not limit population, x, 167; price of, 203-7; price of materials of, 165-6

Clothing (see also Apparel, Dress)

Clotho, Dante on, xx, 230

CLOUD, THE, by Shelley, xli, 852-4

Clouds, on the Corcovado, xxix, 37; lesson from the, xv, 235

Clough, Arthur Hugh, POEMS by, xlii, 1119-22; reviser of Plutarch's Lives, xii, 4

Clover, and bees, xi, 81-2, 101-2

Clubs, established by Cato, ix, 61

Clusius, Charles, xxxv, 241

Clymene, in Hades, xxii, 153; mother of Phaëton, xx, 357 note 1; reference to, iv, 376

Clytemnestra, in HOUSE OF ATREUS, viii, 17-20, 29-30; Ægisthus and, 74-5; Agamemnon and, 39-40; 62-70, 98;

Cassandra and, 45-6; dream of, 99-100; ghost of, 126-7; Homer on, xxii, 39-40, 155; Orestes and, viii, 104-5, 113-17; Voltaire on, xxxix, 364

Clytius, Cydon and, xiii, 332; death of, 319

Clytoneus, in the ODYSSEY, xxii, 102

Cnossus, Governor of, and Epictetus, ii, 151 (93)

Coadjutors, Luther on, xxxvi, 283, 288

Coal, heat from burning of, xxx, 201; price of, x, 169-71

Coal-gas, cause of brightness of, xxx, 110-1; carbon in, 161

Coal-mines, rent of, x, 169, 171

Coan, Hippocrates called, xx, 266 note 15

Coati, Dana on the, xxiii, 152

Coats of Arms, Hobbes on, xxxiv, 367

Cobbett, William, Carlyle on, xxv, 408, 445

Cobham, Raynold, in Crecy campaign, xxxv, 8, 11, 19, 24, 30, 33; at Poitiers, 42, 51, 52, 54

Cobites, alimentary canal of, xi, 185

Cock, lesson on the, xv, 251-2

Cock, Thoreau on the, xxviii, 424

COCK AND FOX, fable of, xvii, 34

COCK AND HORSES, fable of, xxvii, 133

COCK AND PEARL, fable of, xvii, 11; Bacon on, iii, 33

Cock-Fights, Blake on, xli, 587

Cockatrix, fabulous serpent, xlvii, 836 note 3

Cockburn, Alexander, in Jamaica case, xxv, 183

Cockburn, Alison R., FLOWERS OF THE FOREST, xli, 482

COCKPEN, THE LAIRD O', xli, 563-4

Cocles, Horatius, Virgil on, xiii, 289

Cocoanut Trees, Francis Pretty on, xxxiii, 202

Cocoanuts, Biggs on, xxxiii, 236

Cocytus, Dante on the, xx, 60; Homer on, xxii, 143; Milton on, iv, 123; Plato on, ii, 109; Virgil on, xiii, 212

Codes, the conscience of nations, v, 246

Codfish, Hayes on the, xxxiii, 275

Cœlius, at Actium, xii, 372

Coffee, Burke on the taste for, xxiv, 15

Cog-wheels, considered as levers, xxx, 183-4

Cohesion, Faraday on, xxx, 25-43

Cohn, on bacteria, xxxviii, 326 note

Coila, Burns on, vi, 87-8, 239

Coilus, king of Picts, vi, 175 note 7

Coinage, expense of, x, 358, 454; origin of, 30; regulation of, by Congress, xliii, 163-4, 165, 184 (5)

Coke, Sir Edward, Burke on, xxiv, 170

Colbert, Jean Baptiste, administration of, x, 426; policy of, 347

Colchians, Herodotus on the, xxxiii, 50-1

Cold, Locke on endurance of, xxxvii, 10, 11, 14

COLD'S THE WIND, xl, 318

Coleman, Mr., EPILOGUE by, xviii, 196-7

Coleman, William, i, 58, 61, 62

Coleridge, Hartley, SHE IS NOT FAIR, xli, 912

Coleridge, Samuel Taylor, Arnold on, xxviii, 81; Bagehot on, 203; Emerson on, v, 318-21; 440-1; on fancy, xxxix, 307; on French Language, v, 388-9; life and works of, xxvii, 254; Mill on, xxv, 51, 102-3; on Milton's Satan, xxviii, 199; POEMS by, xli, 682-732; ON POESY OR ART, xxvii, 255-63; Wordsworth on, v, 325

Colewort, only medicine in Rome, xxxv, 240

Colgrevance, Sir, xxxv, 176-7

Coligni, Burke on, xxiv, 186

Coliseum, Byron's lines on the, xviii, 445

COLLAR, THE, xl, 343-4

Colleagues, Confucius on sordid, xliv, 59 (15)

College Men, Franklin on, i, 15

College of the Six Days' Works (see Solomon's House)

Colleges, Carlyle on use of, xxv, 364; genius and, v, 423; office of, 11; study of dead matter in, 257

Collier, Jeremy, xxxix, 157 note 6, 173-4

Collingwood, Admiral, Emerson on, v, 348, 358, 377

Collins, Anthony, Burke on, xxiv, 225

Collins, John, friend of Franklin, i, 15, 22, 28, 31, 32-4, 37

Collins, John, the poet, TO-MORROW, xli, 592-3

Collins, Michael, case of, xxviii, 121-3

Collins, William, POEMS by, xli, 475-81; Wordsworth on poems of, xxxix, 325

Collinson, Peter, Franklin on, i, 146-7, 159

Colnett, on discolored sea, xxix, 26-7; on lizards, 389-90; on Galapagos Islands, 395-6

Colonia del Sacramento, xxix, 149

Colonies, Bacon on, iii, 85-7; motive of

establishing, x, 395-404; in subject states, xxxvi, 10-11; wages and profits in, x, 94

Colonna, Fabrizio, xxvii, 392

Colonna, House of, and Clement VII, xxxi, 69 note

Colonna, Stefano, xxxi, 367 note

Colonna Infame, story of, xxi, 4-6

Colonnades, Burke on, xxiv, 64, 113

Colonnesi, Alexander VI and the, xxxvi, 23-4; Orsini and, 39-40; Valentino and, 24

Color, beauty and, xxiv, 95-6, 127-8; Berkeley and, xxxvii, 202-3, 265; cause of, xxxiv, 122-3; climate and, xi, 139; constitutional peculiarities and, 27-8; Goethe on operation of, xxxix, 257; Hume on, xxxvii, 302; importance of, to animals, xi, 92, 199; nature of, illustrated, xxx, 261-2; as source of the sublime, xxiv, 69

Colpoda, Pasteur on, xxxviii, 337, 342

Columba, Renan on, xxxii, 172, 174

Columbus, Christopher, Emerson on, v, 81; Smith on, x, 398; Voltaire on, xxxiv, 100

COLUMBUS, LETTER OF, xliii, 21-7

COLUMBUS, PRAYER OF, xlii, 1420-2

Columbus, Realdus, on the circulation, xxxviii, 97; on the heart, 70; on the lungs, 67

Columella, on agriculture, xxvii, 64-5; on country life, 61; on enclosures, x, 157; on flowers, xxxv, 238; on vineyards, x, 158

Combe, George, xxviii, 210 note

Combination, of capitalists, x, 68; Mill on liberty of, xxv, 206; to fix wages, x, 145; of workmen, 69

Combustion, of carbon and other substances compared, xxx, 161-2, 168-9; chemical affinity, the cause of, 56-7; with and without flame, 105-6; heat generated by, 200-1; oxygen necessary to, 57-8, 104-5; illustrations of, in oxygen, 48-9, 55-6, 137-8; water produced by, 113-5

COME, LET ME TAKE THEE TO MY BREAST, vi, 470-1

COME UNDER MY PLAIDIE, xli, 577-8

Comedy, burlesque and, xxxix, 177-8; Cervantes on, xiv, 477-82; Fielding on epic, xxxix, 176; Hugo on, 346-51, 356; Hume on standards of, xxvii, 218-9; Johnson on, xxxix, 213, 223;

Macaulay on wit in, xxvii, 383-4; M. Aurelius on, ii, 286 (6); popular notions of, xxxix, 214-5; Sidney on, xxvii, 27, 45-6; Voltaire on translations of, xxxiv, 139-40

Comenius, John Amos, iii, 236 note

Comestor, Petrus, xx, 338 note 33

Comets, Bacon on effects of, iii, 137; nature and motion of, xxxiv, 118

Comfort, Confucius on, xliv, 45 (3); Kempis on, vii, 237 (9), 239 (4), 247-9, 269-78

COMIC EPIC IN PROSE, Fielding's, xxxix, 176-81

Comines, Philip de, on England, v, 356; Montaigne on, xxxii, 101

Cominius, Roman consul, xii, 152-3, 154; names Coriolanus, 156

Comitatus, institution of the, xlix, 77 note 2

Commandments, The Ten, Locke on, xxxvii, 132; Milton on giving of, iv, 348; More on, xxxvi, 150

Commendams, Luther on, xxxvi, 283, 288

Commendation, St. Augustine on, vii, 56

Commentators, Johnson on, xxxix, 241-9; Locke on, xxxvii, 169; Montaigne on, xxxii, 107; Voltaire on, xxxiv, 132

Commerce, in agricultural system, x, 431-5, 438-42; Bacon on, in ancient times, iii, 156-7, 159; capital used in, x, 290, 292, 295-302; domestic, sacrificed to foreign, 316; favored above agriculture, 6; foreign (see Foreign Commerce); Harrison on, xxxv, 224-5; honor and, xli, 522-3; interferences with, by landed nations, x, 436; internal, 304, 444-5; language and, xxxix, 202; military spirit and, xxvii, 373-4; necessity of, x, 23-4, 288; regulation of (U. S.), xliii, 184 (3), 185 (6); Wordsworth on, xli, 677; works and institutions for facilitating, x, 453-63 (see also Trade)

Commercial Policy, Washington on our, xliii, 246-7

Commercial Pursuits, Emerson on, v, 45

Commercial System, x, 311-31; Channing on the, xxviii, 361; Emerson on the, v, 45-7; false relations under, 255, Harrison on, xxxv, 225; More on, xxxvi, 181; origin of, x, 27; producers and consumers under, 424-5; results of, v, 400-1; Ruskin on the, xxviii, 116;

Tennyson on the, xlii, 1015-16; ways of trade under, v, 45-6

Commercial Treaties, Smith on, x, 389-94

COMMISSARY GOLDIE'S BRAINS, vi, 459

Commissions, Bacon on standing, iii, 55

Commodus, Machiavelli on, xxxvi, 64, 66, 68; statue called, xxxi, 318 note 1

Common, Dorothy (see Dol Common)

Common Law, suits at, in U. S., xliii, 195 (7); Winthrop on the, 104

Common Sense, Dryden on, xxxix, 163; Epictetus on, ii, 150 (90); limitations of, xxviii, 415; Montaigne on, xlviii, 392, 395; in morals, Kant on, xxxii, 316-7

Common Things, Emerson on, v, 20; Penn on, i, 329 (68)

Commons, House of, Voltaire on, xxxiv, 89-91

Commonwealth, English (see Instrument of Government)

Commonwealths, More on, xxxvi, 236

Commotions, Calvin on, xxxix, 43-5

Communion, holy, Bunyan on, xv, 233-4; Calvin on, xxxix, 37; Kempis on, vii, 335-64; St. Paul on, xlv, 503 (16-17); Quakers on, xxxiv, 67; Rousseau on, 303

Communism, Emerson on, v, 259-60; instituted by Christ, xxxvi, 226; Lowell on, xxviii, 469; More on, xxxvi, 167-9, 184-5, 186, 189-90, 236, 238-9, 240

Commutative Justice, Hobbes on, xxxiv, 406

Como, Lake, Manzoni on, xxi, 7

Compacts, Mohammed on, xlv, 916

Companies, regulated and joint-stock, x, 458-9

Company, Confucius on, xliv, 29 (29), 54 (39); determines manners, xxxvii, 124-5; Epictetus on choice of, ii, 166 (137); Epictetus on vulgar, 153 (99), 156 (107), 175 (167); Kempis on, vii, 212; Locke on importance of, xxxvii, 50, 127; Massinger on, xlvii, 870; Pascal on choice of, xlviii, 12 (6); St. Paul on, with evil-doers, xlv, 497 (9-13); Penn on, i, 335 (128); of strong and weak, xvii, 31

Comparison, necessary to criticism, xxxix, 208-9

Comparisons, Goethe on, xxxix, 256; Hume on, xxvii, 213; Wordsworth on, xxxix, 313

Compass, of the Phœnicians, v, 458

Compass-flower, xlii, 1333

Compassion, Augustine, St., on, vii, 32; Bacon on, iii, 34; Hobbes on, xxxiv, 342-3; Pliny on, ix, 353 note (see also Pity, Sympathy)

Compensation, Darwin on growth of, xi, 150-2; Epictetus on, ii, 126 (27); Gray on, xl, 461-2; Pope on, in nature, 412; of pleasure and pain, Socrates on, ii, 48; Whitman on, xxxix, 404-5

COMPENSATION, ESSAY ON, Emerson's, v, 85-103

Competition, as cause of quarrels, xxxiv, 388-9; excessive, generates fraud, xxviii, 316; Hobbes on, xxxiv, 370; of labor, restraints on, x, 121-33, 137-46; of labor, unnaturally encouraged, 133-38; Mazzini on, xxxii, 380-1; necessary to good management, x, 150-1; in professions, 133-6; as regulator of prices, 57-8; results of, v, 400

Competitive Prices, tendency to minimum, x, 63

Competitive System, Ruskin on the, xxviii, 132

Complacency, Penn on, i, 337

COMPLAINT OF THE ABSENCE OF HER LOVER, xl, 193-4

Complaints, of children, xxxvii, 90; Kempis on, vii, 228 (6)

Complaisance, Hobbes on, xxxiv, 407

Compleat Angler, Walton's, xv, 322

Compliance, Cicero on, ix, 39-40; Locke on, xxxvii, 122

Compliments, Bacon on, iii, 126

Compositæ, Darwin on, xi, 149, 215, 470

Composition, Hume on, xxvii, 206

Compositions, Luther on papal, xxxvi, 286

Compound Animals, Darwin on, xxix, 207

Compound Fractures, Lister on, xxxviii, 257-9, 262-3

Compound Words, Johnson on, xxxix, 189-90

Comprehension, Raleigh on, xxxix, 103 note

Compromise of 1850, xliii, 306 note

Compromises, Lowell on, xxviii, 462; Mill on, xxv, 57; with sin, xlii, 1371

Compulsion, Locke on, in education, xxxvii, 57, 174

Compunction, Kempis on, vii, 225 (5), 226-7

Comte, Auguste, Mill on, xxv, 104-5, 131-3, 152 note 3, 208

Comus: A Mask, iv, 44-72; Bagehot on, xxviii, 205-6; at Ludlow Castle, v, 411

Conaire, story of, xlix, 202-47

Conall Cernach, xlix, 226-7, 231-2, 243, 244, 247-8

Conceit, Æsop's fable of, xvii, 20; Epictetus on, ii, 143 (72); results of, xxxiv, 353; Smith on, of mankind, x, 109

Conceit, country of, in PILGRIM'S PROGRESS, xv, 126

Concentration, Buddha on, xlv, 702-4, 705, 728

Concepcion, Chili, earthquake at, xxix, 307-13

Conception, Point, Dana on, xxiii, 69; gale off, 212-19

Conceptions, Berkeley on, xxxvii, 219-20; Descartes on reality of, xxxiv, 29, 34; Hobbes on impossible, 323; Taine on various kinds of, xxxix, 419-20

Conchenn, the giant, xlix, 239

Concini, wife of, v, 186

Concino, Bartolommeo, xxxi, 430 note

Conciseness, Pliny on, ix, 204; Pope on, xl, 407

Concord, even among devils, iv, 121

CONCORD HYMN, xlii, 1245-6

Concrete Qualities, due to participation in abstracts, ii, 94-5

Concy, Raoul of, xxxv, 35-6

Condé, Prince of (Louis I of Bourbon), constable at Bourges, xxxviii, 46; at Danvilliers, 19-20; in Germany, 18-19; at Metz, 23; at Turin, 9; wounded at St. Denis, 50; wounded at St. Quentin, 44-5

Condé "the Great," before Rocroi, xxi, 25; at Seneffee, xxxix, 174

Condell, Henry, PREFACE TO SHAKESPEARE, xxxix, 148-9

Condillac, Abbé de, on languages, xxxiv, 180; Mill on, xxv, 43-7

Condiments, Locke on, xxxvii, 16-17

Conditions of Life, direct and indirect effects of, xi, 24-6, 138-40; effect of changed, on fertility, 302; law of, 207; slight changes in, beneficial, 303; Taine on, xxxix, 423-5

Condolence, Sulpicius on, ix, 165; Pliny on, 274

Condor, Darwin on the, xxix, 187-191

Condorcet, Burke on, xxiv, 420; death of,

alluded to, 216 note; Life of Turgot by, xxv, 73

Conduct, Buddha on, xlv, 702-4; not motives, to be judged, xxv, 35-6; Penn's rules of, i, 334

Confectionery, Locke on, xxxvii, 21

CONFEDERATION, ARTICLES OF, xliii, 158-68

Conference, maketh a ready man, iii, 122

Confervæ, Darwin on, xxix, 24-7

Confession, Augustine, St., on, vii, 62; Dante on, xx, 272 (note 2); Herbert on, xv, 400; Kempis on, vii, 281 (1); Luther on, xxxvi, 306, 364; Pascal on, xlviii, 44

CONFESSIONS OF ST. AUGUSTINE, vii, 5-197

Confidence, between parents and children, xxxvii, 81-2; daughter of fortune, iii, 100; Hobbes on, xxxiv, 340-1, 365; Kempis on over-, vii, 225 (4); in self, Emerson on, v, 59-63, 67; Epictetus on, ii, 120 (9)

Confiscations, Burke on, xxiv, 288, 289; Machiavelli on, xxxvi, 55, 59

Conformity, Burke on, xxiv, 44; Emerson on, v, 62, 64-5; Mill on, xxv, 157, 251, 253, 256, 264-5; Milton on, in religion, iii, 228-9; Penn on, i, 392-3

Confucius, the basket-bearer on, xliv, 49; Chi Huan and, 61 (4), note 3; Chieh-yü and, 61 (5); Duke Ching and, 61 (3); the gate-keeper on, 49 (41); habits and character of, 6 (10), 21 (4), 22 (9-12-13), 22 (17), 23 (20), 23 (26), 24 (31), 24 (37), 27 (4, 9), 30-2; on himself, 7 (4), 17-8 (25, 27), 21 (1), 21 (2, 3, 5, 7, 8), 22 (10, 11), 22 (16), 22-3 (18), 23 (19, 20, 22, 23), 23 (27, 29), 24 (32), 24 (33), 27 (2), 27 (6, 7, 8), 28 (15), 32 (1), 42 (10), 48 (30), 49 (37), 51 (2), 63 (8); in K'nang, 28 note, 35 (22); life and works, 3; Sainte-Beuve on, xxxii, 130; story of, v, 454; on his teachings, xliv, 13 (15), 16 (12), 23 (23), 23 (24), 27 (1); on tiger-skins, xxviii, 416; Tzu-kung on, xliv, 65 (22) note 6, 65-6 (23), 66 (24-5); the warden of Yi on, 12 (24); wanderings of, 61-2

CONFUCIUS, SAYINGS OF, xliv, 5-67; remarks on SAYINGS, 3

Confusion, and grandeur, xxiv, 66; worse confounded, iv, 133

Congregation Day, Mohammedan, xlv, 942 note 2

Congress, power to propose amendments, xliii, 191 (5); power to incorporate banks, 209-10, 212-16, 222-4; under the Confederation, 159-60 (5), 162-5 (9); under the Constitution, 180-6; power to establish courts, 189 (1); powers forbidden to, 194 (1); implied powers of, 212-22; relations with President, 189; power to prescribe proofs of state records, 190; power to admit new states, 191 (1); power over territories, 191 (2); power to punish treason, 190

Congress of 1774, xliii, 206-7

Congreve, William, comedies of, xxxix, 233; Dryden and, xiii, 67; Macaulay on, xxvii, 383-4; Voltaire on, xxxiv, 139; Wordsworth on, xxxix, 330

Conio, Alberigo of, xxxvi, 44

Conjectural Criticism, Johnson on, xxxix, 246-7

Connate Ones, the seven, xlv, 612

CONNECTICUT, THE FUNDAMENTAL ORDERS OF, xliii, 60-5

Conon, at Ægospotami, xii, 144

Conquered States, arms in, xxxvi, 69; factions in, 69-70; Machiavelli on, 8-12, 18

Conquerors, Jesus on, iv, 386

Conquerors, Locke on, xxxvii, 102

Conquest, Hobbes on right of, xxxiv, 388; More on foreign, xxxvi, 159-60; Rousseau on right of, xxxiv, 213; vanity of, xl, 253

Conrad III. and Cacciaguida, xx, 351 note 15

Conradino, of Naples, xx, 227 note 10

Conrayer, Father, xxxiv, 80, 96

Conscience, Bacon on matters of, iii, 14; Beaumont on, xlvii, 672; Carlyle on, xxv, 325; Cenci on, xviii, 326; Dante on, xx, 118, 153; Emerson on, v, 62; Epictetus on power of good, ii, 161 (119); Goethe on persistency of, xix, 21; Hobbes on, xxxiv, 347; intellect and, xxviii, 323; Kempis on good, vii, 244; liberty and, v, 246; liberty of, Vane on, xliii, 122-4; Mill on liberty of, xxv, 210-49; Milton on liberty of, iii, 221-7; Pascal on rest and security of, xlviii, 312; Raleigh on, xxxix, 70; Rousseau on, xxxiv, 239-40, 268-75; Webster on guilty, xlvii, 830, 851

Consciousness, Carlyle on, xxv, 332; in death and rebirth, xlv, 681-2; of modern society, xxv, 334; origin of, xxxii, 263

Consecration, Luther on, xxxvi, 266

CONSERVATION OF FORCE, Helmholtz on, xxx, 171-210; discovery of the law, 175; statement of the law, 176, 208-9

Conservatism, Burke on, xxiv, 290, 377; Emerson on, v, 264; Lowell on, xxviii, 470

Conservatism, false, Smith on, xxvii, 225-51

Consideration, Penn on, want of, i, 325, 345 (263)

Considius, the Senator, Cæsar and, xii, 275-6

Consigne, Queen, and the mastiff, xxxv, 354

Consistency, Confucius on, xliv, 53 (36); Emerson on, v, 66-7

Consolation, fallacy of false, xxvii, 242; for death, God alone can give, vi, 273; Kempis on, vii, 252 (3), 217-8; Kempis on inward, 258-334; Pascal on, xlviii, 331, 338-9; Pliny on, ix, 274; in public calamities, xxxii, 117; Sulpicius on, ix, 165

Conspicuousness, why honorable, xxxiv, 366

Conspiracies, Machiavelli on, xxxvi, 60-1

Constable, Henry, DIAPHENIA, xl, 228-9

Constable, Thomas, translator of Corneille, xxvi, 75

Constance, Council of, xxxvi, 317-8

Constance, wife of Henry VI, xx, 296 note 7

Constancy, hyacinth, the flower of, vi, 407; Penn on, i, 334 (119)

CONSTANT LOVER, THE, xl, 353

CONSTANT TIN SOLDIER, THE, xvii, 293-7

Constantine the Great, and Council of Nicæa, xxxvi, 273; Dante on, xx, 80 note 10; 278 note 11, 305 note 1, 371 notes 7, 8; the Donation of, xxxvi, 295 note; and the nails of the cross, iii, 280; sons of, 50; Sylvester and, xx, 80 note 10, 113

Constitution, first written, xliii, 60 note; Lowell on an unwritten, xxviii, 468

Constitution, Holmes on the frigate, xlii, 1366 note

CONSTITUTION OF UNITED STATES, xliii, 180-98; the act of the people, not of States, 210-11, 212; defended in Fed-

eralist, 199-207; Hamilton on the, 199-203; implied powers under the, 212-22; Lincoln on the, 316, 317-18, 320-1; Lowell on framers of the, xxviii, 461-2; powers of nation and state under, xliii, 208-9, 210-12, 215, 216, 224; Washington on the, 239, 240

Constitutional Convention, Jay on, xliii, 205-6, 207; suggested by Vane, 133

"Constitutional Society," Burke on the, xxiv, 145

Consulates, expense of, x, 458

Consumers, sacrificed in Commercial System, x, 424

Consumption, annual, dependent on annual labor, x, 5; the end of production, 424; immediate and durable, 275; productive and unproductive, 259, 266-70; taxes on, 517-48; unproductive, More on, xxxvi, 181; unproductive, Smith on, x, 233

Contagious Diseases, Holmes on, xxxviii, 226 (3); Jenner on, 163-4

Contemplation, activity and, ii, 125 (24); Buddha on, xlv, 705, 729; Burke on, xxiv, 39, 46-7; Epictetus on duty of, ii, 121 (13, 14), 141 (68); Hindu ideal of, xlv, 814-5; Kempis on, vii, 250 (3), 296 (3), 320 (1); Mill on, xxv, 94; Montaigne on, xxxii, 9; More on, xxxvi, 206-7, 229; Pascal on, xlviii, 59 (146); Plutarch on proper objects of, xii, 35-6; Rousseau on, xxxiv, 279; Schiller on, xxxii, 280; two ways of, xxxix, 117

Contempt, Bacon on, iii, 135-6; Hobbes on, xxxiv, 338, 364; Kempis on self, vii, 274 (1); Locke on, xxxvii, 121; Rousseau on beginnings of, xxxiv, 204-5

CONTENT, by Greene, xl, 282-3

CONTENT AND RESOLUTE, xl, 329

CONTENT, O SWEET, xl, 318-19

CONTENTED WI' LITTLE AND CANTIE WI' MAIR, vi, 507-8

Contentment, Epictetus on, ii, 118 (6), 121 (14), 127 (31), 159 (114), 163 (127), 165 (133), 179 (182), 184 (17)

CONTENTMENT, by Holmes, xlii, 1368-70

Contentment, Kempis on, vii, 211 (2), 286 (5); Marcus Aurelius on, ii, 201 (5), 204 (13), 211 (16), 211 (3), 216 (23), 216 (25), 233 (11), 241-2 (49, 50), 247 (27), 255 (7), 257 (26), 274 (1), 283 (35), 286 (7), 292 (20); Rousseau on, xxxiv, 261; Shelley on,

xli, 827; wealth and, 522-3; Woolman on, i, 214; work necessary to, 141 (see also Acquiescence, Independence of Circumstances, Tranquillity)

Contiguity of ideas, xxxvii, 304, 327-8

Continental Congress, xliii, 150 note, 158 note

CONTINENTAL DRAMA, xxvi

Continents, Darwin on, xi, 347; Geikie on evolution of, xxx, 328-51; are rising areas, xxix, 484; species, affinity of, in same, xi, 380-1

Continuity, Pascal on, xlviii, 119-20

Contracts, Descartes on, xxxiv, 22; Hobbes on, 394-400, 414; known only to man, x, 18; laws impairing, forbidden in U. S., xliii, 186; Mill on freedom of, xxv, 298-300

Contradiction, Locke on, xxxvii, 122, 125; Montaigne on, xxxii, 41; Pascal on, xlviii, 126; Penn on, i, 337 (149)

Contraries, the life of each other, iii, 316; in temper and distemper, 49

Contrast of ideas, xxxvii, 305 (note 4)

Contrite, Mr., in PILGRIM'S PROGRESS, xv, 280-1, 283

Contrition, Dante on, xx, 272 note 2; Kempis on, vii, 321; Luther on, xxxvi, 252-3; Pascal on, xlviii, 317 (923)

Controversies, Bacon on, iii, 12; Browne on religious, 256-7; Franklin on habit of, i, 15, 126; Penn on, 340 (184); truth and, xxxiv, 54; uncertainty indicated by, xlviii, 310 (902); unsettled, iii, 314-5

Contumely, Hobbes on, xxxiv, 408

Conveniences, Rousseau on, xxxiv, 202

Convention, society loves, v, 210

Conventionalities, Lowell on xxviii, 439

Convents, Luther on, xxxvi, 301-2, 305-6, 326

Convergence of Character, xi, 132-3

Conversation, attention to, ii, 243 (4), 247 (30); Bacon on, iii, 83-5; Emerson on, v, 154; Epictetus's rules of, ii, 175 (164), 176 (171), 177 (175); Franklin on the ends of, i, 18; Goethe on, xxxix, 253; Kempis on, vii, 213; one to one, v, 113-4; Penn on, i, 335-6 (see also Intercourse)

CONVERSATION, ESSAY ON, Swift's, xxvii, 91-8

Conversini, Benedetto, governor of Rome, xxxi, 203-4, 224

Conversion, joy in, of men, vii, 122;

Pascal on, xlviii, 383-6; true, Emerson on, v, 32

Conveyances, in Massachusetts, xliii, 68 (14, 15)

Conviction, Epictetus on, ii, 153-4 (99); is genius, v, 60; necessary to persuasion, xix, 30

Convicts, children of, moral sentiment of, v, 244-5; More on, xxxvi, 151-4

Conway, Gen., i, 136

Cook, Chaucer's, xl, 21; Dryden on Chaucer's, xxxix, 166-7

Cook, Capt., on kelp, xxix, 244

Cook, Lady (see Danvers, Jane), xv (418)

Cook, Sir Robert, xv, 418

Cookery, Penn on, i, 329 (61)

Cooper, Fenimore, Carlyle on, xxv, 393-4, 397

Cooper, Joseph, i, 54

COOPER O' CUDDY, vi, 527

Coöperation, conscious and unconscious, ii, 240 (42); of labor (see Division of Labor); man made for, ii, 200 (1); in nature, 219 (40, 45), 239 (38), 240 (43), 244 (9)

Cope, Prof., on reproduction period, xi, 187

Copenhagen, battle of, v, 345; industries of, x, 264

Copernicus, Nicolaus, life and works, xxxix, 52 note; misunderstood, v, 66; Pascal on opinion of, xlviii, 80 (218); REVOLUTIONS OF HEAVENLY BODIES, xxxix, 52-7

Copiapo, town of, xxix, 358; valley of, 353-4

Copiers, Horace on, xiii, 39

Copland, on puerperal fever, xxxviii, 254

Copley Medal, given to Franklin, i, 149

Copper, action of nitric acid on, xxx, 128

Copulation, unnatural, in Massachusetts law, xliii, 80 (7, 8)

Copyrights, provision for, xliii, 184 (8)

Coquimbo, earthquake at, xxix, 346-7; terraces at, 347; town of, 346

Coral formations, Darwin on, xxix, 406, 456-85; Lyell on, xxxviii, 406, 409-10

Corallines, Darwin on, xxix, 206

Corals, fish feeding on, xxix, 468; stinging, 468; unable to live out of water, 465

Coras, ally of Turnus, xiii, 262

Corbet, Richard, FAREWELL, REWARDS AND FAIRIES, xl, 315-16

CORBIES, THE TWA, xl, 74

Corcovado, Mount, Brazil, xxix, 37-8; Chiloe, 279, 295

Cord, proverb of the, iii, 39

Cordelia, in KING LEAR, xlvi, 217; disowned by father, 218-9, 223; rejected by Burgundy, 223; grief for father's misfortunes, 287-8; her suitors, 216-7, 221-2; letter to Kent, 251; ordered to be hanged, 316; remarks on character of, 214; taken by France, 223; taken prisoner, 306; with doctor in French camp, 288-9; with Kent, 300; with father at his awakening, 301-3

Cordilleras (see Andes)

Cordova, Gonzalo Fernandez de, in Mantuan contest, xxi, 434-6, 466-8

Corellia, Pliny and, ix, 256-7, 303-4

Corellius, Pliny on, ix, 256-7, 261, 340

Corfinius, in Civil War, xii, 300; house of, 306

Cori, Smith on the, x, 399

CORIDON, PHILLIDA AND, xl, 196-7

CORINNA SINGS, xl, 285

CORINNA'S MAYING, xl, 339-40

CORINNA TO TANAGRA, xli, 899-900

Corinth, Christian Church of, xlv, 489

CORINTHIANS, EPISTLES TO THE, xlv, 489-532

Corinthians, crafts most respected among, xxxiii, 83

Coriolanus, accusations against, xii, 162-3; ALCIBIADES, COMPARED WITH, 186-90; Antiates, inroad of, into, 158; banishment of, 165-7; character of, 147-8; consulship, defeat of, for, 158-9; Johnson on, xxxix, 239; love of, for mother, xii, 150; on the multitude, 161; name, origin of, 156; reprieved, 163-5; Rome, in war against, 171-7; seditions of the poor and, 150-1, 152, 158-9; training of, to arms, 148; trial and death of, 184; among the Volscians, 167-9; in Volscian War, 152-6; war, first experience in, 148-9

CORIOLANUS, PLUTARCH'S LIFE OF, xii, 147-85

Cormac Condlongas, xlix, 218-9, 244-5

Cormac, King of Ulaid, xlix, 201

Cormorant, Harrison on the, xxxv, 340

Cormorants, habits of, xxix, 203-4

Corn, Cicero on growth of, ix, 63-4; duties on importation of, x, 522, 340-1; as measure of value, 38-9, 42; parable of the, xv, 205; price of, as affected by bounties, x, 375-6, 382-3; prices of, 12;

real value of, 385; Rousseau on, xxxiv, 206

Cornaro, Francesco, xxxi, 144 note, 145, 170, 212, 221-2, 227-8

Cornaro, Marco, xxxi, 46 note

Cornaro, Pietro, xxxi, 112 note 4

Cornbury, Lord, lines to, xxvii, 273

Corneille, and his critics, xxxix, 361-3; Hugo on, 372-3; Hugo on *Athalie* of, 354; Hume on POLYEUCTE of, xxvii, 221; on length of the drama, xiii, 7; life and works, xxvi, 76; on love, xlviii, 62-3 (162); Macaulay on, xxvii, 383; POLYEUCTE, xxvi, 77-130; Sainte-Beuve on, xxxii, 124; Shakespeare and, xxxix, 357; Voltaire and, 426; Voltaire on *Pompey* of, xxxiv, 135

Cornelia, vestal virgin, ix, 253-4

Cornelia, in Dante's Limbo, xx, 20

Cornelia, wife of Cæsar, xii, 264, 267

Cornelianus, letter to, ix, 294-7

Cornelius, Caius, prophecy of Pharsalia, xii, 303

Cornelius, the centurion, xliv, 444-6 (1-48)

Cornelius, in DR. FAUSTUS, xix, 209-11

Cornelius, in HAMLET, xlvi, 100, 126-7

Corners, of corn, in Elizabethan England, xxxv, 245-7, 249-50

Cornhill Magazine, xxviii, 5

Cornificius, in Civil War, xii, 300 note; fellow candidate of Cicero, ix, 81

Cornwall, tin-mines of, x, 172

Cornwall, Duke of, in LEAR, xlvi, given part of kingdom, 215, 216, 219; at Gloucester's, 244-5; with Kent and Oswald, 246-9; death of, reported, 285-6, 303; Edmund and, with Gloucester's letter, 273; reported war with Albany, 242, 262; with Gloucester, 277-80; with Lear, 255, 257, 258, 261

Cornwall, in SHOEMAKER'S HOLIDAY, xlvii, 532

Cornwallis, Burns on, vi, 51; surrender of, xliii, 169-73

Corœbus, builder of Eleusis, xii, 50; death of, xiii, 114; in sack of Troy, 111-4

CORONACH, by Scott, xli, 747

Coroner's Juries, in Massachusetts, xliii, 74 (57)

Corporal Punishment, of children, xxxii, 56; xxxvii, 35-7, 38-40, 41, 56, 60-3, 65-6, 67-8, 93-4; in Massachusetts, xliii, 73 (46)

Corporations, Burke on punishment of,

xxiv, 274-5; Hobbes on, xxxiv, 415-6; power of Congress to create, xliii, 212-16, 222-3; Smith on, x, 460-2; trade, 121-33

Corpre, son of Conaire, xlix, 224

Corpse, in THE FROGS, viii, 444

Corpuscularians, xxxvii, 165

Correcting, Pascal on, xlviii, 12 (9)

Correction, acceptance of, ii, 236 (21); advantages of, xlviii, 172 (535); in anger, i, 346 (271), 347 (289-90); of children, xxxvii, 103-4; Marcus Aurelius on, of others, ii, 195 (10), 275 (4), 290-1; reason of anger under, xlviii, 35 (80) (see also Punishment)

Corrections, Locke on, xxxvii, 125

Correggio, Hazlitt on, xxvii, 278

Correlated Variation, xi, 27-8, 147-50; instances of, 199

CORRELATION OF PHYSICAL FORCES, Faraday on, xxx, 73-85

Corruption, implies goodness, vii, 111; Locke on, xxxvii, 54; in public affairs, iii, 29-30

Corsablis, King, xlix, 123, 133

Corsets, Locke on, xxxvii, 15

Corsica, Freeman on, xxviii, 256

Corso Donati (see Donati)

Cortese, Tommaso, xxxi, 94 note, 108 note

Cortez, Keats on, xli, 896; Raleigh on, xxxiii, 317, 330

Coruncanius, Tiberius, ix, 15, 24, 60

Coruncanius, Titus, ix, 55

Corvées, defined, x, 457

Corvus, M. Valerius, old age of, ix, 67

Cory, William Johnson, poems by, xlii, 1113-14

Corybantes, reference to the, viii, 373

Corycian Rock, the, viii, 123

Corydon, and Thyrsis, iv, 32

Corynæus, xiii, 215, 400

Coseguina, eruption of, xxix, 295-6

Cosimo, St., xxxi, 156 note 1

Cosington, Sir Thomas, xxxv, 65

Cosmography, Hobbes on, xxxiv, 363

Cosmos, the, ii, 236 (25); Milton's ideas of, iv, 245-7 (see also Universe)

Cosmus, Duke of Florence, on faithless friends, iii, 15; calm nature of, iii, 104-5

Cossus, Virgil on, xiii, 236

Cost of Living (see Food-supply)

Costanza, Queen of Arragon, xx, 156 note 5, 174 note 14

Costiveness, Locke on, xxxvii, 23-5
Costume (see Dress)
Cotta, Lucius, Cicero on, xii, 240
Cotta, Publius, Cicero on, xii, 239
Cottage, and palace, vi, 139
Cotters, life of, Burns on, vi, 152-4;
　Scotch, x, 119
COTTER'S SATURDAY NIGHT, THE, vi, 134-
　40; an idyllic poem, xxxix, 299; remark
　on, vi, 16
Cottius (see Spurinna)
Cotton, Charles, and Walton, xv, 322;
　Wordsworth on *Winter* of, xxxix, 309-
　10
Cotytto, goddess of nocturnal sport, iv, 48
Coulson, Walter, xxv, 58, 76
Councillors, of kings, iii, 53-4; of kings,
　More on, xxxvi, 141-2; Penn on, i, 352
　(360); Webster on duty of, xlvii, 756
Councils, Church, Luther on, xxxvi, 265;
　Pascal on, xlviii, 304 (871)
Councils, Ecclesiastical, Luther on, xxxvi,
　272-5, 290
Counsel, boldness in, iii, 32; of friends,
　70-1, 120; good, excels wealth, viii,
　289; right of legal, in U. S., xliii, 194-
　5 (6); safer to receive than to give, vii,
　213 (3)
COUNSEL, ESSAY ON, Bacon's, iii, 52-6
Counsellors, Confucius on, xliv, 56 (6);
　evil, in Dante's HELL, xx, 106-14; of
　kings, xxxvi, 157-8; Machiavelli on,
　77-8
Count, meaning of, xxxiv, 368
Countenance, expressions of the, xxviii,
　279-81
Counterfeiters, in Dante's HELL, xx, 124-
　5
Counterfeiting, punishable by Congress,
　xliii, 184 (6)
Country, pleasures of the, iv, 30-3; and
　town, relations of, x, 127-31, 304-7
COUNTRY GLEE, xl, 317-18
COUNTRY LAIRD, EPIGRAM ON A, vi, 498-9
COUNTRY LASS, THE, vi, 440-1
Country Life, Bacon on, iii, 88-9; Cicero
　on, ix, 63-6; Cowley on, xxvii, 61-9;
　Emerson on, v, 50; Locke on, xxxvii,
　174-5; Penn on, i, 342-3; Smith on, x,
　129-31; Smith on attractiveness of, 306;
　Wordsworth on, xxxix, 271
COUNTRY LIFE, ESSAY ON, Cowley's, xxvii,
　61-9
COUNTRY SEAT, ON A BEAUTIFUL, vi, 499
Country Workmen, Smith on, x, 22-3

Courage, Buddha on, xlv, 595-6; Con-
　fucius on, xliv, 44 (27), 48 (30), 58
　(8), 60 (23, 24); Hobbes on, xxxiv,
　340, 365; in Latin the same as virtue,
　xii, 148; Locke on, xxxvii, 95-101; and
　oppression, iii, 38-9; not roughness,
　xxxvii, 51; without courtesy, xliv, 25
　(2), 60 (24); without good breeding,
　xxxvii, 72; worldly, Socrates on, ii, 57
Court, fees of, x, 451-2
Court Mantle, trial by, xxxii, 146 note
Court Records, in Massachusetts, xliii, 73
　(48), 75 (64)
COURT OF SESSION, EXTEMPORE IN, vi,
　256-7
Courtesy, Bacon on, iii, 34; benevolence
　of, v, 211, 217; first point of, is truth,
　208; intellectual quality in, 209-10; oft
　found in lowly sheds, iv, 53; Yu-tzu
　on, xliv, 6 (12, 13); Confucius on, 6
　(15), 7 (3), 10 (8), 11 (18), 12 (22),
　13 (13), 21 (25), 25 (2, 8), 37 (1),
　39 (15), 41 (3), 50 (44), 53 (32), 57
　(13), 59 (11), 67 (3)
Courtiers, Burns on, vi, 222; Confucius
　on, xliv, 55 (2); Montaigne on, xxxii,
　42-3; Simon Eyre on, xlvii, 503
COURTIN', THE, xlii, 1376-9
Courts, Bacon on, xl, 349; congressional
　regulation of, xliii, 184 (9); pleasures
　of, iv, 33; Raleigh on, xl, 204-5; United
　States, xliii, 189, 190; Webster on
　princes', xlvii, 755-6 (see Judicature)
Courtship, naturally done by men, xlviii,
　419
Couthony, Mr., on coral-reefs, xxix, 478
　note
Covenants, Hobbes on, xxiv, 394-401,
　414; the keeping of, 401-6
Coventry, Sir William, and Pepys, xxviii,
　302
Coventry, Bishop of, in EDWARD II, xlvi,
　12-13
Coventry, Countess of, beauty of, v, 305
Covered, chapter of the, xlv, 879-81
Coverley, Sir Roger de, xxvii, 83-4; Ad-
　dison's and Steele's parts in, 82, 163-5
Covetousness, Buddha on, xlv, 669; free-
　dom from, 670-1; the cause of war,
　xxviii, 130-1; Epictetus on, ii, 152
　(95); Hobbes on, xxxiv, 340, 366;
　Jesus on, xliv, 387 (15); Locke on,
　xxxvii, 91; Mohammed on, xlv, 971;
　More on cause of, xxxvi, 185; Pascal
　on, xlviii, 188, 220 (663); Penn on, i,

331-2, 373 (4); Paul, St., on, xlv, 497 (11, 10); the sin of, in FAUSTUS, xix, 227 (see Avarice)

Cowardice, Locke on, xxxvii, 95-6; how developed, 97-8

Cowards, insult dying majesty, xvii, 14-15

Cowley, Abraham, OF AGRICULTURE, xxvii, 61-9; on Chaucer, xxviii, 81; xxxix, 168-9; Dryden on, xiii, 62, 427; Dryden on, xxxix, 162 note 13; life and works, xxvii, 60; Poems by, xl, 365-9; *Pindaric Odes* of, xxxix, 320; popularity of works of, 320

Cowper, William, Hymns by, xlv, 562, 563; Poems by, xli, 533-53; Emerson on, v, 21; Mill on works of, xxv, 16; *Verses of Selkirk*, xxxix, 295-6; *The Task* of, 299

Cowpox, first appearance of, xxxviii, 167-8; inoculation for, 169-70, 190-1, 199-202, 203-15, 216-17, 220; Jenner on, 142, 143-220; not fatal or infectious, 168-9, 178-9, 210-11, 215-17; origin and symptoms of, 146, 155-60, 161-3, 170, 180-3, 184-191, 198-203, 204-6, 209, 212, 216-17; return of, 151-2, 162-4; scarlatina and, 215-16; and measles, 215 note; smallpox and, 147-154, 156-7, 160-1, 172, 174, 186 note, 187, 193, 196-199, 200-1, 202-3, 206 note, 209, 210, 212-14, 216, 219-20; sources of spurious, 172-83; treatment of, 186-7, 187-9, 200-1, 208-9, 212, 217-18

Cows, held sacred in Egypt, xxxiii, 25-6

Cox, William, xxxiii, 274, 288, 289

COXCOMB, EPITAPH ON A NOTED, vi, 487

Coya (see Peru)

Crabs, at St. Paul's, xxix, 20; hermit, 461 and note; notopod, 166

Crabs, giant, of Keeling Islands, xxix, 466-7

CRABS, FABLE OF THE, xvii, 30

Crabtree, in SCHOOL FOR SCANDAL, uncle of Backbite, xviii, 119; at Lady Sneerwell's, 122-25; on Backbite's epigram, 131-2; in gossip at Sneerwell's, 132-3, 134-5; at Teazle's, after the scandal, 182-5

Crabwinch, the, xxx, 184

Craft, Hobbes on, xxxiv, 352, 366; Revenge's scheming child, viii, 116

Craftiness, Eliphaz on, xliv, 77 (12-14); Locke on, xxxvii, 119 (see Cunning)

Craigdarroch, Burns on, vi, 363-5, 381

CRAIGIEBURN WOOD, vi, 403, 512

Crane, in FAUST, xix, 187; the prudent, iv, 238

CRANE AND WOLF, fable of the, xvii, 12-13

Cranes, war with dwarfs alluded to, iv, 102

Cranmer, Archbishop of Canterbury, xxxvi, 114, 117, 120

Craon, Lord, xxxv, 35

Crashaw, Richard, WISHES FOR MISTRESS, xl, 359-63; ON SAINT TERESA, 363-4

Crassipes, son-in-law of Cicero, ix, 129

Crassus, Gaius Licinius, law of, ix, 41

Crassus, Lucius, the orator, Sidney on, xxvii, 48

Crassus, Marcus Licinius, Asia contract, ix, 93; Catiline's Conspiracy and, xii, 229-30; Cicero and, ix, 121, 128-9; xii, 238-9, 242, 246; death of, 288; Dryden on, xiii, 16; influence of, xii, 224; Milo and, ix, 98; and the Parthians, xxxiii, 113-14; Pompey and, ix, 99; reference to, xx, 229 note 20

Crassus, Publius, Roman jurisconsult, ix, 55, 63, 67; son of Marcus, admirer of Cicero, xii, 246; killed in Parthia, 247

Crassus, brother of Piso Galba's adopted son, victim of Nero, ix, 189 note 4

Crassinius, Caius, at Pharsalia, xii, 301

Cratais, mother of Scylla, xxii, 165

Craters, of Galapagos Islands, xxix, 376; of elevation, 487

Cratinus, reference to, viii, 449

Cratinus, on Aspasia, xii, 61; on Pericles, 37-8, 50

Cratippus, Cicero and, xii, 237; Cicero the Younger, and, ix, 174

Craving, Buddha on noble and ignoble, xlv, 715

Cravings, of children, xxxvii, 86-8

Creation, Bacon on the, iii, 8; Berkeley on the, xxxvii, 272-8; Calvin on the, xxxix, 47-8; centres of, xi, 383-6; Dante on manner of, xx, 313-14 note 9; Descartes on, xxxiv, 38-9; Dryden on the, xl, 389; Emerson on the, xlii, 1260-1; greater than destruction, iv, 242; Hume on, of matter, xxxvii, 419 note; Job, description of, in, xliv, 132 (4-11); March, date of, xl, 44; Mill on problem of, xxv, 32; Mohammed on the, xlv, 888-9, 899; Mohammed on, of man, 879, 885, 889, 891, 900; music on morning of, iv, 11 (12); Owen on,

xi, 13-14; Pascal on the, xlviii, 82-3, 207 (625); prophecy of, iv, 104, 117; Raleigh on the, xxxix, 99, 101-6, 107-11; reason of the, iii, 287; of the soul, 288-9; special, objections to, xi, 399, 413-14, 417, 418-19, 427, 453-4, 455, 472-3, 488-9, 490, 491, 493, 494, 495, 496, 499-500; special, of species, objections to, 67-8, 102-3, 136-7, 143, 144, 154, 157, 159-60, 166, 180, 192, 196, 247-50, 296, 315; special, Owen on, 13-14; Raphael relates story of, iv, 232-43; Uriel describes the, 153-4

Creative Genius, Aristophanes on, viii, 442

Creator, Addison on the, xlv, 535

Crecy, battle of, xxxv, 27-31; losses at, 32-3 and note; order of the English at, 24-5; order of French, 25-6

CRECY, THE CAMPAIGN OF, xxxv, 7-33

Credit, Bacon on assuming, iii, 100-1; Franklin on assuming, i, 75; Luther on, xxxvi, 331-2 (see also Loans)

Credits, cash, in Scotland, x, 237, 244-5

Credulity, Hobbes on, xxxiv, 374; reason of, human, xxiv, 18

CREECH, WILLIAM, LAMENT FOR, vi, 267-9

Creeds, best when clearest, xxxiv, 289; Brontë on, xlii, 1110; decline of, reason of, xxv, 233-7; xxxiv, 383-7; determined by accident of birth, 284 note; Emerson on modern, v, 77; Hobbes on belief in, xxxiv, 348; Locke on, xxxvii, 127-8; origin of, xxxiv, 375; Pope on religious, xl, 430; Rousseau on usefulness of, xxxiv, 302-3; truth of, impossibility to finding, 292-8; of Utopia, xxxvi, 223-36

Creeper, the, in Tierra del Fuego, xxix, 242

Creighton, Robert, Bishop of Wells, xv, 392

Cremona, reference to, iv, 24 (4)

Creon, brother of Jocasta, sent to Delphi by Œdipus, viii, 211; returns, 211-13; suspected by Œdipus, 221; disclaims guilt, 224-8; last scene with Œdipus, 251-4; King of Thebes, forbids burial of Polynices, 256, 260-3; hears of burial, 263-5; condemns Antigone, 267-74; with Hæmon, 276-80; warned against his crimes, 287-91; sees death of son, 295-6; death of wife, 297-8

Cresceus, Attilius, Pliny on, ix, 281-2

Crespino, the Bargello, xxxi, 203

Cressy, Drayton on, xl, 224 (see Crecy)

Cretaceous Era, in Europe, xxx, 346-7

Crete, Anchises on, xiii, 131-2; Homer on, xxii, 261-2

Creteus, death of, xiii, 319

Cretheus, son of Æolus, xxii, 150

Creüsa, ghost appears to Æneas, xiii, 126-7; in sack of Troy, 123, 125

Crevasses, formation of, xxx, 226-7, 237; in glaciers, 215, 220-2

Crewe, Mrs., lines addressed to, xviii, 108-12

Crichton, Admirable, Hazlitt on, xxvii, 277

CRICKET AND GRASSHOPPER, by Keats, xli, 895

Crifford, John, xxxv, 381

Crime, reasons of, Augustine, St., on, vii, 27-30; Confucius on causes of, xliv, 25 (10); and law, xlviii, 104 note 2; made by distrust, v, 56; nature hostile to, 97; prevention of, laws for, xxv, 291-2; and punishment, inseparable, v, 90; retribution of, 100; retribution of (see Retribution); Stoic doctrine of, ix, 317 note 1; trials of, in U. S., xliii, 194 (5), 194-5 (6) (see also Penology)

Crimes, great, never single, xxvi, 176

Criminal Codes, sanguinary, Emerson on, v, 89

Criminals, equality of, v, 116; public and private, 279; proper treatment of, ii, 150 (88); real punishment of, 120 (12)

Crinisus, father of Acestes, xiii, 179

Crises, Lowell on, xlii, 1371

Crisis, the, shows the man, ii, 173 (157)

Crispinus, and Horace, xviii, 18

Crispus, xliv, 463 (8); baptism of, xlv, 491 (14); destruction of, iii, 50

Cristoforo, Father, in THE BETROTHED, Attilio and, xxi, 181; death, 623; life and character, 53-67; Lucia and, 38-9, 50-1, 123, 130-3, 604-11; Renzo and, 582-91, 609-11; Rodrigo and, 83-7

Critias, and Alcibiades, xii, 139, 145

Critical Periods, xxv, 103-5

Criticism, of art, xxiv, 28; of art, Goethe on, xxxix, 261-3, 264; Bagehot on, xxviii, 194-5; comparison necessary to, xxvii, 213; xxviii, 73-4; xxxix, 208-9; delicacy requisite to just, xxvii, 209-11; false method of, xxxix, 289-90; fallacies of poetic, xxviii, 67-72; Hugo on, xxxix, 383-5; Hume on, xxxvii, 297, 359, 420; Johnson's ideas of, xxxix,

242-8; Johnson on conjectural, 244-5, 246, 247-8; of manners, morals, and religion, xxvii, 219-21; Mazzini on mission of, xxxii, 396; Montaigne on, xlviii, 390-1; need of negative, xxv, 239; of others (see Censoriousness); Pascal's method of, xlviii, 17-18; physical organs in relation to, xxvii, 209; practice necessary to, 211-12; prejudice fatal to, 213-14; of poetry, xxxix, 311-16; possibility of fixing standard of, xxvii, 216-19; reason in, 215-16 (see also Taste)

Critics, Burke on mistake of, xxiv, 48; Burns on, vi, 321; Dryden on, xviii, 15-17, 21; Johnson on, xxxix, 239; knowledge requisite to, xxiv, 18-21; qualifications of, xxvii, 208-16; xxxix, 315-16

Crito, friend of Socrates, ii, 22, 26, 47, 51-2, 110-13

CRITO, Plato's, ii, 31-43

Critobulos, of Cyrene, xxxiii, 89

Critobulus, and Socrates, ii, 22, 26, 47

Critolaus, in Rome, iii, 194

Crobylus, the orator, xii, 204

Croce, Baccino della, xxxi, 98, 126

Crocodile, in Book of Job, xliv, 138 note 1; the, creation of, iv, 239; Herodotus on the, xxxiii, 37-8

Crocker, Mrs., and More, xxxvi, 116

Crocus, David on the, xli, 494

Crœsus, Chaucer on dream of, xl, 43; death of, xxxii, 5; and Solon, iii, 74

Croghan, George, and Braddock, i, 134

Croll, on age of earth, xi, 344; on geological time, 324-5; on glacial period, 401

Cromwell, Burke on, xxiv, 186; Carlyle on, xxv, 366-7, 368-70; Carlyle's Life of, xxxix, 415; Defoe on, xxvii, 135; Emerson on, v, 239; his fast proclamation, xliii, 118 note; Hazlitt on, xxvii, 275; Hugo on, xxxix, 356, 376-80; as Lord Protector, xliii, 106 note, 115 (33); Milton on, xxviii, 188-9; Pascal on, xlviii, 65 (176); Pope on, xl, 437; and the Quakers, xxxiv, 72, 73; quotation from, v, 159-60; Swift on, xxvii, 96; Waller's elegy on, xxxiv, 145-6

Cromwell, preface to Hugo's, xxxix, 337-87

CROMWELL, SONNET TO, iv, 82-3

CROMWELL'S RETURN, ODE UPON, xl, 372-6

Cromwell, Sir Richard, xxxvi, 121

Cromwell, Sir Thomas, and More, xxxvi, 113, 117, 120

Cronion, father of Venus, xxii, 106; name of Zeus, 160; references to, 35, 36, 51

Cronos, his curse on Zeus, viii, 199-200; overthrown by Zeus, reference to, 148; the war against, 173-4

Crosfield, George, i, 306

Crosfield, Jane, i, 308

Cross, the, in architecture, xxiv, 63-4

Cross, of Jesus, exhortation to bear the, vii, 329; few bearers of, 251-2; royal way of the, 253-7; spell of the, xix, 56

Cross Breeding (see Intercrosses)

Cross Lies, iii, 128

Cross, Robert, xxxiii, 230, 245

Crossbow, Helmholtz on the, xxx, 188-9

Crossing (see Intercrossing)

CROSSING THE BAR, xlii, 1057

Crossley, Hastings, translator of Epictetus, ii, 115

Crossness, founded in Vinland, xliii, 13

CROW AND FOX, fable of, xvii, 14

CROW AND PITCHER, fable of, xvii, 32

CROWDIE EVER MAIR, vi, 543

Crowds, not company, iii, 66

Crown Servants, Confucius on, xliv, 43 (20); Tzu-hsia on, 64 (13)

Crowns, Hippolytus on usurped, viii, 347-8; Jesus on, iv, 383

Crucifixion, The, xliv, 415-16

Cruelty, in children, xxxvii, 102-3; in commanders, xxxvi, 55-6; Hobbes on, xxxiv, 343, 408; in princes, xxxvi, 53-5; of single and married men, iii, 22; well and ill employed, xxxvi, 32

Cruelty, Mr., juryman in PILGRIM'S PROGRESS, xv, 100

Crüger, Dr., on orchids, xi, 194-5

CRUIKSHANK, MISS, TO, vi, 331

CRUIKSHANK, MR., EPITAPH FOR, vi, 288

Crusaders, in Dante's PARADISE, xx, 362

Crustacea, South American, xxix, 166-7

Crying, of children, Locke on, xxxvii, 92-5

Crystallization, different forms of, xxx, 30-2, 37

Crystals, perforated, xxix, 154

Ctesias, son of Ormenus, xxii, 210

Ctesiphon, Emerson on, v, 226; indictment of, xii, 210

Ctesippus, xxii, 303; death of, 303; and Demosthenes, xii, 203; with Socrates, ii, 47; and Ulysses, xxii, 280-1

Ctimene, daughter of Anticleia, xxii, 209
Cuba, Independence of, xliii, 440-1, 443 (1), 448-9 (16); slavery in, v, 45-6
Cucao, Chiloe Islands, xxix, 298-9
Cuccagua, land of the, xxi, 193 note
Cúchulainn, xlix, 239
Cuckoo, habits of the, xxix, 60-1; instincts of, xi, 259-62; Wordsworth on the, xxxix, 303
CUCKOO, To THE, by Michael Bruce, xli, 450-1
CUCKOO, To THE, by Wordsworth, xli, 641-2
Cudworth, Dr., xiii, 30; xxxvii, 166
Cudworth's Risk, v, 273
Cuentas, Sierra de las, xxix, 154
Cuevas, Luis Gonzaga, xliii, 289
Culan, Baron de, xxxviii, 37
Cultivated Classes, rage of the, v, 65
Culture, Arnold on, xxviii, 213-14; Confucius on, xliv, 16 (14); Huxley on, xxviii, 214; and morality, Rousseau on, xxxiv, 162; necessity of valor in our, v, 123-4; Rousseau on progress of, xxxiv, 177; proper aim of, xxxii, 276; in relation to freedom and virtue, 219, 236-7, 254-5, 266-7, 271-4; Schiller on office of, 244; Thoreau on, xxviii, 417-18; timidity of our, v, 95
CULTURE AND SCIENCE, Huxley's, xxviii, 207-23
Cumberland, Goldsmith on, xli, 505-7
Cuming, on shells, xxix, 395, 396, 492
Cunizza, xx, 320 note 6
Cunning, Bacon on, iii, 57-60; fable on, xvii, 34; Locke on, xxxvii, 119; Penn on, i, 337 (150-1); Webster on, xlvii, 765
CUNNINGHAM, ALEX., To, vi, 308-9
CUNNINGHAM, ALEXANDER, song to, vi, 538-9
Cunningham, Allan, poems by, xli, 782-4
Cupavo, son of Cycnus, xiii, 328
Cupentus, death of, xiii, 409
Cupid, assumes form of Ascanius, xiii, 97-8; blindness of, v, 301; Dante on worship of, xx, 314; and Psyche, iv, 71
CUPID AND CAMPASPE, xl, 209
Cupidity (see Covetousness)
Curan, in KING LEAR, xlvi, 242
Curianus, Assidius, ix, 260-2
Curiatii, reference to the, xx, 306 note 9
Curio, Gaius Scribonius, xx, 117 note 11; and Antony, xii, 322-3, 325; and Cæsar,

270, 289, 291; and Memmius, ix, 150; and Pompey, 98, 99
Curiosity, Augustine, St., on, vii, 28, 189-90; Burke on, xxiv, 29-30; in children, xxxvii, 104-7; folly of, vii, 207 (1); Goethe on, xix, 19, 339, 340; Hobbes on, xxxiv, 341, 375; Kempis on, vii, 262 (4), 288 (1); Locke on, in children, xxxvii, 89; Marcus Aurelius on, ii, 206 (4); Montaigne on, xxxii, 43; noble and mean, xxviii, 114; Pascal on, xlviii, 15 (18), 60 (152); Penn on, i, 384 (135); Tzu-kung on, xliv, 60 (24)
Curious-impertinent, history of the, xiv, 305-46, 351-5
Curious Persons, envious, iii, 22-3
Curius, Manius, Cicero on, ix, 15, 19, 81; and Coruncanius, 23; old age of, 65; reference to, iv, 383; in war with Pyrrhus, ix, 60
Curle, Dr., xv, 393
Curnach, xlix, 220
Currency, debasement of the, x, 32; depreciation of the, 563-4; effect of debasement on rents, 38-9 (see Money)
Curricle, Lady Betty, epigram on, xviii, 132
Curse, of Faust, xix, 66-7
Curses, Chaucer on, xl, 29
Curtius, Quintus, on Alexander, xxxvii, 354; Cicero and, ix, 114
Curtis, John, i, 265
Curule-chair, defined, xx, 427
Curves, more beautiful than angles, xxiv, 94-5, 98
Cusco, Milton on, iv, 329
Cuscrad, son of Conchobar, xlix, 233-4
Cush, the Benjamite, Psalm concerning words of, xliv, 150-1
Cushing's Battery, at Gettysburg, xliii, 337, 351, 375, 381, 382
Custom, Calvin on, xxxix, 38-9; Descartes on ease of following, xxxiv, 14; Emerson on defiance of, v, 68-9; Harvey on, xxxviii, 101; "honored in breach," xlvi, 112; Hume on, xxxvii, 309, 321-2, 330, 373; and innovations, iii, 62; and justice, xlviii, 104, 105 (297), 108 (309), 109 (312); and manners, xxxviii, 355-6; Mill on, xxv, 199-200, 265-6; in modes of living, v, 51-2; and nature, iii, 96; obedience to, xlviii, 112 (325); obedience to, a result of ignorance, xxxiv, 373-4; overcome by custom, vii, 227 (2); Pascal on, xlviii,

40 (89, 90), 41 (92, 93), 42 (97); in religion, 91 (245), 93 (252); not resisted, becomes necessity, vii, 124; Shakespeare on, xlvi, 167-8; Winthrop on, xliii, 85 (see also Conformity, Habit, Precedent)

CUSTOM, Bacon's ESSAY ON, iii, 98-9

Customs, Augustine, St., on, vii, 39; Burke on, xxiv, 85, 289-90; Goethe on, xix, 80; Woolman on, i, 192 (see Duties)

Customary Conjunction, xxxvii, 324, 330, 346-7, 415

Cuttle-fish, Darwin on habits of, xxix, 16-18; eyes of, xi, 190-1; supposed to have no heart, xii, 16 note

Cuvier, on conditions of life, xi, 207-8; on the Diodon, xxix, 23-4; on monkeys, xi, 341; reference to, v, 18

Cybele, mother of the Gods, iv, 42; viii, 371, ix, 385 note; xiii, 132; and the ships of Æneas, 295-6

Cyclades, the, described, xiii, 132

Cyclic-Uproar, xlv, 603

Cycloid, invention of the, xxxiv, 126

Cyclops, the, in the ÆNEID, xiii, 148-50; and the Phæacians, xxii, 81; of Sindbad, xvi, 252-5; and Ulysses, xxii, 117-29; at Vulcan's forge, xiii, 282

Cycnus, and Phaeton, xiii, 328

Cydon, and Clytius, xiii, 332

Cyllene, hoar, iv, 44

Cyllenius, messenger of Jove, xiii, 83 (see also Mercury)

Cymodoce, the nymph, xiii, 329

Cymothoe, reference to, xiii, 78

Cynemernes, in Utopia, xxxvi, 232

Cynesians (see Kynesians)

Cynicism, Comus on, iv, 63; Epictetus on true, ii, 157-61; tolerated in Athens, iii, 193

Cynics (see Diogenes, Demetrius, Antisthenes)

Cynosarges, at Athens, xii, 5

Cynthia, and the boar of Calydon, xiii, 249; and the Latmian shepherd, xl, 244; the moon called, 232, 244, 248; name of Diana, xxxix, 63; reference to, iv, 35 (see also Artemis, Diana)

Cyprian Epic, of Homer, Herodotus on, xxxiii, 57

Cyprian, St., xxxix, 37 note 30; xxxvi, 134; Luther on, 280; on sin, xxxix, 39-40

Cypris (see Aphrodite)

Cyprus, conquered first by Amasis, xxxiii, 90

Cyrene, Amasis and, xxxiii, 88-9; School of, iii, 193

Cyrus, the Elder, Bacon on, iii, 129-30; and Cassandane, xxxiii, 7; the cities of, iv, 391; first post ascribed to, ix, 368 note; gardening of, xxxvii, 175; on immortality, ix, 73-4; and the Jews, xxxii, 194 (39); xlviii, 210 (633); liberality of, xxxvi, 53; Machiavelli on, 20, 21, 83; on his old age, ix, 55-6; Pascal on, xlviii, 234 (701); prophecy of, 240-1; and Scipio, xxxvi, 50; Sidney on, xxvii, 10-11, 18; and Tomyris, xx, 192; the young soldier of, xxxii, 82

Cyrus, the Younger, and Aspasia, xii, 61; park of, ix, 66-7; Xenophon on, 66-7

Cytheris, and Antony, xii, 328

DÁ DERGA'S HOSTEL, DESTRUCTION OF, xlix, 197-248

Dacia, Freeman on, xxviii, 265

Dacier, Dryden on, xiii, 12

Dædalus, Dante on, xx, 318 note 15; Virgil on, xiii, 207

Dæghrefn, death of, xlix, 73-4

DAER, LORD, LINES ON MEETING, vi, 240-2

DAFFODILS, THE, xli, 639

DAFFODILS, TO, xl, 337-8

Dag, son of Hogni, xlix, 361-3

Dagon, god of the Philistines, iv, 99, 414, 425-6

Dahish, the 'Efrit, xvi, 306-10

Daigne, the apothecary, xxxviii, 23

DAINTY DAVIE, vi, 471

Dairy Products, price of, x, 190-1

Daisies, Shelley on, xli, 842-3; for simplicity, vi, 407, 470

DAISY, STORY OF THE, xvii, 297-301

DAISY, TO THE, xli, 640-1

Dalibard, M., i, 147, 148

Dalila, wife of Samson, iv, 420, 424-5, 428, 432-8

Dalmatia, Freeman on, xxviii, 256

Dalrymple, Dr., reference to, vi, 351

Damaris, xliv, 462 (34)

Damiano, Pietro, xx, 377 and note 13

Damiano, St., xxxi, 156 note 1

Damien, reference to, xli, 531

Damis, in TARTUFFE, disinherited, xxvi, 259; Dorine and, 208, 244-5; Loyal and, 288, 289; Pernelle and, 200, 201-2; Tartuffe and, 248, 253-4, 255-8, 281

Damœtas, reference to, iv, 73

Damon, ostracism of, xii, 79; Pythias and, Browne on, iii, 318; teacher of Pericles, xii, 38

DAMON AND SYLVIA, vi, 414

Damonides, of Œa, xii, 44

Dampier, on gold countries, xiii, 60

Dana, Francis, xxiii, 3

Dana, Richard Henry, Jr., life and works, xxiii, 3-4; TWO YEARS BEFORE THE MAST, 5-374; TWENTY-FOUR YEARS AFTER, 375-405

Danae, founder of Ardua, xiii, 253; Jove and, vii, 18; xlvi, 55; xlvii, 612; Marlowe on, xlvi, 33; Sophocles on, viii, 286; Carew on, xl, 352; Tennyson on, xlii, 974

Danaos, an Egyptian, xxxiii, 45; daughters of, viii, 197-8; xiii, 338; xxxiii, 85, 90

Danby, Earl of, Dedication to, xviii, 7-11; George Herbert and, xv, 391-2

Dancer, in FAUST, xix, 188

Dancing, Confucius on, xliv, 9 (1); Cowley on, xxvii, 65; Emerson on beauty of, v, 303; among the Germans, xxxiii, 106; Locke on, xxxvii, 47, 170

Dancing-Master, in FAUST, xix, 188

Dandini, on Socrates, etc., v, 268

Danger, admiration excited by, ix, 347; Bacon on, iii, 56; Goethe on, xix, 341; Locke on insensibility to, xxxvii, 95; of others, pleasure in, xxiv, 42-3; passions excited by, 35; way of, in PILGRIM'S PROGRESS, xv, 45, 218

Daniel, the prophet, Dante on, xx, 238 and note 12; on dreams, xl, 43; on God, xxxvi, 328; learning of, iii, 199; Luther on, xxxvi, 329; Milton on, iv, 380; Nebuchadnezzar and, xx, 297 note 1; Pascal on, xlviii, 232; prophecies of, 245 (722-3), 254

Daniel, Arnault, Dante on, xx, 253 and note 2

Daniel, Samuel, sonnets by, xl, 219-22

Daniel, the Saxon, xxxiii, 285, 290

Dante Alighieri, ancestry of, xx, 349 notes 1 and 2; Arnold on selections from, xxviii, 72, 79; banishment of, xx, 178 and note 10, 227 note 12; banishment predicted, 42, 63-5, 356-60; Beatrice and (see Beatrice); Browning on the painting of, xlii, 1095-6, at Campaldino, xx, 164 note 8; Carlyle on, xxv, 444; Casella and, iv, 81; Cavalcanti and, xx, 42 note 6; Cellini on line of,

xxxi, 303; date of descent into Hell, xx, 88 note; DIVINE COMEDY, xx; Dryden on, xxxix, 155; Emerson on, v, 179; English love of, 433; father of, xx, 349 note 2; as a Franciscan, 68 note 9; Goethe on, xxxii, 389; Hazlitt on, xxvii, 272; Hugo on, xxxix, 349, 354-5; Huxley on, xxviii, 217; life and works, xx, 3-4; Macaulay on, xxvii, 370; Milton on, xxviii, 174; on the ocean, xliii, 30; on St. Peter's keys, xxviii, 110; in poet's band, xx, 19; religious belief of, 390, 396; rescue of child from drowning, 77 note; Ruskin on creed of, xxviii, 112; Sainte-Beuve on, xxxii, 122, 128, 132; Shelley on, xxvii, 332, 335, 347, 348, 349, 350; Sidney on, 6; Thoreau on, xxviii, 420; Wordsworth on sonnets of, xli, 681

Danti, Vincenzo, xxxi, 420 note

Danube, Herodotus on the (Ister), xxxiii, 22; Tacitus on the, 93

Danvers, Charles, and George Herbert, xv, 392-3

Danvers, Jane, wife of George Herbert, xv, 392, 396, 397, 407-8, 418

Danvilliers, siege of, xxxviii, 19-21

Daphne, and Apollo, xl, 378; iv, 62; grove of, iv, 161; Webster on, xlvii, 794

Daphne, in TARTUFFE, xxvi, 204

Dapper, in THE ALCHEMIST, xlvii, 550-58, 602, 604, 607-11, 649-50, 651-53

Darby, Earl of, and Dryden, xiii, 425

Dardanus, born in Italy, xiii, 133; Electra's son, 272; founder of Troy, xx, 19 note 5; Virgil on, xiii, 246

Dare-not-lye, Mr., xv, 282, 283

Dares, death of, xiii, 402; and Entellus, 190-4; xxxix, 173

Dares, Trojan priest, Caxton on, xxxix, 9

Daring, Graham on, xl, 359; Locke on, xxxvii, 96; Shakespeare on, xlvi, 336

Darius, prophecy of, xlviii, 248

Darius III, Dryden on, xl, 393; empire of, xxxvi, 17; Greek cities and, 22; Raleigh on, xxxix, 98

Dark Ages, Shelley on the, xxvii, 345-6

Dark-land, in PILGRIM'S PROGRESS, xv, 297

Darkness, in architecture, xxiv, 68; children's fear of, xxxvii, 118; sublimity and, xxiv, 67-8; sublimity of, 114-18; terror in idea of, 60-1; usefulness of, xxviii, 418; "visible," iv, 89

DARKNESS, Byron's poem, xli, 796-8

Darkness, Our Lady of, xxvii, 324

Darley, George, LOVELINESS OF LOVE, xli, 913-14

DARNING-NEEDLE, THE, xvii, 315-18

Darwin, Charles Robert, ORIGIN OF SPE-CIES, xi; sketch of life and works, 5-8; VOYAGE OF BEAGLE, xxix

Darwin, Erasmus, xi, 5, 10 note

Darwin, George, on lunar disturbances, xxx, 282-3; on long period tides, 298

Darwin, Horace, on lunar disturbances, xxx, 282-3

Darwinism, Lowell on, xxviii, 462 note

Datarius, Papal, xxxvi, 284 note, 285

Dathan, reference to, xliv, 278 (17)

Datis, general of Darius, xii, 82

Dativo, the pedagogue, xxxviii, 14-15

DATUR HORA QUIETI, xli, 754

DAUNTON ME, TO, vi, 303

Dauphin, heir-apparent of France, xxxv, 217

Davaine, Dr., xxxviii, 364

Davenant, Dr., Bishop of Salisbury, xv, 394

D'Avenant, Sir William, DAWN SONG, xl, 354; Swift on, xxvii, 109

David, and the Amorites, xliii, 103; Bage-hot on, xxviii, 169-70; Burns on, vi, 229; on Christ, xliv, 426-7 (25-31); Dante on, xx, 184-5; in Dante's PARA-DISE, 371; faults of, xv, 260; God's covenant with, xliv, 254 (3), 255 (4), 256 (20-37), 257 (38-51); Goliath and, xxxvi, 46-7; Kempis on, vii, 337 (8); Locke on stories of, xxxvii, 133; Mephibosheth and, xliii, 104; Milton on, iv, 350, 393-4; Mohammed on, xlv, 917; Nathan and, xxvii, 25; one of nine worthies, xxxix, 20; Pascal on, xlviii, 91 (243), 230 (690), 231-2, 264 (752); Paul on, xliv, 451 (22); on the Sabbath, xliv, 368 (3-4); sword of, xxxv, 187-8; and the tabernacle, xliv, 313-14; and the temple, 438 (46); in valley of death, xv, 66, 134-5; water, story of, i, 285-6; v, 126; Win-throp on, xliii, 94

DAVID, PSALMS OF, xliv, 146-94, 205-30, 251-2, 268, 271-2, 283-87, 307-8, 308-9, 312-13, 314-15, 319-32; remarks on, 144; Sidney on, xxvii, 9, 11

DAVID, SONG TO, xli, 484-98

David, King, of Britain, xxxv, 252

DAVIE, EPISTLE TO, vi, 66-70

DAVIE, SECOND EPISTLE TO, vi, 107-8

DAVIES, CHARMS OF LOVELY, vi, 405

DAVIES, MISS, EPIGRAM ON, vi, 404

Davies, Mr., on puerperal fever, xxxviii, 229

Davies, Tom, Lamb on, xxvii, 300 note

Davy, Sir Humphry, and conservation, law of, xxx, 175; Faraday and, 5; on frictional heat, 197; potassium, discov-ered by, 119 note

DAWN SONG, by D'Avenant, xl, 354

DAWN SONG, by Shakespeare, xl, 268

DAY IS COMING, THE, xlii, 1195-7

DAY IS DONE, THE, xlii, 1274-5

DAY IS PAST AND OVER, THE, xlv, 542-3

DAY RETURNS, vi, 314

DAYS, by Emerson, xlii, 1243-4

DAYS THAT WERE, THE, xlii, 1197-8

Dead, Brynhild on the, xlix, 370; Calvin on masses for the, xxxix, 36-7; grief for, xxvii, 286; knowledge of the, xxxix, 92; Luther on masses for, xxxvi, 306-7; Pascal on prayers for the, xlviii, 339-40

Dead Man's Lane, in PILGRIM'S PROGRESS, xv, 128

DEAN OF FACULTY, THE, vi, 545-6

Death, Adam's first view of, iv, 330; Addison on contemplation of, xxvii, 80; Æschylus on, viii, 80; Arabian in-scriptions on, xvi, 300-4, 312, 317, 320-1, 425, 441; Aristophanes on, viii, 483; Aristotle on, xxxviii, 84; Barbauld on, xli, 555; Beaumont on, xlvii, 707; Beowulf on, xlix, 43; Browne on, iii, 251, 290, 291-2, 295-6, 322; Browning, Robert, on, xlii, 1065; Browning, Eliz-abeth B., on, xli, 941-2; Bryant on, xlii, 1213-15; Buddhist ideas of, xlv, 662, 681, 683-4, 736; Bunyan's allegory of, xv, 158-60, 310-18; Burke on idea of, xxiv, 35; Burns on, vi, 62, 297; Byron on fear of, xviii, 427; Calderon on, xxvi, 70; children mitigate, iii, 20; Cicero on, ix, 69-72; Clough on, xlii, 1120; comes to all alike, xxvii, 78 note 2; Confucius on, xlv, 34 (11); Diog-enes on, ii, 180 (187); Drummond on, xl, 326; Dryden on, viii, 98, 99-100; Ecclesiastes on, xliv, 341 (1), 345 (5), 346 (6); Emerson on, v, 131, 293-4; Epictetus on, ii, 131 (44), 132 (45), 135 (55), 158 (112), 164 (130, 131), 165 (132, 134, 135), 167 (139), 174 (161), 181 (188); Euripides on, in misery, viii, 349; Faust on, xix, 66; fear of, disposes to peace, xxxiv, 370;

"felicity of wretched men," xlvi, 72; Fitzgerald on, xli, 945-7, 950, 952; friends lessen fear of, iii, 71; friendship takes sting from, ix, 17; Goethe on, xix, 401-2; Gray on, xl, 446, 454; Grenville on, xlii, 1010; Hamlet's soliloquy on, xlvi, 144; xxxiv, 132-3; the happiest, ii, 181 (189); Harvey on cause of, xxxviii, 122; Harvey on two kinds of, 109; Henley's wish for, xlii, 1210; Herbert on, xl, 342; Hindu conception of, xlv, 792; Job on, xliv, 74-5, 92 (10-12), 104 (23), 105 (24-6); Kempis on meditations of, vii, 230-2; knowledge of world after, xxxix, 96-7; Longfellow on, xlii, 1278; love and, 1036; Marcus Aurelius on, ii, 202 (11, 12), 203 (14), 204 (17), 206 (3), 208 (7), 213 (5, 6), 214 (14), 220 (47, 48), 221 (50), 223 (4), 230 (29), 232 (2), 236 (24), 237 (28), 241 (47), 244 (10), 245 (19), 247 (32), 249 (50), 256 (18), 257 (25), 258 (31), 264 (58), 265-6 (3), 268 (21), 271 (33), 281 (29), 284 (36), 285 (3), 296 (5), 298 (23), 300 (31), 301 (34, 35, 36); Milton on, iv, 165, 320, 356, 454; Mohammed on, xlv, 975; Montaigne on, xxxii, 5-8, 9-28; Montaigne's conceptions, Pascal on, xlviii, 25, 395; More on, xxxvi, 120; Nashe on, xl, 260-1; to be overcome by Christ, iv, 141-2; Pascal on, xlviii, 63 (166, 168), 64 (169), 65 (175), 71, 79 (210), 80 (215-16), 150 (447), 330-8; Penn on, i, 363 (500-5); Pope on knowledge of, xl, 424; Raleigh on, xxxix, 94, 98; Raleigh on thoughts of, xl, 204; Roman expression for, xii, 235; Rossetti, C. G., on xlii, 1181, 1182; Rousseau on, xxxiv, 261-2; Schiller on, xxvi, 473; scholar's dread of, xix, 30-1; Shakespeare on, xl, 269, 270; Shakespeare on fear of, xlvi, 313; Shelley on, xviii, 308-9, 310, 353-4; xli, 833, 869; Shirley on, xl, 349, 350; Socrates on, ii, 16-17, 25, 27, 28-9, 50-9, 60-1; Sophocles on, v, 121-2; viii, 272; Stevenson on, xlii, 1213; Swinburne on, 1205; terror of animals, xxxiv, 177; Utopian ideas of, xxxvi, 228; Valley of Shadow of, xv, 65-9, 245-9; Vaughan on, xl, 347; "where is thy victory," xlv, 513 (55); White on, xli, 913; Whitman on, xlii, 1417-18, 1422; "who

kings and tars dispatches," xli, 503-4; Woolman on nearness to, i, 198
Death, in PARADISE LOST, iv, 125-8, 134, 296-301, 305-7; Burke on, xxiv, 50-1
DEATH, ESSAY ON, Bacon's, iii, 9-10
DEATH BED, THE, xli, 910
DEATH AND DOCTOR HORNBOOK, vi, 74-9
DEATH, by Donne, xl, 305-6
DEATH OF A FAIR INFANT, ON THE, iv, 18-20
DEATH AND THE OLD MAN, a fable, xvii, 39
DEATH OF POOR MAILIE, vi, 41-2
DEATH, PRAYER IN PROSPECT OF, vi, 34-5
DEATH, SONG OF, vi, 426
DEATH STANDS ABOVE ME, xli, 905
DEATH, THE TERROR OF, xli, 897
DEATH'S MESSENGERS, xlv, 685-92
DEATHS OF LITTLE CHILDREN, Hunt's, xxvii, 285-8
Debasement, of currency, x, 31-2; effect on money rents, 38
Debates, Penn on, i, 335 (133-5), 336 (136)
Debauchery, Burns on, vi, 185; courage and, xxxvii, 54
De Bouillon, Cardinal Retz on, v, 307
Debt, Emerson on, v, 96; Franklin on, i, 91; imprisonment for, in Massachusetts, xliii, 71 (33); Penn on collecting, i, 327 (48); in Utopia, xxxvi, 190
Decebalus, King of Dacia, ix, 369 note 2, 370 note 4
Deceit, Pascal on sources of, xlviii, 37-8; punishment of, in Hell, xx, 46-7; Whitman on, xxxix, 402-3
DECEMBER, THOU GLOOMY, vi, 430
Decemviri, Roman, ix, 277 note 2
Decency, Mill on offences against, xxv, 294
Decii, deaths of the, ix, 72
Decius, Publius, Cicero on, ix, 60
Decius, Roman Emperor, persecutions under, xxxviii, 392
Decker (see Dekker)
DECLARATION OF INDEPENDENCE, xliii, 150-5; Lincoln on, 316
DECLARATION, THE MECKLENBURG, xliii, 156-7
Declaration of Right, Burke on, xxiv, 156-7, 171-2
DECLARATION OF RIGHTS, xliii, 147-9
Decow, Isaac, i, 54-5
Decurii, Roman, ix, 194 note
DEDICATION, A, by Burns, vi, 211-14

Dee, Dr., the magician, xlvii, 589 note 4
Deer, ages, various of the, xxxv, 343; in Brazil, xxix, 56-7
Defects, compensation for, v, 98; Hugo on, xxxix, 385-6; Shakespeare on single, xlvi, 112
Defence, national, expense of, x, 447-50
Deference, Emerson on, v, 209; Pascal on, xlviii, 110 (317)
Definitions, Burke on, xxiv, 12; Goethe on, xix, 132; Hobbes on, xxxiv, 326-7, 333; Hume on, xxxvii, 351-2; Johnson on, xxxix, 191-5; Pascal on, xlviii, 404, 405, 422-4, 425-8, 433-4
Defoe, Daniel, EDUCATION OF WOMEN, xxvii, 148-51; Emerson on, v, 433; on Englishmen, 340; Essay on Projects, i, 14; Franklin on, i, 23; life and works, xxvii, 132; SHORTEST WAY WITH DISSENTERS, xxvii, 133-47
DEFORMITY, BACON'S ESSAY ON, iii, 107-8
Deformity, Browne on, iii, 267-8; Burke on, xxiv, 83-4; envy and, iii, 23
Degerando, Landor on, v, 317
Deglutition, Harvey on, xxxviii, 87
Degradation, geological (see Denudation)
Deïanira, and Nessus, xx, 50 and note
Deïdamia, Dante on, xx, 108, 237
DEIL, ADDRESS TO THE, vi, 140-3
DEIL'S AWA WI' THE EXCISEMAN, vi, 439
Deiotarus, Cicero in, ix, 136, 137, 140, 143, 147; in war of Antony and Octavius, xii, 370
Deïphile, in Limbo, xx, 237
Deïphobe, the Sibyl, and Æneas, xiii, 207-38
Deïphobus, in Hades, xiii, 223-5; at Trojan horse, xxii, 53
Deism, Franklin on, i, 55; Mill on, xxv, 33-4, 47-8; Pascal on, xlviii, 181, 183; Rousseau on, xxxiv, 280, 282-3, 284, 288-9, 299-300
Dejection, Coleridge on, xxv, 86; defined by Hobbes, xxxiv, 342; results of, 353
DEJECTION: AN ODE, xli, 728-32
DEJECTION, STANZAS WRITTEN IN, xli, 827-8
Dekker, Thomas, Hazlitt on, xxvii, 276; life and works, xlvii, 468; POEMS BY, xl, 317-19; SHOEMAKER'S HOLIDAY, xlvii, 469-537
Delaware, Lord, at Crecy, xxxv, 24; at Poitiers, 42
Delay, Bacon on, iii, 56-7; Penn on, i, 354 (390); Shakespeare on, xl, 262

Delectable Mountains, in PILGRIM'S PROGRESS, xv, 58, 122-3
DELIA, AN ODE, vi, 340
Deliberation, Hobbes on, xxxiv, 343; language of, 344
Delicacy, as cause of beauty, xxiv, 95; of imagination, Hume on, xxvii, 209-12
Delight, Burke on, xxiv, 33-4; Hobbes on, xxxiv, 339-40; how caused by pain, xxiv, 107-8; Shelley on, xli, 825-7
Delilah (see Dalila)
Delille, Hugo on, xxxix, 369-70
Delio, in DUCHESS OF MALFI, xlvii, 755, 757; in presence-chamber scene, 757, 759-61; learns Antonio's marriage, 774; advises Antonio, 777; despatched to Rome, 780; with Antonio, after interval, 789-91; on Malatesti, 804-5; on Bosola, 805-6; with Julia in Rome, 785-6; on Antonio's betrayal, 786; with Antonio in Milan, 831-4, 845-7; in final scene, 854-5
Dellius, and Cleopatra, xii, 339-40, 368
Delos, island of, xiii, 133
Delphi, navel of earth, v, 334; building of temple of, xxxiii, 88
Delphian Oracle, Æschylus on ambiguity of, viii, 56; Emerson on, xlii, 1248; prophets of, viii, 122-23
Delphos, King, viii, 123
Delrio, Manzoni on, xxi, 532
Deltas, Lyell on, xxxviii, 401
DELUDED SWAIN, THE PLEASURE, vi, 474-5
Deluge, Calvin on the, xxxix, 39; Locke on, xxxvii, 165; Milton on, iv, 337-40; Pascal on, xlviii, 207 (625), 215-16 (644)
Deluges, Bacon on, iii, 136-7
Demades, Alexander and, xii, 210; death of, 217; Demosthenes and, 197, 200, 214; fickleness of, 201
Demagogues, Hamilton on, xliii, 201-2
Demand, effectual and absolute, x, 57
Demand and Supply, equalization of, x, 58; of laborers in regard to population, 82; as regulators of price, 57-8
Demaratus, the Spartan, xii, 31
Demas, in PILGRIM'S PROGRESS, xv, 110-11, 309
Dêmêtêr, functions of, viii, 379; Hades, ruler of, xxxiii, 62; hymn to, viii, 450-1; Iasion and, xxii, 71; the Isis of Egyptians, xxxiii, 34, 79; mystic rites of, 85; Rhampsinitos and, 62

Demetrius, the Cynic, and Nero, ii, 132 (45)

Demetrius, the Grammarian, and the philosophers, xxxii, 49-50

Demetrius, of Phaleron, and Æsop, xvii, 8; on Aristides, xii, 78, 79

Demetrius, son of Philip II, iii, 51

Demetrius, the silversmith, xliv, 465, 466

Democracy, Aristotle on, xxiv, 260 note; Burke on, 229-30, 259-60; education and, xxv, 108; Emerson on, v, 243; justified by example of Lincoln, xxviii, 448; Machiavelli on, xxv, 368-9; Mill on, 107, 120, 144, 196-8, 261; James Mill on, 68-9; nobility and, iii, 35; Rousseau on, xxxiv, 221; supposed shortcomings of, xxviii, 431

DEMOCRACY, ESSAY ON, Lowell's, xxviii, 451-70

Democracy in America, Mill on, xxv, 120-1; James Mill on, 126

Democritus, Browne on, iii, 316; death of, ii, 206 (3); Huxley on, xxviii, 219; on kitchen gardens, x, 157; in Limbo, xx, 20 note 9

Demodocus, the minstrel, xxii, 100, 101, 105, 111-12; Milton on, iv, 22

Demogorgon, xlvii, 567 note 13; Milton on, iv, 132

Demoleüs, and Æneas, xiii, 187

Demons, Hobbes on possession by, xxxiv, 355-6; Milton on, ∶·, 36

Demonstration, Hume on, xxxvii, 332 note, 418-19; judgment and fancy in, xxxiv, 351; Pascal's method of, xlviii, 404-7, 421-37

Demophon, steward of Alexander, xxxii, 57

Demophoon, Dante on, xx, 323

Demosthenes, on action, iii, 31; Æschines on, ix, 215; Alexander demands, xii, 209-10; early ambition, 194; opposes Antipater, 213; compared with other Athenian orators, 197; Athens honors, 216-17; birth and education, 193; Carlyle on, xxv, 378; Cicero compared with, xii, 192-3, 258-9; COMPARISON OF CICERO AND, 260-3; xxxix, 159; Cicero on, xii, 237; condemnation and banishment, 212-13; courage in resisting populace, 202; on the Crown, 210-11; death of, 215-16, 263; iv, 79; determined disposition, xii, 194; fiery eloquence of, ix, 348-9; not an extempore speaker, xii, 196-7; faults,

201-2; flight from battle, 206-7; pronounces funeral oration, 207; suit against guardians, 194-5; Harpalus and, 211-12; forms new league, 209; Midias and, 200; Mill on, xxv, 18; nicknames, xii, 193-4; old woman and, ix, 346; orations, xii, 202-3; Philip of Macedon and, 200-1, 203-7, 208-9; Pliny on, ix, 187, 205; Plutarch's LIFE OF, xii, 191-217; first entry on public business, 194-5, 200; on public speaking, ix, 251; recalled to Athens, xii, 213-14; Sainte-Beuve on, xxxii, 131; urged to new studies, xii, 196; style, 199-200; teachers, 194; methods of training himself, 199-200

Dempster, George, Burns on, vi, 159, 170, 177

Denham, Sir John, Dryden on, xxxix, 163; on Henry VIII, xxiv, 252

Denham, Mr., and Franklin, i, 39, 40, 41, 48, 48-50

Denial, not scepticism, xxxvii, 191-2

Denman (see Denham)

Dennis, John, on Addison's *Cato,* xxvii, 166, 167, 168, 185-96; on Shakespeare, xxxix, 212, 231-2

Denny, Gov., Franklin on, i, 127, 146, 149-50, 161, 162

Dente, Vitaliano del, xx, 71 note 6

Denudation, Darwin on geological, xi, 322-3, 325, 330-1; xxix, 319-20; Giekie on, xxx, 340-1; Lyell on, xxxviii, 400, 414

DEPARTURE, by Patmore, xlii, 1112-13

Dependencies, Machiavelli on, xxxvi, 8-12, 18-19; arms in, 69; factions in, 69-70

Dependent Origination, xlv, 625, 664-5

Deposition, Rousseau on right of, xxxiv, 220, 226

Depravity, Dante on human, xx, 209-11; Emerson on doctrine of, v, 267

Depth, grander than other dimensions, xxiv, 60-2

De Quincey, Thomas, life and works, xxvii, 318; LEVANA AND LADIES OF SORROW, 319-25

Dercennus, in ÆNEID, xiii, 386

Dercetæus, and Antony, xii, 382

Descartes, René, on comets, xxxiv, 118; geometry, work in, 112, 125; on God, xxxvii, 345 note; life and works of, xxxiv, 3; on light, 122; Locke on system of, xxxvii, 165; ON THE METHOD,

xxxiv, 5-62; reasons for and against publishing METHOD, 49-62; remarks on METHOD, 3-4; provisory code of morals, 21-5; compared with Newton, 108-13; Pascal on, xlviii, 34, 408; beginning of new philosophy, xxxiv, 28-34; physical investigations, 35-48, 51-3; idea of planetary motions, 114; on rainbow, 122; Rousseau on, 249; scepticism of, xxxvii, 407-8; on the soul, xxxiv, 103; on telescopes, 124; travels, 10-11, 25-7; Voltaire on, 108-13

Descent, in classification, xi, 441-2

Description, Burke on verbal, xxiv, 51-4; Wordsworth on powers of, xxxix, 297

Desdemona, Lamb on, xxvii, 312

DESERTED VILLAGE, THE, xli, 509-19; an idyllic poem, xxxix, 299

Deserters, article on, in Spanish Treaty, xliii, 275 (13)

Deserters, the Egyptian, xxxiii, 19-20

Desert, "use man after his," xlvi, 139

Deserts, Burton on, xxviii, 411

DESIDERIA, xli, 674-5

Desire, defined by Hobbes, xxxiv, 337; love contrasted with, 337-8; xxiv, 74; Milton on, iv, 167; offences through, ii, 201 (10)

Desires, Augustine, St., on worldly, vii, 182-94; Bacon on, and fears, iii, 48; Buddha on noble and ignoble, xlv, 715; Dante on, xx, 215-18; Descartes on limitation of, xxxiv, 23-4; Emerson on unbridled, v, 92; Epictetus on, ii, 170 (145); Hindu reward of righteous, xlv, 817; Hobbes on, xxxiv, 336-40, 352-3, 369-71; Kempis on, vii, 211, 272, 276, 291, 317 (6); language of, xxxiv, 344; Locke on, xxxvii, 109; Locke on, of children, 86-90; Marcus Aurelius on, ii, 211 (16); Mill on, xxv, 254

Despair, defined by Hobbes, xxxiv, 340; Epictetus on, ii, 173 (156); in music, Collins on, xli, 477

Despair, the giant, in PILGRIM'S PROGRESS, xv, 116-22, 287-9

Despoblado, valley of, interesting features of, xxix, 359

DESPONDENCY: AN ODE, vi, 197-9

Despondency (see Disponency)

Despotism, legitimate with barbarians, xxv, 204; origin of, xxxiv, 215-19; Rousseau on, 225-6; secrecy surrounding, xxiv, 50

De Staël, Madame, and the Emperor, xxvii, 235; on herself, v, 432

Destinies, in MANFRED, xviii, 428-33

DESTRUCTION OF DÁ DERGA'S HOSTEL, xlix, 197-248

Destruction, Way of, in PILGRIM'S PROGRESS, xv, 45-6

Determination, why honorable, xxxiv, 366; Pliny on, ix, 250

Determinism (see Free Will)

Detraction, Jesus on, xliv, 369 (22); Kempis on, vii, 292, 310 (5), 323-4; Penn on, i, 345-6, 380-1 (85-89); Socrates on, ii, 16; superiority to, ii, 119 (7)

DETRACTION, ON THE, WHICH FOLLOWED CERTAIN TREATISES, iv, 79-80

Detritus (see Denudation)

Detroit, River, navigation of, xliii, 286 (7)

Deucalion, son of Minos, xxii, 262

DEUKS, DANG O'ER MY DADDIE, vi, 439

DEUS, EGO AMO TE, xlv, 556

De Vere, Sir Aubrey, GLENGARIFF, xli, 911-12

De Vere, Edward, A RENUNCIATION, xl, 289

DeVere, house of, its motto, v, 374

Devereux, Col., at Gettysburg, xliii, 385, 387

Devereux, Penelope, and Sidney, xxvii, 3-4

Devereux, Robert, A PASSION, xl, 287

Devil, Bacon on, enviousness of the, iii, 26; Bunyan on, xv, 195; Dante on, xx, 164 note 12; Goethe on, xix, 22; Kempis on, vii, 266 (7); More on, xxxvi, 100-1; Penn on, i, 345 (267)

DEVON, BANKS OF THE, vi, 288

Devonshire, Duke of, Emerson on, v, 412-13

DEVOTED WIFE, THE, xlv, 693-6

Devotion, false, Kempis on, vii, 262-3 (5); Molière on false, xxvi, 213, 214

Dexter, Afranius, case of, ix, 322-4

Dexter, H. M., translator of hymn, xlv, 541-2

Dexterity, favored by division of labor, x, 13

Dextro-Tartrate of Lime, fermentation of, xxxviii, 316-23

Dhanañjaya, xlv, 754, 755-6, 760-5

Dhritirashtra, xlv, 785

Diadematus, surname of Metellus, xii, 156

Dialects, Johnson on, xxxix, 183-4

Dialogue, Franklin on, i, 23

DIALOGUE SONG: PHILLY AND WILLY, vi, 506-7

DIALOGUES OF HYLAS AND PHILONOUS, ETC., xxxvii, 185-285; remarks on, 186

DIALOGUES OF PLATO, ii, 5-113

Diamonds, same as charcoal, xxx, 29; pounded, as means of death, xxxi, 246

Diana, Camilla and, xiii, 375-7; chastity of, iv, 56; goddess of childbirth (called Cinthia), xl, 244; Latmian Shepherd and (Cinthia), 244; worship of, at Ephesus, xliv, 465-6 (see also Artemis, Cynthia)

DIANA, HYMN TO, xl, 299

Diana of Foix, Montaigne to, xxxii, 29

DIANEME, TO, xl, 336

DIAPHENIA, xl, 228-9

Diaries, in travel, iii, 46-7

Diastole (see Systole and Diastole)

Diaz, Ruy (see Cid)

Dibdin, Charles, TOM BOWLING, xli, 502

Dicearcus, Montaigne on, xxxii, 20

Dicers, More on, xxxvi, 200

Dichogamous Plants, xi, 105

Dickens, Charles, Emerson on, v, 439, 471; THE IVY GREEN, xlii, 1147-8

Dickie of Dryhope, xl, 111

Dickson, J. F., paper by, xlv, 740

Dicomes, king of the Getæ, xii, 371

Dictes, Caxton on, xxxix, 9

DICTES AND SAYINGS OF THE PHILOSOPHERS, xxxix, 9-13, 5 note

DICTIONARY, PREFACE TO JOHNSON'S, xxxix, 182-206

Didactic Art, Schiller on, xxxii, 270-1

Didactic Poetry, Poe on, xxviii, 375; Wordsworth on, xxxix, 299

Diderot, Carlyle on, xxv, 353; Hobbes and, xxxiv, 308

Didias, Julianus (see Julianus)

Dido, Æneas and, xiii, 83-175; Calypso and, xxxix, 157; Carthage founded by, xiii, 86; Chaucer's picture of, v, 276-7; death of, xiii, 176-7; Dryden on, 29-37; harshness of her reign, xxxvi, 54; in Hell, xx, 23; in the Mournful Fields, xiii, 222-3

Didymus, Newman on, xxviii, 38

Diego, the negro, with Drake, xxxiii, 139, 143, 148, 152

DIES IRÆ, DIES ILLA, xlv, 551-3

Diet, Bacon on changes of, iii, 81; of children, Locke on, xxxvii, 16-21

Difficulty, Burke on, xxiv, 299; Channing on value of, xxviii, 314-15; source of the sublime, xxiv, 65

Difficulty, hill of, in PILGRIM'S PROGRESS, xv, 45, 218

Diffidence, Browning on, xviii, 364; Hobbes on, xxxiv, 340, 365; Pliny on, ix, 275; quarrels caused by, xxxiv, 388, 389

Diffidence, wife of Despair, in PILGRIM'S PROGRESS, xv, 117, 120-1, 287

Digby, Sir Kenelm, v, 354-5; Pope on, xl, 433

Diggory, in SHE STOOPS TO CONQUER, xviii, 216-17, 252

Dignity, Confucius on, xliv, 53 (32); Emerson on, v, 208-9; Hobbes on, xxxiv, 361; Kant on, xxxii, 345; morality alone possesses, 345

Digressions, Raleigh on, xxxix, 112

Dilettantes, Emerson on, v, 161

Diligence, Carlyle on, xxv, 361-2; Penn on, i, 343 (234)

Dimorphism, Darwin on, xi, 57; reciprocal, 305-8

Dinas Bren, eagles of, xxxv, 338

Dinmont, Dandie, Ruskin on, xxviii, 140

Dinomache, mother of Alcibiades, xii, 106

Diocles, son of Orsilochus, xxii, 45, 204

Diocletian, Bacon on, iii, 49; miracles under, xlviii, 288 (832)

Dioclides, accuser of Alcibiades, xii, 124

Diodon Antennatus, habits of, xxix, 23-4

Diodorus, on Themistocles, xii, 34

Diogenes of Apollonia, on the soul, xxxiv, 103

Diogenes, the Cynic, Browne on, iii, 306; on comedies, ii, 286 (6); Dandini on, v, 268; Emerson on, 203; Epictetus on, ii, 163 (128); freedom of, 168 (141); on friends, xxxii, 81; health of, ii, 160-1 (118); Hegesias and, xxxii, 59; on indifference of circumstances, ii, 180-1 (187); in Limbo, xx, 20; lines on, xxv, 438; Marcus Aurelius on, ii, 254 (3); mission of, 157 (108); Philip and, 158-9 (113); on philosophy, xxxii, 59; on recommendations, ii, 136 (57); Rome, Ambassador to, x, 137; in Rome, iii, 194; ix, 53; Rousseau on, xxxiv, 226; and the statues, ii, 177 note; on strength of soul, 138 (62); tub of, referred to, vi, 189; Voltaire on, xxxiv, 103; will of, iii, 292 note

Diognetus, Aurelius's debt to, ii, 193 (6)

Diogoras, iii, 43

Diomede, in Hell, xx, 108; Minerva and, xiii, 105; reference to, 89; return of, from Troy, xxii, 37

Diomedes, Dryden on, xiii, 25; in Italy, 268; refuses aid to Latinus, 364-6

Diomedes, friend of Alcibiades, xii, 114-15

Dion, Cocceianus, ix, 399-401

Dion, in PHILASTER, xlvii; in presence chamber scene, 667-77; before Phara-mond's house, 692-9; scene with Philaster, 699-703; at the hunt, 714-16, 718-21, 725, 727-31; on Philaster, 733; on Arethusa, 735; in the sedition, 736, 737-8; in final scene, 744, 746-8

Dion Prusœus, and the Rhodians, iii, 191

Dion, of Syracuse, and Plato, xii, 78

Dione, mother of Venus, xx, 314 note 1, 382 note 13

Dionysius, the Elder, in Hell, xx, 51; and tragedy, iv, 412

Dionysius, the Younger, Plato and, iii, 194, 206; xxvii, 38; xxxvi, 157; as a poet, xviii, 17

Dionysius, St., of Alexandria, xx, 328 note 22; on God, xxxix, 103; quoted, xxxv, 328; vision of, iii, 200

Dionysius, the Areopagite, xx, 406 notes 3 and 5; xliv, 462 (34)

Dionysius, king of Portugal, xx, 369 note 15

Dionysius, school of, ix, 158

Dionysius, surnamed Thrax, Cicero on, ix, 146-7

Dionysus, in the BACCHÆ, viii, 368-436; Dryas's son and, 286-7; Euripides on, 377, 379, 391-3; festivals of, 438; in the FROGS, 439-87; Hades, ruler of, xxxiii, 62; Osiris and, identified by Herodotus, 26, 29-30, 72-3, 79 (see also Bacchus)

Diophantus, at Athens, xxviii, 59

Diopithes, decree of, xii, 68-9

Diores, death of, xiii, 407; in the foot-race, 188-9

Dioscorides, Dante on, xx, 20

Dioscuroi, unknown in Egypt, xxiii, 27 (see Castor and Pollux)

Diotimus, ii, 257 (25), 259-60 (37)

Dipamkara, xlv, 582-4; Buddha and, 585-7, 599-600

Diphilides, and Themistocles, xii, 9

Diphilus, Cicero on, ix, 110-11; xxvii, 386 note 8

Diræ, the, xiii, 420

Dircê, daughter of Achelous, viii, 391

Dircê, river, Bacchus bathed in, viii, 391

DIRCE, by Landor, xli, 899

Direct Taxes, apportionment of, xliii, 180-1 (3), 185 (4), 191 (5); under the Confederation, 162

DIRGE, by Sidney, xl, 211-12

DIRGE, Fidele's, xl, 269

DIRGE OF LOVE, Shakespeare's, xl, 268-9

DIRGE, A SEA, xl, 270

Dis, in Scandinavian mythology, xlix, 291 note; Proserpine and, iv, 161

Dis, Pluto called, xlvi, 446

Dis, city of, xx, 34 et seq.

Disappointment, defined by Burke, xxiv, 34; Penn on, i, 325 (32), 385 (152)

Disasters, bring out leaders, xix, 374

Disciples, chorus of, in FAUST, xix, 38; Pascal on, xlviii, 169 (519); Woolman on, i, 201

Discipline, Kempis on, vii, 236 (7); Penn on, i, 328; Plutarch on lack of, xii, 147; self, Epictetus on, ii, 154 (100)

Discontent, cause of, xxviii, 456-7; Emer-son on, v, 77; Penn on, i, 326 (38-40)

Discontent, in PILGRIM'S PROGRESS, xv, 75

Discontentment, Epictetus on, ii, 123-4 (20), 127 (31, 32), 128 (35), 133 (49), 167 (140); Marcus Aurelius on, 211-2 (3), 224-5 (8), 233 (11), 256 (17), 259 (34), 280 (25), 281 (28), 292 (20), 299 (26); public, iii, 25-6, 36, 38, 40-1

Discord, Burke on Homer's figure of, xxiv, 54; in chaos, iv, 133; daughter of sin, 308; Pope on, xl, 415; proclaims itself, xxv, 319

Discouragement, easy, Emerson on, v, 75-6

Discourse, absurdities of, xxxiv, 358-9; discretion and fancy in, 351; excessive length or brevity of, xlviii, 29; Hobbes on ends of, xxxiv, 346-8; Kempis on proper, vii, 212; Pascal on natural, xlviii, 14 (14) (see also Conversation, Inquiry, Reasoning)

DISCOURSE, ESSAY ON, Bacon's, iii, 83-5

Discretion, better than daring pride, xlix, 153; defined by Hobbes, xxxiv, 350; in discourse, 351

Discretion, damsel in PILGRIM'S PROGRESS, xv, 50

Discussion, liberty of, James Mill on, xxv, 69, 210-11, 250

Disease, Browne on, iii, 295; carried by

Europeans, xxix, 439-40; cause of, Rousseau on, xxxiv, 172-3; caused by animals, xxxviii, 145; contagious, Jenner on, 163-4; death's messenger, xlv, 686; Emerson on, v, 123; germ theory of, xxxviii, 364-82; Herodotus on cause of, xxxiii, 40; inheritance of, Pliny on, ix, 198; sign of sanitary neglect, xxviii, 457; source of error, xlviii, 38

Diseases, Adam's vision of, iv, 331; cure of desperate, xlvi, 172; effects of, different, xxix, 438 note; incurable, in Utopia, xxxvi, 208

Disgrace, fear of, in children, xxxvii, 39-41; Locke on fear of, 96

Dishonesty, for gain, i, 387 (184)

Disinterestedness, Hume on, xxxvii, 355

Dislike (see Aversion)

Disobedience, Locke on, xxxvii, 61-3

Disorder, and grandeur, xxiv, 66

DISORDER, A SWEET, xl, 336

Dispatch, Bacon on, iii, 62-4; in public business, i, 354-5

Dispensations, Luther on, xxxvi, 309, 315-16

Dispersal, means of, of plants and animals, xi, 386-94; during glacial period, 394-9, 404-8; of fresh-water species, 409-13

Dispondency, Mr., in PILGRIM'S PROGRESS, xv, 288-9, 290, 302; parts with Christiana, 312; death, 314-16

Disposition, Locke on, xxxvii, 57-8; not inherited, xx, 318-19

Dispositions, of children, xxxvii, 44-5, 84-5, 90

Disputes, passion in, iii, 314-15

Disputing, Franklin on habit of, i, 15, 126; Locke on habit of, xxxvii, 125, 126-7, 159-60; Montaigne on, xxxii, 41-2, 43; Penn on, i, 335 (133-5), 336 (136), 340 (184)

Disrespect, Locke on, xxxvii, 119-20

Dissatisfaction, Pascal on human, xlviii, 47 (109)

Dissections, Harvey on, xxxviii, 106-7, 139

Dissent, dishonoring, a way of, xxxiv, 364; Locke on, xxxvii, 125-6

Dissenters, Mill on duty of, xxv, 33; Milton on value of, iii, 224, 230; Price on duty of, xxiv, 152 note 3 (see Nonconformity)

DISSENTERS, SHORTEST WAY WITH, Defoe's, xxvii, 133-47

Dissertation on Liberty and Necessity, i, 42, 55

Dissimulation, Bacon on, iii, 19 (see also Hypocrisy); in Hell, xx, 46; Pascal on, xlviii, 43; Penn on, i, 374 (15-16), 376 (37-44), 377 (44-6); Raleigh on, xxxix, 68-9; Stevenson on, xxviii, 281-2

Distance, Berkeley on idea of, xxxvii, 220-2

DISTANT FRIEND, TO A, xli, 674

Distinction, Carlyle on love of, xxv, 393-5; human thirst for, xxviii, 94-5; Rousseau on love of, xxxiv, 224

Distinctions, Locke on, xxxvii, 170; nice, Bacon on, iii, 64-5

Distress, goods taken in, xliii, 71 (35)

Distresses, of others, pleasure in, xxiv, 40-3

Distribution, Hobbes on, xxxiv, 409-10; importance of just, xxviii, 350-1; in agricultural systems, x, 437; in Utopia, xxxvi, 184-5, 189-90; Mill on laws of, xxv, 152; progress of wealth dependent on, x, 54-5; of produce (see Wages, Rent, Profits)

Distributive Justice, Hobbes on, xxxiv, 406, 409; Hume on, xxxvii, 400-1

District of Columbia, slave-trade in, xliii, 306 note; under Congress, 185 (17)

Distrust, Emerson on, v, 278-9; expensiveness of, 56; opponent of reform, xxvii, 239; Webster on, xlvii, 762-3

Disturbances, charges of creating, xxxix, 43-5

Disuse, of parts, effects of, xi, 140-4

DITTY, by Sidney, xl, 212

DITTY IN PRAISE OF ELIZA, xl, 245-7

Divergence of Character, xi, 115-19; how it leads to formation of species, etc., 119-23; limits to, 133-5

Diversification, of structure and habits, xi, 116-19; limits to, 133-5

Diversion, Pascal on, xlviii, 52-8, 63 (167-8), 64 (170-1), 112 (324)

Diversity, Mill on need of, xxv, 266-7

Dives, and Lazarus, xv, 35; xliv, 397 (19-25), 398 (26-31)

Divination, Augustine, St., on, vii, 106; in Egypt, xxxiii, 42; among the Germans, 98; pagan methods of, xxxiv, 381-2; Pascal on, xlviii, 282-3; Prometheus first teacher of, viii, 184 and note 35; Vindicianus on, vii, 47-8, 104

DIVINE COMEDY, Dante's, xx; Arnold on selections from, xxviii, 72; Carlyle on, xxv, 444; Cellini on line of, xxxi, 303; its relation to Celtic myths, xxxii, 180; Dante on, xx, 360, 391; Hugo on, xxxix, 349, 354; Macaulay on the, xxvii, 370; remarks on, xx, 3-4; Shelley on, xxvii, 347, 349

DIVINE IMAGE, THE, xli, 591

Divine Laws, Emerson on, v, 26-7

Divine Men, Emerson on, v, 193

Divine Mercy, in DIVINE COMEDY, xx, 11 note 5

Divine Nature, attributed to only one or two, v, 29

Divine Right, Rousseau on, xxxiv, 220

DIVINE SERVICE AT LAMINGTON, vi, 427

Divine Spirit (see Over-soul)

Divine Things, judged by human, iii, 46; iv, 195

Divine Truths, Pascal on, xlviii, 400-1

Diviners, punishment of, in Hell, xx, 81-4

Divinity, Emerson on, in man, v, 70-3; study of, Faustus on, xix, 207-8, 210

DIVINITY STUDENTS, ADDRESS TO, v, 25-41

Divisibility, infinite, Hume on, xxxvii, 413-14 note; Pascal on, xlviii, 430-7

Division of Labor, advantages of, x, 9-17, 21; dependent on amount of capital, 213; Kant on, xxxii, 300; limits to, x, 22-6; mischief of, v, 400; in nature, xi, 100; origin of, x, 18-21

Divisions, fable on, xvii, 31

Divorce, among Arabs, xlv, 985 note; Bagehot on, xxviii, 183-4; Jesus on marriage after, xliv, 397 (18); Mill on, xxv, 300-1; Milton on, xxviii, 183-6; Paul, St., on, xlv, 498-9 (10-11); in Utopia, xxxvi, 210-11

DO YOU REMEMBER ME, xli, 904

Dobell, Sydney, BALLAD by, xlii, 1114-16

Dobrizhoffen, on hail-stones, xxix, 121; on ostriches, 100

Dobson, story of, xlv, 689-92

Docility, Pascal on, xlviii, 94 (254)

Doctor, Chaucer's, xl, 22

Doctors (see Physicians)

Doctrinaires, Lowell on, xxviii, 437

Doctrines, Confucius on strange, xliv, 8 (16); traditional, absence of vitality in, xxv, 236

Dodger, in SHOEMAKER'S HOLIDAY, xlvii, 475, 491-3, 496, 526

Dodington, George Bubb, SHORTEN SAIL, xl, 463-4

Dodona, Oracle of, Æschylus on, viii, 196; Herodotus on, xxxiii, 32; origin of, 33

DOE, ONE-EYED, fable of, xvii, 37

Doeg, the Edomite, xliv, 206

DOES HAUGHTY GAUL INVASION THREAT, vi, 530-1

DOG IN THE MANGER, fable of, xvii, 27

DOG AND SHADOW, fable of, xvii, 12

DOG AND WOLF, fable of, xvii, 22

Dog Watches, explained, xxiii, 18

Dogmas, Dunkers' attitude towards, i, 110-1; Emerson on, v, 35; Goethe on, xix, 132

Dogmatism, Franklin on, in speech, i, 18-19; Hume on, xxxvii, 417; Pascal on, xlviii, 129 (395), 144; Rousseau on, xxxiv, 289-92

Dogmatist, in FAUST, xix, 188

Dogs, associative instinct in, xxix, 155-6; Burke on our contempt for, xxiv, 57; Darwin on instincts of, xi, 256, 257; held sacred in Egypt, xxxiii, 37; Harrison on, xxxv, 350-6; Hunter on descent of, xxxviii, 145 note; man, love of, in, iii, 44; xi, 258; origin of, 31, 33, 34, 45-6

Dol Common, in THE ALCHEMIST, Dapper and, xlvii, 602, 609, 652-3; Face and, 543, 546-50, 563-4, 655-7; Mammon and, 579, 584, 610, 613-18, 629-36; Spanish don and, 599-602; Subtle and, 543, 546-50, 563, 654-5

Dolabella, Cornelius, accusation of, xii, 299; Antony and, 328, 330; Cæsar and, 329; Cicero and, ix, 157; Cleopatra and, xii, 386; extravagance of, 306

Dolabella, in ALL FOR LOVE, Antony and, xviii, 25, 56, 59-65, 69-70, 83-7; Cleopatra and, 56, 58-9, 71, 77

Dolben, Gilbert, and Dryden, xiii, 426

Dolcino, the friar, xx, 116 note 6

Dolius, in the ODYSSEY, xxii, 65, 325, 329, 332

Dolphin, Dana on the, xxiii, 22; of Hippo, Pliny's story of, ix, 351-2

Domat, Burke on, xxiv, 285 note

Domestic Animals, adaptability of, to climate, xi, 145-6; breeding of, 42-3; descent of, 31-41; diseases from, xxxviii, 145-6; fertility of, xi, 291-2, 309-10; mental qualities of, 255-8

Domestic Industries, capital naturally seeks, x, 332-4; protection of (see Protective Duties)

Domestic Races, improvement not limited, xi, 51-2; adapted to use of man, 48-9; origin of, 32-3, 41, 42-3, 49-50, 53

Domestic Trade, capital used in, x, 295-6; limit of, 301-2

Domestication, improves fertility, xi, 291-2; eliminates sterility of species, 39; variation under, 23-53

Dominant, technical definition of, xi, 65-6

Dominic, St., Dante on, xx, 330 note 8, 335-7; Luther on, xxxvi, 300

Dominica, Drake at, xxxiii, 226, 239

Dominicans, Dante on the, xx, 333 note 30; Milton on the, iv, 147

Dominis, Antonio de, on the rainbow, xxxiv, 122

Domitian, as an archer, iii, 48; dream of, 91; Helvidius and, ix, 338 and note 1; philosophers and, ii, 116; ix, 239 note; Pliny on, 253-4, 261 note, 314, 320 and note 1; spiders, toys of, xxxv, 348; Tiberius and, xxxvi, 3; the turbot of, xxxix, 356

Domitius, and Antony, xii, 370; Cicero on, ix, 116; xii, 249; in Civil War, 293, 299, 300; Pharnaces and, 305

Donalbain, in MACBETH, xlvi, 322, 334, 341, 346, 347, 349, 383

DONALD THE BLACK, GATHERING SONG OF, xli, 745-6

Donatello, his "Judith," xxxi, 342 note 3, 343 note 5; Cellini on, 343, 358, 359

Donati, Corso, enemy of Dante, xx, 239 note 3; death of, 244 and note 6; head of Neri faction, 27 note 5; Piccarda and, 296 note 6

Donati, Simon, and Schicchi, xx, 124 note

Donatists, Calvin on the, xxxix, 34; Pascal on the, xlviii, 284 (822)

Don Galaor, Cervantes on, xiv, 18, 95

Don John of Austria, xiv, 385, 386, 387; Raleigh on, xxxix, 87-8

Donkey (see Ass)

DONKEY, MAN, AND BOY, fable of, xvii, 35-6

Donn Désa, xlix, 202; sons of, 202, 204, 211, 212, 216, 232

Donne, John, advowsons presented to, xv, 344; appearance and character, 369; benefice declined by, 330-2; birth and education, 323-5; *Book of Devotions* by, 353; burial of, 366-7; charity in life of, 358-9; conduct of Deanery,

359-60; Dean of St. Paul's, 347; death of, 366-7; domestic sorrows, 333-4; Ellesmere, Lord, and, 325-6, 327; embassy to Bohemia, 346; in France, 335; friends of, 353; Hazlitt on, xxvii, 269-70; Herbert and, xv, 354-5, 383-4; Mrs. Herbert and, 376-8; HYMN TO GOD, 355-6; James the First and, 339-40, 342, 348-9; King, Dr., and, 349-50; last sickness of, 351, 361-4; lecturer of Lincoln's Inn, 345; LINES TO GEORGE HERBERT, 354-5; LINES ON HIS MISTRESS, xxvii, 270-1; lines from *Epithalamion* of, 269; marriage of, xv, 326-8, 351; monument of, 365, 368; More, Sir George, and, 327-8; mother of, 359; ordination of, 341-2; POEMS by, 338-9, 354-5; xxvii, 270; xl, 303-13; as a poet, xv, 352; preaching of, 343; Prolocutor of the Convocation, 348; *Pseudo-Martyr* of, 339-40; studies and writings, 356-7; travels of, 323-5; VALEDICTION by, 338-9; vision of, 335-7; Walton and, 322; Walton's LIFE OF, 323-69; wife's death, 344; will of, 357-8; Wolly, Francis, and, 329

Don Quixote, Amadis of Gaul imitated by, xiv, 226-8; on arms and learning, 374-80; balsam prepared by, 128; Biscaine squire and, 66-7, 70-2; calling and manner of life of, 17; at Chrysostom's funeral, 108-9; countryman and his boy and, 36-9; disciplinants and, 507-9; Dorothea and, 270-7, 280-3, 368-70, 459; dream of triumph of, 170-3; Dulcinea and, 96-7, 213-19, 222; encaged, 63-72, 482-7; epitaphs on, 513-14, 515; first sally, 23; friars and, 63-5; galley slaves and, 176-86; goatherds and, 78-90; hearse, adventure of, 145-8; Holy Brotherhood and, 455-7; home, returning to, 510-13; at the inn, 25-8, 117-19, 125-6, 129-31, 430; innkeeper and, 445-6; knighting of, 29-35; on knight errantry, 92-6; knightly tales read by, 17-19; "Knight of the Ill-favoured Face", 149-50; library burnt, 48-54; Mambrino's helmet and, 165-7, 448-51; Maritornes and, 120-2, 435-40; merchants of Toledo and, 40-2; on romances, 489-95; Sancho Panza and, 58-9, 73-7, 284-7, etc.; sheep and, 136-41; sickness of, 55; sonnets in praise of, 11-14; windmills, adventure of, with, 60-1; wine-

bags and, 347-50; Yanguesian carriers and, 110-16

DON QUIXOTE OF THE MANCHA, Cervantes's, xiv; Lowell on, xxviii, 438

DOON, THE BANKS O', vi, 398-400

Doria, Branca, xx, 139 note 6

Dorian Music, described, iv, 102

Dorigen, and Sophocles, v, 121

Dorine, in TARTUFFE, Cleante and, xxvi, 206-7, 264-5; Damis and, 208, 244-5; Elmire and, 268-9; Loyal and, 285-6, 288-9, 290; Mariane and, 228-33, 239-43; Orgon and, 209-10, 219-28, 282, 284, 290-1; Mme. Pernelle and, 200, 202-3, 204-5; Tartuffe and, 245-7, 293-4

Doris, eggs of the, xxix, 205 note

Dorothea, in DON QUIXOTE, xiv, 252-77, 280-3, 356-65, 368-70

Dorothea, in HERMANN AND DOROTHEA, with the fugitives, xix, 345-6; described by Hermann, 372; in the French invasion, 379; found by the doctor, 380-1; the magistrate on, 382; with Hermann at the fountain, 387-90; returns to bid farewell to companions, 391-4; goes home with Hermann, 395-9; presented to his parents, 402-3; reproved in play by the pastor, 403-4; resolves to return to companions, 405-6; Hermann tells her his love, 407; begs father's forgiveness, 407-8; betrothed to Hermann, 408; tells of her first lover, 408-9

Dorset, Earl of, Raleigh on, xxxix, 75; Voltaire on, xxxiv, 147

Doson, name of, xii, 156 note

Dotage, Rousseau on, xxxiv, 176

Doubleday, Gen., at Gettysburg, xliii, 329, 350, 365, 384

Doubt, Blake on, xli, 589; Carlyle on, xxv, 346; Dante on, xx, 301; Descartes on state of, xxxiv, 15, 21-4, 28, 32-3; Hobbes's definition of, 346; Krishna on, xlv, 808 (see also Scepticism)

Doubting Castle, xv, 116, 287-9

Doughty, Master, with Drake, xxxiii, 201, 202, 204, 205-6

Douglas, Burns on family of, vi, 374; family and arms of, xxxv, 99-100

Douglas, Sir Archambault, xxxv, 93, 100

Douglas, Earl James, burial of, xxxv, 99; at Otterburn, 86, 88-9, 90-1; Percy and, 82-4; raid of, 81 (see also ballads of OTTERBURN and CHEVY CHASE)

Douglas, John, the author, Goldsmith on, xli, 505, 507

Douglas, John, ship's master, with Raleigh, xxxiii, 334-5, 336, 337

Douglas, Katherine (see Barlass)

Douglas, Lord, at Poitiers, xxxv, 47

Douglas, Lady Margaret (see DOUGLAS TRAGEDY)

Douglas, Stephen A., Lowell on, xxviii, 440

DOUGLAS TRAGEDY, THE, xl, 51-4

DOVE, JOHN, EPITAPH ON, vi, 120

Dove-house, Blake on a, xli, 587

DOVER BEACH, xlii, 1137-8

DOVER CLIFFS, by Bowles, xli, 682

DOWN THE BURN, DAVIE, vi, 473

DOWY HOUMS O YARROW, xl, 115-16

Draghinazzo, the demon, xx, 88, 91

DRAKE, SIR FRANCIS, REVIVED, xxxiii, 121-96

DRAKE'S FAMOUS VOYAGE ROUND THE WORLD, xxxiii, 199-224

DRAKE'S GREAT ARMADA, xxxiii, 229-259

Drake, Sir Francis, armadas of, xxxiii, 226-7; on Barbary Coasts, 199-200; at Cape Blanco, 200; Cacafuego pursuit, 211; in Canaries, 233; at Canno, 212; at Cape Verde Islands, 201-2, 234-8; Cartagena, expeditions against, 144-5, 155-60, 244-53; Chagres Fleet and, 185; Chili, on coast of, 209-11; Cimaroons and, 152-5; in Cuba, 253; death of, 227; DEDICATORY EPISTLE TO ELIZABETH, 126-7; at Dominica, 239; at Ferro and Cape Blanco, 233-4; fleet of, and commanders of, 229-30; at Fogo and Brava Islands, 202-3; French captain and, 186-8; Garret, John, and, 132; at Guatulco, 212; Harrison on, xxxv, 321; at Isle of Pinos, xxxiii, 134, 143; at Isle of Victuals, 141-2; at La Mocha, 208; life of, chief events, 122, 128; at Lima, 210-11; in Malay Islands, 218-24; in New Albion, 213-7; at Nombre de Dios, 135-40, 166; in Pacific Ocean, 171, 207, 217; in Panama, 166-78; at Port Pheasant, 131-3; at Port St. Julian, 205-6; prizes and losses of, 258-9; Raleigh's colony and, 256-8; Resolution of Land-Captains, 248-50; Rio Grande expedition, 149-51; at St. Augustine, 254-6, 258; at St. Christopher's, 239; at St. Domingo, 240-4; 258-9; at St. Helena, 256; at Santiago, 202-3; at Santa Marta, 161; in Sound

of Darien, 148; on coast of S. America, 203-5; on coast of Spain, 230-3; Spanish prize, 163; Spanish treasure train taken by, 187-9; stores of, 151-2, 160-1; in Strait of Magellan, 206-7; at Venta Cruz, 178-9; plan against Veragua, 182-5; wound of, 140-1; wrongs and purpose to avenge, 129-30

Drake, Sir Francis (nephew) xxxiii, 123; DEDICATION TO CHARLES I, 125; DEDICATION TO THE READER, 128

Drake, Dr., James, xxxix, 165

Drake, John, brother of Sir Francis, xxxiii, 130, 136, 138, 139, 143, 146-7, 152, 155; death of, 164

Drake, Joseph, brother of Francis, xxxiii, 165

Drake, Thomas, brother of Francis, xxxiii, 205, 230 and note

Drama, in Athens, xxvii, 339, 340; Burns on imported, vi, 374; Dryden on, xiii, 6-10, 13; Goethe on, xxxix, 260; Hugo on, 352-75; Hugo on Greek, 341, 346-7; language in, correctness of, xxix, 374-5; length of, 382-3; love as basis of, 211; Macaulay on, xxvii, 383; influence of, on morals, 339-40; narrations in, xxxix, 218; originality in, 364-6; pleasure in, reason of, 222-3; popular and poetical ideas of, xix, 11-17; reading of, xxxix, 223; reality in, 366-9; refinement in false, 370-1; Shelley on, xviii, 276, 278; xxvii, 339-40; Sidney on place and time in, 43-4; society, state of, and 339-42; tragedy and comedy in, mingled, xxxix, 213; unities of, 220-4, 258-63; verse in, 369, 371-4

DRAMAS, CONTINENTAL, xxvi

DRAMAS, ELIZABETHAN, xlvi, xlvii

DRAMAS, GREEK, viii

DRAMAS, MODERN ENGLISH, xviii

Dramatic Poetry, Wordsworth on, xxxix, 298

Dramatists, Aristophanes on duty of, viii, 470, 472

Drances, and Æneas, xiii, 359-60; denounces Turnus, 363, 368-9

Drawbacks, Smith on, x, 330-1; called bounties, 357; on exports, 371-3

Drawing, Locke on knowledge of, xxxvii, 135

Drayton, Michael, poems by, xl, 222-8

DREAM, A, by Burns, vi, 207-11

DREAM, A, OF THE UNKNOWN, xli, 842-3

DREAM, THE, by Donne, xl, 306

Dreams, Adam on, iv, 183; Augustine, St., on, vii, 182; Bunyan on, xv, 226-7; Calderon on, xxvi, 52-5, 56, 67-8; Chaucer on, xl, 37-8 note 34, 39-43; Descartes on, xxxiv, 33-4; Elihu on, xliv, 123-4 (15-17); Hobbes on, xxxiv, 315-17; Homer on, xxii, 271; Hume on, xxxvii, 304; Pascal on, xlviii, 127 (386); Pliny on, ix, 202-3; Tennyson on, xlii, 1004

Dress, in ancient Egypt, xxxiii, 41-2; in Elizabethan England, xxxv, 289-92; of the Germans, xxxiii, 102; Herrick on disorder in, xl, 336; Locke on, xxxvii, 10, 15-16, 29-30; Luther on luxury in, xxxvi, 331; Pascal on, xlviii, 37-8, 110 (315-16); Shakespeare on, xlvi, 109; in Utopia, xxxvi, 178-9, 182-3, 193-4, 199 (see also Apparel)

Dreux, battle of, xxxviii, 48-9

Dreux, Earl of, xxxv, 16

Drewry, Sir Robert, and Dr. Donne, xv, 335, 353

Drinking, Burns on, vi, 100, 185; Brynhild on, xlix, 369; of children, xxxvii, 19-20, 30; Cotton on, xxxix, 309; Dryden on, xl, 392-3; Johnson on, xxxvii, 179; Locke on, xxxvii, 14, 176-7; More on, xxxvi, 203; Omar Khayyam on, xli, 943, 946, 976, 950-2, 954-5, 956-7; Penn on, i, 329 (65-7); Shakespeare on, xlvi, 343-4

DRINKING, by Cowley, xl, 366-7

Drinking Song, by Jordan, xl, 364-5

DRINKING SONG, by Sheridan, xli, 567

Drinking Song (16th century), xl, 190-2

Drinking Song, of Tony Lumpkin, xviii, 211-12

Dris, fosterer of Conaire, xlix, 229; effects of, xxix, 137-9

Drought, Bacon on, iii, 136; Darwin on effects of, xxix, 137-9

Drugger, in THE ALCHEMIST, xlvii, 558-62, 589-91, 603, 606-7, 638, 640, 653-4, 656, 662

Druids, Burke on, xxiv, 50; Milton on, iv, 73; Voltaire on, xxxiv, 88

DRUMLANRIG, ON DESTRUCTION OF WOODS OF, vi, 411-12

Drummond, William, poems by, xl, 326-30

Drunkenness, as a crime, xxv, 294; Hobbes on, xxxiv, 354; St. Paul on, xlv, 497 (10), 497 (11); Penn on, i,

329 (72); price of wine and, x, 364; Woolman on, i, 196-7

Drusilla, wife of Felix, xliv, 477 (24)

Drusus, in Germany, xxxiii, 114; marriage of, xii, 388; Pillars of Hercules and, xxxiii, 112

Dryden, John, translation of ÆNEIS and DEDICATION, xiii; ALL FOR LOVE, xviii, 7-106; Arnold on, xxviii, 81-3; CHARLEMAGNE, HYMN OF, translation of, xlv, 547-8; on Chaucer, xxviii, 77-81; as a critic, xxvii, 197; on his critics, xxxix, 172-5; Gray on, xl, 456; Hazlitt on, xxvii, 274; life and works, xxxix, 153 note; xviii, 5-6; Locke and, xxxvii, 3; Macaulay on, xxvii, 383; Mill on, xxv, 16; on Milton, xxviii, 203; Pepys and, 304-5; PREFACE TO FABLES, xxxix, 153-75; remarks on his work, xiii, 424; l, 47; on Shakespeare, xxxix, 249, 317; SHORT POEMS by, xl, 384-96; Taine on, xxxix, 428; Voltaire on, xxxiv, 134; Wordsworth on *Indian Emperor* of, xxxix, 323-4 and note

Dryops, death of, xiii, 333

Duad, of St. Augustine, vii, 58

Dualism, in nature (see Polarity)

Duan, meaning of, vi, 172 note

Duban, the Sage, story of, xvi, 30-9

Dubartas, *The Creation* of, xxxix, 317

Dubthach Chafer, xlix, 238, 245

Duca, Guido del, in Purgatory, xx, 199-201, 205 note

Ducato, value of the, xxxi, 37 note 1

DUCHESS, MY LAST, xlii, 1074-5

DUCHESS OF MALFI, xlvii, 755-855; remarks on, 754

DUCKLING, THE UGLY, xvii, 221-30

Ducks, descent of, xi, 33; non-flying, 140; shoveller, 226-7; steamer, xxix, 204-5; wild and domestic, compared, xi, 27

Duclaux, M., Pasteur and, xxxviii, 273

DUDDON RIVER, VALEDICTORY SONNET TO, xli, 679

Duelling, Hobbes on, xxxiv, 367; Locke on, xxxvii, 172-3; Swift on, xxvii, 100

Duera, family of, xx, 134 note 10

Dufferin, Lady, LAMENT by, xli, 919-20

Dugong, Owen on the, xi, 434

Du Guesclin, saying of, v, 307

Duilius, Gaius, Cato on, ix, 61

Duke, meaning of, xxxiv, 368

Dulcinea del Toboso, mistress of Don Quixote, xiv, 22, 70; Don Quixote and, 96-7, 221; epitaph on, 515; Oriana to, 13; Sancho Panza and, 219-20, 290-1; Solis Dan on, 12-3; Sonnet on, 514

Dull, in PILGRIM'S PROGRESS, xv, 217

Dumas, M., on fermentation, xxxviii, 351

Dumont, Pierre Etienne, on Bentham's works, xxv, 44, 45; *Traité des Judicaires*, xxv, 74

DUMOURIER, GENERAL, IMPROMPTU ON DESERTION OF, vi, 461

Dunbar, Col., Franklin on, i, 132, 135, 137, 145-6

Dunbar, William, lines to, vi, 256 note

Duncan, in MACBETH, in camp near Forres, xlvi, 322-4; horses of, 348; Lady Macbeth and, 332, 333, 334-5, 340; Macbeth and, 330-1, 334, 355; murder of, 337

DUNCAN DAVISON, vi, 301

DUNCAN GRAY, vi, 448-9

Duncon, Edmund, xv, 409-10, 413-14

DUNDAS, ROBERT, ON THE DEATH OF, vi, 292-3

Dundee, Burns on, vi, 291

DUNDEE, BONIE, by Burns, vi, 256

DUNDEE, BONNY, by Scott, xli, 752-4

Dunkers, beliefs of the, i, 110-11

Dunlop, John, poem by, xli, 581-2

Dunning, Mr., Burke on, xxiv, 396

Dunstan, St., Harrison on, xxxv, 253

Dunyzad, in ARABIAN NIGHTS, xvi, 10

Duport, Dr., Dean of Peterborough, xv, 382

Duppa, Dr., Walton on, xv, 353

Duquesne, Fort, attack on, i, 134-5, 137

Duranti, Durante, xxxi, 180 note, 245

Duras, Robert of, xxxv, 45

Dürer, Albert, method of, iii, 106

Duress, in Massachusetts, xliii, 72 (40)

Durham, Bishop of, at Otterburn, xxxv, 85, 94, 95-6, 97-8

Durham, John George Lambton, Lord, xxv, 134-5

Durindana, sword of Roland, xlix, 119, 128, 130, 145, 171-2

Duris, the Samian, on Alcibiades, xii, 138; Cicero on, ix, 149; on Pericles, xii, 64

Dust, infusorial, in St. Jago, xxix, 14-5

Dutch, Goldsmith on the, xli, 528

Duties, Customs, administration of, best, x, 528-30; discriminating, 353-70; excise and customs, 524; exemption from, 389, 406; high, effect of, 527; historically considered, 524; on importation of necessities, 516; name, origin of,

524; origin of, 458; of passage, 533-4;
protective, on foreign goods, 332-42;
removal of, 348; retaliatory, 347; for
revenue, 352, 372; to equal taxes, 334-
5; under U. S. Constitution, xliii, 181
(1), 185 (5, 6), 186 (2, 3); for war
purposes, x, 342-3

Duty, Channing on, xxviii, 335-6; Confucius on, xliv, 52 (23); defined, xxxii,
344, 349-50; Emerson on, v, 26, 41,
75, 290; Epictetus on, ii, 117 (2), 150
(91), 162 (124), 165 (132), 176 (170,
172), 183 (22); Hindu doctrine of, xlv,
800; Hobbes on natural, xxxiv, 392,
401-12; imperatives of, xxxii, 332-44,
363-4; Kant on, 309-16, 317, 318-24,
336-7; Kempis on, vii, 223 (5); Lælius
on, ix, 11-12; Locke on, xxxvii, 57, 59,
129; M. Aurelius on, ii, 201 (5), 216
(24), 218 (33), 222 (1), 223 (6), 232
(2), 236 (22), 237 (26), 248 (45);
Mill on compulsion to, xxv, 205; Pascal
on reminders of, xlviii, 46 (104); perfect and imperfect, xxxii, 332 note; Poe
on sense of, xxviii, 376; poetry, as the
subject of, 376, 378; principles of, xxxii,
350-4, 342-3; Ruskin on, xxviii, 96,
157; Vishnu Purana on, 420; Woolman on, i, 189; worth of, intrinsic,
xxxii, 345-6, 350

Duty, Ode to, by Wordsworth, xli, 649-
51

Dyer, Chaucer's, xl, 21

Dyer, Sir Edward, My Mind to Me, xl,
207-9

Dyes, Woolman on, i, 309-10

Dying Man in His Garden, xli, 481

Dymas, in Æneid, xiii, 111, 113, 114

Dyslogistic Fallacies, xxvii, 245-6

Eadgils, xlix, 70 note 3, 71 note

Eagerness, Confucius on, xliv, 26 (16)

Eagle and Arrow, fable of, xvii, 41

Eagle(s), in old England, xxxv, 338;
Job's description of, xliv, 136-7; Manfred on, xviii, 416-7

Eanmund, xlix, 70 note 3, 77

Earle, John, letter of, xxxviii, 176-7

Early Piety, xlv, 563-4

Early Rising, Locke on, xxxvii, 21-2

Earnest Cry and Prayer, vi, 157-63

Earnestness, Confucius on, xliv, 58 (6);
Kempis on, vii, 236 (7)

Ears, drooping, cause of, xi, 27

Earth, age of, xi, 321-5, 344-5, 394-5;
ancient opinions of its motion, xxxix,

55; changes in, xi, 345-7, 387; xxxviii,
385-418; Copernicus on motion of the,
xxxix, 52-7; Descartes on the, xxxiv,
37; Faraday on, xxx, 9-10; Geikie on
past history of, 338-9; interior of the,
299-300, 305-6; Lactantius on the,
xxxix, 56; Milton on, iv, 169, 195,
245-7, 263, 307-8; motion of poles of,
xxxiv, 128-9; palpitation of, xxx, 283;
Raleigh on changes in the, xxxix, 107;
rigidity of the, xxx, 299, 300, 305-6;
Socrates's idea of the, ii, 104-8; temperature of, changes in, xxxviii, 395

Earth-Spirit, in Faust, xix, 27

Earthly Paradise, Prologue of the,
xlii, 1193-4

Earthquakes, Darwin on, xxix, 305-16,
507; effect of, on the weather, 355-6;
Lyell on, xxxviii, 406-7; oblivion in,
iii, 136; rain and, xxix, 355-6; Woolman on, as judgments of God, i, 237

Ease, after pain, iv, 61; Confucius on,
xliv, 6 (14); deliciousness of, due to
toil, xxviii, 314-5; Hobbes on desire
for, xxxiv, 370-1; Tennyson on, xlii,
994-8; Yutzu on, xliv, 6 (12)

Ease, Plain of, in Pilgrim's Progress,
xv, 109

East India Company, end of, xxv, 154;
forts of, x, 457; Mill on, xxv, 212;
mismanagement of, x, 470

Eastburn, Samuel, i, 234, 239, 249

Easter, celebration of, xv, 403

Easter, Spenser's, xl, 249

Easter Choruses, in Faust, xix, 36

Easter Song, by Herbert, xl, 345

Eating, Augustine, St., on continency in,
vii, 183; Confucius on excessive, xliv,
60 (22); Locke on children's, xxxvii,
16-21, 31; Luther on freedom of,
xxxvi, 309-10; More on pleasure of,
203; Penn on, i, 328 (59)

Ebusus, and Corynæus, xiii, 400

Ecbatan, reference to, iv, 329

Eccentricity, Mill on, xxv, 262

Eccentrics, defined, iii, 45 note

Eccius, John, xxxvi, 340-1

Ecclesiastes, Book of, Buddha, resemblances of, to, xlv, 574; xliv, 335-49;
remarks on, 334; l, 29

Ecclesiastical Princedoms, xxxvi, 38-40

Ecgtheow, xlix, 12, 15, 18 note 3

Echecrates of Phlius, ii, 45-7, 81, 95-6

Echeneus, in the Odyssey, xxii, 94, 153

Echephron, son of Nestor, xxii, 43

Echetus, the king, xxii, 247, 292

Echinades, Herodotus on the, xxxiii, 11

Echion, father of Pentheus, viii, 390, 392; husband of Agave, 429

Echo, the nymph, Dante on, xx, 334 note 3; Milton on, iv, 50-1; Shelley on, xli, 860

ECHOES, by Moore, xli, 821-2

Eclipses, foretold by ancient philosophers, vii, 64; Pericles on the, xii, 72; signs of ill, xlviii, 65 (173)

Economical Table, of Quesnai, x, 438, 444

Economists, of France, x, 443-4; on land taxes, 481

Economy, beauty in, v, 304; Burke on true, xxiv, 397; Emerson on, v, 52; of nature, xi, 151-2

ECSTASY, AN, xl, 341

Ector, Sir, in the HOLY GRAIL, xxxv, 156-8, 159, 160-1, 162, 179-80, 203-4

Ed-Dejjal, Muslim Antichrist, xvi, 239 note

Ed-Dimiryat, king of the Jinn, xvi, 308, 309, 310

EDDA, ELDER, SONGS FROM THE, xlix, 359-438; remarks on, 250-2

Edelfla, the tree, xxxix, 12

Eden, Burns on, vi, 142; Dante in, xx, 258-84; Milton on, iv, 158, 160-2

Edgar, king of England, navy of, xxxv, 361; and the wolves, 341

Edgar, in KING LEAR, Edmund and, xlvi, 226-9, 310-4; flight of, 242-3, 251-2; Gloucester and, 281-3, 291-3, 297-300, 306; Goneril's letter found by, 299, 305; Lear and, 273-7; as madman, 269-72; madness of, remarks on, 214; soliloquy of, 280-1

Edh-Dhubyani, Arab poet, xvi, 297 note 1

Edinborough, Franklin on men of, i, 15

Edinburgh, built of foreign timber, x, 170; industries of, 264

EDINBURGH, ADDRESS TO, vi, 252-3

Edinburgh Review, Emerson on the, v, 315; establishment of, xxvii, 225; Mill on, xxv, 61-62, 137; Whig organ, xxvii, 362; Wordsworth on, v, 464

Editors, Carlyle on, xxv, 446; Johnson on, xxxix, 235-6, 242-8; Stevenson on duty of, xxviii, 285

Edmund, in KING LEAR, bastard son of Gloucester, xlvi, 216; Albany and, 305, 308-10; before battle, 305; character

of, 214; confession of, 312-15; Curan and, 242; death of, 316; Edgar and, 225-9, 242-3, 311; Gloucester and, 267, 273; Goneril and, 277, 283-4, 299; Lear and Cordelia with, 306-7; Regan and, 290, 303-4

Education, Channing on, xxviii, 358-60; Confucius on, xliv, 45 (28), 53 (38); Emerson on, v, 7-15, 48-50, 191-2, 256-7, 261-2; Epictetus on lack of, ii, 156 (105); Franklin on female, i, 15, 93; Goethe on, xxv, 381-2; Goethe on, of artists, xxxix, 252, 255-7, 264-6; Hippocrates on, xxxviii, 4; Hume on importance of, xxxvii, 355-6; Huxley on, xxviii, 210-23; Kant on moral, xxxii, 322 note 2; Luther on, xxxvi, 321-7; Marcus Aurelius on, ii, 193 (4); Mill on, xxv, 9, 28, 29, 37-8, 70, 87-8, 108, 111, 115, 302-5; Newman on, xxviii, 31-8; Pascal on, xlviii, 19 (34), 38, 41 (95); Penn on, i, 321-3; Pliny on, ix, 301-3, 320-1; Ruskin on, xxviii, 94, 102-3, 111, 135, 136, 146-56; Schiller on, xxxii, 207-95; Smith on, x, 133-7, 219, 463-4; in Utopia, xxxvi, 231-2; Vaughan on, i, 69-70; Washington on need of public, xliii, 243; Wordsworth on, v, 323

EDUCATION, ESSAY ON, Bacon's, iii, 98-9

EDUCATION, LOCKE'S THOUGHTS CONCERNING, xxxvii, 5-183; remarks on, 3-4

EDUCATION, MILTON'S TRACTATE ON, iii, 235-47; remarks on, 234

EDUCATION OF CHILDREN, Montaigne's, xxxii, 29-71

EDUCATION OF THE HUMAN RACE, xxxii, 185-206; remarks on, 184; l, 32, 36-7

EDUCATION OF WOMEN, by Defoe, xxvii, 148-51; remarks on, l, 36

EDWARD, a ballad, xl, 56-8

Edward I, of England, Dante on, xx, 174 note 16, 368 note 8

Edward the Second, of England, in EDWARD THE SECOND, in abbey, xlvi, 65; at Berkeley, 72-3, 82-3; at Boroughbridge, 52-3; capture of, 66-8; crown yielded by, 68-70; delights of, 9; death of, 84-6; flight of, 84; Gaveston and, 7-8, 9-21, 26-7, 31-4, 38-9, 43, 50-1; Gurney and Matrevis with, 74-5, 77-9; Isabella, Queen, and, 20-2, 25-7, 38; iii, 50; in Kenilworth Castle, xlvi, 68-70; nobles' quarrel with, 35-8, 54-5, 59-60; Normandy lost by, 49; Raleigh

on murder of, xxxix, 72; Spencer and, xlvi, 47-8, 51-2; at Tynemouth, 40

EDWARD THE SECOND, xlvi, 7-89; remarks on, 5; Lamb on, 6

Edward the Third, in EDWARD THE SECOND, xlvi, 49, 56-9, 63-4, 81-2, 87-9; in France (see Crecy); St. Patrick's Purgatory and, xxxii, 178; Raleigh on, xxxix, 72; victories over kings, xxxv, 221

Edward IV, beauty of, iii, 106; census of England under, xxxv, 231; founder of King's College, 380; licence to sheep exporters, 328-9; Raleigh on, xxxix, 74-5

Edward V, murder of, xxxix, 75-6

Edward the Confessor, miracles of, xlvi, 377-8

Edward, the Black Prince (see Black Prince)

Edwardes, Richard, AMANTIUM IRÆ, xl, 201-2

Edwards, Jonathan, Hazlitt on, xxvii, 277

Edwards, Milne, on organization, xi, 129; on physiological division of labor, 118; on types, 451

Eels, in Egypt, xxxiii, 39

Effects, Pascal on reason of, xlviii, 110 (315)

Effiat, Marquis d', and Bacon, xxxiv, 98-9

Effort, Channing on value of, xxviii, 314-15; Confucius on, xliv, 20 (20); ECCLESIASTES on uselessness of, xliv, 335-8, 341 (15-16); Johnson on high, xxxix, 198-9

Efrits, species of genii, xvi, 9

Egbert, the navy of, xxxv, 361

Egerton, Lady Alice, in COMUS, iv, 44

Egerton, Lord, Jonson on, xxvii, 56-7

Egerton, Thomas, in COMUS, iv, 44

Eggs, number of, as security against destruction, xi, 75-6

Egidio, in THE BETROTHED, xxi, 173-4, 321, 323

Egidius, the disciple, xx, 332 note 18

Egil, Emerson on, v, 344

Eglemore, Sir, xiv, 93

Eglentyne, Madame, in CANTERBURY TALES, xl, 14

EGMONT, Goethe's, xix, 253-334; remarks on, 252

Egmont, Count, Alva and, xix, 298, 303, 305, 307-14; arrested, 313-14; Clara and, 267-8, 291-6, 315-18; Ferdinand and, 305, 326-32; historically, 252; Machiavel and, 262-4; Netherlanders' love of, 254, 255; with Orange, 283-8; in prison, 318-20; Raleigh on, xxxix, 89; rashness of, xix, 281-2; rioters and, 276-7; on way to scaffold, 333-4; with secretary, 278-83; hears his sentence, 326; sleep and vision, 332

Ego, Berkeley on the, xxxvii, 254-5; Buddhist denial of the, xlv, 653-60; Pascal on, xlviii, 111 (323), 155 (469); Schiller on, xxxii, 238-41

Egotism, Emerson on value of, v, 232-3; Kant on, xxxii, 334, 341; Pascal on, xlviii, 152 (457)

Egremont, Earl of, i, 49

Egypt, agriculture of, xxxiii, 12-13; artificial lake in, 75-6; canals of, 52-3, 79-80; civilization of, why early, x, 25; "Deserters" of, xxxiii, 19-20; fathers and sons in, x, 64; freedom in ancient, v, 89; gods in, xxxiii, 72-3; xxxviii, 387; history of, xxxiii, 48-89; Israel in, xliv, 435-8; kings of, xxxiii, 9, 48-89; labyrinth of, 74-5; land of, nature and extent, 9-15; pigeons in ancient, xi, 40; plagues of, iv, 346; xliv, 242 (43-51), 276 (27-36); pyramids of, xxxiii, 63-5, 67, 68-9; Rousseau on arts of, xxxiv, 177; shipping in ancient, iii, 157; species in, unchanged, xi, 210; wealth of ancient, x, 295; wonders of, xxxiii, 22

EGYPT, ACCOUNT OF, Herodotus's, xxxiii, 7-90; remarks on, 5-6; l, 19

Egyptian Feasts, skeleton at, xxxii, 16, 19

Egyptians, anointing among, xxxiii, 47; antiquity of the, 7-8, 13-4; athletics among, 45; boats and navigation of, 47-8; calendar of the, 9; chronology of the, xxxiv, 127; circumcision among, xxxiii, 23, 51; classes among the, 82-3; costumes, 41-2; diet and feasts of, 40-1, 45-6; divination among, 42; of the fens, 45-7; gnats, manner of protection from, 47; gods of the, 9, 26-31, 72-3, 78-9; health, care of, 40; hero-worship not practised by, 31; lotos and papyrus eaters, 45-6; manners and customs of the, 22-3; medical skill of, Homer on, xxii, 52; medicine among, xxxiii, 42; memory of, 40; mode of greeting, 41; monogamy practised by, 45; mourning and burial customs, 42-4; old age, respect for, 41; oracles of, 33, 42, 78-9;

Perseus worshipped by, 44-5; religious celebrations of, 33-5; religious customs, 23-4; sacred animals of, 24-30, 36-40; sanctity of temples, 35-6; song of, 41; transmigration believed in by, 62

Ehrenberg, on infusoria, xxix, 15; on phosphorescence of sea, 168

Eichthal, Gustave d', xxv, 105

Eidothëe, daughter of Proteus, xxii, 55-7

Eimeo, island of, xxix, 410

Ekphantus, on motion of earth, xxxix, 55

Elaine, mother of Galahad, xxxv, 203 (see Galahad, birth of); Renan on, xxxii, 153

Eland, Cumming on the, xxviii, 409

Elasticity, force of, xxx, 188-92

Elater, Darwin on the, xxix, 39-40

Elatreus, in the games, xxii, 102

El-Bakbuk, story of, xvi, 164-8

Elbe, Tacitus on the, xxxiii, 116

Elbo, island of Anysis, xxxiii, 70

ELDER EDDA, SONGS FROM THE, xlix, 359-438

Eldon, Lord, and the cartoons, v, 417; Holdship and, 370; on impressment, 364; never "ratted," 377

El Dorado, city of, Milton on, iv, 329; Smith on, x, 403 (see also Manoa)

Elect, Pascal on the, xlviii, 189 (575, 577)

Election, doctrine of eternal, xxxix, 49-50

ELECTION BALLAD, vi, 379-383

ELECTION BALLAD FOR WESTERHA', vi, 370-1

Election Expenses, Mill on, xxv, 173

Elective Franchise, Emerson on the, v, 241; Mill on the, xxv, 159-60; in U. S., xliii, 197 (15), 198 (19), (see also Suffrage)

Electoral College, first provision of, xliii, 187 (2, 3); amended provisions 195-6 (12), 196-7 (14), 197-8 (17)

Electra, daughter of Atlas, xiii, 272; Dante on, xx, 19 and note 5; in THE LIBATION-BEARERS, viii, 79-101; Voltaire on, xxxix, 364

Electric Fish, xi, 188-90

Electricity, and the ether, xxx, 263, 264; Franklin on, i, 146-8; magnetism and, xxx, 82-5, 206; motive force of, 203-7; production of, 61-4, 74-81, 203, 204; transferability of, 66-72

Electro-magnetism, xxx, 83, 206

Elegance, born, not bred, v, 214; Burke on, xxiv, 98; true, in few wants, v, 53

Elegiac Poets, Milton on, xxviii, 173-4

Elegy, Sidney on the, xxvii, 29; Wordsworth on the, xxxix, 298

ELEGY, by Byron, xli, 790

ELEGY IN A COUNTRY CHURCHYARD, Gray's, xl, 443-7

Eleians, in Egypt, xxxiii, 80-1

Elements, creation of the, xx, 313-14

Elephantinē, Herodotus on, xxxiii, 11

Elephants, habits of, xxix, 91; increase of, xi, 74; insects and, 355; seldom destroyed by beasts of prey, 77; weight of, xxix, 94

ELEU LORO, xli, 742-3

Eleusis, chapel of, at Athens, xii, 50

Eleutheria, establishment of the, xii, 99

Elevation, coral reefs and land, xxix, 483; Lyell on, of land, xxxviii, 401, 406, 409, 411

El-Fadl, the vizier, xvi, 193-9

El-Feshsharf, story of, xvi, 177-84

ELFIN MOUND, THE, xvii, 259-65

Elfmounds, champions of the, xlix, 240-1

Elgin, song of, Burns on, vi, 138

Elgin, Lord, and the Greek remains, v, 361

El-Heddar, story of, xvi, 168-71

Eli, name of Chief Good, xx, 398; sons of, iv, 100

Elian le Blank, xxxv, 163

Elias, Calvin on, xxxix, 40, 44; St. James on, xlviii, 303 (868)

Eliazar, and Argustus, xxxv, 154; son of Pelles, 206-7, 208

Eligius, St., xl, 14 note 68

Elihu, son of Barachel, xliv, 121-32; remarks on speech of, 72

Elijah, Augustine on, vii, 185; Bunyan on, xv, 159; Jesus and, xliv, 379 (30); Milton on, iv, 368, 372, 378; Zarephath and, xliv, 364 (25-6)

Eliot, John, BRIEF NARRATIVE, xliii, 138-46; life and works of, 138 note; on wine, v, 126

Eliott, Sir Thomas, xxxvi, 134

Eliphaz, the Temanite, xliv, 73, 75, 93, 105, 141

Elisabat, the barber, xiv, 207, 210

Elisabeth, mother of John, xliv, 353 (5, 7, 13), 354 (24-5), 359 (36, 41-5), 356 (57-60)

Elisha, and Naaman, xliv, 364 (27)

Eliwlod, xxxii, 168-9

Elixir, Sir Mammon on the, xlvii, 565-6

ELIXIR, THE, xl, 342-3

ELIZA, FAREWELL TO, vi, 218

ELIZA, QUEEN OF THE SHEPHERDS, xl, 245-7

ELIZABETH, L. H., EPITAPH ON, xl, 297

Elizabeth, of Bohemia, Walton on, xv, 347

ELIZABETH OF BOHEMIA, xl, 287-8

Elizabeth, Queen of England, Drake and, xxxiii, 122, 126-7; in *The Faerie Queene*, xxxix, 63; Harrison on progresses of, xxxv, 327; Hugo on, xxxix, 356; Johnson on times of, 218; literary age of, xviii, 5; Mary Queen of Scots on, vi, 396-7; the navy of, xxxv, 357-9; Philip II and, xxxiii, 226; pictures of, xxxix, 80; Raleigh and, 67 note 1; xxxiii, 300; secretaries of, stories of, iii, 57, 59; Sidney and, xv, 384; stockings first worn by, x, 206

Elizabethan Age, Emerson on the, v, 434-8

ELIZABETHAN DRAMAS, xlvi, xlvii

Elizabethan England, ale-drinking in, xxxv, 285-6; ale-houses in, 245; apparel and attire, 289-92; the church in, 252, 256-70; cities, towns, bishoprics, parishes, and estates of, 230-5; climate, soil, and products, 307-17; commerce of, 224-6; customs of, 330-1; degrees of people in, 217-29; dishes of, 298-9, 321-2; dogs in, 350-6; fairs and markets, 244-51, 327; food and diet in, 271-88; fowls, wild and tame, 334-40; gardens and orchards of, 236-43; holidays in, 266; houses and furniture in, 293-8, 309-10; interest in, 299-300; laws and licences in, 315; learning in, xxxix, 225-6, 229; live stock of, xxxv, 325-33; luxuries of life in, 297-9, 321-2; manners in, 223, 226-7, 232, 273-5, 277-9, 286-8; minerals and metals, 318-24; navy and shipping of, 357-62; poor relief, beggars, vagabonds, and jugglers, 301-6; punishment of vagabonds, 305-6; punishments of crime in, 363-70; rents and tenures, 299, 300; universities of, 371-83; wealth of, 299, 300; wild beasts, vermin, and insects, 341-9; woolen manufactures in, 328-9

ELIZABETHAN ENGLAND, DESCRIPTION OF, xxxv, 215-383

Elizabethan Language, Johnson on, xxxix, 196-7

El-Kuz el Aswani, story of, xvi, 174-7

Ellesmere, Lord, relations with John Donne, xv, 325-6, 327

Elliot, Sir Gilbert, xl, 110

Elliot, Jane, LAMENT FOR FLODDEN, xli, 483

Elliot of Lariston, xli, 768

Elliott, Willie, and Scott, xxv, 414

Ellis, Sarah, wife of Woolman, i, 187

Ellis, William, xxv, 54, 63, 78, 80

El-Mihraj, the king, xvi, 239

Elmire, in TARTUFFE, Cleante and, xxvi, 208; Orgon and, 266-70, 278; Pernelle and, 199-201, 206; Tartuffe and, 247-54, 270-6, 284, 291, 293-4, 296

El-Móin, the vizier, xvi, 193-209, 225-7, 229

El-Muntasir bi-llah, Caliph, xvi, 162-3

Eloquence, Augustine, St., on, vii, 67; Burke on, xxiv, 29-40, 299; Carlyle on, xxv, 377; Descartes on study of, xxxiv, 8-9; Hobbes on, 360, 373; Hume on, xxxvii, 381-3; Milton on, iv, 122; Montaigne on, xxxii, 62, 64; Pascal on, xlviii, 12, 14-15, 17 (25-6); Penn on, i, 336; Pliny on, ix, 346-8; Woolman on, i, 311

Elpenor, and Artemidora, xli, 902; Homer on, xxii, 144, 146-7, 162

ELPHINSTONE'S TRANSLATIONS, ON, vi, 264

Elpinice, sister of Cimon, xii, 45; Pericles and, 64

Elsbeth, in WILLIAM TELL, xxvi, 437, 440

ELSIE, CLEVER, story of, xvii, 121

Ely, Island of, xxxv, 314, 317

Elymas, the sorcerer, xliv, 450 (8-11)

Elysian Fields, Æneas's visit to, xiii, 229; Britain reputed locality of, xxxv, 307; Homer on the, xxii, 60

Elysium, Socrates on, ii, 105-6, 109

Emancipation, Lincoln and, xxviii, 442-7

EMANCIPATION PROCLAMATION, xliii, 323-5; Emerson on the, xlii, 1261 note

Emathian Conqueror, Alexander called the, iv, 78

Embalming, in ancient Egypt, xxxiii, 42-4

Embassies, origin of, x, 457-8

Embellishment, is deformity, v, 302

Emblems, use of, v, 167-9, 175-6

Embryo Spirit, in FAUST, xix, 185

Embryological Characters, in classification, xi, 437

Embryological Resemblances, xi, 249-50

Embryology, Darwin on, xi, 457-69

Embryos, early death of, xi, 301-2; in Milton's Limbo, iv, 147; pictures of past, xi, 371-2

Emendation, Johnson on, xxxix, 243-8

Emeria, country of, xxxiii, 325 note 23, 331

Emerson, Ralph Waldo, Carlyle and, xxv, 316-17; ENGLISH TRAITS, v, 315-474; Essays of, 5-310; life and work of, 3-4; Lowell on, xxviii, 467; personal acquaintances in England, v, 462-6; Poems by, xlii, 1241-64; remarks on, l, 36; SPEECH AT MANCHESTER, v, 471-4; visit to Stonehenge, 453-62

EMIGRANTS IN BERMUDA, xl, 376-7

Emilius, Paulus (see Æmilius)

Eminence, Confucius on, xliv, 40 (20); verses on, xvi, 235

Emlen, Samuel, i, 289-91, 301

Emmet, Æsop's fable of the, xxxiii, 129

Emmets (see Ants)

Emonides, death of, xiii, 339-40

Emotions, Emerson on the, v, 66-70; Mill on the, xxv, 35-6; Stevenson on display of, xxviii, 280-1

Empedocles, Bacon on, iii, 66; in Dante's Limbo, xx, 20; on evolution, xi, 6; in Milton's Limbo, iv, 147; Sainte-Beuve on, xxxii, 116; Sidney on, xxvii, 7; sphere of, ii, 295 (3); on the world, xxxix, 104

EMPEROR'S NEW CLOTHES, THE, xvii, 234

EMPIRE, ESSAY ON, Bacon's, iii, 48-52

Employers (see Capitalists)

Employment, necessary to contentment, i, 141; Woolman on, 236

Employments, Johnson on the lower, xxxix, 182; Smith on, x, 63-4, 102-46

Empty Sack, proverb of the, i, 91

Emulation, Bacon on, between brothers, iii, 20; envy and, xl, 420; defined by Hobbes, xxxiv, 343

Enceladus, and Ætna, xiii, 147

Enchanted Ground, in PILGRIM'S PROGRESS, xv, 138-9, 301-5

Enclos, Ninon de l', xxvii, 274

Enclosures, advantage of, x, 154; Democritus and Columella on, 157; effect of, xi, 80

Encolpius, reader to Pliny, ix, 316

Encyclopædists, Burke on the, xxiv, 246; Carlyle on the, xxv, 335

END OF THE PLAY, xlii, 1058-60

Endicott, Gov., xliii, 88

Endor, Witch of, iii, 90; xviii, 428

Endowments, Carlyle on, xxv, 374-5; Mill on, 114-15

Ends, Kant's kingdom of, xxxii, 343-4, 347 note, 348-9

Endurance, Locke on, xxxvii, 94-5, 99-101

Endymion, called Latmian shepherd, xl, 244

Enemies, fable of despicable, xvii, 18: fable on promises of, 29; Jesus on loving, xliv, 369 (27, 35)

Energy, Hume on idea of, xxxvii, 336-50; ill-temper and, xxviii, 175-6 (see also Force)

Engagements, Mill on liberty of, xxv, 299

En-gedi, reference to, xli, 485

Engelier, the Gascon, xlix, 120, 135, 138, 144, 167

Enghien, Duc d', xxxviii, 23

Engines, Helmholtz on, xxx, 190-4; improvement in, due to boy, x, 15

England, Alfieri, on, v, 331; in American Civil War, xxv, 166-7; xxviii, 115; apprenticeships in, x, 122; artificiality of, v, 362-3; Carlyle on history of, xxv, 366; Catholic Church in, xxxv, 252-6, 266, 267; climate and situation, v, 331-6; coasts of, action of sea on, xxxv, 319; commercial laws of, x, 405-25; country of contradictions, v, 362-3; Elizabethan (see Elizabethan England); estates of, 404-7; first book in, xxxix, 5 note; food in, xxxv, 237, 245, 330-3, 335, 336, 347; foreign policy, v, 467-8; France and, in trade, x, 367-8; France and, in war, iii, 75; free trade movement in, xxv, 65; Goldsmith on, xli, 528-31; influence of, v, 332-3; interest, rates of, in, x, 91; liberalism in, xxv, 64-5; liberty, ideas of, in, 202-3; luxury and rioting in, xxxvi, 147-8; Milton on, iii, 215, 222-4, 225-6; minerals and metals, xxxv, 319-24; money of, x, 43; More on causes of theft in, xxxvi, 143-8; names of places in, v, 405; Norman, navy of, xxxv, 361; peerage of, Carlyle on, xxv, 371; penalties in, xliii, 92; poor laws of, x, 139-41; post-office established in, ix, 368 note 4; press of, v, 447-53; prices in, i, 304; x, 195-6, 205; xxxv, 224-5, 228, 247-9; progress of wealth of, x, 272-3; races of, v, 352-3; Raleigh on,

xxxix, 72-80; Royal Society and Acade-
mies of, xxxiv, 154-9; Saxon, x, 30,
194; xxxv, 361; sea-power of, iii, 80;
serving men in, xxxvi, 144-6; sheep-
raising in, 146-7; stage-coaches in
(1772), i, 304-5; state of (1782), xxiv,
387-9; Tennyson on, xlii, 998; Thomson on, xl, 442-3; trade treaty with
Portugal, x, 390-4; universities of, v,
415-23; wages in, i, 304; x, 77, 143-4;
weights and measures in, xxxv, 249;
Winthrop on government of, xliii, 91;
Wordsworth on, xli, 675, 677; work-
manship in, xxxv, 228, 321-2

ENGLAND AND SWITZERLAND, xli, 675-6

England, Bank of, operations of, x, 241-3;
power of, v, 396; privileges of, x, 461;
profits of, 469

England, Church of, Browne on, iii, 255-
6; Burke on, xxiv, 235-40; Defoe on
establishment of, xxvii, 133-47; under
Elizabeth, xxxv, 252, 256-70; Emerson
on, v, 424-32; Voltaire on, xxxiv, 78-
81

ENGLAND, MY ENGLAND, xlii, 1210-12

ENGLAND, YE MARINERS OF, xli, 777-8

English, ability of the, v, 361; American
interest in the, 50; aristocracy, 402-15;
Austin on the, xxv, 111; belles lettres
among the, xxxiv, 140-54; brutality
among the, v, 346-7; Burke on the,
xxiv, 222-3; character of the, v, 379-
87; character summarized, 466-71;
close union of the, 365; cockayne, 387-
92; constitutional force, 381; courage
and tenderness of, 348; diet of, 349;
dinner among the, 372; domestic life of
the, 369; dulness of the, 377; freedom
of, 355; Goldsmith on the, xli, 528-9;
government of the, xxxiv, 85-92; hatred
of pretension, v, 372; horsemanship of,
350; industry and machinery, 394-6;
literature of, 432-46; love of custom,
370; love of home, 369; love of private
independence, 387; machinery, results
of, on, 399-400; maritime inclinations
of the, 347; mechanical tendencies of
the, 367; Mill on the, xxv, 41-2, 96-7,
148-9; Mirabeau on the, xxviii, 468;
moroseness, v, 379; narrow patriotism
of, 388-9; natural sincerity of the,
373-9; patience of the, 359-60; perti-
nacity of the, 360-1; physique of, 347;
plain-dealing of the, 354; pluck of the,
366; practicalness of, 355; pride in

wealth, 392-4; propriety of the, 371-2;
prosperity, love of, 359; the race, 336-
51, 352-3; religion of, 423-32; xxiv,
226-7; religious sects among the, xxxiv,
65-85; respect for property, v, 397-8;
Ruskin on the, xxviii, 116-27; sea
supremacy of the, v, 330; self-esteem,
389-90; social system, artificiality of,
364; sports of, 350; stoutness of mind
of the, 381; Taine on the, xxxix, 416,
421, 425; testiness of the, v, 384-5;
thoroughness of the, 360; trade of the,
xxxiv, 92-3; travellers, v, 382; under-
lying strength, 386; universities, 415-
23; utility, love of, 357, 443-4; vigor
of the, 367-8; in war, 358; wars of the,
xxxiv, 85-7; wealth of the, v, 396;
wealth, use of, 400-1; Wordsworth on
the, xli, 676-7

ENGLISH, LETTERS ON THE, Voltaire's,
xxxiv, 65-159

English Channel, tides of, xxx, 287-8

English Civil War, Marvell on, xl, 370-1;
Vane on, xliii, 121

English Comedy, Voltaire on, xxxiv, 136-
40

English Commonwealth, Milton on the,
xxviii, 188-9; discussion under the,
189-90 (see also INSTRUMENT OF GOV-
ERNMENT)

English Drama, blank verse in, xix, 204;
gentility in, v, 121; Shakespeare and,
xxxix, 229-30, 231-3; Shakespearized,
v, 10; in Shakespeare's time, xxxix,
230; (16th century) Sidney on, xxvii,
43-6; Voltaire on, xxxiv, 130-40

ENGLISH DRAMAS, MODERN, xviii

ENGLISH ESSAYS, xxvii

English Language, Caxton on old, xxxix,
24-5; Dryden on, xiii, 54; Johnson on,
xxxix, 182-96; Locke on study of,
xxxvii, 162-3; Milton on, iii, 197; iv,
20-1; Sidney on, xxvii, 49-50; Whitman on the, xxxix, 408

English Law, Mill on, xxv, 44

English Literature, Bagehot on, xxviii,
176-7; Emerson on, v, 432-46; in 17th
century, xxxix, 427-8; Taine on, 436-7;
Thoreau on, xxviii, 413

ENGLISH LITERATURE, INTRODUCTION TO
TAINE'S, xxxix, 410-37

English Money, Smith on, x, 30-2

ENGLISH PHILOSOPHERS, xxxiv, 307-417;
xxxvii

English Poetry, Arnold's review of, xxviii,

75-90; Eliot on, l, 4; Emerson on, v, 180; Wordsworth's retrospect of, xxxix, 316-30

ENGLISH POETRY, xl, xli, xlii

English Revolution, Burke on principles of, xxiv, 155-172; Price on the, 155

English Tragedy, Voltaire on, xxxiv, 130-6

ENGLISH TRAITS, Emerson's, v, 315-474; remarks on, l, 45

ENID'S SONG, xlii, 976-7

Enipeus, and Tyro, xxii, 150-1

Enis-el-Jelis, story of, xvi, 193-230

Enjoyment, of the present, xliv, 337 (24), 338 (12-13), 341 (18-19), 345 (15); social, ii, 118 (3); temperance in, 198

Enlightenment, Kempis's prayer for, vii, 287-8

Enna, field of, iv, 161

En-Nabighah, Arab poet, xvi, 297 note 1

Ennius, on death, ix, 71; Dryden on, xxxix, 163; on Fabius, ix, 49; old age of, 50; on principles of nature, xxvii, 61; quoted, ix, 17-31; Shelley on, xxvii, 344; Sidney on, 6, 36-7

Enoch, Bunyan on, xv, 159; identified with Idris, xlv, 911 note 5; Pascal on, xlviii, 201; book of, 210

Enoch's Pillars, iii, 276 note 53

Ens, father of the Predicaments, iv, 22

Entellus, character of, xiii, 60; Dares and, 191-4

Enteritis, Holmes on, xxxviii, 247

Enthusiasm, Emerson on, v, 55, 159; method of divination, xxxiv, 381

ENVIER AND ENVIED, story of, xvi, 78-81

ENVIOUS WEZIR, story of, xvi, 35-6

Environment, of a race, Taine on, xxxix, 423-5

ENVY, ESSAY ON, Bacon's iii, 22-6

Envy, Æschylus on, viii, 38; Augustine, St., on, vii, 28; Bacon on extinguishing of, iii, 129; beginnings of, xxxiv, 204; Blake on, xli, 588; Burns on, vi, 89; Dante on, xx, 201; in Dante's PURGATORY, 195; death and, iii, 10; defined by Hobbes, xxxiv, 343; Emerson on, v, 60; emulation and, xl, 420; fable on, xvii, 32; Molière on, xxvi, 282; physical effects of, xxxviii, 124; Penn on, i, 345-6 (267-9), 380-1; public, Penn on, 353 (367); sin of, in FAUSTUS, xix, 228; Socrates on, results of, ii, 16; the vice of republics, xlii, 1301

Envy, in PILGRIM'S PROGRESS, xv, 97

Eocene Period, in Europe, xxx, 347

Eocene Strata, Lyell on, xxxviii, 404

Eochaid Feidlech, xlix, 199-201

Eofor, xlix, 73 note 1, 86-7

Eomer, in BEOWULF, xlix, 58

Eôs, and Kephalos, viii, 323

Eotens, sword of, xlix, 48, 49, 50-1, 76

Eozoon, Darwin on the, xi, 345

Epaminondas, Bacon on, iii, 101; Cicero on death of, ix, 103; on death, xxxii, 7; Emerson on, v, 128, 203; Pascal on, xlviii, 119 (353); Plutarch on, xii, 150, 189; poverty of, 78; Sidney on, xxvii, 41

Epaphos, child of Zeus and Io, viii, 197; the same as Apis, xxxiii, 77

Epaphroditus, freedman of Octavius, xii, 383

Epaphroditus, master of Epictetus, ii, 116; and the shoemaker, 130 (40)

Epeius (Epeüs), and the horse of Troy, xiii, 108-9; xxii, 112

Ephesian Books, burning of the, iii, 201

Ephesians, on examples of virtue, ii, 293 (26)

Ephesus, Herodotus on plains about, xxxiii, 11

Ephialtes, the Athenian, xii, 42, 44; murder of, 46

Ephialtes, the giant, in Dante's HELL, xx, 129, 130; Homer on, xxii, 152-3 (see also Alæan Twins)

Ephorus, and Theopompus, ix, 146

Ephraim, children of, xliv, 240 (9); Milton on, iv, 421; son of Jacob, xlviii, 237

EPIC AND SAGA, xlix

Epic Poetry, Dryden on, xiii, 5-11, 14; xxxix, 158; Fielding on, 176; Hugo on, 340-2, 352, 353-4; Milton on, v, 175; Poe on, xxviii, 372; Shelley's, xxvii, 349; Sidney on, xxvii, 28-9; Wordsworth on, xxxix, 298

Epicaste, in Hades, xxii, 151

Epicharmus, rule of, ix, 118; on the understanding, xxxii, 38

Epicles, of Hermione, xii, 9

Epicrates of Acharnæ, xii, 26-7; Cicero the Younger on, ix, 174

Epics, prose, xxxix, 176-7

Epictetus, on anger, xlviii, 35 (80); banishment of, ix, 239 note; on changes, ii, 293 (35); on consistency, xlviii, 118-19 (350); corn-superintendent and, ii, 125 (24); on desire and avoidance,

293-4 (37); on free will, 293 (36); GOLDEN SAYINGS OF, 117-85; Governor of Cnossus and, 151-2 (93); on himself, 159 (114); Hume on philosophy of, xxxvii, 319; on impossibilities, ii, 293 (33); life and teachings of, 116; Marcus Aurelius's acquaintance with, 194 (7); Pascal on, xlviii, 13 (18), 142 (431), 155 (466-7), 388-9, 396-400; priest of Augustus and, ii, 131 (43); the rich man and, 126 (25); on soul and body, 219 (41); the thief and, 120 (11); on words of bad omen, 293 (34); the young man and, 140 (65)

Epicureans, Bacon on, iii, 8

Epicurism, Locke on, xxxvii, 30-1

Epicurus, Aristophanes on, xxxii, 64-5; in Athens, iii, 193; xxviii, 58; xxxvii, 393; Augustine, St., on, vii, 97; Chaucer on, xl, 20; Dante on, xx, 40; freedom from citations, xxxii, 31; on God, iii, 43; Hugo on, xxxix, 343; on man as proper study of self, iii, 27; Mill on, xxv, 35; not an atheist, iii, 272; on pain, ii, 251 (64); on philosophy, xxxii, 54; property of, xxviii, 59; quotation from, xxxix, 114; religious principles of, xxxvii, 394-401; on sickness, ii, 272-3 (41); on the soul, xxxiv, 103

Epicycles, defined, iii, 45 note

Epicydes, and Themistocles, xii, 10

Epidaurian Giant, xxvi, 136

Epidaurus (see Æsculapius)

Epidemics, as a check to increase, xi, 78-9

Epigenes, with Socrates, ii, 22, 47

EPIGRAM, by Prior, xl, 398

EPILOGUE, by Browning, xlii, 1109-10

Epimenides, iii, 66; viii, 184 note 34

Epimetheus, fable of, iii, 40; Pandora and, iv, 172

Epiphanius, leader of Arabic school, xxviii, 59; Milton on, iii, 203

EPIPHANY, xlv, 565

Epirot, Pyrrhus called the, iv, 83

Epitaphs, Wordsworth on poetic, xxxix, 299

EPITHALAMION, Spenser's, xl, 234-45

Epitomes, Shelley on, xxvii, 335

Epixyes, and Themistocles, xii, 31

Epoch, Taine on importance of, xxxix, 422, 426-7

EPODE, by Jonson, xl, 294-7

Epuremei, Raleigh on the, xxxiii, 354-5, 358, 365; religion of, 374

Equability, is piety, xlv, 795

Equality, among low races, xxix, 234; ants pattern of, iv, 239; Ball, John, on, xxxv, 61; Burke on, xxiv, 175-6, 187; envy of, iii, 24; of fortune, 33; v, 88; of goods, Milton on, iv, 65; Hobbes on, xxxiv, 387-8, 408-10; Jefferson on, xliii, 150; Lowell on, xxviii, 469; Montaigne on, xxxii, 25; More on, xxxvi, 167, 168; natural, of men, v, 268; x, 21; Pascal on, xlviii, 106 (299), 378-80; Paul, St., on, xlv, 525 (14); principle of, discovered by Plato, xxvii, 346; realized in æsthetics, xxxii, 295; of rights, v, 240-1; sedition bred by, iii, 36; Spartan principle of, v, 241; of trades, x, 116-21

Equanimity, Hindu doctrine of, xlv, 855; Marcus Aurelius on the term, ii, 277 (8)

Equestrian Order, of Rome, ix, 204 note 2

Equipage, demand for, x, 167-8

Equity, Hobbes on, xxxiv, 409; Mohammed on, xlv, 986

Equivocation, Penn on, i, 336 (144)

Erasistratus, xxxviii, 67, 88-9

Erasmus, on the English universities, xxxv, 374; on folly, xxvii, 31; More on, xxxvi, 89; at Oxford, v, 416

Eraso, secretary of Charles V, xv, 327

Erastus, the disciple, xliv, 465 (22)

Erato, reference to, xiii, 240

Ercilla, Alonso de, Cervantes on, xiv, 54

Ercoco, reference to, iv, 329

Erechtheus, Athens the city of, viii, 352; references to, 157; xxvi, 153

Eric the Red, xliii, 5, 6, 8, 11, 13

Ericetes, death of, xiii, 347

Erichtho, Dante on, xx, 36

Erichthonius, reference to, xiii, 70

Erinyes, reference to the, viii, 290

Eriphyle, Homer on, xxii, 153; in the Mournful Fields, xiii, 222; slain by son, xx, 300 note 12, 192

Erisichthon, Dante on, xx, 239

Eristics, Socrates on the, ii, 95

Ermine, hunting of the, xiv, 316; Smart on the, xli, 494

Ernst, H. C., translator of Pasteur, xxxviii, 269

Erôs, and Anteros, xii, 109 note 3; xviii, 425; song to, viii, 326-8

Eros, servant of Antony, xii, 381

Erosion, Darwin on, xxix, 320-1; Geikie on, xxx, 341 (see also Denudation)

Erotic Poetry, Shelley on, xxvii, 342-3

Erp, son of Gudrun, xlix, 353, 357, 418, 426-7, 430

Erpingham, at Agincourt, xl, 224

Error, Augustine, St., on origin of, vii, 58; Berkeley on, xxxvii, 228; Emerson on, v, 17, Euripides on, viii, 325; hill of, in PILGRIM'S PROGRESS, xv, 123; Hobbes on, xxxiv, 332-3; knowledge of, necessary to truth, iii, 202; Milton on, iv, 401; Pascal on sources of, xlviii, 38-9; Sophocles on correction of, viii, 289

Erskine, Thomas, Lord, Burns on, vi, 159, 256-7, 449

Ertanax, the fish, xxxv, 183

Erymanthus, death of, xiii, 317

Erymanthus (region), and Hercules, xiii, 234

Erynnis, references to the, xx, 37; xxii, 206

Erysipelas, and puerperal fever, xxxviii, 236-7, 240 note, 242, 248-9, 252, 253

Erythrabolos, city of, xxxiii, 54

Erythræan Sea, Herodotus on, xxxiii, 10, 11; Milton on, iv, 16

Esau, Augustine, St., on, vii, 185; Bunyan on, xv, 125, 130-1; Woolman on, i, 298

Eschilus (see Æschylus)

Escobar, Pascal on, xlviii, 313 (915)

Escovedo, Raleigh on, xxxix, 88

Escremis, xlix, 124, 135

Escurial, Bacon on the, iii, 109

Esdras, Pascal on, xlviii, 209-10; Raleigh on, xxxix, 100

ESOPUS TO MARIA, vi, 485-7

Espanola, Drake at, xxxiii, 226

Esquife, friend of Don Quixote, xiv, 46

Esquimaux, Darwin on the, xxix, 234

ESSAY ON MAN, Pope's, xl, 406-40; l, 32

Essays, founded by Montaigne, xxxii, 3

ESSAYS, AMERICAN, xxviii, 307-470

ESSAYS, Bacon's, iii, 7-142

ESSAYS, Emerson's, v, 5-310

ESSAYS, ENGLISH, xxvii, xxviii

ESSAYS, FRENCH, GERMAN, etc., xxxii

Essence, defined, ii, 70; knowledge of, 64-5 (see also Real Existence)

Essex, Earl of, and Bacon, iii, 3; Emerson on, v, 183; Jonson on, xxvii, 56; A PASSION, xl, 287

ES-SINDIBAD OF THE SEA, xvi, 231-95

Es-Sindibad, the Porter, xvi, 231-4, 294-5

Establishment, misuse of word, xxvii, 245

Estampes, M. d', governor of Brittany, xxxviii, 13-14, 15

Este, Azzo da, and Del Cassero, xx, 163 note 5

Este, Ippolito d', Cardinal of Ferrara, xxxi, 197 note 5, 201-2, 249, 258-61, 267, 274-6, 278, 282-3, 284-5, 294, 319-20, 334-5

Este, Obizzo da, and Ghisola, xx, 74 note 2; murder of, 52 note 9

Esteem, love of, in children, xxxvii, 39-41; Pascal on, xlviii, 60 (148-9), 61 (153), 115 (333), 131 (404); Penn on, i, 348 (313); for rank, Pascal on, xlviii, 381

ESTEEM FOR CHLORIS, vi, 500

Esther, reference to, xx, 213

Estorause, King, xxxv, 211

Estorgan, in SONG OF ROLAND, xlix, 124, 135

Estouteville, Jean d', xxxi, 279 note

Estramarin, xlix, 97, 124, 135

Estrella, in LIFE A DREAM, with Astolfo, xxvi, 21-3; her claim to throne, 22-3; agrees to king's plan, 28-9; with Segismund, 43-4; chosen queen of Segismund, 73

Estrés, M. d', Paré on, xxxviii, 25, 43

Etáin, daughter of Eochaid, xlix, 201-2

Etáin, daughter of Etar, xlix, 200-1

Etampes, Madame d', mistress of Francis I, xxxi, 283 note, 328 note; Cellini and, 292-3, 296-8, 300-1, 310, 322, 325-6, 329-30, 333

Etearchos, king of Ammonians, xxxiii, 20-2

Eteocles, and Polynices, xx, 107 note; viii, 255, 260, 261-2; sung by Statius, xx, 235 note 3

Eteoneus, squire of Menelaus, xxii, 46-7, 202

ETERNAL GOODNESS, THE, xlii, 1338-41

Eternal Life, Kempis on desire of, vii, 315

Eternity, Browne on, iii, 262; Burke on idea of, xxiv, 52-3; Hindu doctrine of, xlv, 791-2; in an hour, xli, 586; human life and, ii, 271 (32); ocean of, in MIRZA, xxvii, 74, 76-7; Pascal on, xlviii, 31; shadows of, xl, 348; time and, iv, 39

Eterscél, King, xlix, 201, 202

Ethan the Ezrahite, Maschil of, xliv, 254-7

Ethelred, navy of, xxxv, 361

Ethelwald, at Winborne, v, 354

Ether, luminiferous, Kelvin on, xxx, 255, 263-6, 271-3

Ethics, common rational basis of, xxxii, 305-17; empirical and metaphysical bases of, 318-55; Hobbes on, xxxiv, 363; Hume on standard of, xxvii, 204-5; Kant on science of, xxxii, 299-300; Mill on Christian, xxv, 242-3; need of metaphysic of, xxxii, 300-3; need of philosophical basis, 316-7; Pascal on, xlviii, 25-6 (67), 313 (912); Pope on study of, xl, 406-7 (see also Morals)

Ethiopia, Herodotus on, xxxiii, 16, 19-20

ETHIOPIA SALUTING THE COLORS, xlii, 1407-8

Ethiopian Eunuch, xliv, 440-1 (27-40)

Ethiopians, circumcision among, xxxiii, 51; Homer on the, xxii, 9-10

Ethnology, importance of, xxviii, 230-4; a physical science, 235-6 (see also Race)

Etna (see Ætna)

ETON COLLEGE, ON A DISTANT PROSPECT OF, xl, 447-50

Ettrick Forest, men of, at Flodden, xli, 482 note

Etymology, Johnson on English, xxxix, 186-8

Eu, Comte d', at Dreux, xxxviii, 48

Eu, Earl of, in English wars, xxxv, 13, 50

Eucharist, Calvin on the, xxxix, 37, 50; institution of the, xliv, 410 (19-20); Kempis on, vii, 335-64; Luther on the, xxxvi, 320; Newman on doctrine of the, xxviii, 38; Pascal on the, xlviii, 81 (224), 218 (654), 220 (666), 223 (670), 273 (789), 301-2, 335, 348-9; St. Paul on the, xlv, 505-6 (23-9)

Euchidas, the Platæan, xii, 99

Euclia, the goddess, xii, 99

Euclid, the mathematician, Huxley on, xxviii, 219; in Limbo, xx, 20; on unity, xlviii, 434-5

Euclid, friend of Socrates, ii, 47

Eudæmon, name of, xii, 156 note

Eudamidas, will of, xxxii, 81, 82

Eudes, Mayor of Palace, xxxix, 83

Euergetes, name of, xii, 156 note

EUGANEAN HILLS, LINES WRITTEN AMONG, xli, 835-41

Eugene, Prince, xli, 734; and the English merchants, xxxiv, 92-3; story of, xxvii, 102

Eugenio, the goatherd, in DON QUIXOTE, xiv, 499-507

Eugenius, Calvin on, xxxix, 42, 43

Eulogies, fancy and judgment in, xxxiv, 350

Eulogistic Fallacies, xxvii, 245-6

Eumæus, swineherd of Odysseus, xxii, 186-99, 207-12, 215-19, 228, 232-6, 236, 241-4, 289-90, 293-4, 298-309; Cowley on, xxvii, 68

Eumedes, death of, xiii, 402

Eumenides, Hugo on the, xxxix, 348; name of, xxvii, 324

Eumenius, death of, xiii, 379

Eumolpus, Pliny on, ix, 399-400

Eunapius, at Athens, xxviii, 53-4

Eunoë, river, xx, 261-2

Eunomus, and Demosthenes, xii, 195

Eunuchs, envy of, iii, 23; king's favor for, 108

Euodius, conversion of, vii, 147; at funeral of Monnica, 155

Eupeithes, father of Antinous, xxii, 330-1; death of, 333

Euphelia, and Cloe, xl, 397-8

Euphrantides, the Prophet, xii, 17

Euphrasia, in PHILASTER (see Bellario)

Euphrates, the philosopher, ix, 195-6; quoted, ii, 172-3 (154)

Euphrosyne, reference to, iv, 30

Eupolis, and Alcibiades, ix, 149; on Pericles, ix, 207 note; xii, 38

Euripides, and Æschylus, xxxix, 426; Aristophanes on, viii, 438, 441; BACCHÆ of, 368-436; defeats of, xxxix, 317; dispute with Æschylus in THE FROGS, viii, 462-85; domestic relations of, 472; on hiding wickedness, xxxix, 70; HIPPOLYTUS of, viii, 303-67; Hugo on, xxxix, 347; Hugo on Suppliants of, 341; Johnson on, 210; on liberty of speech, iii, 183; life and works, viii, 302; in Limbo, xx, 236 note 6; Milton on, iv, 413; Shelley on, xxvii, 338; Sophocles, compared with, viii, 208; on the Spartans, iii, 194; verses of, in Syracuse, xxvii, 37

Euripus, the flux of, xxxviii, 75, 98, 99

Europa, reference to, xx, 401

Europe, American policy toward, xliii, 278-9; "better fifty years of," xlii, 985; civilization of, cause of, xxxiv, 206; eastern, Freeman on, xxviii, 262-72; growth of continent of, xxx, 342-51; races of, xxviii, 257-73

Europeans, contact of, with native races, xxix, 439-40

Eurus, reference to, xiii, 77

Euryades, death of, xxii, 303

Euryalus, and Nisus, xiii, 188, 298-308

Euryalus, in the ODYSSEY, xxii, 102, 103, 109-10

Eurybates, henchman of Ulysses, xxii, 263

Eurybiades, Admiral of Greeks, xii, 11; given rewards for valor, 20; at Salamis, 86; Themistocles and, 15-16

Eurycleia, nurse of Telemachus, xxii, 20, 30, 65, 228-9, 266-70, 306-7, 310-12

Eurycles, and Antony, xii, 374

Eurydamas, in the ODYSSEY, xxii, 252, 303

Eurydice, wife of Creon, viii, 294-6, 298-9

Eurydice, wife of Nestor, xxii, 44

Eurydice, wife of Orpheus, iv, 34

Eurylochus, in Circe's isle, xxii, 135-7, 141; at island of Helios, 169, 170-1

Eurymachus, suitor of Penelope, xxii, 19-20, 25-6, 62, 200, 213, 251-2; death of, 297-8; Melantho and, 253; Telemachus and, 226; Theoclymenus and, 282; Ulysses and, 254-5, 289-93

Eurymedon, in the ODYSSEY, xxii, 91

Eurymedusa, Homer on, xxii, 90

Eurynome, in ODYSSEY, xxii, 241, 249-50, 259, 314

Eurynomus, wooer of Penelope, xxii, 21, 302

Eurypilus, Dante on, xx, 84

Euryptolemus, and Pericles, xii, 41-2

Eurypylus, in ÆNEID, xiii, 104

Eurystheus, Epictetus on, ii, 142-3 (71)

Eurythmus, freedman of Trajan, ix, 295

Eurytion, in ÆNEID, xiii, 194, 196

Eurytion, the Centaur, xxii, 291

Eurytus, Homer on, xxii, 105

Eusebius, at Athens, xxviii, 60; on the Creation, xxxix 102; Milton on, iii, 203

Eustochium, vision of, iii, 200

Euterpe, mother of Themistocles, xii, 5

Eutyches, on Christ, xx, 306 note 5

Eutychus, and Octavius, xii, 372 note

Eutychus, and St. Paul, xliv, 467 (9-12)

Evadne, and Laodamia, xiii, 222

Evandale, Lord, character of, v, 122-3

Evander, and Æneas, xiii, 271-280, 283-7; Cowley on Virgil's, xxvii, 68; in Italy, xiii, 270; lament over Pallas, 361-2

EVANGELINE, Longfellow's, xlii, 1300-38; its debt to HERMANN AND DOROTHEA, xix, 336

Evangeline, daughter of Benedict Bellefontaine, xlii, 1301-2; her suitors, 1303; her love for Gabriel, 1303-4; her heifer, 1305; on evening of betrothal, 1306, 1307, 1309-10; at feast of betrothal, 1311; waiting for father's return, 1313-14; on day of expulsion, 1315, 1316, 1317-18; in exile, 1319; her search for Gabriel, 1319-34; in Philadelphia, as Sister of Mercy, 1334-5; during the plague, 1335-6; with Gabriel at last, 1336-7

Evangelist, in PILGRIM'S PROGRESS, xv, 14-15, 24-8, 89-91

Evangelus, servant of Pericles, xii, 54

Evans, mate of the "Alert," xxiii, 401

Eve, Adam accuses, iv, 287-9; Adam, first meeting with, 165-7, 255-7; Adam, her dependence on, 170-1; Adam, evening meal with, 163; Adam denounces, 312-14; Adam's love besought by, 314; Adam tempted by, 280-7; appearance of, at the feast, 190, 191-2; Bagehot on Milton's, xxviii, 192, 202-3; beauty of, v, 305; Browne on creation of, iii, 274; Bunyan on apple of, xv, 237; creation of, iv, 255-6; Dante on, in PARADISE, xx, 419 note 1; death suggested by, iv, 315-6; departs from Eden, 358; description of, 162; dream of, 181-3; feast prepared by, for Raphael, 188-9; hides from God, 293-4; judged, 294-6; labors of, 186; lamentation of, at loss of Eden, 325-6; prayer of, 184-6; temptation of, 273-80; tree of, xxxv, 186, 188

EVE OF ST. AGNES, xli, 883-93

Evelake, King, xxxv, 118-20, 138, 151, 207, 209

EVELYN HOPE, xlii, 1078-80

Evening, Goethe on influence of, xix, 52, 53; Milton's description of, iv, 169-70

EVENING, TO, xli, 479-81

EVENING STAR, TO THE, xli, 771, 776-7

Events, cause of, Whewell on, xi, 1; Emerson on origin of, v, 133; relation of, to causes, xxxvii, 352-7; tests of worth of, v, 187-88

Evenus, the Parian, ii, 8, 48, 49

Everett, Edward, oration at Gettysburg, xliii, 415 note

Evil, Augustine, St., on, vii, 37, 58, 74, 101-3, 111; Buddha on, xlv, 661; Carlyle on, xxv, 343; Dante on cause of, xx, 209-10; Emerson on, v, 27; Epictetus on, ii, 174 (162); Hobbes on,

xxxiv, 338-9; Hume on problem of, xxxvii, 368-70, 398; knowledge of, Mrs. Herbert on, xv, 376; knowledge of, Milton on, iii, 202; iv, 278; last infirmity of, xviii, 416; made by thought, xlvi, 132; Marcus Aurelius on, ii, 202 (11), 204 (17), 213 (7), 214 (8), 219 (39), 232 (1), 268 (13), 271 (35); Omar Khayyam on, xli, 955; Pascal on, xlviii, 132 (408), 332; Pope on, xl, 409-15, 433; Rousseau on, xxxiv, 260-2, 278-9; seeds of, fable on, xvii, 16; Socrates on, ii, 37-8; speaking and believing, vii, 209 (1); Woolman on, i, 256

Evils, as benefactors, v, 98; choose less of two, vii, 273; Goethe on imagined, xix, 33; Milton on imagined, iv, 54

Evolution, antiquity of idea of, xi, 6; Descartes on growth by, xxxiv, 12-3; generally accepted, xi, 246; growth of idea of, xi, 9-24

Evolution, Geographical, xxx, 328-51

Ewaipanoma, the, xxxiii, 359-60

Ewell, Gen., at Gettysburg, xliii, 343, 344, 355-6, 362-3

Exaggeration, Emerson on, v, 231

Example, best precept, xvii, 30; Chaucer on, and precept, xl, 25; Confucius on guiding by, xliv, 7 (3); education by, ix, 320; Epictetus on, and precept, ii, 177 (175); Epictetus on teaching by, 154 (102); Locke on teaching by, xxxvii, 55-6, 59, 65-6, 69-70; Spenser on teaching by, xxxix, 62

Examples, Bacon on use of, xxxix, 140; great men as, xlviii, 45-6 (103); Machiavelli on high, xxxvi, 19; Pascal on effect of, xlviii, 49 (117); Raleigh on historical, xxxix, 70-2, 89; true and feigned, xxvii, 20; use of good and evil, iii, 29

Excalibur, sword of Arthur, xlii, 986-90

Excess, causes defect, v, 87; Confucius on, xliv, 34 (15); Epictetus on, ii, 184 (12); Pascal on, xlviii, 30

Exchange, advantages of, x, 21; ancient media of, 28; effects of high price of, 315; medium of (see Money); power of, limits division of labor, 22; propensity to, 18; rates of, as criterion of balance of trade, 355-8; rates of international, 314-5

Excise, Duties, vexation of, x, 539

Excises under U. S. Constitution, xliii, 184 (1)

Excisemen, Kirk and State, vi, 460

Excitement, man's sphere, xix, 72; Pascal on quest of, xlviii, 54, 55, 56; Wordsworth on thirst for, xxxix, 273-4

Exclusionists, Emerson on, v, 94

Excommunication, Chaucer on, xl, 29 note 330; Dante on, xx, 364 note 10; Luther on, xxxvi, 275, 291, 292, 307-8; in Utopia, 230-1

Excuses, Confucius on, xliv, 54 (1); fable of, xvii, 11; Locke on, xxxvii, 114-15, 118; Marcus Aurelius on, ii, 124 (12); Pascal on, xlviii, 23 (58); Penn on, i, 337 (150); Thackeray on, xxviii, 11; Tzu-hsia on, xliv, 64 (8)

Executive Power (U. S.), xliii, 186-9

Exercise, Burke on necessity of, xxiv, 108-9; Cicero on, ix, 58

Existence, annihilation of, heresy of, xlv, 657-8, 664; definition of, impossible, xlviii, 425-6; Hindu doctrine of persistent, xlv, 791-2; persistent, heresy of, 657-8, 664; struggle for (see Struggle for Existence) (see also Real Existence)

Exorcism, Pascal on, xlviii, 284 (820)

Expectation, Manzoni on, xxi, 639; never satisfied, v, 232

Expediency, St. Paul on, xlv, 498 (12), 504 (23)

Expenditure (see Consumption)

Expense, Bacon on, iii, 72; educational, xxxvii, 70-1; immediate and durable, x, 274-7

Experience, in animals, xxxvii, 371-2; Bacon on analysis of, xxxix, 134, 137-40; Bunyan on, xv, 293; Descartes on value of, xxxiv, 10, 13; education by actual, v, 12-15; faith superior to, 133; Hobbes on, xxxiv, 314, 320; Hume on, xxxvii, 300-303, 308-11, 354-5, 375-6, 400-1; Hume on conclusions from, 312-18, 320, 321-3, 330; mother of sciences, xiv, 165; necessity of moral, xxviii, 172; of others, i, 70; Raleigh on, xxxix, 100; reason and, 127; xxxvii, 322 note; teacher of wisdom, best, xxviii, 339; thought and, Thoreau on, 399

Experience, the shepherd, in Pilgrim's Progress, xv, 123-6

Experiment, Bacon on necessity of, xxxix, 125, 127, 134, 135-6; Descartes on truth by, xxxiv, 12-3, 51

Explanations, actions the only true, v, 190-91

Expletives, Johnson on, xxxix, 192

Exports, and Exportation, bounties on, x, 374-88, 522; drawbacks on, 371-2; encouragement of, 330; of materials, discouraged, 405, 410-22; taxes on, from U. S., xliii, 185 (5)

Ex Post Facto Laws, xliii, 185 (3), 186 (10)

Expression, Locke on correct, xxxvii, 160-2; means of, other than words, xxviii, 280-1; necessary to beauty, v, 306-7

EXTEMPORANEOUS EFFUSION, vi, 355

EXTEMPORE IN COURT OF SESSION, vi, 256-7

Extempore Speaking, Locke on, xxxvii, 148

Extempore Writing, Carlyle on, xxv, 443-7

Extension, Berkeley on, xxxvii, 207-9, 211-2, 265; Hume on idea of, 411-2; infinite divisibility of, xlviii, 430-7; as source of grandeur, xxiv, 61-7

External Circumstances, independence of (see Independence of C.)

Extinction of Species, Darwin on, xi, 113-4, 124-5, 353-7; xxix, 179-81; Lyell on causes of, xxxviii, 403-4

Extortioners, St. Paul on, xlv, 497 (11), 497 (10)

Extradition, between U. S. and Great Britain, xliii, 281, 287-8; under Confederation, 159

Extravagance, economically considered, x, 266-8; public, 269-70

Extremes, Molière on man's tendency to, xxvi, 213-4; Pascal on, xlviii, 29-30; Plutarch on, xii, 148

Eye, beauty of the, xxiv, 97; development of the, xi, 181-4; Helmholtz on the, 203-4; interpreter of the heart, xlviii, 415

Eyes, temptation of, St. Augustine on, vii, 187-8

Eylimi, King, xlix, 278, 279

Eyre, Gov., prosecution of, xxv, 182

Eyre, Margery, in SHOEMAKER'S HOLIDAY, xlvii, 473-5, 480-3, 488-91, 497-504, 530

Eyre, Simon, in SHOEMAKER'S HOLIDAY, character of, xlvii, 468; king and, 531-2, 534-7; Leadenhall built by, 535 note; Lord Mayor and, 496, 501-4; Mayor, 514, 521, 528-31; Ralph and, 473-6; Rowland and, 482-3, 520, 525-

6; sheriff, 500-1; ship bought by, 489-91; at his shop, 479-83, 488-9

Eyre's Sound, glaciers in, xxix, 251

Eystein, and Sigurd, v, 344

Eyvind, and Olaf, v, 276

Ezekiel, and Æschylus, viii, 5; Pascal on, xlviii, 307 (886); vision of, iv, 99

Ezra, and the ass, xvi, 116 note

Ezzelin, reference to, xviii, 301

Fa, Jacques de la, xxxi, 310 note 1

Fabatus, letters to, ix, 248, 293, 303

Faber, Frederick William, HYMN BY, xlv, 571-2

Fabian, in POLYEUCTE, xxvi, 87-90, 118

Fabius Maximus, Cicero on, ix, 48-9; Pericles and, compared, xii, 37; Scipio and, xxxvi, 56; Virgil on, xiii, 236

FABLES AND FOLK-LORE, xvii

FABLES, PREFACE TO, Dryden's, xxxix, 153-75

Fables, law of compensation in, v, 91-2; remarks on, xvii, 8-9

Fabricius, Gaius, Cicero on, ix, 19; Dante on, xx, 225; on Epicurus, ix, 60; Milton on, iv, 383; More on, xxxvi, 162; Virgil on, xiii, 236

Fabricius, Hieronymus, Harvey on, xxxviii, 76; on lungs, 65, 71; on veins, 117-8

Face, Burke on beauty of the, xxiv, 96-7; character in the, iii, 312; expressions of the, xxviii, 280-1; ideal, rare, v, 305-6; sign of mind, as, Shakespeare on, xlvi, 330

Face, in THE ALCHEMIST, confederates betrayed by, xlvii, 655-7; Dame Pliant and, 591-2, 618, 620-1, 625-9; Dapper with, 551-8, 602, 607-10, 651-2, 653; Drugger and, 559-62, 589-91, 603-607; as Jeremy the servant, 645-50; Lovewit and, 650-1; Mammon and, 564, 567-70, 572, 574-5, 579-83, 611-2, 613-4, 617-18, 630-1, 632-3; Subtle and, 543-50, 621-2; Surly and, 582-3, 584, 622-5, 636-8

Facing-both-ways, Mr., in PILGRIM'S PROGRESS, xv, 102

Fact, Hume on matters of, xxxvii, 306-18, 321-3, 330-1, 415, 418-9

FACTION, ESSAY ON, Bacon's, iii, 123-4

Factions, Bacon on, iii, 37, 39; Franklin on, i, 89

Facts, Burns on, vi, 208; Emerson on, v, 183; worship of, 187

Fadl-ed-Din, the vizier, xvi, 193-9

Faerie Queene, LEAR, story of, in, xlvi, 214; Shelley on, xxvii, 349

FAERIE QUEENE, PREFATORY LETTER ON, xxxix, 61-5

Fafnir, xlix, 284, 285, 286, 292-5; the heart of, 296

Failure, M. Aurelius on, ii, 225 (9), 242 (50)

Faint-Heart, in PILGRIM'S PROGRESS, xv, 128, 133

Fainting, Harvey on cause of, xxxviii, 113

FAIR ANNET, LORD THOMAS AND, xl, 61-5

FAIR INES, xli, 905-7; Poe on, xxviii, 384-6

FAIR IS MY LOVE, xl, 250

FAIR YOUNG LADY, SONG TO A, xl, 388-9

FAIREST MAID ON DEVON BANKS, vi, 553

Fairfax, motto of house of, v, 374

Fairfax, Edward, Dryden on, xxxix, 154, 163

FAIRFAX, LORD GENERAL, AT SIEGE OF COLCHESTER, iv, 82

FAIRIES, THE, by Allingham, xlii, 1116-17

Fairness, and fitness, Augustine, St., on, vii, 57

Fair-speech, Lord, in PILGRIM'S PROGRESS, xv, 102-3

Fair-speech, town of, in PILGRIM'S PROGRESS, xv, 102

Faith, American lack of, v, 54; Arnold on decline of, xlii, 1138; Augustine, St., on, in Scripture, vii, 82; Bacon on, and suspicion, iii, 82-3; Blake on children's, xli, 589; Browne on, iii, 260 (9, 10), 271, 309; Bunyan's allegory of, xv, 33-4; Calvin on, xxxix, 30-1, 49-50; Carlyle on, xxv, 343; Dante on, xx, 388-9; Dante's allegory of, 265 note 11; Dante's star of, 177 note 9; decline of, modern, v, 37, 277; xxv, 343-5; Emerson on, v, 133, 147, 274, 281, 298; Hindu doctrine of, xlv, 846, 848, 863, 865; Hobbes on, xxxiv, 347-8; Hume on Christian, xxxvii, 392; Isidore on, xxxix, 110-11; Jesus on, xliv, 398 (5-6); justification by, xxxvi, 346-59, 362-3, 363-4, 367-8, 375; justification by, Hindu idea of, xlv, 794; Kempis on necessity of, vii, 363-4 (2), 364 (5); Longfellow on, xlii, 1333; Luther on Christian, xxxvi, 344-5, 351-7, 372-3; Milton on, iii, 217-20; iv, 50, 352; More on, under difficulties, xxxvi, 100; Pascal on, xlviii, 92 (248), 96 (265-7), 99 (278-9), 136, 165

(504), 168 (516), 301; Paul, St., on, xlv, 508 (2, 13); Penn on, i, 359 (454); Pope on modes of, xl, 430; Rousseau on, articles of, xxxiv, 289; Tzu-chang on, xliv, 63 (2); Voltaire on, and reason, xxxiv, 107; Whitman on, xxxix, 392-3; Wordsworth on, 314-15; of youth, xix, 37 (see also Fidelity, Promises)

Faithful, in PILGRIM'S PROGRESS, xv, 59, 70, 72-90, 93-101

FAITHFUL JOHN, tale of, xvii, 57-64

Faithfulness, Confucius on, xliv, 5 (8), 13 (15), 29 (24), 39 (10), 45 (8), 51 (5); Jesus on, 397 (10-12)

Falada, the speaking horse, xvii, 173-7

Falconer, Hugh, on crocodiles, xi, 349-50; on elephants, 355; on periods of modification, 337

Falconer, the Jesuit, xxix, 112-3

Falkland Islands, climate and productions of, xxix, 247-8; Darwin on, 55-6, 193-208; peat in, 291; tameness of birds in, 404

Falkland, Lord, on ceremony, v, 202; Pope on, xl, 433

FALL OF FYERS, LINES ON THE, vi, 281

FALL OF THE LEAF, vi, 315-6

FALLACIES OF ANTI-REFORMERS, Smith's, xxvii, 225-51

Fallen Angels, in PARADISE LOST, muster of, iv, 100-2; names on earth of, 97; number of, 95-7; in Pandemonium, 107-8; pastimes of the, 121-4; punishment of, yearly, 304-5; rebellion of, 198, 206-7, 209-26

Falling Bodies, law of, xxx, 19-21

Falloppio, system of, xxxviii, 388

Falsaron, xlix, 123, 133

False accusers, branded in Rome, ix, 296 note 8

False Opinions, injuriousness of, ii, 242 (57)

False Prosecutions, in Massachusetts, xliii, 72 (37)

False Witness, punished by death, xliii, 81 (11)

Falsehood, Bacon on, iii, 7-9, 128; Dante places, in Hell, xx, 46; Emerson on, v, 27, 100; Hobbes on, xxxiv, 326; Kant on, xxxii, 314-5, 330, 333, 351; Locke on early training in, xxxvii, 30; Marcus Aurelius on, ii, 264 (1); Montaigne on, iii, 8-9; Penn on, i, 336 (144); semblance of, to be avoided, xx, 69;

Spanish proverb on, iii, 19; Whitman on, xxxix, 402

Fame, Augustine, St., on, vii, 56; Bacon on, iii, 36, 126; Burns on, vi, 260, 308; Byron on, xli, 789-80; Carlyle on, xxv, 419; Confucius on, xliv, 5 (1), 7 (16), 13 (14), 40 (20), 48 (32); Dante on, xx, 99, 189, 309 note 25; death and, iii, 10; Diogenes on, ii, 180 (187); Epictetus on, 131 (43); Huxley on, xxviii, 209; "infirmity of noble minds," last, iv, 74; Marcus Aurelius on, ii, 202 (12), 204 (17), 209 (10), 211-2 (3), 215 (19), 218 (33, 35), 235 (16, 18), 242 (51), 244 (6), 247 (34), 261 (44); Milton on, iv, 74, 336, 384-7; Pascal on love of, xlviii, 60 (148), 61 (153, 158); Pliny on, ix, 291, 351; Pope on, xl, 436-8; results of desire for, xxxiv, 371; Seneca on, xxxix, 67; Virgil's figure of, xiii, 158-9; Virgil's figure of, Burke on, xxiv, 54

Fame, Essay on, Bacon's, iii, 140-2

Familiarity, Bacon on, iii, 125; breeds contempt, xvii, 25; defeats dignity, xii, 42; Emerson on, v, 208-9; in friendship, 115; Kempis on, vii, 212; Locke on, of children, xxxvii, 80-3; Marcus Aurelius on, ii, 219 (44), 243 (1), 254 (6); Penn on, i, 334 (119); Shakespeare on, xlvi, 109; wonder destroyed by, xlviii, 40 (90)

Familiars, defined, xlvii, 763

Family, Feast of, in New Atlantis, iii, 163-6; founders of a, indulgent, 20, 35; origin of the, xxxiv, 202; Taine on the, xxxix, 429-30; in Utopia, xxxvi, 183-4

Famine, Woolman on, as a judgment, i, 237

Fan Ch'ih, disciple of Confucius, xliv, 7 (5), 20 (20), 40 (21, 22), 41-2 (4), 43 (19)

Fanaticism, Burke on, xxiv, 286-7

Fancy, feeling and, xlviii, 98 (274-5); imagination and, xxxix, 301, 307-9; Hobbes on, xxxiv, 83; Milton on, iv, 83; Pascal on, xlviii, 39 (86), 40 (87); Wordsworth on, xxxix, 301-2, 307-9 (see also Imagination)

Fancy, by Shakespeare, xl, 263

Fancy, The Realm of, xli, 871-3

Fannia, mother-in-law of Helvidius, ix, 338, 341

Fannia, wife of Helvidius, ix, 307-8

Fannius, contemporary of Pliny, ix, 264

Fannius, Gaius, in Cicero's essay on Friendship, ix, 9-10

Fano, Ludovico da, xxxi, 97 note 5, 162, 166

Faraday, Michael, Chemical History of a Candle, xxx, 86-170; Forces of Matter, 7-85; life and work of, 5-6; on regulation of ice, 233, 243, 245

Fare Thee Well, by Byron, xli, 799-801

Farewell, The, by Burns, vi, 215-6, 224

Farewell, Love's, xl, 228

Farewell, Rewards and Fairies, xl, 315-16

Farewell Thou Stream, vi, 508

Farewell to Eliza, vi, 218

Farewell to the World, xl, 292-3

Farfarello, the demon, xx, 88, 91

Farinata degli Uberti, Dante on, xx, 41-4

Farmer, In the Character of a Ruined, vi, 22-3

Farmers, in agricultural system, x, 427-8, 440-1; capital of, 216; indolence of, reason for, 14; monopoly unknown among, 342; pleasures of, ix, 63-6; studies for, xxviii, 327-8

Farming (see Agriculture)

Farnese, Alessandro, xxxi, 74 note, 75, 249 note (see also Paul III)

Farnese, Pier Luigi, xxxi, 147 note 2, 340 note 2; Cellini and, 149, 202-3, 207, 225, 245, 257 note 11, 339; prevision of his murder, 251, 257 note 8; wife of, 232 note

Farrel, Capt., at Gettysburg, xliii, 370, 385

Farrer, Nicholas, xv, 410-2; George Herbert and, 388, 409, 412, 413-15; letter from Herbert to, 413

Farrington, Abraham, i, 179, 183

Fashion, Channing on, xxviii, 317-8; classes of, v, 203-6, 210-15; Emerson on, 201, 204, 211-12, 217; Goldsmith on pleasures of, xli, 515

Fastidiousness, in love, xlviii, 415-16; Penn on, i, 384 (135-46)

Fasts, Calvin on, xxxix, 38; Luther on, xxxvi, 309-10

Fatalism (see Necessity)

Fata Morgana, references to, xvii, 273; xlii, 1330

Fate, Academics, the, on, xxxix, 108; Calderon on, xxvi, 72; Chaucer on, xl, 45-6, 48; fable on, xvii, 37; Herodotus's

belief in, xxxiii, 6; irremovable, by prescience, xiii, 304; lines on, v, 273; Machiavelli on, xxxvi, 80; Marcus Aurelius on, ii, 200 (3), 213 (6), 214 (9), 216 (26), 224 (8), 253 (75), 275 (5); Omar Khayyam on, xli, 953-4; ordained of old, viii, 96; superior to gods, 45; unavoidable rather than unexpected, xii, 315 (see also Necessity)

Fates, the, iv, 43; Æschylus on the, viii, 161-2; De Quincey on the, xxvii, 320; guides of necessity, viii, 185; of Norse mythology, xlix, 272 note (see also Destinies)

Father, loss of a, Plutarch on, xii, 147

Father Abraham's Sermon, i, 3, 92

Fathers, honored in NEW ATLANTIS, iii, 165; tyrannical, Shelley on, xviii, 302 (see also Parents)

Fathers of the Church, Calvin on, xxxix, 35-38; Milton on, iv, 210

Fatimeh, in story of Ala-ed-Din, xvi, 418-20

Fattore, Il, xxxi, 34 note 3, 39, 57

Faucon, Capt., xxiii, 161, 162, 185; (in 1859), 383; in Boston, 400

Faulkner, F., translator of Pasteur, xxxviii, 269

Fault-finding (see Censoriousness)

Faults, compensation for, v, 98; Confucius on, xliv, 13 (7), 53 (29); man's dislike to hear own, ii, 140-1 (67); Pascal on hiding of, xlviii, 43-4; Penn on, i, 335 (123); pointing out of, xlviii, 172 (535); Shakespeare on single, xlvi, 112; uncorrected, become habits, ii, 144 (75)

Faults, geological, xi, 323-4

Fauns, referred to, iv, 73

Faunus, Latin god, xiii, 417; father of Latinus, 241

Faust, Doctor, historical character, original of Goethe's tragedy, xix, 6

Faust, in Goethe's FAUST, at Auerbach's wine-cellar, xix, 90, 96; in witches' kitchen, 100-1; vision of Helena, 104; restored to youth, 108-9; before Margaret's door, 158-9; kills Valentine, 162; compact with Mephistopheles, 64-75; curse of, 66-7; starts out, 83-4; dissatisfied, calls on spirits, 23-9; interrupted by Wagner, 29-31; first sight of Margaret, 112; demands her from Mephistopheles, 112-14; in Margaret's

chamber, 115-18; his corruption undertaken by Mephistopheles, 20-2; in despair, attempts suicide, 33-6; in forest cavern, 142-5; urged by Mephistopheles to return to Margaret, 145-7; in study, Mephistopheles appears, 57-66; learns appointment with Margaret, 130-4; with Margaret in garden, 133-9; in summer-house, 141-2; learns casket given to church, 121-2; on Walpurgis'-Night, 167-82; vision of Margaret, 181-2; learns her imprisonment and determines to free her, 190-3; on way to prison, 192-4; in dungeon with Margaret, 193-202; with Margaret, on his religion, 149-51; on Mephistopheles, 152; plans secret meeting with Margaret, 153; with Mephistopheles, 155-6; with Wagner before the gate, 43-8; his aspirations, 49; with the dog, 51-2

Faust, tragedy of, Goethe's, xix, 9-202; remarks on, 5-8

Faustina, wife of Marcus Aurelius, ii, 199 (17)

Faustus, in Marlowe's FAUSTUS, and the horse-courser, xix, 239-41; at court of Vanholt, 241-2; recalls spirit of Helen of Troy, 243; birth, education, and practise of magic, 205-6; dissatisfied with human learning, takes to magic, 206-7; half repents, 224; discusses astronomy, 225; calls on Christ, 226; with Lucifer, 226-227; with Seven Sins, 227-8; promised to see Hell, 229; studies astronomy on Olympus, 229; remarks on dying utterance of, 204; remarks on speech to Helen, 204; renounces God for Belzebub, 218; compact with Mephistophilis, 219-24; travels of, 229; in Rome, at Pope's feast, 231-2; returns home, his fame, 233; at Emperor's court, 236-8; urged to repent, 244; renews compact, 245; wins Helen of Troy for paramour, 245-6; last hours, 246-7; taken by devils, 249-50; with Valdes and Cornelius, 208-9; conjures Mephistophilis, 213-15

Faustus, Dr., Marlowe's, xix, 205-50; remarks on, 204

Faustus, Bishop of Manichees, vii, 63; St. Augustine on, 67-9

Favonius, iv, 84; ix, 96; Cæsar, opposed by, xii, 282; Pompey and, 292-3, 299

Favorinus, ii, 179 note

Favorites, Marlowe on, xlvi, 28; royal, Bacon on, iii, 66-7, 94

Favors, apt to be repeated, i, 98; Cicero on, ix, 34; claim returns, xix, 131; Emerson on receiving, v, 95-6; Hobbes on, xxxiv, 371; Marcus Aurelius on, ii, 194 (8); Mohammed on, xlv, 880, 884; Socrates on, ii, 293 (25); Woolman on, i, 245

FAVOUR, ON RECEIVING A, vi, 354

FAVOURITE CAT, ON A, xl, 462-3

Fawcett, Mr., xxv, 184

Fawkener, Everard, postmaster-general, i, 145

Fawkes, Guy, Hazlitt on, xxvii, 280

Fawn, defined, xxxv, 343

Fay, Godemar du, xxxv, 21-2

Fazio, Friar, in THE BETROTHED, xxi, 131

Fear, Augustine, St., on, vii, 28; Burke on, xxiv, 49-50; cause of, 105-7; critic, the most rigid, ix, 307; darkness, cause of, xxiv, 68, 114-17; David on use of, xli, 491; delight caused by, xxiv, 109; dishonorableness of, 362; Emerson on, v, 94; Epictetus on, ii, 135 (55); eyes of, to see under the ground, xiv, 154; of God, Bunyan on, xv, 152-3; of God, necessary to grace, guide to duty, v, 129; Hobbes's definition of, xxxiv, 341; honoring, a way of, 364; hope and, iv, 55; ignorance, cause of, v, 17; instinctive, xi, 255; judge of souls, viii, 143; Locke on, xxxvii, 95-6, 98; loudness, cause of, xxiv, 69-70; love and, xxxvi, 54-6; Marcus Aurelius on, ii, 280 (25), 283 (34); music and, xli, 476; obscurity cause of, xxiv, 50-1; Pascal on religious, xlviii, 95 (262); power, idea of, cause of, xxiv, 55-60; in privation, 60; sounds, intermitting, cause of, 70-1; suddenness, cause of, 70; vastness, in idea of, 61-2, 109-110 (see also Sublime)

Fearing, in PILGRIM'S PROGRESS, xv, 174, 253-9, 273

Fearlessness, Confucius on, xliv, 45 (4), 47 (21)

Fears, and desires, iii, 48; make us traitors, xlvi, 370; may be liars, xlii, 1119

Feasts, in New Atlantis, iii, 166

FEATHERS, THE THREE, xvii, 156-9

Feathers, fine, and fine birds, xvii, 20

Febo, Cavalier del, xiv, 114

Federal Government and state governments, xliii, 208-9, 210-13, 215-16, 224; Jay's argument for a, 203-7

FEDERALIST, THE (Nos. I and II), xliii, 199-207

Federigo, Cardinal, in THE BETROTHED, xxi, 351-60; with the Unnamed, 361-72; visits Lucia, 396-401; visits Lucia's village, 406-9; advises Lucia, 414; reprimands Abbondio, 415-25; in Milan famine, 456-8, 465; in plague, 505, 527-8, 531, 533

Feeble-mind, in PILGRIM'S PROGRESS, xv, 174, 271-4, 275-6, 281-2, 284, 288, 290, 302; parts with Christiana, 312; death, 314

Feejee Islanders, cannibalism of, v, 199

Feeling, the beautiful in, xxiv, 98-9; fancy and, xlviii, 98 (274-5); Longfellow on, xlii, 1323; Mill, James, on, xxv, 71; necessary to persuasion, xix, 30; reason and, xlviii, 98 (276-8), 99 (282); reason and, Schiller on, xxxii, 243-9; reasoning and, xlviii, 10; virtue, basis of, xxxii, 352; Ruskin on, xxviii, 113-15; sense of, as source of sublime, xxiv, 73; Wordsworth on need of developing, xxxix, 273-4

Feelings, Mill on the, xxv, 36, 91-2, 254; thoughts and, xxxix, 272-3; undermined by analysis, xxv, 88

Fees, in New Atlantis, not permitted, iii, 148, 149

Feet, Locke on care of the, xxxvii, 11-12

Feigning, Lady, in PILGRIM'S PROGRESS, xv, 102

Felice, Father (see Casati Felice), xxi

Felice, partner of Cellini, xxxi, 132, 165-7, 169-70, 171-2, 176

Felician, Father, in EVANGELINE, xlii, 1303; in the church, 1312-13; on day of exile, 1316, 1317, 1318; with Evangeline in wanderings, 1320, 1323, 1326; at Basil's, 1327, 1329

Felician of Silva, books of, xiv, 18

Felicion, the shoemaker, ii, 130 (40)

Felicity, Hobbes on, xxxiv, 345; lies in progress, 370

Felix, Roman governor, xliv, with Paul, 475 (24-35), 477 (22-7)

Felix, governor of Armenia, in POLYEUCTE, tells Pauline of Severus's approach, xxvi, 84-7; his wrath at Polyeucte, 102-6; his dilemma, 107-8; determines not to pardon Polyeucte, 119-21; with Polyeucte, 121-3, 125;

condemns Polyeucte to death, 126-7; becomes a convert, 129-30

Felix V, Pope (see Amadeus, Cardinal)

Felixmarte of Hircania, xiv, 92, 303-4

Fellowes, Sir Charles, researches of, v, 361

Fellow-feeling, Confucius on, xliv, 52 (23)

Fellowship, in pain, divides not smart, iv, 369

Felon, origin of word, xxxv, 364

Felons, children of, v, 346

Felony, crimes included under, xxxv, 364-5

Feltro, Bishop of, xx, 321 note 15

Fencing, Locke on, xxxvii, 171-2; Milton on, iii, 244

Fenelon, Hume on ethics of, xxvii, 204

Fennians, Tacitus on the, xxxiii, 119-20

Feoblas, balsam of (see Balsam of Fierebias)

Fer Caille, xlix, 209, 214, 232, 241

Fer Gair, xlix, 202, 210, 217, 232

Fer Le, xlix, 202, 210, 232

Fer Rogain, xlix, 202, 210, 212, 215, 217-8 et seq.

Ferdinand II, in THE BETROTHED, in Mantuan contest, xxi, 78

Ferdinand IV, Dante on, xx, 368 note 9

Ferdinand V, of Spain, Machiavelli on, xxxvi, 72-3; Pope Julius and, 45; Raleigh on, xxxix, 85-6

Ferdinand, son of Alva, in EGMONT, xix, 303, 304-6, 313-14; final scene with Egmont, 326-32

Ferdinand of Naples, iii, 50

Ferdinand, in DUCHESS OF MALFI, in presence chamber scene, xlvii, 758-9; hires Bosola to watch Duchess, 761-4; Antonio on, 760; at court of Malfi, 791; with Duchess, 791; with Bosola, 792-3; in Milan, his frenzy, 833, 834-6; death, 853; learns flight of Duchess, 806; letter to Duchess, 809-10; on Malatesti, 804; parting counsel to Duchess, 764-6; learns her fault, 787-9; with Bosola after murder, 818-30; with Bosola at Malfi, 813-14; with Duchess in prison, 814-15; his purposes of vengeance, 818-19; with Duchess in chamber, 795-7; his return to Rome, 799

Ferdinand, in THE TEMPEST, in shipwreck, xlvi, 398, 406; led by Ariel's song, 412-13; meeting with Miranda

and Prospero, 413; at his task, 432; with Miranda, 432-5; betrothed to Miranda, 443-9; at chess with Miranda, 458; reunion with father, 458-9

Ferguson, Sir Adam, vi, 159 and note 4; Carlyle on, xxv, 366

Ferguson, Sir Samuel, FAIR HILLS OF IRELAND, xli, 921-2

Fergusson, Robert, vi, 16; Burns on, 81, 87; INSCRIPTION FOR HEADSTONE OF, 257; INSCRIPTION UNDER PORTRAIT OF, 257; LINES ON THE POET, 431

Fermentation, Pasteur's Theory of, xxxviii, 275-363

Fermo, Oliverotto of, xxxvi, 30-2

Fernando Noronha, Darwin on, xxix, 21

Fernando, in Cardenio's story, xiv, 203-5, 240-7

Fernando, and Dorothea, xiv, 257-79

Fernando, and Lucinda, xiv, 264-5

Fernando, Don, reunion with Dorothea, xiv, 356-65

Ferragosto, the, xxxi, 40 note 2

Ferrante, Don, in THE BETROTHED, xxi, 410, 413; learning of, 444-8; in the plague, 623-5

Ferrara, Cardinal (see Este, Ippolito d')

Ferrara, Duke of, xxxvi, 8; and Cellini, xxxi, 199, 268, 271, 273; and Louis, xxxvi, 13; and Paul III, xxxi, 268

Ferrara, Marquis of, xx, 52 note 9

Ferrer, Antonio, at Milan, xxi, 197-8, 199, 214-24

FERRIER, MISS, TO, vi, 275

Ferro, Drake at, xxxiii, 233

Fertility, as distinction between varieties and species, xi, 312 (see also Sterility)

Fertilization, methods of, xi, 193-4; remarks on, 103-7

Fesque, defined, xxvii, 105

Festino, Mrs., xviii, 121

Festus, Porcius, xliv, 477 (27); and Paul, 477-9 (1-27), 481 (24, 30-1)

FETE CHAMPETRE, THE, vi, 309-11

Feudal Laws, of succession, x, 506

Feure, Raoul le, xxxix, 5

Fevers, Indian treatment of, xliii, 35

Fèvre, le, Dryden on, xiii, 14

"Few sometimes may know when thousands err," iv, 208

Fewster, Mr., xxxviii, 183, 194, 213

Fiad sceme, the giant, xlix, 239

Fiaschino, the chamberlain, xxxi, 270, 273

Fichte, Mazzini on, xxxii, 380; patriotism of, 386-7; on silent work, xxv, 417

Ficinus, on nature, xxxix, 109
FICKLE FORTUNE: A FRAGMENT, vi, 36
Fickleness of man, vii, 297-8 (1)
Fiddler, in FAUST, xix, 188
FIDDLER, A, IN THE NORTH, 479-80
Fiddler's Song, from JOLLY BEGGARS, vi, 127-8
FIDELE, by Collins, xli, 475
FIDELE'S DIRGE, xl, 269
Fidelity, Penn on, i, 340; of princes, xxxvi, 56-7; worth of, intrinsic, xxxii, 345
Field, Barron, in Hazlitt's discussion, xxvii, 275
Field, parable of the, xv, 205
Fielding, Henry, Hazlitt on, xxvii, 275; HUNTING SONG, xli, 501-2; his *Joseph Andrews*, xiv, 3; PREFACE TO JOSEPH ANDREWS, xxxix, 176-81; sketch of life and works, 176 note; religion of, xxviii, 17-8; Thackeray on, 9, 19
Fiennes, house of, motto of, v, 374
Fierabras, xiv, 489
Fierebras, Balsam of, xiv, 74-5
Fieschi, Bonifazio de', xx, 243 note 4
FIESOLE, EPITAPH AT, xli, 904
Fife, in LIFE IS A DREAM, with Rosaura, arrival in Poland, xxvi, 7-13; with Segismund, 14-7; arrested, 18-9; in the tower, 56-8; found by soldiers, 59-61; with Rosaura again, 66-7; in the battle, 69-70; death, 70
Fig-tree, Indian, iv, 288; parable of, xliv, 390 (6-9); proverb of the, v, 10
Figulus, C. Marcius, mention of, ix, 83
Figures, Berkeley on, xxxvii, 207-8; Plato's definition of, v, 175-6
FILE AND SERPENT, fable of, xvii, 22
Filippo, Francesco di (see Lippi Francesco)
Final Causes (see First Cause)
Finance, Burke on science of, xxiv, 358
Finches, in Galapagos Islands, xxix, 383
Findlater, Andrew, xxv, 188
Findlay, song on, vi, 48
Fineness, defined by Burke, xxiv, 98, 125
Fines, excessive, forbidden, xliii, 195 (8); More on, xxxvi, 160, 163
Fingers, in story of DARNING-NEEDLE, xvii, 316
Finite, the, a manifestation of the infinite, xxviii, 341
Finitude, Kelvin on, xxx, 258
Finn, story of, xlix, 34 note 5, 35, 36, 37

Finnbogi, the Norseman, xliii, 17-18
Finns, sailors' notion of, xxiii, 41-2
Fiorentino, Giuliano, xxxi, 70
Fiorino of Cellino, xxxi, 6
Fiornir (see Fjolnir)
Firdousi, Sainte-Beuve on, xxxii, 130
Fire, lesson of the, xv, 235; Marcus Aurelius on, ii, 267 (9); methods of producing, xxx, 59; methods of producing, by friction, xxix, 413-4
Fire-arms, and civilization, x, 450
Fire Bells, Poe on, xlii, 1234
Fire-engines, ancient, ix, 377 note
Fireflies, Darwin on, xxix, 38-9
Firenzuola, Giovanni of, xxxi, 26-7
Fireside, to make a happy, vi, 367
Firk, in SHOEMAKER'S HOLIDAY, at Ralph's departure, xlvii, 473-6; at Eyre's, 480-3, 487-91, 497-8; announces Eyre's appointment, 500-1; at Old Ford, 503-4; before shop, 509-10; with Ralph, 512-13; at Lord Mayor's, 516-17; at Hammon's wedding, 521-2; at Eyre's dinner, 528-9, 531, 535
Firmament, Addison on the, xl, 400; xlv, 535; Habington on the, xl, 253
Firminus, and his astrology, vii, 104-5
Firmus, Romanus, letter to, ix, 204, 259
First Cause, Hume on the, xxxvii, 309-10; ideas of different, xxxix, 101, 103; Marcus Aurelius on the, ii, 253 (75), 265 (1), 269-70 (28); Pascal on knowledge of, xlviii, 27-8, 331; Rousseau on, xxxiv, 249
First Fruits (see Annates)
First Principles, Pascal on, xlviii, 99 (282)
Fish, creation of, iv, 237; electric organs of, xi, 188-9; flying, 177; flying, Pretty on, xxxiii, 203; fresh-water, distribution of, xi, 409; heart in, xxxviii, 69, 90, 131-2; Herodotus on breeding of, xxxiii, 46-7; Mohammed on eating of, xlv, 1004; price of, by what determined, x, 52, 200; price of, rent as element in, 148; respiration of, xxx, 168; teleostean, xi, 343
Fisher, Bishop of Rochester, xxxvi, 114-5
FISHER, THE, fable of, xvii, 27-8
FISHER AND LITTLE FISH, fable of, xvii, 31-2
Fisher Boy, song of, in WILLIAM TELL, xxvi, 379-80
Fisheries, produce of, source of capital, x, 221

FISHERMAN, THE, AND HIS WIFE, xvii, 83-90

FISHERMAN, THE, story of, xvi, 25-54

Fishes, hearts in, xxxviii, 77, 84; Smart on, xli, 488

Fishing, Franklin's early ideas of, i, 35

Fistinghound, the, xxxv, 351

Fitch, the shop-keeper, xxiii, 390

Fitela, and Sigemund, xlix, 29

Fitness, Augustine, St., on, vii, 57; beauty and, v, 301-2; cause of beauty, xxiv, 85-7; in works of art, 87-8; Penn on, i, 338 (161)

Fitzgerald, Edward, RUBAIYAT OF OMAR KHAYYAM, xli, 943-58

Fitz-James, Lord, xxxvi, 130

Fitz Roy, Capt., Darwin on, xxix, 9

Five, Nature's love of number, xlii, 1250

FIVE CARLINS, THE, vi, 367-70

Fixed Capital, defined, x, 216; depends on circulating capital, 220; expense of maintaining, 224-6, 230; kinds of, four, 218; resemblance to money, 226, 230

Fjolnir, xlix, 289-90, 345, 409

Flaccus, Gaius Valerius, Dante on, xx, 19

Flaccus, M. Lænius, Cicero on, ix, 89

Flame, direction of, xxx, 97; Faraday on, 95; forms of, 96-7; illumination from, cause of, 106-12, 157; structure of, in candles, 101-4

Flamens, Roman, ix, 218 note 1

Flamingoes, Darwin on, xxix, 73

Flamininus, Lucius, expelled from Senate, ix, 60

Flat-fish, peculiarities of, xi, 229-32

Flatterer, in PILGRIM'S PROGRESS, xv, 135-6

Flatterers, Epictetus on, ii, 183 (4), 184 (13); fable of, xvii, 14; in Hell, xx, 46, 76

Flatteries, the four, xii, 343 note

Flattery, Bacon on, iii, 126-7; Burke on, xxiv, 45, 148; Chaucer on, xl, 48; Cicero on, ix, 39-42; Confucius on, xliv, 5 (3), 17 (24), 59 (17); Hobbes on, xxxiv, 373; Kempis on avoiding, vii, 292 (5); love of, reason for, v, 219; Machiavelli on, xxxvi, 76-7; parasite of Luxury, vi, 250; Shakespeare on, xlvi, 149; a way of honoring, xxxiv, 361, 364

Flavius, the tribune, and Cæsar, xii, 313-4; Cicero on, ix, 145, 149

Fleance, in MACBETH, xlvi, 338-9, 354, 356-7, 363

Fleetness, limits of, xi, 52

Fleetwood, Dr., and the Spectator, xxvii, 162

Fletcher, John, ASPATIA'S SONG, xl, 321-2; Custom of the Country, xxxix, 174; life and works, xlvii, 666; Massinger and, 858; MELANCHOLY, xl, 322 (see also Beaumont and Fletcher)

Fletcher, Master, with Drake, xxxiii, 206, 209

Flibbertigibbet, xlvi, 270

Flies, Harrison on, and spiders, xxxv, 348; Pascal on, xlviii, 122 (367)

Flipotte, in TARTUFFE, xxvi, 199, 206

FLODDEN, LAMENT FOR, xli, 483

Flodden, men of Ettrick Forest at, xli, 482 note

Flogging, Dana on, xxiii, 363-4; in England, v, 346

Florence, arms of commune of, xxxi, 13 note 3; auxiliaries employed by, xxxvi, 45; built in imitation of Rome, xxxi, 5-6; Dante on, xx, 43 note 12, 106 note, 117 note 12, 169-70, 350-7; dress in (16th century), xxxi, 29 note 2; the "Eight" of, 16 note 2; factions in, xx, 26-7, 101-2 and notes; Guelfi and Ghibellini in, 66 notes 1, 2; guilds of, xxxi, 12 note 2; Macaulay on, xxvii, 372; mercenaries of, xxxvi, 42-4; name, origin of, xxxi, 5; patrons of, xx, 57 note 5; Pistoja and, xxxvi, 54-5; the plague in, xxxi, 84 note 6; policy towards Pisa and Pistoja, xxxvi, 69; republican party of, xxxi, 30 note 2, 32 note 1; subjugation of, xxvii, 392, 400; wealth of (14th century), 369, 370

Florida, cession of, xliii, 268-76

Florimell, Spenser's, xxxix, 65

Florio, John, translator of Montaigne, xxxii, 3

Floripes, Princess, xiv, 489

Florismarte of Hircania, xiv, 49

Florus, and Agrippinus, ii, 119 (8)

Flower, Prof., on conformity of type, xi, 453

FLOWER IN THE CRANNIED WALL, xlii, 1005

FLOWER, THE, by Herbert, xl, 344-5

Flowers, Bacon on, iii, 112-3; beauty of, Burke on, xxiv, 77; beauty of, Darwin on, xi, 201; Columella on, xxxv, 238; correlation in, xi, 149-50; Emerson on,

as gifts, v, 219, 230; insects and, re-
lations of, xi, 99-100, 101-2; parable
of the, xv, 205
FLOWERS OF THE FOREST, xli, 482
FLOWERS, LITTLE IDA'S, xvii, 334-41
FLOWERY BANKS OF CREE, vi, 483-4
Flue, Klaus von der, in WILLIAM TELL,
xxvi, 412-3, 423
Flute, Alcibiades on the, xii, 107-8; Dry-
den on the, xl 390
Fluxions, invented by Newton, xxxiv,
125-6
Fly, on the chariot-wheel, iii, 127
FLY AND BALD MAN, fable of, xvii, 18
Flycatchers, tyrant, Darwin on, xi, 178
Flying-fish, Darwin on, xi, 177-8; Pretty
on, xxxiii, 203
FLYING TRUNK, THE, xvii, 344-9
Focaccia of Cancellieri, xx, 132 note 4
Fœtus, blood in the, xxxviii, 72-3; cir-
culation in the, 92-4; Harvey on forma-
tion of the, 127; heart in the, 84, 131,
135-6; liver in the, 127
Fogliani, Giovanni, xxxvi, 30, 31
Fogo, Island of, xxxiii, 202-3
Foiano, Benedetto da, xxxi, 237 note
Foix, Diana of, Montaigne to, xxxii, 29
Foix, Gaston de, xlvii, 757
Folco, of Genoa, xx, 320 note 8, 322
Folger, Peter, i, 9
FOLK-LORE AND FABLE, xvii
FOLLOW THY FAIR SUN, xl, 285
FOLLOWERS, ESSAY ON, Bacon's, iii, 119-20
Folly, Burns on, vi, 184; ECCLESIASTES on,
xliv, 346 (1-3), 347 (12-15)
FOLLY, HUMAN, xl, 327
FOLLY, RAPTURES OF, vi, 460
Folques, of Marseilles (see Folco)
Fonblanque, Mill on, xxv, 59, 63, 67, 81,
109, 123
Fondness, Confucius on, xliv, 58 (8)
Fontaine, M. de, xxxviii, 50
Fontainebleau, Cellini's work on, xxxi,
294
Fontana, Domenico, xxxi, 136
Fontanes, Sainte-Beuve on, xxxii, 130
Fontenelle, M., on affectation in nature,
v, 335; on Newton, xxxiv, 109, 119
Fontenelle, Miss, addresses spoken by, vi,
446-7, 477-8; EPIGRAM on, 447
Food, in ancient Egypt, xxxiii, 40, 45;
animal, Darwin on, xxix, 122-3; as
circulating capital, x, 219; labor in re-
lation to, 149; Locke on, of children,

xxxvii, 15-21; materials and, comparative values of, x, 178-9; Mohammed on lawful, xlv, 994-5, 1003;
necessity of, iv, 191; Penn on selection
of, i, 328-9 (59-62); rent of land
used for, x, 149-65; of rich and poor,
167-8; variability due to excess of, xi,
23
Food-supply, industry and, x, 83-4, 84-5,
86-7; population and, 81-3, 167; wages
and, 75-6, 85, 87
Fool, in KING LEAR, xlvi, 233-6, 239-41,
252-5, 264-70, 274-6; remarks on character of, 214
Fool, in PILGRIM'S PROGRESS, xv, 292
Fool, song of, from JOLLY BEGGARS, vi,
125
Fool-hardiness, Locke on, xxxvii, 95
Fools, disclosed by words, xvii, 30;
Browne on, iii, 270 (18); Paradise of,
iv, 148; Pascal on, xlviii, 35 (80);
"rush in where angels fear," xxiv,
183-4; Solomon on, xxxvi, 156; test
of, iii, 57; in Utopia, xxxvi, 211; wise
men and, 260-1
Foot-pound, defined, xxx, 179
FOOTSTEPS OF ANGELS, xlii, 1267-9
Foppa, Ambrogio, xxxi, 48 note
FOR A' THAT, vi, 133-4
Forbearance, Brynhild on, xlix, 304; Epic-
tetus on, ii, 179 (183); Locke on habit
of, xxxvii, 19
Forbes, Edward, on Atlantic Islands, xi,
386; on distribution, 395, 399; on fossils, 326; on glaciers, xxx, 224, 228,
231; on shells, xi, 139
Force, Bacon on, iii, 96; Emerson on, v,
247; Hume on idea of, xxxvii, 336-50;
Milton on, iv, 104, 445; Pascal on,
xlviii, 115 (334)
Force, in PROMETHEUS BOUND, viii, 166
FORCE, CONSERVATION OF, xxx, 173-210
FORCES, CORRELATION OF, xxx, 73-85;
Helmholtz on, 188, 206, 208
FORCES OF MATTER, Faraday on, xxx, 7-85
Foreign Commerce, advantages of, x,
326-7, 359-63; of agricultural states,
435-6; capital least attracted to, 308;
capital used in, 295-9; disadvantages
of, 306; gains in, 359-63; government
interferences in, 330-88; Luther on,
xxxvi, 331, 332; Mun on, x, 313; necessity of, 300-1
Foreign Competition, Emerson on, v, 286

Foreign Conquests, More on, xxxvi, 159-60

Foreign Dominions, Bacon on, iii, 76-7; Machiavelli on, xxxvi, 7-12, 18-19; arms in, 68-9; factions in, 69-70

Foreign Missions, "pious editor's" view of, xlii, 1373-4

Foreign Nations, Washington on relations with, xliii, 243-8

Foreign Things, Emerson on love of, v, 79; Harrison on love of, xxxv, 236-7, 239; Holinshed on love of, 318

Foreigners, liberty of, in Massachusetts, xliii, 79

Foreknowledge, Chaucer on, xl, 45 note 146, 46 note 149; is fore-sorrow, viii, 16; Milton on, iv, 138; not necessity, xx, 358 note 7

Forel, on tides, xxx, 283

Forese, in Purgatory, xx, 239-41

Foresight, Hobbes on, xxxiv, 320, 345; Machiavelli on, xxxvi, 47; may be vain, vi, 120

Foresters, Emerson on, xlii, 1254, 1255

Forests, Darwin on sublimity of, xxix, 506; Emerson on beauty of, v, 223-4; Geikie on destruction of, xxx, 350-1; growth of, checked by cattle, x, 169-70; rent of, 170; Thoreau on, xxviii, 411-12

Forgers, in Dante's HELL, xx, 120

Forgetful Green, in PILGRIM'S PROGRESS, xv, 243

Forgetfulness, Augustine, St., on, vii, 172-3; Keats on, xli, 875; Pascal on, xlviii, 123 (372)

Forgiveness, Bacon on, iii, 15, 16, 34; Jesus on, xliv, 398 (3-4); Marcus Aurelius on, ii, 194 (7); Pittacus on, 153 (96)

Forli, Countess of, xxxvi, 13, 72

FORLORN, MY LOVE, NO COMFORT NEAR, vi, 535

Formal, and material, ii, 216 (21), 227 (13), 244 (10), 247 (29)

Formal Instinct, Schiller on the, xxxii, 242-8

Formalist, in PILGRIM'S PROGRESS, xv, 43-5

Formality, Bacon on, iii, 125-6; Pascal on, xlviii, 92 (249-51), 93 (252); Penn on, i, 334 (119), 386; as source of power, xxxiv, 360; Swift on, xxvii, 103

Fornication, Mohammed on, xlv, 916; Mohammedan punishment of, 969 note 6, 971; Paul, St., on, 496-7, 498 (13-18); punishment of, in old England, xxxv, 365-6; punishment of, in Utopia, xxxvi, 208-9; Spirit of, iii, 168

FORSAKEN GARDEN, A, xlii, 1207-9

FORSAKEN MERMAN, THE, xlii, 1123-6

Fort George, massacre of, i, 153

Fort William Henry, attack on, i, 220

Fortebraccio (see Braccio)

Fortescue, George, xxxiii, 230, 258

Fortinbras, in HAMLET, xlvi, 96, 99, 127, 174, 209-11; not in original story, 92

Fortitude, Dante's star of, xx, 146 note 5; defined by Hobbes, xxxiv, 341; Locke on, xxxvii, 96-7, 98-101; the virtue of adversity, iii, 16-17

Fortresses, Machiavelli in, xxxvi, 71

Fortunatus, xlv, 514 (17)

FORTUNE, ESSAY ON, Bacon's, iii, 99-101

Fortune, Browne on, iii, 268-70; Burns on fading, vi, 170; changes of, xxxix, 96, 98; Chaucer on, xl, 50; Cicero on, ix, 28, 103; Cockburn on, xli, 482; Dante on, xx, 30-1; Descartes on, xxxiv, 23; Emerson on, v, 83, 88; favors the brave, ix, 286; good, honorable, xxxiv, 365; inequality of, verses on, xvi, 232; injustice of, lines on, vi, 431; life entangled with, ii, 183 (1); love and, xlvi, 153-4; Machiavelli on, xxxvi, 80-2; Marcus Aurelius on good, ii, 232 (36); Montaigne on changes of, xxxii, 5-6; More's lines on, xxxvi, 124-5; Mortimer on, xlvi, 88; Pope on gifts of, xl, 432-7; Raleigh on, xxxix, 91-2, 96-7; Shakespeare on, xlvi, 131-2, 138-9; Tennyson on, xlii, 976-7; Vespucci on, xliii, 29; virtue and, xxxi, 12

FORTUNE, FICKLE, a fragment, vi, 36

FORTUNE, RAGING, a fragment, vi, 36

FORTUNE, To, by Thomson, xl, 443

Fosco, Bernardin di, xx, 202 note 18

Fosians, Tacitus on the, xxxiii, 113

Fossiliferous Strata, Lyell on formation of, xxxviii, 400-3, 407-8, 411, 413-15

Fossils, Falloppio on, xxxviii, 388; old ideas of, xi, 166; xxxviii, 396 (see Palæontological Collections)

Fothergill, Dr., i, 120, 147, 159, 160

Fouche's Police, v, 450

Foulk, Samuel, i, 256, 257, 269

Foundations, Pascal on, xlviii, 114 (330)

Founders of States, Bacon on, iii, 129-30; Machiavelli on, xxxvi, 19-22
Fountain, The, xli, 602-4
Fountains, Bacon on, iii, 115-16
Fourier, Mill on, xxv, 106
Fowl, descent of, xi, 33
Fox, Bishop, and More, xxxvi, 91; quoted, xxxv, 378
Fox, Charles J., and Burke, xxiv, 5; v, 211; Burns on, vi, 52, 161, 338-9; the debt of honor, v, 211; Emerson on, 265; Napoleon on, 211
Fox, Dr., and John Donne, xv, 364-5
Fox, George, Emerson on, v, 141, 232-3; Penn and, xxxiv, 75; on slavery, i, 168; Voltaire on, xxxiv, 71-3
Fox and Cat, fable of, xvii, 26
Fox and Crow, fable of, xvii, 14
Fox and Goat, fable of, xvii, 44
Fox and Grapes, fable of, xvii, 24
Fox and Lion, fable of, xvii, 25
Fox and Mask, fable of, xvii, 19
Fox and Mosquitoes, fable of, xvii, 36-7
Fox and Stork, fable of, xvii, 19
Fox and Wolf, Grimm's story of, xvii, 167-8
Fox, Cock, and Dog, fable of, xvii, 34
Fox Without a Tail, fable of, xvii, 37
Foxes, in San Pedro Island, xxix, 284
Fox-goose, the, in Egypt, xxxiii, 39
Fracastorius, on the heart, xxxviii, 75
Fragment of Song, vi, 237, 443
Frailty, Burns on, vi, 185
Framms, of the Germans, xxxiii, 95
France, apprenticeships in, x, 124; armies of, xxxvi, 47; belles lettres in (18th century), xxxiv, 140; Burke on old régime in, xxiv, 261-6; Calvinism in, xxxix, 27-47; church property, confiscation of, in, xxiv, 241-56; clergy of, under old régime, 273-80; departments, communes, and cantons in, 305-6, 314-15; economists of, x, 443-4; England and, trade of, 367-8; England and, in war, iii, 75; Goldsmith on, xli, 526-7; interest, rates of, in, x, 92-3; Machiavelli on, xxxvi, 8-9, 16-17, 61-2; More on kingdom of, 159; nobility of, under the old régime, xxiv, 269; parliaments, abolition of, 161-2; parliaments, old, of, 338; poetry, early, of, xxviii, 75-6; Raleigh on kings of, xxxix, 80-1; revenue laws of, x, 541-2; Swiss mercenaries in, xxxvi, 47; Taine on,

xxxix, 430-1; taxation in (18th century), x, 545-7; theatre in (18th century), xxxiv, 154; treaty with U. S., xliii, 250-4; Voltaire on civil wars of, xxxiv, 87
France, King of, in Lear, in love with Cordelia, xlvi, 216, 222-3; notified of Lear's misfortunes, 262-3; his invasion of England, 286-7, 289
Francesca di Rimini, in Hell, xx, 23-4
Francesco, Gian (see Penni)
Franchise, qualifications for the, v, 241
Francis, Mr., Attorney-General of Pennsylvania, i, 113
Francis I, Andrea del Sarto and, xlii, 1091, 1093; Calvin to, xxxix, 27-8, 45-7; at Camp Marolle, xxxviii, 13; Charles V and, xxxi, 68 note, 321, 328 note 1, 334 note 1; Cellini and, 91, 196, 201-7, 212, 249, 261, 269, 274-5, 278-82, 282-6, 289-99, 291-2, 292-6, 299, 300, 301, 309-10, 312, 317, 319-22, 322-3, 324-6, 327-8, 329-35, 348, 350-2, 374; Clement and, 119; expedition against Turin, xxxviii, 9; Guido Guidi and, xxxi, 298 note 1; at Landresy, xxxviii, 17; Piero Strozzi and, xxxi, 291-2; and poets, xxvii, 40; Raleigh on, xxxix, 83; in triumvirate of kings, iii, 50; war with England, xxxi, 334 and note 1
Francis II, Raleigh on, xxxix, 83
Francis, St., Dante on, xx, 330-3; Luther on, xxxvi, 300; in Paradise, xx, 420; quoted, vii, 320
Francis, St., Xavier, hymn attributed to, xlv, 556
Franciscans, Dante on the, xx, 337 note 28; in Limbo, iv, 147
Francisco, in Hamlet, xlvi, 93-4
Francisco, in The Tempest, xlvi, 420, 441
Franco of Bologna, xx, 189 note 3
Franklin, Chaucer's, xl, 20-1
Franklin, Abiah, mother of Benjamin, i, 9, 12-13
Franklin, Benjamin, ability to write, advantages gained by, i, 60, 63; aids his workmen to start in business, 93, 104; ancestry and family of, 6-10; anecdote of fish, 35; anecdote of wharf, 11; Art of Virtue, 86-7; as Assembly's commissioner to England, 150-62, 164; assists Braddock, 128-34, 136-7; Autobiography of, 5-162; becomes printer,

14; becomes vegetarian, 17; birth of, 3, 9, 163; Bond, the Doctors, and, 137-8; Boston, departure from, 22; Boston, first return to, 29-30; Bradford, work for, 22, 27; in business with Meredith, 53-4, 56, 59, 60-2; in business for self, 62-4; in charge of frontier defences, 139-43; city-watch, suggests reform of, 98-9; clerk of Assembly, 97, 107, 115; colonel of militia, 144-6; commissioner to the Indians, 115-16; daily program of, 83; death of, 165; degrees conferred on, 123, 164; *Dialogue* advocating a militia, 138-9, 144; disputatious turn of, 15; *Dissertation on Liberty and Necessity*, 42, 55; domestic life of, 66, 76; Denham, Mr., work for, 48-50; early occupations of, 3, 10-11, 13-14; education of, 3, 10, 12, 17-8; felicity of his life, 5, 85; "fire" engine, 110; five kings and, 76; food, indifference to, 12; Hemphill and, 94; hospital, 116-18; industry of, 46, 49, 59, 64, 75; influence of, 116-17; influence of Abel James on, 68; intrigues of, 66; Journal of, 49 note; journalist, 92-3; Junto formed by, 57-8; at Keimer's, 26-8, 35-6, 50-4, 56; Keimer's new religion and, 35-6; Keith, Sir William, relations with, 28-31, 34-5, 39-41, 49-50; languages studied by, 95; letters of, as Busy Body, 60; library, founds first public, 66-7, 74-5; life of, 3-4; life of, chief events in, 163-5; in London, 40-9; on London streets, 120-2; marriage of, 66; match for, projected by Mrs. Godfrey, 65-6; member Royal Society, 148-9; moderation of, 87, 18; moral living, plan of, 78-86; *New England Courant,* connection of, with, 3, 19-21; open stove invented by, 111-2; organizes fire company, 99-100; organizes militia, 105-7; paper money discussion, 62-3; parents of, 11-13; Party for Virtue projected by, 89-91; *Pennsylvania Gazette* established by, 59-60, 104; Philadelphia, arrival at, 25-6; Philadelphia, second trip to, 31-3; Philosophical Society founded by, 105; *Plain Truth,* 105; *Plan of Union,* 124-6; poetry of, juvenile, 14-15; *Poor Richard's Almanac,* 91-2; postmaster, 98; postmaster-general, 123, 145, 165;

prayers used by, 78, 82-3; Presbyterian Church and, 76-8; proprietary quarrels, 126-8, 144-6, 149-51; prose writing, practise in, 15-17; public offices, 3-4, 114-15; public printer, 60, 63, 97-8; Read, Miss, and, 25, 28, 36, 39, 42, 50, 66; reading, love of, 13-18, 42-3, 75; James, relations with brother, 3, 14, 17, 19-22, 30, 96; religious belief of, 6, 18, 42, 55-6, 76-7, 82-3, 90; Revolution, share in, 4, 165; scientist, 3, 114, 146-9; settlement of claims, 155; son, death of, 96; street-lamps improved by, 120; streets, moves improvement of, 119-23; Socratic method adopted by, 17-18, 35-6; success, reason of, 87-8; surname, origin of, 6; swimming abilities of, 47-8, 49; temperance of, 44; tyranny, hatred of, 20; University of Pennsylvania founded by, 105, 112-14; Vaughan on character and influence of, 69-73; *Way to Wealth,* 164; Whitefield and, 101-4; Woolman's book on slavery published by, 189 note

Franklin, Benjamin, uncle of the preceding, i, 7, 8, 10

Franklin, Benjamin, Mrs. (see Read, Miss)

Franklin, James, establishes *New England Courant,* i, 19-21; relations of, with Benjamin, 3, 14, 17, 19-22, 30, 96

Franklin, John, brother of Benjamin, i, 13, 31

Franklin, John, uncle of Benjamin, i, 7

Franklin, Josiah, brother of Benjamin, i, 13

Franklin, Josiah, father of Benjamin, i, 3, 9, 10-13

Franklin, Matthew, i, 194

Franklin, Samuel, i, 7, 13

Franklin, Sir John, equipment of, v, 81; Parry on, 349; search for, 361

Franklin, Thomas, grandfather of Benjamin, i, 7

Franklin, Thomas, uncle of Benjamin, i, 7

Franklin, William, son of Benjamin, i, 115, 129, 131, 133, 139, 158

Frankness, Bacon on, iii, 8, 17; Cicero on, ix, 39-41; Confucius on, xliv, 35 (20); Emerson on, v, 62

Franzesi, Matio, xxxi, 165

Franziska, in MINNA VON BARNHELM, with Minna, xxvi, 313-15; with land-

lord, 315-19; with Minna on finding Tellheim's ring, 319-21; with Just, 321-3; prepares Minna to receive Tellheim, 323; drags off landlord, 324; with Just, agrees to meet Tellheim, 327-30; with the landlord, 330-2; warned to beware of the landlord, 332; with Werner, talk of Tellheim, 333-4; with Tellheim, 340-2; with Werner again, 342-3; with Minna, the plot to win Tellheim, 343-4; in scene with Riccaut, 344-5, 347, 348-9; growing interest in Werner, 350-1; tells her mistress's misfortunes, 358-9; with Tellheim, in the plot, 360-2; at interview of Minna and Tellheim, 363, 365, 370, 372-3; tries to explain to Werner, 371; reconciliation with Werner, 374-5

Fraser, on Berkeley's DIALOGUES, xxxvii, 186

Fraser, General, reference to, vi, 51

Fraser's Magazine, Carlyle on, v, 321

Fraternities, ancient, ix, 404 note 2

Fraud, Dante on, xx, 69 note; punishment of, in Hell, 46, 73-144

Freawaru, xlix, 60 and note, 61 note

Frederick I, Luther on, xxxvi, 263; and Milan, xx, 219-20 note 8

Frederick II, birth of, xx, 296 note 7; in Hell, 44 note 14; Luther on, xxxvi, 263; Parma, defeat at, xx, 211 note 6; Pierro delle Vigne and, 54 note 2, 55; treason punished by, 95 note 3

Frederick of Sicily, Dante on, xx, 368 note 12

Frederick the Great, Mill's interest in, xxv, 11; and Voltaire, xxxiv, 64

Freedom, Æschylus on uncontrolled, viii, 143; from care, Cicero on, ix, 26; definition of perfect, v, 17; Emerson on, xlii, 1262; Epictetus on, ii, 148 (83), 166 (136), 168 (141), 169 (142), 184 (10, 15); fable on, xvii, 22-3; Goethe on, xix, 378; insolence and, vi, 261; inward slaves, impossible to, iv, 398; of labor, Smith on, x, 124-5; law of nature, xxvi, 14; necessary to true allegiance, iv, 138; Penn on use of, i, 393 (253); from worldly things, vii, 290

FREEDOM AND LOVE, xli, 782

Freeman, Edward A., life and works, xxviii, 226; RACE AND LANGUAGE, 225-73; l, 22

Freeport, Sir Andrew, xxvii, 85; Johnson on, 165

Freethinkers, Burke on, xxiv, 225; Carlyle on, xxv, 354

Free Trade, Bacon on, iii, 86-7; Emerson on, v, 255; Mill on, xxv, 65, 291-2; Smith on, x, 4, 332-52, 368-9, 433-4

Free-Will, Adam's, iv, 186; beauty and, xxxii, 266-7; Berkeley on, xxxvii, 258; cause of evil, vii, 101; Channing on, xxviii, 332; Confucius on, xliv, 29 (25); Dante on, xx, 210, 218, 302 and note 2; distinguishes man from beasts, xxxiv, 175-6; Epictetus on, ii, 124 (20, 22), 127 (29), 148 (83); given to man, iv, 138-9; human, 291-2; Hume on, xxxvii, 351-2, 363-4, 366, 369-74; Kant on, xxxii, 356-68; Machiavelli on, xxxvi, 80, 84; Mill on doctrine of, xxv, 107; Raphael on, iv, 194-5; Rousseau on, xxxiv, 259-60; Schiller on, xxxii, 262-3 (see also Autonomy of the Will)

Freezing-point, of water, xxx, 231-2

Freke, Dr., on origin of species, xi, 15

Fremont, John C., Dana on, xxiii, 391

Fremy, M., xxxviii, 307-9, 352-3

French, Colonel, i, 29, 40

French, in American Revolution, i, 136; Burke on the, xxiv, 224-5; descent from Hector, claimed for, xiii, 19; Dryden on the, 23; Goldsmith on the, xli, 526-7; influence of the, v, 378; military abilities of the, xxv, 309; polite rather than true, v, 375; sentiments of the, xxv, 41; sociability of the, 42; Taine on the, xxxix, 416, 425, 430; wiser than they seem, iii, 64

French Academy, Voltaire on, xxxiv, 154-9

French Civil War, Burke on the, xxiv, 186-7

French Classical Drama, Pellisson on, xxviii, 68

French Classics, xxxii, 122-3, 124-6, 129-30

FRENCH DRAMAS, xxvi, 75-296; Dryden on, xviii, 14-15

FRENCH ESSAYS, xxxii, 3-182

French Language, Burke on the, xxiv, 140; Dryden on, xiii, 54; Hugo on changes in, xxxix, 374-5; Huxley on study of, xxviii, 220; Johnson on changes in, xxxix, 204; Locke on study

of, xxxvii, 136, 153-4; Sainte-Beuve
on, xxxii, 119; Sidney on, xxvii, 50
French Literature, Hugo on, xxxix, 384;
Taine on, 427-8
French and Indian War, in America, i,
127-43; Woolman on, 220-2, 232, 262-
3, 264
French Money, Smith on, x, 31-2
French Nation, Freeman on the, xxviii,
255, 257-8
FRENCH PHILOSOPHERS, xxxiv, 3-305
French Revolution, aristocrats in, xxiv,
410-11; army under, 341-53; assignats
of, 256-8, 322-7, 364-71; church-lands
sale, 257-8, 323-4; church property
confiscated in, 240-56, 281-95; clergy
in, 273-4; clergy, civil constitution of
the, 281-2; completeness of, 382; population and wealth, decline of, under,
266-8; executive power, constitution of,
330-7; fanaticism and proselytism of,
247, 286-7; finances of, 357-78; Goethe
on, xix, 336, 376-9; good of the, xxiv,
376; gunpowder, making of, in, 414
note; inconsistencies of, 353-6; invasion
of Holland, 419-20; judicial power,
constitution of, 337-41; leaders of, 299-
300; letters, men of, in, 246-8, 411-12;
Lowell on, xxviii, 435; Mill on, xxv,
43, 84, 197; mistakes of, xxiv, 174-9;
monied interest in, 244-5; municipal
guards, 356-7; Napoleon on, xxviii,
468; National Assembly in, xxiv, 178-
88, 205-8, 296-9, 329-30, 353-6; nobility in, 268-73, 418-19; October sixth
and, 208-17; paper currency of, 322-
7, 364-71; Paris, preeminence of, in,
328-9; parliaments abolished by, 257;
public debts, care of, 242-50; representation under, 305-22; revenue system of, 357-74; Sheridan on, xviii, 108;
spread of principles of, xxiv, 390-2;
sympathy of English clubs with, 144-
50; Washington's policy toward, xliii,
247-8
FRENCH REVOLUTION, REFLECTIONS ON
THE, Burke's, xxiv, 141-378
Freneda, counselor of Philip II, xix, 290
Frenzy, first of ills, viii, 15
Fresh-water Productions, Darwin on, xi,
111-12; distribution of, 409-13
Frestron, the enchanter, xiv, 57, 61
Fretting, uselessness of, David on, xliv,
186 (7, 8)

Freydis, daughter of Eric the Red, xliii,
6; in Vinland, 17-19
Freyia, the goddess, xlix, 259
Freyr, Germanic god, xlix, 13 note 2
Friar, Chaucer's, xl, 16-18; Dryden on
Chaucer's, xxxix, 164
Friars, in Milton's Limbo, iv, 148; More
on, xxxvi, 155-6
FRIARS' CARSE HERMITAGE, INSCRIPTION
AT, vi, 514
FRIARS' CARSE HERMITAGE, LINES WRIT-
TEN IN, vi, 307-8
FRIARS' CARSE HERMITAGE, WRITTEN IN,
vi, 319-20
Friction, chemical effects of, xxx, 197;
heat generated by, 59, 196-7
FRIEND, TO A DISTANT, xli, 674
Friends, Confucius on, xliv, 55 (4); Con-
fucius on choice of, 5-6; Emerson on
love of, v, 152; faithful, rare, vii, 309
(2); falling out of faithful, xl, 201-2;
forgiveness of, iii, 15; little, may prove
great, xvii, 16; many, equal to none,
39; no whit worse than brothers, xxii,
114: Pascal on advantage of, xlviii, 61
(155); Ruskin on impossibility of
choosing, xxviii, 96-7; Samson on, iv,
419; Shakespeare on, xlvi, 109-10;
Shelley on false, xviii, 302-3; single
men best, iii, 21
Friends, Society of (see Quakers)
FRIENDS, FOLLOWERS AND, ESSAY ON, Bacon's, iii, 119-20
FRIENDS AND LAND I LOVE, FRAE THE, vi,
419-20
Friendship, Augustine, St., on false and
true, vii, 52; Blair on, vi, 167; Browne
on, iii, 318-9; Burns on, vi, 181; Coleridge on, xli, 703-4; Confucius on,
xliv, 41 (23); Confucius on false,
17 (24); Emerson on, v, 195; Epictetus
on true, ii, 148 (82); excess in, ix, 314
and note; Goethe on, xxxix, 252-3;
xix, 381; Hume on, xxxvii, 399; immortality of, i, 383 (127-31), 384 (132-
4); Kempis on true, vii, 306; Locke on,
xxxvii, 6-7; Lothario on, xiv, 312;
Machiavelli on, xxxvi, 55; Manzoni on,
xxi, 186; Marcus Aurelius on false, ii,
289 (15); of parents and children,
xxxvii, 81-2; Pascal on, xlviii, 44-5,
45 (101); Penn on, i, 334 (111-17);
pity and, xxxiv, 189; seldom between
equals, iii, 120; Shakespeare on, xlvi,

109; Swift on, xxvii, 91; toast to, xli, 582; Tzu-chang on, xliv, 63 (3)

FRIENDSHIP, ESSAY ON, Bacon's, iii, 65-71

FRIENDSHIP, ESSAY ON, Emerson's, v, 105-19

FRIENDSHIP, ESSAY ON, Montaigne's, xxxii, 72-86; remarks on, 3

FRIENDSHIP, SONNET ON, xiv, 238

FRIENDSHIP, TREATISE ON, Cicero's, ix, 9-44

Friesshardt, in WILLIAM TELL, xxvi, 436-41, 468-9

Frigate-bird, Darwin on the, xi, 180, 181

Frights, Locke on, xxxvii, 97-9, 116-18

Fringing-reefs, Darwin on, xxix, 475-81

Frisians, Tacitus on the, xxxiii, 111-12

Frivolousness, Confucius on, xliv, 5 (8)

Frobisher, John, Harrison on, xxxv, 321

Frobisher, Martin, death of, xxxiii, 227; with Drake, 226, 229, 239-40, 245, 255; northwest passage and, 262

Froda, xlix, 60 note, 61 note

Frog, story of, who became a god, xlv, 706-7

Frog and Mouse, fable of, xx, 93 note

FROG AND OX, fable of, xvii, 20

FROG-KING, tale of the, xvii, 47-50

Frogs, in Brazil, xxix, 38; hearts in, xxxviii, 83; in oceanic islands, xi, 417; snakes and, xxxv, 345; on volcanic islands, xxix, 386

FROGS, THE, of Aristophanes, viii, 439-87; remarks on, 438

FROGS AND HARES, fable of, xvii, 17-18

FROGS DESIRING A KING, fable of, xvii, 16-17

Froissart, Jean, BATTLE OF OTTERBURN, xxxv, 81-101; BATTLE OF POITIERS, 34-59; CAMPAIGN OF CRECY, 7-33; CHRONICLES of, remarks on, l, 22; on the English, v, 379; life and works, xxxv, 5-6; Montaigne on, xxxii, 98; in Scotland, xxxv, 86-7; WAT TYLER'S REBELLION, 60-80

Fronde, Pascal on the, xlviii, 306 (878)

Frondeurs, the, xxxiv, 87 note

Frontinus, Roman lawyer, ix, 261

Fronto, teacher of Marcus Aurelius, ii, 192, 195 (11)

Frosch, in FAUST, xix, 84-99

Froth, in NEW WAY TO PAY OLD DEBTS, xlvii, 859-63, 919-22

Frothingham, Ellen, translator of Goethe, xix, 335

Frugal, Master, in NEW WAY TO PAY OLD DEBTS, xlvii, 877-8

Frugality, Bacon on, iii, 72; economically considered, x, 265; Franklin on, i, 85, 91; Franklin's rule of, 79, 80; Hobbes on, xxxiv, 373; motives of, x, 269, 270; Penn on, i, 327-8

Fruits, beauty of, reason for, xi, 201-2; cultivation of, in Elizabethan England, xxxv, 241-2; fermentation of, xxxviii, 275, 310; fermentation of, in carbonic acid gas, 302-12; as gifts, v, 219; importance of down and color of, xi, 92; Locke on eating of, xxxvii, 20-1; ripening of, xxxviii, 306

FRUITS OF SOLITUDE, Penn's, i, 317-97

Fucci, Vanni, in Hell, xx, 101-2

Fuegians, Darwin on the, xi, 47; xxix, 209-14, 217-21, 223-8, 230-5, 238-9

Fuentes, Darwin on, xxix, 13-14

Fugger, commercial house of, xxxvi, 286 note 15, 332

FUGITIVE SLAVE ACT, xliii, 306-12

Fugitive Slaves, constitutional provision for, xliii, 191; Lincoln on, 314-15, 319; Whittier on, xlii, 1345-7

Fugitives, usually single men, iii, 21

Fulgentio, and Dr. Donne, xv, 357

Fullarton, Col., vi, 176 note, 177, 182

Fuller's Teazel, xi, 42

Fulvia, wife of Antony, xviii, 48; xii, 329; Cicero and, 230; death of, 344-5; Octavius and, 341, 344; son of, 388

Fulvius, and Ennius, xxvii, 36-7

Functions, conversion of, xi, 185-7

FUNDAMENTAL ORDERS OF CONNECTICUT, xliii, 60-5

Fundanus, daughter of, ix, 273-4

FUNDEVOGEL, story of, xvii, 140-2

Funding, system of, x, 555, 558-9 (see National Debt)

FUNERAL, THE, xl, 303

Funerals, in ancient Egypt, xxxiii, 42-4; German, 107; Indian, xliii, 34-5; in Utopia, xxxvi, 228

Fungi, Pasteur on, xxxviii, 296, 298 and note

Fungus, edible, in Tierra del Fuego, xxix, 240-1

Fur, thickness of, to what due, xi, 139

Furies, Dante on the, xx, 37; De Quincey on the, xxvii, 320; Emerson on, v, 92; Virgil on the, xiii, 419-20

FURIES, THE, of Æschylus, viii, 122-65; Voltaire on, xxxix, 364

Furnace, in NEW WAY TO PAY OLD DEBTS, xlvii, 866-8, 871-2, 873, 875, 876, 881-2, 883-4, 885-8, 923, 941

Furnius, and Antony, xii, 367

Furnivall, Dr., xxxv, 216

Fürst, Walter, in WILLIAM TELL, friend of Stauffacher, xxvi, 391; Melchthal and, 395-6, 400-1; with Stauffacher, 397-9; begins revolt, 401-5; at the rendezvous, 417-27; with Tell at Altdorf, 440-9; at death of Attinghausen, 456-61; with Rudenz, 462-4; at destruction of Keep, 474-7; hears death of Emperor, 478-81; in final scene, 488-9

Furuncles, Pasteur on, xxxviii, 371-4

Fusconi, Francesco, xxxi, 164 note, 166-7, 170

Fuscus, letters to, ix, 353, 355

Fusella, Ambrogio, in THE BETROTHED, xxi, 236, 246-7

Future, Confucius on knowledge of the, xliv, 9 (23); Hobbes on the, xxxiv, 320-1; Kempis on care of the, vii, 294 (2, 3); Milton on foreknowledge of the, iv, 338; Pascal on the, xlviii, 356; Pascal on our care for, 64 (172); past to, reasonings from, xxxvii, 316-17; Pope on blindness to, xl, 409; uncertainty of the, xxxix, 96-7; veil of the, v, 142; worry over the, ii, 123 (19), 244 (8)

Future Life (see Immortality, Hereafter)

FUTURE PEACE AND GLORY OF THE CHURCH, 563

FYERS, FALL OF, LINES ON THE, vi, 281

Gabinia, Lex, Cicero on, ix, 24

Gabinius, Aulus, campaigns of, xii, 323-4; Cicero and, 244; in Civil War, 327; Crassus and, ix, 128; return to Rome, 118; suit against, 115; Syria given to, xii, 242

Gabriel, Archangel, song of, in FAUST, xix, 18; in Luke's gospel, xliv, 354 (19, 26-30), 355 (31-8); Mohammed and, xlv, 897 note 1; Gabriel in PARADISE LOST, iv, 169, 174, 176-80, 205, 213, 291; in PARADISE REGAINED, iv, 362

Gabriel, in EVANGELINE (see Lajeunesse)

Gadarenes, xliv, 375 note 5

Gaddi, Agnolino, xxxi, 128-30

Gaddi, Cardinal de', xxxi, 73, 201-2

Gaddi, Giovanni, xxxi, 97-8 note 4, 111, 133-4, 160, 164, 167

Gaddi, Niccolo, xxxi, 73 note

Gaia, daughter of Gherardo, xx, 212 note 10

Gain, Confucius on pursuit of, xliv, 12, 56 (10); Penn on thirst for, i, 335 (127), 344 (252); Smith on hope of, x, 109-10; Tennyson on lust of, xlii, 1016

Gaius, friend of Paul, xliv, 466 (29), 467 (4); baptism of, xlv, 491 (14)

Gaius, in PILGRIM'S PROGRESS, xv, 263-75

Galahad, Sir, in HOLY GRAIL, at Abblasoure, xxxv, 124-5; Arthur and, 110, 115, 210; bed of, 186-7; birth of, 109-10, 112, 115, 152; Bors and, 206; buried at Sarras, 196; adventure of burning tomb, 205-6; at castle of Carbonek, 206-7; at castle of Carteloise, 190-2; at court, 108-9; death, 211-12; Gawaine and, 156-7, 179-80; at abbey of Gore, 205-6; Guenever and, 114-15; sees hart and four lions, 192-3; Holy Grail and, 104, 207-8; made king, 211-12; knighting of, 105-6; Launcelot and, 128-9, 198-9; at castle of Maidens, 124-5, 128; Sir Melias and, 120-1, 122-3; Mordrains and, 205-6; at Mortaise, 144; at parting of the roads, 122; Percival and, 128, 138, 197-8; prayer for death, 209-10; thrown into prison, 211; at Sarras, 210-11; shield of, 117-19; led to ship of Faith, 181-2; Siege Perilous and, 109-10; at castle of strange custom, 193-7; sword of, 182-6, 189-90; adventure of the tomb, 119-20; at tourney, 112-13; at hermitage of Ulfin, 180; virginity of, 160, 205; and queen of Waste Lands, 135; at the well, 205; at the White Abbey, 116

GALAHAD, SIR, by Tennyson, xlii, 1002-4

Galaor, Don, mistress of, xiv, 95-6

Galapagos Archipelago, Darwin on, xxix, 376-405; health conditions in, 369; species of, xi, 414, 421-5

Galatea, in PHILASTER, xlvii, 668-9; Arethusa and, 690-1; at the hunt, 714-21; Pharamond and, 686-8, 689, 690, 692-3; on Philaster, 674, 675

Galaxy, Milton on, iv, 241 (see also Milky Way)

Galba, Emperor, death of, iii, 10; em-

pire foretold to, 91; speech of, 41; Tacitus on, 30

Galdino, Father, in I PROMESSI SPOSI, xxi, 48-51, 297-9

Galeazzo de' Visconti, xx, 177 notes 5 and 7

Gale-Jones, Mill and, xxv, 80

Galen, on the arteries, xxxviii, 65, 66, 68, 81, 94-5; on the blood, 88-9; Browne on, iii, 265 (14); on the circulation, xxxviii, 97-100; on the heart, 82, 136; Huxley on, xxviii, 219; immortality doubted by, iii, 273; ostentation of, 128; on the pulse, xxxviii, 65, 69

Galesus, in ÆNEID, xiii, 257-8

Galfridus, on Arthur, xxxix, 21

Galileo, Emerson on, v, 66, 81; heliocentric theory and, xxxix, 52 note; the Inquisition and, xxxiv, 111; Milton on, iii, 215; on tides, xxx, 280; "Tuscan artist," iv, 95

Galitta, case of, ix, 294

GALLA WATER, BRAW LADS O', vi, 452

Galland, Antoine, translator of ARABIAN NIGHTS, xvi, 3

GALLANT WEAVER, THE, vi, 412

Gallatin, Albert, in Treaty of 1814, xliii, 255, 264

Galleotti, Pietro Pagolo, xxxi, 157, 158 note 7, 160, 174, 262, 266, 267, 277, 279, 304, 335, 348, 351

Galleys, of the Germans, xxxiii, 117

Gallinazo, Darwin on the, xxix, 66

Gallio, proconsul of Achaia, xliv, 463 (12-17)

Gallipoli, description of, xxviii, 55

GALLOWAY, EARL OF, EPIGRAMS ON, vi, 466

Gallura, Nino di, in Purgatory, xx, 176 and note 2; Ugolino and, 135-6 note

Gallus, Cornelius, Cicero on, ix, 62-3; death of, xxxii, 13-14; Lælius on, ix, 12

Gallus, Flavius, xii, 354-5

Gallus, M. Fadius, letter to, ix, 105

Gallus, friend of Pliny, letters to, ix, 221, 329

Galluzzi, Bernardo, xxxi, 250

GALLUPI'S, A TOCCATA OF, xlii, 1080-1

Galvanic Batteries, xxx, 203-4

Gama, Vasco de, x, 398

Gamaliel, xliv, 433 (34), 434 (35-9); Paul and, 472 (3)

Gambier, James, Lord, xliii, 255, 264

Gambling, Blake on, xli, 589; Locke on,

xxxvii, 176; Pascal on pleasure of, xlviii, 55-6

Gambling Laws, Mill on, xxv, 296-7

Games, five, of skill, xii, 73 note; in Utopia, xxxvi, 180

Gandaline, squire of Amadis, xiv, 163; sonnet to Sancho Panza, 13

Ganelon, in Charlemagne's Council, xlix, 100, 101-2; sent to King Marsil, 103-6; death of, 194; Count Walter on, 139; embassy and crime, 106-18, 121, 122; in Hell, xx, 134 note 13; Marsil and, xlix, 103-6; Roland and, 127, 131, 142, 154; trial of, 186, 187-90

Ganges, Harrison on, xxxv, 233-4

Ganymede, and Jove, xiii, 186; xx, 179

Garba, Pedro, xiv, 490

Garcia, Diego, xiv, 302-3

GARDEN, A, by Marvell, xl, 370-1

Garden of Delight, Harun Er-Rashid's, xvi, 210-12

GARDEN, THE DYING MAN IN HIS, xli, 481

GARDEN, A FORSAKEN, xlii, 1207-9

GARDEN, MY, by Brown, xlii, 1148

Garden, parable of the, xv, 205-6

GARDEN OF PARADISE, THE, xvii, 280-93

GARDEN OF PROSERPINE, xlii, 1203-5

GARDEN, THOUGHTS IN A, xl, 377-9

Gardening, Locke on, xxxvii, 174-5

GARDENS, ESSAY ON, Bacon's, iii, 4, 112-17

Gardens, kitchen, Smith on, x, 156-7; proportion in, xxiv, 82-3; in Utopia, xxxvi, 176

GARD'NER WI' HIS PAIDLE, vi, 340-1

Gareth, Sir, xxxv, 126, 127; xxxix, 23

Garget, superstition of the, xxxv, 311

Garland, Hugo on, xxxix, 380

Garnett, on THE PRINCE, xxxvi, 3-4

Garret, John, and Drake, xxxiii, 132

Garrick, David, epitaph on, xxvii, 299; Goldsmith on, xli, 505, 507-8; as Hamlet, xxvii, 303-4; Hazlitt on, 275-6; Lamb on, 308-9; PROLOGUES by, xviii, 113-14, 203-4

Garrison, William Lloyd, Mill on, xxv, 165

Garter, Order of the, xxxv, 221-2

Gärtner, Joseph, on sterility of hybrids, xi, 287-8; on mongrels and hybrids, 313-14; on prepotency, 104; on reciprocal crosses, 294, 295; on sterility of species, 285-6, 300-1, 309; on varieties, 311-12

Gas, cause of brightness of illuminating, xxx, 110-11

Gasabel, squire of Don Galaor, xiv, 163

Gascoigne, George, LOVER'S LULLABY, xl, 195-6

Gascony, Machiavelli on, xxxvi, 9

Gases, expansion of, Joule on, xxx, 198; expansion of, measurement of, 189; transparency of, 44-5; vapors and, difference of, 102-3; volume of, 43; weighing, method of, 144-6

GATHERING SONG OF DONALD THE BLACK, xli, 745-6

Gatta, Il, Cellini on, xxxi, 304

Gattinara, Giovanni Bartolommeo di, xxxi, 206 and note 2

Gauchos, character of, xxix, 161-2; compared with Guasos, 263; riding skill of, 157-8

Gaudry, M., on fossils, xi, 362

Gaufred, and Richard, xl, 48

Gaul, Cæsar's campaigns in, xii, 279-88

Gauls, risings of, repeated, xxxvi, 17; in Rome, xiii, 290; Tacitus on, xxxiii, 108

Gautama, Siddhartha, xlv, 574

Gaveston, in EDWARD THE SECOND, banishment, xlvi, 16-21; conspiracies against, 13-16, 34; Coventry and, 12-13; Edward and, 11-13, 16-17, 18, 19-21, 33, 38-9, 40; flight and capture, 42-6; historically, 5; preparations for marriage, 39; Mortimer and, 28, 38-9; nobles and, 9-11, 16; return, 33-4; Spencer and, 29; in Tynemouth, 40; Warwick and, 46-7

Gawaine, Sir, in HOLY GRAIL, meets Aglovale, xxxv, 128; nephew of Arthur, 110; Bagdemagus and, 204; dream of, 156-7, 159-60; Galahad and, 126, 179-80; Guenevere and, xlii, 1184, 1185, 1188-9, 1192; at hermitage, xxxv, 127-8; Holy Grail and, 113, 115, 156, 158; mother of, xlii, 1188-9; at Nacien, xxxv, 159-62; return home, 204; meets Seven Knights, 127; skull of, xxxix, 21; and the sword, xxxv, 108; Uwaine and, 158-9

Gay, John, Addison and, xxvii, 175-6; Eclogues of, xxxix, 322; Hazlitt on, xxvii, 278; POEMS by, xl, 402-3; Swift and, xxviii, 17

GAY GOSS-HAWK, THE, xl, 69-73

Gay-Lussac, on fermentation, xxxviii, 299

Gazehounds, Harrison, xxxv, 350

GAZELLE, THE SHEYKH AND THE, xvi, 17-18

Geary, General, at Gettysburg, xliii, 362

Geese, of Falkland Islands, xxix, 204-5; Harrison on, xxxv, 336

Gehenna, Hinnom called, iv, 98

Geikie, Sir Archibald, GEOGRAPHICAL EVOLUTION, xxx, 325-51; life and works, 324

Gellius, Aulus, on classics, xxxii, 121

Gellius, Lucius, xii, 239

Gellius, Marcus, Cicero on, xii, 240

Gelon, gift of, xii, 160; Macaulay on, xxvii, 399

Gemellinus, Virdius, ix, 374

Gemini, sign of, Dante on, xx, 381 note 8

Geminius, and Antony, xii, 367-8

Geminius, friend of Pliny, ix, 309, 337, 367

Genera, formation of, illustrated, xi, 119-22, 127; in geological record, 340-4, 352-3; large, vary most, 66-8; species in, resemble each other, 68-9

General Principles, Hume on, xxxvii, 297

Generalization, Bacon on, xxxix, 134; Bentham on, xxvii, 245; Emerson on, v, 151-3; Hume on, xxxvii, 373 (6), 414 note

Generation, alternate, xi, 458; artificial, in New Atlantis, iii, 175; death and, xxxviii, 84; economic aspect of, x, 80; Heraclitus on, ii, 220 (46); Marcus Aurelius on, 213 (4, 5), 227 (13); passions of, xxiv, 36-8; Socrates on, ii, 59-61; spontaneous, Harrison on, xxxv, 346

Genesis, Bagehot on, xxviii, 204; Browne on, iii, 286; Hugo on, xxxix, 340; Milton on events of, iv, 329 et seq.; selection, principle of, in, xi, 45

Geneva, Lake, sedimentary deposits in, xxxviii, 401

Genii, ancient belief in, v, 300; species of different, xvi, 9 note

Genitor, Julius, letters to, ix, 239, 343

Genius, Carlyle on, xxv, 322-3; colleges and, v, 422; Emerson on, 10, 59, 135, 143-6, 171-2, 263, 281-2; excesses and, 174-5; freedom requisite to, xxv, 260; Hugo on, xxxix, 365, 369, 385-6; Pascal on, xlviii, 274-5 (793); penalty of, v, 87-8; Poe on, xxviii, 373; recognition of, v, 197; Sainte-Beuve on, xxxii, 125; Schiller on, 237; talent and,

v, 165; Thoreau on, xxviii, 413; trade and, v, 45, 185; tragedy of, 51; Wordsworth on, xxxix, 333

GENIUS IN BEAUTY, xlii, 1179

Gens, nature of the, xxviii, 246

Gentilesse, Chaucer on, v, 176; Emerson on word, 201

Gentility, Emerson on word, v, 201; in English drama, 121

Gentillis, Albericus, at Oxford, v, 416

GENTLEMAN, LINES TO A, vi, 375-6

Gentlemen, Chi Tzu-ch'eng on, xliv, 38 (8); Confucius on, 5 (1), 8 (12, 13, 14), 10 (7), 13 (5, 10, 11), 14 (16, 24), 16 (15), 18 (3), 20 (16, 24), 23 (25), 24 (36), 27 (6), 28 (13), 37 (4), 38 (5, 8), 45 (7), 48 (24, 29), 50 (45, 1), 52 (17-22), 53 (31, 33, 36), 56 (7, 8, 10), 60 (23, 24), 67 (2, 3); Emerson on, v, 200-3, 210-13; Locke on making of, xxxvii, 72, 77; Newman on education of, xxviii, 34; Pascal on, xlviii, 19 (35), 26 (68); Ruskin on production of, xxviii, 133-4; Tseng-tzu on, xliv, 25 (4, 6), 41 (24), 48 (28); Tzu-hsia on, 64 (9, 10, 12); Yu-tzu on, 5 (2)

Gentleness, ECCLESIASTES on, xliv, 347 (4); manliness of, ii, 291

Gentry, Burns on the, vi, 152-6, 235; Confucius on example of, xliv, 25 (2); Hobbes on, xxxiv, 368

Gentucca, Dante on, xx, 243, 272 note 3

Genus (see Genera)

Geoffrey of Anjou, in SONG OF ROLAND, xlix, 98, 180, 182

Geoffrey of Monmouth, on Arthur, xxxii, 155; chronicle of, 161; legend of Lear in, xlvi, 214

Geographical Changes, Darwin on, xi, 387

Geographical Distribution, xi, 378-430; in classification, 437-8

GEOGRAPHICAL EVOLUTION, by Geikie, xxx, 323-51

Geography, Geikie on study of, xxx, 325-6; geology, relations to, 326-7; Hobbes on, xxxiv, 363; Hume on, xxxvii, 419-20; Locke on study of, 138, 147, 153-4, 155-6; Milton on study of, iii, 241

Geological Evolution, Geikie on, xxx, 324, 328-51

Geological Formations, age of, xxx, 335-6; Darwin on, xi, 332-5; Lyell on, xxxviii, 398-415

Geological Record, Darwin on the, xi, 319-77; Lyell on imperfections in, xxxviii, 399-415

Geology, Emerson on, v, 228-9, 297; Geikie on importance of, xxx, 327-8; Lyell on, xi, 102; xxxviii, 384, 418; papers on, 383-418; species, theory of, in relation to, xi, 504-5

GEOLOGY, PROGRESS OF, Lyell's, xxxviii, 385-97

Geometrical Spirit, Pascal on the, xlviii, 421-37

Geometry, beginning of, xxxiii, 53; Descartes on, xxxiv, 16, 17, 18, 31; Descartes's work on, 3, 112, 125; Hobbes on, 326, 363; Hume on, xxxvii, 306, 311, 413-14 note; Locke on study of, 138, 153, 155; Newton on, xxxix, 150-1; Pascal on, xlviii, 28, 409-10, 421-3 note, 424, 428

George, St., Carlyle on, xxv, 421; Emerson on, v, 392

George II, and Pitt, xxiv, 332

George III, and American Colonies, xliii, 151-3, 174; Burns to, vi, 207-11

George IV, debauchery of, v, 412; picture ships of, 302

George, Henry, Lowell on, xxviii, 469

GEORGE CAMPBELL, BONNIE, xl, 114

Georgia, island of, vegetation in, xxix, 253

Georgia, State of, settlement of, i, 101

Geraint, saint of Brittany, xxxii, 161

Geraldine, in CHRISTABEL, xli, 712-27

Gerard, in A BLOT IN THE 'SCUTCHEON, xviii, 359-61, 362, 377-80

Gerard of Roussillon, xlix, 120, 158, 167

Gérard, Balthazar, murderer of William of Orange, iii, 98

Gereia, in ROLAND, xlix, 98, 100, 120, 134, 138, 146, 167

Gergonne, M., Mill on, xxv, 40

Geri of Bello, in Hell, xx, 119 and note

Gerier, in SONG OF ROLAND, xlix, 98, 100, 120, 134, 138, 146, 167

GERM THEORY, Pasteur's, xxxviii, 364-82

German Empire, Freeman on the, xxviii, 259-60; language as factor in forming of, 256

GERMAN ESSAYS, xxxii, 185-373

GERMAN NOBILITY, ADDRESS TO, Luther's, xxxvi, 260-335; remarks on, 246

German Language, Huxley on study of, xxviii, 220

German Literature, established by Luther, xxxvi, 246; in 19th century, xxxix, 427-8; Taine on, two centuries of blankness in, 436

German Philosophy, Carlyle on, xxv, 353-4

Germanic Peoples, works dealing with early, l, 21, 24-5

Germanic Races, Taine on, xxxix, 420, 424, 430

Germanicus, Cæsar, hatred of cocks, xxxii, 57; descent and children of, xii, 388-9; in Germany, xxxiii, 114

Germanicus, Caius (see Caligula)

Germans, agriculture of, xxxiii, 101, 107, 118-19, 120; arms and practices of war, 96, 97, 98, 100-1, 109-10, 114, 117, 118; assemblies of, 99; bathing of ancient, cold, xxxvii, 13; boats of, xxxiii, 117; Cæsar's campaign against the, xii, 279-80, 283-4; chastity of, xxxiii, 103-4; children of, 104; coats of arms among, xxxiv, 368; crimes, penalties of, xxxiii, 99, 105; dances and games, 106; divination among, 97-8; dress of, 102, 114; Emerson on, v, 338, 342, 373; family ties and hospitality, xxxiii, 104-5; feasts, broils, and reconciliations, 105; food and drink, 106; funerals among, 107; gifts, their delight in, 101, 105; habitations of, 102; heroes and battle-songs, 94; inheritance, laws of, 104; kings and generals, 96, 117-18; lands, herds, and use of metals, 95-6, 107, 118; life, daily, 105-6; marriage among, 103-4; origin of, 93; physical character of, 94-5; priesthood, power of, among, 96-7; princes among the, 99-102; purity of race, 94-5; queen among, only, 119; religion of the, 97-8, 114-5, 117, 118; Romans and, 113-4; seasons of, 107; slavery among, 106-7; slavery among, Harrison on, xxxv, 226-7; Taine on, xxxix, 416, 420, 424; time, reckoning of, xxxiii, 99; tribes and name of, 93-4, 108-20; usury unknown to, 107; village chiefs, 99-100; women, 97, 102

Germany, classes in, v, 365; Emerson on science of, 438, 443; geography of, xxxiii, 93, 95; Luther on temporal state of, xxxvi, 331-4; Machiavelli on cities of, 36-7; monasteries in, 315; papal power in, 276-81, 288-9, 293-6,

306-7, 327-30; pilgrimages in, 310; Romans in, xxxiii, 113-14

GERMANY, by Tacitus, xxxiii, 93-120; remarks on, 92

Germs, defined by Pasteur, xxxviii, 343

Gerson, Jean de, as author of IMITATION OF CHRIST, vii, 200

Gertrude, the Signora, in THE BETROTHED, xxi, 139-75, 295-6, 323-5, 622-3

Gertrude, Queen, in HAMLET, Claudius and, xlvi, 99, 102-3; death, 208; Hamlet and, 101, 102, 162-9; Laertes and, 180; Ophelia and, 143, 176-8; at Ophelia's funeral, 196, 197, 198; at the play, 150, 154, 155; with Polonius, 127-30

Gertrude, in WILLIAM TELL, xxvi, 387-91

Gertrude of Wyoming, Mill on, xxv, 16

Gervase, in THE BETROTHED, xxi, 94-5, 109-12, 114, 117-18, 119, 125, 183

Gervais of Tilbury, xxxii, 153 note 8

Gervasius, the martyr, vii, 147

Geryon, monster, Dante on, xx, 69-70, 73; Virgil on, xiii, 217, 262

Gessler, in WILLIAM TELL, Armgart and, xxvi, 469-72; cap of, 393, 476; death of, 472-3; Rudenz and, 445-6; Stauffacher and, 388-9, 426; Tell and, 430-1, 441-9, 452, 453-4, 464-7, 471-2; tyranny of, 389

GET UP AND BAR THE DOOR, a ballad, xl, 87-8

GETTYSBURG, BATTLE OF, xliii, 326-414

GETTYSBURG ADDRESS, Lincoln's, xliii, 415

GHENT, TREATY OF, xliii, 255-64

Gherardeschi, Ugolino de', xx, 135-38

Ghibellines, Dante on, xx, 308 note 23; in Florence, 66 note 1; friends of Papacy, 306 note 7; Guelfs and (see numerous notes to DIVINE COMEDY)

Ghirlandajo, Hazlitt on, xxvii, 279, 281

Ghosts, Browne on, iii, 289-90; Burke on fear of, xxiv, 50; Hobbes on, xxxiv, 316-17, 377; Locke on, xxxvii, 117-18, 163-4; Milton on, iv, 56; Pliny on, ix, 311-14; Socrates on, ii, 73-4

GHULEH, THE PRINCE AND THE, xvi, 35-6

Gianciotto, Lord of Rimini, xx, 24 note 3

Giangiacomo of Cesena, xxxi, 40-1

Giannotti, Giannotto, xxxi, 26

Giants, Burke on, xxiv, 126; in Dante's HELL, xx, 128-31; in Milton's Limbo, iv, 147

Gibbon, Edward, Carlyle on, v, 322; on changes in human affairs, xxxviii, 392-3; style of, v, 21; on Tacitus, xxxiii, 92; Wordsworth on, v, 464

Gibbon, General John, at Gettysburg, xliii, 326 note, 331, 332, 335, 336, 345, 348, 350, 352, 358, 359, 360, 361, 368, 369, 370, 371, 372, 376, 377, 379, 380, 381, 391, 402, 403, 406, 407

Gibeah, the Levite woman in, iv, 100

Giberti, Gianmatteo, xxxi, 98 note

Giddiness, defined, xxxiv, 352-3

Gideon, Locke on, xxxvii, 175; Milton on, iv, 382, 421; Pascal on, xlviii, 284 (822), 298

Giese, Tidemann, xxxix, 53

Gifford, George, with Raleigh, xxxiii, 315, 336, 337, 342, 343, 345, 351, 357, 369, 372

Gifts, Burns on, vi, 191; among the Germans, xxxiii, 105; Hobbes on, xxxiv, 364, 395, 396; Kempis on, vii, 265 (4); Krishna on, xlv, 865; in law, xxxiv, 395-6; Penn on, i, 323-4 (20); Plutarch on accepting, xii, 78; Shakespeare on, xlvi, 145; Stella's definition of, xxvii, 127-8; Woolman on, i, 201; worth of, lies in giver, xlv, 807

GIFTS, by Thomson, xlii, 1149

GIFTS, EMERSON'S ESSAY ON, v, 219-22

GIFTS, HER, by Rossetti, xlii, 1181

Gila River, navigation of, xliii, 294-5

Gilbert, Sir Humphrey, life of, xxxiii, 262; Spaniards, expeditions against, 300; VOYAGE TO NEWFOUNDLAND, 263-98; remarks on voyage of, 226

Gilbert, Sir John, xxxiii, 297, 337, 351, 356

Gildas, and the bards, xxxii, 168

Giles, St., on Archbishop Turpin, xlix, 165-6

Giles, Peter, on More's UTOPIA, xxxvi, 136, 241-3

Giliolo, Girolamo, xxxi, 268, 270

Gill, Mr., on changes of drainage, xxix, 362-3

GILPIN, JOHN, DIVERTING HISTORY OF, xli, 546-54

Gines, of Passamonte, xiv, 181-2, 184-5, 188-9, 287

Ginn, Mohammed on the, xlv, 900

Ginori, Federigo, xxxi, 85-6, 91

Giotto, Dante on, xx, 189 note 4; Hazlitt on, xxvii, 279, 281

Giovanna, Queen of Naples, xxxvi, 42

Giovanni, Pier, xxxi, 121

Gipsies, Browne on, iii, 313

Giraffe, development of, xi, 219-22; tail of, 196

Giraldus Cambrensis, narratives of, xxxii, 177

GIRDLE, ON A, xl, 357

GIRL WITHOUT HANDS, THE, xvii, 116-21

Girls, Confucius on, xliv, 61 (25); Locke on training of, xxxvii, 11, 14, 51; Ruskin on education of, xxviii, 146-56

Giuki, King, xlix, 309, 313-14; daughter of, 297, 309

Giukings (see Niblungs)

Giulio, value of the, xxxi, 156 note 3

GIVE ALL TO LOVE, xlii, 1244-5

GIVE ME MORE LOVE, xl, 352-3

GIVE ME THE SPLENDID SILENT SUN, xlii, 1410-12

Giver, "God loveth a cheerful," xlv, 526 (7)

Glacial Period, Darwin on, xi, 399-401; distribution of life, effect of, on, 394-9, 404-8; in Europe, xxx, 349; species, effect of, on, xxxviii, 409

Glaciers, of the Alps, xxx, 214; appearance of, 215-23; bending and bursting of, explained, 231-9; boulders, distribution of, by, 227-8, 229-30; cause of, 214-15; crevasses in (see Crevasses); Darwin on, xxix, 250-3; dirt-bands of, xxx, 228-9; extent of former, 229-30; longitudinal rifts explained, 238; movement of, 224-6; origin of name, 215; purity of waters from, 241; effect of, on rocks, 229-30; structure of ice of, 239-40; temperature of, 232; utility of, 241-2

Gladstone, and free trade, xxv, 65; on King of Naples, v, 278

Glass, discovery of, xxxv, 295-6

Glaucus, Dante on, xx, 287; death of, xiii, 402; in Hades, 223

Glaumvor, wife of Gunnar, xlix, 343, 344, 345

Gleichen, Baron de, xxv, 224 note 4

GLENCAIRN, EARL OF, LAMENT FOR, vi, 400-2

Glendowyn, Simon, at Otterburn, xxxv, 92, 99

GLENGARIFF, by De Vere, xli, 911-12

GLENRIDDELL'S FOX, ON, vi, 407-9

Glibness, Confucius on, xliv, 15 (4), 35 (24), 49 (34), 51 (10), 55 (4)

GLOOMY WINTER'S NOW AWA', xli, 594

GLORIA IN EXCELSIS, xlv, 541

GLORIES OF OUR BLOOD AND STATE, xl, 349-50

Glory, Byron on, xli, 789-90; Hobbes on desire for, xxxiv, 389; Kempis on, vii, 244 (2), 305 (5); Milton on, iv, 377, 385-8; Pascal on love of, xlviii, 60 (150-1), 112 (324), 131 (404); "paths of," xl, 444; Pliny on, ix, 194; Plutarch on desire of, xii, 245; Tennyson on, xlii, 1005; Walton on, xv, 364; Webster on, xlvii, 823

Glosses, Luther on, xxxvi, 284

Gloucester, Earl of, in KING LEAR, blinded, xlvi, 279; Cornwall and, 277-80; Edgar and, 216, 272, 281-3, 291-3, 297-300, 306, 313; Edmund and, 216, 225-8, 243-6, 267, 273; Kent and, 247, 248, 250; Lear and, 254-5, 261, 267, 271-2, 276, 294-6; Oswald and, 298

Glub, Charles, xxxiii, 163

Gluttony, Dante's punishment of, xx, 25-6, 238-40; examples of, 245; Kempis on punishment of, vii, 233 (3); sin of, in FAUSTUS, xix, 228

Glycerin, production of, xxx, 88

GLYNN, THE MARSHES OF, xlii, 1390-3

Gmelin, on independent creations, xi, 394

Gnadenhut, Franklin fortifies, i, 140-2; massacre at, 139

Gnatho, Sidney on, xxvii, 17, 27

Gnomon, learned from Babylon, xxxiii, 53

GO, LOVELY ROSE, xl, 357-8

GO ON, SWEET BIRD, AND SOOTH MY CARE, vi, 295

GOAT AND Fox, fable of, xvii, 44

Goatherd, in DON QUIXOTE, xiv, 499-504

Goats, sacred to Mendesians, xxxiii, 28-9

GOBLET, INSCRIPTION ON A, vi, 513

Goblins, Burke on fear of, xxiv, 50; Locke on, xxxvii, 117-18, 164

God, Aristotle on, xxxix, 104; Augustine, St., on, vii, 5-10, 38, 59-60, 74-5, 98-103, 115-16, 164-5, 174-81; v, 149; Bacon on unworthy ideas of, iii, 43, 45; Berkeley on existence and nature of, xxxvii, 232-5, 252-4, 257-8, 260-2, 265, 275-6, 279; Browne on, iii, 262, 263, 265-6, 281; Burke on, xxiv, 39, 57-60;

Calvin on knowledge of, xxxix, 47-8; Channing on study of, xxviii, 329, 331; Cowper on ways of, xlv, 562; Dante on, xx, 298, 390; Descartes on existence and nature of, xxxiv, 29-33; "dice of, always loaded," v, 90; Emerson on, 146-7; Emerson on ideas of, 275; Emerson on knowledge of, 70-1; Epictetus on, ii, 137 (59-61), 141 (68); "helps those who help themselves," xvii, 35; Hobbes on, xxxiv, 375; Hume on, xxxvii, 301, 343-5, 367-70, 396-404; Locke on, 116, 118; Marcus Aurelius on existence of, ii, 300 (28); Mill on common notions of, xxv, 30-1; Mill on worship of, 170; Milton on, iv, 145, 231, 253-4, 422; Montaigne on existence of, xlviii, 391-2; morality and idea of, xxxii, 353; Pascal on existence and nature of, xlviii, 82, 84-6, 90-1, 159-61, 190 (580); Pascal on misery of man without, 24, 67, 128 (389); Penn on low ideas of, i, 387; Pope on knowledge of, xl, 408; Raleigh on, xxxix, 109-11; Raleigh on, as the Creator, 101-2, 103-4, 105-6, 107-8; Rousseau on, xxxiv, 249, 251-5, 266-8, 289, 377 (see also Providence, Sacred Books)

God, in FAUST, xix, 19-22

God, in PARADISE LOST, iv, 137-41, 142-4, 195-6, 199, 221-2, 231, 306-7, 321-2; Bagehot on Milton's, xxviii, 200

GOD, A MIGHTY FORTRESS IS OUR, xlv, 557-8

GOD, NOW THANK WE ALL OUR, xlv, 558

GOD THE FATHER, HYMN TO, xl, 304

Godfrey de Bouillon, in Dante's PARADISE, xx, 362 note 5; "one of nine worthies," xxxix, 21

Godfrey, Thomas, i, 56, 58, 65

Godlyman, Mr., in PILGRIM'S PROGRESS, xv, 291

Godolphin, Lord, and Addison, xxvii, 159-60

Gods, date of, on earth, xxxiii, 71-2, 73; first named in Egypt, 9, 26-7, 30-2; Herodotus on the, 8-9; Plutarch on, xii, 76; Roman and Greek, Dryden on, xiii, 46, 47

Godwin, Mary, second wife of Shelley, xviii, 272

Goethe, Johann Wolfgang von, Arnold on, xlii, 1135, 1136, 1137; on the

beautiful, v, 301; Byron compared with, xxxii, 388-92; Carlyle and, xxv, 315-16; Carlyle on, v, 454; xxv, 324, 387, 424, 444; characteristics of, xxxii, 380, 385-9; charities of, v, 191; on classics, xxxii, 127; on compensation of growth, xi, 150; as a critic, xxxii, 124; device of, xxv, 103; EGMONT, xix, 253-334; Emerson on, v, 21; on evolution, xi, 6, 10 note; FAUST, xix, 9-202; HERMANN AND DOROTHEA, 335-410; on himself, xxv, 408; honor due to, xxxii, 393; the *Iphigenia* of, xxxix, 415; life and works, xix, 5-8; loneliness of, xxviii, 19; MAHOMET'S SONG, xxx, 241-2; on Manzoni's drama, xxi, 3; Mazzini on, xxxii, 377-8; PROPYLAEN, INTRODUCTION TO, xxxix, 251-66; remarks on PROPYLAEN, l, 47-8; reaction against, xxxii, 378; Schiller and, xxvi, 378; on self-development, xxv, 158; Taine on, xxxix, 428; *Wilhelm Meister,* xxv, 380-2; on the will, v, 290
GOETHE AND BYRON, ESSAY ON, Mazzini's, xxxii, 377-96
Goeze, J. M., and Lessing, xxxii, 184
Goguier, M. de, and Paré, xxxviii, 23, 43
Gold, "all not, that glitters," xviii, 203; all doth lure, xix, 120; found generally virgin, x, 175; good to buy gold, v, 239; Harrison on, xxxv, 321; man's god, i, 331 (87); More on, xxxvi, 191-2, 193-4; not "all that glisters," xl, 463; "sacred hunger of pernicious," xiii, 130; type of wisdom, xxviii, 101-2 (see also Precious Metals)
GOLD, FOR LACK OF, xli, 532-3
Gold-mining, in Chili, xxix, 270-1
Golden Age, Don Quixote on the, xiv, 79; Hume on, xxxvii, 398; Milton on, iv, 11
Golden Calf, xliv, 278 (19), 437 (41); Milton on, iv, 100
Golden Fleece, Stukeley on, v, 457-8
GOLDEN GOOSE, story of the, xvii, 159-62
Golden Hind, Drake's ship, xxxiii, 206 note 5; in Gilbert's voyage 262, 274, 296
Golden Legend, iii, 42 note; PROLOGUE TO, xxxix, 13-14
Golden Rule, of Confucius, xliv, 37 (2), 52 (23); of Jesus, 369 (31); Kant on the, xxxii, 340 note; of Tzu-kung, xliv, 16 (11)

GOLDEN SAYINGS OF EPICTETUS, ii, 117-87
Golden Years, Luther on, xxxvi, 298-9 and note
GOLDIE, JOHN, EPISTLE TO, vi, 94-5
GOLDIE'S BRAINS, ON COMMISSARY, vi, 459
Goldsmith, Oliver, DESERTED VILLAGE, xli, 509-19; Emerson on, v, 21; to Johnson, xviii, 201; life and works, 200; RETALIATION, xli, 505-9; Sainte-Beuve on, xxxii, 128; SHE STOOPS TO CONQUER, xviii, 199-269; Thackeray on, xxviii, 9, 11, 19; THE TRAVELLER, xli, 520-31; WHEN LOVELY WOMAN, 505
Goleta, loss of, xiv, 387-8; sonnet on, 391
Goliath, Cervantes on, xiv, 8; Mohammed on, xlv, 914 note
Gomez, in EGMONT, xix, 301-3
Gomita, the friar, in Hell, xx, 91 and note 4
Gomorrah, Browne on, iii, 272
Goneril, in KING LEAR, Albany and, xlvi, 284-5, 309, 311-12; before battle, 304; Cordelia and, 223-4; death of, 314; Edmund and, 283-4, 289-90, 299, 305, 311; Lear and, 217, 224, 229-30, 235-40, 256-7; Regan and, 240, 253, 258-61, 286, 308-9; Ruskin on, xxviii, 139
Gonzaga, Carlo, xxi, 434
Gonzaga, Ercole, xxxi, 83 note 3
Gonzaga, Ippolito, xxxi, 335, 339
Gonzaga, Ludovic, death of, xxxii, 14
Gonzaga, Vincenzo, xxi, 434
Gonzago, Federigo, xxxi, 82 note 2
Gonzales, Mariano, companion of Darwin, xxix, 318, 365
Gonzalo, in THE TEMPEST, Ariel and, xlvi, 426-7; at banquet, 440-1, 443; in island after wreck, 417-22, 439-40; Prospero and, 405, 454-6, 459; in shipwreck, 398, 399
Gonzalo, Don, xxi, 434-7, 466-8
Gooch, Dr., on puerperal fever, xxxviii, 229
Good, Arabian verse on sowing, xvi, 24; Browning on, xlii, 1102; Confucius on, xliv, 14 (25), 52 (12), 56 (11); for evil, ii, 153 (96); xliv, 49 (36), 369 (27-35); for good's sake, ii, 163 (126); i, 358 (441); nature of, ii, 137 (59, 60); Pascal on search for, xlviii, 136-7, 154 (462); unlimited, xx, 205-6
Good and evil, Augustine, St., on, vii,

58; Emerson on, v, 218; Euripides on, viii, 352; Hobbes on, xxxiv, 388-9, 412; Marcus Aurelius on, ii, 219 (39), 239-40 (41), 253-4 (1), 280 (20), 289 (16); Milton on, iii, 201-2; Pope on, xl, 409-15; Shakespeare on, xlvi, 132

Good Breeding, Locke on, xxxvii, 72-3, 77, 78, 79-80, 121, 122, 123; Swift on, xxvii, 99-103 (see also Manners)

GOOD-BYE, by Emerson, xlii, 1241-2

Good-conscience, in PILGRIM'S PROGRESS, xv, 315

Good Friday, Walton on, xv, 403

Good Hope, Cape of, xxxiii, 224

GOOD MANNERS AND GOOD BREEDING, ESSAY ON, xxvii, 99-103

GOOD MORROW, THE, xl, 312-13

Good Nature, Emerson on, v, 210; Hobbes's definition of, xxxiv, 340; Locke on, xxxvii, 72, 118

Goodness, Cicero on, ix, 15, 16; Emerson on, v, 62; Pliny on, ix, 263; sensuous and ascetic, xxviii, 169-72; "thinks no ill," iv, 153; Tzu-chang on, xliv, 63 (2)

GOODNESS AND GOODNESS OF NATURE, iii, 32-4

Good Sense, Descartes on, xxxiv, 5

Good-Will, Buddha on, xlv, 598; Hobbes on, xxxiv, 340; Kant on, xxxii, 305-6, 325, 347-8, 350

Good-Will in PILGRIM'S PROGRESS, xv, 29, 31

Goody, Blake, tale of, xxxix, 268

Gookins, Capt., xliii, 143, 145

GOOSE WITH GOLDEN EGGS, fable of, xvii, 33

GOOSE-GIRL, THE, xvii, 173-8

Gorboduc, Sidney on, xxvii, 43

GORDON CASTLE, vi, 282-3

Gordon, Dr., on puerperal fever, xxxviii, 227-8

Gordon, Lord George, in Newgate, xxiv, 220

Gordon, Thomas, translator of Tacitus, xxxiii, 91

Gorges, Butshead, xxxiii, 337, 351, 357

Gorgias, Cicero on, xii, 237-8; native of Sicily, xxviii, 58; old age of, ix, 50; Plato on, ii, 7; riches of, x, 137

Gorgons, Æschylus on the, viii, 195

Goring, John, xxxiii, 229, 236, 237, 247, 250

Gorini, Lattanzio, xxxi, 345-6, 364, 393

Gorner Glacier, xxx, 219, 226

Gosan, fertility of, xxxv, 312

Gospel, Bunyan's parable of the, xv, 33-4; Calvin on the, xxxix, 49; Jesus on the, xliv, 397 (16); Luther on the, xxxvi, 255, 256, 325-7, 346-7; Mohammed on the, xlv, 999; Pascal on the, xlviii, 186 (568), 218 (658), 262 (742), 277 (798-800), 397, 398; Paul, St., on the, xxxix, 45

GOSPEL ACCORDING TO LUKE, xliv, 353, 419

GOSS-HAWK, THE GAY, xl, 69-73

Gosson, Stephen, and Sidney, xxvii, 4

Gothel, Dame, the enchantress, xvii, 68-9

Gothinians, Tacitus on the, xxxiii, 116

Gothones, Tacitus on the, xxxiii, 117

Goths, learning despised by, xxxv, 383; on poetry, xxvii, 36

Gouast, Capt., xxxviii, 45-6

Goulburn, Henry, xliii, 255, 264

Goujon, Jean, Hugo on, xxxix, 349

Gould, John, on cuckoos, xi, 261; on colour of birds, 139

Gournay, Mlle. de, xlviii, 25 note; Montaigne and, xxxii, 105

Gournou, husbandry of, v, 199

Goveanus, Andreas, xxxii, 70

Government, Bacon on, iii, 14, 37-8; Bentham on criticism of, xxvii, 239-1, 244-5; better no, than cruel, xvii, 17; Burke on, xxiv, 197-8, 199, 393; Calvin on civil, xxxix, 50; checks to evil, v, 88-9; Confucius on, xliv, 7 (1), 8 (19), 42 (11), 67 (2); dangers of money-power in, xxv, 108; by discussion, xxviii, 464; duties of, x, 445-6; Emerson on, v, 240-4, 246-8, 249-50, 255; expenses of, x, 447-67; expenses of, unproductive, 270-1; Goldsmith on, and human happiness, xli, 529; Hamilton on efficiency of, xliii, 201-2; importance of, overrated, xxviii, 320; Jay on necessity of, xliii, 203; Jefferson on, 150; Lincoln on perpetuity of, 315; Lowell on forms of, xxviii, 464; Machiavelli on kinds of, xxxvi, 7; Marshall on powers of, xliii, 213, 214, 215, 216; Mill on form of, xxv, 107-8; Mill on science of, 100-2; Milton's plan of, xxviii, 189; not an end, i, 348 (311); "of, by, for the people," xliii, 415; Pascal on foundations of, xlviii, 107 (304), 109 (311); Penn on, i, 350-53;

Pope on, xl, 429, 430; revenue of, x, 468-564; Rousseau on origin and forms of, xxxiv, 214-22; Ruskin on visible, xxviii, 128; self-defence first duty of, 434; superstition and, iii, 45; Swift on perfect form of, xxvii, 91; Vane on, xliii, 121; Washington on duty to, 239; Washington on, and liberty, 240

GOVERNMENT, ARBITRARY, by Winthrop, xliii, 85-105

Government Intervention, with capital, x, 335-6; with education, xxv, 302-5; with equality of employments, x, 121-46; with foreign commerce, 330-94; with freedom of contract, xxv, 299-301; with individual liberty, 202-9, 270-289; with industry, x, 445-6; with marriage, xxv, 305; with movements of precious metals, x, 313-19, 380-3; objections to, xxv, 306-12; with rates of interest, x, 97-8, 284-6; De Tocqueville on, xxv, 120; with trade, 290-9; with wages, x, 79-80, 144

Government Ownership, Mill on, xxv, 307-10; Smith on, x, 468-76

GOWDEN LOCKS OF ANNA, vi, 377

Gower, John, Dryden on, xxxix, 163; Johnson on, xxviii, 77; Sidney on, xxvii, 6

Gracchi, conciseness of the, ix, 205; Emerson on the, v, 183; Machiavelli on the, xxxvi, 35

Gracchus, Caius, with Tiberius, ix, 23; his tribuneship, 24

Gracchus, Tiberius, Blosius and, xxxii, 79; friends of, ix, 22-3; revolution of, 24

Grace, Bunyan on, xv, 36, 84-7, 216; Dante on reception of, xx, 408; Kempis on, vii, 250, 323-27, 264-5; Milton on, iv, 139-40, 141; misinterpretations of doctrine of, xxxix, 45; Pascal on, xlviii, 140, 146, 165 (508), 168 (517), 169 (520-2), 214-15 (643), 328, 367-8; Penn on, i, 365 (528)

GRACE, A CHILD'S, xl, 334

GRACE AFTER DINNER, vi, 428

GRACE AFTER MEAT, vi, 460

GRACE BEFORE AND AFTER MEAT, vi, 461

GRACE BEFORE DINNER, vi, 427

Grace, in PILGRIM'S PROGRESS, xv, 279, 283

GRACE, JAMES, EPIGRAM ON, vi, 513

Grace, Robert, i, 58, 61, 62, 111

Gracefulness, beauty without, v, 306; Burke on, xxiv, 98

Graceless, Christian first named, xv, 50

Graces, De Quincey on the, xxvii, 320

Gradation, necessity of, in change, v, 303

Graeme, Sir John, and Barbara Allan, xl, 68-9

Graeme, Sir Robert, xlii, 1156-7, 1168-9, 1173, 1174-5, 1177

Graffiacane, the demon, xx, 88, 90

Grafting, xi, 297; Cicero on, ix, 65; in Elizabethan England, xxxv, 242; Webster on, xlvii, 776

Graham, George, xxv, 54, 63, 78

Graham, Marquis of, Burns on, vi, 159

GRAHAM, MISS, INSCRIPTION TO, vi, 494

Graham, James, MY DEAR AND ONLY LOVE, xl, 358-9

Graham, Robert, of Gartmore, IF DOUGHTY DEEDS, xli, 531-2

GRAHAM, ROBERT, of Fintry, EPISTLE TO, vi, 311-13

GRAHAM, ROBERT, SECOND EPISTLE TO, vi, 423

GRAHAM, ROBERT, BURNS TO, vi, 354

GRAHAM, WILLIAM, LINES ON, vi, 487

GRAHAME, BEWICK AND, a ballad, xl, 121-8

Gram, the sword, xlix, 280, 287-8, 291, 306, 316-17, 327-8

Gramimond, horse of Valdabrun, xlix, 145

Grammar, Augustine, St., on rules of, vii, 20; of foreign languages, xxxvii, 137, 140, 143-6; Locke on study of, 143-6; Montaigne on study of, xxxii, 60-1; Penn on teaching, i, 322 (6, 8)

GRAMMARIAN'S FUNERAL, A, xlii, 1083-7

Granacci, Elisabetta, mother of Cellini, xxxi, 8-9

Granacci, Stefano, xxxi, 8

Grand, M. le, xxxviii, 12

Grand-Pré, village of, xlii, 1300, 1300-1; burning of, 1317, 1318

Grand Jury, in U. S., xliii, 194 (5)

Grandeur (see Sublime)

Grandgent, Prof., on Dante, xx, 4

Grandison, Sir Charles, xxvii, 275

Grandonie, xlix, 143, 146-7

Grani, Sigurd's horse, xlix, 284, 299, 315-16, 338, 397

Granite, Darwin on, xxix, 287-8

Granmar, King, xlix, 273

GRANT, DAVID, LINES ON, vi, 352-3

Grant, Prof., on origin of species, xi, 11-12

Grant, Sir Robert, Hymn by, xlv, 540

Grant, U. S., terms of surrender at Appomattox, xliii, 421-2

Granulations, Lister on, xxxviii, 260-1

Granville, Lord, Burns on, vi, 52; on America, i, 159-60

Granville, Cardinal, xxxix, 87

Grape, Cicero on the, ix, 64

Grapes, Locke on, xxxvii, 20

GRAPES, SOUR, fable of, xvii, 24

Grasse, Count de, xliii, 169, 173

GRASSHOPPER AND ANT, fable of, xvii, 25

GRASSHOPPER AND CRICKET, by Keats, xli, 895

Grasshoppers, Harrison on, xxxv, 349

Grassuccio, Il, xxxi, 33

Gratian, the monk, xx, 327 note 17

Gratilla, wife of Rusticus, ix, 262 note

Gratitude, Burns on emotions of, vi, 285 note; benefits, for small, iii, 34; to God, Kempis on, vii, 250; greed, go not together, and, xvii, 13; Hobbes on xxxiv, 371, 406-7; Milton on, iv, 156; no, in the wicked, xvii, 18; rich, the tribute of, vi, 494; sign of noble souls, xvii, 21; Wordsworth on, xli, 649

Grave, Bryant's choice of a, xlii, 1219-20

Grave-digger, riddle of the, xlvi, 191-2

Gravelines, battle of, xix, 255-6

Gravitation, Bacon on, xxxiv, 101; Cartesian idea of, 114; Faraday on, xxx, 11-24; Helmholtz on law of, 174; illustrations of, 11, 12-13; universality of, 14-16, 19-21; illustration of laws of, 22-4; Kelvin on, 281-2, 301-3; Leibnitz on theory of, xi, 498; Locke on, xxxvii, 164-5; Newton's discovery of universal, xxxiv, 115-21; Newton on, xxxvii, 345 note; Newton's Principia, expounded in, xxxix, 150 note (see also Gravity)

Gravity, centre of, xxx, 16-20; moving force, 178-81, 188; old view of, xxxiv, 313

Gravity, the quality, Cicero on, in age, ix, 69; Hobbes on, xxxiv, 366; Penn on, i, 334 (119)

Gray, Asa, on holly, xi, 101; Manual of Flora, 118; on plants of New and Old Worlds, 398-9; on sexes in trees, 106; on spores, 501

Gray, Farquhar, vi, 182 note 9

Gray, Thomas, Arnold on, xxviii, 83-4; Bagehot on, 192-3; THE BARD of, James Mill on, xxv, 16; Burns on, vi, 178; Hazlitt on, xxvii, 278; poems by, xxxix, 275; poems by, xl, 443-63; quoted, vi, 134; Wordsworth on, xxxix, 275, 294

Grease, and cow-pox, xxxviii, 145-7 and note, 181-3; disease of horses, 145, 147 note 3; and smallpox, 153-5, 183, 197-8

Great Acts require great means, iv, 382

Great Britain, Burke on crown of, xxiv, 154-73; Freeman on, xxviii, 257-8; naval forces on Great Lakes, xliii, 265-7; realm of, iv, 45; Treaty of 1783 with, xliii, 174-9; Treaty of 1814 with, 255-64; Treaty of 1842 with, 280-8; wages in, x, 75-9; cost of living in, 79-80

Great-grace, in PILGRIM'S PROGRESS, xv, 129, 132-3

Great Harry, Longfellow on the, xlii, 1281

Great-Heart, in PILGRIM'S PROGRESS, xv, 174; at Mnason's house, 278, 281-2, 286-90; fight with Monster, 283-4; kills Giant Despair, 286-90; encounter with Slay-good, 271-2; with Feeble-mind, 274-6; on Christian and Faithful, 277; experience with Mr. Fearing, 253-8; on Self-will, 259-61; with Gaius, 263-5; his riddle, 269; in Delectable Mountains, 289-90; meets Valiant, 295-302; in the Enchanted Ground, 301-5; on Madam Bubble, 308; parts with Christiana, 311; in PILGRIM'S PROGRESS, conducts the women, 211-22; fights with Grim the giant, 222-3; leaves the pilgrims, 224; returns to pilgrims, 238; in valley of Humiliation, 240-4; in valley of Death, 245-9; with Mr. Honest, 251-2

Great Lakes, naval forces on, xliii, 265-7

Great Men, acquiescence of, v, 60; Aristotle on, 383; belief in, natural, 193; Confucius on, xliv, 10 (9); illustrate their places, v, 128; independence of, 64; love and, iii, 27; love of, xlviii, 420; make great things, v, 18; obligations of, i, 393-5; Pascal on vices of, xlviii, 45-6 (103); past and present, v, 81; smiles of, vi, 189; worship of, Carlyle on, xxv, 393-5; worship of, meaning of, v, 18

Great Place, Bacon on, iii, 28-31 (see also Ambition); Confucius on, xliv, 13

(14); Dyer on, xl, 207-8; Epictetus on,
ii, 131 (43); Penn on, i, 381; penalty
of, v, 87-8

Great Riches, Luther on, xxxvi, 332

Great Sacrifice, Confucius on the, xliv,
10 (10, 11)

GREAT SPIRITS NOW ON EARTH SOJOURN-
ING, xli, 897

Great works, from childless men, iii, 20,
21

Greatness, appeals to future, v, 67; Burns
on, vi, 85; domesticity and, i, 70;
essence of, v, 126; known by accident,
xxv, 409; latent, 417; Mammon on, iv,
115; original, always, v, 193; pleasure
of, xlviii, 108 (310); Pascal on, 66
(180), 119 (353), 125 (378), 130
(397), 274 (793), 378-83, 412; Pope on,
xl, 436; Seneca on, iii, 16; Shakespeare
on, xlvi, 175-6; transitoriness of, xvi,
300-4, 312, 317, 320-1; true, Kempis
on, vii, 209 (6); unconsciousness of,
xxv, 406; unpopularity of, 403-4; Webster's fable of, xlvii, 813; quest of, 850;
worldly price of, xviii, 440-1

GREATNESS, TRUE, by Watts, xl, 398

GRECIAN URN, ODE ON A, xli, 878-9

Greco, Giovanni, xxxi, 97 note 5

Greece, Ancient, works dealing with, l,
19-20, 25; Caxton on women of, xxxix,
11; Collins on music in, xli, 479;
colonies of, x, 395; decline of military
spirit in, xxvii, 373-4; decline of morality in, 378; freedom of speech in ancient, iii, 191, 193-4; history of, Carlyle on, xxv, 365-6 (see also Plutarch's
Lives of Themistocles, Pericles, Aristides, Alcibiades, and Demosthenes);
languages, study of, in, xxxvii, 146,
162-3; letters and arts of, v, 149;
literature of, later, xxvii, 342-3; literature of, Jesus on, iv, 403-4; patriotism
in, strength of, xxvii, 396; Pliny on,
ix, 332; religion, philosophy and art
of, xxxix, 431; Roman dominion in,
xxxvi, 17; Romans in, 11-12, 18-19,
73-4; Rousseau on cause of arts of,
xxxiv, 177; Schiller on culture of,
xxxii, 220, 224-5, 235; the Turkish
dominion in, xxxvi, 10; Turkish power in, beginning of, 45 (see also Hellas)

GREECE, THE ISLES OF, xli, 812-15; remarks on, l, 24, 28

Greed, Confucius on, xliv, 56 (7); FABLE

OF, xvii, 33; "goes not with gratitude,"
13 (see also Covetousness)

Greedy, Justice, in NEW WAY TO PAY OLD
DEBTS, xlvii, Furnace on, 867; at Lady
Allworth's 871-2; Marrall and Over-
reach on, 876-7; at Overreach's, 895-6,
898-9, 901, 903-4, 905, 906, 907; with
Tapwell, 921-2

Greek Church, Freeman on, xxviii, 232;
Luther on, xxxvi, 302

Greek Classics, xxxii, 121-2

Greek Comedy, Hugo on, xxxix, 346-8

Greek Drama, debt of, to Homer, xiii, 7;
Hugo on, xxxix, 341-2, 347, 359, 383;
Voltaire on, 364

Greek Dramas, l, 20, 29

GREEK HYMNS, xlv, 541-5

Greek Language, Carlyle on, xxv, 365;
Emerson on, v, 256-7; Huxley on,
xxviii, 213-20; Locke on, xxxvii, 68,
77, 127, 145, 162-3, 167-9; Mill on,
xxv, 24; Montaigne on, xxxii, 65, 67;
Milton on, iii, 237, 241-2; More on,
xxxvi, 137; study of, Augustine, St.,
on, vii, 16

Greek Learning, study of, iii, 199-200

Greek Literature, Hugo on, xxxix, 340-2,
346-8

Greek Names, xii, 156-7

Greek Philosophers, Cudworth on, xxxvii,
166

Greek Philosophy, divisions of, xxxii, 299

Greek Science, Huxley on, xxviii, 219

Greek Tragic Dance, Coleridge on, xxvii,
258

Greek Tragedy, decay of, viii, 438 (see
THE FROGS)

Greeks, and barbarians, xxxvii, 146,
162-3; calendar of the, xxxiii, 8-9;
chronology of the, xxxiv, 127; in Egypt,
xxxiii, 88; Freeman on the modern,
xxviii, 263-4, 265-6, 271; Goethe on
culture of the, xxxix, 251-2; poetry
among the, xxvii, 9-10; Schiller on art
of the, xxxii, 252; Taine on the, xxxix,
412, 424

GREEN GROW THE RASHES, vi, 47-8

GREEN LINNET, THE, xli, 642-3

Greene, Robert, CONTENT, xl, 282-3

Greenhead Ghyll, xli, 615, 627

Greenland, Christianity in, xliii, 13, 14;
colonized by Eric the Red, 56; subsidence in, xxxviii, 406

Greenough, Horatio, Emerson on, v, 316-
17

Greenvile, John, xxxiii, 337, 351, 356

Greenville, Sir Richard, xxxiii, 226

GREENWOOD TREE, UNDER, THE, xl, 263

Gregory I, St., the Great, on angels, xx, 406; and the Angles, v, 348; xxviii, 48; and England, xxxvi, 130; heathen antiquities destroyed by, iii, 137; on sin, xxxvi, 270

Gregory, St., Nazianzen, Basil, St., and, students at Athens, xxviii, 52-3, 54-61; *Christ Suffering*, iv, 412

Gregory VII, and Henry IV, xxxvi, 294 note 25

Gregory Bay, the climate at, xxix, 236

Gregson, Mr., on puerperal fever, xxxviii, 228

Grendel, in BEOWULF, ravages of, xlix, 8-10, 13, 17; and Beowulf, 16-17, 21, 23-8, 31, 40, 59-60, 62; hand of, 27-8, 31-2, 41; head of, 49, 50; mother of, 40-8, 63

Grenville, Lord, and Burke, xxiv, 382

Grenville, Sir Richard, xlii, 1007-10

Gresham, Mr., and More, xxxvi, 116

Gretchen, in FAUST (see Margaret)

GRETHEL, HÄNSEL AND, xvii, 76-83

Greville, Fulke (see Brooke, Lord)

Grey, half brother to Richard III, xxxix, 75, 76

Grey, Dr., on Shakespeare, xxxix, 240

Greyhounds, in hunting, Harrison on, xxxv, 350

Grief, alone and with mates, xlvi, 276; Augustine, St., on, vii, 28, 50; beauty's canker, xlvi, 413; Browning, E. B., on, xli, 937; Burke on, xxiv, 34-5; Coleridge on, xli, 729; desires to be alone, xlvii, 509; Hobbes on, xxiv, 340; instructs the wise, xviii, 407; Marcus Aurelius on, ii, 280 (25), 281 (28), 283 (34); physical effects of, xxxviii, 124; Shakespeare on, and joy, xlvi, 153; Shakespeare on silent, 380; and tears, xxvii, 285; "what need a man forestall his," iv, 54

Griefs, reduced by sympathy, iii, 68

Griego, John, xxxiii, 209

Grieve, James, Epitaph on, vi, 50

Griffith, John, i, 183

Grifir, prophecy of, xlix, 288; in the Edda, 251

Griflet, Sir, xxxv, 108

Grifolino, of Arezzo, in Hell, xx, 122 and note

Grignapoco, the bravo, xxi, 122

Grignon, R. S., translator of Luther, xxxvi, 2

Grim, the giant, xv, 222-3

Grimes, Sir Thomas, and Dr. Donne, xv, 357

Grimhild, wife of Giuki, xlix, 310; and Sigurd, 312, 313-14; and Brynhild, 314, 317, 320, 321; and Gudrun, 338, 339-40, 339, 400-1, 403; remarks on magic potion of, 251

Grimm, Baron, on Shakespeare, xxxix, 318

Grimm, Hermann, Emerson and, v, 4

Grimm, Jakob, xvii, 46

Grimm, Wilhelm, xvii, 46

Grimms' HOUSEHOLD TALES, xvii, 45-218; remarks on, 8

Gripe-man, the schoolmaster, xv, 104

Gripir (see Grifir)

Grisi, Julia, in England, v, 413

Griso, in THE BETROTHED, xxi, 106-9, 121-4, 179-80, 183, 185; despatched to Monza, 186-8; finds Lucia, 291; with Rodrigo in the plague, 536-7, 539-41; his death, 541

Grisolan, in DUCHESS OF MALFI, xlvii, 759, 778, 779, 847-8, 851

Grocyn, Doctor, xxxvi, 90

Grolier, Jean, xxxi, 323 note 1

Grose, Francis, Capt., epigram on, vi, 350-1; lines on, 349-51, 387-8

Grote, George, xxv, 77, 78; Mill on, 49-50, 188; in Parliament, 122; and *Westminster Review*, 63, 64

Grotesque, Hugo on the, xxxix, 346-52, 356-7; origin of word, xxxi, 61

Ground-rent, how determined, x, 489; taxes on, 491-2

Groups, of organic beings, xi, 136-7; sudden appearance of specific, 340-3

Grout, Sir Jenken, epitaph of, v, 213

Grove's Battery, xxx, 76

Growth, compensation of, xi, 150-2; laws of, defined, 212; laws of, effects of, 215-17; law of nature, v, 101-2

Grub Street, Swift on necessity of a, xxvii, 117

Gryphon, symbol of Christ, xx, 265 note 10; Æschylus on the, viii, 195 and note 55

Grypus, name of, xii, 156 note

Guadagni, Felice, xxxi, 175-6, 188, 200

GUADALUPE HIDALGO, TREATY OF, xliii, 289-305

Gualdrada, Dante on, xx, 66 note 1

Guam, cession of, xliii, 443 (2), 444 (5), 445-6 (8)

Guanaco, Darwin on the, xxix, 170-3

Guardian Angels (see Tutelary A.)

Guardians, Hobbes on power of, xxxiv, 415; Mohammed on duties of, xlv, 967-8

Guascar, xxxiii, 303, 317, 321, 330

Guascontis, the, and Cellini, xxxi, 28-31

Guasos, of Chili, xxix, 263

Guayatecas, Darwin on, xxix, 285-94

Guayna-capac, xxxiii, 307, 317, 318-19

GUDE ALE KEEPS THE HEART ABOON, vi, 515

GUDEWIFE, COUNT THE LAWIN, vi, 378

Gudrid, the Norsewoman, xliii, 11, 13, 14, 15, 16, 20

Gudrun, at Alfscourt, xlix, 338, 399; Atli and, 340-1, 350-3, 402-6, 415-17, 425-6; Brynhild, quarrel with, 318-20, 322-3; daughter by Sigurd, 336; death of, 356, 419-23; dream of, 310-12; drink of, 339, 400-1; future foretold, 336-7, 383-5; Gunnar and, 349-50, 414; married to Jonaker, 353, 418; Morris on, 255; Renan on, xxxii, 142; runes to brethren, xlix, 342, 409-11; Sigurd, her marriage to, 314-15, 371-95; at Sigurd's death, 328-35, 376-7, 392, 393, 397-8; story of, remarks on, 251, 252; Swanhild avenged by, 355-6, 420, 424-6

GUDRUN, FIRST LAY OF, xlix, 329-35; remarks on, 251

GUDRUN, SECOND LAY OF, xlix, 396-406

GUDRUN, THE WHETTING OF, xlix, 418-23; remarks on, 252

Guelfs, and Ghibellines in Italy (see numerous notes to Dante); opposed to papacy, xx, 306 note 8, 308 note 21

Guenevere (see Guinevere)

GUENEVERE, THE DEFENCE OF, xlii, 1183-93

Guenevor (see Guinevere)

Guerra, Pablo de la, xxiii, 385, 393

Guest, Lady Charlotte, xxxii, 138-9, 148

Guevarra, Fernando de, xiv, 490

GUIANA, DISCOVERY OF, Raleigh's, xxxiii, 301-80

Guiana, advantages of, xxxiii, 377-8; drunkenness in, 322; extent of, 354; first knowledge of, 302; French attempts on, 326; gold of, 305-7, 358, 366-7; Milton on, iv, 329; productions and climate of, xxxiii, 375-6; Raleigh's

exploration of, 335-73; religions and customs of, 374-5; riches of, 317, 321, 324, 326, 358; settled from Peru, 317, 319-20; slave and other trades to, 334-5; Spanish attempts to conquer, 319-25, 327-35; tribes of, 373; wealth of, 303, 374-5

Guicciardini, Francesco, Cellini and, xxxi, 407 note 1; Montaigne on, xxxii, 100-1

Guid-guid, Darwin on the, xxix, 292

Guidi, Giacopo, xxxi, 406

Guidi, Guido, xxxi, 298, 319, 336, 348

Guido, Da Vinci and, xxxix, 426; Hazlitt on, xxvii, 278; portrait of Beatrice Cenci, xviii, 278

Guidoguerra, in Hell, xx, 66 and note 1

Guildenstern, in HAMLET, xlvi, 124-6, 131-5, 140, 142-3, 149, 156-8, 159-60, 170, 171, 184, 200, 210

Guilds, labor, x, 121-32

Guillotine, in Elizabethan England, xxxv, 366-7

Guilt, Manzoni on, xxi, 324; Shakespeare on, xlvi, 177; what quick eyes has, xviii, 76

Guilt, in PILGRIM'S PROGRESS, xv, 128, 132-4

Guines, Earl of, Constable of France, at Caen, xxxv, 9, 13-16

Guinevere, and Launcelot, xiv, 92, 489; xx, 352 note 2; xxxv, 105-6, 115-16, 132-3 (see also GUENEVERE, DEFENCE OF); in HOLY GRAIL, xxxv, 109-10, 114, 115-16; Renan on, xxxii, 142

Guinicelli, Guido, xx, 189 note 5, 252-3

Guion, type of temperance, iii, 202

Guiscard, Robert, xx, 114 note; in Paradise, 362

Guise, Duke of, at Boulogne, xxxviii, 18; at Danvilliers, 20; at Metz, 23, 24, 25, 26, 27-8, 29, 30, 31, 32, 33; at Moncontour, 51; murder of, xxxix, 359

Guittone, Dante on, xx, 253

Guizot, M., in England, v, 376

Gulf Stream, Dana on the, xxiii, 345-6

Gulliver's Travels, Thackeray on, xxviii, 20-3

Gulike, country of, xxxvi, 137, 138

Gumila, the Jesuit, x, 403

Gummere, Francis B., translator of BEOWULF, xlix, 3-4

Gun-cotton, xxx, 58 note 20

Gunnar, son of Giuki, xlix, 310; Atli and, 341-3, 344, 407-10; Brynhild and, 315-16, 317, 319-20, 321-2, 324, 335-7,

378-86, 393-5; editor's remarks on story of, 251; Gudrun and, 338, 339, 383, 400; imprisoned, 348-9, 412, 413-14; Oddrun and, 336, 431, 433, 435-8; Sigurd and, 313, 314, 325-7, 328, 333-4, 373-5, 377-8, 391-2, 425; in the worm-close, 350, 414, 437-8

Gunning, Elizabeth and Maria, v, 305

Gunpowder, combustibility of, compared with iron, xxx, 74; force of, 189; invention of, Don Quixote on, xiv, 379; invention of, effect on civilization, x, 450

Gunpowder Plot, attributed to Machiavelli, xxvii, 363; discovery of, iii, 268-9 and note 33

Gunshot Wounds, Lister on, xxxviii, 265-6; Paré on, 11-12, 38-9, 52

Günther, Dr., authority on fishes, xi, 231; on fish, 409-10

Gurney, in EDWARD THE SECOND, xlvi, 75, 78-9, 82-4, 86

Gusman, Felix, father of St. Dominic, xx, 336 note 18

Gustavus Adolphus, hymn attributed to, xlv, 559

Guthlaf, xlix, 34 note 5, 37

Gutters, Franklin on, i, 121-2

Guttorm, son of Giuki, xlix, 310, 326-7, 337, 375-6, 391-2; on royalty of truth, v, 374

Guy of Warwick, xiv, 93

Guyard, the groom, xxxviii, 21

Guyon, Sir, xxxix, 63, 64

Guyot, quoted, xxviii, 406

Gwendolen, chess-board of, xxxii, 145-6

Gwrhyr Gwalstawd Ieithoedd, xxxii, 150-2

Gyara, ii, 132 (45) note

Gyas, the Latin, xiii, 332

Gyas, the Trojan, xiii, 81, 95, 182-7

Gyges, death of, xiii, 318

Gylippus, Plutarch on, xii, 59, 127; sons of, in the ÆNEID, xiii, 399

Gynæcea, goddess, xii, 271

Habbâb, xlv, 912 note 8

Habeas Corpus, Johnson on writ of, xliii, 429-30; privilege of, 185 (2)

Haberdasher, Chaucer's, xl, 21

Habington, William, POEMS by, xl, 252-4

Habit(s), Bacon on, formation of, iii, 97; Burke on, xxiv, 84; changed, exhibited by insects, xi, 178; changed without change of structure, 180-1; diversification of, 116-18, 178-80; in eating,

xxxvii, 17-19; endurance of cold and heat as a, 10-11; Epictetus on evil, ii, 144 (75); errors due to, xlviii, 38; Goethe on, xix, 77; hereditary, in plants, xi, 144-5; Hume on, xxxvii, 321-2, 330, 373; inherited, effect of, xi, 27, 255-8; instinct, compared with, 251-2; Kempis on, vii, 274 (5); Locke on importance of, xxxvii, 4, 14, 19, 43, 88, 92, 103-13; perfects qualities of mind, xlviii, 416; Shakespeare on, xlvi, 167-8; of sleeping, xxxvii, 21-2; teaching of, 44; ten times nature, v, 371; transitional, xi, 175-8; variation due to, 10

Had I a Cave, vi, 467-8

Had I the Wyte? She Bade Me, vi, 529-30

Hades, Æneas's visit to, xiii, 216-28; Rhampsinitos in, xxxiii, 62; Socrates's description of, ii, 108-9; Ulysses's visit to, xxii, 145-61 (see also Hell)

'Hadīgah, wife of Mohammed, xlv, 876

Hadley's Quadrant, inventor of, i, 58

Hadrian, Emperor, enviousness of, iii, 24; Marcus Aurelius on, ii, 257 (25), 259 (37)

Haeckel, Prof., on phylogeny, xi, 452

Haemmerlein, Thomas (see Kempis, Thomas à)

Hæmon, in ÆNEID, xiii, 316, 326; in ANTIGONE, viii, 274, 276-80, 294, 295

Hæthcyn, in BEOWULF, xlix, 71-2, 73, 85

Hafiz, quotation from, v, 290, 445

Hafsah, wife of Mohammed, xlv, 992 note 1

Haggai, prophecies of, xlviii, 254-5

Haggis, Address to a, vi, 253-5

Haidinger's, Brushes, xxx, 266-7

Haies, Edward, captain of "Golden Hind," xxxiii, 262, 274, 291-7; VOYAGE TO NEWFOUNDLAND, 263-98

Hail-storms, Darwin on, xxix, 121

Hainault, John of, in Crecy campaign, xxxv, 12, 17, 22, 29, 30-1; in EDWARD THE SECOND, xlvi, 57-9, 60, 62

Hair, To a Lock of, xli, 740

Hair, St. Paul on long, xlv, 505 (14-15); teeth and, relation of, xi, 28, 148-9

Hake, King, death of, v, 344

Hakewill, Wordsworth on, xxxix, 318 note

Hakluyt, Richard, Drayton on, xl, 228; on geography and chronology, xxx, 325

Haldeman, Prof., on species, xi, 12

Halden, Henry of the, in WILLIAM TELL, xxvi, 398-9

Haldor, character of, v, 386

Haldudo, John, in DON QUIXOTE, xiv, 38

Hales, Chief Justice, on cost of living, x, 79

Hales, the irrefragable, xxviii, 47

Halesus, in ÆNEID, xiii, 264, 333, 335-6

Halifax, punishment of theft in, xxxv, 366-7

Halifax, Lord, and Addison, xxvii, 159-60; Voltaire on, xxxiv, 147

Halitherium, Darwin on, xi, 363

Halitherses, in ODYSSEY, xxii, 25, 229, 331

Halius, son of Alcinous, xxii, 102; dance of, 108

Halket, George, LOGIE O' BUCHAN, xli, 571-2

Hall, Bishop, Encomium of, iii, 190 and note; Walton on, xv, 353

Hall, David, partner of Franklin, i, 114

Hall, Jim, in TWO YEARS BEFORE THE MAST, xxiii, 25-6, 397

Hall, Sir John, xlii, 1174

Hallam, Henry, Emerson on, v, 439

Halley, Edmund, on comets, xxxiv, 118; Newton on, xxxix, 152

HALLOWEEN, vi, 110-19

Halonesus, speech on, xii, 198 note 5

Ham, son of Noah, Burns on, vi, 164; Milton on, iv, 344

Haman, minister of Pharaoh, xvi, 320 note 9; Mohammed on, xlv, 932, 933

Hamburgh (Hamburg), taxation at, x, 499; trading enterprises of, 469, 471

Hamdir, in the VOLSUNG TALE, xlix, 353, 356, 357; in the Edda, 418, 419, 420

HAMDIR, THE LAY OF, xlix, 424-30; remarks on, 252

HAME, HAME, HAME, xli, 782-3

Hamilcar, and Agathocles, xxxvi, 29

Hamilton, Alexander, article in the Federalist, xliii, 199-203; and Washington's Farewell Address, 233 note

Hamilton, Andrew, i, 40, 41, 60, 63

Hamilton, Duchess of, beauty of, v, 305

Hamilton, Gavin, Burns on, vi, 70, 72, 105; EPITAPH for, 219; DEDICATION to, 211-14; farewell to, 224; STANZAS ON NAETHING, epistle to, 222-3

HAMILTON, GAVIN, vi, 119-200

HAMILTON, MARY: a ballad, xl, 117-19

Hamilton, William, THE BRAES OF YARROW, xli, 572-6

Hamilton, Sir William, Mill on philosophy of, xxv, 167-70

HAMISH, THE REVENGE OF, xlii, 1393-8

Hamlet, Prince of Denmark, Arnold on, xxviii, 73; Bagehot on, 192; in churchyard, xlvi, 192-8; Claudius and, 161-2, 172-3, 185-9, 203-4, 208; death of, 209; scene with Gertrude, 162-9; the ghost and, 112-18; Guildenstern's report on, 142; Horatio and, 111-12, 149-50, 183-4, 199-201; Laertes, duel with, 205-7; pretended madness, 123-4; Ophelia and, 107-8, 110-11, 128, 144-6; at Ophelia's funeral, 197-8; in the original story, 92; Osric and, 201-4; at the play, 150-2, 153-6; players and, 136-40, 147-8; Polonius and, 130-1, 135-6, 162-3; with Rosencrantz and Guildenstern, 131-5; Ruskin on, xxviii, 137; soliloquy of, xlvi, 144; soliloquy, Lamb on, xxvii, 301; soliloquy translated by Voltaire, xxxiv, 132-3

HAMLET, TRAGEDY OF, xlvi, 93-211; editorial remarks on, 92; Johnson on, xxxix, 215, 226; Lamb on stage representation of, xxvii, 303-4, 306-7, 316; Thoreau on, xxviii, 413; Voltaire on, xxxiv, 131

Hammon, Master, in SHOEMAKER'S HOLIDAY, xlvii, 484, 485-6, 493-5, 505-9, 512, 522-4

Hammon, the god, iv, 13 (22)

Hamor, and Jacob, xv, 108

Hananiah, death of, xlviii, 286 (827)

Hancock, Gen., at Gettysburg, xliii, 331, 332, 333, 334, 339, 345, 350, 352, 358, 359, 361, 364, 367, 369, 370, 391, 406-7; Haskell on, 359, 403

Hancock, John, signer of Declaration, xliii, 153

HANDSOME NELL, vi, 19-20

Hanmer, Sir Thomas, xxxix, 237

Hannibal, Cervantes on, xiv, 488; Cicero on, ix, 20; Fabius and, 48-9; Machiavelli on, xxxvi, 55-6; story of, before Rome, iii, 225

HANS IN LUCK, story of, xvii, 168-73

HÄNSEL AND GRETHEL, xvii, 76-83

Happiness, Augustine, St., on, vii, 176-8; Bacon on highest, iii, 8; Browne on, 331-2; Burns on, vi, 308; Dante's allegory of, xx, 221; Epictetus on, ii, 118 (3), 152 (94), 162 (122), 163 (129), 171 (147), 171 (151); Franklin on, i, 56, 86, 123; Goldsmith on, xli, 515,

521-2, 531; Kant on, xxxii, 305, 307, 310-11, 326, 328-9; Kempis on, vii, 278; Locke on, xxxvii, 9; Marcus Aurelius on ii, 201 (8), 210 (12), 221 (51), 231 (34); Mill's theory of, xxv, 90-1; More on, xxxvi, 196-204; Pascal on, xlviii, 54, 55, 58, 63 (165), 64 (170), 136, 147 (437), 154, 412; Penn on, i, 343-4; Pliny, on greatest, ix, 334; Pope on, xl, 405, 430-40; Rousseau on search for, xxxiv, 279; Shakespeare on, xlvi, 131; Surrey on, xl, 194-5; Washington on, and virtue, xliii, 227; Wotton on, xl, 288-9

HAPPINESSE, THAT WE SHOULD NOT JUDGE OF OUR, UNTILL AFTER OUR DEATH, xxxii, 5-8

HAPPY INSENSIBILITY, xli, 875-6

HAPPY LIFE, CHARACTER OF A, xl, 288-9

HAPPY LIFE, MEANS TO ATTAIN, xl, 194-5

HAPPY WARRIOR, CHARACTER OF THE, xli, 656-8

Hardiness, Locke on, xxxvii, 94, 100-1

Haquin, king of Norway, xx, 369 note 16

Harapha, of Gath, with Samson, iv, 441-6

Harbors, expense of maintaining, x, 454

Harcourt, Godfrey of, in French invasion, xxxv, 7-10, 14-16, 17, 19, 20, 24, 30

Hardcastle, in SHE STOOPS TO CONQUER, with Mrs. Hardcastle and Tony, xviii, 205-8; with Kate, 208-9; trains his servants, 216-17; receives Marlow and Hastings, 219-24; discusses Marlow with Kate, 233-5, 243-4; catches Marlow with Kate, 243-4; with Marlow and his servants, 247-8; with Sir Charles Marlow, 256-9; with Tony and wife in the garden, 262-3; sees Kate and Marlow, 265-6; reconciled to Marlow, 267; to Hastings, 268; gives Kate to Marlow, 268-9

Hardcastle, Kate, in SHE STOOPS TO CONQUER, with father, hears of young Marlow, xviii, 208-10; with Miss Neville, 210; meets Marlow, 226-9; discusses him with her father, 233-5; pretends to be barmaid, 239-40; with Marlow as barmaid, 240-3; caught by her father, 243-4; undeceives Marlow and tries to detain him, 249-50; tells of Marlow's love for her, 259; besought by Marlow, 265-6; makes herself known, 266-7; united to Marlow, 268-9

Hardcastle, Mrs., in SHE STOOPS TO CONQUER, at home with Hardcastle and Tony, xviii, 205-8; with Hastings, 229-30; with Tony and Miss Neville, 230-2, 251-2; and Miss Neville's jewels, 236-9; Tony's letter and, 252-3; orders Constance to aunt's, 253, 255-6; fooled by Tony, 261-3; plans finally upset, 267-9

Hardness, Berkeley on, xxxvii, 210

Hardships, Channing on value of, xxviii, 314-15

Hardwicke, Dr., xxxviii, 166

Hare, Mr., system of personal representation, xxv, 159-60

HARE AND TORTOISE, fable of, xvii, 38

HARE WITH MANY FRIENDS, fable of, xvii, 39

HARE-MARK IN MOON, story of, xlv, 697-701

HARES AND FROGS, fable of, xvii, 17-18

Hargreaves, James, inventor of spinning-jenny, v, 395

Harleian Miscellanies, Emerson on, v, 123

Harlequin, Thackeray on, xxviii, 7

Harley, Burns on, vi, 261

Harm, Marcus Aurelius on, ii, 213 (7), 228 (22)

Harmonia, wife of Cadmus, viii, 433

Harmony, Confucius on, xliv, 59 (11); Dryden on, xl, 389

HARP OF THE NORTH, FAREWELL, xli, 755-6

HARP THAT ONCE THROUGH TARA'S HALLS, xli, 819

Harpalus, Demosthenes and, xii, 211

Harpalyce, in ÆNEID, xiii, 84

Harpies, Æneas and the, xiii, 135-6; in Dante's HELL, xx, 53

Harpocras, physician, ix, 359, 360

Harras, Rudolph der, in WILLIAM TELL, xxvi, 441-8, 469-73

Harriers, Harrison on, xxxv, 350

Harris, John, with Drake, xxxiii, 177

Harris, Tom, friend of Dana, xxiii, 180, 189-94, 261, 267, 396-7

Harrison, Benjamin, and Hawaii, xliii, 437 headnote

Harrison, William, collaborator of Holinshed, xxxv, 216; DESCRIPTION OF ELIZABETHAN ENGLAND, 215-383

Harrowing, origin of word, ix, 63

Harry, David, i, 51, 64

Harsnett, Dr., and Dr. Donne, xv, 343-4

Hart, Christ, typified by a, xxxv, 193; defined, 343

HART AND HUNTER, fable of, xvii, 21-2

HART IN THE OX-STALL, fable of, xvii, 23

Hart, Sir Robert, at Otterburn, xxxv, 90, 99

Harte, Bret, THE REVEILLE, xlii, 1401-2

Hartley, David, Hazlitt on, xxvii, 277; Mill on philosophy of, xxv, 46-7

Hartlib, Samuel, iii, 234; Cowley on, xxvii, 66; Milton on, iii, 235

Hartsocher, Voltaire on, xxxiv, 126

Harun, Er-Rashid, in ARABIAN NIGHTS, xvi, 60-5, 99-100, 112-14, 210, 215-25, 228-30, 288-91

Harut, the fallen angel, xvi, 56 note

HARVARD CLASSICS, Editor's Introduction, l, 3-14; Reader's Guide to, 17-72

HARVARD COMMEMORATION ODE, xlii, 1379-90

Harvey, William, discoverer of circulation of blood, xxxiv, 126; Descartes on, 41 note; life and works of, xxxviii, 60; ON MOTION OF HEART AND BLOOD, 61-139

Hasdrubal, Chaucer on wife of, xl, 49

'Hâsîy Ibn Wâil, xlv, 912 note

Haskell, Frank A., ACCOUNT OF GETTYSBURG, xliii, 326-414; life of, 326 note

Haste, half-sister of delay, xlii, 1001; "from the Devil," xvi, 156; "make, slowly," xix, 369; Penn on excessive, i, 348 (300), 379 (76), 380 (77); "that mars all decency," xx, 153

Hastings, in SHE STOOPS TO CONQUER, admirer of Miss Neville, xviii, 210, 217-19; at the ale-house, 213-15; arrival at Hardcastle's, 217-19; with Mr. Hardcastle, 219-20; with Miss Neville, 224-5; carries on jest with Marlow, 225-6; presents Marlow to Kate, 226-7; with Mrs. Hardcastle, 229-30; with Tony, 231-3, 236; plans to elope with Constance, 244; learns loss of jewels, 245-6; his letter to Tony, 253-4; denounces Tony, 254-5; and Marlow, 255; hears Miss Neville gone, 256; recovers Constance through Tony, 260; with Miss Neville, 264; wins consent to marriage, 268-9

Hastings, Lord, Raleigh on, xxxix, 75, 76

Hastings, Warren, Burke on, xxiv, 6; on Oriental literature, v, 446; Sheridan and, xviii, 108

Hatch, mate on "Alert," xxiii, 402-3

Hate-good, Lord, in PILGRIM'S PROGRESS, xv, 96-101

Hate-light, Mr., in PILGRIM'S PROGRESS, xv, 100

Haterius, Augustus on, xxvii, 55

Hatred, Buddha on, xlv, 669-71; Confucius on, xliv, 60 (24); Hume on, xxxvii, 324; Marcus Aurelius on, ii, 286-7 (8); Pascal on, xlviii, 151 (451); Penn on, i, 346 (269)

Hats, Locke on, xxxvii, 11, 14

HAUNTED PALACE, THE, xlii, 1225-6

Hauteclere, sword of Oliver, xlix, 137, 142, 151

Havre de Grace, siege of, xxxviii, 49

Hawaiian Islands, Annexation of, xliii, 437-9

Hawker, Robert Stephen, poem by, xlii, 1111-12

Hawkins, Sir John Drake and, xxxiii, 122, 129, 227; Melendez and, 256; at San Juan, 323-4

Hawkins, William, in Cape Verde Islands, xxxiii, 238

Hawks, carrion, xxix, 62-7; guided to prey by sight, xi, 92; sacred in Egypt, xxxiii, 36, 37

Hay, John, Convention with Panama, xliii, 451, 461, 462

Hay, Lord, ambassador of King James, xv, 335, 346

Hays, Gen. Alex., at Gettysburg, xliii, 336, 342, 384

Hazard, Capt., at Gettysburg, xliii, 372

Hazing, on board ship, xxiii, 53 note

Hazlitt, William, Carlyle on, xxv, 345-6; life and writings, xxvii, 266; PERSONS ONE WOULD WISH TO HAVE SEEN, 267-81; Stevenson on, xxviii, 289

Head, and limbs, related, xi, 27; Locke on coverings for the, xxxvii, 11-14

Head, Sir Francis, on America, xxviii, 406-7

Heady, Mr., in PILGRIM'S PROGRESS, xv, 100

Healfdene, xlix, 6

HEALING QUESTION, A, xliii, 118-37

Health, Antonius's care of, ii, 197; Burke on pleasure in enjoyment of, xxiv, 35-6, 37; Carlyle on, xxv, 407-8, 418-19; Carlyle on care of, 385-6; Channing on, xxviii, 353-5; Descartes on, xxxiv, 50; Epictetus on, care of, ii, 160-1 (118); Hunt on, xxvii, 291-2; More

on, xxxvi, 201-2, 203; Locke on importance of, xxxvii, 9-10; Pascal on use and misuse of, xlviii, 370; Pope on, xl, 432; rules of, xxxvii, 10-26; unconsciousness of, xxv, 319-34; Woolman on, care of, i, 235-6

HEALTH, by Pinkney, xxviii, 382-3
HEALTH, TO ANE I LOE DEAR, vi, 551
HEALTH, HERE'S HIS, IN WATER, vi, 183
HEALTH, HERE'S TO THY, vi, 27-8
HEALTH, REGIMEN OF, Bacon's, iii, 81-2
HEALTH TO THEM THAT'S AWA, vi, 449-50

Heardred, xlix, 65, 70 and note 3
Hearing, art of, ii, 146-8 (81); speaking and, 183 (6)
Heart, auricles of the, the seat of life, xxxviii, 84-6; Descartes on motion of the, xxxiv, 39-44; in the fœtus, xxxviii, 127, 128, 131, 135-6; Harvey on motion and uses of the, 60-139; Harvey on structure of the, 130-7, 139; importance of the, 137; in lower animals, 129-131, 132-3; lungs and, 65, 69-73, 88, 90, 91-4, 99-100, 131-2; nourishment through the, 102, 103

HEART'S COMPASS, xlii, 1180
HEART'S HOPE, xlii, 1178-9
Hearth-money, x, 494
Heat, Berkeley on real existence of, xxxvii, 193-9; chemical action of, xxx, 207-8; dependent on expansion and compression, 212-13; Descartes on, xxxiv, 37; effect of, on cohesion, xxx, 39-43; evolved from chemical affinity, 79-80; Faraday on, 58-9; generated by friction and impact, 195-7; Locke on endurance of, xxxvii, 10-11, 14; mechanical equivalent of, xxx, 197-9; mechanical power produced by, 188-97; mechanical theory of, 199-200, 231-2; from moonlight, 260-1; as motion, theory of, 199-200; old theory of, 192-4; Pascal on, xlviii, 123 (368); produced by combustion of carbon, xxx, 200-1; produced by combustion of hydrogen, 202-5; produced by electrical currents, 206; production of, in New Atlantis, iii, 176; radiant, xxx, 259; transference and conduction of, 69-70

Heaven, Augustine, St., on, vii, 152; Bernard of Morlaix on, xlv, 548-9; Browne on, iii, 300-1; Browne on hope of, 298-9, 303-4; Browning on, xlii,

1073; Bunyan on, xv, 17-18, 161-2, 229; Burns on, vi, 138-9; compared to mustard seed, iii, 74; Darwin on, xxix, 288; Fitzgerald on, xli, 953; gate of, Milton on, iv, 147-8; Hobbes on, xxxiv, 345; Kempis on, vii, 312 (3, 4), 313-17; Luther on, xxxvi, 252 (16); Milton on, iv, 195, 196-7, 204; Rousseau on, xxxiv, 264-5; saints in, xii, 332-3

HEAVENLY BODIES, REVOLUTIONS OF THE, xxxix, 52-7
Heavens, Dante's ten, xx, 292 note 3
Hebe, and Heracles, xxii, 160; Keats on, xli, 873; references to, iv, 21, 31; xl, 244
Heber, Reginald, Hymns by, xlv, 563-5
Hebrew Literature, Milton on, iv, 403-4; Wordsworth on, xxxix, 306
Hebrew Prophets, piety and grossness of the, v, 169
HEBREW SACRED WRITINGS, xliv, 69-349
Hebrews, Raleigh on history of, xxxix, 112 (see also Israelites, Jews)
Hebron, seat of giants, iv, 418
Hecataios, the historian, xxxiii, 72
Hecate, in MACBETH, xlvi, 362-3; Virgil on, xiii, 216
Hectic Fever, Machiavelli on, xxxvi, 12
Hector, and Ajax, v, 93; Burke on, xix, 127; Caxton on, xxxix, 20; Chaucer on, xl, 43; in Dante's HELL, xx, 19; Dares Phrygius on, xiii, 33; ghost of, appears to Æneas, 109-10; Shelley on Homer's, xxvii, 336
Hecuba, at death of Priam, xlvi, 138-9; madness of, xx, 123; in sack of Troy, xiii, 117-18
Hedge, F. H., translator of Luther's Hymn, xlv, 557
Hedwig, in WILLIAM TELL, xxvi, 428-32, 456-8, 482-4, 488
Heedless, in PILGRIM'S PROGRESS, xv, 248, 303-5
Hegel, on civil history, v, 437; on planetary motions, xxx, 281; Taine on, xxxix, 428
Hegesias, and Diogenes, xxxii, 59
Height, less grand than depth, xxiv, 61
Heimer of Hlymdale, xlix, 306-7, 315
Heimskringla, Emerson on the, v, 343
Heine, Taine on, xxxix, 411-12
Heineccius, on Roman Law, xxv, 44
Heinsius, on Horace, xiii, 12
HELEN, TO, xlii, 1226

HELEN OF KIRCONNELL, xl, 324-5

Helen of Troy, Æschylus on, viii, 9, 22-3, 33-5, 36; Burke on Homer's description of, xxiv, 136; Dante on, xx, 22; Darley on, xli, 914; Deïphobus and, xiii, 224-5; in FAUSTUS, xix, 243-4, 245-6; Herodotus on, xxxiii, 54-8; in the ODYSSEY, xxii, 49-53; 202-3, 204; Proteus and, xxxiii, 54-6; Theseus and, xxvi, 136-7; in siege of Troy, xiii, 119-20; xxii, 51-3; vest of, xiii, 96; wife of Thone and, iv, 62

Helena, Jove-born, iv, 62 (see Helen of Troy)

Helenor, the Trojan, death of, xiii, 311

Helenus, in ÆNEID, xiii, 137, 139, 140-3; Dryden on, 20

Helgi Hunding's-Bane, in the VOLSUNG TALE, xlix, 272-4, 275-6; SECOND LAY OF, 361-7; remarks on LAY of, 250

Helgi, the Norseman, xliii, 17-19

Helias le Grose, xxxv, 151

Helice, reference to, xx, 416 note 5

Heliocentric Theory, xxxix, 52 note

Heliodorus, Dante on, xx, 229; and note 18; Sidney on, xxvii, 13

Heliogabalus, Machiavelli on, xxxvi, 67

Heliometer, Newcomb on the, xxx, 315-16

Heliopolis, city of, xxxiii, 10, 34, 35

Helios, giver of light, xxii, 133; herds of, 147, 165, 170-2; wrath of, at the Greeks, 171-2; worshipped in Egypt, xxxiii, 34

Helizeus, More on, xxxvi, 156

Hell, Æneas's visit to, xiii, 216-28; Browne on, iii, 301-3; Browne on, fear of, 298-9, 303-4; Buddhist ideas of, xlv, 685-8; Bunyan on, xv, 229; Burke on paintings of, xxiv, 54; Burke on Virgil's picture of, 60-1; Burns on the fear of, vi, 204; Burns on, orthodox ideas of, 101; Dante's, xx, 5-144; Kempis on, vii, 233 (3, 4); Kempis on fear of, 234 (7); Luther on, xxxvi, 252 (16); Marlowe on, xix, 222; Mill on notion of, xxv, 30-1; Milton's description of, iv, 88-90, 94, 123-4, 125, 130-1, 225-6; Milton's, Burke on, xxiv, 138-9; Mohammed on, xlv, 880-1, 884, 886, 888, 892, 893, 896-7, 901, 912, 934, 946, 973-4; Omar Khayyam on, xli, 953, 956; Pascal on belief in, xlviii, 88 (239); Raleigh on thoughts of, xl, 204; Rousseau on, xxxiv, 264-6

Hell, How Love Looked for, xlii, 1398-1401

Hellas, by Shelley, xli, 824-5

Hellenes, John de, xxxv, 49-50

Hellenion, in Egypt, xxxiii, 88

Hellenora, Spenser's, xxxix, 65

Hellespont, Dante on the, xx, 260

Hellusians, Tacitus on the, xxxiii, 120

Helm Gunnar, xlix, 300, 388

Helmholtz, ON CONSERVATION OF FORCE, xxx, 173-210; on the eye, xi, 203-4; ICE AND GLACIERS, xxx, 211-48; life and works, 172

Help, in PILGRIM'S PROGRESS, xv, 19

Help, must come from self, v, 22; to those who help themselves, xvii, 35

Helper, yonder aids the helper here, xix, 46

Helpidius, vii, 75

Helvetians, Tacitus on the, xxxiii, 108

Helvetius, Mill's abstract of, xxv, 46

Helvia, mother of Cicero, xii, 218

Helvicus, tables of, xxxvii, 157

Helvidius, contemporaneity, ii, 320; death of, ix, 239; Life, by Senecio, 308; Pliny on, 338-9

Hely, Mrs., and Pepys, xxviii, 289

Helymus, in the ÆNEID, xiii, 180, 188-9

Heman the Ezrahite, maschil of, xliv, 253-4

Hemi-organism, xxxviii, 306-8, 352-3

Heminge, John, PREFACE TO SHAKESPEARE, xxxix, 148-9

Hemionus, descent of the, xi, 163-6

Hemistichs, Dryden on, xiii, 63-4

Hemorrhages, Harvey on, xxxviii, 107

Hempe in prophecy indicating sovereigns of England, iii, 92

Hemphill, Franklin on, i, 94

Hen, and chickens, parable of the, xv, 204-5

Henchman, Humphrey, on George Herbert, xv, 398

Henderson, Matthew, Elegy on, vi, 383-7

Hengest, the Dane, xlix, 34 note 5, 35, 36-7; Vortizem weds daughter of, v, 276

Henley, William Ernest, Poems by, xlii, 1209-12

Hennings, in FAUST, xix, 187

Henpecked Country Squire, Epigrams on a, vi, 58

Henpecked Husband, The, vi, 324-5

Henriquez, Don Martin, xxxiii, 129-30

Henry I, Raleigh on, xxxix, 72

Henry II, of England, and Becket, xxxix, 165 note 21; sons of, iii, 51

Henry II, of France, Cellini on, 283 note 1, 300; death foretold, iii, 91; expedition against Hesdin, xxxviii, 21-2; expedition to Germany, 18-19; Montgomery and, xxxiii, 186; Paré a ', xxxviii, 22-3, 34, 43, 44; siege of Danvilliers, 19-20

Henry III, of England, Dante on, xx, 174 and note 15; and the Jews, v, 346-7; Oxford students and, xxxv, 373

Henry III, of France, Bacon on, iii, 37; Montaigne on régime of, xxxii, 116; Raleigh on, xxxix, 74, 83; Voltaire on, xxxiv, 87

Henry IV, Emperor, and Gregory VII, xxxvi, 294 note 25

Henry IV, of England, and Chaucer, xxxix, 163-4; Raleigh on, 73

Henry IV, of France, and Acevedo, xxi, 12; Bacon on, iii, 130; Burke on, xxiv, 186, 270; compared with Lincoln, xxviii, 437-9; on manly exer ' e, v, 350; murder of, xxxix, 359; plots against, xxxiv, 87

Henry V, at Agincourt, xl, 223-4, 225, 226; Falstaff and, vi, 210; Macaulay on, xxvii, 377-8; Raleigh on, xxxix, 73-4

Henry VI, of England, colleges at Cambridge founded by, xxxv, 380; death of, xxxix, 74-5; Raleigh on, 74

Henry VII, of Cyprus, xx, 369 note 21

Henry VII, Emperor, Dante on, xx, 415 note 6; death of, xxxiv, 87; married to Constance, xx, 296 note 7

Henry VII, of England, and John Cabot, xliii, 45 and note, 46, 47-8; chapel of, xxxv, 374; councillors of, iii, 54; greatness of, foretold, 91; King's College founded by, xxxv, 380; law of farmers, iii, 75; liberator, 130; mastiffs and falcon killed at behest of, xxxv, 353; Sir Thomas More and, xxxvi, 91; nobility and, iii, 51; Perkin Warbeck and, xxxiv, 101-2; Raleigh on, xxxix, 76-7; suspiciousness of, iii, 82; Voltaire on, xxxiv, 90

Henry VIII, and the abbeys, xxiv, 251-2; Anne Bullen an.i, xxxvi, 102, 111, 114; Bentham on times of, xxvii, 228; Burke on, xxiv, 401-4; Canterbury nun and, xxxvi, 114-15, Catherine, legality of marriage with, 102-4, 105; Christ's Church, Oxford, founded by, xxxv, 381; Latimer and, v, 376; Sir Thomas More and, xxxvi, 92-5, 97-8, 99, 106, 110-12, 113-14, 115, 117-20, 121-2, 123, 124, 125, 126-9, 132-3, 134; More on, 135; More on marriage of, 99, 102-3, 105, 110-11, 114; More on Supremacy Act of, 123, 129-30; Protestantism in England not founded by, iii, 256; Raleigh on, xxxix, 77-8; Sacraments, his book on the, xxxvi, 118; severity of, xxxv, 369; studdery of, 328; on subversion of colleges, 382-3; on supremacy of the Pope, xxxvi, 118; Trinity College, Cambridge, founded by, xxxv, 380; in triumvirate of kings, iii, 50; Wolsey and, xxxvi, 105-6

Henry of the Halden, xxvi, 398-9

Henry of Luxemburg, xx, 168 note 11

Henry of Navarre, Dante on, xx, 173 note 8

Henry, son of Richard of Almaine, xx, 52 note 10

Henslowe, Philip, Dekker and, xlvii, 468; Massinger and, 858; Webster and, 468

Heorogar, xlix, 6, 18, 64

Heorot, the hall of Hrothgar, xlix, 7 note 1

Hephæstion, and Proæresius, xxviii, 53; proctor of Oriental school, 59

Hephæstos, Prometheus and, viii, 167 note 2 and 4; in PROMETHEUS BOUND, 166-9; the snare of, xxii, 106-8; temple of, in Memphis, xxxiii, 49, 53, 58-9, 68, 70, 71, 77 (see also Vulcan)

Hephestion, and Alexander, xlvi, 28

HER FLOWING LOCKS, vi, 110

HER GIFTS, xlii, 1181

Hera, guardian of marriage-bed, viii, 130-1; the peacock sacred to, 187 note 37 (see also Juno)

Heracleon, the Megarian, xxxii, 49-50

Heracles (see Hercules)

Heracles, in THE FROGS, viii, 440-3

Heraclides Ponticus, philosopher, xxxii, 59; on motion of earth, xxxix, 55

Heraclitus, death of, ii, 206 (3); Democritus and, iii, 316; on generation, ii, 220 (46); on incredulity, xii, 183; to judges, ii, 135 (54); in Limbo, xx, 20; Marcus Aurelius on, ii, 254 (3); on the sleepers, 240 (42)

HERACLITUS, by Cory, xlii, 1113

Heraldry, the boast of, xl, 444; remarks on, xxviii, 415

Herbert, George, birth and family of, xv, 373-4; charity of, 407-8; childhood and education, 375; church at Layton Ecclesia, 387-8; church services by, 399-404; clerk of Bemerton, 393-5, 396, 397, 398; academic career, 380-1; consumption of, 391-2, 408-9, 414, 415, 416; deacon, 387; death of, 415, 416, 417-18; Emerson on, v, 143; Farrer, Nicholas, letter to, xv, 413; friendships with Bacon, Andrews, Wotton, and Donne, 383; health, infirmity of, 384; on Holy Days, 403-4; LIFE OF, by Walton, 373-418; life, sanctity of his, 394-5; marriage, 392-3; mother, letter to his, 389-91; music, love of, 405-6; parson, rules as, 398-9; Poems by, 379-80, 385, 398, 416; xl, 341-6; poor woman and, xv, 397; prayer, habits of, 404-5; Sacred Poems, 354, 396, 414-15; Salisbury walks, incidents of, 406-7; sermons, 399-400; sinecure given by James, 384; successor, lines to his, 398; as university orator, 380-1; wife of (see Danvers, Jane)

Herbert, Henry, xv, 374, 388, 391

Herbert, Magdalen, mother of George, xv, 373-4, 375-6; death of, 392; Donne, friendship with, 376-8; letter to, 389-91; son, relations with her, 384-5, 387-8

Herbert, Thomas, xv, 374

Herbert, Rev. W., on hybrids, xi, 288-90; on origin of species, 11; on struggle among plants, 72

Herborg, Queen, xlix, 330-1

Herbs, Harrison on, xxxv, 239-40

Hercules, Alcestis and, xli, 664; amours of, xii, 349; Antæus and, iv, 409; xiv, 19; xx, 130 note 6; birth of, xxii, 151; Cacus and, xiii, 274-7; Cerberus and, xx, 38 note; viii, 442, 453; character of, v, 184; compass, and the, 458; date of, xxxiii, 72-3; as Egyptian god, xxxiii, 26-8, 42; as king of Egypt, xxxviii, 387; envenomed robe of, iv, 122; Epictetus on, ii, 143 (71); faith of, 162 (124); genealogy of, viii, 194 note 50, 198; as a German god, xxxiii, 97; in Germany, 94; in Hades, xxii, 160; Hylas and, xlvi, 11, 28; Iole and, xx, 323; Iphitus and, xxii, 284-5; the Mænad and, viii, 327; Nessus and, xx,

50 note; parentage of, xii, 5; the pigmies and, xxxix, 347; Pillars of, Tacitus on, xxxiii, 112; Prometheus and, iii, 16; viii, 193-4, 198 note 63; Rhea and, xiii, 262; Virgil on, 234, 277-8; Waller on death of, xxxiv, 146; Zeus and, xxxiii, 26-7

HERCULES AND THE WAGGONER, fable of, xvii, 35

Herder, quotation from, xxxii, 386

Herdsman's Song, from WILLIAM TELL, xxvi, 380

Hereafter, Buddha on questions of the, xlv, 647-52, 660; Emerson on popular views of the, v, 85-6; Epictetus on the, ii, 158 (112), 181 (188); Epicurus on the, xxxvii, 400-1; Euripides on the, viii, 311; Goethe on the xix, 69; Hindu idea of, xlv, 822-4, 827-8, 854-5; hope of the, xl, 410; Kempis on the, vii, 232-3, 312; Mohammed on, xlv, 882, 883-4, 885-6, 915; Montaigne on the, xxxii, 25; Omar Khayyam on the, xli, 944, 948, 950-1, 952, 953, 954, 955, 958; Pascal on question of, xlviii, 70 2, 75-6, 77 (200), 79 (213), 80 (217); the philosopher's, ii, 75-7; Pope on the, xl, 435; Raleigh on the, xxxix, 92-3; Rousseau on the, xxxiv, 264-6, 277-8; sailors' idea of, xxiii, 39-40; Shakespeare on the, xlvi, 144; Shelley on, xviii, 353-4; Socrates on, ii, 29, 51, 58, 103-4, 108-10; Vaughan on the, xl, 346-7 (see also Heaven, Hell, Paradise, Purgatory, Hades)

Hereditary Princedoms, Machiavelli on, xxxvi, 7-8; Pascal on, xlviii, 111 (320)

Heredity, Darwin on laws of, xi, 29; in habit and instinct, 255-8; in individual differences, 55; in mutilations, 141; in variations, 28-9

Heremod, xlix, 29-30, 52

Herennius, and Cicero, xii, 258-9

HERE'S A HEALTH TO KING CHARLES, xli, 754-5

HERE'S A HEALTH TO THEM THAT'S AWA, vi, 449-50

HERE'S HIS HEALTH IN WATER, vi, 183

HERE'S TO THY HEALTH, vi, 27-8

Heresies, Augustine, St., on, vii, 115; Bacon on, iii, 11-12; Browne on, 257-60; Hobbes on, xxxiv, 373; Mill on, xxv, 240-2; Pascal on, xlviii, 301, 302; speculative, iii, 138

Heretics, Burns on, vi, 213; in Dante's

HELL, xx, 39, 115-16; Hobbes on covenants with, xxxiv, 404; Luther on, xxxvi, 318-19; Pascal on, xlviii, 291 (841), 295 (845), 298, 301, 302

Héricault, Charles d', on classics, xxviii, 68-9

Herilus, and Evander, xiii, 286-7

Heriulf, the Norseman, xliii, 5, 6

Herman, in MANFRED, xviii, 436-7, 442, 443-5

HERMANN AND DOROTHEA, Goethe's, xix, 335-410; remarks on, 336; l, 24

Hermaphrodites, Darwin on, xi, 103, 106-7

Hermes, guard of the dead, viii, 102, 106; herald of heaven, 26, 81; Herodotus on worship of, xxxiii, 31; in the ODYSSEY, xxii, 10, 69-72, 107-8, 137-8, 320; in PROMETHEUS BOUND, viii, 201-5; rod of, ii, 156 (106); iv, 322; slayer of Argos, xxii, 11; Ulysses and, iv, 61

Hermes Trismegistus (see Trismegistus)

Herminius, death of, xiii, 379

Hermione, Homer on, xxii, 46; Milton on, iv, 273

Herminones, Tacitus on the, xxxiii, 93

Hermippus, accuser of Aspasia, xii, 68

Hermits, Burns on life of, vi, 198-9; in Milton's Limbo, iv, 147-8

Hermodius, and Aristogiton, xxxii, 77

Hermogenes, precocity of, iii, 105-6; with Socrates, ii, 47

Hermon, murderer of Phrynichus, xii, 131

Hermondurians, Tacitus on the, xxxiii, 116

Hernandez, Gonzalo, xiv, 302-3, 488

Hernox, Earl, xxxv, 191-2

Herodes Atticus, teacher of M. Aurelius Antoninus, ii, 302

Hero-worship, Carlyle on, xxv, 394-5

Herod, the king, xliv, 448 (1), 449 (19-23); believed to be Messiah, xlviii, 264 (753); gold raised, iv, 382; Pascal on, xlviii, 234 (700-1); persecution of, xliv, 448 (1); son of, xlviii, 66 (179); in war of Antony and Octavius, xii, 369, 377, 378-9

Herod, tetrarch of Galilee, xliv, 360 (1), 361-2 (19), 377 (7-9); Jesus and, 392 (31-2), 413 (7-11); Pilate and, 414 (12)

Herodes Atticus, xxviii, 59-60

Herodias, and John the Baptist, xliv, 361-2 (19)

Herodicus, and Hippocrates, xxxviii, 2

Herodotus, AN ACCOUNT OF EGYPT, xxxiii, 7-90; editorial remarks on Account of, l, 19; Hugo on, xxxix, 341; life and histories, xxxiii, 5-6; Shelley on, xxvii, 335; Sidney on, 7; Themistocles and, ix, 104

Heroes, Emerson on our love of, v, 18; Lowell on, xlii, 1372; of poems, Dryden on, xviii, 13; Pope on, xl, 436; Thoreau on, xxviii, 408; Yu-tzu on, xliv, 6 (13)

Heroic Poetry, Sidney on, xxvii, 28-9

HEROISM, ESSAY ON, v, 121-31

Heron, Mr., son-in-law of More, xxxvi, 107

HERON ELECTION BALLADS, vi, 520-6, 548-9

Herrick, Robert, Poems by, xl, 334-40

Herschel, Sir John, work of, v, 360-1

Herthum, German goddess, xxxiii, 115

HERVEY, WILLIAM, ON THE DEATH OF, xl, 367-9

HE'S OWER THE HILLS THAT I LO'E WEEL, xli, 560-1

Hesdin, siege of, xxxviii, 34-7; destruction of, 43

Hesiod, Cicero on, ix, 64; Clauserus on, xxvii, 50-1; on his estate, 67; Greek theogony due to, xxxiii, 32; Herodotus on time of, 32; quoted, ii, 293 (32); Sainte-Beuve on, xxxii, 130; Sidney on, xxvii, 6; Socrates on, ii, 29; teachings of, viii, 471

Hesione, wife of Prometheus, viii, 178 note 20, 186-7

Hesperian Tree, Milton on the, iv, 55

Hesperus, gardens of, iv, 71, 150

Hesperus, the star, iv, 170, 261

HESPERUS, THE WRECK OF THE, xlii, 1269-71

HESTER, by Lamb, xli, 735-6

Heteronomy of the Will, xxxii, 343; spurious principles of morality due to, 342-3, 351-4

Hetwaras, xlix, 70 note 2, 84

Heuer, Sir Roger, xl, 99

Heusinger, on effects of color, xi, 27

HEY, CA' THRO', boat song, vi, 265

Heyne, Carlyle on, xxv, 376

Heywood, Thomas, Hazlitt on, xxvii, 276; PACK CLOUDS, AWAY, xl, 316-17

Hezekiah, Bunyan on, xv, 133; in Dante's PARADISE, xx, 371 note 5; Walton on, xv, 356

Hibernation, Darwin on, xxix, 104-5; Harvey on, xxxviii, 85, 130

Hic Breve Vivitur, xlv, 548-9

Hickey, Goldsmith on, xli, 505, 508

Hickson, Mr., Mill on, xxv, 137

Hide-curing, Dana on, xxiii, 148-9

Hides, price of, x, 193-9

Hiera, and Alcanor, xiii, 316

Hierius, Augustine, St., on, vii, 56

Hiero of Syracuse, Machiavelli on, xxxvi, 22; the poets and, xxvii, 38; Themistocles and, xii, 26-7; troops of, xxxvi, 46

Hierocles, the pedant in, xxxix, 210

Hierome, St., and Paula, xv, 377

Hieronymus Fabricius, xxxviii, 65, 71

Highland Balou, The, vi, 490

Highland Girl, To the, xli, 652-4

Highland Harry Back Again, vi, 357

Highland Mary, vi, 444-5

Highland Widow's Lament, vi, 490-1

Highlands, In the, xlii, 1212

High-mind, Mr., in Pilgrim's Progress, xv, 100

Highways (see Roads)

Hilarity, of heroism, v, 127

Hilarius, a Bithynian, xxviii, 58

Hilary, on the true church, xxxix, 41

Hildeburh, xlix, 34 note 5, 36, 37

Hildegard, in William Tell, xxvi, 437, 440

Hill, Gen. A. P., at Gettysburg, xliii, 343, 344, 347

Hilton, Walter, as author of Imitation of Christ, vii, 200

Himeraeus, death of, xii, 214

Hind Horn, a ballad, xl, 59-61

Hindoos, Freeman on name of, xxviii, 271; idea of world, 415; Taine on the, xxxix, 421

Hinduism, xlv, 784 (see also Bhagavad-Gita)

Hinny, origin of the, xi, 315

Hipparchus, Huxley on, xxviii, 219; Marcus Aurelius on, ii, 241 (47); on precession of equinoxes, xxxiv, 128-9

Hipparchus, freedman of Antony, xii, 374

Hipparete, wife of Alcibiades, xii, 112-3

Hipparion, Darwin on the, xi, 363

Hippias, the comedian, xii, 328

Hippias of Elis, ii, 7; wealth of, x, 137

Hippo, the dolphin of, ix, 351-2

Hippocoön, in the Æneid, xiii, 194-5

Hippocrates, Dante on, xx, 266 note 15;

editor's remarks on writings of, l, 39; first aphorism of, xxxviii, 2, 37; on the heart, 136; Law of, 4-5; life and works, 2; in Limbo, xx, 20; Marcus Aurelius on, ii, 206 (3); Oath of, xxxviii, 3; remarks on Oath, 2

Hippodamus, Cicero on, ix, 113, 117

Hippolytus, Virgil on, xiii, 265

Hippolytus, of Euripides, viii, 303-67

Hippolytus, in Tragedy of Hippolytus, Aphrodite's hatred of, viii, 303-5; Artemis and, 305-6; death of, 355-8, 361-7; huntsman and, 306-8; innocence told by Artemis, 359-61; Phædra and, 328-32; Theseus and, 342-52; Voltaire on, xxxix, 364

Hippolytus, in Phædra, Aricia and, xxvi, 135-7, 150-1, 152-6, 185-7; death of, related by Theramenes, 191-4; denounced by Œnone, 173-4; Dryden on, xviii, 15; Phædra and, xxvi, 134-5, 144-6, 156-61; Theramenes, scenes with, 133-8, 161-2, 172; Theseus and, 170-1, 174-8

Hipponicus, and Alcibiades, xii, 112

Hippopotamus, described in Job, xliv, 137-8; Herodotus on the, xxxiii, 38-9

Hippotades, Æolus called, iv, 74

Hircania, dogs of, xxxv, 355

Hire, Confucius on, xliv, 45 (1)

Hirtius, and Cicero, xii, 254; death of, 256

Hisbo, death of, xiii, 334

Hispaniola, Columbus on, xliii, 22, 24, 25; Drake in, xxxiii, 239-43; sheep in, x, 194

Hispulla, letter to, ix, 258

Historians, Dryden on, xviii, 7; Montaigne on, xxxii, 97-9; as teachers of virtue, xxvii, 15, 16, 19-22

History, Bacon on study of, iii, 122; Burke on use and misuse of, xxiv, 289; Carlyle on reading of, xxv, 365; Cervantes on, xiv, 71; Channing on study of, xxviii, 329, 336, 359; Comte's ages of, xxv, 104; Descartes on study of, xxxiv, 7-8; Emerson on, v, 11, 68, 71, 73, 93; Franklin's observations on, i, 89, 125; Freeman on science of, xxviii, 244; Goethe on study of, xix, 31-2; Hume on, xxxvii, 354, 359, 419; judgment and fancy in, xxxiv, 350; lessons of, xvi, 15; Locke on study of, xxxvii, 138, 153, 156, 157, 170; Montaigne on study of, xxxii, 44-7, 97;

natural and civil, xxxiv, 359; organic and critical periods of, xxv, 103-4; Pliny on, ix, 305, 316; poetry and, compared, xxviii, 74; xxxix, 279-80; politics and, xxi, 446; Raleigh on, xxxix, 69-71, 113-14; repetitions of, ii, 249 (49), 268 (14), 281 (27); iii, 257-8; right reading of, xxvii, 380; Rousseau on business of, xxxiv, 196; Ruskin on study of, xxviii, 148-9; Taine on study of, xxxix, 410-37

History of civilization, reading course in, l, 19-28

HISTORY OF THE WORLD, PREFACE TO, Raleigh's, xxxix, 66-115

Hive-Bees, instincts of, xi, 268-76

Hixom, Ellis, with Drake, xxxiii, 123, 143, 163, 166, 181

Hjalli, the thrall, xlix, 349, 412

Hjalprek, King, xlix, 281, 282

Hjordis, wife of Sigmund, xlix, 278, 279, 280, 281-2; wife of Alf, 283; remarks on story of, 250

Hnæf the Scylding, xlix, 34 note 5, 36 note 9

Hnikar, xlix, 289-91

Hobart Town, Darwin on, xxix, 450

Hobbes, Thomas, Berkeley on, xxxvii, 233; Hazlitt on, xxvii, 277; *Iliad,* translation of, by, xxxix, 158; *Leviathan* burned at Oxford, v, 417; life and works, xxxiv, 308; *Logic* of, Mill on, xxv, 17; OF MAN, xxxiv, 311-417; on natural viciousness of man, 187-8; style of, v, 433

Hodbrod, King, xlix, 273, 275

Hodge, in SHOEMAKER'S HOLIDAY, at Ralph's departure, xlvii, 473; at Eyre's, 480-3, 487-91, 497-501; at Old Ford, 503; before shop, 509-11; at Hammon's wedding, 521-7; at Eyre's dinner, 528-9, 535

Hoel, Renan on, xxxii, 162

Hofe, Jorg im, in WILLIAM TELL, xxvi, 418, 421

Hoffman, M., xxvii, 102

Hogarth, on beauty, xxiv, 94; Fielding on, xxxix, 179

Hogg, James, poems by, xli, 756-69

Hogni, King, xlix, 273, 275, 361 note 2

Hogni, son of Giuki, xlix, 310; Atli and, 342-6, 408-10; in battle, 346-7, 348, 349, 411; Brynhild and, 322, 323, 336, 380-1; death of, 349, 412-13; Sigurd

and, 313, 326-7, 328, 374-5, 391-2, 397-8, 419, 425

Hogs, price of, x, 189

HOHENLINDEN, xli, 781

Hold-the-world, Mr., in PILGRIM'S PROGRESS, xv, 104-8

Holidays, Herbert on sacred, xv, 403-4; Luther on, xxxvi, 308; Mill on, xxv, 27; in Utopia, xxxvi, 232

Holinshed, Raphael, his *Chronicles,* xxxv, 216; selection from *Chronicles,* 217-383

Holland, Burke on French invasion of, xxiv, 419-20; Burke on nobility of, 419; Goldsmith on, xli, 527-8; interest in, x, 93; republican government, importance of, to, 547-8; taxation in, 500-1; trade, attitude toward, in, 98

Holland, Lord, anecdote of, v, 189

Holland, Sir John, xxxv, 72

Holland, Sir Thomas, xxxv, 11, 14, 16, 19, 24

Holly-trees, and bees, xi, 100

Holmes, Oliver Wendell, life and works, xxxviii, 222; Poems by, xlii, 1365-70; ON PUERPERAL FEVER, xxxviii, 223-53; editor's remarks on PUERPERAL FEVER of, l, 40; SUN-DAY HYMN, xlv, 570

Holmes, Robert, i, 28, 50

HOLY CROSS, ROYAL WAY OF THE, vii, 253-7

Holy Communion (see Communion)

HOLY FAIR, THE, vi, 95-102

Holy Ghost, Calvin on the, xxxix, 49-50; Charlemagne on, xlv, 547-8; Hobbes on the, xxxiv, 415

HOLY GRAIL, THE, by Malory, xxxv, 105-214; Caxton on, xxxix, 23

Holy Grail, Don Quixote on quest of, xiv, 489; legends of the, xxxii, 163-6

Holy-man, Mr., in PILGRIM'S PROGRESS, xv, 282, 283

Holy Roman Empire, Luther on, xxxvi, 327-30

HOLY THING, THAT, xlii, 1118

Holy Things, Tsai Wo on, xliv, 11-12 (21)

Holy Thursday, Walton on, xv, 404

HOLY THURSDAY, xli, 590-1

HOLY TULYIE, THE, vi, 63-6

HOLY WILLIE, EPITAPH ON, vi, 73

HOLY WILLIE'S PRAYER, vi, 70-3

Holyoake, George Jacob, xxv, 224 note 3

Holystones, described, xxiii, 177

Homage, Pascal on, xlviii, 381

Home, Locke on education at, xxxvii,

50-5; prized first at evening, xix, 50;
Ruskin on, xxviii, 145-6

HOME THEY BROUGHT HER WARRIOR
DEAD, xlii, 973-4

HOME-THOUGHTS, FROM ABROAD, xlii,
1068-9

HOME-THOUGHTS, FROM THE SEA, xlii,
1069

Homer, accused of drunkenness, xxvii,
357; on agriculture, ix, 64-5; Aristophanes on, viii, 471; Arnold on, xxviii,
71-2, 79; Augustine, St., on, vii, 16-17;
Bacon on, iii, 101; Burke on, xxiv, 127;
Burke on similes of, 18; Caxton on,
xxxix, 9; claimed by seven cities, xxvii,
37; Clauserus on, 50-1; on country
life, 67-8; Dante on, xxxix, 352-3; the
dramatists and, xiii, 5-7; Dryden on,
15, 24, 26, 33, 43; xl, 396; Emerson
on, v, 144, 180-1; Greek theogony due
to, xxxiii, 31-2; Fielding on, xxxix,
176; the fisherman and, iii, 322; Greek
tragedies and, xxxix, 342, 347; Herodotus on time of, xxxiii, 32; heroes of,
xxxix, 343; Hugo on, 340, 352, 253,
386; Hume on ethics of, xxvii, 204;
intelligibleness of, xxxix, 248; Johnson on, 209; Keats on Chapman's
translation of, xli, 895-6; Lang on,
xxii, 335; life of, 3; in Limbo, xx, 19;
the Margites of, iii, 200; Milton on, iv,
401; THE ODYSSEY of, xxii, oldest ballad singer, vi, 130 note; on Paris,
xxxiii, 55-6; Pascal on, xlviii, 208
(628); Pliny on, ix, 271, 347-8; Sainte-
Beuve on, xxxii, 127, 130; Shelley on,
xxvii, 336-7, 342; Sidney on, 6, 11,
36; Spenser on, xxxix, 62; Socrates on,
ii, 29; universal admiration of, xxvii,
208; Virgil and, xiii, 5-6, 38-40, 46;
xxxix, 157-9

Homologies, serial, xi, 454-6

Homologous Parts, xi, 148

Honest, in PILGRIM'S PROGRESS, xv, 174,
251-63, 269, 276-9, 280-1, 287, 305-8,
312, 315

Honest Man, Burns on the, vi, 105, 511;
"the noblest work of God," 139, 254;
xl, 436

Honesty, Bacon on, iii, 8; forced, i, 387;
fortune and, iii, 100; Hamlet on, xlvi,
130, 132; instruction in, xxxvii, 92;
Kant on pure, xxxii, 309-10; Mohammed on, xlv, 916; want and, i, 91

Honeycomb, Will, xxvii, 86-7

HONOR, ESSAY ON, Bacon's, iii, 129-30

Honor, Burns on, vi, 204; commerce
and, xli, 522; Dante on love of, xx,
309 note 25; Dryden on, xl, 394; Hobbes on, xxxiv, 361-9; Kempis on temporal, vii, 305-6; Lessing on, xxvi,
357; Pascal on, xlviii, 59-60 (147);
Pliny on loss of, ix, 334; venerableness
of, v, 67

Honors, Confucius on, xliv, 13 (5), 22
(15), 26 (13); desire for, the strongest
of motives, xxviii, 94-5; More on
worldly, xxxvi, 199; Pope on, xl, 435,
437; Raleigh on, xxxix, 91, 93, 96

Hood, Thomas, BRIDGE OF SIGHS, xxviii,
386-9; Poe on FAIR INES of, 384-6;
Poe on The Haunted House of, 386;
Poems by, xli, 905-11

HOOD, WILLIAM, EPITAPH ON, vi, 50

Hooke, saying of, v, 307

Hooker, General, xliii, 327, 413

Hooker, Thomas, on change, xxxix, 185-
6; Jonson on, xxvii, 56; language of,
xxxix, 196

Hooker, Sir William J., on Australian
species, xi, 134; on correlation in flowers, 149; Darwin and, 20; on descent
of species, 17; on Galapagos species,
421-2; xxix, 400-1; on glacial period,
xi, 400, 402; on ovules, 213-4; on
sexes in trees, 106

Hope, allegory of, xx, 265 note 11;
American lack of, v, 54; Burns on, vi,
428; Coleridge on, xxv, 89; Dante on,
xx, 393; Dante's star of, 177 note 9;
Dryden on, xxxiv, 134; fear and, iv,
55; eternal fort of, xli, 491; Hobbes
on, xxxiv, 340, 365; life on a single,
ii, 184 (16); in music, xli, 477; "never
comes that comes to all," iv, 89; Penn
on, i, 343 (235); Pope on, xl, 410,
422, 424; Shelley's Beatrice on, xviii,
354; sweetness of, viii, 186; white-
handed, iv, 50

Hope, Thomas, xxv, 319 note 1, 341;
Carlyle on Essay on Man of, 347-51

Hopeful, in PILGRIM'S PROGRESS, xv, 101,
110, 112-25, 127-8, 129-33, 136, 138-
46, 156-65

Horace, accused of cowardice, xxvii, 357;
on affecting the passions, xxiv, 52; on
art of poetry, xxvii, 108; an astrologer,
xxxix, 159; Augustus and, 164; on
changes, xlviii, 119 note; cold baths
of, xxxvii, 13; Dryden on, xiii, 51;

Dryden on, epistles of, 12; Dryden on translators of, xviii, 17-18; Greek examples followed by, 19; on happiness, xlviii, 33 note 7; on himself, xxvii, 183; on instruction in taste, xxiv, 22; Locke on, xxxvii, 157; love of country life, xxvii, 69; Montaigne on, xxxii, 90; Newman on, xxviii, 53; on poetry, xxxii, 62; Sainte-Beuve on, 131; as a soldier, 111; on terror caused by wonders of nature, xxiv, 58-9; Voltaire on, xxxii, 133

Horace, Duke, at Metz, xxxviii, 25; at Hesdin, 34, 36

Horatii, Dante on the, xx, 306 note 9

Horatio, in HAMLET, xlvi, on watch at Elsinore, 94-9; tells Hamlet of ghost, 104-6; on watch with Hamlet, 111-14; sworn to secrecy, 118-20; with Hamlet, told to watch king, 149-50; with Hamlet after play, 156; on Ophelia, 176; letter from Hamlet, 183-4; with Hamlet in grave-yard, 192-5; at Ophelia's funeral, 197; with Hamlet, hears of king's plot, 199-201; with Osric, 202, 203; on the wager, 204; at the duel, 207, 208-9; with Fortinbras, 209-10; in the original story, 92

Horatius, called Cocles, xiii, 289

Horn, Cape, Darwin on, xxix, 216

Horn, Count, xix, 252

Hornbills, instinct of, xi, 284

HORNBOOK, DOCTOR, DEATH AND, vi, 74-9

Horner, Francis, and Edinburgh Review, xxvii, 224

Hornets, Harrison on, xxxv, 346

Horoscopy, defined, xxxiv, 381-2

HORSE AND Ass, fable of, xvii, 42-3

HORSE, HUNTER, AND STAG, fable of, xvii, 24

Horse(s), descent of, xi, 163-5; described in Job, xliv, 136; of England, Harrison on, xxxv, 326-7; in Falkland Islands, xxix, 196; used by Germans in augury, xxxiii, 98; grease disease of, xxxviii, 145, 147 note 3; Pugliano on, xxvii, 5; races of, xi, 33; remains of, in S. America, xxix, 135-6; S. American, how broken, 156-9; among the Tencterians, xxxiii, 111; swimming power of, xxix, 148; why not sublime, xxiv, 56

Horsemanship, Locke on, xxxvii, 171; Pugliano on, xxvii, 5; Webster on, xlvii, 759

HORSES AND COCK, fable of, xxvii, 133

Hortensius, and Cæsar, xii, 291; and Caius Antonius, brother of Mark Antony, 337; Cicero on, ix, 94; iii, 106; at trial of Murena, xii, 247; Verres and, 223

Hosea, prophecy of, xlviii, 228

Hoskins, Jane, i, 183-4, 194

Hospitality, Emerson on modern, v, 51; of heroism, 125; Homer on, xxii, 201-2; obligations from, i, 201, 245; Penn on, 328 (54); Socrates on, ii, 179 (181)

Hospitals, antiseptic treatment in, xxxviii, 266-7; in Utopia, xxxvi, 185-6

Host, Chaucer's, xl, 31-2

HOST, EPIGRAM ON A KIND, vi, 281

Hottentots, food of, xxviii, 409; sight of, xxxiv, 174

Houghton, Lord, SONNET, xlii, 1057-8

Hounds, Harrison on, xxxv, 350-1

HOUSE OF ATREUS, Æschylus's, viii, 7-165; only extant tragic trilogy, 5; remarks on, 5-6

House-rent, taxes on, x, 488-95

House, George, i, 56

House of Commons, Burke on, xxiv, 182, 183, 189-90

House of Lords, Burke on, xxiv, 189

House of Representatives, xliii, 180-1, 182-3, 196-7; election of president by, 187, 196

Houses, Buddha on defects of, xlv, 581 note 11; taxes, on transfer of, x, 505, 509; in Utopia, xxxvi, 176-7, 182

HOW CRUEL ARE THE PARENTS, vi, 532-3

HOW LANG AND DREARY IS THE NIGHT, vi, 501

HOW LONG AND DREARY IS THE NIGHT, vi, 300

HOW LOVE LOOKED FOR HELL, xlii, 1398-1401

HOW THEY BROUGHT THE GOOD NEWS, xlii, 1066-7

Howard, Charles, dedication to, xxxiii, 301-4

Howard, Elizabeth, wife of Dryden, xviii, 5

Howard, Gen., at Fredericksburg, xliii, 403; at Gettysburg, 330, 333, 336, 357, 358, 397-8; Haskell on, 358, 359, 398, 413

Howard, Henrietta, Countess of Suffolk, xl, 406

Howard, Henry, poems by, xl, 193-5

Howard, Sir Robert, xiii, 29

Howard, Lord Thomas, xlii, 1007
Howe, William, Burns on, vi, 51-2
Hreidmar, xlix, 284-5, 286
Hrethel, the king, xlix, 72-3
Hrethric, son of Hrothgar, xlix, 38, 55
Hrimnir, the giant, xlix, 259
Hrodland (see Roland)
Hrothgar, xlix, 7-8; banquet of, 32-9;
  Beowulf and, 13, 15-19, 23, 30-1, 33,
  51-6, 60; daughter of, 60 and note;
  Grendel and, 9-11; Grendel's mother
  and, 40-5
Hrothglod, xlix, 428-9
Hrothmund, son of Hrothgar, xlix, 38
Hrunting, the sword, xlix, 45-6, 47 note,
  50-1, 54
Hsien, xliv, 47 (19)
Huan of Chi, xliv, 47 (16, 17, 18) note 4
Huan Túi, xliv, 23 note 6
Huber, Pierre, on ants, xi, 264; on bees,
  272-3; on caterpillars, 252; on Oxford,
  xxviii, 48-9
Huckster-Witch, in FAUST, xix, 177-8
Hudibras, Voltaire on, xxxiv, 147-8
Hudson, Hendrik, Emerson on, v, 81
Hugh, St., patron of shoemakers, xlvii,
  481 note
HUGH OF LINCOLN: a ballad, xl, 81-3
Hughes, Mr., and Addison's Cato, xxvii,
  165-6
Hugo, Victor, PREFACE TO CROMWELL,
  xxxix, 337-87; Taine on, 411; work
  of, 337 note
Huguenots, in France, xxxix, 83-4; Pas-
  cal on the, xlviii, 270 (775), 305 (874)
Hugues, of St. Victor, xx, 338 note 32
Hui (see Yen Yüan)
Human Body, in art, xxxix, 255-6, 258;
  beauty of the, v, 304, 307-8; cause of
  beauty of, xxiv, 79-80; Whitman on
  the, xlii, 1402; Whitman on the, in
  art, xxxix, 402
HUMAN FOLLY, xl, 327
Human Nature, Austin on pliability of,
  xxv, 112; benevolence in, i, 170; iii,
  28; best studied in the family, xxviii,
  341; Burke on study of, xxiv, 9, 46-8;
  Channing on, xxviii, 365; Channing
  on study of, 331-2; corruption of, vii,
  326-7; education and, xxxvii, 85; Epictetus on, ii, 149 (86); goodness in, iii,
  32-4; Hume on science of, xxxvii,
  289-90; in laws, v, 246; love of appreciation in, ii, 223 (6); love of mankind in, 207 (4); malignity in, iii, 34;

more foolish than wise, 31; Pascal on,
  xlviii, 41 (92, 93, 94), 42 (97), 50
  (125-7); Pope on science of, xl, 406;
  represented by Prometheus, iii, 16;
  Schiller on, xxxii, 238-49; is social, ix,
  38; three ideas of, xxviii, 308; truth
  the sovereign good of, iii, 8; uniform-
  ity of, xxxvii, 353-61; most virtuous
  when uncultivated, v, 280 (see also
  Nature in Men)
HUMAN SEASONS, THE, xli, 896-7
HUMAN UNDERSTANDING, AN ENQUIRY
  CONCERNING, xxxvii, 287-420
Humanists, Huxley on the, xxviii, 217
Humanity, Locke on development of,
  xxxvii, 103
HUMBLE-BEE, THE, xlii, 1246-7
Humble-mind, the damsel, xv, 224
HUMBLE PETITION OF BRUAR WATER, vi,
  278-81
Humboldt, Alexander von, Darwin on
  Narrative of, xxix, 506; on earth-
  quakes and the weather, 355-6; on
  granitic regions, xi, 330-1; on marshes,
  xxix, 369-70; Thoreau on, xxviii, 406
Humboldt, Wilhelm von, on individual-
  ity, xxv, 252; on liberty, 158; on
  marriage, 300-1; on public degrees,
  305
Hume, David, Carlyle on philosophy of,
  xxv, 353-4; Emerson on, v, 438; EN-
  QUIRY CONCERNING THE UNDERSTAND-
  ING, xxxvii, 287-420; Franklin and, i,
  136; Hazlitt on, xxvii, 277; life and
  works, 202; xxxvii, 288; Locke and, 4;
  Mill on, xxv, 38; in Parliament, 65;
  on rate of interest, x, 282; ON STAND-
  ARD OF TASTE, xxvii, 203-21; Wordsworth on, xxxix, 321 note
Humiliation, Valley of, xv, 59, 240-4
Humility, Bunyan on, xv, 75; Franklin's
  rule of, i, 80, 87; Goethe on, xix, 135;
  Jesus on, xliv, 393 (11), 401 (14);
  Kempis on, vii, 207 (4), 211 (7), 240
  (2), 250-1 (4), 251-2, 261-3, 266-8,
  274-5; Pascal on discourses of, xlviii,
  125 (377); Penn on, i, 334 (119), 348
  (307), 382 (116), 392 (247); song on,
  xv, 242; Woolman on, i, 199
Humming-birds, in Chili, xxix, 276
Humor, Bagehot on, xxviii, 176-9; has
  only fancy value, xxxii, 345
Humorists, Thackeray on, xxviii, 7
Humors, the four, xl, 37 note 38; iii, 93
  note

Humpback, story of the, xvi, 115-20, 190-2

Hunding, King, xlix, 272-3; sons of, 291, 292

Hundred, the, of the Germans, xxxiii, 96

Hungarians, and Turks, xxviii, 227-9

Hungary, Freeman on, xxviii, 270

Hunger, Homer on, xxii, 235; rebellions caused by, iii, 38; thirst and, powerful persuaders, iv, 275

Hunn, Conrad, in WILLIAM TELL, xxvi, 416, 417, 423-4

Hunt, Gen., at Gettysburg, xliii, 379

Hunt, James Henry Leigh, DEATHS OF LITTLE CHILDREN, xxvii, 285-8; dedication to, xviii, 273; in Hazlitt's discussion, xxvii, 277, 279-80; life and writings, 284; POEMS by, xli, 870-1; REALITIES OF IMAGINATION, xxvii, 289-95

Hunt, William, Woolman on, i, 309

Hunter, Anne, poem by, xli, 581

Hunter, John, axiom of, xxxviii, 206 note 2

Hunter's Song, from WILLIAM TELL, xxvi, 380-1

Hunting, Harrison on, xxxv, 343; Locke on, xxxvii, 175; More on, xxxvi, 200-1; Pascal on, xlviii, 54

HUNTING SONG, by Fielding, xli, 501-2

HUNTING SONG, by Scott, xli, 750

Hunting Song, from WILLIAM TELL, xxvi, 428

Huntingdon, Earl of, in Crecy campaign, xxxv, 10, 13

Hurlame, King, xxxv, 183

HUSBAND, THE, AND THE PARROT, xvi, 33-5

Husband-honorer, story of, xlv, 693-6

Husbandry (see Agriculture)

Husbands and wives, Oberon's counsel to, xix, 184; Paul, St., on, xlv, 498; Ruskin on, xxviii, 144-6; Tennyson on, xlii, 980; understanding of, xxviii, 283-4

Huskisson, and free trade, xxv, 65

Huss, John, Browne on, iii, 278-9; Luther on, xxxvi, 317-18; rise of, iii, 196; Woolman on, i, 222-3; Wyclif and, iii, 223

Hussites, Luther on the, xxxvi, 320

Hutcheson, Francis, and Adam Smith, x, 3; on moral sense, xxxii, 352 note

Hutchinson, Mrs., Hazlitt on, xxvii, 279

Hutchison, W. G., translator of Renan, xxxii, 135

Huxley, Thomas Henry, life and works of, xxviii, 208; SCIENCE AND CULTURE, 209-23; on species, xi, 17

Huygens, and Hartsocher, xxxiv, 126

Hyacinth, and Apollo, iv, 18-19 (4); reference to, xli, 860

Hyacinth, flower, for constancy, vi, 407; Milton on the, iv, 74

Hyades, the rainy, xlii, 977; Virgil on the, xiii, 145

Hyarba, and Dido, xiii, 159-60

Hybernation (see Hibernation)

Hybreas, and Antony, xii, 339

Hybridism, xi, 285-318

Hyde Park Affair, Mill in, xxv, 178-9

Hydra, digestion of the, xi, 185; reference to, iv, 82

Hydrogen, its affinity for oxygen, xxx, 139-40; Faraday on, 47-9, 50-3; Helmholtz on, 202-4; production of, 120-4, 134-5; water produced by combustion of, 126; weight of, 124-5, 137

Hydrophobia, origin and spread of, Darwin on, xxix, 357-8

Hydrostatic Paradox, the, v, 268

Hydrostatics, Pascal on, xlviii, 11

Hygd, Queen, xlix, 58, 59, 64, 70, 91 note

Hygelac in BEOWULF, xlix, 57, 59, 64, 65; death of, 65 note 3, 70, 84; historical basis of, 3-4; kinsman of Beowulf, 17, 47; Ongentheow and, 86; the ring of, 38-9

Hylas, and Hercules, xlvi, 11, 28; reference to, xlvii, 742

HYLAS, NYMPH'S SONG TO, xlii, 1194-5

HYLAS AND PHILONOUS, DIALOGUES OF, xxxvii, 187-285; remarks on, 186

Hyllus, death of, xiii, 408

Hymen, references to, iv, 33, 334

Hymettus, reference to, iv, 401

HYMN, by Addison, xl, 400

HYMN BEFORE SUNRISE, xli, 707-9

HYMN OF CLEANTHES, ii, 186-7

HYMN TO DIANA, xl, 299

HYMN TO GOD THE FATHER, xl, 304

HYMN ON THE MORNING OF THE NATIVITY, iv, 7-15

Hymns, of Christian Church, xl, 533-72; Augustine, St., on, vii, 146-7; Herbert on, xv, 400-1

Hypanis, Virgil on, xiii, 111-12, 114

Hyperbolus, Aristophanes on, viii, 456;

banishment of, xii, 85; ostracism of, 115-16

Hyperides, the orator, ix, 205 note 2; death of, xii, 214; Demosthenes and, 201

Hyperion, reference to, xx, 382

Hypermnæstra, and Lynceus, viii, 198 note

Hypocrisy, in Burn's HOLY FAIR, vi, 97; Fielding on, xxxix, 180; Jesus on, xliv, 385-6 (37-44), 386-7 (1-3); Marcus Aurelius on, ii, 208 (7); Milton on, iv, 152; Mohammed on, xlv, 981; in PILGRIM'S PROGRESS, xv, 43-6; in religion, vi, 95-6; Webster on, xlvii, 765

HYPOCRITE, THE, by Molière, xxvi, 199-296

Hypocrites, in Dante's HELL, xx, 95-7; Molière on, xxvi, 213-15, 280

Hypotheses, Rousseau on, xxxiv, 196-7

Hypsipyle, and Jason, xx, 75; in Limbo, 237 note 8; Lycurgus and, 252 note

Hythloday, Raphael, xxxvi, 88, 135, 137 et seq.; Peter Giles on, 241, 243

I DO CONFESS THOU ART SAE FAIR, vi, 431

I DREAMED A LAY, vi, 21

I FEAR T - KISSES, xli, 828

I GAED A WAEFU' GATE YESTREEN, vi, 356-7

I HAE A WIFE O' MY AIN, vi, 307

I HAE BEEN AT CROOKIEDEN, vi, 421

I LO'ED NE'ER A LADDIE BUT ANE, xli, 576-7

I LOVE MY LOVE IN SECRET, vi, 343-4

I LOVED A LASS, xl, 331-2

I MURDER HATE, vi, 378

I PROMESSI SPOSI, Manzoni's, xxi

I REIGN IN JEANIE'S BOSOM, vi, 316

Iacchus, hymn to, viii, 451; song to, in THE FROGS, 448-9

Iadmon, master of Æsop and Rhodope, xxxiii, 67

Iago, Macaulay on, xxvii, 377-8

Iambic Poetry, Sidney on, xxvii, 26

Iapis, in the ÆNEID, xiii, 403-4

Iasion, and Demeter, xxii, 71

Iasius, born in Italy, xiii, 133

Ibis, sacred in Egypt, xxxiii, 37; described, 40

Iblis, name of Satan, xvi, 9 note; xlv, 918

Ibn-'Abbas, companion of Mohammed, xvi, 153 note

Ibn Hankal, on Sogd, v, 125-6

Ibn Roschd, xx, 20 note

Ibn-Sina (see Avicenna)

Ibrahim, the sheykh, xvi, 210-24

Icarius, father of Penelope, xxii, 17, 66

Ice, structure of compressed, xxx, 239-40, 246-8; expansive power of, 116-19; pliability of, 236-9, 246-7; regulation of, 233, 243-5; snow transformed to, 234-5; temperature of, affected by pressure, 231-2

ICE AND GLACIERS, by Helmholtz, xxx, 211-48

Icebergs, Dana's description of, xxiii, 297-8, 311-12; action of, on rocks, xxix, 256 note; use of, in disseminating seeds, xi, 392-3

Iceland, birds of, xxix, 253; Christianity in, xxxii, 171, 175

Iceland Spar, crystallization of, xxx, 31-2; effect of, on polarized light, 34-5

Ictinus, builder of Parthenon, xii, 50

Idæus, in Hades, xiii, 223

Idealism, Berkeley's, xxxvii, 189-285; Emerson on, v, 44, 153, 435

Idealist, in FAUST, xix, 188

Ideals, Lowell on, xlii, 1380, 1382, 1384-5; xxviii, 460

Ideas, abstract (see Abstract Ideas); association of, xxxvii, 304-5, 327-9, 330, 331; Berkeley on reality of, 189-285; Channing on, xxviii, 333-5; defined by Hume, xxxvii, 299-300; defined by Locke, 303 note; Descartes on reality of, xxxiv, 29, 34; Goethe on exchange of, xxxix, 252-3; Hume on origin of, xxxvii, 301-3, 336-7, 349-50; Innate, Hume on, 303 note; Plato on, ii, 93-5; power of originating, xxxvii, 341-2, 344; Relations of, 306; Rousseau on general, xxxiv, 183-4, 250-1; test of, xxxvii, 302-3, 337

Ides, of March, xii, 315

Idiots, in Limbo, iv, 147-8; Mohammed on care of, xlv, 968 note 4

Idleness, Caxton on, xxxix, 5-6, 13-14; as a crime, xxv, 294; discontentment and, i, 141; More on, xxxvi, 180-1; Penn on, i, 328 (57); Smith on, x, 263-5

Idol, fable of the, xvii, 27

Idolatry, David on, xliv, 158 (4); Lessing on, xxxii, 186; Milton on, iv, 344-5; Mohammed on, xlv, 915, 916, 917, 918; Pascal on, xlviii, 325; Paul, St., on, xlv, 501 (4-5)

Idomeneus, in the ÆNEID, xiii, 132, 141, 365

Idomeneus, historian, on Pericles, xii, 46

Idris, Mohammed on, xlv, 911

Idyllic Poetry, Wordsworth on, xxxix, 298-9

IF DOUGHTY DEEDS, xli, 531-2

Ignatius, and the lions, xv, 265; and Trajan, ii, 312 and note

Igneous Rocks, production of, xxxviii, 393-4, 395, 418

Ignis, Fatuus, in FAUST, xix, 168-9; Milton on, iv, 276

Ignorance, Augustine, St., on, vii, 28; is bliss, xl, 450; Epictetus on, ii, 138-9 (63); Hindu Krishna on, xlv, 853-4, 864, 869; Hobbes on, xxxiv, 373-4; karma depends on, xlv, 625, 661-2, 667-8; Pascal on, xlviii, 113 (327); Penn on, i, 321; Socrates's three kinds of, xxxix, 11

Ignorance, in PILGRIM'S PROGRESS, xv, 126-7, 146-51, 164-5

Iguana, Vespucci on the, xliii, 38 note

IL PENSEROSO, iv, 34-8; Wordsworth on, xxxix, 299

Ilia, mother of Romulus and Remus, xiii, 82

Iliad, Arnold on selections from the, xxviii, 71-2; Burke on heroes of the, xxiv, 126-7; Dryden on, xiii, 14-15; editorial remarks on, xxii, 3-4, 6; Mill on the, xxv, 12; Pascal on, xlviii, 208 (628); Poe on, xxviii, 372; Thoreau on, 413

Ilioneus, in the ÆNEID, xiii, 77, 91-3, 94, 246-7, 312

I'LL AYE CA' IN BY YON TOWN, vi, 518

I'LL GO AND BE A SODGER, vi, 36

I'LL MEET THEE ON THE LEA RIG, vi, 443

Illumination, cause of, from flame, xxx, 106-11, 157

Illuminato, Dante on, xx, 338 note 31

Ill-will, in PILGRIM'S PROGRESS, xv, 291

Illyrians, the modern Albanians, xxviii, 264

Ilus, son of Mermerus, xxii, 16; in Hades, xiii, 229

I'M O'ER YOUNG TO MARRY YET, vi, 295-6

Imagery, Burke on, xxiv, 51

Images, Calvin on, xxxix, 36-7; Jamblichus on, v, 166-7; Pascal on, xlviii, 325-6; not allowed in Utopia, xxxvi, 233

Imagination, Bagehot on the, xxviii, 177-8; Berkeley on, xxxvii, 256, 268; Burke on, xxiv, 8-9, 16-22; Descartes on train of, xxxiv, 318-22; Emerson on, v, 173, 177, 308-9; fancy and, xxxix, 301; Hobbes on, xxxiv, 313-18; Hume on, xxxvii, 299, 300, 324-5, 417; Kant on, xxxii, 345; Marcus Aurelius on, ii, 245 (17), 247 (29); Mill on, xxv, 96; Pascal on, xlviii, 35-9; reason and, xxvii, 351, 353; Renan on, xxxii, 143, 182; Schiller on, 290; Shelley on, xxvii, 329; Wordsworth on, xxxix, 301-9, 332

IMAGINATION, REALITIES OF, xxvii, 289-95

Imitation, Bacon on, iii, 29; Burke on passion of, xxiv, 43-4; Coleridge on, xxvii, 257; Emerson on, v, 38-9, 60, 79; fable of, xvii, 43; Hobbes on, xxxiv, 364; Jonson on, xxvii, 56; in nature, xi, 224-5, 445-6; pleasure and pain from, xxxix, 223; power of, among savages, xxix, 211

IMITATION OF CHRIST, vii, 201-364, remarks on, 200; l, 30

Immanuel's Land, xv, 58-9, 122-3

Immaterialism, advantages of, xxxvii, 279-80; possible objections to, 281-2

Immodesty, Epictetus on, ii, 124 (23), 164 (130)

Immorality, commentaries on, xxxix, 173-4

Immortality, Arnold on unbelief in, xlii, 1138-9; Browne on, iii, 258 (7), 289-90, 291; Browning on, xlii, 1081; Buddha on question of, xlv, 647-52, 675-6; Burns on, vi, 316, 373; Carlyle on, v, 323; Cicero on, ix, 13, 72-4; Dante on certainty of, xx, 314; Descartes on, xxxiv, 47-8; Egyptian belief in, xxxiii, 62; Emerson on, v, 237, 293, 304; Franklin on, i, 77, 90; Hindu idea of, xlv, 791-2; Hume on, xxxvii, 399-400; Lessing on belief in, xxxii, 189-92, 195, 197-8, 200; Marcus Aurelius on possibility of, ii, 215 (21), 249 (50); More on, xxxvi, 196-7, 227; Omar Khayyam on, xli, 952, 955-6; Pascal on question of, xlviii, 70-1, 80 (218-20); Paul, St., on, xlv, 511 (12-55); Penn on, i, 362 (487-502); Rousseau on, xxxiv, 262-5; Shelley on, xli, 861; Socrates on, ii, 29, 59-63, 68-73, 78-81, 84-103; Voltaire on, xxxiv, 105-6; Xenophon on, ix, 73-4

IMMORTALITY, ODE ON INTIMATIONS OF, xli, 595-600

Impact, heat produced by, xxx, 196-7; mechanical effects of inelastic, 196-7

Impartiality, Penn on, i, 355-6

Impeachments, in United States, xliii, 181 (5), 182 (6, 7), 189 (4)

Imperatives, defined, xxxii, 324; hypothetical and categorical, 325; of skill, prudence, and morality, 325-49; possibility of categorical, 363-5, 371, 373

Imperfection, Pope on, xl, 409, 410, 412, 414

Impetuosity, Machiavelli on, xxxvi, 82

Implacable, Mr., in PILGRIM'S PROGRESS, xv, 100

Importation, of instruments and materials encouraged, x, 405-10; restraints on, 330, 332-52, 353-70, 424

Impossibilities, Marcus Aurelius on, ii, 228 (17)

Impostors, in Dante's HELL, xx, 123-6

Imposts, under U. S. Constitution, xliii, 184 (1), 186 (2)

Impressions, of childhood, xlviii, 38; defined by Hume, xxxvii, 300; the basis of ideas, 301-2, 336-7, 349-50

Imprisonment, Pascal on, xlviii, 53-4

Improvement, Goethe on spirit of, xix, 354, 356, 367; Penn on, i, 343 (227-32); Rousseau on faculty of, xxxiv, 175-6; Woolman on, i, 214

Impudence, defined by Hobbes, xxxiv, 342

Impulses, Mill on, xxv, 254

Imran's Family, chapter of, xlv, 949-66

In Cæna Domini, papal bull, xxxvi, 292 note 21

Ina, and Peter's Pence, xxxiv, 89

Inachus, river-god, viii, 76, 189 note

Incas Bridge, in the Andes, xxix, 338

Incarnation, Pascal on the, xlviii, 170 (526)

Incivility, Locke on, xxxvii, 119-23

Inclination(s), of children, xxxvii, 56-8, 83-5, 87-8, 90-1; Goethe on following, xxxix, 264-5; defined by Kant, xxxii, 325 note; distinguished from propensities, xxxii, 336 note

Income (see Revenue)

Incomprehensible Truths, Pascal on, xlviii, 140, 431-2

Inconsiderate, in PILGRIM'S PROGRESS, xv, 296

Inconsiderate, Mrs., in PILGRIM'S PROGRESS, xv, 187

Inconsistency, Emerson on, v, 61, 65-6;

Lowell on, xxviii, 441 (see also Consistency)

Inconstancy, Pascal on, xlviii, 47 (110), 48 (112)

INCONSTANCY IN LOVE, vi, 502

Incontinence, in Dante's HELL, xx, 21-4; in PURGATORY, 249-50

Incorporatio, defined, xxxvi, 283-4

Increase, of organic beings, xi, 73-6; checks to, 76-9

Incredulity, Heraclitus on, xii, 183

Incrustations, Darwin on, xxix, 18-19

Incubators, in Utopia, xxxvi, 173

Incubus, invoked by Faust, xix, 56

Incurables, in Utopia, xxxvi, 209

Independence, Emerson on, v, 64, 65, 67, 68, 73-4; of heroism, 130; verses on, by Burns, vi, 307

INDEPENDENCE, INSCRIPTION FOR ALTAR OF, vi, 526

INDEPENDENCE AND RESOLUTION, xli, 658-62

Independence of Circumstances, Epictetus on, ii, 121 (14), 123 (19, 20), 126 (25), 127 (31), 130 (38), 133 (49), 168 (141), 169 (144), 170 (145), 171 (148), 172 (151), 180 (187), 180 (188); Kempis on, vii, 213-14, 240, 243-4, 295, 307-8, 322; Marcus Aurelius on, ii, 201 (7, 9), 208 (6), 211 (16), 212 (3), 222 (2), 228 (18, 19, 20), 230 (29), 231 (35, 36), 234-5 (16), 245 (16), 247 (29), 250 (55), 252 (67, 68), 258 (32), 259 (35), 260 (41), 261 (45, 47), 262 (51), 268 (13, 15), 271 (31, 32), 279 (13), 282 (32, 33), 288 (11), 294 (1, 2), 295 (3)

Index, of Roman Church, iii, 196

Indexing, Swift on, xxvii, 110-11

India, British rule in, v, 469; cause of early civilization of, x, 25-6; rates of interest in, 96; under the mercantile company, 74-5; religion, philosophy, and art of, xxxix, 430-1; shells as money in, x, 28; wealth of, ancient, 295

INDIAN AIR, LINES TO AN, xli, 828-9

Indian Mutiny, incident of, xlii, 1183

Indian Summer, description of, v, 223

Indians, Bacon on barbarism of, iii, 136; Chilian, xxix, 280, 283, 302-4; civility of, xxxvii, 126-7; Columbus on, xliii, 22, 23-4, 25-6; under control of Congress, 163-4, 184 (3); drunkenness

among, 144; Eliot on Christianity among, 138-46; fires, method of making, among, i, 141-2; houses of ancient, xxix, 360-1; medicines of, xxxv, 240; myths of, xvii, 7; Norsemen and (see Skrellings); Peruvian, xxix, 362, 371-2; poets of, xxvii, 8; religion of, iii, 43; v, 276; xl, 410; rum among, i, 115-16, 258; on servants, 304 (268); S. American, xxix, 71-2, 75-6, 79-80, 107-8, 174, 361, 374-5; Vespucci on, xliii, 31-44; Woolman's visit to, i, 255-70

Indictments, in U. S., xliii, 194 (5)

Indifference, Buddha on, xlv, 598-9, 658, 712, 728-9; Burke on, xxiv, 34; in Dante's HELL, xx, 14-15, 219; Epictetus on, ii, 119 (8), 133 (51); Hindu teaching of, xlv, 791, 796, 811, 855; Marcus Aurelius on, ii, 202 (11, 12), 203 (14), 211 (1), 214 (8, 15), 219 (39), 220 (49), 228 (20), 229 (23), 238 (32), 239 (41), 242 (52), 243 (3), 245 (14), 247 (27, 31), 254 (4), 257 (20), 261 (46), 268 (17), 269 (28), 279 (15), 280 (22, 23), 283 (34), 289 (16); Pascal on, xlviii, 75-7, 77 (200), 80 (217); Penn on, i, 357; Tennyson on, xlii, 1020; Whitman on, xxxix, 394-5

Indignation, Drake on, xxxiii, 129; Eliphaz on, xliv, 77 (2) note 1; defined by Hobbes, xxxiv, 340; language of, 344-5

Individual, Franklin on power of the, i, 91; state and, ii, 228 (22), 242 (54); v, 248

Individual Differences, Darwin on, xi, 55-8, 87-99

Individuality, Channing on, xxviii, 333; Cicero on, xlviii, 121 note 7; democracy and, xxviii, 466-7; Emerson on, v, 22-3, 114, 11, 18, 128-9, 186-7; Epictetus on, ii, 119 (8), 120 (9); Marcus Aurelius on, ii, 220 (49), 222 (3), 245 (15); Mazzini on, xxxii, 380; Mill on, xxv, 157-8, 203-9, 250-89; Schiller on need of, xxxii, 223 (see also Self-reliance)

Induction, Bacon on, xxxix, 133-4, 136; Mill on, xxv, 101

Indulgence, Locke on, xxxvii, 27-9, 31-2

Indulgences, sale of, xxxvi, 281 note; 287 note 16, 299 note; Dante on sale of, xx, 410 note 7; Luther on, xxxvi, 247, 251-9, 315-16

Industrial Problems, Smith on solution of, x, 3-4

Industrial Schools, proposed by Ticknor, xxviii, 367

Industries, domestic, capital naturally seeks, x, 332-5; infant, protection of, 336-7

Industry, climate and, xxxiv, 177-8; food-supply in relation to, x, 84-5; Franklin on, i, 59, 75-6, 85, 91; Franklin's rule of, 79, 80; Huxley on, xxviii, 222; paper money in relation to, x, 234-5, 247, 250-2; Penn on, 1, 328, 343; quantity of, on what dependent, x, 233, 262-3, 332-3; wages in relation to, 83

INEQUALITY, ON THE, AMONG MANKIND, xxxiv, 165-228

Inequality, Emerson on, v, 101; Hobbes on, xxxiv, 408-9; immortality and, xxxii, 191; More on, xxxvi, 167-8, 236-7; Pascal on, xlviii, 125-6 (380); Penn on, i, 393 (255-8); Pope on, xl, 431-2

Inertia, of matter, Hobbes on, xxxiv, 313; Hume on, xxxvii, 345-6 note; Kelvin on, xxx, 302

INES, FAIR, xli, 905-7

Inexperience, Hippocrates on, xxxviii, 5

Infallibility, Pascal on, xlviii, 305 (876), 306 (880)

Infancy, Augustine, St., on, vii, 9-11; Locke on impressions of, xxxvii, 9, 27, 32-3; nonconformity of, v, 61; Pope on, xl, 425; Wordsworth on, xli, 596-7

INFANT, ON AN, DYING AS SOON AS BORN, xli, 736-8

Infatuation, Buddha on, xlv, 669; freedom from, 670-1

INFERNO, Dante's, xx, 5-144

Infinite Divisibility, Hume on, xxxvii, 413-14 note

Infinities, in geometry, xxxiv, 125-6; Hume on, xxxvii, 413 note

Infinity, artificial, xxiv, 62-3; Burke on, 52-3, 65; Burke on sublimity of, 62-3, 111-14; Hobbes on, xxxiv, 321-2; Kelvin on, xxx, 258; Pascal on, xlviii, 27-8, 49-50 (121), 78 (206), 83 (231-3), 429-37

Infusoria, in air of St. Jago, xxix, 15; on surface of ocean, 24-7

Inga, emperor of Guiana, xxxiii, 321

Ingævones, Tacitus on the, xxxiii, 93

Ingcél, the One-eyed, xlix, 205, 210-14, 215-16, 217-46

Ingeld, and Freawaru, xlix, 60 note, 61 note

Ingenhousz, Dr., xxxviii, 172

Ingenuity, Penn on, i, 343 (229)

Ingenuousness, Locke on, xxxvii, 114

Ingolf, the Norseman, xliii, 5

Ingratitude, Cervantes on, xiv, 184; Hobbes on, xxxiv, 407; Shakespeare on, xl, 268; Shakespeare on, of children, xlvi, 237-8, 268; Sheridan on, xviii, 169

Inheritance, Bacon on riches by, iii, 88, 90; Burke on principle of, xxiv, 172; Emerson on, v, 49, 241; freedom of, in BODY OF LIBERTIES, xliii, 68 (10); in Massachusetts, 77 (81), 78 (82); Mill on, xxv, 143-4; Mohammedan laws of, xlv, 968-70, 971, 984; Pascal on, xlviii, 378-9 (see also Heredity)

Inheritance Taxes, Smith on, x, 506, 508

Injuries, Browne on, iii, 153; Franklin on repaying, ii, 153; Franklin on resenting, i, 79; Hobbes on, xxxiv, 372, 393; Machiavelli on, xxxvi, 10; Marcus Aurelius on, ii, 229 (25), 236 (20), 289 (18); Penn's maxim on, i, 348 (298); Socrates on, ii, 37-8

Injustice, Hobbes on, xxxiv, 393, 401-6, 409-10; Marcus Aurelius on, ii, 264 (1); Pascal on, xlviii, 79 (214), 151 (454); Socrates on, ii, 38

Innate Ideas, Hume on, xxxvii, 303 note; Voltaire on, xxxiv, 104-5

Inner Life, admonitions concerning the, vii, 238-57

Inner Light, Kempis on the, vii, 258; Woolman on, i, 174, 175-6, 194, 214, 224, 248-9

INNER VISION, THE, xli, 672-3

Innis, anecdote of, i, 152-3

INNKEEPER, NICKNAMED "THE MARQUIS," vi, 499

Innocence, Goethe on, xix, 135; Marvell on, xl, 377; Sheridan on consciousness of, xviii, 165-6; virtue and, i, 358 (443-4)

INNOCENCE, AUGURIES OF, xli, 586-90

Innocent VI, and King John, xxxv, 34

Innocent, in PILGRIM'S PROGRESS, xv, 201

Innocent, Mount, xv, 291

Innovation, Bacon on, iii, 61-2; Berkeley on, xxxvii, 265; Burke on spirit of,

xxiv, 171-2; Gallus on, xxxv, 315 note; Machiavelli on, xxxvi, 8, 20-1; Penn on, i, 343 (230-1); reform contrasted with, xxiv, 391; Smith on, xxvii, 239; Washington on, xliii, 240

Inns of the Court, xxxv, 379-80

Ino, in the BACCHÆ, viii, 399, 421; in the ODYSSEY, xxii, 76

Inoculation, Franklin on, i, 96; extended by Pasteur, xxxviii, 270; Voltaire on, xxxiv, 93-7; Woolman on, i, 237-8 (see also Vaccination)

Inquiry, Bacon on, xi, 1; Bacon's method of, xxxix, 132-40; 143-6; Browne on, iii, 264-5; Burke on, xxiv, 7-9, 46-8; Buddha on useless subjects of, xlv, 647-52; Carlyle on, xxv, 320, 346; Channing on, xxviii, 325; Emerson on, v, 20-1; Hobbes on ends of, xxxiv, 346-7; 374-5; judgment and fancy in, 350-1; Hume on limits of, xxxvii, 418-20; Kempis on, vii, 262 (4), 363 (1, 2), 364 (5); Marcus Aurelius on, ii, 209 (11), 232 (3), 243 (4), 247 (30), 255 (11), 284 (37), 300 (29); Penn on, i, 338, 386 (164); Plutarch on improper love of, xii, 35

Inquisition, censorship of press by the, iii, 193, 196, 198; Galileo and, xxxiv, 111; in the Netherlands, xix, 257; Pascal on the, xlviii, 315

Inquisitiveness, of children, xxxvii, 104-7; Horace on, xxvii, 32 note 33

Insects, color of, xi, 139; flowers and, 99-100, 101-2, 104-5; Harrison on, xxxv, 346-7; hearts in, xxxviii, 85, 86, 130; imitation among, xi, 224-5, 446-8; luminous, 188, 190; neuter and sterile, 278-83; phosphorescent, xxix, 38-9; respiration in, xxxviii, 134-5; at sea, xxix, 164-5; wings of, developed from tracheæ, xi, 187

Insensibility, Pascal on, xlviii, 77 (197-8)

INSENSIBILITY, HAPPY, xli, 875-6

Insight, Confucius on, xliv, 38 (6)

Insincerity, Marcus Aurelius on, ii, 204 (16)

Inspiration, Emerson on, v, 28-9, 43, 59, 70; Epictetus on, ii, 134 (53); Hobbes on, xxxiv, 354; Pascal on, xlviii, 91 (245); Plutarch on, xii, 177-8; Quaker doctrine of, xxxiv, 70-1

Instævones, Tacitus on the, xxxiii, 93

INSTAURATIO MAGNA, PREFACES TO, xxxix, 116-42; editorial remarks on, 3

Instigation, Mill on liberty of, xxv, 250, 295-7

Instinct, Burke on, xxiv, 406; Darwin on, xi, 251-84; Emerson on, v, 69-70; of giant crab, xxix, 466-7; Hume on, xxxvii, 374; Pascal on, xlviii, 117 (344), 129 (396). 441; Pope on, xl, 413, 424-5; Rousseau on, xxxiv, 268-9 note

INSTITUTES, DEDICATION OF CALVIN'S, xxxix, 27-51

Institutions, Burke on sudden changes in, xxiv, 290; Emerson on, v, 10, 68, 190

Institutions, Public, expense of, x, 452-67

Instruction, Emerson on, v, 237; Epictetus on need of, ii, 156 (105); expense of public, x, 463-4

Instructions, in Slough of Dispond, xv, 19-20

INSTRUMENT OF GOVERNMENT, THE, xliii, 106-17

Instruments, Berkeley on, xxxvii, 238-9; Smith on, x, 218, 405, 422

Insurance, Smith on, x, 110

Insurance Corporations, x, 461-2

Insurrections, congressional control of, xliii, 185 (15)

INTEGER VITÆ, xl, 286-7

Integrity, Franklin on, i, 87

Intellect, Archytas on, ix, 59; beauty and, xxxii, 266-7, 272; Carlyle on unconsciousness of high, xxv, 322; Channing on the, xxviii, 323, 324, 326; Emerson on the, v, 135, 190, 281, 282; good, marred and evil, xlv, 869; Hobbes on, xxxiv, 349-59; love and, xlviii, 415-16; Marcus Aurelius on, ii, 213 (4); as measure of organization, xi, 129-30; Pascal on, xlviii, 11, 12 (7), 125 (378), 275; Rousseau on, xxxiv, 245-7

Intellectual Growth, Emerson on, v, 137-8

Intelligence, three scales of, xxxvi, 75-76

Intemperance, taught to children, xxxvii, 30; fruits of, iv, 331; Luther on, xxxv, 332-3; a tyranny, xlvi, 375; Woolman on, i, 196-7 (see also Drunkenness)

Intention(s), Kant on, xxxii, 305-13; Kempis on purity of, vii, 298 (2); Locke on, xxxvii, 103; James Mill on, xxv, 35-6

Interbreeding, Darwin on close, xi, 103, 134, 304

INTERCOURSE, TRUTH OF, by Stevenson, xxviii, 277-84

Intercrossing, compared with change of

conditions, xi, 303-4; importance of, 53; necessity of, 103-7; reciprocal, 294-5; between species, 285-305; species kept true by, 109; varieties, how affected by, 98-9, 107-9

Interdicts, Luther on, xxxvi, 269 note 4

Interest (ethical), as source of errors, xlviii, 38-9; as basis of friendship, ix, 27; Hobbes on, xxxiv, 269, 374; Kant on, xxxii, 325 note, 359 note, 370 note

Interest (monetary), defined, x, 53; in Elizabethan England, xxxv, 299-300; unknown among ancient Germans, xxxiii, 107; legal regulation of, x, 284-5; Luther on, xxxvi, 331-2; in early Massachusetts, xliii, 70 (23); Penn on, i, 337; price of land dependent on rate of, x, 286; rates of, historically considered, x, 91-2, 96; rate of, on what dependent, 280-2; rate of, affected by taxes on profits, 504-5; rate of, due to insecurity, 97-8; rate of, determines building rent, 488; rates of, as index of profits, 98; taxes on, 496-7 (see also Usury)

Intermediate Varieties, absence of, xi, 169-75; in geological formations, 332-40

Intermitting, Burke on, xxiv, 70-1, 111-12

International Law, offences against, xliii, 184 (10)

International Relations, Washington on, xliii, 243-8

Interpreter, in PILGRIM'S PROGRESS, xv, 32-41, 202-12

Interruptions, Bacon on, iii, 63; Locke on, xxxvii, 125, 126

Interstate Commerce, xliii, 184 (3), 185 (6)

INTIMATIONS OF IMMORTALITY, xli, 595-600; Mill on, xxv, 95

Intolerance, Mill on, xxv, 37, 226-8; in politics, Hamilton on, xliii, 201

Introspection, Burke on value of xxiv, 9

Introversion, Emerson on, v, 20

Intuition, Emerson on, v, 59, 62, 69; Mill on doctrine of, xxv, 168-9; Mill on knowledge by, 141; Pascal on, xlviii, 41 (95), 99-100, 143 (434)

Intuitive Mind, Pascal on the, xlviii, 9-12

Invective(s), Browne on religious, iii, 256; Hobbes on, xxxiv, 350; Luther on, xxxvi, 337; Swift on, xxvii, 115

nventions, monopolies of, in BODY OF LIBERTIES, xliii, 68 (9); Emerson on, v, 81; Franklin on patenting, i, 112; Penn on, 343 (230-2); profits of, x, 61-2; Voltaire on, xxxiv, 100-1; Woolman on, i, 214-5

nventors, honors for, Channing on, xxviii, 357-8; in New Atlantis, iii, 180-1

NVENTORY, THE, vi, 186-8

NVERARY, THE BARD AT, vi, 272

NVEREY, in THE BARON OF BRACKLEY, xl, 119-21

nvestigation (see Inquiry)

nvestitures, Luther on, xxxvi, 294

nvestments, Smith on imprudent, x, 269

NVICTUS, xlii, 1210

NVITATION, THE, by Shelley, xli, 843-4

NVITATION, APOLOGY FOR DECLINING AN, vi, 513

NVITATION, EXTEMPORE REPLY TO AN, vi, 460

NVITATION, VERSIFIED REPLY TO AN, vi, 201

NVOCATION, by Shelley, xli, 825-7

nward Consolation, Kempis on, vii, 258-334

o, in PROMETHEUS BOUND, viii, 187-98

odine, vapor of, xxx, 43

olas, in the ÆNEID, xiii, 379, 409

ole, Dante on, xx, 323; on Hercules, v, 184

on, on Pericles, xii, 39

onian Sea, named from Io, viii, 197

onians, in Egypt, xxxiii, 77-8, 82

opas, in the ÆNEID, xiii, 99

ophon, son of Sophocles, viii, 208, 303, 441

phicles, th kine of, xxii, 152

PHIGENEIA, by Landor, xli, 903-4

phigenia, Æschylus on sacrifice of, viii, 15-16; Dante on, xx, 303; Landor on, xli, 903-4; Lucretius on, iii, 14; Ruskin on, xxviii, 142

phimedeia, in Hades, xxii, 152

phitus, son of Eurytus, xxii, 284-5; in sack of Troy, xiii, 111, 115

quique, town of, xxix, 365-7

ras, Cleopatra and, xii, 368, 387; in ALL FOR LOVE, xv˙. 39-40, 72, 75, 89, 90, 102-4

reland, candle-eating in, xxxv, 354; Christianity in, xxxii, 170, 171, 172, 173-81; Emerson on, v, 341; epic literature of, xlix, 198; Freeman on,

xxviii, 258, 266; Mill on, xxv, 146, 180-1; Newman on, xxviii, 50; poetry in, xxvii, 7-8, 117-21; Renan on, xxxii, 137, 140; woolen manufactures of, x, 195-6

IRELAND, THE FAIR HILLS OF, xli, 921-2

Irenæus, St., on early converts, xxviii, 37-8; Milton on, iii, 203

IRESON'S RIDE, xlii, 1357-60

Iris, Juno and, xiii, 46, 177; Milton on, iv, 46, 71, 325; in THE TEMPEST, xlvi, 445-7, 448

Irish, cold baths among the, xxxvii, 13; Thackeray on the, xxviii, 16 (see also Celtic Races)

Irish Channel, tides in, xxx, 288

IRISH EMIGRANT, LAMENT OF THE, xli, 919-20

Irish Rebel, story of the, iii, 98-9

Iron, beginnings of use of, xxxiv, 206; More on, xxxvi, 191; combustion of, in oxygen, xxx, 138; action of, on water, 120-2

Iron Brigade, at Gettysburg, xliii, 326 note, 330, 331

IRON HENRY, tale of, xvii, 47-50

IROQUOIS INDIANS, TREATY WITH, xliii, 229-32

Irresolution, Hobbes on, xxxiv, 366-72

Irrevocable Laws, fallacy of, xxvii, 229-35

Irus, the beggar, Ulysses and, xxii, 245-8

Irving, Edward, Carlyle and, xxv, 315

Isaac, son of Abraham, xliv, 436 (8); Augustine, St., on, vii, 187; Mohammed on, xlv, 910; Pascal on, xlviii, 201

Isabella, Queen, of Castile, on forms, iii, 125; Raleigh on, xxxix, 85, 86

Isabella, Queen of Edward II, her griefs, xlvi, 15, 21-2; sues for Gaveston's recall, 21-5; reconciled to king, 26-7; at Gaveston's return, 31-4, accused by king, 38; in Tynemouth, 40-2; sent to France, 49, 55, 56-9; return with Mortimer, 61-4; Edward on, 69, 71, 72; her triumph with Mortimer, 73; her part in king's death, 74-5; with Prince Edward, 76-82; at death of Kent, 82; accused of king's murder, 87; committed to Tower, 88-9

Isæus, Demosthenes and, xii, 194; Pliny on, ix, 213-14

Isaiah, Augustine, St., on, vii, 145; Burns on, vi, 138; prophecy of Eucharist, xlviii, 349; murder of xlv, 914 note

Isauricus, Servilius, xii, 295

Iscantinaro, Cesare, xxxi, 206-7

Iselastic Games, ix, 415 note

Iseult, Renan on, xxxii, 142

Ishmael, xlii, 1310; Mohammed on, xlv, 911

Isidore, Archbishop of Seville, xx, 329 note 26

Isis, the Egyptian Demeter, xxxiii, 79; Herodotus on, 26, 34; temple of, at Memphis, 87; Milton on, iv, 14, 100; as Suevian goddess, xxxiii, 97-8

Islam, xlv, 951, 956 (see also Mohammedanism)

Islands, species of oceanic, xi, 413-25

Isle of France, Darwin on, xxix, 486-9

ISLES OF GREECE, xli, 812-15

Ismael the Sophy, beauty of, iii, 106

Ismarus, in the ÆNEID, xiii, 326

Ismene, in ANTIGONE, viii, 256-8, 272-4; in Dante's Limbo, xx, 237; in ŒDIPUS THE KING, viii, 253-4; in PHÆDRA, xxvi, 148-51

Ismenias, Plutarch on, xii, 36

Isocrates, Demosthenes and, xii, 194; Logos Arepagiticos of, iii, 184, 191; old age of, ix, 50; oration for son of Alcibiades, xii, 115; on oratory at feasts, xxxii, 55; school of, iii, 244; on teachers, x, 136

Isodorus, C., slaves of, ix, 374 note 2

Isolation, Cicero on, ix, 38; Emerson on, v, 73, 208; Kempis on need of, vii, 322-3; qualities of mind due to, xxviii, 171-2, 186-7, 190; species in regard to, xi, 109-10

Israelites (see Jews)

Ister, Herodotus on the, xxxiii, 22

IT WAS A' FOR OUR RIGHTFU' KING, vi, 491-2

Italian Classics, xxxii, 122

ITALIAN ESSAYS, xxxii, 377-396

Italian Language, change in, xxxix, 202; Milton on study of, iii, 242; Sidney on, xxvii, 50

Italian Literature, Arnold on, xxviii, 75; Taine on, xxxix, 436

Italicus, Silius, Pliny on, ix, 236-7

Italy, Alfieri on, v, 331, 346; two civilizations of, xxxix, 424; Dante on distractions of, xx, 168-9; Goethe on art of, xxxix, 259-60, 265-6; Goldsmith on, xli, 522-4; Harrison on, xxxv, 223, 311; named Hesperia of old, xiii, 92, 133; language as factor in reuniting,

xxviii, 256-7; Louis XII in, xxxvi, 13-15, 24; Macaulay on mediæval, xxvii, 366-76, 382; Machiavelli on princes of, xxxvi, 78-9; Machiavelli's plea for freedom of, 83-6; mercenaries in, 43-4; papal power in, 276-7; politics of, after Charles VIII, xxvii, 387-8; Renaissance in, l, 23; Taine on mediæval, xxxix, 424; Turner on travels in, xxxv, 378; Virgil on ancient, iii, 76

Ithaca, Homer on, xxii, 61, 115

Ithacus (see Ulysses)

Ithuriel, in PARADISE LOST, iv, 174-5

Itinerant Preachers, Franklin on, i, 103; Penn on, 359 (461)

Itylus, and Philomela, xx, 213 note; Homer on, xxii, 270

ITYLUS, by Swinburne, xlii, 1201-3

Iulus (see Ascanius)

Ivon, and Ivor, xlix, 158, 167, 174

IVY GREEN, THE, xlii, 1147-8

Ixion, Æschylus on, viii, 140, 151; Virgil on, xiii, 228

Iwarawaqueri, the, xxxiii, 354, 356, 358

Jackson, Lidian, second wife of Emerson, v, 3

Jackson, Stonewall, and Barbara Frietchie, xlii, 1363-4

Jacob, and the angel, xlii, 1304; Augustine, St., on, vii, 187; Bunyan on dissimulation of, xv, 260; Milton on, iv, 148, 324, 345; Mohammed on, xlv, 910-11, 922, 926-9; Pascal on, xlviii, 201, 203, 237; the Psalmist on, xliv, 275 (10), 276 (23); Stephen on, 436 (8, 12, 14-16)

Jacob's Ladder, Bunyan on, xv, 237

JACOBITE'S EPITAPH, A, xli, 917

JACOBITES, YE, BY NAME, vi, 420-1

Jacobs, Joseph, compiler of Æsop's Fables, xvii, 9

Jacobus de Benedictis, hymn by, xlv, 553-5

Jael, Sisera and, iv, 439; xv, 58

Ja'far, vizier of Harun Er-Rashid, xvi, 60-1, 62, 63, 64, 65, 99-100, 215-18, 220, 221, 228, 229-30

Jaguar, flesh of the, xxix, 122; habits of, 140-1

Jaïrus, the daughter of, xliv, 376 (41-2), 377 (49-56)

Jamaica, disturbance in, xxv, 181-4

James, St., the Great, xliv, 366 (10-11), 368 (14), 377 (51), 379 (28), 380 (54), 424 (13), 448 (2); disillusion-

ment of, ii, 324; in Dante's PARADISE, xx, 391-4; on faith, ii, 342

James, St., son of Alphæus, xliv, 368 (15), 424 (13), 455-6 (13-21)

James II, of Aragon, xx, 369 note 14

James I, King of England, Bacon to, xxxix, 119-20; Bentham on, xxvii, 228-9; Bohemia and, xv, 346-7; Dr. Donne and, 339-40, 342, 343, 347, 348; Harvey and, xxxviii, 60; George Herbert and, xv, 381, 382-3, 384, 386; marriage bed of, x, 275; Andrew Melvin and, xv, 381-2; Puritans and, xxvii, 135, 136; Raleigh on, xxxix, 78-80; charter to Virginia, xliii, 49-58

James II, Bentham on abdication of, xxvii, 235; Burke on, xxiv, 162-3, 166 and note; Dissenters and, xxvii, 137; William Penn and, xxxiv, 77

James I, of Scotland, xlii, 1153-78; his imprisonment in England, xxxv, 272

James, king of Majorca, xx, 369 note 13

James, in PILGRIM'S PROGRESS, xv, 220, 224, 228, 245, 253, 259, 274, 287

James, Abel, letter of, to Franklin, i, 68

James Island, Darwin on, xxix, 380-1

JAMIE, COME TRY ME, vi, 343

Jan Yu, xliv, 10 (6) note 4, 15 (7) note 5, 19 (6, 10) notes 10 and 13, 22 (14), 33 (2), 34 (12, 16) note 11, 35 (21, 23) notes 19 and 22, 36 (25) note 24, 43 (14) note 2, 54 (1) note 6

Jane, in SHOEMAKER'S HOLIDAY, xlvii, 473, 475-6, 499, 505-9, 512, 522-5

Janizaries, Bacon on, iii, 52 and note

Jann, species of genii, xvi, 9 note

Jansenists, xlviii, 5; Pascal on the, 302 (865), 307 (887)

Jansenius, Cornelius, xlviii, 5, 288 (834)

Janus, Milton on, iv, 322; Virgil on, xiii, 83, 245, 260

Jarjaris, the 'Efrit, xvi, 74-8, 80-1, 84-7

Jason, son of Æson, in Dante's HELL, xx, 75

Jason, brother of Onias, xx, 79 note 5

Jason, the Christian, xliv, 460 (5-9)

Java, Drake at, xxxiii, 223-4

Jaws, and limbs, related, xi, 148

JAY AND PEACOCK, fable of, xvii, 19-20

Jay, John, article in the FEDERALIST, xliii, 203-7

Jealousy, Æschylus on, viii, 38; Bacon on, of husbands, iii, 22; Campion on, xl, 286; defined by Hobbes, xxxiv, 341; Dryden on, xviii, 71; Eliphaz on, xliv,

77 (2); music and, xli, 477; Pascal on, xlviii, 164 (502); Penn on, i, 341, 388; rage and, xxxiv, 353

JEAN, THY BONIE FACE, IT IS NA, vi, 316

Jefferson, Thomas, author of DECLARATION OF INDEPENDENCE, xliii, 150 note; the Mecklenburg Declaration and, 156 note

Jeffrey, Francis, Carlyle and, xxv, 316; Edinburgh Review and, xxvii, 224

Jehoshaphat, Last Judgment in, xx, 40 note 1

Jehovah, name of God (see JOB, BOOK OF, and PSALMS)

Jellaladeen, parable of, xxviii, 460

Jemimah, daughter of Job, xliv, 141

Jenner, Edward, life and works, xxxviii, 142; ON VACCINATION, 143-220

Jenner, Henry, xxxviii, 154, 160-1, 202, 211, 216

Jenner, Rev. G. C., xxxviii, 213-14

JENNY KISS'D ME, xli, 870

Jephthah, Dante on, xx, 303; daughter of, xlvi, 136; Milton on, iv, 382, 421

Jeremiah, Burns's paraphrase of, vi, 24; Calvin on, xxxix, 42; worshipped in Egypt, 35; imprisonment of, xlv, 914 note; Pascal on, xlviii, 209; Woolman on, i, 194

Jeremy, in SHE STOOPS TO CONQUER, xviii, 247

Jeroboam, Bunyan on, xv, 309

Jerome, St., apparition of, iii, 199; on angels, xx, 408 note 1; on idleness, xxxix, 13-4

Jerome of Prague, xxxvi, 317

Jerusalem, Dante on destruction of, xx, 232 note 5, 311 note 6; Jesus on, xliv, 392 (34-5), 404-5 (41-4); Jews on situation of, v, 334; lament over destruction of, xliv, 244-5; Paré on destruction of, xxxviii, 31; Pascal on ruin of, xlviii, 217-8 (654); prayer for peace of, 307-8; prophecy of destruction of, xliv, 408 (20-4); temple of, washed with alum, xxxv, 319; Woolman on wickedness of, i, 206

JERUSALEM, THE GOLDEN, xlv, 549

JESSIE, THE FLOWER O' DUNBLANE, xli, 593-4

Jester's Song, from JOLLY BEGGARS, vi, 125-6

Jesting, Bacon on limits of, iii, 83; clumsy, no joke, xvii, 15; with malice, Sheridan on, xviii, 120

Jesu, Dulcedo Cordium, xlv, 550-1
Jesu, Dulcis Memoria, xlv, 550
Jesuits, Bacon on cunning of, iii, 57; miracles performed by, 279-80 (27); Pascal on, xlviii, 7, 298, 299 (854), 302 (865), 306 (882), 309 (891), 310-11 (902), 314 (919), 315
Jesus, apostles of, xliv, 368 (13-16); baptism of, 362 (21-2); birth of, 358 (7); birth of, hymns on, eclipse at death of, iii, 281 (29); Bunyan on, xv, 143; Calderon on death of, xxvi, 24; centurion and, xliv, 371 (2-10); Chaucer on language of, xl, 31; circumcision of, xliv, 358 (21); circumcision of, Milton on, iv, 40-1; coming of the Lord, xliv, 388-90 (35-59), 399 (22-37), 400 (8), 408 (8-11), 409 (25-36); Dante on darkness at death of, xx, 409-10; cures demoniacs, xliv, 379 (38-43), 384-5 (14-26); heals dropsy, 392 (1-6); Emerson on, v, 29-30, 66, 68, 141, 144, 147, 153, 197; feasts in commemoration of, xv, 403-4; feeds five thousand, xliv, 378 (11-17); the fig-tree and, xxxv, 133; Francis, St., on love of, xlv, 556; Franklin on, i, 80; Gadarene miracle, xliv, 375-6 (27-39); genealogy of, 362 (23-38); Herod and, 377 (7-9); Hume on miracles of, xxxvii, 375; infirm woman cured by, xliv, 390-1 (11-17); Jairus's daughter raised by, 376 (41-2); Jerusalem, entry into, 404-5 (28-44); Jerusalem, foretells destruction of, 408 (20-4); John the Baptist and, 372; Kempis on cross of, vii, 251; Kempis on loving, 245-6; Lamb on, xxvii, 280; last supper, xliv, 410 (14-37); lepers healed by, 366 (12-15), 399 (11-19); lullaby for infant, xl, 256-60; MacDonald on, xlii, 1118; Martha and Mary with, xliv, 383 (38-42); Mary Magdalene and, 373 (37-50); Mill on persecution of, xxv, 219-20; Mill on teachings of, 244; miraculous draught of fishes, xliv, 365-6 (4-11); Mohammed on, xlv, 910, 953-4, 966, 983-4, 999, 1002, 1005-6; More on teachings of, xxxvi, 165-6; palsied man healed by, xliv, 366-7 (18-26); parable of fig-tree, 390 (6-9); parable of Good Samaritan, 382-3 (25-37); parable of great supper, 393 (15-24); parable of the importunate widow, 400 (1-5); parable of Lazarus,

397-8 (19-31); parable of lost sheep, 394 (3-7); parable of marriage feast, 392-3 (8-11); parable of old and new garments and wines, 367 (36-9); parable of the Pharisee and publican, 400-1 (9-14); parable of piece of silver, 394-5 (8-10); parable of prodigal son, 395-6 (11-32); parable of rich man, 387 (16-21); parable of sower, 374 (4-15); parable of ten servants, 403 (11-26); parable of unjust steward, 396-7 (1-13); parable of vineyard, 405-6 (9-18); in Paradise Regained, iv, 359 et seq.; Pascal on, xlviii, 80 (222-3), 175-8, 180 (554), 263 (744), 273-4 (786-92), 275; Pascal on miracles of, 280-1 (808-13), 285 (826), 286-7 (829), 288 (834), 289-90 (838, 839), 292-3, 294; passion and death, xliv, 411-16; passion of, Milton on, iv, 23-5; Paul, St., on resurrection of, xlv, 511 (3-11); Peter and, xliv, 412 (55-62); Peter and, 426-7 (22-36), 428, 430 (10-12); Pharisees and, 385-6 (37-44), 397 (14-17); Plato and, xxvii, 346; teaches prayer, xliv, 383-4 (1-13); public ministry, 363-409; resurrection of, 416-17; Rousseau on, xxxiv, 301; on the Sabbath, xliv, 368 (1-11), 390-1 (14-16), 392 (1-6); Sadducees and, 406-7 (27-40); casts sellers out of temple, 405 (45-6); sermon on the mount, 369-70 (20-49); sends out seventy disciples, 381-2 (1-24); Shelley on, xxvii, 345; Sidney on parables of, 18; storm stilled by, xliv, 375 (22-5); temptation of, 362-3 (1-13); transfiguration of, 379 (29-36); on tribute money, 406 (22-6); xxxvi, 370; Watts on, xlv, 537-8; Wesley on, 559-60; widow of Nain and, xliv, 371 (11-17); on the widow's mite, 407 (1-4); women and, 374 (2-3); xv, 266; Woolman on, i, 279-80; Zacchaeus and, xliv, 402-3 (1-10) (see also Christ)
Jethro, daughter of, xlii, 1097
Jetter, in Egmont, xix, 253-9, 271-7, 296-301, 316-17
Jevons, on Herodotus, xxxiii, 6
Jewish Physician, story of the, xvi, 142-9
Jews, Browne on the, iii, 277-8 (25); in England, v, 346; German, cold baths of, xxxvii, 13; Justine on the, in Egypt,

iii, 281; Lessing on the, xxxii, 186-
97; Lowell on the, xxviii, 458-9;
Luther on the, xxxvi, 301, 311, 317,
331, 333; Milton on history of the, iv,
345-51; Mohammed on the, xlv, 902-
4, 913-14, 921, 942, 954, 957, 982-3,
995, 998-9, 1001-2; in New Atlantis,
iii, 167; orange-tawny worn by, 101
note; permanence of the, v, 338; Pascal on the, xlviii, 187, 192 (592), 203
(618), 204-9, 210-11 (633), 211-13,
216 (645-6), 219-20 (662-4), 222-3
(670-1), 224-5, 234 (701), 235 (702-
4), 236-7, 238 (713), 243 (714),
256-7, 258-9 (735), 260, 262-3 (745-
50), 266-7 (759-63), 269 (774), 280
(808), 284 (822), 286-7 (829), 349;
in Roman Empire, ii, 312; Winthrop
on commonwealth of the, xliii, 90

ezebel, Raleigh on, xxxix, 70

HANSI, IN THE ROUND TOWER AT, xlii,
1183

inni, defined, xvi, 9 note

oab, Edomites and, xliv, 215; Winthrop
on, xliii, 95

oabin, merchant of New Atlantis, iii,
167

oachim, Abbot of Flora, xx, 339 note 38

oan of Arc, burning of, xxxix, 359;
education of, xxviii, 153-4; Renan on,
xxxii, 154-5

oanna, wife of Chuzas, xliv, 374 (3),
416 (10)

ob, Browne on, iii, 295 (44), 317;
Burke on, xxiv, 406; Milton on, iv,
362, 368, 385; Pascal on, xlviii, 65
(174)

ob, THE BOOK OF, xliv, 71-141; compared with Æschylus, viii, 5; Burke
on passages from, xxiv, 54, 56-7; editorial remarks on, xliv, 70; l, 18-19,
29; Hugo on, xxxix, 353; Lessing on,
xxxii, 191; Pascal on, xlviii, 261 (741);
Shelley on, xxvii, 332

ocasta, in ŒDIPUS THE KING, viii, 228-
32, 236-8, 240-1, 246-8; called Epicaste, xxii, 151

OCK OF HAZELDEAN, xli, 741

OCKEY'S TAEN THE PARTING KISS, vi,
544

oel, prophecy of, xliv, 425 (16-17),
426 (18-21)

ohannes Parricida (see John of Suabia)

ohn, St., disciple of Jesus, xliv, 366 (10-
11), 368 (14), 377 (51), 379 (28),
380 (49, 54), 410 (8-13), 424 (13),
428 (1), 429-30; apocalypse of, iv,
154; v, 176; vi, 138; on the Eucharist,
xlviii, 349; Gospel of, translated by
Faust, xix, 54; Milton on, iii, 231;
in PARADISE of Dante, xx, 394-7, 422
note 7; in Samaria, xliv, 439 (14-16),
440 (17-25)

John, St., of Damascus, hymn by, xlv,
543

John, called Mark, xliv, 449 (12), 450
(25), 450 (5), 451 (13), 457 (37-9)

JOHN BAPTIST, SAINT, by Drummond, xl,
326

John the Baptist, birth prophesied, xliv,
353 (13), 354 (14-17); birth of, 356
(57-63); childhood in desert, 357
(80); Dante on, xx, 238, 365 note 12,
420; Herod and, xliv, 361 (19), 362
(20), 377 (9); Jesus and, 371 (18-
19), 372 (20-8); Kempis on, vii, 362
(3); Milton on, iv, 359-60, 363-6; Mohammed on, xlv, 908, 909, 914 note
4; Pascal on, xlviii, 264 (752), 272
(784); Paul, St., on, xliv, 451 (24-5);
preaching of, 360 (2-4), 361 (5-18)

John XXI, Pope, xx, 338 note 34

John XXII, Pope, xx, 400 note 8; annates established by, xxxvi, 278 note

John of Austria, xxxix, 87

John, King of Bohemia, in Crecy campaign, xxxv, 12, 17, 22, 28-9

John of Burgogne, xxxix, 85

John, King of England, Bertrand and,
xx, 118 note; Cistertians and, xxxv,
255-6; fowling laws of, 334; Voltaire
on, xxxiv, 89

John, King of France, Black Prince and,
xxxv, 54, 55-6, 58; capture of, 51, 58-
9; cardinal of Perigord and, 39-42; at
Poitiers, 34-9, 47-8, 48-50; prisoner in
England, 221

John of Gaunt, and Chaucer, xxxix, 163

John of Hainault, in EDWARD II, xlvi,
57-9, 62

John, King of Portugal, xxxix, 86

John, Duke of Suabia, xxvi, 424 and
note; murders Emperor, 478; as monk
in WILLIAM TELL, 482-8

John the Swede, in TWO YEARS BEFORE
THE MAST, xxiii, 33-4, 42, 100, 101-3,
107, 126, 397

JOHN ANDERSON, MY JO, vi, 345

JOHN BARLEYCORN: A BALLAD, vi, 39-
40

JOHN GILPIN, THE DIVERTING HISTORY OF, xli, 546-54
JOHNIE ARMSTRONG, xl, 101-3
JOHNIE LAD, COCK UP YOUR BEAVER, vi, 414
Johnson, Andrew, PROCLAMATION OF 1866, xliii, 426-31
JOHNSON, ESTHER, ON DEATH OF, xxvii, 122-30
Johnson, Esther, and Swift, xxviii, 8, 9, 14, 23-6, 27-8; xxvii, 90; Thackeray on, xxviii, 23-4; on Vanessa, 27
Johnson, Samuel, LIFE OF ADDISON, xxvii, 155-99; Carlyle on, xxv, 409; LETTER TO CHESTERFIELD, xxxix, 206-7; PREFACE TO DICTIONARY, 182-206; editorial remarks on works of, 182 note; l, 47-8; Emerson on, v, 355, 438-9; Goldsmith to, xviii, 201; on Gower, xxviii, 77; Hazlitt on, xxvii, 268, 272-3; ON ROBERT LEVET, xli, 503-4; life and works of, xxvii, 154; on Milton, xxviii, 206; xxxix, 319-21; on PARADISE LOST, xxviii, 203; paraphrase on Proverbs, xxxix, 294-5; parody by, xxxix, 288-9; on persecution, xxv, 221-2; on Percy's Reliques, xxxix, 325-6; on Pope, 322; on primogeniture, v, 414; A SATIRE, xli, 504; PREFACE TO SHAKESPEARE, xxxix, 208-50; style of, v, 21; as biographer of Swift, xxviii, 8-9; Thackeray on, 9; Wordsworth on Prefatory Lives of, xxxix, 330
Johnson, Sir William, treaty with Senecas, xliii, 230
Joint-stock Companies, x, 460-3
JOLLY BEGGARS, THE, vi, 122-34; Arnold on, xxviii, 88; editorial remarks on, vi, 17
JOLLY GOOD ALE AND OLD, xl, 190-2
Jonadab, son of Rechab, xliii, 96
Jonah, Ninevites and, xliv, 385 (30, 32)
Jonakr, King, xlix, 336, 353, 354, 384, 418
Jonas, ancestor of Launcelot, xxxv, 151
Jonathan, David, and, xli, 486; Saul and, xliii, 104
Jones, Owen, Renan on, xxxii, 138
Jones, Paul, and Franklin, i, 165
Jones, Sir William, poems by, xli, 579-80
Jonson, Ben, THE ALCHEMIST, xlvii, 541-664; ON BACON, xxvii, 56-7; BEAUMONT'S LETTER TO, xl, 319-21; on beauty, xxviii, 410; Devil is an Ass, by, xxvii, 387; Explorata of, 54; Field-

ing on, xxxix, 180; Hazlitt on, xxvii, 276-7; life and works, 54; xlvii, 540; poems by, xl, 290-303; ON SHAKESPEARE, xxvii, 55
Jordan, Thomas, LET US DRINK, xl, 364-5
Jorge, Alvaro, xxxiii, 315 note
Jormunrek, King, xlix, 336, 354, 355-6, 357, 385, 418, 428, 420
Josaphat (see Jehoshaphat)
Joseph of Arimathæa, xliv, 416 (50-3); in Holy Grail legend, xxxv, 118-19, 137, 151, 205, 212
Joseph, husband of Mary, xliv, 354 (27), 357 (4), 362 (23); xl, 260
Joseph, Kaiser, as Count Lorraine, xxv, 427
Joseph, in PILGRIM'S PROGRESS, xv, 228-9, 245, 247, 282, 287
Joseph, son of Jacob, Chaucer on dreams of, xl, 43; the harlot and, v, 66; xv, 72, 85; Locke on story of, xxxvii, 133; Mohammed on, xlv, 922-30, 933; Pascal on, xlviii, 207 (623), 234 (698), 237, 268 (768); the Psalmist on, xliv, 276 (17-22); Stephen on, 436 (9-15)
JOSEPH ANDREWS, PREFACE TO, xxxix, 176-81
Josephus, silence of, on Christ, xlviii, 273 (787); on Jewish Law, 205-206, 209, 211; Pascal on, 208 (629); on spirits, xli, 686 note
Joshua, Gibeonites and, vii, 303 (2); Milton on, iv, 348, 349; one of nine worthies, xxxix, 20; in Paradise, xx, 362; Pascal on, xlviii, 207 (627)
Joule, James Prescott, law of conservation and, xxx, 175-6; on mechanical equivalent of heat, xxx, 198; on expansion of gases, 199
Jourbert, THE GERM THEORY, xxxviii, 269, 364-70
JOURNAL OF JOHN WOOLMAN, i, 169-312
Journalism, Franklin's ideas of, i, 92-3
JOURNEY ONWARDS, THE, xli, 820
JOURNEYS IN DIVERSE PLACES, xxxviii, 9-58; remarks on, 8
Jousts, Bacon on, iii, 96
Jove, in the ÆNEID, xiii, 82-3, 121, 160-1, 200-1, 321, 325, 342, 417-18; Alcmena and, xl, 242; Amalthea and, iv, 161; Augustine, St., on, vii, 17-18; bird of, iv, 323; Danæ and, xlvi, 55; Leda and, xl, 230; Maia and, 242; Milton on, iv, 66, 273 (see also Jupiter)

Jowett, Benjamin, translator of Plato, ii

Joy, Augustine, St., on, vii, 122, 178; Blake on, and grief, xli, 588; Chaucer on, xl, 45; of Christians, Pascal on, xlviii, 354-5; Confucius on, xliv, 55 (5); contrasted with relief from pain, xxiv, 34

Joy, Goethe on, xix, 126; Hobbes on, xxxiv, 340-2; Jonson on unshared, xl, 293; in music, xli, 478-9; Shakespeare on, and grief, xlvi, 153; son of Cupid and Psyche, iv, 71

Joyeuse, sword of Charlemagne, xlix, 177

Joyous Friars, the, xx, 96 note 4

Juan Fernandez, Dana on, xxiii, 43-9; earthquake at, xxix, 314

Juba, Plutarch on, xii, 306-8, 388

Juba, in Cato, xxvii, 187, 189, 193-5; son of, xii, 308

Jubal, Dryden on, xl, 389

Jubilees, Papal, xxxvi, 299 note

Judæa, Christian Church in, xliv, 443 (31)

Judah, tribe of, xliv, 243 (68)

Judaism, Hobbes on, xxxiv, 383-4; Lessing on, xxxii, 186-96; Pascal on, xlviii, 195-6 (601-3), 197-200, 223 (673), 224 (675), 371; Rousseau on, xxxiv, 294-5

Judas, called Barsabbas, xliv, 456 (22, 27), 457 (32)

Judas, son of James, xliv, 368 (16), 424 (13)

Judas of Galilee, xliv, 434 (37)

Judas Iscariot, xliv, 368 (16), 409-10 (3-6), 412 (47-8), 424 (16-20); St. Brandan and, xxxii, 148; Bunyan on, xv, 109, 309; in Dante's HELL, xx, 142; death of, iii, 275; Hazlitt on, xxvii, 280; Pascal on, xlviii, 271 (780); tilting with Jesus, xx, 227 note 13

Judges, Bacon on, iii, 130-4; Burke on elective, xxiv, 338; Epictetus on, ii, 184 (8); Heraclitus on, 135 (54); marriage of, iii, 21; in Massachusetts, xliii, 69 (20); righteous, in Paradise, xx, 363-6; Pascal on, xlviii, 108 (307); pay of, x, 451-2; Pliny on, ix, 279; Shelley on false, xviii, 302; Socrates on, ii, 24; Tseng-tzu on, xliv, 65 (19); United States, xliii, 189; Winthrop on discretionary power of, 91-105

Judgment, Burke on standards of, xxiv, 11; Dante on hasty, xx, 342-3; intellect and, xlviii, 12; Hobbes on, xxxiv, 346, 349-50, 351-2; human and divine, vii, 296 (5), 311; Kempis on rash, 217-18; Massinger on, xlvii, 929; Penn's rule of, i, 385-6; necessary to poets, xxxix, 297; Pascal on, xlviii, 126 (381, 383); Rousseau on the, xxxiv, 245-7; sentiment compared with, xxvii, 205-6, 216; taste and, xxiv, 22-6; wit compared with, i, 339 (171-3); xxiv, 17

Judgment Day (see Last Judgment)

JUDICATURE, ESSAY ON, Bacon's, iii, 130-4

Judicature, expenses of, x, 450-2, 465; Hobbes on, xxxiv, 410-11; in U. S., xliii, 194 (5), 194-5 (6), 195 (7, 8); in Utopia, xxxvi, 212-13

Judicial Penalties, Winthrop on, xliii, 90-100, 101, 102, 103, 104-5

Judicial Power, of U. S., xliii, 189-90, 195 (11)

Judicial Proceedings, in Massachusetts, xliii, 69-74, 77 (76)

Judith, the Jewess, in Paradise, xx, 419

Judith, wife of Louis Debonnaire, xxxix, 82

Jugglery, Woolman on, i, 271-2

Julia, mother of Antony, xii, 322, 336

Julia, daughter of Cæsar, xii, 275, 284; in Dante's Limbo, xx, 20

Julia, wife of Marius, xii, 267

Julia, in DUCHESS OF MALFI, wife of Castruccio, her jests, xlvii, 758-9; with Cardinal, 783-5; with Delio, 785-6; with Pescara, 832; on Bosola, 837; with Bosola, 838-41; last scene with Cardinal, 841-3

Julian, St., patron saint of hospitality, xl, 20 note 178

Julian, Emperor, at Athens, xxviii, 60; laws against Christians, vii, 124; iii, 199

Julianus, death of, xxxvi, 64; Machiavelli on, 67

Julienne, name of Bramimonde, xlix, 195

Juliers, Duke of, xxxv, 101

Julius II, Pope, his aggrandizement of the papacy, xxxvi, 39-40; auxiliaries of, 45; Cæsar Borgia and, 28; economy of, 52-3; Ferrara and, 8; impetuosity of, 81-2; Luther and, 264, 336

Julius III, Pope, Cellini and, xxxi, 385; election of, 383 note 1

Julius, Caius, the physician, xxxii, 14

Julius, the centurion, xliv, 481 (1, 3)

JULLANAR OF THE SEA, story of, xvi, 326-40

JUNE, Bryant's, xlii, 1219-20; Poe on, xxviii, 380-1

Junior, letter to, ix, 337

Junius, author of *Letters*, Hazlitt on, xxvii, 274

Junius, etymologist, Johnson on, xxxix, 187-8

Junius, Franciscus, xxvii, 11

Junius, governor of Asia, xii, 265

Juno, in the ÆNEID, xiii, 75-6, 88-9, 121, 155-6, 198, 204, 249-50, 322-24, 343-4, 394-5, 417-9; Hercules and, iii, 198 and note; Iris attendant of, xiii, 46; goddess of marriage, 154; xl, 244; in the TEMPEST, xlvi, 447

Juno Ludovici, Schiller on the, xxxii, 252

JUNO, PEACOCK AND, fable of, xvii, 24

Junto, Franklin's, i, 57-9, 96-7

Ju Pei, Confucius and, xliv, 60 (20)

Jupiter, adulteries of, xxxiv, 367; attendants of, xiii, 46; Briareus and, iii, 40; Emerson on fable of, v, 92; infancy of, viii, 373; Juno and, iv, 167; Metis and, iii, 53 (see also Jove)

Jupiter, Dante's sixth Heaven, xx, 363-4

Jupiter Ammon, worship of, xxxiii, 26

Jurassic Period, in Europe, xxx, 250

Jurfalez, son of Marsil, xlix, 110, 158

Juries, arbitrary damages of, xliii, 91; Pliny on, ix, 206

Jurisprudence, Burke on science of, xxiv, 231; Descartes on, xxxiv, 8; Goethe on, xix, 80; Marlowe on, 207, 209; Milton on study of, iii, 242; Pascal on, xlviii, 104

Jurors, in Massachusetts, xliii, 73 (49, 50); private offences of, 74 (61)

Jury Trial, in Massachusetts, xliii, 70 (29), 70-1 (30), 71 (31), 77 (76); right of, 148 (7); in U. S., 190, 194-5 (6), 195 (7)

Just, in MINNA VON BARNHELM, xxvi, 299-305, 307-12, 321-3, 327-30, 370, 374

Justice, Æschylus on, viii, 143, 151; Burke on, xxiv, 219, 289; among children, xxxvii, 91-2; Dante on divine, xx, 366-7; Dante's star of, 146 note 5; Dennis on poetical, xxvii, 186; distributive and commutative, iii, 329; Emerson on, v, 156, 186-7; expense of administration of, x, 450-2, 465; Franklin's

rule of, i, 79; Hobbes on, xxxiv, 401-7, 409; human and divine, xlviii, 83 (233); Manzoni on, xxi, 52; Marcus Aurelius on, ii, 287 (10), 341-2; More on, xxxvi, 213; of nature, v, 26, 90; Pascal on, xlviii, 38, 103 (294), 105-6 (297-9), 108 (309), 109 (312), 124 (375), 305 (878); Penn on benefit of, i, 387-8; Penn on delays of, 354-5 (390-4); Penn's maxim of, 337; Plutarch on, xii, 83-4; Pope on origin of, xl, 429; Shakespeare on human, xlvi, 295; story of statue of, xlii, 1308-9; Winthrop on, xliii, 92-3, 97

Justification, Bunyan on, xv, 27, 213-14; Calvin on, xxxix, 49; Ignorance's idea of, xv, 149-50; Luther on, xxxvi, 346-78

Justin of Val Ferrée, xlix, 137

Justina and St. Ambrose, vii, 146

Justinian, Dante on, xx, 168, 305-6; Marlowe on *Institutes* of, xix, 207

Justin Martyr, *Apology* of, ii, 309-10, 312, 313

Justus, Fabius, letter to, ix, 197

Justus, Titus, xliv, 462-3 (7)

Juturna, in the ÆNEID, xiii, 394-5, 397-9, 405, 406, 417, 420-1

Juvenal, authorship of *Satires* doubted, ii, 320 note 2; contemporaneity, ii, 320; on death, iii, 10; the grotesque in, xxxix, 350; George Long, on, ii, 320-1

Juvenale, Latino (see Manetti)

Kaabah, the, xlv, 876, 893 note, 1004

Kalm, Peter, on American colonies, x, 186-7

Kamadûk, xlv, 800, 832

Kanakas, the, xxiii, 139-40, 143-8, 242-4

Kangaroo, young of the, xi, 234

Kant, Immanuel, Emerson on, v, 143; life and works, xxxii, 298; METAPHYSIC OF MORALS, 299-373; Schiller on system of, 210

Kao Ch'ai, xliv, 34 note 12

Kao-tsung, xliv, 50 (43)

Kao-yao, xliv, 40

Kara, daughter of Halfdan, xlix, 367

Karen, in THE RED SHOES, xvii, 329-34

Karlsefni, Thorfinn, xliii, 14-17, 19-20

Karma, cessation of, xlv, 731; fruitful and barren, 669-74; good and bad, 675-6; kinds of, 666-8; meritorious and bodily, 666-8; on ignorance depends, 625, 661-2, 667-8; proximate, 654 note

Karmabandh, xlv, 828

Kasim, brother of 'Ali Baba, xvi, 424, 426-9, 430, 432, 437

Kassapa, xlv, 748, 749

Kastrill, in THE ALCHEMIST, xlvii, 603-7, 618-20, 625-9, 637-9, 648-9, 658-9, 662-3

Kastriota, John, xlvii, 489 note 9

Katherine (see Catherine)

Kauri Pines, Darwin on, xxix, 431

Kay, Sir, steward of Arthur, xxxv, 107-8

Keats, John, Arnold on, xxviii, 77, 78, 79; Browning on, xlii, 1099; buried in Rome, xxiii, 4; elegy on death of, xli, 856-70; poems by, xli, 871-98

Keble, John, hymn by, xlv, 565-6

KEEKIN-GLASS, THE, vi, 427

Keeling Islands, Darwin on, xxix, 456-69

Keightley, Thomas, remarks on his Life of Milton, xxviii, 168

Keimer, friend of Franklin, i, 26-8, 35-6, 50-4, 56; goes to Barbadoes, i, 64; paper of, 59-60

KEITH OF RAVELSTON, BALLAD OF, xlii, 1114-16

Keith, George, i, 22

Keith, Sir William, character of, i, 40-1, 55; Franklin and, 28-31, 34-5, 39-41, 49

KELLY BURN BRAES, vi, 436

Kelp, Darwin on, xxix, 243-5; Smith on, x, 148

Kelvin (see Thomson, Sir William)

KEMBLE, MRS., ON SEEING, IN YARICO, vi, 498

Kempenfelt, Cowper on, xli, 533-4

Kempis, Thomas à, IMITATION OF CHRIST, vii, 201-364; life of, 200; Woolman on, i, 222-3

Kenelm, St., xl, 42

KENMURE'S ON AND AWA, WILLIE, vi, 422

KENNEDY, JOHN, LINES TO, vi, 221

KENNEDY, JOHN, DUMFRIES HOUSE, vi, 188-9

Kennet, Bishop, on Swift, xxviii, 16

Kent, Earl of, in EDWARD II, in quarrels of king and nobles, xlvi, 10-3, 17, 33-4, 36; quarrel with king, 37-8; joins nobles, 39-40; a captive, 54; banished to France, 56, 57-8; return with Mortimer, 61, 62; his relenting, 62-3; suspected by Mortimer, 75-6; attempts rescue of king, 76-7, 78-9; death, 81-2

Kent, in KING LEAR, with Gloucester and his son, xlvi, 215-16; banished by

Lear, 219-21; with Lear in disguise, 230-1; with Oswald, 233; and Fool, 233-4; sent to Gloucester, 240; at Gloucester's, quarrel with Oswald, 246-9; in stocks, 249-51; set at liberty, 256; in the storm, 262-4; finds Lear, 265-6; at the hovel, 267-9, 271, 272; with Lear in his madness, 273-6; flight with Lear, 286; with gentleman in French camp, 286-8; with Cordelia, 300; at Lear's awakening, 301, 302; Edgar on, 313-14; final scene with Lear, 314, 315-16, 317; editor's remarks on character of, 214; Ruskin on character of, xxviii, 137-8

Kephalos, and Eos, viii, 323

Kepler, Johann, Emerson on, v, 177; heliocentric theory of, xxxix, 52 note; on tides, xxx, 280

Keppel, Lord, Burke on, xxiv, 416-20

Kerguelen Land, species of, xi, 422

Kerim, the fisherman, xvi, 219-20

Kethe, William, hymn by, xlv, 539

Kevin, St., and the birds, xxxii, 152-3

Keymis, Capt., xxxiii, 315, 337, 368, 371

Keyserling, Count, on origin of species, xi, 16

Keziah, daughter of Job, xliv, 141

Khemā, disciple of Buddha, xlv, 586

Khoja Hoseyn, in ALI BABA, xvi, 437-40

KID AND WOLF, fable of, xvii, 18

Kidron, reference to, xli, 486

Kilhwch and Olwen, tale of, xxxii, 146, 149-52

Kilissa, in THE LIBATION-BEARERS, viii, 106-8

KILLED AT THE FORD, xlii, 1299-1300

KILLIECRANKIE, THE BRAES O', vi, 359-60

KILLIGREW, MRS. ANNE, ODE TO, xl, 384-8

KILMENY, by Hogg, xli, 756-65

Kin, are less than kind, viii, 87; strange the power of, 167

Kindness, apt to be repeated, i, 98; Burns on, vi, 83, 252; Confucius on, xliv, 58 (6); defined by Hobbes, xxxiv, 341; the power of, v, 57; reward of, ii, 133 (50); stronger than severity, xvii, 35

King, Archbishop, and Swift, xxviii, 23

King, Dr., Bishop of London, xv, 341; relations with Dr. Donne, 349-50, 357; Walton on, 353

King, Gregory, on laborers' income, x, 78

KING LEAR, TRAGEDY OF, xlvi, 213-317;

Ruskin on, xxviii, 137-8; Shelley on, xviii, 276; stage representation of, xxvii, 310-11

KING THRUSHBEARD, story of, xvii, 142-6

Kingcraft, Confucius on, xliv, 38 (7), 39 (11, 14, 19), 43 (15, 16)

Kingdom of Ends, Kant's, xxxii, 343-7 note, 348-9

KINGDOMS, TRUE GREATNESS OF, iii, 73-80

Kingdoms, all have graves, xl, 253; Raleigh on ruin of, xxxix, 71 (see also Princedoms)

Kingfishers, in Cape Verd Islands, xxix, 12; S. American, 143

Kings, councillors of, iii, 52-5; Burke on, xxiv, 165-6, 168-70; Confucius on, xliv, 42 (11); ECCLESIASTES on, 340 (13-16); Emerson on, v, 68-9; friendships of, iii, 66-7; More on enrichment of, xxxvi, 160-3; Penn on government of, i, 350-3; Raleigh on, xl, 205; Ruskin on false and true, xxviii, 128-9; such divinity doth hedge, xlvi, 180 (see also Princes, Rulers)

KINGS' CHILDREN, THE TWO, xvii, 196-203

KING'S COLLEGE CHAPEL, CAMBRIDGE, xli, 678

King's Evil, reference to, xlvi, 378

KING'S TRAGEDY, THE, xlii, 1153-78; remarks on, l, 23, 26

Kingship, Calvin on true, xxxix, 30; Milton on, iv, 383; Pascal on, xlviii, 53, 57-8, 108 (307-8, 310), 114 (330); Pope on beginning of, xl, 428; Rousseau on origin of, xxxiv, 215-21; Shakespeare on, xlvi, 159-60

Kingsley, Charles, POEMS by, xlii, 1060-4

Kingston, Sir William, xxxvi, 131

KINMONT WILLIE, a ballad, xl, 108-14

Kinnersley, Mr., i, 146-7

KIRK AND STATE EXCISEMEN, vi, 460

KIRK OF SCOTLAND'S ALARM, THE, vi, 351-4

KISS, THE PARTING, vi, 318

Kisses, E. B. Browning on, xli, 937-8; Burns on, vi, 438; of love, Goethe on, xix, 407

Kitchen God, xliv, 11 note 6

Klopstock, on Bürger, xxxix, 326

Knavery, origin of, xxxiv, 209

Knight, Chaucer's, xl, 12-13, 34

Knight of the Redcrosse, Spenser's, xxxix, 63-4

Knight, Andrew, on bees, xi, 255; on

hermaphrodites, 103; on cause of variability, 23

Knight-errantry, Cervantes on tales of, xiv, 473-6, 481, 487-95; Don Quixote on, 92-6; expenses of, 130-1; literature of, 3, 9-10, 48-54; Manzoni on, xxi, 545-6; Sancho Panza on, xiv, 118-19

Knighthood, in Elizabethan England, xxxv, 219-22

Knolles, Francis, xxxiii, 229

Knolles, Sir Robert, xxxv, 70, 78, 79

KNOW, CELIA, xl, 352

Knowing Ones, in FAUST, xix, 189

Knowledge, action and, xxxii, 58-9; Augustine, St., on, vii, 65-6, 189-90; on authority, xxv, 229-39; xxxii, 36-9; xxxix, 124; Bacon on, 128-9, 141-2, 143; beauty and, xxxii, 266-7, 272; Berkeley on reality of, xxxvii, 248-52, 267-8, 279-81; Browne on, iii, 313-14, 321-2; Browne on, of self, 263, 266; Bunyan on two kinds of, xv, 85-6; Carlyle on, xxv, 320; Channing on little, xxviii, 341; Comte's three ages of, xxv, 104; always conditional, xxxiv, 346; Confucius on, xliv, 20 (18), 58 (8); Dante on, xx, 302; desire of, inclines to peace, xxxiv, 371; ECCLESIASTES on, xliv, 336 (18), 342 (12); Epictetus on acquisition of, ii, 132 (46), 140 (65), 143 (72); of evil, Mrs. Herbert on, xv, 376; of evil, Milton on, iii, 202-3; iv, 277-8; is not happiness, xviii, 433; Harvey on advance of, xxxviii, 76; Harvey on pursuit of, 63; Hindu doctrine of, xlv, 808, 849; Hippocrates on requisites of, xxxviii, 4-5; Hobbes on attainment of, xxxiv, 352; intuitive and rational, xlviii, 99-100; Kempis on worldly and spiritual, vii, 295-6 (2), 307-8; Locke on, xxxvii, 104-5; Marcus Aurelius on, ii, 230-1 (32); Mill on à priori view of, xxv, 140-1; Milton on, iv, 167-8, 400-1; Pascal on impossibility of certain, xlviii, 30-2; Pascal on universality in, 20 (37); Paul, St., on, xlv, 500-1 (1-2); Penn on, i, 338, 348 (307); pleasure the basis of, xxxix, 280-1; Pope on human, xl, 409; power from, xxxiv, 360-1; xxxix, 142; pride in, ii, 178 (177); xlviii, 153 (460); progress of, due to passions and wants, xxxiv, 177; progress of, requires liberty, iii, 221-2, 229-30; quantity and quality of, xxviii,

330; as recollection, ii, 63-8; Ruskin on impossibility of, xxviii, 111; of self, Shelley on, xviii, 276; of sense and understanding, xxxii, 361-2; Sidney on object of, xxvii, 13-14; Socrates on, ii, 8-9; is sorrow, xviii, 407; taste dependent on, xxiv, 19-20, 25; temperance in, iv, 230; timidity of, xix, 32; Tennyson on, and wisdom, xlii, 984; Thoreau on, xxviii, 419-20; true and false, xlv, 868; two kinds of, xxxiv, 359; vanity of human, vii, 205-6 (3), 206-7, 208-9; xix, 24, 48, 74-5; xlviii, 113; Washington on diffusion of, xliii, 243; of the world, Locke on, xxxvii, 52, 75-8, 80 (see also Learning)

Knowledge, the shepherd, in PILGRIM'S PROGRESS, xv, 123-6

Know-nothing, Mrs., in PILGRIM'S PROGRESS, xv, 187

Knox, John, Carlyle on, xxv, 367, 386, 411-12; life and works, xxxix, 58 note; PREFACE TO REFORMATION IN SCOTLAND, 58-60

Kolita, disciple of Buddha, xlv, 586

Kölreuter, on the barberry, xi, 104-5; on fertility of varieties, 312-13; on hermaphrodites, 103; on reciprocal crosses, 294; on sterility of species, 286-300

Konghelle, town of, v, 345

Korah, Psalms of sons of, xliv, 194-203, 249-51, 252-4

Koran, Bacon on the, iii, 42 note; Browne on the, 276; editor's remarks on, l, 21; Hume on morals of the, xxvii, 204-5; on duty of governors, xxv, 244; legend of Seven Sleepers in, xxxviii, 391-2; Pascal on the, xlviii, 194 (597)

KORAN, CHAPTERS FROM THE, xlv, 879-1007

Kostbera, wife of Hogni, xlix, 343-4, 345

Kotzebue, August, Carlyle on, xxv, 404; on Tahiti, xxix, 417-18

Krishna (see BHAGAVAD-GITA)

Kuan Chung, xliv, 12 note, 46 (10), 47 (17, 18) note

KUBLA KHAN, xli, 701-3

Kung-hsi Hua, xliv, 15 note 6, 18 note 3, 18 note 4, 35 (21), 36 (25), note 25

Kung-ming Chia, xliv, 46 (14)

Kung-shan Fu-jao, xliv, 58 (5)

Kung-shu Wen, xliv, 46 (14), 47 (19)

Kung-sun Ch'ao, xliv, 65 (22)

K'ung wen, xliv, 16 (14)

Kung-yeh Ch'ang, xliv, 14 (1)

Kunz of Gersau, in WILLIAM TELL, xxvi, 449-50

Kuoni, in WILLIAM TELL, xxvi, 381-6, 405-6

Kush, son of Sheddad, inscription of, xvi, 302-4

Kusinārā, city of, xlv, 638, 639

Kuteyt, the jailer, xvi, 226-7

Kynesians, Herodotus on, xxxiii, 22

Kypris, reference to, viii, 198

Kyrenē (see Cyrene)

LA BELLE DAME SANS MERCI, xli, 893-5

Labdacus, father of Laius, viii, 216

Laberius, quoted, xxxii, 6

Labienus, lieutenant of Cæsar, xii, 279; death of, 346; in eastern campaign, 341, 344; goes over to Pompey, 293; story of, 250

Labor, Burke on necessity of, xxiv, 108; capital and, x, 6, 67-8, 212-13, 271, 289-303, 333; Channing on value of, xxviii, 314-17; children sweeten, iii, 19-20; competition of, restraints on, x, 121-32, 137-46; competition of, unnaturally increased, 132-7; demand for (see Wages); division of (see Division of Labor); division of, dwarfs the mind, xxviii, 316; ECCLESIASTES on vanity of, xliv, 335 (3), 336 (11), 337 (18-23), 339 (4-5), 341 (15-16), 342 (7); Emerson on, v, 47-51, 95-6, 286; excessive, results of, i, 197, 251-3; x, 84; xxviii, 315-16; exchange value of, x, 48; free and slave, cost of, 82; Hindu doctrine of, xlv, 799-801, 805-6, 813; independent and wage, x, 85-6; Luther on, xxxvi, 314; Marcus Aurelius on, ii, 207 (5), 222 (1), 238 (33), 268 (12); More on condition of, xxxvi, 180-3; original state of, x, 66; Penn on, i, 328; prices of, real and nominal, x, 37-8; productive and unproductive, 258-65; productive and unproductive in agricultural system, 428-33; productive power of, 9-26; products of, its natural recompense, 66-7; real ends of, v, 96; the real measure of value, x, 34-5, 37, 40-1. 50-1; real recompense of, 79; as recreation, xxxvii, 173-8; remuneration of (see Wages); respect due to, xxviii, 399; rest and, iv, 170; skilled and common, x, 103-4; talents of, fixed capital, 219; Tennyson on, xlii, 994, 995; Thoreau on value of, xxviii, 399; thought needed

in, 327-8; in Utopia, xxxvi, 178-9, 181-3, 188-9; value of, how determined, x, 35; value of, to the scholar, v, 14-15; wages of (see Wages)

Labor, King, xxxv, 183

LABORING CLASSES, ELEVATION OF THE, Channing's, xxviii, 307-67; editorial remarks on, l, 37

LABOURER AND NIGHTINGALE, fable of, xvii, 33-4

Labourers, combinations of, x, 68-9

La Bruyère, Burke on, xxiv, 365 note; Hume on, xxxvii, 291; on his Characters, xxvii, 162, 163; Sainte-Beuve on, xxxii, 130-1

Labyrinth, of Egypt, xxxiii, 74-5

Lacedæmonians, hospitality of the, ii, 293 (24)

Lacedæmonius, son of Cimon, xii, 65

Lacey, Father, Wood on, v, 349

Lachares, and Antony, xii, 374

Lachesis, reference to, xx, 230 note 4

LACK OF GOLD, xli, 532-3

Lactate of Lime, fermentation of, xxxviii, 324

Lactantius, Copernicus on, xxxix, 56; on doers, 108-9; on following authorities, 100; on Providence, 101

Lacy, Sir Hugh, in SHOEMAKER'S HOLIDAY, with Mayor, xlvii, 469-72; with Rowland, 471-2; with Dodger, learns Rowland not in France, 491-3, 496; seeks nephew at Lord Mayor's, 515-16; hears flight of Rose, 516; with Firk, 517-18; plans to stop wedding, 519; mistakes Ralph for Rowland, 524-6; learns of wedding, 525-6; with the king, 532-4

Lacy, Rowland, in SHOEMAKER'S HOLIDAY, in love with Rose Oateley, xlvii, 469-70; his travels, 470; appointed colonel, 470-1; with Sir Hugh, 471-2; delays departure for France, 472; Ralph and, 473-4; summoned by Dodger, 475; Sybil on, 477-8; as Dutch shoemaker, 479; takes service with Eyre, 481-3; the skipper and, 487, 490-1; plot discovered by uncle, 492-3, 496; with Margery, as Hans, 497, 498, 499; with Eyre as sheriff, 500-1; at Mayor's, as Hans, 503-4; at Hodge's, 509-10; goes to Rose with Sybil, 510-1; with Rose, as Hans, 513-5; flight with Rose, 516; with Rose at Eyre's, 520-1; marriage, 526; pardoned by king, 530-1;

denounced by uncle, 532-3; marriage confirmed, 534; knighted, 534; on the shoemakers, 535

LAD THEY CA' JUMPIN JOHN, vi, 302

LADDIE'S DEAR SEL', vi, 347-8

LADIES OF BAGHDAD, stories of the, xvi, 55-66, 100-112

Ladike, wife of Amasis, xxxiii, 89

Ladislaus V, King, xxxvi, 317

Lady, Ruskin on title of, xxviii, 157-8

LADY, TO A, WITH A GUITAR, xli, 848-50

LADY MARY ANN, vi, 435-6

LADY ONLIE, HONEST LUCKY, vi, 283

LADY OF SHALOTT, THE, xlii, 967-71

LADY'S POCKET ALMANAC, LINES IN A, vi, 459

Lælius, called the wise, ix, 10; in Cicero's FRIENDSHIP, 9-10; in Cicero's OLD AGE, 46; Scipio and, 10, 11-14, 20, 43; Sidney on, xxvii, 39

Laertes, in Hamlet, gets leave to go to France, xlvi, 101; farewell to Ophelia, 107-9, 110; and Polonius, 109-10; Reynaldo sent to watch, 121-3; return of, 179-83; with king, plans vengeance on Hamlet, 184-9; learns Ophelia's death, 189-90; at Ophelia's funeral, 196; Osric on, 202-3; duel with Hamlet, 205-7; confesses and dies, 208; not in original story, 92

Laertes, in the ODYSSEY, xxii, 14, 149, 209, 218-9, 325-30, 333; Cowley on, xxvii, 67; Plutarch on, xii, 252 note

Laertius, Diogenes, iii, 242 note 39; Montaigne on, xxxii, 97

Laestrygons, and Ulysses, xxii, 132-3

Lafayette, Burke on, xxiv, 418, 420

La Fontaine, Sainte-Beuve on, xxxii, 123, 129-30, 131

LAGGAN, LAIRD OF, EPIGRAM ON, vi, 467

Lagoon Islands, Darwin on, xxix, 463-4, 469-72; gradually formed from fringing-reefs, 477-81

Lagus, death of, xiii, 334

La Harpe, Hugo on, xxxix, 363, 366

Laing, Malcolm, on Macpherson, xxxix, 328

LAIRD O' COCKPEN, xli, 563-4

LAIRD OF LAGGAN, EPIGRAM ON, vi, 467

Lais, daughter of Timandra, xii, 146

Laius, death of, viii, 212-3, 230-1; Œdipus accused of killing, 222-3; prophecy of death of, 230-1

Lajeunesse, Basil, in EVANGELINE, xlii, 1303; at Benedict's house, 1306-7,

1308, 1309; denounces the English, 1312; in exile, 1315-6, 1319; as herdsman, 1325-8; with Evangeline, 1329, 1330-2

Lajeunesse, Gabriel, lover of Evangeline, xlii, 1303-4; at feast of betrothal, 1311; on day of expulsion, 1315; his wanderings in exile, 1319, 1321, 1323, 1325-6, 1328-9, 1330, 1332, 1333; found by Evangeline in plague, 1336-7

Lake, Dr., Walton on, xv, 407

Lake-dwellers, domestic plants and animals of, xi, 32

L'ALLEGRO, iv, 30-4; Bagehot on, xxviii, 180; an idyllic poem, xxxix, 299

Lalli, Gianstefano, xxxi, 421 note 4

Lally, letter on October Sixth, xxiv, 210-11 note

Lamachus, general in Sicilian expedition, xii, 121, 124, 126

Lamachus, the Myrinæan, xii, 197

Lamarck, on adaptive resemblances, xi, 443; on blind animals, xxix, 59; on evolution, xi, 6; on innate tendency to perfection, 130; objection to his theory of inherited habit, 283; on origin of species, 10

Lamartine, Taine on, xxxix, 411

Lamb, Charles, Hazlitt on, xxxvii, 267; in Hazlitt's discussion, 267-81; on imagination, xxxix, 306 note; life and writings, xxvii, 298; poems by, xli, 735-8; ON TRAGEDIES OF SHAKESPEARE, xxvii, 299-316

LAMB AND WOLF, fable of, xvii, 11

Lambert, Hugo on, xxxix, 379

Lambertaccio, xx, 202 note 17

Lamberti, Mosca de' (see Uberti)

Lambwell, Sir David, xl, 99

Lamech, Pascal on, xlviii, 201

LAMENT, A, by Shelley, xli, 842

LAMENT, THE, by Burns, vi, 195-7

LAMENT FOR JAMES, EARL OF GLENCAIRN, vi, 400-2

LAMENT OF MARY QUEEN OF SCOTS, vi, 396-7

LAMENT, BURLESQUE, FOR WILLIAM CREECH, vi, 267-9

Lamentone, Il, xxxi, 150-1, 152-3

Lamias, in story of WILD SWANS, xvii, 277

Lampedo, queen of Amazons, xxxiii, 327

Lampetie, the nymph, xxii, 165, 171

Lampon, the diviner, xii, 40

Lampus, steed of the sun, xxii, 316

Lancaster, in EDWARD THE SECOND, his opposition to Gaveston, xlvi, 9-12, 13-16; in exiling of Gaveston, 16-18; consents to his return, 22-6; on Gaveston's return, 31-4; quarrel with king, 35-8; in attack on Tynemouth, 40-2; at capture of Gaveston, 43-4; in battle, 53; capture and death, 54-5

Lancaster, Capt., explanation of story of, xxix, 106-7

Lancaster, Duke of, in Tyler's Rebellion, xxxv, 67

Lancelet, simplicity of the, xi, 131

Lancelot, Sir, the best knight next to Galahad, xxxv, 111; Bors and, 213; at castle of the Grail, 199-203; at chapel of the dead man, 147-9; Chaucer on story of, xl, 45; departure on quest of Grail, xxxv, 114, 115-6; Ector's vision of, 157, 161; at the forest chapel, 129; Galahad's father, 109-10, 115, 152; Galahad and, 106, 128-9, 198-9; Gawaine on, 156; Guinevere and, xiv, 92; xx, 24 note 4, 352 note 2; xxxv, 132-3; xlii, 1185-8, 1191-3; at the hermitage, xxxv, 132-4; horse of, smitten, 155; loses horse and arms, 131; Lady of Shalott and, xlii, 969-70, 971; lineage of, xxxv, 117, 151; the marvelous sword and, 107; Mellyagraunce and, xlii, 1189-90; Nacien on, xxxv, 162; Renan on, xxxii, 163; returns home, xxxv, 204; robber knight and, 150-1; the Siege Perilous and, 107; sorrow of, 131-2; sword of, xxxix, 21; at the tourney, xxxv, 112; vision of, 150-2; white knights and, 153-5

Land, building of the, xxx, 239-46; elevation and subsidence of (see Elevation, Subsidence); final source of all capital, x, 221-2; has existed in all ages, xxxviii, 401; improvements in, constitute fixed capital, x, 219; Lowell on ownership of, xxviii, 469; made of river silt, xxxiii, 9, 11, 12; materials of, xxx, 328-35; price of; price of, dependent on rate of interest, x, 285-6; price of, and usury, iii, 102, 103-4; produce of, source of capital, x, 221; as property, effect on wages, 67; rent of (see Rent); returns of, greater than labor, x, 150; Rousseau on property in, xxxiv, 198; Ruskin on ownership of, xxviii, 132; taxes on, proportioned to produce, x,

486-8; proportioned to rent, 479-486; taxes on transfer of, 505-8

LAND O' THE LEAL, xli, 560

Landas, John of, at Poitiers, xxxv, 37, 39, 46, 47, 48

Landenberg, Berenger von, xxvi, 396 note 6; Henry of Halden and, 398; flight of, 476

Landi, Antonio, xxxi, 352-3, 361

Landi, Pierro di Giovanni, xxxi, 32, 84, 87, 171

Landino, on poets, xxvii, 51

Landlord, in MINNA VON BARNHELM, xxvi, 299-303, 315-21, 321-3, 324, 330-3, 365

Landlords, interest of, x, 208

Landor, Walter Savage, Emerson on, v, 317-8; poems by, xli, 898-05

Landresy, Francis I at, xxxviii, 17

Landscape Gardens, poetic sentiment in, xxviii, 377

Lane, Edw. William, translator of ARA-BIAN NIGHTS, xvi, 4

Lane-Poole, Stanley, reviser of ARABIAN NIGHTS, xvi, 4

Lane, Ralph, governor of Virginia, xxxiii, 257-8

Lang, A., translator of Homer, xxii; LINES ON THE ODYSSEY by, 7; SONNET ON HOMER, 335

Langland, Bishop of Lincoln, xxxvi, 102

Langley, Samuel Pierpont, on heat from the moon, xxx, 259-60; on radiant heat, 260

Langobards, Tacitus on the, xxxiii, 115

Language, anomalies and absurdities of, xxxix, 183; Augustine, St., on acquisi-tion of, vii, 11-12; command of, its importance, xxviii, 278-9; custom and, xxxix, 169 note; Emerson on, v, 171; Hobbes on, xxxiv, 322-30; Johnson on uses of, xxxix, 186; a means, not an end, iii, 234; natural, xxxix, 215-6; Pascal on, xlviii, 313 (912); Pascal's rules of, 16-17, 21-3; of the passions, xxxiv, 345; poets the authors of, xxvii, 331-2; race test, xxviii, 235-45, 252-72; Rousseau on origin of, xxxiv, 179-185, 201, 203; Shelley on use of familiar, xviii, 278; Stevenson on, xxviii, 278-80; superiority of, xxvii, 333; in va-rious civilizations, xxxix, 419, 420-1 (see also Words)

LANGUAGE, AND RACE, xxviii, 227-73

Languages, classification of, xi, 440; con-tinual change of, xxxix, 201-4; dead, study of, v, 256-7; Descartes on study of ancient, xxxiv, 7; Franklin on study of, i, 95-6; Hugo on change in, xxxix, 374-5; Huxley on study of, xxviii, 220-1; Locke on study of, xxxvii, 136-53, 162-3, 167-9, 179-80; Milton on study of, iii, 236-7; Montaigne on study of, xxxii, 65-6; Pascal on, xlviii, 21 (45); Penn on teaching, i, 322-3; Taine on, xxxix, 411

Langue d'oc and d'oil, xxviii, 75

Languet, Hubert, and Philip Sidney, xxvii, 3

Lanier, Sidney, poems by, xlii, 1390-1401

Lankester, E. Ray, on homogeneity, xi, 456-7; on longevity, 210

Lannoy, reference to, xlvii, 804

Lano, Dante on, xx, 56 and note 3

Laocoön, death of, xiii, 107; statue of, xxxi, 318; the Trojan horse and, xiii, 101-2

Laodamas, in the ODYSSEY, xxii, 94, 102, 103, 108

Laodamia, and Evadne, xiii, 222

LAODAMIA, xli, 662-7; Emerson on, v, 122

Laodiceans, Bacon on, iii, 12

Laomedon, the Orchomenian, xii, 195; Emerson on, v, 276

LAP-DOG, EPITAPH ON A, vi, 466

LAPDOG AND ASS, fable of, xvii, 15

Laplace, on tides, xxx, 284, 288

LAPRAIK, J., EPISTLES TO, vi, 79-86, 102-4

Lares, Hobbes on, xxxiv, 380

Largeness (see Vastness)

Largus, Julius, ix, 396

Laris, and Thymbrus, xiii, 335

Lark, Milton on the, iv, 31, 379

La Rochefoucauld, Sainte-Beuve on, xxxii, 130

Lartius, Titus, xii, 153

Las Vargas, counsellor of Philip II, xix, 290

LASCELLES, CAPTAIN, LINES ON, vi, 487

LASS O' BALLOCHMYLE, vi, 220-1

LASS OF CESSNOCK BANKS, vi, 28-30

LASS OF ECCLEFECHAN, vi, 516

LASS THAT MADE THE BED TO ME, vi, 527-9

LASS WI' A TOCHER, vi, 548

LASSIE WI' THE LINT-WHITE LOCKS, vi, 505-6

LAST CONQUEROR, THE, xl, 350

LAST DUCHESS, THE, xlii, 1074-5

LAST INVOCATION, THE, xlii, 1422

Last Judgment, à Celano on, xlv, 551-3; Browne on the, iii, 296-8; Bunyan on, xv, 39, 83-4; Dante on kings at, xx, 368-9; Emerson on doctrine of, v, 85-6; Kempis on the, vii, 232-3, 306-7; location of, belief concerning, xx, 40 note 1; Milton on the, iv, 12, 143-4, 353; Mohammed on, xlv, 880, 881-2, 886-97, 900-1, 912

Last Leaf, The, xlii, 1366-8

Last Lines, xlii, 1110-11

Last Ride Together, The, xlii, 1070-3

Last Rose of Summer, xli, 818

Last Supper, xliv, 410-11 (14-37); Pascal on, xlviii, 180 (554)

Last Time I Came o'er the Moor, vi, 461-2

Last Wish, The, xlii, 1119

Last Word, The, xlii, 1139-40

Latagus, death of, xiii, 345

Lateran, the, given to Sylvester, xx, 80 note 10

Latimer, and Henry VIII, v, 376

Latin, Augustine, St., on study of, vii, 15-18; Carlyle on, xxv, 365; Emerson on study of, v, 257; Franklin on study of, i, 95-6; Huxley on study of, xxviii, 213-20; Locke on study of, xxxvii, 68, 77, 127, 136-53, 157, 162-3, 167-9; Mill on study of, xxv, 24; Milton on way to study, iii, 239-41; Montaigne on study of, xxxii, 65-6; Penn on study of, i, 323 (15); wrong way to study, iii, 236-7

Latin Classics, xxxii, 122

Latin Hymns, xlv, 546-56

Latin Literature, More on, xxxvi, 205; Taine on, xxxix, 436

Latin Philosophers, More on, xxxvi, 137

Latini, Brunetto, Arnold on, xxviii, 75; in Dante's Hell, xx, 20

Latinus, in the Æneid, xiii, 241-3, 245-8, 359, 366-8, 390-1, 395-7; in Dante's Limbo, xx, 20; Dryden on, xiii, 20-1

Latinus, Titus, dream of, xii, 169

Latitudinarian, Penn's, i, 393

Latmian Shepherd, Endymion called, xl, 244

Latona, and the frogs, iv, 80; references to, xiii, 91; xx, 229

Laud, and George Herbert, xv, 394; and the Star Chamber, iii, 184

Laudatory Personalities, Bentham on, xxvii, 235-6

Lauderdale, Earl of, and Burke, xxiv, 380; translator of Virgil, xiii, 66-7

Laughter, Ecclesiastes on, xliv, 336 (2); Epictetus on, ii, 175 (165); Hobbes on, xxxiv, 342

Launcelot (see Lancelot)

Laurence, the martyr, vii, 248 (2); Dante on, xx, 299 and note 10

Laurentia, honors of, ix, 179

Laurentius, Andreas, xxxviii, 73; on the heart, 75

Lausus, in the Æneid, xiii, 261, 336, 346, 349-50

Lautizio, xxxi, 47, 259

Laval, M. de, xxxviii, 13, 15; xlviii, 347 note 2

Laval, Pyrard de, on atolls, xxix, 469

Lavinia, in the Æneid, xiii, 241, 248, 391; in Dante's Limbo, xx, 20

Law(s), Bentham on opposition to reform of, xxvii, 225-51; correction the purpose of, ii, 150 (88); defined in Hindoo Scriptures, v, 284; Goethe on human, xix, 80; highest, is welfare of people, iii, 133; Hume on foundation of, xxxvii, 365; inadequacy of, and revenge, iii, 15; the intention of lawgiver is the, xliii, 314; Jones, Sir William, on, xli, 579; language of the, how corrupted, x, 452; Locke on study of, xxxvii, 158; Luther on, xxxvi, 323-4; Machiavelli on good, 40; Marlowe on study of, xix, 207, 209; Milton on study of, iii, 242; Montaigne on multiplicity of, xlviii, 390-1; More on, xxxvi, 212-13; More on antiquated, 160, 163; natural, superior to statutes, v, 242, 246; necessity of, to control officials, xxvii, 235; needless where not eluded, xxxiv, 222; numerous, effect of, xxxv, 315; Pascal on, xlviii, 104-5, 113 (325-6), 205-6; Pliny on spirit and letter of, ix, 252, 272; Pope on origin of, xl, 429; Raleigh on, 206; Rousseau on origin of, xxxiv, 211-15; Ruskin on, xxviii, 133; Schiller on substitution of, for force, xxxii, 214-18; Smith on, and men, xxvii, 236-7; Socrates on obedience to, ii, 38-41; Winthrop on penal, xliii, 91-105 (see also Government Intervention)

Law, John Burke on, xxiv, 371

Lawes, Mr. H., To, on His Airs, iv, 81

Lawgivers, great, iii, 130

Lawmakers, Winthrop on, xliii, 98

Lawrence, St., on the Church, xxxvi, 255-6

LAWRENCE, TO MR., iv, 84

Lawsuits, Confucius on, xliv, 39 (13); St. Paul on, xlv, 497 (1-7)

Lawyer, Chaucer's, xl, 19-20

Lawyers, excluded from Utopia, xxxvi, 212; Franklin on, i, 15; Jesus on, xliv, 386 (45-52); judges and, iii, 130-2; Milton on mercenary, 250; remuneration of (see Professions); Sidney on, xxvii, 16

Laxness, Confucius on, xliv, 18 (1)

Lay, nautical term, xxiii, 28 note

LAY THY LOOF IN MINE, LASS, vi, 550

Lazarus, xliv, 397 (20-5); Browne on, iii, 273; Dives and, xv, 35; the Jews and, vii, 298 (2); Pascal on, xlviii, 218-19 (658), 264-5 (754)

Laziness, Locke on, xxxvii, 107-10, 177-8

Lazo, Darwin on the, xxix, 52

Lazzaretto, in Milan plague, xxi, 578-81

Lead Pyrophorus, xxx, 56 note; combustion of, 161, 168-9; how made, 168 note

Lead-trees, xxx, 81 note

LEADER, THE LOST, xlii, 1067-8

Leaders, developed by disaster, xix, 374; of sedition, iii, 41

Leagues, More on, xxxvi, 214-15

Leah, type of active life, xx, 256 note 4

Leander, reference to, xx, 260

Leandra, in the goatherd's story, xiv, 500-4

LEAR, KING, TRAGEDY OF, xlvi, 215-317; editorial remarks on, 214; Ruskin on, xxviii, 137; Shelley on, xviii, 276, 358; stage representations of, xxvii, 310-11

Lear, in KING LEAR, divides kingdom between daughters, xlvi, 216-18; disowns Cordelia, 218-19; resigns power, 219; quarrel with Kent, 219-20; with France and Burgundy, 221-3; coldly treated by Goneril, 229-30, 232; with Kent in disguise, 230-1; with Oswald, 232-3; and the Fool, 233-5; scene with Goneril, 235-9; departure for Gloucester, 240-1; arrival at Gloucester's, 252-4; with Gloucester, 254-5; with Regan and Cornwall, 255-7; refused hospitality by both daughters, 258-61; goes out into storm, 262-3; in the storm, 264-6; at Edgar's hovel, 267-72; his madness, 274-6; warned to fly, 276; conveyed to Dover, 277; refuses

to see Cordelia, 288; in fields near Dover, mad, 294-7; taken by Cordelia's messengers, 297; awakening from sleep, with Cordelia, 301-2; taken prisoner, 306-7; ordered to be killed by Edmund, 315; with body of Cordelia, 315-6; with Kent, 316; death, 316-7

Lear, Bagehot on character of, xxviii, 192; editorial remarks on character of, xlvi, 214

Learchus, Dante on, xx, 123

Learning, and actions, xxxii, 59-60; arms compared with, xiv, 374-9; Confucius on, xliv, 5 (1), 6 (14), 26 (13), 48 (25); end of, iii, 236; four ages of, 140; Hume on, xxxvii, 293-4; Locke on, 72, 77-8, 127-52; Montaigne on, xxxii, 34; Sidney on object of, xxvii, 13-14; Tzu-hsia on, xliv, 5 (7), 64 (5, 6); (see also Knowledge)

Leaves of Grass, PREFACE TO, xxxix, 388-409; remarks on, 3

Leblanc, Baptiste, xlii, 1319

Leblanc, René, the notary in EVANGELINE, xlii, 1307-9, 1334

Lechartier, M., xxxviii, 305-6 notes

Lechery, the sin, in FAUSTUS, xix, 228

Lechery, Mr., in PILGRIM'S PROGRESS, xv, 188

Leda, mother of Castor and Pollux, xx, 402 note 14; in Homer's Hades, xxii, 152; and Jove, xl, 230

Lee, E., translator of Sainte-Beuve, xxxii, 103

Lee, Fitzhugh, at Gettysburg, xliii, 343

Lee, Richard Henry, xliii, 150 note

Lee, Gen. Robert E., FAREWELL TO HIS ARMY, xliii, 423; at Gettysburg, 379, 400; terms of surrender at Appomattox, 421-2

LEEZIE LINDSAY, vi, 542

Lé fri flaith, xlix, 207, 231, 244, 247

Legacy-taxes, x, 506, 508-9

Legal Language, corruption of, x, 452

Legal Penalties, Winthrop on, xliii, 90-100, 101-2, 104-5

Legal Pleading, Pliny on, ix, 204-9, 226-7

Legal Tender, in England, x, 43; in United States, xliii, 186 (10)

Legal Technicalities, More on, xxxvi, 213

Legality, Mr., in PILGRIM'S PROGRESS, xv, 23, 27

Legislation, Burke on methods of, xxiv, 302-3; does not make the state, v, 239-40; by experience and fiat, xxxiv, 13;

Lowell on, xxviii, 441; in Utopia, xxxvi, 177-8

Legislative Commissions, Mill on, xxv, 163-4

Legislative Powers, in United States, xliii, 180-6

Legislators, Burke on qualities of, xxiv, 301-2; fame of, compared with poets, xxvii, 333

Legouvé, M., xxxix, 371

Leibnitz, Hazlitt on, xxvii, 277; Hobbes and, xxxiv, 308; supposed inventor of fluxions, 126; on theory of gravitation, xi, 498

Leicester, in EDWARD II, xlvi, 66-7, 68-73

Leicester, Earl of, on Chaucer, xxxix, 168, 169

Leif the Lucky, his baptism, xliii, 5; his expedition of discovery, 8-11; Gudrid, and, 13-14; his house in Vinland, 14, 17; Freydis and, 19

Leiodes, and the bow of Ulysses, xxii, 288; death of, 304

Leisure, Milton on, iv, 35; Penn on, employment of, i, 328; Rufus on, ii, 118 (v)

Lela Zoraida, xiv, 373

Leland, on copper mines, xxxv, 323; on England, 231, 233

Lelius, and Blosius, xxxii, 79

Lemnos, crime of, viii, 103

Lemovians, Tacitus on the, xxxiii, 117

Lemur, Darwin on the flying, xi, 176-7

Lemures, mentioned, iv, 13 (21)

Lending, Penn on, i, 327 (47)

Length, less striking than depth, xxiv, 61

Lennox, in MACBETH, xlvi, in camp with Duncan, 323; at Macbeth's, 344-5, 346; at the banquet, 357-8, 361; conversation with lord, 363-5; with Macbeth, 369-70; in war against Macbeth, 383-4

LENORE, by Poe, xlii, 1224-5

Lent, Calvin on meat in, xxxix, 36; Herbert on, xv, 403

Lentulus Spinther, the consul, consulship of, xii, 246; letter to, ix, 118; property of, 150; recall of, 97, 99

Lentulus Sura, the consul, Antony and, xii, 322, 326; Cæsar and, 289, 290; in Catiline conspiracy, 231-3, 269; Cicero on death of, ix, 159; executed, xii, 235, 243

Leo X, Pope, xxvii, 390; Cellini and, xxxi, 13; Luther to, xxxvi, 336-44; Machiavelli on, 40

Leo, Valerius, and Cæsar, xii, 278

Leocritus, in the ODYSSEY, xxii, 27, 303

Leolin, imprisonment of, xxxii, 145

Leoline, Sir, (see CHRISTABEL)

Leon, St., on God, xlviii, 352

Leon of Salamis, ii, 21; Socrates and, 251-2 (66)

Leonardo da Vinci (see Vinci)

Leonela, in story of CURIOUS-IMPERTI-NENT, xiv, 325-45, 351-3

Leoni, Leone, xxxi, 246 note 3

Leosthenes, xii, 213

Leotychides, son of Alcibiades, xii, 128

Lepanto, battle of, iii, 79; Cervantes at, xiv, 3; Cervantes on, 385-6

Lepidotos, Herodotus on the, xxxiii, 39

Lepidus, Catius, letter to, ix, 250-1

Lepidus, Marcus Æmilius, xii, 315, 318; Africa allotted to, 344; Antony and, 334-5; Brutus and, 331; Cicero on, ix, 67, 177, 179, 180; consul with Cæsar, xii, 329; death of, xxxii, 13; left in Rome by Cæsar, xii, 326; put out of government, 364-5; in the triumvirate, 257, 335-6

Lerna, Lake, viii, 191 note 40

Leroux, Paul, his article on God, v, 278

Lessing, Gotthold Ephraim, and Burke, xxiv, 28; EDUCATION OF THE HUMAN RACE, xxxii, 183-206; life and works, xxvi, 298; MINNA VON BARNHELM, 299-375; Taine on, xxxix, 414

LESSON, A, xli, 614-15

LET ME IN THIS AE NIGHT, vi, 517

LET THERE BE LIGHT, xlv, 572

LET US DRINK AND BE MERRY, xl, 364-5

Lethe, Dante on, xx, 61, 261; Milton on, iv, 123-4

Létiche, story of, xlii, 1307

Leto, in Egyptian mythology, xxxiii, 78-9; oracle of, xxxiii, 42, 78; Tityos and, xxii, 159; worshipped in Egypt, xxxiii, 34

Letters, Hobbes on invention of, xxxiv, 322; invented by Prometheus, viii, 183

Letters, men of, why so called, xxviii, 102

Letters, Bacon on business, iii, 117; Goethe on, xxxix, 253; Locke on writing of, xxxvii, 161; Pliny on unsatisfactoriness of, ix, 273; Stevenson on, xxviii, 280

LETTERS OF CICERO, ix, 81-181; remarks on, 7, 79-80

LETTERS OF PLINY, ix, 183-416; remarks on, 185-6

LETTERS ON ÆSTHETIC EDUCATION, Schiller, xxxii, 207-295

LETTERS ON THE ENGLISH, Voltaire's, xxxiv, 65-159

LETTY'S GLOBE, xli, 921

Leucaspis, in Hades, xiii, 218

Leucippus, school of, iii, 42

Leucothea, Milton on, iv, 68, 322; in the ODYSSEY, xxii, 76

Leuthold, in WILLIAM TELL, xxvi, 437-40, 447, 449

Leuwenhoek, Voltaire on, xxxiv, 126

LEVANA AND OUR LADIES OF SORROW, xxvii, DeQuincey, 319-25

Level, Lyell on changes of, xxxviii, 406-9, 411-12 (see also Elevation, Subsidence)

Leveridge, Mr., xliii, 139

Levers, velocity and power in, xxx, 183-4

LEVET, DR. ROBERT, ON THE DEATH OF, xli, 503-4

Levi, and Jesus, xliv, 367 (27-9)

Leviathan, in BOOK OF JOB, xliv, 138-40 (1-34); Job's description of, Burke on, xxiv, 57; old Irish idea of, xlix, 213; references to, iv, 93, 237; xv, 133, 134; xliv, 235 (14), 274 (26)

LEVIATHAN, FIRST PART OF, Hobbes's, xxxiv, 307-417

Levune, in EDWARD THE SECOND, xlvi, 49, 55, 60

Lexicographers, Johnson on, xxxix, 182

Lexington, battle of, xliii, 156; Longfellow on battle of, xlii, 1298

LEWARS, JESSIE, COMPLIMENTARY VERSICLES TO, vi, 550

LEWARS, JESSY, INSCRIPTION TO, vi, 552

Lewes, G. H., on Egyptian races, xi, 210

LEY, LADY MARGARET, TO THE, iv, 79

Li, son of Confucius, xliv, 33 (7) and note 5

Liandolo, Loderingo di, xx, 96 note 4

Lianour, Duke, xxxv, 126

Liar, Mr., in PILGRIM'S PROGRESS, xv, 100

Liars, fable on, xvii, 28

LIBATION-BEARERS, Æschylus', viii, 76-121; Voltaire on, xxxix, 364

LIBELLER'S SELF-REPROOF, vi, 276

Libels, in Athens, iii, 193-4; in Rome, 195; Franklin on, i, 92-3

Liberality, in children, xxxvii, 91, 92; Hobbes on, xxxiv, 341, 371; Penn on, i, 327; of princes, xxxvi, 52-4; proverb on, xvi, 202

Liberators, great, iii, 130

LIBERTIES, THE BODY OF, xliii, 66-84

Liberty, art and, xxxii, 210-12; Burke on, xxiv, 148-9, 197-200, 375-6; Byron on, xli, 811; contentment and, 522; duty of respecting others, xxxii, 340; Emerson on, v, 245-6, 249; extreme ideas of, iii, 21; Goldsmith on ills of, xli, 529-30; government and, xliii, 201-2, 240; Hamilton on jealousy of, 201; history of doctrine of, xxv, 158; Hume on religious, xxxvii, 405; inequality not inconsistent with, iv, 200; intellectual growth and, xxviii, 360; Kempis on, vii, 227 (2), 286, 296 (1); of labor, Smith on, x, 124; licence and, iv, 80; love of, in children, xxxvii, 57-8, 85, 110-11; Lovelace on, xl, 355-6; Milton on, iii, 189, 221-7; iv, 4, 115, 344; natural, Hobbes on, xxxiv, 391-2; natural, Smith's theory of, x, 3, 251-2; necessity and, Hume on, xxxvii, 351-70; Pascal on excessive, xlviii, 125 (379); philosophy and, xxxvii, 393, 405; "pious editor's" creed of, xlii, 1373-6; refinement and, xxxii, 236-7, 254; Rousseau on love of, xxxiv, 215-16; Rousseau on renunciation of, 217-18; Schiller on, xxxii, 264-5; Smith on, x, 445-6; social, xxxiv, 393-4, 408-9; of speech and press in U. S., xliii, 194 (1); standing armies and, x, 448-9; Tennyson on, xlii, 998; on trial in America, xliii, 227-8; Vane, Sir Henry, on, 120-1, 122-3; Ward, Nathaniel, on, 66; Washington on love of, 235-6; of the will (see Free Will); Whitman on, xxxix, 399-401; Woolman on, i, 203; works on, xxv, 5

LIBERTY, ESSAY ON, Mill's, xxv, 195-312; remarks on, 155-8

LIBERTY, CHRISTIAN, Luther on, xxxvi, 344-78

Liberty of the Press, Franklin on, i, 92-3; James Mill on, xxv, 69; John Stuart Mill on, 210-49; Milton on (see AREOPAGITICA); in U. S., xliii, 194 (1)

Libicocco, the demon, xx, 88, 91

Libo, and Antony, xii, 327

Libra, the constellation, referred to, xx, 149 note 2

Libraries, Hunt on, xxvii, 294; invention of, xxviii, 56; Ruskin on public, 131; subscription, proposed by Franklin, i, 67

Libya, Herodotus on, xxxiii, 13-15, 21-2

Licences, Smith on, x, 501-2

Lichas, in the Æneid, xiii, 332

Lichas, servant of Alcides, iv, 122

Licinianus, Valerius, Pliny on, ix, 253-5

Licinus, Largius, and professional applauders, ix, 220-1

Lidgate, Dan John, xxxix, 7

Lie, The, xl, 204-6

Liebig, on fermentation, xxxviii, 345-57

Liemer, Harrison on the, xxxv, 350

Lies, cross, iii, 128; some, never penned, vi, 74; Stevenson on, xxviii, 277, 282 (see also Falsehood)

Life, advancement in, Ruskin on, xxviii, 94, 127-8; Arabian proverb on, xvi, 16; Bacon on monotony of, iii, 10; beginning of, on the earth, xi, 345-6; the best teacher, xxviii, 339; bridge of, in Mirza, xxvii, 74-6; Browne on length of, iii, 293 (42), 294 (43); Buddha on, xlv, 578, 658, 694-5; Burke on pleasure in idea of, xxiv, 35, 36; Burns on, vi, 144-5, 169-70, 195, 308, 316, 475, 547; Carlyle on, xxv, 320-2; Cicero on, ix, 74-6; Cicero on various ages of, 56-8; Cory on, xlii, 1114; Dante on, xx, 5 note 1; Darwin's tree of, xi, 137; Dryden's lines on, xxxiv, 134; Ecclesiastes on vanity of, xliv, 335-8, 341 (15-17), 341 (3-6); Emerson on, v, 26, 29, 63, 71-2; Epictetus on, ii, 141 (68), 162 (125), 174 (159), 181 (189), 183 (1), 184 (9), 185 (20); Goethe on false study of, xix, 79; Gray on, xl, 453; Greek dramatists on, viii, 293, 311, 411; Harvey on cause of, xxxviii, 85, 86, 102; Herrick on, xl, 337, 338, 340; Hindu conception of, xlv, 791, 849, 851; Job on, xliv, 92; Jonson on worth of, xl, 291; Keats's seasons of, xli, 896-7; Kempis on, vii, 283 (3), 284 (4), 313-14; Kempis on the inward, 238-40; Longfellow on, xlii, 1278, 1288-9; Lowell on, 1381; Marcus Aurelius on, ii, 204 (17), 209 (10), 212 (3), 221 (50), 229 (24), 231 (33), 234 (16), 241 (46), 248 (40), 251 (61), 257 (24), 270 (30), 271 (36), 272 (37), 300 (31); Mill on, xxv, 35; Milton on, iv, 81, 332-3; Montaigne on, xxxii, 23, 24, 26, 27; not the result of chance, xxxiv, 252-3; Omar Khayyam on, xli, 944, 945, 952, 953; Pascal on, xlviii, 61 (156), 71, 79 (213), 127 (386);

Penn on, i, 381; Plato on, ii, 249 (48); Pliny on, ix, 237; Poe on, xlii, 1240-1; Pope on, xl, 407; preservation of, as a duty, xxxii, 309-10; Psalm on vanity of, xliv, 190-1; Pythagoras on, xxxii, 46; Rossetti, C. G., on, xlii, 1182; Scott on, xli, 748; Shakespeare on, xlvi, 144, 388; Shelley on, xli, 869; Socrates on value of, ii, 37; Spencer on principle of, xi, 304-5; struggle for (see Struggle for Existence); Thackeray on, xlii, 1059; universal interest in, xix, 15; Webster on, xlvii, 850; without air (see Anærobian Life); without light, xxxviii, 363 (see also Organic Beings)

Life, by Bacon, xl, 348-9

Life, by Barbauld, xli, 555

Life, by Drummond, xl, 327

Life, A Psalm of, xlii, 1264-5

Life, The River of, xli, 775

Life, The Stream of, xlii, 1120

Life, What Is Our, xl, 207

Life is a Dream, Calderon's, xxvi, 7-74; remarks on, 6

Ligarius, Quintus, trial of, xii, 251

Ligatures, Harvey on, xxxviii, 110-15; Lister on, 266-7

Ligea, reference to, iv, 68

Liger, in the Æneid, xiii, 312, 341-2

Light, in architecture, xiv, 68-9; Berkeley on, xxxvii, 205-6; composition of white, xxx, 261-2; Descartes on, xxxiv, 36, 37; diffraction of, xxx, 268; effects of various waves of, 260-1; frequency of vibration, 270; from flame, its cause, 107-11, 157; heat from, 260; intermitting, effects of, xxiv, 71; invisible, xxx, 258; knowledge of, 260; Milton on, iv, 135-6; Newton's discoveries in, xxxiv, 121-4; Noël's definition of, xlviii, 426 note; Pascal on, 123 (368); photographer's or actinic, xxx, 260; polarization of, 264-6; produced by chemical affinity, 78; refraction of, Faraday on, 32-6; sublimity of, xxiv, 67-8; velocity of, xxx, 270; vibrations of, 256-8, 263; wave lengths of, 267-70

Light, The Wave Theory of, xxx, 251-73

Light Brigade, Charge of the, xlii, 1005-7

Light of Other Days, xli, 816-17

Light of Stars, The, xlii, 1265-6

Light Shining Out of Darkness, xlv, 562

Lightborn, in EDWARD THE SECOND, xlvi, 79-80, 83-6

Lighthouses, Franklin on, i, 157-8

Light-mind, Mrs., in PILGRIM'S PROGRESS, xv, 187-8

Lightning, Burke on grandeur of, xxiv, 67; Darwin on effects of, xxix, 69; Franklin on, i, 146-8; tubes formed by, xxix, 67-9

Lightning Legion (see Thundering)

Like, buys like, v, 239; cures like, iv, 412

LIKE AS THE CULVER, xl, 251-2

Likeness, of all things, v, 230; attracts likeness, ii, 267 (9); ix, 26-7; in unlikeness, xxxix, 286

Lilies, Jesus on the, xliv, 388 (27)

LILIES OF QUEENS' GARDENS, xxviii, 135-62

Lilinau, story of, xlii, 1331

Lilith, Adam's wife, xix, 178-9

Liliuokalani, Queen, xliii, 437 note

Lilla, Hafiz on, v, 216

Lilly, Johnson on, xxxix, 225

Lima, Darwin on, xxix, 371-2

Limbo, Dante's, xx, 16-20; Milton's, iv, 147-8; spirits in, xx, 10 note 3

Limbs, and jaws, related, xi, 148

Lime Light, Faraday on, xxx, 108

Limestone, composition of, xxx, 329

Lime-water, composition of, xxx, 151

Limitations, Emerson on, v, 152

Linacer, Johnson on, xxxix, 225

LINCOLN, ABRAHAM, by Lowell, xxviii, 429-50

Lincoln, Abraham, absence of demagogism, xxviii, 449; his Americanism, 439; AMNESTY PROCLAMATIONS, xliii, 416-19; difficulties of, xxviii, 434-6; EMANCIPATION PROCLAMATION, xliii, 323-5; FIRST INAUGURAL ADDRESS, 313-22; GETTYSBURG ADDRESS, 415; Henry IV compared with, xxviii, 437-8; LETTER TO MRS. BIXBY, xliii, 420; Lowell's lines on, xlii, 1383-4; not a ready-made ruler, xxviii, 439-40; power and fame at death, 450; SECOND INAUGURAL ADDRESS, xliii, 424-5; self-unconsciousness, xxviii, 449; slavery problem and, 442-7 (see also EMANCIPATION PROCLAMATION); statesmanlike qualities of, 433; tentative policy, 436-7, 440-1; trustfulness in the people, 448-9; Whitman on death of, xlii, 1412

LINCOLN, DEATH OF, by Bryant, xlii, 1223-4

Lincoln, Earl of (see Lacy, Sir Hugh)

Lindsay, Lady Anne, AULD ROBIN GRAY, xli, 557-8

Lindsay, Sir James, and Bishop of Durham, xxxv, 95-6; and Matthew Redman, 94-5, 97; at Otterburn, 92

Lindsey, Earl of, Dryden on, xviii, 11

Lineage, Don Quixote's two manners of, xiv, 173-4

Ling, Duke of Wei, xliv, 47 (20), 50 (1)

Lingende, on miracles, xlviii, 295 (846)

Linnæus, on American plants, xxviii, 407; Emerson on, v, 18; on genus, xi, 433; on increase of plants, 14; mistake of, 443

LINNET, THE GREEN, xli, 642-3

Linos, song of, xxxiii, 41

Linus, in Dante's Limbo, xx, 20; Sidney on, xxvii, 6

Lion, flesh of the, xxix, 122

LION AND FOUR OXEN, fable of, xvii, 31

LION AND FOX, fable of, xvii, 25

LION AND MOUSE, fable of, xvii, 15-16

LION AND STATUE, fable of, xvii, 25

LION, FOX, AND OTHER BEASTS, fable of, xvii, 40-1

LION IN LOVE, fable of, xvii, 40

LION, THE SICK, xvii, 14-15

LION'S SHARE, THE, fable of, xvii, 12

Lion-ant, of Australia, xxix, 445 note

Lionel, Sir, at the Abbey, xxxv, 106; at court, 107; in captivity, 167; believed to be dead, 169; his character, 173; attempts to slay Sir Bors, 175; combat with Sir Colgrevance, 175-6; combat with Bors prevented by miracle, 177-8; his return home, 204

Lippi, Filippino, xxxi, 24 note 3

Lippi, Francesco, and Cellini, xxxi, 24, 28

Lipsius, on criticism, xxxix, 248; Montaigne on, xxxii, 32

Liquefaction, cold caused by, xxx, 39

Liquids, cohesion of, xxx, 40-1

Liquor Trade, Mill on regulation of, xxv, 297-8

Liquors, duties on, x, 364

Liris, death of, xiii, 380

Listening, the art of, ii, 147 (81)

Lister, Joseph, ON ANTISEPTIC PRINCIPLE, xxxviii, 257-67; life and work, 256; Pasteur on, 370

Lister, William, in Tyler's Rebellion, xxxv, 73-4

Listlessness, Locke on, xxxvii, 107-10, 177

LITERARY AND PHILOSOPHICAL ESSAYS, xxxii

Literature, Arnold on good, xxviii, 90; Carlyle on, xxv, 441, 447; Carlyle on modern, 338-40; classical and romantic, xxxix, 346; criticism of manners, morals, and religion in, xxvii, 219-21; effeminacy of our, v, 51; Emerson on, 154-5; Huxley on ancient, xxviii, 213-20; Ruskin on encouragement of, 130; Seneca on, xlviii, 121 note 6; for subsistence, remarks on, xxv, 55; Taine on study of, xxxix, 410-17, 435-6; Taine on, as transcript of its times, 410-17, 435-6; tested by time, 208-9; Thoreau on nature in, xxviii, 414; Whitman on simplicity in, xxxix, 396-7; why so called, xxviii, 102

Litigation, enemy of right and wrong, vi, 292

LITTLE BRIAR-ROSE, story of, xvii, 137-40

Little-Faith, in PILGRIM'S PROGRESS, xv, 128-35

LITTLE IDA'S FLOWERS, xvii, 334-41

Little John, in ROBYN HODE, in adventure with sorrowful knight, xl, 129, 130-2, 133-4, 136, 138, 139; with sheriff of Nottingham, 147-53; in adventure with monks, 154-8, 160; at archery contest, 165-6; saved by Robyn Hode, 167; returns to green wood, 170, 179; with Robyn at court, 183

LITTLE RED CAP, xvii, 109-13

Little Round Top, at Gettysburg, xliii, 335

LITTLE SEA-MAID, THE, xvii, 238-59

LITTLE SNOW-WHITE, xvii, 146-54

Littleness, as cause of beauty, xxiv, 92-3, 125-7; infinite, is sublime, 62

Littlewit, John, xxxix, 161

Liu-hsia Hui, xliv, 52 note, 61 (2), 63 (8)

Live-loose, Mr., in PILGRIM'S PROGRESS, xv, 100

Liver, Harvey on the, xxxviii, 96-7, 127

Livermore, Thomas L., xliii, 326 headnote

Livia, Augustus and, iii, 50; the sons of, xii, 388; Tacitus on, iii, 17; Tiberius and, 141

LIVING TOO LONG, ON, xli, 905

Livingston, Robert R., in Louisiana Purchase, xliii, 250 note

Livre, French coin x, 31

Livy, citizen of Cadiz and, ix, 214-15; on

fall of the great, xxxix, 71 note; Macaulay on, xxvii, 394-5; Mill's delight in, xxv, 13; on prophecy of Pharsalia, xii, 303; Shelley on, xxvii, 335, 344; the Spaniard and, xxviii, 57

Liwarc'h Hên, Celtic bard, xxxii, 166

LIZ, by Buchanan, xlii, 1199

Lizards, of Galapagos Islands, xxix, 389-95; S. American, 104

Ljod, daughter of Hrimnir, xlix, 259-60

Llama, Darwin on the wild, xxix, 170-3; Francis Pretty on, xxxiii, 210

Lloyd, Captain, in Mauritius, xxix, 488

Loadstones, Faraday on, xxx, 65

Loans, bank, x, 243-6; in Scotland, 236-7; Shakespeare on, xlvi, 109; Smith on, x, 278-80; by states, 470-1

Lobineau, Dom, Saints of Brittany, xxxii, 173

Local Administration, abuses of, x, 456

Local Expenses, x, 465-7

LOCHINVAR, xli, 751-2

LOCK OF HAIR, TO A, xli, 740

LOCK THE DOOR, LARISTON, xli, 767-9

Locke, John, on arguments, xxxvii, 332 note; Berkeley and, 186; on darkness, xxiv, 114-15; Emerson on, v, 143, 436, 438; on general words, xxiv, 131; Hazlitt on, xxvii, 267-8; On Human Understanding, i, 17; Hume on, xxxvii, 291, 303 note; on innate ideas, 303; life and works, 3-4; on matter, 345 note; Mill on, xxv, 47; Mill's abstract of, 46; on money, x, 312; on pleasure and pain, xxiv, 32 note; on power, xxxvii, 338 note; on property, xxxiv, 205; THOUGHTS CONCERNING EDUCATION, xxxvii, 5-183; Unitarianism and, xxxiv, 84; Voltaire on, 102-8; on wit and judgment, xxiv, 17

Lockhart, Life of Scott, Carlyle on, xxv, 396-403

LOCKSLEY HALL, xlii, 979-86

Locrians, legislation of the, xxv, 222

Locrine, son of Brutus, iv, 66

Locusts, Darwin on, xxix, 333; Harrison on, xxxv, 348-9; the plague of, iv, 96; swarms of, blown by winds, xi, 391

Loderingo, (see Liandolo)

Lodge, Thomas, Poems by, xl, 214-17

Lodging, materials of, Smith on, x, 166-8, 178-9

Loe, Thomas, and William Penn, xxxiv, 74 note

Lofraso, Anthony, Cervantes on, xiv, 53

Logan, James, anecdote of, i, 109

Logan, John, BRAES OF YARROW, xli, 500-1

LOGAN, MAJOR, EPISTLE TO, vi, 245-8

LOGAN, MISS, TO, vi, 255

Logan, Sir W., on Canadian strata, xi, 345

LOGAN BRAES, vi, 462-3

Logic, Bacon on, xxxix, 125, 132-3, 134-5, 144, 145; Bacon on study of, iii, 122; Carlyle on, xxv, 323-4; Descartes on, xxxiv, 16-17; Goethe on, xix, 78-9; Hobbes on, xxxiv, 363; Hume on, xxxvii, 297; Kant on, xxxii, 299; Locke on study of, xxxvii, 138, 158-60; Marlowe on, xix, 206 and note 10; Mill on study of, xix, 206 and note 10; Mill on study of, xxv, 17-18; Mill's work in, 100-1, 113-14, 129-30, 138-41; Milton on study of, iii, 237, 243; Montaigne on, xxxii, 63; Pascal on, xlviii, 409-10

Logicians, Pascal on, xlviii, 129 (393)

LOGIE O' BUCHAN, xli, 571-2

Logris, realm of, xxxv, 183

Lokabyuhas, xlv, 603

Loki, in STORY OF VOLSUNGS AND NIBLUNGS, xlix, 285, 286

Lombardi, commentator of Dante, xx, 145 note 2, et seq

Lombardo, Marco, xx, 209 note

Lombardo, Pietro, xx, 328 note 19

Lomna Drúth, xlix, 217, 219, 220, 223, 226, 230, 231, 233, 238, 240, 241, 243

LONDON, MDCCCII, xli, 676

London, Carlyle on, v, 323; Emerson on, 361, 466; Franklin on streets of, i, 120-3; Harrison on Lord Mayors of, xxxv, 278; Herschel on, v, 334; industries of, x, 264-5; rent and lodging in, 120-1

London Punch, Emerson on, v, 452

London Review, The, xxv, 4, 125-6, 129, 133-7

LONDON SQUARE, IN A, xlii, 1121

London Times, The, Emerson on, v, 448

London University, Harrison on, xxxv, 371-2, 379, 382

Long, George, LIFE OF M. AURELIUS ANTONINUS, ii, 302-19; PHILOSOPHY OF ANTONINUS, 320-45; translator of M. Aurelius Antoninus, 191

Long Parliament, free printing suppressed by, iii, 184, 185-7; Milton on the, 190-2, 226-7, 231; xxviii, 187-8; theatres closed by, xviii, 5

LONG PARLIAMENT, NEW FORCERS OF CONSCIENCE UNDER THE, iv, 80-1

Longevity, Browne on, iii, 294 (43); Cicero on, ix, 69-70; Darwin on, xi, 209-10; its effect on traditions, xlvii, 207

Longfellow, Henry Wadsworth, poems by, xlii, 1264-1338; Poe on Waif of, xxviii, 378-80

LONGING, xli, 798-9

Longinus, Hugo on, xxxix, 345; quoted, xxiv, 45

Longstreet, Gen., at Gettysburg, xliii, 343, 347

Lope Ruyz, tale of, xiv, 156

Lope de Vega, quoted, xxxix, 365

Lopez, Dr., xix, 240 note 1

Lopez, Francisco, xxxiii, 317, 318-19

LORD GREGORY, vi, 454-5

LORD THOMAS AND FAIR ANNET, xl, 61-5

LORD ULLIN'S DAUGHTER, xli, 773-5

Lord's Prayer, The, xliv, 383 (2-4); Dante on, xx, 186-7; Herbert on the, xv, 402-3; Locke on the, xxxvii, 132

Lords of Articles (Scotland), xxiv, 254 note

Lords of Trade, and Albany Convention, i, 124

Lorenzo the Magnificent, age of, xxvii, 371-2

LORIMER, MISS, INSCRIPTION TO, vi, 541

Lorraine, Cardinal of, Cellini on, xxxi, 283 note, 284, 297, 298; in FAUSTUS, xix, 231

Lorraine, François de, at Boulogne, xxxviii, 18

Losses, and crosses, lessons from, vi, 68; Epictetus on, ii, 120 (11), 126 (27); Smith on fear of, x, 110

LOST LEADER, THE, xlii, 1067-8

LOST MISTRESS, THE, xlii, 1069-70

LOST YOUTH, MY, xlii, 1290-3

Lot, Jesus on, xliv, 399-400 (28-9); Jesus on wife of, 400 (32); Mohammed on, xlv, 906-993; wife of, xv, 112-13

Lothair, son of Louis Debonnaire, xxxix, 82

Lothario, and Anselmo, xiv, 307-46, 351-5

Lothario, gay, reference to, xix, 113

Lotos-Eaters, in Egypt, xxxiii, 45; Ulysses and the, xxii, 17

LOTOS-EATERS, THE, xlii, 993-8; editor's remarks on, l, 20

Lotteries, Smith on, x, 109; Woolman on, i, 243-4

Lotto, Pier Maria di, xxxi, 80 note

Lotus-Eaters (see Lotos-Eaters)

Loudness, as source of the sublime, xxiv, 69-70

Loudoun, Lord, administration of, i, 154-5; attack on Louisburg, 153; death of, vi, 299 note; indecision of, i, 152-4; in proprietary quarrels, 151

Louis, of Bavaria, son of Debonnaire; xxxix, 82

Louis le Bègue, xxxix, 82

Louis the Debonnaire, Raleigh on, xxxix, 80-3

Louis, son of Charles the Simple, xxxix, 83

Louis, Saint, wife of, xx, 174 note 14

Louis XI, barber of, xxxix, 356; Henry VII and, 77; leaden god of, 95; mercenaries of, xxxvi, 47; postal service established by, ix, 368 note 4; secrecy of, iii, 68

Louis XII, Macaulay on, xxvii, 388; Machiavelli on, xxxvi, 8-9, 12-15, 24

Louis XIII, Richelieu and, xxiv, 332

Louis XIV, Burke on reign of, xxiv, 246; Dryden on, xiii, 55; on duties of sovereign, xxxiv, 217-18; Emerson on, v, 390; English dislike of, xxxiv, 86; literature under, xxxix, 428; Mazarin and, xxiv, 332; Scarron and, xxxix, 351; Voltaire on, xxxiv, 151

Louis XVI, Burke on, xxiv, 202-3, 208-12, 218-20, 266, 269, 281; king under the Constitution, 331-4; on October Sixth, 208-12; place of execution of, xxxix, 359-60

Louis, Don, in DON QUIXOTE, xiv, 431-5, 442-7

LOUISIANA, CESSION OF, xliii, 250-4

LOUSE, TO A, vi, 190-1

Louvain, Lipsius on, xxviii, 46

Louviers, town of, xxxv, 16

Louvois, and Louis, xxiv, 332

Love, Alcibiades on, xii, 109 note 2; among angels, iv, 259; Beaumont on, xlvii, 692; beginnings of conjugal and paternal, xxxiv, 202; Blake on, xli, 591; Brome on, xl, 369-70; Browning, E. B., on, xli, 927-8, 928-9, 931-2, 934, 939, 940; Browning, Robert on, xlii, 1099-1100, 1109; Browning, Robert, on fraternal, xviii, 383-4; Burke on, xxiv, 36-8; Burns on, vi, 136-7, 181, 204, 475; business and, xl, 311; Byron on, xli, 800; Campbell on, 782; "can tame the wildest," xvii, 40; comfort in

strength of, xli, 626; Confucius on, xliv, 9 (3), 12-13 (1-7), 16 (18), 20 (20, 21), 21 (28, 6), 23 (29), 29 (28), 37, 40 (22), 43 (19), 45 (2, 5, 7, 8), 47 (17), 48 (30), 51 (8, 9), 53 (34, 35), 58 (6, 8); Corneille on causes and effects of, xlviii, 62-3; a cureless sorrow, xl, 248; death and, iii, 9; xlii, 1036; Hobbes's definition of, xxxiv, 341; desire contrasted with, xxiv, 74; Donne on, xl, 312-13; echoes of, xli, 822; Emerson on blindness of, v, 301; Envy compared with, iii, 22, 26; Euripides on, viii, 313, 323, 327, 331, 359; excited by theatre, xlviii, 13 (11); fear and, xxxvi, 55-6; xlvi, 152-3; friendship and, ix, 42; xxxii, 75-6; Goethe on, xix, 67, 132-3, 139-40, 291-2, 369; Greek epigram on, v, 306-7; Hume on, xxxvii, 324; inspired by virtue, ix, 19; is love forever, xlii, 981; jealousy and, xl, 286; Jonson on, 295-7; Kant on practical, xxxii, 311; Kempis on, vii, 247 (4), 263-5; Longfellow on, xlii, 1283; Marcus Aurelius on the universal, ii, 280 (21); mathematically just, v, 97; Milton on, iv, 258, 266; Milton on misfortunes of, 313; Milton on wedded, 173-4; of misanthropes, ii, 185 (23); Moore on, xxviii, 384; More on, xxxvi, 212; music and, xli, 479; the panacea, v, 56-7; Pascal on decay of, xlviii, 50 (123); Pascal on passion of, 411-21; Paul, St., on, xlv, 508-9 (1-13), 514 (14); Penn on, i, 330 (82-3), 366-7 (545-56); physical cause of, xxiv, 119-20; physical effects of, xxxviii, 124; pity and, xl, 393-4; Poe on, xxviii, 391, 392; poets of, xxvii, 347-8; Raleigh on, xl, 205; refined by sense of beauty, xxxii, 292-3; remedy of all blunders, v, 282; Scott on, xli, 743-4, 751-2; Shakespeare on, xl, 262, 281, 282; xlvi, 124, 153-4, 223; Shelley on, xli, 826-7 850-1; "short word that says much," xviii, 390; Sidney on, xxvii, 34; Sophocles on, viii, 281; in state of nature, xxxiv, 191-4; Stevenson on, xxviii, 283-4; Stoic definition of, xxxii, 77-8; Swinburne on, xlii, 1208; Tennyson on, 980, 1020, 1028; Tennyson on faith in, 976; Thomson on, 1149; time and, xlvi, 188; Tzu-hsia on, xliv, 64 (6); unlawful, punished in Hell, xx, 22-4; un-

requited, impossibility of, v, 118-19; Walton on, xv, 326; Webster on, xlvii, 797; Wordsworth on, xli, 664-6; in young men, xiv, 204; Yu-tzu on roots of, xliv, 5 (2)

Love, Essay on, Bacon's, iii, 26-8

Love, by Coleridge, xli, 704-7

Love, by Herbert, xl, 341-2

Love, All for, xli, 789-90

Love, Dirge for, by Sidney, xl, 211-12

Love, Dirge of, by Shakespeare, xl, 268-9

Love, The Flight of, xli, 851-2

Love, Give All to, xlii, 1244-5

Love, Give Me More, xl, 352-3

Love, Summons to, xl, 329-30

Love for Love, vi, 442

Love Gregor: a ballad, xl, 65-8

Love in Her Eyes Sits Playing, xl, 402

Love in the Guise of Friendship, vi, 294

Love in the Valley, xlii, 1140-5

Love Lies A-Bleeding, xlvii, 667-751

Love Looked for Hell, How, xlii, 1398-1401

Love Not Me, xl, 325-6

Love Thou Thy Land, xlii, 999-1001

Love Will Find Out the Way, xl, 379-80

Love-Begotten Daughter, To a, vi, 55-7

Love-gain, town of, xv, 104

Love-lust, Mr., in Pilgrim's Progress, xv, 100

Love-Potions, Webster on, xlvii, 791-2

Love-saint, Mr., in Pilgrim's Progress, xv, 282

Love-Sweetness, xlii, 1180

Love-the-flesh, Mrs., in Pilgrim's Progress, xv, 188

Love's Deity, xl, 309-10

Love's Farewell, xl, 228

Love's Omnipresence, xl, 314

Love's Perjuries, xl, 266-7

Love's Philosophy, xli, 832

Lovejoy, Emerson on, v, 130

Lovelace, Richard, poems by, xl, 354-6

Loveliness of Love, The, xli, 913-14

Lovell, in Shoemaker's Holiday, xlvii, 471

Lovell, Lord, in New Way to Pay Old Debts, xlvii, master of Allworth, 868-9; Overreach's plan to win, 878, 892, 899-900; with Allworth on way to Overreach's, 892; Overreach on, 898;

arrival at Overreach's, 901-2; with Margaret, 902-3; 909; with Lady Allworth at Overreach's, 905, 906; departure, 909; discharges Allworth, 911; with Overreach at Allworth's, 912-15; with Lady Allworth, 916-19; reconciliation with Lady Allworth, 928-30; with Wellborn, 931; in final scene, 937, 939, 941, 942-3

Lovely Lass of Inverness, vi, 488-9

Lovely Polly Stewart, vi, 413-14

Lovely Young Jessie, vi, 455-6

Lover, The Constant, xl, 353

Lover and His Lass, xl, 263-4

Lover's Appeal, xl, 192-3

Lover's Infiniteness, xl, 308-9

Lover's Lullaby, A, xl, 195-6

Lover's Morning Salute to His Mistress, vi, 502-3

Lover's Resolution, The, xl, 332-3

Lovesight, by Rossetti, xlii, 1178

Lovewit, in The Alchemist, xlvii, 642-51, 657-64

Loving in Truth, xl, 212-13

Low Archipelago, Darwin on, xxix, 406

Lowell, James Russell, Abraham Lincoln, xxviii, 429-50; Democracy, 451-70; life and works, 428; Poems by, xlii, 1370-90

Loxias, Apollo called, viii, 100, 119, 123

Loyal, Mr., in Tartuffe, xxvi, 285-90

Lubbock, Sir John, on linking species, xi, 337; on sexual characters, 158-9; on variability in Coccus, 56

Lucagnolo, xxxi, 34, 35-8, 42

Lucagus, death of, xiii, 341-2

Lucan, Browne on, iii, 294-5 (44); in Dante's Hell, xx, 19; Montaigne on, xxxii, 90; Nero and, xviii, 17; Shelley on, xxvii, 338, 349; xli, 867; Sidney on, xxvii, 12

Lucanus, Domitius, ix, 327-8

Lucas, Prosper, on inheritance, xi, 28; on resemblances, 315

Lucasta, To, Going Beyond the Seas, xl, 356

Lucasta, To, on Going to the Wars, xl, 354-5

Lucceius, Cicero on, ix, 88, 150; letter to, 101

Lucchesini, Girolamo, xxxi, 418 note

Lucetius, death of, xiii, 312

Luchdonn, the satirist, xlix, 212

Lucia, Dante on, xx, 11 note 6, 180, 422

Lucia, in THE BETROTHED (see Mondella, Lucia)

Lucia, Sainte, xxxi, 374 note

Lucian, Alexander the prophet and, xxxvii, 384-5; atheism of, iii, 43; dispute of S. and T. in, 314-15; on love of lies, 7

Lucianus, in HAMLET, xlvi, 155

Lucifer, in Dante's HELL, xx, 140, 141-2; in FAUSTUS, xix, 226-7, 228-9; Marlowe on fall of, 214-15; pictured in Purgatory, xx, 191; Satan called, iv, 301; called the worm, xx, 25 note 1

Lucilius, and Brutus, xii, 375-6

Lucinda, in DON QUIXOTE, xiv, 201-6, 240-8, 264-5, 356-65

Lucius of Cyrene, xliv, 450 (1)

Luck, Hobbes on, xxxiv, 360; Gudrun on the trust in, xlix, 354; shallow men believe in, v, 283

LUCKNOW, THE PIPES AT, xlii, 1360-2

Lucre Hill, in PILGRIM'S PROGRESS, xv, 109, 285

Lucretia, in Dante's Limbo, xx, 20; reference to, 306

Lucretius, Cicero on, ix, 110; Claudian and, xxxix, 426; Montaigne on, xxxii, 90-1; on pleasure of truth, iii, 8; on religion, 14; xxiv, 136-7; xxv, 30; in Rome, iii, 195; Sainte-Beuve on, xxxii, 132; Shelley on, xxvii, 344; Sidney on, 12; Swift on, 106; on terror caused by wonder of nature, xxiv, 59; Wordsworth on, v, 324

Lucullus, Cicero and, xii, 244; Clodius and, 241-2; faction of, iii, 123; Pompey and, 109

LUCY: by Wordsworth, xli, 669-72

LUCY ASHTON'S SONG, xli, 748

LUCY, COUNTESS OF BEDFORD, xl, 297

Ludlow, Hugo on, xxxix, 380

Luisens, Duke de, and Edw. Herbert, xv, 374

Luke, St., Dante on, xx, 266 and note 14; vocation and nationality of, xliv, 352

LUKE, GOSPEL ACCORDING TO, xliv, 351-419; Pascal on, xlviii, 190 (578)

Luke Dosa, iron crown of, xli, 531

LULLABY, by Shakespeare, xl, 265

LULLABY, A LOVER'S, xl, 195-6

LULLABY, A SWEET, xl, 197-8

LULLABY, OUR BLESSED LADY'S, xl, 256-60

Lully, Raymond, iii, 199 note; xlvii, 585 note

Lumpkin, Tony, in SHE STOOPS TO CONQUER. Hardcastle, xviii, 206; his pranks, 206-7; Miss Neville and, 210; goes to ale-house, 207; at the ale-house, 211-13; with Marlow and Hastings, 213-15; with Constance Neville, 229, 230-1; with his mother, 231; with Hastings, 232-3; steals Miss Neville's jewels for her, 235-6, 237-9; with Miss Neville in the plot, 250-2; and the letter from Hastings, 252-4; denounced by all, 254; takes leave, 256; as driver in elopement plot, 260-3; finally releases Miss Neville, 268

Luned, in Arthurian legends, xxxii, 166 note

Lungs, developed from swimbladder, xi, 186; Fabricius on the, xxxviii, 65; Harvey on, 138, 139; heart and, relations of, 65, 69-72, 88, 90, 90-4, 100, 131; passage of blood through, 94-7, 99-100

Lupercalia, feast of, xii, 313

Luperci, Virgil on the, xiii, 290

Lupercus, letter to, ix, 346-50

Lupus, Nymphidius, Pliny on, ix, 371

Luscinius, Gaius, and Æmilius, ix, 23

Lust, Dante on, xx, 50; in Dante's HELL, 22-4; defined by Hobbes, xxxiv, 341; of the eyes, vii, 189; Hindu Krishna on, xlv, 862; love and, i, 330 (82-3); xl, 419; Milton on, iv, 56-7; Pascal on three kinds of, xlviii, 152-3 (458), 153-4 (460-1); Shakespeare on, xl, 281 (135); xlvi, 116; Webster on, xlvii, 783

Lutatius, Catulus, xii, 235; Cæsar and, 268-9

LUTE, TO HIS, William Drummond's, xl, 328

Luther, Martin, ADDRESS TO GERMAN NOBILITY, xxxvi, 263-335; Browne on, iii, 253-4 (2); Carlyle on, xxv, 324; CHRISTIAN LIBERTY, xxxvi, 344-78; Emerson on, v, 66; hymn by, xlv, 557-8; letter to Archbishop Albert, xxxvi, 247; letter to Leo X, 336-44; letter to Nicholas Amsdorff, 260-1; life and works, 246; NINETY-FIVE THESES, 251-59; Taine on table-talk of, xxxix, 435; Voltaire on, xxxiv, 84; on wisemen, v, 232; Wyclif and, iii, 223

Luxuries, defined by Smith, x, 517-18; Emerson on, v, 51; Milton on, iv, 63, 65; taxes on, Penn on, i, 327-8, 391;

taxes on, Smith on, x, 518-21, 533-39; taxes on, when best paid, 477-8 (3)

Luxury, Burns on, vi, 139, 250; defined by Hobbes, xxxiv, 341; of doing good, xli, 520; Epictetus on, ii, 176 (168); generation and, x, 80; Goldsmith on, xli, 516, 518; Jonson on, xl, 295-6; Penn on, i, 325, 330; Pliny on, ix, 216; Woolman on, i, 196-7, 290-1

Luynes, Duke de, xlviii, 346 note 2

Lycas, in the ÆNEID, xiii, 340

Lyceian King, Apollo called, viii, 215, 236

Lychnocaia, religious festival, xxxiii, 34-5

LYCIDAS, Milton's, iv, 72-77; Ruskin on, xxviii, 105-10

Lycis, reference to, viii, 439

Lycomedes, and Neoptolemus, ix, 34; at Salamis, xii, 19

Lycon, accuser of Socrates, ii, 11

Lycopodium, xxx, 106 note

Lycurgus, Aristides and, xii, 79; Bacon on, iii, 130; learning of, 194; young law-breaker and, ii, 150 (88)

Lycurgus, and Hypsipile, xx, 252 note

Lycus, in the ÆNEID, xiii, 81, 311-12

Lydgate, Dryden on, xxxix, 163

Lydia, the Christian, xliv, 458 (14-15)

Lyell, Sir Charles, on colonies of Barrande, xi, 350; Darwin to, xxix, 7; editor's remarks on papers of, l, 40; on geology, xi, 102-3; geology, works on, 321-2; life and works of, xxxviii, 384; on means of dispersal, xi, 386; on origin of species and geological record, 347-8; PROGRESS OF GEOLOGY, xxxviii, 385-97; on struggle for life, xi, 72; on subsidence of Pacific, xxix, 472 note; on succession of species, xi, 349; UNIFORMITY OF CHANGE, xxxviii, 398-418

Lygians, Tacitus on the, xxxiii, 117

Lying, Locke on, xxxvii, 114, 115

Lying-in Hospitals, Lee on, xxxviii, 248

Lyly, John, CUPID AND CAMPASPE, xl, 209; SPRING'S WELCOME, 209; Jonson on, 301-3

Lyncæus, eyes of, v, 170

Lynceus, in the ÆNEID, xiii, 319

Lynceus, and Hypermnæstra, viii, 198 note

Lyngi, King, xlix, 278, 280, 291, 292

Lyon, Richard, and Wat Tyler, xxxv, 69

Lyric Poetry, Hugo on age of, xxxix, 339-40, 352-3, 354; Milton on, v, 175;

Sidney on, xxvii, 28; Wordsworth on, xxxix, 298

Lysander, admiral of Sparta, xii, 142, 144; Alcibiades and, 145; Cyrus and, ix, 67; on Spartan respect for age, 67-8

Lysanias of Sphettus, ii, 22

Lysanias, tetrarch of Abilene, xliv, 360 (1)

Lysias, Claudius, xliv, 475 (26), 477 (22)

Lysias, the orator, ix, 205 note 1

Lysicles, and Aspasia, xii, 60

Lysimachus, son of Aristides, xii, 105

Lysippus, and Alexander, ix, 104

Lyso, Cicero on, ix, 154

Lyte, Henry Francis, ABIDE WITH ME, xlv, 566-7

Lytton, Edward Earl, THE LAST WISH, xlii, 1119

Mab, fairy, Milton on, iv, 32

Mabinogion, The, xxxii, 139 note, 145-65

Mabon, son of Modron, xxxii, 150-2

M'ADAM, TO MR., vi, 189-90

Macariens, law of the, xxxvi, 163

Macario, Father, miracle of, xxi, 49-50

Macarius, the monk, xx, 379 note 4

Macaroni, Pagolo, xxxi, 304, 308

Macaulay, G. C., Editor of Froissart, xxxv, i; translator of Herodotus, xxxiii, 1

Macaulay, Thomas Babington, Emerson on, v, 440; life and works, xxvii, 362; ON MACHIAVELLI, 363-401; Mill on, xxv, 51-2, 81, 100, 101; poems by, xli, 915-17; in Union Debating Society, xxv, 51

Macaulay, Zachary, xxvii, 362

MACBETH, TRAGEDY OF, xlvi, 319-94; Hugo on witches in, xxxix, 348; Lamb on staging of, xxvii, 309-11, 312-6

Macbeth, general of Duncan, xlvi, 322-3; made Thane of Cawdor, 324; with the witches, 324-7; with king's messengers, 327-9; received by king, 330-1; hatred of Malcolm, Prince of Cumberland, 331; letter to wife, 331; Lady Macbeth on, 331-2; return home, 333; hesitates to kill Duncan, 335-6; urged on by Lady Macbeth, 336-7; with Banquo before murder, 338-9; vision of dagger, 339; goes to murder, 340; with Lady Macbeth after murder, 340-2; with Macduff and Lennox, 344-5; on discovery of murder, 345, 346-7; chosen king, 349; with Banquo, 350-1;

plots to kill Banquo, 351-4; tells Lady
Macbeth, 354-6; at the banquet, 357-
62; Lennox on, 363-4; with witches,
shown apparitions, 366-9; learns Macduff's flight, 370; Macduff on, 375; in
Dunsinane Castle, 384-7, 388; hears
death of wife, 388; learns forest moving, 389; fights with young Siward,
390; and Macduff, 391-2; death, 393

Macbeth, Lady, letter from husband, xlvi,
331; plans to kill king, 332-3; receives husband, 333; welcomes king to
castle, 334; urges husband to murder,
336-8; Duncan's gift to, 338; during
murder, 340; with husband after murder, 340-3; on discovery of murder,
345, 347; with Banquo, 350; with husband, concerning Banquo's murder,
354-6; at banquet, 357-8, 360-2; walks
in sleep, 382-3; doctor on, 386; her
death, 388, 394; Ruskin on, xxviii, 139

Maccabæus, Judas, Dante on, xx, 362 note
3; Milton on, iv, 388; one of nine
worthies, xxxix, 20

Maccabees, Pascal on the, xlviii, 208-9
(630)

MacCarthy, D. F., translator of STABAT
MATER, xlv, 553-5

Maccecht, son of Snade, xlix, 206-7, 212,
213, 222-3; 225, 243, 244, 245-6, 247

M'Culloch, Mill on, xxv, 63, 65, 80-1

McCULLOCH vs. MARYLAND, xliii, 208-24

MacDonald, George, poems by, xlii,
1118-9

M'Dougal, Sir George, xxv, 413

Macduff, in MACBETH, xlvi, 334; with the
porter, 343-44; discovers king's murder, 344-7; with Ross, 348-9; his flight
to England, 364, 370; at English court,
with Malcolm, 373-7; with Ross, learns
death of family, 378-81; in war on
Macbeth, 383, 387, 390; fight with
Macbeth, 390-2; his victory, 393

Macduff, Lady, xlvi, 370-2

Macedo, Largius, and his slaves, ix, 240-
41

Macedonia, Raleigh on, xxxix, 71, 113

Macer, Baebius, letters to, ix, 231-309

Macer, Calpurnius, ix, 382, 392

Macer, Licinius, death of, xii, 225

M'Gill, Dr. William, vi, 337 note, 351

Machabeus (see Maccabæus)

Macherone, Cesare, xxxi, 110

Machiavel, in EGMONT, xix, 260-5, 288-
91

Machiavelli, *Art of War*, xxvii, 392-4;
Bacon on, iii, 98; *Belphegor*, xxvii,
387; Cæsar Borgia and, 388-9; on
Christianity, iii, 33; *Clizia* of, xxvii,
386; on democracy, xxv, 368; deserts
of, xxvii, 400-1; *Discourses on Livy*,
394-5; efforts to relieve Italy, 390-3;
life and works of, xxxvi, 3-4; *Mandragola* of, xxvii, 382-6; obloquy following death, 400; odiousness of, 363-5;
political correspondence of, 387-8; THE
PRINCE, xxxvi, 5-86; THE PRINCE,
Macaulay on, xxvii, 363-5, 394, 395;
representative of Italian Renaissance, l,
23; his times, xxvii, 366-82; works of,
Macaulay on, 382-7, 397-400

MACHIAVELLI, ESSAY ON, xxvii, 363-401

Machinery, advantages of, x, 225; fixed
capital, 219; division of labor and, 14-
15; Emerson on, v, 81, 399; power and
velocity in, xxx, 181-4; in woollen
manufactures, x, 206-7; work of, xxx,
176-7

MACKENZIE, DR., NOTE TO, vi, 215

M'Kenzie, Mr., of Applecross, vi, 205

Mackinlay, Rev. James, Burns on, vi, 163,
166, 242, 352

McKinley, William, Cuba and, xliii, 440
note; Hawaii and, 437 note

Mackintosh, Sir James, Emerson on, v,
143, 439

Maclean of Lochbuy, xlii, 1394-7

M'Lehose, Mrs., Burns and, vi, 293, 295

M'Leod, Isabella, verses on, vi, 299

M'LEOD, JOHN, ON THE DEATH OF, vi,
272-3

M'MATH, JOHN, EPISTLE TO, vi, 104-7

M'MURDO, JOHN, LINES ON, vi, 466

M'MURDO, JOHN, LINES TO, vi, 329

MacNeil, Hector, poems by, xli, 576-8

Maçon, Antoine de, xxxi, 291 note 2

Macpherson, James, Goldsmith on, xli,
507; Wordsworth on, xxxix, 328-9

M'PHERSON'S FAREWELL, vi, 297-8

Macrauchenia Patachonica, xxix, 177

Macready, and Browning, xviii, 358

Macrinius, letters to, ix, 216-7, 299-301

Macrinus, Emperor, Machiavelli on,
xxxvi, 67

Macrinus, Minutius, letter to, ix, 326-7;
Pliny on, 201

Macro, and Sejanus, iii, 94

Macrobius, on dreams, xl, 43; on Virgil,
xiii, 14

Macrocosmus, sign of, xix, 25

Macronians, circumcision among, xxxiii, 51

Macureguarai, town of, xxxiii, 355, 363

MAD MAID'S SONG, xl, 334-5

Madasinia, Queen, xiv, 207, 210

Madeira, flora of, xi, 111; species of, 415-6, 424

Madeline, and Porphyro, xli, 884-93

Madison, James, papers for FEDERALIST, xliii, 199 note

Madness, cause of, xxiv, 37; Hobbes on, xxxiv, 353-8; Pascal on, xlviii, 133 (414); Shakespeare on, xlvi, 127-8, 130-1

MADRIGAL, by Drummond, xl, 326

MADRIGAL, by Shakespeare, xl, 267

Mæcenas, Antony and, xviii, 25; Dryden on, 17; Pliny and, xliii, 29; Plutarch on, xii, 348; Virgil and, xiii, 3; xxxix, 164

Maecianus, Lucius V., teacher of M. Aurelius Antoninus, ii, 303

Maël, and Lancelot, xxxii, 163

Mælius, Spurius, death of, ix, 65

Mænads, Bacchus and the, viii, 215; Pentheus and the, 123; son of Dryas and, 286

Mæon, death of, xiii, 332-3

Mæonides, Homer called, iv, 136

Mævius, Dryden on, xiii, 13; Shelley on, xxvii, 358

Magæus, and Alcibiades, xii, 145-6

Magalotti, Gregorio, xxxi, 122 note

Magdalena, Drake at, xxxiii, 149

Magdalene, Mary, xliv, 373 (37-50), 374 (2), 416 (10); John Donne on, xv, 378; Kempis on, vii, 246 (1)

MAGDALENE, FOR THE, xl, 328

Magdolos, battle of, xxxiii, 80

Magellan, first to circumnavigate globe, xxxiii, 122; at Port St. Julian, 205

Magellan Clouds, described, xxiii, 30

Magellan, Straits of, Darwin on, xxix, 236; Pretty on, xxxiii, 207-8

Magic, Browne on, iii, 282 (31); Faust on, xix, 24; Faustus on, 208

Magicians, in Dante's HELL, xx, 84

Magistrates, expenses of, x, 465; marriage of, iii, 21; Vane on duties of, xliii, 122-3

Magna Charta, Burke on, xxiv, 170-1; Voltaire on, xxxiv, 90; Winthrop on, xliii, 96

MAGNA, INSTAURATIO (see INSTAURATIO MAGNA)

Magnane, M. de, xxxviii, 24

Magnanimity, friendship requires, v, 114; Hobbes on, xxxiv, 341, 365; Marcus Aurelius on term, ii, 277 (8); Ruskin on, xxviii, 127

Magnetism, Faraday on, xxx, 65-8; illustrated, 25; produced by electricity, 82-5, 206

Magneto-electrical Machines, xxx, 206

Magneto-electricity, discovered by Faraday, xxx, 5

Magnificence, a source of the sublime, xxiv, 66

Magnitude, in architecture, xxiv, 64-5; Pliny on, ix, 205; sublimity of, xxiv, 61-2, 109-11

Magnússon, Eirikr, xlix, 249

Magus, death of, xiii, 339

Magyars, Freeman on the, xxviii, 268-9; Turks and, 227-9

Maha Bharata, The, remarks on, xlv, 784

Maha-Brahma, xlv, 610, 613-14, 618

Maha-Maya, mother of Buddha, xlv, 606-10

Mahatmas, xlv, 823, 826

Mahew, Mr., among the Indians, xliii, 138, 140

Mahmúd, Omar Khayyam on, xli, 952

Mahomet (see Mohammed)

Maia, daughter of Atlas, xiii, 272; Jove and, xl, 242; mother of Mercury, xx, 382 note 13

Maiander, River, Herodotus on, xxxiii, 11

MAID OF ATHENS, xli, 795-6

Maimonides, Moses, on prophets, xlviii, 214 (2)

Mairet, and Corneille, xxxix, 361

Mâisar, game of, xlv, 994 note 3

Majority, Burke on tyranny of the, xxiv, 259-60; Lincoln on rule of the, xliii, 318-19; Lowell on government by, xxviii, 464; Mill on tyranny of the, xxv, 198; Pascal on rule of, xlviii, 106 (301), 305-6 (878)

Mál, son of Telband, xlix, 225-6

Malacoda, in Dante's HELL, xx, 87

Malaspina, Alagia, xx, 224 note

Malaspina, Archbishop of Genoa, xxxi, 45 note 1

Malaspina, Conrad, in Purgatory, xx, 178

Malaspina, Marcello, and Dante, xx, 224 note

Malaspina, Morello, Dante and, xx, 102 note 5, 178 note 10

Malatesti, Count, in DUCHESS OF MALFI, xlvii, 791, 804-5, 835, 847-8, 851-4

Malavolti, Catalano de, xx, 96 note 4

Malay Archipelago, Darwin on, xi, 338, 418-19

Malays, superstition of the, xxix, 462

Malaysia, Drake in, xxxiii, 218-24

Malchus, and St. Peter, xlviii, 262 (744)

Malcolm, in MACBETH, with Duncan in camp, xlvi, 322, 323; reports death of Cawdor, 329; made Prince of Cumberland, 330-1; after father's murder, 346, 347-8; suspected of murder, 349; at English court, 363-4; with Macduff, 373-7; and Ross, 378-9; comforts Macduff, 380-1; in war on Macbeth, 383, 387, 389-91; with Siward, 392-3; hailed as king, 393-4

Maldiva, Archipelago, Darwin on, xxix, 481-2

Maldonado, town, Darwin on, xxix, 48-9

Maldonado, Lopez, Cervantes on, xiv, 53-4

Malebolge, in Hell, xx, 73

Malebranche, Nicholas, Berkeley on, xxxvii, 234; on God, 345-6 note; xxxiv, 104; Hume on, xxxvii, 291; Montesquieu on, xxxii, 118; Voltaire on, xxxiv, 71

Malfi, Duchess of, in DUCHESS OF MALFI, Antonio on, xlvii, 761; in presence-chamber scene, 761; Bosola hired to watch, 763-4; with brothers, advised against marriage, 765-6; scene with Antonio, 767-72; Bosola on condition of, 774, 778; with Bosola, 775-77; plans to hide her condition, 777; birth of son, 780, 782-3; her unchastity believed by brothers, 787-9; with Ferdinand after interval, 791; plan to force confession, 792; with Antonio in chamber, 793-5; with Ferdinand, 795-8; with Bosola, 799; covers flight of Antonio, 799-802; confesses marriage to Bosola, 802; plans for flight, 803-4; betrayed by Bosola, 804, 805-6; banished from Ancona, 807-8; with Antonio near Loretto, 808-9; letter from brother, 809-10; parting from Antonio, 810-11; arrested by Bosola, 812-13; in imprisonment, 813-18; with Cariola, 818-20; with madmen, 821-22; with Bosola as old man, 822-5; death, 826, 830

Malice, Burns on, vi, 106; Emerson on

limits of, v, 131; Martial on, xlviii, 21 (41); More on, xxxvi, 128; Woolman on, i, 274

Malice, Mr., in PILGRIM'S PROGRESS, xv, 100

Malignity, Bacon on, iii, 34

Malin, Admiral, at Gravelines, xix, 256

Mallon, Col., at Gettysburg, xliii, 385, 387

MALLY'S MEEK, MALLY'S SWEET, vi, 543

Malory, Sir Thomas, THE HOLY GRAIL, xxxv, 105-214; life and book, 104; PROLOGUE TO KING ARTHUR of, xxxix, 20-4

Malprimis, in SONG OF ROLAND, xlix, 123, 134

Malquiant, son of Malcus, xlix, 146

Malseron, in SONG OF ROLAND, xlix, 137

Malt, Harrison on making of, xxxv, 282-3

Malta, Coleridge on government of, v, 320; heat of, xxxvii, 10-11; Knights of, Mill on, xxv, 10

Malthus, debt of Darwin to, xi, 6; Emerson on, v, 248, 393; Mill on, xxv, 68

Maluco Islands, Drake in, xxxiii, 218-21

Malunkyaputta, xlv, 647-52

Mambrino's Helmet, xiv, 75, 165-67, 448-51

Mammals, first appearance of, xi, 341; in oceanic islands, 417-18

Mammary Glands, development of the, xi, 233-4

Mammon, Burns on followers of, vi, 86, 325-6; Jesus on, xliv, 397 (13); in PARADISE LOST, iv, 105, 114-15

Mammon, Sir Epicure, in THE ALCHEMIST, Subtle on, xlvii, 563-4; visit to Subtle's 564-83; plot against, 584-5; his return, 610, 611-12; with Dol, 613-18, 629-31; with Subtle, 631-2; hears loss of Subtle's works, 632-4; returns with Surly, 647-8; with officers, 657-61

MAN, OF, by Hobbes, xxxiv, 307-417

Man, animals and, difference between, xxxiv, 175-7; antiquity of, xi, 32-3; xxxviii, 387-8, 404-5; Augustine, St., on, vii, 56-7, 82-3; Bacon on, and God, iii, 44; Bildad on, xliv, 110 (4-6); Browne on, iii, 286, 325-6; Burns on, vi, 34, 231, 249, 285, 308, 339, 507; Byron on, xviii, 416; Channing on study of, xxviii, 331-3; Confucius on, xliv, 20 (17); David on, 151 (4-8),

325 (3-4); defined by Plato, xlviii, 425; Descartes on creation of, xxxiv, 38-9; Emerson on, v, 26, 69-72, 135, 228, 264, 267, 274, 288, 298; Epictetus on, ii, 120 (9), 122 (16), 137 (60-1), 162 (124), 166 (136); "folly's microcosm," xix, 58; Franklin on, i, 72-3; God's ways to, iv, 431-2; Goethe on state of, xix, 19; Homer on littleness of, xxii, 248; Kant on, xxxii, 338-41; Kempis on, vii, 303-4; littleness of, xliv, 132-4 (3-41), 135-7 (1-30), 137 (1-14), 138-9 (1-11); Marcus Aurelius on, ii, 243 (3), 255 (7), 258 (27), 259 (34), 275 (6), 288 (14), 301 (32); Minerva on, v, 218; Mohammed on creation of, xlv, 879, 885, 889, 891, 899-900, 935; natural state of, xxxiv, 166, 168-97, 204-5, 387-91; Pascal on state of, xlviii, 26-32, 48 (111), 50 (125-7), 52-4, 56-7 (140), 63 (165), 77 (199), 78-9 (205-8), 120 (358), 128 (389-90), 130 (397), 130-1 (398-404), 132 (409), 132-5 (411-23), 137 (427), 144-5, 146, 147-9, 160 (486), 166 (510-11), 191 (584), 219 (660), 396-7, 437; Pascal on study of, 58-9; Penn on, i, 323-5, 342 (220-2); Poe's tragedy of, xlii, 1241; proper study of himself, i, 77, 96; iii, 27, 264, 266; "proposeth, God disposeth," vii, 222; Rousseau on, xxxiv, 255-6; Rousseau on early, 168; Schiller on person and condition of, xxxii, 238-41; Schiller on what constitutes, 211-13; self-torture is the lot of, xix, 34; Shakespeare on, xlvi, 133-4, 175, 270; a social being, ii, 128 (34), 136 (56), 162 (123), 228 (16), 243 (5), 244 (13), 250 (55), 264 (59), 267 (9), 287 (8); ix, 38; xxiv, 39; xxv, 327-9; Socrates on mediocrity of, ii, 82; supreme in strangeness, viii, 265-6; the temple of God, xlv, 494 (16-17), 523 (16); Tennyson on, xlii, 1019-20; thought requisite to, xlviii, 117 (339), 118 (346-8); Timæus on, v, 176; transitoriness of, xliv, 258, 271 (15-16); twofold nature of, xxxvi, 345; universal and particular, v, 6; Zophar on, xliv, 87 (12)

MAN AND SATYR, fable of, xvii, 33
MAN AND SERPENT, fable of, xvii, 13
MAN AND TWO WIVES, fable of, xvii, 29
MAN AND THE WOOD, fable of, xvii, 22
MAN AND WOODEN GOD, fable of, xvii, 27

MAN, BOY, AND DONKEY, fable of, xvii, 35-6
MAN, ESSAY ON, by Pope, xl, 406-40
MAN THE REFORMER, Emerson's, v, 43-58
MAN WAS MADE TO MOURN, vi, 60-2
MAN'S A MAN FOR A' THAT, vi, 511-12; Arnold on, xxviii, 85-6
Manardi, Arrigo, xx, 202 note 16
Manasseh, Pascal on, xlviii, 237
Manchet, a kind of bread, xxxv, 280
Mandeville, Bernard, Addison and, xxvii, 179; on pity, xxxiv, 189
Mandeville, Sir John, on headless men, xxxiii, 359
Mandioca, Darwin on, xxix, 32
Mandrake, superstition of the, xlvii, 786 note 2
Maneros, song of, xxxiii, 41
Manetho, on Egypt, xxxviii, 387
Manetti, Latino Giovenale de, xxxi, 145 note, 178-9, 184
MANFRED: A DRAMATIC POEM, xviii, 407-50; remarks on, 406
Manfred, in MANFRED, with the spirits, xviii, 407-13; spell pronounced on, 413-15; on the mountain, 415-19; saved by chamois-hunter, 419; in hunter's cottage, 419-22; with Witch, relates his life, 423-27; determines to learn what death is, 427-8; in Hall of Arimanes, 432-3; calls up Astarte, 434-6; in castle, his calmness, 436-7; with Abbot of St. Maurice, 437-42; address to the sun, 442-3; Herman on, 443; Astarte and, 444; on beauties of night and the Coliseum, 445-6; summoned by spirits, 447-9; death, 450
Manfredi, Alberigo de', xx, 139 and note 4
Manfredi, King of Naples, Dante on, xx, 156-7 and note 3
Manfredi, Tribaldello de', xx, 134 note 14
Mangiadore, Pietro, xx, 338 note 33
Mangona, Alberto da, xx, 166 note 6
Manhood, Channing on true, xxviii, 331-2; Emerson on, v, 18-19, 82; Lowell on, xxviii, 439; xlii, 1387; Pascal on, xlviii, 19-20
Manichæans, vii, 3; Augustine, St., on the, 35-42, 63-69, 74-5, 132-3; Mill on, xxv, 30; Nebridius's argument against, vii, 100
Manilius, case of, xii, 225

Mankind, uniformity of, xxxvii, 353-60; unity of, v, 18-19

Manlius, Capitolinus, Virgil on, xiii, 290

Manlius, Marcus, in Catiline's conspiracy, xii, 229, 230; defeat of, xxxiii, 113-14

Manlius, Titus, Corneille on, xxvi, 127

Manna, Browne on, iii, 272

Mannellini, Bernardino, xxxi, 349-50, 378

Manners, in authors, criticism of, xxvii, 219; Hobbes on, xxxiv, 369-75; Hume on, of different ages, xxxvii, 355; Locke on, 47-50, 72-4, 120-6

MANNERS, ESSAY ON, by Emerson, v, 199-218

MANNERS, TREATISE ON GOOD, by Swift, xxvii, 99-103

Mannus, god of the Germans, xxxiii, 93

Manoa, city of, xxxiii, 302-3, 317, 320, 321-2

Manoa, in SAMSON AGONISTES, iv, 422-3, 425-6, 429, 451-2, 453-5, 457-8

Mansfeld, Count, xxxviii, 50-1

Mansfield, Lord, Pope on, xxvii, 273; on the press, v, 447

Mantius, son of Melampus, xxii, 206

Manto, Dante on, xx, 82-3; in Limbo, 237 note 9

Mantrap, Mrs., in SHE STOOPS TO CONQUER, xviii, 242, 267

Mantua, contest over Duchy of, xxi, 78, 434-6, 466-71; origin of, xx, 83; Virgil on, xiii, 328

Mantua, Marquis of, in DON QUIXOTE, xiv, 43, 75

Manual Labor, Emerson on, v, 47, 50; Locke on, xxxvii, 173-8

Manuel, in MANFRED, xviii, 443-5

Manufacturers, interests of, x, 210-11

Manufactures, agriculture and, x, 11-12, 220-2, 304-7; in agricultural system, 430-6, 439-42; capital used in, 290, 292-3; commerce compared with, 307-8; division of labor in, 9-10; foreign competition keenest in, 338-9; favored by laws, 128-31; materials of, importation and exportation of, 405-22; military spirit and, iii, 77; xxvii, 373-4; monopolies in, x, 342; necessity of, 288, 444-5; prices of, 52, 202-7; protection of new, 337-8

Manzoni, Alessandro, I PROMESSI SPOSI, xxi; life and works, 3-5

Māra, the god, xlv, 618-22, 728-29

Maranon, river, xxxiii, 317 note 11, 319

Marat, Burke on, xxiv, 420

Marathon, battle of, xii, 82-3; Byron on, xli, 812

Marble, composition of, xxx, 152 note; crystallization of, 239-40; experiments with, 14-16

Marbois, Francis Barbé, xliii, 250-1

Marcela, and Chrysostom, xiv, 85-90, 104-8

Marcellinus, Pliny to, ix, 273

Marcellus, brother-in-law of Octavius, xii, 254-5

Marcellus, Caius, first husband of Octavia, xii, 344, 388

Marcellus, Marcus Claudius (d. 208 B. C.), Virgil on, xiii, 236

Marcellus, Marcus Claudius (d. 46 B. C.), Antony and, xii, 325; Cæsar and, ix, 164; xii, 289; Catiline and, 229; death of, ix, 72; Milo and, 97

Marcellus, Marcus Claudius (d. 23 B. C.), son of Octavia, xii, 388; Virgil on, xiii, 32, 237

Marcellus, in HAMLET, xlvi, 94-9, 104-7, 111, 113-4, 118-9

March, month of Creation, xl, 44; twenty-fifth of, xv, 403

MARCH, WRITTEN IN, xli, 604-5

March, George, Earl of, his raid into England, xxxv, 81-2; at Otterburn, 88, 90; Ralph Percy and, 98

Marchant, Chaucer's, xl, 18-19

Marcia, wife of Cato, in Cato, xxvii, 194-5; in Dante's Limbo, xx, 20, 147

Marcii, house of the, xii, 147

Marcius, and Cicero, xii, 230, 250

Marcius, Caius (see Coriolanus)

Marco Polo on China, xx, 73

Marco of the Serbs, xxxii, 157 note 12

Marcomanians, M. Aurelius Antoninus' war with, ii, 305, 307; Tacitus on the, xxxiii, 116

Marcone, the goldsmith, xxxi, 14, 15, 21, 22

Marcus Antoninus (see Aurelius)

Marcus Aurelius (see Aurelius)

Mardion, the eunuch, xii, 368

Mardonius, general of Xerxes, xii, 8, 87, 88, 91, 92-3, 94, 95; death of, 97; at Platæa, 20

MARE, SALUTATION TO AN AULD, vi, 147-50

Margano, Pietro, xxxi, 98 note 1

Margaret, in FAUST, first meeting with Faust, xix, 112; wonders who he is,

115-6; in chamber, finds casket, 118-9; grieves for loss of casket, 122; finds second casket, 122-3; meets Mephistopheles at Martha's, 124-31; with Faust in garden, 133-9; in summer-house, 141-2; song of, 148-9; with Faust, on his religion, 149-51; dislike of Mephistopheles, 152; plans meeting with Faust, 153-4; with Bessy at the well, 155-7; prayer of, 157-8; Valentine on, 158-9; with Valentine, 162-5; in the cathedral, 165-7; vision of, seen by Faust, 181; imprisoned and doomed to death, 190-91; in the dungeon, with Faust, 193-202; remarks on story of, 7

MARGARET, THE AFFLICTION OF, xli, 644-6

Margaret d'Alençon, xxxi, 334 note 2

Margaret of Anjou, Raleigh on, xxxix, 74, 75

Margaret of Austria, xxxi, 157 note 6, 221 note

Margaret of Burgundy, xxxix, 5, 6-7, 8; Warbeck and, xxxiv, 102

Margaret of Parma, xix, 252; Raleigh on, xxxix, 87

Margaret of Parma, in EGMONT, regent of Netherlands, xix, 256-7; on the iconoclasts, 259-60; with Machiavel, on state of Netherlands, 260-2; suspects Egmont and Orange, 263-5; Egmont and Orange on, 283-4, 294-5; determines to abdicate, 288-91; her departure, 298

Margaris, in SONG OF ROLAND, xlix, 125, 136, 141

MARGARITÆ SORORI, xlii, 1209-10

Marginal Notes, Cervantes on, xiv, 6-9

Margites, of Homer, iii, 200; xii, 209 note

MARGUERITE, To, xlii, 1128-9

Marguerite de Valois, xxxi, 283 note, 300

Maria, in SCHOOL FOR SCANDAL, in love with Charles Surface, xviii, 117, 118, 127; at Lady Sneerwell's, 119-25, 132-3; with Joseph Surface, 132, 137-8; Sir Peter and, 145; toasted by Charles, 151; reconciled to Charles, 192-4

Maria, the widow, in I PROMESSI SPOSI, xxi, 392, 479

Mariane, in TARTUFFE, and Mme. Pernelle, xxvi, 200; in love with Valère, 208, 229; marriage put off by father, 216-17; with her father, ordered to marry Tartuffe, 218-28; with Dorine, 228-33; with Valère, 233-43; protests against marriage with Tartuffe, 264-66; in final scene, 293, 296; promised to Valère, 296

Marids, a kind of genii, xvi, 9 note

Marie Antoinette, Burke on, xxiv, 212-13; on October Sixth, 208-9

Marine Currents, Lyell on, xxxviii, 401, 403

Marine Species, the simultaneous changes in, xi, 359

MARINERS OF ENGLAND, YE, Thomas Campbell's, xli, 777-8

Marini, Dryden on, xiii, 59

Mario, in England, v, 413

MARION'S MEN, SONG OF, xlii, 1217-19

Maritornes, the Asturian wench, xiv, 118, 119-23, 132-3; on knightly tales, 302; plot of, against Quixote, 435-9

Marius, Caius, Burke on confiscations of, xxiv, 250-1; Cæsar and, xii, 264, 267, 268; death of, xxvii, 21; Dryden on, xiii, 15

Marius, M., letter to, ix, 107

Marjaneh, in story of ALI-BABA, xvi, 429-30, 432, 435-6, 439-41

Mark, John surnamed, xliv, 449 (12), 450 (25), 457 (37-9)

Mark, St., Pascal on 13th chapter of, xlviii, 357-8

MARK YONDER POMP OF COSTLY FASHION, vi, 533-4

Market, extent of, limits division of labor, x, 22

Market Price, defined, x, 57; as determined by demand and supply, 57-9; effect of fluctuations on rent, wages, and profits, 59-61; natural price compared with, 59-64

Markets, in Utopia, xxxvi, 184-5

Markland, Leif Ericsson's, xliii, 8-9

Marl, Harrison on, xxxv, 308

Marlborough, Duke of, Addison on, xxvii, 183; Bolingbroke on, xxxiv, 99

MARLBOROUGH ROAD, THE OLD, xxviii, 401-3

Marliniere, Riccant de la, xxvi, 344-9

Marloff, Madame, in MINNA VON BARNHELM, xxvi, 305-7

Marlow, Sir Charles, in SHE STOOPS TO CONQUER, xviii, 256-9, 265-9

Marlow, Young, in SHE STOOPS TO CONQUER, selected as husband for Kate Hardcastle, xviii, 208-9; Miss Neville on, 210; at the ale-house, 213-15; ar-

rival at Hardcastle's, 217-19; with Mr. Hardcastle, 219-24, 225-6; meets Miss Hardcastle, 226-9; discussed by Kate and her father, 233-5, 243-4; with Kate as the barmaid, 239-43; with Miss Neville's jewels, 244-6; with Hardcastle and his servants, 246-8; ordered to leave house, 247-8; learns inn is Mr. Hardcastle's, 249; parting with Kate, 250; denounces Tony and Hastings, 254-5; protests against loving Kate, 257-8; love scene with Kate, 265-6; learns who she is, 267; united to Kate, 268-9

Marlowe, Christopher, EDWARD THE SECOND, xlvi, 5-89; DOCTOR FAUSTUS, xix, 205-50; influence on Goethe, 6; Hazlitt on, xxvii, 276; Jonson on, xl, 301; life and works, xix, 204; THE PASSIONATE SHEPHERD, xl, 254-5

Marmagne, Seigneur de, xxxi, 281 note

Marmontel, Mill on *Memoirs* of, xxv, 90

Maron, son of Euanthes, xxii, 120

Marque and Reprisal, Letters of, xliii, 161, 162, 184 (11), 186 (10)

Marquis, meaning of, xxxiv, 368

Marrall, in NEW WAY TO PAY OLD DEBTS, xlvii, 871-2; scene with Overreach, 876-79; with Wellborn, 879-81; with Wellborn at Allworth's, 883-5; with Wellborn after dinner, 888-90; reports to Overreach, 890-2; at Overreach's, 896, 901, 905, 906, 907, 908; at Allworth's, 911-12; with Wellborn on way to Lady Allworth's, 920-21, 923-4; with Overreach, 931-2, 934, 935-7; in final scene, 940-1

Marriage, Augustine, St., on, vii, 23, 46; Browne on, iii, 323; Cervantes on, xiv, 318-19; dispensations, xxxvi, 309; of divorced persons, Jesus on, xliv, 397 (18); from economic standpoint, x, 72, 80-1; Epictetus on, ii, 159-60 (116); equality in, viii, 198-9, 198 note; Euripides on, 331; among Germans, xxxiii, 103; Goethe on, xix, 348; Locke on, xxxvii, 182; Luther on, xxxvi, 333; Massinger on, xlvii, 917-18; Mill on, contracts of, xxv, 300-1; Milton on, iv, 173, 313-14; xxviii, 183-4; Mohammed on, xlv, 968, 970-1, 980; Moliere on, without love, xxvi, 223; Montaigne on, xxxii, 76; among Moravians, i, 143; in New Atlantis, iii, 167-70; Pascal on, xlviii, 127 (385),

341-2; Paul, St., on, xlv, 498-9, 499-500 (27-8, 33-40); Penn on, i, 330-1, 332-3 (92-105); Pliny on, for wealth, ix, 201; of priests, Calvin on, xxxix, 38; of priests, Luther on, xxxvi, 301-5; prostitution and, iii, 168-9; Rousseau on effect of indissoluble, xxxiv, 193; Ruskin on, xxviii, 144-5; sanctity of, Æschylus on, viii, 131; sanctity of, Emerson on, v, 245; Shakespeare on, xlvi, 146; Shakespeare on second, 153; state control of, xxv, 305; Stevenson on, xxviii, 283-4; Swift on, xxvii, 91; in Utopia, xxxvi, 208-11; Walton on, xv, 326-7; Webster's Antonio on, xlvii, 768

MARRIAGE AND SINGLE LIFE, Bacon on, iii, 21-2

Marriott, John, hymn by, xlv, 572

Mars, as German god, xxxiii, 97 (see also Ares)

Mars, the planet, xlii, 1266; Dante's fifth heaven, xx, 346

Marsh, George, on the "Alert," xxiii, 199-202, 252; (in 1859), 386

Marshall, John, OPINION IN CASE OF McCULLOCH, xliii, 208-24

Marshall, Mr., of Leeds, xxv, 76

MARSHES OF GLYNN, xlii, 1390-1

Marsians, Tacitus on the, xxxiii, 94

Marsignians, Tacitus on the, xxxiii, 116

Marsil, King, in SONG OF ROLAND, xlix, 95-8, 100-5, 108-15, 141-3, 148-50, 158, 183-4

Marsyas, Apollo and, xx, 285

Martel, Charles, king of Hungary, xx, 315-19

Martha, and Jesus, xliv, 383

Martha, in FAUST, with Margaret, xix, 123-4; learns husband's death, 125-30; with Mephistopheles in garden, 134, 137-8, 140; with Valentine, 162-4

Martha, in PILGRIM'S PROGRESS, xv, 282

Marthesia, Queen of the Amazons, xxxiii, 327

Martial, Elphinstone's translation of, vi, 264; Montaigne on, xxxii, 92; Pascal on epigrams of, xlviii, 21; Pliny on, ix, 247-8; on the ugly man, v, 306

Martigues, M. de, at Metz, xxxviii, 25; at Hesdin, 36, 37, 38-40

Martin IV, in Purgatory, xx, 242 and note 2

Martin V, Milton on, iii, 196

Martin, Sir, xx, 343 note 24

Martin, Theodore, translator of Schiller, xxvi, 377

Martineau, Harriet, Emerson and, v, 464

Martinez, Juan, xxxiii, 320-22

Martini, Luca, xxxi, 172 note; Capitolo addressed to, 251-7

Martius, and Sophocles, v, 121

Martyrs, Bacon on, iii, 138; Browne on, 278-9; Bunyan on Christian, xv, 264-5; Emerson on, v, 99; Goethe on, of truth, xix, 32; Lowell on, xlii, 1372; under M. Aurelius Antoninus, ii, 306-7, 311-15; Pascal on the, xlviii, 159 (481), 294-5 (844)

Marullus, the tribune, Cæsar and, xii, 313-14

Marut, the fallen angel, xvi, 57 note

Marvel, Mount, xv, 291

Marvell, Andrew, poems by, xl, 370-9

Marvellous, human love of the, xxxvii, 380-3

Mary, mother of Jesus, xliv, 354-6, 357-8 (5-7), 358 (19), 360 (48-51), 375 (19-21), 416 (10), 424 (14); at the cross (see STABAT MATER); Dante on, xx, 184, 225; in Dante's PARADISE, 385-6, 418-9, 423; LULLABY for, xl, 256-60; Luther on, xxxvi, 369; Milton on, iv, 190, 362, 365, 373-4; Mohammed on, xlv, 909-10, 952 note, 953, 983, 993, 1002, 1006; Pascal on virginity of, xlviii, 81 (222-3), 262 (742)

Mary, mother of John, xliv, 449 (12)

Mary, sister of Martha, xliv, 383

Mary of Brabant, and Brosse, xx, 166 note 7

Mary, Queen of Scots, Burns on, vi, 374

MARY, QUEEN OF SCOTS, LAMENT OF, vi, 396-7

Mary Tudor, Queen, Raleigh on, xxxix, 86

Mary, the Coptic girl, xlv, 992 note 1

MARY, TO, IN HEAVEN, vi, 365

MARY HAMILTON, a ballad, xl, 117-19

Mary Magdalene (see Magdalene)

MARY MORISON, vi, 31

MARY UNWIN, TO, xli, 536-8

Maryland, Quakers in, i, 276-7

MARYLAND vs. McCULLOCH, xliii, 208-24

Marzio, in THE CENCI, xviii, 319, 327-8, 328-9, 330, 333-4, 340-5

Masaccio, frescoes of, xxxi, 24 note 1

Mascheroni, Sassol, xx, 133 note 5

Masinissa, old age of, ix, 57

Masistius, Plutarch on, xii, 92

MASK AND FOX, fable of, xvii, 19

Mason, Sir Josiah, xxviii, 209-10, 211-12

MASONIC SONG, vi, 242

Masons, Burns on, vi, 37

Masorah, Pascal on the, xlviii, 208-9 (630)

MASQUES AND TRIUMPHS, ESSAY ON, Bacon's, iii, 95-6

Mass (in physics), measured by inertia, xxx, 301-2

Mass (in Roman Church), Calvin on, xxxix, 37; Luther on, xxxvi, 314-15; Luther on, for the dead, 306-7; Rousseau on, xxxiv, 303

Massa, Boebius, impeachment of, ix, 315-16

Massachusetts, Folger on persecutions in, i, 9; Winthrop on government of, xliii, 85-105

MASSACHUSETTS BODY OF LIBERTIES, xliii, 66-84

MASSACHUSETTS TO VIRGINIA, xlii, 1344-7

Massena, Napoleon on, v, 40

Massicus, ally of Æneas, xiii, 327

Massinger, Philip, life and works, xlvii, 858; NEW WAY TO PAY OLD DEBTS, 859-943

Massive Ones, in FAUST, xix, 190

Masson, David, Bagehot on Life of Milton by, xxviii, 165-8

Masters, Epictetus's advice to, ii, 178-9 (180); Penn's counsel to, i, 340-1; single men best, iii, 21

Master's Eye, fable of the, xvii, 23

Mastic, Columbus on, xliii, 26

Mastication, Locke on, xxxvii, 16

Mastiff, Harrison on the, xxxv, 352-4, 355; cross between bear and, 355

Masurius, Epictetus on, ii, 169 (144)

MATCH, A, xlii, 1205-7

Matches, story of the, xvii, 345-9

Materialism, Berkeley on, xxxvii, 250, 270, 276-81; Channing on, xxviii, 321-2; Rousseau on, xxxiv, 250-4, 258-9; Schiller on, xxxii, 222-3; Voltaire on, xxxiv, 105-7

Materials, as circulating capital, x, 219-20; of manufacture, importation, and exportation of, 405-22; rent of land used to produce, 165-78; value of, compared with food, 178-80

Mathematical Mind, Pascal on the, xlviii, 8-11

Mathematicians, Franklin on, i, 58

Mathematics, ancient, xxviii, 219; Bacon on study of, iii, 122; Berkeley on the, xxxvii, 280; Burke on, xxiv, 21, 75; Descartes on study of, xxxiv, 8, 9, 18-19; Hobbes on, 363; Hume on the, xxxvii, 306, 311; Mill on, compared with logic, xxv, 17-18; Mill on indisputableness of, 230; Milton on study of, iii, 240, 241; moral sciences compared with, xxxvii, 335-6; Newton on, xxxix, 150-1; Pascal on, xlviii, 11

Mather, Cotton, church history of, i, 9; *Essays to do Good*, 14

Matilda, in Dante's PURGATORY, xx, 259 note; Ruskin on, xxviii, 161-2

Matius, Caius, xii, 305 note

Matrevis, in EDWARD II, xlvi, 74-5, 77-9, 82-4, 86

Matter, M. Aurelius Antoninus on, ii, 326; Berkeley on existence of, xxxvii, 190-1, 193-5, 214-26, 235-47, 250-1, 253-5, 258-61, 263-5, 268, 270, 273, 277-9, 281-3; cause and effect in, 352-3; defined by Faraday, xxx, 10; idea of eternity of, xxxix, 102-3; Hume on creation of, xxxvii, 419 note; Hume on energy in, 338; Hume on inertia of, 345-6 note; Hume on reality of, 409-12; Locke on, 164-5; mind and, Channing on, xxviii, 321-2; not endowed with motion, xxxiv, 247-9, 250-1; qualities of, Bacon on, xxxix, 138-9; qualities of, Berkeley on, xxxvii, 193-214, 349 note; qualities of, Hume on, 411-12; as self-created, xxxix, 103; spirit and, Hindu doctrine of, xlv, 852, 853

MATTER, FORCES OF, Faraday's, xxx, 7-85

Matters of Fact, Hume on, xxxvii, 306-8, 320-4, 330, 331, 415, 419; Raleigh on, xxxix, 100

Matthew, the apostle, xliv, 368 (15), 424 (13); Mahomet on, xlviii, 194 (597)

Matthew, in PILGRIM'S PROGRESS, xv, 229-30, 232-6, 250, 252-3, 250, 265, 266, 267, 268, 287

Matthews, Fuegian missionary, xxix, 212, 226, 228, 230

Matthias, the disciple, xliv, 424 (23-6)

Mattiacians, Tacitus on the, xxxiii, 109

MAUCHLINE, THE BELLES OF, vi, 58

MAUCHLINE LADY, THE, vi, 57

MAUD, Tennyson's, xlii, 1015-57

Maud, Queen, and the Pope, xxxv, 254

MAUD MULLER, xlii, 1351-55

Mauer, Hans auf der, in WILLIAM TELL, xxvi, 416, 418, 420, 423-4

Maugridge, William, i, 58

Maul, the giant, xv, 248-9

Maunciple, Chaucer's, xl, 26-7

Maupertius, axiom of least action, xi, 500

Maurice, F. D., Carlyle and, xxv, 316; in London Club, 82; Mill and, 3, 97-8

Maurice of Saxony, Machiavelli and, xxvii, 363

Mauricus, Junius, ix, 190 note; letter to, 200-2; Pliny on, 191

Mauritius, Darwin on, xxix, 486-9

Maurizio, Ser, xxxi, 150 note 4

Maurus, Rabanus, xx, 339 note 37

Maxim, defined by Kant, xxxii, 312 note 2, 331 note 7

Maximilian, Emperor, Macaulay on, xxvii, 388; Machiavelli on, xxxvi, 77

Maximilla, Antonia, ix, 359

Maximinus, Machiavelli on, xxxvi, 66-7, 68

Maxims, Macaulay on general, xxvii, 395

Maximus, Fabius (see Fabius)

Maximus, freedman of Trajan, ix, 369, 374

Maximus, Nonius, letters to, ix, 219-20, 264-5, 283, 297, 310-11, 332-4, 345-6

Maximus, Q., and his son, ix, 168

Maximus, teacher of Aurelius, ii, 195-6 (15), 199

MAXWELL, DR., TO, vi, 498

MAXWELL, JOHN, EPISTLE TO, vi, 422-3

Maxwell, Sir John, at Otterburn, xxxv, 89-90

Maxwell, Lord, xl, 100

MAY MOON, THE YOUNG, xli, 821

MAY MORNING, SONG ON, iv, 39

MAY, THE CHARMING MONTH OF, vi, 504-5

MAY, THY MORN, vi, 428

Maya, mother of Buddha, xlv, 586

Mayer, Julius Robert, on law of conservation, xxx, 175

Mayflower, Lowell on the, xlii, 1372

MAYFLOWER COMPACT, THE, xliii, 59

Mazarin, Louis XIV and, xxiv, 332; motto of, xxviii, 436; Pascal on, xlviii, 23 (56)

Mazzaroth, xliv, 134 note 15

Mazzini, Giuseppe, BYRON AND GOETHE, xxxii, 377-96; editorial remarks on paper of, l, 49; life of, xxxii, 376

Mead, Harrison on, xxxv, 286

Meade, General, seizes Gettysburg, xliii, 329; in battle of Gettysburg, 331, 332, 333, 334, 335, 339, 345, 357, 358, 362, 364, 366-7, 370, 371, 381, 391-2, 396, 397, 399; Haskell on, 328, 358, 359

Meals, Locke on, xxxvii, 17-18; of children, 18

Meanness, Confucius on, xliv, 24 (35), 26 (11); punishment of, v, 26

Means, and ends, Emerson on, v, 90; Penn on, i, 348 (310-19)

Measles, cowpox and, xxxviii, 215 note; Jenner on, 164-5; small-pox and, 202-3

Measure, Emerson on love of, v, 209-10

Measures, English and metric system of, xxx, 253

Meat, Augustine, St., on eating of, vii, 185; Darwin on eating of, xxix, 123; Locke on eating of, xxxvii, 16, 18; Mohammed on eating of, xlv, 994, 1004; price of, Smith on, x, 151-2, 154-5, 183, 187-8, 189, 198

Mecca, the House of, xlv, 957 note 14

Mecca Suras, in Koran, xlv, 879-941

Mechanic Arts Schools, proposed by Ticknor, xxviii, 367

Mechanical Arts, Bacon on, xxxix, 122; poetry and, compared in usefulness, xxvii, 350-3

Mechanics, compensation in, v, 87; Hobbes on, xxxiv, 363; Newton on science of, xxxix, 150-1; Penn on, i, 323 (16)

Mechthild, in WILLIAM TELL, xxvi, 437, 440

MECKLENBURG DECLARATION, xliii, 156-7

Meddling, Kempis on, vii, 227 (3), 243 (2), 288 (1); Marcus Aurelius on, ii, 203 (13); Penn on, i, 357 (435)

Medea and Æson, xli, 664

Medes, Raleigh on history of, xxxix, 113

Mediæval Architecture, Hugo on, xxxix, 350-1

Medici, Alessandro, de', xxxi, 84-5 note, 98, 101, 105; Cellini and, 149, 156-60, 172, 173; reputed son of Pope Clement, 174; murder of, 158 note 9, 177

Medici, Bernardo de', xxxi, 144 note 3

Medici, Caterina de', xxxi, 283 note; cupbearer to, 411 note; Count Mansfeld and, xxxviii, 51; King of Navarre and, 47-8

Medici, Cosimo de', xxxi, 15 note 1, 178 note 4; Almeni and, 366 note; Cellini

and, 341-4, 347-8, 350, 353-5, 357, 358-63, 364, 366-72, 373-6, 383, 387, 388-92, 392-3, 395-8, 400-2, 404-5, 405-7, 409-19, 421, 429-31, 433-5, 436; diamond of, 352-4, 361-2; Michaelangelo and, 384-7; mother of, 407 note; in Siennese war, 392-3, 406; Tasso and, 25 note 4

Medici Family, arms of, xxxi, 13 note 3; banishment and return of, 13; xxvii, 392

Medici, Francesco de', xxxi, 428

Medici, Giovanni de', xxxi, 68, 83 note 4

Medici, Giovannino de, xxxi, 15

Medici, Giuliano de', xxxi, 16 note, 84 note

Medici, Giulio de', xxxi, 16 note, 86 note 4 (see also Clement VII)

Medici, Ippolito de', xxxi, 84-5 note, 134 note; Cellini and, 137, 139-40, 144-5

Medici, Isabella de', xxxi, 201 note

Medici, Lorenzino de', xxxi, 85 note, 158 note 9, 160, 174-5, 177, 356 and note

Medici, Lorenzo de, Bacon on, iii, 50; Cellini and, xxxi, 11; descendants of, 84 note; mercantile enterprises of, x, 470

Medici, Lorenzo Di Piero de, Machiavelli to, xxxvi, 5-6, 83-6

Medici, Mary of, the wife of Concini and, v, 186

Medici, Ottaviano de, xxxi, 158 note 1, 172, 174

Medici, Pallone de, xxxi, 70

Medici, Piero de, father-in-law of Strozzi, xxxi, 78 note 1; monument of, 134 note 4

Medici, Pietro de, xxxi, 11 note 1, 12

Medicina, Piero de, xx, 116-17

Medicine(s), for children, Locke on, xxxvii, 26; Descartes on science of, xxxiv, 50-1; Descartes on study of, 8; in ancient Egypt, xxxiii, 42; external, xxxviii, 126; the germ theory in, 364; Goethe on profession of, xix, 82; in Greece, xxxviii, 2, 3, 4; Harrison on, xxxv, 238-40; Hippocrates on practise and study of, xxxviii, 2, 3, 4-5; Marlowe on study of, xix, 206-7, 209; practise of, among Indians, xliii, 35; Milton on study of, iii, 241; More on study of, xxxvi, 206, 208; in New Atlantis, iii, 176; papers on, xxxviii, 3-5, 145-220, 223-54, 364-82; Prome-

theus inventor of, viii, 184; Rousseau on, xxxiv, 172-3

Medina, origin of name, xlv, 986 note 7; siege of, 985 note, 986 note 6

Medina Suras, in Koran, xlv, 942-1007

Mediocrity, abhorred by the sublime, xxiv, 68

Meditation, Carlyle on, xxv, 322; Hindu doctrine of, xlv, 795-6, 799, 846; Kempis on, vii, 224 (1); Pascal on, xlviii, 63 (168); Plutarch on proper objects of, xii, 35-6; Rousseau on, xxxiv, 172

MEDITATIONS OF MARCUS AURELIUS, ii, 193-301; remarks on, 192

Mediterranean Sea, countries about, earliest in civilization, x, 24-5; Shelley on the, xli, 834; Taine on the, xxxix, 412

Medon, in ODYSSEY, xxii, 63-4, 221, 232, 305, 331

Medoro, and Angelica, xiv, 213, 226

Medusa, Dante on, xx, 37; Milton on, iv, 123-4

Medusa, queen of amazons, xxxiii, 327

Medwin, story from, v, 346

Meekness, Confucius on, xliv, 44 (27); Goethe on, xix, 135; Woolman on, i, 174

MEETING OF THE WATERS, xli, 817-18

MEG O' THE MILL, vi, 456-7

Megaenetus, pupil of Æschylus, viii, 468

Megaera, Dante on, xx, 37; Milton on, iv, 305

Megapenthes, son of Menelaus, xxii, 46, 202, 203

Megara, in Homer's Hades, xxii, 151

Megara, city of, xii, 65-7

Megatheroid Animals, habits of, xxix, 90-1

Megra, in PHILASTER, xlvii, 668-9; on Pharamond, 674, 675; with Pharamond, 688-90; before Pharamond's house, 692-3; caught with Pharamond, 695-7; accuses Arethusa, 698; at the hunt, 714-15, 716, 721; denounces Arethusa, 745; arrested, 748; freed, 750

Meinrad, of Hohenzollern, xxvi, 397 note 7

Melampus, Dionysus and, xxxiii, 30; Iphicles and, xxii, 152 note; story of, 206

Melancholy, Christianity and, xxxix, 343; Hobbes on, xxxiv, 353; in music, xli, 478; pleasures of, iv, 34-8

MELANCHOLY, by Fletcher, xl, 322

MELANCHOLY, ODE TO, xli, 882-3

Melancthon, on poetry, xxvii, 40

Melanopus, Callistratus and, xii, 201

Melanthius, in the ODYSSEY, xxii, 233-4, 237, 277-8, 288-9, 299-300, 301, 308

Melantho, daughter of Dolius, xxii, 253, 259

Melchthal, Arnold von, in WILLIAM TELL, at house of Fürst, xxvi, 395-6; hears father's blinding, 399-401; enters league with Fürst and Stauffacher, 402-5; at the rendezvous, 412-27; with Tell at Altdorf, 440, 443, 444; at death of Attinghausen, 459; with Rudenz, 462-4; reports progress of revolt, 475-6; hears death of Emperor, 477-81

Melcombe, Lord, SHORTEN SAIL, xl, 463-4

Meleager, son of Althea, viii, 102; Dante on, xx, 247 and note 2

Melendez, Pedro, governor of Florida, xxxiii, 256

Melesigenes, Homer called, iv, 401

Meletus, accuser of Socrates, ii, 7, 12-16, 22, 24, 27

Melias, Sir, knighting of, xxxv, 121; adventures of, 122-3; promises to follow Galahad, 124

Meliboeus, Milton on, iv, 66; Sidney on, xxvii, 25

Melissus, of Samos, xii, 62, 63; Dante on, xx, 343 note 20; Themistocles and, xii, 6; on the world, xxxix, 104

Melito, and M. Aurelius Antoninus, ii, 313

Melitene (see Thundering)

Mellus, Henry, xxiii, 387, 398

Mellyagraunce, and Launcelot, xlii, 1189-90

Melmoth, William, translator of Pliny, ix, 183

Melo, John de, Don Quixote on, xiv, 490

Melvin, Andrew, xv, 381-2, 417

Memmius, C., Gabinius and, ix, 116

Memnon, reference to, xiii, 90

MEMORABILIA, xlii, 1082

MEMORIAL VERSES, by Arnold, xlii, 1135-7

Memories, Homer on, of griefs, xxii, 210; Moore on, xli, 816; of pleasures, xvii, 43-44; Tennyson on, xlii, 981

Memorizing, Confucius on, xliv, 42 (5); Locke on, xxxvii, 150-2; of poetry, Eliot on, l, 8

Memory, Augustine, St., on the, vii, 166-

74; Calderon on, xxvi, 39; Hobbes on, xxxiv, 314; Hume on the, xxxvii, 299, 322-4; Locke on exercising the, 150-3; in old age, ix, 52-3; Pascal on, xlviii, 41 (95), 123 (369); Raleigh on, xxxix, 96-7; reliance on the, v, 66; verse and, xxvii, 31-2

Memphis, statues of Amasis at, xxxiii, 87; embankments at, 48-9; temple of Isis at, 87; founded by Min, 48; camp of Tyrians in, 54

Men, Confucius on study of, xliv, 7 (16), 8 (10); constitute states, xli, 579; divine and undivine, xlv, 861-2; two kinds of, xlviii, 171 (534); women and, Ruskin on, xxviii, 145

Ménage, Abbé, on Le Bailleul, v, 306

Menalippus, reference to, xx, 135

Menander, on his comedy, xxxii, 62-3, on friendship, 83-4

Menas, the pirate, xii, 345-6

Mendesians, sacred animals of, xxxiii, 25, 29

Mendicant, Ideal, of Buddhism, xlv, 748-50

MENDICANTS, THE ROYAL, xvi, 66, 99

Mendoza, city of, xxix, 334

Menelaus, Æschylus on, viii, 23, 30-3; Burke on grief of, xxiv, 34-5; in Egypt, Herodotus on, xxxiii, 57; in Egypt, Virgil on, xiii, 365; in ODYSSEY, xxii, 16, 36-7, 40-1, 46-62, 201-4; Pliny on, ix, 208 note 10; in Trojan horse, xiii, 108

Menenius, the senator, xxxix, 212

Menes (see Min)

Menexenus, with Socrates, ii, 47

Meng Chih-fan, xliv, 20 (13)

Meng Ching, xliv, 25 (4) note 3

Meng Chuang, xliv, 65 (18)

Meng Kung-Ch'o, xliv, 46 (12)

Meng Wu, Confucius and, xliv, 7 (6), 15 (7)

Meng Yi, disciple of Confucius, xliv, 7 (5)

Menico, in THE BETROTHED, xxi, 101, 123-4, 126, 129-30, 184

Menippus, Plutarch on, xii, 51

Menjot, M., Pascal on, xlviii, 342

Mennonists, on slavery, i, 215

Menœkeus, son of (see Creon)

Menœtes, in the ÆNEID, xiii, 183-4, 408

Menon, and Phidias, xii, 68

Mental Discourse, Hobbes on, xxxiv, 318-21; ends of, 346

Mental Powers, of animals, xi, 224-5

Mental Sciences, Helmholtz on, xxx, 173-4

Menteith, in MACBETH, xlvi, 383-4, 387

Mentes, form assumed by Pallas, xxii, 12, 14

Mentor, in ODYSSEY, xxii, 27, 229

Mephibosheth, and David, xli, 486; xliii, 104

Mephistopheles, in Goethe's FAUST, undertakes Faust's downfall, xix, 19-22; appears to Faust in shape of dog, 51; in Faust's study, appears as scholar, 52-64; as youth of high degree, 65; compact with Faust, 66-75; with the student, 76-83; starts with Faust, 83-4; at the wine-cellar, 88-98; in Witches' Kitchen, 100-12; promises Margaret to Faust, 113-15; in Margaret's chamber, 115-8; learns casket given to church, 121-2; visit to Martha's, 124-31; tells Faust of appointment, 131-3; with Martha in garden, 133-4, 137-8, 140; with Faust in cavern, 142-7; urges return to Margaret, 145-7; disliked by Margaret, 152-7; taunts Faust, 154-5; before Margaret's door, 160-1; with Valentine, 161-2; on Walpurgis-Night, 167-83; with Faust in the Plain, 190-3; in Open Country, 193; in dungeon, takes Faust, 202; Hugo on, xxxix, 348, 357

Mephistophilis, in Marlowe's FAUSTUS, conjured by Faustus, xix, 213-6; compact with Faustus, 219-24; with Faustus, on Heaven, astrology, etc., 224-6; with Faustus in Rome, 230-2; with Robin and Ralph, 235; with horse-courser, 239-40; renews compact with Faustus, 245

Mer de Glace, of Chamouni, xxx, 216-20, 223; movement of, 223-6, 228

Mercantile System, effect of, on revenue of the state, x, 526; principle of the, 311-31; producers and consumers under, 424-5

Mercator, work of, in mathematics, xxxiv, 125

Mercenary Soldiers, Bacon on, iii, 75; Machiavelli on, xxxvi, 45-6; More on, 219

Merchant, Chaucer's (see Marchant)

Merchant, the natural, v, 185

MERCHANT AND THE JINNI, story of, xvi, 15-17

MERCHANT AND HIS WIFE, story of, xvi, 12-13

Merchantman, duties on a, xxiii, 16-21

Merchants, in agricultural system, x, 431-5, 439-42; Bacon on, iii, 51; Harrison on, xxxv, 224; interests of, x, 210-11; in war (agreement with Mexico), xliii, 303

Mercurius, the spirit in the battle, xvii, 183

Mercurius Aulicus, royalist paper, iii, 208 note

Mercury, in the ÆNEID, xiii, 33-4, 83, 161-2, 172; frauds of, xxxiv, 367; as German god, xxxiii, 97; son of Maia, xiii, 272

Mercury (the metal), supposed parent of metals, xlvii, 577

Mercury (the planet), Dante's second Heaven, xx, 305

Mercy, Blake on, xli, 591; Bunyan on name and practice of, xv, 231-2; Cowper on, xli, 536; Dryden on, xviii, 86-7; Hobbes on, xxxiv, 407; Jesus on, xliv, 369 (36); Luther on acts of, xxxvi, 254; Milton on, iv, 19-20 (8); in princes, xxxvi, 53; Shakespeare on, xlvi, 160-1; Solomon on, xliii, 95; Mercy, in PILGRIM'S PROGRESS, xv, 174; neighbor of Christiana, 186, 188-90; in Slough of Dispond, 190-1; admitted at the gate, 192-3; conversation with Christiana, 194; asks about the Dog, 195-6; her innocency, 200; at the Interpreter's House, 202-4; why she went on pilgrimage, 209-10; on Difficulty Hill, 218; in Beautiful Palace, 225; her dream, 226-7; her suitor, Mr. Brisk, 230-1; in Valley of Humiliation, 242; in Valley of Death, 246-7; and Mr. Honest and, 253; on Mr. Fearing, 259; married to Matthew, 265-6, 268; in Vanity Fair, 282; at By-way to Hell, 292; the looking-glass and, 293-4

Meredith, George, LOVE IN THE VALLEY, xlii, 1140-5

Meredith, Hugh, i, 50-1, 58; Franklin in business with, 53-4, 56-7, 59, 60-2; goes south, 62

Merit, contrasted with worthiness, xxxiv, 369; Hobbes on, 396-7; not envied, iii, 24; Pascal on word, xlviii, 167

Merlin, on Arthur, xlii, 986-7; converted by St. Columba, xxxii, 170; Keats on, xli, 888; legend of, xxxii, 153; Renan

on, 168; the Round Table and, xxxv, 135-6

MERMAID TAVERN, THE, xli, 874-5

Mermaid's, Chaucer on, xl, 46

MERMAN, THE FORSAKEN, xlii, 1123-6

Meroe, Herodotus on city of, xxxiii, 19

Merope, daughter of Pandareüs, in the ODYSSEY, xx, 274

Merriman, Dr., xxxviii, 246

MERRY ANDREW'S SONG, vi, 125-6

MERRY HAE I BEEN TEETHIN' A HECKLE, vi, 134

Merryman, in FAUST, xix, 12-16

Merton, Walter, xxxv, 381

Mertoun, Earl, in A BLOT IN THE 'SCUTCHEON, suitor of Mildred Tresham, xviii, 259-60; described by retainers, 361; arrival at Tresham's 363; his love for Mildred, 364-6; secret visit to Mildred, 372-7; discovered, unknown, by Gerard, 377-80; under Mildred's window the last time, 392-3; killed by Tresham, 394-8

Mesaulius, Homer on, xxii, 197

Mescidius, Cicero on, ix, 110

Mesrur, the executioner, xvi, 60

Messalla, and Cicero, ix, 116; Cicero on, 94, 176

Messapus, in the ÆNEID, Æneas and, xiii, 406; ally of Turnus, 263, 268, 294, 298, 310, 347, 372, 374, 409, 413; Aulestes and, 400

Messiah, Milton on prophecies of the, iv, 348, 350-1; Mohammed on the, xlv, 984, 996, 1002; Pascal on prophecies of the, xlviii, 186-9, 201, 202 (616-17), 203-4, 214, 219 (662), 236 (707)

Metabus, father of Camilla, xiii, 375-6

Metagenes, of Xypete, xii, 50

Metallurgy, beginnings of, xxxiv, 206

Metals, artificial, in New Atlantis, iii, 172; Harrison on source of, xxxv, 320-1; as medium of exchange, x, 28-9; prices of, 171-6, 179, 200-1

Metamorphic Rocks, xxx, 334-5

Metaphors, Bunyan on, xv, 7-8; Burke on pleasure from, xxiv, 18; Hobbes on, xxxiv, 351; Lowell on, xxviii, 458; Pliny on, ix, 348-50; Wordsworth on, xxxix, 302-4

Metamorphoses, of insects, xi, 457-8

Metamorphosis, Browne on, iii, 289, 291-2

Metaphysic of Morals, necessity of a, xxxii, 299-303, 319-24

Metaphysical Reasoning, Franklin on, i, 55

Metaphysicians, Burke on, xxiv, 412

Metaphysics, Aryan and Semitic, xxxix, 420; Bacon's attitude toward, iii, 144; Berkeley on, xxxvii, 280; Carlyle on, xxv, 340-2; Carlyle on German, 353-4; Channing on study of, xxviii, 329; Cowley on, xxvii, 64-5; defined by Kant, xxxii, 299; Goethe on, xix, 79-80; Hume on, xxxvii, 292-8, 336, 420; Locke on study of, 138; Milton on study of, iii, 237-8; Rousseau on, xxxiv, 250-1

Metelli, names of the, xii, 156

Metellus, the tribune, xii, 294

Metellus Quintus, Cicero on, ix, 125; free from resentment, xii, 189

Metempsychosis, Browne on, iii, 289 (37); Lessing on, xxxii, 205-6; of opinions, iii, 257; Socrates on, ii, 59-62, 73-4 (see also Transmigration)

Meteorology, Hobbes on, xxxiv, 363; origin of term, xii, 68 note; in Utopia, xxxvi, 195

Metheglin, Welsh drink, xxxv, 286

Method, in business, i, 355 (403); Goethe on, xix, 78; Locke on, xxxvii, 169-70

Methon, observations of, xxxiv, 129

Methuen, treaty drawn by, x, 390

Methusalem, Browne on, iii, 275

Metius, the traitor, xiii, 289

Meton, the astrologer, xii, 121

Metoposcopy, xlvii, 592; defined by Hobbes, xxxiv, 382

Metras, restored by Cicero, ix, 136

Metre, Shelley on, xxvii, 342-3; Whitman on, xxxix, 394; Wordsworth on, 283-4, 285-6, 287, 293, 296

Metric System, Kelvin on the, xxx, 253

Metrical Novels, Wordsworth on, xxxix, 298

Metrodorus, xii, 338

Metropolis, every, a university, xxviii, 36, 37, 38

Metz, Paré on expedition against, xxxviii, 19; siege of, 23-33

Mexican War, cause of, xliii, 289 note

Mexico, ancient, iii, 157; Johnson on palaces of, xxxix, 225; Raleigh on conquest of, xxxiii, 330; seat of Montezume, iv, 329; TREATY WITH U. S., xliii, 289-305

Meyer, Heinrich, xxxix, 251 note

Meyer von Sarnen, in WILLIAM TELL, xxvi, 412-25

Meymum, the son of Demdem, xvi, 79

Mezentius, ally of Turnus, xiii, 261, 268; in attack on Trojan town, 310; in the battle, 345-8; wounded by Æneas, 348-9; his death, 350-4; Dryden on, 20, 33

Miasma, source of, xxix, 369

Miaulina, xiv, 137

Mica, crystallization of, xxx, 30; effect on polarized light, 34

Micaiah, Calvin on, xxxix, 42; Milton on, iii, 228

Micceri, Pagolo, xxxi, 304-5, 306, 312-14, 318

Mice, bees and, xi, 82; country and town, ii, 292 (22); country and town, fable of, xvii, 13-14; Darwin on, xxix, 363; in Galapagos Islands, 382; range of, xi, 146; use of ears of, 213

Michael, Archangel, in FAUST, xix, 18-19; in PARADISE LOST, iv, 205, 210-12, 321-2, 325-6, 327-55, 357

Michael, the fiddler in EVANGELINE, xlii, 1311, 1326

MICHAEL: A PASTORAL POEM, xli, 615-27

Michal, references to, xli, 486, 488

Michaux, on American trees, xxviii, 406

Michelangelo, Andrea del Sarto and, xlii, 1091-2; on Baccio d'Agnolo's cupola, xxxi, 412 note 3; on beauty, v, 304; Bugiardini and, xxxi, 86 note; cartoon on taking of Pisa, 23 and note 2; Cellini and, 3-4, 24, 85-6, 384; Cellini on, 343, 359, 418; Cosimo de' Medici and, 384, 385-6; "David" of, 342 note 3; "David" of, Bandinello on, 401-2; "The Fair" of, xxxix, 200; Hazlitt on, xxvii, 278; Hugo on "Last Judgment" of, xxxix, 352; Luigi Pulci and, xxxi, 62; Rossetti on, xlii, 1179; model for a "Samson," xxxi, 416; Torrigiani and, 23-4; work in S. Lorenzo Sacristy, 368-9 note 2; his man Urbino, 386 note

Michelet, Taine on, xxxix, 414

Micheletto, the engraver, xxxi, 91-2

MICHIE, WILLIAM, EPITAPH FOR, vi, 265

Michol, reference to, xx, 184

Mickle, Samuel, i, 57

Micocolembo, xiv, 137

Micomicona, Princess, xiv, 280-3

Microbe, origin of term, xxxviii, 364

Microscopic Organisms, Pasteur on, xxxviii, 343

Midas, Dante on, xx, 228; ears of, iv, 81

Midias, and Demosthenes, xii, 200

Middle Ages, classics of, xxxii, 122; the grotesque in the, xxxix, 350-1; Hugo on architecture of, 350; philosophy of, xxviii, 215; poetry of the, xxvii, 346-8; Taine on, xxxix, 426, 433; works dealing with, l, 22-3, 26

Middle Doctrine of Buddha, xlv, 661-5

Middleton, Newman on, xxviii, 47

Midian, reference to, xliv, 248 (9)

Midianites, Mohammed on the, xlv, 907 note

Midwifery, Holmes on, xxxviii, 252-3

Mien, the music-master, xliv, 54 (41)

Migāra, the treasurer, xlv, 756, 760, 764-5, 766-72

Might, and justice, xlviii, 106 (198-300), 305 (878); opinion and, 107 (303), 109 (311)

MIGHTY FORTRESS IS OUR GOD, xlv, 557-8

Migratory Birds, Milton on, iv, 238

Milan, Cathedral of, the eighth wonder, xxi, 190; corn scarcity in (1628), 196-9; fall of, xxxvi, 79; famine in, xxi, 450-65; insurrection of, 199-226, 267-71; Lazzaretto of, 461-2; Louis XII at, xxxvi, 8-9; Machiavelli on princedom of, 7; plague of, xxi, 467-8, 500-35, 557-70, 612; power of, before French invasion, xxxvi, 38; Sforza at, 42

Milbanke, Miss, wife of Byron, xviii, 406

Milbourne, Luke, xxxix, 172 note 34, 172-3

Mildmay, Sir Walter, xxxv, 381

Milinda, the king, xlv, 653-6

Military Affairs, Machiavelli on, xxxvi, 40-50, 68-9, 71-2

Military Service, in BODY OF LIBERTIES, xliii, 67

Military Spirit, in different states of society, xxvii, 372-4

Military Training, in Milton's Academy, iii, 244-6

Militia, Bacon on a, iii, 52; congressional control of, xliii, 185 (15, 16); provision for, under Confederation, 161; standing army and, x, 447-8; in United States, xliii, 194 (2)

Milk, Burke on composition of, xxiv, 123; Harrison on, xxxv, 330

MILKMAID AND PAIL, fable of, xvii, 42

Milky Way, ancient idea of, xlviii, 442; Bacon on the, iii, 100; Newcomb on the, xxx, 313, 318, 319-20; reference to the, iv, 241

Mill, James, xxv, 3; Analysis of Human Mind, 47, 188-9; death of, 127; early life of, 8; Elements of Political Economy, 23, 43; English law, abhorrence of, 44; ethics and psychology of, 69-70; examiner of Indian correspondence, 21-2; on feeling, 71-2; friendships, 38-9, 49-50; History of India, 9, 21-2; influence of, 60; influence among Benthamites, 65-9; criticized by Macaulay, 100; on Mackintosh and Tocqueville, 126; moral convictions, 34-7; on poetry and poets, 15-16; political belief, 69-70; political philosophy mistaken, 101-2; religious belief of, 29-32; son's education, 7-28; later relations with son, 113; tenderness lacking, 37; unpublished dialogue on government, 44; Westminster Review, connection with, 60-3, 83-4; work, estimation of, 127-8; writings for London Review, 125-6

Mill, John Stuart, address at St. Andrews, xxv, 188; on American Civil War, 164-7; AUTOBIOGRAPHY, of, 7-192; AUTOBIOGRAPHY, reasons for writing, 7-8; a Benthamite, 44-6, 66-73; birth of, 8; Carlyle and, 110-11, 316; Comte and Positivism, 171; correspondence with Comte, 131-3; Council, offered seat in, 154-5; on Demosthenes and Plato, 18-19; dissatisfaction with present aims, 86-90, 93; Dissertations, 161-2; early essays, 48; early ideas of the poets, 16; early wish to be a reformer, 85; edits Bentham's work on evidence, 74-5; edits father's Analysis, 188; edits London Review, 124-6, 129, 133-7; education, 9-14, 16-17; education in political economy, 22-4; his education, remarks on, 24-8; elocution studied by, 20; Examination of Hamilton's Philosophy, 167-70; the Examiner, writings in, 109; as examiner in India House, 154; on fatalism, 106-7; father's relations with, 37-8, 113; father's friends, relations with, 38-9; feelings cultivated, 91-2; first newspaper articles, 58-9; France, visit to, 39-42; on French Revolution, 43, 84;

friendship with Grote and the Austins, 49-53, 111; friendship with Maurice and Sterling, 97-9; happiness, new theory of, 90-1; his *History of Roman Government*, 14; hopes of human improvement, 147-8; in Hyde Park affair, 178; improvement club, 77-9; India Company, with, 54-7; in Jamaica Committee, 181-3; law read by, 44; ON LIBERTY, 195-312; remarks on, 155-8; life and works, 3-5; logic studied by, 17-18; logic, his work on, 101-2, 113-14, 130-1, 138-41, 152 note 2; London club formed, 80-3; love of the heroic, 73; marginal notes made for father, 43; marriage to Mrs. Taylor, 149; music, pleasure in, 92-3; Owenites debated with, 79-80; in Parliament, 172-92; *Parliamentary Reform*, pamphlet on, 159; *Parliamentary Review*, writings in, 76-7; philosophical studies, 45-8; on poetry, 72-3; his *Political Economy*, 145-7, 151-3; political philosophy of, 99-106, 107-8, 120-1, 143-5, 163-4; popular editions of works, 171-2; private reading, 13-14; religious and moral influences, 29-36; *Representative Government*, 163-4; Roebuck and, 95-7; his *Spirit of the Age*, 109-10; on his step-daughter, 163; *Subjection of Women*, 164; Taylor, Mrs., and, 116-19, 142-3, 149-54, 155-6; *Utilitarianism*, 164; Utilitarian Society formed by, 53-4; on verse writing, 15; *Westminster Review*, connection with, 61, 62 note, 63-4, 83-4; woman suffrage and, 68, 151 note 1; Wordsworth, acquaintance with, 93-5; writing, his method of, 138-9; writings (1830-2), 113-15; writings (1833-4), 123-5; on his writings, 150-2

Millar's *Historical View of English Government*, xxv, 11

Miller, Chaucer's, xl, 26-7; Dryden on Chaucer's, xxxix, 166

MILLER, HEY THE DUSTY, vi, 300-1

Miller, Rev. Alex., Burns on, vi, 100

Miller, Hugh, THE BABIE, xli, 918

Mills, wind and water, introduction of, x, 206

Milnes, Richard Monckton, SONNET, xlii, 1057-8

Milo, Titus Annius, Clodius and, xii, 246; defence of, by Cicero, ix, 6; trial of, 97; xii, 246-7

Milo of Croton, Cicero on, ix, 55; his feat at Olympia, 56

Miltiades, Aristides and, xii, 82; Byron on, xli, 814; in fetters, xxvii, 21; Themistocles and, xii, 7-8

Miltitz, Charles, xxxvi, 341-342

Milto, concubine of Cyrus, xii, 61

Milton, John, father of the poet, iv, 3

Milton, John, the poet, AREOPAGITICA, iii, 189-232; Arnold on, xxviii, 77, 80; Arnold on lines from, 73-4; Arnold on prose of, 81-2; austere goodness of, 172-4; Bagehot on COMUS, 205-6; Bagehot on PARADISE LOST, 194-205; Bagehot on SAMSON AGONISTES of, 178-9; blindness of, iv, 3, 4-5, 84, 85, 86, 136-7; books of, burned at Oxford, v, 417; Browning on, xlii, 1068; Burke on, xxiv, 50-1, 53, 68, 100; Burke on his picture of Hell, 138-9; Carlyle on, xxv, 322, 444; on Charles II, xxvii, 171; daughters of, iv, 4, 5; on divorce, xxviii, 183-6; Dryden on, xiii, 13, 49, 57; xxxix, 154; xl, 396; early desires to write a great epic, iv, 21-2; Eliot on POEMS of, l, 7; Emerson on, v, 128, 144, 180, 433, 438; Gray on, xl, 456; Hazlitt on, xxvii, 268; highest merit of, v, 59; Hugo on, xxxix, 354-5; Hugo on Paradise of, 349; humor and knowledge of ordinary life lacking in, xxviii, 176-80; Johnson on, 206; Keightley's *Life* of, remarks on, 168; liberty, his passion for, iv, 4; life and works, 3-6; marriage to Mary Powell, xxviii, 180-4, 186; Masson's *Life* of, review of, 165-8; mention of, in *Cromwell*, xxxix, 380; James Mill on, xxv, 16; outline of life, xxviii, 168-9; Pascal on, xlviii, 69 (192), 150 (448), 152 (455); personal beauty, xxviii, 174-5; POEMS of, iv; poetry of, remarks on, xxviii, 191-4; on poets, v, 175; political relations, xxviii, 190-1; political writings, 189-90; Ruskin on, 106-7, 111-12; Sainte-Beuve on, xxxii, 128; sensibility of, xxviii, 180-1; Severity, 175-6; Shelley on, xxvii, 335, 341, 348-9; xli, 857; Shelley on PARADISE LOST of, xxvii, 354-5; strength of his nature, xxviii, 175; his studiousness, 176; Swift on, xxvii, 112; Thoreau on, xxviii, 413; TRACTATE ON EDUCATION, iii, 235-47; at twenty-three, iv, 29; ON HIS DECEASED WIFE, iv, 86; Wordsworth on,

xxxix, 306, 319-21; xli, 675, 677; Wordsworth on sonnets of, xli, 681; Wright on, xxviii, 191-2

MILTON, ESSAY ON, Bagehot's, xxviii, 165-206

Mimas, death of, xiii, 346

MIMNERMUS IN CHURCH, xlii, 1114

Mimosa, Longfellow on the, xlii, 1321

Min, first king of Egypt, xxxiii, 9, 48-9

Min Tzu-ch'ien, xliv, 19 (7), 33 (2, 4), 34 (12, 13)

Mincius, smooth-sliding, iv, 74

Mincius, the Triton, xiii, 328

Mind, anticipation of the, xxxix, 146; Bacon on operations of the, 134-5, 136, 144; Berkeley on the, xxxvii, 252, 254-5, 271; body and, connection between, xxiv, 108; body and, Pascal on, xlviii, 32; Burke on study of the, xxiv, 46-7; Byron on the, xviii, 449; xxxii, 383; Channing on improvement of the, xxviii, 328-36; Channing on power of, 350; Descartes on reality of the, xxxiv, 29; diffusion of, ii, 264 (57, 60); diseases of the, 144 (75); as the first cause, 91; geometrical and imaginative, xlviii, 412-13; heart and, relations of, v, 282-3; its hell, xlii, 1399-1400; Helmholtz on sciences of, xxx, 173-4; Hume on perceptions of the, xxxvii, 299-300; Hume on study of the, 295-8; Locke on a sound, 9; Locke on training the, 27 et seq., 70-1; Marvell on the, xl, 378; materialistic ideas of, xxxiv, 104-8; Marcus Aurelius on the, ii, 261 (48); mathematical and intuitive, compared, xlviii, 9-12; memory and, St. Augustine on, vii, 171; More on pleasures of, xxxvi, 201-3; native propensities of the, xxxvii, 84-5; Penn on pleasures of the, i, 332 (96-8); perturbations of the, vii, 171-2; Pope on study of the, xl, 406-7; religiousness of, xlv, 865; Rousseau on the, xxxiv, 258-9; Schiller on nature of the, xxxii, 261-3; Shakespeare on diseases of, xlvi, 386; Shelley on the, xli, 856; troubled, no medicine for, xlvii, 708; virtues and defects of, xxxiv, 349-59; Watts on the, xl, 398 (see also Understanding)

MIND, MY, TO ME A KINGDOM IS, xl, 207-9

Mindarus, xii, 133-5

Mineralogy, Locke on study of, xxxvii, 147; in New Atlantis, iii, 177

Minerva, Jove's keys and, v, 92; on mankind, 218; the shield of, iv, 56 (see also Athena)

Mines, discovery of, in Chili, xxix, 321-2; fertility of, x, 169; produce of, a source of capital, 221; rent of, 169, 171-7

Minicianus, Cornelius, letter to, ix, 253

Mining, in Chili, xxix, 264-5, 270-1, 342-5, 349-50; Smith on projects of, x, 402-3

Minister, in FAUST, xix, 177

Ministers, Burns on "whids" of, vi, 74; Chaucer on, xl, 24-5; Penn on, i, 359 (457-467); who change to better their income, xv, 106-7; Woolman on true, i, 176, 245-6; Woolman's counsel to, 310-12

Ministers (of state), Bacon on, iii, 95; Confucius on, xliv, 11 (19); Henry VII's policy toward, xxxix, 77; Machiavelli on, xxxvi, 75-6; Penn on, i, 351-3

Ministry, Emerson on the, v, 33-40; Sidney on the, xxvii, 16; Walton on the, xv, 340-1

MINNA VON BARNHELM, Lessing's, xxvi, 299-375; remarks on, 298

Minnesingers, Poe on the, xxviii, 378

Minorities, Lincoln on duty of, xliii, 318-19

Minority Representation, Mill on, xxv, 160

Minos, in Crete, xxii, 261-2; Dante on, xx, 21; Homer on, xxii, 159; judge of the dead, xiii, 221; judge in Hades, xxvi, 183; Scylla and, viii, 102

Minotaur, Dante on the, xx, 49; reference to the, xxvi, 136

Minshull, Elizabeth, wife of Milton, iv, 5

MINSTREL, THE, AT LINCLUDEN, vi, 480-1

Minstrels, Homer on, xxii, 111-12

Minutius Æmilianus, ix, 200-2

Miocene, Upper, Lyell on the, xxxviii, 412

Mirabeau, Carlyle's estimate of, v, 183; Emerson on, 265; on the French aristocracy, 406; on October sixth, xxiv, 211 note; on political societies, x, 444; ugliness of, v, 306

Miracles, Bacon on, iii, 153-4; of Bible, Browne on, 259-61, 271-5, 279 (27); Calvin on, xxxix, 33-5; Dante on Christian, xx, 389; Emerson on, v, 30, 32, 293; Hobbes on, xxxiv, 385; Hume on, xxxvii, 375-92; Marcus Aurelius on, ii, 193 (6); of Old Testament, Lessing on, xxxii, 189; only in ancient

history, v, 29; Pascal on, xlviii, 279-99, 348, 358; Plutarch on, xii, 182-3; Rousseau on, xxxiv, 286-8; in Utopia, xxxvi, 229; Walton on, xv, 326-7; Whitman on, xxxix, 399

Miranda, in THE TEMPEST, with Prospero on island, xlvi, 399-405, 410; first meeting with Ferdinand, 413-6; with Ferdinand, at his task, 432-5; betrothed to Ferdinand, 443-9; discovered to Alonso, etc., 458-9; Hunt on, xxvii, 294; Shelley on, and Ariel, xli, 848-9

Miranda, Francesco, expedition of, xliii, 273

Mirandola, Galeotto della, xxxi, 339-40

Mirandola, Pico della, xlviii, 28 note

Mirandola, Picus, xv, 323

Mirrors, ancient, xxxv, 322

Mirth, ECCLESIASTES on, xliv, 336 (2), 342 (4), 345 (15); in music, xli, 478; parentage of, iv, 30; pleasures of, 30-4; religion and, Herbert on, xv, 406

MIRZA, VISION OF, by Addison, xxvii, 73-7

Misael, Luther on, xxxvi, 329

Misanthropy, Bacon on, iii, 34; Socrates on, ii, 82

Misbelievers, Mohammed on, xlv, 883, 931-2, 946, 947-8, 949-50, 957, 959, 977-8, 981-2, 984, 998

Miscelin, a kind of bread, xxxv, 281, 312

Misenus, death and burial of, xiii, 213, 214; the Harpies and, 136

Miserliness, Blake on, xli, 588; contrasted with avarice, xxxvi, 51; More on, 200; in princes, 52-4

Misers, Burns on, vi, 221; fable of, xvii, 36; Penn on the, i, 327 (45), 331 (88-91)

Misery, "acquaints with strange bedfellows," xlvi, 428; contemplation of, vii, 228-9; death's harbinger, iv, 260; islands in sea of, xli, 835; Kempis on bearing of, vii, 279; miracles and, xlvi, 251; origin and cessation of, xlv, 625-6, 661-2, 674; Pascal on human, xlviii, 130, 131 (405); truth and, iv, 371

Misfortune(s), Arabian verses on, xvi, 16; Burns on, vi, 68; children and, iii, 19-20; compensation for, v, 98, 101-2; envy bred by, iii, 23; indifferency of, ii, 135-6 (56); Marcus Aurelius on bearing, 220 (49), 224 (8), 228 (18); of others, pleasure in, xxiv, 40-3; Penn on use of, i, 385 (150); profit from, ii,

156 (106); Woolman on, i, 256 (see also Adversity)

Misology, Kant on, xxxii, 307; Socrates on, ii, 82-3

Mississippi River, provision for navigation of, xliii, 179; sediment of, xxxviii, 402; Thoreau on the, xxviii, 408

MISTAKES OF A NIGHT (see SHE STOOPS TO CONQUER)

Mistletoe, origin of the, xi, 20

MISTRESS, HIS SUPPOSED, xl, 300

MISTRESS, LINES TO HIS, xxvii, 270-1

MISTRESS, THE LOST, xlii, 1069-70

MISTRESS MINE, xl, 262

MISTRESS, WISHES FOR THE SUPPOSED, xl, 359-63

Mistrust, in PILGRIM'S PROGRESS, xv, 46-7, 128; Christian on, 132-3; punishment of, 221

Misunderstanding, Emerson on, v, 66

Misuse, of good things, iv, 159-60; is loss, i, 329 (70); Sidney on, xxvii, 35

Mitchel, Dr., i, 147

MITCHELL, COLLECTOR, VERSES TO, vi, 544-5

Mites, Pascal on, xlviii, 27

Mitford, exposed by Grote, xxv, 63; Mill on history of, 13

Mithra, Utopian name of God, xxxvi, 225, 233

Mithridates, and Antony, xii, 358, 359

Mithridates, Chrysippus, ix, 361

Mithridates of Pontus, water-wheel of, xxx, 181

Mithropaustes, and Demaratus, xii, 31

Mitscherlich, on fermentation, xxxviii, 345, 349-50 and note

Mivart, St. George, objections to Natural Selection, xi, 218-50

Mlithe, the jester, xlix, 242

Mnason of Cyprus, xliv, 470 (16)

Mnason, Mr., in PILGRIM'S PROGRESS, xv, 278-9

Mnesicles, Athenian architect, xii, 50

Mnesiphilus and Themistocles, xii, 6

Mnesiptolema, daughter of Themistocles, xii, 32, 33

Mnesitheus, of Athens, xxxv, 274

Mnestheus, in the ÆNEID, in archery contest, xiii, 194-5; in battle, 409; at the combat, 394; in defence of town, 319, 326; in Trojan camp, 298, 303; in Trojan games, 182-6

Mobs, Emerson on, v, 99, 206; Manzoni on, xxi, 214-16; Ruskin on, xxviii, 114

Mocking-birds, in Brazil, xxix, 62; Longfellow on, xlii, 1324

Moderation, Confucius on, xliv, 21 (27); Descartes on, xxxiv, 22; Franklin on, i, 79; Hamilton on, xliii, 200; Hume on, xxxvii, 399; Kant on, xxxii, 306; Penn on, i, 346

MODERN ENGLISH DRAMA, xviii

Modern Europe, works dealing with, l, 27-8

Modern Man, Whitman on the, xlii, 1402

Modestus, Metius, Pliny on, ix, 189, 252; Regulus and, 191

Modesty, Burke on amiability of, xxiv, 90; Confucius on, xliv, 58 (6); Dryden on excessive, xviii, 11; Epictetus on, ii, 158 (111); Hobbes on, xxxiv, 409; impudence and, xviii, 218; resides with other virtues, 209; in speech, Franklin on, i, 18-9, 87; Steele on, xxvii, 176-7; violets for, vi, 407; virtue and, ix, 250

Modification (see Variation)

Modred, Gray on, xl, 457

Mogador, island of, xxxiii, 199

Moggallana, xlv, 701, 710, 711, 777

Mohammad, son of Suleyman Ez-Zeyni, xvi, 193, 223, 225, 229

Mohammed, the prophet, Abu Ghal and, xlv, 879 note 3; the believers and, 908 note; the blind man and, 885 note; the caravan and, 942-3 notes 2, 3; Dante on, xx, 278 note 12; in Dante's HELL, 115; the hill and, iii, 32; on himself, xlv, 989; Hobbes on, xxxiv, 382; Hume on ethics of, xxvii, 205; Jews and, xlv, 964 notes; on learning and folly, v, 294; liaison with Mary, xlv, 992 note 1; life, 876; the Meccans and, 944 note 5; at Ohod, 959 note; Pascal on, xlviii, 194-6 (595-601); the Quráish and, xlv, 994 note 1; at siege of Medina, 986 note 6; on the spoils, 992 note 32; the sun and, xvi, 31 note; supposed prophecy of, in the Bible, xlv, 966 note 2; Thoreau on, xxviii, 420; Voltaire on, xxxiv, 84; wives of, xlv, 985 note 2, 987 note 16, 989 note 20; on his wives, 987-8, 990, 991, 992-3

Mohammed Aben Alhamar, xxxix, 84

Mohammedan Literature, l, 21-2, 26

Mohammedanism, xlv, 855; Bacon on rise of, iii, 138; Browne on, 278;

Rousseau on, xxxiv, 294; Taine on, xxxix, 432 (see also Koran)

Mohun, at Crecy, xxxv, 24

Moine, Le, Dryden on, xiii, 13

Moiris, king of Egypt, xxxiii, 12, 49

Moiris, Lake, built by Moiris the king, xxxiii, 49-50; Herodotus on, 9, 75

Molecular Forces, Newton on, xxxix, 151-2

Moles, eyes of, xi, 142; xxix, 59

Molesworth, Sir William, xxv, 122, 123, 124-5, 129

Molière, Jean Baptiste Poquelin, English dramatists and, xxxiv, 139; Goethe on, xxxii, 124; Hazlitt on, xxvii, 279-80; Hugo on, xxxix, 357, 372, 373; life and works, xxvi, 198; as Orgon in TARTUFFE, 199; Sainte-Beuve on, xxxii, 124, 129, 131; TARTUFFE, xxvi, 199-296; Voltaire on *Misanthrope* of, xxxiv, 136

Molinera, Lady, in DON QUIXOTE, xiv, 35

Moloch, in PARADISE LOST, iv, 98, 109, 213; reference to, 13-4 (23)

Molothrus, Darwin on the, xxix, 60; instincts of, xi, 262-3

Moluccas, Drake in the, xxxiii, 218-21

Momemphis, battle of, xxxiii, 84

Moment, the, alone is decisive, xix, 368

Monad, Augustine, St., on the, vii, 58

Monaeses and Antony, xii, 349, 358

Monaldi, Sandrino, xxxi, 234 note, 237-8

Monarchy, Burke on, xxiv, 261-2; Emerson on, v, 243; Pope on, xl, 428-9; republics compared with, v, 245-6; Rousseau on origin of, xxxiv, 215-21 (see also Princedoms)

Monasteries, Harrison on, xxxv, 232; Luther on, xxxvi, 300-1, 305-6, 315, 326

Monatunkanet, xliii, 143, 146

Moncontour, battle of, xxxviii, 50

Mondella, Agnese, in I PROMESSI SPOSI, mother of Lucia, xxi, 37; advises Renzo, 40; with Father Galdino, 48-52; advised by Father Cristoforo, 68-70; plans marriage of Lucia, 89-92, 95-6; with Menico, 101-2; at Abbondio's, 114, 116, 124-6; goes to convent, 129-33; to Monza, 133-44, 176-7; reunion with Lucia, 393-5; with Cardinal Federigo, 397-8; at the tailor's, 409-11; receives gift from the Unnamed, 426-7; learns Lucia's vow, 427-31; tries to find Renzo, 431-2;

corresponds with Renzo, 437-41; flight to castle of Unnamed, 474-80, 487-91; at the castle, 493-6; learns Lucia's safety from Renzo, 617-8; returns home, 620-1; with her grandchildren, 642

Mondella, Lucia, in I PROMESSI SPOSI, marriage of, forbidden, xxi, 14; with Renzo, 36-7; confesses Rodrigo's persecution, 38-40; sends for Father Cristoforo, 48-51; advised by Father Cristoforo, 68-71; plans for marriage with Renzo, 89-92, 95-6; consents to plan, 100-1; plot to carry off, 106-8; at Abbondio's with Renzo, 114, 116-7, 118-9, 125-6; goes to convent, 130-3; flight to Monza, 133-8; at the convent, 139-44, 175-7; discovered by Rodrigo, 291; learns of Renzo's mishaps, 293-6; abduction of, 323-34; in castle of the Unnamed, 336-43; release planned, 367-70; taken to village, 380-92; reunion with mother, 394-5; visited by Cardinal, 397-400; life at the tailor's, 409-10; Donna Prassede and, 411-13; return home, 414-5; goes with Donna Prassede, 425-6; confesses vow to mother, 427-31; at Prassede's, unable to forget Renzo, 441-3; taken with plague, 571; found by Renzo, 597-603; absolved from vow, 606-10; returns home, 622, 626-7; married to Renzo, 636-7; her daughter, 642; lesson of her life, 643

Mondrames, xxxv, 119

Money, Bacon on need of spreading, iii, 40; Burns on, thirst for, vi, 82; in Chiloe, xxix, 278; as circulating capital, x, 219; congressional right of borrowing, xliii, 183 (2); Emerson on, strife for, v, 18; evils from use of, 255-6; of ancient Germans, xxxiii, 95; increase of, in relation to wages and profits, x, 283-4; justice and, Shakespeare on, xlvi, 296; makes money, x, 95; as measure of value, 36, 40-1, 46; Milton on power of, iv, 382; Mirabeau on, x, 444; More on wrongs due to, xxxvi, 238; need of continual supply of, x, 228; origin and use of, 27-33; paper (see Paper Money); Penn on love of, i, 335 (127), 390; Plutarch on use of, xii, 156; prolific nature of, i, 104; its proportion to produce circulated by its means, x, 234-5; quantity of, de-

pendent on consumable goods, 267-8; quantity of, in relation to industry, 234; regulation of, under Confederation, xliii, 163-4; regulation of, by Congress, 184 (5); revenue and, x, 227-9; as reward for services, xxiv, 305; Ruskin on love of, xxviii, 115-16; scarcity of, x, 319; Sophocles on power of, viii, 264; standards of, x, 42-3; states forbidden to coin, xliii, 186 (10); Tennyson on power of, xlii, 982; Tennyson on strife for, 1015-7; trade does not require, x, 319; variation in value of, 36-7, 45; as wealth, 227-8, 311-31; Woolman on, pursuit of, i, 297, 298, 304

Money-love, Mr., in PILGRIM'S PROGRESS, xv, 104-9

Money Prices, remark on, x, 46

Mongrels, compared with hybrids, xi, 312-15

Monicongo, epitaph by, on DON QUIXOTE, xiv, 513

Monied Interest, defined, x, 280; increase of, 280-1; remarks on the, xxiv, 245-6

Monimus, the Cynic, ii, 203 (15)

Monk, Chaucer's, xl, 15-16; Dryden on Chaucer's, xxxix, 164

Monkeys, first appearance of, xi, 341; tails of, 232-3

Monkeys, in FAUST, xix, 99-106

Monks, Calvin on, xxxix, 36; Dante on corruption of the, xx, 380-1; Harrison on the, xxxv, 234; irregular, xxxvi, 306 note; Luther on, 300-2, 313, 333; Luther on confession of, 306; in Milton's Limbo, iv, 147-8; Pascal on corruptions of, xlviii, 308 (889); proverb on, xxxvi, 260

Monnica, mother of St. Augustine, vii, 3; cares for son, 24-5, 70-1, 95, 136, 142; funeral of, 155; last sickness and death of, 147, 151-5; life and character of, 148-52; in Milan, 79-80; in the Milan troubles, 146; offerings to the churches, 80; piety of, 14-15; prayer for, 157-8; vision of, 42; Walton on visions of, xv, 336

Monody, by Burns, vi, 484

Monogamy, among the Germans, xxxiii, 103; of Greeks and Egyptians, 45

Monolith of Amasis, xxxiii, 87-8

Monopoly, enemy of good management, x, 151; forbidden, in BODY OF LIBERTIES, xliii, 68 (9); in manufactures and

agriculture, x, 341-2; as means to riches, iii, 89

Monopoly Prices, x, 63

Monotony, of life, Bacon on, iii, 10; Marcus Aurelius on, ii, 241 (46)

Monroe, James, in Louisiana Purchase, xliii, 250 note

MONROE DOCTRINE, THE, xliii, 277-9; Russia and the, 432 note

Monstrosities, beauty in, iii, 267-8; Darwin on, xi, 25, 247; definition of, 54; under nature and domestication, 54-5

Montagu, Earl of Huntingdon, xxxix, 73

Montague, and Addison, xxvii, 158

Montague, Bishop, xv, 339

Montague, Lady Wortley, xxxiv, 96

Montague, picture-dealer, v, 320-1

Montagues and Capulets, xx, 169 note 13

Montaigne, Michel Eyguem de, *Art of Conversation*, xlviii, 407-8; OF BOOKES, xxxii, 87-102; on Castalio, xxxvii, 71; on ceremony, xviii, 14-15; character of, xxxii, 107-8; on his character, 69-70; in the civil wars, 115-17; commentators of, 106-7; devotees of, 105; Dryden on, xxxix, 160; on his education, xxxii, 65-9; on his essays, 4, 72, 87-8; OF FRIENDSHIP, 72-86; Hazlitt on, xxvii, 279; Hugo on language of, xxxix, 374; INSTITUTION AND EDUCATION OF CHILDREN, xxxii, 29-71; ON JUDGMENT OF HAPPINESS, 5-8; on his learning, 29-30; on lies, iii, 8-9; his life, résumé of, xxxii, 108-9; life and works, 3; literary style of, 117-20; as mayor of Bordeaux, 117-20; men of his time, 111; Pascal on, xlviii, 15 (18), 24-5, 33, (74), 80 (220), 87, 110 (315), 112-13 (325), 281 (813), 389-400; TO PHILOSOPHIZE IS TO LEARN HOW TO DIE, xxxii, 9-28; on his reading, 89-102; recovered letters of, 106; Rousseau on, xxxiv, 272-3; Sainte-Beuve on, xxxii, 105-20, 129, 131; Steven de la Boetie, and, 72-3, 78, 83-6; on Tacitus, xxxiii, 92; times of, xxxii, 109-10; travels in Italy, v, 208; Voltaire on Essays of, xxxiv, 101

MONTAIGNE, ESSAY ON, Sainte-Beuve's, xxxii, 105-20

Montanarolo, in THE BETROTHED, xxi, 319

Montanus, Calvin on, xxxix, 38

Montaperto, battle of, xx, 133 note 8

Montefeltro, Buonconte da, xx, 164 and note 8

Montefeltro, Guido da, xx, 111 note 4; in Dante's HELL, 110-14

Montejan, M. de, xxxviii, 9, 12

Montelupo, Raffaello da, xxxi, 71 note 7, 206

Monterey, Dana on, xxiii, 71-2, 81-4, 227-8, 384

Montesquieu, on classification of citizens, xxiv, 317; inventor of national workshops, xxviii, 456; *Le Temple de Gnide*, xxxix, 384; Sainte-Beuve on, xxxii, 123; Sainte-Beuve on *Spirit of Laws*, 126; Taine on, xxxix, 434

Montevideo, Darwin on, xxix, 147

Montevarchi, Francesco da, xxxi, 427

Montferrat, William, Marquis of, Dante on, xx, 174 and note 17

Montgomerie, James, Burns on, vi, 181 note

MONTGOMERIE'S PEGGY, vi, 25

Montgomery, M., and Henry II, xxxiii, 186

Montgomery, Sir Hugh, in CHEVY CHASE, xl, 98-9; at Otterburn, xxxv, 91; xl, 91, 92, 93

Montgomery, Richard, Burns on, vi, 51

Montjoie, origin of cry of, xlix, 177

Montluc, Jean de, xxxi, 207 note 1, 248-9

Montmorency, Maréchal de, xxxviii, 51

Montone, Andrea de (see Braccio)

Montone, river, Dante on, xx, 68 and notes

Montorsoli, Giovanni Angelo, xxxi, 403 note

Montrose, Marquis of, MY DEAR AND ONLY LOVE, xl, 358-9

Moodie, Rev. Alexander, Burns on, vi, 98-9, 352 (see also TWA HERDS)

Moods, Pascal on, xlviii, 47 (107)

Moon, Addison on the, xlv, 535; xl, 400; Browning on the, xlii, 1098-9; Dante on the, xx, 290-5; as Egyptian goddess, xxxiii, 29; Faust's apostrophe to the, xix, 24; heat from the, xxx, 260-1; Milton on the, iv, 236, 247, 307; motions and distance of, xxx, 303-4; motion of, Copernicus on, xxxix, 54; motion of, Voltaire on, xxxiv, 116-17, 118; Pascal on superstitions concerning, xlviii, 15 (18); Raleigh on the, xxxix, 107-8; Shelley on the, xli, 853, 856; tides and, xxx, 280-2, 291-2, 303-5; tides and Descartes on, xxxiv, 37; tides

and, Voltaire on, 108, 118; weather influenced by, xxx, 298-9

Moon, To the, by Shelley, xli, 847-8

Moon, To the, by Sidney, xl, 214

Moone, Thomas, with Drake, xxxiii, 146, 209, 212, 230, 250-1, 258

Moor-Hen, The Bonie, vi, 261-2

Moore, Sir John, Burial of, xli, 822-3

Moore, Thomas, Poe on, xxviii, 378, 384; poems by, xli, 816-22

Mora, Giangiacomo, the barber, xxi, 5, 566

Moraines, lateral, central, and terminal, xxx, 215-16, 227-8

Moral, meaning of word, v, 281

Moral Causes, Taine on, xxxix, 417

Moral Education, Locke on, xxxvii, 27-56, 60-7, 78-118, 134, 157; Mill on, xxv, 34; Milton on, iii, 240, 242

Moral Instruction, Kant on, xxxii, 322 note 2

Moral Life, Buddhist precepts of, xlv, 743

Moral Perfection, Franklin on, i, 78, 85

Moral Philosophy, Hobbes on, xxxiv, 412; Hume on, xxxvii, 289-90, 297, 335-6, 419-20 (see also Ethics)

Moral Progress, Emerson on, v, 137

Moral Sciences, Channing on study of, xxviii, 329; Helmholtz on, xxx, 173-4; Taine on, xxxix, 426-7

Moral Sense, Bentham on term, xxv, 44; Emerson on the, v, 26-8, 284; Kant on, xxxii, 352, 370; Poe on the, xxviii, 376

Moralists, Sidney on, xxvii, 15-18, 22

Morality, autonomy the supreme principle of, xxxii, 343, 349-50, 354-5; Bacon on, and atheism, iii, 45; Bagehot on positive, xxviii, 205; beauty and, v, 310; belief in Providence and, xxxvii, 399-400, 404-5; in books, criticism of, xxvii, 219-20; Burke on beauty as basis of, xxiv, 91-2; Burns on, vi, 212; censorship of, iii, 206-8; charge of danger to, xxxvii, 364; common rational notions of, xxxii, 305-17; criticism of defects in, xxvii, 244; culture and, Rousseau on, xxxiv, 162; Descartes's code of, 21-4; Descartes on study of, 8, 9; defined, xxxii, 349; empirical and metaphysical bases of, 318-24, 336-7; empirical and rational bases of, 351-4; equalizes all, v, 291; esthetics and, xxxii, 267-8, 271-4; first manifestations of, 278-9; Franklin's

plan of, i, 78-86; free will and, xxxii, 357, 358-63, 364-5; Hume on standard of, xxvii, 204-5; immaterialism and, xxxvii, 280; immortality and, xlviii, 80 (219); imperatives of, xxxii, 328, 330-50, 363-5 (see also Categorical Imperative); interest attaching to ideas of, 359-60, 369-70; intrinsic worth of, 345-6, 349; Locke on popular, xxxvii, 127; love the secret of, xxvii, 337; Marcus Aurelius on the highest, ii, 253 (69); Mill on Christian, xxv, 242-6; Mill on standards of, 200-1; natural to man, xxxiv, 269-74; necessity and liberty in regard to, xxxvii, 363-70; need of metaphysic of, xxxii, 299-303; refinement and, 236-7, 254; Pascal on standard of, xlviii, 126 (383); Pascal on true, 11 (4); Penn on true, i, 373-4; philosophical basis of, need of, xxxii, 317; pleasure inseparable from, v, 91; poetry as teacher of, xxvii, 337-8, 340-1; religion and, Mill on, xxv, 30-1; revelation and, Dryden on, xiii, 30; of rugged countries, xli, 526; among savages, xxxiv, 186-91; spurious principles of, due to Heteronomy of Will, xxxii, 343, 351; unconscious of itself, xxv, 324-7; of youth and age, iii, 105-6; Washington on, xliii, 242-3

Morals, Fundamental Principles of, Kant's, xxxii, 299-373

Morangis, Abbé, Burke on, xxiv, 280

Moravians, attitude of, toward war, i, 140; marriage among, 143-4; practices of, 143-4

Moray, Earl John, his raid into England, xxxv, 81-2; at Otterburn, 89-90, 91

Morebeke, Sir Denis, xxxv, 51, 58

Mordecai, Dante on, xx, 213; honors of, xxxiv, 365

Mordrains, King, xxxv, 185; Galahad and, 205

Mordred, son of Arthur, xx, 132 note 3

More and Less, tragedy of, v, 101

More, Sir George, and Dr. Donne, xv, 326-8, 332, 347

More, Hannah, On a Work of, vi, 191

More, Sir Thomas, accused of taking bribes, xxxvi, 115-16; accused of treason, 117-21; affection for his father, 107-8; ambassador to Cambray, 104-5; ambassador for merchants, 92; Anne Boleyn and, 114; ascetic practices, 109-10; on Augustine, St., 90; barrister,

90; burgess in Parliament, 91; the Canterbury nun and, 115; chancellor of Lancaster, 97; Charles V on, 134; at Charterhouse, 90; conviction of, 130-1; counsel for Pope, 92-3; Cromwell advised by, 113-14; daughters of, 90, 100-1; education and youthful wit, 89-90; embassies to Flanders and France, 98; on his embassy to Flanders, 135; embassy to Spain offered to, 97; on English Church, 104; freedom from anger, 104; Furnival's Inn and, 90; gentleness toward opponents, 98; Peter Giles on, 241; Henry VII, troubles with, 91; Henry VIII and, 92, 93-4, 97, 98, 99, 102-3, 105, 110-11, 113-14, 117-19; heroism of, v, 127; imprisoned in tower, xxxvi, 121-5; indictment and trial, 126-31; Jonson on, xxvii, 56; Johnson on, xxxix, 225; justice of, xxxvi, 107; on king's marriage and supremacy, 114, 117; lands of, 123; last days and death, 132-4; lawyer, 91-2; learning and power of speaking, 98; LIFE by Roper, 89-134; Lord Chancellor, 105, 106-8, 111-13, 115-16; manner of dress, 110; marriage, 90; patience with slanders of merchants, 98-9; piety of, 99-101, 109, 111, 113, 120, 122; poverty, 113; reader at Furnival's Inn, 90; religious writings and present from clergy, 109-10; Lord Rich with, 126; Sidney on, xxvii, 18; speaker of Parliament, xxxvi, 93-6; three wishes of, 99; under-sheriff of London, 91; unselfishness of his aims, 99; UTOPIA, 135-243; remarks on UTOPIA of, 88; virtues and wisdom of, 89; Walton on, xv, 323; Wolsey and, xxxvi, 95-7

Morelli, Dr., Dryden on, xiii, 56
Morequito, King, of Aromaia, xxxiii, 332-3, 355-6
Morgan, chariot of, xxxii, 146
Morgan, Col., at Gettysburg, xliii, 393
Morgan, Matthew, xxxiii, 229, 247, 254
Morgan, Miles, xxxiii, 268
Morgant, the giant, xiv, 19
Morley, his work on liberty, xxv, 5
Morluc (see Montluc)
Mormons, Mill on persecution of, xxv, 287-9
Morning, Berkeley on, xxxvii, 189; Gray on, xxxix, 275-6; Milton on, iv, 37, 170

Moro, Raffaello del, xxxi, 88, 96-8, 183
Morone, Macaulay on, xxvii, 390
Morpheus, reference to, iv, 171
Morphology, Darwin on, xi, 452-7
Morrell, Sir Charles, xl, 99
MORRIS, AULD ROB, vi, 445-6
Morris, Captain, i, 151
Morris, Gov., and Franklin, i, 126-7, 145; love of dispute, 126; quarrel with Assembly, 127-8, 138; retirement of, 127, 145-6
Morris, James, i, 108
Morris, William, POEMS by, xlii, 1183-98; PROLOGUE TO NIBLUNGS AND VOLSUNGS, xlix, 255-6; translator of songs from the EDDA, 360; translator of VOLSUNGA SAGA, 249
Morshead, E. D. A., translator of HOUSE OF ATREUS, viii, 1
Morsimus, reference to, viii, 443
Mortality (see Death)
Morte d'Arthur, favorite in old England, xxxix, 225; Holy Grail, story of, from Malory's, xxxv, 104-214; PROLOGUE to Malory's, xxxix, 20-4
MORTE D'ARTHUR, Tennyson's, xlii, 986-92
Mortification, Ruskin on, xxviii, 95
Mortimer the elder, in EDWARD II, xlvi, 9-11, 14-15, 16-19, 22-8, 35
Mortimer, the younger, in EDWARD THE SECOND, in opposition to Gaveston, xlvi, 9-11, 14-15, 16-19; consents to his return, 22-5; made Marshal, 26-7; on Gaveston, 28; at Gaveston's return, 31-4; quarrel with king, 34-7; Edward on, 37-8; in attack on Tynemouth, 39-40, 41; at capture of Gaveston, 43-5; in battle, 53; captured, 54-5; escapes to France, 56, 57-9; his return in arms, 61, 63-4; the Queen and, 63, 66, 69; his triumph, 73; plots king's death, 74-5; with Kent, 75-6; new plots against king, 79-80; made Protector, 80-1; puts Kent to death, 81-2; suspected of king's death, 86-7; condemned to death, 88; Edward Third on, 89
Morton, Bishop of Durham, relations with Dr. Donne, xv, 329-30; Walton on, 330
Morton, Cardinal, xxxvi, 89
Morton, John, More on, xxxvi, 142
Mosca degli Uberti, in Hell, xx, 27, 117-18

Mosca, II, xxxi, 420 note

Moschino, II, xxxi, 420 note

Moses, Browning on, xlii, 1099; Bunyan on, xv, 74, 134; on clean beasts, 83; in Dante's PARADISE, xx, 422; on his own death, iii, 281 (29); Defoe on, xxvii, 142; Jesus and, xliv, 379 (30); Jesus on, xlviii, 272 (782); learning of, iii, 199; Lessing on, xxxii, 190; Machiavelli on, xxxvi, 20, 21, 83; meekness of, xv, 341; Milton on, iv, 88, 347-8, 349; on miracles, xlviii, 279 (803); Mohammed on, xlv, 888, 902-4, 911, 913, 921, 932, 966, 982, 983, 992 note 32, 996-7; More on law of, xxxvi, 150; Pascal on, xlviii, 189-90, 201, 203, 206 (622), 207 (624), 208 (629), 209 (631), 218 (657), 230 (690), 232, 238, 243 (714), 261 (741), 264 (752), 269 (774); Paul, St., on, xlv, 519 (13); prayers of, vii, 303 (2); his prophecy of Christ, xlviii, 285 (826); xliv, 429 (22-3); the Psalmist on, 267 (6-8), 276 (26), 278 (16), 279 (23, 32); Psalms attributed to, 144, 258-9; on resurrection, 407 (37-8); Stephen on, 436-7 (20-40); taken from Limbo, xx, 18; wish of, iii, 224

Moses, in SCHOOL FOR SCANDAL, xviii, 142-4, 149-50, 153-61, 163

MOSQUITOES AND FOX, fable of, xvii, 36-7

Mosquitoes, Drake on, xxxiii, 149-50

MOTHER, I CANNOT MIND MY WHEEL, xli, 901

MOTHER, TO MY, by Poe, xlii, 1236

MOTHER HOLLE, story of, xvii, 104-7

MOTHER'S LAMENT, A, vi, 315

MOTHER'S PICTURE, ON HIS, by Cowper, xli, 543-6

Motherhood, Holmes on, xxxviii, 251-2

Mothers (see Parents)

Motherwell, SONG OF THE CAVALIER, xxviii, 392

Motion, Berkeley on, xxxvii, 209-10, 211-13, 237, 265; first law of nature, v, 229, 231; Pascal on, xlviii, 428-30; Rousseau on, xxxiv, 247-9, 251

Motives, and actions, xxxvii, 353-8, 362-3 note, 365-6; James Mill on, xxv, 36; Ruskin on human, xxviii, 94-6

Motte, Andrew, translator of Newton, xxxix, 1

MOTTO TO BURNS'S FIRST BOOK, vi, 221

Moulds, bacteria and, xxxviii, 342; Pasteur on, 295, 297, 298 and note

Mounier, on October Sixth, xxiv, 211 note

Mountain-chains, formation of, xxix, 316; Geikie on, xxx, 338-9

MOUNTAIN DAISY, TO A, vi, 193-4

Mountain of the Congregation, iv, 200

Mountain-torrents, Darwin on, xxix, 320-1

Mountains, as barriers of species, xxix, 330; difficulty of judging distances on, 329; Helmholtz on low temperature of, xxx, 212-13; resemblance of species of, xi, 394-6

MOUNTAINS IN LABOR, fable of, xvii, 17

Mountjoy, Lord, Harrison on, xxxv, 319 note

Mourning, in ancient Egypt, xxxiii, 42; Bacon on, iii, 9; Byron on, xli, 790; Confucius on, xliv, 12 (26), 60 (21), 65 (17); Dekker on, xlvii, 508; ECCLESIASTES on, xliv, 342 (2, 4); Ennius on, ix, 71; Hamlet on, xlvi, 101-2; Pascal on, xlviii, 338, 339; Rossetti, C. G., on, xlii, 1181, 1182; Shakespeare on, xl, 275; Tzu-yu on, xliv, 65 (14)

MOURNING, VALEDICTION FORBIDDING, xl, 304-5

MOUSE, TO A, vi, 119-20; remarks on, 16

MOUSE AND LION, fable of, xvii, 14-15

MOUSE, THE TOWN, AND THE COUNTRY MOUSE, xvii, 13-14

Movement, definitions of, xlviii, 427-8

Moving Pictures, in New Atlantis, iii, 178-9

Mowis, tale of the, xlii, 1331

Mozzi, Andrea de', xx, 64 and note 5

Mozzi, Rocco di, xx, 57 note

Mucalinda, xlv, 627-8

Much, the miller's son, in adventure with knight, xl, 129, 130, 136, 137, 138; with monks, 155, 156, 157; at archery contest, 165, 167

Much-afraid, in PILGRIM'S PROGRESS, xv, 175; daughter of Dispondency, 288-9, 290; parts with Christiana, 312; death of, 314-15

Mucianus, Tacitus on, iii, 128; on Vitellius, 17, 141

Mucii, Plutarch on the, xii, 219

Muck-rake, man with, in PILGRIM'S PROGRESS, xv, 202-3

Muggins, Dick, in SHE STOOPS TO CONQUER, xviii, 207, 212

Muhagerin, xlv, 949 note 14

MUIR, WILLIAM, EPITAPH ON, vi, 50

Muirkirk, John Shepherd, Burns on, vi, 353 and note

Mulciber, his fall from Heaven, iv, 106; architect of Pandemonium, 106 (see also Vulcan)

Mule, Darwin on the, xxix, 319

MULE, THE SHEYKH AND THE, xvi, 24

Muley, Hameda, xiv, 387

Mulius, Homer on, xxii, 256

Müller, Fritz, on air-breathing crustaceans, xi, 191-2; on classification, 437; on crustaceans, 282; on dimorphism, 57; on larval stage, 466; on twining plants, 242

Müller, John, Browne on, iii, 266 note

Müller, Max, quoted, xxviii, 240

Multiple Organs, variable, xi, 152

Multitudes, effect of shouting of, xxiv, 69-70

Multrie, Rev. John, Burns on, vi, 165 and note 11

Mummius, at Corinth, xiii, 235-6

Mun, Mr., book of, x, 316; on foreign trade, 313

Munatius, and Cicero, xii, 238

Munday, Anthony, BEAUTY BATHING, xl, 201

Munificence, proverb on, xvi, 201

Munremar, son of Gerrchenn, xlix, 225-6

Muralt, M. de, xxxiv, 136

Murder, Chaucer on, xl, 41; in Massachusetts law, xliii, 80; Mohammed on, xlv, 916, 976-7; punishment of, in old England, xxxv, 364, 365; Shakespeare on, xlvi, 141; Webster on, xlvii, 827

Murderers, in Dante's HELL, xx, 46, 51

Murena Licinius, defence of, xii, 261; trial of, 247

Muret, Mark Antony, xxxii, 66

Murillo, Hugo on, xxxix, 352

Murmuring, Penn on, i, 326

Murranus, death of, xiii, 408, 412

MURRAY, BONNY EARL OF, xl, 107-8

MURRAY, MISS EUPHEMIA, LINES ON, vi, 286-7

Murray, Gilbert, translator of Euripides, viii, 1

Musa, Arab general, xvi, 298 note 3 in story of CITY OF BRASS, 298-325

Musæus, Aristophanes on, viii, 471; Marlowe on, xix, 210; Milton on, iv, 36; Sidney on, xxvii, 6; Socrates on, ii, 29; in Virgil's Hades, xiii, 229-30

Musaget, in FAUST, xix, 187

Muses, Aristophanes on the, viii, 465; De

Quincey on the, xxvii, 320; Milton on the, iv, 35, 72

Mushroom, Emerson on the, v, 57

Mushtari, reference to, xli, 954

Music, beauty in, xxiv, 100-1; Browne on, iii, 323; Browning on, xlii, 1072, 1101; Coleridge on, xxvii, 255, 262; Collins on, xli, 479; Confucius on, xliv, 12 (23), 25 (8), 41 (3); Dorian, Milton on, iv, 102; Dryden on power of, xl, 390; Herbert on, xv, 380; Hobbes on, xxxiv, 363; instrumental, power of, xxiv, 51; Locke on study of, xxxvii, 170-1; Mill on effects of, xxv, 92; Mill on limitations of, 93; Milton on, iv, 40, 43; as recreation, iii, 245; the passions and, xli, 476-9; Poe on, xxviii, 377, 378; Ruskin on best, xxviii, 152; Schiller on, xxxii, 269-70

MUSIC, FOR, by Byron, xli, 788-9

MUSIC, THE POWER OF, xl, 391-6

MUSIC, WHEN SOFT VOICES DIE, xli, 855

MUSICAL INSTRUMENT, A, xli, 922-3

Musical Notes, rates of vibration of, xxx, 252-4

Musicians, Browning on, xlii, 1102

Musing, a deadly happiness, viii, 321

Musonius Rufus, teacher of Epictetus, ii, 310, 320, 321

Mussato, Albertino, xx, 51 note 8

Mussels, no heart in, xxxviii, 129

Musset, De, Taine on, xxxix, 411

Mustapha, and Roxalana, iii, 50

Mustard-seed, parable of the, xliv, 391 (18-19)

Mutilations, inheritance of, xi, 141

Mutual Aid Societies, ancient, ix, 404 note 2

MY BONIE BELL, vi, 417

MY BONIE MARY, vi, 318

MY COLLIER LADDIE, vi, 433-4

MY DEAR AND ONLY LOVE, xl, 358-9

MY EPPIE ADAIR, vi, 348

MY EPPIE MACNAB, vi, 414

MY FAITH LOOKS UP TO THEE, xlv, 569-70

MY FATHER WAS A FARMER, vi, 38-9

MY GIRL SHE'S AIRY, vi, 58

MY HEART LEAPS UP, xli, 600

MY HEART'S IN THE HIGHLANDS, vi, 362

MY HIGHLAND LASSIE, O, vi, 202

MY HOGGIE, vi, 298

MY LAST DUCHESS, xlii, 1074-5

MY LORD A-HUNTING, vi, 262-3

MY LOVE IN HER ATTIRE, xl, 325

My Love, She's but a Lassie Yet, vi, 345

My Mother Bids Me Bind My Hair, xli, 581

My Nanie O, vi, 46-7

My Nanie's Awa, vi, 509

My Native Land Sae Far Awa, vi, 430-1

My Peggy's Charms, vi, 289

My Spouse Nancy, vi, 476-7

My Tocher's the Jewel, vi, 415

My Wife's a Winsome Wee Thing, vi, 444

Mycene, reference to, xxii, 24

Mykerinos, king of Egypt, xxxiii, 65-7

Mylodon, Darwin on the, xxix, 91

Myopotamus, Darwin on the, xxix, 291

Myris, in All for Love, xviii, 24-5

Myrmex, Aristophanes on, viii, 486

Myrmidons, return of, from Troy, xxii, 37

Myrrha, in Dante's Hell, xx, 124

Myrtle, David on the, xli, 494

Myrto, granddaughter of Aristides, xii, 105

Mysteries, Egyptian, xxxiii, 84-5; in religion, Browne on, iii, 259 (9), 260 (10)

Mystery, Carlyle on, xxv, 332-3; many shapes of, viii, 436

Mysticism, Emerson on, v, 178

Mystics, songs of, in The Frogs, viii, 449-52

Mythology, Celtic, xxxii, 153-5; Descartes on study of, xxxiv, 7-8; Renan on Classical, xxxii, 160; Taine on, xxxix, 411; Thoreau on, xxviii, 414

Myths, law of compensation in, v, 91-2; remarks of, xvii, 7

Naaman, the Syrian, xliv, 364 (27)

Nabal, Winthrop on, xliii, 93

Nabis, Prince of Sparta, xxxvi, 35, 60

Nachoran, Abraham's son, iii, 167

Nacien, the hermit, xxxv, 111, 114, 120, 151, 158, 159-61, 184-5

Nadab, Browning on, xlii, 1099

Naegling, the sword, xlix, 78

Naething, Stanzas on, vi, 222-3

Naevius, Roman poet, iii, 195; quoted, ix, 52; old age of, 63

Nāga, the Great, xlv, 732-3

Nāgasena, and Milinda, xlv, 653-6, 677-80

Nägeli, on plants, xi, 212

Naharvalians, Tacitus on the, xxxiii, 117

Naiads, Homer on the, xxii, 176; Milton on the, iv, 51

Nails, as money in Scotland, x, 28; making of, 13

Naimes, Duke, xlix, 102, 116, 119, 121, 154, 155, 174, 175, 180

Nain, widow of, xliv, 371 (12-15)

Nairne, Lady (see Oliphant, Carolina)

Name, good, a precious ointment, iii, 5

Names, among the Bornoos, v, 200; Epictetus on, ii, 172 (154); Goethe on, xix, 57; Hobbes on, xxxiv, 324-30; independence of, v, 128; Thoreau on, xxviii, 417

Namur, William of, xxxv, 12

Nan Jung, Confucius on, xliv, 14 (1), 33 (5)

Nan-kung Kuo, xliv, 45 (6)

Nantucket, Praying Indians of, xliii, 140; Woolman's description of, i, 247-8

Nan-tzu, xliv, 21 (26), 22 note 3

Naphtha, Browne on, iii, 272

Naples, betrayed by Ferdinand, xxxix, 85; conquest of, xxxvi, 14, 27; described by Marlowe, xix, 230; in 16th century, xxvii, 392; Machiavelli on kingdom of, xxxvi, 7; papal authority in, 296; power of, before French invasion, 38-9; reasons of fall of, 79

Naples, Stanzas written near, by Shelley, xli, 827-8

Napoleon, aristocracy courted by, v, 204; art of war of, 342-3; Bagehot on, xxviii, 199; Carlyle on, xxv, 324, 406; on charlatanism, xxviii, 66; compared with Milton's Satan, 199; Emerson on, 265; Empire of, 375; etiquette of, 208; on French Revolution, xxviii, 468; on the heaviest battalions, v, 358; Hugo on, xxxix, 377; Louisiana sold by, xliii, 250 headnote; Mazzini on, xxxii, 382, 389; method of, v, 81; at the pest house, 290; the royal armies and, 97; on sublime and ridiculous, xxxix, 357; Wellington on French and, v, 375; the wounded officer and, xxv, 336

Napoleon III, Mill on, xxv, 147-8

Nár, the Squinter, xlix, 242-3

Narahs, evil genii, xvi, 9 note 4

Naraka, xlv, 862

Narcissus, cunning of, iii, 58; Dante on, xx, 293 note 2; Milton on, iv, 51; Shelley on, xli, 860

Nardi, Jacopo, xxxi, 150-1 note 5

Nariscans, Tacitus on the, xxxiii, 116

Narrative Poetry, forms of, xxxix, 298
Narrowness, of mind, Confucius on, xliv, 56 (9)
Narses, Bacon on, iii, 23
Narvaez, Roderick, and the Moor, xiv, 44
Nasamonians, Herodotus on the, xxxiii, 21
Nashe, Thomas, POEMS by, xl, 260-1
Nashope, Indian town, xliii, 144
Nasidius, reference to, xx, 104
Naso, banished by Augustus, iii, 195; Dante on, xx, 19
Nassaro, Matteo del, xxxi, 305 note
Nathan, and David, xliv, 205; Luther on, xxxvi, 330; Sidney on, xxvii, 25
Natick, Eliot on, xliii, 142
National Antipathies, Browne on, iii, 315-16; Pascal on, xlviii, 103-4; Washington on, xliii, 244
National Armies, Machiavelli on need of, xxxvi, 47-8
National Banks, Marshall on, xliii, 209, 212-15, 223-4 (see also United States Bank)
National Debt, congressional right to contract a, xliii, 184 (2); Washington on, 243
National Debts, Smith on, x, 549-64
National Property, regulation of, xliii, 185 (17)
National Wealth, Bacon on sources and distribution of, iii, 39-40
Nationality, Freeman on sentiment of, xxviii, 231-2
Nations, amorousness of different, xlviii, 420; as determined by language, xxviii, 252-73; origin of, 245-9; Pascal on division of world into, xlviii, 103-4; Rousseau on division of mankind into, xxxiv, 213; Rousseau on origin of, 203; splendor of, how judged, v, 435; Taine on differences of, xxxix, 422-32; Washington on relations with foreign, xliii, 243-6; Woolman on prosperity of, i, 231 (see also Races)
NATIONS, WEALTH OF, Smith's, x
NATIVITY, HYMN ON THE, iv, 7-15
Naturæ Encheiresis, xix, 79
Natural, and artificial, xxv, 330; definition of word, xi, 1
Natural History, Bacon on, xxxix, 137-40; Darwin's theory, its effect on, xi, 502-5; defined by Hobbes, xxxiv, 359
Natural Laws, Descartes on, xxxiv, 36-8;

suppose an intelligent agent, xi, 1; Whewell on, 1
Natural Liberty, Hobbes on, xxxiv, 391 (see also Natural State)
Natural Objects, Burke on effects of, xxiv, 129
Natural Philosophy, Bacon on study of, iii, 122; Berkeley on, xxxvii, 279-80; Hobbes on, xxxiv, 362; Hume on limits of, xxxvii, 311, 336, 419; Huxley on study of, xxviii, 221; Kant on, xxxii, 299; Locke on, xxxvii, 163-7; Milton on study of, iii, 240-1; Newton on, xxxix, 151-2; Socrates on, ii, 7, 90
Natural Price, defined, x, 56-7; market price tends to equal, 59; tends to minimum, 63
Natural Principles, Pascal on, xlviii, 41 (92, 94)
Natural Rectitude, Bentham on term, xxv, 44
Natural Religion (see Religion)
Natural Rights, Hobbes on, xxxiv, 391-2, 401-13
Natural Science, Bacon on, xxxix, 128-9; Helmholtz on, xxx, 173-5
Natural Selection, xi, 87-137; Aristotle's idea of, 9 note; difficulties of theory, 169-250, 276-83, 298-300, 319-20; meaning of, 72; progress of idea of, 11-22; recapitulation of theory, 478-506; theory of, briefly stated, 21
Natural State, advancement of man from, xxxii, 284, 292-3; Hobbes on, xxxiv, 387-91; Pope on the, xl, 426; Rousseau on man in, xxxiv, 166, 168-95, 204-5; Schiller on, xxxii, 275-6
Natural Style, Pascal on, xlviii, 17 (29)
Naturalization, Bacon on, iii, 76; Freeman on, xxviii, 247-8; of plants, xi, 118; under control of Congress, xliii, 184 (4); of words, Johnson on, xxxix, 189
Naturalness, Locke on, xxxvii, 45-7
Nature, adaptations in, xi, 71-2, 84-5; art and, xxvii, 10; art and, Confucius on, xliv, 20 (16), 38 (8); art and, Goethe on, xxxix, 255-8, 260-1; art and, Hugo, on, 366-7; art and, Whitman on, 402; M. Aurelius Antoninus on, ii, 326-7, 335-6; Bacon on interpretation of, 132-40, 143-6; Bacon on observation of, xxxix, 141-2; Berkeley on beauties of, xxxvii, 230-1; Berkeley on laws of, 252; Browne on, iii, 263

(12), 266-8 (15, 16); Browne on study of, 264-5, 266-8; Bryant on, xlii, 1213-15; Burke on study of, xxiv, 7-8; Burns on, vi, 67, 88-9, 320-1, 502, 504; Bishop Joseph Butler on, ii, 327; Channing on study of, xxviii, 328-9; Channing on unity of, 324-5; Cicero on accordance with, ix, 70; Cicero on rebellion against, 46; Coleridge on wisdom in, xxvii, 258-9; complexity of, xi, 79-86; contemners of, in Dante's HELL, xx, 46, 61-5; Darwin on, xi, 89, 203-4, 209; Descartes's method of studying, xxxiv, 51-3; economy of, xi, 151-2; education by, v, 59, 192; xxviii, 153-4; Emerson on, v, 25, 27-8, 54, 89, 101, 152, 167, 171, 173, 189, 192, 193, 240, 275, 301; xlii, 1250, 1253, 1257-8; Epictetus on, ii, 164 (130); God and, St. Augustine on, vii, 164; God and, Hume on, xxxvii, 396-404; God and, Pascal on, xlviii, 82 (229), 90-1, 137 (428), 190 (580), 325-6; God and, Raleigh on, xxxix, 104, 108-10; God and, Rousseau on, xxxiv, 253-4; God and, Tennyson on, xlii, 1004-5; Goethe on study of, xxxix, 251; Goethe on unity of, xix, 24; Goldsmith on gifts of, xli, 522; Hindu doctrine of, xlv, 851; Hume on knowledge of, xxxvii, 309-10, 311-12; Hunt on love of, xxvii, 293; institutions influenced by, v, 339; interdependence of, xxx, 168; lessons of, xlii, 1243; living according to, ii, 253 (74), 275 (2); xxxvi, 197-8; Locke on works of, xxxvii, 163, 165; Lyell on laws of, xxxviii, 386; Marcus Aurelius on study of, ii, 205 (2); Milton on gifts of, iv, 63-5; Milton on unity and degrees of, 192-3; "never betrayed the heart that loved her," xli, 638; Newton on phenomena of, xxxix, 151-2; "non facit saltum," xi, 195-6, 207; offences against, vii, 39-40; opposition in, ii, 59-61; original meaning of, 326-7; Pascal on, xlviii, 26-8, 40 (91), 49-50 (119-21); Penn on life next to, i, 342-3; Penn on study of, 321 (3), 322-3; pleasure the plan of, xli, 643-4; Pope on, xl, 414, 422-3, 425, 433; proverb on, v, 91; Raleigh on, xxxix, 108-10; Ruskin on our carelessness of, xxviii, 120-1; Shelley on love of, xli, 826; Thoreau on attractions and benefits of,

xxviii, 395-425; Whitman on life with, xlii, 1410; "will out," xvii, 42; Wordsworth on love of, xli, 600, 636-9, 678
NATURE, ESSAY ON, Emerson's, v, 223-37
NATURE, GOODNESS OF, essay on, iii, 32-4
NATURE, HYMN TO THE SPIRIT OF, xli, 841-2
NATURE IN MEN, Bacon's essay, iii, 96-8
NATURE, THE INFLUENCES OF, xli, 607-14
NATURE AND THE POET, xli, 605-7
NATURE'S LAW: A POEM, vi, 225-7
Naturlangsamkeit, v, 110
Naucratis, city of, xxxiii, 88
Naudin, M., on origin of species, xi, 15-16; on reversion, 314
Naunton, Sir Robert, xv, 380-1
Nausicaa, daughter of Alcinous, xxii, 81-9; farewell to Ulysses, 111; Ruskin on, xxviii, 142
Nausithous, son of Poseidon, xxii, 91; reference to, 81
Nautes, in the ÆNEID, xiii, 201
Navagero, Bernardo, quoted, xxviii, 455
Navarre, King of, at Hesdin, xxxviii 21-2; at Rouen, 47-8
Navidad, city of, xliii, 25
Navigation, ancient, iii, 156-7, 159; Emerson on, v, 339; Hobbes on, xxxiv, 363; power of, necessary to civilization, x, 24-6
Navigation Act of Great Britain, x, 342-4
Navy, Harrison on need of a, xxxv, 360
Navy, United States commander-in-chief of, xliii, 188 (1); under the Confederation, 161, 164, 165; under Constitution, 184-5 (13, 14)
Naxos, famed for vintage, xiii, 132
Naylor, James, Woolman on, i, 292; worshipped as Christ, v, 233
Neaera, and Helios, xxii, 165; reference to, iv, 74
Nealces, Virgil on, xiii, 347-8
Neale, Dr., Dean of Westminster, xv, 375
Neale, J. M., translator of hymns, xlv, 542, 543, 544, 548
Nearchus, in POLYEUCTE, urges Polyeucte to be baptised, xxvi, 77-80; persuaded to go to temple with Polyeucte, 95-7; blamed by Pauline, 99-100; doomed by Felix, 102-3; his death, 106
Nearchus of Tarentum, ix, 59
NEARER, MY GOD, TO THEE, xlv, 568-9
Nebaioth, in the Wilderness, iv, 379
Nebridius, friend of St. Augustine, vii,

48, 92, 100, 126; conversion of, 141; on divination, 104

Nebuchadnezzar, Bunyan on, xv, 99; Daniel and, xx, 297, note 1; dream of, xlviii, 245-6; image of, iii, 13; the Jews and, xlviii, 212; reference to, xlv, 914 note

Nebulæ, composition of, xxx, 314

Necessaries of life, defined, x, 517-18; Kempis on, vii, 290 (4); Shakespeare on, xlvi, 260; taxes on, x, 518, 520-3, 547 (see also Food-Supply)

Necessary, Marshall on word, xliii, 217

Necessary Connexion, Idea of, xxxvii, 335-50, 353

Necessity, Burns on, vi, 366; Chaucer on, xl, 46; Dante on, xx, 210; defined by Kant, xxxii, 356, 365; foreknowledge not, xx, 358, note 7; Goethe on, xxv, 379; Hume on doctrine of, xxxvii, 351-70; makes vile things precious, xlvi, 266; Mill on doctrine of, xxv, 106-7; Pascal on belief in, xlviii, 40 (91), 83-4 (233); Sophocles on, viii, 291; the spur of knowledge, xxxiv, 178; the tyrant's plea, iv, 164

Necker, M., on assignats, xxiv, 370; Burke on, 336-7; on French finances, 253; on population of France, 262-3; on wealth of France, 264-5

Necos, king of Egypt, xxxiii, 79-80

Necromancy, Cellini on, xxxi, 127-30, 136; Hobbes on, xxxiv, 382

Neglect, excuses for, ii, 195 (12); a way of dishonoring, xxxiv, 364

NEGOTIATING, ESSAY ON, Bacon's, iii, 117-18

Negus, empire of, iv, 329

Nehemiah, and the Sabbath-breakers, xliii, 94, 95

NEIDPATH, THE MAID OF, by Campbell, xli, 777

NEIDPATH, THE MAID OF, by Scott, xli, 744-5

NEIDPATH CASTLE, LINES COMPOSED AT, xli, 679

Neighbors, Confucius on love of, xliv, 44 (24); Jesus on, 382-3 (29-37)

Neleus, birth of, xxii, 151; Chloris and, 152; Homer on, 43; Melampus and, 206

Nelson, in the Baltic, v, 358; xli, 779-80; courage of his sailors, v, 381-2; death of, 348; Emerson on, 366; expecting duty, 387; feat of doubling, 358; at Trafalgar, 414; want of fortune, 393

Nemesianus, on hounds, xxxv, 350-1

Nemesis, Emerson on doctrine of, v, 92-3; Herodotus's belief in, xxxiii, 5-6; in MANFRED, xviii, 430-2, 433-6; Pliny on, ix, 272 note

Nemetes, Tacitus on the, xxxiii, 108

Némglan, and Conaire, xlix, 203

Nemours, Duc de, at Metz, xxxviii, 23

Nennius, on Arthur, xxxii, 155-6

Neocles, father of Themistocles, xii, 5

Neo-Druidism, xxxii, 168

Neoptolemus, and Lycomedes, ix, 34

Neoptolemus, son of Achilles (see Pyrrhus)

Nepenthes, reference to, iv, 62

Nephelogetes, and Alaopolitanes, xxxvi, 216

Nepoios, Raleigh on the, xxxiii, 349

Nepos, Licinius, Pliny on, ix, 259

Nepos, Metellus, Cicero on, xii, 239-40

Nepos, friend of Pliny, ix, 213, 242

Nepos, the prætor, decree of, ix, 277-8

Nepos, Proconsul of Spain, and Cæsar, xii, 282

Neptune, in the ÆNEID, xiii, 77-9; 204-5; Milton on, iv, 21, 45, 67; in sack of Troy, xiii, 121

Neptune, the planet, discovery of, xxx, 23

Nereids, reference to the, xiii, 79

Nereus, references to, iv, 66-7; xiii, 114

Neri, beginning of party, xx, 132 note 4; faction in Florence, 26 note 3, 101-2 and notes

Neri, St. Philip, and the nun, v, 287-8

Nerius, Cn., informer, ix, 99

Nero, Drusus, ix, 232 note 2

Nero, Emperor, Apollonius on, iii, 48; Carlyle on death of, v, 322; Demetrius and, ii, 132 (45); descent of, xii, 389; harp of, iii, 49; Epaphroditus, patron of, ii, 321; Marcus Aurelius on, ii, 211 (16); Pliny on reign of, ix, 320-2; as a poet, xviii, 17; Rome burned by, xl, 49; and Seneca, ii, 320 note; Spintrian recreations of, iii, 320

Nero, Francesco del, xxxi, 108 note 2

Nero, Tiberius, and Gabinius, ix, 115

Nerva, edict of, ix, 390; Pliny on, 212, 316; Trajan and, 356 note 2

Nervians, Tacitus on the origin of, xxxiii, 108

Nervii, Cæsar's campaign against the, xii, 281

Nesle, Castle of, xxxi, 327 note 2

Nessus, Dante on, xx, 50 and note

Nestor, Achilles and, xxii, 321; birth of, 152; Cicero on, ix, 56; in the ODYSSEY, xxii, 34-45

Netherlands, Bacon on government of, iii, 35; Browne on success of the, 269; under Charles V, xix, 252; manufactures of the, iii, 40; under Margaret of Parma, xix, 256-8; periodic returns in, iii, 137; Philip II and the, xxxix, 86-9; revolt of the, Mill on, xxv, 10-11

Nethersole, Sir Francis, xv, 380-1

Neufville, Nicholas de, xxxi, 281 note

Neuri, Herodotus on the, xlix, 268 note

Neuter Insects, Darwin on, xi, 278-83; sterility of, how developed, 299-300

Neutrality, Machiavelli on, xxxvi, 73-4; Pascal on, xlviii, 310 (899); Penn on, i, 357; Washington on policy of, xliii, 246, 248

NEVER THE TIME AND THE PLACE, xlii, 1108

Nevers, Duke of, and Mantua, xxi, 78, 434-5, 466

Nevil, Dr., and George Herbert, xv, 375, 380

Nevill, Sir Robert, xxxv, 24

Neville, Constance, in SHE STOOPS TO CONQUER, with Kate Hardcastle, xviii, 209-10; with Hastings at Hardcastle's, 224-5; carries on joke with Marlow, 226; with Tony Lumpkin, 229, 231; Tony's description of, 232; tries to get her jewels, 236-8; plans to elope, 244; with Tony in elopement plot, 250-1; Tony's letter and, 252-3; denounces Tony, 254; ordered to aunt's by Mrs. Hardcastle, 253, 255-6; refuses to elope, 264; wins consent to marry Hastings, 268

New Academy, xii, 220 note

New Albion, Drake's, xxxiii, 213-17

NEW ATLANTIS, Bacon's, iii, 145-81; editorial remarks on, 144; l, 42

New Atlantis, acoustics in, iii, 178; air and water machines, 178-9; ancient commerce of, 156-7, 159-60; ancient expeditions against, 157-8; arrival at, 145-8; Christianity in, 153-5; dress in, 147, 151, 165, 170-2; Feast of Family in, 163-6; food in, 149-50, 175-6; health, care of, in, 148, 173-4; instruments of warfare in, 178; Jews in, 167; jugglery in, 179; machines and engines

in, 178-9; manufactures in, 176; marriage in, 168-70; medicine in, 176; mineralogy in, 177; optics in, 177; production of heat in, 176-7; production of odors and tastes, 178; scientific expeditions from, 162; self-sufficiency of, 159-60; Salomon's House in, 161 (see further Salomon's House); Stranger's House in, 149; treatment of visitors in, 151-2, 160-1; why unknown, 155-6 et seq.

NEW-BORN CHILD, ON PARENT KNEES A, xli, 580

New Caledonia, barrier-reef of, xxix, 477, 481

New England, historical documents of early, xliii, 59-105, 138-46

New England Courant, i, 3, 19, 21

NEW ENGLAND REFORMERS, v, 253-71

NEW FORCERS OF CONSCIENCE UNDER LONG PARLIAMENT, iv, 80-1

Newfoundland, American rights in fisheries of, xliii, 177; colonization of, xxxiii, 262; description of, 281-6; exploration of coast, 287-8; Hayes on banks of, 275

NEWFOUNDLAND, GILBERT'S VOYAGE TO, xxxiii, 263-98

New Jersey, settlement of, i, 276; slaves in, 178 note

New Light, party of, vi, 16; Burns on, 89-90

New South Wales, Darwin on, xxix, 436-49

NEW TESTAMENT, SELECTED BOOKS FROM, xliv, 351-486

New Testament, adversity the blessing of, iii, 16; corruption of, St. Augustine on, vii, 75; Goethe on, xix, 53-4; Lessing on the, xxxii, 199-200; Luther on, xxxvi, 350; Mill on, xxv, 243; Pascal on, xlviii, 214, 220-1 (666), 261 (740), 288-9 (835), 298-9 (852); Rousseau on the, xxxiv, 300-2 (see also Gospel)

NEW WAY TO PAY OLD DEBTS, xlvii, 857-943; remarks on, 858

New Year's Day, why celebrated, xv, 403

NEW YEAR'S DAY: A SKETCH, vi, 372-3

New Zealand, Darwin on, xxix, 420-34; fauna and flora of, xi, 371; ferns in, xxix, 249; as an oceanic island, xi, 416; species of, 403, 414, 422

New Zealanders, health of the, v, 80

Newby, Samuel, i, 213

Newcomb, Simon, sketch of life and

works, xxx, 310; EXTENT OF THE UNI-
VERSE, 311-21

Newlights, American society called, i, 207

Newman, Col., on humble-bees, xi, 82

Newman, John Henry, *Call of David*
quoted, xxviii, 170; HYMN by, xlv,
567-8; IDEA OF A UNIVERSITY, xxviii,
31-61; sketch of life and works, 30

Newport, Magdalen, mother of George
Herbert, xv, 373-4, 375-9, 384, 387-8;
letter to, 389-1; death, 392

News, Arabian proverb on, xvi, 158; evil
and good, iv, 453; suspense in, 454

NEWS, LASSIES, NEWS, vi, 542

Newspapers, American, i, 19; Bentham
on power of, xxvii, 229; Carlyle on
writing for, xxv, 446; Ruskin on,
xxviii, 98; Wordsworth on taxation of,
v, 324

Newton, Sir Isaac, Burke on, xxiv, 103;
Cartesian vortices disproved by, xxxiv,
114-5; chronology of, 126-30; Emerson on, v, 66; gravitation, universal,
discovered by, xxxiv, 115-21; on gravitation, v, 310; xxx, 301-4; xxxvii, 345-
6 note; Hazlitt on, xxvii, 267-8; the
heliocentric theory and, xxxix, 52 note;
honors paid him, xxxiv, 152; law of
conservation and, xxx, 175; Leibnitz
on, xi, 498; life and works, xxxix, 150
note; Locke on, xxxvii, 166; mathematical discoveries of, xxxiv, 125-7;
optics, discoveries in, 121-4; Pepys and,
xxviii, 304; on polarity in nature, v, 14;
PREFACE TO *Principia*, xxxix, 150-2; remarks on, l, 39; Rousseau on, xxxiv,
249; spectrum discovered by, xxx,
261-2; on tides, 280-1; Unitarianism
and, xxxiv, 83, 84; Voltaire on, 98,
108-13; Warden of Mint, 152; Wordsworth on theory of, v, 326

Newton, Gen. John, at Gettysburg, xliii,
336, 358, 370; Haskell on, 359

Newton, Sir John, xxxv, 64, 66, 68

New York, Whitman on, xlii, 1411-2

Nia, the waiter, xlix, 237

Niata, Cattle, xxix, 150-1

Nibbio, in THE BETROTHED, xxi, 323,
326-9, 333-5

Niblung, son of Hogni, xlix, 352

Niblungs, names of the, xlix, 253-4

NIBLUNGS AND VOLSUNGS, story of, xlix,
249-358

Nicæa, Council of, xxxvi, 273, 290

Nicagoras, xii, 14

Nicandra, priestess of Dodona, xxxiii,
32-3

Nicanor, xliv, 434 (5)

Nicely, Miss, marriage of, xviii, 123

Nicephorius, steward of Q. Cicero, ix,
112

Niceta, on motion of the earth, xxxix, 55

Niceta of Remisiana, TE DEUM, xlv, 546

Nicety, is depraved modesty, xviii, 14

Nicholas, the gift of, xx, 225 note 3

Nicholas III, in Dante's HELL, xx, 79-80

Nicholas, in TWO YEARS BEFORE THE
MAST, xxiii, 141-2

Nicholas, the barber, in DON QUIXOTE,
xiv, 45, 48-54, 229-36, 276, 300-1

Nicholas, Harry, xlvii, 662 note 10

Nichols, Joseph, i, 276

Nichols, Philip, editor of DRAKE REVIVED,
xxxiii, 123

Nichomedes, the mastiff of, xxxv, 354

Nicias, Alcibiades and, xii, 85, 116-18;
Cicero on, ix, 107; Hyperbolus and,
xii, 116; peace of, 116; power of, 115;
in Sicilian expedition, 121, 124, 126

Nicias, in *Mandragola*, xxvii, 384-5

Nicodemus, the Jew, on Jesus, xlviii, 280
(808), 286-7 (829)

Nicodemus, the Messenian, fickleness of,
xii, 201

Nicogenes, and Themistocles, xii, 27-8

NICOL, WILLIAM, EPITAPH FOR, vi, 265

Nicol Prism, the, xxx, 265

Nicolaüs of Antioch, xliv, 434 (5)

Nicomachus, Aristophanes on, viii, 486

Nicomedia, aqueduct of, ix, 378; fire at,
377; lake near, 382, 391-2; temple at,
384

Nicopolis, school of Epictetus at, ii, 116

Nicors, xlix, 17 note 1, 44-5

Nicostratus, Plato on, ii, 22

Nidau, Earl at Poitiers, xxxv, 46

Niépce, discoverer of actinism, xxviii, 418

Nieuwentheit, Rousseau on, xxxiv, 253

Niger, name of, xii, 157

Niger, rival of Severus, xxxvi, 64-5

Night, Byron on beauties of, xviii, 445;
Carlyle on, xxv, 332; Dryden's description of, xxxix, 323 note; Habington
on, xl, 252-4; Milton on, iv, 131,
132-3, 170-1, 181, 311-312; Mohammed on the, xlv, 881; patroness of
grief, iv, 24 (5); Shakespeare on, xl,
276; xlvi, 159; terrors, why greater at,
xxiv, 50

NIGHT, by Blake, xli, 585-6

NIGHT, TO THE, by Shelley, xli, 832-3
NIGHT, TO, by White, xli, 913
NIGHT, AT THE MID HOUR OF, xli, 822
NIGHT, HYMN TO THE, xlii, 1267
Night-hag, Milton on the, iv, 125
Nightingale, Æschylus on the, viii, 51; Homer on the, xxii, 270; Milton on the, iv, 35, 50, 170, 238; Swinburne on the, xlii, 1202
NIGHTINGALE AND LABORER, fable of, xvii, 33-4
NIGHTINGALE, ODE TO A, by Keats, xli, 876-8
NIGHTINGALE, SONNET TO THE, Milton's, iv, 38-9
NIGHTINGALE, THE, by Barnfield, xl, 283
NIGHTINGALE, THE, story of, xvii, 301-10
Night-Watchers, Psalm of, xliv. 314-15
Nigidius, Publius, friend of Cicero, xii, 234
Nigrinus, counsel against Varenus, ix, 299
Nihilism, philosophy of, xix, 58; philosophical, Buddha on, xlv, 664-5
Nile, Æschylus on the, viii, 196; breezes, why without, xxxiii, 18; delta of the, 14; Egypt a gift of the, 9, 11-13; Egyptian civilization due to, x, 25; embankments of, made by Min, xxxiii, 48-9; fish of the, 46-7; Lang on the, xxii, 335; Milton on the, iv, 345-6; mouths of the, xxxiii, 14-15; overflows of the, 15-16, 48; rise of the, cause of, 16-18; sacred animals of the, 38-9; sources of the, 18-22
Nimeguen, Peace of, x, 347
Nimrod, Burns on, vi, 408; in Dante's HELL, xx, 129; the mighty hunter, iv, 342-3; pictured in Purgatory, xx, 191
Nine Worthies, the, xxxix, 20
NINETY-FIVE THESES, Luther's, xxxvi, 251-9; remarks on, 246
Ninevah, Milton on kingdom of, iv, 391
Ning Wu, xliv, 17 note 9
Nino di Gallura (see Gallura, Nino di)
Ninus, Raleigh on, xxxix, 112
Niobe, Dante on, xx, 191-2; daughter of Tantalus, viii, 282
Niphæus, death of, xiii, 341
Niphates, Satan alights first on, iv, 154
Nirvana, attainment of, xlv, 738-9; Buddha on, 720; Buddha's passage into, 646; Buddha's search for, 578-80; the craving for, 715; Hindu doctrine of, 814

Nisroch, in PARADISE LOST, iv, 215
Nisus, in the ÆNEID, xiii, 188-90; Dante on, xx, 8; Euryalis and, xiii, 298-308; Euryalis and, Sidney on, xxvii, 17
Nisus of Dulichmin, xxii, 248
NITH, THE BANKS OF, vi, 342-3
NITHSDALE'S WELCOME HAME, vi, 419
Nitrate of silver, under voltaic current, xxx, 129 note
Nitrocris, queen of Egypt, xxxiii, 49
Nitrogen, in air, xxx, 143-4; binoxide of, 44 note; weight of, 144
Niuthones, Tacitus on the, xxxiii, 115
No CHURCHMAN AM I, vi, 37
No, MY OWN LOVE, xli, 901
Noah, Adam's vision of, iv, 336-41; Browne on story of, iii, 274; Jesus on days of, xliv, 399 (26-7); Kempis on, vii, 336 (4); Mohammed on, xlv, 905, 913; Pascal on, xlviii, 201, 215-16 (644); progeny of, iv, 341; taken from Limbo by Christ, xx, 18; wife of, xlv, 993
Noailles, Count of, Burke on, xxiv, 418
Noailles, family of, xxiv, 249-50
Nobili, Antonio de', xxxi, 408 note
Nobility, Bacon on the, iii, 34-6, 51; Browne on the true, 311; Burke on a, xxiv, 273; Burns on, vi, 511-12, 520-1; Goldsmith on, xli, 510; Hobbes on, xxxiv, 360; Keppel on a, xxiv, 417-18; Machiavelli on a, xxxvi, 16, 33-5; More on, 199; origin of hereditary, xxxiv, 221-2; Pascal on, xlviii, 379-380, 381-3; titles of, forbidden in United States, xliii, 160, 186 (8, 10); of Vanity Fair, xv, 98
Noble, C., on rhododendrons, xi, 290
NOBLE EARL'S PICTURE, VERSES FOR A, vi, 260
NOBLE LORD, LETTER TO A, xxiv, 379-421
NOBLE NATURE, THE, xl, 291
Noddy, Darwin on the, xxix, 20
Nodier, on school of Alexandria, xxxix, 366
Noël, Father, on light, xlviii, 425 note
Noëmon, son of Phronius, in the ODYSSEY, xxii, 31, 62-3
No-good, Mr., in PILGRIM'S PROGRESS, xv, 100
No-heart, in PILGRIM'S PROGRESS, xv, 217
Noise, much, little outcome, xvii, 17
NOISY POLEMIC, EPITAPH ON A, vi, 58
Nollet, Abbe, theory of electricity, i, 147-8

Nombre de Dios, account of expedition against, xxxiii, 122-3, 130-41; taking of, 226-7

Nominalism, Buddha on, xlv, 665

Nominations, in early Connecticut, xliii, 62

Nomphon, the sachem, xliii, 145

Non-combatants, agreement with Mexico concerning, xliii, 303-4

Non-conformists, called atheists, iii, 43

Non-conformity, of heroism, v, 129; of infancy, 61; Mill on, xxv, 143, 240-2, 261-2; Milton on, iii, 224-5; Montaigne on, xxxii, 41-2; necessary to manhood, v, 62-3; penalty of, 65; popular ideas of, 74-5; power of, 189; source of sanctity, 192; Whitman on, xxxix, 397; (see also Individuality)

Non-existence, Buddha on, xlv, 578, 661

Nonianus, and Claudius, ix, 199

Nonius, story of, xii, 250

Non-resistance, Emerson on, v, 460

Nonsuits, in Massachusetts, xliii, 70

NOON, SILENT, xlii, 1179-80

Norcia, Francesco da (see Fusconi)

Norfolk, 3d Duke of, imprisonment of, xxxix, 78; Thomas More and, xxxvi, 111, 117, 120, 125

Norfolk, Dukedom of, v, 405

Noriego, Senor, xxiii, 235, 385

Norman Conquest, Vane on the, xliii, 121

Norman Islands, Freeman on, xxviii, 254-5

Normanby, Marquis of, dedication to, xiii, 5-71

Normandy, Duke of, at Poitiers, xxxv, 46

Normandy, Edward III's invasion of, xxxv, 8-11, 11-16; Machiavelli on, xxxvi, 9

Normans, eating of the, xxxv, 287; Emerson on the, v, 345; Renan on the, xxxii, 160

Nornir, northern fates, xlix, 272 note, 294

Norris, Mr., speaker of Penn. Assembly, i, 115, 124

Norris of Bemerton, xxxix, 320

North, Goethe on the, xix, 74; Tennyson on the, xlii, 974-5

North, Lord, Burke and, xxiv, 5; Burke on, 387

North America, Asia formerly united to, xxix, 137; glacial period in, xi, 400; productions of, related to European, 398-9, 401-2; zoology of, 178-9; zoology of, changes in, xxix, 178-9; zoology of, compared with South America, 136

NORTH-EAST WIND, ODE TO THE, xlii, 1062-4

Northampton, Earl of, xxxv, 24, 27

Northburgh, Michael of, xxxv, 11 note, 13 note

Northern Hemisphere, climate of, xxix, 253-4

Northmen, Charlemagne and the, v, 342; government and people, 343-4

Northumberland, Earl of, xl, 93 (see Percy)

Norway, early depopulation of, v, 345; Freeman on, xxviii, 259

Nostradamus, reference to, xix, 25

Notes (see Annotations)

NOTHING, STANZAS ON (see NAETHING, STANZAS ON)

Not-right, Mr., in PILGRIM'S PROGRESS, xv, 274

Nottingham, Samuel, i, 183

Nourishment, Pascal on, xlviii, 120 (356)

Nova Albion (see New Albion)

Novello, Alessandro, xx, 321 note 18

Novello, Frederic, xx, 166 note 4

Novello, Guido, xx, 43 note 12

Novels, Burns on, vi, 57; Fielding on, xxxix, 176-81; Ruskin on, xxviii, 150-1

Novelty, Bacon on, iii, 136; human thirst for, xxiv, 29-30; Pascal on, xlviii, 38; wonder and, 40 (90)

Novum Organum, Bacon's, iii, 3

NOVUM ORGANUM, PREFACE TO, xxxix, 143-7

NOW SLEEPS THE CRIMSON PETAL, xlii, 974

NOW THANK WE ALL OUR GOD, xlv, 558

Nowell, Master, xxxv, 380

NOX NOCTI INDICAT SCIENTIAM, xl, 252-4

Numa, Bacon on, iii, 66; Hobbes on, xxxiv, 382; intercalary month of, xii, 312; on religious processions, 170;

Numa, in the ÆNEID, xiii, 340

Numantia, destruction of, xxxvi, 18

Numanus, death of, xiii, 313-14

Numbers, in battle, iii, 74; xliii, 341; effect of, in struggle for existence, xi, 78-9; Emerson on our respect for, v, 82; grandeur in, xxiv, 66; Hobbes on, xxxiv, 325-6; Pascal on, xlviii, 428-30; Prometheus as inventor of, viii, 183

Numitor, and Maeon, xiii, 332-3; Virgil on, xiii, 233

Nun, Chaucer's, xl, 14-15

Nun's Priest's Tale, xl, 34-51; remarks on, 10

Nur-ed-Din, Story of, xvi, 193-230

Nurse and Wolf, fable of, xvii, 29

Nurse's Song, xli, 590

Nymph's Song to Hylas, xlii, 1194-5

Nymph's Passion, A, xl, 293-4

Nymphs, references to, iv, 13 (20), 37

Nyseian Isle, iv, 161

Oak, Plutarch on the, xii, 149; species of, xi, 62

Oateley, Sir Roger, in Shoemaker's Holiday, with Lincoln, xlvii, 469-71; with Rowland Lacy, 471; with Hammon and daughter, 486, 493, 494-5; with Eyre, 496; learns Rowland Lacy is in London, 496-7; with Eyre at Old Ford, 501-4; finds Hans with Rose, 514; visited by Lincoln, 515-16; learns flight of Rose, 516; with Firk, 516-18; plans to stop wedding, 516-19; mistakes wedding, 524-5; hears daughter married, 526; with the king, 533-4

Oateley, Rose, in Shoemaker's Holiday, in love with Rowland Lacy, xlvii, 469-70; in the garden, her lament, 477; with Sybil, 477-8; the hunters and, 484-6; Hammon and, 493-5; with Eyre and wife, 503; discovers Rowland as Hans, 503-4; with Rowland, as Hans, 513-15; her flight, 516; with Rowland at Eyre's, 520-1; her marriage, 526; pardoned by king, 531; marriage confirmed, 533-4

Oaths, are but tools to deceive, xxvi, 120; Brynhild on, xlix, 305, 368; continuity of law by, xxvii, 232-5; Epictetus on, ii, 175 (166); Hobbes on, xxxiv, 400-1; Luther on sanctity of, xxxvi, 316-17; Mohammed on, xlv, 1003; Quaker attitude toward, xxxiv, 68; shall not enforce the wrong, viii, 140

Oaths of Office, Marshall on, xliii, 219

Oball, son of Conaire, xlix, 224

Obedience, Confucius on, xliv, 7 (5); is honor, xxxiv, 361; Kempis on, vii, 212, 274; Locke on, in children, xxxvii, 32-4, 61-2; Milton on, of subjects, iv, 208; Penn on, to parents, i, 339; Taine on sentiments of, xxxix, 429-30

Oberon, in Faust, xix, 183

Obizzo of Este, Dante on, xx, 52 and note 9, 74 note 2

Object, and sensation, xxxvii, 213-14

Objects, two kinds of, xxxvii, 222

Obligation, defined by Kant, xxxii, 324, 350; epigram on, xl, 398; Franklin on, from favors, i, 98; Hobbes on, xxxiv, 371; Machiavelli on, xxxvi, 37; Pliny on, ix, 200; Woolman on, from gifts, i, 201

Oblin, son of Conaire, xlix, 224

Oblivion, Lowell on, xlii, 1386; Marcus Aurelius on, ii, 217 (33), 246 (21)

Obscenity, Shelley on, xxvii, 341

Obscurity, brings safety, xvii, 26; Confucius on, xliv, 7 (16), 48 (32); Greene on, xl, 283; Hobbes on, why dishonorable, xxxiv, 366-7; Hume on, xxxvii, 294; more affecting than clearness, xxiv, 51-4; terror caused by, 50-1

Observation, Confucius on, xliv, 8 (18), 23 (27); Goethe on, xxxix, 252, 256; misuse of, xii, 35; necessary to poets, xxxix, 297; unhonored task of, v, 15

Obsolete Words, Johnson on, xxxix, 190, 203-4

Obstacles, Channing on value of, xxviii, 315; Marcus Aurelius on, ii, 260 (41), 261 (47)

Obstinacy, constancy and, iii, 277; Epictetus on, in opinion, ii, 124 (23), 132 (47), 142 (69); Locke on, xxxvii, 61, 62, 63, 66, 68; Penn on, in opinion, i, 385 (155-8)

Obstinate, in Pilgrim's Progress, xv, 15-17

Occam, Newman on, xxviii, 47

Occasion, Arabian verse on, iii, 56; Milton on awaiting, iv, 388-9

Occupation, Kempis on, vii, 223 (4); necessary to happiness, xlviii, 140-1

Occupations, Plutarch on mean, xii, 36

Ocean, currents of the, due to wind, xxx, 277-8; Darwin on the, xi, 347; xxix, 504-5; Geikie on floor of the, xxx, 330-2; organic discoloration of the, xxix, 24-7; Socrates's idea of, ii, 108; a sinking area, xxix, 484

Ocean Nymphs, Chorus of (see Prometheus Bound)

Oceanus, Herodotus on river, xxxiii, 17; Homer on, xxii, 145; Milton on, iv, 67 (see also Okeanos)

Ochre, Widow, in School for Scandal, xviii, 133

Ockley, Simon, History of Saracens, v, 127

Ocnus, ally of Æneas, xiii, 328

Octavia, Antony's wife, xii, 344-5, 346,

348, 362, 363, 366; children of, 388;
Virgil and, xiii, 32

Octavia, in ALL FOR LOVE, xviii, 13-14;
scene with Antony, 61-5; with Cleopatra, 67-8; discovers Dolabella with
Cleopatra, 76-7; tells Antony, 79; farewell to Antony, 82-3

Octavius, at Actium, xii, 372; xiii, 290;
Actium, triumph after, 292; Antony
and, xii, 254, 256, 333, 346, 348,
364-5; Antony, war with, 366-74, 379,
380-1, 382; Cæsar's heir, 255; Cæsarion
killed by, 384; Cicero and, 254-6, 259;
xlvi, 28; Cicero on, ix, 178; clemency
to Alexandria, xii, 383; Cleopatra and,
378-9, 382, 384-6; xvii, 51; Dolabella
and, 55; Dryden on, 42-3, 60; Empire
of, xii, 344; prophecy of his greatness,
255; in Rome, 338; in second triumvirate, 335-6; in war with republicans,
336-7 (see also Augustus)

Octavius, the African, xii, 239

Octavius, Caius at Cæsar's death, xii, 319

Octavius, Cnæus, ix, 133

Octavius, Marcus, at Actium, xii, 372

October Sixth, Burke on, xxiv, 208-17

Octopus, habits of the, xxix, 16-17

Oddrun, and Gunnar, xlix, 336, 383-4

ODDRUN, THE LAMENT OF, xlix, 431-8;
remarks on LAMENT, 252

Ode, Hugo on the, xxxix, 340, 352, 353,
354

ODE, by O'Shaughnessy, xlii, 1198-9

ODE IN IMITATION OF ALCÆUS, xli, 579

ODE ON INTIMATIONS OF IMMORTALITY, xli,
595-600; Emerson on, v, 466

ODE, WRITTEN IN MDCCXLVI, xli, 476

Oderigi, in Dante's PURGATORY, xx, 188
and note 2

Odeum, of Athens, xii, 50

O DEUS, EGO AMO TE, xlv, 556

Odin, in the EDDA, xlix, 361, 363, 429
note; Emerson on, v, 344; in the VOL-
SUNGA SAGA, xlix, 257; 258, 259, 261
note, 277 note, 279 note, 284, 285,
286, 300, 358 note 1

Odiousness, contrasted with sublimity,
xxiv, 72-3

Odors, Berkeley on, xxxvii, 199-200, 206,
207

Odysseus (Ulysses), Achilles and, xxii,
101; Æneas and, xxxix, 157; Æolus
and, xxii, 130-2; Agamemnon's praise
of, viii, 38; Aias and, xxii, 158-9;
Alcinous and, 90-102, 108-11, 113-15;

Amphinomus and, 248-9; Antinous
and, 237-41; Athene and, 38-9, 179-
85; as beggar, 228, 233-4, 236-8; the
boar and, 268-9; bow of, 284-5, 290-5;
on Calypso's isle, 9, 10, 60, 71-5, 173;
Charybdis and, 167-8, 172-3; Charybdis and, Milton on, iv, 134; the
Cicones and, xxii, 116; on Circe's island, 133-43; Circe's prophecy for,
162-6; Ctesippus and, 280-1; in the
land of the Cyclopes, 117-29; Cyclops
and, Virgil on, xiii, 148-9; Dante on,
xx, 107-10 and note 7; Demodocus
and, xxii, 111-12; dog of, 235-6; dog
of, Pliny on, ix, 352-3 note 2; Don
Quixote on, xiv, 212; Eumæus, swineherd of, xxii, 186-99, 207-12, 277-9,
289-90; Eurycleia recognizes, 266-70;
Eurymachus and, 254-5; faithful servants received by, 309; in the games,
102-5; in Germany, xxxiii, 94; on God,
ii, 126 (28); Hades, his visit to, xxii,
142-61; on island of Helios, 168-72;
Hermes and, iv, 61; Iphitus and, xxii,
284-5; Irus and, 245-8; Ithaca, arrival
in, 177, 178-81; Laertes and, 325-9; at
Læstrygonia, 132-3; Lotus-eaters and,
117 (see Lotos-eaters); the mantle and,
197-9; Melantho and, 253; Milton on,
iv, 22, 261; Minerva and, xiii, 105-6;
named by Autolycus, xxii, 267; Nausicaa and, 83-9; Nestor on, 35-8; omens
of his success, 275-6; Palamedes and,
xiii, 102-3; Penelope and, xxii, 241-3,
258-66, 270-2, 310-19; Penelope and,
Bacon on, iii, 22; in Phæacia, xxii, 79-
80; Phæacia, departure from, 174-6;
Philomeleides and, 54; Pliny on, ix,
208 note 9; Poseidon and, xxii, 11;
return home decreed by Zeus, 69-71;
righteousness of, 63; at Scylla and
Charybdis, 167-8; Shelley on Homer's,
xxvii, 336; Sidney on, 17; the Sirens
and, xxii, 166-7; the Siren and, Dante
on, xx, 221 note 4; Socrates on, ii, 29;
Spenser on, xxxix, 62; in the storm,
xxii, 75-8; Telemachus and, 215-23,
279-80; in Troy, 112; in Troy as a
beggar, 52; in Trojan horse, xiii, 108;
xxii, 53; Virgil on wanderings of, xiii,
365; the wooers and, xxii, 273-4, 296-
307; wooers' friends and, 330-4;
wrecked, 172-3 (see also Ulysses)

ODYSSEY, Homer's, xxii; ÆNEID compared
with, xiii, 38-40; xxxix, 157; Burke on,

xxiv, 34-5; editor's remarks on, l, 19-20; lines on, by Lang, xxii, 7, 335; reference to the, iv, 261

Œbalus, ally of Turnus, xiii, 264

ŒDIPUS THE KING, viii, 209-54; Æschylus's supposed criticism of, 476-7; Shelley on, xviii, 276

Œdipus, birth of, viii, 243-4; blinds himself, 247; Creon and, 211-13, 220-1, 224-30, 251-4; daughters of, 252-8, 270, 272-4; elected king of Corinth, 237; exile of, 254; exposed as infant by father, 230; father's death described to, 230-1; grief of, 236; Homer on, xxii, 151; Laius's murderer sought by, viii, 213, 216-17; life related by, 232-3; marriage to wife of Laius, 217; called Œdipodes, xxii, 151; in plague of the city, viii, 209-13; Polybus and, 237-9; Prynne on tragedies on, xxxiv, 153; remorse of, viii, 248-51; Sidney on example of, xxvii, 17; the sphinx and, iv, 409; viii, 221, 224, 254; Teiresias denounces, 220-3; Voltaire on, xxxix, 364

Œnone, in PHÆDRA, with Phædra, learns of her love, xxvi, 138-46; urges Phædra to live, 139, 140, 141, 147-8; prevents Phædra's death, 161; urges Phædra to assume throne, 163; announces Theseus's return, 166; urges Phædra to accuse Hippolytus, 168-9; accuses Hippolytus, 172-4; hears Hippolytus in love with Aricia, 180-2; denounced by Phædra, 184; kills herself, 190

Œnone AND PARIS, xl, 217-18

Offa, reference to, xlix, 58

Offences, against nature and custom, vii, 39; Jesus on, xliv, 398 (1-2)

Offenders, patience toward, ii, 289 (18)

Office (see Public Office)

Office Work, for literary workers, xxv, 55

Officials, Bacon's advice to, iii, 29-30; Bentham on criticism of, xxvii, 239-41; corruption of, inevitable under property system, xxxvi, 168; expences of, x, 465; legal responsibility of, xxvii, 234-5; private offences of, xliii, 74 (61); Penn on public, i, 353-6 (see also Public Office)

Offspring, universal love of, xl, 425-6

Og, king of Bashan, xliv, 315 (11); Milton on, iv, 17

Ogier, the Dane, xlix, 118, 120, 191

Ogle, Mrs., in SCHOOL FOR SCANDAL, xviii, 135

Ogygia, isle of Calypso, xxii, 96

O'Hagan, J., translator of DIES IRÆ, xlv, 551; translator of ROLAND, xlix, 93

O'Higgins, family of, in Chili, xxix, 353

Ohlenschlager, on Danish readers, v, 365

Ohod, battle of, xlv, 959 note, 963 note

Ohtere, son of Ongentheow, xlix, 85; sons of, 70-1

Oïcles, son of Antiphates, xxii, 206

Oil, as vehicle of taste, xxiv, 122

Okeanos, Æschylus on, viii, 171; in PROMETHEUS BOUND, 176-9

O'Kearney, Nicholas, xlix, 198

Oken, Emerson on, v, 177

Olaf, and Eyvind, v, 276

Olaf Tryggvason, and Leif Ericsson, xliii, 5

OLD AGE, ON, by Cicero, ix, 45-76; remarks on treatise, 7, 10

Old Age, Æschylus on, viii, 10; Aristophanes on, 428; beauty of, iii, 107; Browne on, 293-4; Browning on, xlii, 1103, 1106; Buddha on, xlv, 662; Burns on, vi, 169, 503; childishness of, xix, 16; Coleridge on, xli, 703-4; Collins's wish for, 592-3; comeliness of, ii, 206 (2); envy of, iii, 23; Goldsmith on best, xli, 511; Kingsley on, xlii, 1062; messenger of death, xlv, 685; Mill on happiness in, xxv, 35; Milton on, iv, 332; Pliny on order in, ix, 230; Rousseau on, xxxiv, 221; Shakespeare on, xl, 267; talkativeness of, i, 6; Wordsworth on, xli, 615

OLD AGE AND YOUTH, ESSAY ON, Bacon's, iii, 104-6

OLD CLOAK, THE, xl, 188-9

OLD FAMILIAR FACES, xli, 735

OLD IRONSIDES, xlii, 1366; remarks on, xxxviii, 222

OLD MAN AND DEATH, fable of, xvii, 39

Old Man of the Sea, the, xvi, 275-7

OLD MARLBOROUGH ROAD, xxviii, 401-3

OLD STOIC, THE, xlii, 1111

OLD SWEETHEART, LINES TO AN, vi, 221

OLD TESTAMENT, BOOKS FROM, xliv, 69-349

Old Testament, Calvin on the, xxxix, 493; Jesus on, xliv, 397 (16); Lessing on the, xxxii, 189-96; Luther on, xxxvi, 349; Mill on, xxv, 243; miracles of, xlviii, 286 (827), 288 (835), 299

(852); Mohammed on, xlv, 998; Pascal on, xlviii, 206, 207, 209 (631), 209-11, 214-19, 220 (666), 222 (670), 225, 226, 227-9, 230 (691), 231, 243 (714-16), 261 (740); Pascal on prophecies of, 186-8, 189 (576, 578); prosperity, the blessing of, iii, 16

OLD WOMAN AND WINE-JAR, fable of, xvii, 43

Oldfield, Mrs., the actress, xxxiv, 153

Oldmixon, on story of the exiled princes, xxvii, 171

Oley, Barnabas, xv, 399

Olimpio, in THE CENCI, xviii, 319, 327-9, 330, 333

Oliphant, Carolina, POEMS by, xli, 560-6

Oliphant, Rev. James, Burns on, vi, 163

Oliva, Count, in EGMONT, xix, 280-1

Olivares, Count D', xxi, 78

Oliver, friend of Roland, xlix, 94 (see also Olivier)

Oliver, Andrew, Franklin and, i, 4

Oliverotto of Fermo, xxxvi, 30-1

Olivier, in SONG OF ROLAND, xlix, 98, 100, 103; Ganelon on, 112-13; with Roland in return, 120, 126; at Roncesvalles, 127-30, 131-2, 133, 134, 136, 137, 139, 142, 144-5, 149-50, 151, 152-3, 157; his death, 159-62; blessed by Archbishop, 167; found by Charlemagne, 182-3; burial, 186-7

Olwen and Kilhwch, tale of, xxxii, 146, 149-52

Olympia, and Jove, iv, 273; xl, 391

Olympias, and St. Chrysostom, xv, 377

Olympic Games, Egyptians on the, xxxiii, 80-1

Olympiodorus, Plutarch on, xii, 92

Olympus, Mount, Homer on, xxii, 82

Olympus, physician of Cleopatra, xii, 385

Om, Hindu sacred syllable, xlv, 832

Omar, the Caliph, simplicity of, v, 55-6

OMAR KHAYYAM, RUBAIYAT OF, xli, 943-58; editorial remarks on, l, 22

Omberto, Count, in Dante's PURGATORY, xx, 188

Omens, Browne on, iii, 283; Hobbes on, xxxiv, 382; reading of, taught by Prometheus, viii, 184 and note 35

Omnipresence, Emerson on doctrine of, v, 89

ONE DAY I WROTE HER NAME, xl, 251

ONE-EYE, TWO-EYES, AND THREE-EYES, xvii, 206-13

ONE-EYED DOE, fable of the, xvii, 37

ONE NIGHT AS I DID WANDER, vi, 91-2

ONE WORD IS TOO OFTEN PROFANED, xli, 850-1

ONE WORD MORE, xlii, 1094-1100

ONE'S-SELF I SING, xlii, 1402

Onela, xlix, 70 note 3, 71 note, 77, 85

Onesti, Pietro degli, xx, 377 note 14

Ongentheow, xlix, 73 and note 1, 85-7; offspring of, 73; son of, 70 note 3

Onis, Luis de, xliii, 268

Ontario, Lake, naval forces on, xliii, 265

Onund, King, referred to, v, 344

Onythes, death of, xiii, 407

Opaqueness, cause of, xxxiv, 123

Open Air, Locke on the, xxxvii, 14

Open Sesame, xvi, 425

OPEN THE DOOR TO ME, OH, vi, 455

Opera, Wordsworth on the, xxxix, 298

Ophelia, in HAMLET, farewell to Laertes, xlvi, 107-10; advised by Polonius against Hamlet, 110-11; relates Hamlet's madness, 123; letter from Hamlet, 128; in plot to test Hamlet, 143; meeting with Hamlet, 145-6; at the play, 151-2, 155; her madness, 176-9, 181-2; death, 189-90; funeral, 196-7; Lamb on acting of, xxvii, 306-7; in the original story, xlvi, 92; Ruskin on, xxviii, 139

OPHELIA'S SONG, xl, 266

Ophion, Milton on fable of, iv, 305

Ophir, Milton on, iv, 329

Ophiuchus, constellation, mentioned, iv, 126

Ophiusa, alluded to, iv, 304

Opinion, all is, ii, 203 (15), 298 (22), 299 (25); Bacon on change of, iii, 30; Berkeley on, xxxvii, 234-5; bondage to, of others, iii, 33; confirmation of, 257; current, generally false, xx, 342; defined by Hobbes, xxxiv, 347; Descartes on grounds of, 16; diversity of, reason for, 5; earnestness of, not intolerance, xxv, 36-7; fable of yielding to others', xvii, 35-6; Hume on differences of, xxvii, 203; knowledge and, xxxviii, 5; is knowledge in the making, iii, 223; liberty of, Mill on, xxv, 210-49, 250; life is, ii, 213 (3); Lowell on confidence of, xxviii, 451; Marcus Aurelius on change of, ii, 214 (12), 236 (21), 256 (16); Marcus Aurelius on freedom from, 242 (52), 243 (2), 260 (40), 262 (49), 289 (16); metempsychosis of, iii, 257; might and, xlviii,

107 (303), 109 (313); Milton on formation of, iv, 183; Milton on variety of, iii, 223-5; Montaigne on willingness to change, xxxii, 43; of others, may be best, vii, 212-13 (2, 3); prevailing, not necessarily true, xxxiv, 15-16; "queen of world," xlviii, 38 note; spoken, reacts on speaker, v, 94; Ruskin on, xxviii, 111; Seneca on slanderous, xxxix, 67 note 2; Socrates on, ii, 35-6; Tennyson on liberty of, xlii, 998 (see also Public Opinion)

Opis, reference to, xiii, 375

Opium, Burke on taste for, xxiv, 15-16

Opium Trade, Ruskin on, xxviii, 115

Oppius, Atticus and, ix, 133; Cæsar and, xii, 279; Cicero on, ix, 171; Publius and, 116

Opportunities, Bacon on, iii, 56; finding and making, 125; Penn on, i, 348 (303)

Opposites, in nature (see Polarity); Socrates on, ii, 60-1, 97-100

Opposition, attitude toward, ii, 287 (9); some men's strength is in, iii, 124

Oppression, daunts courage, iii, 38-9; Ecclesiastes on, xliv, 339 (1), 340 (8); Hobbes on fear of, xxxiv, 372; impossible in state of nature, 195-6; Penn on, i, 352 (365)

Oppressors, Job on, xliv, 108-9 (1-12)

Ops, mother of the gods, ix, 385 note

Ops, son of Peisenor, xxii, 20

Optics, Hobbes on, xxxiv, 363; in New Atlantis, iii, 177; Newton's discoveries in, xxxiv, 121-4

Oracles, Browne on, iii, 281 (29); Herodotus on founding of, xxxiii, 32-3; Hobbes on pagan, xxxiv, 381; Milton on, iv, 12-13; Pascal on, xlviii, 195 (601); Satan as giver of, iv, 370

Oral Teaching, Newman on, xxviii, 32-8

Orange, Prince of, in sack of Rome, xxxi, 79

Orange, William of (see William of O.)

Orante, in Tartuffe, xxvi, 204-5

Orators, Penn on qualities of, i, 339 (173)

Oratory, action in, iii, 31; Cicero's book on, ix, 130; judgment and fancy in, xxxiv, 350; old age and, ix, 55; Pliny on, 205-9, 226-7, 346-8; rhetoric contrasted with, xxv, 324

Orbec, Vicomte d', xxxi, 282 note, 285

Orchard-making, in Chiloe, xxix, 301-2

Orchids, fertilization of, xi, 194-5; origin of, 239-40

Orco, Remiro d', xxxvi, 25-6

Ordas, Diego, xxxiii, 319-20

Order, as cloak for misgovernment, xxvii, 244-5; Franklin's rule of, i, 79, 80, 83-5; Heaven's first law, xl, 431; in nature, M. Aurelius Antoninus on, ii, 335-6; Pascal on, xlviii, 123 (373); Penn on, in homes, i, 328 (55-6); Pliny on, ix, 230

Order, in New Way to Pay Old Debts, xlvii, 866-8, 871, 872, 875, 876, 882, 884, 885-8, 923, 941

Ordination, Catholic doctrine of, xxxvi, 267 note; Luther on, 266; of Buddhist priests, xlv, 740-7

Ordination, The, by Burns, vi, 163-6

Ordnance, antiquity of, iii, 139; Don Quixote on, xiv, 379-80

Oreb, references to, iv, 88; xliv, 249 (11)

O'Reilly, John Boyle, A White Rose, xlii, 1198

Orejones, Raleigh on the, xxxiii, 354

Orellana, Raleigh on, xxxiii, 319-20, 322

Orenoqueponi, Raleigh on the, xxxiii, 321 note, 354, 373, 393

Orestes, in The Furies, viii, 124-5, 132-41, 145-54; Homer on, xxii, 10, 16-17, 38, 40-1, 60

Orestes, in The Libation-Bearers, viii, 76-7, 85-101, 103-5, 113-20; Mnesitheus and, xxxv, 274; Pylades and, vii, 50; ix, 18; Pyrrhus and, xiii, 139; Virgil on, 169

Organ, antiquity of the, xx, 183 note; Dryden on the, xl, 389-90

Organic Beings, affinities of, xi, 431-77; animal or vegetable, xxxviii, 340-2; classification of, xi, 431-43; increase of, 73-6; increase of, checks on, 76-9; complex relations among, 79-86; geographical distribution of, 378-430; geographical distribution of, Browne on, iii, 275; geological succession of, xi, 349-77 (see also Species)

Organic Periods, of history, xxv, 103-4

Organization, advance of, xi, 129-32; degree of, of ancient and living beings, 368-72; low, highly variable, 152; not the result of chance, xxxiv, 252-3; repetition a sign of low, xi, 152; standard of, defined, 218, 368, 370

Organs, with distinct functions, xi, 185-6; of extreme perfection, how developed,

181-96; highly developed, are variable, 153-6; incipient stages of useful, 219-44; of little importance, 196-9; multiple, variable, 152; rudimentary, atrophied, and aborted, 469-75; rudimentary, are variable, 152; with simultaneous functions, 185-6; specific and generic, compared, 156-9; use or beauty of, 199-204

Orgon, in TARTUFFE, relations with Tartuffe, xxvi, 207; returns home, 208-11; with Cleante, on Tartuffe, 211-16; on daughter's marriage, 216-18; Mariane with, 218-28; with Tartuffe after latter denounced, 254-61; prepares for marriage of Tartuffe and Marlane, 265-6; refuses to believe Tartuffe false, 267-8; at meeting of Tartuffe and Elmire, 269, 276-7; orders Tartuffe away, 277; repents gifts to Tartuffe, 278; with Cleante, 278-80; with Madame Pernelle, 281-4; advised to pretend peace with Tartuffe, 285; ordered to vacate house, 287-91; warned to fly, 291-2; stopped by Tartuffe, 292-3; his property restored, 295

Oria, Pagan de, death of, xiv, 388
Oriana, Lady, Amadis and, xiv, 116, 212-13, 227; to Dulcinea, 13
Orient, Tennyson on the, xlii, 984-5
Oriental Languages, Burke on, xxiv, 140
Oriental Literature, Hastings on, v, 446
Oriental States, Taine on, xxxix, 430
Origen, heresy of, iii, 258
ORIGIN OF SPECIES, Darwin's, xi
Original Sin, Bunyan's parable of, xv, 33-4; Burns on, vi, 70; Calvin on, xxxix, 48; Kempis on, vii, 326 (2); Lessing on doctrine of, xxxii, 201 (74); Milton on, iv, 143, 329; Pascal on, xlviii, 83 (230), 145, 148 (445-7), 264 (752)
Originality, Bacon on, iii, 129; Emerson on, v, 59, 60, 79; Hugo on, xxxix, 385; Johnson on, 232; Mill on, xxv, 259-61; Pascal on perception of, xlviii, 12 (7), 107 (302); in poetry, Hugo on, xxxix, 365-6; in poetry, Wordsworth on, 331-4; Whitman on, 397 (see also Individuality)
Orinda, reference to, xl, 387
Orinoco, Raleigh on the, xxxiii, 328, 330, 339, 350, 361-2; tributaries of the, 371
Orion, Aurora and, xxii, 71; Homer on, 152, 159; mentioned in JOB, xliv, 83,

134; Milton on, iv, 95; Virgil on, xiii, 45-7, 145, 348
Orithea, and Boreas, xxvii, 270
Orlando, Dante on, xx, 127 and note; in Dante's PARADISE, 362; Don Quixote on, xiv, 213, 226, 490; to Don Quixote, 12; Sidney on, xxvii, 10 (see also Roland)
Orlando Furioso, composition of, xxvii, 355; Montaigne on, xxxii, 92; Shelley on, xxvii, 349
Orleans, Duke of, at Poitiers, xxxv, 37, 46
Orleans, Duke of (Egalité), Burke on, xxiv, 381, 418
Orme, Captain, on Braddock, i, 136
Ormond, Hugo on, xxxix, 379
Ornaments, Whitman on, xxxix, 402
Ornithology, Emerson on science of, v, 297
Ornithorhynchus Paradoxus, xxix, 445
Ornithus, death of, xiii, 380
Orodes, death of, xiii, 347
Oronte, Molière on, xxvi, 215
Orontes, in the ÆNEID, xiii, 77, 93
Oropus, case of, xii, 194
Oros, as king of Egypt, xxxiii, 72
Orosius, Paulus, xx, 328 note 23; on Christian persecutions, ii, 315 note
Orphan House, Whitefield's, i, 101-2, 103
Orphans in Massachusetts, xliii, 78 (84); Mohammed on, xlv, 883, 884, 916, 967-8
Orpheus, Æschylus on, viii, 73; Aristophanes on, 471; in Dante's Limbo, xx, 20; Dryden on, xl, 390; Euripides on, viii, 393; on hoariness, v, 176; Milton on, iv, 33-4, 36, 73, 228; Sidney on, xxvii, 6, 11; Socrates on, ii, 29; Virgil on, xiii, 211; in Virgil's Hades, 229
Orphic Mysteries, Herodotus on the, xxxiii, 42
Orses, death of, xiii, 347
Orsilochus, in the ÆNEID, xiii, 378, 380; in the ODYSSEY, xxii, 45, 180, 204
Orsini, Alexander VI and the, xxxvi, 24; Burke on, xxiv, 269; Colonnesi and, xxxvi, 39, 40; Duke Valentine and, 24-5, 27, 31, 46
Orsini, Franciotto, xxxi, 79 note 3
Orsino, Gierolimo, xxxi, 201 note 2
Orsino, in THE CENCI, with Beatrice, xviii, 286-7; plots against Beatrice, 287-8; returns petition, 295; with

Giacomo, 301-3, 318-20; plans to win Beatrice, 303-4; learns Beatrice's wrong, 309-10; in plot to kill Cenci, 310-16; letter to Beatrice found, 334; with Giacomo after murder, 337-9; flight of, 339-40; accused by Marzio, 341

Orso, Count da Cerbaia, xx, 166 note 6

Orsono, volcano of, xxix, 279, 295

Orsua, Pedro de, xxxiii, 322, 361

Ortal, Jeronimo, xxxiii, 324

Orthodox, in FAUST, xix, 185

Orthodoxy, Burns on, vi, 212; Copernicus on, xxxix, 52; Penn on, i, 360 (472)

Orthography, Johnson on English, xxxix, 183-6

Ortolans, in France, x, 188

Ortygius, Virgil on, xiii, 312

Orus, the god, Milton on, iv, 14, 100

Osborne, Charles, friend of Franklin, i, 37-8

Osbrit Longhand, xlix, 234

O'Shaughnessy, Arthur, ODE by, xlii, 1198-9

Osians, Tacitus on the, xxxiii, 108, 116

Osiris, Dionysus called, xxxiii, 26, 72-3; Milton on, iv, 14 (24), 100; story of, iii, 221

Oslaf, xlix, 34 note 5, 37

Osman, humanity of, v, 217-18

Osprey, Harrison on the, xxxv, 339-40

Osric, in HAMLET, xlvi, 201-3, 206, 207

Ossa, and Pelion, Homer on, xxii, 152

Ossa, Jacques d' (see John XXII)

Ossar, Conaire's dog, xlix, 228

Ossian, and St. Patrick, xxxii, 169-70; Wordsworth on Books of, xxxix, 327-9

Ostenta, defined, xxxiv, 382

Ostentation, Bacon on, iii, 25; Penn on, i, 358; of virtue, ii, 177 (176) (see also Vainglory)

Osteomyelitis, Pasteur on, xxxviii, 374-5

Ostracism, at Athens, xii, 25; directed against persons of reputation, 79, 84; manner of, 84-5; remarks on, 115-16

Ostrich, Darwin on the, xi, 140; described in JOB, xliv, 135-6; eggs of the, xi, 263; xxix, 119; parasitical habits of the, xxix, 61; the S. American, 96-100, 118

Oswald, in DA DERGA'S HOSTEL, xlix, 234

Oswald, in KING LEAR, xlvi, 229-30, 231, 232-3, 240, 246-9, 257, 277, 283-4, 289-90, 298

Oswald, MRS., ODE TO, vi, 325-6

Othello, and Desdemona, Lamb on, xxvii, 302, 312; Macaulay on, 378; Ruskin on, xxviii, 138, 139; Voltaire on, xxxiv, 131

Otho, Count, in SONG OF ROLAND, xlix, 120, 135, 167

Otho, Emperor, death of, xviii, 439; followers of, iii, 9-10

Otho IV, and Gualdrada, xx, 66 note 1

Otho, Marcus, xii, 228

Otos (see Otus)

Otter, son of Hreidmar, xlix, 285

OTTERBURN, THE BATTLE OF, xxxv, 81-101

OTTERBURN: A BALLAD, xl, 88-93

Ottergild, gold called, xlix, 287

Otters, in Chonos Islands, xxix, 291; in the Nile, xxxiii, 39; sanctity of, xlix, 285 note

Ottocar, King of Bohemia, Dante on, xx, 173 and note 6

Ottoman, Bacon on, iii, 130

Ottomans (see Turks)

Otus, Homer on, xxii, 152

Otway, Sylvester, Burns on, vi, 340

Otway, Thomas, Hazlitt on, xxvii, 278; Venice Preserved of, xxxiv, 131

OUR BLESSED LADY'S LULLABY, xl, 256-60

OUR LADY'S CHILD, tale of, xvii, 50-4

OUT OVER THE FORTH, vi, 398

Outcry, much, little outcome, xvii, 17

Outdoor Life, and love of beauty, xxxix, 393-4; Locke on, xxxvii, 14

OUTLAW, THE, xli, 738-40

Oven-bird, Darwin on the, xxix, 101-2

Over-population, leads to wars, iii, 139

Overreach, Sir Giles, in NEW WAY TO PAY OLD DEBTS, character of, xlvii, 858; uncle of Wellborn, 861; Wellborn on, 865; at Allworth's, 871-2; with Wellborn, 872; scene with Marrall, 876-9; Furnace on, 886; with Marrall after the dinner, 890-2; preparations for Lord Lovell, 895-6; with Margaret, 896-901; with Lovell, 901-2; at meeting of Lovell and Margaret, 902, 903-5, 909; receives Lady Allworth and Wellborn, 905-6; believes Lady Allworth in love with Wellborn, 908; conference with Wellborn, 909-10; with Lovell at Allworth's, 911-16; his plot against Wellborn, 923, 928; with Allworth and Margaret, 925-8; at Allworth's in search of daughter, 932;

with Wellborn, 932-7; learns daughter's marriage, 938-9; with Lovell, 939-40; crazed, 841-2

Overreach, Margaret, in NEW WAY TO PAY OLD DEBTS, Allworth and, xlvii, 864; intended for Lord Lovell, 878-9, 891-2; Lovell and Allworth on, 892-5; scene with father, 896-901; with Lovell, 902-4; with Allworth, 905; parting with Lovell, 909; Lady Allworth on, 917; scene with Allworth, 924-8; announces marriage to Allworth, 938-9; in final scene, 942

Overshot Wheels, xxx, 180-1

OVER-SOUL, ESSAY ON THE, v, 133-48

Over-soul, Aristotle's idea of an, xxxiv, 103; exhibited in laws of compensation, v, 85; Hindu doctrine of, xlv, 803, 815-16, 818-41, 851-2, 858-9; Pythagorean doctrine of the, ix, 73; relations of man to the, v, 71; Virgil on the, xiii, 231-2

Overton, Colonel, character of, Hugo on, xxxix, 380

Over-trading, cause of scarcity of money, x, 319

Overwork, More on causes of, xxxvi, 180-1; Smith on results of, x, 84; Woolman on, i, 197, 251-2

Ovid, Chaucer compared with, xxxix, 154, 159-62; Dante on, xx, 104; Dryden on, xiii, 35, 36, 37, 52, 54-5; Dryden on Metamorphoses of, xxxix, 153; on himself in love, xxiv, 24; Montaigne on *Metamorphoses* of, xxxii, 68, 90

Ovieda, Gonzalo de, xxxiii, 322 note 18

Ovules, position of, xi, 213-14

Owannamug, the Indian, xliii, 144

Owen, Aneurin, xxxii, 138

Owen, Knight, in Purgatory, xxxii, 177; Renan on, 143

Owen, Prof. Richard, on cuttle-fish, xi, 461-2; on disadvantages of size, 354-5; on the dugong, 434; Emerson on, v, 443; on fossils, xi, 372; on generalized forms, 362-3; on highly developed parts, 153; on limbs, 453; on Megatheroid animals, xxix, 90-1; Mill on, xxv, 106; on non-flying birds, xi, 140; on origin of species, 13-14; the Solenhofen fossils and, xxviii, 119; on turkey-buzzards, xxix, 189

Owl, Darwin on the little, xxix, 130-1

OX AND FROG, fable of, xvii, 20

Oxen, English, Harrison on, xxxv, 326; German, Tacitus on, xxxiii, 95; More on, xxxvi, 173; sacred in Egypt, xxxiii, 24-6; why not grand, xxiv, 56

OXEN AND LION, fable of, xvii, 31

Oxenham, John, with Drake, xxxiii, 136, 139, 158, 171, 174, 183, 192

Oxford, Earl of, A RENUNCIATION, xl, 289

Oxford, Earldom of, v, 405

Oxford University, Emerson on, v, 416-7; Harrison on, xxxv, 371-9, 381; Huber on, xxviii, 48-9; Newman on, 47-50

Oxidrakes, cannon of, iii, 139

Oxiones, Tacitus on the, xxxiii, 120

Oxnam, John (see Oxenham)

Oxygen, absorbed by bacteria, xxxviii, 326; absorbed by fruits, 305; in air, xxx, 141-44; breathing requires, 163-4; combustion in, 137-39; combustion requires, 56-9; Faraday on, 48-9; Helmholtz on, 203; hydrogen and, 53, 139; produced from water, 135; production of, easy method, 136-7; tested by nitrous oxide, 148; weight of, 137, 144; yeast and, xxxviii, 275-302, 313-16

Oysters, no heart in, xxxviii, 129; Raleigh on, xxxiii, 312

Ozeyr, and the ass, xvi, 116 note

OZYMANDIAS OF EGYPT, xli, 851

Paches, death of, xii, 104-5

Pacific Islanders, Pretty on, xxxiii, 217

Pacific Ocean, Darwin on, xxix, 406, 420; Drake and the, xxxiii, 122, 171

PACK, CLOUDS, AWAY, xl, 316-17

PACK OF RAGAMUFFINS, THE, xvii, 64-6

Pacorus, death of, xii, 347

Pacuvius, play of, ix, 18; works of, lost, xxvii, 344

Padarn, coat of, xxxii, 146

Padilla, story of, xxi, 5

Padumuttara, xlv, 780

Pæëon, in ODYSSEY, xxii, 52

Pætus, Cæcinna, Arria and, ix, 242-4

Pætus, L. Papirius, letters to, ix, 155, 158, 159

Pagan, in PILGRIM'S PROGRESS, xv, 69

Pagan, Isobel, CA' THE YOWES, xli, 556

Pagan Learning, Milton on study of, iii, 199-200

Pagan Philosophy, Hugo on, xxxix, 342

Pagan Poets, Wordsworth on the, xxxix, 306

Pagani, Dante on the, xx, 202 note 27

Paganism, Bacon on, iii, 11; Hobbes on,

xxxiv, 379-83; Hugo on, xxxix, 343; Pascal on, xlviii, 195 (601)

Pagano, Machinardo, xx, 112 note 8

Pagans, in Hell, Browne on, iii, 305; Dante on, xx, 17-20

Pagasus, death of, xiii, 380

Page, Curtis Hidden, translator of Molière, xxvi, 197

Paget, Stephen, translator of Paré, xxxviii, 7, 9 note

Pagno, Maestro, Zanobi di, bell-founder, xxxi, 358

Pagolo, Pietro (see Galleotti)

Pain, Berkeley on idea of, xxxvii, 195, 198-9; Burke on standards of, xxiv, 11-12; cause of, 105-7; darkness as cause of, 116-19; of death, iii, 9; delight caused by, xxiv, 107-8; endurance of, xxxvii, 94-5, 99-101; Epictetus on, ii, 135 (55); fear of, xxxvii, 97, 99; Hunt on, xxvii, 287; of the imagination, xxiv, 16-21; from imitations, xxxix, 223; infinity as cause of, xxiv, 111-12; of the judgment, 21-4; Locke on, xxxvii, 86; Marcus Aurelius on, ii, 229 (26), 247 (33), 251 (64), 258 (28), 260 (42), 261 (47), 264-5 (1); of others, pleasure in, xxiv, 39-43; Pascal on yielding to, xlviii, 62 (160); passions excited by, xxiv, 35; philosophic attitude toward, ii, 75; pleasure in relation to, xxiv, 30-1, 36; removal of, not positive pleasure, 31-4, 35; Rousseau on, xxxiv, 261; of the senses, xxiv, 13-16; sensibility to, 23-5; Socrates on, and pleasure, ii, 48; sublimity always produced by, xxiv, 73; vastness as cause of, 110-11; Webster on, xlvii, 853

Paine, Thomas, Burke on, xxiv, 420; Franklin and, i, 165

Painting, Burke on effects of, xxiv, 129; Coleridge on, xxvii, 261; color in, xxxix, 257; color in historical, xxiv, 69; defined as mute poesy, xxvii, 256-7; Locke on study of, xxxvii, 174; knowledge of minerals needed in, xxxix, 256; Pascal on, xlviii, 51 (134); plastic art strives toward, xxxix, 260; poetry compared with, xxiv, 53-4, 138; reason of power of, 40, 44

Palace, Bacon's idea of a, iii, 109-12

Palæontological Collections, poorness of, xi, 326-32

Palamedes, Trojan War and, xiii, 102-3

Palamon and Arcite, story of, xxxix, 160, 161, 172

Palazzo, Currado da, xx, 211 note 8

Pales, Milton on, iv, 270

Palgrave, Francis T., Golden Treasury of, xl, 10

Palinurus, in Æneid, xiii, 134, 145, 146, 178, 205, 218, 220

Pallas Athene, in the Æneid, xiii, 121; in Trojan War, 74, 106 (see also Athene)

Pallas, son of Evander, in the Æneid, xiii, 271-2, 285, 287, 334-5, 336, 337, 339, 356-9, 360-2, 423

Pallavicini, Cellini on, xxxi, 209 note, 209-211

Pallium, the, xxxvi, 282 note

Palmer, E. H., translator of Koran, xlv, 875

Palmer, Ray, hymn by, xlv, 569; translator of hymn, 550-1

Palmer, London printer, i, 42

Palmerin of England, xiv, 51

Palmerin de Oliva, xiv, 51

Palmerston, Lord, on English troops, v, 358

Palmus, death of, xiii, 345

Pampas, S. American, Darwin on, xxix, 82-139; changes of animals and plants in, 125-6; geology of, 134-5; view of the, from the Andes, 331; formation of the, 332

Pan, Browning on, xli, 922-3; date of, xxxiii, 72-3; as Egyptian god, 29; Emerson on, v, 227; Milton on, iv, 10 (8), 376; Syrinx and, xl, 378

Pan, Hymn of, xli, 823-4

Panætius, on Aristides, xii, 78-9; Plutarch on, 17

Panama, Convention of U. S. with, xliii, 450-62

Panama Canal, xliii, 450 note

Panama, Isthmus of, Drake at, xxxiii, 172-173; formerly open, xi, 379-80

Panatuket, Eliot on, xliii, 145

Pandafilando of the Dusky Sight, the giant, xiv, 281

Pandar, Chaucer's, xxvii, 17

Pandareüs, daughters of, in the Odyssey, xxii, 270, 274

Pandarus, in the Æneid, xiii, 316, 317-8

Pandemonium, palace of Satan, iv, 106; council in, 108-21

Pandora, Milton on, iv, 172

Panegyric, Pliny on, ix, 192-3; Swift on, xxvii, 115

Paniagando on Dulcinea del Toboso, xiv, 514

Panic, Hobbes on, xxxiv, 341

Panope, Milton on, iv, 74; in PHÆDRA, xxvi, 146-7, 190

Panopea, in the ÆNEID, xiii, 186, 188-9

Pansa, Cicero and, xii, 254; death of, 256

Pantasilea, mistress of Cellini, xxxi, 55, 62-8

PANTHEISM, THE HIGHER, xlii, 1004

Pantheus, priest of Apollo, xiii, 111; death of, 114-15

Panthers, said to be marked with constellations, xxvi, 15 and note

Paoli, of Corsica, Mill on, xxv, 11

Paolo, Padre, iii, 196; Dr. Donne and, xv, 357

Paolo of Rimini, xx, 24 note 3

Papacy, Dante's allegory of, xx, 264-6, 275, 277-9, 281; Dante on temporal authority of the, 211, 399-401; Henry VIII on the, xxxvi, 118; Luther on corruption of the, 338-40, 341; Machiavelli on temporal power of the, 38-40; Milton on the, iv, 354-5; More on supremacy of the, xxxvi, 129; Pascal on the, xlviii, 304-5 (871-7), 306 (880) (see also Popes)

Papal Pardons (see Indulgences)

Papamene River, xxxiii, 319 note, 325

Paper Money, advantages of, x, 230-8; limits to circulation of, 238-9; dangers of, 248-9; Franklin on, i, 62-3; effect on value of gold and silver, x, 256; effect on industry, 248; effect of increase on prices, 252

Paphlagonia, Pliny on, ix, 374 note 1

Paphos, island of Venus, viii, 384; xiii, 87; Emerson on, v, 226

Papian Law, the, ix, 409 note

Papin, Pierres, xiv, 138

Papirius, Gaius, flatteries of, ix, 40

Pappus, historian, xii, 216

Papremis, worship at, xxxiii, 34, 35, 38-9

Papunehang, the Indian, i, 266, 267

Papyrus, eaten in Egypt, xxxiii, 46

Parables, Bunyan on, xv, 8-9

Paracelsus, on creation of man, iii, 288; Emerson on, v, 177

Paraclete, Holy Ghost called, xlv, 547

PARADISE, Dante's, xx, 285-426

Paradise, Marvell on, xl, 378-9; Mohammedan, xlv, 888, 892, 893, 895-6, 900-1, 911, 940, 950, 960-1

PARADISE, THE GARDEN OF, xvii, 280-93

Paradise of Fools, iv, 148

PARADISE LOST, Milton's, iv, 87-358; Arnold on selections from, xxviii, 73; Bagehot on, 194-6; composition of, iv, 5; Dryden on, xiii, 13; Hugo on, xxxix, 354; Poe on, xxxviii, 371-2; Shelley on, xxvii, 348-9; subject compared with other great epics, iv, 260-1; Wordsworth on, xxxix, 320-1

PARADISE REGAINED, Milton's, iv, 359-411; date of, 5

Paradoxes, Berkeley on, xxxvii, 190; Goethe on, xix, 110

Paræus, on Revelations, iv, 412

Parallax, of stars, xxx, 315-16

Paralus, Plato on, ii, 22

Parana River, Darwin on the, xxix, 131-2, 139, 144; sediment of, xxxviii, 402

Parasitic Insects, xi, 263

Parceval, romance of, xxxii, 164-6

Parcitati, Montagna de', xx, 111 note 6

Pardon, right of, in early Massachusetts, xliii, 76

Pardoner, Chaucer's, xl, 29-31

Pardoning Power, of President, xliii, 188 (1)

Pardons, Hobbes on, xxxiv, 407

Pardoning, the honorablest revenge, xlvii, 815; proverb on, xvi, 65

Paré, Ambroise, JOURNEYS IN DIVERSE PLACES, xxxviii, 9-58; remarks on JOURNEYS of, l, 23, 39; life and works, xxxviii, 8

Paredes, Garcia de, xiv, 488

Parents, and children, intercourse between, xxviii, 283; and children, Locke on, xxxvii, 27-31, 32-45, 49-50, 50 note, 55-6, 60-7, 80-2, 83-91, 104-11; and children, Montaigne on, xxxii, 73-4; Confucius on duty to, xliv, 6 (11), 7 (5, 6, 7, 8), 14 (18-21), 43 (18); Mohammed on inheritances of, xlv, 968-9; Mohammed on kindness to, 915; Montaigne on education by, xxxii, 39; Penn on obedience to, i, 339; Tzu-hsia on duty to, xliv, 5 (7); Yu-tzu on duty to, xliv, 5 (2)

PARENTS AND CHILDREN, ESSAY ON, Bacon's, iii, 19-21

Parigi, Piera de Salvadore, wife of Cellini, xxxi, 4

Paris, son of Priam, in Dante's HELL, xx, 22; Dares and, xiii, 190; Helen and, viii, 22-3; Mimas and, xiii, 346; King Proteus and, xxxiii, 54-7; punishment

of, viii, 27; Webster on judgment of, xlvii, 794

Paris (city), industries of, x, 264; pre-eminence of, in French Revolution, xxiv, 328-9

Paris, Parliament of, on National Assembly, xxiv, 177

Paris, University of, site of, xxviii, 45-6

PARIS, TREATY OF, xliii, 174-9

Paris, Abbé, miracles of, xxxvii, 387

Paris, Ferdinand John, i, 160-2

PARIS AND ŒNONE, xl, 217-8

Park, Mungo, on desire for salt, xxix, 116

PARKER, HUGH, EPISTLE TO, vi, 305

Parker, Theodore, on democracy, xxviii, 460

Parliament, burgesses in, xxxv, 224; under the Commonwealth, xliii, 106-13; More's plea for freedom of, xxxvi, 94-6; Voltaire on, xxxiv, 85-8, 91

Parliament of Man, xlii, 983

Parma, Duchess of (see Margaret of Parma)

Parma, Prince of, xix, 209 note 26

Parmenas, the deacon, xliv, 434 (5)

Parmenides, Dante on, xx, 343; Sidney on, xxvii, 7

Parmenius, Stephen, xxxiii, 290 note

PARNASSUS HILL, O WERE I ON, vi, 314-15

Parnell, More and, xxxvi, 115-16

Paros, marbles of, xiii, 132

Parrot, South American, xxix, 143

PARROT AND THE HUSBAND, story of, xvi, 33-5

Parry, C. H., Jenner to, xxxviii, 143

Parsees, of Bombay, xxv, 281 note; Freeman on the, xxviii, 271

Parsifal, legend of, xxxii, 165

Parsimony, Bacon on, iii, 88; Burke on, xxiv, 397; defined by Hobbes, xxxiv, 341; why dishonorable, 365; economically considered, x, 265-6; motives of, 269, 270

Parson, Chaucer's, xl, 24-5; Dryden on Chaucer's, xxxix, 164

Parson, Goldsmith's, xli, 512-13

Parsons, William, i, 58

Parthenon, built by Ictinus and Callicrates, xii, 50; Emerson on the, xlii, 1248

Parthenope, Milton on, iv, 68

Parthia, Antony's war with, xii, 349-61; M. Aurelius Antoninus' war with, ii, 304; Cicero in, ix, 136-7, 147; Milton on, iv, 391

Parthians, Tacitus on the, xxxiii, 113-14

Partiality, Penn on, i, 355-6

Participles, Johnson on, xxxix, 190

Particles, Johnson on, xxxix, 192

Parties, political, Emerson on, v, 244-5; Franklin's observations on, i, 89; Washington on, xliii, 238, 239, 240-1

PARTING AT MORNING, xlii, 1069

PARTING KISS, THE, vi, 318

Partisanship, of principle, i, 357 (432-8); of rulers, iii, 37

Partnerships, Franklin on, i, 104

Partridges, in Brazil, xxix, 53

Parvenu, in FAUST, xix, 177

Parvenus, envy of, iii, 23

Parvin, Benj., Woolman's companion to Indians, i, 257-69

Parwin, Omar Khayyam on, xli, 954

Pascal, Blaise, language of, xxxix, 374; LETTERS, xlviii, 321-61; life and works, 7-8; MINOR WORKS, 365-444; M. de Saci on, 387; THOUGHTS, 9-317; remarks on THOUGHTS, 8; l, 31

Pascal, Jacqueline, sister of Blaise, xlviii, 321-30, 341; letters of, 323-30; letter to, 321-3; profession of, 341

Pascal, pere, epitaph on, xlviii, 365; letter on death of, 330-41

"Pascha, The," Drake's flagship, xxxiii, 130

Paschal, St., Luther on, xxxvi, 253 (29)

Pascucci, Girolamo, the Perugian, xxxi, 188-9, 200-1, 202-3, 213

Pasenadi, the Kosalan, xlv, 675, 755-7

Pasiphaë, Dante on, xx, 49 note 3, 251; Massinger on, xlvii, 909; in the Mournful Fields, xiii, 222

Pasqualigo, Lorenzo, letter of, xliii, 45-6

Passion, Blake on, xli, 589; Bunyan's allegory of, xv, 34-5; Confucius on, xliv, 16 (10); in Dante's HELL, xx, 31-2, 47; Hindu Krishna on, xlv, 802-3, 853-4, 864, 868, 869; Kempis on, vii, 241 (1); nature seen in moments of, iii, 97; Penn on, i, 346-7; Poe on, xxviii, 391; reason and, iii, 271; in religion, i, 365 (533-40); simulation of, xlviii, 420 (see also Anger)

PASSION, THE, Milton, iv, 23-5

Passions, Burke on study of the, xxiv, 46-8; Burke on taste in the, 22; clearness not necessary to affect the, 51-2; David on the, xli, 491; Epictetus on

correction of, ii, 184 (14); Harvey on physical effects of the, xxxviii, 124; Hobbes on the, xxxiv, 336-46; Hume on the, xxxvii, 353; infinity, its effect on the, xxiv, 62-3; intellectual differences caused by, xxxiv, 352-3; of love, xxiv, 36-7, 38-9; Pascal on the, xlviii, 133 (412-13), 411, 164 (502); physical causes of the, xxiv, 103-28; poetry, its effect on the, 51-4; Pope on the, xl, 418; power, its effect on the, xxiv, 55-60; privation, its effect on the, 60-1; Rousseau on the, xxxiv, 177; Ruskin on the, xxviii, 112-15; reason and, xxiv, 40; of self-preservation, 35, 37-8; of society, 36-45; strong, most creditable to conquer, vii, 235-6 (4); sublimity, its effect on the, xxiv, 49-73; thoughts and, xxxvii, 299, 301; vastness, its effect on the, xxiv, 61-2; words, their power over the, 129-40; Wordsworth on, xxxix, 332-3

PASSIONS, THE, by Collins, xli, 476-9
PASSIONATE SHEPHERD, Marlowe's, xl, 254-5
Passivity, and activity, ii, 268 (16)
Passover, feast of the, xliv, 409 (1)
Past, America's attitude toward the, xxxix, 388; Bacon on the, iii, 15, 62; Bentham on veneration of the, xxvii, 226-32; Byron on, xxviii, 390-1; Carlyle on, xxv, 351-2; Confucius on, xliv, 11-12 (21); Descartes on rejection of the, xxxiv, 15; ECCLESIASTES on the, xliv, 342-3 (10); Emerson on the, v, 8, 70-1, 102; Goethe on study of, xix, 31; Hobbes on the, xxxiv, 320; Lowell on worship of the, xli, 1372; Pascal on the, xlviii, 355; Raleigh on the, xxxix, 96-7, 100; reasoning from, to future, xxxvii, 316; Tennyson on the, xlii, 972-3 (see also Antiquity)
PAST, THE, by Bryant, xlii, 1221-2
PAST AND PRESENT, by Hood, xli, 910-11
Pasteur, Louis, on bacteria, xxxviii, 257; editorial remarks on papers of, l, 40; to his father, xxxviii, 271; GERM THEORY, 364-82; life and works, 270; THEORY OF FERMENTATION, 273-363
Pastimes, dangerousness of, Locke on, xxxvii, 176
Pastoral Poetry, Sidney on, xxvii, 25-6
PASTORAL POETRY, by Burns, vi, 409-11
Pastoureaux, the, xxxv, 63 note
Pasture, rent of, x, 151-2, 154

Patagonia, Darwin on, xxix, 169-77, 184-93, 506
Patagonians, Darwin on the, xxix, 236-7
Patarbemis, and Amasis, xxxiii, 82
Patents, under control of Congress, xliii, 184 (8); Franklin on, i, 112
Paternus, Pliny to, ix, 209, 325-6
Pathos, Wordsworth on, in poetry, xxxix, 333-4
Patience, Bacon on lack of, iii, 134; better than pride, xliv, 342 (8); Buddha on, xlv, 596; Bunyan's allegory of, xv, 35; Byron's Manfred on, xviii, 420; Epictetus on, ii, 128 (34), 130 (39), 176 (170), 177 (174); Ferdinand's lesson in, xlvii, 835; Goethe on, xix, 367; Goethe's apothecary's lesson in, 400-1; instances of, given by Dante, xx, 206-7; Kempis on, vii, 219, 249 (6), 273, 280-1, 329-30; Manzoni on, xxi, 98; Marcus Aurelius, ii, 199 (1), 211 (3), 251 (63), 253 (70), 256 (14), 264 (59), 268 (11), 269 (27), 273 (42), 275 (3), 281 (30), 287 (9), 289 (18); Penn on, i, 334 (119), 339-40, 343 (234), 347 (294); in public office, 355; Rousseau on reason for, xxxiv, 277-8 (see also Bearing)
Patmore, Coventry, DEPARTURE, xlii, 1112-13; Ruskin on, xxviii, 144 note
Patriarchal Age, Hugo on, xxxix, 339-40; Pope on the, xl, 428
Patriarchs, Pascal on the, xlviii, 207; the twelve, xliv, 436 (8-9)
Patricians, Roman, ix, 292 note; Marcus Aurelius on, ii, 195 (11)
Patricius, father of St. Augustine, vii, 3, 150-1; St. Augustine and, 24; conversion of, 151; death of, 34; an unbeliever, 14
Patrick, St., on Gælic heroes, xxxii, 138; Ossian and, 169-70; Purgatory of, 177-8
PATRIOT, THE, by Browning, 1082-3
Patriotism, Burke on, xxiv, 329; extreme, not fortunate, iii, 100; superior to friendship, ix, 25; Locke on, xxxvii, 5; Lowell on mock, xlii, 1373; Socrates on, ii, 39-40; universality of, xli, 521-2
Patroclus, and Achilles, Æschylus on, xxxii, 77; Homer on, xxii, 36, 156, 322; Marlowe on, xlvi, 28
Patron, in the ÆNEID, xiii, 188
Patronage, Johnson on, xxxix, 207
Paul, St., before Agrippa, xliv, 478-81;

at Athens, 461-2 (15-34); in Antioch, 448 (25-6, 30), 450 (25, 1); at Antioch of Pisidia, 451 (14-52); Augustine, St., on, vii, 116, 124; Bacon on, iii, 13, 34; Barnabas and, xliv, 450-1, 457; at Berœa, 460-1 (10-14); conversion of, v, 141; vii, 124; xliv, 441 (3-19); at Corinth, 462; Dante on, xx, 266 note 14; editorial remarks on teachings of, xliv, 422; Emerson on, v, 239; at Ephesus, xliv, 464; EPISTLES TO CORINTHIANS, xlv, 489-532; Euripides quoted by, iv, 412; Felix and, xliv, 477 (24-27); before Festus, 477-81; on forgiveness, ii, 339; accused before Gallio, xliv, 463 (12-17); Greek poets quoted by, ii, 330; on himself, xlv, 493 (1-5), 501 (1-27), 511 (9-10), 516 (8-9), 519-22, 523 (5), 527-31; in Iconium, xliv, 453 (1-5); at Jerusalem, 470-81; at council of Jerusalem, 455; Kempis on, vii, 301; learning of, iii, 199; visit to Limbo, xx, 9 note 2; Luke and, xliv, 352; at Lystra, 453-4; in Macedonia, 466 (1-5); in Melita, 484; at Miletus, 467-8 (17-36); Mill on, xxv, 220, 242; misinterpretations of, xxxix, 44-5; missionary journeys, xliv, 450-70; Pascal on, xlviii, 100 (283), 192 (588), 222 (670), 224 (673, 674), 227 (683), 297 (851), 299 (853), 351; in persecution of Christians, xliv, 439 (3), 441 (1-2); at Philippi, 458-60; in Rome, 485-6; Taine on epistles of, xxxix, 435; at Thessalonica, xliv, 460 (1-9); at Troas, 467 (6-12)

Paul III, Pope, Cellini and, xxxi, 145-7, 159, 163-4, 178-80, 183-5, 202-3, 207-9, 212, 213, 222-3, 225-6, 227-8, 232, 239, 243, 244-5, 248-50; Charles V and, 178-81; children of, 147 note 2, 185 note; Copernicus to, xxxix, 52, 56-7; election of, xxxi, 145 note 3; escape from early imprisonment, 223-4; Duke of Ferrara and, 268-9; in sack of Rome, 74 note

PAUL REVERE'S RIDE, xlii, 1295-9

Paula, St. Hierome and, xv, 377

Paulet, Sir Amyas, iii, 3

Pauline, in POLYEUCTE, her dream referred to, xxvi, 77; begs Polyeucte to stay, 80-1; with Stratonice, tells her old love for Severus, 81-3; her marriage to Polyeucte, 83; her dream, 83-4; learns Severus's approach, 84-7; with

Severus, 90-3; with Polyeucte on his return, 94-5; her fears for Polyeucte, 97-9; learns Polyeucte a Christian, 99-102; pleads for Polyeucte with father, 102-6; with Polyeucte in prison, 111-15; asks Severus to save Polyeucte, 116-17; last appeal for Polyeucte, 123-5; follows him to death, 126-7; announces herself a Christian, 128; Saint-Victor on character of, 76

Paulino, Cellini's boy, xxxi, 39-40, 42

Paulinus, Valerius, letters to, ix, 255, 275, 334, 354

Paullus, Lucius, and his sons, ix, 168

Paulus, Lucius, Æmilius (d. 216 B. C.), death of, ix, 72

Paulus, Lucius, Æmilius (d. 160 B. C.), xxxii, 16

Paulus, Passienus, Priscus and, ix, 284

Paulus, Sergius, xliv, 450 (7, 12)

Paulus, the consul, and Cæsar, xii, 289

Pausanias, the Spartan monarch, Cleonice and, xviii, 428; haughtiness of, xii, 101-2; at Platæa, 89, 91, 93, 94, 95-6; treason of, 25

Pavia, Bishop of (see Rossi, Girolamo de')

Pavy, Salathiel, xl, 299-300

Paxton Affair, Franklin in, i, 4

Payen, Dr., on Montaigne, xxxii, 105-7

Pazzi, Camiccione de', xx, 133 and note 6

Pazzi, Carlino de, xx, 133 note 7

Pazzo, in Dante's HELL, xx, 52 and note 12

Peace, Blake on, xli, 591; Burns on, vi, 308; chamber of, in PILGRIM'S PROGRESS, xv, 57; "hath her victories," iv, 83; Hobbes on, xxxiv, 371, 391, 392; Milton on descent of, iv, 8; oversecurity in times of, vii, 268 (4); Pope on, xl, 432; the sovereign good, xlviii, 106 (299); temporal and eternal, vii, 300 (2); Tennyson on, xlii, 1015-17, 1055-6; the true end of war, xiv, 375; Washington on, xliii, 243-4

Peaceableness, Kempis on, vii, 241

Peacock, Milton on the, iv, 238; sacred to Hera, viii, 187 note 37

PEACOCK AND JAY, fable of, xvii, 19-20

PEACOCK AND JUNO, fable of, xvii, 24

Pearcy (see Percy)

PEARL AND COCK, fable of, xvii, 11

Pears, Darwin on improvement of, xi, 47-8; Locke on eating of, xxxvii, 21

Pearson, Dr. G., xxxviii, 171-2, 199

Peasantry, Goldsmith on the, xli, 510-11

Peasants, and lords, xlii, 1254
Peasants' Song, in FAUST, xix, 44-5
PEASANT'S WISE DAUGHTER, THE, xvii, 178-21
Peat, formation of, xxix, 291
Pébrine, Pasteur on, xxxviii, 270
Pecci, Pier Antonio, xxxi, 139 note
Peckham, Sir George, xxxiii, 269
Pectoralis Reservatio, xxxvi, 285-92
Peculators, in Dante's HELL, xx, 86, 89-92
Pedantry, Confucius on, xliv, 20 (16); Hobbes on, xxxiv, 336; Locke on, xxxvii, 150; Swift on, xxvii, 94, 101
Pediculi, Harvey on, xxxviii, 130
Pedro of Castile, xxxix, 84
Peebles, Rev. William, Burns on, vi, 99-100, 352 note
Peel, Sir Robert, blue books and, v, 360; law reform and, xxv, 65; model Englishman, v, 395
Peele, George, PARIS AND ŒNONE, xl, 217-18
Peele Castle, Wordsworth on, xli, 605-7
Peerage, English, Carlyle on the, xxv, 371-3
Peewit, habits of the, xxix, 120
PEG-A-RAMSAY, BONIE, vi, 514
PEGASUS AT WAULOCKHEAD, vi, 326
PEGGY, by Ramsay, xl, 401
PEGGY ALISON, BONIE, vi, 30
Peiræus, and Theoclymenus, xxii, 282-3
Peirson, Dr., on puerperal fever, xxxviii, 233
Peisander, in ODYSSEY, xxii, 252, 302, 303
Peisenor, the herald, xxii, 22
Peisistratus, in ODYSSEY, xxii, 34, 43, 50, 201, 203-5
Pelagianism, Pascal on, xlviii, 169 (521), 270 (777); Renan on, xxxii, 172
Pelagius, the monk, xxxv, 371
Pelasgians, gods of the, xxxiii, 31-2
Pelasgos, king of the Apian land, viii, 197 note 61
Peleus, father of Achilles, xxii, 157-8
Pelias, birth of, xxii, 151; in sack of Troy, xiii, 115
Pelican, habits of the, xlvi, 269 note 6; lesson of the, xv, 236; Shakespeare on the, xlvi, 181
Pelides (see Achilles)
Pelion, and Ossa, xxii, 152-3
Pella, studdery of, xxxv, 328
Pellean Conqueror, Alexander called, iv, 376

Pelles, King, Balin and, xxxv, 111; Sir Ector and, 203; at feast of Grail, 207-8; grandsire of Galahad, 109; Launcelot and, 203; the sword and, 185-6
Pellinore, father of Percivale, xxxv, 182
Pellisson, on French classical poetry, xxviii, 68
Pelopïdas, and Epaminondas, xii, 78
Peloponnesian War, xii, 65-92
Pelops, Cicero's letter to, xii, 238
Pelorus, references to, iv, 94; xx, 200 note 5
Pembroke, in EDWARD THE SECOND, xlvi, 16, 22-6, 33-4, 39, 45-6, 53
Pembroke, Countess of, epitaph on, xl, 333
Pembroke, Earl of, George Herbert and, xv, 381, 388
Penagwog Indians, xliii, 145
Penal Code, Marshall on, xliii, 219-20
Penalties, Winthrop on prescribed, xliii, 90-102, 104-5
Penance, Krishna on, xlv, 863, 866; Luther on, xxxvi, 251-2; Pascal on, xlviii, 234 (698)
Penarius, T., Cicero and, ix, 117
PENCIL, VERSES WRITTEN WITH A, vi, 276-7
Pendulum, Faraday on the, xxx, 13; Helmholtz on the, 186-7
Penelope, in the ODYSSEY, the minstrel and, xxii, 17-18; web of, 23-4, 261; learns plot against Telemachus, 63-5; her dream, 66-7; grief of, 149; told of Telemachus's return, 223; rebukes the suitors, 225-6; with Telemachus on his return, 229, 230-2; sends for Ulysses, 241-4; goes among the wooers, 249-50; draws gifts from wooers, 250-3; talks with Ulysses as a beggar, 258-66; relates her dream, 269-71; prepares contest for the suitors, 271-2; longs to die, 274-5; at feast of the suitors, 283; brings forth bow of Ulysses, 284-6; wishes Ulysses to shoot, 292-3; told of Ulysses's return, 310-12; reunion with Ulysses, 312-19; fame of, 325; Bacon on, iii, 22; Ruskin on, xxviii, 142
P'eng, xliv, 21 note 1
Penguin, habits of the, xxix, 204; Hayes on, xxxiii, 276; wings of, xi, 341
Penitence, David's prayer in, xliv, 188-90; Luther on, xxxvi, 251-2, 364-5; Pascal on, xlviii, 219 (661); Webster on, xlvii, 845

Penitent, Mr., in PILGRIM'S PROGRESS, xv, 282, 283

Penn, Thomas, i, 124, 160

Penn, Vice-Admiral, xxxiv, 74-5, 76

Penn, William, anecdote of, i, 109; FRUITS OF SOLITUDE, 317-97; editor's remarks on FRUITS OF SOLITUDE, l, 31; Helmholtz descended from, xxx, 172; life of, i, 316; Pepys and, xxviii, 300; Voltaire on, xxxiv, 74-8

Penni, Gian Francesco, xxxi, 34 note 3, 38-9, 55

Pennsylvania, in French and Indian War, i, 127-42; land conveyed to, by United States, xliii, 230; loans of, x, 471; paper money in colonial, 255; Penn and, i, 316; quarrels between Assembly and governors of, 126-8, 131, 138-9, 149-51, 160-2, 165; settlement of, 276-7; Voltaire on, xxxiv, 76

Pennsylvania Assembly, on Franklin's plan of union, i, 125; in French War, 127-9, 133, 138; Philadelphia Hospital and, 117-18; votes powder as "other grain," 110

Pennsylvania Gazette, i, 60, 92, 104

Penology, correction the purpose of, ii, 150 (88); in Elizabethan England, xxxv, 305-6, 363-70; Hobbes on, xxxiv, 408; More on, xxxvi, 143-4, 149-54, 210-11

Pensions, Burke on, xxiv, 396; Ruskin on, xxviii, 123

Pentapolin, and Alifamfaron, xiv, 136

Pentateuch, Hume on miracles of the, xxxvii, 392

Pentheus, in the BACCHÆ, opposes Dionysus, viii, 370; hears of bacchanals, 377-8; orders arrest of Dionysus, 381-2; with Dionysus, 385-91; house destroyed, 396-7; determines to go to bacchanals, 402-8; led by Dionysus, 411-15; death, 418-21; Cadmus on, 432; Mænads and, Æschylus on, 123; Virgil on distraction of, xiii, 169

Penthiselea, in ÆNEID, xiii, 90, 379

People, Confucius on the, xliv, 5 (5), 8 (19, 20), 25 (9); Lincoln on government by the, xliii, 415; Lincoln on justice of the, 321; Pascal on opinions of the, xlviii, 112 (324), 113 (327), 114 (328-30), 116 (335); Vane on sovereignty of the, xliii, 129-32 (see also Populace, Public Opinion)

Peor, Milton on, iv, 13 (22), 98

Pepin, son of Charlemagne, xxxix, 81, 82

Pepin, son of Louis Debonair, xxxix, 81-2

Pepin, of Aquitaine, xxxix, 82

Pepper-plant, Sindbad on the, xvi, 281

Pepys, Samuel, as a critic, xxviii, 299; Diary of, 286-92; editorial remarks on Diary of, 276; xxxi, 3; domestic troubles, xxviii, 303-4; Emerson on stories from, v, 411-12; musical compositions, xxviii, 298-9; old age of, 304-5; portrait by Hales, 292-3; on praise of God, v, 428; public services of, xxviii, 286-7, 302; respectability of, 299-302; his unique position, 285-6; versatility of his desires and pleasures, 292-7; as a writer, 297-9

PEPYS, SAMUEL, ESSAY ON, Stevenson's, xxviii, 285-305

Perception(s), Augustine, St., on inward, vii, 169-70; Berkeley on, xxxvii, 192-224, 228-30, 232, 234, 235, 245, 248-51, 255-6, 259-60, 264, 266-70, 273; Buddha on, xlv, 731; Hume on, xxxvii, 299-300, 410-12; involuntary, Emerson on, v, 70; belongs to judgment, xlviii, 11; mediate and immediate, xxxvii, 192-3, 222-3, 224-5; reality of, 193-4

Perceval, Spencer, popularity of, v, 370

Percivale, Sir, in the HOLY GRAIL, the sword and, xxxv, 108; at the tourney, 112; meeting with Galahad, 128-9; at the hermitage, 129; with his aunt, 134-6; follows Galahad, 136; at monastery at King Evelake, 137-8; encounter with men at arms, rescued by Galahad, 138-9; the robber knight and, 139-40; how he got a horse, 140; how he helped the lion, 141; his dream, 142-3; tempted by devil in woman's shape, 143-7; Gawaine on, 156; virginity of, 160; meeting with Sir Bors, 178; meeting with Galahad, 181; meeting with sister, 182; in ship of Faith, 181-2, 189; at castle Carteloise, 190-2; sees hart and lions, 192-3; at castle of strange custom, 194-5; meets Galahad and Bors, 206; comes to castle of Carbonek, 206-7; fed by Holy Grail, 208-9; commanded to go to Sarras, 209; goes to Sarras, 210-11; in prison, 211-12; farewell to Galahad, 212; becomes hermit, 213; death and burial, 213; Renan on, xxxii, 158; sister of, xxxv, 181-90, 194-6, 198, 210-11

Percy, Lord Henry, in Scots' raid, xxxv, 82; loses pennon to Douglas, 82-3; follows Douglas, 84-6; in battle of Otterburn, 87, 91 (see also ballads of OTTERBURN and CHEVY CHASE)

Percy, Sir Ralph, in Scots' raid, xxxv, 82, 84; at battle of Otterburn, 87, 89-90; Earl March and, 98

Percy's Reliques, Wordsworth on, xxxix, 325-7, 329

Perdiccas, Socrates and, ii, 293 (25)

Peredur, legend of, xxxii, 163-4, 165; Renan on, 142, 147

Perez, Anthony, xxxix, 88

Perez, John, of Viedma, xiv, 426

Perez, Pero, the curate in DON QUIXOTE, xiv, 45, 48-54, 229-33, 239, 271

Perez, Ruy, of Viedma, the Captive in DON QUIXOTE, xiv, 382-423

Perfection, as cause of beauty, xxiv, 90; Descartes on attainment of, xxxiv, 12-13; degree of, in nature, xi, 203-4, 209; Franklin on moral, i, 78, 84; doctrine of innate tendency to (see Progressive Development); Kant on conceptions of, xxxii, 353; Pascal on, xlviii, 326; Rousseau on attainment of, xxxiv, 214

Perfections, of Buddhism, xlv, 593-9, 619, 621

Périandre, Molière on, xxvi, 215

Peribœa, daughter of Eurymedon, xxii, 91; reference to, xxvi, 136

PERICLES, LIFE OF, Plutarch's, xii, 35-77

Pericles, Alcibiades and, xii, 106, 108, 111; Anaxagoras and, 55; v, 437; Aspasia and, xii, 60-1; Athens beautified by, 47-52; birth of, 37; character of, 39-40, 76-7; charges against, 51; Cimon and, 44-6; convention of Greeks proposed by, 55-6; death, 75-6; domestic economy of, 54; domestic troubles, 73-4; education of, 38-40; Ephialtes and, 46; government of, 43-5, 46-7; his large head, 37-8; marriage of, 60; military conduct of, 56-60, 61-5; Mill on, xxv, 257; Newman on, xxviii, 41, 57; as an orator, ix, 207-8; in Peloponnesian War, xii, 65-72; in public life, 41-2; removed from command, 72; sayings of, 43; his supremacy, 52-4

Pericles, the younger, xii, 75

Periclymenus, Homer on, xxii, 152

Pericoli, Niccolo de', xxxi, 149 note 1

Perier, Madame, letters to, xlviii, 323, 326, 330, 341, 344, 346

Perier, M., country house of, xlviii, 329 note; letters to, 330, 341, 342-4

Perigord, Bertrand, Cardinal of, xxxv, 34-5, 39-42, 45, 58

PERIGOT AND WILLIE'S ROUNDELAY, xl, 247-9

Perillus, and the Sicilian bull, xx, 110 note 1

Periodicals, Mill on, xxv, 61

Peripatetics, Locke on the, xxxvii, 165-6

Periphantes, tutor of Ascanius, xiii, 196

Periphas, in sack of Troy, xiii, 116

Peris, good jinn, xvi, 9 note

Perithoüs, in Tartarus, xiii, 227

Perjury, punishment of, in old England, xxxv, 365

Permanence, a word of degrees, v, 149-50

Pernambuco, Darwin on, xxix, 500-2

Pernelle, Madame, in TARTUFFE, leaves Orgon's house, xxvi, 199-206; refuses to credit Tartuffe's falseness, 282-4; convinced, 290, 295-6

Pero, Homer on, xxii, 152

Perpendiculars, grander than inclines, xxiv, 61

Perpetua, in THE BETROTHED, with Abbondio, xxi, 21-4; with Renzo, 30-1; on night of Renzo's intended marriage, 114-16, 124-5; her anger, 183; in German invasion, 473-80, 487-91; at castle of Unnamed, 493-5; returns home, 495-9; dies in plague, 549

Perpetual Motion, Helmholtz on, xxx, 209-10

Perpignan, camp of, xxxviii, 15-17

Perrault, discoverer of circulation of sap, xxxiv, 126

Perry, English drink, xxxv, 286

Perse, mother of Circe, xxii, 133

Persecutions, Bacon on, iii, 14; Browne on, 278; Emerson on folly of, v, 99; examples of religious, xxv, 219-21; Hume on, xxxvii, 393; Johnson on, xxv, 222; Mill on, 222-6; Rousseau on, xxxiv, 303 note; Voltaire on, 72-3

Persephone, Ceres's daughter, xli, 873; hymn to, viii, 450; maid-servant of, 454

Perseus, king of Macedon, xlviii, 132 (409, 410)

Perseus, son of Danae, worship of, in Chemmis, xxxiii, 44-5

"Perseus," Cellini's statue of, xxxi, 342 notes 3, 4; 354, 373-4, 375-8, 379-83, 397, 400-2

Perseverance, not genius, xxviii, 373; proverb on, xv, 207; Zoroaster on, v, 77

Persia, cities of, shown to Jesus, iv, 390-1; Raleigh on, xxxix, 71, 113

Persistency, Epictetus on, ii, 173 (156); of heroism, v, 129

Personal Cautions, Penn's, i, 347-8

Personal Force, Emerson on, v, 201-2

Personal Instruction, Newman on, xxviii, 32-8

Personal Representation, Hare's, xxv, 159-60

Personal Rights, equality of, v, 240

Personalities, defamatory, xxvii, 237-9; laudatory, 235-7

Personality, and condition, Schiller on, xxxii, 238-41; extinction of (see Nirvana); reality of (see Ego)

Personifications, Wordsworth on, xxxix, 274

Persons, natural and artificial, xxxiv, 413-17; as the object of government, v, 240-2

PERSONS ONE WOULD WISH TO HAVE SEEN, xxvii, 267-81

Persuasion, Æschylus on, viii, 162; Franklin on methods of, i, 18; Pascal on, xlviii, 13 (10), 400-11

Pertelote, in NUN'S PRIEST'S TALE, xl, 36-49

Pertinax, Machiavelli on, xxxvi, 63, 68; slain by Pretorian Guards, 64

Pertness, Locke on, xxxvii, 106-7

Peru, ancient, iii, 157-8; conquest of, xxxiii, 330; Darwin in, xxix, 365-75; empire of, xxxiii, 317; Johnson on palaces of, xxxix, 225; Lopez on, xxxiii, 318-19; mines of, x, 173-4; religion of the Incas, xxxiii, 374; riches of, 303-4, 374

Pescara, Macaulay on, xxvii, 390

Pescara, Marquis, in DUCHESS OF MALFI, xlvii, 805-6, 831, 832-3, 834-7, 847-8, 852, 853-4

Pescennius, Cicero and, ix, 90

Pestalozzi, on help, v, 22; Mill on work of, xxv, 158

Pestilence, as a judgment of God, i, 237

PESTILENCE, IN TIME OF, xl, 260-1

Petar, "hoist with own," xlvi, 169

Peter, St., Æneas healed by, xliv, 443

(32-5); with Ananias and Sapphira, 432; angel of, xv, 337; Bunyan on, 133, 134; chosen apostle, xliv, 368 (14); on circumcision, 455 (7-11); Cornelius and, 444 (1-33); his defence, 446 (1-18); his denial of Jesus, 411 (34), 412 (54-62); editorial remarks on teachings of, 422; imprisoned, 429 (1-12), 448 (3-6); with Jesus, 376 (45), 377 (51), 378 (20), 379 (28, 32-6), 389 (41), 401 (28), 410 (8-13), 411 (31-4); at Jesus's tomb, 416 (12); keys of, xx, 182 note 8; lame man cured by, xliv, 428 (1-16); Luther on keys of, xxxvi, 271; Malchus and, xlviii, 262 (744); miracles done by, xliv, 432 (15); in Paradise, xx, 386-90, 399-401, 422; Paul, St., and, xxxvi, 272; on day of Pentecost, xliv, 425-7; in Samaria, 439 (14), 440 (25); Tabitha and, 443 (36-43); Tansillo on, xiv, 315

Peter, Prince, of Arragon, Dante on, xx, 174 and note 12

Peter III, of Arragon, Dante on, xx, 173 and note 10

Peter the Great, standing army of, x, 448

Peter Lombard, Sentences of, xxxvi, 324 note

Peter of Provence, Don Quixote on, xiv, 490

Peterborough, Lord, Berkeley and, xxxvii, 186; Dryden and, xiii, 425

Petermann, the sacristan in WILLIAM TELL, xxvi, 417, 418, 425, 437, 439, 480

Peters, Rev. Hugh, Burke on, xxiv, 151, 203

Peters, Secretary, i, 124

Petition, right of, in United States, xliii, 194 (1)

Petition of Right (English), Burke on, xxiv, 171

Petrarch, Chaucer and, xxxix, 159-60; Hume on, xxvii, 221; on spirit of Italy, xxxvi, 86; Macaulay on, xxvii, 370; Milton on, xxviii, 174; Shelley on, xxvii, 347; Sidney on, 6; Wordsworth on sonnets of, xli, 681

Petrella, Castle of, xviii, 279, 312

Petrels, Darwin on, xxix, 293-4; habits of, xi, 179-80

Petro, Granius, xii, 277

Petronius, arbiter of revels to Nero, iii, 203; on poetry, xxvii, 106, 109

Petrucci, Pandolfo, xxxvi, 70; minister of, 75

Pets, animal, Augustus on, xii, 35; Harrison on, xxxv, 351-2

Pettinagno, Piero, xx, 198 note 6

Peucinians, Tacitus on the, xxxiii, 119-20

PEYSTER, COLONEL DE, EPISTLE TO, vi, 546-7

Pezoro, Signior, xxxiii, 182-3, 184

Pfeiffer, in WILLIAM TELL, xxvi, 386-7

Phæax, and Alcibiades, xii, 115, 116

Phaedimus, king of Sidon, xxii, 62

PHÆDO, Plato's, ii, 45-113

Phædondes, ii, 47

PHÆDRA, Racine's, xxvi, 133-96; Dryden on, xviii, 14-15; editorial remarks on, xxvi, 132

Phædra, in HIPPOLYTUS, daughter of Minos, her love for Hippolytus, viii, 304; song of her woes, 309-10; her illness, 310-20; tells her shame, 321-2; urged to love on, 324-6; hears Hippolytus tempted, 328-9; anger at nurse, 333; determines to die, 335; death of, 337; her innocence told by Artemis, 361

Phædra, in PHÆDRA, apparent hatred of Hippolytus, xxvi, 134-5, 144-6; her malady, 138-43; confesses love for Hippolytus, 144-6; hears of Theseus's death, 146; urged to live for son, 147-8; interview with Hippolytus, 156-61; her son chosen king, 162; her grief, 162-4; sends to offer Hippolytus the crown, 165; her prayer to Venus, 165-6; learns Theseus's return, 166-7; urged to accuse Hippolytus, 168-9; tells Theseus his wrong, 169; begs Theseus to spare Hippolytus, 179; learns love of Hippolytus for Aricia, 179-83; denounces Œnone, 184; Panope tells despair of, 190; confesses to Theseus, 195-6

Phædra, in Homer's Hades, xxii, 153; Virgil on, xiii, 223, 265

Phædrus, translator of Æsop, xvii, 8

Phaëthon, steed of the sun, xxii, 316

Phæthusa, the nymph, xxii, 165

Phaeton, references to, xx, 72, 357 note 1; xlvi, 17

Phalaris, in ÆNEID, death of, xiii, 319

Phalaris, the tyrant, bull of, iii, 306; xx, 110 note 1; Marcus Aurelius on, ii, 211 (16)

Phanias the Lesbian, xii, 18

Pharamond, in PHILASTER, suitor of Arethusa, xlvii, 667-8; with the King and Arethusa, 669-71; denounced by Philaster, 672-5; with Arethusa and Philaster, 683-4; with Galatea, 686-8; and Megra, 688-90; his fault reported to Arethusa, 691; before his lodging, 693; caught with Megra, 694-7; at the hunt, 714-15, 720-1; finding of Arethusa, 724-5; finds Bellario wounded, 727-8; arrests Philaster, 728-30; taken prisoner by citizens, 736, 738, 739-41; rescued by Philaster, 742-3; sent home, 750

Pharaoh (of Exodus), Mohammed on, xlv, 881, 888, 891, 902-4, 921, 932-4

Pharaoh (time of Joseph), dreams of, xl, 43; Joseph and, xliv, 436 (10)

Pharaoh, wife of, Mohammed on, xlv, 993

Pharisaism, leads to superstition, iii, 45-6

Pharisees, beliefs of the, xliv, 474 (8); Bunyan on, xv, 108; Jesus on the, xliv, 372-3 (30-5), 385-6 (37-44), 397 (14-17), 400-1 (10-14); Pascal on the, xlviii, 287 (829), 290 (839), 292, 294

Pharnabazus, Alcibiades and, xii, 144, 145; Plutarch on, 133, 134, 135, 137

Pharnaces, and Cæsar, xii, 305

Pharnapates, Plutarch on, xii, 346

Pharos, death of, xiii, 332

Pharsalia, battle of, xii, 299-303; Antony at, 327-8

Phebe, daughter of Gaius, xv, 274, 283

Phegeus, death of, xiii, 403

Phelps, Oliver, xliii, 230

Phemius, in ODYSSEY, xxii, 13, 17-18, 234, 304-6

Pheræus, Alexander, xxvii, 27-8

Pheres, birth of, xxii, 151; death of, xiii, 335

Pheros, king of Egypt, xxxiii, 53-4

Phidias, accusation and death of, xii, 67-8; beautifies Athens, 50; Epictetus on, works of, ii, 138 (61); the "Jove" of, xlii, 1248; statue of Minerva, xii, 51

Philadelphia, city-watch of, i, 98-9; fire company formed by Franklin, 99-100; Library, founded by Franklin, 66-7, 74-5; Longfellow on, xlii, 1334; public hospital established, i, 116-18; situation of, v, 334; streets of, improved by Franklin, i, 119-20; University of (see University of Pennsylvania)

Philadelphia Catechism, xxiii, 21

Philadelphia Experiment, the, i, 148

Philadelphus, name of, xii, 156 note

Philagrus, tutor of Nepos, xii, 240

Philanthropy, Bacon on, iii, 32-4; Emerson on false, v, 63; Epictetus on true, ii, 185 (18); Marcus Aurelius on, 209-10 (11); moral worth of, xxxii, 310

Philarch, officer of Utopia, xxxvi, 177

PHILASTER, Beaumont and Fletcher's, xlvii, 667-751; remarks on, 666

Philaster, in PHILASTER, heir to Sicily, xlvii, 668; with king and Pharamond, 671-5; with the courtiers, 675-6; sent for by princess, 677; Arethusa on, 678; scene with Arethusa, 679-82; with Pharamond, 683-4; Bellario and, 684-6; with courtiers, hears Arethusa faithless, 700-4; questions Bellario, 704-8; with Arethusa, concerning Bellario, 710-13; in the woods, 717; meeting with Bellario, 717-18; finds Bellario with Arethusa, 721-3; attempts to kill Arethusa, 722; his regrets, 726; wounds Bellario, 726; saves Bellario, 729-30; in arrest, 730; summoned to death, 731; in prison, 731-3; married to Arethusa, 734-5; condemned by king, 735-6; sent to quiet rebels, 738-9; rescues Pharamond, 742-3; in final scene, 744-6, 748-50

Philip, the apostle, xliv, 368 (14), 424 (13)

Philip, the deacon, xliv, 434 (5), 439 (5-13), 440-1 (26-40), 469 (8)

Philip, tetrarch of Ituræa, xliv, 360 (1)

Philip II, King of Macedon, Alexander and, xii, 36; v, 317; Demetrius and, iii, 51; Demosthenes and, xii, 200-1, 203-7; death of, 208-9; dream of, iii, 91; forces of, xxxvi, 48; love of horse races, xxvii, 28; Marcus Aurelius on, ii, 270 (29); the poor woman and, v, 263; Thebes and, xxxvi, 42

Philip II, King of Spain, Drake and, xxxiii, 129; Elizabeth and, 226; the Netherlands and, xix, 254-5, 261-2; Raleigh on, xxxix, 86-8; wealth of, xxxiii, 307-8, 319

Philip III, King of France, Dante on, xx, 173 and note 7

Philip IV, King of France, beauty of, iii, 106; Pope Clement and, xx, 79 note 6, 368 note 7, 173 and note 9, 226 notes 4 and 5, 228 notes 15 and 16, 279 note 15

Philip IV, King of Spain, Calderon and, xxvi, 5

Philip V, King of Madecon, Machiavelli on, xxxvi, 79; the Romans and, 12

Philip VI, King of France, in Crecy campaign, xxxv, 12, 17, 19-31

Philip of Burgundy, xix, 252

Philippa, Queen, Froissart and, xxxv, 5

Philippi, battle of, xii, 321; Antony at, xviii, 38

Philippi, Dr. A., xxxviii, 405

Philippine Islands, cession of, xliii, 443-9

Philippus, stepfather of Octavius, xii, 254-5

Philips, Ambrose, To CHARLOTTE PULTENEY, xl, 440-1

Philiscus, at Athens, xxviii, 58

Philistines, festival of, iv, 425; Samson and, 420-1

Philitis, the shepherd, xxxiii, 65

PHILLADA FLOUTS ME, xl, 380-3

PHILLIDA AND CORIDON, xl, 196-7

Phillips, Erasmus, in Hazlitt's discussion, xxvii, 274

Phillips, Wendell, Mill on, xxv, 165

Phillis, Milton on, iv, 32

PHILLIS, by Lodge, xl, 216-17

PHILLIS THE FAIR, by Burns, vi, 467

PHILLIS THE QUEEN OF THE FAIR, vi, 469-70

PHILLY AND WILLY, vi, 506-7

Philo, the Academic, xii, 219

Philo, the Jew, xlviii, 206

Philoctetes, in ODYSSEY, xxii, 37, 104

Philoetius, in ODYSSEY, xxii, 278-9, 289-90, 293-4, 299-309

Philolaus, on motion of earth, xxxix, 55; Plato on, ii, 49

Philologus, Cicero and, xii, 258; death of, 259

Philology, an historical science, xxviii, 236-7; important results of, 229-30 (see also Language)

Philomela, Milton on, iv, 35; story of, xx, 213 note 1

Philomeleides, and Ulysses, xxii, 54

Philon, the shepherd, xl, 199-200

PHILONOUS AND HYLAS, DIALOGUES OF, xxxvii, 187-285

Philopœmon, Prince of Achaia, xxxvi, 49-50

Philosophers, Augustine, St., on, vii, 64-6; Burns on, vi, 334-6; charges against, ii, 11; Cicero on, xlviii, 121 note 4; Comte's rule of, xxv, 132-3; Dante on

unskilful, xx, 343; death and, ii, 53-7;
Epictetus on, 142, 143, 152, 155-6,
158-62; French, Burke on, xxiv, 246-7;
Harvey on true, xxxviii, 62-3; the hereafter desired by, ii, 76-7; Marcus Aurelius on true, 217 (30); moral, Sidney
on, xxvii, 14-19, 22-3; Pascal on, xlviii,
11, 138 (430), 139, 164 (503), 170;
attitude toward pleasure and pain, ii,
75-6; poets compared with in usefulness, xxvii, 350-3; Rousseau on, xxxiv,
242-3; sacred and literary, v, 143; Sidney on, xxvii, 13-14; statesmen and,
Plutarch on, xii, 54

PHILOSOPHERS, ENGLISH, xxxvii

PHILOSOPHERS, FRENCH AND ENGLISH,
xxxiv

Philosopher's Candles, xxx, 123-5

Philosopher's Stone, Sir Epicure Mammon
on the, xlvii, 566; Milton on, iv, 150

Philosophia Prima, xxxiv, 363

Philosophic Radicalism, Mill on, xxv, 68-
71

Philosophic Radicals, in Parliament, xxv,
122-24, 133-35

PHILOSOPHICAL ESSAYS, xxxii

PHILOSOPHISE, THAT TO, IS TO LEARNE
HOW TO DIE, xxxii, 9-28

Philosophy, Arnold on our, xxviii, 66;
Athenian, Milton on, iv, 402-3, 8; M.
AURELIUS ANTONINUS, LIFE OF, ii, 302-
19; authority and, xxxix, 100, 122-123;
Berkeley on innovations in, xxxvii,
265; Browne on righteousness of, iii,
264-5; Byron on, xviii, 436-437; Carlyle on, xxv, 340; Cicero on, ix, 45;
Cowley on, xxvii, 61; Dante's allegory
on, xx, 221; Descartes on study of,
xxxiv, 8, 10; empirical and pure, xxxii,
299-300; as an employment, x, 15;
Epictetus on, ii, 132 (56), 143 (72);
need of, in ethics, xxxii, 316-17, 319-
20; extreme limits of practical, 367-9,
372; Faustus on, xix, 206, 209; Hume
on different species of, xxxvii, 289-98,
310-11, 312, 319-20; irreligion and, iii,
42; Kant on divisions of, xxxii, 299;
knowledge of consequences, xxxiv,
362; liberty needed by, xxxvii, 400-1,
412-13; magic and, iii, 282; Marcus
Aurelius on, ii, 204 (17), 225 (9), 233
(12); Montaigne on study of, xxxii,
48-51, 53-4; "more things than dreamt
of in," xlvi, 120; PHILOSOPHY OF M.
AURELIUS ANTONINUS, ii, 320-45; Plato

on true, xxxii, 38; practical, best, ix,
196; Raleigh on, xxxix, 109; reading
course in, l, 29-35; religion and, Voltaire on, xxxiv, 107-8; school and
practical, xxxvi, 164-6; several branches
of, xxxiv, 362-3; Socrates on, ii, 48,
72-3, 74-6; Taine on, xxxix, 429, 430,
431; Tasso on, xxxii, 34-5; tran-
scendental, 302; of various races, xxxix,
419, 420

Philostratus, and Octavius, xii, 384

Philotas, on Antony, xii, 342-343

Philotimus, Cicero on, ix, 113, 149

Phineas, Burns on, vi, 164

Phinehas, xliv, 279 (30)

Phlebotomy, Harvey on, xxxviii, 115, 116,
117

Phlegethon, river, xiii, 225; source of the,
xx, 61

Phlegyas, Dante on, xx, 32-3; in Tartarus,
xiii, 228

Phocion, Carlyle on, xxv, 378; courage
and honesty of, xii, 202; death of,
xxvii, 21; on the event of the battle,
v, 129; Landor on, 318; Marcus Aurelius on, ii, 288 (13); as orator, xii, 199

Phocylides, Sidney on, xxvii, 7, 12

Phœbe, name of Diana, viii, 122; xxxix,
63

Phœbe, the deaconess, ix, 406 note

Phœbus, Milton on, iv, 24 (4), 46, 74;
wain of, 49 (see also Apollo)

Phœnicians, circumcision among, xxxiii,
51

Phœnix, Æsop on the, xvii, 285; Dante
on, xx, 100; Herodotus on, xxxiii, 39;
Milton on, iv, 187, 457; Virgil on the
Greek, xiii, 126, 187

Pholus, Dante on, xx, 50; death of, xiii,
402

Phorcys, Homer on, xxii, 11

Phorkides, the, viii, 195

Phormisius, pupil of Æschylus, viii, 468

Phosphorescence, of the sea, xxix, 167-8

Phosphorescent Insects, Darwin on, xxix,
38-40

Phosphorus, combustion of, in oxygen,
xxx, 138; flame of, 109

Phosphorus (youth), statue of, v, 172

Photographic Light, xxx, 260

Phraates, king of Parthia, in war with
Antony, xii, 349-50, 351-3, 356; in
war with Media, 362

Phrontis, the pilot, xxii, 40

Phrygians, antiquity of the, xxxiii, 7-8

Phrynichus, accuser of Alcibiades, xii, 124, 130-1

Phyllis, Dante on, xx, 323 note 30

Phylogeny, defined, xi, 452

Physcon, name of, xii, 156 note

Physic (see Medicine)

Physical Science, Channing on study of, xxviii, 327-8; Descartes on, xxxiv, 50; Faraday on, xxx, 85; Huxley on, xxviii, 210-21; Pascal on, xlviii, 25 (67), 439-41

Physical Training, of children, xxxvii, 10-27; Milton on, iii, 244-6; Montaigne on, xxxii, 40, 55, 57; for women, xxviii, 146-8

Physicians, atheism of, iii, 253 note; Bacon on best, 82; early guilds of, xxxviii, 2, 3; Hippocrates on, 2, 3, 4-5; Pascal on costumes of, xlviii, 37

Physics (see Natural Philosophy)

Physiognomy, beauty of the, xxiv, 96-7; Browne on, iii, 312-3; of religious sects, v, 338; science of, 288; Webster on, xlvii, 762

Physiology, papers on, xxxviii, 75-139

Phytophagic Species, xi, 60-1

Pia, of Sienna, xx, 165 and note

Piazza, the anointer of Milan, xxi, 4-5

Picard, M., xxxiv, 116

Piccarda, in Paradise, xx, 294-7 and note

Piccolomini, Alfonso, xxxi, 266 note 1

Pickering, Timothy, xliii, 229

Pickett's Charge at Gettysburg, xliii, 379-90, 402

Pickthank, in PILGRIM'S PROGRESS, xv, 98-9

Pico, Don Andres, xxiii, 393

Pico, Galeotto, xxxi, 292 note 1

Pictet, Prof., on birds, xi, 341; on chalk formations, 367-8; palæontology, work on, 341

Picture-books, Locke on, xxxvii, 132

PICTURE OF LITTLE T. C., xl, 371-2

Pictures, less affecting than words, xxiv, 51-4; moving, in New Atlantis, iii, 179

Picus Mirandola, xv, 323

Picus, son of Saturn, xiii, 241; Circe and, 245

Piedmont, Prince of, xxxviii, 36

PIEMONT, SONNET ON MASSACRE OF, iv, 83-4

Pienne, M. de, xxxviii, 25

Pierce, Mr., on wolves, xi, 97

Piercy (see Percy)

Pierino, and Cellini, xxxi, 17-20

Pierres, Mosen, xiv, 490

Pierus, daughters of, xx, 145 note 1

Pietra, Nello della, xx, 165 note

Piety, in PILGRIM'S PROGRESS, xv, 51-3, 239-40

PIETY, EARLY, xlv, 563-4

Piety, of act, speech and mind, xlv, 864-5; Carlyle on, xxv, 386; Dryden on, xiii, 24; Epictetus on true, ii, 175 (163); false, a double sin, xlviii, 316; Herbert on decay of, xv, 406-7; Hindu conception of, xlv, 795, 814; Pascal on, xlviii, 94 (255), 162 (496), 354-5; Penn on, i, 360 (470); Segrais on, xiii, 24

Piffero, Ercole del, xxxi, 17

Pigeons, analogous variations of, xi, 159-60; breeds of domestic, 34-6; circumstances favorable to breeding of, 51; correlation in, 28, 148; descent of, 36, 39-40, 49; in Elizabethan England, xxxv, 335; in history, xi, 40; instincts of tumblers, 257; reversion of, 161, 162

Pigray, the surgeon, xxxviii, 49, 50

Pigs, held abominable in Egypt, xxxiii, 29-30

Pi Hsi, xliv, 58 (7)

Pilate, Pontius, governor of Judæa, xliv, 360 (1); and the Galilæans, 390 (1); and Jesus, 413 (1-7), 413-14 (11-25); Pascal on, xlviii, 262 (744), 273-4 (791)

PILGRIMAGE, Raleigh's, xl, 203-4

Pilgrimages, Luther on, xxxvi, 298-300, 310; Milton on, iv, 147

PILGRIM'S PROGRESS, Bunyan's, xv, 5-319; authorship of, 319; Franklin on, i, 13, 22-3; remarks on, xv, 4; l, 31; widespread influence of, xv, 171-2

Pilgrims, Lowell on the, xlii, 1372

PILGRIMS OF THE NIGHT, xlv, 571-2

PILLAR OF CLOUD, xlv, 567-8

Pilli, Raffaello, de', xxxi, 373, 427

Pillows, in old England, xxxv, 298

Piloto, Cellini on, xxxi, 63 note, 144

Pin, M. du, Burke on, xxiv, 341-2; on French army, 342-4

Pinabel of Sorrence, xlix, 106, 189, 190-3

Pincheira, Darwin on, xxix, 269

Pindar, Alexander and, iv, 78; Browning on, xli, 931; the English, xiii, 62; Hiero and, xxvii, 38; Horace on, 183; house of, spared, iv, 78; Hugo on, xxxix, 340; Sidney on, xxvii, 28

Pindaric Line, Dryden on the, xiii, 54
Pindarus, freedman of Cassius, xii, 337
Pindenissus, siege of, ix, 138
Pineda, Juan de, iii, 277 note
Pine-tree, Emerson on the, xlii, 1253-61
Pinkney, Edward C., HEALTH by, xxviii, 382-3
Pins, manufacture of, x, 10-11
Piombo, Sebastian del, xxxi, 97 note 6, 113 note 2
PIONEERS! O PIONEERS! xlii, 1404-7
PIOUS EDITOR'S CREED, xlii, 1373-6
PIPES AT LUCKNOW, xlii, 1360-2
PIPPA'S SONG, xlii, 1073
Piracy, punishment of, in old England, xxxv, 368; under control of Congress, xliii, 162, 184 (10)
Piræus, companion of Telemachus, xxii, 213-14, 229-30
Piræus, port of, established by Themistocles, xii, 22
Pirithoüs, Racine on, xxvi, 171
Pisa, and Florence, xxxvi, 18
Pisistratus, and his daughter's lover, xx, 206 note 4; Emerson on, v, 239; Macaulay on, xxvii, 399; Newman on, xxviii, 40; Solon and, ix, 71
Piso, Calpurnius, Pliny on, ix, 274-5
Piso, Julius, ix, 411
Piso, Cæsonius, Lucius Calpurnius, Cicero on, iii, 64-5; Cicero and, xii, 243; Clodius and, 242; made consul, 275
Piso, son-in-law of Cicero, xii, 243-4
Pissuthnes, the Persian, xii, 61-2
PITCHER AND CROW, fable of, xvii, 32
Pitigliano, Count of, xxxvi, 43; Cellini on, xxxi, 292, note 1
Pitt, William, Earl of Chatham, George II and, xxiv, 332
Pitt, William, and Burke, xxiv, 380; Burns on, vi, 52, 161, 209, 409; Mazzini on, xxxii, 382
Pittacos, maxim of marriage, viii, 198 note
Pittacus, on forgiveness, ii, 153 (96)
Pittheus, and Hippolytus, xxvi, 176
Pity, Bacon on, iii, 9-10, 34; Blake on, xli, 591; Burke on passion of, xxiv, 41; envy and, iii, 24; Hobbes on, xxxiv, 342-3; language of, 344-5; love and, xl, 393-4; a natural feeling, xxxiv, 188-90; Pascal on, xlviii, 151 (452); without power to relieve, xviii, 179
Pizarro, Francisco, xxxiii, 302-3, 319; Raleigh on, 317, 330

Place, independence of, v, 127-8; no sanctity in, iv, 340; showeth the man, iii, 30; virtue indifferent to, xii, 191
Plagiarism, Montaigne on, xxxii, 32
Plagues, of Egypt, Milton on, iv, 346
Plain Truth, Franklin's pamphlet, i, 105
Planariæ, Darwin on, xxix, 35-6
Plancus, Munatius, xii, 335, 367
Planets, Bacon on motion of, iii, 37; Berkeley on the, xxxvii, 230-1; cause of movements of, xxxiv, 113-18, 119-21; Copernicus on motions of the, xxix, 54-7; Dante on the, xx, 382; Dante on motions of, 325 and note 3; Locke on motion of, xxxvii, 155; Marlowe on movements of, xix, 225-6; Milton on motion of the, iv, 246, 307-8; Raleigh on the, xxxix, 107-8; Rousseau on movement of the, xxxiv, 248-9
Plans, road long from, to acts, xxvi, 244
Planta, Pompeius, governor of Egypt, ix, 360
Plantain, Biggs on the, xxxiii, 236
PLANTATIONS, ESSAY ON, Bacon's, iii, 85-7
Plants, advantages of diversity of character, xi, 117; of all seasons, iii, 112-13; breeding of, xi, 43-5; checks on increase of, 76-9; complex relations with animals, 79-86; distribution of, 388-94; divided into groups, 136-7; domestic, descent of, 32, 41; experiments on, in New Atlantis, iii, 174; fertilization of, xi, 104-6; most fragrant, iii, 113; freshwater, distribution of, xi, 411-13; habits of, hereditary, 144-5; rate of increase of, 73-6; insects and, relations of, 99-100, 101-2, 104-5; live on carbonic acid, xxx, 168; sexes in, separation of, xi, 100-1; the young of the world, v, 229
Plastering, in Elizabethan England, xxxv, 294
Plastic Arts, Goethe on, xxxix, 255-6, 257, 259-60, 262, 265
Plata River, Darwin on the, xxix, 147; Drake at, xxxiii, 204
Platæa, annual sacrifice at, xii, 99-100; battle of, 20; campaign of, 89-98
Plathane, in THE FROGS, viii, 455-6
Platinum, weight of, xxx, 11 note 1, 52
Plato, Academy of (see Academy of Plato); APOLOGY OF, ii, 5-30; cause and effect, effect on doctrine of, ii, 329-30; on censorship of books, iii, 205-6; on children, xxxii, 53; on chil-

dren of the gods, v, 194; Christianity and, xxvii, 346; Cicero on, xii, 237; CRITO of, ii, 31-43; in Dante's Limbo, xx, 20; DIALOGUES of, remarks on, l, 29; Dionysius and, iii, 194, 205-6; xxvii, 38; on disease, xxxiv, 172-3; ideas of education, xxxii, 57; Emerson on, v, 239; on principle of equality, xxvii, 346; on faith and sincerity, xxxii, 38; four flatteries of, xii, 343 note; on freedom of the will, ii, 169 (142); on happiest state, xii, 262 and note; on indifference of places, ii, 280 (23); influence of, on English thought, v, 435; on kings and philosophers, xxxvi, 157-8; on life and death, ii, 248 (35, 44, 45); life and works, 3-4; Lowell on, xxviii, 452; man defined by, xlviii, 425; Mill on, xxv, 19-20, 34; Montaigne on *Commonwealth* of, xxxii, 34; Montaigne on DIALOGUES of, 95; Montesquieu on, 118; More on *Republic* of, xxxvi, 165; Newman on, xxviii, 57; old age of, ix, 50; Pascal on, xlviii, 15-16 (20), 80 (219), 114-15 (331), 268 (769); PHÆDO of, ii, 45-113; on pleasure, ix, 61; on the poets, xiii, 32, 38-41; preferences of, xxxix, 93; Sainte-Beuve on, xxxii, 131; school of, xxviii, 59; Shelley on, xxvii, 334; shows of, xii, 78; Sidney on, xxvii, 7, 24; on socialism, xxxvi, 167; at Socrates's trial, ii, 22, 26; on the soul, xxxiv, 103; on souls in the stars, xx, 298 note 3; on speculation, v, 436; Spenser on, xxxix, 62; spirits, belief in, iii, 284 (33); on training of body and mind, xxxii, 56; two horses of the soul, xii, 349 note; on the universe, v, 310; on viewing life, ii, 249 (48); wealth of, xxviii, 59; x, 137; on wise men and the public, xxxvi, 166; on words and deeds, xl, 31; on the world, xxxix, 104-5

Plato's Year, iii, 137 note, 258 note

Platonism, Emerson on, v, 436

Platonists, on Christ, vii, 107-9; Mill on title of, xxv, 19-20

Plautianus, and Severus, iii, 68

Plautus, the *Casina,* of, xxvii, 386; Dryden on, xxxix, 174; Hugo on, 347; in Limbo, xx, 236; *Menæchmi* of, xxxix, 228; Montaigne on, xxxii, 91; Sidney on, xxvii, 44, 45

Play, of adults, xxxvii, 176; of children,

89, 111-12, 113; instinct of, Schiller on, xxxii, 248-52, 290-2; out-door, xxxvii, 14

PLAY, THE END OF THE, xlii, 1058-60

Playhouses, Swift on, xxvii, 119-20

Playthings, Locke on, xxxvii, 112-13, 129-30

Pleading, Pliny on conciseness in legal, ix, 204-5; Shelley on, xviii, 354-5

Pleasanton, Gen., at Gettysburg, xliii, 358, 360, 370, 397-8; Haskell on, 359

Pleasing, Pascal on art of, xlviii, 403

Pleasure, analysis of, ii, 285 (2); Archytas on sensual, ix, 59; Berkeley on idea of, xxxvii, 195, 198-9; Burke on standards of, xxiv, 11-12; Cicero on, ix, 60; Confucius on, xliv, 5 (1); Cowper on, xli, 535; effects of cessation of, xxiv, 34-5; as the end of life, xliv, 336 (1), 338 (12-13), 339 (22), 341 (18), 345 (15), 346 (7-10); xlv, 861; Epictetus on indifference to, ii, 117 (2); Epictetus on use of, 149 (86); of farmers, ix, 63-5; Goldsmith on lowly, vi, 110; highest, after danger or pain, vii, 122-3; Hobbes on, xxxiv, 339-40; of the imagination, xxiv, 15-21; in imitations, xxxix, 223; inseparable from morality, v, 90; of the judgment, xxiv, 21-4; Keats on, xli, 871, 873; Kempis on worldly, vii, 273 (4); Krishna on, xlv, 870; of love, xxiv, 36, 37-9; Marcus Aurelius on, ii, 202 (12), 204 (16), 229 (26), 238 (34), 255 (10); may be spared, iv, 215; of melancholy, 34-8; Mill on, xxv, 35; of mirth, iv, 30-4; Montaigne on, xxxii, 9-10; More on, xxxvi, 196, 197-204; not the end of man, ii, 256 (19); of old age, ix, 60-1; in one thing, ii, 232 (7); the order of nature, xli, 643; pain in relation to, xxiv, 30-1; pain and, Shelley on, xxvii, 352; pain and, Socrates on, ii, 48; Pascal on, xlviii, 66 (181), 372, 414; Pascal on principles of, 403; Pascal on yielding to, 62 (160); philosophic attitude toward, ii, 73-6; physical action of, xxiv, 120; physical causes of, 120-8; Pope on, xl, 418; power and, xxiv, 55; rare, ii, 184 (11); removal of, not like positive pain, xxiv, 31-5, 36-7; of the senses, 13-16; sensibility to, 23-5; of society, 36-45; two kinds of, xxvii, 351; Utopian idea of, xxxvi, 188; Vaughan on innocent, i, 73;

wants and, Goldsmith on, xli, 525-6; a weaker idea than pain, xxiv, 35; Wordsworth on principle of, xxxix, 280

PLEASURE ARISING FROM VICISSITUDE, xl, 460-2

Pleiad, Taine on the, xxxix, 428

Pleiades, called Atlantic Sisters, iv, 308; mentioned in Job, xliv, 83, 134; Milton on the, iv, 236; Tennyson on the, xlii, 979

Pliable, in PILGRIM'S PROGRESS, xv, 15-21, 71-2

Pliant, Dame, in THE ALCHEMIST, xlvii, 618-20, 625-9, 635, 654, 659-60, 662-3

Pliny, the Elder, on animal breeding among savages, xi, 45; on bees, xxxv, 347; death of, ix, 185-6, 284-8; habits of, 232-4; on lead mines of Wales, xxxv, 322-3; Mæcenas and, xliii, 29; on marl of Britain, xxxv, 308; on pears, xi, 47; on pigeons in Rome, 40; Sainte-Beuve on, xxxii, 116; on sugar, xxxv, 276; on torrid zone, xxxix, 106; on the viper, xxxv, 344 note, 345 note; works of, ix, 231-2

Pliny, the Younger, on his abstemiousness in sickness, ix, 297-8; attends recitations, 200; as augur, 251-2; as counsel for Bætica, 315-16; on boldness in writings, 346-50; on the Christians, 404-7; clemency of, 344-5; Corellius on, 257; his dealings with merchants, 317-18; description of inundation, 326; dream of, 203; equal hospitality of, 215-16; fame of, during his life, 345-6; on his friendships, 314; his belief in ghosts, 311-14; on giving library to his town, 192-5; as governor of Bithynia, 364 et seq.; grief for Corellius Rufus, 199; humanity of, 352 note; in the Hundred Court, 219-21, 255-6, 345-6; indulgence of others' levity, 343-4; on interpretation of a will, 252, 272; as lawyer and judge, 206-7, 227, 252, 256-7, 259, 277, 279, 283, 299-301, 345, 358; legacy from Curianus, 260; LETTERS OF, 187-416; LETTERS, editor's remarks on, l, 20; life and works, ix, 185-6; life in Laurentum, 355; life in Tuscum villa, 353-4; occupations of, 196; on poetry, 302-3; made a privileged citizen, 356; prosecution of Certus, 341-3; on purchasing a new property, 246-7; on

reason for reciting his works, 305-7; on reciting his writings, 331-2; Regulus, relations with, 189-91; seeks office of augur or septemvir, 363; on selling an estate, 303-4; as a senator, 319-25; slaves and servants, relations with, 209, 275-6, 316-17, 325; on the spring, 259; statue purchased by, 235; method of study, 191-2; a supper of, 202; Tacitus and, xxxiii, 92; ix, 345; the temple of, 362; with his tenants, 355; town under his patronage, 248-9; correspondence with Trajan, 356-416; ii, 311-12; speech on Trajan, ix, 244-6, 292-3; to Trajan, on princes, xxxiv, 215; made treasurer of Saturn, ix, 358, 362 note 1; vanity of, iii, 128-9; verses by, ix, 302; verses on, 248; during eruption of Vesuvius, 288-91; villa of, 222-6; villa in Tuscany, 265-72; villas on Larian Lake, 336; wealth of, 362 note 2; wife of (see Calpurnia); wish to live in history, 315-16; on his works, 337; on his writings and lectures, 263; Zosimus, servant of, 276

Pliocene Strata, Lyell on, xxxviii, 404

Plistoanax, king of Sparta, xii, 58-9

Plodding, wins the race, xvii, 38

Plotinus, Emerson on, v, 125; on the soul, ii, 332-3; the "union" of, v, 141

PLOUGHMAN'S LIFE, THE, vi, 25

Plover, long-legged, xxix, 120

Plowman, Chaucer's, xl, 25-6

Plumptre, E. H., translator of Greek Dramas, viii, 1

Plums, Locke on, xxxvii, 20

Pluralities, Harrison on, xxxv, 260-1; Luther on, xxxvi, 315; Milton on, iv, 80; iii, 210

Plutarch, on dissimulation, xxxix, 68-9; on Elysian Fields, xxxv, 307; Emerson on heroes of, v, 183; historian of Heroism, 123; Irish myths and, xxxii, 179; on his knowledge of Latin, xii, 192; life and works of, 3-4; Montaigne on, xxxii, 30, 44-5, 93-4; on motion of the earth, xxxix, 55; on poets, xxvii, 39; on Saturn, iii, 45; Shelley on, xxvii, 335; study of advised, iii, 239-40; on victors of the games, xxxiv, 263

PLUTARCH'S LIVES, xii; editor's remarks on, l, 20, 42; Franklin on, i, 14; Mill on influence of, xxv, 73; Shakespeare and, xxxix, 226

Pluto, in THE FROGS, viii, 483-7; helmet of, iii, 56-7; Hugo on, xxxix, 348

Plutocracy, Mill on dangers of, xxv, 108

Plutus, Dante on, xx, 28-9; fable of, iii, 88; Webster on, xlvii, 801

Plymouth, settlement of (see also MAY-FLOWER COMPACT)

Plymouth Rock, Lowell on, xlii, 1372

Plynteria, feast of, xii, 140

Po-niu, disciple of Confucius, xliv, 19 (8)

Po-yi, xliv, 17 note 10, 22 (14), 56 (12), 63 (8)

Po-yü, son of Confucius, xliv, 56 (13), 59 (10)

Podalirius, and Alsus, xiii, 400

Podesta, in I PROMESSI SPOSI, xxi, 74-81, 289, 405-6, 554

Podolia, honey of, xxxv, 347

Poe, Edgar Allan, life and works of, xxviii, 370; poems by, xlii, 1224-41; THE POETIC PRINCIPLE, xxviii, 369-92

Poems, Poe on length of, xxviii, 371-4

POESY OR ART, Coleridge on, xxvii, 255-63

POESY, DEFENSE OF, by Sidney, xxvii, 5-51

POESY, THE PROGRESS OF, xl, 453-6

POET, THE, by Emerson, v, 161-82

POET, ADVICE TO A YOUNG, xxvii, 104-21

Poetic Diction, Wordsworth on, xxxix, 283-4, 292-6

POETIC PRINCIPLE, THE, by Poe, xxviii, 369-92

Poetical Beauty, Pascal on, xlviii, 18 (33)

Poetical Justice, Dennis on, xxvii, 186-7

Poetry, advantages of, over prose, xxxix, 285-7; in America, Whitman on, 338-409; Aristotle on, xiii, 35; xxvii, 19; Arnold, STUDY OF, xxviii, 65-90; the aspiration for supernal beauty, 377-9; Bentham on, xxv, 72; Burke on cause of power of, xxiv, 129-40; Byron's definition of, xxxii, 394; characteristics of high, xxviii, 73-4; classes of readers of, xxxix, 311-16; Coleridge on, xxvii, 255-6; comic, 26-8; common life in, xxxix, 271-2; compared with history and biography, 279-80; compared with painting in effect on the passions, xxiv, 51-4; compared with reason in usefulness, xxvii, 350-3; Confucius on, xliv, 25 (8), 56 (13), 59 (9); contemptible subjects in, xxxix, 289; criticism of, 311-16; defined, xxvii, 329; Descartes on study of, xxxiv, 8, 9; didactic, xxviii, 375; Dryden on, epic and dramatic,

xiii, 5-11, 13; Dryden on virtues of, xxxix, 158; earliest form of teaching, xxvii, 6-8; effects of, on society, 335-50; elegiac, 26; Eliot on reading of, l, 7-8; Eliot on translations of, 4; Emerson on power of, v, 155; enervating, xxvii, 35-7; English (16th century), 40-50; English, retrospect of, xxxix, 316-30; English, review of, xxviii, 75-90; estimate of, by comparison, 72-4; exhortation to honor, xxvii, 50-1; expression of high delights, 330; false criticism of, xxxix, 290-1; fancy and imagination in, 301-10; fancy and judgment in, xxxiv, 350; favored by eminent men, xxvii, 104; Franklin on usefulness of writing, i, 16; future of, xxviii, 65-6; Goldsmith on, xli, 519; habits of order produced by, xxvii, 357; heroic, 28-9; high standards necessary in, xxviii, 66-7; hints for encouragement of, xxvii, 116-21; historic and personal estimates of, xxviii, 67-72; Hobbes on, xxxiv, 363; honored by great men, xxvii, 39-40; Hugo on taste in, xxxix, 384-5; Hugo on originality in, 364-6; Hugo on rules in, 363-6, 387; Hume on rules of, xxvii, 206-7; iambic, 26; inspiration of, 354-5; lack of appreciation of high, xxxix, 315-30; language of, 267-8, 269, 271-2, 274-9, 282-4, 288-9, 292-6, 395-7; learning unnecessary to, xxvii, 108-9; Locke on, xxxvii, 149-50; of love, xxvii, 347-8; lyric, 28; Mazzini on, xxxii, 379-80; Mazzini on Goethe's conception of, 387-8; measure in, xxvii, 332-5; merit of, as measured by length, xxviii, 371-5; James Mill on, xxv, 15; Milton on study of, iii, 243; Montaigne on, xxxii, 30, 62-3; music and, xxxix, 300; national awakening influenced by, xxvii, 359; nature and, xxxix, 401-2; its need of giving immediate pleasure, 280; need of, in periods of wealth, xxvii, 353; not an imitative art, xxiv, 137-9; observation of order and relations in, xxvii, 331; originality in, xxxix, 331-4, 397; pastoral, xxvii, 25; Plato on, 38-9; Plato's banishment of, 37-38; Pliny on, as method of study, ix, 302-3; popularity as test of, xxxix, 333-36; reason of power of, xxiv, 40, 44; powers requisite for producing, xxxix, 297; primitive, ancient, and

modern, 339-55; profitableness of, xxvii, 32-3; prose and, xxxix, 276 note; purpose in, 272; record of best moments, xxvii, 355-6; relation of feeling and action in, xxxix, 273-4; relation of substance and style in, xxviii, 74; religion and, xxvii, 105-8; xxxix, 313-14; requirements of, 393-5; restricted meaning of, xxvii, 332; rhyme in, 111; rhythm in, xxviii, 378; Romans and, xxvii, 8-9; romantic and classical, xxxix, 345-6; rural life and, xxvii, 65-7; Sainte-Beuve on reason in, xxxii, 125; satiric, xxvii, 26; Schiller on, xxxii, 269-70; science compared with, xxxix, 280-1; science related to, 282; similes in, xxvii, 112; source of all knowledge and virtue, 354; sources of, xxviii, 391-2; stories compared with, xxvii, 335; STUDY OF, Arnold's, xxviii, 65-90; superiority of, to other arts, xxvii, 333; taste in, xxxix, 268; Thoreau on nature in, xxviii, 414; three classes of readers of, xiii, 58-60; three general kinds of, xxvii, 11-12; tragic, 27-8; truth and, xxxix, 402-3; truth and duty may be introduced incidentally, xxviii, 378, 391; truth its object, xxxix, 279, 281; turns all things to loveliness, xxvii, 356; universality of, 332-5; xxxix, 281-2; as untruth, xxvii, 33-4; various kinds of, 25-9; xxxix, 298-9; of various races, 420-1; verse and rhyme in, xxvii, 31-2, 49; as teacher of virtue, 13-25; as promoting wantonness, 34-5; Whitman on future, xxxix, 388-409; word from the Greek, xxvii, 9-11; Wordsworth on, xxxix, 267-8, 269-91, 292-6, 297-310, 311-36; Wordsworth on materials of, 267; world created anew by, xxvii, 355-7

POETRY OF THE CELTIC RACES, xxxii, 135-82

POETRY, ENGLISH, xl, xli, xlii

POETRY, SHELLEY'S DEFENCE OF, xxvii, 327-59

POETRY, STUDY OF, Arnold's, xxviii, 65-90

Poets, Aristophanes on duty of, viii, 469-470, 472; authors of language, xxvii, 331-2; banished by Plato, 37-9; Browning on, xlii, 1072; Burke on narrowness of, xxiv, 48; Burns on, vi, 80-1, 85, 108, 312-13, 321, 424-5; called vates, xxvii, 8-9; defined in universal

sense, 331; Dryden on, xviii, 7; Emerson on great, v, 144; fame of, xxvii, 333; happiest and best of men, 356-8; historians as, 335; Jonson on, xl, 302-3; to be judged only by time, xxvii, 336; as legislators and prophets, xxvii, 332; Manzoni on advice of, xxi, 467; meaning a maker, xxvii, 9, 30; O'Shaughnessy on, xlii, 1198-9; Pascal on, xlviii, 19 (34), 20 (39); philosophers as, xxvii, 334-5; philosophers, compared with, 350-3; qualifications requisite to, xxxix, 297; shoemakers and, xxvii, 112; Socrates on wisdom of, ii, 10; Tasso on, xxvii, 356 note; unacknowledged legislators of the world, 359; Whitman on, xxxix, 391-409; Wordsworth on, 278-84, 300-1; xli, 659

POET'S DREAM, THE, xli, 855-6

POET'S PROGRESS, THE, vi, 320-3

POET'S WELCOME TO HIS LOVE-BEGOTTEN DAUGHTER, vi, 55-7

POETS, ODE ON THE, xli, 873-4

Poggini, Domenico, xxxi, 350, 360, 362

Poggini, Gianpagolo, xxxi, 350 note, 360, 362

Pogius of Florence, xxxix, 16

Pointers, instincts of, xi, 256, 257

Poisoning, Harvey on, xxxviii, 125; punishment of, in old England, xxxv, 364-5

Poisons, regulation of sale of, xxv, 292, 293-4

POITIERS, THE BATTLE OF, xxxv, 34-59

Poix, Edward III at, xxxv, 18

Polarity, in affairs of government, v, 246; in nature, 14, 87-8

Polarization of Light, xxx, 264-7

Pole, Cardinal, and Machiavelli, xxvii, 366

POLEMIC, EPITAPH ON A NOISY, vi, 58

Polemo, the sophist, xxviii, 60

Polemon, King, capture of, xii, 351

Polenta, Guido da, xx, 111 note 3

Policy, and justice, xxiv, 289-90; Penn on, i, 337 (152-4)

Polite Letters, Hume on, xxxvii, 292-3

Politeness, Character and, xxxii, 236, 254; Locke on, xxxvii, 47-8, 124-5; origin of, xxxiv, 204; the ritual of society, v, 409; Swift on ceremonial, xxvii, 100-1 (see also Manners)

Polites, and Circe, xxii, 135-6; death of, xiii, 118

Politian, mentioned, xxvii, 372

Political Economy, Burke on beginnings of, xxiv, 394; effects of a mistaken, x, 437-8; human nature in, xxviii, 469; Mill on, xxv, 146-7; need of imagination in, xxvii, 351, 353; objects of, x, 310; systems of (see Commercial S., Agricultural S.)

Political Institutions, dependent on circumstances, xxiv, 148; Hamilton on, xliii, 199; Mill on choice of, xxv, 107-8

Political Parties, Washington on, xliii, 238, 239, 240-1

Politicians, Smith on, x, 348; Socrates on, ii, 9-10; Webster on, xlvii, 804

POLITICS, ESSAY ON, Emerson's, v, 239-51

POLITICS, ON, by Burns, vi, 452

Politics, Burke on science of, xxiv, 198-9; Channing on, xxviii, 318-20; corruption in, under property system, xxxvi, 168; friendship in, ix, 23-5, 30-1; Hamilton on intolerance in, xliii, 201; Hobbes on science of, xxxiv, 362; Hume on science of, xxxvii, 297, 359, 419; Lowell on science of, xxviii, 439; Mill on science of, xxv, 99-103; Milton on study of, iii, 242; reading course in, l, 42-4; Thoreau on, xxviii, 400

Poll-taxes, Smith on, x, 503-4, 514-15

Pollio, Asinius, orator, ix, 205 note 3; in African War, xii, 307; Cæsar, and, 292; on Cæsar, xxxii, 99

Polonius, in HAMLET, the prototype of, xlvi, 92; Laertes, and, 100-1; farewell advice to Laertes, 109; counsels Ophelia against Hamlet, 110-11; sends Reynaldo to Laertes, 120-3; hears Hamlet's madness, 123-4; reports to king, 126, 127-30; scene with Hamlet, 130-1; announces players, 136, 138-9; asks king to play, 142, 149; plan to test Hamlet's madness, 143, 147; at the play, 150-1, 155; summons Hamlet to queen, 158; in hiding at Hamlet's meeting with mother, 160, 162; death, 163; Hamlet on, 163, 169, 172-3

Polus, the actor, xii, 191 note, 214

Polyalces, Plutarch on, xii, 66

Polybus, in the ODYSSEY, xxii, 49, 302; death of, 303

Polycarp, M. Aurelius Antoninus, in reign of, ii, 310-11 and note 3; Bunyan on, xv, 265

Polycaste, daughter of Nestor, xxii, 45

Polycrates, tyrant of Samos, xii, 63;

Anacreon and, xli, 814; death of, prophesied, iii, 91; Emerson on, v, 95

Polydamna, wife of Thon, xxii, 52; Helen and, xxxiii, 56

Polydeuces, and Castor, xxii, 152

Polydore, Molière on, xxvi, 215; murder of, xiii, 129-30

POLYEUCTE, Corneille's, xxvi, 77-130; remarks on, 76

Polyeucte, in POLYEUCTE, goes to be baptized, xxvi, 77-81; Pauline on, 83; Severus on, 88-9; returns to Pauline, 93-4; determines to go to temple, 95-7; his deeds in temple, 101-2; his conduct at death of Nearchus, 105, 106; in prison, 108-11; with Pauline in prison, 111-15; with Felix, 121-3; last scene with Pauline, 123-4; refuses to yield and condemned, 125-7

Polygamy, Browne on, iii, 323; Mill on, xxv, 287-8

Polylerites, More on the, xxxvi, 151

Polymnestor, Dante on, xx, 229 note 19

Polymorphic Genera, xi, 56-7

Polynices, and Eteocles, xx, 107 note; references to, in ANTIGONE, viii, 255, 258-60, 263-4, 294-5

Polypheides, son of Mantius, xxii, 206

Polypheme, the Cyclops, xiii, 149-50; reference to, xli, 939

Polyphemus, Burke on, xxiv, 126; remarks on story of, xxii, 3; Ulysses and, 11, 119-29

Polytheism, Lessing on, xxxii, 186

Pomarre, Queen, of Tahiti, xxix, 419-20

Pomham, the Indian, xliii, 146

Pommiers, Aymenion of, xxxv, 36, 42, 47

Pomona, reference to, iv, 190; Vertumnus and, 270

Pomp, Milton on, iv, 189; Penn on, i, 388-9

Pompeia, wife of Cæsar, xii, 267; Clodius and, 241-2, 270-2

Pompeius, Quintus, quarrel with Sulpicius, ix, 9

Pompeius Saturninus, letter to, ix, 192

Pompeius, Sextus, xii, 345-6 (see Pompey, Sextus)

Pompeo, xxxi, 91-2, 121, 125-6, 133, 135, 142-3, 145-6

Pompey, accusations against, ix, 98-9; Cæsar and, iii, 123, 141; ix, 5-6; xii, 248-50, 252, 274, 275-6, 281, 282, 284, 285; Cæsar and, Cicero on, ix, 162-3; Cæsar, final contest with, xii,

288-302; Cæsar killed beside statue of, 318; Cæsar presented with head of, 303; Cicero and, ix, 88, 113, 115-16, 120, 122, 123-4, 162-3; xii, 224, 242-3, 244, 246, 248-50; Cicero on, ix, 82, 94, 122-3; Cicero on death of, 159; Clodius and, xii, 245; Crassus and, 274; Dryden on, xiii, 16; in Egypt, xxxii, 5-6; as manager of corn supplies, ix, 96; marries Cæsar's daughter, xii, 267, 275; at Milo's trial, ix, 97-8; xii, 246; Milton on, iv, 385; in Parthian war, ix, 147; Pascal on, xlviii, 235 (701); preparations of, ix, 99; provincial laws of, 398 note 2; sea-power of, iii, 79; sons of, xii, 309; temperate life of, 336; Sylla and, iii, 67; Webster on death of, xlvii, 853

Pompey, Sextus, Erichtho and, xx, 36 note 2; refuses to break word, xii, 345-6; in Sicily, 345; war on, 348

Pomponia, and Q. Cicero, ix, 134; Philologus and, xii, 259

Ponkipog, Eliot on, xliii, 142

Pontanus, Sidney on, xxvii, 12

Pontitianus, and St. Augustine, vii, 126-8

Pontonous, in the ODYSSEY, xxii, 94

Pontormo, Jacopo Carrucci da, xxxi, 401 note

Pooley, Thomas, persecution of, xxv, 223 note 2

Poor, Burns on life of the (see THE TWA DOGS); Luther on care of the, xxxvi, 313-14; Montaigne on the, xxxii, 117

Poor Laws, in Elizabethan England, xxxv, 301-3; of England, x, 139-44; Ruskin on, xxviii, 123 and note 17

POOR MAILIE, DEATH OF, vi, 41-2

POOR MAILIE'S ELEGY, vi, 43-4; remarks on, 16

Poor Richard's Almanac, i, 3, 91-2, 163

POORTITH CAULD AND RESTLESS LOVE, vi, 451-2

Pope, Alexander, on Addison, xxvii, 172, 173, 177, 178; Addison's *Cato* and, 166, 167; Arnold on, xxviii, 81-3; Burns on, vi, 338; Byron on, xxxii, 128; as editor of Shakespeare, xxxix, 235-6, 318; Emerson on, v, 444; ESSAY ON MAN, xl, 406-40; Hazlitt on, xxvii, 273-4; ON A LADY AT COURT, xl, 406; lines by, on friends, xxvii, 273-4; Milton and, xxxix, 319; on Milton's God, xxvii, 200; on modesty in speech, i, 18-19; Ralph and, 38, 150; Sainte-

Beuve on, xxxii, 127-8, 131; on Shakespeare, xxxix, 211-12, 218, 229; SOLITUDE by, xl, 405-6; Swift and, xxviii, 17, 28; Swift on, 16; on Swift, 15; on Thomson, xxxix, 325; Voltaire on, xxxiv, 148-50, 152; Wordsworth on xxxix, 322; Wordsworth on *Iliad* of, 323-4; Wordsworth on *Windsor Forest* of, 323

Pope, Sir Thomas, xxxvi, 132-3

Pope, in PILGRIM'S PROGRESS, xv, 69

Pope's Months, xxxvi, 280, 288

Popery, Milton on, iii, 229-30

Popes, benefices and the, xxxvi, 280-5; bishoprics and, 281-2, 288-9, 294; bulls of the, 312-13; Calvin on the, xxxix, 41-2; court of the, xxxvi, 278, 293; custom of kissing their feet, 296-7; Dante on covetousness of the, xx, 399-401; Dante on temporal authority of the, 211; Datarius of the, xxxvi, 284 note, 285-6; encroachments in Germany, 277-9, 288, 293-4; England and, xxxiv, 89; how regarded in Italy, xxvii, 367-8; jubilees of the, xxxvi, 299 note; legates of, 316; attitude toward liberty of press, iii, 195-8; Luther on pomp of the, xxxvi, 275-6, 281, 293, 297; Luther on powers of the, 251-2, 253, 256, 256-7, 309; Luther on right of punishing, 269-70, 272-3; Luther on vices and encroachments of the, 275-98, 316-17, 321, 323-4; monasticism encouraged by, 300; Pascal on the, xlviii, 304-5 (871-7), 306 (880, 882); their relation with temporal power, xxxvi, 265-70, 290-1, 294-6; relations with empire, 294-6, 327-30; their right to interpret Bible, 270-2; their rights over councils, 272-5; saints and, 311-12; as vicars of Christ, 343-4 (see also Papacy)

Popillius, and Cicero, xii, 258

POPLAR FIELD, THE, xli, 534-5

Poplicola, Plutarch on, xii, 178

Poppy-water, Locke on, xxxvii, 26

Populace, Bacon on movements of the, iii, 39-40; Browne on the, 311; disapproval of the, v, 65-6; kings and, iii, 51-2; nobility and, xxxvi, 32; praises of the, iii, 126; in princedoms, xxxvi, 33-6; Shakespeare on likes of the, xlvi, 172; superstition of, iii, 45-6

Popular Science, Freeman on, xxviii, 235

Popularity, Carlyle on, xxv, 403-4; Hob-

bes on, xxxiv, 360; Milton on, iv, 385; Pe**n** on, i, 349; as test of poetry, xxxix, 333-6

Population, Bacon on need of limiting, iii, 39; laws of, in Utopia, xxxvi, 183-4; limited only by food supply, x, 167; Mill on restriction of, xxv, 68; regulated by demand for labor, x, 81-2; relation of, to poverty, 80-1

Poquelin (see Molière)

Porphyro, and Madeline, xli, 885-93

Porphyry, the vision of, v, 141

Porpoises, Darwin on, xxix, 47

Port Famine, Darwin on, xxix, 236, 238

Port Pheasant, xxxiii, 131-2

Port Plenty, Drake at, xxxiii, 143, 151

Port Royal, Pascal on nuns of, xlviii, 291 (841)

Portail, Antoine, xxxviii, 46

Portents, defined, xxxiv, 382; study of, in Egypt, xxxiii, 42

Porter, in MACBETH, xlvi, 343-4

PORTER, THE, AND THE LADIES OF BAGHDAD, xvi, 55-66

Porter, Edward, xxxiii, 337, 351, 371

Portia, death of, xlvii, 816 note

Portillo Pass, Darwin on, xxix, 317-18; origin of name, 329

Portinari, Folco, Father of Beatrice, xx, 3

Porto Praya, Darwin on, xxix, 11-12

Porto Rico, cession of, xliii, 443 (2), 445-8

PORTRAIT, A, Sheridan's, xviii, 109-12

Portraits, Coleridge on, xxvii, 259-60

Portugal, discoveries of, x, 398; reading and writing in, xxxvii, 128-9; taxes on precious metals in, x, 380-1; trade treaty with England, 390-4

PORTUGUESE, SONNETS FROM THE, xli, 923-41

PORTUGUESE CHAPEL HYMN, xlv, 555-6

Portunus, reference to, xiii, 186

Porzia, Madonna (see Chigi, Porzia)

Poseidon, among the Ethiopians, xxii, 9; origin of name of, xxxiii, 31; in the ODYSSEY, xxii, 9-10, 11, 75-7, 108, 177-8; Tyro and, 150-1

Posidonius, on tides, xxx, 279

POSIE, THE, vi, 406-7

Positiveness, Franklin on, i, 18-19

Possession, better than prospect, xvii, 32; use the only, xix, 34

Possibilities, Aurelius on, ii, 235 (19)

Post-office, expense of maintaining, x, 454; government ownership of, 469

Post-offices, under Confederation, xliii, 164; under Constitution, 184 (7)

Postal Service, Marshall on, xliii, 219; progress of, ix, 368 note

Posterity, Bacon on care of, iii, 20, 21-2; Penn on care of, i, 342; Raleigh on greatening, xxxix, 92-4; Woolman on care of, i, 233

POSTHUMOUS CHILD, ON A, vi, 394-5

Postponement, Marcus Aurelius on, ii, 205 (1), 210 (14), 214 (17)

Postumus, name of, xii, 156-7

Potassium, tester of water, xxx, 114, 120 note; why it decomposes water, 140

Potatoes, cultivation of, x, 163-4; introduced into England by Drake, xxxiii, 122; nourishment in, x, 163-4; wild, in Chonos Islands, xxix, 289

Potentates, Raleigh on, xl, 205

Pothinus, the eunuch, xii, 304-5

Potiphar's wife, in Dante's HELL, xx, 125 note 6

Pots, fable of the, xvii, 31

Potts, Stephen, i, 51, 58

Poultry, price of, x, 188-9; in Utopia, xxxvi, 173

Pourceaugnac, Hugo on, xxxix, 356

Poverty, Arabian verses on, xvi, 128; Browne on, iii, 330; Burns on, vi, 511; Carlyle on, xxv, 336-7; Confucius on, xliv, 6 (15), 46 (11), 55; and crime, Confucius on, 25 (10); and crime, Shakespeare on, xlvi, 295; Goldsmith on, xli, 516; Hobbes on, xxxiv, 365; Jesus on, xliv, 369 (20); Kempis on, vii, 285-6 (4); Lear on hardships of, xlvi, 268; Lucan on, xx, 331 note 16; money and, xxxvi, 238; More on fear of, 185; old age and, ix, 48; Penn on, i, 328 (52); relation of, to marriage and generation, x, 80-1; due to property system, xxxvi, 167-8; a cause of sedition, iii, 38, 39; in subjects, xxxvi, 162; unmerited, makes proud, xix, 384

Powell, Anthony, with Drake, xxxiii, 229; in Drake's Armada, 226, 241, 247, 250, 256, 258

Powell, Mary, first wife of Milton, xxviii, 181-4, 185-6; iv, 4

Power, Burke on idea of, xxiv, 55-60; Confucius on, xliv, 9; the desire for, xxxiv, 370; different kinds of, xxx, 9-12; education confers the only true, xxviii, 135-6; Emerson on thirst for,

v, 18; force is not, viii, 380; gives no true claim to obedience, xxviii, 198; Hobbes on sources of, xxxiv, 359-61; honor in relation to, 361, 365-69; Hume on idea of, xxxvii, 336-50; love of, in children, 85-6; Pascal on, xlviii, 108-9 (310); penalties of, v, 88-9; political, Washington on distribution of, xliii, 242-3; the pomp of, xl, 444; real and imaginary, xlviii, 108 (307, 308); resides in transition, v, 72; Ruskin on love of, xxviii, 157; Shelley on fear of, xviii, 337; thirst for, iii, 25-6, 33; velocity and, in machines, xxx, 182-5; worldly, price of, xviii, 441; worldly, transitoriness of, xvi, 301-4, 311-12, 316-17, 319-21

Pozzobonelli, Michele, xxi, 511, 526

Practicalness, More on, xxxvi, 164-6

Practice, Bacon on, iii, 96-7; early, makes the master, xxvi, 428; Locke on teaching by, xxxvii, 44, 47-8; Marcus Aurelius on, ii, 296 (6)

Praed, Mill on, xxv, 81

Prætors, Roman, ix, 277 note 2

Pragmatic, defined by Kant, xxxii, 328 note

Pragmatick, in PILGRIM'S PROGRESS, xv, 296

PRAISE, ESSAY ON, Bacon's, iii, 126-7

Praise, Augustine, St., on, vii, 57, 67; Augustine, St., on desire of, 191-4; belongeth to God alone, 247 (4); children's love of, xxxvii, 39-42, 173; Cicero on, ix, 104, 153; danger from, v, 98; desire of, i, 349 (320-1); Emerson on the highest, v, 40; "foolish face of," 65; Goldsmith on love of, xli, 527; Hobbes on, xxxiv, 345-6; independence of, vii, 244 (2, 3); Jesus on, xliv, 369 (26); Jonson on, xl, 301-2; Kempis on danger of, vii, 310 (5); Kempis on love of, 304-5; Locke on, of children, xxxvii, 105; love of, the strongest motive, xxviii, 94-6; Marcus Aurelius on, ii, 215 (19, 20), 234-5 (16), 251 (62), 257 (21), 263 (53), 271 (34); as means of training, xxv, 87-8; Milton on, iii, 190; Milton on popular, iv, 385; Pascal on, xlviii, 121 note 10; Penn on, i, 382; Pliny on, iii, 129; Pliny on, ix, 247; Raleigh on, xxxix, 91; results of competition for, xxxiv, 370; results of desire of, 371; Rufus on leisure for, ii, 118 (5); of

self, Pliny on, ix, 195; superiority to, v, 192

Praising, the delight of, xli, 902

Prassede, Donna, in I PROMESSI SPOSI, xxi, 410-13, 425, 441-4, 623

Prato, Giovanni of, xxxi, 216, 245, 248

Prayer, in affliction, vii, 293; allegory of, xv, 191-2; Browne's, iii, 328-9; Calvin on, xxxix, 49; for cleansing the heart, vii, 291; Coleridge on the best, xli, 701; by Dante, xx, 186-7; David on, xli, 495, 496-7; xliv, 179 (6); for the dead, Browne on, iii, 258; for the dead, Dante on, xx, 166-7; Emerson on, v, 35, 76; for enlightenment, vii, 287-8; Epictetus on, ii, 136 (58); against evil thoughts, vii, 287; Franklin's, i, 82-3; to do God's will, vii, 277; gratitude the most perfect, xxvi, 323; Jesus on, xliv, 383-4 (1-13), 400 (1-7); Kempis on proper, vii, 276; Luther on, xxxvi, 307; Marcus Aurelius on, ii, 224 (7), 272 (40); Milton on, iv, 319-20, 322-3; Mohammed on, xlv, 883, 919, 921, 972, 978, 995; Pascal on, xlviii, 167-8 (513-14), 340; Penn on formal, i, 361 (478); Raleigh on dying, xxxix, 94-5; Rousseau on, xxxiv, 279; Shakespeare on, xlvi, 161, 162; in sickness, by Pascal, xlviii, 366-74; for the spirit of devotion, vii, 261; Tennyson on, xlii, 992; Thomson's, i, 83; in times of doubt, vii, 303 (2); in Utopia, xxxvi, 233, 235; Woolman on, i, 175, 288

PRAYER, A, IN PROSPECT OF DEATH, vi, 34-5

PRAYER: O THOU DREAD POWER, vi, 238

PRAYER, A, UNDER PRESSURE OF VIOLENT ANGUISH, vi, 32

Preacher, Goldsmith's, xli, 512-14

Preaching, Emerson on, v, 34-6, 41; Luther on Christian, xxxvi, 357-8

Precedents, Hobbes on, xxxiv, 373-4; Lowell on, xxviii, 440

Precepts, the Buddhist, xlv, 743

Precious Metals, demand for, x, 175, 178; effect of increase and decrease of, 201-2; exportation and importation of, 268; in foreign trade, 298; movements of the, 267-8, 313-17; not indispensable to trade, 318; price of, 171-5, 200; steadiness of price of, 313-14; taxes on exportation of, 380, 382; in Utopia, xxxvi, 191-2; value of, compared with

corn, x, 179; value of, reason for, 402-3; variation in value of, 36-7, 45-6; effect of variation on rents, 38; as wealth, 319-30

Precious Stones, prices of, x, 176-7, 178, 179; reason for high prices of, iii, 88; in Utopia, xxxvi, 191-3, 199-200

Precious Things, David on, xli, 497; for those that prize them, xvii, 11

Precision, excessive, v, 210

Precocity, Bacon on, iii, 105

Preconception, Seneca on, xlviii, 121 note 5

Predecessors, the memory of, iii, 31

Predestination, St. Augustine on, vii, 47; Browne on, iii, 262, 308-9; Calvin on, xxxix, 49-50; Dante on, xx, 373; Hume on doctrine of, xxxvii, 368-70; Jansenist doctrine of, xlviii, 7; Omar Khayyam on, xli, 954, 955

Predicaments, of Aristotle, St. Augustine on, vii, 59-60; sons of Ens, iv, 22

Predictions (see Prophecies)

Pre-existence, Augustine, St., on, vii, 9; Cicero on proofs of, ix, 73-4; Lessing on, xxxii, 205-6; Socrates on, ii, 63-8; Wordsworth on intimations of, xli, 595-600

Prefaces, Hugo on, xxxix, 337-8; remarks on, 3; to speeches, a waste of time, iii, 63

Prefaces to Famous Books, xxxix

Prejudice, Burke on, xxiv, 223-4; fatal to a critic, xxvii, 213; Pascal on, xlviii, 42 (98); in Pilgrim's Progress, xv, 291; Tennyson on, xlii, 999

Prelates, and kings, iii, 51

Premium, Mr., in School for Scandal, xviii, 143; Sir Oliver Surface as, 149, 153-60

Premiums, for encouragement of industry, x, 387-8

Premunire, defined, xlvii, 877 note

Preparations, a poem, xl, 198-9

Prepotency, in animals, xi, 314; instances of, 306

Presage, defined, xxxiv, 381-2

Presbyter, is but priest writ large, iv, 81

Presbyterianism, Franklin on, i, 76-7; Voltaire on, xxxiv, 81-2

Prescott, Mill on, xxv, 77, 78

Prescription, rights by, Burke on, xxiv, 285-6

Present, the, alone can be lost, ii, 203 (14); Emerson on the, v, 20; Hobbes

on the, xxxiv, 320; Longfellow on the, xlii, 1265; Omar Khayyam on enjoyment of the, xli, 945, 946, 947, 954; Pascal on the, xlviii, 355; Pascal on neglect of the, 64 (172); a point in eternity, ii, 239 (36); Raleigh on the, xxxix, 89; represents all eternity, ii, 239 (37), 259 (36); Shakespeare on the, xl, 262, 264; Thoreau on the, xxviii, 423-4; use of the, ii, 205 (1), 210 (14), 214 (17), 216-17 (26)

Present in Absence, xl, 313

Present Crisis, The, xlii, 1370-3

Presents, defined by Stella, xxvii, 127-8 (see also Gifts)

Presidency, price of the, v, 88

Press, liberty and licentiousness of the, xxvii, 245-6; Franklin on liberty of, i, 92-3; Mill on liberty of the, xxv, 210-49; pious editor's idea of liberty of, xlii, 1374; liberty of, in U. S., xliii, 194 (1); Mill on writing for, xxv, 55

Pressure, effect of, on temperature, xxx, 233

Preston, Captain, xxxiii, 303, 311, 316, 324

Presumption, of mankind, Smith on, x, 109; Pascal on, xlviii, 79 (214)

Presumption, in Pilgrim's Progress, xv, 42, 216-17

Pretas, xlv, 863 note 2

Pretences, Cicero on, ix, 39-40; Raleigh on, xxxix, 70

Pretexts, Thackeray on, xxviii, 11

Pretino, Il, xxxi, 157 note 5

Pretty, Francis, Drake's Voyage, xxxiii, 199-224

Pretty Peg, vi, 500

Prevention, better than cure, i, 348 (304)

Priam, Burke on, xxiv, 127; character of, xiii, 20; death of, 119; in sack of Troy, 117-18; Shakespeare on death of, xlvi, 137; visit to Arcadia, xiii, 273

Priam, grandson of King Priam, xiii, 196

President of United States, xliii, 186-9; duties and powers, 188-9; election, early method, 187 (2, 3); election, amended method of, 196-7; impeachment of, 182 (6), 189 (4); his part in legislation, 183-4; Lincoln on duty of, 321; oath, 188 (7); qualifications, 187-8 (4); removal or death of, 188 (5); salary, 188 (6); term of, 186 (1); veto power of, 183-4

Price, Dr. Richard, Burke on, xxiv, 150-71, 191, 193-4, 202-4

Price, Thomas, xxxii, 138

Price, everything has its, v, 96

Prices, of agricultural products, x, 12; of bread and meat, 151-2, 154-5; bounties, their effect on, 378-9, 383; of cattle, 183-4; of clothing, 203-7; of coal and wood, 169-71; of commodities made by employments, 119-20; comparative, of food and materials, 178-80; component parts of, 48-55; of dairy produce, 190-1; as dependent on wages and profits, 99-100; in England (1772), i, 304; of fish, x, 199-200; of hogs, 189; of limited or uncertain products, 192-202; of manufactures, as affected by progress, 202-7; of meat, as dependent on price of hides, 198; of metals, 172-6, 200-2; of metal manufactures, 202-3; natural and market, 55-65; of necessaries in relation to wages, 75-6, 84-5, 87-8; paper currency, its effect on, 252; of poultry, 188-9; of precious stones, 176-7; of produce determine progress of cultivation, 192; of produce, effect on rents, 207-8; of producible things, 183-92; progress of society, its effect on, 180-207; real and nominal, 34-47; regulated by corn, 379; regulation of, by law, 145-6; rent and, relations of, 149; scarcity, 181-2; taxes on consumption, in relation to, 520-1; variations in, 118-19; of venison, 187-8; of wool and hides, 193-8 (see also Values)

Pridam le Noire, xxxv, 164-5; his fight with Sir Bors, 165-6

Pride, Augustine, St., on temptations of, vii, 191-2; Browne on, iii, 321-2; Burke on, v, 94; Confucius on, xliv, 26 (11); folly of, vii, 211; fosterer of inequality, xxxvi, 239; Franklin on, i, 88; Hunt on, xxvii, 291; instances of, given by Dante, xx, 191-2; Jesus on, xliv, 393 (11), 401 (14); Marcus Aurelius on, ii, 278 (10), 299-300 (27); Mohammed on, xlv, 916; Pascal on human, xlviii, 131 (405-7); i, 323-5; provokes envy, iii, 25; punishment of, in Purgatory, xx, 186-90; results of, xxxiv, 353; the sin, in Faustus, xix, 227; Sophocles on, viii, 235; Tennyson on, xlii, 1023; virtue and, xl, 419-20; in one's virtues, ii, 177-8 (176);

womanly, xl, 250-1; Woolman on, i, 274

Pride of Life, daughter of Adam, xv, 73

Pride of Youth, xli, 746-7

Priestley, Huxley on, xxviii, 209; Lowell on, 458-9

Priestman, Thomas, i, 313

Priests, actors and, xix, 29-30; Buddhist, ordination of, xlv, 740-7; Caxton's tale of two, xxxix, 17-18; Chaucer on, xl, 25; Dryden on satires of, xxxix, 164-5; Emerson on, v, 33-40; false, Shelley on, xviii, 302; Kempis on qualities of, vii, 345-6, 355 (6, 7); Luther on, xxxvi, 266, 267, 269, 333-4, 354-5, 357-8; marriage of, Calvin on, xxxix, 38; marriage of, Luther on, xxxvi, 302-5; Pascal on, xlviii, 307 (885); punishments of, xxxvi, 307-8 note; Quaker attitude toward, xxxiv, 70; in Utopia, xxxvi, 231-2, 234-5; Whitman on, xxxix, 407

Primal Four, the, xix, 55

Primary Qualities, xxxvii, 206-7, 210-11

Primary Schools, origin of, xxviii, 366-7

Primaticcio, Francesco (Il Bologna), xxxi, 301 note, 309-12, 314, 318, 324

Prime, the, in Low Countries, iii, 137

Primogeniture, Hobbes on, xxxiv, 410; Johnson on, v, 414; Pascal on, xlviii, 103 (291), 111 (320)

Primum Mobile, iii, 37 note

Prince, etymology of word, xxxv, 217

Prince, The, Machiavelli's, xxxvi, 5-86; editorial remarks on, 3; Garnett on, 3-4; influence of. xxvii, 363-4; Macaulay on, 365, 394-5

Prince and the Ghuleh, The, xvi, 35-6

Prince Rupert's Drops, xxx, 29 note 9

Prince of Wales, title of heir of England, xxxv, 217

Princes, need of adaptability in, xxxvi, 81-2; clemency and cruelty, 54, 55-6; counsellors of, 77-8; Duke Chon on, xliv, 63 (10); expedients of, for security, xxxvi, 68-72; faith of, 57; flatterers of, 76-7; Goldsmith on, xli, 510; liberality and miserliness in, xxxvi, 52-4; duty of, in military affairs, 48-50, 68-9, 71-2; More on, 140-1; Pliny on praise of, ix, 244; means of acquiring reputation, xxxvi, 71-5; secretaries of, 75-6; should avoid contempt and hatred, 59-67; should not depend on fortune, 80-1; should they

excite love or fear, 54-6; Tzu-kung on, xliv, 65 (20, 21); virtues and vices of, xxxvi, 50-1, 57-9; Webster on, xlvii, 775 (see also Kings, Rulers)

Princedoms, absolute and limited by nobility, xxxvi, 15-16; acquired by crimes, 29-32; acquired by fortune, 22-8; advantages of new, 78-9; arms in new, 68-9; arms and factions in mixed, 69-70; best friends in new, 70; civil, 33-5, 70-1; ecclesiastical, 38-40; hereditary, 7-8; military affairs of, 40-50, 68-9, 71-2; mixed, 8-19; new, acquired by merit, 19-22; the several kinds of, 7; strength of, 36-7

Principal and Agent, Hobbes on, xxxiv, 413-14

Principia, Newton's, Locke on, xxxvii, 166-7

PRINCIPIA, PREFACE TO NEWTON's, xxxix, 150-2

Principles, assertorial, problematical, and apodictic, xxxii, 326; Emerson on, v, 83; Epictetus on, ii, 127 (30); Marcus Aurelius on, 210 (13), 212, 216 (16), 286 (5); Pascal on intuitive, xlviii, 99-100

Printing, Hobbes on invention of, xxxiv, 322

Printing-houses, Franklin on, i, 45 note

Prior, Matthew, poems by, xl, 396-8; Voltaire on, xxxiv, 147, 156

Prioress, Chaucer's, xl, 14-15; Dryden on, xxxix, 166

Priscian, in Dante's HELL, xx, 64

Priscilla, wife of Aquila, xliv, 462 (2-4), 463 (18), 464 (26)

Priscus, Cornelius, letters to, ix, 218, 247, 281, 307

Priscus, Javolenus, anecdote of, ix, 284

Priscus, Vibius, xxxv, 348

PRISONER OF CHILLON, xli, 801-11

Prisoners of War, in agreement with Mexico, xliii, 304-5

Prisons, Cellini in praise of, xxxi, 251-4; Emerson on, v, 56

Pritchard, Mrs., Hazlitt on, xxvii, 275

Privacy, Penn on, i, 349-50, 353

Private Property (see Property)

Privation, Burke on terror in, xxiv, 61

Privernus, death of, xiii, 312-13

PRO PATRIA MORI, xli, 817

Proæresius, leader of Attic school, xxviii, 59; Hephæstion and, 53

Proairesis, Milton on, iii, 242 note

Probability, Hume on, xxxvii, 332-3, 376-7; Pascal on doctrine of, xlviii, 312 (908), 314 (917-18, 920), 316 (922)

Probity, Franklin on usefulness of, i, 87

PROBLEM, THE, by Drummond, xl, 327-8

PROBLEM, THE, by Emerson, xlii, 1247-9

Problematical Principles, xxxii, 326

Probus, the soldiers and, iii, 41

Prochorus, xliv, 434 (5)

Procula, Serrana, Pliny on, ix, 201

Proclus, on beauty, v, 308; on God and the world, xxxix, 106; on the universe, v, 167, 176

Procopius, xxxii, 179 note 30, 180

Procrastination, Bentham on, xxvii, 243; Machiavelli on, xxxvi, 12

Procris, in Homer's Hades, xxii, 153; in the Mournful Fields, xiii, 222

Proctophantasmist, in FAUST, xix, 180-1

Proculeius, Cleopatra and, xii, 382-3

Proculus, meaning of name of, xii, 156

Proculus, Vettius, ix, 340

Procurators, Roman, ix, 295 note 5

Prodicus of Ceos, ii, 7

Prodigal Son, parable of the, xliv, 395 (11-32)

Prodigality, Augustine, St., on, vii, 28; economically considered, x, 266-9; liberality and, i, 327-8; motives of, x, 269; public, 270; punishment of, in Dante's HELL, xx, 29, 47

Prodigies, Plutarch on, xii, 40-1

Prodius, character of, iii, 65

Production, bounties on, x, 385-6; consumption the object of, 424; on what dependent, 5-6, 271-2; improvement in, causes of, 9-26; improvement in, dependent on capital, 213; improvements in, effect on prices, 178-207; improvements in, raise rents, 207-8; effects of increase in, on wages, profits, and interest, 284; less important than intellectual improvement, xxviii, 350-1; a means, not an end, 222; Mill on laws of, xxv, 152-3; taxes on, x, 486-8

Productive Labor, in agricultural system, x, 429-30; defined, 258; employment of capital is, 289-92; maintenance of, 259-60; proportion of, on what dependent, 261-5

Professions, competition in, unnaturally increased, x, 133-142; liberal, remuneration of, 102, 104, 107-9

Profitableness, Aurelius on, ii, 241 (45), 249 (53)

Profit(s), in by-employments, x, 120-1;
capital and, 90, 96, 97; of city and
country, 115; clear and gross, 98; as
fixed by competition, 281; defined, 53;
dependent on prices, 118; by what determined, 56; tendency of, to equality,
101; extraordinary, 61; effect of increase of commodities on, 284; effect
of increase of money on rate of, 183-4;
inequalities, natural, 103, 104-5, 107,
112-13; inequalities due to government interference, 121-46; as indicated
by rate of interest, 90-6, 98-9; as affected by market fluctuations, 60-1;
maximum of, 98-9; minimum of, 98;
an element in natural price, 56-7; in
new trades, 117; effect of high, on
prices, 99-100; as affected by progress,
262-3; proportion in different employments, 64-5; of speculators, 116; of
stock, as element in prices of commodities, 49-52; taxes on, 496-501;
wages and, 113-14; of wholesale and
retail trade, 113-16
Profusion, a source of grandeur, xxiv, 66
Progne, changed to swallow, xx, 179 note
4
Prognostics, Browne on, iii, 283; Hobbes
on, xxxiv, 379, 381-2
Progress, dependent on art, xxxii, 231
et seq.; Emerson on, v, 149-60; Goethe
on, xix, 354, 366, 367-8; Pascal on,
xlviii, 119 (354), 120 (355); effect of,
on landlords, capitalists, and wage-
earners, x, 207-11; effect on prices,
178-207; liberty necessary to, iii, 221
et seq.; Tennyson on, xlii, 985; due to
wants, xxxiv, 177-8; of wealth, x, 54-
5, 304-9
Progressive Development, Darwin on, xi,
217, 218-19; objection to law of, 209-
10
Progressive State, effect of, on profits, x,
90; effect of, on wages, 71-3, 83
Prohibition, Mill on, xxv, 284-5; in
United States, xliii, 198 (18)
Projects, Franklin on new, i, 125; imprudent, economically considered, x,
268-9; Penn on, i, 343
Prologue, A, by Burns, vi, 260-1
Prologue Spoken at Dumfries, vi, 371-2
Prologues to Famous Books, xxxix
Promeneia, the priestess, xxxiii, 33
Prometheus, crime and punishment of,
viii, 166-9; fire stolen by, 167 note,

170 note; Heracles and, 194, 198 note
63; Hobbes on, xxxiv, 376-7; Io and,
viii, 188-9; Jove and, v, 92; lament of,
viii, 169-71; marriage with Hesione,
178, 186-7; Mazzini on, xxxii, 395;
with ocean nymphs, viii, 171-6; with
Okeanos, 176-80; his services to man,
175-6, 182-4; type of human nature,
iii, 16; Zeus and, viii, 193-4, 199-206
Prometheus Bound, viii, 166-206; editorial remarks on, 5; Voltaire on,
xxxix, 364
Promises, of captives, fable of, xvii, 33-4;
Descartes on, xxxiv, 22; of enemies,
fable on, xvii, 29; Goethe on written,
xix, 71; Kant on, xxxii, 314-15, 330,
333, 340; in law, xxxiv, 395-401;
Marcus Aurelius on breaking, ii, 208
(7); Penn on, i, 340; of princes, xxxvi,
57-8; of princes, Beaumont on, xlvii,
669; Yu-tzu on, xliv, 6 (13)
Promissory Notes, as money, x, 251-3
Promessi Sposi, I (see Betrothed, The)
Proofs, Hume on, xxxvii, 332 note, 376;
Pascal on, xlviii, 20 (40)
Propagation (see Population)
Propensity, and inclination, xxxii, 336
note
Property, Burke on representation of,
xxiv, 189-90; under democracy, xxviii,
453-4; denunciations of, their origin,
455-6; elective franchise based on, v,
241-2; xxviii, 453-4; Emerson on cares
and uses of, v, 48-9, 50; Emerson on
the institution of, 46-7, 242; Emerson
on reforms of, 258-9; Emerson on
wrongs of, 95; by gift or inheritance,
241; in labor, x, 124; in land, effect
on wages, 67; Locke on, xxxiv, 205;
Locke on love of, xxxvii, 85, 91; Lowell
on rights of, xxviii, 463, 470; Mill on
private, xxv, 143-4; More on system of,
xxxvi, 166-8, 236-9; Pascal on private,
xlviii, 105 (295); Pascal on rights of,
378-9; reliance on, is want of self-
reliance; v, 82; Rousseau on, xxxiv,
198; Rousseau on origin of, 201-2, 208;
Rousseau on effects of system, 210;
secures private, U. S. Constitution,
xliii, 194-5; weight of, in government,
v, 243
Prophecies, Bacon on, iii, 90-3; Browne
on, 297; Hume on, xxxvii, 392; not
miracles, xlviii, 280-1; among Pagans;
xxxiv, 380-2; Pascal on, xlviii, 214-19,

225-6, 231-59, 282-3; Rousseau on, xxxiv, 291

Prophesying, St. Paul on, xlv, 508 (1-6), 509 (22-5), 510 (37-9)

Prophets, armed and unarmed, xxxvi, 21; God's compact with the, xlv, 956 note; Lessing on Hebrew, xxxii, 189; Milton on Hebrew, iv, 404; not acceptable in own country, xliv, 364 (24)

Proportion, as cause of beauty, xxiv, 75-85; Emerson on love of, v, 209-10; in works of art, xxiv, 87-9

Proportional Representation, xxv, 159-60, 185-6

Proprietors, in agricultural system, x, 428

Propriety, Tzu-hsia on, xliv, 64 (11); works on, xxvii, 162-3

PROPYLAEN, INTRODUCTION TO THE, xxxix, 251-66

Prose, in the drama, xxxix, 373-4; poetry and, Wordsworth on, 276-7; qualities of fit, xxviii, 82

Proserpine, Dis and, iv, 161; the moon called, xx, 42 note 9 (see also Persephone)

PROSERPINE, THE GARDEN OF, xlii, 1203-5

Prosopitis, island of, xxxiii, 26

Prosper, on idleness, xxxix, 14

Prosperity, Arabian verses on, xvi, 203; Bacon on, iii, 16; its dependence on virtue, xliii, 227; dependent on God, xliv, 310-11; ECCLESIASTES on, 343 (14); excessive, punished by Nemesis, ix, 272 note; happiness and, i, 343, 344; Kempis on, vii, 228 (2), 267 (3), 268 (4); love and, iii, 27-8; Machiavelli on blindness of, xxxvi, 80; Marcus Aurelius on, ii, 259 (33); Pascal on, xlviii, 47 (107), 354; Raleigh on, xxxix, 67, 96; religion and, iii, 44

Prospero, in THE TEMPEST, with Miranda, tells his story, xlvi, 399-405; with Ariel, 406-10; with Caliban, 410-13; with Ferdinand, 413-14; in scene of Ferdinand and Miranda, 432, 434, 435; plot against, 436-7; invisible at banquet, 440, 441, 442-3; betroths Miranda to Ferdinand, 443-8; in the conspiracy of Caliban, 448-50, 452; in final scene, 452-63; epilogue spoken by, 462-3

PROSPICE, by Browning, xlii, 1065

Prostitution, Bacon on, iii, 168-9; Blake on, xli, 589; in ancient Germany, xxxiii, 103-4; Luther on houses of,

xxxvi, 333; punishment of, in old England, xxxv, 365-6

Protagoras, banishment of, xxxvii, 393; books burned in Athens, iii, 193; wealth of, x, 137

Protasius, the martyr, vii, 147

Protean Genera, xi, 56-7

Protective Duties, Smith on, x, 332-48; removal of, 348-50

Protectorate, The English (see INSTRUMENT OF GOVERNMENT)

Proteic Matter, formation of, xxxviii, 362

Protesilaus and Laodamia, xli, 663-7

Protestant Church, music of, xxxix, 417

Protestantism, Catholicism and, iii, 254-5 (3), 255-6 (5); Shelley on, xviii, 277 (see also Reformation)

Proteus, king of Egypt, xxxiii, 54-6; called Carpathian Wizard, iv, 67; Menelaus and, xxii, 56-60; Milton on, iv, 150; iii, 228; representative of, nature, v, 228

PROTHALAMION, Spenser's, xl, 229-34

PROUD WORD YOU NEVER SPOKE, xli, 899

Proudhon, not the first against property, xxviii, 455

Proverbs, Don Quixote on, xiv, 165; Emerson on, v, 93-4; law of compensation in, 94; Manzoni on, xxi, 74-5; the ready money of experience, xxviii, 438

Proverbs, Book of, paraphrase from, xxxix, 294-5

Providence, academics on, xxxix, 108; Browne on, iii, 265, 268-70; Calvin on, xxxix, 48-9; epic poetry requires belief in, xiii, 47; Epictetus on, ii, 126 (28), 129 (36), 134-5 (53), 157-8 (110), 162 (124), 185 (24); Franklin on, i, 6, 56, 77, 90; Hume on, xxxvii, 342-5, 399; Marcus Aurelius on, ii, 200 (3), 333; More on, xxxvi, 227; Pascal on, xlviii, 331; Raleigh on, xxxix, 70-89, 98-103; Washington on, xliii, 226; Woolman on, i, 176

Provinces, Machiavelli on acquired, xxxvi, 8-11, 18-19; arms in acquired, 69; factions in, 69

Provisions (see Food-supply)

Proxenus, office of, xii, 116 note

Prudence, Burns on, in enjoyment, vi, 319; Dante's allegory of, xx, 266 note 13; Dante's star of, 146 note 5; Emerson on, v, 57-8, 125, 156; Hobbes on, xxxiv, 320-1, 335-6, 351-2, 360, 387;

Kant on imperatives of, xxxii, 327, 328-30; Kempis on, vii, 209; Locke on, xxxvii, 77; of speech, Burke on, xxiv, 149; Whitman on, xxxix, 403-6; in youth, Sheridan on, xviii, 141

Prudence, in PILGRIM'S PROGRESS, xv, 53-4, 228-30, 235-6

Prudentius, Walton on, xv, 356

Prusa, baths at, ix, 394-5

Prynne, on the drama, xxxiv, 153-4

PSALM, FIRST, PARAPHRASED, vi, 33

PSALM, NINETEENTH, VERSIFIED, vi, 33-4

PSALM CXIV, PARAPHRASE OF, iv, 15

PSALM CXXXVI, PARAPHRASE OF, iv, 15-18

PSALM FOR THE CHAPEL OF KILMARNOCK, vi, 336-7

PSALM OF LIFE, xlii, 1264-5

Psalm-singing, origin of, vii, 146-7

PSALMS, THE BOOK OF, xliv, 145-332; Augustine, St., on, vii, 142-3; editorial remarks on, xliv, 144; l, 29; Esdras and, xlviii, 210; idea of God in, xxiv, 59; Herbert on, xv, 400; HYMNS based on, xlv, 535-40; Pascal on, xlviii, 194 (596); Sidney on, xxvii, 9; Smart on, xli, 487-98

Psammetichos, king of Egypt, xxxiii, 7-8, 18, 20, 76-9

Psammis, king of Egypt, xxxiii, 80-1

Psellus, Michael, xli, 686

Pseudo-Martyr, of Dr. Donne, xv, 324-40

Psyche, Cupid and, Milton on, iv, 71

PSYCHE, ODE TO, xlii, 880-2

Psychology, future of, xi, 505

Ptolemy, and Gabinius, xii, 323, 324

Ptolemy Ceraunus, xii, 84 note

Ptolemy Epiphanes, xlviii, 249

Ptolemy Euergetes, xlviii, 249

Ptolemy Philadelphus, xlviii, 248

Ptolemy Philopator, xlviii, 249

Ptolemy Soter, xlviii, 248-9

Ptolemy, son of Abubus, xx, 139 note 5

Ptolomea, round of, in Hell, xx, 139 note 5

Public Affairs, boldness in, iii, 31-2

Public Buildings, in war (agreement with Mexico), xliii, 303

Public, flattery of the, not equal to truth, ix, 40-1; ingratitude of, xix, 177; Mill on the, xxv, 215 (see also People, Populace)

Public Debts, Burke on, xxiv, 243, 248, 288; Smith on, x, 549-64

Public Duties, Christianity and, xxv, 244

Public Education, Mill on, xxv, 302-3

Public Hospitals, idea of Thomas Bond, i, 116

Public Institutions, expence of, x, 452-67

Public Interests, in relation to landlords, capitalists, and wage-earners, x, 209-11

Public Lands, as source of revenue, x, 472-6

Public Libraries, Carlyle on, xxv, 374; proposed by Franklin, i, 67

Public Life, character in, v, 184-5; Epictetus on, ii, 160 (117); Penn on, i, 353

Public Measures, Franklin on, i, 125

Public Men, complaints of, iii, 25; Franklin on, i, 89

Public Office, Bacon on, iii, 28-31; Channing on, xxviii, 319; Cicero on conduct of, ix, 129; Confucius on, xliv, 43-4 (20), 48 (27); often held in contempt, ix, 37; Emerson on corruption in, v, 278-9; Franklin on holding, i, 107; in New Atlantis, iii, 148, 149; qualifications for, i, 354-7; xxiv, 188-9; Tzu-lu on, xliv, 62-3 (see also Officials)

Public Opinion, Emerson on independence of, v, 64, 65; Epictetus on dread of, ii, 171 (150), 174 (158), 176 (172); government by, xxviii, 468; improper field for, xxv, 279-80; Kempis on independence of, vii, 244-5; Marcus Aurelius on, ii, 206-7 (4), 268 (18), 269 (27), 271 (34), 295 (4); Socrates on, 292 (23); Mill on, xxv, 157, 261, 264, 268; Pliny on weight of, ix, 306; Plutarch on desire of, xii, 245 and note; proper field of, xxv, 271-3, 279; Raleigh on, xxxix, 67, 69; Socrates on, ii, 33-4, 35-7; tyranny of, xxv, 199-202, 226-7; Wordsworth on, xxxix, 336

Public Ownership, objections to, xxv, 307-10

Public Peculators, in Dante's HELL, xx, 86, 89-90

Public Revenges, Bacon on, iii, 15

Public Schools, Locke on, xxxvii, 50-4

Public Service, in BODY OF LIBERTIES, xliii, 67

Public Spiritedness, Mill on, xxv, 66-7

Public Works, expence of, x, 452-7

Public Worship, Franklin on, i, 77; Penn on, 360 (473)

Publicans, xliv, 362 note 2

Publicola, at Actium, xii, 372, 373

Publilia, wife of Cicero, ix, 6, 79-80; xii, 252-3

Publius, Paul and, xliv, 484 (7-8)

Pucci, Antonio, xxxi, 212 note

Pucci, Roberto, xxxi, 114 note 4, 222

Puck, in FAUST, xix, 184, 190

Pudens, Servilius, legate to Pliny, ix, 366

PUERPERAL FEVER, CONTAGIOUSNESS OF, xxxviii, 223-54

Puerperal Fever, relations with erysipelas, xxxviii, 227, 240 note, 242, 249, 253-4; with other fevers, 249; Pasteur on, 375-81

Puffendorf, on liberty, xxxiv, 218; works of, xxxvii, 157-8

Pugliano, John Pietro, xxvii, 5

Pulci, Luigi, xxxi, 63-8; Dryden on, xiii, 13; reference to, xxvii, 372

PULLEY, THE, by Herbert, xl, 345-6

Pulleys, power and velocity in, xxx, 182-3

Pulmonary Artery, Harvey on the, xxxviii, 70, 71, 80, 88-9, 91, 92-3, 97, 137, 138-9

Pulmonary Veins, uses of, xxxviii, 71-2, 88, 91, 137, 139

Pulse, Galen on the, xxxviii, 65; Harvey on the, 65-9, 77, 79-81, 87-8, 122, 128, 138

PULTENEY, CHARLOTTE, LINES TO, xl, 440-1

Puma, habits of the, xxix, 273-4; meat of the, 122

Punch, Emerson on London, v, 452, 471-2

Punctuality, Swift on, xxvii, 103

Punishment, of children, xxxvii, 34-43, 45-6, 60-4, 65-9, 93-4, 103; Confucius on, xliv, 7 (3); judicial, in Massachusetts, xliii, 72, 73 (46); Marshall on power of, 219-20; as means of association, xxv, 87-8; Montaigne on corporal, xxxii, 56

Punishments, cruel, forbidden in United States, xliii, 195 (8); prescribed, Winthrop on, 90-100, 101-2, 104-5

Punnā, the slave-girl, xlv, 614-15

Punnavaddhana, xlv, 756

Punta Alta, remains at, xxix, 88-9

Purana, Taine on the Indian, xxxix, 412-13

Purdie, Tom, description of, xxv, 431-2

Purgatory, Dante's visit to, xx, 145-284; gate of, guarded by St. Peter's angel, 8 note 11; Luther on, xxxvi, 252, 253; Pascal on, xlviii, 169 (518), 339; of St. Patrick, xxxii, 177-8; Shakespeare on, xlvi, 115; Socrates's idea of, ii, 108-9

Purification, Dante on, xx, 231

Purist, in FAUST, xix, 185

Puritans, Defoe on the, xxvii, 135-6; editorial remarks on the, iv, 6; Emerson on the, v, 37; on secular music, vi, 17

Purity, Kempis on, vii, 242

PURITY, THE WAY OF, xlv, 702-4

Purpose, Epictetus on, in life, ii, 117-18 (2); lack of, 201 (7), 204 (16), 206-7 (4); Marcus Aurelius on, 210 (14), 211 (2); Shakespeare on, xlvi, 153

Pursuits, Mohammed on ill-chosen, xlv, 916

Pursy, Mrs., in SCHOOL FOR SCANDAL, xviii, 134

Purusha, xlv, 851

Purushottama, xlv, 859

Pus, due to bacteria, xxxviii, 256; Pasteur on microbe of, 369 (see also Suppuration)

Pusey, Edward B., translator of St. Augustine, vii

Pusillanimity, defined by Hobbes, xxxiv, 341; why dishonorable, 365; irresolution and, 372

Putijma, the cacique, xxxiii, 368, 371

Putrefaction, cause of, xxxviii, 257

Putyma, lord of Aromaia, xxxiii, 350

Pygmalion, king of Tyre, xiii, 85; Dante on, xx, 228

Pygmies, war of, with cranes, iv, 101-2

Pylades, in THE LIBATION-BEARERS, viii, 113; Orestes and, vii, 50; ix, 18; Sidney on, xxvii, 10

Pyramids, of Egypt, Herodotus on, xxxiii, 63-5, 67, 68-9; Emerson on, xlii, 1248; Milton on, iv, 105

Pyramus, and Thisbe, xx, 255

Pyrgo, the nurse, xiii, 199

Pyrilampes, and Pericles, xii, 51

Pyriphlegethon, Homer on the, xxii, 143; Plato on, ii, 108, 109

Pyrrha, and Deucalion, iv, 319

Pyrrhic Dance, Byron on the, xli, 814

Pyrrhonism, Carlyle on, xxv, 341; Hume on, xxxvii, 415-16; of Montaigne, xlviii, 389-90

Pyrrhus, king of Epirus, Appius's speech against, ix, 51; Cicero on, 20; in Dante's HELL, xx, 52; Decius on, ix, 60; called Epirot prince, xx, 306 note 11; Machiavelli on, xxxvi, 17; Pascal on, xlviii, 54; surnamed the Eagle, xii, 84 note

Pyrrhus, son of Achilles, Andromache and, xiii, 138-9; Chaucer on, xl, 49; Homer on (Neoptolemus), xxii, 157; Priam killed by, xiii, 118-19; Priam and, Shakespeare on, xlvi, 137-9; slain by Orestes, xiii, 139; in Trojan horse, 108; in sack of Troy, 116-17

Pythagoras, Dandini on, v, 268; Emerson on, 66, 177; *Golden Verses* of, i, 81; on guardian spirits, iii, 284 (33); Hugo on, xxxix, 343; on life, xxxii, 46; Marcus Aurelius on, ii, 241 (47); proverb of, iii, 68; school of, 244; Sidney on, xxvii, 7; on the soul, ix, 73; on suicide, 71

Pythagoreans, custom of the, xxxix, 52-3; alleged debt to British philosophy, iii, 222; on the stars, ii, 293 (27)

Pytheas, the orator, Antipater and, xii, 213; on Demosthenes, 197

Pythian Lord, Apollo called the, viii, 26

Pythoclides, teacher of Pericles, xii, 38

Python, the Byzantine, xii, 197

Python, the serpent, Milton on, iv, 304

Qarûn, xlv, 932

QUA CURSUM VENTUS, xlii, 1121-2

Quadians, M. Aurel s Antoninus' war with, ii, 304, 307-8; Tacitus on the, xxxiii, 116

Quadratilla, Numidia, Pliny on, ix, 309-10

Quadratus, Numidius, Pliny on, ix, 283, 309-10

Quagga, descent of the, xi, 163-5

Quail, falling sickness of, xxxv, 334

Quakers, attitude of, toward lotteries, i, 108, 243-4; attitude of, toward war, 107-10, 190-2, 217-20; duty toward unwise laws, 282; in England, 305; epistle of (1759), 230-4; Folger on persecution of, 9; in French and Indian War, 220-1; history of, xxxiv, 71-8; Lamb on, xli, 736; principles of, i, 227; settlements of, in America, 230-1; shifts to support their principles, 109-10; slavery and, 168, 206-7, 208-9, 212, 224-5, 229, 251, 273; Smith on decline of, 272; Voltaire on doctrines of, xxxiv, 65-71 (see also Woolman, Penn)

Qualities, of Hinduism, xlv, 853-6, 870-1; primary and secondary, xxxvii, 206-7, 210-11, 411-12

Quarles, Francis, AN ECSTASY, xl, 341

Quarrels, causes of, xxxiv, 389; Shakespeare on, xlvi, 109

Quasir, god of poetry, xlix, 401 note

Quatrefages, M., on hybrids, xi, 291

Queens, Bacon on, iii, 50; Confucius on, xliv, 57

QUEEN'S RETURN FROM LOW COUNTRIES, xl, 358

Queintanonina, Lady, Don Quixote on, xiv, 490

Quesnai, Mr., on agricultural system, x, 437-8, 443

Questions, Bacon on habit of asking, iii, 83-4; Buddha on useless, xlv, 647-52; of children, xxxvii, 104, 105-7; Stevenson on, xxviii, 282; sudden, iii, 59

Quiescence, Buddha on, xlv, 705

Quillota, Chili, Darwin on, xxix, 259

Quinault, Voltaire on, xxxiv, 145

Quintilian, on the body in speaking, ix, 226 note; Mill on, xxv, 19; teacher of Pliny, ix, 185

Quintius, Titus, conqueror of Macedon, xxxvi, 79; Milton on, iv, 383

Quirinius, governor of Syria, xliv, 357 (2)

Quiriquina, earthquake at, xxix, 306-13

Quixada, Guttierre, xiv, 490

Quotations, Cervantes on, xiv, 6-9; Locke on, xxxvii, 150-1; Montaigne on, xxxii, 30-1

Rabaud, M., on National Assembly, xxiv, 300 note

RABBI BEN EZRA, xlii, 1103-8

Rabbinism, chronology of, xlviii, 211

Rabbits, descent of, xi, 33; in Falkland Islands, xxix, 197-8

Rabelais, Hazlitt on, xxvii, 279; Hugo on, xxxix, 351; language of, 374; Montaigne on, xxxii, 89; *Morris-Dance of Heretics*, iii, 12; Sainte-Beuve on, xxxii, 105, 129; Voltaire on, xxxiv, 148

Rabirius Posthumus, his desire for riches, iii, 88

Race, the, is not to the swift, xliv, 346 (11)

Race, blood relationship, as tested by, xxviii, 242-3, 245-51; counteracting forces to, v, 338-9; Emerson on influence of, 337-8; extension of ties of, xxviii, 272-3; language and, editor's remarks on, l, 19; language not a proof of, xxviii, 235-40; language a practical test of, 252-73; language as a presumption of, 239-46; meaning of word, 226; not a fixed thing, v, 339; sentiment of,

its growing importance, xxviii, 227-34; Taine on, xxxix, 422-3 (see also Races)
RACE AND LANGUAGE, Freeman's, xxviii, 225-73
Race, Cape, Hayes on, xxxiii, 287
Races, Emerson on human, v, 336; origin of, xxviii, 245-9; political divisions and, 252-3; Taine on differences of, xxxix, 419-32
Rachel, in Dante's Limbo, xx, 11, 18; in Dante's PARADISE, 420; Milton on, iv, 28; references to, xxvii, 321-2; xlii, 1277; type of contemplative life, xx, 256 note 4
Racine, Jean Baptiste, Hugo on, xxxix, 363, 370-2; Hugo on *Athalie* of, 354; Hume on *Athalia* of, xxvii, 221; life and works, xxvi, 132; PHÆDRA, 133-96; Sainte-Beuve on *Athalie* of, xxxii, 125-6; Taine on, xxxix, 412
Radcliffe, Dr., on electric fish, xi, 189
Radicalism, Emerson on, v, 264
Raffael (see Raphael)
Rafinesque, on species, xi, 12
RAGAMUFFINS, THE PACK OF, xvii, 64-5
Rage, Hobbes on, xxxiv, 353
RAGING FORTUNE, a fragment, vi, 36
Rahab, in Dante's PARADISE, xx, 323; lies of, xv, 260
Raillery, in conversation, xviii, 120; Locke on, xxxvii, 122; Swift on, xxvii, 95
Raimbaud, Dante on xx, 362 note 4
Rainbow, cause of the, xxxiv, 122; the first, iv, 340-1; lesson of the, xv, 235
RAINY DAY, THE, xlii, 1273-4
Rajas, xlv, 853, 863, 865, 868-70
Rakshasas, xlv, 863 note
Raleigh, Sir Walter, colony of, xxxiii, 226-7, 257; DISCOVERY OF GUIANA, 301-80; dream of Eldorado, x, 403; Emerson on, v, 183; Gilbert and, xxxiii, 262, 273-4; HIS PILGRIMAGE, xl, 203-4; Jonson on, xxvii, 56; language of, xxxix, 196; life and works, xxxiii, 300; xxxix, 66 note; THE LIE, xl, 204-6; PREFACE TO HISTORY OF WORLD, xxxix, 66-115; editor's remarks on PREFACE, 3; l, 23, 30; REPLY TO MARLOWE'S PASSIONATE SHEPHERD, xl, 254-5; St. Joseph captured by, xxxiii, 315; Spenser's letter to, xxxix, 61-5; Trinidad explored by, xxxiii, 311-12; VERSES, xl, 207; WHAT IS OUR LIFE, 207
Ralph, in FAUSTUS, xix, 233-6
Ralph, in SHOEMAKER'S HOLIDAY, sent to the wars, xlvii, 473-6; his return, 498-9; at Lord Mayor's, 503-4; reported dead, 507-8; at Hodge's shop, 510-11; with wife's shoe, 511-13; stops Hammon's wedding, 521-2; reunited to Jane, 522-4; mistaken for Rowland, 525; at Lord Mayor's dinner, 529, 535
Ralph, James, i, 37-9, 39-40, 41-2, 43-4, 49, 150
Rama, teachings of, xlv, 719
Ramath-lechi, Samson at, iv, 418
Ramayana, The, remarks on, xlv, 784
Ramazan, reference to, xli, 955
Rambler, Johnson's, xxvii, 154
Ram-Dass, Carlyle on, xxv, 405-6
Ramiel, in PARADISE LOST, iv, 213
Rammaka, monastery of, xlv, 714
Ramsay, Sir Andrew Crombie, on the cuckoo, xi, 261; on degradation, 322; on faults, 323-4
Ramsay, Allan, PEGGY, xl, 401; Burns on, vi, 16, 81, 87, 410
Ramuzzini, on diseases of overwork, x, 83
Ran, the goddess, xlix, 286 note
Rand, and the adder, v, 276
RANDOLPH OF ROANOKE, xlii, 1341-4
Randver, son of Jormunrek, xlix, 354, 418, 427 note
Rank(s), Channing on, xxviii, 343-4; is but the guinea's stamp, vi, 511; not inconsistent with liberty, iv, 200; Pascal on, xlviii, 378-80, 382; without bounty, xliv, 12 (26)
RANKINE, JOHN, EPISTLE TO, vi, 53-5
RANKINE, JOHN, EPITAPH ON, vi, 59-60
RANKINE, JOHN, REPLY TO ANNOUNCEMENT OF, vi, 53
Ranse, James, xxxiii, 133-5, 143
RANTIN' DOG, THE, vi, 182-3
RANTIN', ROVIN' ROBIN, vi, 92-3
Ranulph, of Chester, xxxv, 231
Rapacity, Machiavelli on, xxxvi, 54, 59
Raphael, the archangel, in FAUST, xix, 18; in PARADISE LOST, iv, 180-260
Raphael, the painter, accused of immorality, xxvii, 357; Agostino Chigi and, xxxi, 34 note 4; Andrea del Sarto and, xlii, 1090; Emerson on, v, 181; Hazlitt on, xxvii, 278; Il Fattore and, xxxi, 34 note 3; Madonnas of, xlii, 1094-5; sonnets of, 1094-6
Rapture, David on, xli, 491; so deep, its ecstasy was pain, xix, 16
RAPUNZEL, story of, xvii, 66-9

Rare Things, Penn on, i, 329 (69)
Rarity, forerunner of extinction, xxix, 181
Rashness, belongs to youth, ix, 52; Emerson on, v, 110; Penn on, i, 334 (119)
RASSELAS, Johnson's, xxvii, 154
Rastall, Judge, Walton on, xv, 323
Rastelli, Giacomo, xxxi, 96 note 3
Rat, Brander's song of the, xix, 87
Rational, term, ii, 277 (8)
Rational Soul, Marcus Aurelius on the, ii, 285 (1)
Rationalism, Rousseau on, xxxiv, 289-92
Rats, range of, xi, 146
Ratsey, Gamaliel, xlvii, 547 note 19
Rattlesnakes, Dana on, xxiii, 153-4; Darwin on, xi, 202-3
RATTLIN' ROARIN' WILLIE, vi, 256
Raulin, Jules, xxxviii, 359 note
RAVEN, THE, by Poe, xlii, 1227-30
Ravenna, battle of, Macaulay on, xxvii, 393; Machiavelli on, xxxvi, 85
Ravens, Epictetus on, ii, 134-5 (53); Harrison on, xxxv, 339
RAVENS, THE THREE, xl, 73-4
RAVENS, THE SEVEN, xvii, 107-9
Ravillac, murderer of Henry IV, iii, 98
RAVING WINDS AROUND HER BLOWING, vi, 299
Ravishment, divine enchanting, iv, 51
Rawley, Dr., Bacon's literary executor, iii, 144
Reaction, in human affairs, v, 283-5 (see also Polarity)
Read, Rebecca, first marriage of, i, 50; Franklin and, 25, 28, 36, 39, 42, 66, 76
Readers, of poetry, three classes of, xiii, 58-9
Reading, Bacon on, iii, 122-3; Carlyle on, xxv, 364, 373; Channing on, xxviii, 337-8; for children, xxxvii, 131-3; choice of, xxviii, 99-100; Confucius on, xliv, 19 (11), 21 (25), 39 (15); Emerson on our, v, 68-9; Emerson on right, 11; Epictetus on, ii, 170 (145); folly of trying to limit, iii, 199-205; for girls, xxviii, 150-2; Kempis on, vii, 210; Locke on instruction in, xxxvii, 128-31; Marcus Aurelius on, ii, 194 (7); Milton on, iv, 403; Newman on education by, xxviii, 31-2, 33-8; Pascal on, xlviii, 26 (69); Pliny on, ix, 303; power given by, xxviii, 135-6; preparation for, 99-100; proper method

of, 101-13; true, impossible under modern conditions, 116 (see also Books)
Ready-to-halt, in PILGRIM'S PROGRESS, xv, 174, 276, 284, 288, 312, 313
Ready-writing, Carlyle on, xxv, 443-7; Dryden on, xxxix, 156
Real Existence, Berkeley on, xxxvii, 193-257, 264-8, 270-85; Buddhist denial of, xlv, 657-8, 661; Descartes on, xxxiv, 29; ECCLESIASTES on, xliv, 343 (24); Emerson on, v, 99-100; Hume on evidences of, xxxvii, 306-18, 324, 330-1, 409, 414-15, 419; Montaigne on, xlviii, 389-92; Rousseau on, xxxiv, 244; Schiller on, xxxii, 239-40; Socrates on, ii, 90-6
Real Presence, Pascal on, xlviii, 301-2; Tillotson on, xxxvii, 375
Realist, in FAUST, xix, 188
REALITIES OF IMAGINATION, Hunt's, xxvii, 289-95
Reality, alone beautiful, v, 301-2; in art, Hugo on, xxxix, 366-7
REAPER, THE SOLITARY, xli, 654-5
Reason, in animals, Darwin on, xi, 251; in animals, Descartes on, xxix, 46-8; of animals, Hume on, xxxvii, 371-4; Bacon on the, iii, 8; Boileau on human, xxxiv, 142-3; Browne on the, iii, 257, 264-5, 306; Burke on standards of, xxiv, 11; Calderon on the, xxvi, 56; Carlyle on, xxv, 323-4; Chénier on, xxxii, 125; in criticism of art, xxvii, 215; Dante on, xx, 218; Descartes on conduct of the, xxxiv, 5-6, 17-20; Descartes on equal distribution of, 5-6; direct and indirect interests of, xxxii, 370 note; discursive and intuitive, iv, 193; Epictetus on, ii, 118 (6), 128 (33), 129 (37), 137 (59), 169 (144); experience and, xxxvii, 322 note; faith and, Browne on, iii, 261, 271-2; faith and, Kempis on, vii, 364 (4, 5); faith and, Voltaire on, xxxiv, 107; Franklin on, i, 35; Goethe on, xix, 76; habit and, xxxvii, 92; happiness in obedience to, ii, 201 (8), 207 (4), 208 (6, 7), 210 (12), 221 (51); Helmholtz on the, xxx, 175; Hobbes saying on, xxv, 100; Hume on objects of, xxxvii, 306; imagination and, xxvii, 350-3; instinct and, Pascal on, 117 (344); instinct and, Pope on, xl, 425-6; Kant on faculty of, xxxii, 361-2;

Kant on purposes of, 307-8; Kempis on natural, vii, 326 (2); limits of practical, xxxii, 368-9, 373; Locke on the, xxxvii, 107; love and, xlviii, 419; man's misuse of, xix, 19; Marcus Aurelius on the, ii, 210 (15), 211 (1), 214 (13, 16), 216 (22), 226 (10), 227 (14), 228 (16), 229 (27), 238 (35), 267 (10), 278 (12), 282 (33), 284 (38); Milton on, iv, 269; Montaigne on the, xlviii, 392-3; morality from, xxxii, 316-17, 319-21, 323; More on the, xxxvi, 197; "our affections' king," xl, 294; Pascal on, xlviii, 32-3, 35, 118 (345); the passions and, xxiv, 40; xxxiv, 177; xlviii, 133 (412-13); Penn on, i, 385-6; pity and, xxxiv, 190; in poetry, Sainte-Beuve on, xxxii, 125; Pope on, xl, 417, 420; possibility of pure, practical, xxxii, 371-2; the province of, xlviii, 439-42; Raleigh on, xxxix, 99, 111 note; in religion, xxxii, 193 (37), 201-3; in religion, Pascal on, xlviii, 81 (226), 84, 91 (245), 93 (252-3), 94 (259), 95 (260), 96 (263), 97 (267, 270, 272), 98 (273-82), 184 (561), 185 (563), 311 (903); in religion, Raleigh on, xxxix, 110-11; in religion, Renan on, xxxii, 181; Rochester on, xxxiv, 143-4; Schiller on the, xxxii, 276-7; Shelley on, xxvii, 329, 351; sensation and, Schiller on, xxxii, 243-9; the senses and, Pascal on, xlviii, 39 (83); senses do not limit, xxxiv, 32; sentiment and, xxxvii, 293; Shakespeare on, xlvi, 175; in sleep, St. Augustine on the, vii, 182; speech and, xxxiv, 327; "what a wretched aid," xviii, 93; will and, xxxii, 324

Reasoning, from analogy, xxxvii, 371, 374 (7); Bacon on, in matters of fact, xxxix, 130, 133-4, 136, 144-5; Buddha on, xlv, 731; with children, xxxvii, 64, 83, 89-90; difference in powers of, 373 note; different kinds of, 332 note; ends of, xxxiv, 346-8; feeling and, xlviii, 11-12; Hobbes on, xxxiv, 330; Hume on accurate, xxxvii, 293-5, 412-15; Hume on demonstrative, 306, 314, 413, 418-19; Hume on, in matters of fact, 306-18, 320-2, 323-4, 331, 372-4, 376-8, 415, 419-20; Locke on, 159; Pascal on, xlviii, 404-7; Raleigh on, in matters of fact, xxxix, 100; Socrates on, ii, 83

Rebbye, Sir Ralph, xl, 99

Rebecca, in Dante's PARADISE, xx, 419

Rebellion, a capital crime in early Massachusetts, xliii, 81; Hobbes on, xxxiv, 403-4; Machiavelli on, xxxvi, 9; Penn on, i, 339 (178); punishment of, in United States, xliii, 197

Rebellions, Bacon on, iii, 36-42

Rebels, the vanquished only are, xxvi, 69

Rebirth, Buddhist doctrine of, xlv, 677-84, 738; Hindu doctrine of, 817, 823-4, 854, 862; old belief in, xlix, 367

Rebours, M., xlviii, 322

Recalcati, Ambrogio, xxxi, 145 note 5

Recklessness, Confucius on, xliv, 22 (10); Locke on, xxxvii, 95-6

Recollection, Augustine, St., on, vii, 166-74; Hobbes on, xxxiv, 319-20; knowledge as, ii, 63-8; of sorrow pleasant, ix, 103

RECOLLECTION, THE, by Shelley, xli, 845-7

Recombes, Louis de, xxxv, 43

Recommendations, Diogenes on, ii, 136 (57)

Recompense, Jesus on, xliv, 393 (12-14)

Reconstruction, Johnson's plan of, xliii, 428-31; Lincoln's plan of, 416 note

Recreation, labor as, xxxvii, 175-7 (see also Diversion)

Recreations, of children, xxxvii, 89-90, 111, 171

Rectitude, beauty and power from, v, 281; a perpetual victory, 188; Pliny on doubtful, ix, 203

RECUYELL OF HISTORIES OF TROY, xxxix, 5-9

RED, RED ROSE, vi, 482-3

Red River, sediment of, xxxviii, 402-3

Red Rowan, in KINMONT WILLIE, xl, 113

Red Sea, origin of name, xxix, 24; passage of the, xliv, 278 (9), 317 (13-15); Milton on passage of the, iv, 16-17, 95-6, 346-7; Mohammed on passage of, xlv, 904; Pascal on passage of, xlviii, 214-15, 224

RED SHOES, THE, xvii, 329-34

Redemption, Dante on human, xx, 311-14; Pascal on types of, xlviii, 271 (781); typified by Red Sea, 214-15, 224

Reding, Itel, in WILLIAM TELL, xxvi, 413-28

Redman, Sir Matthew, at Otterburn, xxxv, 92; Lindsay and, 94-5, 97

Redman, Mercy, i, 242, 246, 248

Redress, for every wrong, xviii, 311

REED AND TREE, fable of, xvii, 26

REEDS OF INNOCENCE, xli, 584-5

Reefs, coral, Darwin on, xxix, 469-83; as showing areas of subsidence, 483-4

Rees, William, xxxii, 138; on saints of Wales, 173

Reeve, Chaucer's, xl, 27-8; Dryden on Chaucer's, xxxix, 166

Refinement, Channing on, xxviii, 345-6 (see also Culture)

Reflection, Buddha on, xlv, 731; Epictetus on, ii, 159 (115); Goethe on, xxxix, 252; Locke on habit of, xxxvii, 152; Marcus Aurelius on, ii, 251 (59); necessary to poets, xxxix, 297; Rousseau on faculty of, xxxiv, 245-7; Schiller on, xxxii, 280-1

Reform, Bacon's advice on, iii, 29; Bacon on popular, 46; Burke on methods of, xxiv, 301-3; Descartes on political, xxxiv, 14-15; destruction and, Burke on, xxiv, 290; false methods of opposing, xxvii, 225-51; innovation contrasted with, xxiv, 391; Lowell on, xxviii, 469-70; Lowell on opposition to, 458-9; More on, xxxvi, 142, 164-6; Tennyson on, xlii, 999-1001

Reform Bill, English, Emerson on, v, 364; Wordsworth on, 324

Reformation, Browne on the, iii, 253-4 (2), 255 (4); early attempts at, xxv, 222-3; in England, iii, 222-3; Hobbes on causes of the, xxxiv, 386-7; Lowell on the, xxviii, 456; LUTHER'S ARTICLES OF, xxxvi, 288-335; Luther's part in the, 246; James Mill on the, xxv, 32; Taine on the, xxxix, 432-3; Woolman on the, i, 277; works concerning the, l, 23

REFORMATION IN SCOTLAND, PREFACE TO KNOX'S, xxxix, 58-60

REFORMER, MAN THE, v, 43-58

Reformers, Burke on, xxiv, 201; Emerson on, v, 258-9

REFORMERS, FALLACIES OF ANTI-, xxvii, 225-51

REFORMERS, NEW ENGLAND, v, 253-71

Regan, in KING LEAR, xlvi, 217; farewell to Cordelia, 223-4; plot against father, 224-5; at Gloucester's, 244-6, 247, 250; with father, 255-61; with Gloucester, 277-80; with Oswald, her love for Edmund, 289-90; with Edmund, before battle, 303-4; after battle, quarrel over Edmund, 308-9; her sickness, 309-10; poisoned by Goneril, 314-15; Ruskin on, xxviii, 139

Regelation of Ice, xxx, 233, 243-4

REGENCY BILL, ODE ON THE DEPARTED, vi, 332-4

REGIMENT OF HEALTH, ESSAY ON, Bacon's, iii, 81-2

Regin, the Lay of, xlix, 250; Sigurd and, 283-92; slaying of, 295-6

Regiomontanus, prophecy of, iii, 92 (see Müller, John)

Registration Duties, x, 505-11

Regnault, on mechanical equivalent of heat, xxx, 199-200

Regnault's Apparatus, xxx, 189

Regnier, Mathurin, Sainte-Beuve on, xxxii, 129

Regrets, Emerson on, v, 77

Regulus, Marcus, Aurelia and, ix, 229; Blaesus and, 229; Pliny on, 188-91, 207, 229, 249-51, 278-9; his son, 249-51; Verania and, 228

Regulus, Marcus Atilius, Bacon on, iii, 130; death of, ix, 72; Milton on, iv, 383

Rehoboam, Dante on, xx, 192

Reinauld, of Mount Alban, xiv, 19

Reincarnation, Lessing on, xxxii, 205-6

Relations, and friends, Cicero on, ix, 15-16

Relations of Ideas, xxxvii, 306

Relaxation, Amasis on need of, xxxiii, 85-6; Pascal on, xlviii, 16 (24), 126 (380); sudden, effect of, xxiv, 118

Relevancy, in writing, Pliny on, ix, 271

Relics, Browne on, iii, 280 (28); Hume on, xxxvii, 329; Pascal on, xlviii, 290 (839), 335, 358

Reliefs, feudal, x, 506-7

RELIGIO MEDICI, Browne's, iii, 251-332; editorial remarks on, l, 31

Religion, of ascetic natures, xxviii, 171-3; on authority, Channing on, 342-3; on authority, Emerson on, v, 147-8; on authority, Lessing on, xxxii, 192-3; on authority, Mill on, xxv, 229-37; on authority, Milton on, iii, 218-20, 229; iv, 355; on authority, Pascal on, xlviii, 438-40; on authority, Rousseau on, xxxiv, 285-6; in authors, criticism of, xxvii, 220-1; Bacon on, iii, 42-6; Bentham on criticism of faults in, xxvii, 244; Browne on doubts in, iii, 257; Buddha on useless questions of, xlv,

647-52; Bunyan on, xv, 76-7, 83, 106-9; Bunyan on backsliding in, 154-5; Burke on fear in, xxiv, 59; Burns on, vi, 138-9, 205; Carlyle on, xxv, 337-8, 366; changes in, iii, 137-8; xxxiv, 384-7; Cowper on, xxxix, 295; decline of, v, 277-8, 280; determined by accident of birth, xxxiv, 284 note; duties of, 305; Emerson on, v, 27-8, 147-8, 197, 428-9; force in matters of, iii, 13-14; freedom of, in U. S., xliii, 194 (1); freedom of, Vane on, 121-2; of the future, Emerson on, v, 294-5; of the future, Lessing on, xxxii, 204-5; geography in, iii, 253 (2); Goethe on, xix, 150-1; Herbert on, music and, xv, 405-7; Hobbes on, xxxiv, 341, 376-87; Hume on revealed, xxxvii, 385; hypocrisy in, vi, 95-6; xxvi, 214-15; individualism and, v, 280; Mill on, xxv, 47-8, 148; Mill on dissenters in, 33-4; miracles in, xxxvii, 381-2, 385-6, 388-91; morality and, xiii, 30; xxv, 30-1; xxxvii, 399-400, 404-5; mysteries in, Browne on, iii, 259-60 (9, 10); Newman on teaching of, xxviii, 37-8; origin of, xxxiv, 375; Pascal on, xlviii, 68, 91 (245), 93 (252), 95 (260), 97 (268), 98 (273-90), 156 (470), 181, 189 (574); Pascal on the true, 138 (430), 142 (433), 155 (468), 161 (487, 489, 491-4), 185 (565), 191 (585), 192, 196 (605), 197 (606), 282-3, 294 (844); Penn on, i, 359-67, 348; iii, 42; philosophy and, xxxiv, 107-8; poetry and, xxvii, 105; xxxix, 313-15; Raleigh on, 90, 110-11; reason and, xxxii, 201-4; xxxvii, 395-9; xlviii, 81 (226), 84; Rousseau on natural, xxxiv, 280, 282-4, 289, 300-1; scepticism in, xlviii, 72-7, 82 (230); science and, iii, 271-3; xxx, 5; xxxix, 128; self-reliance in, v, 38-40; of sensuous natures, xxviii, 169-70; Shelley on, xxvii, 332; state, Burke on need of, xxiv, 228-35; Taine on, xxxix, 429, 430-1, 432-3; virtue the essence of, v, 26; wars of, xiii, 15; xxxiv, 85; Washington on, xliii, 242; Woolman on, i, 173-4; Woolman on unity in, 230

RELIGION, UNITY IN, ESSAY ON, Bacon's, iii, 11-14

Religion and Philosophy, reading course in, l, 29-35

Religions, come from imaginative men, v, 177; the four, iii, 277 note 58; national, remarks on, v, 423; original, allegorical, xxvii, 332; of Utopia, xxxvi, 224-36; represent culture of votaries, v, 275-7

Religious Errors, origin of, v, 178

Religious Exercises, Kempis on, vii, 222-4

Religious Instruction, expense of, x, 464, 466; Locke on, xxxvii, 116, 132-3

Religious Liberty, Mill on, xxv, 202, 217-37, 242-6

Religious Life, Buddha on the, xlv, 651, 662-3, 671, 674; Kempis on a, vii, 220; Pascal on the, xlviii, 312 (906)

Religious Sympathy, Freeman on, xxviii, 230-1

Religious Teachers, compared with poets, xxvii, 333

Religious Tests, forbidden in U. S., xliii, 192 (3); Mill on, xxv, 223-5

Religious Writings, base tone of, v, 86

Religiousness, of act, speech and mind, xlv, 864-5

Rembrandt, Hazlitt on, xxvii, 279

Remedies, fable on impossible, xvii, 38; Pascal on belief in, xlviii, 282

Remedy, things without, xlvi, 354

REMEMBER, by C. G. Rossetti, xlii, 1182

Remembrance, Hobbes on, xxxiv, 320; rosemary for, xlvi, 182

Remonstrances, Cicero on, ix, 39

Remorse, Byron on, xviii, 439; Shelley on, 337

REMORSE: A FRAGMENT, vi, 49-50

REMORSEFUL APOLOGY, vi, 479

Remulus, and Cædicus, xiii, 305; death of, 378

Remus, the Latian, killed by Nisus, xiii, 304

Remus, twin of Romulus, Virgil on, xiii, 82-3, 289

Renaissance, Huxley on the, xxviii, 217, 219; in Italy, xxvii, 369-72; Taine on the, xxxix, 427; works of and concerning the, l, 23-4, 26-7

Renan, Ernest, life and works, xxxii, 136; POETRY OF CELTIC RACES, 137-82

Rendu, Pere, on glaciers, xxx, 231

Renfusa, city of New Atlantis, iii, 153

Rengger, on cattle in Paraguay, xi, 81

Reni, Guido, Raphael's sonnets and, xlii, 1094-5 (see also Guido)

Renous, the German collector, xxix, 272

Rent(s), in agricultural system, x, 428, 429; building and ground, 488-9;

Burke on, xxiv, 293; of coal mines, x, 169, 171; considered as produce of nature, 290-1; corn, 39-40; corn, in Elizabethan England, xxxv, 249; defined, x, 53; by what determined, 56; extraordinary, 62; of forests, 169-70; gross and neat, 223-4; of houses, taxes on, 488-95; in kind, Pliny on, ix, 355; of land, by what determined in general, x, 147-9; of land cultivated for food, 149-65, 177; of land used to produce materials, 165-8, 177; of land, taxes on, 479-86; market prices, their effect on, 60; of metallic mines, 171-5; money, affected by variation of value of gold, 38; of precious stone mines, 176-7; prices and, relations between, 149; prices of commodities, as determined by, 50; profits and wages, confounded with, 54; progress of society in relation to, 208, 262; taxes on, 479-86, 488-95; taxes on, when best paid, 477 (3)

RENTON, MR., NOTE TO, vi, 269

Renty, Sir Oudart of, at Poitiers, xxxv, 48-9

Renunciation, Buddha on, xlv, 594; Emerson on, v, 27; Hindu doctrine of, xlv, 799, 809, 813, 847, 866; Kempis on, vii, 296 (1); Pascal on, xlviii, 89 (240)

RENUNCIATION, A, by De Vere, xl, 289

Renzo Tramaglino (see Tramaglino)

Reparation, Penn on, i, 334-5

Repentance, Calvin on, xxxix, 49-50; Cenci on, xviii, 321; Jesus on, xliv, 394 (7), 395 (10), 398 (3-4); Marcus Aurelius on, ii, 255 (10); Raleigh on, xxxix, 81; time for, xv, 262

Repetition, Burke on effects of, xxiv, 62-3, 70; Darwin on effects of, xxix, 321; Pascal on, xlviii, 22 (48); sublimity of, its cause, xxiv, 111-14

Rephan, xliv, 438 (43)

Replevin, in Massachusetts, xliii, 71 (32)

Repose, our foster-nurse of nature, xlvi, 289

Representation, Jefferson on right of, xliii, 151; of minorities, Mill on, xxv, 159-60; personal, Mill on, 159-60; principles of, adopted by French Revolution, xxiv, 305-22; of property, Burke on, 189-90

Representative Government, Mill on, xxv, 69

Representatives, Congressional, xliii, 180-1, 182 (1), 183 (6, 7), 192 (3), 197-8; qualities needed by, v, 184-5 (see also Agents)

Reproach, independence of, vii, 244 (2, 3); worse than violence, iv, 205

Reproduction, period of, change in, xi, 187-8

Reproductive System, affected by conditions of life, xi, 302; sensitiveness of, 256

Reproofs, in anger, i, 347 (289-92); Cicero on, ix, 38-9; usefulness of, xliii, 94; vain, i, 358 (446-7)

Reproval, our fear of, vii, 310-11

Republican Government, on trial in America, xliii, 227

Republics, Dryden on, xviii, 8-9; limitation of authority in, xxv, 196-8; Machiavelli on difficulty of conquering, xxxvi, 19; military affairs of, 42; monarchies compared with, v, 245

REPUTATION, ESSAY ON, Bacon's, iii, 129-30

Reputation, daughter of fortune, iii, 100; the desire for, ii, 253 (73); Locke on, xxxvii, 42, 78, 115; a matter of imagination, xlviii, 36; Pascal on desire of, 59 (147); Plutarch on desire of, xii, 245; as power, xxxiv, 360; Rousseau on love of, 223-4; Webster on, xlvii, 797 (see also Fame)

Reputations, of great men, beyond their acts, v, 183

REQUIEM, by Stevenson, xlii, 1213

REQUIESCAT, by Arnold, xlii, 1129

Requisition, right of, under Confederation, xliii, 159; under Constitution, 190-1

Rerir, son of Sigi, xlix, 258-9

Resemblance of ideas, Hume on, xxxvii, 304-5, 327-8

Resemblances, analogical, xi, 443-8; Browne on, iii, 313; deformity and, 46; embryonic, xi, 459-60; family, iii, 20; in nature, xi, 452-7; Pascal on, xlviii, 51 (133); pleasure in finding, xxiv, 17-20

Resentment, Pascal on, xlviii, 112 (324); Penn on, i, 339-40 (182-5); 346 (270-1)

Reservation, in speech, Penn on, i, 383 (120)

Reservations, Papal, xxxvi, 285, 288, 291-2

Reserved Cases (Catholic Church), xxxvi, 292-3

Residences, Bacon on, iii, 108-12

RESIGNATION, by Longfellow, xlii, 1277-9

Resignation, Burns on, vi, 32; Penn on, i, 325-6 (see also Acquiescence)

Resolution, Buddha on, xlv, 597; from despair, iv, 92; Franklin's maxim on, i, 79, 80; why honorable, xxxiv, 366; Kempis on, vii, 222 (2)

RESOLUTION AND INDEPENDENCE, xli, 658-62

Resolutions, hasty, Penn on, i, 340

RESOLVE, THE, by Brome, xl, 369-70

Respect, ceremonious and natural, xlviii, 380-2; Dryden on, xviii, 41; friendship and, ix, 36-7; an inferior degree of astonishment, xxiv, 49; Kant on, xxxii, 313 note 3; Locke on want of, xxxvii, 120-3; love and, xlviii, 418, 419

Respectability, Penn on, i, 345; religion of, xxviii, 301; Stevenson on, 299-300; virtue and, 301-2

RESPECTS, CEREMONIES AND, ESSAY ON, iii, 124-6

Respiration, compared with combustion of a candle, xxx, 162-70; Descartes on use of, xxxiv, 43-4; Galen on, xxxviii, 65; in high altitudes, xxix, 325-6; pulse and, xxxviii, 65, 69

Rest, Burke on state of, xxiv, 107-8; complete, is death, xlviii, 51 (129); Cowper on, xli, 542; after good works, iii, 29; Herbert on, xl, 345-6; labor and, vii, 281 (4); xxviii, 314-16; needed by man, iv, 170; Pascal on complete, xlviii, 51 (129), 51 (131); second law of nature, v, 229, 236; temporal and eternal, vii, 300 (2); Tennyson on, xlii, 994-6

Restitutus, letter to, ix, 297-8

Restlessness, Herbert on, xl, 345-6; Pascal on, xlviii, 51 (130), 52-5

Restoration, English, drama of the, xviii, 5; Milton on, iv, 5

Results, Arabian proverb on, xvi, 33; Machiavelli on, xxxvi, 59; Webster on weighing, xlvii, 786; Whitman on certainty of, xxxix, 404-6

Resurrection, Browne on the, iii, 299-300; Bunyan on, xv, 230; celebration of the, 403; Dante on certainty of, xx, 314; Jesus on, xliv, 406-7 (27-40); Milton on the, iv, 352; Mohammed on the, xlv, 890-1, 912; Pascal on, xlviii, 80-1

(222-3); Paul, St., on, xlv, 511 (12-55); Sadducees on, xliv, 406-7 (27-36); songs of the, xix, 36-8

RESURRECTION, THE DAY OF, xlv, 543-4

Retail Trade, profits in, why greater than in wholesale, x, 114-15

Retailing, capital used in, x, 289-90, 291; necessity of, 288-9

RETALIATION, by Goldsmith, xli, 505-9

Retaliation, Mohammed on law of, xlv, 999; Shelley on, xviii, 276-7; Socrates on, ii, 38-9

Retaliatory Duties, x, 346-8

Retirement, Goldsmith on, xli, 511; Kempis on, vii, 225 (5)

RETREAT, THE, xl, 347-8

Retribution, Æschylus on, viii, 21-2, 24-5, 35, 70, 78, 89-90, 92, 93, 94, 98, 103, 116, 133-4, 144, 160; Asaph on, xliv, 233 (17-20); Bildad on, 98 (5-21); Buddhist doctrine of, xlv, 669-70, 671-4, 675-6, 678-80; Christ, the teacher of, xxxii, 198 (61); David on, xliv, 150 (12-16), 155 (5-6), 182 (16, 21), 186 (1, 2, 9-38), 213 (6-11); doctrine of, among the Jews, xxxii, 189-92; ECCLESIASTES on, xliv, 344 (11-13); Elihu on, 126 (21-30); Eliphaz on, 75 (8), 94 (20-35); Emerson on, v, 90, 99-100; Franklin on, i, 77, 90; future needlessness of doctrine, xxxii, 203 (85); Hindu doctrine of, xlv, 861-2; Jesus on, xliv, 369 (21-6), 370 (38), 397 (25); Hobbes on legal, xxxiv, 408; Job on, xliv, 104-5 (17-33), 109-10 (18-25), 112-13 (13-23), 119 (3); Kempis on, vii, 232-4; More on doctrine of, xxxvi, 196, 227; Omar Khayyam on, xli, 955, 956; ORESTEIA deals with subject of, viii, 5-6; popular ideas of, v, 85-6; Whitman on, xxix, 404-5; Zophar on, xliv, 101 (5-29)

Retz, Cardinal de, miracle related by, xxxvii, 386-7; Voltaire on, xxxiv, 87

Reuben, Winthrop on, xliii, 94

REVEILLE, THE, xlii, 1401-2

Revelation, Bunyan on, xv, 99, 151; Emerson on, v, 32-3, 140-2; Franklin on, i, 55, 56; Lessing on, xxxii, 185-202; Pascal on, xlviii, 283 (818); Rousseau on, xxxiv, 282-302; superior to morality, xiii, 30; yearning for, xix, 53

Revelation, Book of, Paræus on, iv, 412

REVENGE, ESSAY ON, Bacon's, iii, 15-16

Revenge, Burns on, vi, 106; contempt the best, iii, 320; Epictetus on, ii, 169 (143); forgiveness and, 153 (96); Hobbes on desire of, xxxiv, 353, 408; Marcus Aurelius on best, ii, 232 (6); masters fear of death, iii, 9; music and, xli, 477; Schiller on, xxvi, 479; Shelley on, xviii, 276-7; what will not, descend to, iv, 264

REVENGE, THE, xlii, 1007-10

Revengefulness, defined by Hobbes, xxxiv, 341; language of, 344-5

Revenue, capital and, as determining industry, x, 263-5; composed of wages, profits, and rent, 223; duties for, 352, 372; gross and neat, 224-9; as measured by money, 227-9; public, Burke on, xxiv, 357; sources of, x, 53; sources of public, 468-564

Revenue Bills, under Constitution, xliii, 183

RÉVERE, PAUL, RIDE OF, xlii, 1295-9

Reverence, Burke on, xxiv, 49; Goethe on, xxv, 381; Locke on, xxxvii, 84; Tennyson on, xlii, 999

REVERIE OF POOR SUSAN, xli, 655

Reversion, Darwin on, xi, 161-2; instance of, among pigeons, 38; of mongrels and hybrids, 314-15; remarks on, 39; tendency to, 28-9; tendency to, does not prevail against selection, 107-8

Reviewers, Carlyle on, xxv, 339-40

Reviews, Smith on, xxvii, 225

Reviling, ECCLESIASTES on, xliv, 347 (20)

Revilius, Caninius, xii, 310

Revision, of writings, Pliny on, ix, 307-8

Revolution, ages of, Emerson on, v, 20; Burke on, xxiv, 170, 289-90; Franklin on, i, 89; Jefferson on right of, xliii, 150-1; Pascal on, xlviii, 105; reform contrasted with, xxiv, 390-1

Revolution Society, Burke on the, xxiv, 144-5, 204; answer to doctrines of, 155-72, 193-6

Revolutionists, Burke on, xxiv, 200-1, 297-8

REVOLUTIONS OF HEAVENLY BODIES, DEDICATION OF, xxxix, 52-7

Rewards, as means of association, xxv, 87; for children, xxxvii, 37-9, 40, 42, 56, 88; Emerson on, v, 269-70, 289; Marcus Aurelius on, ii, 273 (42)

Reynaldo, in HAMLET, xlvi, 120-1

Reynard the Fox, Locke on, xxxvii, 132

Reynolds, Sir Joshua, Goldsmith on, xli,

505, 508; Hazlitt on, xxvii, 279; Sheridan on, xviii, 106; on taste, xxxix, 268, 289-90

Reynolds, General, at Gettysburg, xliii, 329, 331, 332; Haskell on, 332-3

Reynolds, Mr., More and, xxxvi, 124

Reynolds, Mrs., in Hazlitt's discussion, xxvii, 272, 274

Rhadamanthus, Homer on, xxii, 60, 98; Socrates on, ii, 29; Virgil on, xiii, 226

Rhamnes, death of, xiii, 304

Rhamnus, and Antony, xii, 360

Rhampsinitos, king of Egypt, xxxiii, 58-63

Rhapsodies, Montaigne on, xxxii, 32

Rhea, mother of the gods, ix, 385 note; Bacchus and, viii, 370; Hercules and, xiii, 262; Jove and, xx, 60

Rhesus, reference to, xiii, 89

Rhetoric, Burke on, xxiv, 137; Carlyle on, xxv, 376-9; Descartes on study of, xxxiv, 9; Goethe on, xix, 30; Hobbes on, xxxiv, 363; Locke on study of, xxxvii, 158-9, 160-1; Marcus Aurelius on, ii, 207 (5); Montaigne on study of, xxxii, 59-60; oratory contrasted with, xxv, 324; Penn on, i, 336 (137-41), 383 (126); Plutarch on, xii, 53; simplicity in, v, 304

Rhetoricians, Pliny on, ix, 214

Rhexenor, son of Nausithous, xxii, 91

Rhine, Byron on the, xli, 798-9; Cæsar's bridge over, xii, 283; Tacitus on the, xxxiii, 93; Thoreau on the, xxviii, 408

Rhinoceros, old Arabian idea of the, xvi, 249

Rhode, the maid, xliv, 449 (13-15); St. Peter and, xv, 337

Rhodius, Apollonius, xxvii, 349

Rhodon, tutor of Cæsarion, xii, 384

Rhodopis, Herodotus on, xxxiii, 67-8

Rhœtus, in the ÆNEID, xiii, 304, 335

Rhone, sediment of the, xxxviii, 401

Rhorty's Battery, at Gettysburg, xliii, 337, 351, 382

Rhyme, Dryden on, xiii, 55-6; Hugo on, xxxix, 373; Milton on, iv, 87; Montaigne on, xxxii, 62; Pope on advantages of, xl, 407; Sidney on, xxvii, 28; Swift on, 112; Whitman on, xxxix, 394

Rhymer, on Shakespeare, xxxix, 212, 215

Rhythm, Poe on, xxviii, 378; Shelley on, xxvii, 334; Sidney on, 49; universal inclination to, iii, 323-4

Ribeira Grande, Darwin on, xxix, 12

Ribemont, Eustace, at Poitiers, xxxv, 37-8, 48

Ricardo, David, Emerson on, v, 248; as member of Parliament, xxv, 65; Mill and, 22, 38, 65

Ricardo, Duke, in Cardenio's story, xiv, 202-3

Riccaut, in MINNA VON BARNHELM, xxvi, 344-9

Ricci, Federigo de', xxxi, 429, 431-2

Riccio, Pier Francesco, xxxi, 345, 346-7, 355, 382, 386-7

Rice, cultivation of, x, 163-4

Rice ap Howell, in EDWARD II, xlvi, 63-8

Rice, Hugh ap, xxxv, 381

Rich, Lord, and More, xxxvi, 126

Richard I, accusations of God, v, 276

Richard II, Chaucer and, xxxix, 163; Raleigh on, 73; in Tyler's Rebellion, xxxv, 63, 66, 68, 70-3, 75-80

Richard III, Raleigh on, xxxix, 75-6; reference to, xl, 458

Richard the Third, stage presentation of, xxvii, 309

Richard, Archbishop of Canterbury, xxxv, 258

Richard of St. Victor, xx, 329 note 28

Richard of the Lea, the knight in ROBYN HODE, xl, 131-46, 162-4, 168, 170-3, 174, 180, 183

RICHARDSON, GABRIEL, EPITAPH FOR, vi, 513

Richardson, Samuel, Franklin on style of, i, 23; Hazlitt on, xxvii, 275

Richelet, Hugo on, xxxix, 365

Richelieu, Burke on, xxiv, 186; Joseph the Capuchin and, xxxix, 356; Louis XIII and, xxiv, 332-3; in Mantua contest, xxi, 78, 435, 466

RICHES, ESSAY ON, Bacon's, iii, 87-90

Riches, advantage of, remains to maker, v, 48; Burns on, vi, 48, 85, 204, 326; Cicero on, ix, 37; compensation of v, 88; Confucius on, xliv, 6 (15); Curius, Manlius, on, ix, 65; death and, xvi, 303-4, 312, 321; Dekker on, xl, 318-19; ECCLESIASTES on, xliv, 340 (10-14), 341 (1, 2), 346 (11); Emerson on true, v, 217-18; Epictetus on true, ii, 179 (182); friendship and, ix, 27; good and evil, xlvii, 801; grow in Hell, iv, 105; happiness and, i, 343, 344; xix, 364; heirs to, v, 49; Herbert on, xv, 390; why honorable, xxxiv, 365; in-

dependence of, v, 54; Jesus on, xliv, 369 (24), 387 (16-21), 401 (24-5); Job on, xliv, 120 (24-5, 28); Kempis on, vii, 273 (4); loss of, no misfortune, ii, 126 (25); Massinger on, xlvii, 917; Milton on, iv, 382-3; Morris on, xlii, 1196; Nashe on, xl, 260; Pascal on property of, xlviii, 109 (310); Penn on pursuit of, i, 390; poetical idea of, v, 226; Pope on, xl, 435, 437-8; as power, xxxiv, 360; Psalm on folly of trust in, xliv, 201-3; Raleigh on, xxxix, 90-1, 96; Raleigh on pursuit of, 90, 92-4; results of competition of, xxxiv, 370; Stoic dictum of, ix, 133; Thoreau's idea of, xxviii, 394; Utopian opinion of, xxxvi, 194, 200; virtue and, i, 342 (219); Walton on, xv, 329; Webster on, xlvii, 764; Woodnot on, xv, 388; Woolman on, i, 196 note, 211, 233 (see also Wealth)

Richmond, Duke of, and George Herbert, xv, 386

RIDDELL, CAPTAIN, LINES TO, vi, 328-9

RIDDELL, CAPTAIN, RHYMING REPLY TO, vi, 329

RIDDELL, MARIA, EPIGRAM ON, vi, 478

RIDDELL, MRS., ON BIRTHDAY OF, vi, 475-6

RIDDELL, ROBERT, LINES TO MEMORY OF, vi, 514

RIDDELL, ROBERT, SONNET ON, vi, 488

RIDDELL, WALTER, EPITAPH FOR, vi, 485

RIDDELL, MRS. WALTER, ON THE CARRIAGE OF, vi, 485

Ridiculous, Fielding on the, xxxix, 179

Riding, Locke on, xxxvii, 171, 172

Ridolfi, Niccolo, xxxi, 45-6 note 2

Riemer, on Goethe, v, 191

Rigby, Dr., xxxviii, 223, 245, 248

Right, Augustine, St., on wrong and, vii, 38-9; Confucius on seeing and doing, xliv, 9 (24); disputes on wrong and, xxxiv, 374; "doth its own likeness breed," viii, 35; Emerson on, v, 62, 283; Franklin's early view of, i, 55; "gives way to delight," viii, 321; Kant on tests of, xxxii, 332-5; law and, xxxiv, 391-2; "makes room where weapons want," xlvi, 58; Manzoni on, xxi, 19-20; James Mill on, xxv, 35-6; Pope on, xl, 408-15; for right's sake, xlv, 795; Rousseau on, xxxiv, 268; success as the measure of, ix, 278; of

the sword, Pascal on, xlviii, 305-6 (878)

Right Reason, Bentham on phrase, xxv, 44

Right-Timing, Penn on, i, 338

Righteousness, Æschylus on, viii, 36; Augustine, St., on, vii, 37-9; Burns on rigid, vi, 183; Confucius on, xliv, 52 (17), 55 (2); David on, 182 (15-22), 187-88, 213 (10-11); ECCLESIASTES on, 343 (15-16), (20), 344 (12, 14), 345 (2); Elihu on, 127-8 (2-8), 129 (6-7); Eliphaz on, 105 (3); of God, Elihu on, 128-9 (2-7); Justice compared with, xxxiv, 404-5; Pascal on hunger after, xlviii, 96 (264); "the path of," xl, 77; the Psalmist on, xliv, 288 (4-9); reward of, 261 (12-15); reward of desire for, xlv, 817; wickedness, contrasted with, xliv, 145, 232-4, 237 (10); Woolman on, i, 189

Rights, Burke on, of man, xxiv, 196-200; Hobbes on, natural, xxxiv, 391-2; Jefferson on, xliii, 150; of persons and of property, v, 240-3; renunciation and transference of, xxxiv, 392-3; social, 392-3, 408-9

RIGHTS OF WOMAN, THE, vi, 446-7

Rigogli, Giovanni, xxxi, 53-4

Rigor, pushed too far, xxvii, 445

RIGS O' BARLEY, vi, 44-5

Rimini, Francesca da, xx, 24; Hugo on, xxxix, 349

Rimini, Malatestino da, xx, 111 note 5; Cassero and, 116 note 9

Rimmon, the god, iv, 99

Rimsky-Korsakoff, influence of ARABIAN NIGHTS on, xvi, 4

Rinaldo, Dante on, xx, 362 note 4; Spenser on, xxxix, 62

Rinaldo d'Este, Dryden on, xiii, 33

RING AND THE BOOK, DEDICATION OF, xlii, 1109-10

Ringrave, Captain, xxxviii, 18

Ringrave, Count, death of, xxxviii, 51

Rinkart, Martin, hymn by, xlv, 558

Rio Grande River, xliii, 292, 294

Rio Negro, Darwin on, xxix, 70-1

Rio Sauce, Darwin on the, xxix, 112-3

Riolan, John, on the heart, xxxviii, 82

Riolanus, on arteries, xxxviii, 69

Riou, reference to, xli, 780

Ripamonti, on plague of Milan, xxi, 500

Ripheus, in Dante's PARADISE, xx, 372-3;

death of, xiii, 114; in sack of Troy, 111-3

Ripley, George, xlvii, 585 note 3

Riquet, and the Languedoc canal, x, 455

Risks, human contempt of, x, 110; Penn on, i, 345

Rites, Bacon on religious, iii, 45-6; Luther on religious, xxxvi, 372-3; Penn on religious, i, 363 (507), 387 (175)

Ritter, Heinrich, commentator on Antoninus and Epictetus, ii, 323

Ritter, Karl, Geikie on, xxx, 325

Rituals, without reverence, xliv, 12 (26)

Rivalry, friendship and, ix, 21-22; fruits of, xxvi, 98; Pliny on, happy, ix, 237

RIVER OF LIFE, by Campbell, xli, 775-6

Rivers, second Earl of, xxxix, 9-10, 13; death of, 75-6

Rivers, John, xxxiii, 230

Rivers, Pascal on, xlviii, 15 (17)

Riviere, Mercier de la, x, 444

RIZPAH, by Tennyson, xlii, 1011-14

Rizzio, murder of, xxxix, 359

Roads, expence of maintaining, x, 453-6; Smith on good, 150-1

ROADS, ROUGH, EPIGRAM ON, vi, 237

Roannez, Charlotte Gouffier de, xlviii, 346 note 2; letters to, 346-7

Roannez, M. de, on reason, xlviii, 98 (276)

Roanoak, colony of, xxxiii, 226-7, 257

ROB MORRIS, AULD, vi, 445

Robb, D. C., translator of Pasteur, xxxviii, 269

Robbers, in Dante's HELL, xx, 46, 52-3, 100-1; rich and poor, xlv, 673

Robert, of Normandy, Henry I and, xxxix, 72

Robert, king of Sicily, Dante on, xx, 317 note 11, 319 note 2; poets and, xxvii, 40

ROBERT OF LINCOLN, xlii, 1215-17

Roberton, Mr., on puerperal fever, xxxviii, 230-1, 244-5

Roberts, inventor of the mule, v, 395

Robertson, F. W., translator of Lessing, xxxii, 183

Robertson, Rev. John, Burns on, vi, 165, 242

Robertson, Joseph, of London Review, xxv, 129; Wordsworth on, v, 464

Robin, parable of the, xv, 206

Robin, M. Ch., xxxviii, 340-4

ROBIN GRAY, AULD, xli, 557-8

Robin Hood, Emerson on character of, v,

349; Maid Marian and, xli, 875 (see also Robyn Hode)

Robin the Ostler, in FAUSTUS, xix, 233-6

ROBIN-REDBREAST, CALL FOR THE, xl, 322-3

ROBIN SHURE IN HAIRST, vi, 324

Robinson, Mr. Alfred, marriage of, xxiii, 235-40; (in 1859), 385

Robinson, Gen., at Gettysburg, xliii, 329-30

Robinson, Henry Crabbe, and story of THE FISHERMAN, xvii, 83 note

Robinson, Ralph, translator of UTOPIA, xxxvi, 2

Robyn Hode, in ROBYN HODE, his friends and customs, xl, 129-32; the knight and, 132-9, 146, 162-4, 168-9; welcomes Little John, 151; with the Sheriff, 153-4; and the monk, 155, 157-61; at archery contest, 164-7; in knight's castle, 167-8; returns to greenwood, 170; rescues knight, 170-2; the king and, 173-83; at court, 183-4; returns to greenwood, 184-5; death, 185-6

ROBYN HODE, A GEST OF, xl, 128-86

Rochambeau, Count de, xliii, 169

Roche-sur-Yon, at Metz, xxxviii, 23, 24, 25; Navarre and, 47-8

Rochefoucauld, Duke de, Burke on, xxiv, 250, 418-19; Voltaire on Maxims of, xxxiv, 101

Rochester, Earl of, ON CHARLES II, xl, 383; Hugo on, xxxix, 380; Voltaire on, xxxiv, 142-4

Rockingham, Lord, Burns on, vi, 52; Burke and, xxiv, 5

Rocks, Geikie on, xxx, 328-9, 337-8; Lyell on volcanic, xxxviii, 396-7; metamorphic, xxx, 334-5; sedimentary, 330-1, 339-40; stratified and crystalline, xxxviii, 395

Rocks Wandering, the, xxii, 163

Roc's Egg, Aladdin and the, xvi, 421-2; story of the, 244-5, 274-5

RODDICK, WILLIAM, EPITAPH ON, vi, 487

Roderigo, in DUCHESS OF MALFI, xlvii, 758, 778-9, 847-8, 851, 852, 853

Roderigo, counsellor of Philip, xix, 290

Rodney, Emerson on character of, v, 349

RODNEY'S VICTORY, LINES ON, vi, 459-60

Rodolph, Emperor, Dante on, xx, 168 and note 12, 172-3

Rodrigo, Don, in I PROMESSI SPOSI, bravoes of, xxi, 15; relations with Ab-

bondio, 20-1; Lucia and, 38; palace and friends of, 71-82; conference with Cristoforo, 83-7; plans of vengeance, 103-4; rallied by Attilio, 105-6; plans to carry off Lucia, 106-8; learns failure of plans, 178-80; advises with Attilio, 181-3; plans to have Renzo banished, 188-9; learns Lucia's whereabouts, 291-2; determines to seek aid of the Unnamed, 292-3, 313-17; conference with Unnamed, 318-21; goes to Milan, 405-6; takes the plague, 536-8; taken to the Lazzaretto, 540-2; in the Lazzaretto, 590; death of, 629-30

Roebuck, John Arthur, Mill on, xxv, 54, 78, 79, 82, 95-7; in Parliament, 122; in Westminster Review, 63

Roger, in SHE STOOPS TO CONQUER, xviii, 216-17

Roger, in SHOEMAKER'S HOLIDAY (see Hodge)

Roger of Doncaster, xl, 186

Rogers, B. B., translator of Aristophanes, viii, 1

Rogers, Mr., first husband of Miss Read, i, 50, 66

Rogers, Samuel, POEMS by, xli, 582-3

Rohan, M. de, xxxviii, 13, 15, 18-19

Roland, in SONG OF ROLAND, with Charlemagne at Cordres, xlix, 98, 100; advises against Marsil, 101; offers to go to Marsil, 103; quarrel with Ganelon, 103-4, 105; Ganelon on, 107, 112; plot against, 108, 112-15; in return to France, 117; given rear guard, 118-21; prodigies preceding death of, 140; before battle of Roncesvalles, 126, 127, 128-30, 131; in the battle, 132, 135, 136-7, 138, 139, 142, 143-6, 147, 148, 149-50, 151; the horn of, 152-5, 170, 186; renews fight, 156-8, 159; with Olivier, 160-2; with Walter, 162-3; last fight, 163-6; with Archbishop Turpin, 166-9; his death, 169-73; body of, found by Charlemagne, 179-83; his tomb, 186; Renan on, xxxii, 158 (see also Orlando)

ROLAND, SONG OF, xlix, 95-195; remarks on, 94; l, 22

Roland de Vaux of Tryermaine, xli, 721, 723-4

Roman Catholic Church, Augustine, St., on the, vii, 83, 84; Bacon on, iii, 130; Browne on, 254 (3), 256 (5); Calvin on, xxxix, 32-3, 35-8, 41-3; cardinals

of, xxxvi, 276-7; Dante on, xx, 211, 377-8; in England, xxxv, 252-6, 266, 267; Hobbes on revolt from, xxxiv, 386-7; Hume on ceremonies of, xxxvii, 328; Knox on the, xxxix, 58; liberty of the press under, iii, 195-7; Luther on, xxxvi, 276-70; Machiavelli on temporal power of, 38-40; Mill on, xxv, 232-3; Pascal on, xlviii, 296 (849, 850), 300 (857-62), 303 (867), 304 (869-70), 306 (878, 881), 307 (885), 309 (890, 896), 311 (905), 315, 347, 348; services in, xxxv, 265; Shelley on, in Italy, xviii, 277 (see also Papacy)

Roman Classics, Sainte-Beuve on, xxxii, 122

Roman Empire, Bacon on fall of, iii, 139; decline of, xxxviii, 391-2; Hugo on fall of, xxxix, 344-5; liberty of press in, iii, 195-6; life in early (see Pliny, LETTERS); literary works of, l, 20, 25; Luther on, xxxvi, 327-8; Machiavelli on cause of overthrow of, 47; power of the soldiery in, 62-3

Roman Names, Plutarch on, xii, 155-6

Roman Provinces, ix, 396 note 1

Roman Time, ix, 233 note 4

ROMANCE AND CHRONICLE, xxxv

Romance-poetry, Arnold on the, xxviii, 75-7

Romances, Cervantes on, xiv, 474-7, 481, 487-8; defended by Don Quixote, 488-95; Fielding on, xxxix, 176-81; Whitman on, 402

Romanianus, friend of Augustine, vii, 95-6

Romano, Giulio, xxxi, 34 note 3, 55, 58, 60, 82

Romano, Ezzolino di, xx, 51 note 8

Romans, Caxton on the, xxxix, 15; eating customs of the, xxxv, 288; xxxvii, 17-18; education among the, 50 note; Emerson on the, v, 52; houses and public buildings of early, 52; poetry among the, xxvii, 8-9; swimming among, xxxvii, 13; Taine on the, xxxix, 421, 424

Romantic Literature, Hugo on, xxxix, 346

Romantic Movement, Hugo in, xxxix, 337 note; Wordsworth in, 268 note

Romanus, the martyr, xv, 265

Romanus, Voconius, Pliny on, ix, 218-19, 357-8; Pliny's letters to, 188, 211, 284, 318, 336

Rome, agrarian law of, x, 395-6; allies of, iii, 78; America and, ix, 7; assimilation of other nations by, xxviii, 248-9; Bacon on, v, 362; Bacon on triumphs of, iii, 80; bribery in, xii, 159-60; burning of, Chaucer on, xl, 49; custom of candidates in early, xii, 158-9; Carthage and, Virgil on, xiii, 174; Cicero on success of, iii, 44-5; civil war in, 38; xii, 292-4, 308-9; colonies of, x, 397; corn importations in, 153-4; England compared with, xxxiv, 85-6; of Evander's time, xiii, 279-80; foreign policy of, xxxvi, 19; freedom of, due to her arms, 41-2; freedom of press in, iii, 193-4; galleys of, xxxv, 357 note; the Germans and, xxxiii, 113-14; Goethe and Byron on, xxxii, 390 note; greatness of, prophesied, iii, 90; conquest of Greece, xxxvi, 11-12, 18; Grecian art in, xxxii, 237; history of, Carlyle on, xxv, 365-6; history of, Dante on, xx, 306-8; history of, Virgil on, xiii, 289-92; interest in, x, 96; kings of, Virgil on, xiii, 234-5; Luther on, xxxvi, 298; Marlowe on, xix, 230; medicine in, xxxv, 240; Milton on, iv, 396-9; money in, x, 29, 30, 31, 43; More on standing armies of, xxxvi, 145; naturalization policy of, iii, 76-7; penology in, xxxvi, 151; pigeons in ancient, xi, 40; poetry of, Shelley on, xxvii, 344; Prætorian emperors of, xxxvi, 22; present level of, xxx, 350; provincial policy of, xxxvi, 11-12, 17, 73-4; Raleigh on, xxxix, 71; religion and philosophy of, 431-2; religious matters in early, xii, 170; religious toleration in, xxxiv, 383; xxxvii, 393; republic of, Machiavelli on, xxv, 368-9; Republican, works dealing with, l, 20, 25; sack of, by Imperialists, xxxi, 68-80; seditions in early, xii, 150-2, 157-8; See of (see Papacy); selection known in, xi, 45; Shelley on, xli, 868; value of silver in, x, 182; slavery in early, xii, 169-70; study of language in, xxxvii, 146, 162; Taine on, xxxix, 424; turdi cultivated in, x, 188; of Virgil's time, Dryden on, xiii, 15-17; Volscian Wars of, xii, 152-4, 171-82

Romeo, steward of Raymond Berenger, xx, 309 note 26

Romeo and Juliet, Lamb on, xxvii, 302; Ruskin on, xxviii, 138

Romilly, Sir Samuel, apprentice bill of, v,

393; on buying seat in Parliament, 364
note; on chancery, 364; on English
laws, 347; his love for his wife, 370;
Mill and, xxv, 67; on public speaking,
v, 360

Romilly, Edward, xxv, 122

Romilly, John, xxv, 122

Romoaldo, S., xx, 379 note 5

Romoli, Vincenzio, xxxi, 127, 128, 129,
161, 163, 169

Romulus, the asylum of, xiii, 279; Dryden on, 17; Machiavelli on, xxxvi, 20,
21; ordered Romans to live in arms,
iii, 77-8; parentage of, xx, 318 note 16;
prophecy of, xiii, 82; suckled by Wolf,
289; Virgil on, 233; Waller on, xxxiv,
146

RONALDS OF THE BENNALS, THE, vi, 25-7

Roncesvalles, battle of, xlix, 94 127-73

Roncevaux (see Roncesvalles)

Ronsard on the ÆNEID, xiii, 43, 44; Montaigne on, xxxii, 62; Taine on, xxxix,
428-9

Roosevelt, Theodore, CONVENTION WITH
PANAMA, xliii, 450-62

Roper, William, son-in-law of More,
xxxvi, 88; LIFE OF MORE, 89-134

Ropes, Henry, at Gettysburg, xliii, 367

Rosa, Vincent de la, in the goatherd's
story, xiv, 500-2

ROSABELLE, xli, 748-50

ROSALIND'S MADRIGAL, xl, 214-15

ROSALINE, by Lodge, xl, 215-16

Rosas, General, xxix, 74, 78, 80-1, 109-
10, 146

Rosaura, in LIFE IS A DREAM, arrival in
Poland, xxvi, 7-13; with Segismund,
14-17; with Clotaldo, 18-21; at palace,
with Segismund, 41; reason of coming
to Poland, 66-7; returns to tower, with
Segismund, 67-8; reunited with Astolfo, 73

Roscius, case of, xii, 219-20

Roscommon, Lord, Silenus of, xiii, 57;
Voltaire on, xxxiv, 147; Wordsworth
on, xxxix, 330

Rose, in SHOEMAKER'S HOLIDAY (see Oateley)

ROSE, A WHITE, xlii, 1198

ROSE, THE RED, RED, vi, 482-3

Rose, Aquila, i, 22; elegy on, 27; son of,
64

ROSE AYLMER, xli, 898

ROSE-BUD, A, BY MY EARLY WALK, vi,
287

ROSE-RED AND SNOW-WHITE, xvii, 213-18

Rosegli, Mariano, xxxi, 424

Rosemary, flower of remembrance, xli,
481; xlvi, 182

Rosencrantz, in HAMLET, xlvi, 124-5,
131-5, 140, 142-3, 149, 150, 156-7,
159-60, 169, 170, 172-3, 175, 184,
200, 210

Roses, Harrison on, xxxv, 242-3; Massinger on, xlvii, 864

ROSES IN THE BOSOM OF CASTARA, xl, 252

Roses, Wars of the, Raleigh on, xxxix, 79

ROSLIN INN, EPIGRAM AT, vi, 263

Ross, in MACBETH, reports victory to
Duncan, xlvi, 323-4; messenger to
Macbeth, 327; and the old man, 348;
with Macduff, 348-9; at the banquet,
357, 359, 361; with Lady Macduff,
370-1; at English Court, 378-80; with
Siward, 393

Ross, Alexander, WOOED AND MARRIED,
xli, 567-8

Ross, Captain, at Keeling Island, xxix,
456, 461

Rösselmann, the priest in WILLIAM TELL,
at Rooth league, xxvi, 417-28; before
Gessler's cap, 437; with Tell at Altdorf,
439-48; reports murder of emperor,
477-8

Rossetti, Christina Georgina, poems by,
xlii, 1181-3

Rossetti, Dante Gabriel, poems by, xlii,
1149-83

Rossi, Girolamo de', xxxi, 247 note 1,
298-9, 335-6

Rosso, Il, xxxi, 46 note 1, 54, 195-6, 301
and note, 324

Rotund, the, in building, xxiv, 63 and
note

Rouen, capture of, xxxviii, 47; Smith on,
x, 263-4

ROUGH ROADS, EPIGRAM ON, vi, 237

Roughness, of manners, xxxvii, 121; more
sublime than smoothness, xxiv, 61;
why not beautiful, 120-1

Roumania, Freeman on, xxviii, 264-6

Round Table, The, xxxv, 135-6; why
founded, 168; knights of the, xiv,
92; Renan on the, xxxii, 157-8; Tennyson on the, xlii, 992; seen at Winchester, xxxix, 21

Round Top, at Gettysburg, xliii, 333, 335

ROUND TOWER AT JHANSI, xlii, 1183

Rous, Sir Francis, xxv, 369-70

Rousseau, Jean Jacques, his principles of

composition, xxiv, 303-4; remarks on *Confessions* of, xxxi, 3; editor's remarks on DISCOURSE of, l, 32; Emerson on, v, 265; Hume and, xxvii, 202; Hazlitt on, 279-80; Hobbes and, xxxiv, 308; ON INEQUALITY, 164-228; life and works, 162-3; Mill on work of, xxv, 241; SAVOYARD VICAR, xxxiv, 229-305; Sainte-Beuve on SAVOYARD VICAR of, xxxii, 123; Stevenson on, xxviii, 289

Roux, Maitre, xxxi, 46 note 1, 54

ROVER, THE, by Scott, xli, 743-4

Rovere, Francesco Maria della, xxxi, 73 note 1

ROWAN TREE, THE, xli, 564

Rowe, Nicholas, editor of Shakespeare, xxxix, 234-5, 244; Johnson on, 232; on Shakespeare, 229

Rowlands, Richard, OUR BLESSED LADY'S LULLABY, xl, 256-60

Rowley, in SCHOOL FOR SCANDAL, with Sir Peter, xviii, 126-8; with Sir Oliver, 139; plans to try Charles and Joseph Surface, 141-2; with Charles Surface, 162; with Sir Oliver, 163; in visit to Joseph Surface, 177; announces arrival of Sir Oliver, 180; with Sir Peter after scandal, 185-7; at Joseph Surface's, 190-5

Roxalana, Solyman's wife, iii, 50

Roxanes, and Themistocles, xii, 30

Roy, M. le, i, 148

ROYAL GEORGE, LOSS OF THE, xli, 533-4

Royal Society of England, Franklin and, i, 146, 148-9

Royalty, Calvin on true, xxxix, 29-30

Roye, Lord, xxxv, 56-7

Royer-Collard, Rémusat on, xxxii, 125

Rozinante, horse of Don Quixote, dialogue with Babieca, xiv, 13-14; Don Quixote on, 216; the mares and, 110-11; named, 20-1, 70-1; sonnet on, 514-15

Ruæus, commentator of Virgil, xiii, 43, 44, 50, 56-7

RUBAIYAT OF OMAR KHAYYAM, xli, 943-58

Rubens, Hazlitt on, xxvii, 279; Hugo on, xxxix, 348, 352

Rubicant, the demon, xx, 88, 90

Rubicon, passage of the, xii, 291-2

Rucellai, Cosimo, xxvii, 392-3

Rucellai, Luigi, xxxi, 144

RUDELY THOU WRONGEST MY HEART'S DESIRE, xl, 250-1

Rudeness, grandeur and, xxiv, 66

Rudenz, Ulrich of, in WILLIAM TELL, with Attinghausen, xxvi, 405-10; in love with Bertha, 411; with Bertha in the forest, 432-6; with Gessler in Altdorf, 441; defies Gessler, 445-6; joins the League, 461-4; takes Sarnen keep, 475; recovers Bertha, 475-6; in final scene, 488-9

Rudeyneh, xvi, 326 note

Rudimentary Organs, xi, 469-77; in classification, 434-5; highly variable, 152

Ruffo, John, Cervantes on, xiv, 54

Rufinus, letter to, ix, 327-9

Rufus, C. Musonius, ii, 116, 118 (5) and note

Rufus, Calvisius, letter to, ix, 246-7

Rufus, Caninius, letter to, ix, 236-7

Rufus, Corellius, Pliny on, ix, 197-9

Rufus, Curtius, story of ghost and, ix, 311-12

Rufus, Satrius, in Certus's case, ix, 341

Rufus, Verginius, Pliny on, ix, 211-13, 282-3

RUGBY CHAPEL, xlii, 1130-5

Ruggieri, Archbishop, xx, 135-6 note 1

Rugians, Tacitus on the, xxxiii, 117-18

RUIN, To, by Burns, vi, 194-5

RUINED FARMER, IN THE CHARACTER OF A, vi, 22-3

RUISSEAUX, ROBERT, ELEGY ON THE DEATH OF, vi, 93-4

Rukh's Egg, story of the, xvi, 244-5, 274-5; Aladdin and, 421-2

RULE, BRITANNIA, xl, 442-3

Rulers, Bacon on, iii, 48-52; Confucius's advice to, xliv, 5 (5), 7 (1, 3), 8 (19, 20), 9 (21), 38 (9), 39 (17, 19), 41 (1, 2, 3), 42 (6, 13), 43 (15, 17), 50 (44), 51 (4, 10), 67 (2); Epictetus to, ii, 128 (34); Franklin on, i, 125; partisanship of, iii, 37; reverence for, 37-8 (see also Princes)

Rules, for children, xxxvii, 43-4; laying down, for others, ii, 293 (29)

Rum, Indians and, i, 116; Woolman on selling, 258-9

Ruminants, and pachyderms, xi, 362

Rumor, Æschylus on, viii, 18; Bacon on, iii, 140-2; false, a sign of sedition, 36; in Milton's Chaos, iv, 132-3; Raleigh on, xxxix, 67; Virgil on, xiii, 158-9

RUMPELSTILTSKIN, story of, xvii, 154-6

Ruodi, in WILLIAM TELL, xxvi, 381-6, 474, 476, 477

Rupilius, Publius, made consul by Scipio, ix, 34

Rush, Richard, correspondence with Bagot, xliii, 265-7

Ruskin, John, Greenough and, v, 316-17; life and works of, xxviii, 92; SESAME AND LILIES, 93-162

Russel, the fox, xl, 48

Russell, first Baron, xxiv, 401-4

Russell, Lord John, pluck of, v, 366-7

Russell, Rev., John, Burns on, vi, 94-5, 101, 163, 166, 351

Russell, Jonathan, xliii, 255

Russell, Mr., in Two YEARS BEFORE THE MAST, xxiii, 94, 99, 141, 245-6

Russell, W. Clark, on Dana's work, xxiii, 4

Russia, the bureaucracy of, xxv, 308-9; monks in, iii, 99; TREATY WITH UNITED STATES, xliii, 432-6

Rusticity, Burns on, vi, 248; Locke on, xxxvii, 72

Rusticucci, Giacopo, xx, 66 and note 3; in Hell, 27

Rusticus, Q. Junius, teacher of Marcus Aurelius, ii, 193-4 (7), 199, 303, 321

Rusticus Arulenus, his death, ix, 188 note, 190 note; wife of, 261 note

Rustum, reference to, xli, 944

Ruth, Bunyan on, xv, 210; in Dante's PARADISE, xx, 419 note 2; Keats on, xli, 878; Milton on, iv, 78

RUTH: OR THE INFLUENCES OF NATURE, xli, 607-14

Rutherford, Milton on, iv, 80

Rütimeyer, on cattle, xi, 33

Ruysum, in EGMONT, xix, 254-9

Rymer, Dryden on, xxxix, 155

Saadi, on the ugly schoolmaster, v, 306

Saavedra, the captive, xiv, 394 (see Cervantes)

Sabacos, king of Egypt, xxxiii, 69-70, 77

Sabæans, Mohammed on, xlv, 1001

Sabbath, Emerson on the, v, 34, 41; Jesus on the, xliv, 368 (1-11), 391 (14-16), 392 (1-6); Pascal on the, xlviii, 198

Sabbath, Laws, Mill on, xxv, 286-7

Sabellius, Dante on, xx, 343 note 21

Sabinian, and heathen antiquities, iii, 137

Sabinianus, letters to, ix, 344, 346

Sabines, rape of the, alluded to, xiii, 289

Sabinus, Statius, letter to, ix, 252

Sable, Marchioness de, letter to, xlviii, 342

Sabrina, in COMUS, iv, 66-9

Sachems, Indian, xliii, 142

Sacheverell, Henry, xxvii, 157

Saci, M. de, conversation with Pascal, xlviii, 387-400

Sackville, Lord, Burns on, vi, 52

Sacrament, of the Altar, Kempis on, vii, 335-64

Sacraments, Quakers on the, xxxiv, 67

Sacred Poetry, Sidney on, xxvii, 11-12

SACRED WRITINGS, xliv, xlv

Sacrifices, Confucius on, xliv, 10 (12), 11 (17); Hindu doctrine of, xlv, 800, 806, 864; Pascal on, xlviii, 333

Sacrilege, Dr. Donne on, xv, 350

Sadducees, xliv, 406-7 (27-40), 433 (17), 474 (7-8); Hobbes on the, xxxiv, 357

Sadness, connection of, with beauty, xxviii, 382

SAGA AND EPIC, xlix

Sagacity, Mr., in PILGRIM'S PROGRESS, xv, 178, 191

Sagas, Emerson on the, v, 343-4

Sages, in the ÆNEID, xiii, 412

Saibah, xlv, 1004 note

Sailing, Franklin on, i, 157

Sailors, Dana on life of, xxiii, 356-7; duties of, 18-21; how to improve their condition, 357-74; Woolman on hardships and depravity of, i, 292-5, 301

Sailor Songs, Dana on, xxiii, 259

ST. AGNES, THE EVE OF, xli, 883-93

St. André, Louis of, xxxviii, 21

St. Andrea, Giacomo da, xx, 56 note 4

St. Aubin, Capt., xxxviii, 46

St. Augustine (see Augustine)

St. Augustine, Drake at, xxxiii, 256, 259

St. Bartholomew, massacre of, Bacon on, iii, 14; Capt. Tetu on, xxxiii, 186

Sainte-Beuve, Charles Augustin, on charlatanism, xxviii, 66; as a critic, l, 48-9; life and writings, xxxii, 104; ON MONTAIGNE, 105-20; Port Royal of, xxxix, 415-16; Taine on, 417; WHAT IS A CLASSIC, xxxii, 121-33

ST. CECILIA'S DAY, SONG FOR, xl, 389-90

St. Clair, Sir John, i, 132

Saint-Cyran, letter of, xlviii, 323-4

St. Denis, battle of, xxxviii, 50

St. Domingo, Drake at, xxxiii, 227, 240-4, 258-9; productions of, x, 399-401; village of, xxix, 13

St. Elmo's Light, xxix, 47

St. Etienne, Raband de, on National Assembly, xxiv, 300 note

St. Helena, island of, xxix, 489-94; species of, xi, 414

Saint-Hilaire, Geoffroy, on compensation of growth, xi, 150-1; on homologous parts, 453; on origin of species, 10, 15-16

St. John, H. (see Bolingbroke)

St. John, Newfoundland, settlement of, xxxiii, 262, 279-80

St. John's River, navigation of, xliii, 284

St. Jago, Darwin on, xxix, 11-16; health conditions at, 369-70

St. Lawrence River, navigation of, xliii, 286

Saint-Lo, Edward III at, xxxv, 13; importance of, 12 note

Saint-Martin, Capt., xxxii, 14

St. Omer, the iconoclasts at, xix, 260

St. Paul's Rocks, Darwin on, xxix, 18-19

St. Peter's, the building of, xxxvi, 247, 255, 258

St. Quentin, the wounded of, xxxviii, 44-5

Saint-Simon, Mill on, xxv, 42; Mill on school of, 103-6

St. Winifred's Well, xxxvii, 13

SAINT, FOLLOW YOUR, xl, 284

Saintré, John of, xxxv, 46, 47, 50-1

Saints, Bunyan on the, xv, 57; canonization of, xxv, 215-16; disputes on the merits of, vii, 331-3; Hume on relics of, xxxvii, 330-2; Kempis on the, vii, 220-2; Luther on glorification of, xxxvi, 310-13; Pascal on, xlviii, 275, 303 (868), 358-9; patience of the, vii, 300 (3)

Saint's Days, Luther on, xxxvi, 308-9

Saïs, city of, xxxiii, 34-5, 82, 84, 88

Sakelde, in KINMONT WILLIE, xl, 108, 110-11

Saki, reference to the, xli, 949

Sakka, the god, xlv, 611, 613-14, 618, 699-700

Saladin, Emerson on, v, 202; in Limbo, xx, 20 and note 7

Salamanca, Bishop of (see Bobadilla)

Salamander, Cellini and the, xxxi, 10-11; invoked by Faust, xix, 55

Salamis, Æschylus at, viii, 5; Aristides at, xii, 86; battle of, 16-17; Byron on, xli, 813; drama on, viii, 5

Salaries, of public officials, l, 354 (385-6); taxes on, x, 513-14

SALATHIEL PAVY, ON, xl, 299-300

Sale, Sir Robert, in Tyler's Rebellion, xxxv, 73-4

Salem, reference to, iv, 25 (6)

Salih, brother of Jullanar, xvi, 330-7

Salimbene, Francesco, xxxi, 24, 28

Salimbeni, Niccoli, xx, 122 and note

Salinator, and Fabius, ix, 49

Salinator, Fuscus, Pliny on, ix, 283, 292

Salius, death of, xiii, 347; in the foot-race, 188-9

Salisbury Cathedral, Emerson on, v, 459-60

Salisbury, Earl of, in Tyler's Rebellion, xxxv, 68, 70, 79

Salisbury, university of, xxxv, 371

Sallust, on the viper, xxxv, 345 note

Sallust, on war, xxxvi, 145

Sallustius, Cicero on, ix, 110

Sallutio, Scipio, xii, 306-7

SALLY IN OUR ALLEY, xl, 403-5

Salmanassar, reference to, iv, 391

Salmasius, defender of Charles the First, iv, 4

Salmon and Dog-fish, tale of, xlvii, 813

Salmoneus, in Tartarus, xiii, 226-7

Salmydessos, viii, 192-3 and note 46

Salomon's House (see Solomon's House)

Salt, crystallization of common, xxx, 31 note 12; the desire of vegetarians for, xxix, 116; incrustations of, in Patagonia, 84-5; Locke on use of, xxxvii, 17; used to melt ice, xxx, 30

Salt-lakes, in South America, xxix, 72-4

Salterello, Lapo, xx, 351 note 12

Salutations, Mohammed on, xlv, 976

Salvani, Provenzano, xx, 190 and note

Salvation, Browne on, iii, 305-9; Bunyan on means of, xv, 228; Calvin on, xxxix, 32-3, 48-51; Dante on requisites of, xx, 311-13, 367-8, 421; Jesus on, xliv, 382, 401-2 (18-30); Lessing on, xxxii, 201; Luther on, xxxvi, 247-8, 255, 258, 347, 348, 351, 352, 362-3; meaning of, xv, 228; of non-Christians, xx, 367, 372-3; Peter on, xliv, 430 (12); Ruskin on false ideas of, xxviii, 109; the Wall of, in PILGRIM'S PROGRESS, xv, 41

Salviati, Alamanno, xxxi, 408 note

Salviati, Cardinal, xxxi, 114-15, 119, 273 note

Salviati, Giovanni, xxxi, 45 note 2

Salviati, Jacopo, xxxi, 14 note 4, 68-9, 74, 75

Salviati, Piero, xxxi, 413

Salzburg, Archbishop of, xix, 336

Sam, in Two Years Before the Mast, xxiii, 99-101, 107, 126, 397

Sama-Ved, xlv, 832

Samarchand, Temir's throne, iv, 328

Samaria, founding of church in, xliv, 439 (5-8); the woman of, xx, 230

Samaritan, the good, xliv, 382-3 (33-5)

Samaritans, belief confined to Pentateuch, iii, 277 (25)

Samos, war with Athens, xii, 61-4

Sampson, John, xxxiii, 229, 231-2, 234-5, 237, 247, 250, 254

Samson, Browne on, iii, 273; Delilah and, iv, 287; slays with the jaw-bone of an ass, xv, 296

Samson, in Samson Agonistes, lament of, iv, 414-17; his deeds sung by chorus, 417-19; his marriages, 420; his victory over Philistines, 421; Manoa's lament over, 423-4; reveals secret to Dalila, 424-5; hears of feast, 425; relates how shorn by Dalila, 428; his despair, 428-31; rejects reconcilement with Dalila, 432-9; with Harapha, 441-6; summoned to show feats of strength, 447; goes to temple, 450; his feat there, 455-9

Samson, Duke, in Song of Roland, xlix, 98, 120, 134-5, 145, 167

Samson Agonistes, iv, 414-59; Bagehot on, xxviii, 178-9; date of, iv, 5; introduction to, 412-13

Samuel, Luther on, xxxvi, 330; the Psalmist on, xliv, 267 (6-8); Saul and, xv, 336-7

Samuel, in Pilgrim's Progress, xv, 229, 247, 253, 282, 287

San Carlo, plague of, xxi, 502

San Diego (1834), xxiii, 96; in (1859), 388-90; Dana on, 120

San Francisco (1834), Dana on, xxiii, 220, 226-7; (in 1835), 375-6; (in 1859), 376-82; Drake in Bay of, xxxiii, 213; history of, xxiii, 392-3

San Gallo, Antonio da, xxxi, 196 note 1

San Gallo, Francesco da, xxxi, 392 and note

San Juan, Dana on, xxiii, 136-7

San Lorenzo, island of, xxix, 373

San Pedro (in 1859), xxiii, 386

San Pedro Island, Darwin on, xxix, 284-5

San Severino, Roberto of, xxxvi, 43

San Salvador, Columbus on, xliii, 21

Sanacharib, expedition against Egypt, xxxiii, 71

Sancho, Panza, Cervantes on, xiv, 10; Gandaline to, 13; becomes squire to Don Quixote, 58-9; promises not to aid master against knights, 63; beaten by the lackeys, 65; asks for promised island, 73; reason of name, 71; conversation with Don Quixote, 73-7; prefers to eat without ceremony, 78-9; the carriers and, 110-11; his doubts, 111-16; relates the adventure, 118; his idea of knight-errantry, 118-19; adventure with Maritornes, 122-7; takes Don Quixote's balsam, 128-9; refuses to pay innkeeper and is tossed in blanket, 131-3; discouraged, 134-5; in adventure of hearse, 145-7; tries to dissuade Don Quixote from perilous adventure, 153-4; his tale, 155-7; his distress, 158-60; rebuked for his merriment, 162-4; plans for his future earldom, 174-5; loses his ass, 189; finds wallet, 189-90; rebels, 209-11; despatched with letter to Dulcinea, 222-5, 288-93; his embassy, 229-32; returns with curate and barber, 235-6; does not wish to become a churchman, 271; nor a ruler of Moors, 274; becomes vassal of Micomicona, 283; quarrel with Quixote over Dulcinea, 300-3; recovers his ass, 284-6; in wine-bags adventure, 347-51; the barber and, 447-9; 451-4; enchanted, 462; promised his wages, 465; the curate and, 473; proves his master not enchanted, 483-5; plans for his earldom, 495-6; lament over Don Quixote, 509; his return home, 511-12; sonnet to, 515; epitaph on, 515; Lowell on, xxviii, 438; story of wine, xxvii, 209-10

Sanctuary, right of, among Romans, ix, 369 note 1

Sand Dunes, Darwin on, xxix, 82

Sandauce, children of, xii, 17, 87

Sanderson, Robert, Walton's life of, xv, 322

Sands of Dee, xlii, 1061

Sandwich Islanders, belief of, v, 98; Dana on, xxiii, 141-7, 242

Sandwich Islands, Dana on, xxiii, 242

Sandwich Land, snow in, xxix, 253

Sandys, Sir Edwin, xxvii, 56

Sandys, George, Dryden on, xxxix, 154

Sanga, Battista, xxxi, 98 note 7

Sangreal (see Holy Grail)

Sanhedrin, Pascal on the, xlviii, 237

Sanjaya, xlv, 785, 790, 791, 835-6, 840, 844, 874

Sañjiva, xlv, 733

Sankara, xlv, 832

Sânkhya, xlv, 794, 799, 820-1

Sanna, in story of FUNDEVOGEL, xvii, 140-2

Sannayâs, xlv, 866

Sansovino, Giacopo del, xxxi, 149 note 2, 153-4, 356

Sant Angel, Luis de, xliii, 21

Santa Barbara, xxiii, 57-9; (in 1859), 384-6; fandango at, 236-40; funeral at, 129-30

Santa Croce, Paolo, referred to, xviii, 352

Santa Cruz River, Darwin on, xxix, 182-5

Santacroce, Antonio, xxxi, 71, 72, 79

Santi, the goldsmith, xxxi, 33

Santiago, Cape Verde Islands, Drake at, xxxiii, 226, 258

Santiago, Chili, Darwin on, xxix, 266-7; Drake at, xxxiii, 209

Santiago, Island of, xxxiii, 202

Santiago de Tolou, xxxiii, 132; Drake at, 155-6

Santini, Giovan Battista, xxxi, 425

Sapia, of Sienna, xx, 197 and note 3

Sapor, and Valerian, xxxix, 98

Sapphira, wife of Ananias, xliv, 432 (1-10); Bunyan on, xv, 125; Dante on, xx, 228

Sappho, Byron on, xli, 812

SAPPHO REDIVIVUS, vi, 327-8

Saragossa, Charlemagne at, xlix, 95, 184-5

Sarah, and Abraham, xxxvi, 272; lies of, xv, 260; in Paradise, xx, 419

Sarandib, island of, xvi, 288

Sardanapalus, xx, 350 note 6; Calvin on, xxxix, 43-4; city-building of, xxxv, 359; stealing of treasures of, xxxiii, 76

Sarepta (see Zarephath)

Sāriputta, xlv, 701, 733; the Demons and, 710-11

Sark, battle of, vi, 175 note 5

Sarlabous, Captain, xxxviii, 49

Sarmatia, ix, 368 note 3

Sarmatians, Tacitus on the, xxxiii, 119-20

Sarmentus, Octavius's page, xii, 368

Sarmiento, Don Juan, xxxiii, 323, 331

Sarmiento, Mount, xxix, 246

Sarmen, Meyer von, in WILLIAM TELL, xxvi, 412-25

Sarpedon, death of, xiii, 337; reference to, 76

Sarrebruck, Earl of, xxxv, 12, 36, 38, 46

SARTO, ANDREA DEL, xlii, 1087-94

Satan, in BOOK OF JOB, xliv, 71-2

Satan, in PARADISE LOST, seducer of mankind, iv, 88; his fall and awakening in Hell, 89-90; speech with Beelzebub, 90-2; rises and wakens the fallen angels, 93-6; raising of his standard, 101; speech to the angels, 103-4; proposes man's seduction, 104, 117; in council of fallen angels, 108-9; undertakes to find out man and his world, 118-20; issues from council, 121; wings to gates of Hell, 124; meets Sin and Death, 125-8; voyage through chaos to the world, 132-5; seen by God flying to earth, 137; on outer sphere of world, 146; beholds interior of world, 149; in the sun, 150-1; inquires way to earth, 152; first view of earth, 153-154; alights on Niphates, 154; his remorse, 155-7; decides against submission, 157; his perturbation betrays him, 157-8; arrives at Eden, 158-9; sees Adam and Eve, 162; resolves to work fall of man, 164-5, 168; found at Eve's ear, 175; before Gabriel, 177-80; stirs rebellion in Heaven, 197-8, 199-200; rebuked by Abdiel, 201; asserts self-existence of angels, 202; in the rebel forces, 206; combat with Abdiel, 207-9; encounter with Michael, 210-12; encourages his forces, 214-5; proposes infernal engines, 216; in second day's battle, 218, 219; returns to Eden, 262; assumes form of serpent, 262, 265; his spite, 262-5; tempts Eve, 271-80; returns to Hell, 299-303; announces his success, 302-3; changed to a serpent, 303-4; how overcome by Christ, 351-3

Satan, in PARADISE REGAINED, undertakes to ensnare Christ, iv, 360-2; tempts him in guise of old man, 367-71; appeals to fellows for aid, 374-5; undertakes to tempt Christ again, 377; tempts Jesus to eat, 379-82; tempts with riches, 382-4; tempts by glory, 384-7; tempts Jesus to assume his throne, 387-395; shows him kingdoms of earth, 390-2; shows Rome, 396-7; demands that Christ worship him, 399; tempts by offer of wisdom, 400-4; warns him of sorrows in store, 404-5; tempts by fear, 405-10; carries Jesus

above Jerusalem, 408-9; his fall, 409; overcome by Christ, 410-11

Satan, Bagehot on Milton's, xxviii, 191-2, 198-202; Burke on Milton's portrait of, xxiv, 53; Calvin on, xxxix, 43; Goethe on name of, xix, 107; the grotesque in ideas of, xxxix, 347-8; Mohammedan (see Iblis); meaning of name of, iv, 300; Shelley on Milton's, xxvii, 348-9

Satiety, and fear of death, iii, 10

SATIRE, A, by Johnson, xli, 504-5

Satires, Sidney on, xxvii, 26-7; Swift on, 115-16; Wordsworth on, xxxix, 299

Satirists, Dryden on, xviii, 16-18

Satisfaction, Bacon on, xxxix, 121; Johnson on, 198-9; never attained, v, 232-3, 235

Sattwan, xlv, 853, 863-69

Saturn, Dante on reign of, xx, 375 note 5; in Italy, xiii, 278; Jove and, iv, 66; Milton on, 101; Plutarch on, iii, 45; Vesta and, iv, 34

Saturn, the planet, Dante's seventh Heaven, xx, 374

Saturnalia, feast of, ix, 226 note 3

Saturnia, Virgil on, xiii, 319

Saturninus, bequest of, ix, 272

SATYR AND MAN, fable of, xvii, 33

Satyric Drama, xii, 40 note

Satyrs, reference to the, iv, 73

Satyrus, the actor, and Demosthenes, xii, 196

Satyrus, A. Caninius, relations with Cicero, ix, 82

Saufeius, Cicero on, ix, 146

Saul, king of Israel, xliv, 451 (21); Dante on, xx, 192; David and, xli, 488; xliv, 213; Jonathan and, xliii, 98, 104; Psalms on David's deliverance from, xliv, 160-4, 211-12; his vision of Samuel, xv, 337; the witch of Endor and, iii, 90

SAUL, SONG OF, BEFORE HIS LAST BATTLE, xli, 812

Saul, the apostle (see Paul)

Saunderson, Mr., Burke on, xxiv, 134

Sauntering, origin of word, xxviii, 395

Saurophagus, Darwin on the, xxix, 61-2

Saussure, in the Alps, xxx, 224

Saut-perdu, horse of Malquiant, xlix, 146

Savage, James, Channing on, xxviii, 366

Savage State, progress of man from, xxxii, 284, 292; Rousseau on the, xxxiv, 168-95, 204

Savages, Darwin on, xxix, 506-7; poverty of, x, 5-6; power of imitation among, xxix, 211

Save-all, Mr., in PILGRIM'S PROGRESS, xv, 104-9

Savella, in THE CENCI, comes to summon Cenci, xviii, 331; finds him dead, 332-3; finds Orsino's letter, 334; with Beatrice and Lucretia, 334-7

Savelli, Giovan Battista, xxxi, 134 note 3

Saveself, in PILGRIM'S PROGRESS, xv, 154

Savile, Sir Henry, xxvii, 56

Saving, economically considered, x, 266-7; motives of, 269, 270; not happiness, xix, 364

Savonarola, Machiavelli on, xxxvi, 21; the party of, xxxi, 30 note 1, 32 note 1

Savoyard, story of the, xxxii, 45

SAVOYARD VICAR, FAITH OF A, xxxiv, 229-305; editorial remarks on, 162-3; Sainte-Beuve on, xxxii, 123

SAW YE BONIE LESLEY, vi, 442-3

SAW YE MY DEAR, MY PHILLY, vi, 501

Saxo Grammaticus, xlvi, 92

Saxon Race, Emerson on the, v, 472

Saxons, Celts and, v, 338; in England, 352-3

Saxony, breeding in, xi, 43

Say, M., Mill on, xxv, 42

SAY NOT THE STRUGGLE NAUGHT AVAILETH, xlii, 1119

Say-well, in PILGRIM'S PROGRESS, xv, 81

Sayce, Mr., quoted, xxviii, 240, 242

Saying, and Doing, Bunyan on, xv, 83

Sbietta, Lo, xxxi, 421-7, 428-30, 431-3

Scæva, Cassius, xii, 277

Scævola Pontifex, Cicero on, ix, 9

Scævola, Quintus Mucius, his part in Cicero's essay on Friendship, ix, 9-11; the publicani and, 132

Scala, Alberto della, xx, 219 note 9

Scala, Can Grande della, Dante on, xx, 359 note 14; leader of Ghibellines, 281 note 6; patron of Dante, 3; reference to, 7 note 6

Scales (constellation), Milton on, iv, 180

Scali, Giorgio, xxxvi, 35

Scaliger, and M. Aurelius Antoninus, ii, 308; on his emendations, xxxix, 248-9; on poets, xxvii, 38-40; Sainte-Beuve on, xxxii, 125; on Virgil, xiii, 37-8; xxvii, 50

Scandal, Garrick on, xviii, 113-14; punishment of, in Dante's HELL, xx, 115-18; Sheridan's Maria on, xviii, 120

Scander Beg, xlvii, 489 note 9

Scaptius, M., ix, 143-4

Scaramouch, xlviii, 13 note 1

Scarborough, John, i, 194

SCARING SOME WATER-FOWL, ON, vi, 285-6

Scarlatina, and cowpox, xxxviii, 215-16

Scarlet Fever, Jenner on the, xxxviii, 164

Scarlok, in ROBYN HODE, in adventure with knight, xl, 129, 131, 136, 137-8; with monk, 155; at archery contest, 165; at shoot in forest, 179; with Robyn at court, 183

Scarmiglione, Dante on, xx, 87

Scarron, Goldsmith on feasts of, xli, 505; Hugo on, xxxix, 351

Scatheloke (see Scarlok)

Scelidotherium, Darwin on the, xxix, 88-9, 90

Sceptic, in FAUST, xix, 189

Sceptical Philosophy, Hume on, xxxvii, 319-20, 407-20

Scepticism, Bacon on, xxxix, 141, 143; Bacon on contemporary, iii, 7; Berkeley on, xxxvii, 190-2, 231-2, 267-8, 270-1; Carlyle on, xxv, 353; defence of, xxxvii, 319-20; Descartes on, xxxiv, 28; Emerson on, v, 274, 283-4; Hume on, xxxvii, 306-20, 407-20; of Montaigne, xlviii, 389-93, 395-6; Pascal on, 71-7, 78 (202), 82-3 (230), 123-5, 128 (387), 128-9 (390-2), 129 (395), 142 (432), 143 (434); Rousseau on, xxxiv, 241; Socrates on, ii, 82-3

Sceptics, Browne on the, iii, 306; Mill on, xxv, 33; Pascal on, xlviii, 99 (282)

Sceva, sons of, xliv, 465 (14-16)

Schedo (see Schio)

Scheggia, Raffaellone, xxxi, 431-2

Schelling, philosophy of, v, 437

Schicchi, Gianni, xx, 124 note 1

Schiller, Carlyle on, xxv, 444; Emerson on, v, 183; Goethe and, xix, 5; Goethe on, xxv, 99; LETTERS ON ÆSTHETIC EDUCATION, xxxii, 207-95; life and works, xxvi, 378; on truth, xxv, 351; WILLIAM TELL, xxvi, 379-489; work of, xxxii, 208

Schio, Girolamo, xxxi, 108 note

Schismatics, in Dante's HELL, xx, 115-18

Schisms, Bacon on, iii, 11-12; breed atheism, 44; Milton on, 222, 224-5, 229-31; Pascal on, xlviii, 295 (846), 297; Paul, St., on, xlv, 491 (10) (see also Heresies)

Schlegel, Friedrich, Carlyle on, xxv, 345; Carlyle on Lectures of, 348-9

Schoine, Egyptian measure, xxxiii, 9-10

SCHOLAR, THE, by Southey, xli, 734-5

SCHOLAR, THE AMERICAN, v, 5-23

Scholars, Browne on power of, iii, 315; Confucius on, xliv, 13 (9), 40 (20), 45 (3); Goethe on closet, xix, 29-30; manual labor and, v, 50-1; soldiers and, Don Quixote on, xiv, 373-9; Tseng-tzu on, xliv, 25 (7); Tzu-chang on, 63 (1); Tzu-hsia on, 64-5 (13); unteachable, ii, 146 (80)

Scholarships, Smith on, x, 133-6

Scholasticism, attacks on, xxxvii, 4

Scholiasts, Johnson on, xxxix, 241

Schomberg, Nicolas, xxxi, 89 note 2; xxxix, 53

School, Locke on going away to, xxxvii, 50-4

SCHOOL FOR SCANDAL, Sheridan's, xviii, 115-97; remarks on, 108

Schoolmaster, Goldsmith's, xli, 514

Schoolmen, Bacon on the, iii, 123; Carlyle on the, xxv, 323; debt of, to St. Augustine, vii, 4; Hobbes on the, xxxiv, 358; Hume on the, xxxvii, 303 note; Mill on, xxv, 238-9; Reformation as caused by the, xxxiv, 386; subtlety of, iii, 45-6; Voltaire on the, xxxiv, 105; on war, iii, 50

Schultz, J. M., M. Aurelius Antoninus, essay on, referred to, ii, 323, 326, 333; editor of Antoninus, 317

Schützenberger, M., xxxviii, 290-2

Schurz, Carl, at Gettysburg, xliii, 330

Sciancato, in Dante's HELL, xx, 106

Science, another kind of ignorance, xviii, 433; Augustine, St., on irreligious, vii, 64-5; on authority, xxxix, 122-5; Bacon on popular, 123-4; Carlyle on, xxv, 320; Channing on study of, xxviii, 327-9; defined by Hobbes, xxxiv, 359; Emerson on our, v, 297-9; need of experiment in, xxxix, 125-7; faith and, Browne on, iii, 271-5; Faraday on study of, xxx, 85; the finding of analogy, xi, 7; Helmholtz on study of, xxx, 173; Hobbes on, xxxiv, 335-6; Hume on, xxxvii, 292, 293; Huxley on applied, xxviii, 229-30; literary study compared with, 211-20; logical method in, xxxix, 125-6, 134-5; Montaigne on study of, xxxii, 47-8; natural and mental, compared, xxx, 173-5; Pascal on

false, xlviii, 196 (604); Pasteur on, xxxviii, 275, 355; poetry and, xxviii, 65-6; xxxix, 398; Pope on, xl, 415-16; public attitude toward, xxviii, 118-19; reading course in, l, 39-41; reason and authority in, xlviii, 439-42; religion and, Bacon on, xxxix, 128-9; religion and, Faraday on, xxx, 5; sensuality of our, v, 167; several branches of, xxxiv, 362-3; teaching of, Emerson on, v, 256-7; as source of power, xxxiv, 361; value of, xxviii, 210-13

SCIENCE AND CULTURE, Huxley's, xxviii, 209-23; editorial remarks on, l, 458

Sciences, Bacon on divisions of, xxxix, 131-2; deductive and experimental, xxv, 101-2; Locke on study of, xxxvii, 139; Montaigne on the, xlviii, 392-3; Pascal on the, 439; Pascal on infinity of the, 27-8; Sidney on object of, xxvii, 14

Scientific Congresses, Newman on, xxviii, 35-6

SCIENTIFIC PAPERS, xxx, xxxviii

Scientists, Emerson on our, v, 299

Sciography, Hobbes on, xxxiv, 363

Sciorina, Giacopa della, xxxi, 86-8

Scipio Africanus, Antiochus and, xlviii, 249-50; charged with peculation, v, 127; Cicero on, ix, 52; Cyrus and, xxxvi, 50; Ennius and, xxvii, 37; "the highth of Rome," iv, 273; the Iberian maid and, 376; leniency of, xxxvi, 56; Livy on, iii, 106; Milton on, iv, 385, 386; statue of, ix, 148-9

Scipio Asiaticus, results of conquests of, ix, 343 note 1

Scipio, father-in-law of Pompey, xxxii, 7; xii, 290, 298, 299, 301; speech of, on tribune law, ix, 40-1; war against Cæsar, xii, 306-7

Scipio, Publius, argument for justice, ix, 18; in Cicero's essay on OLD AGE, 46; on friendship, 21-2, 29-30; his friendships, 34; the Greek philosophers and, iii, 194-5; his belief in immortality, ix, 14-15; Laelius and, 10, 14, 20; Laelius on, 12-13; made Pontifex Maximus, 63; Q. Pompeius and, 35

Scipios, Caxton on the, xxxix, 15; Virgil on the, xiii, 236

Sciro, reference to, xxvi, 136

Scissor-beak, Darwin's description of the, xxix, 141-3

Scissor-tail, Darwin on the, xxix, 143

Scoffers, Goethe on, xix, 21-2; Sidney on, xxvii, 30-1

Scoffing, habit of, in discourse, iii, 84-5; at religion, 43-4

Scolds, punishment of, in old England, xxxv, 366-7

Scoresby, on color of water, xxix, 27

Scornigiani, Farinata de', xx, 166 note 5

Scorpion, Harrison on the, xxxv, 346

Scorzone, Jeanne, xxxi, 318-19

Scotch, Burns on the, vi, 162; Carlyle on character of the, xxv, 410-12; Harrison on diet of the, xxxv, 271-3, 288

SCOTCH BARD, ON A, vi, 216-18

SCOTCH DRINK, vi, 144-7

Scotland, agriculture of, xxxv, 310; apprenticeships in, x, 124; banking operations in, 235-8, 241-2, 244-6, 253; Burns on, vi, 161-2; Burns on learning of, 260-1; Burns' vision of, 174-6; Emerson on, v, 341; Harrison on eating in, xxxv, 271-2; Knox on Reformation in, xxxix, 58-60; quarries and mines in, xxxv, 309; Raleigh on union with England, xxxix, 79; rate of interest in, x, 92; soil of, xxxv, 308; union with England, economic effect of, x, 186, 199; wages in, 78; wolves and foxes in, xxxv, 341; Wordsworth on critics of, xxxix, 321 note (see also Caledonia)

SCOTLAND, PREFACE TO HISTORY OF THE REFORMATION IN, xxxix, 58-60

SCOTS PROLOGUE FOR SUTHERLAND, vi, 374-5

Scott, Master, in SHOEMAKER'S HOLIDAY, xlvii, 493, 494, 495

Scott, Michael, Dante on, xx, 84 and note 6

SCOTT, MISS JEAN, EPIGRAM TO, vi, 272

SCOTT, MRS., EPISTLE TO, vi, 258-9

SCOTT, ESSAY ON, Carlyle's, xxv, 393-451; remarks on, 317

Scott, Sir Walter, ambition of, xxv, 438; babyhood, incidents of, 412-13; Ballantyne and, 429-30; biographer of Swift, xxviii, 8; Byron and, xxxii, 378-9; Carlyle on Lockhart's Life of, xxv, 396-403; death of wife, 449-51; dinner with the Regent, 428-9; Emerson on, v, 214, 444; fame, indifference to, xxv, 419-20; financial ruin and last writings, 447-8; a genuine, healthy man, 406-7; Goethe's influence on, 424-5; lameness, 410; last days, 451; letters of,

427; *Liddesdale Raids,* 413-14; life at Abbotsford, 431-7; life up to thirty, 410; life, middle period of, 418-19; *Life of Napoleon,* Mill on, 84; love of animals for, 435-6 and note; Mill on, 94; *Minstrelsy of Scottish Border,* 417-18; national influences, 410-11; not a great man, 402-7; POEMS by, xli, 738-56; poems criticized, xxv, 422-4; popularity of, 395-6; in printing business, 420-1; productive faculty of, 445; Ruskin on heroes and heroines of, xxviii, 139-40; success in literature, xxv, 417-18; Taine on, xxxix, 414; unconsciousness of, xxv, 421-2; *Waverley Novels,* 426, 439-43; Wordsworth on, xli, 633

Scotus, Duns, Hazlitt on, xxvii, 278; the subtle doctor, xxviii, 47

Scowling, Marcus Aurelius on, ii, 246 (24)

Scribes, Jesus on the, xliv, 407 (45-7)

Scribonia, and Augustus, xiii, 37

Scribonianus, and his wife, ix, 243

Scriptures (see Bible)

Scrofa, Cicero on, ix, 146

Scrofula, and inoculation, xxxviii, 169, 193, 219

SCROGGAM, MY DEARIE, vi, 433

Scroop, Lord, xl, 108-9, 113

Scrope, P., on earthquakes, xxix, 356

Scrovigni, arms of the, xx, 71 note 5

Scuda, value of the, xxxi, 37 note 1

Scudamour, Sir, xxxix, 64-5

Scudéri, Corneille and, xxxix, 361-2

Scudéry, Mlle. de, on Chaucer, xxxix, 170; Dryden on, xiii, 13; Pascal on *Artamène* of, xlviii, 14 note 2

Scull, Nicholas, i, 58

Sculpture, Browning on, xlii, 1072; Coleridge on, xxvii, 261-2; Emerson on, v, 193; Goethe on, xxxix, 255-6, 257, 259-60, 262, 265; Schiller on, xxxii, 269-70; training for, xxxix, 265

Scurvy, Dana on, xxiii, 341-2

Scyld the Scefing, xlix, 5-6

Scylla, Æschylus on, viii, 55; Bacon on fable of, xxxix, 122; Homer on, xxii, 164-5; Milton on, iv, 51, 125; slaying of her father, viii, 102; Ulysses at, xxii, 167-8; Virgil on, xiii, 141-2

Scythian, and the Athenian, xxxvii, 10

Sea, discoloration of the, xxix, 20-7; Emerson on the, v, 329; geological changes under the, xxxviii, 394, 396; Longfellow on the, xlii, 1284; phosphorescent, xxix, 167-9; sunrise at, xxiii, 13 (see also Ocean)

SEA, BY THE, xli, 673

SEA DIRGE, xl, 270

Sea Stories, Dana on, xxiii, 5

Sea-captains, Dana on, xxiii, 358-60, 364; religious, 371-2

Sea-fire, Emerson on, v, 328

SEA-MAID, THE LITTLE, xvii, 238-59

Sea-pen, Darwin on the, xxix, 105-6

Sea-power, Bacon on, iii, 79-80; Emerson on, v, 342-3

Sea-sawdust, Darwin on, xxix, 24

Sea-slugs, Darwin on, xxix, 16

Sea-urchins, forceps of, xi, 235-6

Sea-weed, Darwin on, xxix, 243-5

Seals, Darwin on, xxix, 288; Francis Pretty on, xxxiii, 204

Seamen (see Sailors)

Search Warrants, in U. S., xliii, 194 (4)

SEAS, ON THE, AND FAR AWAY, vi, 494-6

Seasons, Burns on the, vi, 385-6; Campbell on, xli, 771-2

Seasons, Thomson's, Wordsworth on, xxxix, 322-25

SEASONS, THE HUMAN, xli, 896-7

Sebastian, in THE TEMPEST, xlvi, in shipwreck, 398-9; on island after wreck, 417-22; in plot with Antonio, 423-6, 440; at the banquet, 440, 441; denounced by Ariel, 441-3; imprisoned by Ariel, 453; before Prospero, 454-5, 456, 457-8; in final scene, 461, 462

Sebastian del Piombo, xxxi, 97 note 6, 113 note 2

Sebright, Sir J., on crossing, xi, 34

Secession, Johnson, on right of, xliii, 429; Lincoln on, 316, 318-19, 320, 321; Lowell on doctrine of, xxviii, 444-5

Second Sight, of Bards, vi, 232

Second Thought, the wiser, viii, 323

Secondary Qualities, Berkeley on, xxxvii, 206-7, 210-11; Hume on, 411

Secrecy, Bacon on habit of, iii, 18; Marcus Aurelius on, ii, 208 (7); Penn on, i, 337

Secret, in PILGRIM'S PROGRESS, xv, 182-3

Secrets, Manzoni on spread of, xxi, 186; never kept, vii, 309-10 (4); Milton on, iv, 427; proverb on, xvi, 57-8; Webster on, xlvii, 841-2

Sects, Bacon on religious, iii, 11-12; Browne on new, 259; Franklin on positiveness of, i, 111; Milton on, iii, 222, 223-4, 229-30; physiognomy of,

v, 338; rise of new, iii, 137-8; Ruskin on, xxviii, 109-10

Secundus, Gaius Plinius Cæcilius (see Pliny the Younger)

Secundus, Pomponius, ix, 232 note 1; on public opinion, 305-6

Security, Jonson on, xl, 298; Kempis on over-, vii, 268 (4); suburb of hell, xlvii, 845

Sedgwick, Gen., at Antietam, xliii, 403; at Gettysburg, 338, 358, 397; Haskell on, 358

Sedgwick, Prof., xxxviii, 412; Mill on, xxv, 125-6

Sedillot, M., xxxviii, 364, 370

Sedimentary Deposits, Lyell on, xxxviii, 400-2, 409, 411-2

Sedimentary Formations, rate of, xi, 324-5; manner of, 329-30

Sedimentary Rocks, Geikie on, xxx, 330-1, 339-40

Sedition, Calvin on charges of, xxxix, 44-5; Hobbes on, xxxiv, 372

SEDITIONS AND TROUBLES, ESSAY ON, Bacon's, iii, 36-42

Sedley, Sir Charles, POEMS by, xl, 383-4

Seducers, in Dante's HELL, xx, 46, 73-5

Seeds, Darwin on destruction of, xi, 77; dissemination of, 193, 388-94, 412-13; fable of, xvii, 16; plants without, Dante on, xx, 261 and note; plumed, xi, 84; transportation of, xxix, 458-9; use of nutriment in, xi, 85; winged, Darwin on, 150

Seeley, Thomas, xxxiii, 230

SEEMING WISE, ESSAY ON, Bacon's, iii, 64-5

Segismund, in LIFE IS A DREAM, as prisoner in chains, xxvi, 13-15; with Rosaura, 14-17; birth of, related by Basilio, 24-5; reason of imprisonment, 25-6; plan to try, 26-7; his awakening in palace, 30-4; with chamberlain, 34-7; with Clotaldo, 36-7; second sight of Rosaura, 41; with Astolfo, 41-3; with Estrella, 43-4; quarrels with Astolfo, 44-5; with the king, 46-52; in the tower again, 52-5; rescued by soldiers, 58-68; sends Clotaldo back, 68; in the battle, 70; on his father, 71-2; made king, 74

Segrais, on the ÆNEID, xiii, 22-31, 34, 35, 38, 43-6, 55; on readers of poetry, 58-9; Voltaire on, xxxiv, 145

Seiches of Forel, xxx, 283

Seius, nightingale of, x, 182

Sejanus, Tiberius and, iii, 67-8, 94

Selden, Burke on, xxiv, 171; Milton on work of, iii, 200-1

Seldius, Charles V and, xxxix, 91

Selection, by man, Darwin on, xi, 42-5, 50-3; by man, in Elizabethan England, xxxv, 241-2; by man and nature, compared, xi, 89-91; by man, in New Atlantis, iii, 174-5; Natural, xi, 87-137; Sexual, 94-6; unconscious, 45-50

Seleucus I, prophecy of, xlviii, 248

Seleucus Callinicus, xlviii, 249

Seleucus, Ceraunus, xlviii, 249

Seleucus Philopator, xlviii, 250

Self, Emerson on meaning of, v, 69-70; fear of, xlviii, 122 note 12; Pascal on, 152 (455); Shelley on principle of, xxvii, 353

Self-analyzing, Shelley on, xviii, 303

Self-assertion, Sterling on, xxv, 257 note

Self-conceit, fable on, xvii, 20

Self-condemnation, Byron on, xviii, 439

Self-confidence, Locke on, xxxvii, 120-1

Self-contempt, Kempis on, vii, 274 (1)

Self-control, Confucius on, xliv, 14 (23), 37 (1), 42 (13); Epictetus on, ii, 154 (100), 184 (15); Hindu teaching of, xlv, 796-8, 811, 813, 815, 816; Kant on, xxxii, 306-7; Kempis on, vii, 208 (3), 302-3 (1), 323; Locke on, xxxvii, 35, 58, 88, 172-3; Milton on, iv, 383; Pascal on, xlviii, 62 (160)

Self-defence, a natural right, xxxiv, 392; a social right, 394, 399

Self-denial, Epictetus on, ii, 154 (100, 101), 174 (159); Franklin on, i, 92; Kempis on, vii, 272 (4), 296-7, 304 (4), 323 (3), 328 (1); Locke on, xxxvii, 27, 31, 35; training in, 31-2, 35, 87-8

Self-dependence, Confucius on, xliv, 52 (14); Pascal on, xlviii, 120 (359)

Self-education, Franklin's example of, i, 69-70

Self-esteem, Kempis on, vii, 243; Milton on, iv, 258

Self-examination, Bacon on, iii, 69-70; Burke on value of, xxiv, 9; Carlyle on, xxv, 325; Epictetus on, ii, 145 (76), 151-2 (93), 153 (98), 170 (146), 183 (7); Franklin's plan of, i, 81-4; Kempis on, vii, 223 (4); Marcus Aurelius on, ii, 226 (11), 230 (31), 284 (37)

Self-fertilization, preventives of, xi, 104-5

Self-help, Emerson on, v, 53

Self-importance, Emerson on, v, 233

Self-interest, Carlyle on doctrine of, xxv, 354; Franklin on, i, 89; God's providence, x, 3; as the mover of society, 20; Pascal on, xlviii, 38; Rousseau on, xxxiv, 269-70, 273

Self-knowledge, Pascal on, xlviii, 25 (66); Shelley on, xviii, 276

Self-love, Kempis on, vii, 291 (1); Pascal on, xlviii, 43-5, 157 (474-7), 160, 162 (492), 336, 415; Pope on, xl, 416-17, 422, 429, 430, 439; Raleigh on, xxxix, 112; reason of, ix, 36; Sidney on, xxvii, 5

Self-mastery (see Self-control)

Self-possession, Goethe on, xix, 84

Self-praise, Pliny on, ix, 194

Self-preservation, Kant on duty of, xxxii, 309-10, 332-3, 340; passions of, xxiv, 35; passions of, contrasted with those of sex, 37

Self-regarding Conduct, Mill on, xxv, 268-71

Self-Reliance, Essay on, Emerson's, v, 59-83

Self-reliance, in children, xxxvii, 52; Epictetus on, ii, 118 (4), 120 (9), 137-8 (61), 153 (98), 155 (103), 159 (115), 166 (137); of heroism, v, 128-9; Kempis on, vii, 212 (2), 309 (3); Luther on, xxxvi, 263-4; Marcus Aurelius on, ii, 201 (6, 8), 207 (5), 212 (3), 201 (18), 217 (29), 244 (12), 247 (28); necessity of religious, v, 29, 37-40

Self-respect, Channing on, xxviii, 333; Locke on, xxxvii, 121; Marcus Aurelius on, ii, 208 (7)

Self-restraint, Hindu doctrine of, xlv, 813

Self-reverence, the bridle of vice, iii, 169

Self-sacrifice, Bacon on, iii, 34

Self-satisfaction, Pascal on, xlviii, 163 (499); Pope on, xl, 421

Self-sufficingness, Emerson on, v, 188

Self-trumpeters, fallacy of, xxvii, 235

Self-trust, the essence of heroism, v, 125; of the scholar, 15-16

Self-truth, Shakespeare on, xlvi, 109

Self-will, Pascal on, xlviii, 156 (472), 157 (475-6), 159 (482); Plato on, xii, 160

Self-will, Mr., in Pilgrim's Progress, xv, 259-62

Selfishness, Bacon on, iii, 60-1; Kant on,

xxxii, 334, 341; Mill on limiting, xxv, 257-8; Pascal on, xlviii, 152 (456-7), 157 (477), 159 (483); Rousseau on, xxxiv, 270, 273

Selina, Helen, Lament by, xli, 919-20

Selkirk, Alexander, Solitude of, xli, 535-6

Selkirk, Alexander, supposed lines by, xxxix, 295

Selwyn Correspondence, Emerson on the, v, 412

Selymus I, Bajazet and, iii, 51

Selymus II, Bacon on, iii, 50

Semele, mother of Bacchus, viii, 292, 327, 368-9

Seminary Ridge, at Gettysburg, xliii, 330

Semiramis, Burns on, vi, 408; Dante on, xx, 22

Semitic Races, Taine on the, xxxix, 420

Semnones, Tacitus on the, xxxiii, 114-15

Sempronius, in Cato, xxvii, 188, 189, 190-1, 192-3

Senate, Burke on necessity of a, xxiv, 330; origin of name, ix, 51

Senate, United States, xliii, 181-3; equal suffrage in, 191 (5); powers with the President, 188 (2); election of Vice-President by, 187, 197

Senators, oath and qualifications of, xliii, 192 (3), 198

Sencha, son of Ailill, xlix, 237-8, 245

Seneca, on adversity, iii, 16-17; cold baths of, xxxvii, 12; Dante on, xx, 20; on death, iii, 9, 10; xlviii, 332; diet of, xxxvii, 17; on education, 78-9; on evil opinions, xxxix, 67 note; on fame, 67; method of avoiding vice, iii, 298; Milton on tragedies of, iv, 412; Montaigne on, xxxii, 30, 93-4; quotations from, xlviii, 121 note 2, 3, 6, 122 note 16; as a Stoic, ii, 320 note; on suicide, 344; Tacitus on, iii, 90; vanity of, 128

Seneca Indians, xliii, 230

Senecio, Herennius, as counsel for Baetica, ix, 315; death of, life of Helvidius by, 308; on Licinianus, 255; on orators, 251; Regulus on, 188

Senecio, Sempronius, accused of forgery, ix, 295

Senecio, Socius, letter to, ix, 199

Senjer, the chamberlain, xvi, 208

Sennacherib, Dante on, xx, 192; Mohammed on, xlv, 914 note 4 (see also Sanacharib)

Sennacherib, Destruction of, xli, 785

Sennet, defined, xix, 231 note

Sensation(s), Berkeley on, xxxvii, 192-224, 228-30, 232-3, 235, 245, 248-51, 256, 259-60, 265-71, 282-3; Buddha on, xlv, 731; as the Ego, 658-60; Hobbes on, xxxiv, 311-12; Hume on, xxxvii, 299, 301-3, 322-4, 343-4; Rousseau on, xxxiv, 244-7; Ruskin on, xxviii, 112-15; same in all men, xxiv, 13-16

Sense(s), Bacon on, xxxix, 128, 134-5, 144; as source of the beautiful, xxiv, 92-102; Calderon on, xxvi, 56; Descartes on uncertainty of, xxxiv, 28, 34; Goethe on, xix, 54; the Hell of, xlii, 1398-9; Hindu teachings on world of, xlv, 796; Hobbes on, xxxiv, 311-12; Hume on evidence of, xxxvii, 408-12; Kant on knowledge through, xxxii, 360-1; More on pleasures of, xxxvi, 203-4; Petrarch on, xxxix, 98 note; pleasures of, xxxiv, 339; Pope on scale of, xl, 412; reason and, xxxiv, 32; xlviii, 39 (83); satisfactions of the, i, 332 (96); Socrates on the, ii, 53-5; as source of the sublime, xxiv, 67-73

Sensibility, Bagehot on, xxviii, 170-1; requisite to poets, xxxix, 297, 298 note; Schiller on education of, xxxii, 229-30; taste and, xxiv, 22, 23-4

SENSIBILITY, FRAGMENT ON, vi, 248

SENSIBILITY, POEM ON, vi, 426-7

Sensible Qualities, Berkeley on, xxxvii, 192-213, 219, 237, 248-9, 251; Hume on, 411

Sensible Things, Berkeley on, xxxvii, 192-26, 228-30, 233, 244-5, 251-2, 255, 282

Sensitiveness, Cicero on, ix, 86; Ruskin on, xxviii, 113

Sensual Pleasure, Archytas on, ix, 59; Buddha on, xlv, 727-9

Sensuous Goodness, Bagehot on, xxviii, 169-71

Sensuous Instinct, Schiller on the, xxxii, 241-9

Sensuousness, Schiller on, xxxii, 275-7

Sentiment, Hume on standard of, xxvii, 205-9, 216-17; Lowell on dangers of misplaced, xxviii, 435; James Mill on, xxv, 71; reason and, xxxvii, 292; thought and, 299, 301-2

Sentimentality, Carlyle on, xxv, 326-7

Sentry, Captain, xxvii, 85-6

Senzeille, Thierry of, xxxv, 29

Seppi, in WILLIAM TELL, xxvi, 381, 386

Septemvirs, Roman, ix, 363 note 1

Septicemia, Pasteur on, xxxviii, 364-70

Septimus Severus (see Severus)

Septitius, letters to, ix, 187, 314, 316

Seraphim, Milton on the, iv, 40

Serapion, in ALL FOR LOVE, xviii, 23-7, 90-2, 104-5

Serbonian Marsh, xii, 323; Milton on the, iv, 123

SERENADE, by Scott, xli, 743

SERENADE, by Shelley, xxviii, 373-4

SERENADE, FROM THE SPANISH STUDENT, xlii, 1273

Serestus (Seresthus), xiii, 95, 298, 319

Sergeant of the Law, Chaucer's, xl, 19-20

Sergestus (Sergesthus), in ÆNEID, xiii, 91, 182, 184-5, 187

Sergius, and Antony, xii, 328

Sermon on the Mount, xliv, 369 (20-49)

Sermons, Pascal on, xlviii, 12 (8)

Serpa, Pedro Hernandez de, xxxiii, 324, 351

SERPENT AND FILE, fable of, xvii, 22

SERPENT AND MAN, fable of, xvii, 13

SERPENT AND WOODMAN, fable of, xvii, 18

Serpents, winged, in Egypt, xxxiii, 39-40

Serranus, in the ÆNEID, xiii, 304

Serristori, Averardo, xxxi, 385 note, 429

Servants, children and, xxxvii, 40-1, 49-50, 69-70, 88, 103, 117; Confucius on, xliv, 61 (25); Epictetus on, ii, 178-9 (179, 180); Indians on, i, 394 (268); Job on, xliv, 119 (13-15); liberties of, in Massachusetts, xliii, 78; Penn on, i, 389; Penn's counsel to, 341; single men best, iii, 21; taxes on, x, 504; troubles with, v, 56; unproductive laborers, x, 248

Servianus, letter to, ix, 292

Servibilis, in FAUST, xix, 183

Service, Confucius on true, xliv, 48 (23), 53 (37); Emerson on honest, v, 99; Marcus Aurelius on, ii, 223 (6), 274

Services, Cicero on mentioning, ix, 33; Emerson on, v, 221

Servility, Penn on, i, 334 (119)

Servilius, Publius, ix, 117

Serving-men, More on, xxxvi, 144, 145

Servitude, impossible in state of nature, xxxiv, 195; involuntary, prohibited in

United States, xliii, 197; Milton on, iv, 208

Servius Tullius, first coiner of money in Rome, x, 30

SESAME AND LILIES, Ruskin's, xxviii, 93-162; remarks on, 92

Sesostris, king of Egypt, xxxiii, 50-3

Sestius, Bestia and, ix, 99-100; charged with bribery, 99; Pompey and, 121

Setebos, xlvi, 412

Sethos, king of Egypt, xxxiii, 70-1

Settala, Lodovico, xxi, 502, 508-9, 512

Settlement, Act of, Burke on the, xxiv, 163-4

Settlement Laws, of England, x, 139-44

SEVEN RAVENS, THE, xvii, 107-9

Seven Sages, the, ix, 11

Seven Sleepers, legend of, xxxviii, 391-3

SEVEN SWABIANS, THE, xvii, 203

Seven Years' War, America in, i, 127-43

Severinus, St., xxxvi, 253 (29)

Severity, with children, xxxvii, 34, 37, 63-4, 80; kindness stronger than, xvii, 35

Severus, Alexander, Machiavelli on, xxxvi, 63, 64, 68

Severus, Annius, letters to, ix, 235, 260

Severus, brother of Marcus Aurelius, ii, 195 (14), 198

Severus, Catilius, letters to, ix, 209, 240, 244, 292

Severus, Septimus, Bacon on, iii, 104; death of, 10; Machiavelli on, xxxvi, 64-5, 68; Plautianus and, iii, 68; Sidney on, xxvii, 21

Severus, in POLYEUCTE, Pauline on, xxvi, 82-3; reported to be coming to Armenia, 84-5; his love for Pauline, 87-8; learns Pauline's marriage, 88-9; with Pauline, 90-3; with Pauline in Polyeucte's prison, 116; determines to save Polyeucte, 117-19; denounces Felix, 128-9; won by Christians, 130

Sewa, Arnold von, in WILLIAM TELL, xxvi, 412-13, 423

Sewell, George, DYING MAN IN HIS GARDEN, xli, 481

Seward, William H., Alaska Purchase and, xliii, 432

Sexes, Hume on difference of the, xxxvii, 355-6; James Mill on relations between, xxv, 70; in plants, separation of, xi, 100-1

Sextius, Publius, Cicero and, xii, 239

Sextus, Bishop, xx, 400 note 5

Sextus, teacher of Marcus Aurelius, ii, 194 (9), 303

Sexual Characters, secondary, defined, xi, 153; their variability, 153, 157-9

Sexual Passion, Burke on the, xxiv, 37, 38-9; in state of nature, xxxiv, 191-4; Wordsworth on origin of, xxxix, 286

Sexual Selection, xi, 94-6; beauty and, 202

Seyton, in MACBETH, xlvi, 385-6, 388

Sforza, Ascanio, xxxi, 225 note

Sforza, Francesco, citadel of, xxxvi, 71; Macaulay on, xxvii, 377; Machiavelli on, xxxvi, 23, 44, 48; the Milanese and, 42

Sforza, Ludovico, Bacon on, iii, 50; at Milan, xxxvi, 8-9; Montaigne on, xxxii, 6

Sforza, Sforza, xxxi, 185 note

Sguazzella, the painter, xxxi, 196 note 2

SHADOW, THE, story of, xvii, 318-29

Shadow of Death, valley of, xv, 245-9; xliv, 169 (4)

Shadows, Celtic Isle of, xxxii, 179

Shadrach, the slave, Dana and, xxiii, 3

Shadwell, Dryden and, xviii, 5; Voltaire on, xxxiv, 136; Wordsworth on, xxxix, 317

Shaftesbury, Earl of, on burlesque, xxxix, 178; on English poetry, 321; Locke and, xxxvii, 3; Montesquieu on, xxxii, 118; satire on, xviii, 5

Shahrazad, xvi, 10-13

Shah-Zeman, king of Samarkand, xvi, 5-10; Jullanar and, 326-40

Shahriyar, King, xvi, 5-13

Shakalik, story of, xvi, 184-90

Shakers, Emerson on the, v, 274, 292

Shakespeare, Arnold on, xxviii, 77, 79, 80; Arnold on selections from, 73; Bagehot on, 178; carelessness of future fame, xxxix, 233; Carlyle on, xxv, 322, 409, 421-2, 440, 444; the Celtic element in, xxxii, 160; Coleridge on, xxvii, 254; inclination to comedy, xxxix, 216; defects of, 217-20, 233; Dryden on, xviii, 19; early editions of, xxxix, 321; Emerson on, v, 15, 144, 181, 214, 433, 434, 435, 438; English drama, indebted to, 10; Gray on, xl, 455; HAMLET, xlvi, 91-211; Hazlitt on, xxvii, 268; his debt to Holinshed's *Chronicles*, xxxv, 216; Hugo on, xxxix, 352, 354, 355, 357, 374, 382, 386; KING LEAR, xlvi, 213-317; KING LEAR,

Shelley on, xxvii, 339; lack of learning, xxxix, 227-9; Landor on, xli, 902; language of, xxxix, 196, 216-17; Macaulay on comedies of, xxvii, 384, 385; MACBETH, xlvi, 319-94; James Mill on, xxv, 16; Milton on, iv, 33; miscellaneous poems of, xxxix, 319; originality of his genius, 229-32; as a player, xxvii, 308; action in his plots, xxxix, 226-7; the poet of nature, 210-12; publications of his works, 233-50; Ruskin on creed of, xxviii, 112; Ruskin on heroes and heroines of, 137-9; Sainte-Beuve on, xxxii, 127, 130; Shelley on, xxvii, 335; SHORT POEMS by, xl, 262-82; the sonnet and, xli, 681; Swift on, xxvii, 109; THE TEMPEST, xlvi, 395-463; THE TEMPEST, Hunt on, xxvii, 294; Thackeray on, xxviii, 9-19; Thoreau on, 413; his times and sources, xxxix, 225-6; tragedy and comedy mixed, 213-14; unities neglected by, 220-4; Voltaire on, xxxiv, 130-2; Wordsworth on, xxxix, 285, 306, 317-19, 330; Wordsworth on Sonnets, 318-19 note

SHAKESPEARE, Arnold's sonnet on, xlii, 1129-30

SHAKESPEARE, ON, by Jonson, xxvii, 55

SHAKESPEARE, ON, by Milton, iv, 25-6

SHAKESPEARE, ON THE TRAGEDIES OF, by Lamb, xxvii, 299-316

SHAKESPEARE, PREFACE TO, by Johnson, xxxix, 182 note, 208-50

SHAKESPEARE, PREFACE TO FIRST FOLIO OF, xxxix, 148-9

SHAKESPEARE, TO THE MEMORY OF, by Jonson, xl, 301-3

Shakiriyeh, the, xvi, 239

Shallowness, Confucius on, xliv, 26 (16)

SHALOTT, THE LADY OF, xlii, 967-71

Shame, Burke on, xxiv, 251; Confucius on, xliv, 45 (1); Dante on, xx, 71; defined by Hobbes, xxxiv, 342; Milton on, iv, 162, 288; sense of, in children, xxxvii, 39-42, 60-1, 67, 173; a slow poison, viii, 321; the only grief without redress, xxvi, 86; Pope on, xl, 435; virtue and, 420; Webster on, xlvii, 796

Shame, character in PILGRIM'S PROGRESS, xv, 75-8

Shamelessness, Epictetus on, ii, 124 (23)

Shamgar, the goad of, xv, 58

Shandy, Walter, xxv, 323

Shang, and Shih, xliv, 34 (15)

Shao, Confucius on, xliv, 22; music of, 12 (25)

Shao Hu, xliv, 47 (17) note

Shao-lien, xliv, 63

Shaving, Franklin on, at home, i, 123

She, Duke of, xliv, 43 (16, 18)

SHE IS NOT FAIR, xli, 912

SHE SAYS SHE LOES ME BEST OF A', vi, 497

SHE STOOPS TO CONQUER, Goldsmith's, xviii, 199-269

SHE WAS A PHANTOM OF DELIGHT, xli, 651-2

SHE WALKS IN BEAUTY, xli, 789

SHE'S FAIR AND FAUSE, vi, 328

Sheba, Queen of, reference to, xix, 223

Shechem, Bunyan on, xv, 108

Sheep, appeal of a, vi, 41-2; destruction of, for wool, x, 194; parable of the, xv, 205; sacred in Thebes, xxxiii, 27

Sheffield, the mercer, xxxix, 25

Shelburne, Burns on, vi, 52

Shelley, Percy Bysshe, Arnold on, xxviii, 89; Browning's debt to, xviii, 358; buried in Rome, xxiii, 4; Byron and, xxxii, 378; Carlyle on, xxv, 345; THE CENCI, xviii, 271-356; death of, xxvii, 284; DEFENCE OF POETRY, 327-59; remarks on DEFENCE of, l, 48; life and works, xviii, 272; Mazzini on, xxxii, 386; on Milton's Satan, xxviii, 198; poems by, xli, 823-70; SERENADE by, xxviii, 373-4; on his own works, xviii, 273

Shell-fish, the heart in, xxxviii, 130

Shells, color of, xi, 139; fresh-water, distribution of, 410-11; Lyell on, xxxviii, 404, 405; Tennyson on, xlii, 1046; transportation of land, xi, 420

Shelton, Thos., translator of Cervantes, xiv, 3; dedication by, 5

Shem, Pascal on, xlviii, 207 (625)

Shemei, Winthrop on, xliii, 94

Shen Ch'ang, xliv, 16 (10)

Shenstone, Burns on, vi, 179; Wordsworth on Schoolmistress of, xxxix, 326 note

Sheol, references to, xliv, 81 (9), 87 (8), 92 (13), 98 (13), 104 (13), 110 (19), 111 (6), 149 (5), 158 (10), 176 (3), 178 (17), 202 (14), 253 (3), 257 (48), 291 (3), 323 (7), 346 (10)

Shepherd, in ŒDIPUS, viii, 242-4

SHEPHERD, THE PASSIONATE, xl, 254-5

SHEPHERD OF TENDER YOUTH, xlv, 541-2

SHEPHERD'S BOY, fable of the, xvii, 28

Shepherd's Calendar, Sidney on, xxvii, 42

Shepherd-dogs, S. American, xxix, 154-6

SHEPHERDESS, THE UNFAITHFUL, xl, 199-200

Sherbrooke, Lord, quoted, xxviii, 468-9

Sheridan, Richard B., DRINKING SONG, xli, 554; on easy writing, xxv, 445; Goldsmith on, xli, 505, 506; life and works, xviii, 108; Macaulay on, xxvii, 383-4; A PORTRAIT, xviii, 109-12; SCHOOL FOR SCANDAL, 115-97; Swift and, xxviii, 28

Sheridan, Thomas, xviii, 108

Sheriff of Nottingham, in ROBYN HODE, xl, 130; with Little John, 147-8; brought before Robyn Hode, 151-4; holds archery contest, 164-5, 166; attempts to capture Robyn Hode, 168-70; captures knight, 170; killed by Robyn Hode, 172-3

Sherman, Roger, xliii, 150 note

Sherman, Wm. T., march of, to the sea, xlii, 1407

SHERRAMUIR, THE BATTLE OF, vi, 358

Sherwell, Thomas, xxxiii, 192

SHEYKH AND THE GAZELLE, story of the, xvi, 17-21

SHEYKH AND THE HOUNDS, story of the, xvi, 21-4

SHEYKH AND THE MULE, story of the, xvi, 24

Sheytans, species of genii, xvi, 9 note

Shiftiness, Hobbes on, xxxiv, 352, 366; lines on, viii, 455

Shifts, Penn on, i, 337

Shih, and Shang, xliv, 34 (15)

Shimei, reference to, xli, 485

SHIP, THE BUILDING OF THE, xlii, 1280-90

Ship-masters, Dana on, xxiii, 357-9, 363-6; religious, 371-2

Ship Money, case of, v, 347

Shipley, Jonathan, i, 5

Shipman, Chaucer's, xl, 22

Shippen, quoted, xxxiv, 85

Ships, Franklin on speed of, i, 156-7; invented by Prometheus, viii, 183

Shirley, Braddock's secretary, i, 135

Shirley, Gen., Franklin on, i, 137, 154-5

Shirley, James, poems by, xl, 349-50

Sho'hâib, xlv, 907

SHOEMAKER'S HOLIDAY, THE, xlvii, 469-537; remarks on, 468

Shoes, Locke on, xxxvii, 11

SHOES, THE RED, xvii, 329-34

Sholts, Harrison on, xxxv, 354

Shongi, Zealand chief, xxix, 423-4, 433

Shooting Star, in FAUST, xix, 190

SHORTEN SAIL, xl, 463-4

Short-hand, Franklin's, i, 8; Locke on, xxxvii, 135

Shortreed, Mr., and Scott, xxv, 414-6

Short-wind, in PILGRIM'S PROGRESS, xv, 217

Shovel, Sir Cloudesly, monument of, xxvii, 79

Show, a poor substitute for worth, xvii, 19

Shrewdness (see Cunning)

Shrewsbury, Duke of, Dryden on, xiii, 426-7

Shrimps, Harvey on, xxxviii, 86; the heart in, 130

SHROUD, THE, a story, xvii, 195-6

SHRUBBERY, THE, xli, 542-3

Shu-ch'i, xliv, 17 note 10, 22 (14), 56 (12), 63 (8)

Shu-sun Wu-shu, xliv, 65 (23), 66 (24)

Shuckburgh, E. S., translator of Cicero, ix

Shun, Emperor, xliv, 21 (28), 26 (18, 20, 21), 40 (22), 50 (45), 51 (4), 66 (1) note

Shusy Pye, xl, 84

Shuter, Mr., the actor, xviii, 203

Siberia, remains in, xxix, 254-5

Sibyl, Virgil on the, xiii, 142-3 (see Deïphobe)

Sibylline Books, Bacon on the, iii, 56; Hobbes on, xxxiv, 381; Pascal on, xlviii, 208 (628)

SIC A WIFE AS WILLIE HAD, vi, 434-5

Sichæus, and Dido, xiii, 85, 153; in Virgil's Hades, 223

Sicilian Bull, the, xx, 110 note 1

Sicilian Vespers, reference to, xx, 316 note 10

Sicily, changes of species in, xxxviii, 405; Coleridge on government of, v, 320; geology of, xxxviii, 405; popes in, xxxvi, 296; Raleigh on history of, xxxix, 113

Sicinnus, Plutarch on, xii, 16-7

SICK LION, THE, fable of, xvii, 14-5

Sickles, Gen., at Gettysburg, xliii, 334, 337, 345-8, 400, 413; Haskell on, 329, 345

Sickness, Epicurus on, ii, 272-3 (41); lessens fear of death, xxxii, 20-1; Pascal

on use of, xlviii, 366-74; Pliny on virtue in, ix, 310; Rousseau on causes of, xxxiv, 172-3; Woolman on, i, 198, 235-6

Siddhartha Gautama, xlv, 574

Sidney, Sir Philip, *Arcadia* of, xlvi, 214; *Arcadia* of, Johnson on, xxxix, 218; *Arcadia,* written at Wilton House, v, 411; DEFENSE OF POESY, xxvii, 5-51; Elizabeth and, xv, 384; Emerson on, v, 183; Johnson on language of, xxxix, 196; Jonson on, xxvii, 56; life and works, 3-4; poems by, xl, 210-14; Pope on, 433; Pugliano and, xxvii, 5; Shelley on, xli, 867; ugliness of, v, 307; Wotton on, 372

Siebel, in FAUST, xix, 85-99

Siege Perilous, the, xxxv, 107-8, 109-10; made by Merlin, 136

Siegfried, mortality of, v, 92

Sienna, the Brigata Godereccia of, xx, 122 note 7

Siennese, Dante on the, xx, 122 note 6, 198 note 8

Sierra Leone, Pretty on, xxxiii, 224

Sieve, superstition of the, xix, 103

Sieyès, Burke on, xxiv, 413

Sigebert, the monk, xx, 329 note 29

SIGEDRIFA, THE LAY OF, xlix, 368-70; remarks on, 251

Sigemund, saga of, xlix, 29-30

Siggeir, king of Gothland, xlix, 260-4; sons of, 265; with Sigmund and Sinfjotli, 269-70; his death, 271-2

Sighs, De Quincey's Lady of, xxvii, 322-4

Sight, Berkeley on realities of, xxxvii, 221-2; Burke on means of, xxiv, 109-10; Burke on pleasures of the, 14-15; Milton on sense of, iv, 416; Whitman on the, xxxix, 393

Sigi, son of Odin, xlix, 257-8

Sigismund, Emperor, and Huss, xxxvi, 317

Sigismund, father of Manfred, xviii, 443

Siglorel, the wizard, xlix, 138

Sigmund, in VOLSUNGA SAGA, xlix, 260; the sword of, 261; King Siggeir and, 261; the wolf and, 264-5; Signy's children and, 265-6; his son Sinfjotli, 267-9; his revenge on Siggeir, 269-71; marriage to Borghild, 272; at death of Sinfjotli, 277; last battle, 278-9; the avenging of, 289-92; remarks on story of, 250

SIGN-POSTS, VERSICLES ON, vi, 325

Signora, the, in I PROMESSI SPOSI (see Gertrude)

Signy, daughter of Volsung, xlix, 260, 262-7, 269, 270, 271

Sigrun, Queen, xlix, 273, 274, 275-6, 361-3, 364-7

Sigurd Fafnir's-Bane, birth and growth of, xlix, 282-4; his sword, 287-8; Grifir's prophecy, 288; avenges his father, 289-92; slays Fafnir, 292-5; Regin and, 295-7; hears of Brynhild, 297-8; takes gold of Fafnir, 298; meeting with Brynhild, 299-305; his semblance and array, 305-6; at Hlymdale, 306-7; renews troth to Brynhild, 307-9; Brynhild on, 311-12; his marriage to Gudrun, 312-15, 371, 396; his wooing of Brynhild for Gunnar, 316-17, 371-2, 389-90, 395; with Gudrun, 318; his visit to Brynhild in grief, 323-25; slaying of, 326-9, 373-7, 391-2, 395, 396-7; lament for, 329-35; his daughter, 336; burned beside Brynhild, 337, 385-6, 387; fame of, 337; Morris on, 256; remarks on story of, 251, 252

Sigurd, King, and Eystein, v, 344

SIGURD, SHORT LAY OF, xlix, 371-86; remarks on, 251

Sihon, king of Amorites, xliv, 315 (11)

Silanus, Julius, in Catiline conspiracy, xii, 232, 234; Cicero on, ix, 81

Silas, the disciple, xliv, 456 (22, 27), 457 (32); with Paul, 457 (40), 458-61, 462 (5)

Silence, Bacon on habits of, iii, 18; Carlyle on, xxv, 332-3, 377; Confucius on, xliv, 8 (18), 51 (7), 59 (19); Emerson on, v, 154; Franklin's maxim of, i, 79, 80; Kempis on, vii, 224; in love, xlviii, 418; may be a lie, xxviii, 282; Montaigne on, xxxii, 41; Pascal on, xlviii, 21 (44): Penn on, i, 335 (129), 383 (118-20); Shakespeare on, xlvi, 109; sole cure of wrong, viii, 28; speech and, Carlyle on, xxv, 397; terror in, xxiv, 60

Silenus, Don Quixote on, xiv, 115; Hugo on, xxxix, 347

Silicified Trees, Darwin on, xxix, 335-6, 356

Siloa, reference to, iv, 88

Siloam, tower in, xliv, 390 (4)

Silurian Period, in Europe, xxx, 343

Silva, Pedro de, xxxiii, 324

Silva, in EGMONT, xix, 301-4, 306, 325-6

Silvanus, xlv, 517 (19)

Silver, demand for, x, 175; as measure of value, 41; More on, xxxvi, 191-2; price of, x, 175; reason of value of, 403; seldom found pure, 175; value of, compared with corn, 178; variation in value of, 36, 40, 45; variation, effect of, on rents, 38 (see also Precious Metals)

Silvia, daughter of Tyrrheus, xiii, 256

SILVIA, by Shakespeare, xl, 264

Silvio, in DUCHESS OF MALFI, xlvii, 758, 759, 761-2, 805, 806

Silvius Æneas, Virgil on, xiii, 233

Silvius, Jacobus, on veins, xxxviii, 118

Simeon, xliv, 359 (25-35); finds Jesus in the temple, iv, 365; Herbert on song of, xv, 401; prophecy of, iv, 374

Similes, Bunyan on, xv, 172-3; Burke on pleasure from, xxiv, 17-18; Dryden on use of, xiii, 41-2; Johnson on, xxvii, 183-4; Sidney on, 48; Swift on, 112

Similitudes, Bacon on, xxvii, 331

Simmias, with Socrates in prison (see PHÆDO, Plato's)

Simoisius, Burke on, xxiv, 127

Simon, Archbishop of Canterbury, xxxv, 71

Simon of Cyrene, xliv, 414 (26)

Simon, the Indian, xliii, 146

SIMON LEE, THE OLD HUNTSMAN, xli, 647-9

Simon Peter, chosen apostle, xliv, 368 (14); Jesus and, 365 (3-11), 373 (40); mother-in-law of, 365 (38-9); in PARADISE REGAINED, iv, 372

Simon, son of Onias, panegyric on, xxiv, 67

Simon, the sorcerer, xliv, 439 (9-13), 440 (18-24); Bunyan on, xv, 109; Dante on, xx, 77

Simon, the tanner, xliv, 443 (43)

Simon of Tours, xx, 242 note 2

Simon, the Zealot, xliv, 368 (15), 424 (13)

Simonides, of Ceos, xii, 191 note; Hiero and, xxvii, 38; Themistocles and, xii, 9

Simony, defined, xxxvi, 284; punishment of, in Dante's HELL, xx, 46, 77-80

Simple, in PILGRIM'S PROGRESS, xv, 42; hanged, 216-18

SIMPLEX MUNDITIIS, by Ben Jonson, xl, 290

Simplicianus, St. Augustine on, vii, 118, 124

Simplicity, Confucius on, xliv, 44 (27); Goethe on, xix, 135; Jonson on, xl, 290; Kempis on, vii, 242; necessary to friendship, ix, 31; reward of, vi, 232; Whitman on, xxxix, 396

Simplicius, Commentary on the Enchiridion of Epictetus, ii, 318, 321, 337

Sims, and Dana, xxiii, 3

SIMSON, WILLIAM, EPISTLE TO, vi, 86-91

Simulation, Bacon on, iii, 17-19; of love, xlviii, 420 (see also Hypocrisy)

Sin, Augustine, St., on, vii, 26-30, 73, 101-3; Berkeley on, xxxvii, 258; Bunyan on living in, xv, 207; denouncing and abhorring, 85; future punishment of, vii, 232-4; in gold and in rags, xlvi, 296; knowledge of, necessary to virtue, iii, 202; man not compelled to, xxxiv, 278; Omar Khayyam on, xli, 955; Pascal on, xlviii, 221, 326; Pascal on source of, 336, 340, 352; problem of (see Evil); retribution of (see Retribution)

Sin, in PARADISE LOST, at the gates of Hell, iv, 124-5; announces herself to Satan, 127-8; opens gates, 130; paves road to world, 134; journeys to earth, 296-301; arrives in Paradise, 305-7

Sinai, Mount, cause of sounds on, xxix, 365; references to, iv, 12 (17), 347; xv, 24

Sincere, the shepherd, in PILGRIM'S PROGRESS, xv, 123-6, 293-4

Sincerity, Franklin on, i, 56, 79; in friendship, v, 111-12

Sinclair, Sir John, at Otterburn, xxxv, 90-1

Sindibad (see Es-Sindibad)

Sinfjotli, son of Sigmund, xlix, 267-72, 274-5, 276-7

Singers, high reward of, x, 109

Single Life, St. Paul on, xlv, 500 (32, 34)

SINGLE LIFE AND MARRIAGE, ESSAY ON, iii, 21-2

Single Men, greatest, iii, 20

Sinking Funds, misapplication of, x, 557

Sinnis, reference to, xxvi, 136

Sinon, betrays Troy, xiii, 102-8; Chaucer on, xl, 45; in Dante's HELL, xx, 125-6

Sinope, water supply of, ix, 402-3

Sins, the Seven Deadly, in FAUSTUS, xix, 227-8

Sion (see Zion)

Siracides, on beggary, xxxix, 93; on God, 103-4; quoted, 67

Sirens, the, xxii, 163; Dante on the, xx, 221; Milton on the, iv, 68; Ulysses and the, xxii, 166-7

Siret, the surgeon, xxxviii, 50

Sirius, distance of, xxx, 316; references to, xiii, 133, 330; worshipped by Arabs, xlv, 899 note 4

Sisera, and Jael, iv, 439; reference to, xliv, 248 (9)

Sismondi, and Manzoni, xxi, 3

Sisters, and brothers, Browning on, xviii, 383-4

SISTERS, THE TWA, xl, 54-6

Sisyphus, Homer on, xxii, 159-60; Jonson on, xlvii, 579; Socrates on, ii, 29

Sitones, Tacitus on the, xxxiii, 119

Siward, in MACBETH, in war against Macbeth, xlvi, 379, 383, 387, 390, 391; on his son, 393

Siward, the younger, in MACBETH, xlvi, 390, 393

SIX NATIONS, TREATY WITH THE, xliii, 229-32

SIX SWANS, THE, xvii, 132-7

Sixtus, Laurence and, vii, 248 (2)

Sixtus the Fifth, erects statue of St. Paul, ii, 307

Skadi, xlix, 257

Skanda, xlv, 832

Skanderbeg, xlvii, 489 note 9

Skeletons, at Egyptian banquets, xxxii, 16, 19

Skelton, John, xxxix, 26; Milton on, iii, 203 and note 44

Skene, and his wife, xlii, 1183

Skepticism (see Scepticism)

SKETCH IN VERSE, vi, 338-9

Sketches, unfinished, why pleasing, xxiv, 65

Skill, Kant on imperatives of, xxxii, 326, 327-8

Skill, Mr., in PILGRIM'S PROGRESS, xv, 232-5

Skin-changers, xlix, 268 note 1

SKINNER, CYRIACK, SONNETS TO, iv, 85

Skinner, John, Johnson on, xxxix, 187-8; TULLOCHGORUM, xli, 568-70

SKIPPER IRESON'S RIDE, xlii, 1357-60

Skrellings, the, xliii, 13, 15-17

Skunks, Darwin on, xxix, 87

Sky, Kelvin on color of the, xxx, 270-2; Omar Khayyam on the, xli, 954

SKYLARK, THE, by Hogg, xli, 767

SKYLARK, TO A, by Shelley, xli, 829-32

SKYLARK, TO THE, by Wordsworth, xli, 644

Slander, Penn on, i, 337 (145); proper attitude toward, ii, 176 (169); Shakespeare on, xlvi, 170-1; superiority to, ii, 119 (7) (see also Detraction)

Slanderers, Sheridan on male, xviii, 120

Slang, Jack, in SHE STOOPS TO CONQUER, xviii, 207, 212

Slave Labor, compared with free, x, 82; Woolman on, products of, i, 286

Slave-making Ants, xi, 264-8

Slave Trade, in Treaty of Ghent, xliii, 263; in Webster-Ashburton Treaty, 280-1, 287; Woolman on, i, 241, 242-3, 296

Slavery, abolition of, in America, xxviii, 442-7; abolition of, in rebellious states, xliii, 323-25; attempted justification of, i, 203-5; congressional control of, xliii, 185 (1), 191 (5); Darwin on, xxix, 502-3; Darwin on instances of, 33-4; Emerson on, xlii, 1263-4; Epictetus on, ii, 131 (41); among the Germans, xxxiii, 106-7; in Greece and Rome, iii, 77; Homer on, xxii, 236; impossible in state of nature, xxxiv, 195; Lincoln on, xliii, 424-5; Lincoln's attitude toward, 313, 319; Lowell on, xlii, 1371; in Massachusetts, xliii, 79; in New Jersey, i, 178 note; origin of, xxxiv, 210; Pascal on, xlviii, 79 (209); the peace of, iv, 116-17; production and, i, 203; prohibited in U. S., xliii, 196-7; Quakers and, i, 168, 206-9, 212, 225, 228-9, 251, 272-3; in southern colonies, 206-7; in the territories, xliii, 318; Whittier on, xlii, 1345-7

Slavery Contracts, illegal, xxv, 299-300

SLAVE'S LAMENT, THE, vi, 437-8

Slavonic Race, Freeman on the, xxviii, 267

Slay-good, the giant, xv, 271-2

Sleep, Browne on, iii, 327-8; Burke on, xxiv, 118; of children, Locke on, xxxvii, 21-3; Coleridge on, xli, 691; Goethe's Egmont on, xix, 332; of impostors, Shelley on, xviii, 326; Milton on, iv, 37, 59; Shakespeare on, xlvi, 341, 362, 422-3; Shelley on, xli, 833

SLEEP, THE, by E. B. Browning, xli, 941-2

SLEEP, To, by Daniel, xl, 222
SLEEP, To, by Keats, xli, 896
SLEEP, To, by Sidney, xl, 213
SLEEP, To, by Wordsworth, xli, 680
SLEEPING BEAUTY, by Rogers, xli, 582-3
Sleeping Beauty, story of, in LITTLE BRIAR-ROSE, xvii, 137-40
Sleepy-head, in PILGRIM'S PROGRESS, xv, 217
Sleigh-bells, Poe on, xlii, 1233
Sloane, Sir Hans, i, 43
Sloane, Sir John, Museum of, v, 333
Slocum, Gen., at Gettysburg, xliii, 334, 336, 358, 397; Haskell on, 358
Sloth, the sin, in FAUSTUS, xix, 228
Sloth, in PILGRIM'S PROGRESS, xv, 42; hanged, 216-18
Slothfulness, ECCLESIASTES on, xliv, 347 (18)
Slough of Despond, xv, 18-20, 190-1
Slow-pace, in PILGRIM'S PROGRESS, xv, 217
Slow-worm, Harrison on the, xxxv, 345-6
Sluggishness, in children, xxxvii, 107-10; lines on, xxxix, 294-5
Smallness, as source of beauty, xxiv, 92-3, 125-7
Small-pox, chicken-pox and, xxxviii, 173; cow-pox and, 147-54, 160-1, 172, 174, 178, 186 note, 187, 193, 196-9, 200-1, 202-3, 204, 206 note, 209, 210, 212-15, 216, 219-20; heel-disease of horses and, 154-5, 183-4, 197-8; inoculated, 169, 192-3; mortality from, 226; propagated by contagion, 226; cases of return of, 193-5, 218-19; scrofula and, 219; source of, 145, 163-4; spurious, 175-8; treatment of, 190, 214; varieties of, 164, 189
SMALLPOX, VACCINATION AGAINST, xxxviii, 145-220
Smart, Christopher, SONG TO DAVID, xli, 484-98
SMELLIE, WILLIAM: A SKETCH, vi, 255
Smells, beauty in, xxiv, 101; Berkeley on, xxxvii, 199-200, 206; as sources of the sublime, xxiv, 71-3
Smiles, of villainy, xlvi, 117
Smith, Adam, life and works, x, 3-4; Mazzini on, xxxii, 380; Mill on, xxv, 23; WEALTH OF NATIONS, x; Wordsworth on, xxxix, 321 note
Smith, Alexander, BARBARA, xlii, 1146-7
Smith, Dr., Andrew on African animals, xxix, 92-3

Smith, F., on ants, xi, 264, 281
Smith, Rev. George, Burns on, vi, 99
Smith, Goldwin, on Jamaica Committee, xxv, 183 note
SMITH, JAMES, EPITAPH ON, vi, 120-1; EPISTLE TO, 167-71
Smith, John, with Drake, xxxiii, 190
Smith, John, the Quaker, i, 272
Smith, Captain John, his books, ii, 318-19
Smith, Sydney, FALLACIES OF ANTI-REFORMERS, xxvii, 225-51; life and works, 224; quoted, v, 415
Smith, Sir Thomas, on the English, xxxv, 363
Smooth-man, Mr., in PILGRIM'S PROGRESS, xv, 102
Smoothness, as cause of beauty, xxiv, 93, 99, 120-4
Smugglers, Smith on, x, 538-9
Smyrdis, prophecy of, xlviii, 248
Snails, Harvey on, xxxviii, 86; the heart in, 130
Snake, in SCHOOL FOR SCANDAL, with Lady Sneerwell, xviii, 115-17; suspected of treason, 119; detected in forgery, 142; employed by Lady Sneerwell in plot, 188; confesses, 193-4
Snakes, Buddhist ideas of, xlv, 708-9; Darwin on, xi, 202-3; South American, xxix, 103
Sneerwell, Lady, in SCHOOL FOR SCANDAL, conversation with Snake, xviii, 115-17; with Joseph Surface, 118-19; on slander, 120; plots against Maria, 126; in gossip with friends, 132-6; at Lady Teazle's after the scandal, 181-3; with Joseph Surface, 188-9; accuses Charles, 192-3
Sneezing, Pascal on, xlviii, 62 (160)
Snorri, son of Karlsefni, xliii, 15, 20
Snow, Darwin on red, xxix, 326-7; effect of, on rocks, 322-3; height of perpetual, 249; structure of frozen, 328 note; transformation of, to ice, xxx, 234-5, 240
Snowdon, Ruskin on, xxviii, 155
Snow-line, Helmholtz on the, xxx, 213-14
SNOW-WHITE AND ROSE-RED, xvii, 213-18
SNOW-WHITE, LITTLE, xvii, 146-54
SO OFT AS I HER BEAUTY DO BEHOLD, xl, 250
Soap-bubbles, experiments with, xxx, 41, 51-2

Soaring, of birds, Darwin on, xxix, 190-1

Sociability, Hobbes on, xxxiv, 407

Social Acts, natural, ii, 223-4 (6), 286 (4), 292 (21), 298 (20)

Social Contract, Rousseau on the, xxxiv, 219-20

Social Improvement, dependent on art, xxxii, 230 et seq.

Social Phenomena, Huxley on, xxviii, 223

Social Pleasures, Burns on, vi, 83; Epictetus on, ii, 118 (3)

Social Reform, Emerson on, v, 259-61; possibility of, 55; to come through love, 56-7

Social Relations, penalty of false, v, 94

Social Science, Comte's stages of, xxv, 104

Social Virtues, and self-love, xl, 429, 431, 439

Socialism, Austin on, xxv, 112; of early Christians, xliv, 427 (44-5), 431 (32-6); Emerson on, v, 259-60; Lowell on, xxviii, 469-70; Mill on, xxv, 143-5; of Moravians, i, 143-4; More on, xxxvi, 167, 168-9, 184-5, 186, 189-90, 236, 238, 239, 240; Morris on, xlii, 1195-7; St. Simonian, xxv, 105; Woolman on, i, 158

Society, aimlessness of, v, 234; Bacon on aversion to, iii, 65-6; Burke on civil, xxiv, 197-8; Carlyle on, xxv, 327-30; Carlyle on modern, 334-46; as a contract, Burke on, xxiv, 232-3; desires that dispose to, xxxiv, 370-1; Emerson on the state of, v, 6, 75; the end of man, ii, 227-8 (16), 230 (30), 234 (14); founded on mutual deceit, xlviii, 45; frivolousness of, v, 189; good, defined, 200-1; the individual and, xxv, 203-9, 270-89, 290-1; individuality and, v, 62; interests of, in relation to landlords, wage-earners, and capitalists, x, 208-11; man in relation to, xl, 422-30; Mill on so-called, xxv, 141-2; Mill on tyranny of, 198-202; natural and ideal, xxxii, 213-17; necessary to man, ix, 38; never advances, v, 80; Pascal on, xlviii, 79 (211); Pascal on ties of, 107 (304); passions which belong to, xxiv, 36-46; passions that incline to, xxxiv, 391; a perpetual disappointment, v, 109; rights and duties of man in, xxxiv, 392-4, 401-13; Rousseau on origin of, 166, 185-6, 198-220; Rousseau on spirit of, 226-8; Rousseau on state of, 257; state of, effect on profits, x, 90, 96-7; state of, effect on wages, 71-2, 82-3; state of, in relation to its poetry, xxxix, 339-53; worst, is some relief, xix, 68

SOCIETY, A PROSPECT OF, xli, 520-31

Sociology, Huxley on study of, xxviii, 223

Socinians, Voltaire on the, xxxiv, 83-4

SOCRATES, APOLOGY OF, ii, 5-30

Socrates, on absolutes, ii, 96-7; Alcibiades and, xii, 106, 108-9, 110, 111-12; xlvi, 28; Aristophanes on, viii, 486; ii, 7; Aspasia and, xii, 60; Browne on, iii, 279; calmness of, ii, 139-40 (64), 149 (85); on causes, 90-6; charges against, 3, 6, 7, 12; Cicero on, ix, 11, 12, 13-14; the cook and, xxxix, 356; as corrupter of youth, ii, 22; Dandini on, v, 268; in Dante's Limbo, xx, 20; on death, ii, 17-18, 25, 27, 29, 50-9, 62; on death and the Thirty, xxxii, 22; death of, why delayed, ii, 45-6; deformity of, iii, 108; demands reward for his services, ii, 25; on discontents, 294 (39); divinities revealed through works, 331; dress of, 293 (28); on duty, 165 (132); idea of earth, 104-9; eloquence of, 5; Emerson on, v, 66, 127, 141, 203; Epictetus on, ii, 124 (21), 127 (32), 134 (52), 150 (91), 154 (99), 177 (175), 180 (185); on essential opposites, 97-100; Euripides and, viii, 302; on doing evil, ii, 37-8; on God, 126 (28); on forgiveness, 339; hatred against, its origin, 3, 6, 9, 12; on the hereafter, 103-4, 108-10; on hospitality, 179 (181); Hugo on, xxxix, 343; Hume on death of, xxxvii, 393; as example of humility, i, 80; on immortality, ii, 58-62, 67-73, 84-103; on incantations, v, 176; inward voice of, ii, 20; on knowledge as recollection, 62-7; last hours of, 46-113; life and philosophy, 3-4; the lyre of, ix, 54; Marcus Aurelius on, ii, 198, 206 (3), 208 (6), 251-2 (66), 254 (3), 343; Meletus and, 11-16; Mill on, xxv, 34; Mill on condemnation of, 218-19; Milton on, iv, 386, 402; on misology, ii, 82-3; mission of, 157 (108); on his mission, 20-1, 24-5; Myrto and, xii, 105; early studies in natural science, ii, 90; on obedience to laws, 39-41; ostentation of, iii, 128; Pascal on, xlviii, 268 (769), 332; Penn on, i, 343 (227);

Perdiccas and, ii, 293 (25); on pleasure and pain, 48; on his pleasure, 172 (153); as a poet, 48-9; xxvii, 39; Pope on, xl, 436; in prison, ii, 180 (185); prophesy on accusers, 27-8; as public officer, 20-1; on public opinion, 35-7, 292 (23); on his readiness for trial, 133 (48); refuses to beg mercy, 22-4, 26-8; refuses to escape, 37-43; refuses to be silent, 26-7; religion of, 14-16, 24; Rousseau on, xxxiv, 301-2; against Sicilian expedition, xii, 121; sons of, ii, 23, 30, 33-4, 43, 111; on the soul, xxxiv, 103; on suicide, ii, 49-50; method of teaching, xxxii, 36; teachings of, ii, 3, 17-18; xxviii, 86; virtue's chief favorite, xxxii, 52; vision of, ii, 32; wealth of, xii, 79; wisdom of, ii, 8-10, 17; on women, xxxix, 10-12; world-citizenship of, ii, 121-2 (15); xxxii, 45

Socrates, the historian, iii, 199
Socratic Method, Franklin and the, i, 17-18, 35-6; Mill on the, xxv, 19, 238-9
Soderini, Francesco, xxxi, 174, 177
Soderini, Piero, xxxi, 12 note 1; Vespucci's letter to, xliii, 28
Sodom, Browne on, iii, 272; Bunyan on, xv, 113; Milton on wickedness of, iv, 100; Mohammed on, xlv, 891 note, 899 note 5
SODGER, I'LL GO AND BE A, vi, 36
Soest, in EGMONT, xix, 253-9, 271-7, 297-300, 316
Sofala, Milton on, iv, 329
Softness, beauty in, xxiv, 99
Sogd, hospitality of, v, 125-6
Sogdiana, mentioned, iv, 391
Soger, term applied to sailors, xxiii, 123 note
Sogliani, Giovanbattista, xxxi, 28
Soirées, Carlyle on, xxv, 393-4
Solace, God the true, vii, 277-8
Solamona, king of Atlantis, iii, 160
Solar Spectrum, xxx, 261
Solar System, motion of the, xxx, 312
Soldanieri, Gianni, xx, 134 note 12
Soldiers, ambition of, iii, 93-4; love of, 28; Machiavelli on different kinds of, xxxvi, 40-8; marriage of, iii, 21; Massinger on qualities of, xlvii, 869-70; pay of, why low, x, 111; quartering of, in United States, xliii, 194 (3); students compared with, by Don Quixote, xiv, 374-9

SOLDIER'S DREAM, xli, 770-1
SOLDIER'S FORTUNE, THE, xxvi, 299-375
SOLDIER'S RETURN, THE, vi, 457-9
Soldiers' Song, in FAUST, xix, 42-3
Soldiers' Song, from JOLLY BEGGARS, vi, 123
SOLEMN LEAGUE AND COVENANT, vi, 512
SOLEMN MUSIC, AT A, iv, 40
Solicitation, liberty of, xxv, 294-7
Solidification, heat evolved in, xxx, 39-40
Solidity, Berkeley on, xxxvii, 210
Solinus, Milton on, iii, 241 note 35
Solis Dan, to Don Quixote, xiv, 12-13
SOLITARY REAPER, THE, xli, 654-5
SOLITUDE, by Pope, xl, 405-6
Solitude, Bacon on real, iii, 65-6; Burke on, xxiv, 39; contrary to human nature, ix, 38; delight in, iii, 65-6; impossible, 324; Kempis on, vii, 224-6; Marvell on, xl, 377, 379; Milton on, iv, 35-6, 37, 252, 266; Pascal on, xlviii, 53; Penn on, i, 319; Selkirk on, xli, 535-6; terror in idea of, xxiv, 60-1
Solomon, Arabian idea of power of, xvi, 296-8; in the Arthurian Legends, xxxv, 187-90; Browne on salvation of, iii, 308; Bunyan on, xv, 106; Burns on loves of, vi, 48; Burns on Proverbs of, 144; in story of CITY OF BRASS, xvi, 306-10; Cowley on, xxvii, 61; Dante on, xx, 328 and notes 20, 21; Dante on salvation of, 343 note 23; Dante on wisdom of, 342 and notes; as author of ECCLESIASTES, xliv, 334; on fools, xxxvi, 156; the genii and, xvi, 26 note; the harlots and, xliii, 93-4; idolatry of, iv, 99, 376; Kempis on, vii, 336 (4); his largeness of heart, xxxix, 80; lost book of, iii, 276 (24); magic palace of, xlii, 1100; on mercy, xliii, 95; Milton on, iv, 271, 350; mines of, xxxv, 321; Pascal on, xlviii, 65 (174), 217 (651), 268 (769); Psalms attributed to, xliv, 144, 231-2, 310-11; Sainte-Beuve on, xxxii, 130; Sidney on Songs of, xxvii, 11; temple of, iv, 98; xliv, 438 (47); versified, vi, 183-4; on violence, xxxix, 94; on wisdom and riches, 90; wives of, iv, 376-7; xv, 260; works of, in New Atlantis, iii, 161
Solomon's House, in New Atlantis, iii, 153, 161-2, 171-81; comment on, 144; a father of, 170-1
Solon, Croesus and, iii, 74; on custom, xxxvii, 27; epitaph of, ix, 71; on

happiness, xxxii, 5, 6; old age of, ix, 54; Pisistratus and, 71; on reward and punishment, 177; Sainte-Beuve on, xxxii, 130; Sidney on, xxvii, 7

Solosmeo, Antonio, xxxi, 134 note 4, 135, 138

SOMEBODY, FOR THE SAKE OF, vi, 510

Somerby, George, xxiii, 402

Somers, Lord, xxiv, 158; Addison and, xxvii, 158; on PARADISE LOST, xxxix, 321 note

Somerset, Duke of, on colleges, xxxv, 383

Somerset, Earl of, and Dr. Donne, xv, 340

Son of the Vine, in New Atlantis, iii, 164, 165

Soncino, Raimondo di, despatches of, xliii, 46-8

SONG, by Blake, xli, 591-2

SONG, by Donne, xl, 307

SONG, by C. G. Rossetti, xlii, 1181

SONG, by Sidney, xl, 210-11

SONG OF ROLAND, xlix, 93-195

Songs, Milton on, iv, 33, 35, 40, 122

SONNET, THE, by Wordsworth, xli, 681

Sonnets, Pascal on false, xlviii, 18; Taine on study of, xxxix, 411-12; Wordsworth on, 299

SONNETS FROM THE PORTUGUESE, xli, 923-41

Sons, Yu-tzu on duties of, xliv, 5 (2); Confucius on duty of, 6 (11), 7 (5, 6, 7, 8), 14 (20), 43 (18)

Soothfastness, xlv, 853-4, 863, 864, 869

Sopater of Beroea, xliv, 467 (4)

Sophia, Princess, title of, xxiv, 163

Sophists, the, xii, 6

Sophocles, the Ægæan and, xlii, 1138; Æschylus and, viii, 462; ANTIGONE, 255-99; Aristophanes on, 441, 486; Carlyle on tragedies of, xxv, 366; Hugo on, xxxix, 347; life and works, viii, 208; Milton on, iv, 413; ŒDIPUS THE KING, viii, 209-54; old age of, ix, 53; Pericles and, xii, 43; Sainte-Beuve on, xxxii, 131

Sophocles, duke of Athens, v, 121

Sophronius, and Basil, xxviii, 60

Sorcery, Pascal on, xlviii, 282-3

Sordello, in Dante's PURGATORY, xx, 168 and note 9

Sorli, son of Gudrun, xlix, 353, 357, 418, 426, 428, 429-30

SORROW, LEVANA AND OUR LADIES OF, xxvii, 321-5

Sorrow(s), Augustine, St., vii, 50; better than laughter, xliv, 342 (3); come in battalions, xlvi, 178; folly of, ii, 123 (19); godly and worldly, xlv, 524 (10); joy and, xix, 126; knowledge is, xviii, 407; Pascal on, xlviii, 371-2; past and future, xlvii, 804; pleasure of, xxvii, 352; Pliny on feeling and bearing, ix, 325-6; Raleigh on two sorts of, xxxix, 97; tears and, xxvii, 285

Sorrows of Werther, Goethe's, xix, 5; Carlyle on, xxv, 339

Sosicles, the Pedian, xii, 18

Sosthenes, xliv, 463 (17); xlv, 491

Sot, fable of the, v, 68

Sotthiya, the grass-cutter, xlv, 616

Soul, ancient ideas of the, xxxiv, 102-4; Arabian belief of the, iii, 258 (7); Augustine, St., on the, vii, 58; M. Aurelius Antoninus on, ii, 331-2; Berkeley on the, xxxvii, 252-5; body and, Buddha on, xlv, 647-52, 662-3; body and, Epictetus on, ii, 178 (178), 120 (10); body and, Hume on, xxxvii, 339, 343-4; body and, Marcus Aurelius on, ii, 199 (2), 206 (3), 211 (16), 211 (3), 237 (29); Cicero on the, ix, 72; creation and transmission of the, iii, 287-90; Dante on the, xx, 248; Descartes on creation of the, xxxiv, 47-8; Descartes on existence of the, 29, 32, 38; Emerson on the, v, 9, 135; Emerson on laws of the, 26; Epictetus on care of the, ii, 139 (64); as a harmony of the body, 78-9, 85-9; immortality of the (see Immortality); Hindu doctrine of the, xlv, 792, 849, 853; Locke on the, xxxiv, 104-5; Lowell on the, xlii, 1387; Montaigne on the, xlviii, 391-2; nature and, v, 8; Omar Khayyam on the, xli, 953; Pascal on the, xlviii, 82 (230), 83 (233); Pascal on immateriality of the, 118 (349); Plato's two horses of the, xii, 349 note; pre-existence of the (see Pre-existence); Prior on the, xl, 398 (269); progressiveness of the, v, 72; Raleigh on the, xxxix, 101; reality of the, v, 99-100; relations of the, to the divine spirit, 71; Rousseau on the, xxxiv, 257-9, 263-4; Shakespeare on the, xl, 281 (136); spherical form of the, ii, 288 (12); strength of, Diogenes on, 138 (62); transmigration of (see

Transmigration); Voltaire on the, xxxiv, 105-7; Whitman on the, xxxix, 396

Soul-sides, the two, xlii, 1099

Soul of the World (see Over-soul)

Sound, More on pleasures of, xxxvi, 203-4; as source of the sublime, xxiv, 69-71; velocity of, xxx, 253-4; vibrations of, compared with light, 256-8, 262-3; wave theory of, 251-5

Sounds, beauty in, xxiv, 100-1; Berkeley on, xxxvii, 200-2, 206-7, 265; Burke on intermitting, xxiv, 70-1; repetition of, cause of sublimity in, 112

South, Tennyson on the, xlii, 974-5

South America, Darwin on, xxix, 21-375; Drake in, xxxiii, 203-12; geology of west coast, xi, 328-9; species of, 399, 401-2; zoology of, compared with North, xxix, 136-7; zoology, changes in, 178-80

South American Republics, Monroe on, xliii, 278-9

South Shetland Islands, vegetation of, xxix, 253

South Wind, Kingsley on the, xlii, 1063

Southampton, tides at, xxx, 275

Southern Cross, Dana on the, xxiii, 30; Darwin on the, xxix, 507

Southern Hemisphere, climate and productions of, xxix, 253-6; leaving in, 437

Southern, Henry, xxv, 62, 83

Southey, Robert, POEMS by, xli, 732-5; on romance-poetry, xxviii, 75-6

Southwell, Sir Richard, xxxvi, 126, 129

Southwell, Robert, THE BURNING BABE, xl, 218-19

Sovereignty, Hobbes on rights of, xxxiv, 397; Vane on popular, xliii, 129-31

Sower, parable of the, xliv, 374 (4-15)

Space, abolished by the soul, v, 136; Aristotle on, 175; Hume on idea of, xxxvii, 412-13; Pascal on, xlviii, 78 (206), 428-30; Pascal on infinite divisibility of, 430-7

Spain, Bacon on empire of, iii, 77; Freeman on, xxviii, 258-9; Goethe on, xix, 91; Monroe on affairs of, xliii, 277, 279; in New World, x, 401-4; Raleigh on kings of, xxxix, 84-9; Raleigh on wealth of, xxxiii, 307-9, 318-20; under Roman dominion, xxvi, 17; Taine on history of, xxxix, 425; taxes on precious metals in, x, 380-2; TREATY OF U. S.

WITH (1819), xliii, 268-79; TREATY OF U. S. with (1898), 442-9

Spangenberg, Bishop, i, 139

Spaniards, Paré on cruelty of, xxxviii, 32, 37; slowness of, iii, 63; wisdom of, 64

Spaniels, Harrison on, xxxv, 350, 351-2

Spanish Armada, Drake and the, xxxiii, 122; Macaulay on the, xli, 915-16; prophesied, iii, 92; Providence in defeat of, 269

Spanish Infantry, Machiavelli on, xxxvi, 85

Spanish Language, Sidney on, xxvii, 50

Spanish Literature, Taine on, xxxix, 436

Spanish Student, Serenade from the, xlii, 1273

Spanish War, Treaty ending, xliii, 442-9

Sparhawk, Harrison on the, xxxv, 338-9

Sparks, Jared, ordination of, xxviii, 308

Sparrow, Francis, xxxiii, 366, 367

Sparta, age honored at, ix, 68; boys in, iii, 98; Dante on, xx, 169-70; Descartes on pre-eminence of, xxxiv, 13; education in, iii, 244; elders of, ix, 52; reason of freedom of, xxxvi, 41-2; iron money of, x, 29; a military state, iii, 78; military spirit of, xxvii, 374; Milton on, iii, 194; policy of, toward Athens and Thebes, xxxvi, 18; precious metals in, x, 318; Rousseau on laws of, xxxiv, 222; warriors most honored in, xxxiii, 83

Spartans, Bacon on the, iii, 76-7; Emerson on the, v, 50; lyrics among the, xxvii, 28; respect for seniority, xxxiii, 41; Taine on the, xxxix, 421 (see also Lacedemonians)

Spay, defined, xxxv, 343

Speaking, Locke on good, xxxvii, 160-1; Manzoni on thinking before, xxi, 517; Pascal on, xlviii, 22 (47)

Species, aberrant, xi, 448-9; allied, struggle with each other, 84; ancient and modern compared in organization, 368-72; resemblance of ancient and modern, 372-4; centres of creation of, 383-6; connected by extinct links, 362-6; why distinct, 319-20; doubtful, 58-64; duration of, 332-3; geographical distribution of, 378-430; groups of, appearance and disappearance, 352-3; intercrossing between, 105-6, 109; of large genera, vary most frequently, 66-8; of large genera, resemble each other, 68-9; lost, do not reappear, 350, 351-2;

Lyell on changes of, xxxviii, 403-5, 409, 412-13; Lyell on extinction of, 403, 405, 409; meaning of, xi, 54; new, appear gradually, 349, 350; favorable conditions for production of new, 107-13; production of new, in New Atlantis, iii, 174; number of, limits to, xi, 133-5; origin of, progress of opinion on, 9-22; past, present, and future, 128; evidence of their being permanent varieties, 67, 68-9, 156, 315; Rousseau on immutability of, xxxiv, 253; simultaneous changes of, xi, 357-62; special creation of, objections to doctrine, 67, 102-3, 136, 143, 144, 154, 157, 160, 166, 180, 192, 196, 247-50, 315, 399, 414, 417, 418, 419, 427, 453-4, 455, 472-3, 489, 491, 492, 494, 495, 496-7, 499-500; sterility between, 39, 285-305; sterility does not determine, 287, 307-8; succession of, in geological record, 349-77; sudden appearance of, in geological record, 340-3; varieties compared with, 308-9, 311, 334-5; how varieties become, 115-24; why well defined without intermediate forms, 170-5; wide-ranging, vary most, 65-6; in wide-ranging genera, 425-6

SPECIES, ORIGIN OF, DARWIN'S, xi

Specific Characters, more variable than generic, xi, 156-9

Speciousness, beauty contrasted with, xxiv, 98

Spectator, The, xxvii, 162, 163-5, 170; Addison and Steele's parts in, 82; Franklin's use of the, i, 16; selections from the, xxvii, 73-80, 83-7

SPECTATOR CLUB, Steele's, xxvii, 83-7

Spectrum, the diffraction, xxx, 267-8; Faraday on the, 33; the prismatic, 261; solar, 261; Voltaire on the, xxxiv, 122

Speculation (financial), in Elizabethan England, xxxv, 245-8; profits of, x, 115-16

Speculation (philosophical), Bacon on, iii, 89-90; Browne on, 264; Buddha on useless, xlv, 647-52; Carlyle on, xxv, 340-2, 353; Hume on, xxxvii, 417-18; Kempis on, vii, 207 (1), 262 (4); Lessing on religious, xxxii, 202; Milton on, iv, 245; Rousseau on, xxxiv, 242, 243, 254; Scepticism and, xxxvii, 319; Adam Smith on, x, 15; Sydney Smith on, xxvii, 247-8

Speculative Men, Goethe on, xix, 75

Spedding, J., editor of Bacon, xxxix, 1

Speech, Bacon on, iii, 106; Burke on, xxiv, 51-4, 150; Carlyle on, xxv, 376-9, 397; Coleridge on, xxvii, 257; Confucius on, xliv, 45 (4), 47 (21), 51 (7), 54 (40), 56 (6); Epictetus on, ii, 146-7 (81), 175 (164), 183 (5, 6); Franklin on, i, 18-19, 79; Hobbes on, xxxiv, 322-30; liberty of, Mill on, xxv, 206, 210-49, 250; liberty of in U. S., xliii, 194 (1); Marcus Aurelius's rule of, ii, 258 (30), 297 (17); Montaigne on, xxxii, 63-5; Pascal on freedom of, xlviii, 314-15; Penn's rules of, i, 335-6, 383; Quaker idea of, 184, 227; religiousness of, xlv, 864; rules of, vii, 213; Sidney on, xxvii, 31; Themistocles on, iii, 69

Speght, editor of Chaucer, xxxix, 163 note 16

Spelling, learned by play, xxxvii, 130

Spence, Dr., i, 146; apparatus purchased by Franklin, 114

Spence, William, on Blacklock, xxiv, 133-4; on England, v, 391

SPENCE, SIR PATRICK: a ballad, xl, 74-6; Coleridge on, xli, 728

Spencer, Earl of Kent, xxxix, 73

Spencer, Herbert, on beginning of organization, xi, 132; idea of evolution and, 6; on origin of species, 15; on principle of life, 304-5; inventor of term "Survival of Fittest," 72

Spencer, the elder, in EDWARD THE SECOND, xlvi, 48, 52-3, 63-4

Spencer, the younger, in EDWARD THE SECOND, xlvi, 29-31; presented to king, 39; advice to king, 47-8; on Gaveston's death, 50; adopted by king, 51, 52; in the battle, 53; sends Levune to France, 55; with Edward after battle, 59-60; in Edward's flight, 62, 64; in the abbey, 65; captured, 67-8

Spenser, Edmund, Arnold on, xxviii, 77; Burke on Belphebe of, xxiv, 136; creed of, v, 437; A DITTY, xl, 245; Dryden on, xiii, 13, 26, 54, 55, 57, 62, 63; Emerson on, v, 144, 433; EPITHALAMION, xl, 234-45; Hazlitt on, xxvii, 272; heroes and heroines of, xxviii, 142; Johnson on, xxxix, 232; language of, 196; life and works, 61 note; James Mill on, xxv, 16; Milton on, iii, 202; PERIGOT, xl, 247; PREFATORY LETTER

ON FAERIE QUEENE, xxxix, 61-5; *Prince Arthur* of, xiii, 19; PROTHALAMION, xl, 229-34; Shelley on, xxvii, 338; SONNETS, xl, 249-52; Thoreau on, xxviii, 413; Wordsworth on, xxxix, 306, 317; Wordsworth on sonnets of, xli, 681

Spensippus, death of, xxxii, 14; school-house of, 56

Spermatozoa, nature of, xxxviii, 342

Sphinx, Œdipus and the, iv, 409

Spices, Locke on use of, xxxvii, 16

Spider, parable of the, xv, 203-4

Spiders, aëronautic, xxix, 164-6; Browne on, iii, 266 (15); in Brazil, xxix, 44-6; flies and, Harrison on, xxxv, 348; Pope on instinct of, xl, 425

SPINNERS, THE THREE, xvii, 74-6

Spinola, Ambrogio, xxi, 468, 504, 518

Spinoza, Berkeley on, xxxvii, 233; Emerson on, v, 143; Hobbes and, xxxiv, 308

Spinther, Lentulus, death of, xii, 319

Spiridion, Calvin on, xxxix, 36 note 24

Spirit, superior to intellect, v, 190

Spirit of the Times, Goethe on, xix, 31

SPIRIT, THE, IN THE BOTTLE, xvii, 182-5

Spirits, Browne on, iii, 281-5; Hobbes on possession by, xxxiv, 355-8; of the impure, ii, 73-4; Locke on, xxxvii, 116-18, 163-4; Milton on, iv, 98-9, 171-2, 192-3, 212-13; terror of, 50

Spiritual, true meaning of, v, 281

Spiritual Delights, Kempis on, vii, 250 (1)

Spiritual Enlightenment, prayer for, vii, 287-8

Spiritual Estate, Luther on the, xxxvi, 265-70

Spiritual Gifts, St. Paul on, xlv, 506 (1-31)

Spiritual Knowledge, Channing on, xxviii, 329-30

Spiritual Life, admonitions profitable for the, vii, 205-37

Spiritual Progress, Kempis on, vii, 213-15

Spiritualism, in Utopia, xxxvi, 229

Spite, repaid by spite, iv, 265

Spleen, Harvey on the, xxxviii, 128-9

Splendor, Goldsmith on, happiness and, 515-17

Sponges, no heart in, xxxviii, 129

Spontaneity, Emerson on, v, 10, 69

Spontaneous Generation, Frémy on, xxxviii, 353; Lamarck on, xi, 10, 130; Pasteur on, xxxviii, 337, 364

Spontaneous Impressions, Emerson on, v, 10

Spontaneous Variation, Darwin on, xi, 213; instances of, 211-13

Sportfulness, of heroism, v, 127

Sporting Plants, xi, 26

Spotswood, Col., i, 98

Sprengel, on flowers, xi, 149; on hermaphrodites, 103; on fertilization, 104-5

Spring, Burke on pleasantness of, xxiv, 65; Campbell on, xli, 771-2; Collins on evenings in, 480; Goethe on, xix, 43-4; Milton on, iv, 71; Shelley on the, xli, 834; Shakespeare on, xl, 263; Tennyson on the, xlii, 979; Swinburne on, 1199-1201

SPRING, by Nashe, xl, 261

SPRING, by Shakespeare, xl, 264-5

SPRING, EARLY, by Wordsworth, xli, 643-4

SPRING, ODE ON, by Gray, xl, 452-3

SPRING, SONG COMPOSED IN, by Burns, vi, 192-3

SPRING, To, by Blake, xli, 584

SPRING'S WELCOME, xl, 209

Springs, as motive force, xxx, 188

Spruceness, Pascal on, xlviii, 110 (316)

Spur-kites, xxxiii, 155

Spurinna, Cottius, Pliny on, ix, 217

Spurinna, Vestricius, Pliny on, ix, 216-17, 229-30; letters to, 238, 274

Squinternotto, bravo in THE BETROTHED, xxi, 320

Squire, Chaucer's, xl, 13-14

Squirrels, flying, origin of, xi, 176

Srubdaire, the giant, xlix, 239

Ssu-ma Niu, xliv, 37 (3, 4, 5)

STABAT MATER, xlv, 553-5

Staël, Mme. de, on English poets, xxxix, 328

Stafford, Edward, 3rd Duke of Buckingham, (of earlier creation), (1478-1521), xxxv, 381

Stafford, Humphrey, 1st Duke of Buckingham, (earlier creation), (1402-1460), xxxix, 74, 75-6

Stafford, Lord, at Crecy, xxxv, 24, 33

Stag, defined, xxxv, 343; fable of the, v, 98

Stagirite, reference to the, xx, 154

Staig, Jessie, lines on, vi, 498

Stamford, university of, xxxv, 371

Stamp Act, xliii, 147 headnote, 148; Franklin on the, i, 4, 165

Stamp-duties, x, 505-11; legal, 452

Stand-fast, in Pilgrim's Progress, xv, 305-9, 311, 316-18

Standing Armies, advantages of, iii, 79; danger of, 52; Johnson on, xliii, 429; Macaulay on, xxvii, 375; Machiavelli on, xxxvi, 40-8; More on, 145; need and dangers of, x, 448-9; Vane on a, xliii, 125-7; Washington on, 237

Standish, John, and Wat Tyler, xxxv, 77; made a knight, 78

Standley, William, i, 206, 214

Stanhope, Earl, on French Revolution, xxiv, 151

Stanley, Mr., in School for Scandal, xviii, 141; Sir Oliver Surface as, 176-9

Stanley, Lord, Mill on, xxv, 284-5

Stanton, Daniel, i, 226-7

Stanton, Richard, xxxiii, 229

Stanzas, by Shelley, xli, 854-5

Stanzas on Naething, vi, 222-3

Star-Chamber, on unlicensed printing, iii, 184

Star-fish, eyes of, xi, 182; forceps of, 235-7

Star-form, in nature, xlii, 1250

Stars, Addison on the, xl, 400; Berkeley on the, xxxvii, 231; Burke on grandeur of the, xxiv, 66; composition of, xxx, 313; dark, 320-1; distance of, 314-16, 318-20; distribution of, in space, 316, 317-18; Emerson on beauty of the, v, 25; the forget-me-nots of angels, xlii, 1309; Habington on the, xl, 252-4; influence of, Cellini on, xxxi, 230; influence of, Milton on, iv, 307-8; Marcus Aurelius on lesson of the, ii, 293 (27); Milton on the, iv, 47, 49-50, 171, 185, 244-7; Newcomb on contemplation of the, xxx, 311-12; number of, 320-1; proper motions of, 314, 317, 319; Raleigh on the, xxxix, 107; Shelley on the, xli, 856; Wotton on the, xl, 287-8

Stars, The Light of, xlii, 1265-6

State, Burke on the, xxiv, 232-3; church and, xliii, 74 (58-60); duties and expenses of the, x, 426-67; education by the, xxv, 302-5; Emerson on the, v, 239-40, 250; Hobbes on the, xxxiv, 309; the individual and the, ii, 39-41, 228-9 (22), 242 (54), 283 (33); v, 248; natural and ideal, xxxii, 212-17; no, that hangs on one man's will, viii, 279; the perfect lines on, v, 239;

revenue of the, x, 468-564; Ruskin on meaning of, xxviii, 136; Taine on the, xxxix, 429-30; what constitutes a, xli, 579 (see also Society)

State Church, Burke on a, xxiv, 228-58

State Enterprises, Smith on, x, 468-72

State Rights, Lowell on doctrine of, xxviii, 444-5

Stateliness, preferable to fellowship, v, 208; Penn on, i, 388-9

Staten Land, Dana on, xxiii, 319-20

States, Confucius on strength of, xliv, 38 (7); founders of, iii, 129-30; Goldsmith on barren, xli, 524-6; Goldsmith on strength of, 519; Machiavelli on foundations of, xxxvi, 40; Raleigh on ruins of, xxxix, 71; rise and fall of, iii, 269 (17); temporality of, xlviii, 202 (614); three ages of, iii, 140; tributary, xxxvi, 8-12, 18-19, 69; Woolman on prosperity of, i, 231

States, True Greatness of, iii, 73-80

States, of U. S., admission of new, xliii, 191; commerce between, 184 (3); committee of, 164, 165-6 (10); disputes between, 162-3, 189, 190; Federal government and, 208-9, 210-13, 214-15, 224; Hamilton on union of, 202, 203; Jay on union of, 203-7; Johnson on rights of, 429; Lincoln on rights of, 314, 320-1; powers of, 195 (10); relations of, under the Confederation, 158-9; relations of, under the Constitution, 190-1; republican government secured to, 191 (4); rights and powers of, under the Confederation, 158-62, 163, 164, 165-6; rights and powers of, under the Constitution, 185 (16), 185-6 (6), 186 (10), 195 (10), 196 (14), 197 (4, 15), 198 (17, 18, 19); suits against, 195 (11)

States-General, French, Burke on composition of, xxiv, 178-82

Statesmanship, ideal and practical, xxviii, 440; xxxvi, 164-6; Lowell on, xxviii, 433, 437, 439, 440, 441-2, 447; Newman on, 34-5

Statesmen, Bacon on, iii, 73; Burke's standard of, xxiv, 290; Confucius on, xliv, 35 (23); Plutarch on, xii, 54-5; policy of, Goethe on, xix, 262; Raleigh on, xl, 205; Smith on, x, 348

Statianus, Plutarch on, xii, 351

Stationary State, effect of, on profits, x,

96-7; Smith on, 83; effect of, on wages, 72-4, 75, 83

Statius, Dryden on, xiii, 5-6; in Purgatory, xx, 230-57, 275-83; Shelley on, xxvii, 349

STATUE, LION AND, fable of, xvii, 25

Statues, Mohammed on, xlv, 1003; public, Pliny on, ix, 217; speaking, Plutarch on, xii, 182-3

Statute Laws, Winthrop on, xliii, 104-5

Stauffacher, Gertrude, in WILLIAM TELL, xxvi, 387-91

Stauffacher, Werner, in WILLIAM TELL, with Pfeiffer, xxvi, 386-7; with Gertrude, stirred to action, 387-91; at building of keep, 392-3; conversation with Tell, 392-3, 394-5; at Fürst's, 397-405; at the rendezvous, 413-28; with Tell near Altdorf, 440-9; at death of Attinghausen, 456-61; with Rudenz, 461-4; reports murder of Emperor, 477-81; in final scene, 488

STAY, MY CHARMER, vi, 298

STAY, O SWEET, xl, 310-11

Steadfastness, Confucius on, xliv, 23 (25), 44 (22); Hindu doctrine of, xlv, 869

Steam, volume of, xxx, 115-19

Steam-engines, Helmholtz on, xxx, 190-4

Steele, Sir Richard, Addison and, xxvii, 156, 160, 165, 166, 169, 170, 171, 173-5, 178, 179; on Addison, 165-6, 176-7, 178, 180; the *Guardian* of, 168-9; life of, 82; on Peerage Bill, 174; religion of, xxviii, 17-18; the *Spectator* and, xxvii, 161-2, 164, 165, 170; THE SPECTATOR CLUB, 83-7; the *Tatler* of, 161; Thackeray on, xxviii, 11, 19

STEER HER UP AN' HAUD HER GAUN, vi, 516

Steevens, George, editor of Shakespeare, xxxix, 319

Steeving, described, xxiii, 258-9

Stefano, in THE BETROTHED, xxi, 128

Stella, Swift on death of, xxvii, 122-30; Thackeray on, xxviii, 24 (see also Johnson, Esther)

STELLA, ELEGY ON, vi, 269-72

Stenches, Burke on, xxiv, 72

Stendhal, Taine on, xxxix, 434-5

Stephanas, household of, xlv, 492 (16), 514 (15)

Stephano, in THE TEMPEST, xlvi, 428-32, 435-9, 450-2, 461-2

Stephen, St., the Martyr, appointed deacon, xliv, 434 (5); editorial remarks

on teachings of, 422; martyrdom of, 438 (54-60); martyrdom of, Dante on, xx, 206-7; Pascal on death of, xlviii, 277 (800); trial of, xliv, 435 (9-15)

Stephen, St., the Sabaite, HYMN by, xlv, 544-5

Stephen, King, and the Bishop of London, xxxv, 254-5; the tailor and, xl, 189

Stephen, Leslie, on Berkeley's Dialogues, xxxvii, 186; on Hume, xxvii, 202

Stepney, Wordsworth on, xxxix, 330

Stereo-chemistry, Pasteur on, xxxviii, 270

Sterility, cause of, xi, 295-298; in dimorphic plants, 305-8; of first crosses and hybrids, 285-92; laws of, 292-5; origin of, 298-305; in species, eliminated by domestication, 39, 291-2; among varieties, 311-12

Sterling, John, Carlyle and, xxv, 316; in London Club, 82; *London Review* and, 129; Mill and, 3; Mill on, 97-9

Sterne, on readers, xxv, 339

Stesilaus, of Ceos, xii, 7, 80

Stesimbrotus, on Pericles, xii, 51

Steven, Rev. James, Burns' poem to, vi, 225

Stevenson, Robert Louis, life and works, xxviii, 276; poems by, xlii, 1212-13; TRUTH OF INTERCOURSE, xxviii, 277-84; SAMUEL PEPYS, 285-305; remarks on PEPYS of, l, 49

Steward, Chaucer's, xl, 27

Stewart, Jack, Dana on, xxiii, 390

Stewarts (see Stuarts)

Sthenoboeas, references to, viii, 471, 472

Sthenelus, in the ÆNEID, xiii, 108, 402

Stillingfleet, Bishop, Locke and, xxxiv, 105

Stimson, Ben, Dana on, xxiii, 398

Stinging, power of, in marine animals, xxix, 468

Stingo, the Landlord in SHE STOOPS TO CONQUER, xviii, 212-13, 214-15

Stirline, Earl of, To AURORA, xl, 314-15

Stobi, John of, ii, 185 note

Stock, divisions of, x, 215-22; investment of, 221-2; lent at interest, 278-90; taxes on, 505-11 (see also Capital)

Stock, custom of pulling the, vi, 111 note 5

Stock-dove, Wordsworth on the, xxxix, 303

Stockings, invention of, x, 206

Stoeckl, Edward de, xliii, 432

STOIC, THE OLD, xlii, 1111

Stoicism, Epictetus on true, ii, 145 (78); Milton's Comus on, iv, 63; Montaigne on, xlviii, 396; Socrates on, ii, 74-5

Stoics, Browne on the, iii, 305-6; on crimes, ix, 317 note; on death, iii, 10; divisions of, ii, 321-2; good and evil, idea of, 342; on happiness, 344-5; Hume on the, xxxvii, 319; Hume on doctrine of the, 368-9; on matter, ii, 326; Milton on philosophy of, iv, 402-3; on necessity, iii, 272; Pascal on the, xlviii, 118-19, 120 (360), 155 (465); on riches, ix, 133; in Rome, ii, 320-2; on suicide, iii, 294-5 (44) (see also Aurelius, Marcus, and Epictetus)

Stokes, Whitney, translator of DÁ DERGA'S HOSTEL, xlix, 197

Stoksely, Bishop of London, xxxvi, 105-6

Stone Age, as pictured by Æschylus, viii, 182-3 note 29

Stonehenge, Burke on, xxiv, 65; Emerson on, v, 455-8

Stones, knowledge of, necessary to art, xxxix, 256; transportation of, by ice, xxx, 230; transported by trees across water, xxix, 465-6

Storer, John, i, 242, 245

Stories, compared with poems, xxvii, 335; practise of telling, xvii, 7

STORK AND FOX, fable of, xvii, 19

Storks, Pope on, xl, 425

STORKS, THE, story of, xvii, 310-14

Storms, on land and at sea, xxix, 505

Storrs, Robert, on puerperal fever, xxxviii, 253

Stoves, in Elizabethan England, xxxv, 294-5; open, invented by Franklin, i, 111-12

Strabo, on English tin, xxxv, 321; on hounds, 350; on prodigies preceding Cæsar's death, xii, 315; on studdery of Pella, xxxv, 27-8; on tides, xxx, 280; on torrid zone, xxxix, 106

Strafford, Bagehot on trial of, xxviii, 177; Charles I on, v, 385

Stranger's House, in New Atlantis, iii, 149

Strangers, Emerson on, v, 105-6; liberties of, in Massachusetts, xliii, 79

STRATHALLAN'S LAMENT, vi, 281-2

Stratified Rocks, Lyell on, xxxviii, 395

Stratius, Homer on, xxii, 43

Stratonice, in POLYEUCTE, xxvi, 80-4, 93, 99-102

Strauchius, Chronology of, xxxvii, 156-7

Straw, Jack, xxxv, 62, 64, 69, 71, 73, 75; Chaucer on, xl, 50; death of, xxxv, 80

Strawberry, cultivation of the, xi, 51

Stream, Confucius on the, xliv, 28 (16)

STREAM OF LIFE, THE, xlii, 1120

Street-lamps, improved by Franklin, i, 120

Streets, expense of maintaining, x, 456; Franklin on cleanliness of, i, 119, 121-22

Strength, Cicero on, ix, 56-7; Confucius on, xliv, 11 (16), 19 (10), 44 (27), 49 (35), 58 (8); David on, xli, 496; from misfortunes, v, 98; Nashe on, xl, 260; as a cause of the sublime, xxiv, 55-7; what is, without wisdom, iv, 415-16

Strength, in PROMETHEUS BOUND, viii, 166-9

Strenuousness, Mohammed on, xlv, 977

Stricca, Dante on, xx, 122

Strong, the battle is not to the, xliv, 346 (11)

Strophades, abode of the Harpies, xiii, 135

Strophius of Phocis, Clytemnestra and, viii, 40; Orestes and, 103-6

Stroza, on hounds, xxxv, 350-1

Strozzi, Fra Alessio, xxxi, 32

Strozzi, Bernardo degli, xxxi, 99 note 2

Strozzi, Filippo, xxxi, 78 note 1, 113 note 3, 191 note 2

Strozzi, Leone, xxxi, 314 note

Strozzi, Piero, xxxi, 291 note 1, 334, 392 note 1

Strozzi, Prior degli, xxxi, 357

Struggle for Existence, xi, 71-86; Tennyson on, xlii, 1019

Struggle, alone pleases, xlviii, 52 (135)

Strutt, Mill on, xxv, 52, 76; in Parliament, 122

Struve, theory of, xxx, 320

Strymonius, Virgil on, xiii, 335

Stuart, Lady Arabella, xv, 382

Stuart, Charles Edward, Burns on birthday of, vi, 290-1; supposed lament of, 305 (see also HE'S OWER THE HILLS, WHA'LL BE KING BUT CHARLIE, CHARLIE IS MY DARLING)

Stuart, Lady Jane, xxv, 8

Stuart, Sir John, and James Mill, xxv, 8

Stuart, Robert, xlii, 1161, 1166, 1173

Stuarts, Burns on the, vi, 266, 276

Stubbornness, man's worst ill, viii, 296;

Locke on, xxxvii, 61-2, 84; Sophocles on, viii, 270, 278

Stucco, Lady, in SCHOOL FOR SCANDAL, xviii, 135

Student, Chaucer's, xl, 19

Students, Carlyle's advice to, xxv, 361-2; in FAUST, xix, 40-1; soldiers and, Don Quixote on, xiv, 373-9; in Utopia, xxxvi, 181, 183, 194-5

STUDIES, ESSAY ON, Bacon's, iii, 122-3

Studiousness, Bagehot on, xxviii, 176

Study, Burke on methods of, xxiv, 7-8; Burke on object of, 47; of children, xxxvii, 78-9, 128-30, 139-42; Confucius on, xliv, 26 (12, 17); ECCLESIASTES on, 349 (12); Epictetus on, ii, 170 (145); hours for, iii, 97-8; Locke on listlessness in, xxxvii, 107-12; Milton's course of, iii, 239-4; Montaigne on, xxxii, 9; Montaigne on aim of, 38-9; Montaigne on excessive, 53-5; pleasures of, iv, 36, 38; Pliny's method of, ix, 191-2, 301-3; thought and, Confucius on, xliv, 8 (15), 53 (30); Tzu-hsia on, 64 (7)

Stufa, Pandolfo della, xxxi, 411 note 2

Stufa, Prinzivalle della, xxxi, 30 and note 3

Stukeley, on Stonehenge, v, 457-8

Stupidity, town of, in PILGRIM'S PROGRESS, xv, 251, 252

Stussi, in WILLIAM TELL, xxvi, 467-9, 472-3

Stygian Lake, Dante on the, xx, 31-2

Style, Pascal's rules of, xlviii, 14-19, 21-3

Styx, Aristophanes on the, viii, 453; Dante on the, xx, 60; Milton on the, iv, 123; oaths by the, xiii, 296, 418; xxii, 72; xxvi, 178; Socrates on the, ii, 108; Virgil on the, xiii, 222, 296

Subhadda, xlv, 640-4

Subject States, arms in, xxxvi, 68-9; Bacon on, iii, 76-7; factions in, xxxvi, 69-70; Machiavelli on, 8-12, 18-19; More on, 159-60

Subjection, Kempis on, vii, 212-13

Subjects, single men not best, iii, 21

SUBLIME AND BEAUTIFUL, Burke's, xxiv, 29-140; remarks on, 28

Sublimity, in building, xxiv, 63-5; Burke on source of, 35-73; Burke on tests of, 72; color as source of, 69; compared with the beautiful, 101-2; defined, 45; difficulty as a source of, 65; feeling as source of, 73; heightened by the gro-tesque, xxxix, 349; infinity a source of, xxiv, 62-3; light and darkness as sources of, 67-9, 114-19; littleness as cause of, 61-2; magnificence a source of, 66-7; passion caused by, 52; physical causes of, 103-18; pleasure in contemplating, 45; power a cause of, 55-60; privation a source of, 60-1; smells and tastes as sources of, 71-3; sound as source of, 69-71, 111-14; succession and uniformity causes of, 63-4, 111-14; terror the first principle of, 49-50; ugliness and, 97; vastness a cause of, 61-2, 110-11; Wordsworth on, xxxix, 334

Submarine Changes, Lyell on, xxxviii, 393-4, 395, 396

Submarines, in New Atlantis, iii, 179

Submission, Kempis on, vii, 240-1; Pascal on, xlviii, 97 (268-70)

Subscriptions, Franklin's advice on getting, i, 118-19

Subsidence, areas of, as shown by coral reefs, xxix, 483-4; Lyell on, xxxviii, 402, 407, 409, 412; rate of, xxix, 485

Subsidies (see Bounties)

Subsistence, relation of, to population, x, 81 (see Food-Supply)

Substance, son of Ens, iv, 22-3

Subterranean Changes, Lyell on, xxxviii, 394-7

Subterranean Movements, Lyell on, xxxviii, 406-9

Subtle, in the ALCHEMIST, with Face, xlvii, 543-50; with Dapper, 550, 551-8, 601-2; with Dapper as Priest of Fairy, 608-11, 650, 651-3; with Drugger, 558-62, 588-92; with Mammon, 563-4, 571-80; in plot against Mammon, 584; finds Mammon with Dol, 631-4; with Kastrill and Dame Pliant, 618-21; quarrel with Face over Pliant, 621-2; dealings with Puritans, 585-8, 592-3, 593-9, 599-600, 601-2, 638-41; plot against Surly as the Don, 621-9; on Surly and Pliant, 634; denounced by Surly, 635-6; promises coming of Count, 637; renews claims to Pliant, 640; hears Lovewit's return, 641-2; his plot with Dol, 654-5; betrayed by Face, 655-7

Subtlety, Raleigh on, xxxix, 74-5

Success, in business, price of, v, 45, 46-7; requires toil, ii, 173-4 (157); a source of power, xxxiv, 360

Succession, effect of, on the imagination,

xxiv, 63; physical cause of sublimity of, 111-14

Succession Act, Burke on the, xxiv, 163-4

Succession-taxes, x, 506

SUCH A PARCEL OF ROGUES IN A NATION, vi, 420

Suckling, Sir John, POEMS by, xl, 353-4

Sucro, death of, xiii, 407

Sudassana the Great, xlv, 638

Suddenness, disagreeable, xxiv, 99; as source of sublime, 70

Suddhodana, father of Buddha, xlv, 586, 606

Sudra, caste of, xlv, 870

Suevian Sea, Tacitus on the, xxxiii, 118

Suevians, origin of the, xxxiii, 93-4; Tacitus on the, 114-19; worship of Isis by, 97-8

Suffering, alone and with others, xlvi, 276; Longfellow on, xlii, 1266; Shakespeare on, xlvi, 149; strength equal to, iv, 113

Suffolk, Duke of, xxxix, 74

Suffrage, Lowell on universal, xxviii, 453-4, 465-6; Mill on democratic, xxv, 69-70; woman (see Woman S.)

Sugar, in ancient times, xxxv, 276; cause of pleasantness of, xxiv, 122-3; composition of, xxx, 166; potash and, 54 note; profits of cultivation of, x, 160-1

Suicide, Browne on, iii, 294-5 (44); Bunyan on, xv, 118-19; Epictetus on, ii, 122-3 (17, 18); xlviii, 389; Goethe's Faust on, xix, 35; Hamlet on, xlvi, 103, 144; Kant on, xxxii, 332-3, 340; Milton on, iv, 316-17; Mohammed on, xlv, 971; punishment of, in old England, xxxv, 366; Shelley on, xviii, 309; Socrates on, ii, 49-50; in Utopia, xxxvi, 208

SUICIDE, ON A, vi, 499

Suicides, in Dante's HELL, xx, 53-7

Suiones, Tacitus on the, xxxiii, 117-18

SUITORS, ESSAY ON, Bacon's, iii, 120-1

Sujātā, story of, xlv, 613-15

Suleyman (see Solomon)

Sulivan, Capt., on Falkland Islands, xxix, 193 note, 195, 196, 197

Sully, Burke on, xxiv, 186

Sulphindigotic Acid, xxx, 80 note

Sulpicius, Caius, in Catiline conspiracy, xii, 233

Sulpicius, Publius, quarrel with Pompeius, ix, 9

Sulpicius, Servius, letter to Cicero, ix, 165; letter from Cicero, 168

Sultan, Pascal on the, xlviii, 37-8, 48 (113)

SULTAN'S STEWARD, STORY OF THE, xvi, 133-42

Sultans, death of, concealed, iii, 141

SUMEDHA, THE STORY OF, xlv, 577-602

Summer, beauties of, v, 25; Campbell on, xli, 772; evening in, 480; one swallow makes not a, xiv, 95

Summer, of All-Saints, xlii, 1304

Summers, William, xxxviii, 158-9, 161

Summoner, Chaucer's, xl, 28-9

Summons, judicial, in Massachusetts, xliii, 69 (21), 70 (25)

Summum Bonum, Buddhist, xlv, 713-30; Pascal on, xlviii, 121 (361); various ideas of, 32-3

Sumptuary Laws, Penn on, i, 391; Smith on, x, 274

Sun, Addison on the, xl, 400; xlv, 535; Bunyan's lesson from the, xv, 235; Burke on grandeur of the, xxiv, 67-8; Copernicus on motion of, xxxix, 54; Dante's fourth Heaven, xx, 325; David on the, xliv, 163 (4-6); Goethe on the, xix, 18; Herodotus on the, xxxiii, 17-18, 71-2; human mind compared with, ii, 263 (57); Manfred on the, xviii, 442-3; Milton on the, iv, 16, 149-51, 155, 191, 246, 307-8; Pascal on the, xlviii, 26-7; Raleigh on the, xxxix, 107-8; Raleigh on changes in, 107; source of all forces, xxx, 210; started in Aries, xx, 6 note 5; Tacitus on the, xxxiii, 118; tides affected by, xxx, 276-9, 291

Sun-dial, invented in Babylon, xxxiii, 53

Sun-spots, Pascal on, xlviii, 40 (91)

SUN AND WIND, fable of, xvii, 34-5

SUN, FOLLOW THY, xl, 285

SUN OF MY SOUL, THOU SAVIOUR DEAR, xlv, 565-6

SUN-DAY HYMN, xlv, 570

SUN-FLOWER, AH, xli, 584

Sunday Laws, Mill on, xxv, 286-7

Sunderland, Earl of, Peerage Bill of, xxvii, 173-4

Sunrise, lines on, iv, 31; on land and sea, xxiii, 13

Sunset, Thoreau on, xxviii, 424-5; Thoreau's allegory of, 421-2

Superfluities, attitude of Quakers toward, i, 305; Kempis on, vii, 290 (4); Penn

on taxing, i, 328 (53), 390-1; Wool-man on, 252-3, 290

Superfluity, of words, vii, 213

Supernatural Agencies, belief in, xxxviii, 386, 389-91

Supernaturalist, in FAUST, xix, 189

SUPERSTITION, ESSAY ON, Bacon's, iii, 45-6

Superstition, Burke on, xxiv, 292; in Burns's HOLY FAIR, vi, 97; defined by Hobbes, xxxiv, 341; fable on, xvii, 27; in literature, xxvii, 220-1; origin of, xxxiv, 375; piety and, xlviii 94 (255); Pope on, xl, 428-9

Superstition, in PILGRIM'S PROGRESS, xv, 97-8

Suplee, Capt., at Gettysburg, xliii, 387

Suppiyā, xlv, 774-5

SUPPLICATION, A, by Cowley, xl, 365-6

SUPPLICATION, A, by Wyatt, xl, 192

Supply, annual, on what dependent, x, 5-6

SUPPOSED MISTRESS, HIS, by Jonson, xl, 300

SUPPOSED MISTRESS, WISHES FOR THE, xl, 359-63

Suppuration, causes and prevention of, xxxviii, 257-67

Supremacy Act, More on, xxxvi, 129-30

Supreme Court, of United States, xliii, 189-90; appointment of judges, 188 (2); Lincoln on decisions of, 319; Marshall on duties of, 208-9, 224

Sura, Attius, Pliny on, ix, 366

Sura, Licinius, letters to, ix, 259, 311

Sureties, Hobbes on, xxxiv, 417

Surface, Charles, in SCHOOL FOR SCANDAL, in love with Maria, xviii, 117, 118; his bankruptcy, 120, 122, 124-5; Row-ley on, 127; Sir Peter on, 127; Sir Oliver on, 140-1; Sir Oliver plans to try, 141-4; Maria on, 145; at home, 150-2; with Sir Oliver as Premium, 153-7; in the picture room, 158-62; with Rowley, 162; suspected with Lady Teazle, 139, 142, 145, 168, 171-2, 187, 193; at Joseph's, 171-5; mistakes Sir Oliver for Premium, 189-90; reconciled with Sir Oliver, 191-2; reconciled to Maria, 192-5

Surface, Joseph, in SCHOOL FOR SCANDAL, relations with Lady Sneerwell, xviii, 117; calls on Lady Sneerwell, 118-26; Sir Peter on, 127; on Backbite's epi-gram, 131-2; with Maria at Sneer-well's, 132, 137; with Lady Teazle, 137-8; Sir Oliver on, 140; Sir Oliver plans to try, 141; Maria and, 145; with Lady Teazle, 164-6; with Sir Peter, 167-71; with Charles, 171-3; de-nounced by Lady Teazle, 175-6; visited by Sir Oliver as Stanley, 177-9; Lady Sneerwell and, 188-9; expels Sir Oliver as Stanley, 190; denounced by Sir Oliver, Peter, and Lady Teazle, 190-1; accuses Charles with Lady Sneerwell, 192-3; follows Sneerwell, 193

Surface, Sir Oliver, in SCHOOL FOR SCAN-DAL, reported to be coming home, xviii, 124; his return, 128; with Rowley, 139; with Sir Peter, 140-1; plans to try his nephews, 141-4; at Charles's house, 149-50, 153-7; in picture room, 158-62; after the sale, 163; visits Joseph as Stanley, 176-9; mistaken for physician, 184; with Sir Peter after scandal, 186-7; returns to Joseph's as himself, 189-91; denounces Joseph, 190-1; recon-ciled to Charles, 191-2

Surgery, antiseptic principle in, xxxviii, 257-67; the germ theory in, 364, 369-70; papers on, 9-58, 223-54, 257-67, 364-82; in 16th century, 8

Surly, Pertinax, in THE ALCHEMIST, with Mammon at Subtle's, xlvii, 564-7, 571-83; plot against, 584; fails to meet Face, 599; as Spanish don, 599-600; with Face and Subtle, 622-5; presented to Dame Pliant, 627-9; exposes fraud to her, 635; denounces Subtle and Face, 635-6; with Kastrill, 637-8; and Drug-ger, 638; quarrel with Kastrill, 639; returns with Mammon, 647-8; with officers, 658-61

Surprise, Marcus Aurelius on, ii, 256 (15), 297 (13)

Surrey, Earl of, death of, xxxix, 78; Jon-son on, xxvii, 56; poems by, xl, 193-5; Sidney on, xxvii, 45

Surt, the giant, xlix, 295 note

Surtees, Robert, BARTHRAM'S DIRGE, xli, 769-70

Survival of the Fittest, term invented by Spencer, xi, 72 (see also Natural Selec-tion)

Susagus, ix, 369 note 2

SUSAN, THE REVERIE OF POOR, xli, 655

Susanna, friend of Jesus, xliv, 374 (3)

SUSPICION, ESSAY ON, Bacon's, iii, 82-3

Suspicion, simplicity and, iv, 153; Web-ster on, xlvii, 762-3

Suspiciousness, Confucius on, xliv, 49 (33)

SUTHERLAND, MR., PROLOGUE FOR, vi, 374-5

Sutlej, sediment of the, xxxviii, 402-3

Suttee, practise of, iii, 98

SWABIANS, THE SEVEN, xvii, 203-6

Swaflod, the maid, xlix, 322

SWALLOW AND OTHER BIRDS, fable of, xvii, 16

SWALLOW, SWALLOW, O, xlii, 974-5

Swallow, Swinburne on the, xlii, 1201-3

Swamps, Thoreau on, xxviii, 410-11

Swan, Milton on the, iv, 238; Socrates on death-song of the, ii, 77

SWANS, THE SIX, xvii, 132-7

SWANS, THE WILD, xvii, 265-80

Swanhild, daughter of Sigurd, xlix, 353, 418; wedding and slaying of, 354-5, 418, 421-2, 424; her future foretold, 336, 383, 385

Swanwick, Anna, translator of EGMONT, xix, 251

Swarga, xlv, 827, 862

Swearing, Hobbes on, xxxiv, 400-1

SWEARING COXCOMB, ON A, vi, 499

Sweden, Freeman on, xxviii, 259; geological elevation of, xxxviii, 406-7

Swedenborg, Emanuel, Emerson on, v, 21-2, 177, 178; on the English, 388; the illumination of, 141; on time and space, ii, 328 note; on truth, 139-40

SWEET AFTON, vi, 417-18

SWEET DISORDER, xl, 336

SWEET AND LOW, xlii, 972

Sweet-meats, Locke on, xxxvii, 21

SWEET TIBBIE DUNBAR, vi, 344

SWEET WILLIAM'S GHOST, xl, 78-80

SWEETEST LOVE, I DO NOT GO, xl, 307-8

Sweetness, Berkeley on, xxxvii, 198-9; nature of, xxiv, 121-3; relaxing, 123-4

Swift, nest of the, xi, 277

SWIFT, JONATHAN, ESSAY ON, xxviii, 7-28

Swift, Jonathan, academy planned by, xxxiv, 156; Addison and, xxvii, 176, 179-80; ambition of, xxviii, 10-11; attitude toward inferiors and superiors, 9-10; benefactions of, 16; Berkeley and, xxxvii, 186; biographers of, xxviii, 8-9; his bitterness, 11; as a churchman, 17-19; ON CONVERSATION, xxvii, 91-8; at court, xxviii, 15-16; ON DEATH OF STELLA, xxvii, 122-30; Directions to Servants, xxxvi, 3-4; Drapier's Letters, xxviii, 19; Emerson on, v, 433; An

Englishman by all but birth, xxviii, 11-12; Goldsmith on, xli, 505, 506; ON GOOD MANNERS, xxvii, 99-103; Gulliver's Travels, xxviii, 21-3; Hazlitt on, xxvii, 278; life and writings of, 90; xxviii, 7-8; literary style, 12; loneliness and greatness, 27-8; loneliness and suffering, 18-19; on marriage and children, 19-20; Modest Proposal, 19; morality of his times, 10-11; on new and obsolete words, xxxix, 203-4; religion of, xxviii, 17-19; Stella and, 23-7, 28; Temple and, 12-15; his unhappiness, 22-3; Vanessa and, 27; Voltaire on, xxxiv, 148, 152; TO A YOUNG POET, xxvii, 104-21; remarks on YOUNG POET, l, 47

Swim bladder, Darwin on the, xi, 186

Swimming, Locke on, xxxvii, 13-14

Swinburne, Algernon C., POEMS by, xlii, 1199-1209

Swine, abominated in Egypt, xxxiii, 29-30

SWINEHERD, THE, story of, xvii, 230-4

Swine-pox, xxxviii, 197

Swiss, in France, xxxvi, 47; Goldsmith on the, xli, 524; in Italy, xxxvi, 45; Machiavelli on the, 42; Pascal on the, xlviii, 108 (305)

Swiss Cantons, ancient league of, xxvi, 402 note

Swiss Confederation, Freeman on, xxviii, 261-2

Swiss Republic, Bacon on, iii, 35

Swiss Soldiers, Machiavelli on, xxxvi, 85

Switzerland, connection with the German Empire, xxvi, 420-1; first settlement of, 419-20; Goldsmith on, xli, 524-6; taxes in, x, 499-500

SWITZERLAND AND ENGLAND, xli, 675-6

Sybaris, death of, xiii, 402

Sybil, in SHOEMAKER'S HOLIDAY, xlvii, 477-9, 484-6, 504, 510-11, 514, 516, 518

Sycophants, bites of, proverb of, xxxix, 56

Sycorax, the witch, xlvi, 408-9

Sydenham, Locke and, xxxvii, 4

Sydney, Australia, Darwin on, xxix, 435-6

Sykes, Gen., at Gettysburg, xliii, 337, 358, 360, 397; Haskell on, 359

Sykes, John, i, 185, 188, 189-90, 227

Sylla, Faustus, Cicero on, xii, 240-1

Sylla, Lucius, Cornelius, Burke on confiscations of, xxiv, 251; Cæsar and, xii, 264, 267; Cæsar on, iii, 41; called

Felix, 101; Dryden on, xiii, 15; ignorance of, xxvii, 21; name of, xii, 157; Pompey and, iii, 67; the tower of Archelaus at, xxxv, 319

Syllogism, Bacon on the, xxxix, 133; Hobbes on meaning of, xxxiv, 327; Mill's theory of the, xxv, 114; Montaigne on the, xxxii, 63

SYLVANDER TO CLARINDA, vi, 293-4

Sylvester, follower of St. Francis, xx, 332 note 19

Sylvester, Joshua, LOVE'S OMNIPRESENCE, xl, 314

Sylvester, Pope, and the Lateran, xx, 80 note 10

Symbols, Epictetus on, ii, 172-3 (154); expression by, v, 166; mistaken use of, 178; universal use of, 168, 175

SYME, JOHN, COMPLIMENTS OF, vi, 513

Symeon Niger, xliv, 450 (1), 456 (14)

Symmachus, prefect of Rome, vii, 76

Symmetry, Pascal on, xlviii, 17 (28)

Symonds, J. Addington, translator of Cellini, xxxi

Symonds, Thomas, xliii, 169

Sympathy, Bacon on, iii, 68; Browne on, 317-18; Burke on, xxiv, 40-3; Emerson on false, v, 77; excessive, Emerson on, 209; natural to man, xxxiv, 271; pleasure in, xxxix, 280, 281

Synagogue, Pascal on the, xlviii, 297 (851), 298 (852)

Syncope, Paré on, xxxviii, 54

Syndercomb, Hugo on, xxxix, 380

Synods (see Councils)

Syphax, in *Cato*, xxvii, 187, 188, 189, 190-1

Syphogrants, officers in Utopia, xxxvi, 177, 179, 181, 185, 187

Syracuse, expedition against, xii, 120-23, 126, 127

Syria, Raleigh on, xxxix, 71; Sesostris in, xxxiii, 50

Syrians, circumcision among ancient, xxxiii, 51

Syrinx, and Pan, xl, 378; references to, iv, 44, 376; Webster on, xlvii, 794

Systematic Affinity, defined, xi, 293

Systems, Voltaire on, xxxix, 376

Systole and Diastole, of arteries, xxxviii, 65-6, 67-8, 80-1; of the heart, 75, 78-9, 80-1

Tabernacle, references to the, iv, 348; xliv, 438

Tabitha, xliv, 443 (36-42)

Table, Mohammed's chapter on the, xlv, 994-1000

Tabor, the, xx, 89 note

Tabus, xlix, 198

Tacca, Giovan Francesco della, xxxi, 226

Tacca, Giovan Piero della, xxxi, 39

Tacco, Ghino di, xx, 166 note 2

Tachompso, island of, xxxiii, 19

Tacitus, Cornelius, on benefits, xlviii, 30 note; celebrity of, ix, 345; his silence on Christ, xlviii, 273 (787); funeral orator of Verginius, ix, 212; GERMANY, xxxiii, 93-120; remarks on GERMANY of, l, 21; life and works, xxxiii, 92; on miracles of Vespasian, xxxvii, 385-6; Pliny's letters to, ix, 191, 204, 284, 288, 315

Tact, Ruskin on, xxviii, 113

Taddeo, Dante on, xx, 336 note 21

Tadino, Alessandro, xxi, 458, 467; in plague of San Carlo, 502-3, 508, 532-3

Tagarasikkhi, xlv, 675

Tâghût, xlv, 973 note 16

Tagua-tagua, Lake, xxix, 270

Tagus, in the ÆNEID, xiii, 307, 407

Tahattawans, the sachem, xliii, 144

Tahiti, Darwin on, xxix, 407-20

Tahitians, Darwin on the, xxviii, 410

Tai-po, xliv, 24 (1) note

Taillefer, at Hastings, xxviii, 70-1

TAILOR, REPLY TO A, vi, 228-30

TAILOR, STORY TOLD BY THE, xvi, 149-62

TAILOR, THE VALIANT LITTLE, xvii, 90-8

Tails, use and development of, xi, 196-7

Taine, Hippolyte Adolphe, life and works, xxxix, 410 note; INTRODUCTION TO ENGLISH LITERATURE, 410-37; remarks on INTRODUCTION of, l, 49

Take-heed, in PILGRIM'S PROGRESS, xv, 248

TAKE, O TAKE, xl, 267

Tale-bearers, Mrs., Candour on, xviii, 121

Talent, character contrasted with, v, 159; differences of, due to division of labor, x, 20-1; duty of developing, xxxii, 333-4, 340-1; genius contrasted with, v, 144, 165; not good in itself, xxxii, 305; reason brilliantly expressed, 125

Tales, remarks on, xvii, 7-8

Talib, son of Sahl, xvi, 296-7, 298-325

Taliessin, Celtic bard, xxxii, 166; reference to, xl, 460

TALK OF HIM THAT'S FAR AWAY, vi, 302

Talkative, in PILGRIM'S PROGRESS, xv, 78-87

Talkativeness, excessive, ii, 183 (5); vii, 213; Shakespeare's advice against, xlvi, 109

Talkers, Bacon on, iii, 18; Confucius on, xliv, 45 (5)

Talleyrand, on necessity, v, 461

Talmud, the, iii, 42 note; Pascal on the, xlviii, 211

TAM THE CHAPMAN, LINES ON, vi, 59

TAM GLEN, vi, 346

TAM O' SHANTER, vi, 388-94

TAM SAMSON'S ELEGY, vi, 242-5

Tamar, Pascal on story of, xlviii, 262 (743)

Tamas, xlv, 853, 863, 865, 868, 869, 870

Tamerlane, Bacon on, iii, 23; Bajazet and, xxxix, 98

Tanabuso, bravo in THE BETROTHED, xxi, 319-20

Tanais, death of, xiii, 407

Tanagra, Landor on, xli, 899-900

Tancarville, Earl of, at Caen, xxxv, 9, 13-16; at Poitiers, 37, 50, 56

Tang, xliv, 40 note 8, 66 (1) note

Tannahill, Robert, POEMS by, xli, 593-4

Tansillo, Luigi, quoted, xiv, 315

Tan-tai Mieh-ming, xliv, 19 (12)

Tantalus, Cervantes on, xiv, 104; Homer on, xxii, 159; Milton on, iv, 124; Webster on, xlvii, 757

Tanusius, xii, 283 note

Tapacolo, Darwin on the, xxix, 275

Tapalguen, Sierra, xxix, 122

Taprobane, Greek name of Ceylon, xxxv, 227 note

Tapwell, in NEW WAY TO PAY OLD DEBTS, xlvii, 859-63, 919-21

Tarantula, Harrison on the, xxxv, 346

Taratan, herald in New Atlantis, iii, 165

TARBOLTON LASSES, vi, 23-4

Tarchon, Tuscan chief, xiii, 284, 288; ally of Æneas, 326-7; in battle, 382-3

Tarentum, Fabius at, ix, 48-9

Targhetta, Miliano, xxxi, 182

Tariff (see Duties)

Tarlatti Ciacco de', xx, 166 note 3

Tarn, Mount, Darwin on, xxix, 239-40

Tarquin, on his friends, ix, 28; reference to, xlvi, 340

Tarquinius Superbus, attempts to return to Rome, xii, 148-9

Tarquins, Virgil on the, xiii, 235

Tarquitus, death of, xiii, 340

Tartars, raids of, iv, 301-2

Tartarus, Milton on, iv, 205; Socrates's

description of, ii, 107-8, 109; Virgil on, xiii, 225, 226-8

Tartrate of Lime, fermentation of, xxxviii, 316-23

TARTUFFE, Molière's, xxvi, 199-296; editorial remarks on, 198; Goethe on, xxxii, 124; Hugo on, xxxix, 350, 356, 357

Tartuffe, in TARTUFFE, discussed by Mme. Pernelle and others, xxvi, 201-3, 205; relations with Orgon, 207, 209-10; discussed by Orgon and Cleante, 211-15; chosen by Orgon for Mariane's husband, 219-28; sent for, by Elmire, 244; with Dorine, 245-6; with Elmire, 247-52; denounced by Damis, 254; with Orgon, 255-61; with Cleante, 262-4; led on by Elmire, 270-5; caught by Orgon, 277; refuses to leave house, 277; sends Mr. Loyal to claim property, 285-90; the box of Argas and, 279, 291; comes to arrest Orgon, 292; himself arrested, 295

Tar-water, Berkeley on, xxxvii, 186

Tasks, Locke on, xxxvii, 56-7

Tasmania, Darwin on, xxix, 450

Tasso, Battista del, xxxi, 24-5, 27, 345 note 5

Tasso, Torquato, Dryden on, xiii, 23, 24, 26, 33, 43; a madman, xxvii, 357; on philosophy, xxxii, 34; on poets, xxvii, 356-7; Sainte-Beuve on, xxxii, 132; Scudéri on, xxxix, 361; Shelley on, xxvii, 338; the sonnet and, xli, 681; Spenser on, xxxix, 62

TASTE, ESSAY ON, Burke's, xxiv, 11-26

TASTE, THE STANDARD OF, Hume's, xxvii, 203-21

Taste, Burke on standards of, xxiv, 11-12; Burke on study of, 9; constituents of, 22-3; definition of, 12-13; delicacy of, xxvii, 209-11; differences of, due to organs, 209; differences of, due to particular humors, 217-18; differences due to age or country, 218-21; differences of, judged by degree of pleasure, xxiv, 20-1; reason of so-called differences of, 18-21; Emerson on good, v, 209; habits affect sense of, xxiv, 15-16; of the imagination, 16-18; improved by practice, xxvii, 211-13; not a separate faculty, xxiv, 25-6; Poe on, xxviii, 376; in poetry, Hugo on, xxxix, 384-5; possibility of determining a standard of, xxvii, 216-18; prejudice and, 213-14;

as matter of reason, 214-16; Reynolds on, xxxix, 268, 289; Schiller on cultivation of, xxxii, 234-8, 254-5, 266-7, 271-4, 294-5; sense of, Burke on, xxiv, 121-2; sense of, same in all men, 14-15; of the senses, 13-16; for sensible objects and in the passions, 21-2; as matter of the understanding, 22-6; variety of, xxvii, 203-4; want of, its cause, xxiv, 22-3; Wordsworth on, xxxix, 321, 331-4

Tastes, Berkeley on, xxxvii, 198-9, 206; as sources of the sublime, xxiv, 71-3

Taste-that-which-is-good, the cook, xv, in PILGRIM'S PROGRESS, 264

Tathāgata, a name of Buddha, xlv, 633 note

Tatti, Giocopo, xxxi, 149 note 2

Taulchinne, the juggler, xlix, 233

Taureas, and Alcibiades, xii, 120

Taurus, commander for Octavius, xii, 372

Taurus, the sign, reference to, iv, 107

Taxation, equality of, x, 477; general rules of, 477-80; heavy, unfits for empire, iii, 75; popular attitude toward, v, 247; without representation, xliii, 147 (3)

Taxes, on capital, x, 505-10; capitation, 514-7; on commerce, iii, 51; on consumption, x, 517-48; direct apportionment of, xliii, 180-1 (3), 185 (4); duties and, x, 345; farming of, 543; on house rent, 488-95; on interest of money, 496-9; on luxuries, 518-21, 535-9; on luxuries, payment of, 477 (3); on luxuries, Penn on, i, 328 (53), 390-1; national, under the Confederation, xliii, 162; national, under Constitution, 184 (8), 185 (5); on necessaries, x, 518, 520-3, 547-8; on necessaries, as requiring duties on foreign goods, 345-6; on newspapers, Wordsworth on, v, 324; on produce of land, x, 486-7; on profits, 496; on rent of land, 479-86; on rent, payment of, 477 (3); source of, 53; on stimulants, Mill on, xxv, 297; on transfers of property, x, 505-11; on wages, 511; for war, Quakers on, i, 217-20

Taylor, Dr., of Norwich, vi, 94

Taylor, Father, Dana on, xxiii, 111

Taylor, Jeremy, Emerson on, xlii, 1249; Wordsworth on, xxxix, 308-9

Taylor, Thomas, Emerson on, v, 465

Taylor, Mrs., and J. S. Mill, xxv, 4; Mill on, 116-9, 142, 149-54; death of, 155

Taylor, P. A., Mill on, xxv, 183 note

Taylor, W., on fancy and imagination, xxxix, 301

TE DEUM LAUDAMUS, xlv, 546-7

Tea, Burke on taste for, xxiv, 15-16

Teachers, Channing on importance of, xxviii, 358-60; Confucius on, xliv, 8 (11); Locke on, xxxvii, 69-80, 128, 139-42, 153-4, 167-8; Montaigne on, xxxii, 35-6; need of personal, xxviii, 32-7; paid, Socrates on, ii, 7-8; pay and consideration of, x, 135-7; qualities needed by, ii, 157 (108), 161-2 (121); sacred and literary, v, 143

Teaching, Burke on method of, xxiv, 12; Confucius on, xliv, 21 (7, 8); Pope on methods of, i, 18-19 (see also Education)

TEAR-DROP, THE, vi, 510

Tears, Byron on, xli, 790; De Quincey's Lady of, xxvii, 321-2; false, true pity move, xiii, 105; Hunt on, xxvii, 285; Laertes on, xlvi, 190

TEARS, IDLE TEARS, xlii, 972-3

Teazle, Lady, in SCHOOL FOR SCANDAL, marriage with Sir Peter, xviii, 126; scene with Sir Peter, 128-31; at Lady Sneerwell's, 132-7; Joseph Surface and, 137-8, 164-7, 171; suspected with Charles Surface, 139, 142, 145, 168, 171-2, 187, 193; reconcilement and new quarrel with Sir Peter, 146-8; caught behind screen, 175-6; at Joseph Surface's after reconcilement to husband, 190-4; epilogue spoken by, 196

Teazle, Sir Peter, in SCHOOL FOR SCANDAL, guardian of Surface brothers, xviii, 116; on Lady Teazle, 126-7; with Rowley, 126-8; scene with Lady Teazle, 128-31; at Sneerwell's, 134-6; with Sir Oliver, 140-1; his plan to make trial of Charles Surface, 134-45; with Maria, 145; reconcilement and new quarrel with Lady Teazle, 146-8; at Joseph Surface's house, 167-71, 174-6; at home after the scandal, 184-7; at Joseph Surface's, 190-4

Tedaldi, Lionardo, xxxi, 335, 338

Tedmur, inscription of, xvi, 320-1

Teeth, and hair, related, xi, 28, 148-9

Tegan, mantle of, xxxii, 146

Tegetmeier, on bees, xi, 275

Tegghiaio, in Dante's HELL, xx, 27

Teiresias, in ANTIGONE, viii, 287-91; in the BACCHÆ, 374-6, 379-82; Homer on, xxii, 142, 147-8; in ŒDIPUS THE KING, viii, 218-23

Telauges, and Socrates, ii, 251-2 (66)

Teleclides, on Pericles, xii, 38, 53

Telegraph, Helmholtz on the, xxx, 206-7

Telemachus, in the ODYSSEY, roused to action by Pallas, xxii, 12-17; rebukes Penelope, 18; with the suitors, 18-19; complains of suitors in assembly, 22-5; asks for ship to go to Pylos, 26-7; counselled by Pallas, 28; prepares for sailing, 29-31; sails, 32; with Nestor at Pylos, 33-45; with Menelaus at Sparta, 46-62; plotted against by the suitors, 62-3, 66, 67; warned by Athene to return home, 200-1; departs with gifts, 201-5; takes ship at Pylos, 205-7; his landing in Ithaca, 212-14; at Eumæus's hut, 215-19; recognizes Ulysses, 219-20; in plan to destroy the suitors, 221-3; hears return of his enemies, 227; returns to mother, 228-9; relates what he had heard, 230-1; receives Eumæus and Ulysses, 236-7; rebukes Antinous, 238; the sneeze of, 242; warned by Eumæus, 243; protects Ulysses in fight with Irus, 246-7; rebuked by Penelope, 250-1; advises suitors to retire, 255; removes arms from hall, 257-8; goes to assembly-place, 276-7; protects Ulysses from the wooers, 279-81; replies to Agelaus, 282; advised to expel Ulysses, 283; with the bow of Ulysses, 286-7; orders Penelope away, 293; gives Ulysses the bow, 293-4; with Ulysses against the suitors, 297-306; hangs faithless servants, 308; in meeting of father and mother, 312-13; in final fight, 333; Tennyson on, xlii, 978

Telemus, the soothsayer, xxii, 128

Teleology, Kant on, xxxii, 347 note

Telescopes, Newton on, xxxiv, 124

Tell, Walter, in WILLIAM TELL, at home, goes to Altdorf with father, xxvi, 428, 432; at Altdorf, 438-49; reunion with mother, 456; at home again, 482-3

Tell, William, in WILLIAM TELL, residence of, xxvi, 384 note; son-in-law of Fürst, 398; takes Baumgarten across the lake, 384-5; arrival at Stauffacher's, 391; at home, starts for Altdorf, 428-32; at Altdorf with Walter, 438-9;

neglects to bow to Gessler's cap, 439-40; at building of the Keep, 392; conversation with Stauffacher, 394; ordered to shoot apple from son's head, 441-7; arrested by Gessler, 447-9; embarked at Flüelen, 449; escape of, 453-5; in wait for Gessler, 464-7; with Stussi, 467-8; kills Gessler, 471-2; returns home, 483-4; with Duke John, 483-8; in final scene, 488-9

Tellheim, Major von, in MINNA VON BARNHELM, changing of his room referred to, xxvi, 300-2; announces intention to leave inn, 303; with Just, 303-4; with Madame Marloff, 305-7; destroys note, 307; with Just, agrees to keep him, 307-9; pardon asked by Minna, 309; prepares to leave inn, 309-10; Minna on, 314-15; discovered by his ring, 319-20; with Minna, takes leave of her, 324-7; with Werner, 335-40; with Franziska, 340-2; scene with Minna, 351-8; hears her misfortunes, 358-9; borrows money of Werner, 459-60; determines to marry Minna, 360; returns to Minna, with Franziska, 361; seeks reconciliation, 362-4; letter from king, 365-6; offers himself to Minna, 366-9; accuses Minna of faithlessness, 370; refuses Werner's money, 370-1; final reconciliation, 372-3; with Minna's uncle, 373; reconciliation with Werner, 374

Tell-true, in PILGRIM'S PROGRESS, xv, 297

Tellus, reference to, xx, 265

Temminck, on classification, xi, 437-8

Temper, Penn on, i, 336

Temperance, Channing on, xxviii, 351-2; Cicero on, ix, 57; common notion of, ii, 57-8; Dante's star of, xx, 146 note 5; definitions of, i, 79; Epictetus on show of, ii, 177 (176); Franklin on, i, 17, 44, 85; Franklin's rule of, 79-80; Greek idea of, xxv, 35; of heroism, v, 126; instances of, xx, 237-8; Manzoni on habits of, xxi, 237-8; Marcus Aurelius on, ii, 197-8, 260 (39), 297 (15); Milton on, iii, 201-2; iv, 63-4, 65, 332; necessity of, in pleasure, v, 87-8; Penn on, i, 328-9; philosopher's reason of, ii, 74-6; the virtue of prosperity, iii, 16

Temperance Ships, Dana on, xxiii, 300-1

Temperature, production of high, xxx,

108 note; why low, on mountains, 212-13

TEMPEST, THE, xlvi, 395-463; Hunt on, xxvii, 294; stage representation of the, 313-15

Temple, Sir William, Swift and, xxvii, 90; xxviii, 8, 12-15

Temples, pagan, Burke on grandeur of, xxiv, 63-4

Temporal Estate, Luther on the, xxxvi, 265-70

Temporal Happiness, Penn on, i, 343-4

Temporary, in PILGRIM'S PROGRESS, xv, 153-4

Temptation, Burns on, vi, 547; Kempis on, vii, 215-16, 249, 281-2, 299-300; More on, xxxvi, 100; necessary to virtue, iii, 202, 207-8; Pascal on, xlviii, 284 (821); Paul, St., on, xlv, 503 (13); Rousseau on reasons of, xxxiv, 277-8; seek not, iv, 269; supposes fallibility, 268; Winthrop on, xliii, 97; yielding to, Epictetus on, ii, 144 (75); yielding to, Kempis on, vii, 210 (2)

Temptation, In, xlv, 559-60

Temptations, of the flesh, vii, 183-8; of curiosity, 189-91; of pride, 191-4

Temsice, George, xxxvi, 135

Ten Thousand, Emerson on the, v, 189; retreat of the, xii, 357-8

Tencterians, Tacitus on the, xxxiii, 111

Tenderness, in friendship, v, 112

Tenedos, island of, xiii, 101

Tenements, Channing on, xxviii, 354-5

Teneriffe, identified as mountain of Atlas, viii, 178 note 21

TENNANT, JAMES, EPISTLE TO, vi, 334-6

Tennent, Gilbert, Franklin on, i, 118

Tennyson, Alfred Lord, ARABIAN NIGHTS' influence on, xvi, 4; Emerson on, v, 445; Poe on, xxviii, 390; poems by, xlii, 967-1057; Wordsworth on, v, 464

Terah, father of Abraham, iv, 15

Terence, Augustine, St., on, vii, 18; on compliance, ix, 39, 40; in Dante's Limbo, xx, 236; Montaigne on, xxxii, 90-1; quotations from, xlviii, 121 note 11; Scipio and, xiii, 67

Terentia, wife of Cicero, ix, 6; in Catiline conspiracy, xii, 233-4; Clodius and, 241-2; divorce of, ix, 79; xii, 252-3; letter to, ix, 89

TERESA, ST., ON THE BOOK AND PICTURE OF, xl, 363-4

Tereus, and Progne, xx, 179 note 4

Termagant, xlvi, 148 note 3

Tern, the snow-white, xxix, 461

Ternate, Drake at, xxxiii, 218-21

Terray, Abbé, interest under, x, 92

Terrier, Sir Tivy, xviii, 148

Terriers, Harrison on, xxxv, 350

Territories, under control of Congress, xliii, 191

Terror, as a means of authority, ix, 333; Burke on, xxiv, 41, 49-50; cause of, 105-6; darkness, as cause of, 68, 114-17; delight caused by, 109; in idea of infinity, 62-3; intermitting sounds, as cause of, 70-1; loudness, as cause of, 69-70; obscurity, as cause of, 50-1; idea of power, as cause of, 55-60; in privation, 60; suddenness, as cause of, 70; in idea of vastness, 61-2, 109-10 (see also Sublimity)

Terry, Job, Dana on, xxiii, 36-7

Tertian Fever, Harvey on, xxxviii, 125-6

Tertiary Deposits, Lyell on, xxxviii, 404-5

Tertullian, on Christians, xlviii, 354; on the church, 309 (890); on Esdras, 210

Tertullus, Cornutus, colleague of Pliny, ix, 362 note 1; on Certus, 341

Tertullus, the orator, xliv, 476 (1-8)

Teru-tero, Darwin on the, xxix, 120-1

Testa, C. Trebatius, letters to, ix, 132, 173

Testimony, Hobbes on, xxxiv, 399; Hume on, xxxvii, 377-8; Mohammed on, xlv, 1005-6

Tethys, references to, iv, 67; viii, 171

Tetu, French captain, xxxiii, 186-7, 188, 189, 192, 194

Tetzel, xxxvi, 281 note 9

Teucer, accuser of Alcibiades, xii, 123-4

Teucer, and Belus, xiii, 95

Teucrus, Virgil on, xiii, 132

Teuthrania, Herodotus on plains of, xxxiii, 11

Teutonic Literature, Renan on early, xxxii, 147-8

Teutonic Races, Christianity and, xxxii, 171

Teutons, compared with Slavs in, situation, xxviii, 266-7

Texas, history of, xliii, 289 note

Thackeray, William Makepeace, Emerson on, v, 439; END OF THE PLAY, xlii, 1058-60; ESSAY ON SWIFT, 7-28; life and works, xxviii, 5-6; remarks on Essay, l, 50

Thais, Alexander and, xl, 391, 394, 395; in Dante's HELL, xx, 76

Thalberg, and the Queen, v, 372
Thales, in Dante's Limbo, xx, 20; on death, xxxii, 27; Lycurgus and, iii, 194; Sidney on, xxvii, 7
Thames, importance of the, v, 335
Thammuz, Milton on, iv, 99
Thamud, xlv, 891, 906, 918
Thamyris, blind, iv, 136; death of, xiii, 402
THANATOPSIS, xlii, 1213-15
Thankfulness, human, ii, 131 (42); for virtue, 170 (146)
THANKSGIVING, A PSALM OF, xliv, 152-3
THANKSGIVING FOR A NATIONAL VICTORY, vi, 459
Thanksgivings, Roman, Cato on, ix, 152
Thaqif, tribe of, xlv, 919 note
Thargelia, the courtesan, xii, 60
THAT'S THE LASSIE o' MY HEART, vi, 540
Theagenes, Chariclea and, xxvii, 13; Sidney on, 10
Theano, the priestess, xii, 126
Theatre, Hugo on the Greek, xxxix, 341; Hugo on the modern, 381-2; Montaigne on the, xxxii, 70-1; morality and the, xxvii, 339-40; Pascal on the, xlviii, 13 (11); Swift on the, xxvii, 119-20; Voltaire on the, xxxiv, 152-3
Theatrical Representations, Lamb on, xxvii, 301-16
Thebes (Egypt), distance from sea, xxxiii, 10-11; extent of, 14; sacred animals of, 26-7
Thebes (Grecian), building of, xx, 131; founders of, xxii, 151; Philip of Macedon and, xxxvi, 42; Spartan policy toward, 18; the war against, viii, 258-60
Thebez, the prophet of, iv, 379
Theft, Augustine, St., on, vii, 26-7; Confucius on, xliv, 39 (18); Mohammed on, xlv, 997; More on causes and punishment of, xxxvi, 143-54; penalty of, by the Law, xliii, 94-8; punished in second circle of Hell, xx, 46; punishment of, in old England, xxxv, 366-7, 369
THEIR GROVES o' SWEET MYRTLE, vi, 534-5
Themes, Locke on, xxxvii, 54-6, 161-2
Themis, Æschylus on, viii, 174 note, 198; goddess of assemblies, xxii, 23; mother of Prometheus, viii, 167 note; second prophet at Delphi, 122

Themistocles, accused of treason, xii, 25-6; Aristides and, 79-81, 84-5, 86-7, 102, 104; rebuilds Athens, 21-2; is banished, 24-5; birth and boyhood of, 5-7; character of, 7-8, 9-10, 20-1; children of, 33-4; ix, 180; Cicero on, 25, 103; death of, xii, 33; Emerson on, v, 265; escapes death by dream, xii, 31-2; Herodotus and, ix, 104; honors conferred on, xii, 20-1; honors to family, 34; loses favor with confederates, 23; at Marathon, 83; memory of, ix, 52; Montaigne on, xxxii, 33-4; in Persian war, xii, 10-19; proposes destruction of Greek fleet, 22-3; proposes ships, 8; prosperity, 31; public treasury and, 81-2; at Salamis, 85-7; the Seriphian and, ix, 48; the soldier and, iii, 328; incurs displeasure of Sparta, xii, 23-4; the statue and, 32; tomb of, 34; his wanderings, 26-8; Xerxes and, 28-31; iii, 141-2
THEMISTOCLES, LIFE OF, Plutarch's, xii, 5-34
THENIEL MENZIES' BONIE MARY, vi, 283-4
Theobald, Johnson on, xxxix, 238-9
Theoclymenus, in the ODYSSEY, xxii, 207, 213, 231-2, 282
Theocratic Society, Hugo on, xxxix, 340
Theocritus, on husbandry, xxvii, 68; an idyllic poet, xxxix, 299; reference to, xli, 923
Theodoric, Bacon on, iii, 130
Theodorus, death of, xii, 384; high priest of Athens, 139
Theodotus, with Pompey's head, xii, 303-4
Theogenes, the statue of, v, 93
Theogiton, the Megarian, xii, 98
Theognis, Sainte-Beuve on, xxxii, 130-1
Theology, Bagehot on modern, xxviii, 204-5; Carlyle on, xxv, 363-4; Channing on, xxviii, 330; Descartes on, xxxiv, 8, 9-10; Emerson on our, v, 38; false, cure for, 280-1; Goethe on, xix, 80-1; Hume on, xxxvii, 420; Luther on study of, xxxvi, 324-7; Marlowe on, xix, 208, 210; of Middle Ages, xxviii, 215-16; Milton on study of, iii, 242; Milton on true, 222; Pascal on, xlviii, 48 (115), 398, 438; popular, Emerson on, v, 86; women and, xxviii, 149-50
Theomancy, defined, xxxiv, 382
Theophanes, the Lesbian, xii, 249-50

Theophilus, Antony's steward, xii, 373

Theophrastus, on anger and desire, ii, 201 (10); Cicero on, xii, 237; on Demades, 198; Huxley on, xxviii, 219; Milton on study of, iii, 241 note 29; on morals and sickness, xii, 75; Newman on, xxviii, 58; Plutarch on, xii, 113-14; Zaleucus and, ix, 149

Theopompus, Cæsar and, xii, 303; on Demosthenes, xii, 202; Ephorus and, ix, 146

Theoris, the priestess, Theopompus on, xii, 202

Theory, Burke on, xxiv, 8-9, 47-8; Goethe on, xix, 82; practical man's distrust of, v, 55; practise and, Mill on, xxv, 25; Smith on, xxvii, 247-8; test of truth of, xi, 497

Theramenes, in PHÆDRA, xxvi, 133-7, 155, 161-2, 191-4

Theramenes, pupil of Euripides, viii, 468; Aristophanes on, 455

THERE WAS A BONIE LASS, vi, 514

THERE'LL NEVER BE PEACE TILL JAMIE COMES HAME, vi, 398

Theresa, St., Pascal on, xlviii, 163 (499), 303 (868), 314 (917)

Thermo-electric Batteries, xxx, 208

Thermodon, Plutarch on, xii, 206

Thermometers, freezing-point of, xxx, 231-2

Thermopylæ, Byron on, xli, 813

Thermus, Cicero on, ix, 82, 146

Theron, death of, xiii, 332

Thersites, Epictetus on, ii, 158 (110); Pliny on, ix, 209 note 8

Theseus, acts and loves of, xxvi, 136-7, 159; the Amazons and, viii, 150; Ariadne and, xxii, 153; the centaurs and, xx, 245 note 7; in Epirus, xxvi, 171; in Hades, xiii, 220; Hercules compared with, v, 184; Hippolyta and, xiii, 379; Machiavelli on, xxxvi, 20, 21, 83; the Minotaur and, xiii, 208; xx, 49 note 4; ship of, ii, 45-6; in Tartarus, xiii, 228

Theseus, in HIPPOLYTUS, plotted against by Aphrodite, viii, 304; returns to find wife dead, 337-42; dooms Hippolytus, 342-3; scene with Hippolytus, 343-51; hears accident of Hippolytus, 355-8; hears of innocence of Hippolytus, 360; at death of Hippolytus, 364-7

Theseus, in PHÆDRA, his absence referred

to, xxvi, 133-4; reported dead, 146, 148-9; rumored still alive, 162; his return, 166, 169-72; hears dishonor of Hippolytus, 172-4; banishes Hippolytus, 174-8; tells Phædra, 179-80; with Aricia, 188-9; becomes suspicious of wrong, 189-90; learns death of Hippolytus, 191-4; learns his innocence, 194-6

Thesmophoria, the, xxxiii, 85

Thespis, reference to, xxxix, 351

Thessalus, accuser of Alcibiades, xii, 122-3

Thestylis, reference to, iv, 32

Thetford, university of, xxxv, 371

Thetis, Achilles and, v, 92; her flight from Chiron, xx, 180; in Dante's Limbo, 237 note 10; Milton on, iv, 68; Virgil on, xiii, 240; Zeus and, viii, 194 note 49

Theudas, xliv, 434 (36)

Thevet, Andrew, xxxiii, 312, 319, 326

Thibault, king of Navarre, xx, 90 note 3

THIEF AND HIS MOTHER, fable of the, xvii, 28-9

Thief, Epictetus on punishment of the, ii, 120 (12)

Thierry, Augustin, *History of the Conquest*, xxxii, 172 note; Taine on, xxxix, 414

Thierry, in SONG OF ROLAND, xlix, 189, 190-4

THINE AM I, MY FAITHFUL FAIR, vi, 475

Thiodrek, the king, xlix, 396

Thirlwall, Mill on, xxv, 80, 81

THIS IS NO MY AIN LASSIE, vi, 537-8

Thisbe, and Pyramus, xx, 255

Thistles, South American, xxix, 129

THO' CRUEL FATE SHOULD BID US PART, vi, 92

Thoas, in the ÆNEID, xiii, 335-6

Thoas, and Hypsipyle, xx, 75 note 4

Thomas, the apostle, xliv, 368 (15), 424 (13)

Thomas, Gov., Franklin on, i, 105, 110, 112

THOMAS RYMER AND THE QUEEN OF ELF-LAND, xl, 76-8

Thompson, Capt., at San Diego, xxiii, 396-7

Thompson, William, Mill on, xxv, 80

Thomson, C. P., Mill on, xxv, 81

THOMSON, CATHERINE, SONNET ON, iv, 81-2

Thomson, James (1700-48), Burns on,

vi, 179; To FORTUNE, xl, 443; Hazlitt on, xxvii, 278; prayer written by, i, 83; quotation from, vi, 224; RULE BRITANNIA, xl, 442-3; Wordsworth on his *Castle of Indolence,* xxxix, 325; Wordsworth on *Seasons* of, 322-5

THOMSON, ADDRESS TO SHADE OF, vi, 418-19

THOMSON, ON SOME COMMEMORATIONS OF, vi, 447-8

Thomson, James (1834-82), GIFTS, xlii, 1149

Thomson, Dr. James, on chemistry, xxv, 17; on freezing-point, xxx, 232-3; on regelation of ice, 243; on plasticity of ice, 245-6; on tides, 293

Thomson, N. H., translator of THE PRINCE, xxxvi, 1

Thomson, Sir William, on age of earth, xi, 344, 345; on freezing-point, xxx, 232, 233; life and work, 250; THE TIDES, 274-307; WAVE THEORY OF LIGHT, 251-73

Thone, and Helena, iv, 62

Thonis, the Egyptian, xxxiii, 55

Thoösa, daughter of Phorcys, xxii, 11

Thor, at Utgard, v, 360

Thora, daughter of Hakon, xlix, 338, 399

Thórdharson, Jón, xliii, 5

Thoreau, Henry David, sketch of life and works, xxviii, 394; on the truth, 282; ON WALKING, 395-425

Thorfinn Karlsefni, xliii, 14-16, 17, 19-20

Thorgeir, son of Snorri, xliii, 20

Thori, the Norseman, xliii, 11

Thorndike, Herbert, xv, 384

Thorold, Earl Tresham (see Tresham)

Thorough, is no word of peace, viii, 313

Thorstein, son of Eric the Red, xliii, 6, 13-14

Thorstein the Swarthy, xliii, 14

Thorvald, son of Eric the Red, xliii, 6; voyage to Vinland, 11-13

Thorvard the Norseman of Gardar marries Freydis, daughter of Eric the Red, xliii, 6; with Freydis makes voyage to Vinland, 17-20

Thorycion, Aristophanes on, viii, 449-50

THOU FAIR ELIZA, vi, 416-17

THOU HAST LEFT ME EVER, JAMIE, vi, 473-4

Thought, aberrations of, four principal, ii, 291 (19); "act in fancy," xlv, 799; action and, Carlyle on, xxv, 340; Channing on, xxviii, 323-36, 340-2; Des-

cartes on reality of, xxxiv, 29; duty of man, xlviii, 59 (146); Hobbes on, xxxiv, 313-8, 321-2, 346-8; Hume on limits of, xxxvii, 300-5, 327-8; not wisdom, viii, 380; liberty of, Mill on, xxv, 210-49, 250; liberty of, Milton on, iii, 220-7; makes place, vii, 314 (5); man born for, xlviii, 411; Pascal on, 117 (339), 120 (346-8), 122 (365), 123 (370); preventing power of, 94-5 (259); as product of matter, xxxiv, 104-8; Rousseau on, 244-7; Schiller on courage of, xxxii, 230; sensation and, xxxvii, 299-300; Socrates on pure, ii, 53; study and, Confucius on, xliv, 8 (15), 53 (30); swifter than time, xviii, 326; Walton on sympathy of, xv, 336-7

Thoughtlessness, Buddhist idea of, xlv, 687

Thoughts, Bacon on good, iii, 29, Browning on, 401; Bunyan on good, xv, 148-9; chance in, xxxix, 119; character determined by, ii, 227 (16); connection of, xxxix, 155; defined, xxxvii, 300-1; Emerson on, v, 143, 168-9, 419; Emerson on our rejected, 59-60; evil, a prayer against, vii, 287; feelings and, xxxix, 272; Goethe on exchange of, 252-3; Marcus Aurelius on purity of, ii, 216 (4), 209 (8); Penn on government of, i, 378-80; Shakespeare on, xlvi, 109; source of, outside of human will, v, 133-4; two at same time impossible, xlviii, 59 (145); wandering of, Byron on, xviii, 446; wandering, Dante on, xx, 162; worldly and heavenly, vii, 314-15 (5, 6)

THOUGHTS IN A GARDEN, xl, 377-9

THOUSAND AND ONE NIGHTS, xvi

Thrace, the modern Roumania, xxviii, 264-5; Sesostris in, xxxiii, 50

Thrasea, Pætus, contemporaneity, ii, 320; Stoic philosopher, ix, 188 note; Pliny on, 307, 308

Thrasiline, in PHILASTER, xlvii, 667-77, 692-3, 699-703, 714-16, 731, 733, 737

Thraso, Sidney on, xxvii, 27; Thaïs and, xx, 76 note 6

Thrasybulus, of Stiria, xii, 132; accuses Alcibiades, 142

Thrasymedes, son of Nestor, xxii, 34, 43-4

THREE FEATHERS, story of the, xvii, 156-9

THREE LITTLE MEN IN THE WOOD, xvii, 69-74

THREE RAVENS, THE, xl, 73-4
THREE SPINNERS, THE, xvii, 74-6
THREE WARNINGS, THE, xlv, 689-92
Thrift, Confucius on, xliv, 24 (35)
Thrush, nests of the, xi, 284; Whitman on the, xlii, 1413
THRUSHBEARD KING, story of, xvii, 142-6
Thucydides, of Alopece, rival of Pericles, xii, 46-7, 52; on Pericles, 43, 53
Thule, King of, song of, xix, 119
THUMBLING, story of, xvii, 124-8
THUMBLING AS JOURNEYMAN, xvii, 128-32
Thumomancy, defined, xxxiv, 381-2
Thunder, Beaumont on, xlvii, 682; Longfellow on, xlii, 1314
Thundering Legion, and M. Aurelius Antoninus, ii, 308-9
Thunderstorms, Darwin on, xxix, 69
Thurloe, Hugo on, xxxix, 379-80
Thyestes, feast of, viii, 71-2
Thymbræan God, Apollo called, xx, 191 note
Thymbrus, and Laris, xiii, 334-5
Thymœtes, Virgil on, xiii, 101, 326
Thyn, Captain, xxxiii, 337, 345, 351, 356, 369
Thyrsis, and Corydon, iv, 32
Thyrsus, freedman of Octavius, xii, 379
Thyrsus, sacred wand of Bacchus, viii, 370
THYRZA, ELEGY ON, xli, 785-7
TIBBIE, I HAE SEEN THE DAY, vi, 20-1
Tibboos, Emerson on rock, v, 199
Tiber, river, origin of name, xiii, 279
Tiberius, aided by mother, iii, 141; caution of, 17; Dante on victories of, xx, 30 note 19; death of, iii, 10; in Germany, xxxiii, 114; mentioned in Luke, xliv, 360 (1); Marco and, iii, 94; Marcus Aurelius on, ii, 299-300 (27); memoirs of, xxxvi, 3; Milton on, iv, 397; the pictures and, xlvii, 569; Sejanus and, iii, 67-8
Ticino, Freeman on, xxviii, 256
Tickell, on Addison, xxvii, 176
Ticknor, Elisha, xxviii, 367
Tidal Harmonic Analyser, xxx, 293-6
Tidal Waves, Kelvin on, xxx, 275-6
Tide Gauge, the, xxx, 289
Tide Predictors, xxx, 295-6
Tides, ancient knowledge of, xxx, 279-80; declinational, 291-2; defined, 274-7; Descartes on, xxxiv, 37; due to attraction of sun and moon, xxx, 276,

281-2, 291-2, 303-5; dynamic action of, 287-8; elastic, 299, 305; equilibrium theory of, 286-7; harmonic analysis of, 290-5; meteorological, 277-9; moon as cause of, 280-2, 291-2, 303-4; observation of, 288-90; prediction of, 295-7; spring and neap, 284-6; true solar and lunar, how known, 278-9; Voltaire on, xxxiv, 108, 118; weather, influenced by, xxx, 298-9
TIDES, ESSAY ON, Kelvin's, xxx, 274-307
Tierny, Dr., xxxviii, 198, 211-12
Tierra del Fuego, boulders in, xxix, 252; climate and productions of, 247-8; Darwin on, 56, 209-35, 240-7; glaciers of, 229, 250; peat in, 290; snow-line in, 249; trees in, 290
Tigellinus, and Burrhus, iii, 59
TIGER, THE, a poem, xli, 583-4
Tigillinus, death of, xxxii, 14
Tignoso, Federigo, xx, 202 note 21
Tigranes, and the Romans, iii, 74
Tigris, river, in Eden, iv, 262
Tillotson, Dr., on the real presence, xxxvii, 375
Timæa, Alcibiades and, xii, 128
Timæus, on plants and man, v, 176; Plutarch on, xii, 125; on the Pyrrhian War, ix, 102; Timoleon and, 104
Timandra, and Alcibiades, xii, 145, 146
Timarete, the priestess, xxxiii, 33
Time, abolished by the soul, v, 136; Bacon on, xxxix, 123; brings evil and good, xxxvi, 12; cleanses all, viii, 134; consists of two days, xvi, 16; definitions of, xlviii, 426-7; duration of past, xi, 321-4, 344; duration of past, Lyell on, xxxviii, 386-93; element of, in formation of species, xi, 110; eternity and, iii, 262; Hume on idea of, xxxvii, 412-13; the greatest innovator, iii, 61-2; lifter of the veil, viii, 349; like a river, ii, 219 (43); makes manifest the righteous, viii, 227; the measure of business, iii, 63; measures all things, iv, 195; method and, xix, 78; Milton on, iv, 39; numbers motion, 26-7; Pascal on, xlviii, 50 (122); Penn on use of, i, 319-20; Raleigh on, xl, 205, 207; among the Romans, ix, 233 note 4; Shakespeare on, xl, 274; slower than thought, xviii, 326; subtle thief of youth, iv, 29; teaches many a lesson, viii, 202; as the test of books, xxxix, 208-9; unhasting stride of, viii, 410

Time-server, Lord, in PILGRIM's PROGRESS, xv, 102

Timeliness, Bacon on, iii, 63-4; Penn on, i, 338

Timesileus, Plutarch on, xii, 57

Timidity, Hippocrates on, xxxviii, 5; of modern society, v, 75

Timocreon, on Themistocles, xii, 23-4

Timoleon, fortune of, iii, 101; Landor on, v, 318; Timæus and, ix, 104

Timon, of Athens, xii, 376-7; Alcibiades and, 120-1; misanthropy of, ix, 38; tree of, iii, 34

Timon, the deacon, xliv, 434 (5)

Timon of Phlius, on Zeno, xii, 38-9

Timon, teacher of Arthur, xxxix, 62

Timorous, in PILGRIM's PROGRESS, xv, 46-7, 221

Timorous, Mrs., in PILGRIM's PROGRESS, xv, 184-8

Timorousness, Locke on cure of, xxxvii, 97-101

Timotheus, Athenian general, Apollodorus and, xii, 203; Bacon on, iii, 101

Timotheus, musician at Alexander's feast, xl, 391-2

Timothy, at Berœa, xliv, 461 (14); circumcision of, 457 (1-3); xxxvi, 369; at Corinth, xliv, 462 (5); the Corinthians and, xlv, 496 (17), 516 (1), 517 (19); sent to Macedonia, xliv, 465 (22), 467 (4); St. Paul on, xlv, 514 (10-11); Penn on, i, 386 (163)

Timoxena, wife of Plutarch, xii, 3

TIN SOLDIER, THE CONSTANT, xvii, 293-7

TINDER-BOX, THE, story of, xvii, 349-55

Ting, Duke, xliv, 43 (15)

Tinker's Song, from JOLLY BEGGARS, vi, 129

Tinochorus, Darwin on the, xxix, 100-1

TIPPLING BALLAD, A, vi, 450-1

Tiquitoc, on Dulcinea, xiv, 515

Tiradritto, bravo in THE BETROTHED, xxi, 319

Tirante the White, xiv, 52, 93

Tiresias, in Dante's HELL, xx, 82; Milton on, iv, 136

Tiro, freedman of Cicero, ix, 80, 114; Cicero's letter to, 154; letter of Cicero the Younger to, 173; letter of Q. Cicero to, 175

Tiro, Calestrius, letter to, ix, 197

Tiro, Julius, codicils of, ix, 295

Tirsan, father of family in New Atlantis, iii, 163

Tirynthian Groom, Hercules called the, xl, 242

Tisaphernes, and Alcibiades, xii, 129-31, 133

Tisiphon, wreath of, xlvi, 69

Tisiphone, Dante on, xx, 37; in Virgil's Hades, xiii, 226

Tisso, Prince, anecdote of, v, 299

Titania, in FAUST, xix, 184

Titans, Milton on the, iv, 93, 101; sons of Okeanus and Earth, viii, 174 note 14; in Tartarus, xiii, 226; war of, referred to, viii, 174

Tithes, David on, xli, 491; Harrison on, xxxv, 261-2; Hindu doctrine of, xlv, 800

Tithonus, Aurora and, v, 92; xxii, 68; xl, 236; reference to, xx, 179

Titian, Cellini and, xxxi, 356; Hazlitt on, xxvii, 278-9; portraits by, 272

Titius, the quæstor, xii, 355, 367

Titles, Austin on, xli, 532-3; Hobbes on, xxxiv, 368-9; Pope on, xl, 435

Titmouse, habits of the, xi, 178, 277

Titus, Paul, St., and, xxxvi, 369, 374; Paul, St., on, xlv, 518 (13), 523 (6-7), 524 (13-15, 6), 525-6 (16-24), 531 (18)

Titus, the Emperor, beauty of, iii, 106; Jerusalem destroyed by, xx, 232 note 5, 308; xxxv, 319; xxxviii, 31; Pope on, xl, 434

Tityrus, Sidney on, xxvii, 26

Tityus, Homer on, xxii, 159; in Tartarus, xiii, 227

Tivitivans, Raleigh on the, xxxiii, 340, 373

Tmolus, Euripides on, viii, 386; reference to, xli, 823

TOADEATER, THE, vi, 427

Toads, adders and, xxxv, 345; South American, xxix, 103-4

Tobacco, Burke on taste for, xxiv, 15; Harrison on use of, xxxv, 239; introduced into England by Drake, xxxiii, 122; profits of cultivation of, x, 161-2

Tobbia, the goldsmith, xxxi, 119-20, 122, 124-5, 126

Tobias, Augustine, St., on, vii, 187; Milton on, iv, 186

TOCCATA OF GALUPPI'S, A, xlii, 1080-1

Tocqueville, M. de, Mill on his Democracy, xxv, 120

Toledo, Eleonora di, grand duchess of Tuscany, xxxi, 342 note 1; Cellini and,

362, 363, 366, 383, 388-92, 396-8, 407-8, 412, 415-16, 417-18, 420, 426-7, 433-5

Toledo, Pietro Alvarez de, xxxi, 136 note

Toleration, in ancient Athens, iii, 193-4; in ancient nations, xxxvii, 393-4; Lord Brook on, iii, 227; Burke on, without any belief, xxiv, 284; Hume on, xxxvii, 405; Mill on, xxv, 36-7; Mill on popular ideas of, 202; Milton on, iii, 228-9; Pascal on, xlviii, 342-4; in Utopia, xxxvi, 226-7

Tolleme la Feintes, xxxv, 118-19

Tollendal, de Lally, letter on October Sixth, xxiv, 210-11 note

Tolls, Smith on, x, 454-6

Tolmides, Athenian general, xii, 56, 57

Tolosa, Lady, in DON QUIXOTE, xiv, 34

Tolumnius, in the ÆNEID, xiii, 371, 399, 406

TOM BOWLING, xli, 502

TOMB, THE BISHOP ORDERS HIS, xlii, 1075-8

TOMBS IN WESTMINSTER ABBEY, ON THE, xl, 319

TO-MORROW, by Collins, xli, 592-3

To-morrow, Omar Khayyam on, xli, 946; sees undone, what happens not to-day, xix, 16; Shakespeare on, xlvi, 388

Tomyris, Cyrus and, xx, 192

Tonio, in THE BETROTHED, xxi, 93-5, 109-11, 114, 116-18, 125, 183-4, 547

Tonson, on Addison, xxvii, 173

Too-bold, in PILGRIM'S PROGRESS, xv, 303-4

Tooke, Horne, xxvii, 277

Tooke, William Eyton, xxv, 54; free trade petition, 65; in Utilitarian movement, 67; and Westminster Review, 63

TOOTHACHE, ADDRESS TO THE, vi, 239-40

Toparimaca, Raleigh on, xxxiii, 348-9

Tophet, Hinnom named, iv, 98

Topiawari, king of Aromaia, xxxiii, 333, 353-5, 362-7

Torello, Lelio, xxxi, 412 note 1

Torquatus, A., Cicero on, ix, 134; Dante on, xx, 307; Virgil on, xiii, 235

Torralva, Lope Ruyz and, xiv, 156-7

Torrens, Col., Mill on, xxv, 58

Torrigiani, Piero, xxxi, 22-4

TORTOISE AND BIRDS, fable of, xvii, 29-30

TORTOISE, HARE AND, fable of, xvii, 38

Tortoises, on Chatham Island, xxix, 379; Darwin on meat of, 381; of Galapagos Islands, 398, 399; habits of, 386-9

Torture, judicial, Harrison on, xxxv, 363; Hobbes on, xxxiv, 399-400; in Massachusetts, xliii, 73 (45)

Tosa, Cianghella, xx, 351 note 12

Totems, in Ireland, xlix, 202 note

Touch, beauty in sense of, xxiv, 98-9

Touraine, Earl of, at Poitiers, xxxv, 46

Tourneys, Bacon on, iii, 96

Tournon, François de, xxxi, 261-2 and note 2

TOUSSAINT L'OUVERTURE, TO, xli, 655-6

Town, and country, relations of, x, 127-31, 304-7

TOWN MOUSE AND COUNTRY MOUSE, fable of, xvii, 13-14

Town Meetings, disturbers of, xliii, 74 (56)

Towns, Goethe on life in, xix, 368; in Massachusetts, xliii, 75-6; origin of, x, 306

Townshend, Goldsmith on, xli, 506, 507

Toxodon, Darwin on the, xxix, 89

Trade, advantages of, x, 21; Balance of (see Balance of T.); division of labor limited by facilities of, 22-3; Emerson on the ways of, v, 45-6; genius in, 185; Goldsmith on evils of, xli, 510-11, 519; government interference with, xxv, 291-8; home and foreign, x, 333-4; human propensity to, 18-19; Locke on learning a, xxxvii, 173-8; necessity of, x, 27; Penn on ways of, i, 387 (185), 388 (186); tyranny of, v, 400; "the vena porta of wealth," iii, 102; Voltaire on, xxxiv, 92-3; wholesale, three kinds of, x, 295; Woolman on, i, 180, 195-6 and note, 197 (see also Commerce)

Trades, equality of, the requisites to, x, 116-21; exclusive, profits and wages in, 62-4; government interferences with equality of, 121-46; incorporated, 121-33; inequalities, natural, of various, 102-21; inequalities, political, 121-46; Tzu-hsia on, xliv, 64 (4)

Trade-winds, effect of Andes Mountains on, xxix, 327

Trading Companies, x, 458-63

TRADITIONAL BALLADS, xl, 51-186

Traditions, over-reverence of, iii, 46

Tragedy, before Æschylus, viii, 5; Athenian, iv, 401-2; Augustine, St., on, vii, 31-2; better read than seen, xxxix, 223; Cervantes on, xiv, 478; Dennis on unity of place in, xxvii, 192; Dryden

on, compared with epic poetry, xiii, 6-11, 13-14; English, Voltaire on, xxxiv, 130-6; French classical, xxvi, 76; Greek, Hugo on, xxxix, 341-2; 346-7; Johnson on origin of, 214; Lamb on stage representation of, xxvii, 301-16; Macaulay on eloquence in, xxvii, 383; Marcus Aurelius on lessons of, ii, 286 (6); Milton on, iv, 412-13; in periods of decay, xxvii, 341; pleasure in, Burke on, xxiv, 40-2; pleasures of, Milton on, iv, 36; pleasure in, the reason of, xxvii, 351-2; xxxix, 223; popular notions of, 214; requires a comic element, xxviii, 176-7; Schiller on, xxxii, 270; Shelley on, xxvii, 341; Voltaire on translations of, xxxiv, 139-40 (see also Drama)

TRAGIC FRAGMENT, vi, 23

Traitors, Æschylus on, viii, 205; punishment of, in Dante's HELL, xx, 47, 131-42

Trajan, the Christians and, ix, 407 and note; Dante on, xx, 185 and note; in Dante's PARADISE, 371, 372-3; expedition against Decebalus, ix, 370 note 4; the forum of, 365 note 1; the government of, 357 note 1; justice of, 294-6; Pliny and, 185; Pliny on, 244, 292-3; Pliny's correspondence with, 356-416; ii, 311-12; success of empire of, ix, 366 note 1; times of, ii, 217 (32)

Trajano, the chamberlain, xxxi, 120-1, 144, 147

Tramaglino, Renzo, in I PROMESSI SPOSI, marriage of, forbidden, xxi, 14, 20-1; put off by Abbondio, 26-30; learns of Don Rodrigo, 30-2; plans of vengeance, 34-5; with Lucia, 36-7; hears of Rodrigo's persecution, 38-40; with Azzecca-Garbugli, 41-8; returns, 52; promises not to attack Rodrigo, 69-70; plans for marriage with Lucia, 89-96; threatens to kill Rodrigo, 99-100; wins Lucia's consent, 100-1; at the inn, 109-12; at Abbondio's, 113-14, 116-17, 118-20, 125-6; goes to convent, 129-33; to Monza, 133-8; in Milan, 190-5; in the insurrection, 204-5, 205-8; in attack on corn superintendents, 211, 213, 219, 220; proposes appeal to Ferrer, 226-8; at the inn, 229-43; arrested, 248-55; rescued, 256; flight to Bergamo, 257-88; disappearance of, 431-2; actual truth of disappearance, 432-3; demanded by Don Gonzalo,

432-3; corresponds with Agnese, 437-41; returns to Bergamo, 542-3; taken with plague, 543; determines to seek Lucia, 543-6; returns to native village, 547-55; goes to Milan, 555-70; learns Lucia's sickness, 571; suspected of being a prisoner, 572-6; at the Lazzaretto, 577-81; meets Cristoforo, 582-91; search for Lucia, 592-8; finds Lucia, 598-603; leads Cristoforo to her, 605-6; reunited to Lucia, 608-11; returns to tell Agnese, 612-19; preparations for marriage, 620-1, 626; asks Abbondio to perform ceremony, 627-8; outlawry removed, 635-6; married to Lucia, 636-7; at Bergamo, 638-40; in business with Bortolo, 640-1; daughter born to, 642; lessons he had learned, 643

Trance of Cessation, xlv, 731-7

Tranibores, in Utopia, xxxvi, 177, 181

Tranquillity, Epictetus on, ii, 142 (71), 149 (85), 152 (94), 181 (188); Franklin on, i, 80; Marcus Aurelius on, ii, 212 (3), 222 (2), 238 (31), 248 (37, 43)

Tranquillus, Suetonius, letters to, ix, 202, 403-4

Transcendentalists, belief of the, xxviii, 308

Transfers, taxes on, x, 505-11

Transfiguration, the, xliv, 379 (29-36)

Transformations, Browne on, iii, 282

Transition, beauty lies in, v, 303; Darwin on modes of, xi, 185-8

Transitional Habits, xi, 175-8

Transitional Structures, xi, 175-8

Transitional Varieties, absence of, xi, 170-5; in geological formations, 332-40

Transitoriness, of things, v, 149, 153

Translating, as a means of study, ix, 301

Translations, Dryden on, xiii, 64-5; Eliot on, l, 3-4; Johnson on, xxxix, 204; Shelley on vanity of, xxvii, 333-4; Voltaire on, xxxiv, 132-4, 139-40

Transmigration, Egyptian belief in, xxxiii, 62-3; Lessing on, xxxii, 206; rebirth not, xlv, 677, 681-4; Socrates on, ii, 59-62, 74-5; Virgil on, xiii, 231-2

Transparency, cause of, xxxiv, 123-4

Transsilvania, Freeman on, xxviii, 269

Transubstantiation (see Real Presence)

Trapemernes, in Utopia, xxxvi, 232

Traube, Moritz, xxxviii, 315-16 note 1, 344

Travel, Bacon on, iii, 46-8; Confucius on, xliv, 14 (19); Darwin on, xxix, 503-9; Descartes on, xxxiv, 8; education by, iii, 246-7; xxxii, 39, 45; Emerson on, v, 79; Epictetus on thirst for, ii, 121 (14), 142 (70); Locke on, xxxvii, 179-82; Pliny on motives of, ix, 329

TRAVELLER, ADMONITION TO A, xli, 680

TRAVELLER, THE, by Goldsmith, xli, 520-31

TRAVELS AND VOYAGES, xxxiii

Traversaro, Pier, xx, 202 note 16

Treachery, punished in Hell, xx, 131-42

Treason, most horrid where trust is, xviii, 87; punishment of, in Dante's HELL, xx, 47, 131-42; punishment of, in old England, xxxv, 363-4; against United States, xliii, 190

Treasure-trove, Smith on, x, 222

Treaties (United States), under the Confederation, xliii, 162, 165; under Constitution, 186 (10), 188 (2); interpretation of, 189

Treaties of Commerce, Smith on, x, 389-94

Trebatius, Cicero on, ix, 113; Cicero and, xii, 249

Trebellius, Plutarch on, xii, 328

Trebonius, on Antony, xii, 331; Cicero on, ix, 114

Trebúat, son of Hua-Lonsce, xlix, 220

Tree, parable of the rotten, xv, 207-8

TREE AND REED, fable of, xvii, 26

Tree of Knowledge, Milton on, iv, 160, 182-3, 240-1, 251-2, 276-80

Tree of Life, highest in Eden, iv, 159, 160

Trees, as abodes, Buddha on, xlv, 582 note 12; conditions favorable to, xxix, 54-5; experiments on, in New Atlantis, iii, 174-5; fallen, Darwin on, xxix, 304, 305; imperfect men, v, 229; Locke on study of, xxxvii, 147; separated sexes in, xi, 106; silicified, xxix, 356; silicified, in the Andes, 335-6; Thoreau on climbing, xxviii, 422-3

TRELAWNY, DIE, AND SHALL, xlii, 1111-12

Tremellius, Emanuel, xxvii, 11

Trent, city of, Freeman on, xxviii, 256

Trent, Council of, on liberty of press, iii, 196, 198; schoolmen at, 45

Tresham, Austin, in A BLOT IN THE 'SCUTCHEON, betrothed to Guendolen, xviii, 363; on Mertoun's suit, 364, 366; in scene between Earl Tresham and Mildred, 386, 388-9; with brother after duel, 397-8; with Thorold at death, 403-4

Tresham, Earl, in A BLOT IN THE 'SCUTCHEON, described by retainers, xviii, 361-2; welcomes Mertoun and his suit, 363-8; Guendolen on, 369-70; hears Mildred's fault from Gerard, 377-80; with Guendolen, sends for Mildred, 381-2; with Mildred, 382-8; under Mildred's window, 392-3; meeting with Mertoun, 393-7; with Guendolen after duel, 397-9; with Mildred after Mertoun's death, 400-3; death of, 403-4

Tresham, Guendolen, in A BLOT IN THE 'SCUTCHEON, betrothed to Austin, xviii, 363; on Mertoun's suit, 364, 365, 366-8; with Mildred, 369-71; with Earl Tresham, 381-2; in scene between Tresham and Mildred, 386, 388-92; with Earl Tresham after duel, 397-8; with Thorold at death, 403-4

Tresham, Mildred, in A BLOT IN THE 'SCUTCHEON, sought by Mertoun, xviii, 360, 364-6; age of, 367; with Guendolen, 369-71; with Mertoun, 371-7; relations with Mertoun, 374-6; discovered by Gerard, 378-80; with Earl Tresham, 382-8; with Guendolen, confesses Mertoun her lover, 389-91; in chamber, waiting for Mertoun, 399-400; with Thorold after Mertoun's death, 400-3; dies, 403

Trespasses, in Massachusetts, xliii, 70 (24)

Tresvaux, Abbé, Renan on, xxxii, 173

Treverians, Tacitus on the, xxxiii, 108

Treves, Marlowe on, xix, 229

Trials, jury, xliii, 190; right of prompt, 72 (41); in United States, 190, 194 (5), 195 (6, 7); Winthrop on right of, 91

Triassic Period, in Europe, xxx, 345-6

Tribocians, Tacitus on the, xxxiii, 108

Tribulation, Kempis on, vii, 253-7, 280-1, 292-5, 312-13, 316-17; More on, xxxvi, 100-1; Pascal on, xlviii, 353-4

Tribunes, of Rome, xii, 152; power of Roman, ix, 342 note 9

Tributary States, Machiavelli on, xxxvi, 8-12, 18-19, 69; More on, 159-60

Trickery, Penn on, i, 346

Trieste, Freeman on, xxviii, 256

Trifles, Confucius on, xliv, 53 (26, 33); Franklin on, i, 80; Marcus Aurelius on, ii, 217-18 (32); Pascal on, xlviii, 52 (136), 77 (198); Penn on, i, 348 (314); profiting in, iii, 48

Trifling, Locke on, xxxvii, 107

Trimorphism, Darwin on, xi, 57; reciprocal, 305-8

Trina, in WISE FOLKS, xvii, 192-5

Trinculo, in THE TEMPEST, xlvi, 427-31, 435-9, 450-2, 461

Trinidad, Raleigh on, xxxiii, 312

Trinity, Browne on the, iii, 262-3 (12); Coleridge on doctrine of the, v, 319-20; Dante on the, xx, 341 note 15, 390, 425-6; first taught by Moses, xlviii, 264 (752); Lessing on doctrine of the, xxxii, 200-1; Mohammed on the, xlv, 1002; Newman on doctrine of the, xxviii, 38; universal idea of a, v, 163

TRINITY, THE HOLY, xlv, 564-5

Trip, in SCHOOL FOR SCANDAL, xviii, 149-50, 163

Triptolemus, Socrates on, ii, 29

Trismegistus, Hermes, iii, 261 note 12; Milton on, iv, 36; Pascal on, xlviii, 208 (628)

Trist, Nicholas P., xliii, 289

Tristan (Tristram), in Dante's HELL, xx, 22; in Malory's Morte d'Arthur, xxxix, 23; Renan on, xxxii, 163; Ysoude and, xiv, 489

Triton, references to, xiii, 78; xli, 678

TRIUMPH, THE, xl, 290-1

TRIUMPHS, MASQUES AND, ESSAY ON, Bacon's, iii, 95-6

Triumphs, Cato on, ix, 152; Roman, Bacon on, iii, 80

Trivia, name of Diana, xx, 383 note 2; Hippolytus and, xiii, 265-6

Trochilus, and crocodile, xxxiii, 38

Troilus, and Achilles, xiii, 90

Trophimus the Ephesian, xliv, 471 (29)

Tropics, Darwin on scenery of the, xxix, 498-9, 505-6; More on the, xxxvi, 138; not always habitable, xxxix, 106-7

Trotti, Alfonso de', xxxi, 271-3

Troubadours, Arnold on the, xxviii, 75-6

Trouble, man born into, xliv, 77 (7); none free from, vii, 228 (1)

Trotter, W. F., translator of Pascal, xlviii

Troubles, Manzoni on, xxi, 643

Trouvères, Renan on the, xxxii, 161

Troy, Æschylus on siege of, viii, 28-9; Augustus planned to rebuild, xiii, 21; downfall caused by Helen, viii, 33-5; Herodotus on plains about, xxxiii, 11; Herodotus on story of, 56-8; the horse of, Homer on, xxii, 112; the horse of, Virgil on, xiii, 100-9; RECUYELL OF HISTORIES OF, xxxix, 5-9; remarks on siege of, xxii, 3; taking of, related by Æneas, xiii, 100-21; taking of, announced, viii, 8, 18-19

Troyes, ancient fair of, x, 31

TRUE LOYAL NATIVES, THE, vi, 459

Truelove, Edward, xxv, 224 note 3

Trumball, Sir William, and Dryden, xiii, 425

TRUMPETER TAKEN PRISONER, fable of, xvii, 43

Trumpets, Dryden on, xl, 389

TRUNK, THE FLYING, xvii, 344-9

Trussel, in EDWARD II, xlvi, 71

Truth, in art, v, 304; St. Augustine on, love of, vii, 179; on authority, Mill on, xxv, 229-39; Bacon on search for, xxxix, 128-9, 132-40, 143-5; beauty and, Keats on, xli, 879; Berkeley on, xxxvii, 228; Buddha on, xlv, 596-7; Bunyan on, xv, 8-9; Channing on, love of, xxviii, 326-7; with children, xxxvii, 105, 106; commotions due to spread of, xxxix, 43-4; Confucius on, xliv, 9 (22), 13 (8, 9), 29 (24), 51 (5), 53 (28, 31); courtesy and, v, 207; Descartes on, xxxiv, 5, 16-20, 26; diversity of, iii, 228; eloquence and, i, 336; Emerson on, v, 27, 63, 74, 139-40, 186, 187, 288; exact difficulty of, xxviii, 277, 281; of fact and of sentiment, 277-8, 282; Franklin on, i, 56; friendship and, v, 111; historical, Montaigne on, xxxii, 99; Hindu Krishna on, xlv, 807-8, 853-4; Hume on, xxxvii, 319-20, 408; Kempis on, vii, 207-8, 261-2; liberty necessary to progress of, iii, 220-2, 229-30; Locke on inquiry of, xxxvii, 159-60; Lowell on, xlii, 1371, 1372, 1380, 1382-3; Milton on, iii, 217, 227-8; Montaigne on, xlviii, 392-3; men natural lovers of, v, 264-5, 267; in nature, 283, 374; opinions and, xxxiv, 13, 16; Pascal on, xlviii, 16 (21), 29, 38-9, 79 (211), 99 (282), 126-7, 191 (582), 300 (857), 421-2, 431; Penn on, i, 336, 338, 386 (164); persecution and, xxv, 222-3; Poe on

inculcation of, xxviii, 375-6; poetry and, 376, 378, 391; xxxix, 279, 281; Quakers on, i, 191-2; Rousseau's method of seeking, xxxiv, 244-7; Schiller on, xxxii, 231; xxv, 351; search for, ii, 171 (149); Socrates's test of, 93; speaking and hearing, xxviii, 282-3; an attribute of speech, xxxiv, 326; told with bad intent, xli, 588; said to lie in a well, xxviii, 464-5; Whittier on, xlii, 1350

TRUTH, ESSAY ON, Bacon's, iii, 7-9

TRUTH OF INTERCOURSE, Stevenson's, xxviii, 277-84

Truthfulness, Locke on, xxxvii, 118-19; Whitman on, xxxix, 402-3

Truttes, Bernard of, xxxv, 58

Tryon, vegetarian, i, 17, 35

Tsai Wo, disciple of Confucius, xliv, 11 (21), 15 note, 20 (24), 33 (2), 60 (21)

Tsai-Yü, xliv, 15 (9)

Tsang Wen, xliv, 16 (17), 52 (13)

Tsang Wu-chung, xliv, 46 (13, 15)

Tseng-Hsi, xliv, 36 (25)

Tseng-tzu, disciple of Confucius, xliv, 13 note, 5 (4), 6 (9), 25 (3, 4-7), 34 (17) note 13, 41 (24), 48 (28), 65 (16-19)

Tso Ch'in-ming, xliv, 17 (24)

Tubero, Quintus, T. Gracchus and, ix, 22

Tucker, Ellen, wife of Emerson, v, 3

Tucker, Lieut., with Drake, xxxiii, 237, 258

Tucutuco, Darwin on the, xxix, 58-9

Tudwal, grindstone of, xxxii, 146

Tufton, Sir Louis, xxxv, 24-5

Tuidle of Ulaid, xlix, 221-2

Tuisto, god of the Germans, xxxiii, 93

Tulchinne, the juggler, xlix, 232-3

Tullia, daughter of Cicero, ix, 80, 146; death of, 165-9; Plutarch on, xii, 252-3 (see also Tulliola)

Tulliola, letter to, ix, 89; Cicero on, 91

Tullius, M., Cicero on, ix, 99

TULLOCHGORUM, xli, 568-70

Tullus, Domitius, will of, ix, 327-8

Tullus, friend of Cicero, xii, 241

Tullus, the king, xiii, 235

Tultie, Salomon de, xlviii, 15 note 3

Tumefaction, Harvey on, xxxviii, 114-15

Tumors, Harvey on treatment of, xxxviii, 110

Tungrians, the original Germans, xxxiii, 94

Tunstall, Bishop of Durham, xxxvi, 103, 104, 109, 114, 135

Tuppukkoowillin, xliii, 143, 146

Turco, Darwin on the, xxix, 274-5

Turdi, in ancient Rome, x, 187-8

Turenne, Pope on, xl, 433; Sainte-Beuve on, xxxii, 126

Turgis, Count of Tortosa, xlix, 124, 135

Turgot, Mill on, xxv, 73

Turin, Paré on expedition against, xxxviii, 9-11

Turkey, Burke on, xxiv, 261; poets in, xxvii, 7; Smith on, 240-1

Turkey-buzzard, Darwin on the, xxix, 66, 189-90, 288

Turkey-cock, hair of the, xi, 96

Turkish Empire, Freeman on races in, xxviii, 263-70; Machiavelli on the, xxxvi, 15-17; power of soldiery in, 67

Turks, kindness of, to animals, iii, 33; Magyars and, xxviii, 227-9; royalty of the, iii, 50

Turn-about, Lord, in PILGRIM'S PROGRESS, xv, 102

TURN ALL THY THOUGHTS TO EYES, xl, 286

Turnaway, in PILGRIM'S PROGRESS, xv, 128

Turn-back, in PILGRIM'S PROGRESS, xv, 154

TURNER, ANDREW, ON, vi, 500

Turner, Charles Tennyson, LETTY'S GLOBE, xli, 921

Turnspits, Harrison on, xxxv, 354

Turnus, in the ÆNEID, Lavinia and, xiii, 241; descent of, 252; stirred by Alecto against Æneas, 254-5; beginning of war, 259-61; his allies, 261-7; shield of, 266; attacks Trojan fleet and town, 293-8, 309-20; renews battle, 330-1; kills Pallas, 336-8; drawn from battle by Juno, 344-5; challenged by Æneas, 359; denounced by Drances, 363, 368-9; his reply, 369-70; agrees to fight Æneas, 372; in cavalry fight, 373-5, 387; determines to fight Æneas in single combat, 389-93; in Rutulian fight, 401-3, 405-9; final combat with Æneas, 412-23; remarks on duel with Æneas, 48-50; Dante on, xx, 8; Milton on, iv, 260; Sidney on, xxvii, 24

Turpin, Archbishop, in SONG OF ROLAND, xlix, 100, 103; with Roland in return to France, 120; at Roncesvalles, 130-1, 134, 135, 137, 138, 139, 141, 143-4,

146, 149, 153, 157, 162, 163, 164, 165-6; last benediction, 166-9; found by Charlemagne, 182-3; his tomb, 186

Turpio, Ambivius, Cicero on, ix, 62

Turtles, catching of, in Keeling Island, xxix, 463

Tuscany, Pliny's description of, ix, 265-6

Tuscus, Minutius, husband of Corellia, ix, 303-4; letter to, 301

Tutelary Angels, Browne on, iii, 275-6, 284-5; Elihu on, xliv, 124 (23); Walton on, xv, 337

Tutors, Locke on, xxxvii, 69-80, 83, 128, 140-2, 153, 167

TWA CORBIES, THE, xl, 74

TWA DOGS, THE, vi, 151-7; editorial remarks on, 16; an idyllic poem, xxxix, 299

TWA HERDS, THE, vi, 63-6

TWA SISTERS, THE, xl, 54-6

'TWAS NA HER BONIE BLUE E'E, vi, 534

Tweeddale, Marquis of, xxv, 8

Twelfth Day, celebration of, xv, 403

Twelve Peers, Charlemagne's, xlix, 174

Twelve Tables, Law of, xlviii, 205, 206

TWENTY YEARS HENCE, xli, 898-9

TWENTY-FOUR YEARS AFTER, Dana's, xxiii, 375-405

TWENTY-THREE, ON BEING ARRIVED AT THE AGE OF, iv, 29

Twist, Tom, in SHE STOOPS TO CONQUER, xviii, 207

TWO APRIL MORNINGS, xli, 600-2

TWO BLACK HOUNDS, story of the, xvi, 21-4

TWO KINGS' CHILDREN, story of the, xvii, 196-203

Two-tongues, Mr., in PILGRIM'S PROGRESS, xv, 102

TWO YEARS BEFORE THE MAST, xxiii; editorial remarks on, l, 45

Twrch Trwyth, Arthur and, xxxii, 146

Tyaga, xlv, 866

Tybris, reference to, xiii, 279

Tydeus, Athenian general, xii, 143; and Menalippus, xx, 135; Virgil's mention of, in Hades, xiii, 223

Tydides, bravest of the Grecian train, xiii, 76

Tyler, Wat, leader of the rebellion, xxxv, 62, 64, 69, 71, 73, 75, 76; Richard Lyon and, 69; death, 77-8

Tyndall, John, on Faraday, xxx, 6; on glaciers, 225, 227, 229, 231, 236, 240, 247

Tyndareus, Lede and, xxii, 152

Types, law of succession of, xi, 372-4

Typhœus, Dante on, xx, 316 note 8; Virgil on, xiii, 317

Typhon, the giant, viii, 179 and note 22; deposed by Apollo, xxxiii, 72; Milton on, iv, 93

Typology, Pascal on, xlviii, 214-32

Typotherium, Darwin on the, xi, 363

Tyrannicide, Mill on, xxv, 210 note

Tyranny, adage on, xvi, 33; death a gentler lord than, viii, 61; lawlessness and, 143; of majorities, xxv, 196-9; Milton on, iv, 344; of opinion, xxv, 199-202; origin of, xxxiv, 215-19, 225-6; Pascal on, xlviii, 115 (332); Pope on, xl, 428, 429; of rulers, xxv, 195-6

Tyrant Flycatchers, Darwin on, xxix, 61-2

Tyrants, Cicero on, ix, 27-8; in Dante's HELL, xx, 51

Tyre, antiquity of, xxxiii, 27-8

Tyrian Cynosure, referred to, iv, 53

Tyrker, the German, xliii, 8, 10-11

Tyrnog, pot of, xxxii, 146

Tyro, Homer on, xxii, 24, 150-1

Tyrrhene Trump, Æschylus on the, viii, 144

Tyrrhenus, in the ÆNEID, xiii, 378

Tyrrheus, in the ÆNEID, xiii, 256-8

Tyrtæus, Sidney on, xxvii, 7, 12

Tysander, in Trojan horse, xiii, 108

Tythes, Smith on, x, 486-8

TYTLER, WILLIAM, ADDRESS TO, vi, 266-7

Tzetzes, xxxii, 179 note 31

Tzu-Ch'an, xliv, 16 (15), 46 (9, 10)

Tzu-chang, disciple of Confucius, xliv, 8 (18), 9 (23), 16 (18), 34 (17) note 14, 35 (19), 38 (6, 10), 39 (14), 40 (20), 50 (43), 51 (5), 54 (41), 58 (6), 63 (1, 2, 3), 65 (15, 16), 67 (2)

Tzu-ch'in, disciple of Confucius, xliv, 6 (10), 56 (13) note 8, 66 (25)

Tzu-chien, disciple of Confucius, xliv, 14 (2), 33 (2)

Tzu-hsia, disciple of Confucius, xliv, 5 (7), 7 (8), 10 (8), 19 (11), 33 (2), 38 (5), 40 (22), 43 (17), 46 (10), 63 (3-13)

Tzu-kao, xliv, 34 note 7, 35 (24)

Tzu-kung, xliv, 6 (10, 15), 8 (13), 11 (17), 14 (3), 15 (8), 16 (11, 12, 14), 19 (6) note 9, 21 (28), 22 (14), 27 (6), 28 (12), 33 (2), 34 (12, 15), 35 (18), 38 (7, 8), 41 (23), 43 (20), 44

(24), 47 (18), 48 (30, 31), 49 (37), 51 (2, 9), 52 (23), 59 (19), 60 (24), 65 (20-5)

Tzu-lu, disciple of Confucius, xliv, 8 (17) note 5, 15 (6, 7), 16 (13), 17 (25), 19 (6) note 8, 21 (26), 22 (10, 18), 24 (34), 28 (11), 29 (26), 34 (11, 12, 14) note 7, 34 (17) note 15, 35 (21, 23, 24), 36 (25), 39 (12), 41 (1, 3), 45 (28), 46 (13), 47 (17), 48 (23), 49 (38, 41), 50 (45, 1), 52 (3), 54 (1) note 2, 58 (5, 7, 8), 60 (23), 62 (6, 7)

Tzu-sang Po-tzu, xliv, 18 (1)

Tzu-yu, disciple of Confucius, xliv, 7 (7), 14 (26), 19 (12), 33 (2), 46 (9), 57 (4), 64 (12), 65 (14, 15)

Ubaldini, Ottaviano, xx, 44 note 15

Ubaldini, Ruggieri degli, xx, 135 note 1

Ubaldini, Ugolina, xx, 203 note 28

Ubaldini, Ubaldino degli, xx, 242 note 3

Ubaldo, Guido, fortresses of, xxxvi, 71

Ubbriachi, arms of the, xx, 71 note 4

Uberti, family of, xx, 96 note 5

Uberti, Farinata degli, xx, 41-4

Uberti, Mosca degli, in Hell, xx, 27, 117-18

Ubertini, Antonio, xxxi, 56 note 2, 354 note 5

Ubertini, Francesco, xxxi, 56 note 2

Ubians, Tacitus on the, xxxiii, 108

Uchali, king of Algiers, xiv, 385-6, 392

Uddaka, the disciple, xlv, 717-19, 723-4

Udders, developed by use, xi, 27

Ufens, ally to Turnus, xiii, 264-5, 266, 268; death of, 406, 412

Ugliness, Browne on, iii, 267-8; Burke on, xxiv, 97; Emerson on, v, 169, 307

UGLY DUCKLING, THE, xvii, 221-30

Ugo, Marchese, xx, 356 note 25

Ugolina, of Azza, xx, 202 note 20

Ugolini, Antonio, xxxi, 245, 248, 250

Ugolino, Count, xxx, 135 note 1, 203 note 28; Arnold on speech of, xxviii, 72; Hugo on, xxxix, 349

Uladislaus, Dante on, xx, 369 note 17

ULALUME, xlii, 1230-2

Ulfin, Sir, xxxv, 180

Uliades, the Samian, xii, 101

ULLIN'S DAUGHTER, xli, 773-5

Ulubræ, xxvii, 26 note 29

Ulrich of Rudenz (see Rudenz)

Ulrich, the smith in WILLIAM TELL, xxvi, 418

Ulysses (see Odysseus)

Ulysses, by Tennyson, xlii, 977-9; editor's remarks on, l, 20

Umbro, the priest, in the ÆNEID, xiii, 265, 340

Umm Salmâ, xlv, 965 note 26

Unbelievers, Mill on, xxv, 33-4, 224-5; moral teachings of, 245-6; Pascal on, xlviii, 69 (189); salvation of, xx, 367-8, 372-3

Uncertain, town of, in PILGRIM'S PROGRESS, xv, 272

Uncertainty, Burke on terribleness of, xxiv, 70

Uncle Remus, remarks on stories of, xvii, 7

UNCO GUID, ADDRESS TO THE, vi, 183-5

Unconsciousness, as sign of health, xxv, 319-34

Unction, among the ancients, ix, 298 note; Luther on, xxxvi, 266

Undershot Wheels, xxx, 185-6

UNDERSTANDING, ENQUIRY CONCERNING HUMAN, xxxvii, 289-420

Understanding, Bacon on the, xxxix, 135, 136-7, 144-5; body and, xxiv, 108; Confucius on, xliv, 8 (17), 53 (32); feeling and, xlviii, 12 (6); friendship aids, iii, 69; Hobbes on the, xxxiv, 317-18; Job on, xliv, 114 (12-28); Kant on world of, xxxii, 372; knowledge through the, 360, 361; Marcus Aurelius on destruction of the, ii, 265 (2); Pascal on beliefs of the, xlviii, 400-1; petrifaction of, ii, 124-5 (23); reason compared with, xxxii, 361-2; taste and, xxiv, 22-6

Undine, invoked by Faust, xix, 55

Undulation, principle of, in nature, v, 14

UNFAITHFUL SHEPHERDESS, THE, xl, 199-200

Unferth, son of Ecglaf, xlix, 19, 20, 21, 31, 37, 45-6, 54

Unicorn, Job on the, xxiv, 56-7

Uniformity, of human nature, xxxvii, 353-60; effect of, on the imagination, xxiv, 63; cause of sublimity of, 113

UNIFORMITY OF CHANGE, Lyell's, xxxviii, 398-418

Uniformity of Character, how maintained, xi, 109

Unio, defined, xxxvi, 283-4

Union, and division, fable on, xvii, 31; ECCLESIASTES on value of, xliv, 339-40 (9-12); strength in, xvii, 40

Union, American, Hamilton on, xliii, 203;

Jay on, 204-7; Lincoln on, 315-16, 322; Longfellow on, xlii, 1290; Washington on, xliii, 235-9

Union Fire Company, formed by Franklin, i, 99-100

Unitarianism, Coleridge on, v, 319-20; formulation of, xxviii, 308; Voltaire on, xxxiv, 83-4

United States, ARTICLES OF CONFEDERATION, xliii, 158; boundaries of, 256-62, 269-70, 280-3, 286, 292-4; Carlyle on, v, 322; xxviii, 463; CONVENTION WITH PANAMA, xliii, 450-62; Cuba and, 440-1, 443 (1), 448 (16); DECLARATION OF INDEPENDENCE, 150-5; democracy in, xxviii, 453-6, 461-3; Emerson on political institutions in, v, 243-6; foreign population, assimilation of, 462; greatness of nature in, 461-2; annexation of Hawaii, xliii, 437-9; chances for heroism in, v, 130; remarks on history of, xliii, 3; Jay on, 203-5; Longfellow on, xlii, 1290-1; Lowell on, 1390; Marshall on government of, xliii, 210-12; names of places in, v, 405; natural superiority of, 454; naval forces on Great Lakes, xliii, 265-7; original documents in history of, 150-462; its attitude toward the past, xxxix, 388; opportunities for a poet in, v, 179-80; policy of, toward Europe and in America, xliii, 278-9; acquisition of Porto Rico, Guam and Philippines, 443-9; Rome and, comparable, ix, 7; Russia and, xliii, 277; science in, xxx, 310; Taine on sects in, xxxix, 433; Thoreau on, xxviii, 405-6; TREATY WITH FRANCE (1803), xliii, 250-4; TREATY WITH GREAT BRITAIN (1783), 174-9; TREATY OF 1814 WITH GREAT BRITAIN, 255-64; TREATY OF 1842 WITH GREAT BRITAIN, 280-8; TREATY WITH MEXICO, 289-305; TREATY WITH RUSSIA, 432-6; TREATY WITH SIX NATIONS, 229-32; TREATY WITH SPAIN (1819), 268-76; TREATY OF 1898 WITH SPAIN, 442-9; Whitman on poetry in, xxxix, 388-409; Wordsworth on, v, 323-4

United States Bank, Marshall on the, xliii, 208-10, 212-15, 223-4

UNITED STATES CONSTITUTION, xliii, 180-98

Unity, David on excellence of, xliv, 314; enforced, ends progress, iii, 221-5, 229; why excluded from numbers, xlviii,

434; Mohammed's chapter of, xlv, 883; of nature, Emerson on, v, 229-30; of nature, Epictetus on, ii, 129 (36); of nature, Marcus Aurelius on, 219-20 (40, 45), 239 (37, 38), 244 (9), 300 (30); of nature, Pope on, xl, 422-3, 425; in religion, Pascal on, xlviii, 304 (871); in religion, St. Paul on, xlv, 491 (10)

UNITY IN RELIGION, ESSAY ON, Bacon's, iii, 11-14

Unity of Type, defined, xi, 452; law of, 207

Universal-Monarch-Uproar, xlv, 604

Universe, Addison on wonders of, xlv, 535; arrangements of the, prove God, xxxiv, 248-9, 251-4; Berkeley on wonders of the, xxxvii, 230-2; Buddha on question of extent of, xlv, 647-52; Channing on the, xxviii, 324-5; Descartes on growth of the, xxxiv, 36-7; Emerson on, v, 89-90, 167, 175-6, 223; Goethe on the, xix, 26; Hindu idea of, xlv, 853; Hume on man in regard to, xxxvii, 368-9; man with respect to the, xl, 407-15; Aurelius on, cooperation of the, ii, 219 (40), 219-20 (45), 233 (9), 239 (38), 240 (43), 244 (9), 262 (50), 325-6; Milton's ideas of, iv, 245-6; nature of, ii, 217 (27), 233 (10), 236 (25), 275-6 (6); Pascal on greatness of the, xlviii, 26-7; Pope on the, xl, 422-3; unity and symmetry of the, xxx, 312-14

Universities, defined, xxviii, 31; courses at, originally apprenticeships, x, 122-3; Emerson on, v, 415-23; Luther on, xxxvi, 321-7; necessity of, to highest education, xxviii, 32-9; origin of, xxv, 362-3; sites of, xxviii, 40-50; trade corporations formerly called, x, 122

UNIVERSITY, IDEA OF A, by Newman, xxviii, 31-61

UNIVERSITY CARRIER, ON THE, iv, 26-7

UNIVERSITY LIFE AT ATHENS, xxviii, 51-61

University of Paris, site of, xxviii, 45

University of Pennsylvania, founded by Franklin, i, 105, 112-14, 164

Unnamed, the, in I PROMESSI SPOSI, xxi, 313-16; castle of, 318-19; solicited by Rodrigo, 320-3; regrets undertaking against Lucia, 329-32; with Nibbio, 334-5; with Lucia, 336-9; further doubts and regrets, 343-7; visits Cardi-

nal Federigo, 348-50, 361-72; returns to free Lucia, 377-9; takes her to village, 381-8; announces his reformation, 401-4; sends gift to Agnese, 426; his humility, 481-5; during German invasion, 485-6, 490-3

Unproductive Labor, in agricultural system, x, 429-3, 439-42; defined, 258-9; maintenance of, 260-1; More on, xxxvi, 180-1; proportion of, on what dependent, x, 261-5

Unsocial Acts, Marcus Aurelius on, ii, 217 (29), 269 (23)

Unteraar Glacier, xxx, 216; movement of, 224-5

UNWIN, MARY, To, xli, 536-8

UP IN THE MORNING EARLY, vi, 299-30

UP-HILL, xlii, 1182

Upaka, the ascetic, xlv, 724

Upatissa, disciple of Buddha, xlv, 586

Upavāna, xlv, 634-5

Upholsterer, Chaucer's, xl, 21 note 192

Uppalavannā, disciple of Buddha, xlv, 586

Uprightness, Confucius on, xliv, 20 (17); without courtesy, 25 (2); with learning, 58 (8)

Uproars, of Buddhism, xlv, 603-4

Upton, critic of Shakespeare, xxxix, 240

Urania, Dante on, xx, 263; Milton on, iv, 227-8

Urban VIII, in Mantuan contest, xxi, 435

Urbiciani, Buonaggiunta, xx, 242 and note 1

Urbino, Duke of, xxxi, 73 note 1

Urbino, Gian di, xxxi, 77 note 4

URBS SION AUREA, xlv, 549

Urganda, in DON QUIXOTE, xiv, 46-7

Urgel, Nicholas, Cardinal of, xxxv, 34

Uriah, reference to, xliii, 93

Uriel, in PARADISE LOST, iv, 151-2, 153-4, 158, 168-9, 213

Urien, a Breton saint, xxxii, 161

Urim, reference to, iv, 384

Uruguay River, Darwin on the, xxix, 152; sediment of, xxxviii, 402-3

Use, Burke on effects of, xxiv, 84; Darwin on, and disuse, xi, 27, 140-4; Keats on, xli, 873; necessary to true possession, xix, 34; Shakespeare on, xlvi, 168 (see also Habit)

Usefulness, as source of beauty, xxix, 407-8; Marcus Aurelius on, ii, 208 (6), 240-1 (44)

Usipians, Tacitus on the, xxxiii, 111

Uspallata Mountains, Darwin on the, xxix, 335

Usurers, in Dante's HELL, xx, 70-1; Sheridan on, xviii, 143-4

Usurpation, Machiavelli on, xxxvi, 31-2; Pascal on beginning of, xlviii, 105 (295); Washington on, xliii, 242

Usury, Dante on, xx, 47-8; in India and ancient Rome, x, 96; worst method of gain, iii, 89 (see also Interest)

USURY, ESSAY ON, Bacon's, iii, 101-4

Uther Pendragon, xxxix, 23

Utilitarian Doctrine, of structures, xi, 199-204; objections to, 211-13, 218-43

Utilitarian Society, The, xxv, 53-4

Utilitarianism, Carlyle on, xxv, 354; Mill on school of, 66-73; Mill's work in, 4-5; James Mill's, 35-6; origin of name, 53

Utility, beauty and, xxiv, 85-7; in ethics, xxv, 205; Locke on, xxxvii, 170-1; Schiller on, xxxii, 211; as end of science, xxxix, 137-8; Shelley on, xxvii, 350-2; in works of art, xxiv, 87-9

UTOPIA, More's, xxxvi, 135-243; editorial remarks on, 88; l, 42; Peter Giles on, xxxvi, 241-3; Sidney on, xxvii, 18

Utopia, agriculture and live stock in, xxxvi, 172-4, 178-9, 204-5; antiquity of, 169; bondmen in, 207-8, 210-11; its cities, 172-3, 174-5, 177, 183-4; dining-halls, 185, 186-8; distribution in, 184-5, 189-190; dress in, 178-9; drinks of, 174; education and learning in, 195-6, 205-7, 231; families and distribution of population, 183-4; fools and deformed persons, 211-12; foreign trade, 189-90, 207; government and magistrates, 177-8, 212-3; health and prosperity of people, 204; hospitals in, 185-6; the island of, 171-2; language of, 205; laws and justice, 212-3; marriage institutions, 208-10; iii, 169 and note 57, 170; occupations and amusements, xxxvi, 178-83, 188-9; philosophy, 196-204; use of precious metals and stones, 191-4; punishments in, 207-11; readiness of people to learn from others, 169, 205, 206-7; relations with other states, 213-14; religions of, 224-37; sciences, crafts and occupations, 178-83, 189; care of the sick, 208; situation of, 242-3; socialism in, 167-9, 176, 184-5, 186, 189-90, 236, 238-40; statues of good men, 212; strangers in,

186; travelling in, 188-9; wars of, 184, 190, 215-24

Utopus, king of Utopia, xxxvi, 172, 176, 226

Uwaine, Sir, death of, xxxv, 159; Galahad and, 118; Gawaine and, 127, 158-9; Seven Knights and, 127; at the White Abbey, 116

Uzziel, on guard at Eden, iv, 174

VACATION EXERCISE, AT A, iv, 20-3

Vaccination, Franklin on, i, 96; history of, xxxviii, 142, 203-4; Woolman on, i, 237-8

VACCINATION AGAINST SMALLPOX, Jenner's, xxxviii, 145-220

Vacuity, Burke on idea of, xxiv, 60-1

Vacuum, Pascal on the, xlviii, 443-4

Vadimon, Lake, Pliny on, ix, 330-1

Vagabonds, More on, xxxvi, 154

Vagon, xxxv, 116

Vaila, battle of, xxxvi, 43

Vain-confidence, Mr., in PILGRIM'S PROGRESS, xv, 115

VAIN-GLORY, ESSAY ON, Bacon's, iii, 127-9

Vain-glory, Hobbes on, xxxiv, 342, 372; language of, 344-5

Vain-hope, in PILGRIM'S PROGRESS, xv, 165

Vaisya, task of a, xlv, 870

Vajirā, the priestess, xlv, 656

Val-holl, xlix, 274 note

Valdabrun, xlix, 114, 145

Valdes, in DR. FAUSTUS, xix, 209-11

Valdesso, John, Herbert and, xv, 412-13

Valdimagra, Marquis of, xx, 102 note 5

Valdivia, Darwin on, xxix, 301, 302; earthquake at, 305-6

Valdovinos, history of, xiv, 43

Vale, Earl de, xxxv, 148

VALEDICTION, by Donne, xv, 338-9

VALEDICTION, FORBIDDING MOURNING, xl, 304-5

Valentine, in FAUST, xix, 158-65

Valentino, Duke, Cæsar Borgia called, xxxvi, 15

Valère, in TARTUFFE, in love with Mariane, xxvi, 208; marriage put off by Orgon, 216-17; Orgon on, 223; with Mariane, on marriage with Tartuffe, 233-43; advises flight of Orgon, 291-2; promised Mariane, 296

Valeria, and Coriolanus, xii, 178-9

Valerian, and Sapor, xxxix, 98

Valerius, character in SOPHOCLES, v, 121-2

Valiant-for-the-truth, in PILGRIM'S PROGRESS, xv, 175, 295-302, 311, 315-16

VALIANT LITTLE TAILOR, THE, xvii, 90-8

Valkyria, xlix, 274 note

Vallejo, Don Guadalupe, xxiii, 394

VALLEY OF CAUTERETZ, IN THE, xlii, 976

Valley of the Shadow of Death, xv, 65-9

Valmiki, Sainte-Beuve on, xxxii, 130

Valor, Browne on true, iii, 278; defined by Hobbes, xxxiv, 341; Emerson on, v, 153; Segrais on, xiii, 24

Valori, Bartolommeo, xxxi, 113 note 3

Valors, our, the best gods, v, 77

Valparaiso, Darwin on, xxix, 257

Value(s), comparative, of food and materials, x, 178-80; exchange, 34-5, 36-7, 40-1, 48, 50-1; in exchange and use, 32-3; labor as determining, 48, 50-1; of limited or uncertain products, 192-202; measured by corn, 38-41; measured by money, 36-7, 41-2, 46-7; profits as element in, 49-50; rent as element in, 50; scarcity, 181-2; standards of, 42-5; of unlimited productions, 183-92 (see also Prices)

Vampire-bats, in Chile, xxix, 31

Vanbrugh, Sir John, Voltaire on, xxxiv, 138, 139

Vandals, learning despised by, xxxv, 383; origin of the, xxxiii, 94

Van Diemen's Land, climate of, xxix, 249; Darwin on, 449-52

Vandyke, Hazlitt on, xxvii, 279

Vane, Sir Henry, A HEALING QUESTION, xliii, 118-37; SONNET to, iv, 83

Vanessa (see Vanhomrigh)

Vangiones, Tacitus on the, xxxiii, 108

Vanholt, Duke of, in FAUSTUS, xix, 241-2

Vanhomrigh, Esther, Swift and, xxviii, 8, 26-7, 28

Vanini, Berkeley on, xxxvii, 233

Vanities, worldly, vii, 206 (4)

Vanity, all is, xliv, 335-8, 349; Fielding on, xxxix, 180-1; folly of, vii, 211; Franklin on, i, 6; of life, xlviii, 62 (161-2), 63 (164); Pascal on human, 60 (150); Penn on, i, 391-2; in speech, 383 (119); the strongest human motive, xxviii, 94-6; Woolman on, i, 274

Vanity, Limbo of, iv, 146-8

Vanity Fair, in PILGRIM'S PROGRESS, xv, 91-3; altered after Faithful's death, 280

Vansen, in EGMONT, xix, 272-5, 298-301

Vapor, differs from gas in permanency, xxx, 102

Varchi, Benedetto da Monte, xxxi, 33
note 4; sonnet on Cellini, 166, 168
Varenus, and the Bithynians, ix, 299-301
Vargas, Diego Peres of, xiv, 61
Vargas, Garcia Perez de, xiv, 488
Variability, causes of, xi, 23-6, 53; due to
changed conditions, 138-40; due to
use and disuse, 140-4; hereditary, 122;
of highly developed parts, 153-6; in
important organs, 56; of mongrels and
hybrids, 312-13; of multiple, rudimentary or low structures, 152; of secondary sexual characters, 157-9; of specific
and generic organs, 156-9
Variation(s), analogous, xi, 159-62;
Burke on beauty in, xxiv, 94-5, 124-5;
climate not the cause of, xi, 378-9; correlated, 27-8, 147-50; Darwin on
abrupt, 246-50; first appearance of,
462-3; inheritance of, 28-9; of instincts, 254-5; laws of, 138-68; St.
Hilaire on cause of, 10; Spencer on
cause of, 15; spontaneous (see Spontaneous Variation); technical meaning
of, 54; under domestication, 23-53;
under nature, 54-70; Vestiges of Creation in, 12-13
Varieties, classification of, xi, 440-1; compared with species, 58-64; evidence of
their being incipient species, 67-70,
157, 315; extinct intermediate, 320-1,
332-40; fertility of, 308-12; how they
become species, 115-24; intercrossing
between, 105; intermediate, why absent or rare, 170-5; meaning of, 54;
not clearly distinct from species, 335-6;
of same species, struggle with each
other, 84
Variety, of opinion, Milton on, iii, 224-5,
228-9; Pascal on, xlviii, 48 (114);
source of pleasure in, xxvii, 262
Varro, M. Terentius, on country life,
xxvii, 61; Pompey's lieutenant, xii, 294;
works of, lost, xxvii, 344
Varus, and the Germans, xxxiii, 114
Vasari, Giorgio, Cellini and, xxxi, 172,
173, 421 note 3
Vasava, xlv, 832
Vassellario (see Vasari)
Vastness, in architecture, xxiv, 64-5; a
cause of the sublime, 61-2; not lov-
able, 126-7; physical cause of sublimity of, 109-11
Vatable, Professor of Hebrew, xlviii, 283
note 3

Vatinius, Cicero and, ix, 120, 127; xii,
225; Cicero on, 239
Vaudeville, M. de, xxxviii, 41-3
Vaughan, Benj., letter of, to Franklin, i,
69-73
Vaughan, Henry, POEMS by, xl, 346-8
Vauvenargues, Sainte-Beuve on, xxxii,
131
Vedius, P., Cicero on, ix, 151
Vega, Lope de, xxvi, 5; Carlyle on, xxv,
403-4
Vegetable Kingdom, beauty in the, xxiv,
77; distinguished from animal, xxxviii,
340-2
Vegetarianism, Franklin's, i, 17, 35
VEIL, BEYOND THE, xl, 346-7
Veillantif, horse of Roland, xlix, 120, 131
Veins, arteries anciently called, xxxviii,
81; arteries and, 102-3, 109-10, 116,
137-8, 139; communication of, 113;
Harvey on the, 117-21, 137
Vejento, in Certus case, ix, 342
Veleda, worshipped as divinity, xxxiii,
97
Velitræ, colony of, xii, 157-8
Vellutus, condemns Coriolanus, xii, 163,
164; protests against colony of Velitræ,
158; first of the tribunes, 152
Velocity, as a motive force, xxx, 185-7;
measurement of working power of,
186-8; power and, in machines, 182-5
Vena arteriosa, xxxviii, 87
Vena cava, xxxviii, 91-2, 103
Venafro, Antonio of, xxxvi, 75-6
Vendosme, M. de, xxxviii, 21-2
Venedians, Tacitus on the, xxxiii, 119
Veneration, never dies out, v, 28
Venery, Franklin's rule of, i, 80
VENETIAN REPUBLIC, ON THE EXTINCTION
OF THE, xli, 676
Veneziano, Bastiano, xxxi, 111, 113
Venezuela, cities of, xxxiii, 303
Vengeance, Drake on, xxxiii, 129; Raleigh
on divine, xxxix, 69-89 (see also Retri-
bution)
VENI CREATOR SPIRITUS, xlv, 547-8
Venice, Browning on, xlii, 1080-1;
growth and decline of, xxxvi, 43; land-
tax of, x, 482; King Louis and, xxxvi,
13-14, 24, 74; mercenaries of, 43; overthrown by Pope Julius, 39; policy
toward subject cities, 69-70; Pope on,
xl, 438; power of, before French invasion, xxxvi, 38-9; Shelley on, xli,
838-9; situation of, v, 334; in 16th

century, xxvii, 392; trade of, x, 397-8;
Wordsworth on, xli, 676
Venison, price of, x, 187-8
Venner, Thomas, xxxiii, 229, 245
Venta Cruz, Drake at, xxxiii, 178-9
Ventana, Sierra de la, xxix, 113-16
Ventidius, xii, 346, 347; in Parthia,
xxxiii, 113
Ventidius, in ALL FOR LOVE, returns from
East, xviii, 26-9; scene with Antony,
30-8; conversation with Antony on Oc-
tavius, 42-3; on Alexas, 43-4; on Cleopatra's gifts, 44-6; in meeting of An-
tony and Cleopatra, 47-53; advises Antony to seek terms, 54-7; on Antony's
love, 59-60; brings Octavia to Antony,
61-5; in meeting of Dolabella and
Cleopatra, 71, 73-4, 76; tells Antony
of Dolabella's treachery, 77-83; with
Antony after last defeat, 93-8; death,
99; Dryden on character of, 26
Ventilation, need of, xxx, 164-5
Ventricles, of the heart, xxxviii, 79-86,
88, 99-100, 130-5; right and left, 69-
70, 72-3
Venulus, in the ÆNEID, xiii, 268, 364-6,
382
Venus, Adonis and, alluded to, iv, 71;
born of the sea, xl, 364; Emerson on,
fable of, v, 302; Mars's minion, xlvi,
447 note 15; mother of mirth, iv, 30;
statue of, in Vatican, xxxi, 318; zone
of, referred to, iv, 377 (see also Aphrodite)
Venus, in ÆNEID, seeks Jove in Trojans'
behalf, xiii, 81-2; meeting with Æneas,
84-7; persuades Cupid to enter form of
Ascanius, 96-7; warns Æneas to fly,
120-1; plans marriage of Æneas and
Dido, 155-6; seeks Neptune in Æneas's
behalf, 203-4; seeks aid of Vulcan for
Æneas, 280-1; brings Æneas arms, 288;
complains to Jove, 321-3; cures Æneas
of his wound, 404
"Venus de Medici's," Burke on the, xxiv,
98
Venus, the planet, Dante on, xx, 145
note 3, 256; Dante's third Heaven,
314-15
Veracity, in art, v, 304
Veragua, town of, xxxiii, 182
Verania, wife of Piso, Regulus and, ix,
228
Verbal Nouns, Johnson on, xxxix, 189-
90

Verbosity, Montaigne on, xxxii, 45
Vercingetorix, xii, 286 and note, 287-8
Verdi, Francesco and Antonio, xxxi, 56
note 2
Verdicts, special, in Massachusetts, xliii,
71 (31)
Vere, Baron, character of, v, 385
Verecundus, grammarian of Milan, vii,
126; kindness and conversion of, 140
Vergentorix, xii, 286 and note, 287-8
Vergezio, Giovanni, xxxi, 97 note 5
Vergilia, wife of Coriolanus, xii, 179, 180
Vergilius, Caius, Cicero and, xii, 244
Verginius, Rufus, Pliny on, ix, 211-13
Vermilion, Miss, in SCHOOL FOR SCANDAL,
xviii, 132-3
Verneuil, M. de, on changes of species,
xi, 359
Vernon, Franklin and, i, 31, 33, 34, 52,
61
Veronese, Hugo on, xxxix, 352
Verres, Cicero and, ix, 5; prosecution of,
xii, 223-4
Verrocchio, Andrea del, xxxi, 401-2
Verse, in the drama, Hugo on, xxxix,
369, 371-4; Pope on advantages of, xl,
407; Sidney on, xxvii, 12-13, 31-2;
Voice and, sisters, iv, 40
Verses, Locke on making of, xxxvii, 149-
50, 161; James Mill on making of, xxv,
15
Versification, Montaigne on, xxxii, 62-3;
Shelley on, xxvii, 334
Versifying, Sidney on, xxvii, 49-50
Vertumnus, and Pomona, iv, 270
Verulam (see Bacon, Francis)
Verus, Lucius, and M. Aurelius Anto-
ninus, ii, 304, 309
Vesalius, on the heart, xxxviii, 78-9
Vespasian, death of, iii, 10; empire fore-
told to, 91; Jerusalem and, xxxviii, 31;
miracles of, xxxvii, 385-6; night busi-
ness of, ix, 233; Pascal on miracles of,
xlviii, 281 (816); Tacitus on, iii, 30;
times of, ii, 217 (32)
Vesper, Keats on, xli, 880
Vespucci, Amerigo, ACCOUNT OF HIS
FIRST VOYAGE, xliii, 28-44; Emerson
on, v, 392; life of, xliii, 28 note
Vespucci, Giorgio Antonio, xliii, 29
Vesta, reference to, iv, 34
Vestal Virgins, office of, ix, 254 note
Vestiges of Creation, xi, 12-13
Vesuvius, Pliny on the eruption of, ix,
285-7, 288-91

Veto, presidential, xliii, 183-4

Vetus, and Cæsar, xii, 267

Vexation, Eliphaz on, xliv, 77 (2); Marcus Aurelius on, ii, 204 (16), 237 (27), 248 (38)

Vibius, and Cicero, xii, 244

Vibration, frequency of, defined, xxx, 252

Vibrios, xxxviii, 328-42, 365-7; butyric, 327-8; Pasteur on, 322-3

Vibullius, Cicero on, ix, 116

Vice, Augustine, St., on, vii, 57-8; beginnings of, xxxiv, 204; Burns on wretchedness of, vi, 320; degrees of, xxvi, 176; Emerson on, v, 66-7, 100; Epictetus on, ii, 183 (3), 184 (10); false arguments of, iv, 64-5; Franklin on, i, 86, 92; Hobbes on, xxxiv, 412; Jonson on knowledge of, xl, 294; knowledge of, Mrs. Herbert on, xv, 376; knowledge of, necessary to virtue, iii, 201-2; Lessing on worldly retribution of, xxxii, 191-2; Locke on knowledge of, xxxvii, 76-7; not natural to man, xxxiv, 187-8, 269-73, 278-9; nature opposed to, v, 27, 97; necessary to virtue, iii, 316; Pascal on, xlviii, 45 (102); Pope on, xl, 420-1; Pope on supposed prosperity of, 432-9; prosperity and, Bacon on, iii, 16; its own punishment, xvii, 32; public opinion and, xxvii, 379; Rousseau on punishment of, xxxiv, 265-6; Scriptural warrant for, xv, 260-2; taught to children, xxxvii, 29-31; Taine on, xxxix, 417-18; Whitman on punishment of, 403-5

Vice-President (United States), amended method of election, xliii, 196-7; former manner of election, 187 (2, 3); impeachment, 189 (4); president of Senate, 182 (4); succession to presidency, 188 (5), 196 (12); qualifications of electors, 197; term of office, 186 (1)

Vices and Virtues, game of, xxxvi, 180

Vich Ian Vohr, v, 206

Vicissitude, Arabian inscriptions on, xvi, 300-4, 312, 317, 320-1; Browne on, of states, iii, 269-70; Carlyle on, xxv, 350-2; Casaubon on, xxxix, 73-4; Emerson on, v, 149-50; Marcus Aurelius on, ii, 218 (33, 36), 229 (23), 232 (4), 234 (15); Montaigne on, xxxii, 5-6; Raleigh on, xxxix, 70-1, 95-7, 98

VICISSITUDE, ODE ON PLEASURES OF, xl, 460-2

VICISSITUDE OF THINGS, ESSAY ON THE, iii, 136-40

Vicorati, Francesco, da, xxxi, 7

Victorinus, Augustine, St., on, vii, 120-2

Vicuna, Darwin on the, xxix, 363

Vides, governor of Cumana, xxxiii, 332, 333

VIGIL STRANGE I KEPT, xlii, 1403-4

Vigne, Pierro delle, in Dante's HELL, xx, 54-5 and note

Vigo, Drake at, xxxiii, 232

Vigo, John de, xxxviii, 11

Viguiere, Pauline de, v, 305

Vijayuttara, the conch, xlv, 618

VILLAGE BLACKSMITH, THE, xlii, 1271-3

Villagers, Thoreau on, xxviii, 400-1

Villars, Marquis de, xxxviii, 34, 37

Villemarqué, M. de la, xxxii, 139, 167

Villiers, Charles, Mill on, xxv, 52, 80, 81, 82

Villiers, George, Mill on, xxv, 81, 82

Villiers, George, 1st Duke of Buckingham, iii, 5; Voltaire on, xxxiv, 147; Wotton on, v, 405

Villiers, George, 2nd Duke, Clarendon on, v, 349; his house at Cliefden, xxxix, 153 note 1; Voltaire on, xxxiv, 147

Villon, Arnold on, xxviii, 79-80

Vilmund, lover of Borgny, xlix, 431, 432

Vinci, Leonardo da, xxvii, 278; his cartoon of capture of Piso, xxxi, 23 and note 2; Cellini on, 359; Guido and, xxxix, 426

Vincula, San Pietro ad, xxxvi, 28

Vindicianus, St. Augustine and, vii, 47-8, 104

Vindictiveness, Penn on, i, 340 (185) (see Revenge)

Vine, Cicero on culture of the, ix, 64

Vineyards, profits of, x, 159-60; value of, 157-8

Vingi, the messenger, xlix, 342, 343, 345-6

VINLAND, THE VOYAGES TO, xliii, 5-20; remarks on, l, 22

Vintner, in FAUSTUS, xix, 234-5

Violence, punishment of, in HELL, xx, 46, 50-71

Violets, for modesty, vi, 407; Wotton on, xl, 288

Violins, Dryden on, xl, 390

Viper, Harrison on the, xxxv, 344-5

Virbius, son of Hippolytus, xiii, 265-6

Virgil, ÆNEID of, xiii, 73-423; an astrologer, xxxix, 159; Augustine, St., on

study of, vii, 15-16; Augustus and, xiii, 17-18; xxxix, 163-4; on generation of bees, xxxv, 346; birthplace of, xx, 218 note 4; body of, removed to Naples, 153 note; Burke on, xxiv, 72; Burke on his figure of Fame, 54; Burke on his picture of Hell, 60-1; Burke on his picture of Vulcan's forge, 135-6; Caxton on, xxxix, 24-5; Cowley on, xxvii, 61; Dante's guide to HELL and PURGATORY, xx, 7-12; in Dante's Limbo, 170; Dryden on, xiii, 14-71; xl, 396; the *Georgics* of, xxxix, 299; Homer and, xiii, 5-6; xxxix, 157-8; Hugo on, 363; Italicus and, ix, 236-7; life and works, xiii, 3-4; Locke on, xxxvii, 157; machinery of, xiii, 46-50; reputed a magician in Middle Ages, xix, 230 note; Montaigne on, xxxii, 90; morals of his poem, xiii, 19-37; Raleigh on, xxxix, 113; a republican at heart, xiii, 17; on rustic life, xxvii, 68; Sainte-Beuve on, xxxii, 131; Scaliger on, xxvii, 50; Shelley on, 344; Sidney on *Georgics* of, 12; similes of, xiii, 41-2; Spenser on, xxxix, 62; times of, xiii, 15-17; Wordsworth on figures of, xxxix, 302, 304

VIRGIL, To, by Tennyson, xlii, 1014; editor's remarks on, l, 20-1

Virgilianæ, Sortes, xxvii, 8

Virgilius, Bishop, Browne on, iii, 279 and note 60

Virginia, Drayton on, xl, 226-7; Quakers in, i, 276; Winthrop on patent of, xliii, 88

VIRGINIA, FIRST CHARTER OF, xliii, 49-58

VIRGINIA, MASSACHUSETTS TO, xlii, 1344-7

VIRGINIAN VOYAGE, TO THE, xl, 226-8

Virginity, Paul, St., on, xlv, 499 (25-6), 500 (34, 37); Milton on, iv, 56, 65

Virginius, Flavius, story of, ix, 227 note

VIRGINS, To THE, xl, 335

Virgoe, Thomas, xxxviii, 157

Virgularia Patagonica, Darwin on, xxix, 105-7

Virnes, Christopher de, Cervantes on, xiv, 54

Virtue, adversities help unto, vii, 300 (2); in ambition and in authority, iii, 31; Augustine, St., on, vii, 58; Bacon on, iii, 16-17, 99, 100; beauty and, 106-7; Browne on, 306, 325; Burke on beauty in, xxiv, 91-2; Burns on, vi, 320; cannot change at once, xxvi, 176; Chan-

ning on, xxviii, 323; Cicero on, ix, 25-6, 37, 41, 44, 48; the company of, ii, 183 (2); Confucius on highest, xliv, 21 (27), 35 (19); consists in comparison, xxxiv, 349; the chief aim in education, xxxvii, 54-5, 77, 78, 153, 173; Emerson on, v, 26-8, 66-7, 72, 73; an object of envy, ix, 193; Epictetus on, ii, 140 (66), 161 (119); Epicurus on, xxxvii, 399-400; examples of, ii, 293 (26); excessive, xlviii, 119 (353), 120 (357); fortune and, xxxi, 11-12; Franklin on, i, 79-80, 86 note, 87; Franklin's *Art of*, 86; Franklin's party of, 89-91; alone is free, ii, 184 (10); iv, 71-2; friendship and, ix, 16, 19, 23, 26-7, 37, 42; happiness and, Pope on, xl, 432-9; the hereafter, belief in, and, iii, 298-9, 303-4; Hindu ideas of, xlv, 847, 860, 870, 871; Hobbes on, xxxiv, 412; Hume on standards of, xxvii, 204-5; Hume on teaching of, xxxvii, 289; immortality, belief in, and, xxxvi, 228-9; intellectual, xxxiv, 349; intrinsic worth of, xxxii, 364-5; Jonson on, xl, 294; Kant on pure, xxxii, 337 note; knowledge of world and, xxxvii, 51-2; in Latin equivalent to courage, xii, 142; learning and, xxxvii, 128; Locke on, 42, 115, 118; love of, natural to man, xxxiv, 269-74; loveableness of, xxiv, 90-1; Machiavelli on, xxxvi, 51; Machiavelli on appearance of, 57-8; Marcus Aurelius on, ii, 235 (17), 341; measurement of, xlviii, 119 (352); Milnes on pleasures of, xlii, 1057-8; Milton on, iv, 54, 60, 120, 176, 371; Milton on study of, iii, 239, 242; modesty and, ix, 250; Montaigne on, xxxii, 9-10, 51-2; More on, xxxvi, 196-8, 202, 204; nature leagued with, v, 97; no penalty to, 100; not mere absence of vice, xxvii, 263; not virtue if she tumble, xviii, 203; ostentation of, ii, 177 (176); Pascal on maxims of, xlviii, 15-16 (20); passion and, xl, 419-20; Penn on complete, i, 358; pleasure in seeing, ii, 241 (48); Plutarch on, xii, 83-4; Plutarch on contemplation of, 36-7; Pope on vice and, xl, 420-1; popular idea of, v, 63; pure, tests of, xxxii, 309-15; quotations on, i, 82-3; "reason in practice," xxxii, 125; refinement and, 236-7, 254; reward of, xxxiv, 265; reward of, Emerson on, v, 27, 86; reward of,

Jonson on, xl, 298; reward of, Lessing on, xxxii, 191; reward of, Pliny on, ix, 194; reward of, Rousseau on, xxxiv, 263; its own reward, ii, 163 (126), 253 (73); iii, 298; xxxix, 405-6; xlv, 794-5; riches and, iii, 87-8; Rousseau on grounds of, xxxiv, 276-8; Rousseau on natural, 186-90; sensuous and ascetic, xxviii, 169-73; Shakespeare on, xlvi, 116; Sidney on teachers of, xxvii, 14-25; Socrates on, ii, 18-19, 58, 109; Stoics' idea of, ii, 344-5; Taine on, xxxix, 417; Tennyson on wages of, xlii, 1005; through love and fear, xl, 296; trial necessary to, ii, 156 (106); iii, 202, 207-8; unconsciousness of true, xxv, 325-6; vice necessary to, iii, 316; Wordsworth on, xxxix, 316 (see also Morality)

VIRTUE, by Herbert, xl, 342

Virtues, the seven, xx, 171 notes 2 and 3

VIRTUOUS YOUNG LADY, TO A, iv, 78-9

Vis Inertiæ, Hume on, xxxvii, 345 note

Vis Viva, defined, xxx, 186; measure of, 188 note; transformed to weight, 187-8

Visakha, story of, xlv, 754-81

Visconti, Galeazzo de', xx, 177 notes 5 and 7

Vishnu, xlv, 831-2; in the BHAGAVAD-GITA, 784

Vishnu Sarma, quoted, v, 291

Vision, Burke on method of, xxiv, 109-10

VISION, A, by Burns, vi, 481-2

VISION, THE, by Burns, vi, 172-82

VISION OF MIRZA, Addison's, xxvii, 73-7

Visions, Hobbes on, xxxiv, 316-17; Walton on, xv, 336-7

Vitelli, Burke on the, xxiv, 269; Cæsar Borgia and, xxxvi, 27, 31, 46

Vitelli, Niccolo, at Citta di Castello, xxxvi, 71

Vitelli, Paolo, xxxvi, 25, 30, 42

Vitellius, Mucianus and, iii, 141

Vitellozzo, Machiavelli on, xxxvi, 30, 31

Vitet, M., on Chanson de Roland, xxviii, 70-1

Vitruvius, on architecture, v, 176; xxxi, 8

Vittore, Father, in THE BETROTHED, xxi, 583-4

Vivian, Christian king, xlix, 195

Vivien, and Merlin, xxxii, 153

VIVIEN'S SONG, xlii, 976-7

Vivisection, Harvey on, xxxviii, 75; in New Atlantis, iii, 174-5

Vocation, Bacon on choosing, for children, iii, 20-1; content in one's, ii, 217 (31); Epictetus on choice of, 155 (104); Pascal on choice of, xlviii, 42 (97), 49 (116, 117)

Voconius, Cicero on, xii, 240

VOGLER, ABT, Browning's, xlii, 1100-2

Voice, power of human, i, 103; verse and, sisters, iv, 40

Voiture, Voltaire on, xxxiv, 145

Voland, the Devil called, xix, 175

Volcanic Bombs, xxix, 496

Volcanoes, as dependent on changes of surface, xxix, 484-5; earthquakes and, relations of, 314-15; Geikie on, xxx, 333-4; simultaneous eruption of, xxix, 295-6

Volition, Rousseau on, xxxiv, 249-50 (see also Will)

Volscians, Coriolanus with the, xii, 167-9; final defeat, 185; war of Rome against the, 152-4; second war with Rome, 171-82

Volsung, son of Rerir, xlix, 260-1, 262-4

VÖLSUNGA SAGA, xlix, 257-358; PROLOGUE IN VERSE, 255-6; remarks on the, 250-2

Volsungs, names of, xlix, 253; SONGS ABOUT THE, 359-438

VOLSUNGS AND NIBLUNGS, story of the, xlix, 249-358; editor's remarks on, l, 21

Voltaic Batteries, xxx, 76, 203-5; examples of action of, 128-30; power of, 126

Voltaire, Carlyle on, xxv, 421; on circumstances, xxviii, 441; Corneille and, xxxix, 426; on Greek drama, 364; Hazlitt on, xxvii, 279; on Horace, xxxii, 133; Lessing and, xxvi, 298; LETTERS ON THE ENGLISH, xxxiv, 65-159; remarks on LETTERS of, l, 24, 32; life and works, xxxiv, 64; Sainte-Beuve on, xxxii, 123, 131; on Shakespeare, xxxix, 212, 224, 227; on systems, 375-6; on taste, 384; Le Temple du Goût, 384

Volterra, Daniello da, xxxi, 435 note

Volterra, Niccolaio da, xxxi, 19

Voltimand, in HAMLET, xlvi, 100, 126-7

Volumnia, mother of Coriolanus, xii, 150; begs him to desist from war, 179-81

Volusus, in the ÆNEID, xiii, 372

Von Baer, on bees, xi, 370; on embryos, 459; on organization, 129

Vopiscus, name of, xii, 157

Vortigern, Hengist and, v, 276

Voss, on Milton, xxxix, 319

Voters, qualifications of, v, 241

Voting, right of, in United States, xliii, 198 (see also Elective Franchise)

Vows, Dante on, xx, 301-4; ECCLESIASTES on, xliv, 340 (4-5); Hobbes on, xxxiv, 397-8; Shakespeare on, xlvi, 110-11

VOYAGE OF THE BEAGLE, Darwin's, xxix; editor's remarks on, l, 40, 45

Voyages, Darwin on sea, xxix, 503-5

VOYAGES AND TRAVELS, xxxiii

Voyages and Travels, books dealing with, l, 45-6

Vulcan, in the ÆNEID, xiii, 281-3; forge of, 282; forge of, Burke on, xxiv, 135; lameness of, v, 301; sons of, iv, 62

Vulgarity, Confucius on, xliv, 8 (14), 13 (11), 14 (16), 24 (36), 39 (16), 44 (23, 25, 26), 45 (7), 48 (24), 50-1 (1), 52 (20), 53 (33), 56 (8); Ruskin on, xxviii, 113

Vulpius, Christiane, wife of Goethe, xix, 5

Vultures, Harrison on, xxxv, 339

Vyasa, Sainte-Beuve on, xxxii, 130

Wacarima, Mount, xxxiii, 369

Wace, Robert, xxxii, 161

Wadsworth, Gen., at Gettysburg, xliii, 329

Wage-earners, interest of, connected with general interests, x, 209

Wager, Pascal on necessity of the, xlviii, 84-7

Wages, affected by market fluctuations, x, 60-1; in by-employments, 119; relation to cost of living, 75-9, 84-5, 87-9; defined, 53; dependent on state of society, 70-4, 83; determination of, 56; determined by competition, 66-9, 281; determined by time, hardship and skill, 48; in England (1772), i, 304; tendency of, to equality, x, 101; in exclusive trades, 64; increase of money, effect of, on, 283; industry, relation of, to, 83-6; inequalities of, due to government interference, 121-44; natural inequalities of, 102-13; in novel trades, 116-18; population determined by, 80-2; price of commodities, an element in, 48; prices affected by high, 99-100; profits and, confounded, 53-5, 113-14; proportion of, between different employments, 64-5; real, 79-80; regulation of, by law, 144-5; relation of, to rates of interest, 91-3; scarcity, 117-18; taxes on, 511-14; effect of taxes on consumption and, 518-19

Wages, by Tennyson, xlii, 1005

Waggoner, fable of the, xvii, 35

Wagner, in FAUST, xix, 29-32, 43-52

Wagner, in DR. FAUSTUS, xix, 208, 211-12, 216-18, 241, 243

Wagner, Moritz, on isolation of species, xi, 109

WAIF, PROEM TO LONGFELLOW'S, xxviii, 378-80

Wain, constellation of the, xx, 428; Homer on the, xxii, 75

Wainfleet, William, xxxv, 381

Wakan, xliii, 142

Wakes, Luther on, church, xxxvi, 309

Waking, Locke on method of, xxxvii, 22-3

Waldseemuller, Vespucci and, xliii, 28 note

Wales, agriculture of, xxxv, 310; bards of, xxvii, 8; Christianity in, xxxii, 173; education in (1848), xxviii, 155; lead mines of, xxxv, 322-3; literature of, xxxii, 138-9, 144-62; realm of, Milton on, iv, 45; Renan on, xxxii, 137; soil of, xxxv, 308, 310-11

Walid Ibn Mughairah, xlv, 880 note 2, 898 note

WALKING, ESSAY ON, Thoreau's, xxviii, 393-425

Wallace, A. R., Darwin and, xi, 5-6, 19; on origin of species, 385

Wallace, William, Burns on, vi, 88, 139-40, 175, 493-4

Walleechu, Indian god, xxix, 75

Wallenstein, quoted, xxi, 469

Waller, Edmund, Dryden on, xxxix, 154, 163; POEMS by, xl, 357-8; Voltaire on, xxxiv, 144-7

Walls, why less grand than colonnades, xxiv, 113-14

Walpurgis-Night, in FAUST, xix, 167-83; Dream, 183-90; remarks on, 7

Walsh, William, Dryden on, xiii, 426

Walter, Count, in SONG OF ROLAND, xlix, 120, 139, 162-4

Walter, Mr., of the Times, v, 449

Waltham, Thomas, at Otterburn, xxxv, 92

Walton, Izaak, LIFE OF DR. DONNE, xv, 323-69; LIFE OF HERBERT, 373-418; life and works, 322; LIVES, editorial remarks on, l, 31

Walworth, Nicholas, xxxv, 65, 70, 77, 78

WALY, WALY, O, xl, 323-4

Wamesut, town of, xliii, 145

WANDERING WILLIE, vi, 454

Wang-sun Chia, xliv, 11 note 6

Want-wit, in PILGRIM'S PROGRESS, xv, 292

Wanton, Madame, in PILGRIM'S PROGRESS, xv, 72, 188

Wants, and pleasures, xli, 525

Wanuretona, xxxiii, 356

War(s), ancient and modern, iii, 80, 140; Arjuna on, xlv, 787-9; benefit of, iii, 79; Blake on, xli, 588; causes of, iii, 78-9; expenses, x, 447-50; fall of empires always accompanied by, iii, 139; improvements in art of, v, 81; Goethe's Jetter on, xix, 258; Hindu teachings on, xlv, 793-4; Hobbes on causes and state of, xxxiv, 389; Hobbes on desires that lead to, 370-1; a horrid ruthless fiend, xxvi, 390; judgment of God, i, 237; justification of, iii, 49-50; Machiavelli on preparation for, xxxvi, 48-50; maintenance of, x, 322-6; Massinger on school of, xlvii, 869-70; Milton on, iv, 335-6, 393-4; More on, xxxvi, 215-16; More on preparation for, 144-5; overpopulation a cause of, iii, 139; pleasure in distant, 8; provisions for, under the Confederation, xliii, 160-2, 164-5; provisions for, under Constitution, 184-5 (11-16), 186 (3); Quaker attitude toward, i, 107-10, 190-2, 213, 217-20; xxxiv, 68-9; readiness for, of different states of society, xxvii, 372-3; Rousseau on, xxxiv, 213-14; rules of, in treaty with Mexico, xliii, 303-5; Socrates on cause of, ii, 55; Tennyson on, xlii, 1016-17, 1027, 1055-7; true strength in, iii, 74-5; unjust, support of, xxviii, 130-1; Voltaire on religious, xxxiv, 85; Washington on preparation for, xliii, 243; Woolman on, i, 253

War of 1812, Treaty of Peace, xliii, 255-64

Warbeck, Perkin, Bacon on, xxxiv, 101-2

Warburton, William, Lessing on, xxxii, 190; Johnson on, xxxix, 239-40; on Shakespeare's plays, 234, 235

Ward, Nathaniel, xliii, 66 note

Wardlaw, Henry, on the Scotch, xxxv, 271-2

Ware, Rev. Henry, colleague of Emerson, v, 3

Warfare, in Utopia, xxxvi, 215-24

Wargny, Robert of, xxxv, 13

Warner, Master, in SHOEMAKER'S HOLIDAY, xlvii, 484, 485-6

Warrants, in Massachusetts, xliii, 69 (21); in U. S., 194 (4)

Warren, Henry Clarke, translator of Buddhist Writings, xlv, 573

Warrenites, Mill on the, xxv, 158

WARRIOR, THE HAPPY, xli, 656-8

Warton, on Thomson, xxxix, 325

Warwick, Earl of, in Crecy campaign, xxxv, 9-10, 11, 19-20, 24, 30; at Poitiers, 42, 47, 52, 54

Warwick, Earl of, in Edward IV's reign, v, 404

Warwick, Richard Beauchamp, Earl of, v, 403

Warwick, in EDWARD THE SECOND, in quarrel with Gaveston, xlvi, 11, 14-15, 16-19; consents to his return, 22-5, 26, 27; on Gaveston's return, 33-5; in attack on Tynemouth, 40; capture of Gaveston, 43-7; in battle, 53; death, 54-5

Washington, George, Commander-in-Chief, xliii, 169; Emerson on, v, 128, 183, 213; FAREWELL ADDRESS, xliii, 233-49; FIRST INAUGURAL ADDRESS, 225-8; not a great reader, xxviii, 338; president of Constitutional Convention, xliii, 180 note; sweet in his grave, v, 131

WASHINGTON, ODE ON BIRTHDAY OF, vi, 492-4

Wasps, in Brazil, xxix, 44

Wastefulness, Confucius on, xliv, 24 (35); Locke on, xxxvii, 101-2; Mohammed on, xlv, 915

WAT TYLER'S REBELLION, xxxv, 60-80; Chaucer in, xxxix, 163

WAT YE WHA'S IN YON TOWN, vi, 518-20

Watchall, in NEW WAY TO PAY OLD DEBTS, xlvii, 866-7, 872-3, 883

Watches, fall in price of, x, 203

Watches, ship's, xxiii, 17-18

Watchful, the porter, in PILGRIM'S PROGRESS, xv, 49-50, 224, 239

Watchful, the shepherd, in PILGRIM'S PROGRESS, xv, 123-6, 293

Water, action of iron on, xxx, 120-2; decomposition of, 44-8, 126-7 note, 131-5; different states of, 114-19; Faraday on properties of, 10-12; freezing-point of, 231-3; Helmholtz on decomposition of, 202-4; presence of, tested by potassium, 114, 119-20, 140; produced by combustion, 113-15, 126; weight of, 52

Water of Paradise, in New Atlantis, iii, 173

Water-carriage, Adam Smith on, x, 23-4

Water Companies, Smith on, x, 461, 462-3

WATER-FOWL, ON SCARING SOME, vi, 285-6

WATERFOWL, TO A, xlii, 1222-3

Water-hogs, Darwin on, xxix, 57-8

Water-power, Helmholtz on, xxx, 180-1, 185

Watson, Joseph, i, 37-8

Watts, Isaac, hymns by, xlv, 537-9; TRUE GREATNESS, xl, 398

WAUKRIFE MINNIE, vi, 361

Waverley Novels, Carlyle on, xxv, 439-43

Waves, Kelvin on, xxx, 275-6

Wayland, Germanic Vulcan, xlix, 17 note 5

Wazilah, xlv, 1005 note

WE ARE SEVEN, xli, 667-9

WE MUST BE FREE OR DIE, xli, 675

Weak, to be, is miserable, iv, 92

Weakness, as cause of beauty, xxiv, 95; no excuse, iv, 435

Wealhtheow, Queen, xlix, 22, 37, 39, 64

Wealth, aristocracy and, v, 202-3; Burns on, vi, 39; Channing on distinctions of, xxviii, 343-4; Confucius on, xliv, 13, (5), 22 (15), 26 (13), 42 (9), 46 (11); contentment and, xli, 522; death and, xvi, 303-4, 312, 320-1; Emerson on hunger for, v, 234; Goldsmith on accumulation of, xli, 510, 515-16; growth of, not necessarily beneficial, xxviii, 362-3; ignorance of, the best riches, xli, 510; land as source of (see Agricultural System); Lowell on, xxviii, 463, 470; Marcus Aurelius on, ii, 259 (33); a means, not an end, xxviii, 222; measurable by labor it can buy, x, 34-5; Mill on production and distribution of, xxv, 152-3; Milton on, iv, 382-3; money as, x, 228-9, 311-31; Morris on real, xlii, 1196; national, on what dependent, x, 5-6; natural progress of, 304-9; obligations of, i, 393-5; old age and, ix, 48; Pascal on private, xlviii, 378-9; Pascal on pursuit of, 147 (436), 312 (906); Pascal on respect for, 112 (324), 116; on pride in, 153 (460); poverty and, Carlyle on, xxv, 336; Penn on private, i, 390 (221); production and distribution of (see Production, Distribution); progress of, dependent on distribution, x, 54-5; proportioned to neat, not gross, revenue, 224; public and private, connected, 335-6; unused, fable of, xvii, 36; Walton on, xv, 329; Woolman on, i, 180 (see also Capital, Riches)

WEALTH OF NATIONS, Adam Smith's, x; remarks on, 3-4; l, 42-3

Weapons, change and return of, iii, 139-40

Weariness, Pascal on, xlviii, 51 (131)

WEARY PUND O' TOW, vi, 431-2

Weather, influence of moon on, xxx, 298-9

Weathercock, in FAUST, xix, 186

Weaver, Chaucer's, xl, 21 note 191

WEAVERS, TO THE, GIN YE GO, vi, 296-7

Webb, Gen., at Gettysburg, xliii, 383, 384, 387

Webb, George, Franklin on, i, 51-2, 58, 59-60

Weber, Mill on *Oberon* of, xxv, 92

Webster, John, CALL FOR THE ROBIN-REDBREAST, xl, 322-3; DUCHESS OF MALFI, xlvii, 755-855; Hazlitt on, xxvii, 276; life and works, xlvii, 754

WEBSTER-ASHBURTON TREATY, xliii, 280-88

Wedded Love, Milton on, iv, 173-4

Wedding Bells, Poe on, xlii, 1233

Weddings, Webster on secret, xlvii, 765

"WEE JOHNIE," EPITAPH ON, vi, 219

WEE WILLIE GRAY, vi, 514-15

Weeping, Hobbes on, xxxiv, 342; Hunt on, xxvii, 285

Weevil, Harrison on the, xxxv, 282

Wehaloosing, Indian town, i, 268

Wei, King of, xliv, 22 note 3, 41 (3)

Wei-sheng Kao, xliv, 17 (23)

Wei-sheng Mou, xliv, 49 (34)

Weight, measured by inertia, xxx, 301-2; as a motive force, 177-82; transformed to vis viva, 187; used to produce electricity, 208

Weights, English and metric system of, xxx, 253; regulation of, xliii, 164, 184 (5)

Weiler, Jost von, in WILLIAM TELL, xxvi, 413, 423, 425

WELL I REMEMBER, xli, 901

Wellborn, in NEW WAY TO PAY OLD DEBTS, xlvii, at Tapwell's, 859-62; with Allworth, 863-6; at Lady Allworth's, 872-6; Overreach's plot to

ruin, 878; at Overreach's, with Marrall, 879-81; with Marrall at Lady Allworth's, 882-5, 887; with Marrall after dinner, 888-90; thought to be engaged to Lady Allworth, 890-1; at Overreach's with Lady Allworth, 905, 906, 908, 909; conference with Overreach, 909-10; Tapwell and Froth on, 919-20; creditors and, 920-3; advised by Marrall, 923-4; Lady Allworth on, 928-9; with Lovell and Lady Allworth, 931; quarrel with Overreach, 932-7; in final scene, 938, 939-43

Welfare, Michael, i, 110

Wellington, Duke of, on Briscoll, v, 427; Cintra affair and, 377; Emerson on, 375; fear of public creditors, 370; on the life-guards, 381; weighed his soldiers, 358

Wellington, Mount, Darwin on, xxix, 452

Wells, Darwin on ebbing, xxix, 462

Wells, Dr. W. C., and idea of natural selection, xi, 11

Welsh, Jane Baillie, wife of Carlyle, xxv, 315-16, 317

Welsh (see Celtic Races)

Wen, Duke, xliv, 47 (16)

Wen, King, xliv, 24 note, 26-7 and note 8

Wenceslaus, king of Bohemia, Dante on, xx, 173 and note 6, 368 note 10

Weohstan, xlix, 76

Wer-wolves, xlix, 268 note

WERE MY LOVE YON LILAC FAIR, vi, 464

Weregild, xlix, 276 note

WERENA MY HEART LICHT, xl, 398-400

Werner, of Attinghausen, in WILLIAM TELL (see Attinghausen)

Werner, Paul, in MINNA VON BARNHELM, lends money to Tellheim, xxvi, 304; with Just at the inn, 310-12; the landlord and, 332-3; with Franziska, 333-5; plots to give Tellheim money, 335; with Tellheim, 335-40; at meeting of Franziska and Tellheim, 340, 341-2, 343; with Franziska alone, 342-3; announces Tellheim's coming, 350; lends money to Tellheim, 359-60; returns with money, 370-1; reconciliation with Tellheim, 374; with Franziska, 374-5

Werni, in WILLIAM TELL, xxvi, 381-6

WERT THOU IN THE CAULD BLAST, vi, 552

Wesley, Charles, HYMNS by, xlv, 559-62

Wessels, Capt., at Gettysburg, xliii, 373, 379

West, Thoreau on the, xxviii, 404-9

West Indies, absence of atolls in, xxix, 484; Columbus on discovery of, xliii, 21-7; origin of name of, x, 399; Raleigh on disadvantages of, xxxiii, 377-9; zoology of the, xxix, 137

WEST WIND, ODE TO THE, xli, 833-5

Westbrook, Harriet, wife of Shelley, xviii, 272

WESTMINSTER ABBEY, Addison's, xxvii, 78-80

WESTMINSTER ABBEY, ON THE TOMBS IN, xl, 319

WESTMINSTER BRIDGE, UPON, xli, 673-4

Westminster Review, The, xxv, 60-6, 83-4; combined with London Review, 125

Westwood, on insects, xi, 68

WET SHEET, A, AND A FLOWING SEA, xli, 783-4

WHA IS THAT AT MY BOWER-DOOR, vi, 48-9

Whales, Darwin on Greenland, xi, 225-9; jumping out of water, xxix, 228 note

WHA'LL BE KING BUT CHARLIE, xli, 564-5

Whappet, Harrison on the, xxxv, 354

Wharton, Marquis of, Addison and, xxvii, 160-1

WHAT CAN A YOUNG LASSIE DO, vi, 406

WHAT GUILE IS THIS, xl, 249

Whately, Mill on, xxv, 139

Wheat, parable of the, xv, 205-6

Wheatley, Mr., editor of Pepys, xxviii, 285

Wheels, toothed, considered as levers, xxx, 184

Whelks, the heart in, xxxviii, 130

WHEN THE ASSAULT WAS INTENDED TO THE CITY, iv, 78

WHEN I HAVE BORNE, xli, 677

WHEN THE KYE COMES HAME, xli, 765-7

WHEN LILACS LAST IN THE DOOR-YARD, xlii, 1412-20

WHEN LOVELY WOMAN STOOPS, xli, 505

WHEN SHE CAM' BEN SHE BOBBED, vi, 432-3

WHEN WE TWO PARTED, xli, 787-8

WHENAS IN SILKS, xl, 336

WHERE ARE THE JOYS I HAVE MET, vi, 474

WHERE THE BEE SUCKS, xl, 266

WHERE LIES THE LAND, xlii, 1122

Whewell, William, controversy with Mill, xxv, 140; on general laws, xi, 1; Mill on, xxv, 130

Whiddon, Jacob, xxxiii, 303, 313, 316, 335, 336, 337, 357, 358

Whig Party, English, James Mill on, xxv, 62

WHIGS, AWA', vi, 360-1

Whipping, in early Massachusetts, xliii, 72 (43); Locke on, of children, xxxvii, 36-7, 39-40, 41, 56, 60-2, 65-6, 68-9, 93-4

Whisky, Burns on, vi, 147, 162-3

WHISTLE, THE, vi, 362-5

WHISTLE AND I'LL COME TO YOU, MY LAD, vi, 469

WHISTLE O'ER THE LAVE O'T, vi, 348

Whiston, on comets, xxxiv, 118-19

White, Henry, xxxiii, 230, 245

White, Joseph, Woolman on, i, 226, 235, 291

White, Joseph Blanco, TO NIGHT, xli, 913

WHITE ROSE, A, xlii, 1198

Whitefield, Rev. George, i, 101-4; building erected for, 100-1, 113

WHITEFOORD, SIR JOHN, LINES TO, vi, 403

Whitman, Walt, life of, xxxix, 388 note; poems by, xlii, 1402-22; PREFACE TO LEAVES OF GRASS, xxxix, 388-409; PREFACE of, editorial remarks on, 3; l, 48

Whitsunday, xv, 404

Whitsunday Island, xxix, 469-70

Whittier, John Greenleaf, POEMS by, xlii, 1338-64

Wholesale Trade, why smaller profits in, x, 114-15

Wholesaling, capital used in, x, 290, 291-2, 295-6

Wholesome, Tribulation, in the ALCHEMIST, his dealings with the Alchemist, xlvii, 587; scene with Ananias, 592-3; with Subtle, 593-9; returns with Ananias, 649, 658-9, 661-2

WHY SO PALE AND WAN, xl, 353-4

WHY, WHY TELL THE LOVER, vi, 536

Wickedness, Asaph on, xliv, 232-4 (3-12, 17-20); M. Aurelius Antoninus on, ii, 334-5; Bildad on, 98-9 (5-21); Buddha on expiation of, xlv, 671-4; David on, xliv, 144, 182 (16, 21), 186 (1, 2), 186-8 (9-38), 212-13 (1-11); ECCLESIASTES on, 343 (17), 344-5 (11-14), 345 (2); Eliphaz on, 94-5 (20-35); future punishment of, vii, 238-40; xxxiv, 264, 265-6; harms only the doer, ii, 263 (55); Job on, xliv, 84 (24), 88 (6), 103-5 (7-33), 108-9 (2-12), 112-13 (12-23), 119 (3); Kempis on, vii, 244 (1); not free, ii, 166 (136); "the

path of," xl, 77; prayer for overthrow of, xliv, 153-4; Raleigh on punishment of, xxxix, 70-89; righteousness contrasted with, xliv, 145, 232-4, 237 (10); is weakness, iv, 435; Zophar on, xliv, 101-3 (5-29)

WIDOW BIRD, A, xli, 848

Widow's Mite, xliv, 407 (1-4)

Wife of Bath, in Canterbury Tales, xl, 23-4; Dryden on the, xxxix, 166; prologue of, 171

WIFE, THE DEVOTED, xlv, 693-6

WIFE OF USHER'S WELL, xl, 80-1

Wight, O. W., translator of Pascal, xlviii

Wiglaf, xlix, 76-83, 84, 89-90

Wikiri, Raleigh on the, xxxiii, 367, 373

Wilberforce, Samuel, xxv, 81

Wild Ass, in JOB, xliv, 135

Wild-head, in PILGRIM'S PROGRESS, xv, 296

WILD SWANS, THE, xvii, 265-80

Wildness, Thoreau on, xxviii, 409-16

Wilfrid, Bishop, and the slaves, v, 424

Wilfulness, Shakespeare on, xlvi, 261

Wilhelm Meister, Carlyle on, xxv, 380-2; Wordsworth on, v, 324

WILLIAM TELL, Schiller's, xxvi, 379-489; remarks on, 378

Wilkinson, editor of Swedenborg, Emerson on, v, 441

Will, absolute and conditional, xx, 300; autonomy of the (see Autonomy of the Will); belief and, xlviii, 42-3 (99); beliefs of the, 400-1; Coleridge on the, v, 319-20; defined, xxxii, 356; freedom of the (see Free Will); Hobbes on the, xxxiv, 344; Hume on power of the, xxxvii, 338-42, 344, 346; inferior to the soul, v, 139; Kant on absolute value of the, xxxii, 305-15, 347, 349-50; Marcus Aurelius on the, ii, 232 (8); obligations of the, xxxii, 324-42; power of the, v, 290; reason and, xxxii, 324; Rousseau on the, xxxiv, 249-50; Woolman on human, i, 298, 299

Will-o'-the Wisps, in FAUST, xix, 189

WILL YE GO TO THE INDIES, MY MARY, vi, 201

Wills, as evidences of character, ix, 327; Mohammed on, xlv, 1005; Montaigne on men's dislike of, xxxii, 12

Willdo, Parson, xlvii, 927, 937-8, 941, 942

William the Conqueror, census under, xxxv, 231; introduced money payments

of taxes, x, 30; love of deer, v, 351; Vane on, xliii, 121; Voltaire on, xxxiv, 88

William III, king of England, Burke on election of, xxiv, 156-9; Dissenters and, xxvii, 137; Johnson on, 158

William and Mary, Burke on titles of, xxiv, 156-9

William I, of Orange (d. c. 808), xx, 362 note 4

William of Orange (the Silent), anecdote of, v, 290

William of Orange (the Silent), in EGMONT, love of Netherlanders for, xix, 258; suspected by Margaret, 262-3; sent for by Margaret, 265; visit to Egmont, 283-8; gone from Brussels, 298; summoned by Alva, 303; plan to arrest, 305-6; declines to come, 306-7

William II, of Sicily, in Paradise, xx, 371 note 9

William of North Berwick, xxxv, 90

William of Wykeham, Carlyle on, v, 462

WILLIE BREW'D A PECK O' MAUT, vi, 355

WILLIE NICOL'S MARE, ELEGY ON, vi, 376-7

Willis, Nathaniel P., Poe on lines by, xxviii, 374-5

Willoughby, Lord, xxxv, 25, 42, 55

WILLOW-WREN, THE, AND THE BEAR, xvii, 190-2

WILLY DROWNED IN YARROW, xli, 498-9

Wilson, Capt., (in 1859), xxiii, 384-5; in San Diego, 108

Wilson, J., BOAT SONG, xlii, 1064-5

WILT THOU BE MY DEARIE, vi, 479

Wilton Hall, Emerson on, v, 459

Winchester, Bishop of, in EDWARD THE SECOND, xlvi, 69, 71, 74

Winchester Cathedral, Emerson on, v, 461-2

WINCHESTER, MARCHIONESS OF, EPITAPH ON, iv, 27-9

Winckelmann, on the study of beauty, v, 299

Wind, Coleridge on the, xli, 731

WIND AND SUN, fable of, xvii, 34-5

Windmills, Helmholtz on, xxx, 185-6

Winds, Herodotus on cause of, xxxiii, 18; in GARDEN OF PARADISE, xvii, 280-5; names of the, iv, 308

WINDOW, WRITTEN ON A, vi, 276

Window-taxes, x, 494-5

Windows, ancient, ix, 226 note; in old

England, xxxv, 295, 296; in Utopia, xxxvi, 177

Wine(s), Burns on, vi, 146; desire of, which warriors overturn, iv, 428; of Egypt, xxxiii, 40; Eliot on, v, 126; Homer on effects of, xxii, 197, 291-2; invented by Bacchus, viii, 379; manufacture of, Pasteur on, xxxviii, 276, 303 note; misused, sweet poison of, iv, 46; Mohammed on, xlv, 1003; Omar Khayyam on, xli, 943-4, 951, 956, 957; Pascal on, xlviii, 26 (71); price of, in regard to drunkenness, x, 364

Wineland (see Vinland)

Winfield, Sir Richard, xxxvi, 97

Wings, of insects, developed from tracheae, xi, 187; peculiar uses of, 176-7; used for other purposes than flight, xxix, 205; various kinds of, xi, 192-3

Winkelried, Arnold von, at Sempach, xxvi, 460 note

Winkelried, Struth von, in WILLIAM TELL, xxvi, 412-26

Winter, Burns on, vi, 475-6; Collins on, xli, 481; Goethe on departure of, xix, 43; Shelley on, xli, 835

WINTER, Shakespeare's, xl, 262

WINTER: A DIRGE, by Burns, vi, 31-2

WINTER, ODE TO, Campbell's, xli, 771-3

WINTER, ODE ON, Cotton's, xxxix, 309-10

WINTER, THE, IT IS PAST, vi, 303

WINTER NIGHT, A, vi, 248-51

WINTER OF LIFE, vi, 503

WINTER'S, GLOOMY, NOW AWA', xli, 594

Winter, Master, with Drake, xxxiii, 201, 208, 229, 247

Winter, William, with Gilbert, xxxiii, 273, 274

Winterhie, Robert, xxxiii, 205

Winthrop, John, ON ARBITRARY GOVERNMENT, xliii, 85-105

Wisdom, Buddha on, xlv, 595, 702-4, 739; Carlyle on, xxv, 374; Confucius on, xliv, 20 (20, 21), 29 (28), 40 (22), 48 (30), 56 (9); cunning and, i, 337 (151); iii, 57; defined, ii, 71; acquisition of, by discussion, xxv, 215; ECCLESIASTES on, xliv, 336 (17-18), 337 (12-16), 343 (11-12, 16-19), 344 (1), 346 (2), 347 (13-18), 347 (10); Elihu on, 122 (9); Emerson on, v, 11-14, 100, 237; fear of God, the beginning of, xliv, 288 (10); necessary to friendship, ix, 23; highest, M. Aurelius Antoninus on, ii, 335; highest,

Kempis on, vii, 206 (3), 207 (4); highest, Penn on, i, 392 (244-8); Hindu conception of, xlv, 849-50; Job on, xliv, 114-15 (12-28); learning and, xxxvii, 128, 173; needs leisure, xxiv, 188 note 1; Locke on, xxxvii, 119; love and, iii, 27; Marcus Aurelius on, ii, 225 (9); Massinger on, xlvii, 877; Milnes on delights of, xlii, 1057-8; Montaigne on aim of, xxxii, 9; ostentatious, ii, 177 (175); Pascal on pride in, xlviii, 153 (460); Paul, St., on, xlv, 494-5 (18-20); Pope on, xl, 437; profitless with God, vii, 275 (2); pleasures of, iii, 8; Raleigh on, xl, 206; Ruskin on, xxviii, 130; Schiller on love of, xxxii, 230; slow growth of, ii, 173 (155); Socrates on human, 10-11; Solomon on, xxxix, 90-1; spiritual, Kempis on, vii, 295 (2), 297 (4); Tennyson on, xlii, 984; true, attained by death, ii, 54-7; true, Epictetus on, 178 (177); true, Kempis on, vii, 298-9; true, Montaigne on, xxxii, 50; virtue and, Cicero on, ix, 15; way to, vii, 209 (4); ii, 140 (66); Webster on opinion of, xlvii, 774; what else is (song), viii, 409-10; worldly, i, 374-7; only true measure of worth, ii, 58 (see also Knowledge)

Wisdom, Robert, Beaumont on, xl, 320

Wisdom of Ages, Bentham on, xxvii, 226-9

WISDOM FOR A MAN'S SELF, ESSAY ON, iii, 60-1

WISE, SEEMING, ESSAY ON, iii, 64-5

WISE FOLKS, a story, xvii, 192-5

Wise Man, Penn's, i, 377-8, 338 (167)

WISH, A, by Rogers, xli, 582

WISH, THE LAST, xlii, 1119

Wishes, fable on, xvii, 39; oft hide the object we wish for, xix, 369

WISHES FOR SUPPOSED MISTRESS, xl, 359-63

Wit, acquired, xxxiv, 352; Beaumont on, xl, 320-1; cause of differences of, xxxiv, 352; death and, xl, 261; discretion and fancy in, xxxiv, 351; good nature and, Sheridan on, xviii, 136; has only fancy value, xxxii, 345; Hobbes on, xxxiv, 349; judgment compared with, xxiv, 17-18; malice and, Sheridan on, xviii, 120; natural, xxxiv, 349; Penn on, i, 338-9; piety and, Goldsmith on, xviii, 201; puny, can work but puny sin,

viii, 331; Raleigh on, xl, 205; without good breeding, xxxvii, 72

Witch, in MANFRED, xviii, 423-7

Witch, in FAUST, xix, 106-11

Witch, young, in FAUST, xix, 186

Witchcraft, Browne on, iii, 281-3; first English law against, xlvii, 547 note 22; Hobbes on, xxxiv, 382; punishment of, in Dante's HELL, xx, 46, 81-4; punishment of, in old England, xxxv, 366

Witches, Hobbes on, xxxiv, 317; in early Massachusetts, xliii, 80 (2)

Witches, in MACBETH, xlvi, 321-2, 324-6, 365-9

Witford, Mr., Roper on, xxxvi, 91

Wither, George, poems by, xl, 331-3

Witherington, the squire, xl, 96, 99

Withington, Lothrop, xxxv, 216

Witnesses, Hume on evidence of, xxxvii, 377-8; right of summoning, in U. S., xliii, 194-5 (6)

Witticisms, Pascal on, xlviii, 21 (46)

Wives, husbands and, Goethe on, xix, 402-3; husbands and, St. Paul on, xlv, 498, 500 (39); husbands and, Ruskin on, xxviii, 144-6; impediments to great works, iii, 21; Massinger on choice of, xlvii, 918; Milton on, iv, 440-1; Milton on false, 433-4; Penn on choice of, i, 332 (92-3); Oberon's counsel to, xix, 184; "pearls of price," 137; proverb of, i, 76

Wizards, in FAUST, xix, 173

WOE IS ME, MY MOTHER DEAR, vi, 24

Woe, joy and, Blake on, xli, 588; luxury of, Calderon on, xxvi, 9; nothing unscathed by, viii, 275; from too much prosperity, 35-6; springs from wrong, 35, 70

Wolf, F. A., on Homeric question, xxii, 3-4

Wolf, Johann Christian von, xxxii, 302 note

WOLF AND CRANE, fable of, xvii, 12-13

WOLF AND DOG, fable of, xvii, 22-3

WOLF AND FOX, Grimm's tale of, xvii, 167-8

WOLF AND KID, fable of, xvii, 18

WOLF AND LAMB, fable of, xvii, 11

WOLF AND NURSE, fable of, xvii, 29

WOLF AND SEVEN KIDS, a tale, xvii, 54-7

WOLF IN SHEEP'S CLOTHING, fable of, xvii, 27

Wolfe, Charles, BURIAL OF SIR JOHN MOORE, xli, 822-3

Wolfe, Reginald, *Cosmography* of, xxxv, 216

Wolfenschiessen, the, xxvi, 382 note, 398

Wolfram of Eschenbach, Renan on, xxxii, 147

Wolly, Sir Francis, Dr. Donne and, xv, 329, 332

Wolsey, ambition to be Pope, xxxvi, 102; as Chancellor, 106-7; removed from Chancellorship, 106; Charles V and, 102; as commissioner, 103-4; suggests divorce of Queen Catherine, 102; More and, 92, 96-7, 98; Bishop Stoksely and, 105-6

Wolves, Darwin on development of, xi, 97-8; dogs and, xxxv, 355-6; why less despicable than dogs, xxiv, 57; in Egypt, xxxiii, 37; habits of, v, 374; men changed to, xlix, 268 note

Woman(en), adroitness of, xix, 363; Æschylus on insight of, viii, 25; arguing with, xl, 189; Beaumont's Philaster on, xlvii, 712-13; beauty of, as caused by delicacy, xxiv, 95; beauty of, Emerson on, v, 305-6; beauty of, Pascal on, xlviii, 414; beauty of, Ruskin on, xxviii, 146-7; "brief as love of," xlvi, 152; Browne on, iii, 323 (9); Bunyan on, xv, 266; two burdens of, viii, 310; Burns on, vi, 133-4, 169, 220, 259, 328, 474-5; Celtic ideal of, xxxii, 142; Chaucer on, xl, 44; Chaucer on counsel of, 46; counterfeit weakness in, xxiv, 90; creation of, Milton on, iv, 255-6; De Vere on, xl, 289; DIVINE COMEDY, written in praise of, xx, 4; Donne on fickleness of, xl, 307; Don Quixote on affections of, xiv, 157; Dryden on, xviii, 53, 73; ECCLESIASTES on, xliv, 343-4 (26-8); education of, Defoe on, xxvii, 148-51; education of, Franklin on, i, 15, 93; education of, Ruskin on, xxviii, 136, 146-56; Emerson on, v, 215-16; Euripides on, viii, 331; "frailty thy name is," xlvi, 103; Goethe's Dorothea on duties of, xix, 391; happiest knowledge of, iv, 170-1; individuality of, Emerson on, v, 128-9; Lessing on, xxvi, 323; liberties of, in Massachusetts, xliii, 82; in literature, xxviii, 137-43; love of, by what won, iv, 440; love of, Poe on, xxviii, 390, 392; MacNeil on marriages of, xli, 578;

Mephistopheles on creation of, xix, 104; Milton on, iv, 162, 257, 266, 290, 295-6, 334-5, 434, 437; man and, compared in evil, xix, 173; man and, relations of, xlviii, 418; in Mohammedan countries, xlv, 991 note 30; Mohammedan verses on, xvi, 10; Montaigne on friendships of, xxxii, 76; More on idleness of, xxxvi, 180; Patmore on, xxviii, 144; Paul, St., on, xlv, 505 (7-12); as the subject of poetry, xxviii, 392; public duties of, 156-62; Raleigh on, xxxix, 90; Ruskin on sphere of, xxviii, 136-47; to be shielded, not tempted, xiv, 316-17; Socrates on, xxxix, 10-13; Shakespeare on, xlvi, 146; Tennyson on, xlii, 984; in Utopia, xxxvi, 179, 183, 184, 186, 215, 221, 231; Virgil on, xiii, 172; Webster on inconstancy of, xlvii, 784; Webster's Bosola on, 778; Wither on, xl, 332-3

Woman Suffrage, Mill on, xxv, 68, 151 note 1, 186-7; movement started by Mill, 174; in U. S., xliii, 198 (19)

WOMAN, THE RIGHTS OF, vi, 446-7

Woman's Rights, Emerson on, v, 303; Mill on, xxv, 5

WOMEN, EDUCATION OF, by Defoe, xxvii, 148-51

Wonder, mean and noble, xxviii, 114; caused by novelty, xlviii, 40 (90); Wordsworth on, xxxix, 324

Wood, price of, x, 169-70

Wood, Antony, on universities, xxviii, 47

Woodcock, Katherine, wife of Milton, iv, 5; Milton on, 86

WOODEN GOD, fable of the, xvii, 27

WOODLARK, TO THE, vi, 531-2

WOODMAN AND SERPENT, fable of, xvii, 18

Woodnot, Arthur, xv, 388, 394, 395, 415, 416-17

WOODNOTES, xlii, 1249-61

Woodpeckers, color of, xi, 197-8; habits of, 179

Woodruff's Battery, at Gettysburg, xliii, 337, 351, 373, 381, 382

Woods, Emerson on beauty of, v, 223-4

Woods, Mr., Prologue written for, vi, 260-1

Woodville, Dr., xxxviii, 199, 204, 205-6, 209

Woodward, Hezekiah, on Lord's Prayer, v, 381

Woodward, Samuel, on cirripedes, xi, 342; on geological formations, 332

WOOED AND MARRIED AND A', xli, 567-8
WOOER, THE BRAW, vi, 536-7
Wool, price of, x, 193-9
Woolen Manufactures, improvements in, x, 206-7
Woolman, Elizabeth, sister of John Woolman, i, 183
Woolman, John, birth and education of, i, 169-70, 174, 187; business attitude of, 180, 195-6, 235-6; creed of, 172-4, 229-30; death of, 313-4; Delaware, journey to, 185; doubts of, 189-90; manner of dress, 253-4, 302-3 note; duty, incidents of his sense of, 177, 179-80, 194-5, 235, 241, 250, 254; on dyes, 309-10; early occupation, 174-5, 180; East Jersey, journeys to, 179, 183; English journey, 289-308; epistle to Friends in N. Carolina, 209-212; exhortation to follow inner light, 274; first speeches in meeting, 175-6; in the French war, 221-2; on Huss and à Kempis, 222-3; Indian visit of, 255-70; journey to back settlements, 181-2; letter on affliction, 197-9; letter to wife, 240; life and character, 168; in London, 302 and note; Long Island visit of, 194; marriage of, 187; Maryland visited by, 275-81; miraculous appearance of Divine Truth, 200; understanding with a friend, 228; New England journeys of, 183-5, 239-49; parents, his relations with, 169-71, 172; Pennsylvania visit of, 223-4; pleurisy of, 287-8; robins, incident of killing the, 170; Scotch servant and, 176; simplicity of life, 180, 195; on slavery, 202-5, 206-8; slavery, his book on, 187, 189, 250-1; slavery, his first opposition to, 177-8; slavery among Quakers opposed by, 208-9, 211, 225, 273; slaves, education of, moved by, 209; slave-owners visited by, 227-8, 234-5, 244-5, 250; slave-owners' wills, refuses to write, 188-9, 192-3; slave-sale, restitution for assisting in, 281-2, 284; slave-states, uneasiness in, 182-3, 201-3; slave-trade, petition against, 242-4; on the small-pox, 235-8; southern journey, 200-16; spiritual awakening, 164-9; as a tailor, 180-1, 195; trade with Barbadoes, 284-5; vision of death and the slaves, 306-7; West Indian visit, desires and scruples about, 284-7; youthful faults, 171-3

WOOLMAN, JOHN, JOURNAL OF, i, 169-312; editorial remarks on, l, 31
Woolman, Samuel, i, 187-8
Words, acts and, Bunyan on, xv, 83; acts and, Confucius on, xliv, 8 (13), 48 (29), 14 (22, 24), 15-16 (9); acts and, Epictetus on, ii, 177 (175); acts and, Goethe on, xix, 16; acts and, Marcus Aurelius on, ii, 279 (16), 288 (15); aggregate, simple abstract, and compound abstract, xxiv, 129-30; Berkeley on, xxxvii, 236-7, 245-6, 267, 269, 271-2; Burke on, xxiv, 51-4, 129-37, 137-40; Confucius on, xliv, 41 (3), 52 (22), 67 (3); Dryden on antiquated, xxxix, 169; Emerson on, v, 164; Goethe on, xix, 30, 81, 110; Hobbes on use of, xxxiv, 323-6; Johnson on, xxxix, 186; Kempis on, vii, 213, 310 (1); meaning of, xxxiv, 326-7, 329-30, 332-3; Montaigne on, xxxii, 60-6; Pascal on arrangement of, xlviii, 16 (23); Pascal on meanings of, 22 (50); Penn on, i, 383 (123-6); Ruskin on importance of, xxviii, 102-5; Stevenson on, 278-9, 280; Swift on, xxvii, 115; Tzu-kung on, xliv, 66 (25); wise men's counters, money of fools, xxxiv, 327
Wordsworth, William, Arnold on, xlii, 1135, 1136-7; xxviii, 81; his modernization of Chaucer, 78; Emerson on, v, 21, 323-6, 445; Emerson's second visit to, 464-5; Mazzini on, xxxii, 386; Mill on, xxv, 93-5; poems by, xli, 595-681; on poetry, xxviii, 66; PREFACES to poems, xxxix, 267-336; the Romantic Movement and, 267 note; the study of, xxviii, 398
Work, Carlyle on, xxv, 364; Emerson on, v, 286; Goethe on, xxv, 388; Hindu doctrine of, xlv, 799-801, 805-6, 809-10, 813, 866-7, 870-1; without hope, Coleridge on, xxv, 89
Work (mechanical), amount of, defined, xxx, 175-6; amount of, not increased by machines, 181-5; capacity for, exhausted by performance, 177-9, 181, 186, 188, 189, 201, 202, 203-4, 207-8; performed by gravity, 178-81; changed to heat, 196-7; measurement of, 178-9; produced by chemical forces, 200-4; produced by elastic forces, 188-9; produced by electricity, 204-7; produced by heat, 189-94, 195-6; produced

by velocity of moving masses, 185-8; thermal equivalent of, 198-200

Works, Luther on justification by, xxxvi, 346, 347-8, 349, 350-1, 354, 356-7, 359-78; Jesus on, xliv, 370 (47-9); tested by time, xxxix, 209

World, the, Arnold on, xlii, 1138; beauty of, i, 361-2 (485); Browne on, iii, 326; Buddha on eternity of, xlv, 647-52; changes in, xxxix, 107; Drummond on, xl, 327 (196, 197); end of, Browne on, iii, 297-8, 302; end of, Buddhistic, xlv, 603; end of, Hayes on, xxxiii, 266; end of, Raleigh on, xxxix, 105-8; end of, Stoic belief of, ix, 290 note; idea of eternity of, xxxix, 101, 102-7; in a grain of sand, xli, 586; Hume on origin of, xxxvii, 395-6; indestructibility of, xix, 58-9; Socrates's conception of, ii, 104-9; Tennyson on mystery of, xlii, 1020; undivine conceptions of, xlv, 861; visible, a picture of the invisible, iii, 263 (12) (see also Earth, Universe)

WORLD, THE, IS TOO MUCH WITH US, xli, 678

WORLD WELL LOST, Dryden's, xviii, 13-106

World-citizenship, Epictetus on, ii, 121-2 (15, 16); Marcus Aurelius on, 209-10 (11), 213 (4)

Worldliness, aspirations and, xix, 33; Bacon on, iii, 105; Bunyan on, xv, 308-9; Jesus on, xliv, 388 (22-34); Raleigh on, xxxix, 90, 93-5

Worldling, in FAUST, xix, 187

Worldly Goods, Kempis on, vii, 228 (2), 277-8 (1, 2); Marcus Aurelius on, ii, 225-6 (10), 226-7 (12), 227 (15)

WORLDLY PLACE, by Arnold, xlii, 1139

Worldly Things, transitoriness of, xvi, 300-4, 311-12, 316-17, 320-1

Worldly Wisdom, Penn on, i, 374-7

Worldly Wiseman, Mr., in PILGRIM'S PROGRESS, xv, 21-4, 26

WORLD'S WANDERERS, THE, xli, 856

WORM, THE CONQUEROR, xlii, 1240-1

Worm, Shakespeare on the, xlvi, 172-3

Worry, Epictetus on, ii, 123 (19) (see also Anxiety)

Worship, better than knowing, xlv, 847; Calvin on splendor in, xxxix, 35-6; Confucius on, xliv, 10 (12); Emerson on loss of, v, 37-8; natural forms of, xxxiv, 378; Penn on, i, 363-4; Rous-

seau on, xxxiv, 256-7, 282-3; in Utopia, xxxvi, 233-6

WORSHIP, ESSAY ON, v, 273-95

Worth, Confucius on, xliv, 13 (14), 14 (17), 49 (39), 51 (3); Emerson on, v, 188; Jonson on, xl, 291 (152); Hobbes on, xxxiv, 361, 369; moral, tests of, xxxii, 309-15, 349-50; Pope on, xl, 435; is worth wherever found, xxvi, 416

Worthilake, Capt., ballad on, i, 14

Worthington, Dr., xxxvii, 134

Wortley, Mr., quoted, v, 393

Wotton, Edward, xxvii, 5

Wotton, Sir Henry, George Herbert and, xv, 383; poems by, xl, 287-9; Walton on, xv, 353; Walton's *Life* of, 322

WOUND-DRESSER, THE, xlii, 1408-10

WOUNDED HARE, THE, vi, 339-40

Wounds, antiseptic care of, xxxviii, 257-63, 266-7; gunshot, Lister on, 265-6; gunshot, Paré on, 11-12, 38, 52-3; cause of suppuration in, 257

Wrath, Dante on, xx, 50; the sin of, in FAUSTUS, xix, 227-8; punishment of, in HELL, xx, 31, 47 (see also Anger)

Wratislaus, Duke of Bohemia, xxxv, 265-6

WRECK OF THE HESPERUS, xlii, 1269-71

WREN'S NEST, THE, vi, 542

Wrens, nests of, xi, 284

Wrestler, life of a, Epictetus on, ii, 155-6 (104)

Wrestling, Milton advises, iii, 244-5

Wright, Dr., Franklin on, i, 148

Wrightington, Tom, xxiii, 390

Writers, pecuniary rewards of, x, 135-6

Writing, among the Egyptians, xxxiii, 23; extempore, Carlyle on, xxv, 443-7; extempore, Shelley on, xxvii, 354-5; invention of, x, 444; Locke on instruction in, xxxvii, 134-5; maketh an exact man, iii, 122; natural, Pascal on, xlviii, 14 (14); for the press, Mill on, xxv, 55; the primary art, xxvii, 255; for subsistence, Mill on, xxv, 55; Stevenson on difficulty of, xxviii, 278

Writings, Arabian verses on, xvi, 82; Franklin on, i, 103-4; virtue of, tested by time, xxxix, 208-9

Wrong, right and, Emerson on, v, 62; right and, Pope on, xl, 409-15; Rousseau on, xxxiv, 268; Socrates on, ii, 37

Wrong-doing, Manzoni on, xxi, 34; Marcus Aurelius on, ii, 202 (10); Marcus

Aurelius on patience under, 246 (22, 26), 268 (11, 20), 272 (38), 273 (42), 279 (13), 289 (18), 297 (16); Mohammed on punishment of, xlv, 894 note 8; punishment of, Emerson on, v, 100; punishment of, Epictetus on, ii, 120 (12); reason of, iii, 15

Wrongs, "in se," and "prohibita," xxv, 118

Wu, King, xliv, 26 (20), 67 note

Wulf, Eofor and, xlix, 73 note 1, 86-7

Wulfgar, in Beowulf, xlix, 15-16

Wu-ma Ch'i, xliv, 23 (30)

Wyatt, Sir Thomas, Jonson on, xxvii, 56; Lover's Appeal, xl, 192-3; A Supplication, 192

Wycherley, Taine on, xxxix, 428; Voltaire on, xxxiv, 136-8, 139

Wyclif, Milton on, iii, 223; rise of, 196

Wye, lines composed on banks of the, xli, 635-9

Wygate, Franklin and, i, 47-8

Wyndham, Sir William, i, 49

Wyrd, xlix, 17 note 6; references to, 18, 21, 25, 38, 71, 74, 75, 82

Xanthias, in The Frogs, viii, 439-44, 446-59, 461-3

Xanthippe, in prison with Socrates, ii, 47; Socrates and, 293 (28)

Xanthippus, father of Pericles, xii, 37; dog of, 14-15

Xanthippus, son of Pericles, xii, 60; reviles Pericles, 73

Xenien, satirized, xix, 186

Xenocles, of Cholargus, xii, 50

Xenophilus, the Musitian, xxxii, 10-11

Xenophon, on agriculture, ix, 66; Memorabilia, Franklin on, i, 17; Sainte-Beuve on, xxxii, 131; Sidney on, xxvii, 13; Spenser on, xxxix, 62; the Ten Thousand and, xii, 357-8; v, 189

Xerxes, bridge of, iv, 298; Burns on, vi, 408; Dante on, xx, 260 and note 3; defeat of, xii, 8; invasion of, 13-20; memory of, xxxvii, 151-2; prophecy of, xlviii, 248; regrets death of soldiers, ix, 237; Themistocles and, xii, 28-30; iii, 141-2

Ximines, Gonzalez, xxxiii, 325

Xiphias, reference to, xli, 496

Yak Cow, Buddha on the, xlv, 594

Yakshas, xlv, 863 note

Yama, ruler of the dead, xlv, 685, 688

Yang Fu, xliv, 65 (19)

Yang Huo, xliv, 57 (1)

Yao, Emperor, xliv, 21 note 18, 26 (19), 50 (45), 66 (1) note

Yarrow, The Braes of, by Hamilton, xli, 572-6

Yarrow, The Braes of, by Logan, xli, 500-1

Yarrow, The Dowy Houms O, xl, 115-16

Yarrow Revisited, xli, 631-4

Yarrow Unvisited, xli, 627-9

Yarrow Visited, xli, 629-31

Ye Shall Walk in Silk Attire, xli, 580

Year 1788, Elegy on the, vi, 323-4

Year That's Awa', xli, 581-2

Years, cheap and dear, effect on labor, x, 84-8

Yeast, action of, xxxviii, 347-50, 353-4; Liebig on, 352; relations of, to oxygen, 275-302, 314-16; penicillium and, 360-2

Yen P'ing, xliv, 16 (16)

Yen Yüan, disciple of Confucius, xliv, 8, note 4, 15 note 7, 17-18 (25), 18 note 2, 19 (5, 9), 22 (10), 25 note 4, 28 (10), 29 (19, 20), 33 (2, 3, 6, 7, 8, 9, 10), 35 (18, 22), 37 (1), 51-2 (10)

Yeoman, Chaucer's, xl, 14

Yeomen, Harrison on, of England, xxxv, 225-6, 229

Yggdrasil, the tree, xlix, 272 note

Yi, death of, xliv, 45 note

Yi-yi, xliv, 63 (8)

Yi-yin, xliv, 40 note 9

Yngve, Alf and, v, 344

Yôg, xlv, 794, 796, 799, 809, 816

Yon Wild Mossy Mountains, vi, 251-2

Yorick, the skull of, xlvi, 195

York, and Lancaster, xxxix, 74-5

York, the See of, xxxv, 252; archbishop of, 256

York, Minster, the Fuegian, xxix, 212-14, 220, 226, 227, 231, 233-4

Yorktown, Articles of Capitulation at, xliii, 169-73

You Ask Me, Why, xlii, 998

Youatt, on selection, xi, 43, 46-7

You'll Love Me Yet, xl.i, 1073

Young, Edward, Night Thoughts of, xxxix, 299

Young, James, Burns on, vi, 352

Young, Stephen, Burns on, vi, 352

Young Bicham: a ballad, xl, 84-6

Young Friend, Epistle to a, vi, 203-5

Young Highland Rover, vi, 289-90

YOUNG JAMIE, PRIDE OF A' THE PLAIN, vi, 483

YOUNG JOCKIE WAS THE BLYTHEST LAD, vi, 342

YOUNG LADY, TO A, xli, 534

YOUNG MAY MOON, xli, 821

YOUNG AND OLD, xlii, 1062

YOUNG PEGGY BLOOMS, vi, 108-9

Yount, John, xxiii, 397

YOU'RE WELCOME, WILLIE STEWART, vi, 413

Youth, age and, Shakespeare on, xl, 267; aspirations of, xix, 33; beauty of, iii, 107; Byron on glories of, xli, 789; Carlyle on, xxv, 320; confidence of, v, 61; Confucius on, xliv, 29 (22); determines course of life, i, 70; ECCLESIASTES on, xliv, 348 (9-10); education best begun in, iii, 99; faith of, xix, 37-8; Goethe on, 15-16; Kingsley on, xlii, 1062; nature's recipe of, xix, 100; needs guidance, 369; plasticity of, xxv, 361-2; Pliny on leniency with, ix, 337; reason of pleasantness of, xxiv, 65; poetry and, xxxix, 311-12; Shakespeare on, xl, 262; Shakespeare on lightness of, xlvi, 187; son of Cupid and Psyche, iv, 71; Stevenson on, xxviii, 303; virtue and, i, 210; Wordsworth on, xli, 596-7

YOUTH AND AGE, ESSAY ON, Bacon's, iii, 104-6

YOUTH AND AGE, by Byron, xli, 784

YOUTH AND AGE, by Coleridge, xli, 703-4

YOUTH, MY LOST, xlii, 1290-3

Yspaddaden, Penkawr, xxxii, 149

Yü, Emperor, xliv, 66 (1) note

Yü, the historian, xliv, 51 (6)

Yu Jo, disciple of Confucius, xliv, 38 (9)

Yüan Jang, xliv, 50 (46)

Yüan Ssu, disciple of Confucius, xliv, 18 (3), 45 (1) note

Yü-chung, xliv, 63 (8)

Yu-tzu, disciple of Confucius, xliv, 5 (2), 6 (12, 13)

Yukta, xlv, 811, 813, 815

YUNAN, KING, story of, xvi, 30-9

Yunani Sage, story of the, v, 194

Zacchæus, the publican, xliv, 402-3 (1-10)

Zachariah, the prophet, xliv, 386 (51)

Zacharias, the priest, xliv, 353-4, 356; Mohammed on, xlv, 908-9, 952

Zâid, freedman of Mohammed, xlv, 989 note

Zâinab, wife of Mohammed, xlv, 985 note 2, 989 note

Zaleucus, Cicero on, ix, 149

Zâli'h, xlv, 905-6

Zalmunna, reference to, xliv, 249 (11)

Zanche, Michel, in HELL, xx, 91 and note 5; murder of, 139-40 note 6

Zanoguera, John, xiv, 388

Zapoletes, More on the, xxxvi, 219-20

Zarate, Francisco de, xxxiii, 212 note

Zarephath, the widow of, xliv, 364 (26)

Zeal, "excessive, but little wisdom shows," viii, 257; excessive, Browne on, iii, 257; excessive, Penn on, i, 379-80 (76-8), 336 (142-3); knowledge and, Pascal on, xlviii, 303-4 (868); More on, xxxvi, 156; on occasion waits, iv, 388; Raleigh on, xl, 205; without charity, i, 365 (541)

Zebah, reference to, xliv, 249 (11)

Zebra, descent of the, xi, 164-6

Zedechias, physician, xxxix, 82

Zedekiah, King, xxxvi, 317

Zeeb, reference to, xliv, 249 (11)

Zeno, the Eleatic, xii, 38; in Athens, xxviii, 58; in Limbo, xx, 20; mission of, ii, 157 (108); native of Cyprus, xxviii, 58; Newman on, 51-2; on Pericles, xii, 40; Rome, influence in, ii, 320; on two kinds of pupils, xxxii, 65; universe, doctrine of, ii, 325-6

Zephon, in PARADISE LOST, iv, 174-6

Zephyr, and Aurora, iv, 30

Zertusht, and the Yunani sage, v, 194

Zeruiah, sons of, xliii, 95

Zethus, founder of Thebes, xxii, 151

Zeus, Æschylus on, viii, 67; throne of, on Athos, 18; casks of, ii, 336; Cleanthes' hymn to, quoted, 330; Cronos and, viii, 167 note 3; has power over everything but death, 148-9; subject to the Fates, 185; guardian of the hearth and board, 9, 34; Io and, 190-1, 197 and note 59; patron god of marriage, 130-1; Odysseus and, xxii, 10-11, 68, 69, 171-2, 332, 334; overthrow prophesied, viii, 193-4, 199-200; orders Phæacians punished, xxii, 177-8; Prometheus and, viii, 166-8, 170-5, 177-81, 185-6, 189, 193-4, 199-206; why represented with ram's face, xxxiii, 26-7; Semele and, viii, 323; god of strangers and beggars, xxii, 121; Thetis and, viii, 194 note 49; thunderbolts of, controlled by Athena, 156 (see also Jove, Jupiter)

Zeuxidamus, on the Spartans, xxxii, 59

Zeuxis, Agatharchus and, xii, 49; Cervantes on, xiv, 6

Ziba, and David, xli, 486

Zikrs, xvi, 79 note 7

Zinc, action of, on water, xxx, 122-3

"Zingara," statue called, xxxi, 318 note 1

Zion, beauty and glory of, xliv, 200-1; Bernard of Morlaix on, xlv, 549; Bunyan on, xv, 157; chosen of God, xliv, 314 (13-18); description of a citizen of, 157; privileges of citizenship in, 252-3; Milton on, iv, 136

Zion, Mount, xliv, 243 (68)

Ziphites, David on the, xliv, 208

Zipporah, reference to, vi, 164

Zisca, John, skin of, xxiv, 382

Zoilus, Apollo and, xxviii, 383; Cervantes on, xiv, 6

Zoölogy, Locke on study of, xxxvii, 147

Zoöphytes, in Falkland Islands, xxix, 206-8; Harvey on, xxxviii, 129

Zoöspores, Pasteur on, xxxviii, 342

Zophar the Naamathite, xliv, 73, 87, 101, 141

Zophiel, the cherub, iv, 217

Zopyrus, teacher of Alcibiades, xii, 106

Zopyrus, servant of Darius, xxvii, 20

Zoraida, Lela, xiv, 373; story of, 397-423

Zorillo, Darwin on the, xxix, 87

Zoroaster, on God, xxxix, 101; on perseverance, v, 77

Zosimus, freedman of Pliny, ix, 276

Zounds, meaning of, xix, 216 note 1

Zubeydeh, wife of Harun Er-Rashid, xvi, 137

Zuinglius, Voltaire on, xxxiv, 84

CHRONOLOGICAL INDEX

(Names printed in SMALL CAPITALS refer to entries in the *General Index*)

1316–1307 B. C.—Siege of TROY by the Greeks under AGAMEMNON, King of Argos

900–800 B. C.—Birth of HOMER, Greek epic poet. There is great uncertainty regarding both the date and place of his birth

557 B. C.—Birth of Siddhartha GAUTAMA, known as BUDDHA, founder of Buddhism, the "Light of Asia"

551 B. C.—Birth of CONFUCIUS, Chinese philosopher and moralist

550 B. C.—Birth of ÆSOP, Greek fabulist (supposed date)

525 B. C.—Birth of ÆSCHYLUS, father of classic Greek tragedy

500–300 B. C.—The MAHA BHARATA, Hindu epic, probable date of writing, according to the claims of most scholars

495 B. C.—Birth of SOPHOCLES, the "most perfectly balanced among the three great masters of Greek tragedy"

492 B. C.—CORIOLANUS (Gnæus Marcius), defeats the Volsci, an Italic tribe, capturing their town Corioli, whence his surname

491 B. C.—CORIOLANUS banished from Rome for demanding the deposition of the plebeian tribunes

490 B. C.—Battle of MARATHON between the Athenians and Platæans under Miltiades and the Persian army of Darius

490 B. C.—Birth of HERODOTUS, the "father of history" (supposed date)

480 B. C.—Birth of EURIPIDES, Greek tragedian, the youngest of the great trio

479 B. C.—The battle of MYCALE, between the Greeks under Leotychides, King of Sparta, and the army of Xerxes

478 B. C.—Death of CONFUCIUS

477 B. C.—Death of BUDDHA

466 B. C.—PERICLES, General of Athenian forces, subdues revolts in Eubœa and Megara

470–460 B. C.—Birth of HIPPOCRATES, Greek physician, the "father of medicine"

469 B. C.—Birth of SOCRATES, Athenian philosopher, the central figure in the history of Greek thought

468 B. C.—Death of ARISTIDES, called "The Just," Athenian statesman and general (supposed date)

456 B. C.—Death of ÆSCHYLUS (supposed date)

455 B. C.—PERICLES overruns the Peloponnesus

450 B. C.—Birth of ALCIBIADES, Athenian statesman and general

450 B. C.—Birth of ARISTOPHANES, "the greatest of the comic writers in Greek" (supposed date)

444–429 B. C.—PERICLES serves as ruler of the Athenian Commonwealth

428 B. C.—Birth of PLATO, Athenian philosopher, disciple of Socrates

426 B. C.—Death of HERODOTUS (supposed date)

407 B. C.—ALCIBIADES, Athenian statesman, deposed

406 B. C.—Death of EURIPIDES

405 B. C.—Death of SOPHOCLES

404 B. C.—Death of ALCIBIADES

400 B. C.—BOOK OF JOB written, according to many scholars

399 B. C.—Death of SOCRATES

388 B. C.—Death of ARISTOPHANES

384 B. C.—Birth of DEMOSTHENES, Athenian orator

384 B. C.—Birth of ARISTOTLE of Stagira, the famous Greek philosopher, whose theories long dominated the learned world

380–360 B. C.—Death of HIPPOCRATES, Greek physician

356 B. C.—Birth of ALEXANDER THE GREAT, King of Macedon, conqueror of most of the then known world

337 B. C.—DEMOSTHENES chosen as foremost statesman at Athens

323 B. C.—Death of ALEXANDER THE GREAT

322 B. C.—Death of DEMOSTHENES

322 B. C.—Death of ARISTOTLE

106 B. C.—Birth of Marcus Tullius CICERO, the great Roman orator

100 B. C.—Birth of Julius CÆSAR, Roman general and statesman (supposed date)

83 B. C.—Birth of Marcus Antonius (Mark ANTONY), Roman triumvir and general

76 B. C.—CICERO elected quæstor to the province of Lilybæum, Sicily

70 B. C.—Birth of Publius Vergilius Maro (VIRGIL), Roman epic poet; author of the ÆNEID

69 B. C.—Birth of CLEOPATRA, Queen of Egypt, famous for her intrigues and extravagance

64 B. C.—CICERO elected Consul. Crushes the conspiracy of CATILINE

58–50 B. C.—CÆSAR conquers Gaul

58 B. C.—CICERO banished from Rome by the Triumvirate

51 B. C.—CICERO proconsul of Cilicia

49 B. C.—War for supremacy between CÆSAR and POMPEY. Cæsar crosses the Rubicon

48–44 B. C.—Julius CÆSAR made dictator

48 B. C.—POMPEY defeated by CÆSAR in the battle of Pharsalia. Later murdered in Egypt

46 B. C.—CATO kills himself at Utica; CÆSAR dictator for ten years

45 B. C.—CLEOPATRA marries Mark ANTONY

44 B. C.—Julius CÆSAR assassinated in Rome

43 B. C.—CICERO killed by agents of ANTONY

43 B. C.—The second Triumvirate formed by Mark ANTONY, OCTAVIUS and Marcus Æmilius LEPIDUS

42 B. C.—Battle of PHILIPPI; Brutus and Cassius defeated by Antony and Octavius

42 B. C.—CLEOPATRA meets Mark ANTONY by his order at Tarsus

37 B. C.—VIRGIL's "Eclogues" completed

31 B. C.—Battle of ACTIUM between OCTAVIUS and Mark ANTONY

30 B. C.—Death of CLEOPATRA, Queen of Egypt, by suicide at Alexandria. ANTONY commits suicide

30 B. C.—VIRGIL's "Georgics" first issued

19 B. C.—Death of VIRGIL, Roman poet

7–2 B. C.—Birth of CHRIST

46–51 A. D.—Birth of PLUTARCH, Greek biographer—the "great biographer of Antiquity"

50 A. D.—Birth of EPICTETUS, Græco-Roman Stoic philosopher (supposed date)

54–58 A. D.—PAUL's First and Second Epistles to the CORINTHIANS written (supposed date)

62 A. D.—Gaius Plinius Cæcilius Secundus, known as PLINY THE YOUNGER, born

69–70 A. D.—Period covered by the fragments of the "ANNALS" and "Histories" of TACITUS

70 A. D.—The Gospel according to St. LUKE written (supposed date)

80–90 A. D.—ACTS OF THE APOSTLES written, according to accepted chronologies

90 A. D.—EPICTETUS banished from Rome by the Emperor DOMITIAN, who abhorred his Stoic sentiments

100 A. D.—PLINY THE YOUNGER made consul by TRAJAN and governor of Bithynia

113 A. D.—Death of PLINY THE YOUNGER

120–130 A. D.—Death of PLUTARCH, the biographer

121 A. D.—Birth of MARCUS AURELIUS Antoninus, Roman emperor and moralist. Adopted son of the Emperor Aurelius Antoninus

161 A. D.—MARCUS AURELIUS Antoninus succeeds to Imperial throne

170–220 A. D.—Birth of St. CLEMENT of Alexandria, one of the "Fathers" of the Christian Church (supposed date)

180 A. D.—Death of MARCUS AURELIUS Antoninus

354 A. D.—Birth of Aurelius Augustinus, known as Saint AUGUSTINE, Bishop of Hippo, the greatest theologian of the ancient Church

387 A. D.—Saint AUGUSTINE converted to Catholic Christianity from the errors of the Manichæan sect

400 A. D.—GLORIA IN EXCELSIS, great Latin hymn, written (supposed date)

430 A. D.—Death of Saint AUGUSTINE

450–500 A. D.—Birth of BEOWULF, hero of the Saxon epic (supposed date)

571 A. D.—Birth of MOHAMMED, the prophet of Arabia, founder of Mohammedanism

622–624 A. D.—Beginning of the MOHAMMEDAN Era and Holy War

632 A. D.—Death of MOHAMMED

673 A. D.—Birth of the venerable BEDE, Saxon writer in England, most distinguished scholar of his age

676 A. D.—Birth of St. JOHN OF DAMASCUS, great theologian of the Greek Church

725 A. D.—Birth of St. STEPHEN the Sabaite, hymnist

735 A. D.—Death of the Venerable BEDE

742 A. D.—Birth of CHARLEMAGNE (Charles the Great), king of the Franks and Roman Emperor

778 A. D.—CHARLEMAGNE returns from Spain. The rear-guard of his army is annihilated at Roncesvalles by the Basques. Subject of "THE SONG OF ROLAND"

814 A. D.—Death of CHARLEMAGNE

935 A. D.—Birth of FIRDOUSI (Abul Kasim Mausur), Persian epic poet

1000 A. D.—Discovery of North America by LEIF (Ericsson) THE LUCKY (supposed date)

1012 A. D.—Death of FIRDOUSI

1050 A. D.—Birth of OMAR KHAYYAM, Persian astronomer and poet. Author of the "RUBAIYAT"

1091 A. D.—Birth of St. BERNARD OF CLAIRVAUX, mystical theologian and hymnist

1100 A. D.—Period assigned to Irish epic the DESTRUCTION OF DA DERGAS HOSTEL (supposed date)

1112 A. D.—Birth of WACE, Anglo-Norman poet

1125 A. D.—Birth of BERNARD OF MORLAIX (or of Cluny), Benedictine monk; author of Latin poem, basis of JERUSALEM THE GOLDEN (supposed date)

1180 A. D.—Death of WACE, Anglo-Norman poet

1200 A. D.—Period assigned to the composition of the VOLSUNGA SAGA

1200 A. D.—History of the Danes by SAXE GRAMMATICUS written

1200–1275 A. D.—Period of Thomas à CELANO, author of DIES IRÆ

1200–1300 A. D.—Period of JACOBUS DE BENEDICTIS, author of "STABAT MATER"

1265 A. D.—Birth of DANTE Alighieri, Italian poet, author of "THE DIVINE COMEDY"

1300–1350 A. D.—Period of Sir John MANDEVILLE, hero and reputed author of the famous work "Travels of Sir John Mandeville"

1302 A. D.—DANTE Alighieri, condemned to death by his political enemies, saves himself by exile

1313 A. D.—Birth of Giovanni BOCCACCIO, Italian poet and novelist; author of the "Decameron"

1321 A. D.—Death of DANTE Alighieri

1326 A. D.—Birth of John GOWER, English poet (supposed date)

1337 A. D.—Birth of Sir John FROISSART, French poet and historian

1340 A. D.—Birth of Geoffrey CHAUCER, English poet

1346 A. D.—The battle of CRECY in which King EDWARD III of England defeated the French Army under PHILIP VI

1356 A. D.—Battle of POITIERS in which Edward the BLACK PRINCE gained a great victory over the French and captured the French king, JOHN II

1356 A. D.—"Voyage and Travaile of Sir John MANDEVILLE" written

1364 A. D.—CHAUCER's "Canterbury Tales" written

1372 A. D.—Date assigned to death of Sir John MANDEVILLE, hero of book of travels

1375 A. D.—Death of Giovanni BOCCACCIO, "creator of the classic Italian prose and father of the modern novel"

1379–1380 A. D.—Birth of Thomas HAEMMERLEIN, known as Thomas à KEMPIS

1381 A. D.—Wat TYLER's Rebellion. The name usually applied to the English social revolt of 1381, from Wat Tyler, its chief leader

1388 A. D.—Battle of OTTERBURN, between the forces of PERCY, surnamed Hotspur, and DOUGLAS, in which both leaders fell. The battle is commemorated by the ballad "CHEVY CHASE"

1400 A. D.—Death of Geoffrey CHAUCER

1408 A. D.—Death of John GOWER

1410 A. D.—Death of Sir John FROISSART

1422 A. D.—Birth of William CAXTON, the first English printer (supposed date)

1469 A. D.—Birth of Niccolo di Bernardo MACHIAVELLI

1471 A. D.—Death of Thomas à KEMPIS

1471 A. D.—Birth of Albrecht DURER, German painter, engraver and designer, the "greatest master of the German Renaissance"

1472 A. D.—DANTE's "DIVINE COMEDY" first printed

1474 A. D.—CAXTON's translation of "The RECUYELL OF THE HISTORIES OF TROY" published, the first book printed in the English language

1475 A. D.—Birth of Thomas WOLSEY, English Cardinal and statesman (supposed date)

1478 A. D.—Birth of Sir Thomas MORE, English author and statesman

1480–1537 A. D.—Birth of Alessandro de MEDICI, Duke of Florence (supposed date)

1483 A. D.—Birth of Martin LUTHER, the "Founder of Protestant Civilization"

1485 A. D.—Sir Thomas MALORY's "Morte D'Arthur" published

1491 A. D.—Death of William CAXTON

1492 A. D.—The discovery of the West Indies by Christopher COLUMBUS

1495 A. D.—Birth of François RABELAIS, French humorist

1497 A. D.—John CABOT discovers the mainland of North America, probably Labrador

1500 A. D.—Birth of Raphael HOLINSHED, English chronicler

1500 A. D.—Birth of Benvenuto CELLINI, Italian sculptor and goldsmith

1503 A. D.—Birth of Sir Thomas WYATT, English diplomatist and poet (supposed date)

1505 A. D.—Birth of John KNOX, Scottish reformer, statesman and writer

1506 A. D.—Birth of St. FRANCIS XAVIER, Spanish Jesuit missionary

1509 A. D.—Birth of John CALVIN, French reformer and theologian

1513 A. D.—Niccolo MACHIAVELLI imprisoned and tortured

1516 A. D.—Birth of Roger ASCHAM, English classical scholar and author

1516 A. D.—"UTOPIA" by Thomas MORE written

1516 A. D.—"Orlando Furioso" published

1517 A. D.—Birth of Ambroise PARE, French surgeon

1517 A. D.—Birth of Henry HOWARD, Earl of Surrey, English poet (supposed date)

1517 A. D.—Martin LUTHER posts "THE NINETY-FIVE THESES" on the church door at Wittenberg

1519 A. D.—Birth of Cosimo de MEDICI, Grand Duke of Tuscany

1520 A. D.—Martin LUTHER publishes the fundamental principles of the Reformation and is expelled from the Church

1523 A. D.—Pope CLEMENT VII elected

1523 A. D.—Birth of Richard EDWARDS, English dramatist

1526 A. D.—Sack of Rome by the Ghibelline house of Colonna

1527 A. D.—Death of Niccolo MACHIAVELLI

1528 A. D.—Death of Albrecht DÜRER

1529 A. D.—Sir Thomas MORE made Lord Chancellor of England

1530 A. D.—Death of Cardinal WOLSEY

1533 A. D.—Birth of Michel Eyquem de MONTAIGNE, French philosopher and essayist

1533 A. D.—Death of Ludovico ARIOSTO

1533 A. D.—John CALVIN banished from Paris

1534 A. D.—Martin LUTHER's translation of the BIBLE published

1535 A. D.—Birth of George GASCOIGNE, English poet (supposed date)

1535 A. D.—Sir Thomas MORE executed on Tower Hill

1536 A. D.—CALVIN's "INSTITUTES OF THE CHRISTIAN RELIGION" published

1536 A. D.—Birth of Thomas SACKVILLE, Earl of Dorset, English poet

1537 A. D.—Death of Alessandro, Duke de MEDICI

1537 A. D.—Triumphal entry of the Emperor CHARLES V into Rome

1539 A. D.—Birth of Sir Humphrey GILBERT, founder of the first English colony in North America

1540 A. D.—Birth of Sir Francis DRAKE, English navigator (supposed date)

1542 A. D.—John KNOX becomes a convert to Protestant doctrines

1542 A. D.—Death of Sir Thomas WYATT

1544 A. D.—Birth of Torquato TASSO, Italian epic poet

1545 A. D.—Birth of Nicholas BRETON, English poet (supposed date)

1547 A. D.—John KNOX a prisoner in France

1547 A. D.—Birth of Miguel CERVANTES Saavedra, Spanish novelist and poet, author of "DON QUIXOTE"

1547 A. D.—Henry HOWARD, Earl of Surrey, English poet and courtier, beheaded

1549 A. D.—First English prayer-book composed

1550 A. D.—Birth of Edward DE VERE, Earl of Oxford, English poet and courtier

1552 A. D.—Birth of Sir Walter RALEIGH, English navigator, author, courtier and soldier

1552 A. D.—Death of St. FRANCIS XAVIER

1552–1555 A. D.—Period of the War of SIENA, when Piero Strozzi acted as general for Henry II of France against the Spaniards

1553 A. D.—Birth of Anthony MUNDAY, English dramatist, poet and compiler

1553 A. D.—Birth of John FLORIO, English lexicographer, author and translator

1553 A. D.—Birth of Edmund SPENSER, English poet

1553 A. D.—Birth of John LYLY, English dramatist

1553 A. D.—Death of François RABELAIS

1554 A. D.—Birth of Sir Philip SIDNEY, English soldier and author

1556 A. D.—Birth of Thomas LODGE, English novelist, dramatist and poet (supposed date)

1558 A. D.—John KNOX's "First Blast of the Trumpet against the Monstrous Regiment of Women" published

1558 A. D.—Birth of George PEELE, English dramatist and poet

1558–1566 A. D.—Period covered by the "Autobiography of Benvenuto CELLINI"

1558–1603 A. D.—Reign of ELIZABETH, Queen of England

1560 A. D.—Birth of Robert GREENE, English dramatist, novelist and poet (supposed date)

1561 A. D.—Birth of Francis BACON, English philosopher, jurist and statesman

1561 A. D.—Birth of Robert SOUTHWELL, English poet and Jesuit martyr (supposed date)

1562 A. D.—Lope de VEGA, the "Spanish Shakespeare," born

1562 A. D.—Birth of Henry CONSTABLE, English poet

1562 A. D.—Birth of Samuel DANIEL, English poet and historian

1563 A. D.—Birth of Joshua SYLVESTER, English poet

1563 A. D.—Birth of Michael DRAYTON, English poet

1564 A. D.—Death of John CALVIN

1564 A. D.—Birth of William SHAKESPEARE, English poet and dramatist

1564 A. D.—Birth of Christopher MARLOWE, English poet and dramatist

1565 A. D.—Birth of Richard ROWLANDS, English poet

1566 A. D.—Death of Richard EDWARDS

1567 A. D.—Birth of William ALEXANDER, Earl of Stirling, Scottish poet and statesman (supposed date)

1567 A. D.—Sir Francis DRAKE commanding a ship under Sir John Hawkins is defeated by the Spaniards

1567 A. D.—Birth of Robert DEVEREUX, Earl of Essex, English courtier and soldier

1567 A. D.—Birth of Thomas CAMPION, English poet (supposed date)

1568 A. D.—Birth of Sir Henry WOTTON, English diplomatist and author

1568 A. D.—Death of Roger ASCHAM

1569–1574 A. D.—Sir Walter RALEIGH serves in the Huguenot Army in France

1569 A. D.—Death of Bernardo Tasso, Italian poet

1570 A. D.—Birth of Thomas DEKKER, English dramatist (supposed date)

1571 A. D.—Death of Benvenuto CELLINI

1572 A. D.—Death of John KNOX

1573 A. D.—Birth of John DONNE, English poet and divine

1574 A. D.—Birth of Ben JONSON, English dramatist (supposed date)

1574 A. D.—Death of Cosimo de' MEDICI

1574 A. D.—Birth of Richard BARNFIELD, English poet

1575 A. D.—Miguel CERVANTES Saavedra, maimed for life in the battle of Lepanto,
is captured by the Moors. He was a slave for five years among them.

1575 A. D.—Birth of Thomas HEYWOOD, English dramatist and miscellaneous writer
(supposed date)

1577 A. D.—Birth of Robert BURTON, English writer

1577 A. D.—Death of George GASCOIGNE

1577 A. D.—Sir Francis DRAKE's voyage in "The Golden Hind"

1578 A. D.—"Chronicles of England," by Raphael HOLINSHED, published

1578 A. D.—Sir Humphrey GILBERT receives from Queen Elizabeth a charter to plant
a colony in North America

1578 A. D.—Birth of William HARVEY, English physiologist and anatomist

1578 A. D.—Sir Walter RALEIGH engages with his half-brother Sir Humphrey GILBERT
in his first expedition against the Spaniards

1579 A. D.—Birth of John FLETCHER, English dramatist and poet

1579 A. D.—Birth of Captain John SMITH, English adventurer

1579 A. D.—"The Shepherds Calendar," by Edmund SPENSER, published

1580 A. D.—Birth of John WEBSTER, English dramatist (supposed date)

1580 A. D.—Death of Raphael HOLINSHED

1582 A. D.—Birth of Richard CORBET, English prelate and poet

1583 A. D.—Birth of Philip MASSINGER, English dramatist

1584 A. D.—Birth of Francis BEAUMONT, English dramatist and poet

1585 A. D.—Birth of Cornelius JANSEN, who gave his name to the Jansenist school

1585 A. D.—Birth of William DRUMMOND, Scottish poet

1586 A. D.—Birth of Martin RINKART, German hymn writer

1586 A. D.—DRAKE brings home the despairing Virginian colony

1586 A. D.—Death of Sir Philip SIDNEY

1587 A. D.—Christopher MARLOWE's first tragedy "Tamburlaine" produced

1588 A. D.—Birth of George WITHER, English poet

1588 A. D.—Birth of Thomas HOBBES, English philosopher
1588 A. D.—Christopher MARLOWE's "Doctor FAUSTUS" first produced
1590 A. D.—"The FAERIE QUEENE," by Edmund SPENSER, published
1590 A. D.—Death of Ambroise PARÉ
1591 A. D.—Christopher MARLOWE's tragedy of "EDWARD II" is produced
1591 A. D.—Birth of William BROWNE
1591 A. D.—Birth of Robert HERRICK, English lyric poet
1592 A. D.—Death of Michel de MONTAIGNE
1592 A. D.—Birth of Francis QUARLES, English poet
1592 A. D.—Sir Walter RALEIGH a prisoner in the Tower
1592 A. D.—Death of Robert GREENE
1593 A. D.—Death of Christopher MARLOWE
1593 A. D.—Birth of Izaak WALTON, English author; noted for his "Compleat Angler"
1593 A. D.—Birth of George HERBERT, English poet
1594 A. D.—Birth of GUSTAVUS ADOLPHUS, King of Sweden
1595 A. D.—Death of Torquato TASSO at Rome
1595 A. D.—Sir Walter RALEIGH discovers Guiana
1595 A. D.—Death of Robert SOUTHWELL
1596 A. D.—Birth of James SHIRLEY, English dramatist
1596 A. D.—Death of Sir Francis DRAKE
1596 A. D.—Birth of René DESCARTES, French philosopher
1597 A. D.—Death of George PEELE (supposed date)
1597 A. D.—Francis BACON's Essays first published
1598 A. D.—Birth of Thomas CAREW, English poet
1599 A. D.—Thomas DEKKER's play, "The SHOEMAKER'S HOLIDAY," first acted
1599 A. D.—Death of Edmund SPENSER
1600 A. D.—Birth of Don Pedro CALDERON, Spanish dramatist and poet
1601 A. D.—Death of Robert DEVEREUX, second Earl of Essex, chief favorite of Queen Elizabeth
1603 A. D.—First edition of SHAKESPEARE s "HAMLET" published
1604 A. D.—Death of Edward DE VERE, Earl of Oxford
1604 A. D.—Beginning of Sir Walter RALEIGH's imprisonment of twelve years for treason against James I. During this period he wrote his "History of the World"
1605 A. D.—"KING LEAR" first acted
1605 A. D.—The first part of "DON QUIXOTE" published in Madrid
1605 A. D.—Birth of Sir Thomas BROWNE, scholar and antiquary; author of "RELIGIO MEDICI"
1605 A. D.—Birth of William HABINGTON, English poet
1606 A. D.—Birth of Edmund WALLER, English poet
1606 A. D.—Birth of Sir William D'AVENANT, English poet and play-writer
1606 A. D.—Death of John LYLY, English romancer and dramatist
1606 A. D.—Birth of Pierre CORNEILLE, French dramatist. The works of Corneille represent most fully the ideal of French classical tragedy
1608 A. D.—Birth of Thomas FULLER, English author and divine, famous for his work, the "Worthies of England"
1608 A. D.—Birth of John MILTON, English poet and statesman
1608 A. D.—Death of Thomas SACKVILLE, Earl of Dorset, English poet and statesman
1609 A. D.—Birth of Sir John SUCKLING, English poet
1610 A. D.—Ben JONSON's play, "The ALCHEMIST," first acted
1610 A. D.—SHAKESPEARE's tragedy, "MACBETH," first produced
1611 A. D.—Birth of William CARTWRIGHT, English poet and divine
1611 A. D.—SHAKESPEARE's play, "The TEMPEST," first produced
1611 A. D.—First English translation of "DON QUIXOTE" (first part) by Thomas Shelton is published

1612 A. D.—Birth of Thomas JORDAN, English poet

1612 A. D.—Birth of James GRAHAM, first Marquis of Montrose

1612 A. D.—Birth of Samuel BUTLER, English satirist

1613 A. D.—Birth of Duke de LA ROCHEFOUCAULD, French epigrammatic moralist

1613 A. D.—Birth of Richard CRASHAW, English poet (supposed date)

1615 A. D.—CERVANTES's "DON QUIXOTE" (second part) published

1616 A. D.—Death of Francis BEAUMONT, English poet and dramatist. In collaboration with FLETCHER wrote fifty-four plays

1616 A. D.—Death of Miguel CERVANTES Saavedra

1616 A. D.—Death of William SHAKESPEARE

1618 A. D.—Birth of Abraham COWLEY, English poet and essayist

1618 A. D.—Birth of Richard LOVELACE, English poet

1618 A. D.—Execution of Sir Walter RALEIGH

1618 A. D.—Francis BACON, philosopher and statesman, made Lord Chancellor and Baron Verulam

1619 A. D.—Death of Thomas CAMPION

1620 A. D.—Lord BACON's "NOVUM ORGANUM" published

1620 A. D.—The MAYFLOWER COMPACT signed

1620 A. D.—Birth of Alexander BROME, English poet and dramatist

1620 A. D.—Birth of John EVELYN, English author

1621 A. D.—Francis BACON, statesman and philosopher, made Viscount St. Albans; convicted of bribery. Sentenced by House of Lords to loss of offices, imprisonment, and fine

1621 A. D.—Birth of Andrew MARVELL, English poet and politician

1621 A. D.—Birth of Jean de LA FONTAINE, French poet and fable writer

1622 A. D.—Birth of Henry VAUGHAN, English poet

1622 A. D.—Birth of Jean Baptiste MOLIÈRE, the "greatest of French dramatists"

1623 A. D.—Birth of Blaise PASCAL, French philosopher and author

1623 A. D.—John WEBSTER's play, "The DUCHESS OF MALFI," published

1623 A. D.—First folio edition of Shakespeare's plays published by HEMINGE and CONDELL

1624 A. D.—John SMITH's "General Historie of Virginia and New England" published

1625 A. D.—MASSINGER's play, "A NEW WAY TO PAY OLD DEBTS," first acted

1625 A. D.—Death of John WEBSTER (supposed date)

1625 A. D.—Death of John FLETCHER

1625 A. D.—Death of Thomas LODGE

1626 A. D.—Death of Nicholas BRETON (supposed date)

1626 A. D.—Death of Francis BACON

1627 A. D.—Birth of Jacques Benigne BOSSUET, French pulpit orator

1627 A. D.—BACON's "NEW ATLANTIS" published

1628 A. D.—William HARVEY's work on "The Circulation of the Blood" published in Latin at Frankfort

1628 A. D.—Birth of Sir William TEMPLE, English statesman and essayist

1631 A. D.—Death of Michael DRAYTON

1631 A. D.—Death of Captain John SMITH

1631 A. D.—Birth of John DRYDEN English dramatist, poet, and critic

1632 A. D.—Death of GUSTAVUS ADOLPHUS

1632 A. D.—Birth of John LOCKE, English philosopher

1633 A. D.—Birth of Samuel PEPYS, English diarist

1633 A. D.—Death of George HERBERT

1633 A. D.—Death of Anthony MUNDAY

1633 A. D.—Abraham COWLEY's "Poetical Blossoms" published

1635 A. D.—Death of LOPE DE VEGA

1636 A. D.—Birth of Nicolas BOILEAU-Despreaux, greatest French critic of the 17th century

1637 A. D.—Death of Ben JONSON
1637 A. D.—René DESCARTES's "DISCOURSE ON METHOD" published
1639 A. D.—The first American constitution of government, adopted by a popul
    convention of the towns, Windsor, Wethersfield, and Hartford
1639 A. D.—Birth of Sir Charles SEDLEY, English poet and dramatist
1639 A. D.—Birth of Jean Baptiste RACINE, greatest of French classical dramatists
1640 A. D.—Death of Philip MASSINGER
1640 A. D.—Death of Robert BURTON
1641 A. D.—Death of Thomas DEKKER (supposed date)
1641 A. D.—MILTON's "Prelatical Episcopacy" published
1641 A. D.—MILTON's "Reformation of England" published
1641 A. D.—The first code of laws established in New England; known as "THE
    BODY OF LIBERTIES"
1642 A. D.—Death of Sir John SUCKLING (supposed date)
1642 A. D.—Sir Thomas BROWNE's "RELIGIO MEDICI" published
1642 A. D.—The Long Parliament closes the theaters
1642 A. D.—Birth of Sir Isaac NEWTON, "The greatest English mathematician and
    physicist"
1644 A. D.—John WINTHROP, Deputy Governor of Massachusetts, publishes a document
    on "ARBITRARY GOVERNMENT"
1644 A. D.—Birth of William PENN, the founder of Pennsylvania
1644 A. D.—MILTON's "AREOPAGITICA" and "TRACTATE ON EDUCATION" published
1647 A. D.—Abraham COWLEY's "The Wish" published
1649 A. D.—King CHARLES I of England executed
1650 A. D.—Death of René DESCARTES
1651 A. D.—Thomas HOBBES's "LEVIATHAN" published
1653 A. D.—CROMWELL and his council of Officers adopt "The INSTRUMENT OF
    GOVERNMENT"
1653 A. D.—Oliver CROMWELL becomes Lord Protector of England
1653 A. D.—Izaak WALTON's "The Compleat Angler" published
1656 A. D.—Sir Henry VANE published "A HEALING QUESTION" on the subject of civil
    and religious liberty
1656–1657 A. D.—PASCAL's "LETTERS" published
1657 A. D.—Death of William HARVEY
1657 A. D.—Birth of John DENNIS, English critic and dramatist
1660–1672 A. D.—John BUNYAN in prison
1661 A. D.—Birth of Charles Montague, Earl of HALIFAX, English statesman and
    financier
1661 A. D.—Birth of Daniel DEFOE, English novelist, author of "Robinson Crusoe"
1662 A. D.—Death of Blaise PASCAL
1664 A. D.—Birth of Matthew PRIOR, English poet and diplomatist
1665 A. D.—Birth of Lady Grisel BAILLIE, Scottish poet
1666 A. D.—John DRYDEN's "Annus Mirabilis" published. It procured for him in
    1670 the Poet Laureateship
1667 A. D.—Birth of Jonathan SWIFT, "Greatest of English satirists"
1667 A. D.—MILTON's "PARADISE LOST" published
1667 A. D.—Death of Jeremy TAYLOR
1667 A. D.—Death of George WITHER
1668 A. D.—William PENN a prisoner in the Tower
1670 A. D.—John DRYDEN appointed Poet Laureate
1670 A. D.—John ELIOT's "BRIEF NARRATIVE" on the Indians published
1670 A. D.—Izaak WALTON's "LIFE OF GEORGE HERBERT" published
1671 A. D.—Birth of Anthony Ashley Cooper, third Earl of SHAFTESBURY, moralist
1671 A. D.—Birth of Colley CIBBER, English actor and dramatist
1672 A. D.—Birth of Richard STEELE, English essayist and dramatist

1672 A. D.—Birth of Joseph ADDISON, English poet and essayist

1673 A. D.—Death of Jean Baptiste Poquelin MOLIÈRE

1674 A. D.—Birth of Isaac WATTS, English nonconformist theologian, hymn writer and author

1674 A. D.—Death of Robert HERRICK

1674 A. D.—Death of John MILTON

1675 A. D.—Birth of Ambrose PHILIPS, English poet and dramatist (supposed date)

1678 A. D.—Birth of Henry St. John, first Viscount BOLINGBROKE, English statesman, author and orator

1678 A. D.—First edition of John BUNYAN's "PILGRIM'S PROGRESS" appears

1679 A. D.—Death of Thomas HOBBES

1680 A. D.—Death of Samuel BUTLER

1681 A. D.—Birth of Esther JOHNSON, Swift's "Stella"

1681 A. D.—Death of Pedro CALDERON de la Barca

1681 A. D.—William PENN obtains a charter creating him proprietor and governor of East New Jersey and Pennsylvania

1682 A. D.—Death of Sir Thomas BROWNE

1683 A. D.—Death of Izaak WALTON

1684 A. D.—Death of Pierre CORNEILLE

1685 A. D.—Birth of George BERKELEY, Bishop of Cloyne, English metaphysical philosopher

1685 A. D.—Birth of John GAY, English poet

1686 A. D.—Birth of Allan RAMSAY, Scottish pastoral poet

1687 A. D.—Sir Isaac NEWTON's "PRINCIPIA" published

1687 A. D.—Death of Edmund WALLER

1688 A. D.—Birth of Alexander POPE, English poet and critic

1688 A. D.—Death of John BUNYAN

1689 A. D.—Birth of Lady Mary Wortley MONTAGU, English poet and letter writer

1689 A. D.—Birth of Samuel RICHARDSON, "the founder of the English domestic novel"

1690 A. D.—John LOCKE's "Essay Concerning Human Understanding" published

1694 A. D.—Birth of Lord CHESTERFIELD (Philip Dormer Stanhope), English courtier, wit and orator

1694 A. D.—Birth of VOLTAIRE (François Marie Arouet), French philosopher

1695 A. D.—Death of Jean de LA FONTAINE

1699 A. D.—Birth of Alexander Ross, Scottish poet

1699 A. D.—Death of Jean Baptiste RACINE

1700 A. D.—Death of John DRYDEN

1700 A. D.—Birth of James THOMSON, Scottish poet

1703 A. D.—Death of Samuel PEPYS

1704 A. D.—Death of Jacques Benigne BOSSUET

1704 A. D.—Birth of William HAMILTON of Bangour, Scottish poet

1704 A. D.—Death of John LOCKE

1706 A. D.—Birth of Benjamin FRANKLIN, American statesman, scientist and author

1707 A. D.—Birth of Henry FIELDING, English novelist

1707 A. D.—Birth of Charles WESLEY, English hymn writer

1709 A. D.—Birth of Samuel JOHNSON, English lexicographer, essayist and poet

1711 A. D.—Alexander POPE's "Essay on Criticism" written

1711 A. D.—Birth of David HUME, English philosopher and historian

1711 A. D.—"The Spectator" commenced publication

1711 A. D.—Death of Nicolas BOILEAU-Despreaux

1712 A. D.—Birth of Alison Rutherford COCKBURN, Scottish ballad writer

1712 A. D.—Birth of Jean Jacques ROUSSEAU, French author

1713 A. D.—Bishop George BERKELEY's "DIALOGUES BETWEEN HYLAS AND PHILONOUS" published

1713 A. D.—Joseph ADDISON's drama "Cato" appeared

1713 A. D.—Death of Lord SHAFTESBURY (Anthony Ashley Cooper)
1713 A. D.—Birth of Laurence STERNE, English author
1713 A. D.—Jonathan SWIFT appointed Dean of St. Patrick's, Dublin, Ireland
1715 A. D.—Alexander POPE's translations from Homer published
1715 A. D.—Death of Charles Montague, Earl of HALIFAX
1716 A. D.—Birth of Thomas GRAY, English poet
1718 A. D.—Death of William PENN
1719 A. D.—Death of Joseph ADDISON
1720 A. D.—Birth of John WOOLMAN, English Quaker preacher and social reformer
1721 A. D.—Birth of William COLLINS, English poet
1721 A. D.—Birth of John SKINNER, Scottish poet
1721 A. D.—Death of Matthew PRIOR
1722 A. D.—Birth of Christopher SMART, English poet
1723 A. D.—Birth of Adam SMITH, political economist and moral philosopher
1723 A. D.—Death of Esther VANHOMRIGH, Swift's "Vanessa"
1724 A. D.—Birth of Immanuel KANT, German metaphysician
1726 A. D.—Birth of Adam AUSTIN, English poet (supposed date)
1727 A. D.—Birth of Jane ELLIOT, English poet
1727 A. D.—Death of Sir Isaac NEWTON
1728 A. D.—Death of Esther JOHNSON ("Stella")
1728 A. D.—Birth of Oliver GOLDSMITH, English author and poet
1729 A. D.—Birth of Edmund BURKE, English statesman and orator
1729 A. D.—Death of Sir Richard STEELE
1729 A. D.—Birth of Gotthold Ephraim LESSING, German critic and dramatist
1731 A. D.—Death of Daniel DEFOE
1731 A. D.—Birth of William COWPER, English poet
1732 A. D.—"Poor Richard's Almanac" by FRANKLIN is commenced
1732 A. D.—Death of John GAY
1733 A. D.—Alexander POPE's "ESSAY ON MAN" published
1734 A. D.—Death of John DENNIS
1735 A. D.—Birth of Robert GRAHAM of Gartmore
1739-40 A. D.—David HUME's "Treatise of Human Nature" published
1740 A. D.—Birth of James BOSWELL, "the greatest of English biographers"
1741 A. D.—Birth of Isobel PAGAN, Scottish poet
1742 A. D.—Henry FIELDING's "Joseph Andrews" published
1742 A. D.—Birth of Anne HUNTER, English poet
1742 A. D.—David HUME's Essays (first part) published
1743 A. D.—Birth of Anna Letitia BARBAULD, English poet
1744 A. D.—Death of Alexander POPE
1745 A. D.—Birth of Charles DIBDIN, English song writer and dramatist
1745 A. D.—Death of Jonathan SWIFT
1745 A. D.—Birth of Hannah MORE, English religious writer
1746 A. D.—Birth of Sir William JONES, English Orientalist and linguist
1746 A. D.—Birth of Hector MACNEIL, Scottish poet
1747 A. D.—Birth of Susanna BLAMIRE
1748 A. D.—Death of Isaac WATTS
1748 A. D.—Death of James THOMSON
1748 A. D.—Birth of John LOGAN, Scottish poet
1749 A. D.—Birth of Edward JENNER, English physician and discoverer of vaccination
1749 A. D.—Birth of Johann Wolfgang von GOETHE, German poet and critic
1750 A. D.—Birth of Lady Anne LINDSAY
1750 A. D.—Samuel JOHNSON's "Rambler" started
1751 A. D.—Thomas GRAY's "ELEGY WRITTEN IN A COUNTRY CHURCHYARD" published
1751 A. D.—Birth of Richard Brinsley SHERIDAN, English dramatist, orator, and statesman

1751 A. D.—Death of Henry St. John, Viscount BOLINGBROKE

1752 A. D.—Birth of Thomas CHATTERTON, English poet

1753 A. D.—Death of Bishop George BERKELEY

1754 A. D.—Death of Henry FIELDING

1754–1762 A. D.—David HUME's "History of England" published

1755 A. D.—Birth of John DUNLOP, English poet

1755 A. D.—Dr. Samuel JOHNSON's Dictionary published

1756 A. D.—Edmund BURKE's Essay on the "SUBLIME AND BEAUTIFUL" published

1757 A. D.—Thomas GRAY's "Pindaric Odes" published

1757 A. D.—Birth of William BLAKE, English poet and painter

1757 A. D.—Benjamin FRANKLIN is sent to England to protest against the proprietary government of the colony of Pennsylvania

1758 A. D.—Samuel JOHNSON's "Idler" started

1759 A. D.—Birth of Robert BURNS, the greatest of Scottish poets

1759 A. D.—Birth of Johann Christoph Friedrich von SCHILLER, German poet, dramatist, and historian

1761 A. D.—Birth of August Friedrich Ferdinand von KOTZEBUE, German dramatist

1761 A. D.—Death of Samuel RICHARDSON

1762 A. D.—Birth of William COBBETT, English political writer

1762 A. D.—Birth of William Lisle BOWLES, English poet and antiquary

1762 A. D.—J. J. ROUSSEAU's "Contrat Social" published

1762 A. D.—Death of Lady Mary Wortley MONTAGU

1763 A. D.—Birth of Samuel ROGERS, English poet

1764 A. D.—FRANKLIN petitions George III to resume the government of the colony from the hands of the proprietors

1765 A. D.—Samuel JOHNSON's edition of Shakespeare's works published

1766 A. D.—Birth of Caroline Oliphant, Lady NAIRNE, a Scottish poet known as "The Flower of Strathearn"

1766 A. D.—Oliver GOLDSMITH's "Vicar of Wakefield" published

1767 A. D.—Birth of August Wilhelm von SCHLEGEL, German poet and critic; translator of Shakespeare

1768 A. D.—Oliver GOLDSMITH's first dramatic attempt, "The Good-Natured Man," produced

1768 A. D.—Death of Laurence STERNE

1770 A. D.—Oliver Goldsmith's "DESERTED VILLAGE" published

1770 A. D.—Death of Thomas CHATTERTON

1770 A. D.—Birth of James HOGG, Scottish poet

1770 A. D.—Birth of William WORDSWORTH, English poet

1771 A. D.—Birth of Sir Walter SCOTT, Scottish novelist and poet

1771 A. D.—Death of Thomas GRAY

1771 A. D.—Birth of Sydney SMITH, English wit and essayist

1772 A. D.—Death of John WOOLMAN

1772 A. D.—Birth of Samuel Taylor COLERIDGE, English poet, philosopher and critic

1773 A. D.—Johann Wolfgang von GOETHE's first important work, "Goetz von Berlichingen," produced

1773 A. D.—Death of Lord CHESTERFIELD (Philip Dormer Stanhope)

1773 A. D.—Oliver GOLDSMITH's comedy, "SHE STOOPS TO CONQUER," first produced

1774 A. D.—Birth of Robert TANNAHILL, Scottish poet

1774 A. D.—Birth of Robert SOUTHEY, English poet and prose writer

1774 A. D.—Death of Oliver GOLDSMITH

1775 A. D.—Birth of Charles LAMB, English essayist and critic

1775 A. D.—Birth of Joseph Blanco WHITE, English clergyman and author

1775 A. D.—Birth of Walter Savage LANDOR, English poet and prose writer

1775 A. D.—Richard Brinsley SHERIDAN's "The Rivals" first produced

1775 A. D.—Benjamin FRANKLIN chosen a member of the Continental Congress

1776 A. D.—The DECLARATION OF INDEPENDENCE adopted by the second Continental Congress

1776 A. D.—Death of David HUME

1776 A. D.—FRANKLIN sent to France as commissioner for the United States

1776 A. D.—Adam SMITH's "WEALTH OF NATIONS" published

1777 A. D.—Richard Brinsley SHERIDAN's "SCHOOL FOR SCANDAL" produced

1777 A. D.—Birth of Thomas CAMPBELL, English poet

1778 A. D.—Birth of William HAZLITT, English critic and essayist

1778 A. D.—Death of J. J. ROUSSEAU

1778 A. D.—Death of Jean François Marie Arouet, called VOLTAIRE

1779 A. D.—Birth of Robert SURTEES, English author

1779 A. D.—Birth of Thomas MOORE, Irish poet

1780 A. D.—Richard Brinsley SHERIDAN enters Parliament

1780 A. D.—Birth of William Ellery CHANNING, American clergyman, essayist and philanthropist

1781 A. D.—The surrender of Lord CORNWALLIS at Yorktown

1781 A. D.—Immanuel KANT's "Critique of Pure Reason" published

1781 A. D.—Death of Gotthold Ephraim LESSING

1783 A. D.—TREATY OF PEACE BETWEEN THE UNITED STATES AND GREAT BRITAIN, by which the War of the Revolution was ended and the United States recognized by Great Britain as a free and independent nation

1783 A. D.—Birth of Reginald HEBER, English prelate and hymn writer

1783 A. D.—Birth of Washington IRVING, American historian, essayist and novelist

1784 A. D.—Death of Samuel JOHNSON

1784 A. D.—Birth of Allan CUNNINGHAM, Scottish poet and general writer

1784 A. D.—Birth of Leigh HUNT, English essayist and poet

1785 A. D.—Birth of Count Alessandro MANZONI, Italian novelist and poet

1785 A. D.—William COWPER's "Task" published

1785 A. D.—"FUNDAMENTAL PRINCIPLES OF THE METAPHYSICS OF MORALS," by Immanuel KANT, published

1785 A. D.—Birth of Jakob GRIMM, German philologist and writer

1785 A. D.—Birth of Thomas DE QUINCEY, English essayist and miscellaneous writer

1786 A. D.—Birth of Wilhelm GRIMM, German philologist and writer

1787 A. D.—Birth of François Pierre Guillaume GUIZOT, French historian and statesman

1787 A. D.—Johann Wolfgang von GOETHE's play of "EGMONT" begun, published twelve years later

1787 A. D.—"The FEDERALIST," articles by Alexander HAMILTON, James MADISON and John JAY, begun in "The Independent Journal," New York

1787 A. D.—The CONSTITUTION OF THE UNITED STATES is drawn up at Philadelphia

1788 A. D.—Death of Charles WESLEY

1788 A. D.—Birth of Lord BYRON (George Gordon), English poet

1788 A. D.—Birth of Sir Aubrey DE VERE, Irish poet

1788 A. D.—Richard Brinsley SHERIDAN delivers his great speech at the trial of Warren Hastings

1789 A. D.—WASHINGTON delivers his first inaugural address

1789 A. D.—Nine of the thirteen United States ratify the CONSTITUTION

1790 A. D.—Edmund BURKE's "REFLECTIONS ON THE REVOLUTION IN FRANCE" published

1790 A. D.—Death of Benjamin FRANKLIN

1791 A. D.—Birth of Charles WOLFE, British clergyman and poet

1791 A. D.—Birth of Michael FARADAY, English physicist and chemist

1792 A. D.—Birth of John KEBLE, English clergyman and religious poet

1792–1793 A. D.—Johann Wolfgang von GOETHE takes part in the wars against France

1792 A. D.—Birth of Percy Bysshe SHELLEY, English poet
1793 A. D.—Birth of Henry Francis LYTE, British hymn writer
1793 A. D.—Queen MARIE ANTOINETTE of France guillotined
1794 A. D.—Birth of John Gibson LOCKHART, Scottish author
1794 A. D.—The United States TREATY WITH THE SIX NATIONS OF INDIANS concluded
1794 A. D.—Edmund BURKE delivers a nine days' speech in the Warren Hastings trial
1794 A. D.—Birth of William Cullen BRYANT, American poet and journalist
1795 A. D.—Birth of George DARLEY, English poet
1795 A. D.—Birth of Thomas CARLYLE, Scottish essayist and historian
1795 A. D.—Birth of John KEATS, English poet
1795 A. D.—Death of James BOSWELL
1796 A. D.—WASHINGTON'S FAREWELL ADDRESS read in the House of Representatives
1796 A. D.—"A LETTER FROM THE RIGHT HON. EDMUND BURKE TO A NOBLE LORD" appears
1796 A. D.—Edward JENNER makes his first experiment in vaccination
1796 A. D.—Death of Robert BURNS
1796 A. D.—Birth of Hartley COLERIDGE, English poet
1797 A. D.—Birth of Sir Charles LYELL, English geologist
1797 A. D.—Death of Edmund BURKE
1798 A. D.—JENNER'S FIRST TREATISE ON THE SMALL-POX published
1798 A. D.—Birth of Thomas HOOD, English poet and humorist
1798 A. D.—COLERIDGE'S "ANCIENT MARINER" published
1799 A. D.—Birth of Heinrich HEINE, German poet and critic
1800 A. D.—Death of William COWPER
1800 A. D.—Birth of Thomas Babington MACAULAY, English historian, essayist, poet and statesman
1801 A. D.—Birth of Sir Henry LYTTON, Earl Bulwer
1802 A. D.—Birth of Hugh MILLER, Scottish geologist and writer
1802 A. D.—Birth of Victor Marie HUGO, French lyric poet and novelist
1803 A. D.—TREATY WITH FRANCE, FOR THE CESSION OF LOUISIANA, concluded
1803 A. D.—Birth of Ralph Waldo EMERSON, American essayist, lecturer and poet
1804 A. D.—Death of Immanuel KANT
1804 A. D.—Birth of Robert Stephen HAWKER, English poet and divine
1804 A. D.—Birth of Charles Augustin SAINTE-BEUVE, French critic
1805 A. D.—Death of Johann Christoph Friedrich SCHILLER
1805 A. D.—Birth of Sarah Flower ADAMS, English poet, author of "Nearer, my God, to Thee"
1805 A. D.—Birth of Hans Christian ANDERSEN, Danish novelist, poet and writer of fairy tales
1806 A. D.—Birth of Elizabeth Barrett BROWNING, English poet
1806 A. D.—Birth of John Stuart MILL, English philosopher and economist
1807 A. D.—Birth of Lady DUFFERIN, Irish poet
1807 A. D.—Birth of Henry Wadsworth LONGFELLOW, American poet
1807 A. D.—Birth of John Greenleaf WHITTIER, American poet
1808 A. D.—Birth of Ray PALMER, American hymn writer
1808 A. D.—Birth of Giuseppe MAZZINI, Italian patriot and writer
1808 A. D.—Birth of Charles Tennyson TURNER, English poet
1809 A. D.—Birth of Edgar Allan POE, American poet and story writer
1809 A. D.—Birth of Oliver Wendell HOLMES, American poet, essayist and novelist
1809 A. D.—Birth of Richard Monckton MILNES, Lord Houghton, English statesman, poet and miscellaneous writer
1809 A. D.—Birth of Alfred TENNYSON, English poet
1809 A. D.—Birth of Charles Robert DARWIN, English naturalist, founder of the "Darwinian" theory of evolution

1809 A. D.—Birth of Edward FITZGERALD, English poet, translator of the "RUBAIYAT" of Omar Khayyam

1810 A. D.—Birth of Sir Samuel FERGUSON, Irish poet

1811 A. D.—Birth of William Makepeace THACKERAY, English novelist, satirist and critic

1812–1815 A. D.—"Kinder- und Hausmärchen," fairy stories by the Brothers GRIMM, published

1812 A. D.—Birth of Robert BROWNING, English poet and dramatist

1812 A. D.—Birth of Charles DICKENS, English novelist

1813 A. D.—Birth of William Edmondstoune AYTOUN, Scottish lawyer, poet and editor

1814 A. D.—Birth of Frederick William FABER, English hymn writer

1816 A. D.—Death of Richard Brinsley SHERIDAN, English orator, wit and dramatist

1817 A. D.—Lord BYRON's first poetic drama "MANFRED" appears

1817 A. D.—AGREEMENT BETWEEN GREAT BRITAIN AND THE UNITED STATES REGARDING THE NAVAL FORCE TO BE MAINTAINED ON THE GREAT LAKES

1817 A. D.—Birth of Henry David THOREAU, American author

1818 A. D.—Birth of Emily BRONTE, English poet and novelist

1819 A. D.—SPAIN cedes Florida to the United States

1819 A. D.—Birth of Arthur Hugh CLOUGH, English poet

1819 A. D.—Chief Justice John MARSHALL, delivers his opinion in the case of MCCULLOCH VS. MARYLAND

1819 A. D.—Birth of Walt WHITMAN, American poet

1819 A. D.—Birth of James Russell LOWELL, American poet, critic and scholar

1819 A. D.—Birth of John RUSKIN, English art critic

1821 A. D.—Death of John KEATS

1822 A. D.—Death of Percy Bysshe SHELLEY

1822 A. D.—Birth of Louis PASTEUR, French chemist and bacteriologist, founder of modern stereo-chemistry and discoverer of cure for hydrophobia

1822 A. D.—Birth of Matthew ARNOLD, English poet and critic

1823 A. D.—President James MONROE promulgates his doctrine, the so-called MONROE DOCTRINE, against foreign encroachment and interference in the Americas

1823 A. D.—Birth of William Johnson CORY, English poet

1823 A. D.—Birth of Coventry PATMORE, English poet and writer

1823 A. D.—Thomas CARLYLE's first long work, "Life of Schiller" published

1823 A. D.—Death of Edward JENNER

1823 A. D.—Birth of Professor Max MULLER, German-English philologist

1823 A. D.—Birth of Ernest RENAN, French philologist and religious historian

1823 A. D.—Birth of Edward Augustus FREEMAN, English historian

1823 A. D.—Charles LAMB's "Essays of Elia" published

1824 A. D.—Birth of Sydney DOBELL, English poet

1824 A. D.—Death of Lord BYRON

1824 A. D.—Birth of George MACDONALD, Scottish novelist and poet

1824 A. D.—Birth of William ALLINGHAM, Irish poet

1825–1826 A. D.—Alessandro MANZONI's masterpiece, the novel, "I PROMESSI SPOSI" ("The Betrothed"), published

1825 A. D.—Birth of Thomas Henry HUXLEY, English biologist

1825 A. D.—Lord MACAULAY's Essays published

1826 A. D.—Death of Reginald HEBER

1826 A. D.—Birth of Walter BAGEHOT, English economist, publicist and journalist

1827 A. D.—Birth of Joseph LISTER, founder of antiseptic surgery

1828 A. D.—Birth of Dante Gabriel ROSSETTI, English poet and painter

1828 A. D.—Birth of George MEREDITH, English novelist and poet

1828 A. D.—Birth of Hippolyte Adolphe TAINE, French historian

1829 A. D.—Birth of Alexander SMITH, Scottish poet

1830 A. D.—Birth of Thomas Edward Brown, English poet

1830 A. D.—Birth of Christina Rossetti, English poet

1830 A. D.—Lyell's "Principles of Geology" published

1830 A. D.—Death of William Hazlitt

1831 A. D.—Birth of Edward, Earl of Lytton, English poet

1831 A. D.—On the 27th of December Charles Darwin started on his famous voyage around the world in Her Majesty's ship "Beagle"

1832 A. D.—Death of Sir Walter Scott

1832 A. D.—Death of Wolfgang von Goethe

1832 A. D.—Mazzini exiled from France

1833 A. D.—Browning's first published poem, "Pauline," appears

1833 A. D.—John Henry Newman coöperates with Froude and others in founding the "Oxford Movement"

1834 A. D.—Death of Samuel Taylor Coleridge

1834 A. D.—Birth of William Morris, English poet

1834 A. D.—Birth of James Thomson (B. V.), Scottish poet

1834 A. D.—Death of Charles Lamb

1835 A. D.—Birth of Sir Archibald Geikie, Scottish geologist

1835 A. D.—First volume of fairy tales by Hans Christian Andersen is published

1837 A. D.—Birth of Algernon Charles Swinburne, English poet

1839 A. D.—Birth of Francis Bret Harte, American author and poet

1841 A. D.—Birth of Robert Buchanan, English poet and novelist

1841 A. D.—Emerson's Essays published

1842 A. D.—Birth of Sidney Lanier, American poet and author

1842 A. D.—Treaty between the United States and Great Britain on the Boundaries Question, ratified

1842 A. D.—Death of William Ellery Channing

1843 A. D.—John Ruskin's "Modern Painters" (First volume) appears

1843 A. D.—Browning's tragedy, "A Blot in the 'Scutcheon, is published and acted

1843 A. D.—Death of Robert Southey

1844 A. D.—Birth of Arthur O'Shaughnessy, English poet

1844 A. D.—Birth of John Boyle O'Reilly, Irish-American poet and journalist

1845 A. D.—J. H. Newman leaves the Anglican Church for the Catholic

1845 A. D.—Poe's "Raven" published

1845 A. D.—Death of Sydney Smith

1846 A. D.—Thackeray's "Vanity Fair" published

1848–1849 A. D.—Mazzini returns from banishment to join the Italian revolution when the French besieged Rome and ended the Roman Republic

1848 A. D.—Treaty of Peace between the United States and Mexico, ratified

1848 A. D.—Macaulay's "History of England" published

1849 A. D.—Birth of William Ernest Henley, English author

1849 A. D.—Death of Edgar Allan Poe

1850 A. D.—The Fugitive Slave Act passed in the United States

1850 A. D.—Thackeray's "Pendennis" published

1850 A. D.—Death of William Lisle Bowles

1850 A. D.—Birth of Robert Louis Stevenson, Scottish author

1850 A. D.—Death of William Wordsworth

1852 A. D.—Death of Thomas Moore

1853 A. D.—Irish text and English translation of "The Battle of Gabra" by Nicholas O'Kearney first published

1854 A. D.—Thoreau's "Walden" published

1855 A. D.—Walt Whitman's "Leaves of Grass" published

1855 A. D.—Thackeray's "The Newcomes" published

1856 A. D.—Death of Heinrich Heine

1857 A. D.—Mazzini joins the insurrection in Italy fighting under Garibaldi

1857–1859 A. D.—THACKERAY'S "The Virginians" published
1859 A. D.—DARWIN'S "ORIGIN OF SPECIES" published
1859 A. D.—John Stuart MILL'S "ESSAY ON LIBERTY" published
1859 A. D.—Death of Leigh HUNT
1859 A. D.—Death of Lord MACAULAY
1859 A. D.—Death of Thomas DE QUINCEY
1861 A. D.—President LINCOLN delivers his first inaugural address
1861 A. D.—Death of Elizabeth Barrett BROWNING
1862 A. D.—Death of H. D. THOREAU
1863 A. D.—President LINCOLN'S GETTYSBURG ADDRESS
1863 A. D.—President LINCOLN'S PROCLAMATION OF AMNESTY
1863 A. D.—The EMANCIPATION PROCLAMATION issued by President Abraham Lincoln
1863 A. D.—TAINE'S "History of English Literature" published
1863 A. D.—Death of William M. THACKERAY
1864 A. D.—Death of Walter Savage LANDOR
1865 A. D.—General Robert E. LEE surrenders at Appomattox
1865 A. D.—General Lee's FAREWELL TO HIS ARMY
1865 A. D.—President LINCOLN'S SECOND INAUGURAL ADDRESS
1865 A. D.—J. R. LOWELL'S "Commemoration Ode" published
1866 A. D.—President Johnson's PROCLAMATION DECLARING THE INSURRECTION AT AN END
1866 A. D.—Death of John KEBLE
1867 A. D.—The United States concludes a TREATY WITH RUSSIA, ANNEXING ALASKA by purchase
1867 A. D.—Death of Michael FARADAY
1867 A. D.—John Stuart MILL begins his "AUTOBIOGRAPHY"
1867–1879 A. D.—E. A. FREEMAN'S "History of the Norman Conquest" published
1869 A. D.—Death of Charles Augustin SAINTE-BEUVE
1869 A. D.—John Stuart MILL issues his "Subjection of Women," a standard plea for the rights of women
1870 A. D.—Death of Charles DICKENS
1872 A. D.—Death of Giuseppe MAZZINI
1873 A. D.—Death of John Stuart MILL
1874 A. D.—Death of François Pierre GUIZOT
1875 A. D.—Death of Sir Charles LYELL
1875 A. D.—Death of Hans Christian ANDERSEN
1878 A. D.—Death of William Cullen BRYANT
1879 A. D.—John Henry NEWMAN made a Cardinal
1881 A. D.—Death of Thomas CARLYLE
1882 A. D.—Death of Charles DARWIN
1882 A. D.—Death of Henry W. LONGFELLOW
1882 A. D.—Death of Ralph Waldo EMERSON
1882 A. D.—Sir Archibald GEIKIE'S "GEOGRAPHICAL EVOLUTION" published
1885 A. D.—Death of Victor HUGO
1888–1894 A. D.—Ernest RENAN'S "History of Israel" published
1888 A. D.—Death of Matthew ARNOLD
1891 A. D.—Death of James Russell LOWELL
1892 A. D.—Death of Walt WHITMAN
1892 A. D.—Death of John G. WHITTIER
1892 A. D.—Death of Alfred, Lord TENNYSON
1892 A. D.—Death of Ernest RENAN
1892 A. D.—Death of Edward Bulwer, Earl of LYTTON
1893 A. D.—Death of Hippolyte Adolphe TAINE
1894 A. D.—Death of Oliver Wendell HOLMES
1895 A. D.—Death of Louis PASTEUR

"ENCLOSED please find a list of selections from The Harvard Classics which I have prepared in consultation with Dr. Neilson for the use of boys and girls of from twelve to eighteen years of age, in answer to your suggestion of October fourth."

Charles W. Eliot

SELECTIONS FROM THE FIVE-FOOT
SHELF OF BOOKS

For Boys and Girls from Twelve to Eighteen
Years of Age

	VOL.	PAGE
Æsop's Fables	XVII	11–44
Grimm's Tales	XVII	47–218
Andersen's Tales	XVII	221–361
Homer—*The Odyssey*	XXII	
Virgil—*The Æneid*	XIII	
The Arabian Nights	XVI	
The Song of Roland	XLIX	95–195
Robin Hood	XL	128–186
Traditional Ballads—*Selections at pleasure*	XL	
Malory, Sir Thomas—*The Holy Grail* . . .	XXXV	105–214
Voyages and Travels	XXXIII	
Benjamin Franklin—*Autobiography* . . .	I	5–162
John Bunyan—*The Pilgrim's Progress* . . .	XV	5–319
Shakespeare—*Macbeth* and *The Tempest* . .	XLVI	319–463
Thomas Dekker—*The Shoemaker's Holiday* .	XLVII	469–537
Plutarch's Lives	XII	
Froissart	XXXV	7–101
Ambroise Paré—*Journeys*	XXXVIII	9–58
Manzoni—*The Betrothed*	XXI	
R. H. Dana—*Two Years before the Mast* . .	XXIII	
Darwin—*The Voyage of the Beagle*	XXIX	
Joseph Addison—*The Vision of Mirza* . . .	XXVII	73–77
Goldsmith—*She Stoops to Conquer*	XVIII	205–269
The Deserted Village	XLI	509–519
Schiller—*William Tell*	XXVI	379–489
Goethe—*Hermann and Dorothea*	XIX	337–410
Michael Drayton—*Agincourt* and *To the Virginian Voyage*	XL	222–228
Cowper—*John Gilpin*	XLI	546–554
Wordsworth—*Michael*	XLI	615–627
Sir Walter Scott—*Poems*	XLI	738–756

	VOL.	PAGE
Macaulay—*Poems*	XLI	915–917
Coleridge—*The Ancient Mariner*	XLI	682–701
James Hogg—*Kilmeny*	XLI	756–765
Thomas Campbell—*Poems*	XLI	770–781
Lord Byron—*The Prisoner of Chillon*	XLI	801–811
Lord Byron—*The Destruction of Sennacherib*	XLI	785
Lord Byron—*The Isles of Greece*	XLI	812–815
Thomas Moore—*Poems*	XLI	816–822
Leigh Hunt—*Abou Ben Adhem*	XLI	870–871
Keats—*The Eve of St. Agnes*	XLI	883–893
Tennyson—*Morte d'Arthur*	XLII	986–992
Sir Galahad	XLII	1002–1004
The Charge of the Light Brigade	XLII	1005–1007
The Revenge	XLII	1007–1010
Ruskin—*Sesame and Lilies*	XXVIII	93–162
Thackeray—*The End of the Play*	XLII	1058–1060
Robert Browning—*How They Brought the Good News*	XLII	1066–1067
Sydney Dobell—*The Ballad of Keith of Ravelston*	XLII	1114–1116
Dante Gabriel Rossetti—*The King's Tragedy*	XLII	1153–1178
William E. Henley—*England, My England*	XLII	1210–1212
Bryant—*Robert of Lincoln*	XLII	1215–1217
To a Waterfowl	XLII	1222–1223
Henry Wadsworth Longfellow—*Poems*	XLII	1264–1338
John G. Whittier—*Randolph of Roanoke*	XLII	1341–1344
Barclay of Ury	XLII	1347–1351
The Barefoot Boy	XLII	1355–1357
The Pipes at Lucknow	XLII	1360–1362
Barbara Frietchie	XLII	1362–1364
Oliver Wendell Holmes—*The Chambered Nautilus*	XLII	1365–1366
Old Ironsides	XLII	1366
Sidney Lanier—*The Revenge of Hamish*	XLII	1393–1398
Frank A. Haskell—*The Battle of Gettysburg*	XLIII	326
Abraham Lincoln—*Speech at Gettysburg*	XLIII	415
Selections—*From Sacred Writings*	XLIV	
Some representation of each of the six religions	XLV	